Merriam-Webster's

German-English

Dictionary

Merriam-Webster's
German-English
Dictionary

MERRIAM-WEBSTER, INCORPORATED

Springfield, Massachusetts, U.S.A.

First Edition 2010

© HarperCollins Publishers 2010

ISBN: 978-0-87779-857-6

Typeset by Davidson Publishing Solutions, Glasgow

MANAGING EDITOR
Gaëlle Amiot-Cadey

EDITOR
Susanne Reichert

SERIES EDITOR
Rob Scriven

CONTRIBUTOR
Caroline Wilcox Reul

MADE IN THE UNITED STATES OF AMERICA

Printing: 1 World Color Buffalo May 2010

Contents

Preface 6a

Explanatory Notes 8a

Abbreviations in This Work 15a

Regular German Noun Endings 18a

Irregular English Verbs 19a

Irregular German Verbs 23a

Phonetic Symbols 26a

German-English Dictionary 1

English-German Dictionary 203

Preface

MERRIAM-WEBSTER'S GERMAN-ENGLISH DICTIONARY is a new dictionary designed to meet the needs of English and German speakers in a time of ever-expanding communication among the countries of the world. It is intended for language learners, teachers, office workers, tourists, and business travelers – anyone who needs to communicate effectively in the German and English languages as they are spoken and written today.

This dictionary provides accurate and up-to-date coverage of current vocabulary in both languages, as well as abundant examples of words used in context to illustrate usage. The dictionary includes German words and phrases as they are spoken in Germany and other European countries. The English vocabulary and spellings included here reflect American English usage. Entered words that we have reason to believe are trademarks have been designated as such with the symbol ®. However, neither the presence nor absence of such designation should be regarded as affecting the legal status of any trademark.

The front matter of this dictionary begins with a set of Explanatory Notes followed by a list of abbreviations used in the dictionary. The list includes both German and English abbreviations in a single list that gives both the German and the English meanings of all of the abbreviations. This is followed by a section showing regular German nominative and genitive noun endings, a list of English irregular verbs, and German irregular verbs. Finally, this dictionary makes use of the International Phonetic Alphabet (IPA) for showing pronunciations, and a list of the IPA phonetic symbols used in the dictionary and their sounds appears at the end of the front matter immediately before the first page of the dictionary.

This dictionary is the result of a unique collaboration between Collins and Merriam-Webster. It is based on one of the most popular of the Collins German-English databases and reflects the bilingual lexicographical expertise of Collins editors and contributors. In addition, it has been thoroughly reviewed by editors at Merriam-Webster to ensure its accurate treatment of American English spelling, vocabulary, and idioms. The editors of Collins and Merriam-Webster offer this new dictionary in the belief that it will serve well those who want a concise and handy guide to the German and English languages of today.

Explanatory Notes

Entries

1. Main Entries

A boldface letter or letters, word, or phrase appearing flush left with the left-hand margin of each column of type is a main entry or entry word. The main entry may consist of letters set solid, or letters joined by a hyphen, or letters separated by a space:

> *German examples*
> **A** (*abk*) ...
> **Alt-taste** *f* ...
> **bellen** *vi* ...
> **Fahrrad** *nt* ...
> **Hals-Nasen-Ohren-Arzt** *m* ...
>
> *English examples*
> **BA** (*abbr*) ...
> **button** ... *n* ...
> **eye-opener** ... *n* ...
> **let down** *vt*
> **life preserver** ... *n* ...

The main entry, together with the material that follows it on the same line and succeeding indented lines, constitutes a dictionary entry.

2. Order of Main Entries

Words that are spelled alike (homographs) are treated at the same main entry unless they vary in their capitalization, compounding, punctuation, or presence of diacritical marks. In the German-to-English section, homographs beginning with a lowercase letter precede those beginning with an uppercase letter; homographs without diacritical marks precede those with marks, and homographs without hyphens precede those with hyphens:

ah *interj* ...
äh *interj* ...

angeln *vt* ...
Angeln ... *nt* ...

arm *adj* ...
Arm ... *m* ...

dampfen *vi* ...
dämpfen *vt* ...

Ex ...
Ex- ...

In the English-to-German section, homographs beginning with an uppercase letter precede those beginning with a lowercase letter; open compounds precede closed and hyphenated compounds; and homographs without apostrophes precede those with apostrophes:

break down *vi* ...
breakdown ... *n* ...

check in *vt, vi* ...
check-in ... *n* ...

COD ... *abbr* ...
cod ... *n* ...

fall out *vi* ...
fallout ... *n* ...

get together *vi* ...
get-together *n* ...

its ... *pron* ...
it's ... *contr* ...

Lent ... *n*
lent ... *pt, pp* ...

well ... *n*
we'll ... *contr* ...

3. Guide Words

A pair of guide words is printed at the top of each page, indicating the first and last main entries that appear on that page:

Hochsprung • Huhn

4. Variants

Variant forms of headwords are shown in two ways. If the variant form omits an optional letter, letters, or word, those parts are shown in parentheses:

> *German examples*
> **Abgas(sonder)untersuchung**
> **anders(he)rum**
> **Jog(h)urt**

> *English examples*
> **microwave (oven)**
> **toward(s)**
> **whisk(e)y**

If the variants have differing terminal elements but similar beginning elements, both forms are shown in full:

> *German examples*
> **Mikrowelle ..., Mikrowellenherd**
> **Möhre ..., Mohrrübe**
> **Omelett ..., Omelette**

English examples
hose ..., hosepipe
parking place, parking space
yuppie ..., yuppy

In the German-to-English section, parentheses are also used to show the feminine ending for nouns that have both masculine and feminine forms (see Gender Labels, below).

5. Phrases

Common expressions in which the main entry or an inflected form of the entry word appears are shown in a different size of boldface type. The swung dash, ~, represents the main entry word. For example, in the entry for **Mitte**, the phrase "**~ Juni**" should be read "**Mitte Juni**."

Pronunciation

In the English-to-German section, the phonetic spelling for each headword (indicating its pronunciation) is given in square brackets immediately after the headword:

mountain [maʊntən]

A list of these symbols used in these spellings is given on page 26a.

Functional Labels

An italic label indicating a part of speech or some other functional classification follows the pronunciation or, if no pronunciation is given, the main entry:

dark ... *adj* ...
heute *adv* ...

11a

and ... *conj* ...
ach *interj* ...
ink ... *n* ...
mit *prep* ...
neither ... *pron* ...
scheuen *vr* ...

Verbs that are intransitive are labeled *vi*; verbs that are transitive are labeled *vt*; verbs that are reflexive are labeled *vr*; auxiliary verbs are labeled *vb aux*; irregular verbs are labeled *irr*. In the German-to-English section, nouns are labeled *m*, *f*, or *nt*, depending on their gender (see Gender Labels, below).

The full forms of all of these abbreviations are given in the Abbreviations in This Work section on page 15a.

Gender Labels

In German-to-English noun entries, the gender of the entry word is indicated by an italic *m* (masculine), *f* (feminine), or *nt* (neuter), which appear as the functional label of the entry word.

In the case of nouns that have both masculine and feminine forms, parentheses within the main entry word are used to show the feminine ending:

Einwohner(in) ... *m(f)* inhabitant
Lebensretter(in) *m(f)* rescuer
Schauspieler(in) *m(f)* actor/actress

German equivalents of English entry words are also labeled for gender:

anniversary ... *n* Jahrestag *m*
balance sheet *n* Bilanz *f*
ear ... *n* Ohr *nt*

Inflected Forms

1. Nouns

Plurals of English nouns are shown in boldface within parentheses when they are irregular:

> **brother-in-law** ... (*pl* **brothers-in-law**) ...
> **potato** ... (*pl* **-es**) ...
> **tooth** ... (*pl* **teeth**) ...

In German-to-English entries, genitive and plural forms of nouns are shown next to the main entry word:

> **Abend** (*-s, -e*)
> **Abenteuer** (*-s, -*)
> **Abschied** (*-(e)s, -e*)

Nouns listed with an "r" or an "s" in parentheses take the same endings as adjectives (see the section on Regular German Noun Endings on page 18a).

2. Verbs

Principal parts of verbs are given when they are irregular. In English-to-German entries, principal parts are shown at the main entry:

> **break** ... *vt* (**broke, broken**)
> **catch** ... *vt* (**caught, caught**)
> **deal** ... (**dealt, dealt**) *vt, vi*

In German-to-English entries principle parts of common irregular verbs are shown at the main entry. Principle parts of irregular formed by adding a prefix to an irregular verb are labeled *irr*, and information about their principal parts can be found at the entry for the verb to which the prefix has been added. Further information about irregular verbs can be found in the Irregular German Verbs section beginning on page 23a.

backen (backte, gebacken) *vi, vt* ...
ab|hauen (*irr*) ...
hauen (haute, gehauen) ...

3. Adjectives and Adverbs

The comparatives and superlative forms of English adjective and adverb main entries are shown when they are irregular:

bad ... (worse, worst) ...
far ... (further *o* farther, furthest *o* farthest)
good ... (better, best)

Usage

Information about the usage of certain headwords is given in parentheses before the equivalent in the other language. The information appears in abbreviated form and in italics:

Dingsbums ... *nt* (*fam*) thingy, thingamajig
sprühen *vt, vi* to spray; (*fig*) to sparkle
booze ... (*fam*) *n* Alkohol
second-rate ... *adj* (*pej*) zweiklassig

Meanings

Translations of headwords are given in roman type. Where more than one meaning or usage exists, they are separated by a semicolon. When the main entry word functions as more than one part of speech, the translations for its use in each part of speech are separated by the symbol ▷. Words appearing in italics within parentheses before the translation offer contexts in which the headword is likely to appear or provide synonyms.

Abbreviations in This Work

Abkürzungen		Abbreviations
auch	*a.*	also
Abkürzung	*abk, abbr*	abbreviation
Akronym	*acr*	acronym
Adjektiv	*adj*	adjective
Adverb	*adv*	adverb
Landwirtschaft	*Agr*	agriculture
Akkusativ	*akk*	accusative
Akronym	*akr*	acronym
Anatomie	*Anat*	anatomy
Artikel	*art*	article
Bildende Künste	*Art*	fine arts
Astronomie, Astrologie	*Astr*	astronomy, astrology
Auto, Verkehr	*Auto*	automobiles, traffic
Luftfahrt	*Aviat*	aviation
Biologie	*Bio*	biology
Botanik	*Bot*	botany
britisch	*BRIT*	British
schweizerisch	*CH*	Swiss
Chemie	*Chem*	chemistry
Film	*Cine*	cinema
Wirtschaft	*Comm*	commerce
Konjunktion	*conj*	conjunction
Dativ	*dat*	dative
Eisenbahn	*Eisenb*	railways
Elektrizität	*Elek, Elec*	electricity
besonders	*esp*	especially
und so weiter	*etc*	et cetera
etwas	*etw*	
Femininum	*f*	feminine
umgangssprachlich	*fam*	familiar, informal
übertragen	*fig*	figurative
Finanzen, Börse	*Fin*	finance
Fotografie	*Foto*	photography

Abkürzungen		Abbreviations
Gastronomie	Gastr	cooking, gastronomy
Genitiv	*gen*	genitive
Geographie, Geologie	*Geo*	geography, geology
Geschichte	*Hist*	history
Imperativ	*imper*	imperative
Imperfekt	*imperf*	past tense
Informatik und Computer	*Inform*	computing
Interjektion, Ausruf	*interj*	interjection
unveränderlich	*inv*	invariable
unregelmäßig	*irr*	irregular
jemand, jemandem	jd, jdm	
jemanden, jemandes	jdn, jds	
Rechtsprechung	*Jur*	law
Konjunktion	*konj*	conjunction
Bildende Künste	*Kunst*	fine arts
Sprachwissenschaft, Grammatik	*Ling*	linguistics, grammar
Maskulinum	*m*	masculine
Mathematik	*Math*	mathematics
Medizin	*Med*	medicine
Meteorologie	*Meteo*	meteorology
Maskulinum und Femininum	*mf*	masculine and feminine
Militär	*Mil*	military
Musik	*Mus*	music
Substantiv	*n*	noun
Seefahrt	*Naut*	nautical, naval
Neutrum	*nt*	neuter
Zahlwort	*num*	numeral
oder	*o*	or
pejorativ, abwertend	*pej*	pejorative
Physik	*Phys*	physics
Plural	*pl*	plural
Politik	*Pol*	politics
Partizip Perfekt	*pp*	past participle
Präfix	*pref*	prefix

Abkürzungen		Abbreviations
Präposition	*prep*	preposition
Pronomen	*pron*	pronoun
1. Vergangenheit	*pt*	past tense
Eisenbahn	*Rail*	railways
Religion	*Rel*	religion
siehe	*s.*	see
	sb	someone, somebody
schottisch	*Scott*	Scottish
Singular	*sing*	singular
Skisport	*Ski*	skiing
	sth	something
Technik	*Tech*	technology
Nachrichtentechnik	*Tel*	telecommunications
Theater	*Theat*	theater
Fernsehen	*TV*	television
Typographie, Buchdruck	*Typo*	printing
unpersönlich	*unpers*	impersonal
(nord)amerikanisch	*US*	(North) American
Verb	*vb*	verb
Hilfsverb	*vb aux*	auxiliary verb
intransitives Verb	*vi*	intransitive verb
reflexives Verb	*vr*	reflexive verb
transitives Verb	*vt*	transitive verb
vulgär	*vulg*	vulgar
Zoologie	*Zool*	zoology
ungefähre Entsprechung	≈	cultural equivalent
abtrennbares Präfix	|	separable prefix

Regular German noun endings

nominative	genitive	plural	nominative	genitive	plural
-ade *f*	-ade	-aden	-ist *m*	-isten	-isten
-ant *m*	-anten	-anten	-ium *nt*	-iums	-ien
-anz *f*	-anz	-anzen	-ius *m*	-ius	-iusse
-ar *m*	-ars	-are	-ive *f*	-ive	-iven
- r *m*	- rs	- re	-keit *f*	-keit	-keiten
-at *nt*	-at(e)s	-ate	-lein *nt*	-leins	-lein
-atte *f*	-atte	-atten	-ling *m*	-lings	-linge
-chen *nt*	-chens	-chen	-ment *nt*	-ments	-mente
-ei *f*	-ei	-eien	-mus *m*	-mus	-men
-elle *f*	-elle	-ellen	-nis *f*	-nis	-nisse
-ent *m*	-enten	-enten	-nis *nt*	-nisses	-nisse
-enz *f*	-enz	-enzen	-nom *m*	-nomen	-nomen
-ette *f*	-ette	-etten	-rich *m*	-richs	-riche
-eur *m*	-eurs	-eure	-schaft *f*	-schaft	-schaften
-euse *f*	-euse	-eusen	-sel *nt*	-sels	-sel
-heit *f*	-heit	-heiten	-t t *f*	-t t	-t ten
-ie *f*	-ie	-ien	-tiv *nt*, *m*	-tivs	-tive
-ik *f*	-ik	-iken	-tor *m*	-tors	-toren
-in *f*	-in	-innen	-tum *m*, *nt*	-tums	-t mer
-ine *f*	-ine	-inen	-ung *f*	-ung	-ungen
-ion *f*	-ion	-ionen	-ur *f*	-ur	-uren

Substantive, die mit einem geklammerten 'r' oder 's' enden (z.B. **Angestellte(r)** *mf*, **Beamte(r)** *m*, **Gute(s)** *nt*) werden wie Adjektive dekliniert:

Nouns listed with an 'r' or an 's' in parentheses (eg **Angestellte(r)** *mf*, **Beamte(r)** *m*, **Gute(s)** *nt*) take the same endings as adjectives:

der Angestellte *m*	**die Angestellte** *f*	**die Angestellten** *pl*
ein Angestellter *m*	**eine Angestellte** *f*	**Angestellte** *pl*
der Beamte *m*		**die Beamten** *pl*
ein Beamter *m*		**Beamte** *pl*
das Gute *nt*		
ein Gutes *nt*		

Irregular English Verbs

present	past tense	past participle
arise (arising)	arose	arisen
awake (awaking)	awoke	awaked
be (am, is, are; being)	was, were	been
bear	bore	born(e)
beat	beat	beaten
become (becoming)	became	become
begin (beginning)	began	begun
bend	bent	bent
bet (betting)	bet	bet
bid (bidding)	bid	bid
bind	bound	bound
bite (biting)	bit	bitten
bleed	bled	bled
blow	blew	blown
break	broke	broken
breed	bred	bred
bring	brought	brought
build	built	built
burn	burned (*o* burnt)	burned (*o* burnt)
burst	burst	burst
buy	bought	bought
can	could	(been able)
cast	cast	cast
catch	caught	caught
choose (choosing)	chose	chosen
cling	clung	clung
come (coming)	came	come
cost	cost	cost
creep	crept	crept
cut (cutting)	cut	cut
deal	dealt	dealt
dig (digging)	dug	dug
do (does)	did	done
draw	drew	drawn

present	past tense	past participle
dream	dreamed (*o* dreamt)	dreamed (*o* dreamt)
drink	drank	drunk
drive (driving)	drove	driven
eat	ate	eaten
fall	fell	fallen
feed	fed	fed
feel	felt	felt
fight	fought	fought
find	found	found
flee	fled	fled
fling	flung	flung
fly (flies)	flew	flown
forbid (forbidding)	forbade	forbidden
foresee	foresaw	foreseen
forget (forgetting)	forgot	forgotten
forgive (forgiving)	forgave	forgiven
freeze (freezing)	froze	frozen
get (getting)	got	got, (*US*) gotten
give (giving)	gave	given
go (goes)	went	gone
grind	ground	ground
grow	grew	grown
hang	hung (*o* hanged)	hung (*o* hanged)
have (has; having)	had	had
hear	heard	heard
hide (hiding)	hid	hidden
hit (hitting)	hit	hit
hold	held	held
hurt	hurt	hurt
keep	kept	kept
kneel	knelt (*o* kneeled)	knelt (*o* kneeled)
know	knew	known
lay	laid	laid
lead	led	led
lean	leaned (*o* leant)	leaned (*o* leant)
leap	leaped (*o* leapt)	leaped (*o* leapt)
learn	learned (*o* learnt)	learned (*o* learnt)
leave (leaving)	left	left
lend	lent	lent

present	past tense	past participle
let (letting)	let	let
lie (lying)	lay	lain
light	lit (o lighted)	lit (o lighted)
lose (losing)	lost	lost
make (making)	made	made
may	might	–
mean	meant	meant
meet	met	met
mow	mowed	mown (o mowed)
must	(had to)	(had to)
pay	paid	paid
put (putting)	put	put
quit (quitting)	quit (o quitted)	quit (o quitted)
read	read	read
rid (ridding)	rid	rid
ride (riding)	rode	ridden
ring	rang	rung
rise (rising)	rose	risen
run (running)	ran	run
saw	sawed	sawn
say	said	said
see	saw	seen
seek	sought	sought
sell	sold	sold
send	sent	sent
set (setting)	set	set
shake (shaking)	shook	shaken
shall	should	–
shine (shining)	shone	shone
shoot	shot	shot
show	showed	shown
shrink	shrank	shrunk
shut (shutting)	shut	shut
sing	sang	sung
sink	sank	sunk
sit (sitting)	sat	sat
sleep	slept	slept
slide (sliding)	slid	slid
sling	slung	slung
slit (slitting)	slit	slit

present	past tense	past participle
smell	smelled (*o* smelt)	smelled (*o* smelt)
sow	sowed	sown (*o* sowed)
speak	spoke	spoken
speed	sped (*o* speeded)	sped (*o* speeded)
spell	spelled (*o* spelt)	spelled (*o* spelt)
spend	spent	spent
spin (spinning)	spun	spun
spit (spitting)	spat	spat
split (splitting)	split	split
spoil	spoiled (*o* spoilt)	spoiled (*o* spoilt)
spread	spread	spread
spring	sprang	sprung
stand	stood	stood
steal	stole	stolen
stick	stuck	stuck
sting	stung	stung
stink	stank	stunk
strike (striking)	struck	struck
strive (striving)	strove	striven
swear	swore	sworn
sweep	swept	swept
swell	swelled	swollen (*o* swelled)
swim (swimming)	swam	swum
swing	swung	swung
take (taking)	took	taken
teach	taught	taught
tear	tore	torn
tell	told	told
think	thought	thought
throw	threw	thrown
thrust	thrust	thrust
tread	trod	trodden
wake (waking)	woke (*o* waked)	woken (*o* waked)
wear	wore	worn
weave (weaving)	wove (*o* weaved)	woven (*o* weaved)
weep	wept	wept
win (winning)	won	won
wind	wound	wound
write (writing)	wrote	written

Irregular German verbs

Infinitiv	Präsens 2.,3. Singular	Imperfekt	Partizip Perfekt
backen	bäckst, bäckt	backte o buk	gebacken
befehlen	befiehlst, befiehlt	befahl	befohlen
beginnen	beginnst, beginnt	begann	begonnen
beißen	beißt, beißt	biss	gebissen
bergen	birgst, birgt	barg	geborgen
betrügen	betrügst, betrügt	betrog	betrogen
biegen	biegst, biegt	bog	gebogen
bieten	bietest, bietet	bot	geboten
binden	bindest, bindet	band	gebunden
bitten	bittest, bittet	bat	gebeten
blasen	bläst, bläst	blies	geblasen
bleiben	bleibst, bleibt	blieb	geblieben
braten	brätst, brät	briet	gebraten
brechen	brichst, bricht	brach	gebrochen
brennen	brennst, brennt	brannte	gebrannt
bringen	bringst, bringt	brachte	gebracht
denken	denkst, denkt	dachte	gedacht
dringen	dringst, dringt	drang	gedrungen
dürfen	darfst, darf	durfte	gedurft
erschrecken	erschrickst, erschrickt	erschrak	erschrocken
essen	isst, isst	aß	gegessen
fahren	fährst, fährt	fuhr	gefahren
fallen	fällst, fällt	fiel	gefallen
fangen	fängst, fängt	fing	gefangen
finden	findest, findet	fand	gefunden
fliegen	fliegst, fliegt	flog	geflogen
fließen	fließt, fließt	floss	geflossen
fressen	frisst, frisst	fraß	gefressen
frieren	frierst, friert	fror	gefroren
geben	gibst, gibt	gab	gegeben
gehen	gehst, geht	ging	gegangen
gelingen	–, gelingt	gelang	gelungen
gelten	giltst, gilt	galt	gegolten
genießen	genießt, genießt	genoss	genossen
geschehen	–, geschieht	geschah	geschehen
gewinnen	gewinnst, gewinnt	gewann	gewonnen
gießen	gießt, gießt	goss	gegossen
gleichen	gleichst, gleicht	glich	geglichen
gleiten	gleitest, gleitet	glitt	geglitten
graben	gräbst, gräbt	grub	gegraben
greifen	greifst, greift	griff	gegriffen
haben	hast, hat	hatte	gehabt
halten	hältst, hält	hielt	gehalten

Infinitiv	Präsens 2.,3. Singular	Imperfekt	Partizip Perfekt
hängen	hängst, hängt	hing	gehangen
heben	hebst, hebt	hob	gehoben
heißen	heißt, heißt	hieß	geheißen
helfen	hilfst, hilft	half	geholfen
kennen	kennst, kennt	kannte	gekannt
klingen	klingst, klingt	klang	geklungen
kommen	kommst, kommt	kam	gekommen
können	kannst, kann	konnte	gekonnt
kriechen	kriechst, kriecht	kroch	gekrochen
laden	lädst, lädt	lud	geladen
lassen	lässt, lässt	ließ	gelassen
laufen	läufst, läuft	lief	gelaufen
leiden	leidest, leidet	litt	gelitten
leihen	leihst, leiht	lieh	geliehen
lesen	liest, liest	las	gelesen
liegen	liegst, liegt	lag	gelegen
lügen	lügst, lügt	log	gelogen
mahlen	mahlst, mahlt	mahlte	gemahlen
meiden	meidest, meidet	mied	gemieden
messen	misst, misst	maß	gemessen
mögen	magst, mag	mochte	gemocht
müssen	musst, muss	musste	gemusst
nehmen	nimmst, nimmt	nahm	genommen
nennen	nennst, nennt	nannte	genannt
pfeifen	pfeifst, pfeift	pfiff	gepfiffen
raten	rätst, rät	riet	geraten
reiben	reibst, reibt	rieb	gerieben
reißen	reißt, reißt	riss	gerissen
reiten	reitest, reitet	ritt	geritten
rennen	rennst, rennt	rannte	gerannt
riechen	riechst, riecht	roch	gerochen
rufen	rufst, ruft	rief	gerufen
saufen	säufst, säuft	soff	gesoffen
saugen	saugst, saugt	sog *o* saugte	gesogen *o* gesaugt
schaffen	schaffst, schafft	schuf	geschaffen
scheiden	scheidest, scheidet	schied	geschieden
heben	hebst, hebt	hob	gehoben
scheinen	scheinst, scheint	schien	geschienen
schieben	schiebst, schiebt	schob	geschoben
schießen	schießt, schießt	schoss	geschossen
schlafen	schläfst, schläft	schlief	geschlafen
schlagen	schlägst, schlägt	schlug	geschlagen
schleichen	schleichst, schleicht	schlich	geschlichen
schließen	schließt, schließt	schloss	geschlossen
schmeißen	schmeißt, schmeißt	schmiss	geschmissen

schmelzen	schmilzt, schmilzt	schmolz	geschmolzen
schneiden	schneidest, schneidet	schnitt	geschnitten
schreiben	schreibst, schreibt	schrieb	geschrieben
schreien	schreist, schreit	schrie	geschrie(e)n
schweigen	schweigst, schweigt	schwieg	geschwiegen
schwellen	schwillst, schwillt	schwoll	geschwollen
schwimmen	schwimmst, schwimmt	schwamm	geschwommen
schwören	schwörst, schwört	schwor	geschworen
sehen	siehst, sieht	sah	gesehen
sein	bist, ist	war	gewesen
senden	sendest, sendet	sandte	gesandt
singen	singst, singt	sang	gesungen
sinken	sinkst, sinkt	sank	gesunken
sitzen	sitzt, sitzt	saß	gesessen
sollen	sollst, soll	sollte	gesollt
sprechen	sprichst, spricht	sprach	gesprochen
springen	springst, springt	sprang	gesprungen
stechen	stichst, sticht	stach	gestochen
stehen	stehst, steht	stand	gestanden
stehlen	stiehlst, stiehlt	stahl	gestohlen
steigen	steigst, steigt	stieg	gestiegen
sterben	stirbst, stirbt	starb	gestorben
stinken	stinkst, stinkt	stank	gestunken
stoßen	stößt, stößt	stieß	gestoßen
streichen	streichst, streicht	strich	gestrichen
streiten	streitest, streitet	stritt	gestritten
tragen	trägst, trägt	trug	getragen
treffen	triffst, trifft	traf	getroffen
treiben	treibst, treibt	trieb	getrieben
treten	trittst, tritt	trat	getreten
trinken	trinkst, trinkt	trank	getrunken
tun	tust, tut	tat	getan
verderben	verdirbst, verdirbt	verdarb	verdorben
vergessen	vergisst, vergisst	vergaß	vergessen
verlieren	verlierst, verliert	verlor	verloren
verschwinden	verschwindest, verschwindet	verschwand	verschwunden
verzeihen	verzeihst, verzeiht	verzieh	verziehen
wachsen	wächst, wächst	wuchs	gewachsen
wenden	wendest, wendet	wandte	gewandt
werben	wirbst, wirbt	warb	geworben
werden	wirst, wird	wurde	geworden
werfen	wirfst, wirft	warf	geworfen
wiegen	wiegst, wiegt	wog	gewogen
wissen	weißt, weiß	wusste	gewusst
wollen	willst, will	wollte	gewollt
ziehen	ziehst, zieht	zog	gezogen
zwingen	zwingst, zwingt	zwang	gezwungen

Lautschrift

Phonetic symbols

Vokale und Diphthonge

arm, father	[ɑː]	Bahn	it, wish	[ɪ]	Bischof
life	[aɪ]	weit	bee, me, beat, belief	[i]	viel
house	[aʊ]	Haut	here	[ɪə]	Bier
man, sad	[æ]		no, low	[oʊ]	
but, son	[ʌ]	Butler	not, long, law	[ɔ]	Post
get, bed	[ɛ]	Metall	boy, oil	[ɔɪ]	Heu
name, lame	[eɪ]		push, look	[ʊ]	Pult
ago, better	[ə]	bitte	you, do	[uː]	Hut
bird, her	[ɜ]		poor, sure	[ʊə]	
there, care	[ɛə]	mehr			

Konsonanten

been, blind	[b]	Ball	red, dry	[r]	rot
do, had	[d]	dann	stand, sand, yes	[s]	Rasse
jam, object	[dʒ]		ship, station	[ʃ]	Schal
father, wolf	[f]	Fass	tell, fat	[t]	Tal
go, beg	[g]	Gast	thank, death	[θ]	
house	[h]	Herr	this, father	[ð]	
youth	[y]		church, catch	[tʃ]	Rutsch
keep, milk	[k]	kalt	voice, live	[v]	was
lamp, oil, ill	[l]	Last	water, we, which	[w]	
man, am	[m]	Mast	loch	[x]	Bach
no, manner	[n]	Nuss	zeal, these, gaze	[z]	Hase
long, sing	[ŋ]	lang	pleasure	[ʒ]	Genie
paper, happy	[p]	Pakt			

German–English
Dictionary

A

à prep (+akk) at ... each; **vier Tickets à acht Euro** four tickets at eight euros each
A (abk) = **Autobahn** ≈ I
Aal (-(e)s, -e) m eel

ab prep +dat from; **Kinder ab 12 Jahren** children 12 and over; **ab morgen** from tomorrow; **ab sofort** as of now
▷ adv **1** off; **links ab** to the left; **der Knopf ist ab** the button has come off; **ab nach Hause** off you go home
2 (zeitlich): **von da ab** from then on; **von heute ab** from today, as of today
3 (auf Fahrplänen): **München ab 12.20** leaving Munich at 12.20
4: ab und zu o an now and then o again

ab|bauen vt (Zelt) to take down; (verringern) to reduce
ab|beißen (irr) vt to bite off
ab|bestellen vt to cancel
ab|biegen (irr) vi to turn off; (Straße) to bend; **nach links/rechts ~** to turn left/right
Abbildung f illustration
ab|blasen (irr) vt (fig) to call off
ab|blenden vt, vi (Auto): **die Scheinwerfer ~** to dim one's headlights
Abblendlicht nt dimmed headlights pl
ab|brechen (irr) vt to break off; (Gebäude) to tear down; (aufhören) to stop; (Computerprogramm) to abort
ab|bremsen vi to brake, to slow down
ab|bringen (irr) vt: **jdn von einer Idee ~** to talk sb out of an idea; **jdn vom Thema ~** to get sb off the subject; **davon lasse ich mich nicht ~** nothing will make me change my mind about it
ab|buchen vt to debit (von to)
ab|danken vi (König) to abdicate; (Politiker) to resign
ab|drehen vt (Gas, Wasser) to turn off; (Licht) to switch off ▷ vi (Schiff, Flugzeug) to change course
Abend (-s, -e) m evening; **am ~** in the evening; **zu ~ essen** to have dinner; **heute/morgen/gestern ~** this/tomorrow/yesterday evening; **guten ~** good evening
Abendbrot nt supper
Abendessen nt dinner

Abendgarderobe f evening dress
Abendkasse f box office
Abendkleid nt evening dress (o gown)
Abendmahl nt: **das ~** (Holy) Communion
abends adv in the evening; **montags ~** on Monday evenings
Abenteuer (-s, -) nt adventure
aber conj but; (jedoch) however; **oder ~** alternatively; **~ ja!** (but) of course!; **das ist ~ nett von Ihnen** that's really nice of you
abergläubisch adj superstitious
ab|fahren (irr) vi to leave (o to depart) (nach for); (Ski) to ski down
Abfahrt f departure; (von Autobahn) exit; (Ski) descent; (Piste) run
Abfahrtslauf m (Ski) downhill
Abfahrtszeit f departure time
Abfall m waste; (Müll) garbage
Abfalleimer m garbage can
abfällig adj disparaging; **~ von jdm sprechen** to make disparaging remarks about sb
ab|färben vi (Wäsche) to run; (fig) to rub off
ab|fertigen vt (Pakete) to prepare for shipping; (an der Grenze) to clear
Abfertigungsschalter m (am Flughafen) check-in desk
ab|finden (irr) vt to pay off ▷ vr: **sich mit etw ~** to come to terms with sth
Abfindung f (Entschädigung) compensation; (von Angestellten) severance (pay)
ab|fliegen (irr) vi (Flugzeug) to take off; (Passagier a.) to fly off
Abflug m departure; (Start) takeoff
Abflughalle f departure lounge
Abflugzeit f departure time
Abfluss m drain; (am Waschbecken) drain
Abflussrohr nt drainpipe; (außen) downspout
ab|fragen vt to test; (Inform) to call up
ab|führen vi (Med) to have a laxative effect ▷ vt (Steuern, Gebühren) to pay; **jdn ~ lassen** to take sb into custody
Abführmittel nt laxative
Abgabe f handing in; (von Ball) pass; (Steuer) tax; (einer Erklärung) making
abgabenfrei adj tax-free
abgabenpflichtig adj taxable, subject to tax
Abgase pl (Auto) exhaust fumes pl
Abgas(sonder)untersuchung f exhaust

emission test

ab|geben (*irr*) *vt* (*Gepäck, Schlüssel*) to leave (*bei* with); (*Schularbeit etc*) to hand in; (*Wärme*) to give off; (*Erklärung, Urteil*) to make ▷ *vr*: **sich mit jdm ~** to associate with sb; **sich mit etw ~** to occupy oneself with sth

abgebildet *adj*: **wie oben ~** as shown above

ab|gehen (*irr*) *vi* (*Post*) to go; (*Knopf etc*) to come off; (*abgezogen werden*) to be taken off; (*Straße*) to branch off; **von der Schule ~** to leave school; **sie geht mir ab** I really miss her; **was geht denn hier ab?** (*fam*) what's going on here?

abgehetzt *adj* exhausted

abgelaufen *adj* (*Pass*) expired; (*Zeit, Frist*) up; **die Milch ist ~** the milk is past its sell-by date

abgelegen *adj* remote

abgemacht *interj* OK, it's a deal, that's settled, then

abgeneigt *adj*: **einer Sache** (*dat*) **~ sein** to be averse to sth; **ich wäre nicht ~, das zu tun** I wouldn't mind doing that

Abgeordnete(r) *mf* Representative

abgepackt *adj* prepacked

abgerissen *adj*: **der Knopf ist ~** the button has come off

abgesehen *adj*: **es auf jdn/etw ~ haben** to be after sb/sth; **~ von** apart from

abgespannt *adj* (*Person*) exhausted, worn out

abgestanden *adj* stale; (*Bier*) flat

abgestorben *adj* (*Pflanze*) dead; (*Finger*) numb

abgestumpft *adj* (*Person*) insensitive

abgetragen *adj* (*Kleidung*) worn

ab|gewöhnen *vt*: **jdm etw ~** to cure sb of sth; **sich etw ~** to give sth up

ab|haken *vt* to check off; **das Thema ist schon abgehakt** that's been dealt with

ab|halten (*irr*) *vt* (*Versammlung*) to hold; **jdn von etw ~** (*fernhalten*) to keep sb away from sth; (*hindern*) to keep sb from sth

abhanden *adj*: **~ kommen** to get lost

Abhang *m* slope

ab|hängen *vt* (*Bild*) to take down; (*Anhänger*) to uncouple; (*Verfolger*) to shake off ▷ *vi* (*irr*): **von jdm/etw ~** to depend on sb/sth; **das hängt davon ab, ob ...** it depends (on) whether ...

abhängig *adj* dependent (*von* on)

ab|hauen (*irr*) *vt* (*abschlagen*) to cut off ▷ *vi* (*fam: verschwinden*) to run off; **hau ab!** get lost!, beat it!

ab|heben (*irr*) *vt* (*Geld*) to withdraw; (*Telefonhörer, Spielkarte*) to pick up ▷ *vi* (*Flugzeug*) to take off; (*Rakete*) to lift off; (*Karten*) to cut

ab|holen *vt* to collect; (*am Bahnhof etc*) to meet; (*mit dem Auto*) to pick up

Abholmarkt *m* cash and carry

ab|horchen *vt* (*Med*) to listen to

ab|hören *vt* (*Vokabeln*) to test; (*Telefongespräch*) to tap; (*Tonband etc*) to listen to

Abitur (*-s, -e*) *nt* German graduation examination, ≈ High School Diploma

ab|kaufen *vt*: **jdm etw ~** to buy sth from sb; **das kauf ich dir nicht ab!** (*fam: glauben*) I don't believe you

ab|klingen (*irr*) *vi* (*Schmerz*) to ease; (*Wirkung*) to wear off

ab|kommen (*irr*) *vi* to get away; **von der Straße ~** to leave the road; **von einem Plan ~** to give up a plan; **vom Thema ~** to stray from the point

Abkommen (*-s, -*) *nt* agreement

ab|koppeln *vt* (*Anhänger*) to unhitch

ab|kratzen *vt* to scrape off ▷ *vi* (*fam: sterben*) to kick the bucket, to croak

ab|kühlen *vi, vt* to cool down ▷ *vr*: **sich ~** to cool down

ab|kürzen *vt* (*Wort*) to abbreviate; **den Weg ~** to take a short cut

Abkürzung *f* (*Wort*) abbreviation; (*Weg*) short cut

ab|laden (*irr*) *vt* to unload

Ablage *f* (*für Akten*) tray; (*Aktenordnung*) filing system

Ablauf *m* (*Abfluss*) drain; (*von Ereignissen*) course; (*einer Frist, Zeit*) expiration

ab|laufen (*irr*) *vi* (*abfließen*) to drain away; (*Ereignisse*) to happen; (*Frist, Zeit, Pass*) to expire

ab|legen *vt* to put down; (*Kleider*) to take off; (*Gewohnheit*) to get out of; (*Prüfung*) to take; (*Akten*) to file away ▷ *vi* (*Schiff*) to cast off

ab|lehnen *vt* to reject; (*Einladung*) to decline; (*missbilligen*) to disapprove of; (*Bewerber*) to turn down ▷ *vi* to decline

ab|lenken vt to distract; **jdn von der Arbeit ~** to distract sb from their work; **vom Thema ~** to change the subject

Ablenkung f distraction

ab|lesen vt (*Text, Rede*) to read; **das Gas/den Strom ~** to read the gas/electricity meter

ab|liefern vt to deliver

ab|machen vt (*entfernen*) to take off; (*vereinbaren*) to agree

Abmachung f agreement

ab|melden vt (*Zeitung*) to cancel; (*Auto*) to take off the road ▷ vr: **sich ~** to give notice of one's departure; (*im Hotel*) to check out; (*vom Verein*) to cancel one's membership

ab|messen (*irr*) vt to measure

ab|nehmen (*irr*) vt to take off, to remove; (*Hörer*) to pick up; (*Führerschein*) to take away; (*Geld*) to get (*jdm* out of sb); (*kaufen, umg: glauben*) to buy (*jdm* from sb) ▷ vi to decrease; (*schlanker werden*) to lose weight; (*Tel*) to pick up the phone; **fünf Kilo ~** to lose five kilos

Abneigung f dislike (*gegen* of); (*stärker*) aversion (*gegen* to)

ab|nutzen vt to wear out ▷ vr: **sich ~** to wear out

Abonnement (*-s, -s*) nt subscription

Abonnent(in) m(f) subscriber

abonnieren vt to subscribe to

ab|raten (*irr*) vi: **jdm von etw ~** to advise sb against sth

ab|räumen vt: **den Tisch ~** to clear the table; **das Geschirr ~** to clear away the dishes; **sie hat bei der Preisverleihung abgeräumt** (*Preis etc*) she cleaned up at the award ceremony

Abrechnung f settlement; (*Rechnung*) check

ab|regen vr: **sich ~** (*fam*) to calm (*o* to cool) down; **reg dich ab!** take it easy!

Abreise f departure

ab|reisen vi to leave (*nach* for)

Abreisetag m day of departure

ab|reißen (*irr*) vt (*Haus*) to tear down; (*Blatt*) to tear off; **den Kontakt nicht ~ lassen** to stay in touch ▷ vi (*Knopf etc*) to come off

ab|runden vt: **eine Zahl nach oben/unten ~** to round a number up/down

abrupt adj abrupt

ABS nt (*abk*) (= *Antiblockiersystem*) (*Auto*) ABS

Abs. (*abk*) = **Absender** from

ab|sagen vt to cancel, to call off; (*Einladung*) to turn down ▷ vi (*ablehnen*) to decline; **ich muss leider ~** I'm afraid I can't come

Absatz m (*Comm*) sales pl; (*neuer Abschnitt*) paragraph; (*Schuh*) heel

ab|schaffen vt to abolish, to do away with

ab|schalten vt, vi (*a. fig*) to switch off

ab|schätzen vt to estimate; (*Lage*) to assess

abscheulich adj disgusting

ab|schicken vt to send off

ab|schieben (*irr*) vt (*ausweisen*) to deport

Abschied (*-(e)s, -e*) m parting; **~ nehmen** to say good-bye (*von jdm* to sb)

Abschiedsfeier f farewell party

Abschlagszahlung f advance (payment)

ab|schleppen vt to tow

Abschleppseil nt towrope

Abschleppwagen m tow truck

ab|schließen (*irr*) vt (*Tür*) to lock; (*beenden*) to conclude, to finish; (*Vertrag, Handel*) to conclude

Abschluss m (*Beendigung*) close, conclusion; (*von Vertrag, Handel*) conclusion

ab|schmecken vt (*kosten*) to taste; (*würzen*) to season

ab|schminken vr: **sich ~** to take one's make-up off ▷ vt (*fam*): **sich** (*dat*) **etw ~** to get sth out of one's head

ab|schnallen vr: **sich ~** to unbuckle one's seatbelt

ab|schneiden (*irr*) vt to cut off ▷ vi: **gut/schlecht ~** to do well/badly

Abschnitt m (*von Buch, Text*) section; (*Kontrollabschnitt*) stub

ab|schrauben vt to unscrew

ab|schrecken vt to deter, to put off

ab|schreiben (*irr*) vt to copy (*bei, von* from, off); (*verloren geben*) to write off; (*Comm: absetzen*) to deduct

abschüssig adj steep

ab|schwächen vt to lessen; (*Behauptung, Kritik*) to tone down

ab|schwellen (*irr*) vi (*Entzündung*) to go down; (*Lärm*) to die down

absehbar adj foreseeable; **in ~er Zeit** in the foreseeable future

ab|sehen (*irr*) vt (*Ende, Folgen*) to foresee ▷ vi: **von etw ~** to refrain from sth

abseits adv out of the way; (*Sport*) offside ▷ prep (+gen) away from

Abseits nt (*Sport*) offside

Abseitsfalle f (*Sport*) offside trap

ab|senden (*irr*) vt to send off; (*Post*) to mail

Absender(in) (-s, -) *m(f)* sender

ab|setzen *vt* (*Glas, Brille etc*) to put down; (*aussteigen lassen*) to drop (off); (*Comm*) to sell; (*Fin*) to deduct; (*streichen*) to drop ▷ *vr:* **sich ~** (*sich entfernen*) to clear off; (*sich ablagern*) to be deposited

Absicht *f* intention; **mit ~** on purpose

absichtlich *adj* intentional, deliberate

absolut *adj* absolute

ab|specken *vi* (*fam*) to lose weight

ab|speichern *vt* (*Inform*) to save

ab|sperren *vt* to block (*o* to close) off; (*Tür*) to lock

Absperrung *f* (*Vorgang*) blocking (*o* closing) off; (*Sperre*) barricade

ab|spielen *vt* (*CD etc*) to play ▷ *vr:* **sich ~** to happen

ab|springen (*irr*) *vi* to jump down/off; (*von etw Geplantem*) to drop out (*von* of)

ab|spülen *vt* to rinse; (*Geschirr*) to wash (up)

Abstand *m* distance; (*zeitlich*) intermission; **~ halten** to keep one's distance

ab|stauben *vt, vi* to dust; (*fam: stehlen*) to swipe

Abstecher (-s, -) *m* detour

ab|steigen (*irr*) *vi* (*vom Rad etc*) to get off, to dismount; (*in Gasthof*) to stay (*in +dat* at)

ab|stellen *vt* (*niederstellen*) to put down; (*Auto*) to park; (*ausschalten*) to turn (*o* to switch) off; (*Missstand, Unsitte*) to stop

Abstellraum *m* store room

Abstieg (-(e)s, -e) *m* (*vom Berg*) descent

ab|stimmen *vi* to vote ▷ *vt:* **~** (**auf** +*akk*) (*Termine, Ziele*) to fit in (with); **Dinge aufeinander ~** to coordinate things ▷ *vr:* **sich ~** to come to an agreement (*o* arrangement)

abstoßend *adj* repulsive

abstrakt *adj* abstract

ab|streiten (*irr*) *vt* to deny

Abstrich *m* (*Med*) smear; **~e machen** to cut back (*an +dat* on); (*weniger erwarten*) to lower one's sights

Absturz *m* fall; (*Aviat, Inform*) crash

ab|stürzen *vi* to fall; (*Aviat, Inform*) to crash

absurd *adj* absurd

Abszess (-es, -e) *m* abscess

ab|tauen *vt, vi* to thaw; (*Kühlschrank*) to defrost

Abtei (-, -en) *f* abbey

Abteil (-(e)s, -e) *nt* compartment

Abteilung *f* (*in Firma, Kaufhaus*) depart-

ment; (*in Krankenhaus*) section

ab|treiben (*irr*) *vt* (*Kind*) to abort ▷ *vi* to be driven off course; (*Med: Abtreibung vornehmen*) to perform an abortion; (*Abtreibung vornehmen lassen*) to have an abortion

Abtreibung *f* abortion

ab|trocknen *vt* to dry

ab|warten *vt* to wait for; **das bleibt abzuwarten** that remains to be seen ▷ *vi* to wait

abwärts *adv* down

ab|waschen (*irr*) *vt* (*Schmutz*) to wash off; (*Geschirr*) to wash (up)

Abwasser (-s, *Abwässer*) *nt* sewage

ab|wechseln *vr:* **sich ~** to alternate; **sich mit jdm ~** to take turns with sb

abwechselnd *adv* alternately

Abwechslung *f* change; **zur ~** for a change

ab|weisen (*irr*) *vt* to turn away; (*Antrag*) to turn down

abweisend *adj* unfriendly

abwesend *adj* absent

Abwesenheit *f* absence

ab|wiegen (*irr*) *vt* to weigh (out)

ab|wimmeln *vt* (*fam*): **jdn ~** to get rid of sb, to ditch sb

ab|wischen *vt* (*Gesicht, Tisch etc*) to wipe; (*Schmutz*) to wipe off

ab|zählen *vt* to count; (*Geld*) to count out

Abzeichen *nt* badge

ab|zeichnen *vt* to draw, to copy; (*Dokument*) to initial ▷ *vr:* **sich ~** to stand out; (*fig: bevorstehen*) to loom

ab|ziehen (*irr*) *vt* to take off; (*Bett*) to strip; (*Schlüssel*) to take out; (*subtrahieren*) to take away, to subtract ▷ *vi* to go away

Abzug *m* (*Foto*) print; (*Öffnung*) vent; (*Truppen*) withdrawal; (*Betrag*) deduction; **nach ~ der Kosten** after deducting expenses

abzüglich *prep* (+*gen*) minus; **~ 20% Rabatt** less 20% discount

ab|zweigen *vi* to branch off ▷ *vt* to set aside

Abzweigung *f* intersection

Accessoires *pl* accessories *pl*

ach *interj* oh; **ach so!** I see!; **ach was** (*Überraschung*) really?; (*Ärger*) don't talk nonsense

Achse (-, -n) *f* axis; (*Auto*) axle

Achsel (-, -n) *f* shoulder; (*Achselhöhle*) armpit

Achsenbruch *m* (*Auto*) broken axle

acht *num* eight; **heute in ~ Tagen** in a

week('s time), a week from today

Acht (-) *f:* **sich in ~ nehmen** to be careful (*vor +dat* of), to watch out (*vor +dat* for); **etw außer ~ lassen** to disregard sth

achte(r, s) *adj* eighth; *siehe auch* **dritte**

Achtel (-s, -) *nt* (*Bruchteil*) eighth; (*Wein etc*) eighth of a liter; (*Glas Wein*) ≈ small glass

achten *vt* to respect ▷ *vi:* ~ **(auf +akk)** to pay attention (to)

Achterbahn *f* roller coaster

acht|geben (*irr*) *vi:* ~ **(auf +akk)** to take care (of)

achthundert *num* eight hundred

achtmal *adv* eight times

Achtung *f* attention; (*Ehrfurcht*) respect ▷ *interj* look out

achtzehn *num* eighteen

achtzehnte(r, s) *adj* eighteenth; *siehe auch* **dritte**

achtzig *num* eighty; **in den ~er Jahren** in the eighties

achtzigste(r, s) *adj* eightieth

Acker (-s, *Äcker*) *m* field

Action (-, -s) *f* (*fam*) action

Actionfilm *m* action film

Adapter (-s, -) *m* adapter

addieren *vt* to add (up)

Adel (-s) *m* nobility

adelig *adj* noble

Ader (-, -n) *f* vein

Adjektiv *nt* adjective

Adler (-s, -) *m* eagle

adoptieren *vt* to adopt

Adoption *f* adoption

Adoptiveltern *pl* adoptive parents *pl*

Adoptivkind *nt* adopted child

Adrenalin (-s) *nt* adrenalin

Adressbuch *nt* directory; (*persönliches*) address book

Adresse (-, -n) *f* address

adressieren *vt:* ~ **(an +akk)** to address (to)

Advent (-s, -) *m* Advent

Adventskranz *m* Advent wreath

Adverb *nt* adverb

Aerobic (-s) *nt* aerobics *sing*

Affäre (-, -n) *f* affair

Affe (-n, -n) *m* monkey

Afghanistan (-s) *nt* Afghanistan

Afrika (-s) *nt* Africa

Afrikaner(in) (-s, -) *m(f)* African

afrikanisch *adj* African

After (-s, -) *m* anus

Aftershave (-(s), -s) *nt* aftershave

AG (-, -s) *f* (*abk*) = **Aktiengesellschaft** corp.

Agent(in) *m(f)* agent

Agentur *f* agency

aggressiv *adj* aggressive

Ägypten (-s) *nt* Egypt

ah *interj* ah, ooh

äh *interj* (*Sprechpause*) er, um; (*angeekelt*) ugh

aha *interj* I see, aha

ähneln *vi* (+*dat*) to be like, to resemble ▷ *vr:* **sich** ~ to be alike (*o* similar)

ahnen *vt* to suspect; **du ahnst es nicht!** would you believe it?

ähnlich *adj* similar (*dat* to); **jdm ~ sehen** to look like sb

Ähnlichkeit *f* similarity

Ahnung *f* idea; (*Vermutung*) suspicion; **keine ~!** no idea!

ahnungslos *adj* unsuspecting

Ahorn (-s, -e) *m* maple

Aids (-) *nt* AIDS

aidskrank *adj* suffering from AIDS

Aidstest *m* AIDS test

Airbag (-s, -s) *m* (*Auto*) airbag

Airbus *m* airbus

Akademie (-, -n) *f* academy

Akademiker(in) (-s, -) *m(f)* (university) graduate

akklimatisieren *vr:* **sich** ~ to acclimatize oneself

Akkordeon (-s, -s) *nt* accordion

Akku (-s, -s) *m* rechargeable battery

Akkusativ *m* accusative (case)

Akne (-, -) *f* acne

Akrobat(in) (-s, -en) *m(f)* acrobat

Akt (-(e)s, -e) *m* act; (*Kunst*) nude

Akte (-, -n) *f* file; **etw zu den ~n legen** (*a. fig*) to file sth away

Aktenkoffer *m* briefcase

Aktie (-, -n) *f* stock

Aktiengesellschaft *f* corporation

Aktion *f* (*Kampagne*) campaign; (*Einsatz*) operation

Aktionär(in) (-s, -e) *m(f)* stockholder

aktiv *adj* active

aktivieren *vt* to activate

aktualisieren *vt* to update

aktuell *adj* (*Thema*) topical; (*modern*) up-to-date; (*Problem*) current; **nicht mehr ~** no longer relevant

Akupunktur *f* acupuncture

Akustik *f* acoustics *sing*

akustisch *adj* acoustic

akut *adj* acute

AKW (-s, -s) *nt* (*abk*) = **Atomkraftwerk** nuclear power plant

Akzent (-(e)s, -e) m̓ accent; (Betonung) stress; **mit starkem Südstaaten ~** with a strong southern accent

akzeptieren vt to accept

Alarm (-(e)s, -e) m alarm

Alarmanlage f alarm system

alarmieren vt to alarm; **die Polizei ~** to call the police

Albanien (-s) nt Albania

Albatros (-ses, -se) m albatross

albern adj silly

Albtraum m nightmare

Album (-s, Alben) nt album

Algen pl algae pl; (Meeresalgen) seaweed sing

Algerien (-s) nt Algeria

Alibi (-s, -s) nt alibi

Alimente pl child support sing

Alkohol (-s, -e) m alcohol

alkoholfrei adj non-alcoholic; **~es Getränk** soft drink

Alkoholiker(in) (-s, -) m(f) alcoholic

alkoholisch adj alcoholic

Alkoholtest m alcohol test

All (-s) nt universe

SCHLÜSSELWORT

alle(r, s) adj **1** (sämtliche) all; **wir alle** all of us; **alle Kinder waren da** all the children were there; **alle Kinder mögen ...** all children like ...; **alle beide** both of us/them; **sie kamen alle** they all came; **alles Gute** all the best; **alles in allem** all in all

2 (mit Zeit- oder Maßangaben) every; **alle vier Jahre** every four years; **alle fünf Meter** every five meters

▷ pron everything; **alles, was er sagt** everything he says, all that he says

▷ adv (zu Ende, aufgebraucht) finished; **die Milch ist alle** the milk's all gone, there's no milk left; **etw alle machen** to finish sth up

Allee (-, -n) f avenue

allein adj, adv alone; (ohne Hilfe) on one's own, by oneself; **nicht ~** (nicht nur) not only

alleinerziehend adj: **~e Mutter** single mother

Alleinerziehende(r) mf single mother/father/parent

alleinstehend adj single, unmarried

allerbeste(r, s) adj very best

allerdings adv (zwar) admittedly; (gewiss) sure

allererste(r, s) adj very first; **zu allererst** first of all

Allergie f allergy

Allergiker(in) (-s, -) m(f) allergy sufferer

allergisch adj allergic (gegen to)

allerhand adj (inv) (fam) all sorts of; **das ist doch ~!** (Vorwurf) that's the limit!

Allerheiligen (-) nt All Saints' Day

allerhöchste(r, s) adj very highest

allerhöchstens adv at the very most

allerlei adj (inv) all sorts of

allerletzte(r, s) adj very last

allerwenigste(r, s) adj very least

alles pron everything; **~ in allem** all in all; siehe auch **alle**

Alleskleber (-s, -) m all-purpose glue

allgemein adj general; **im A~en** in general

Allgemeinarzt m, **Allgemeinärztin** f family practitioner

Alligator (-s, -en) m alligator

alljährlich adj annual

allmählich adj gradual ▷ adv gradually

Allradantrieb m all-wheel drive

Alltag m everyday life

alltäglich adj everyday; (gewöhnlich) ordinary; (tagtäglich) daily

allzu adv all too

Allzweckreiniger (-s, -) m multi-purpose cleaner

Alpen pl: **die ~** the Alps pl

Alphabet (-(e)s, -e) nt alphabet

alphabetisch adj alphabetical

Alptraum m siehe **Albtraum**

SCHLÜSSELWORT

als konj **1** (zeitlich) when; (gleichzeitig) as; **damals, als ...** (in the days) when ...; **gerade, als ...** just as ...

2 (in der Eigenschaft) than; **als Antwort** as an answer; **als Kind** as a child

3 (bei Vergleichen) than; **ich kam später als er** I came later than he (did) o later than him; **lieber ... als ...** rather ... than ...; **nichts als Ärger** nothing but trouble

4: **als ob/wenn** as if

also konj (folglich) so, therefore ▷ adv, interj so; **~ gut** (o schön) okay then

alt adj old; **wie alt sind Sie?** how old are you?; **28 Jahre alt** 28 years old; **vier Jahre älter** four years older

Altar (-(e)s, Altäre) m altar

Alter (-s, -) nt age; (hohes alter) old age; **im ~ von**

at the age of; **er ist in meinem ~** he's my age

alternativ *adj* alternative; (*umweltbewusst*) ecologically minded; (*Landwirtschaft*) organic

Alternative *f* alternative

Altersheim *nt* assisted-living facility; (*für Pflegebedürftige*) nursing home

Altglas *nt* used glass

altmodisch *adj* old-fashioned

Altpapier *nt* waste paper

Altstadt *f* old town

Alt-Taste *f* Alt key

Alufolie *f* tin foil

Aluminium (-*s*) *nt* aluminum

Alzheimerkrankheit *f* Alzheimer's (disease)

am *kontr von* **an dem; am 2. Januar** on January 2nd; **am Morgen** in the morning; **am Strand** on the beach; **am Bahnhof** at the station; **was gefällt Ihnen am besten?** what do you like best?; **am besten bleiben wir hier** it would be best if we stayed here

Amateur(in) *m(f)* amateur

ambulant *adj* outpatient; **kann ich ~ behandelt werden?** can I have it done as an outpatient?

Ambulanz *f* (*Krankenwagen*) ambulance; (*in der Klinik*) outpatient department

Ameise (-, -*n*) *f* ant

amen *interj* amen

Amerika (-*s*) *nt* America

Amerikaner(in) (-*s*, -) *m(f)* American

amerikanisch *adj* American

Ampel (-, -*n*) *f* traffic light

Amphitheater *nt* amphitheater

Amsel (-, -*n*) *f* blackbird

Amt (-(*e*)*s*, *Ämter*) *nt* (*Dienststelle*) office, department; (*Posten*) post

amtlich *adj* official

Amtszeichen *nt* (*Tel*) dial tone

amüsant *adj* amusing

amüsieren *vt* to amuse ▷ *vr:* **sich ~** to enjoy oneself, to have a good time

SCHLÜSSELWORT

an *prep* +*dat* **1** (*räumlich: wo?*) at; (*auf, bei*) on; (*nahe bei*) near; **an diesem Ort** at this place; **an der Wand** on the wall; **zu nahe an etw** too near to sth; **unten am Fluss** down by the river; **Köln liegt am Rhein** Cologne is on the Rhine

2 (*zeitlich: wann?*) on; **an diesem Tag** on

this day; **an Ostern** at Easter

3: arm an Fett low in fat; **an etw sterben** to die of sth; **an (und für) sich** actually

▷ *prep* +*akk* **1** (*räumlich: wohin?*) to; **er ging ans Fenster** he went (over) to the window; **etw an die Wand hängen/schreiben** to hang/write sth on the wall

2 (*woran?*): **an etw denken** to think of sth

3 (*gerichtet an*) to; **ein Gruß/eine Frage an dich** greetings/a question to you

▷ *adv* **1** (*ungefähr*) about; **an die hundert** about a hundred

2 (*auf Fahrplänen*): **Frankfurt an 18.30** arriving Frankfurt 6:30 p.m.

3 (*ab*): **von dort/heute an** from there/today onwards

4 (*angeschaltet, angezogen*) on; **das Licht ist an** the light is on; **ohne etwas an** with nothing on; *siehe auch* **am**

anal *adj* anal

analog *adj* analogous; (*Inform*) analog

Analyse (-, -*n*) *f* analysis

analysieren *vt* to analyze

Ananas (-, - o -*se*) *f* pineapple

an|baggern *vt* (*fam*) to come on to

Anbau *m* (*Agr*) cultivation; (*Gebäude*) extension, annex; (*Haus*) addition

an|bauen *vt* (*Agr*) to cultivate; (*Gebäudeteil*) to build on

an|behalten (*irr*) *vt* to keep on

anbei *adv* enclosed; **~ sende ich ...** please find enclosed ...

an|beten *vt* to worship

an|bieten (*irr*) *vt* to offer ▷ *vr:* **sich ~** to volunteer

an|binden (*irr*) *vt* to tie up

Anblick *m* sight

an|braten (*irr*) *vt* to brown

an|brechen (*irr*) *vt* to start; (*Vorräte, Ersparnisse*) to break into; (*Flasche, Packung*) to open ▷ *vi* to start; (*Tag*) to break; (*Nacht*) to fall

an|brennen (*irr*) *vt, vi* to burn; **das Fleisch schmeckt angebrannt** the meat tastes burned

an|bringen (*irr*) *vt* (*herbeibringen*) to bring; (*befestigen*) to fix, to attach

Andacht (-, -*en*) *f* devotion; (*Gottesdienst*) prayers *pl*

an|dauern *vi* to continue, to go on

andauernd *adj* continual

Andenken (-*s*, -) *nt* memory; (*Gegenstand*) souvenir

andere(r, s) *adj* (*weitere*) other; (*verschie-*

den) different; (*folgend*) next; **am ~n Tag**
the next day; **von etw/jdm ~m sprechen** to
talk about sth/sb else; **unter ~m** among
other things

andererseits *adv* on the other hand

ändern *vt* to alter, to change ▷ *vr*: **sich ~** to
change

andernfalls *adv* otherwise

anders *adv* differently (*als* from); **jemand/
irgendwo ~** someone/somewhere else; **sie
ist ~ als ihre Schwester** she's not like her
sister; **es geht nicht ~** there's no other
way

anders(he)rum *adv* the other way around

anderswo *adv* somewhere else

anderthalb *num* one and a half

Änderung *f* change, alteration

an|deuten *vt* to indicate; (*Wink geben*) to
hint at

Andorra (*-s*) *nt* Andorra

Andrang *m*: **es herrschte großer ~** there
was a huge crowd

an|drohen *vt*: **jdm etw ~** to threaten sb with
sth

aneinander *adv* at/on/to one another (*o*
each other); **~ denken** to think of each
other; **sich ~ gewöhnen** to get used to
each other

aneinander|geraten (*irr*) *vi* to clash

aneinander|legen *vt* to put together

an|erkennen (*irr*) *vt* (*Staat, Zeugnis etc*) to
recognize; (*würdigen*) to appreciate

Anerkennung *f* recognition; (*Würdigung*)
appreciation

an|fahren (*irr*) *vt* (*fahren gegen*) to run into;
(*Ort, Hafen*) to stop (*o* call) at; (*liefern*) to
deliver; **jdn** ~ (*fig: schimpfen*) to snap at
sb; (*fam*) to lay into sb ▷ *vi* to start; (*losfahren*) to drive off

Anfall *m* (*Med*) attack

anfällig *adj* delicate; (*Maschine*) temperamental; **~ für** prone to

Anfang (*-(e)s, Anfänge*) *m* beginning, start;
zu/am ~ to start with; **~ Mai** at the beginning of May; **sie ist ~ 20** she's in her early
twenties

an|fangen (*irr*) *vt, vi* to begin, to start;
damit kann ich nichts ~ that's no use to
me

Anfänger(in) (*-s, -*) *m(f)* beginner

anfangs *adv* at first

Anfangsbuchstabe *m* first (*o* initial) letter

an|fassen *vt* (*berühren*) to touch ▷ *vi*:
kannst du mal mit ~? can you give me a

hand?

Anflug *m* (*Aviat*) approach; (*Hauch*) trace

an|fordern *vt* to demand

Anforderung *f* request (*von* for); (*Anspruch*)
demand

Anfrage *f* inquiry

an|freunden *vr*: **sich mit jdm ~** to make (*o*
to become) friends with sb

an|fühlen *vr*: **sich ~** to feel; **es fühlt sich
gut an** it feels good

Anführungszeichen *pl* quotation marks
pl

Angabe *f* (*Tech*) specification; (*fam: Prahlerei*) showing off; (*Tennis*) serve; **~n** *pl* (*Auskunft*) particulars *pl*; **die ~n waren falsch**
(*Info*) the information was wrong

an|geben (*irr*) *vt* (*Name, Grund*) to give;
(*zeigen*) to indicate; (*bestimmen*) to set
▷ *vi* (*fam: prahlen*) to boast; (*Sport*) to
serve

Angeber(in) (*-s, -*) *m(f)* (*fam*) show-off

angeblich *adj* alleged

angeboren *adj* inborn

Angebot *nt* offer; (*Comm*) supply (*an +dat*
of); **~ und Nachfrage** supply and demand

angebracht *adj* appropriate

angebunden *adj*: **kurz ~** curt

angeheitert *adj* tipsy

an|gehen (*irr*) *vt* to concern; **das geht dich
nichts an** that's none of your business; **ein
Problem ~** to tackle a problem; **was ihn
angeht** as far as he's concerned, as for him
▷ *vi* (*Feuer*) to catch; (*fam: beginnen*) to
begin

angehend *adj* prospective

Angehörige(r) *mf* relative

Angeklagte(r) *mf* accused, defendant

Angel (*-, -n*) *f* fishing rod; (*an der Tür*)
hinge

Angelegenheit *f* affair, matter

Angelhaken *m* fish hook

angeln *vt* to catch ▷ *vi* to fish

Angeln (*-s*) *nt* angling, fishing

Angelrute (*-, -n*) *f* fishing rod

angemessen *adj* appropriate, suitable

angenehm *adj* pleasant; **~!** (*bei Vorstellung*)
pleased to meet you

angenommen *adj* assumed ▷ *conj*: **~, es
regnet, was machen wir dann?** suppose it
rains, what do we do then?

angesehen *adj* respected

angesichts *prep* (*+gen*) in view of, considering

Angestellte(r) *mf* employee

angetan *adj*: **von jdm/etw ~ sein** to be

a

impressed by (*o* taken with) sb/sth

angewiesen *adj*: **auf jdn/etw ~ sein** to be dependent on sb/sth

an|gewöhnen *vt*: **sich etw ~** to get used to doing sth

Angewohnheit *f* habit

Angina (*-, Anginen*) *f* tonsillitis

Angina Pectoris (*-*) *f* angina

Angler(in) (*-s, -*) *m(f)* angler

Angora (*-s*) *nt* angora

an|greifen (*irr*) *vt* to attack; (*anfassen*) to touch; (*beschädigen*) to damage

Angriff *m* attack; **etw in ~ nehmen** to get started on sth

Angst (*-, Ängste*) *f* fear; **~ haben** to be afraid (*o* scared) (*vor +dat* of); **jdm ~ machen** to scare sb

ängstigen *vt* to frighten ▷ *vr*: **sich ~** to worry (*um, wegen +dat* about)

ängstlich *adj* nervous; (*besorgt*) worried

an|haben (*irr*) *vt* (*Kleidung*) to have on, to wear; (*Licht*) to have on

an|halten (*irr*) *vi* to stop; (*andauern*) to continue

anhaltend *adj* continuous

Anhalter(in) (*-s, -*) *m(f)* hitchhiker; **per ~ fahren** to hitchhike

anhand *prep* (*+gen*) with; **~ von** by means of

an|hängen *vt* to hang up; (*Eisenb: Wagen*) to couple; (*Zusatz*) to add (on); **jdm etw ~** (*fam: unterschieben*) to pin sth on sb; **eine Datei an eine E-Mail ~** (*Inform*) to attach a file to an e-mail

Anhänger (*-s, -*) *m* (*Auto*) trailer; (*am Koffer*) tag; (*Schmuck*) pendant

Anhänger(in) (*-s, -*) *m(f)* supporter

Anhängerkupplung *f* trailer hitch

anhänglich *adj* affectionate; (*pej*) clinging

Anhieb *m*: **auf ~** right away; **das kann ich nicht auf ~ sagen** I can't say offhand

an|himmeln *vt* to worship, to idolize

an|hören *vt* to listen to ▷ *vr*: **sich ~** to sound; **das hört sich gut an** that sounds good

Animateur(in) *m(f)* host/hostess

Anis (*-es, -e*) *m* aniseed

Anker (*-s, -*) *m* anchor

ankern *vt, vi* to anchor

Ankerplatz *m* anchorage

an|klicken *vt* (*Inform*) to click on

an|klopfen *vi*: **~ (an +akk)** to knock (on)

an|kommen (*irr*) *vi* to arrive; **bei jdm gut ~** to go down well with sb; **es kommt darauf an** it depends (*ob* on whether); **darauf**

kommt es nicht an that doesn't matter

an|kreuzen *vt* to mark with a cross

an|kündigen *vt* to announce

Ankunft (*-, Ankünfte*) *f* arrival

Ankunftszeit *f* arrival time

Anlage *f* (*Veranlagung*) disposition; (*Begabung*) talent; (*Park*) gardens *pl*, grounds *pl*; (*zu Brief etc*) enclosure; (*Stereoanlage*) stereo (system); (*Tech*) plant; (*Fin*) investment

Anlass (*-es, Anlässe*) *m* cause (*zu* for); (*Ereignis*) occasion; **aus diesem ~** for this reason

an|lassen (*irr*) *vt* (*Motor*) to start; (*Licht, Kleidung*) to leave on

Anlasser (*-s, -*) *m* (*Auto*) starter

anlässlich *prep* (*+gen*) on the occasion of

Anlauf *m* run-up

an|laufen (*irr*) *vi* to begin; (*Film*) to open; (*Fenster*) to fog up; (*Metall*) to tarnish

an|legen *vt* to put (*an +akk* against/on); (*Schmuck*) to put on; (*Garten*) to lay out; (*Geld*) to invest; (*Gewehr*) to aim (*auf +akk* at); **es auf etw** (*akk*) **~** to be out for sth ▷ *vi* (*Schiff*) to berth, to dock ▷ *vr*: **sich mit jdm ~** (*fam*) to pick a fight with sb

Anlegestelle *f* moorings *pl*

an|lehnen *vt* to lean (*an +akk* against); (*Tür*) to leave ajar ▷ *vr*: **sich ~** to lean (*an +akk* against)

an|leiern *vt*: **etw ~** (*fam*) to get sth going

Anleitung *f* instructions *pl*

Anliegen (*-s, -*) *nt* matter; (*Wunsch*) request

Anlieger(in) (*-s, -*) *m(f)* resident; **~ frei** residents only

an|lügen (*irr*) *vt* to lie to

an|machen *vt* (*befestigen*) to attach; (*einschalten*) to switch on; (*Salat*) to dress; (*fam: aufreizen*) to turn on; (*fam: ansprechen*) to come on to; (*fam: beschimpfen*) to harass

Anmeldeformular *nt* application form; (*bei Amt*) registration form

an|melden *vt* (*Besuch etc*) to announce ▷ *vr*: **sich ~** (*beim Arzt etc*) to make an appointment; (*bei Amt, für Kurs etc*) to register

Anmeldeschluss *m* deadline for applications, registration deadline

Anmeldung *f* registration; (*Antrag*) application

an|nähen *vt*: **einen Knopf an den Mantel ~** to sew a button on (one's coat)

annähernd *adv* roughly; **nicht ~** nowhere near

Annahme (-, -n) *f* acceptance; (*Vermutung*) assumption

annehmbar *adj* acceptable

an|nehmen (*irr*) *vt* to accept; (*Namen*) to take; (*Kind*) to adopt; (*vermuten*) to suppose, to assume

Annonce (-, -n) *f* advertisement

annullieren *vt* to cancel

an|öden *vt* (*fam*) to bore stiff (*o* silly)

anonym *adj* anonymous

Anorak (-s, -s) *m* anorak

an|packen *vt* (*Problem, Aufgabe*) to tackle; **mit ~** to lend a hand

an|passen *vt* (*fig*) to adapt (*dat* to) ▷ *vr*: **sich ~** to adapt (an +*akk* to)

an|pfeifen (*irr*) *vt* (*Fußballspiel*): **das Spiel ~** to start the game

Anpfiff *m* (*Sport*) (starting) whistle; (*Beginn*) kickoff; (*fam: Tadel*) bawling out

an|probieren *vt* to try on

Anrede *f* form of address

an|reden *vt* to address

an|regen *vt* to stimulate

Anregung *f* stimulation; (*Vorschlag*) suggestion

Anreise *f* journey

an|reisen *vi* to arrive

Anreisetag *m* day of arrival

Anreiz *m* incentive

an|richten *vt* (*Speisen*) to prepare; (*Schaden*) to cause

Anruf *m* call

an|rufen (*irr*) *vt* (*Tel*) to call, to phone

ans *kontr von* **an das**

Ansage *f* announcement; (*auf Anrufbeantworter*) recorded message

an|sagen *vt* to announce; **angesagt sein** to be recommended; (*modisch sein*) to be the in thing

an|schaffen *vt* to buy

an|schauen *vt* to look at

Anschein *m* appearance; **dem** *o* **allem ~ nach ...** it looks as if ...; **den ~ erwecken, hart zu arbeiten** to give the impression of working hard

anscheinend *adj* apparent ▷ *adv* apparently

an|schieben (*irr*) *vt*: **könnten Sie mich mal ~?** (*Auto*) could you give me a push?

Anschlag *m* notice; (*Attentat*) attack

an|schlagen (*irr*) *vt* (*Plakat*) to put up; (*beschädigen*) to chip ▷ *vi* (*wirken*) to take effect; **mit etw an etw** (*akk*) **~** to bang sth against sth

an|schließen (*irr*) *vt* (*Elek, Tech*) to connect

(*an* +*akk* to); (*mit Stecker*) to plug in ▷ *vi*, *vr*: **(sich) an etw** (*akk*) **~** (*Gebäude etc*) to adjoin sth; (*zeitlich*) to follow sth ▷ *vr*: **sich ~** to join (*jdm/einer Gruppe* sb/a group)

anschließend *adj* adjacent; (*zeitlich*) subsequent ▷ *adv* afterwards; **~ an** +*akk* following

Anschluss *m* (*Elek, Eisenb*) connection; (*von Wasser, Gas etc*) supply; **im ~ an** +*akk* following; **kein ~ unter dieser Nummer** (*Tel*) the number you have reached is not in service

Anschlussflug *m* connecting flight

an|schnallen *vt* (*Skier*) to put on ▷ *vr*: **sich ~** to fasten one's seat belt

Anschrift *f* address

an|schwellen (*irr*) *vi* to swell (up)

an|sehen (*irr*) *vt* to look at; (*bei etw zuschauen*) to watch; **jdn/etw als etw ~** to look on sb/sth as sth; **das sieht man ihm an** he looks it

an sein (*irr*) *vi siehe* **an**

an|setzen *vt* (*Termin*) to fix; (*zubereiten*) to prepare ▷ *vi* (*anfangen*) to start, to begin; **zu etw ~** to prepare to do sth

Ansicht *f* (*Meinung*) view, opinion; (*Anblick*) sight; **meiner ~ nach** in my opinion; **zur ~** on approval

Ansichtskarte *f* postcard

ansonsten *adv* otherwise

an|spielen *vi*: **auf etw** (*akk*) **~** to allude to sth

Anspielung *f* allusion (*auf* +*akk* to)

an|sprechen (*irr*) *vt* to speak to; (*gefallen*) to appeal to ▷ *vi*: **auf etw** (*akk*) **~** (*Patient*) to respond to sth

ansprechend *adj* attractive

Ansprechpartner(in) *m(f)* contact

an|springen (*irr*) *vi* (*Auto*) to start

Anspruch *m* claim; (*Recht*) right (*auf* +*akk* to); **etw in ~ nehmen** to take advantage of sth; **~ auf etw haben** to be entitled to sth

anspruchslos *adj* undemanding; (*bescheiden*) modest

anspruchsvoll *adj* demanding

Anstalt (-, -en) *f* institution

Anstand *m* decency

anständig *adj* decent; (*fig, fam*) proper; (*groß*) considerable

an|starren *vt* to stare at

anstatt *prep* (+*gen*) instead of

an|stecken *vt* to pin on; (*Med*) to infect; **jdn mit einer Erkältung ~** to pass one's cold on to sb ▷ *vr*: **ich habe mich bei ihm ange-**

steckt I caught it from him ▷ *vi* (*fig*) to be infectious

ansteckend *adj* infectious

Ansteckungsgefahr *f* danger of infection

an|stehen (*irr*) *vi* (*in Warteschlange*) to stand in line; (*erledigt werden müssen*) to be on the agenda

anstelle *prep* (+*gen*) instead of

an|stellen *vt* (*einschalten*) to turn on; (*Arbeit geben*) to employ; (*machen*) to do; **was hast du wieder angestellt?** what have you been up to now? ▷ *vr*: **sich ~** to stand in line; (*fam*): **stell dich nicht so an!** stop making such a fuss!

Anstoß *m* impetus; (*Sport*) kickoff

an|stoßen (*irr*) *vt* to push; (*mit Fuß*) to kick ▷ *vi* to knock, to bump; (*mit Gläsern*) to drink (a toast) (*auf* +*akk* to)

anstößig *adj* offensive; (*Kleidung etc*) indecent

an|strengen *vt* to strain ▷ *vr*: **sich ~** to make an effort

enstrengend *adj* tiring

Antarktis *f* Antarctic

Anteil *m* share (*an* +*dat* in); **~ nehmen an** (+*dat*) (*mitleidig*) to sympathize with; (*sich interessieren*) to take an interest in

Antenne (-, -*n*) *f* antenna

Antibabypille *f*: **die ~** the pill

Antibiotikum (-*s*, *Antibiotika*) *nt* (*Med*) antibiotic

antik *adj* antique

Antilope (-, -*n*) *f* antelope

Antiquariat *nt* (*für Bücher*) second-hand bookstore

Antiquitäten *pl* antiques *pl*

Antiquitätenhändler(in) *m(f)* antique dealer

Antiviren- *adj* (*Inform*) antivirus

Antivirensoftware *f* antivirus software

an|törnen *vt* (*fam*) to turn on

Antrag (-(*e*)*s*, *Anträge*) *m* proposal; (*Pol*) motion; (*Formular*) application form; **einen ~ stellen auf** ((+*akk*)) to make an application for

an|treffen (*irr*) *vt* to find

an|treiben (*irr*) *vt* (*Tech*) to drive; (*anschwemmen*) to wash up; **jdn zur Arbeit ~** to make sb work

an|treten (*irr*) *vt*: **eine Reise ~** to set off on a journey

Antrieb *m* (*Tech*) drive; (*Motivation*) impetus

an|tun (*irr*) *vt*: **jdm etwas ~** to do sth to sb; **sich** (*dat*) **etwas ~** (*Selbstmord begehen*) to kill oneself

Antwort (-, -*en*) *f* answer, reply; **um ~ wird gebeten** RSVP (*répondez s'il vous plaît*)

antworten *vi* to answer, to reply; **jdm ~** to answer sb; **auf etw** (*akk*) **~** to answer sth

an|vertrauen *vt*: **jdm etw ~** to entrust sb with sth

Anwalt (-*s*, *Anwälte*) *m*, **Anwältin** *f* lawyer

an|weisen (*irr*) *vt* (*anleiten*) to instruct; (*zuteilen*) to allocate (*jdm etw* sth to sb)

Anweisung *f* instruction; (*von Geld*) money order

an|wenden (*irr*) *vt* to use; (*Gesetz, Regel*) to apply

Anwender(in) (-*s*, -) *m(f)* user

Anwendung *f* use; (*Inform*) application

anwesend *adj* present

Anwesenheit *f* presence

an|widern *vt* to disgust

Anwohner(in) (-*s*, -) *m(f)* resident

Anzahl *f* number (*an* +*dat* of)

an|zahlen *vt* to pay a deposit on; **100 Euro ~** to put down 100 euros (as a deposit)

Anzahlung *f* deposit, down payment

Anzeichen *nt* sign; (*Med*) symptom

Anzeige (-, -*n*) *f* (*Werbung*) advertisement; (*elektronisch*) display; (*bei Polizei*) report

an|zeigen *vt* (*Temperatur, Zeit*) to indicate, to show; (*elektronisch*) to display; (*bekannt geben*) to announce; **jdn/einen Autodiebstahl bei der Polizei ~** to report sb/a stolen car to the police

an|ziehen (*irr*) *vt* to attract; (*Kleidung*) to put on; (*Schraube, Seil*) to tighten ▷ *vr*: **sich ~** to get dressed

anziehend *adj* attractive

Anzug *m* suit

anzüglich *adj* suggestive

an|zünden *vt* to light; (*Haus etc*) to set fire to

an|zweifeln *vt* to doubt

Aperitif (-*s*, -*s* (o -*e*)) *m* aperitif

Apfel (-*s*, *Äpfel*) *m* apple

Apfelbaum *m* apple tree

Apfelkuchen *m* apple cake

Apfelmus *nt* apple sauce

Apfelsaft *m* apple juice

Apfelsine *f* orange

Apfelwein *m* hard cider

Apostroph (-*s*, -*e*) *m* apostrophe

Apotheke (-, -*n*) *f* pharmacy

apothekenpflichtig *adj* only available at the pharmacy

Apotheker(in) (-*s*, -) *m(f)* pharmacist

Apparat (-(*e*)*s*, -*e*) *m* (piece of) apparatus;

(*Tel*) telephone; (*Radio, TV*) set; **am ~!**
(*Tel*) speaking; **am ~ bleiben** (*Tel*) to hold
the line

Appartement (*-s, -s*) *nt* apartment

Appetit (*-(e)s, -e*) *m* appetite; **guten ~!** bon
appétit!

appetitlich *adj* appetizing

Applaus (*-es, -e*) *m* applause

Aprikose (*-, -n*) *f* apricot

April (*-(s), -e*) *m* April; *siehe auch* **Juni; ~, ~!**
April fool!

Aprilscherz (*-es, -e*) *m* April fool's joke

apropos *adv* by the way; **~ Urlaub ...** while
we're on the subject of vacation ...

Aquajogging *nt* aqua jogging

Aquarell (*-s, -e*) *nt* watercolor

Aquarium (*-s, Aquarien*) *nt* aquarium

Äquator (*-s, -*) *m* equator

Araber(in) (*-s, -*) *m(f)* Arab

arabisch *adj* Arab; (*Ziffer, Sprache*) Arabic;
(*Meer, Wüste*) Arabian

Arbeit (*-, -en*) *f* work; (*Stelle*) job; (*Erzeugnis*) piece of work; (*schriftlich*) paper

arbeiten *vi* to work

Arbeiter(in) (*-s, -*) *m(f)* worker; (*ungelernt*)
laborer

Arbeitgeber(in) (*-s, -*) *m(f)* employer

Arbeitnehmer(in) (*-s, -*) *m(f)* employee

Arbeitsagentur *f* unemployment agency

Arbeitsamt *nt* employment office

Arbeitserlaubnis *f* work permit

arbeitslos *adj* unemployed

Arbeitslose(r) *mf* unemployed person; **die
~n** *pl* the unemployed *pl*

Arbeitslosengeld *nt* (income-related)
unemployment compensation (*o* benefits)

Arbeitslosenhilfe *f* extended unemployment benefits

Arbeitslosigkeit *f* unemployment

Arbeitsplatz *m* job; (*Ort*) workplace

Arbeitsspeicher *m* (*Inform*) main memory

Arbeitszeit *f* working hours *pl*

Arbeitszimmer *nt* study

Archäologe (*-n, -n*) *m*, **Archäologin** *f*
archeologist

Architekt(in) (*-en, -en*) *m(f)* architect

Architektur *f* architecture

Archiv (*-s, -e*) *nt* archives *pl*

ARD *f* (= *Arbeitsgemeinschaft der öffentlich-
rechtlichen Rundfunkanstalten der Bundesrepublik Deutschland*) German broadcasting corporation

arg *adj* bad; (*schrecklich*) awful ▷ *adv* (*sehr*)
terribly

Argentinien (*-s*) *nt* Argentina

Ärger (*-s*) *m* annoyance; (*stärker*) anger;
(*Unannehmlichkeiten*) trouble

ärgerlich *adj* (*zornig*) angry; (*lästig*) annoying

ärgern *vt* to annoy ▷ *vr:* **sich ~** to get
annoyed

Argument (*-s, -e*) *nt* argument

Arktis (*-*) *f* Arctic

arm *adj* poor

Arm (*-(e)s, -e*) *m* arm; (*Fluss*) branch

Armaturenbrett *nt* instrument panel;
(*Auto*) dashboard

Armband *nt* bracelet

Armbanduhr *f* (wrist)watch

Armee (*-, -n*) *f* army

Ärmel (*-s, -*) *m* sleeve

Ärmelkanal *m* (English) Channel

Armut (*-*) *f* poverty

Aroma (*-s, Aromen*) *nt* aroma

arrogant *adj* arrogant

Art (*-, -en*) *f* (*Weise*) way; (*Sorte*) kind, sort;
(*bei Tieren*) species; **nach Art des Hauses**
à la maison; **auf diese Art und Weise** in
this way; **das ist nicht seine Art** that's not
like him

Arterie (*-, -n*) *f* artery

artig *adj* good, well-behaved

Artikel (*-s, -*) *m* (*Ware*) article, item; (*Zeitung*) article

Artischocke (*-, -n*) *f* artichoke

Artist(in) (*-en, -en*) *m(f)* (circus) performer

Arznei *f* medicine

Arzt (*-es, Ärzte*) *m* doctor

Arzthelfer(in) *m(f)* doctor's assistant

Ärztin *f* (female) doctor

ärztlich *adj* medical; **sich ~ behandeln lassen** to undergo medical treatment

Asche (*-, -n*) *f* ashes *pl*; (*von Zigarette*) ash

Aschenbecher *m* ashtray

Aschermittwoch *m* Ash Wednesday

Asiat(in) (*-en, -en*) *m(f)* Asian

asiatisch *adj* Asian

Asien (*-s*) *nt* Asia

Aspekt (*-(e)s, -e*) *m* aspect

Asphalt (*-(e)s, -e*) *m* asphalt

Aspirin® (*-s, -e*) *nt* aspirin

aß *imperf von* **essen**

Ass (*-es, -e*) *nt* (*Karten, Tennis*) ace

Assistent(in) *m(f)* assistant

Ast (*-(e)s, Äste*) *m* branch

Asthma (*-s*) *nt* asthma

Astrologie *f* astrology

Astronaut(in) (*-en, -en*) *m(f)* astronaut

Astronomie *f* astronomy

ASU (-, -s) f (abk) = **Abgassonderuntersu-
chung** exhaust emission test

Asyl (-s, -e) nt asylum; (Heim) home; (für
Obdachlose) shelter

Asylant(in) m(f), **Asylbewerber(in)** m(f)
asylum seeker

Atelier (-s, -s) nt studio

Atem (-s) m breath

atemberaubend adj breathtaking

Atembeschwerden pl breathing difficulties pl

atemlos adj breathless

Atempause f breather

Athen nt Athens

Äthiopien (-s) nt Ethiopia

Athlet(in) (-en, -en) m(f) athlete

Athletik f track and field

Atlantik (-s) m Atlantic (Ocean)

Atlas (- o Atlasses, Atlanten) m atlas

atmen vt, vi to breathe

Atmung f breathing

Atom (-s, -e) nt atom

Atombombe f atom bomb

Atomkraftwerk nt nuclear power plant

Atommüll m nuclear waste

Atomwaffen pl nuclear weapons pl

Attentat (-(e)s, -e) nt assassination (auf +akk
of); (Versuch) assassination attempt

Attest (-(e)s, -e) nt certificate

attraktiv adj attractive

Attrappe (-, -n) f dummy

ätzend adj (fam) revolting; (schlecht)
lousy

au interj ouch; **au ja!** yeah!

Aubergine (-, -n) f eggplant

SCHLÜSSELWORT

auch adv 1 (ebenfalls) also, too, as well; **das
ist auch schön** that's nice too o as well; **er
kommt – ich auch** he's coming – so am I,
me too; **auch nicht** not ... either; **ich auch
nicht** nor I, me neither; **oder auch** or;
auch das noch! not that too!

2 (selbst, sogar) even; **auch wenn das Wetter schlecht ist** even if the weather is bad;
ohne auch nur zu fragen without even
asking

3 (wirklich) really; **du siehst müde aus –
bin ich auch** you look tired – (so) I am; **so
sieht es auch aus** it looks like it too

4 (auch immer): **wer auch** whoever; **was
auch** whatever; **wie dem auch sei** be that
as it may; **wie sehr er sich auch bemühte**
however much he tried

audiovisuell adj audiovisual

SCHLÜSSELWORT

auf prep +dat (wo?) on; **auf dem Tisch** on
the table; **auf der Reise** on the way; **auf
der Post/dem Fest** at the post office/
party; **auf der Straße** on the road; **auf dem
Land/der ganzen Welt** in the country/the
whole world

▷ prep +akk 1 (wohin?) on(to); **auf den
Tisch** on(to) the table; **auf die Post gehen**
to go to the post office; **auf das Land** into
the country; **etw auf einen Zettel schreiben** to write sth on a piece of paper

2: **auf Deutsch** in German; **auf Lebenszeit**
for my/his lifetime; **bis auf ihn** except for
him; **auf einmal** at once; **auf seinen Vorschlag (hin)** at his suggestion

▷ adv 1 (offen) open; **auf sein** (fam: Tür,
Geschäft) to be open; **das Fenster ist auf**
the window is open

2 (hinauf) up; **auf und ab** up and down;
auf und davon up and away; **auf!** (los!)
come on!

3 (aufgestanden) up; **auf sein** to be up; **ist
er schon auf?** is he up yet?

▷ konj: **auf dass** (so) that

auf|atmen vi to breathe a sigh of relief

auf|bauen vt (errichten) to put up; (schaf-
fen) to build up; (gestalten) to construct;
(gründen) to found, to base (auf +akk on);
sich eine Existenz ~ to make a life for
oneself

auf|bewahren vt to keep, to store

auf|bleiben (irr) vi (Tür, Laden etc) to stay
open; (Mensch) to stay up

auf|blenden vi, vt: **die Scheinwerfer ~** to
put on one's high beams (o brights)

auf|brechen (irr) vt to break open ▷ vi to
burst open; (gehen) to leave; (abreisen) to
set off

auf|drängen vt: **jdm etw ~** to force sth on sb
▷ vr: **sich ~** to intrude (jdm on sb)

aufdringlich adj pushy

aufeinander adv (übereinander) on top of
each other; **~ achten** to look after each
other; **~ vertrauen** to trust each other

aufeinander|folgen vi to follow one anoth-
er

aufeinander|prallen vi to crash into one
another

Aufenthalt m stay; (Zug) stop

Aufenthaltsraum m lounge

auf|essen (*irr*) *vt* to eat up

auf|fahren (*irr*) *vi* (*Auto*) to run (*o* to crash) (*auf* +*akk* into); (*herankommen*) to drive up

Auffahrt *f* (*am Haus*) driveway

Auffahrunfall *m* rear-end collision; (*mehrere Fahrzeuge*) pile-up

auf|fallen (*irr*) *vi* to stand out; **jdm ~** to strike sb; **das fällt gar nicht auf** nobody will notice

auffallend *adj* striking

auffällig *adj* conspicuous; (*Kleidung, Farbe*) striking

auf|fangen (*irr*) *vt* (*Ball*) to catch; (*Stoß*) to cushion

auf|fassen *vt* to understand

Auffassung *f* view; (*Meinung*) opinion; (*Auslegung*) concept; (*Auffassungsgabe*) grasp

auf|fordern *vt* (*befehlen*) to call upon; (*bitten*) to ask

auf|frischen *vt* (*Kenntnisse*) to brush up

auf|führen *vt* (*Theat*) to perform; (*in einem Verzeichnis*) to list; (*Beispiel*) to give ▷ *vr*: **sich ~** (*sich benehmen*) to behave

Aufführung *f* (*Theat*) performance

Aufgabe *f* job, task; (*Schule*) exercise; (*Hausaufgabe*) homework

Aufgang *m* (*Treppe*) staircase

auf|geben (*irr*) *vt* (*verzichten auf*) to give up; (*Paket*) to mail; (*Gepäck*) to check in; (*Bestellung, Inserat*) to place; (*Rätsel*) to ask; (*Problem*) to pose ▷ *vi* to give up

auf|gehen (*irr*) *vi* (*Sonne, Teig*) to rise; (*sich öffnen*) to open; (*klar werden*) to dawn (*jdm* on sb)

aufgelegt *adj*: **gut/schlecht ~** in a good/bad mood

aufgeregt *adj* excited

aufgeschlossen *adj* open(minded)

aufgeschmissen *adj*: **~ sein** (*fam*) to be in big trouble

aufgrund, auf Grund *prep* (+*gen*) on the basis of; (*wegen*) because of

auf|haben (*irr*) *vt* (*Hut etc*) to have on; **viel ~** (*Schule*) to have a lot of homework to do ▷ *vi* (*Geschäft*) to be open

auf|halten (*irr*) *vt* (*jdn*) to detain; (*Entwicklung*) to stop; (*Tür, Hand*) to hold open; (*Augen*) to keep open ▷ *vr*: **sich ~** (*wohnen*) to live; (*vorübergehend*) to stay

auf|hängen (*irr*) *vt* to hang up

auf|heben (*irr*) *vt* (*vom Boden etc*) to pick up; (*aufbewahren*) to keep

Aufheiterungen *pl* (*Meteo*) bright periods *pl*

auf|holen *vt* (*Zeit*) to make up ▷ *vi* to catch up

auf|hören *vi* to stop; **~, etw zu tun** to stop doing sth

auf|klären *vt* (*Geheimnis etc*) to clear up; **jdn ~** to enlighten sb; (*sexuell*) to tell sb the facts of life

Aufkleber (*-s, -*) *m* sticker

auf|kommen (*irr*) *vi* (*Wind*) to come up; (*Zweifel, Gefühl*) to arise; (*Mode etc*) to appear on the scene; **für den Schaden ~** to pay for the damage

Aufladegerät *nt* charger

auf|laden (*irr*) *vt* to load; (*Handy etc*) to charge; (*Handykarte etc*) to load

Auflage *f* edition; (*von Zeitung*) circulation; (*Bedingung*) condition

auf|lassen *vt* (*Hut, Brille*) to keep on; (*Tür*) to leave open

Auflauf *m* (*Menschen*) crowd; (*Speise*) casserole

auf|legen *vt* (*CD, Schminke etc*) to put on; (*Hörer*) to put down ▷ *vi* (*Tel*) to hang up

auf|leuchten *vi* to light up

auf|lösen *vt* (*in Flüssigkeit*) to dissolve ▷ *vr*: **sich ~** (*in Flüssigkeit*) to dissolve; **der Stau hat sich aufgelöst** traffic is back to normal

Auflösung *f* (*von Rätsel*) solution; (*von Bildschirm*) resolution

auf|machen *vt* to open; (*Kleidung*) to undo ▷ *vr*: **sich ~** to set out (*nach* for)

aufmerksam *adj* attentive; **jdn auf etw** (*akk*) **~ machen** to draw sb's attention to sth

Aufmerksamkeit *f* attention; (*Konzentration*) attentiveness; (*Geschenk*) small token

auf|muntern *vt* (*ermutigen*) to encourage; (*aufheitern*) to cheer up

Aufnahme (*-, -n*) *f* (*Foto*) photo(graph); (*einzelne*) shot; (*in Verein, Krankenhaus etc*) admission; (*Beginn*) beginning; (*auf Tonband etc*) recording

Aufnahmeprüfung *f* entrance exam

auf|nehmen (*irr*) *vt* (*in Krankenhaus, Verein etc*) to admit; (*Musik*) to record; (*beginnen*) to take up; (*in Liste*) to include; (*begreifen*) to take in; **mit jdm Kontakt ~** to get in touch with sb

auf|passen *vi* (*aufmerksam sein*) to pay attention; (*vorsichtig sein*) to take care; **auf jdn/etw ~** to keep an eye on sb/sth

Aufprall (*-s, -e*) *m* impact

auf|prallen *vi*: **auf etw** (*akk*) **~** to hit sth, to crash into sth

Aufpreis m extra charge
auf|pumpen vt to pump up
Aufputschmittel nt stimulant
auf|räumen vt (Dinge) to clear (o put) away; (Zimmer) to clean up ▷ vi to straighten up
aufrecht adj upright
auf|regen vt to excite; (ärgern) to annoy ▷ vr: **sich ~** to get worked up
aufregend adj exciting
Aufregung f excitement
auf|reißen (irr) vt (Tüte) to tear open; (Tür) to fling open; (fam: Person) to pick up
Aufruf m (Aviat, Inform) call; (öffentlicher) appeal
auf|rufen (irr) vt (auffordern) to call upon (zu for); (Namen) to call out; (Aviat) to call; (Inform) to call up
auf|runden vt (Summe) to round up
aufs kontr von **auf das**
Aufsatz m essay
auf|schieben (irr) vt (verschieben) to postpone; (verzögern) to put off; (Tür) to slide open
Aufschlag m (auf Preis) extra charge; (Tennis) serve
auf|schlagen (irr) vt (öffnen) to open; (verletzen) to cut open; (Zelt) to pitch, to put up; (Lager) to set up ▷ vi (Tennis) to serve; **auf etw** (+akk) ~ (aufprallen) to hit sth
auf|schließen (irr) vt to unlock, to open up ▷ vi (aufrücken) to close the gap
auf|schneiden (irr) vt to cut open; (in Scheiben) to slice ▷ vi (angeben) to boast, to show off
Aufschnitt m cold cuts pl; (bei Käse) (assorted) sliced cheeses pl
auf|schreiben (irr) vt to write down
Aufschrift f inscription; (Etikett) label
Aufschub m (Verzögerung) delay; (Vertagung) postponement
Aufsehen (-s) nt stir; **großes ~ erregen** to cause a sensation
Aufseher(in) (-s, -) m(f) guard; (im Betrieb) supervisor; (im Museum) attendant; (im Park) keeper
auf sein (irr) vi siehe **auf**
auf|setzen vt to put on; (Dokument) to draw up ▷ vi (Flugzeug) to touch down
Aufsicht f supervision; (bei Prüfung) proctoring, monitoring; **die ~ haben** to be in charge
auf|spannen vt (Schirm) to put up
auf|sperren vt (Mund) to open wide; (aufschließen) to unlock

auf|springen (irr) vi to jump (auf +akk onto); (hochspringen) to jump up; (sich öffnen) to spring open
auf|stehen (irr) vi to get up; (Tür) to be open
auf|stellen vt (aufrecht stellen) to put up; (aufreihen) to line up; (nominieren) to nominate; (Liste, Programm) to draw up; (Rekord) to set
Aufstieg (-(e)s, -e) m (auf Berg) ascent; (Fortschritt) rise; (beruflich, im Sport) promotion
Aufstrich m spread
auf|tanken vt, vi (Auto) to tank up; (Flugzeug) to refuel
auf|tauchen vi to turn up; (aus Wasser etc) to surface; (Frage, Problem) to come up
auf|tauen vt (Speisen) to defrost ▷ vi to thaw; (fig: Person) to warm up, to relax
Auftrag (-(e)s, Aufträge) m (Comm) order; (Arbeit) job; (Anweisung) instructions pl; (Aufgabe) task; **im ~ von** on behalf of
auf|tragen (irr) vt (Salbe etc) to apply; (Essen) to serve
auf|treten (irr) vi to appear; (Problem) to come up; (sich verhalten) to behave
Auftritt m (des Schauspielers) entrance; (fig: Szene) scene
auf|wachen vi to wake up
auf|wachsen (irr) vi to grow up
Aufwand (-(e)s) m expenditure; (Kosten a.) expense; (Anstrengung) effort
aufwändig adj siehe **aufwendig**
auf|wärmen vt to warm up ▷ vr: **sich ~** to warm up
aufwärts adv upwards; **mit etw geht es ~** things are looking up for sth
auf|wecken vt to wake up
aufwendig adj costly; **das ist zu aufwändig** that's too much trouble
auf|wischen vt to wipe up; (Fußboden) to wipe
auf|zählen vt to list
auf|zeichnen vt to sketch; (schriftlich) to jot down; (auf Band etc) to record
Aufzeichnung f (schriftlich) note; (Tonband etc) recording; (Film) taping
auf|ziehen (irr) vt (öffnen) to pull open; (Uhr) to wind (up); (fam: necken) to tease; (Kinder) to bring up; (Tiere) to raise ▷ vi (Gewitter) to come up
Aufzug m (Fahrstuhl) elevator; (Kleidung) get-up; (Theat) act
Auge (-s, -n) nt eye; **jdm etw aufs ~ drücken** (fam) to force sth on sb; **ins ~ gehen** (fam)

to go wrong; **unter vier ~n** in private; **etw im ~ behalten** to keep sth in mind

Augenarzt *m*, **Augenärztin** *f* eye doctor

Augenblick *m* moment; **im ~** at the moment

Augenbraue (-, -n) *f* eyebrow

Augenbrauenstift *m* eyebrow pencil

Augenfarbe *f* eye color; **seine ~** the color of his eyes

Augenlid *nt* eyelid

Augenoptiker(in) (-s, -) *m(f)* optometrist

Augentropfen *pl* eyedrops *pl*

Augenzeuge *m*, **Augenzeugin** *f* eyewitness

August (-(e)s o -, -e) *m* August; *siehe auch* **Juni**

Auktion *f* auction

SCHLÜSSELWORT

aus *prep +dat* **1** (*räumlich*) out of; (*von ... her*) from; **er ist aus Berlin** he's from Berlin; **aus dem Fenster** out of the window

2 (*gemacht/hergestellt aus*) made of; **ein Herz aus Stein** a heart of stone

3 (*auf Ursache deutend*) out of; **aus Mitleid** out of sympathy; **aus Erfahrung** from experience; **aus Spaß** for fun

4: aus ihr wird nie etwas she'll never get anywhere

▷ *adv* **1** (*zu Ende*) finished, over; **aus sein** to be over; **aus und vorbei** over and done with

2 (*ausgeschaltet, ausgezogen*) out; (*Aufschrift an Geräten*) off; **aus sein** (*nicht brennen*) to be out; (*abgeschaltet sein: Radio, Herd*) to be off; **Licht aus!** lights out!

3 (*nicht zu Hause*): **aus sein** to be out

4 (*in Verbindung mit von*): **von Rom aus** from Rome; **vom Fenster aus** out of the window; **von sich aus** (*selbstständig*) of one's own accord; **von ihm aus** as far as he's concerned

Aus (-) *nt* (*Sport*) touch; (*fig*) end

aus|atmen *vi* to breathe out

aus|bauen *vt* (*Haus, Straße*) to extend; (*Motor etc*) to remove

aus|bessern *vt* to repair; (*Kleidung*) to mend

aus|bilden *vt* to educate; (*Lehrling etc*) to train; (*Fähigkeiten*) to develop

Ausbildung *f* education; (*von Lehrling etc*) training; (*von Fähigkeiten*) development

Ausblick *m* view; (*fig*) outlook

aus|brechen (*irr*) *vi* to break out; **in Tränen ~** to burst into tears; **in Gelächter ~** to burst out laughing

aus|breiten *vt* to spread (out); (*Arme*) to stretch out ▷ *vr*: **sich ~** to spread

Ausbruch *m* (*Krieg, Seuche etc*) outbreak; (*Vulkan*) eruption; (*Gefühle*) outburst; (*von Gefangenen*) escape

aus|buhen *vt* to boo

Ausdauer *f* perseverance; (*Sport*) stamina

aus|dehnen *vt* to stretch; (*fig: Macht*) to extend

aus|denken (*irr*) *vt*: **sich** (*dat*) **etw ~** to come up with sth

Ausdruck *m* (*Ausdrücke*) expression ▷ *m* (*Ausdrucke, Computerausdruck*) print-out

aus|drucken *vt* (*Inform*) to print (out)

aus|drücken *vt* (*formulieren*) to express; (*Zigarette*) to put out; (*Zitrone etc*) to squeeze ▷ *vr*: **sich ~** to express oneself

ausdrücklich *adj* express ▷ *adv* expressly

auseinander *adv* (*getrennt*) apart; **~ schreiben** to write as separate words

auseinander|gehen (*irr*) *vi* (*Menschen*) to separate; (*Meinungen*) to differ; (*Gegenstand*) to fall apart

auseinander|halten (*irr*) *vt* to tell apart

auseinander|setzen *vt* (*erklären*) to explain ▷ *vr*: **sich ~** (*sich beschäftigen*) to look (*mit* at); (*sich streiten*) to argue (*mit* with)

Auseinandersetzung *f* (*Streit*) argument; (*Diskussion*) debate

Ausfahrt *f* (*des Zuges etc*) departure; (*Autobahn, Garage etc*) exit

aus|fallen (*irr*) *vi* (*Haare*) to fall out; (*nicht stattfinden*) to be canceled; (*nicht funktionieren*) to break down; (*Strom*) to be cut off; (*Resultat haben*) to turn out; **groß/klein ~** (*Kleidung, Schuhe*) to be too big/too small

ausfindig machen *vt* to discover

aus|flippen *vi* (*fam*) to freak out

Ausflug *m* outing; (*Schulausflug*) fiel trip

Ausflugsziel *nt* destination

Ausfluss *m* (*Med*) discharge

aus|fragen *vt* to question

Ausfuhr (-, -en) *f* export

aus|führen *vt* (*verwirklichen*) to carry out; (*Person*) to take out; (*Comm*) to export; (*darlegen*) to explain

ausführlich *adj* detailed ▷ *adv* in detail

aus|füllen *vt* to fill up; (*Fragebogen etc*) to fill out

Ausgabe *f* (*Geld*) expenditure; (*Inform*) output; (*Buch*) edition; (*Nummer*) issue

Ausgang *m* way out, exit; (*Flugsteig*) gate; (*Ende*) end; (*Ergebnis*) result; „kein ~" 'no exit'

aus|geben (*irr*) *vt* (*Geld*) to spend; (*austeilen*) to distribute; **jdm etw ~** (*spendieren*) to buy sb sth ▷ *vr:* **sich für etw/jdn ~** to pass oneself off as sth/sb

ausgebucht *adj* fully booked

ausgefallen *adj* (*ungewöhnlich*) unusual

aus|gehen (*irr*) *vi* (*abends etc*) to go out; (*Benzin, Kaffee etc*) to run out; (*Haare*) to fall out; (*Feuer, Licht etc*) to go out; (*Resultat haben*) to turn out; **davon ~, dass** to assume that; **ihm ging das Geld aus** he ran out of money

ausgelassen *adj* exuberant

ausgeleiert *adj* worn out

ausgenommen *conj, prep* (+*gen o dat*) except

ausgerechnet *adv:* **~ du** you of all people; **~ heute** today of all days

ausgeschildert *adj* signposted

ausgeschlafen *adj:* **bist du ~?** have you had enough sleep?

ausgeschlossen *adj* (*unmöglich*) impossible, out of the question

ausgesprochen *adj* (*absolut*) out-and-out; (*unverkennbar*) marked ▷ *adv* extremely; **~ gut** really good

ausgezeichnet *adj* excellent

ausgiebig *adj* (*Gebrauch*) thorough; (*Essen*) substantial

aus|gießen (*irr*) *vt* (*Getränk*) to pour out; (*Gefäß*) to empty

aus|gleichen (*irr*) *vt* to even out ▷ *vi* (*Sport*) to equalize

Ausguss *m* (*Spüle*) sink; (*Abfluss*) outlet

aus|halten (*irr*) *vt* to bear, to stand; **nicht auszuhalten sein** to be unbearable ▷ *vi* to hold out

aus|händigen *vt:* **jdm etw ~** to hand sth over to sb

Aushang *m* notice

Aushilfe *f* temporary help; (*im Büro*) temp

aus|kennen (*irr*) *vr:* **sich ~** to know a lot (*bei, mit* about); (*an einem Ort*) to know one's way around

aus|kommen (*irr*) *vi:* **gut/schlecht mit jdm ~** to get along well/badly with sb; **mit etw ~** to get by with sth

Auskunft (-, *Auskünfte*) *f* information; (*nähere*) details *pl*; (*Schalter*) information desk; (*Tel*) information

aus|lachen *vt* to laugh at

aus|laden (*irr*) *vt* (*Gepäck etc*) to unload; **jdn ~** (*Gast*) to tell sb not to come

Auslage *f* window display; **~n** *pl* (*Kosten*) expenses *pl*

Ausland *nt* foreign countries *pl*; **im/ins ~** abroad

Ausländer(in) (-*s*, -) *m(f)* foreigner

ausländerfeindlich *adj* hostile to foreigners, xenophobic

ausländisch *adj* foreign

Auslandsgespräch *nt* international call

Auslandskrankenschein *m* health insurance certificate for foreign countries

Auslandsschutzbrief *m* international auto insurance coverage (*documents/pl*)

aus|lassen (*irr*) *vt* to leave out; (*Wort etc a.*) to omit; (*überspringen*) to skip; (*Wut, Ärger*) to vent (*an* +*dat* on) ▷ *vr:* **sich über etw** (*akk*) **~** to speak one's mind about sth

aus|laufen (*irr*) *vi* (*Flüssigkeit*) to run out; (*Tank etc*) to leak; (*Schiff*) to leave port; (*Vertrag*) to expire

aus|legen *vt* (*Waren*) to display; (*Geld*) to lend; (*Text etc*) to interpret; (*technisch ausstatten*) to design (*für, auf* +*akk* for)

aus|leihen (*irr*) *vt* (*verleihen*) to lend; **sich** (*dat*) **etw ~** to borrow sth

aus|loggen *vi* (*Inform*) to log out (*o* off)

aus|lösen *vt* (*Explosion, Alarm*) to set off; (*hervorrufen*) to cause

Auslöser (-*s*, -) *m* (*Foto*) shutter release

aus|machen *vt* (*Licht, Radio*) to turn off; (*Feuer*) to put out; (*Termin*) to make; (*Preis*) to set; (*vereinbaren*) to agree; (*Anteil darstellen, betragen*) to represent; (*bedeuten*) to matter; **macht es Ihnen etwas aus, wenn ...?** would you mind if ...?; **das macht mir nichts aus** I don't mind

Ausmaß *nt* extent

Ausnahme (-, -*n*) *f* exception

ausnahmsweise *adv* as an exception, just this once

aus|nutzen *vt* (*Zeit, Gelegenheit, Einfluss*) to use; (*jdn, Gutmütigkeit*) to take advantage of

aus|packen *vt* to unpack

aus|probieren *vt* to try (out)

Auspuff (-*(e)s*, -*e*) *m* (*Tech*) exhaust

Auspuffrohr *nt* exhaust (pipe)

Auspufftopf *m* (*Auto*) muffler

aus|rauben *vt* to rob

aus|räumen *vt* (*Dinge*) to clear away; (*Schrank, Zimmer*) to empty; (*Bedenken*) to put aside

aus|rechnen vt to calculate, to work out

Ausrede f excuse

aus|reden vi to finish speaking ▷ vt: **jdm etw ~** to talk sb out of sth

ausreichend adj sufficient, satisfactory; (Schulnote) ≈ D

Ausreise f departure; **bei der ~** on leaving the country

Ausreiseerlaubnis f exit visa

aus|reisen vi to leave the country

aus|reißen (irr) vt to tear out ▷ vi to come off; (fam: davonlaufen) to run away

aus|renken vt: **sich** (dat) **den Arm ~** to dislocate one's arm

aus|richten vt (Botschaft) to deliver; (Gruß) to pass on; (erreichen): **ich konnte bei ihr nichts ~** I couldn't get anywhere with her; **jdm etw ~** to tell sb sth

aus|rufen (irr) vt (über Lautsprecher) to announce; **jdn ~ lassen** to page sb

Ausrufezeichen nt exclamation point

aus|ruhen vi to rest ▷ vr: **sich ~** to rest

Ausrüstung f equipment

aus|rutschen vi to slip

aus|schalten vt to switch off; (fig) to eliminate

Ausschau f: **~ halten** to look out (nach for)

aus|scheiden (irr) vt (Med) to give off, to secrete ▷ vi to leave (aus etw sth); (Sport) to be eliminated

aus|schlafen (irr) vi to have a good night's sleep ▷ vr: **sich ~** to have a good night's sleep ▷ vt to sleep off

Ausschlag m (Med) rash; **den ~ geben** (fig) to tip the balance

aus|schlagen (irr) vt (Zahn) to knock out; (Einladung) to turn down ▷ vi (Pferd) to kick out

ausschlaggebend adj decisive

aus|schließen (irr) vt to lock out; (fig) to exclude

ausschließlich adv exclusively ▷ prep (+gen) excluding

Ausschnitt m (Teil) section; (von Kleid) neckline; (aus Zeitung) clipping

Ausschreitungen pl riots pl

aus|schütten vt (Flüssigkeit) to pour out; (Gefäß) to empty

aus|sehen (irr) vi to look; **krank ~** to look sick, to not look well; **gut ~** (Dauerzustand) to be good-looking; (momentan) to look good; **es sieht nach Regen aus** it looks like rain; **es sieht schlecht aus** things look bad

aus sein (irr) vi siehe **aus**

außen adv outside; **nach ~** outwards; **von ~** from (the) outside

Außenbordmotor m outboard motor

Außenminister(in) m(f) ≈ secretary of state; foreign minister

Außenseite f outside

Außenseiter(in) m(f) outsider

Außenspiegel m side mirror

außer prep (+dat) (abgesehen von) except (for); **nichts ~** nothing but; **~ Betrieb** out of order; **~ sich sein** to be beside oneself (vor with); **~ Atem** out of breath ▷ conj (ausgenommen) except; **~ wenn** unless; **~ dass** except

außerdem conj besides

äußere(r, s) adj outer, external

außergewöhnlich adj unusual ▷ adv exceptionally; **~ kalt** exceptionally cold

außerhalb prep (+gen) outside

äußerlich adj external

äußern vt to express; (zeigen) to show ▷ vr: **sich ~** to give one's opinion

außerordentlich adj extraordinary

außerplanmäßig adj unscheduled

äußerst adv extremely

äußerste(r, s) adj utmost; (räumlich) farthest; (Termin) last possible

Äußerung f remark

aus|setzen vt (Kind, Tier) to abandon; (Belohnung) to offer; **ich habe nichts daran auszusetzen** I have no objection to it ▷ vi (aufhören) to stop; (Pause machen) to drop out; (beim Spiel) to miss a turn

Aussicht f (Blick) view; (Chance) prospect

aussichtslos adj hopeless

Aussichtsplattform f observation platform

Aussichtsturm m observation tower

Aussiedler(in) (-s, -) m(f) émigré (person of German descent from Eastern Europe)

aus|spannen vi (erholen) to relax ▷ vt: **du hast mir die Freundin ausgespannt** (fam) you stole my girlfriend

aus|sperren vt to lock out ▷ vr: **sich ~** to lock oneself out

Aussprache f (von Wörtern) pronunciation; (Gespräch) (frank) discussion

aus|sprechen (irr) vt to pronounce; (äußern) to express ▷ vr: **sich ~** to talk (über +akk about) ▷ vi (zu Ende sprechen) to finish speaking

aus|spülen vt to rinse (out)

Ausstattung f (Ausrüstung) equipment; (Einrichtung) furnishings pl

aus|stehen (*irr*) *vt* to endure; **ich kann ihn nicht ~** I can't stand him ▷ *vi* (*noch nicht da sein*) to be outstanding

aus|steigen (*irr*) *vi* to get out (*aus* of); **aus dem Bus/Zug ~** to get off the bus/train

Aussteiger(in) *m(f)* dropout

aus|stellen *vt* to display; (*auf Messe, in Museum etc*) to exhibit; (*fam: ausschalten*) to switch off; (*Scheck etc*) to make out; (*Pass etc*) to issue

Ausstellung *f* exhibition, exhibit

aus|sterben (*irr*) *vi* to die out

aus|strahlen *vt* to radiate; (*Programm*) to broadcast

Ausstrahlung *f* (*Radio, TV*) broadcast; (*fig: von Person*) charisma

aus|strecken *vr:* **sich ~** to stretch out ▷ *vt* (*Hand*) to reach out (*nach* for)

aus|suchen *vt* to choose

Austausch *m* exchange

aus|tauschen *vt* to exchange (*gegen* for)

aus|teilen *vt* to distribute; (*aushändigen*) to hand out

Auster (*-, -n*) *f* oyster

Austernpilz *m* oyster mushroom

aus|tragen (*irr*) *vt* (*Post*) to deliver; (*Wettkampf*) to hold

Australien (*-s*) *nt* Australia

Australier(in) (*-s, -*) *m(f)* Australian

australisch *adj* Australian

aus|trinken (*irr*) *vt* (*Glas*) to drain; (*Getränk*) to drink up ▷ *vi* to finish one's drink

aus|trocknen *vi* to dry out; (*Fluss*) to dry up

aus|üben *vt* (*Beruf, Sport*) to practice; (*Einfluss*) to exert

Ausverkauf *m* sale

ausverkauft *adj* (*Karten, Artikel*) sold out

Auswahl *f* selection, choice (*an +dat* of)

aus|wählen *vt* to select, to choose

aus|wandern *vi* to emigrate

auswärtig *adj* (*nicht am/vom Ort*) not local; (*ausländisch*) foreign

auswärts *adv* (*außerhalb der Stadt*) out of town; (*Sport:*) **~ spielen** to play away

Auswärtsspiel *nt* away game

aus|wechseln *vt* to replace; (*Sport*) to substitute

Ausweg *m* way out

aus|weichen (*irr*) *vi* to get out of the way; **jdm/einer Sache ~** to move aside for sb/ sth; (*fig*) to avoid sb/sth

Ausweis (*-es, -e*) *m* (*Personalausweis*) identification (card), ID; (*für Bibliothek etc*) card

aus|weisen (*irr*) *vt* to expel ▷ *vr:* **sich ~** to prove one's identity

Ausweiskontrolle *f* ID check

Ausweispapiere *pl* identification documents *pl*

auswendig *adv* by heart

aus|wuchten *vt* (*Auto: Räder*) to balance

aus|zahlen *vt* (*Summe*) to pay (out); (*Person*) to pay off ▷ *vr:* **sich ~** to be worth it

aus|zeichnen *vt* (*ehren*) to honor; (*Comm*) to price ▷ *vr:* **sich ~** to distinguish oneself

aus|ziehen (*irr*) *vt* (*Kleidung*) to take off ▷ *vr:* **sich ~** to undress ▷ *vi* (*aus Wohnung*) to move out

Auszubildende(r) *mf* trainee

authentisch *adj* authentic, genuine

Auto (*-s, -s*) *nt* car; **~ fahren** to drive

Autoatlas *m* road atlas

Autobahn *f* highway, freeway

Autobahnauffahrt *f* on-ramp

Autobahnausfahrt *f* off-ramp

Autobahngebühr *f* toll

Autobahnkreuz *nt* highway (*o* freeway) interchange

Autobahnring *m* beltway

Autobombe *f* car bomb

Autofähre *f* car ferry

Autofahrer(in) *m(f)* driver, motorist

Autofahrt *f* drive

Autogramm (*-s, -e*) *nt* autograph

Automarke *f* make of car

Automat (*-en, -en*) *m* vending machine

Automatik (*-, -en*) *f* (*Auto*) automatic transmission

Automatikschaltung *f* automatic gear shift

Automatikwagen *m* automatic

automatisch *adj* automatic ▷ *adv* automatically

Automechaniker(in) *m(f)* car mechanic

Autonummer *f* license number

Autor (*-s, -en*) *m* author

Autoradio *nt* car radio

Autoreifen *m* car tire

Autoreisezug *m* Auto Train

Autorennen *nt* motor racing; (*einzelnes Rennen*) motor race

Autorin *f* (female) author

Autoschlüssel *m* car key

Autotelefon *nt* car phone

Autounfall *m* car accident

Autoverleih *m*, **Autovermietung** *f* car rental; (*Firma*) car rental company

Autowaschanlage *f* car wash
Autowerkstatt *f* car repair shop, garage
Autozubehör *nt* car accessories *pl*

Avocado (-, -s) *f* avocado
Axt (-, *Äxte*) *f* ax
Azubi (-s, -s) *f(m)* (*akr*) = **Auszubildende**

B

B (abk) = Bundesstraße
Baby (-s, -s) nt baby
Babybett nt crib
Babyfläschchen nt baby's bottle
Babynahrung f baby food
Babysitter(in) m(f) babysitter
Babywickelraum m baby-changing room
Bach (-(e)s, Bäche) m stream
Backblech nt cookie sheet
Backbord nt port (side)
Backe (-, -n) f cheek
backen (backte, gebacken) vt, vi to bake
Backenzahn m molar
Bäcker(in) (-s, -) m(f) baker
Bäckerei f bakery; (Laden) baker's (shop)
Backofen m oven
Backpulver nt baking powder
Backspace-Taste f (Inform) backspace key
Backstein m brick
Backwaren pl baked goods pl
Bad (-(e)s, Bäder) nt bath; (Schwimmen) swim; (Ort) spa; **ein Bad nehmen** to have (o take) a bath
Badeanzug m swimsuit
Badehose f swimming trunks pl
Badekappe f bathing cap
Bademantel m bathrobe
Bademeister(in) m(f) pool attendant
Bademütze f swimming cap
baden vi to take a bath; (schwimmen) to swim ▷ vt to bathe
Baden-Württemberg (-s) nt Baden-Württemberg
Badeort m spa
Badesachen pl swimming gear
Badetuch nt bath towel
Badewanne f bath (tub)
Badezeug nt swimming gear
Badezimmer nt bathroom
Badminton nt badminton
baff adj: ~ **sein** (fam) to be flabbergasted
Bagger (-s, -) m excavator
Baggersee m artificial lake in quarry etc, used for bathing
Bahamas pl: **die** ~ the Bahamas pl
Bahn (-, -en) f (Eisenbahn) railroad; (Rennbahn) track; (für Läufer) lane; (Astr) orbit; **Deutsche** ~ Germany's main railroad operator
bahnbrechend adj groundbreaking
BahnCard® (-, -s) f rail card (allowing 50%

or 25% reduction on tickets)
Bahnfahrt f train ride; (Reise) trip on the train
Bahnhof m train station; **am** o **auf dem** ~ at the train station
Bahnlinie f railroad line
Bahnpolizei f railroad police
Bahnsteig (-(e)s, -e) m platform
Bahnstrecke f railroad line
Bahnübergang m railroad (o grade) crossing
Bakterien pl bacteria pl; (fam) germs pl
bald adv (zeitlich) soon; (beinahe) almost; **bis ~!** see you soon (o later)
baldig adj quick, speedy
Balkan (-s) m: **der** ~ the Balkans pl
Balken (-s, -) m beam
Balkon (-s, -s o -e) m balcony
Ball (-(e)s, Bälle) m ball; (Tanz) dance, ball
Ballett (-s) nt ballet
Ballon (-s, -s) m balloon
Ballspiel nt ball game
Ballungsgebiet nt ≈ aggregation of urban communities
Baltikum (-s) nt: **das** ~ the Baltic States pl
Bambus (-ses, -se) m bamboo
Bambussprossen pl bamboo shoots pl
banal adj banal; (Frage, Bemerkung) trite
Banane (-, -n) f banana
band imperf von **binden**
Band (-(e)s, Bände) m (Buch) volume ▷ (-(e)s, Bänder) nt (aus Stoff) ribbon, tape; (Fließband) conveyor belt; (Tonband) tape; (Anat) ligament; **etw auf** ~ **aufnehmen** to tape sth ▷ (-, -s) f (Musikgruppe) band
Bandage (-, -n) f bandage
bandagieren vt to bandage
Bande (-, -n) f (Gruppe) gang
Bänderriss m (Med) torn ligament
Bandscheibe f (Anat) disk
Bandwurm m tapeworm
Bank (-, Bänke) f (Sitzbank) bench ▷ (-, -en) f (Fin) bank
Bankautomat m ATM
Bankkarte f bank card
Bankkonto nt bank account
Bankleitzahl f bank identifier code
Banknote f banknote
Bankverbindung f (Konto) bank account; (Kontonummer etc) bank account information
bar adj: **bares Geld** cash; **etw in bar bezah-**

len (*Summe*) to pay sth (in) cash; (*Ding*) to pay for somethink in cash

Bar (-, -s) *f* bar

Bär (-en, -en) *m* bear

barfuß *adj* barefoot

barg *imperf von* **bergen**

Bargeld *nt* cash

bargeldlos *adj* non-cash

Barkeeper (-s, -) *m*, **Barmann** *m* bartender

barock *adj* baroque

Barometer (-s, -) *m* barometer

barsch *adj* brusque

Barsch (-(e)s, -e) *m* perch

Barscheck *m* cashier's check

Bart (-(e)s, *Bärte*) *m* beard

bärtig *adj* bearded

Barzahlung *f* cash payment

Basar (-s, -e) *m* bazaar

Baseballmütze *f* baseball cap

Basel (-s) *nt* Basel

Basilikum (-s) *nt* basil

Basis (-, *Basen*) *f* basis

Baskenland *nt* Basque region

Basketball *nt* basketball

Bass (-es, *Bässe*) *m* bass

basta *interj*: **und damit ~!** and that's that

basteln *vt* to make ▷ *vi* to make things, to do handicrafts

Bastler (-s, -) *m* do-it-yourselfer

bat *imperf von* **bitten**

Batterie *f* battery

batteriebetrieben *adj* battery-powered

Bau (-(e)s) *m* (*Bauen*) building, construction; (*Aufbau*) structure; (*Baustelle*) building site ▷ *m* (*Baue: von Tier*) burrow ▷ *m* (*Bauten: Gebäude*) building

Bauarbeiten *pl* construction work *sing*; (*Straßenbau*) roadwork *sing*

Bauarbeiter(in) *m(f)* construction worker

Bauch (-(e)s, *Bäuche*) *m* stomach

Bauchnabel *m* navel

Bauchredner(in) *m(f)* ventriloquist

Bauchschmerzen *pl* stomachache *sing*

Bauchspeicheldrüse *f* pancreas

Bauchtanz *m* belly dance; (*das Tanzen*) belly dancing

Bauchweh (-s) *nt* stomachache

bauen *vt, vi* to build; (*Tech*) to construct

Bauer (-n o -s, -n) *m* farmer; (*Schach*) pawn

Bäuerin *f* farmer; (*Frau des Bauern*) farmer's wife

Bauernhof *m* farm

baufällig *adj* dilapidated

Baujahr *nt* year of construction; **der Wagen ist ~ 2002** the car is a 2002 model, the car

was made in 2002

Baum (-(e)s, *Bäume*) *m* tree

Baumwolle *f* cotton

Bauplatz *m* building site

Baustein *m* (*für Haus*) stone; (*Spielzeug*) brick; (*fig*) element; **elektronischer ~** chip

Baustelle *f* construction site; (*bei Straßenbau*) roadwork

Bauteil *nt* prefabricated part

Bauunternehmer(in) *m(f)* building contractor

Bauwerk *nt* building

Bayern (-s) *nt* Bavaria

beabsichtigen *vt* to intend

beachten *vt* (*Aufmerksamkeit schenken*) to pay attention to; (*Vorschrift etc*) to observe; **nicht ~** to ignore

beachtlich *adj* considerable

Beachvolleyball *nt* beach volleyball

Beamte(r) (-n, -n) *m*, **Beamtin** *f* official; (*Staatsbeamter*) civil servant

beanspruchen *vt* to claim; (*Zeit, Platz*) to take up; **jdn ~** to keep sb busy

beanstanden *vt* to complain about

Beanstandung *f* complaint

beantragen *vt* to apply for

beantworten *vt* to answer

bearbeiten *vt* to work; (*Material, Daten*) to process; (*Chem*) to treat; (*Fall etc*) to deal with; (*Buch etc*) to revise; (*fam: beeinflussen wollen*) to work on

Bearbeitungsgebühr *f* handling (*o* service) charge

beatmen *vt*: **jdn ~** to give sb artificial respiration

beaufsichtigen *vt* to supervise; (*bei Prüfung*) to monitor; (*an der Uni*) to proctor

beauftragen *vt* to instruct; **jdn mit etw ~** to give sb the job of doing sth

Becher (-s, -) *m* mug; (*aud Glas*) tumbler, glass; (*für Jogurt*) cup, container

Becken (-s, -) *nt* basin; (*Spüle*) sink; (*zum Schwimmen*) pool; (*Mus*) cymbal; (*Anat*) pelvis

bedanken *vr*: **sich ~** to say thank you; **sich bei jdm für etw ~** to thank sb for sth

Bedarf (-(e)s) *m* need (*an +dat* for); (*Comm*) demand (*an +dat* for); **je nach ~** according to demand; **bei ~** if necessary

Bedarfshaltestelle *f* flag stop

bedauerlich *adj* regrettable

bedauern *vt* to regret; (*bemitleiden*) to feel sorry for

bedauernswert *adj* (*Zustände*) regrettable;

(*Mensch*) unfortunate
bedeckt *adj* covered; (*Himmel*) overcast
bedenken (*irr*) *vt* to consider
Bedenken (*-s, -*) *nt* (*Überlegen*) consideration; (*Zweifel*) doubt; (*Skrupel*) scruples
pl
bedenklich *adj* dubious; (*Zustand*) serious
bedeuten *vt* to mean; **jdm nichts/viel ~** to
mean nothing/a lot to sb
bedeutend *adj* important; (*beträchtlich*)
considerable
Bedeutung *f* meaning; (*Wichtigkeit*) importance
bedienen *vt* to serve; (*Maschine*) to operate
▷ *vr:* **sich ~** (*beim Essen*) to help oneself
Bedienung *f* service; (*Kellner/Kellnerin*)
waiter/waitress; (*Verkäufer(in)*) sales
clerk; (*Zuschlag*) service (charge)
Bedienungsanleitung *f* operating instructions *pl*
Bedienungshandbuch *nt* instruction
manual
Bedingung *f* condition; **unter der ~, dass**
on condition that; **unter diesen ~en** under
these circumstances
bedrohen *vt* to threaten
Bedürfnis *nt* need
Beefsteak (*-s, -s*) *nt* steak
beeilen *vr:* **sich ~** to hurry
beeindrucken *vt* to impress
beeinflussen *vt* to influence
beeinträchtigen *vt* to adversely affect
beenden *vt* to end; (*fertigstellen*) to finish
beerdigen *vt* to bury
Beerdigung *f* burial; (*Feier*) funeral
Beere (*-, -n*) *f* berry; (*Traubenbeere*) grape
Beet (*-(e)s, -e*) *nt* bed
befahl *imperf von* **befehlen**
befahrbar *adj* passable; (*Naut*) navigable
befahren (*irr*) *vt* (*Straße*) to use; (*Pass*) to
drive over; (*Fluss etc*) to navigate ▷ *adj:*
stark/wenig ~ busy/quiet
Befehl (*-(e)s, -e*) *m* order; (*Inform*) command
befehlen (**befahl, befohlen**) *vt* to order;
jdm ~, etw zu tun to order sb to do sth ▷ *vi*
to give orders
befestigen *vt* to fix; (*mit Schnur, Seil*) to
attach; (*mit Klebestoff*) to stick
befeuchten *vt* to moisten
befinden (*irr*) *vr:* **sich ~** to be
befohlen *pp von* **befehlen**
befolgen *vt* (*Rat etc*) to follow
befördern *vt* (*transportieren*) to transport;
(*beruflich*) to promote

Beförderung *f* transport; (*beruflich*) promotion
Beförderungsbedingungen *pl* conditions
pl of carriage
Befragung *f* questioning; (*Umfrage*) opinion poll
befreundet *adj* friendly; **~ sein** to be
friends (*mit jdm* with sb)
befriedigen *vt* to satisfy
befriedigend *adj* satisfactory; (*Schulnote*)
≈ C
Befriedigung *f* satisfaction
befristet *adj* limited (*auf +akk* to)
befruchten *vt* to fertilize; (*fig*) to stimulate
Befund (*-(e)s, -e*) *m* findings *pl*; (*Med*) diagnosis
befürchten *vt* to fear
befürworten *vt* to support
begabt *adj* gifted, talented
Begabung *f* talent, gift
begann *imperf von* **beginnen**
begegnen *vi* to meet (*jdm* sb), to meet with
(*einer Sache dat* sth)
begehen (*irr*) *vt* (*Straftat*) to commit; (*Jubiläum etc*) to celebrate
begehrt *adj* sought-after; (*Junggeselle*) eligible
begeistern *vt* to fill with enthusiasm; (*inspirieren*) to inspire ▷ *vr:* **sich für etw ~** to
be/get enthusiastic about sth
begeistert *adj* enthusiastic
Beginn (*-(e)s*) *m* beginning; **zu ~** at the
beginning
beginnen (**begann, begonnen**) *vt, vi* to
start, to begin
beglaubigen *vt* to certify
Beglaubigung *f* certification
begleiten *vt* to accompany
Begleiter(in) *m(f)* companion
Begleitung *f* company; (*Mus*) accompani-
ment
beglückwünschen *vt* to congratulate (*zu*
on)
begonnen *pp von* **beginnen**
begraben (*irr*) *vt* to bury
Begräbnis *nt* burial; (*Feier*) funeral
begreifen (*irr*) *vt* to understand
Begrenzung *f* boundary; (*fig*) restriction
Begriff (*-(e)s, -e*) *m* concept; (*Vorstellung*)
idea; **im ~ sein, etw zu tun** to be on the
point of doing sth; **schwer von ~ sein** to
be slow on the uptake
begründen *vt* (*rechtfertigen*) to justify
Begründung *f* explanation; (*Rechtferti-*

gung) justification
begrüßen *vt* to greet; (*willkommen heißen*) to welcome
Begrüßung *f* greeting; (*Empfang*) welcome
behaart *adj* hairy
behalten (*irr*) *vt* to keep; (*im Gedächtnis*) to remember; **etw für sich ~** to keep sth to oneself
Behälter (*-s, -*) *m* container
behandeln *vt* to treat
Behandlung *f* treatment
behaupten *vt* to claim, to maintain ▷ *vr*: **sich ~** to assert oneself
Behauptung *f* claim
beheizen *vt* to heat
behelfen (*irr*) *vr*: **sich mit/ohne etw ~** to make do with/without sth
beherbergen *vt* to accommodate
beherrschen *vt* (*Situation, Gefühle*) to control; (*Instrument*) to master ▷ *vr*: **sich ~** to control oneself
Beherrschung *f* control (*über +akk* of); **die ~ verlieren** to lose one's self-control
behilflich *adj* helpful; **jdm ~ sein** to help sb (*bei* with)
behindern *vt* to hinder; (*Verkehr, Sicht*) to obstruct
Behinderte(r) *mf* disabled person
behindertengerecht *adj* handicapped accessible
Behörde (*-, -n*) *f* authority; **die ~n** *pl* the authorities *pl*

bei *prep* (*+dat*) **1** (*nahe bei*) near; (*zum Aufenthalt*) at, with; (*unter, zwischen*) among; **bei München** near Munich; **bei uns** at our place; **beim Friseur** at the hairdresser's; **bei seinen Eltern wohnen** to live with one's parents; **bei einer Firma arbeiten** to work for a company; **etw bei sich haben** to have sth on one; **jdn bei sich haben** to have sb with one; **bei Goethe** in Goethe; **beim Militär** in the army
2 (*zeitlich*) at, on; (*während*) during; (*Zustand, Umstand*) in; **bei Nacht** at night; **bei Nebel** in fog; **bei Regen** if it rains; **bei solcher Hitze** in such heat; **bei meiner Ankunft** on my arrival; **bei der Arbeit** when I'm *etc* working; **beim Fahren** while driving

bei|behalten (*irr*) *vt* to keep

Beiboot *nt* dinghy
bei|bringen (*irr*) *vt*: **jdm etw ~** (*mitteilen*) to break sth to sb; (*lehren*) to teach sb sth
beide(s) *pron* both; **meine ~n Brüder** my two brothers, both my brothers; **wir ~** both (*o* the two) of us; **keiner von ~n** neither of them; **alle ~** both (of them); **~s ist sehr schön** both are very nice; **30 ~** (*beim Tennis*) 30 all
beieinander *adv* together
Beifahrer(in) *m(f)* passenger
Beifahrerairbag *m* passenger airbag
Beifahrersitz *m* passenger seat
Beifall (*-(e)s*) *m* applause
beige *adj* (*inv*) beige
Beigeschmack *m* aftertaste
Beil (*-(e)s, -e*) *nt* ax
Beilage *f* (*Gastr*) side dish; (*Gemüse*) vegetables *pl*; (*zu Buch etc*) supplement
beiläufig *adj* casual ▷ *adv* casually
Beileid *nt* condolences *pl*; **mein herzliches ~** please accept my sincere condolences
beiliegend *adj* enclosed
beim *kontr von* **bei dem**
Bein (*-(e)s, -e*) *nt* leg
beinah(e) *adv* almost, nearly
beinhalten *vt* to contain
Beipackzettel *m* instruction leaflet
beisammen *adv* together
Beisammensein (*-s*) *nt* get-together
beiseite *adv* aside
beiseite|legen *vt*: **etw ~** (*sparen*) to put sth aside
Beispiel (*-(e)s, -e*) *nt* example; **sich** (*dat*) **an jdm/etw ein ~ nehmen** to take sb/sth as an example; **zum ~** for example
beißen (**biss, gebissen**) *vt* to bite ▷ *vi* to bite; (*stechen: Rauch, Säure*) to sting ▷ *vr*: **sich ~** (*Farben*) to clash
Beitrag (*-(e)s, Beiträge*) *m* contribution; (*für Mitgliedschaft*) subscription; (*Versicherung*) premium
bei|tragen (*irr*) *vt, vi* to contribute (*zu* to)
bekannt *adj* well-known; (*nicht fremd*) familiar; **mit jdm ~ sein** to know sb; **~ geben** to announce; **jdn mit jdm ~ machen** to introduce sb to sb
Bekannte(r) *mf* friend; (*entfernter*) acquaintance
bekanntlich *adv* as everyone knows
Bekanntschaft *f* acquaintance
bekiffen *vr*: **sich ~** (*fam*) to get stoned
beklagen *vr*: **sich ~** to complain
Bekleidung *f* clothing
bekommen (*irr*) *vt* to get; (*erhalten*) to

receive; (*Kind*) to have; (*Zug, Grippe*) to catch, to get; **wie viel ~ Sie dafür?** how much is that? ▷ *vi*: **jdm ~** (*Essen*) to agree with sb; **wir ~ schon** (*bedient werden*) we're being served

beladen (*irr*) *vt* to load

Belag (-*(e)s, Beläge*) *m* coating; (*auf Zähnen*) plaque; (*auf Zunge*) fur

belasten *vt* to load; (*Körper*) to strain; (*Umwelt*) to pollute; (*fig: mit Sorgen etc*) to burden; (*Comm: Konto*) to debit; (*Jur*) to incriminate

belästigen *vt* to bother; (*stärker*) to pester; (*sexuell*) to harass

Belästigung *f* annoyance; **sexuelle ~** sexual harassment

belebt *adj* (*Straße etc*) busy

Beleg (-*(e)s, -e*) *m* (*Comm*) receipt; (*Beweis*) proof

belegen *vt* (*Brot*) to spread; (*Platz*) to reserve; (*Kurs, Vorlesung*) to register for; (*beweisen*) to prove

belegt *adj* (*Tel*) busy; (*Hotel*) full; (*Zunge*) coated; **~es Brötchen** sandwich; **der Platz ist ~** this seat is taken

Belegtzeichen *nt* (*Tel*) busy signal

beleidigen *vt* to insult; (*kränken*) to offend

Beleidigung *f* insult; (*Jur*) slander; (*schriftliche*) libel

beleuchten *vt* to light; (*bestrahlen*) to illuminate; (*fig*) to examine

Beleuchtung *f* lighting; (*Bestrahlung*) illumination

Belgien (-*s*) *nt* Belgium

Belgier(in) (-*s, -*) *m(f)* Belgian

belgisch *adj* Belgian

belichten *vt* to expose

Belichtung *f* exposure

Belichtungsmesser (-*s, -*) *m* light meter

Belieben *nt*: **ganz nach ~** (just) as you wish

beliebig *adj*: **jedes ~e Muster** any pattern; **jeder ~e** anyone ▷ *adv*: **~ lange** as long as you like; **~ viel** as many (*o* much) as you like

beliebt *adj* popular; **sich bei jdm ~ machen** to make oneself popular with sb

beliefern *vt* to supply

bellen *vi* to bark

Belohnung *f* reward

Belüftung *f* ventilation

belügen (*irr*) *vt* to lie to

bemerkbar *adj* noticeable; **sich ~ machen** (*Mensch*) to attract attention; (*Zustand*) to become noticeable

bemerken *vt* (*wahrnehmen*) to notice; (*sagen*) to remark

bemerkenswert *adj* remarkable

Bemerkung *f* remark

bemitleiden *vt* to pity

bemühen *vr*: **sich ~** to try (hard), to make an effort

Bemühung *f* effort

bemuttern *vt* to mother

benachbart *adj* neighboring

benachrichtigen *vt* to inform

Benachrichtigung *f* notification

benachteiligen *vt* to (put at a) disadvantage; (*wegen Rasse etc*) to discriminate against

benehmen (*irr*) *vr*: **sich ~** to behave

Benehmen (-*s*) *nt* behavior

beneiden *vt* to envy; **jdn um etw ~** to envy sb sth

Beneluxländer *pl* Benelux countries *pl*

benommen *adj* dazed

benötigen *vt* to need

benutzen *vt* to use

Benutzer(in) (-*s, -*) *m(f)* user

benutzerfreundlich *adj* user-friendly

Benutzerhandbuch *nt* user's guide

Benutzerkennung *f* user ID

Benutzeroberfläche *f* (*Inform*) user/system interface

Benutzung *f* use

Benutzungsgebühr *f* (rental) charge

Benzin (-*s, -e*) *nt* (*Auto*) gasoline, gas

Benzingutschein *m* gasoline (*o* gas) coupon

Benzinkanister *m* gasoline (*o* gas) can

Benzinpumpe *f* gasoline (*o* gas) pump

Benzintank *m* gasoline(*o* gas) tank

Benzinuhr *f* fuel gauge

beobachten *vt* to observe

Beobachtung *f* observation

bequem *adj* comfortable; (*Ausrede*) convenient; (*faul*) lazy; **machen Sie es sich ~** make yourself at home

Bequemlichkeit *f* comfort; (*Faulheit*) laziness

beraten (*irr*) *vt* to advise; (*besprechen*) to discuss ▷ *vr*: **sich ~** to consult

Beratung *f* advice; (*bei Arzt etc*) consultation

berauben *vt* to rob

berechnen *vt* to calculate; (*Comm*) to charge

berechnend *adj* (*Mensch*) calculating

berechtigen *vt* to entitle (*zu* to); (*fig*) to justify

berechtigt adj justified; **zu etw ~ sein** to be entitled to sth

bereden vt (besprechen) to discuss

Bereich (-(e)s, -e) m area; (Ressort, Gebiet) field

bereisen vt to travel through

bereit adj ready; **zu etw ~ sein** to be ready for sth; **sich ~ erklären, etw zu tun** to agree to do sth

bereiten vt to prepare; (Kummer) to cause; (Freude) to give

bereit|legen vt to lay out

bereit|machen vr: **sich ~** to get ready

bereits adv already

Bereitschaft f readiness; **~ haben** (Arzt) to be on call

bereit|stehen vi to be ready

bereuen vt to regret

Berg (-(e)s, -e) m mountain; (kleiner) hill; **in die ~e fahren** to go to the mountains

bergab adv downhill

bergauf adv uphill

Bergbahn f mountain railroad

bergen (barg, geborgen) vt (retten) to rescue; (enthalten) to contain

Bergführer(in) m(f) mountain guide

Berghütte f mountain hut

bergig adj mountainous

Bergschuh m climbing boot

Bergsteigen (-s) nt mountaineering

Bergsteiger(in) (-s, -) m(f) mountaineer

Bergtour f mountain hike

Bergung f (Rettung) rescue; (von Toten, Fahrzeugen) recovery

Bergwacht (-, -en) f mountain rescue service

Bergwerk nt mine

Bericht (-(e)s, -e) m report

berichten vt, vi to report

berichtigen vt to correct

Bermudadreieck nt Bermuda triangle

Bermudainseln pl Bermuda sing

Bermudashorts pl Bermuda shorts pl

Bernstein m amber

berüchtigt adj notorious, infamous

berücksichtigen vt to take into account; (Antrag, Bewerber) to consider

Beruf (-(e)s, -e) m occupation; (akademischer) profession; (Gewerbe) trade; **was sind Sie von ~?** what do you do (for a living)?

beruflich adj professional

Berufsausbildung f vocational training

Berufsschule f vocational college

berufstätig adj employed

Berufsverkehr m commuter traffic

beruhigen vt to calm ▷ vr: **sich ~** (Mensch, Situation) to calm down

beruhigend adj reassuring

Beruhigungsmittel nt sedative

berühmt adj famous

berühren vt to touch; (gefühlsmäßig bewegen) to move; (betreffen) to affect; (flüchtig erwähnen) to mention, to touch on ▷ vr: **sich ~** to touch

besaufen (irr) vr: **sich ~** (fam) to get plastered

beschädigen vt to damage

beschäftigen vt to occupy; (beruflich) to employ ▷ vr: **sich mit etw ~** to occupy oneself with sth; (sich befassen) to deal with sth

beschäftigt adj busy, occupied

Beschäftigung f (Beruf) employment; (Tätigkeit) occupation; (geistige) preoccupation (mit with)

Bescheid (-(e)s, -e) m information; **~ wissen** to be informed (o know) (über +akk about); **ich weiß ~** I know; **jdm ~ geben** o **sagen** to let sb know

bescheiden adj modest

bescheinigen vt to certify; (bestätigen) to acknowledge

Bescheinigung f certificate; (Quittung) receipt

bescheuert adj (fam, pej) stupid

beschimpfen vt (mit Kraftausdrücken) to swear at

beschlagnahmen vt to confiscate

Beschleunigung f acceleration

Beschleunigungsspur f acceleration lane

beschließen (irr) vt to decide on; (beenden) to end

Beschluss m decision

beschränken vt to limit, to restrict (auf +akk to) ▷ vr: **sich ~** to restrict oneself (auf +akk to)

Beschränkung f limitation, restriction

beschreiben (irr) vt to describe; (Papier) to write on

Beschreibung f description

beschuldigen vt to accuse (gen of)

Beschuldigung f accusation

beschummeln vt, vi (fam) to cheat (um out of)

beschützen vt to protect (vor +dat from)

Beschwerde (-, -n) f complaint; **~n** pl (Leiden) trouble sing

beschweren vt to weight down; (fig) to burden ▷ vr: **sich ~** to complain

beschwipst *adj* tipsy
beseitigen *vt* to remove; (*Problem*) to get rid of; (*Müll*) to dispose of
Beseitigung *f* removal; (*von Müll*) disposal
Besen (*-s, -*) *m* broom
besetzen *vt* (*Haus, Land*) to occupy; (*Platz*) to take; (*Posten*) to fill; (*Rolle*) to cast
besetzt *adj* full; (*Tel*) busy; (*Platz*) taken; (*toilet*) occupied
Besetztzeichen *nt* busy signal
besichtigen *vt* (*Museum*) to visit; (*Sehenswürdigkeit*) to have a look at; (*Stadt*) to tour
Besichtigung *f* visit
besiegen *vt* to defeat
Besitz (*-es*) *m* possession; (*Eigentum*) property
besitzen (*irr*) *vt* to own; (*Eigenschaft*) to have
Besitzer(in) (*-s, -*) *m(f)* owner
besoffen *adj* (*fam*) plastered
besondere(r, s) *adj* special; (*bestimmt*) particular; (*eigentümlich*) peculiar; **nichts ~s** nothing special
Besonderheit *f* special feature; (*besondere Eigenschaft*) peculiarity
besonders *adv* especially, particularly; (*getrennt*) separately
besorgen *vt* (*beschaffen*) to get (*jdm* for sb); (*kaufen a.*) to purchase; (*erledigen: Geschäfte*) to deal with
besprechen (*irr*) *vt* to discuss
Besprechung *f* discussion; (*Konferenz*) meeting
Besprechungsraum *m* conference room; (*beim Arzt*) consultation room
besser *adj* better; **es geht ihm ~** he feels better; **~ gesagt** or rather; **~ werden** to improve
bessern *vt* to improve ▷ *vr*: **sich ~** to improve; (*Mensch*) to mend one's ways
Besserung *f* improvement; **gute ~!** get well soon
beständig *adj* constant; (*Wetter*) settled
Bestandteil *m* component
bestätigen *vt* to confirm; (*Empfang, Brief*) to acknowledge
Bestätigung *f* confirmation; (*von Brief*) acknowledgement
beste(r, s) *adj* best; **das ~ wäre, wir ...** it would be best if we ... ▷ *adv*: **sie singt am ~n** she sings best; **so ist es am ~n** it's best that way; **am ~n gehst du gleich** you'd better go at once

bestechen (*irr*) *vt* to bribe
Bestechung *f* bribery
Besteck (*-(e)s, -e*) *nt* silverware
bestehen (*irr*) *vi* to be, to exist; (*andauern*) to last; **~ auf** *+dat* to insist on; **~ aus** to consist of ▷ *vt* (*Probe, Prüfung*) to pass; (*Kampf*) to win
bestehlen (*irr*) *vt* to rob
bestellen *vt* to order; (*reservieren*) to book; (*Grüße, Auftrag*) to pass on (*jdm* to sb); (*kommen lassen*) to send for
Bestellnummer *f* order number
Bestellung *f* (*Comm*) order; (*das Bestellen*) ordering
bestens *adv* very well
bestimmen *vt* to determine; (*Regeln*) to lay down; (*Tag, Ort*) to set; (*ernennen*) to appoint; (*vorsehen*) to mean (*für* for)
bestimmt *adj* definite; (*gewiss*) certain; (*entschlossen*) firm ▷ *adv* definitely; (*wissen*) for sure
Bestimmung *f* (*Verordnung*) regulation; (*Zweck*) purpose
Best.-Nr. (*abk*) = **Bestellnummer** order number
bestrafen *vt* to punish
bestrahlen *vt* to illuminate; (*Med*) to treat with radiotherapy
bestreiten (*irr*) *vt* (*leugnen*) to deny
Bestseller (*-s, -*) *m* bestseller
bestürzt *adj* dismayed
Besuch (*-(e)s, -e*) *m* visit; (*Mensch*) visitor; **~ haben** to have company
besuchen *vt* to visit; (*Schule, Kino etc*) to go to
Besucher(in) (*-s, -*) *m(f)* visitor
Besuchszeit *f* visiting hours *pl*
betäuben *vt* (*Med*) to anesthetize
Betäubung *f* anesthetic; **örtliche ~** local anesthetic
Betäubungsmittel *nt* anesthetic
Bete (*-, -n*) *f*: **Rote ~** beet
beteiligen *vr*: **sich an etw** (*dat*) **~** to take part in sth, to participate in sth ▷ *vt*: **jdn an etw** (*dat*) **~** to involve sb in sth
Beteiligung *f* participation; (*Anteil*) share; (*Besucherzahl*) attendance
beten *vi* to pray
Beton (*-s, -s*) *m* concrete
betonen *vt* to stress; (*hervorheben*) to emphasize
Betonung *f* stress; (*fig*) emphasis
Betr. (*abk*) = **Betreff** re
Betracht *m*: **in ~ ziehen** to take into consideration; **in ~ kommen** to be a possibility;

nicht in ~ kommen to be out of the question

betrachten vt to look at; **~ als** to regard as

beträchtlich adj considerable

Betrag (-(e)s, Beträge) m amount, sum

betragen (irr) vt to amount (o come) to ▷ vr: **sich ~** to behave

betreffen (irr) vt to concern; (Regelung etc) to affect; **was mich betrifft** as far as I'm concerned

betreffend adj relevant, in question

betreten (irr) vt to enter; (Bühne etc) to step onto; **„B~ verboten"** 'keep off/out'

betreuen vt to look after; (Reisegruppe, Abteilung) to be in charge of

Betreuer(in) (-s, -) m(f) (Pfleger) caregiver; (von Reisegruppe) group leader

Betrieb (-(e)s, -e) m (Firma) company; (Anlage) plant; (Tätigkeit) operation; (Treiben) bustle; **außer ~ sein** to be out of order; **in ~ sein** to be in operation

betriebsbereit adj operational

Betriebsrat m (Gremium) works council

Betriebssystem nt (Inform) operating system

betrinken (irr) vr: **sich ~** to get drunk

betroffen adj (bestürzt) shaken; **von etw ~ werden/sein** to be affected by sth

betrog imperf von **betrügen**

betrogen pp von **betrügen**

Betrug (-(e)s) m deception; (Jur) fraud

betrügen (betrog, betrogen) vt to deceive; (Jur) to defraud; (Partner) to cheat on

Betrüger(in) (-s, -) m(f) cheat

betrunken adj drunk

Bett (-(e)s, -en) nt bed; **ins** o **zu ~ gehen** to go to bed; **das ~ machen** to make the bed

Bettbezug m duvet cover

Bettdecke f blanket

betteln vi to beg

Bettlaken nt sheet

Bettler(in) (-s, -) m(f) beggar

Bettsofa nt sofa bed

Betttuch nt sheet

Bettwäsche f bed linens

Bettzeug m bedding

beugen vt to bend ▷ vr: **sich ~** to bend; (sich fügen) to submit (dat to)

Beule (-, -n) f (Schwellung) bump; (Delle) dent

beunruhigen vt to worry ▷ vr: **sich ~** to worry

beurteilen vt to judge

Beute (-) f (von Dieb) loot; (von Tier) prey

Beutel (-s, -) m bag

Bevölkerung f population

bevollmächtigt adj authorized (zu etw to do sth)

bevor conj before

bevor|stehen (irr) vi (Schwierigkeiten) to lie ahead; (Gefahr) to be imminent; **jdm ~** (Überraschung etc) to be in store for sb

bevorstehend adj forthcoming

bevorzugen vt to prefer

bewachen vt to guard

bewacht adj: **~er Parkplatz** guarded parking lot

bewegen vt to move; **jdn dazu ~, etw zu tun** to get sb to do sth ▷ vr: **sich ~** to move; **es bewegt sich etwas** (fig) things are beginning to happen

Bewegung f movement; (Phys) motion; (innere) emotion; (körperlich) exercise

Bewegungsmelder (-s, -) m motion sensor

Beweis (-es, -e) m proof; (Zeugnis) evidence

beweisen (irr) vt to prove; (zeigen) to show

bewerben (irr) vr: **sich ~** to apply (um for)

Bewerbung f application

Bewerbungsunterlagen pl application documents pl

bewilligen vt to allow; (Geld) to grant

bewirken vt to cause, to bring about

bewohnen vt to live in

Bewohner(in) (-s, -) m(f) inhabitant; (von Haus) resident

bewölkt adj cloudy, overcast

Bewölkung f clouds pl

bewundern vt to admire

bewundernswert adj admirable

bewusst adj conscious; (absichtlich) deliberate; **sich** (dat) **einer Sache** (gen) **~ sein** to be aware of sth ▷ adv consciously; (absichtlich) deliberately

bewusstlos adj unconscious

Bewusstlosigkeit f unconsciousness

Bewusstsein (-s) nt consciousness; **bei ~** conscious

bezahlen vt to pay; (Ware, Leistung) to pay for; **kann ich bar/mit Kreditkarte ~?** can I pay cash/by credit card?; **sich bezahlt machen** to be worth it

Bezahlung f payment

bezeichnen vt (kennzeichnen) to mark; (nennen) to call; (beschreiben) to describe

Bezeichnung f (Name) name; (Begriff) term

beziehen (irr) vt (Bett) to change; (Haus, Position) to move into; (erhalten) to receive; (Zeitung) to take; **einen Stand-**

punkt ~ (*fig*) to take up a position ▷ *vr:* **sich** ~ to refer (*auf +akk* to)
Beziehung *f* (*Verbindung*) connection; (*Verhältnis*) relationship; **~en haben** (*vorteilhaft*) to have connections (*o* contacts); **in dieser** ~ in this respect
beziehungsweise *adv* or; (*genauer gesagt*) or rather
Bezirk (*-(e)s, -e*) *m* district
Bezug (*-(e)s, Bezüge*) *m* (*Überzug*) cover; (*von Kopfkissen*) pillowcase; **in** ~ **auf** *+akk* with regard to
bezüglich *prep* (*+gen*) concerning
bezweifeln *vt* to doubt
BH (*-s, -s*) *m* bra
Bhf. (*abk*) = **Bahnhof** station
Biathlon (*-s, -s*) *m* biathlon
Bibel (*-, -n*) *f* Bible
Biber (*-s, -*) *m* beaver
Bibliothek (*-, -en*) *f* library
biegen (**bog, gebogen**) *vt* to bend ▷ *vr:* **sich** ~ to bend ▷ *vi* to turn (*in +akk* into)
Biegung *f* bend
Biene (*-, -n*) *f* bee
Bier (*-(e)s, -e*) *nt* beer; **helles** ~ ≈ beer; **dunkles** ~ ≈ dark beer; **zwei** ~, **bitte!** two beers, please
Biergarten *m* beer garden
Bierzelt *nt* beer tent
bieten (**bot, geboten**) *vt* to offer; (*bei Versteigerung*) to bid; **sich** (*dat*) **etw** ~ **lassen** to put up with sth ▷ *vr:* **sich** ~ (*Gelegenheit*) to present itself (*dat* to)
Bikini (*-s, -s*) *m* bikini
Bild (*-(e)s, -er*) *nt* picture; (*gedankliches*) image; (*Foto*) photo
bilden *vt* to form; (*geistig*) to educate; (*ausmachen*) to constitute ▷ *vr:* **sich** ~ (*entstehen*) to form; (*lernen*) to educate oneself
Bilderbuch *nt* picture book
Bildhauer(in) (*-s, -*) *m(f)* sculptor
Bildschirm *m* screen
Bildschirmschoner (*-s, -*) *m* screen saver
Bildschirmtext *m* viewdata, videotext
Bildung *f* formation; (*Wissen, Benehmen*) education
Bildungsurlaub *m* sabbatical; (*von Firma*) training
Billard *nt* pool
billig *adj* cheap; (*gerecht*) fair
Billigflieger *m* budget airline
Billigflug *m* cheap flight
Binde (*-, -n*) *f* bandage; (*Armbinde*) band; (*Damenbinde*) sanitary napkin
Bindehautentzündung *f* conjunctivitis

binden (**band, gebunden**) *vt* to tie; (*Buch*) to bind; (*Soße*) to thicken
Bindestrich *m* hyphen
Bindfaden *m* string
Bindung *f* bond, tie; (*Skibindung*) binding
Bio- *in zW* bio-
Biokost *f* health food
Bioladen *m* health-food store

Biologie *f* biology
biologisch *adj* biological; (*Anbau*) organic
Birke (*-, -n*) *f* birch
Birne (*-, -n*) *f* (*Obst*) pear; (*Elek*) (light) bulb

SCHLÜSSELWORT

bis *prep* (*+akk*), *adv* **1** (*zeitlich*) till, until; (*bis spätestens*) by; **Sie haben bis Dienstag Zeit** you have until *o* till Tuesday; **bis Dienstag muss es fertig sein** it must be ready by Tuesday; **bis auf Weiteres** until further notice; **bis in die Nacht** into the night; **bis bald/gleich** see you later/soon
2 (*räumlich*) (up) to; **ich fahre bis Köln** I'm going to *o* I'm going as far as Cologne; **bis an unser Grundstück** (right up) to our property (line); **bis hierher** this far
3 (*bei Zahlen*) up to; **bis zu** up to
4: bis auf etw (*akk*) (*außer*) except sth; (*einschließlich*) including sth
▷ *konj* **1** (*mit Zahlen*) to; **10 bis 20** 10 to 20
2 (*zeitlich*) till, until; **bis es dunkel wird** till *o* until it gets dark; **von ... bis ...** from ... to ...

Bischof (*-s, Bischöfe*) *m* bishop
bisher *adv* up to now, so far
Biskuit (*-(e)s, -s o -e*) *nt* sponge
biss *imperf von* **beißen**
Biss (*-es, -e*) *m* bite
bisschen *adj:* **ein** ~ a little (bit of); **ein** ~ **Salz/Liebe** a little salt/love; **ich habe kein** ~ **Hunger** I'm not at all hungry ▷ *adv:* **ein** ~ a little (o bit); **kein** ~ not at all
bissig *adj* (*Hund*) vicious; (*Bemerkung*) cutting

Bit (-s, -s) nt (Inform) bit

bitte interj please; **wie ~?** (I beg your) pardon?; **~ (schön** o **sehr)** (als Antwort auf Dank) you're welcome, that's alright; **hier, ~** here you are

Bitte (-, -n) f request

bitten (**bat, gebeten**) vt, vi to ask (um for)

bitter adj bitter

Blähungen pl (Med) gas sing

blamieren vr: **sich ~** to make a fool of oneself ▷ vt: **jdn ~** to make sb look a fool

Blankoscheck m blank check

Blase (-, -n) f bubble; (Med) blister; (Anat) bladder

blasen (**blies, geblasen**) vi to blow

Blasenentzündung f cystitis

blass adj pale

Blatt (-(e)s, **Blätter**) nt leaf; (von Papier) sheet

blättern vi (Inform) to scroll; **in etw** (dat) **~** to leaf through sth

Blätterteig m puff pastry

Blattsalat m green salad

Blattspinat m spinach

blau adj blue; (fam: betrunken) plastered; **~es Auge** black eye; **~er Fleck** bruise

Blaubeere f blueberry

Blaulicht nt flashing blue light

blau|machen vi to skip work; (in Schule) to skip school

Blauschimmelkäse m blue cheese

Blazer (-s, -) m blazer

Blech (-(e)s, -e) nt sheet metal; (Backblech) cookie sheet

Blechschaden m (Auto) damage to the bodywork

Blei (-(e)s, -e) nt lead

bleiben (**blieb, geblieben**) vi to stay; **lass das ~!** stop it!; **das bleibt unter uns** that's (just) between us; **mir bleibt keine andere Wahl** I have no other choice

bleich adj pale

bleichen vt to bleach

bleifrei adj (Benzin) unleaded

bleihaltig adj (Benzin) leaded

Bleistift m pencil

Blende (-, -n) f (Foto) aperture

Blick (-(e)s, -e) m look; (kurz) glance; (Aussicht) view; **auf den ersten ~** at first sight; **einen ~ auf etw** (akk) **werfen** to take a look at sth

blicken vi to look; **sich ~ lassen** to show up

blieb imperf von **bleiben**

blies imperf von **blasen**

blind adj blind; (Glas etc) dull

Blinddarm m appendix

Blinddarmentzündung f appendicitis

Blinde(r) mf blind person/man/woman; **die ~n** pl the blind pl

Blindenhund m seeing-eye dog

Blindenschrift f braille

blinken vi (Stern, Lichter) to twinkle; (aufleuchten) to flash; (Auto) to signal

Blinker (-s, -) m (Auto) turn signal

blinzeln vi (mit beiden Augen) to blink; (mit einem Auge) to wink

Blitz (-es, -e) m (flash of) lightning; (Foto) flash

blitzen vi (Foto) to use a/the flash; **es blitzte und donnerte** there was thunder and lightning

Blitzlicht nt flash

Block (-(e)s, **Blöcke**) m (a. fig) block; (von Papier) pad

Blockflöte f recorder

Blockhaus nt log cabin

blockieren vt to block ▷ vi to jam; (Räder) to lock

Blockschrift f block letters pl

blöd adj stupid

blödeln vi (fam) to fool around

Blog (-s, -s) nt (Inform) blog

bloggen vi to blog

blond adj blond; (Frau) blonde

bloß adj **1** (unbedeckt) bare; (nackt) naked; **mit der bloßen Hand** with one's bare hand; **mit bloßem Auge** with the naked eye
2 (alleinig, nur) mere; **der bloße Gedanke** the very thought; **bloßer Neid** sheer envy
▷ adv only, merely; **lass das bloß!** just don't do that!; **wie ist das bloß passiert?** how on earth did that happen?

blühen vi to bloom; (fig) to flourish

Blume (-, -n) f flower; (von Wein) bouquet

Blumenbeet nt flower bed

Blumengeschäft nt florist('s), flower shop

Blumenkohl m cauliflower

Blumenladen m florist('s), flower shop

Blumenstrauß m bouquet

Blumentopf m flowerpot

Blumenvase f vase

Bluse (-, -n) f blouse

Blut (-(e)s) nt blood

Blutbild nt blood count

Blutdruck m blood pressure

Blüte (-, -n) f (*Pflanzenteil*) flower, bloom; (*Baumblüte*) blossom; (*fig*) prime
bluten vi to bleed
Blütenstaub m pollen
Bluter (-s, -) m (*Med*) hemophiliac
Bluterguss m hematoma; (*blauer Fleck*) bruise
Blutgruppe f blood group
blutig adj bloody
Blutkonserve f unit of stored blood
Blutorange f blood orange
Blutprobe f blood sample
Blutspende f blood donation
Bluttransfusion f blood transfusion
Blutung f bleeding
Blutvergiftung f blood poisoning
Blutwurst f blood sausage
BLZ (*abk*) = **Bankleitzahl**
Bock (-(e)s, Böcke) m (*Reh*) buck; (*Schaf*) ram; (*Gestell*) trestle; (*Sport*) vaulting horse; **ich hab keinen ~ drauf** (*fam*) I don't feel like it
Boden (-s, Böden) m ground; (*Fußboden*) floor; (*von Meer, Fass*) bottom; (*Speicher*) attic
Bodennebel m ground mist
Bodenpersonal nt ground staff
Bodenschätze pl mineral resources pl
Bodensee m: **der ~** Lake Constance
Body (-s, -s) m bodysuit; (*für Baby*) Onesie®
Bodybuilding (-s) nt bodybuilding
bog imperf von **biegen**
Bogen (-s, -) m (*Biegung*) curve; (*in der Architektur*) arch; (*Waffe, Instrument*) bow; (*Papier*) sheet
Bohne (-, -n) f bean; **grüne ~n** pl green beans pl
Bohnenkaffee m real coffee
Bohnensprosse f bean sprout
bohren vt to drill
Bohrer (-s, -) m drill
Boiler (-s, -) m water heater
Boje (-, -n) f buoy
Bolivien (-s) nt Bolivia
Bombe (-, -n) f bomb
Bon (-s, -s) m (*Kassenzettel*) receipt; (*Gutschein*) voucher, coupon
Bonbon (-s, -s) nt candy
Boot (-(e)s, -e) nt boat
Bootsverleih m boat rental
Bord (-(e)s, -e) m: **an ~ eines Schiffes** on board (a ship); **an ~ gehen** (*Schiff*) to go on board; (*Flugzeug*) to board; **von ~ gehen** to disembark

Bordcomputer m dashboard computer
Bordell (-s, -e) nt brothel
Bordkarte f boarding pass
Bordstein m curb
borgen vt to borrow; **jdm etw ~** to lend sb sth; **sich** (*dat*) **etw ~** to borrow sth
Börse (-, -n) f stock exchange; (*Geldbörse*) wallet
bös adj siehe **böse**
bösartig adj malicious; (*Med*) malignant
Böschung f slope; (*Uferböschung*) embankment
böse adj bad; (*stärker*) evil; (*Wunde*) nasty; (*zornig*) angry; **bist du mir ~?** are you angry with me?
boshaft adj malicious
Bosnien (-s) nt Bosnia
Bosnien-Herzegowina (-s) nt Bosnia-Herzegovina
böswillig adj malicious
bot imperf von **bieten**
botanisch adj: **~er Garten** botanical gardens pl
Botschaft f message; (*Pol*) embassy
Botschafter(in) m(f) ambassador
Botsuana (-s) nt Botswana
Bouillon (-, -s) f stock
Boutique (-, -n) f boutique
Bowle (-, -n) f punch
Box (-, -en) f (*Behälter, Pferdebox*) box; (*Lautsprecher*) speaker; (*bei Autorennen*) pit
boxen vi to box
Boxer (-s, -) m (*Hund, Sportler*) boxer
Boxershorts pl boxers pl
Boxkampf m boxing match
Boykott (-s, -e) m boycott
brach imperf von **brechen**
brachte imperf von **bringen**
Brainstorming (-s) nt brainstorming
Branchenverzeichnis nt Yellow Pages® pl
Brand (-(e)s, Brände) m fire; **einen ~ haben** (*fam*) to be parched
Brandenburg (-s) nt Brandenburg
Brandsalbe f ointment for burns
Brandung f surf
Brandwunde f burn
brannte imperf von **brennen**
Brasilien (-s) nt Brazil
braten (**briet, gebraten**) vt to roast; (*auf dem Rost*) to grill; (*in der Pfanne*) to fry
Braten (-s, -) m roast
Bratensoße f gravy
Brathähnchen nt roast chicken

Bratkartoffeln *pl* fried potatoes *pl*

Bratpfanne *f* frying pan

Bratspieß *m* spit

Bratwurst *f* fried sausage; (*gegrillte*) grilled sausage

Brauch (*-s, Bräuche*) *m* custom

brauchen *vt* (*nötig haben*) to need (*für, zu* for); (*erfordern*) to require; (*Zeit*) to take; (*gebrauchen*) to use; **wie lange wird er ~?** how long will it take him?; **du brauchst es nur zu sagen** you only need to say; **das braucht seine Zeit** it takes time; **ihr braucht es nicht zu tun** you don't have (*o* need) to do it; **sie hätte nicht zu kommen ~** she needn't have come

brauen *vt* to brew

Brauerei *f* brewery

braun *adj* brown; (*von Sonne*) tanned

Bräune (*-, -n*) *f* brownness; (*von Sonne*) tan

Bräunungsstudio *nt* tanning studio

Brause (*-, -n*) *f* (*Dusche*) shower; (*Getränk*) soda

Braut (*-, Bräute*) *f* bride

Bräutigam (*-s, -e*) *m* bridegroom

brav *adj* (*artig*) good, well-behaved

bravo *interj* well done

BRD (*-*) *f* (*abk*) = **Bundesrepublik Deutschland** FRG

BRD

The **BRD** is the official name for the Federal Republic of Germany. It comprises 16 **Länder** (see **Land**). It was the name given to the former West Germany as opposed to East Germany (the **DDR**). The two Germanies were reunited on October 3, 1990.

---

brechen (**brach, gebrochen**) *vt* to break; (*erbrechen*) to throw up; **sich** (*dat*) **den Arm ~** to break one's arm ▷ *vi* to break; (*erbrechen*) to vomit, to be sick

Brechreiz *m* nausea

Brei (*-(e)s, -e*) *m* (*Breimasse*) mush, pulp; (*für Kinder: Getreide*) cereal; (*Gemüse, Obst*) puree

breit *adj* wide; (*Schultern*) broad; **zwei Meter ~** two meters wide

Breite (*-, -n*) *f* breadth; (*bei Maßangaben*) width; (*Geo*) latitude; **der ~ nach** widthways

Breitengrad *m* (degree of) latitude

Bremen (*-s*) *nt* Bremen

Bremsbelag *m* brake lining

Bremse (*-, -n*) *f* brake; (*Zool*) horsefly

bremsen *vi* to brake ▷ *vt* (*Auto*) to brake; (*fig*) to slow down

Bremsflüssigkeit *f* brake fluid

Bremslicht *nt* brake light

Bremspedal *nt* brake pedal

Bremsspur *f* tire marks *pl*

Bremsweg *m* braking distance

brennen (**brannte, gebrannt**) *vi* to burn; (*in Flammen stehen*) to be on fire; **es brennt!** fire!; **mir ~ die Augen** my eyes are smarting; **das Licht ~ lassen** to leave the light on

Brennholz *nt* firewood

Brennnessel *f* stinging nettle

Brennspiritus *m* methylated spirits *pl*

Brennstab *m* fuel rod

Brennstoff *m* fuel

Brett (*-(e)s, -er*) *nt* board; (*länger*) plank; (*Regal*) shelf; (*Spielbrett*) board; **Schwarzes ~** bulletin board; **~er** *pl* (*Skier*) skis *pl*

Brettspiel *nt* board game

Brezel (*-, -n*) *f* pretzel

Brief (*-(e)s, -e*) *m* letter

Briefbombe *f* letter bomb

Brieffreund(in) *m(f)* pen pal

Briefkasten *m* mailbox; **elektronischer ~** e-mail inbox

Briefmarke *f* stamp

Briefpapier *nt* writing paper

Brieftasche *f* billfold

Briefträger(in) *m(f)* mailman/-woman

Briefumschlag *m* envelope

Briefwaage *f* postage meter

briet *imperf von* **braten**

Brille (*-, -n*) *f* glasses *pl*; (*Schutzbrille*) goggles *pl*

Brillenetui *nt* glasses case

bringen (**brachte, gebracht**) *vt* (*herbringen*) to bring; (*mitnehmen, vom Sprecher weg*) to take; (*holen, herbringen*) to get, to fetch; (*Theat, Cine*) to show; (*Radio, TV*) to broadcast; **~ Sie mir bitte noch ein Bier** could you bring me another beer, please?; **jdn nach Hause ~** to take sb home; **jdn dazu ~, etw zu tun** to make sb do sth; **jdn auf eine Idee ~** to give sb an idea

Brise (*-, -n*) *f* breeze

Brite (*-n, -n*) *m*, **Britin** *f* British person, Briton; **er ist ~** he is British; **die ~n** the British

britisch *adj* British

Brocken (*-s, -*) *m* bit; (*größer*) lump, chunk

Brokkoli *m* broccoli

Brombeere *f* blackberry

Bronchitis (-) f bronchitis
Bronze (-, -n) f bronze
Brosche (-, -n) f brooch
Brot (-(e)s, -e) nt bread; (*Laib*) loaf
Brotaufstrich m spread
Brötchen nt roll
Brotzeit f (*Pause*) break; (*Essen*) snack; ~ **machen** to have a snack
Browser (-s, -) m (*Inform*) browser
Bruch (-(e)s, *Brüche*) m (*Brechen*) breaking; (*Bruchstelle; mit Partei, Tradition etc*) break; (*Med: Eingeweidebruch*) rupture, hernia; (*Knochenbruch*) fracture; (*Math*) fraction
brüchig adj brittle
Brücke (-, -n) f bridge
Bruder (-s, *Brüder*) m brother
Brühe (-, -n) f (*Suppe*) (clear) soup; (*Grundlage*) stock; (*pej: Getränk*) dishwater
Brühwürfel m bouillon cube
brüllen vi to roar; (*Stier*) to bellow; (*vor Schmerzen*) to scream (with pain)
brummen vi (*Bär, Mensch*) to growl; (*brummeln*) to mutter; (*Insekt*) to buzz; (*Motor, Radio*) to drone ▷ vt to growl
brünett adj brunette
Brunnen (-s, -) m fountain; (*tief*) well; (*natürlich*) spring
Brust (-, *Brüste*) f breast; (*beim Mann*) chest
Brustschwimmen (-s) nt breaststroke
Brustwarze f nipple
brutal adj brutal
brutto adv gross
BSE (-) nt (*abk*) = **bovine spongiforme Enzephalopathie** BSE
Bube (-n, -n) m boy; (*Karten*) jack
Buch (-(e)s, *Bücher*) nt book
Buche (-, -n) f beech (tree)
buchen vt to book; (*Betrag*) to enter
Bücherei f library
Buchfink m chaffinch
Buchhalter(in) m(f) accountant
Buchhandlung f bookstore
Büchse (-, -n) f can
Buchstabe (-ns, -n) m letter
buchstabieren vt to spell
Bucht (-, -en) f bay
Buchung f booking; (*Comm*) entry
Buckel (-s, -) m hump
bücken vr: **sich ~** to bend down
Buddhismus (-) m Buddhism
Bude (-, -en) f (*auf Markt*) stall; (*fam: Wohnung*) pad, place
Büfett (-s, -s) nt sideboard; **kaltes ~** cold

buffet
Büffel (-s, -) m buffalo
Bügel (-s, -) m (*für Kleidung*) hanger; (*Steigbügel*) stirrup; (*Brille*) sidepiece; (*von Skilift*) T-bar
Bügelbrett nt ironing board
Bügeleisen nt iron
Bügelfalte f crease
bügelfrei adj non-iron
bügeln vt, vi to iron
buh interj boo
Bühne (-, -n) f stage
Bühnenbild nt set
Bulgare (-n, -n) m, **Bulgarin** f Bulgarian
Bulgarien (-s) nt Bulgaria
bulgarisch adj Bulgarian
Bulgarisch nt Bulgarian
Bulimie f bulimia
Bulle (-n, -n) m bull; (*fam: Polizist*) cop
Bummel (-s, -) m stroll
bummeln vi to stroll; (*trödeln*) to dawdle; (*faulenzen*) to loaf around
Bummelzug m slow train
bums interj bang
Bund (-(e)s, *Bünde*) m (*von Hose, Rock*) waistband; (*Freundschaftsbund*) bond; (*Organisation*) association; (*Pol*) confederation; **der ~** (*fam: Bundeswehr*) the army ▷ (-(e)s, -e) nt bunch; (*von Stroh etc*) bundle
Bundes- in zW Federal; (*auf Deutschland bezogen a.*) German
Bundeskanzler(in) m(f) chancellor
Bundesland nt regional unit in Germany similar to a state in the USA, ≈ state
Bundesliga f (*Sport*): **erste/zweite ~** First/Second Division
Bundespräsident(in) m(f) President
Bundesrat m (*in Deutschland*) Upper House (of the German Parliament); (*in der Schweiz*) Council of Ministers
Bundesregierung f Federal-Government
Bundesrepublik f Federal Republic; ~ **Deutschland** Federal Republic of Germany
Bundesstraße f ≈ state highway
Bundestag m Lower House (of the German Parliament)
Bundeswehr f (German) armed forces pl

The **Bundeswehr** is the name for the German armed forces. It was established in 1955, at first for volunteers, but since 1956 there has been compulsory military service for all able-bodied young men of 18. In peacetime the Defence Minister is the head of the 'Bundeswehr', but in wartime the **Bundeskanzler** takes over. The 'Bundeswehr' comes under the jurisdiction of NATO.

Bündnis nt alliance

Bungalow (-s, -s) m bungalow

Bungeejumping (-s) nt bungee jumping

bunt adj colorful; (von Programm etc) varied; ~e Farben bright colors ▷ adv (anstreichen) in bright colors

Buntstift m colored pencil

Burg (-, -en) f castle

Bürger(in) (-s, -) m(f) citizen

bürgerlich adj (Rechte, Ehe etc) civil; (vom Mittelstand) middle-class; (pej) bourgeois

Bürgermeister(in) m(f) mayor

Bürgersteig (-(e)s, -e) m sidewalk

Büro (-s, -s) nt office

Büroklammer f paper clip

Bürokratie f bureaucracy

Bursche (-n, -n) m boy; (Typ) guy

Bürste (-, -n) f brush

bürsten vt to brush

Bus (-ses, -se) m bus

Busbahnhof m bus station

Busch (-(e)s, Büsche) m bush; (Strauch) shrub

Busen (-s, -) m breasts pl, chest, bosom

Busfahrer(in) m(f) bus driver

Bushaltestelle f bus stop

Businessclass (-) f business class

Buslinie f bus route

Busreise f bus tour

Bußgeld nt fine

Büstenhalter (-s, -) m bra

Busverbindung f bus connection

Butter (-) f butter

Butterbrot nt slice of bread and butter

Butterkäse m type of mild, full-fat cheese

Buttermilch f buttermilk

Butterschmalz nt clarified butter

Button (-s, -s) m button

b. w. (abk) = **bitte wenden** pto

Byte (-s, -s) nt byte

bzw. adv (abk) = **beziehungsweise**

C

Cabrio (-s, -s) nt convertible
Café (-s, -s) nt café
Cafeteria (-, -s) f cafeteria
Call-Center (-s, -) nt call center
campen vi to camp
Camping (-s) nt camping
Campingbus m camper
Campingplatz m campground
Cappuccino (-s, -) m cappuccino
Carving (-s) nt (Ski) carving
Carvingski m carving ski
CD (-, -s) f (abk = **Compact Disc**) CD
CD-Brenner (-s, -) m CD burner, CD writer
CD-Player (-s, -) m CD player
CD-ROM (-, -s) f (abk = **Compact Disc Read Only Memory**) CD-ROM
CD-ROM-Laufwerk nt CD-ROM drive
CD-Spieler m CD player
Cello (-s, -s o Celli) nt cello
Celsius nt Celsius; **20 Grad ~** 20 degrees Celsius, 68 degrees Fahrenheit
Cent (-, -s) m (von Dollar und Euro) cent
Chamäleon (-s, -s) nt chameleon
Champagner (-s, -) m champagne
Champignon (-s, -s) m mushroom
Champions League (-, -s) f Champions League
Chance (-, -n) f chance; **die ~n stehen gut** the prospects are good
Chaos (-) nt chaos
Chaot(in) (-en, -en) m(f) (fam) disorganized person, scatterbrain
chaotisch adj chaotic
Charakter (-s, -e) m character
charakteristisch adj characteristic (für of)
Charisma (-s, Charismen o Charismata) nt charisma
charmant adj charming
chartern vt to charter
Chat (-s, -s) m (Inform) chat
chatten vi (Inform) to chat
checken vt (überprüfen) to check; (fam: verstehen) to get
Check-in (-s, -s) m check-in
Check-in-Schalter m check-in desk
Chef(in) (-s, -s) m(f) boss
Chefarzt m, **Chefärztin** f medical director
Chemie (-) f chemistry
chemisch adj chemical; **~e Reinigung** dry cleaning
Chemotherapie f chemotherapy
Chicoree (-s) m endive

Chiffre (-, -n) f (Geheimzeichen) cipher; (in Zeitung) box number
Chile (-s) nt Chile
Chili (-s, -s) m chilli
China (-s) nt China
Chinakohl m bok choy
Chinarestaurant nt Chinese restaurant
Chinese (-n, -n) m Chinese
Chinesin (-, -nen) f Chinese (woman); **sie ist ~** she's Chinese
chinesisch adj Chinese
Chinesisch nt Chinese
Chip (-s, -s) m (Inform) chip
Chipkarte f smart card
Chips pl (Kartoffelchips) chips pl
Chirurg(in) (-en, -en) m(f) surgeon
Chlor (-s) nt chlorine
Choke (-s, -s) m choke
Cholera (-) f cholera
Cholesterin (-s) nt cholesterol
Chor (-(e), Chöre) m choir; (Theat) chorus
Choreografie f choreography
Christ(in) (-en, -en) m(f) Christian
Christbaum m Christmas tree
Christi Himmelfahrt f the Ascension (of Christ)
Christkind nt baby Jesus; (das Geschenke bringt) ≈ Santa Claus
christlich adj Christian
Chrom (-s) nt chrome; (Chem) chromium
chronisch adj chronic
chronologisch adj chronological ▷ adv in chronological order
Chrysantheme (-, -n) f chrysanthemum
circa adv about, approximately
City (-) f downtown
Clementine (-, -n) f clementine
clever adj clever, smart
Clique (-, -n) f group; (pej) clique; **David und seine ~** David and his group o bunch
Clown (-s, -s) m clown
Club (-s, -s) m club
Cluburlaub m club vacation
Cocktail (-s, -s) m cocktail
Cocktailtomate f cherry tomato
Cognac (-s) m cognac
Cola (-, -s) f Coke®, cola
Comic (-s, -s) m comic strip; (Heft) comic
Compact Disc (-, -s) f compact disc
Computer (-s, -) m computer
Computerfreak m computer nerd

computergesteuert *adj* computer-controlled

Computergrafik *f* computer graphics *pl*

computerlesbar *adj* machine-readable

Computerspiel *nt* computer game

Computertomografie *f* computer tomography, scan

Computervirus *m* computer virus

Container (*-s, -*) *m* (*zum Transport*) container; (*für Bauschutt etc*) Dumpster®

Control-Taste *f* control key

Cookie (*-s, -s*) *nt* (*Inform*) cookie

cool *adj* (*fam*) cool

Cornflakes *pl* cornflakes *pl*

Couch (*-, -en*) *f* couch

Couchtisch *m* coffee table

Coupé (*-s, -s*) *nt* coupé

Coupon (*-s, -s*) *m* coupon

Cousin (*-s, -s*) *m* cousin

Cousine *f* cousin

Crack (*-s*) *nt* (*Droge*) crack

Creme (*-, -s*) *f* cream; (*Gastr*) mousse

Creutzfeld-Jakob-Krankheit *f* Creutzfeld-Jakob disease, CJD

Croissant (*-s, -s*) *nt* croissant

Curry (*-s*) *m* curry powder ▷ (*-s*) *nt* (*indisches Gericht*) curry

Currywurst *f* fried sausage with ketchup and curry powder

Cursor (*-, -s*) *m* (*Inform*) cursor

Cybercafé *nt* cybercafé

Cyberspace (*-*) *m* cyberspace

D

da *adv* **1** (*örtlich*) there; (*hier*) here; **da draußen** out there; **da sein** to be there; **da bin ich** here I am; **da, wo** where; **ist noch Milch da?** is there any milk left?
2 (*zeitlich*) then; (*folglich*) so
3: **da haben wir Glück gehabt** we were lucky there; **da kann man nichts machen** nothing can be done about it
▷ *konj* (*weil*) as, since

dabei *adv* (*räumlich*) close to it; (*zeitlich*) at the same time; (*obwohl, doch*) though; **sie hörte Radio und rauchte ~** she was listening to the radio and smoking (at the same time); **~ fällt mir ein ...** that reminds me ...; **~ kam es zu einem Unfall** this led to an accident; **... und ~ hat er gar keine Ahnung** ... even though he has no idea; **ich finde nichts ~** I don't see anything wrong with it; **es bleibt ~** that's settled; **~ sein** (*anwesend*) to be present; (*beteiligt*) to be involved; **ich bin ~!** count me in!; **er war gerade ~ zu gehen** he was just (*o* on the point of) leaving

dabei|bleiben (*irr*) *vi* to stick with it; **ich bleibe dabei** I'm not changing my mind

dabei|haben (*irr*) *vt*: **er hat seine Schwester dabei** he's brought his sister; **ich habe kein Geld dabei** I don't haven any money on me

Dach (*-(e)s, Dächer*) *nt* roof

Dachboden *m* attic, loft

Dachgepäckträger *m* roof rack

Dachrinne *f* gutter

Dachs (*-es, -e*) *m* badger

dachte *imperf von* **denken**

Dackel (*-s, -*) *m* dachshund

dadurch *adv* (*räumlich*) through it; (*durch diesen Umstand*) in that way; (*deshalb*) because of that, for that reason ▷ *konj*: **~, dass** because; **~, dass er hart arbeitete** (*indem*) by working hard

dafür *adv* for it; (*anstatt*) instead; **~ habe ich 50 Euro bezahlt** I paid 50 euros for it; **ich bin ~ zu bleiben** I'm for (*o* in favor of) staying; **~ ist er ja da** that's what he's there for; **er kann nichts ~** he can't help it

dagegen *adv* against it; (*im Vergleich damit*) in comparison; (*bei Tausch*) for it; **ich habe nichts ~** I don't mind

daheim *adv* at home

daher *adv* (*räumlich*) from there; (*Ursache*) that's why ▷ *conj* (*deshalb*) that's why

dahin *adv* (*räumlich*) there; (*zeitlich*) then; (*vergangen*) gone; **bis ~** (*zeitlich*) till then; (*örtlich*) up to there; **bis ~ muss die Arbeit fertig sein** the work must be finished by then

dahinter *adv* behind it

dahinterkommen *vi* to find out

Dahlie *f* dahlia

Dalmatiner (*-s, -*) *m* dalmatian

damals *adv* at that time, then

Dame (*-, -n*) *f* lady; (*Karten*) queen; (*Spiel*) checkers *sing*

Damenbinde *f* sanitary napkin

Damenkleidung *f* ladies' wear

Damentoilette *f* ladies' restroom

damit *adv* with it; (*begründend*) by that; **was meint er ~?** what does he mean by that?; **genug ~!** that's enough! ▷ *conj* so that

Damm (*-(e)s, Dämme*) *m* dyke; (*Staudamm*) dam; (*am Hafen*) mole; (*Bahn-, Straßendamm*) embankment

Dämmerung *f* twilight; (*am Morgen*) dawn; (*am Abend*) dusk

Dampf (*-(e)s, Dämpfe*) *m* steam; (*Dunst*) vapor

Dampfbad *nt* Turkish bath

Dampfbügeleisen *nt* steam iron

dampfen *vi* to steam

dämpfen *vt* (*Gastr*) to steam; (*Geräusch*) to deaden; (*Begeisterung*) to dampen

Dampfer (*-s, -*) *m* steamer

Dampfkochtopf *m* pressure cooker

danach *adv* after that; (*zeitlich a.*) afterwards; (*demgemäß*) accordingly; **mir ist nicht ~** I don't feel like it; **~ sieht es aus** that's what it looks like

Däne (*-n, -n*) *m* Dane

daneben *adv* beside it; (*im Vergleich*) in comparison

Dänemark (*-s*) *nt* Denmark

Dänin *f* Dane, Danish woman/girl

dänisch *adj* Danish

Dänisch *nt* Danish

dank *prep* (+*dat o gen*) thanks to

Dank (*-(e)s*) *m* thanks *pl*; **vielen ~!** thank you very much!; **jdm ~ sagen** to thank sb

dankbar *adj* grateful; (*Aufgabe*) rewarding

danke *interj* thank you, thanks; **~ schön (*o*

sehr) thank you very much; **nein** ~ no, thank you; **~, gerne** yes, please; **~, gleichfalls** thanks, and the same to you

danken *vi:* **jdm für etw** ~ to thank sb for sth; **nichts zu** ~ you're welcome

dann *adv* then; **bis ~!** see you (later)!; **~ eben nicht** okay, forget it, suit yourself

daran *adv* (*räumlich*) on it; (*befestigen*) to it; (*stoßen*) against it; **es liegt ~, dass ...** it's because ...

darauf *adv* (*räumlich*) on it; (*zielgerichtet*) towards it; (*danach*) afterwards; **es kommt ganz ~ an, ob ...** it all depends whether ...; **ich freue mich ~** I'm looking forward to it; **am Tag ~** the next day; **~ folgend** (*Tag, Jahr*) next, following

darauffolgend *adj* (*Tag, Jahr*) next, following

daraus *adv* from it; **was ist ~ geworden?** what became of it?

darin *adv* in it; **das Problem liegt ~, dass ...** the basic problem is that ...

Darlehen (*-s, -*) *nt* loan

Darm (*-(e)s, Därme*) *m* intestine; (*Wurstdarm*) skin, casing

Darmgrippe *f* gastroenteritis

dar|stellen *vt* to represent; (*Theat*) to play; (*beschreiben*) to describe

Darsteller(in) *m(f)* actor/actress

Darstellung *f* representation; (*Beschreibung*) description

darüber *adv* (*räumlich*) above it, over it; (*fahren*) over it; (*mehr*) more; (*währenddessen*) meanwhile; (*sprechen, streiten, sich freuen*) about it

darum *adv* (*deshalb*) that's why; **es geht ~, dass ...** the point (*o* thing) is that ...

darunter *adv* (*räumlich*) under it; (*dazwischen*) among them; (*weniger*) less; **was verstehen Sie ~?** what do you understand by that?

darunterfallen *vi* to be included

das *def art* the; **das Auto da** that car; **er hat sich das Bein gebrochen** he's broken his leg; **vier Euro das Kilo** four euros a kilo ▷ *pron* that (one), this (one); (*relativ, Sache*) that, which; (*relativ, Person*) who, that; (*demonstrativ*) this/that one; **das Auto da** that car; **ich nehme das da** I'll take that one; **das Auto, das er kaufte** the car (that (*o* which)) he bought; **das Mädchen, das nebenan wohnt** the girl who (*o* that) lives next door; **das heißt** that is; **das sind Amerikaner** they're American

da sein (*irr*) *vi siehe* **da**

dass *conj* that; **so** ~ so that; **es sei denn, ~** unless; **ohne** ~ **er grüßte** without saying hello

dasselbe *pron* the same

Datei *f* (*Inform*) file

Dateimanager *m* file manager

Daten *pl* data *pl*

Datenbank *f* database

Datenmissbrauch *m* misuse of data

Datenschutz *m* data protection

Datenträger *m* data carrier

Datenverarbeitung *f* data processing

datieren *vt* to date

Dativ *m* dative (case)

Dattel (*-, -n*) *f* date

Datum (*-s, Daten*) *nt* date

Dauer (*-, -n*) *f* duration; (*Länge*) length; **auf die** ~ in the long run; **für die** ~ **von zwei Jahren** for (a period of) two years

Dauerauftrag *m* (*Fin*) standing order

dauerhaft *adj* lasting; (*Material*) durable

Dauerkarte *f* commutation ticket

dauern *vi* to last; (*Zeit benötigen*) to take; **es hat sehr lange gedauert, bis er ... it** took him a long time to ...; **wie lange dauert es denn noch?** how much longer will it be?; **das dauert mir zu lange** I can't wait that long

dauernd *adj* lasting; (*ständig*) constant ▷ *adv* always, constantly; **er lachte ~** he kept laughing; **unterbrich mich nicht ~** stop interrupting me

Dauerwelle *f* permanent

Daumen (*-s, -*) *m* thumb

Daunendecke *f* down comforter

davon *adv* of it; (*räumlich*) away; (*weg von*) from it; (*Grund*) because of it; **ich hätte gerne ein Kilo ~** I'd like one kilo of that; **~ habe ich gehört** I've heard of it; (*Geschehen*) I've heard about it; **das kommt ~, wenn ...** that's what happens when ...; **was habe ich ~?** what's the point?; **auf und ~** up and away

davon|laufen (*irr*) *vi* to run away

davor *adv* (*räumlich*) in front of it; (*zeitlich*) before; **ich habe Angst ~** I'm afraid of it

dazu *adv* (*zusätzlich*) on top of that, as well; (*zu diesem Zweck*) for it, for that purpose; **ich möchte Reis ~** I'd like rice with it; **und ~ noch** and in addition; **~ fähig sein, etw zu tun** to be capable of doing sth; **wie kam es ~?** how did it happen?

dazu|gehören *vi* to belong to it

dazu|kommen (*irr*) *vi* (*zu jdm dazukommen*) to join sb; **kommt noch etwas dazu?**

anything else?

dazwischen *adv* in between; (*Unterschied etc*) between them; (*in einer Gruppe*) among them

dazwischen|kommen (*irr*) *vi*: **wenn nichts dazwischenkommt** if all goes well; **mir ist etwas dazwischengekommen** something has cropped up

DDR (-) *f* (*abk*) = **Deutsche Demokratische Republik** (*Hist*) GDR

dealen *vi* (*fam: mit Drogen*) to deal in drugs

Dealer(in) (*-s, -*) *m(f)* (*fam*) dealer, pusher

Deck (*-(e)s, -s o -e*) *nt* deck; **an ~** on deck

Decke (*-, -n*) *f* cover; (*für Bett*) blanket; (*für Tisch*) tablecloth; (*von Zimmer*) ceiling

Deckel (*-s, -*) *m* lid

decken *vt* to cover; (*Tisch*) to set ▷ *vr*: **sich ~** (*Interessen*) to coincide; (*Aussagen*) to correspond ▷ *vi* (*den Tisch decken*) to set the table

Decoder (*-s, -*) *m* decoder

defekt *adj* faulty

Defekt (*-(e)s, -e*) *m* fault, defect

definieren *vt* to define

Definition (*-, -en*) *f* definition

deftig *adj* (*Preise*) steep; **ein ~es Essen** a good solid meal

dehnbar *adj* flexible, elastic

dehnen *vt* to stretch ▷ *vr*: **sich ~** to stretch

Deich (*-(e)s, -e*) *m* dyke

dein *pron* (*adjektivisch*) your

deine(r, s) *pron* (*substantivisch*) yours, of you

deiner *pron gen von* **du**; of you

deinetwegen *adv* (*wegen dir*) because of you; (*dir zuliebe*) for your sake; (*um dich*) about you

deinstallieren *vt* (*Programm*) to uninstall

Dekolleté (*-s, -s*) *nt* low neckline

Dekoration *f* decoration; (*in Laden*) window dressing

dekorativ *adj* decorative

dekorieren *vt* to decorate; (*Schaufenster*) to dress

Delfin (*-s, -e*) *m* dolphin

delikat *adj* (*lecker*) delicious; (*heikel*) delicate

Delikatesse (*-, -n*) *f* delicacy

Delle (*-, -en*) *f* (*fam*) dent

Delphin (*-s, -e*) *m* dolphin

dem *dat sing von* **der/das**; **wie dem auch sein mag** be that as it may

demnächst *adv* shortly, soon

Demo (*-, -s*) *f* (*fam*) demo

Demokratie (*-, -n*) *f* democracy

demokratisch *adj* democratic

demolieren *vt* to demolish

Demonstration *f* demonstration[1]

demonstrieren *vt, vi* to demonstrate

den *art akk sing, dat pl von* **der; sie hat sich den Arm gebrochen** she's broken her arm ▷ *pron* him; (*Sache*) that one; (*relativ: Person*) who, that, whom; (*relativ: Sache*) which, that; **den hab ich schon ewig nicht mehr gesehen** I haven't seen him in ages ▷ *pron* (*Person*) who, that, whom; (*Sache*) which, that; **der Typ, auf den sie steht** the guy (who) she likes (*o* is interested in); **der Berg, auf den wir geklettert sind** the mountain (that) we climbed

denkbar *adj*: **das ist ~** that's possible ▷ *adv*: **~ einfach** extremely simple

denken (*dachte, gedacht*) *vt, vi* to think (*über +akk* about); **an jdn/etw ~** to think of sb/sth; (*sich erinnern, berücksichtigen*) to remember sb/sth; **woran denkst du?** what are you thinking about?; **denk an den Kaffee!** don't forget the coffee! ▷ *vr*: **sich ~** (*sich vorstellen*) to imagine; **das kann ich mir ~** I can (well) imagine

Denkmal (*-s, Denkmäler*) *nt* monument

Denkmalschutz *m* historic preservation; **unter ~ stehen** to be a (historic) landmark

denn *conj* for, because ▷ *adv* then; (*nach Komparativ*) than; **was ist ~?** what's wrong?; **ist das ~ so schwierig?** is it really that difficult?

dennoch *conj* still, nevertheless

Deo (*-s, -s*) *nt*, **Deodorant** (*-s, -s*) *nt* deodorant

Deoroller *m* roll-on deodorant

Deospray *m o nt* deodorant spray

Deponie (*-, -n*) *f* waste disposal site, dump

Depressionen *pl*: **an ~ leiden** to suffer from depression *sing*

deprimieren *vt* to depress

SCHLÜSSELWORT

der (*f* **die**, *nt* **das**, *gen* **des, der, des**, *dat* **dem, der, dem**, *akk* **den, die, das**, *pl* **die**) *def art* the; **der Rhein** the Rhine; **der Klaus** (*fam*) Klaus; **die Frau** (*im Allgemeinen*) women; **der Tod/das Leben** death/life; **der Fuß des Berges** the foot of the hill; **gib es der Frau** give it to the woman; **er hat sich die Hand verletzt** he has hurt his hand

▷ *relativ pron* (*bei Menschen*) who, that;

(*bei Tieren, Sachen*) which, that; **der Mann, den ich gesehen habe** the man who *o* whom *o* that I saw
▷ *demonstrativ pron* he/she/it; (*jener, dieser*) that; (*pl*) those; **der/die war es** it was him/her; **der mit der Brille** the one with glasses; **ich will den (da)** I want that one

derart *adv* so; (*solcher Art*) such
derartig *adj*: **ein ~er Fehler** such a mistake, a mistake like that
deren *gen von die* ▷ *pron* (*Person*) her; (*Sache*) its; (*Plural*) their ▷ *pron* (*Person*) whose; (*Sache*) of which; **meine Freundin und ~ Mutter** my friend and her mother; **das sind ~ Sachen** that's their stuff; **die Frau, ~ Tochter ...** the woman whose daughter ...; **ich bin mir ~ bewusst** I'm aware of that
dergleichen *pron*: **und ~ mehr** and the like, and so on; **nichts ~** no such thing
derjenige *pron* the one; **~, der** (*relativ*) the one who (*o* that)
dermaßen *adv* so much; (*mit Adj*) so
derselbe *pron* the same (person/thing)
deshalb *adv* therefore; **~ frage ich ja** that's why I'm asking
Design (*-s, -s*) *nt* design
Designer(in) (*-s, -*) *m(f)* designer
Desinfektionsmittel *nt* disinfectant
desinfizieren *vt* to disinfect
dessen *gen von der, das* ▷ *pron* (*Person*) his; (*Sache*) its; **ich bin mir ~ bewusst** I'm aware of that ▷ *pron* (*Person*) whose; (*Sache*) of which; **mein Freund und ~ Mutter** my friend and his mother; **der Mann, ~ Tochter ...** the man whose daughter ...; **ich bin mir ~ bewusst** I'm aware of that
Dessert (*-s, -s*) *nt* dessert; **zum** *o* **als ~ for** dessert
destilliert *adj* distilled
desto *adv*: **je eher, ~ besser** the sooner, the better
deswegen *conj* therefore
Detail (*-s, -s*) *nt* detail; **ins ~ gehen** to go into detail
Detektiv(in) (*-s, -e*) *m(f)* detective
deutlich *adj* clear; (*Unterschied*) distinct
deutsch *adj* German
Deutsch *nt* German; **auf ~** in German; **ins ~e übersetzen** to translate into German
Deutsche(r) *mf* German
Deutschland *nt* Germany
Devise (*-, -n*) *f* motto; **~n** *pl* (*Fin*) foreign currency *sing*

Devisenkurs *m* exchange rate
Dezember (*-(s), -*) *m* December; *siehe auch* **Juni**
dezent *adj* discreet
d.h. *abk von* **das heißt**; i.e. (*gesprochen: i.e. oder that is*)
Dia (*-s, -s*) *nt* slide
Diabetes (*-, -*) *m* (*Med*) diabetes
Diabetiker(in) (*-s, -*) *m(f)* diabetic
Diagnose (*-, -n*) *f* diagnosis
diagonal *adj* diagonal
Dialekt (*-(e)s, -e*) *m* dialect
Dialog (*-(e)s, -e*) *m* dialogue; (*Inform*) dialog
Dialyse (*-, -n*) *f* (*Med*) dialysis
Diamant *m* diamond
Diaprojektor *m* slide projector
Diät (*-, -en*) *f* diet; **eine ~ machen** to be on a diet; (*anfangen*) to go on a diet
dich *pron akk von* **du**; you; **~ selbst** (*reflexiv*) yourself; **pass auf ~ auf** look after yourself; **reg ~ nicht auf** don't get upset
dicht *adj* dense; (*Nebel*) thick; (*Gewebe*) close; (*wasserdicht*) watertight; (*Verkehr*) heavy ▷ *adv*: **~ an/bei** close to; **~ bevölkert** densely populated
Dichter(in) (*-s, -*) *m(f)* poet; (*Autor*) writer
Dichtung *f* (*Auto*) gasket; (*Dichtungsring*) washer; (*Gedichte*) poetry
Dichtungsring *m* (*Tech*) washer
dick *adj* thick; (*Person*) fat; **jdn ~ haben** to be sick of sb
Dickdarm *m* colon
Dickkopf *m* stubborn (*o* pig-headed) person
Dickmilch *f* sour milk
die *def art* the; **die arme Sarah** poor Sarah ▷ *pron* (*sing, Person, als Subjekt*) she; (*Person, als Subjekt, Plural*) they; (*Person, als Objekt*) her; (*Person, als Objekt, Plural*) them; (*Sache*) that (one), this (one); (*Plural*) those (ones); (*Sache, Plural*) those (ones); (*relativ, auf Person*) who, that; (*relativ, auf Sache*) which, that; **die mit den langen Haaren** the one (*o* her) with the long hair; **sie war die erste, die es erfuhr** she was the first to know; **ich nehme die da** I'll take that one/those *pl* **von der, die, das**
Dieb(in) (*-(e)s, -e*) *m(f)* thief
Diebstahl (*-(e)s, Diebstähle*) *m* theft
Diebstahlsicherung *f* burglar alarm
diejenige *pron* the one; **~, die** (*relativ*) the one who (*o* that); **~n** (*pl*) those *pl*, the ones

Diele (-, -n) *f* hall
Dienst (-(e)s, -e) *m* service; **außer ~** retired; **~ haben** to be on duty
Dienstag *m* Tuesday; *siehe auch* **Mittwoch**
dienstags *adv* on Tuesdays; *siehe auch* **mittwochs**
Dienstbereitschaft *f*: **~ haben** (*Arzt*) to be on call
diensthabend *adj*: **der ~e Arzt** the doctor on duty
Dienstleistung *f* service
dienstlich *adj* official; **er ist ~ unterwegs** he's away on business
Dienstreise *f* business trip
Dienststelle *f* department
Dienstwagen *m* company car
Dienstzeit *f* office hours *pl*; (*Mil*) period of service
diesbezüglich *adj* (*formell*) on this matter
diese(r, s) *pron* this (one); (*pl*) these; **~ Frau** this woman; **~r Mann** this man; **~s Mädchen** this girl; **~ Leute** these people; **ich nehme ~/~n/~s** (*hier*) I'll take this one; (*dort*) I'll take that one; **ich nehme ~** *pl* (*hier*) I'll take these (ones); (*dort*) I'll take those (ones)
Diesel (-s, -) *m* (*Auto*) diesel
dieselbe *pron* the same; **es sind immer ~n** it's always the same people
Dieselmotor *m* diesel engine
Dieselöl *nt* diesel (oil)
diesig *adj* hazy, misty
diesmal *adv* this time
Dietrich (-s, -e) *m* skeleton key
Differenz (-, -en) *f* difference
digital *adj* digital
Digital- *in zW* (*Anzeige etc*) digital
Digitalfernsehen *nt* digital television, digital TV
Digitalkamera *f* digital camera
Diktat (-(e)s, -e) *nt* dictation
Diktatur *f* dictatorship
Dill (-s) *m* dill
DIN (*abk*) = **Deutsche Industrienorm** DIN; **DIN A4** A4
Ding (-(e)s, -e) *nt* thing; **vor allen ~en** above all; **der Stand der ~e** the state of affairs; **das ist nicht mein ~** (*fam*) it's not my sort of thing (*o* cup of tea)
Dingsbums (-) *nt* (*fam*) thingy, thingamajig
Dinkel (-s, -) *m* (*Bot*) spelt
Dinosaurier (-s, -) *m* dinosaur
Diphtherie (-, -n) *f* diphtheria
Diplom (-(e)s, -e) *nt* diploma

Diplomat(in) (-en, -en) *m(f)* diplomat
dir *pron dat von* **du**; (to) you; **hat er dir geholfen?** did he help you?; **ich werde es dir erklären** I'll explain it to you; (*reflexiv*): **wasch dir die Hände** go and wash your hands; **ein Freund von dir** a friend of yours
direkt *adj* direct; (*Frage*) straight; **~e Verbindung** through service ▷ *adv* directly; (*sofort*) immediately; **~ am Bahnhof** right next to the station
Direktflug *m* direct flight
Direktor(in) *m(f)* director; (*Schule*) principal
Direktübertragung *f* live broadcast
Dirigent(in) *m(f)* conductor
dirigieren *vt* to direct; (*Mus*) to conduct
Discman® (-s, -s) *m* Discman®
Diskette *f* disc, diskette
Diskettenlaufwerk *nt* disk drive
Diskjockey (-s, -s) *m* disc jockey
Disko (-, -s) *f* (*fam*) disco, club
Diskothek (-, -en) *f* discotheque, club
diskret *adj* discreet
diskriminieren *vt* to discriminate against
Diskussion *f* discussion
diskutieren *vt, vi* to discuss
Display (-s, -s) *nt* display
disqualifizieren *vt* to disqualify
Distanz *f* distance
Distel (-, -n) *f* thistle
Disziplin (-, -en) *f* discipline
divers *adj* various
dividieren *vt* to divide (*durch* by); **8 dividiert durch 2 ist 4** 8 divided by 2 is 4
DJ (-s, -s) *m* (*abk*) = **Diskjockey** DJ

doch *adv* **1** (*dennoch*) after all; (*sowieso*) anyway; **er kam doch noch** he came after all; **du weißt es ja doch besser** you know better than I do anyway; **und doch ...** and yet ...
2 (*als bejahende Antwort*) yes I do/it does *etc*; **das ist nicht wahr - doch!** that's not true - yes it is!
3 (*auffordernd*): **komm doch** do come; **lass ihn doch** just leave him; **nicht doch!** oh no!
4: **sie ist doch noch so jung** but she's still so young; **Sie wissen doch, wie das ist** you know how it is(, don't you?); **wenn doch** if only
▷ *konj* (*aber*) but; (*trotzdem*) all the same;

und doch hat er es getan but still he did it

Doktor(in) m(f) doctor
Dokument nt document
Dokumentarfilm m documentary (film)
dokumentieren vt to document
Dokumentvorlage f (Inform) document template
Dolch (-(e)s, -e) m dagger
Dollar (-(s), -s) m dollar
dolmetschen vt, vi to interpret
Dolmetscher(in) (-s, -) m(f) interpreter
Dolomiten pl Dolomites pl
Dom (-(e)s, -e) m cathedral
Domäne (-, -n) f domain, province; (Inform: Domain) domain
Dominikanische Republik f Dominican Republic
Domino (-s, -s) nt dominoes sing
Donau (-) f Danube
Donner (-s, -) m thunder
donnern vi: **es donnert** it's thundering
Donnerstag m Thursday; siehe auch Mittwoch
donnerstags adv on Thursdays; siehe auch mittwochs
doof adj (fam) stupid
dopen vt to dope
Doping (-s) nt doping
Dopingkontrolle f drugs test
Doppel (-s, -) nt duplicate; (Sport) doubles sing
Doppelbett nt double bed
Doppeldecker m double-decker
Doppelhaushälfte f duplex
doppelklicken vi to double-click
Doppelname m hyphenated name
Doppelpunkt m colon
Doppelstecker m two-way adaptor
doppelt adj double; **in ~er Ausführung** in duplicate
Doppelzimmer nt double room
Dorf (-(e)s, Dörfer) nt small town, village
Dorn (-(e)s, -en) m (Bot) thorn
Dörrobst nt dried fruit
Dorsch (-(e)s, -e) m cod
dort adv there; **~ drüben** over there
dorther adv from there
Dose (-, -n) f box; (Blechdose) can; (Bierdose) can
dösen vi to doze
Dosenbier nt canned beer
Dosenmilch f canned milk
Dosenöffner m can opener

Dotter (-s, -) m (egg) yolk
downloaden vt to download
Downsyndrom (-(e)s, -e) nt (Med) Down's syndrome
Dozent(in) m(f) lecturer
Dr. (abk) = Doktor Dr.
Drache (-n, -n) m dragon
Drachen (-s, -) m (Spielzeug) kite; (Sport) hang-glider
Drachenfliegen (-s) nt hang-gliding
Drachenflieger(in) (-s, -) m(f) hang-glider
Draht (-(e)s, Drähte) m wire
Drama (-s, Dramen) nt drama
dramatisch adj dramatic
dran adv (fam) kontr von **daran; gut ~ sein** (reich) to be well-off; (glücklich) to be fortunate; (gesundheitlich) to be well; **schlecht ~ sein** to be in a bad way; **wer ist ~?** whose turn is it?; **ich bin ~** it's my turn; **bleib ~!** (Tel) hang on
drang imperf von **dringen**
Drang (-(e)s, Dränge) m (Trieb) urge (nach for); (Druck) pressure
drängeln vt, vi to push
drängen vt (schieben) to push; (antreiben) to urge ▷ vi (eilig sein) to be urgent; (Zeit) to press; **auf etw** (akk) **~** to press for sth
dran|kommen (irr) vi: **wer kommt dran?** who's turn is it?, who's next?
drauf (fam) kontr von **darauf; gut/schlecht ~ sein** to be in a good/bad mood
Draufgänger(in) (-s, -) m(f) daredevil
drauf|kommen (irr) vi to remember; **ich komme nicht drauf** I can't think of it
drauf|machen vi (fam): **einen ~** to go on a binge
draußen adv outside
Dreck (-(e)s) m dirt, filth
dreckig adj dirty, filthy
drehen vt, vi to turn; (Zigaretten) to roll; (Film) to shoot ▷ vr: **sich ~** to turn; (um Achse) to rotate; **sich ~ um** (handeln von) to be about
Drehstrom m three-phase current
Drehtür f revolving door
Drehzahlmesser m rev counter
drei num three; **~ viertel voll** three-quarters full; **es ist ~ viertel neun** it's a quarter to nine
Drei (-, -en) f three; (Schulnote) ≈ C
Dreieck nt triangle
dreieckig adj triangular
dreifach adj triple ▷ adv three times
dreihundert num three hundred
Dreikönigstag m Epiphany

dreimal adv three times
Dreirad nt tricycle
dreispurig adj three-lane
dreißig num thirty
dreißigste(r, s) adj thirtieth; siehe auch dritte
Dreiviertelstunde f: **eine ~** three quarters of an hour
dreizehn num thirteen
dreizehnte(r, s) adj thirteenth; siehe auch dritte
dressieren vt to train
Dressing (-s, -s) nt (salad) dressing
Dressman (-s, Dressmen) m (male) model
Dressur (-, -en) f dressage
drin (fam) kontr von darin; in it; **mehr war nicht ~** that was the best I could do
dringen (drang, gedrungen) vi (Wasser, Licht, Kälte) to penetrate (durch through, in +akk into); **auf etw** (akk) **~** to insist on sth
dringend, dringlich adj urgent
drinnen adv inside
dritt adv: **wir sind zu ~** there are three of us
dritte(r, s) adj third; **die D~ Welt** the Third World; **3. Juni** June 3(rd); (gesprochen: the third of June or June third): **am 3. Juni** on June 3(rd); **München, den 3. Juni** Munich, June 3(rd)
Drittel (-s, -) nt (Bruchteil) third
drittens adv thirdly
Droge (-, -n) f drug
drogenabhängig, drogensüchtig adj addicted to drugs
Drogerie f drugstore
Drogeriemarkt m drugstore

DROGERIE

The **Drogerie** as opposed to the **Apotheke** sells medicines not requiring a prescription. It tends to be cheaper and also sells cosmetics, perfume and toiletries.

drohen vi to threaten (jdm sb); **mit etw ~** to threaten to do sth
dröhnen vi (Motor) to roar; (Stimme, Musik) to boom; (Raum) to resound
Drohung f threat
Drossel (-, -n) f thrush
drüben adv over there; (auf der anderen Seite) on the other side
drüber (fam) kontr von darüber

Druck (-(e)s, Drücke) m (Phys) pressure; (fig: Belastung) stress; **jdn unter ~ setzen** to put sb under pressure ▷ (-(e)s, -e) m (Typo: Vorgang) printing; (Produkt, Schriftart) print
Druckbuchstabe m block letter; **in ~n schreiben** to print
drucken vt, vi to print
drücken vt, vi (Knopf, Hand) to press; (zu eng sein) to pinch; (fig: Preise) to keep down; **jdm etw in die Hand ~** to press sth into sb's hand ▷ vr: **sich vor etw** (dat) **~** to get out of sth
drückend adj oppressive
Drucker (-s, -) m (Inform) printer
Druckertreiber m printer driver
Druckknopf m snap fastener
Drucksache f printed matter
Druckschrift f block capitals pl
drunten adv down there
drunter (fam) kontr von darunter
Drüse (-, -n) f gland
Dschungel (-s, -) m jungle
du pron you; **bist du es?** is it you?; **wir sind per du** we're on first-name terms
Dübel (-s, -) m anchor, dowel
ducken vt to duck ▷ vr: **sich ~** to duck
Dudelsack m bagpipes pl
Duett (-s, -e) nt duet
Duft (-(e)s, Düfte) m scent
duften vi to smell nice; **es duftet nach ...** it smells of ...
dulden vt to tolerate
dumm adj stupid
Dummheit f stupidity; (Tat) stupid thing
Dummkopf m idiot
dumpf adj (Ton) muffled; (Erinnerung) vague; (Schmerz) dull
Düne (-, -n) f dune
Dünger (-s, -) m fertilizer
dunkel adj dark; (Stimme) deep; (Ahnung) vague; (rätselhaft) obscure; (verdächtig) dubious; **im D~n tappen** (fig) to be in the dark
dunkelblau adj dark blue
dunkelblond adj light brown
dunkelhaarig adj dark-haired
Dunkelheit f darkness
dünn adj thin; (Kaffee) weak
Dunst (-es, Dünste) m haze; (leichter Nebel) mist; (Chem) vapor
dünsten vt (Gastr) to steam
Duo (-s, -s) nt duo
Dur (-) nt (Mus) major (key); **in G-Dur** in G major

durch prep +akk **1** (hindurch) through; **durch den Urwald** through the jungle; **durch die ganze Welt reisen** to travel all over the world

2 (mittels) through, by (means of); (aufgrund) due to; **Tod durch Herzschlag/den Strang** death from a heart attack/by hanging; **durch die Post** by mail; **durch seine Bemühungen** through his efforts

▷ adv **1** (hindurch) through; **die ganze Nacht durch** all through the night; **den Sommer durch** during the summer; **8 Uhr durch** past 8 o'clock; **durch und durch** completely

2 (durchgebraten etc): **(gut) durch** well-done

durchaus adv absolutely; ~ **nicht** not at all
Durchblick m view; **den ~ haben** (fig) to know what's going on
durch|blicken vi to look through; (fam: verstehen) to understand (bei etw sth); **etw ~ lassen** (fig) to hint at sth
Durchblutung f circulation
durch|brennen (irr) vi (Sicherung) to blow; (Draht) to burn through; (fam: davonlaufen) to run away
durchdacht adj: **gut ~** well thought-out
durch|drehen vt (Fleisch) to grind ▷ vi (Räder) to spin; (fam: nervlich) to crack up
durcheinander adv in a mess; (fam: verwirrt) confused
Durcheinander (-s) nt (Verwirrung) confusion; (Unordnung) mess
durcheinander|bringen (irr) vt to mess up; (verwirren) to confuse
durcheinander|reden vi to talk all at the same time
durcheinander|trinken (irr) vi to mix one's drinks
Durchfahrt f way through; „~ **verboten!"** 'no thru (o through) traffic'
Durchfall m (Med) diarrhea
durch|fallen (irr) vi to fall through; (in Prüfung) to fail
durch|fragen vr: **sich ~** to ask one's way
durch|führen vt to carry out
Durchgang m passage; (Sport) round; (bei Wahl) ballot
Durchgangsverkehr m through traffic
durchgebraten adj well done
durchgefroren adj frozen to the bone

durch|gehen (irr) vi to go through (durch etw sth); (ausreißen: Pferd) to break loose; (Mensch) to run away
durchgehend adj (Zug) through; ~ **geöffnet** open all day
durch|halten (irr) vi to hold out ▷ vt (Tempo) to keep up; **etw ~** (bis zum Schluss) to see sth through
durch|kommen (irr) vi to get through; (Patient) to pull through
durch|lassen (irr) vt (jdn) to let through; (Wasser) to let in
durch|lesen (irr) vt to read through
durchleuchten vt to X-ray
durch|machen vt to go through; (Entwicklung) to undergo; **die Nacht ~** to make a night of it, to pull an all-nighter
Durchmesser (-s, -) m diameter
Durchreise f journey through; **auf der ~** passing through; (Güter) in transit
Durchreisevisum nt transit visa
durch|reißen (irr) vt, vi to tear (in two)
durchs kontr von **durch das**
Durchsage (-, -n) f announcement
durchschauen vt (jdn, Lüge) to see through
durch|schlagen (irr) vr: **sich ~** to struggle through
durch|schneiden (irr) vt to cut (in two)
Durchschnitt m (Mittelwert) average; **im ~** on average
durchschnittlich adj average ▷ adv (im Durchschnitt) on average
Durchschnittsgeschwindigkeit f average speed
durch|setzen vt to get through ▷ vr: **sich ~** (Erfolg haben) to succeed; (sich behaupten) to get one's way
durchsichtig adj transparent, see-through
durch|stellen vt (Tel) to put through
durch|streichen (irr) vt to cross out
durchsuchen vt to search (nach for)
Durchsuchung f search
durchwachsen adj (Speck) streaky; (fig: mittelmäßig) so-so
Durchwahl f direct dialing; (Nummer) extension
durch|ziehen (irr) vt (Plan) to carry through
Durchzug m draft

dürfen (unreg) vi **1** (Erlaubnis haben) to be allowed to; **ich darf das** I'm allowed to (do that); **darf ich?** may I?; **darf ich ins Kino?** can *o* may I go to the movie theater?; **es darf geraucht werden** you may smoke **2** (*in Verneinungen*): **er darf das nicht** he's not allowed to (do that); **das darf nicht geschehen** that must not happen; **da darf sie sich nicht wundern** that shouldn't surprise her **3** (*in Höflichkeitsformeln*): **darf ich Sie bitten, das zu tun?** may *o* could I ask you to do that?; **was darf es sein?** what can I do for you? **4** (*können*): **das dürfen Sie mir glauben** you can believe me **5** (*Möglichkeit*): **das dürfte genug sein** that should be enough; **es dürfte Ihnen bekannt sein, dass …** as you will probably know …

dürftig *adj* (*ärmlich*) poor; (*unzulänglich*) inadequate
dürr *adj* dried-up; (*Land*) arid; (*mager*) skinny
Durst (-*(e)s*) *m* thirst; **~ haben** to be thirsty

durstig *adj* thirsty
Dusche (-, -*n*) *f* shower
duschen *vi* to take a shower ▷ *vr:* **sich ~** to take a shower
Duschgel *nt* shower gel
Duschvorhang *m* shower curtain
Düse (-, -*n*) *f* nozzle; (*Tech*) jet
Düsenflugzeug *nt* jet (aircraft)
Dussel (-*s*, -) *m* (*fam*) dope
duss(e)lig *adj* (*fam*) stupid
düster *adj* dark; (*Gedanken, Zukunft*) gloomy
Dutyfreeshop (-*s*, -*s*) *m* duty-free store
Dutzend (-*s*, -*e*) *nt* dozen
duzen *vt* to address as 'du' ▷ *vr:* **sich ~ mit jdm** to address each other as 'du', to be on first-name terms
DVD (-, -*s*) *f* (*abk*) = Digital Versatile Disk DVD
DVD-Player (-*s*, -) *m* DVD player
DVD-Rekorder (-*s*, -) *m* DVD recorder
dynamisch *adj* dynamic
Dynamo (-*s*, -*s*) *m* dynamo
D-Zug *m* fast train

d

E

Ebbe (-, -n) *f* low tide
eben *adj* level; (*glatt*) smooth ▷ *adv* just; (*bestätigend*) exactly
Ebene (-, -n) *f* plain; (*fig*) level
ebenfalls *adv* also, as well; (*Antwort: gleichfalls!*) you too
ebenso *adv* just as; ~ **gut** just as well; ~ **viel** just as much
Eber (-s, -) *m* boar
EC (-, -s) *m* (*abk*) = **Eurocityzug**
Echo (-s, -s) *nt* echo
echt *adj* (*Leder, Gold*) real, genuine; **ein ~er Verlust** a real loss
EC-Karte *f* ≈ debit card
Ecke (-, -n) *f* corner; (*Math*) angle; **an der ~** at the corner; **gleich um die ~** just around the corner
eckig *adj* rectangular
Eckzahn *m* canine (tooth)
Economyclass (-) *f* coach (class), economy class
Ecstasy (-) *f* (*Droge*) ecstasy
edel *adj* noble
Edelstein *m* precious stone
EDV (-) *f* (*abk*) = **elektronische Datenverarbeitung** EDP
Efeu (-s) *m* ivy
Effekt (-s, -e) *m* effect
egal *adj*: **das ist ~** it doesn't matter; **das ist mir ~** I don't care, it's all the same to me; **~ wie teuer** no matter how expensive
egoistisch *adj* selfish
ehe *conj* before
Ehe (-, -n) *f* marriage
Ehefrau *f* wife; (*verheiratete Frau*) married woman
Eheleute *pl* married couple *sing*
ehemalig *adj* former
ehemals *adv* formerly
Ehemann *m* husband; (*verheirateter Mann*) married man
Ehepaar *nt* married couple
eher *adv* (*früher*) sooner; (*lieber*) rather, sooner; (*mehr*) more; **je ~, desto besser** the sooner the better
Ehering *f* wedding ring
eheste(r, s) *adj* (*früheste*) first ▷ *adv*: **am ~n** (*am wahrscheinlichsten*) most likely
Ehre (-, -n) *f* honor
ehren *vt* to honor
ehrenamtlich *adj* voluntary
Ehrengast *m* guest of honor

Ehrenwort *nt* word of honor; ~! I promise!; **ich gebe dir mein ~** I give you my word
ehrgeizig *adj* ambitious
ehrlich *adj* honest
Ei (-(e)s, -er) *nt* egg; **hart gekochtes/weiches Ei** hard-boiled/soft-boiled egg
Eiche (-, -n) *f* oak (tree)
Eichel (-, -n) *f* acorn
Eichhörnchen *nt* squirrel
Eid (-(e)s, -e) *m* oath
Eidechse (-, -n) *f* lizard
Eierbecher *m* eggcup
Eierstock *m* ovary
Eieruhr *f* egg timer
Eifersucht *f* jealousy
eifersüchtig *adj* jealous (*auf +akk* of)
Eigelb (-(e)s, -) *nt* egg yolk
eigen *adj* own; (*typisch*) characteristic (*jdm* of sb); (*eigenartig*) peculiar
eigenartig *adj* peculiar
Eigenschaft *f* quality; (*Chem, Phys*) property; (*Merkmal*) characteristic
eigentlich *adj* actual, real ▷ *adv* actually, really; **was denken Sie sich ~ dabei?** what on earth do you think you're doing?
Eigentum *nt* property
Eigentümer(in) *m(f)* owner
Eigentumswohnung *f* condominium
eignen *vr*: **sich ~ für** to be suitable for; **er würde sich als Lehrer ~** he'd make a good teacher
Eilbrief *m* express letter, special-delivery letter
Eile (-) *f* hurry
eilen *vi* (*dringend sein*) to be urgent; **es eilt nicht** there's no hurry
eilig *adj* hurried; (*dringlich*) urgent; **es ~ haben** to be in a hurry
Eimer (-s, -) *m* bucket
ein *adv*: **nicht ein noch aus wissen** not to know what to do; **ein - aus** (*Schalter*) on - off
ein(e) *art* a; (*vor gesprochenem Vokal*) an; **ein Mann** a man; **ein Apfel** an apple; **eine Stunde** an hour; **ein Haus** a house; **ein gewisser Herr Miller** a (certain) Mr. Miller; **eines Tages** one day
einander *pron* one another, each other
ein|arbeiten *vt* to train ▷ *vr*: **sich ~** to get used to the work
ein|atmen *vt, vi* to breathe in
Einbahnstraße *f* one-way street

ein|bauen *vt* to build in; (*Motor etc*) to install, to fit

ein|biegen (*irr*) *vi* to turn (*in +akk* into)

ein|bilden *vt*: **sich** (*dat*) **etw ~** to imagine sth

ein|brechen (*irr*) *vi* (*in Haus*) to break in; (*Dach etc*) to fall in, to collapse

Einbrecher(in) (*-s, -*) *m(f)* burglar

ein|bringen (*irr*) *vt* (*Ernte*) to bring in; (*Gewinn*) to yield; **jdm etw ~** to bring (*o* earn) sb sth ▷ *vr*: **sich in** (*akk*) **etw ~** to make a contribution to sth

Einbruch *m* (*Haus*) break-in, burglary; **bei ~ der Nacht** at nightfall

Einbürgerung *f* naturalization

ein|checken *vt* to check in

ein|cremen *vt* to put some cream on ▷ *vr*: **sich ~** to put some cream on

eindeutig *adj* clear, obvious ▷ *adv* clearly; **~ falsch** clearly wrong

ein|dringen (*irr*) *vi* (*gewaltsam*) to force one's way in (*in +akk* -to); (*in Haus*) to break in (*in +akk* -to); (*Gas, Wasser*) to get in (*in +akk* -to)

Eindruck *m* impression; **großen ~ auf jdn machen** to make a big impression on sb

eine(r, s) *pron* one; (*jemand*) someone; **~r meiner Freunde** one of my friends; **~r nach dem andern** one after the other

eineiig *adj* (*Zwillinge*) identical

eineinhalb *num* one and a half

einerseits *adv* on the one hand

einfach *adj* (*nicht kompliziert*) simple; (*Mensch*) ordinary; (*Essen*) plain; (*nicht mehrfach*) single; **~e Fahrkarte** one-way ticket ▷ *adv* simply; (*nicht mehrfach*) once

Einfahrt *f* (*Vorgang*) driving in; (*eines Zuges*) arrival; (*Ort*) entrance

Einfall *m* (*Idee*) idea

ein|fallen (*irr*) *vi* (*Licht etc*) to fall in; (*einstürzen*) to collapse; **ihm fiel ein, dass ...** it occurred to him that ...; **ich werde mir etwas ~ lassen** I'll think of something; **was fällt Ihnen ein!** what do you think you're doing!

einfarbig *adj* all one color; (*Stoff etc*) self-colored

Einfluss *m* influence

ein|frieren (*irr*) *vt, vi* to freeze

ein|fügen *vt* to fit in; (*zusätzlich*) to add; (*Inform*) to insert

Einfügetaste *f* (*Inform*) insert key

Einfuhr (*-, -en*) *f* import

Einfuhrbestimmungen *pl* import regula-

tions *pl*

ein|führen *vt* to introduce; (*Ware*) to import

Einführung *f* introduction

Eingabe *f* (*Dateneingabe*) input

Eingabetaste *f* (*Inform*) return (*o* enter) key

Eingang *m* entrance

Eingangshalle *f* lobby

ein|geben (*irr*) *vt* (*Daten etc*) to enter, to key in

eingebildet *adj* imaginary; (*eitel*) arrogant

Eingeborene(r) *mf* native

ein|gehen (*irr*) *vi* (*Sendung, Geld*) to come in, to arrive; (*Tier, Pflanze*) to die; (*Stoff*) to shrink; **auf etw** (*akk*) **~** to agree to sth; **auf jdn ~** to respond to sb ▷ *vt* (*Vertrag*) to enter into; (*Wette*) to make; (*Risiko*) to take

eingelegt *adj* (*in Essig*) pickled

eingeschaltet *adj* (switched) on

eingeschlossen *adj* locked in; (*inklusive*) included

ein|gewöhnen *vr*: **sich ~** to settle in

ein|gießen (*irr*) *vt* to pour

ein|greifen (*irr*) *vi* to intervene

Eingriff *m* intervention; (*Operation*) operation

ein|halten (*irr*) *vt* (*Versprechen etc*) to keep

einheimisch *adj* (*Produkt, Mannschaft*) local

Einheimische(r) *mf* local

Einheit *f* (*Geschlossenheit*) unity; (*Maß*) unit

einheitlich *adj* uniform

ein|holen *vt* (*Vorsprung aufholen*) to catch up with; (*Verspätung*) to make up for; (*Rat, Erlaubnis*) to ask for

Einhorn *nt* unicorn

einhundert *num* one (*o* a) hundred

einig *adj* (*vereint*) united; **sich** (*dat*) **~ sein** to agree

einige *pron* (*pl*) some; (*mehrere*) several ▷ *adj* some; **nach ~r Zeit** after some time; **~ hundert Euro** several hundred euros

einigen *vr*: **sich ~** to agree (*auf +akk* on)

einigermaßen *adv* fairly, quite; (*leidlich*) reasonably

einiges *pron* something; (*ziemlich viel*) quite a bit; (*mehreres*) a few things; **es gibt noch ~ zu tun** there's still a fair bit to do

Einkauf *m* purchase; **Einkäufe machen** to do one's shopping

ein|kaufen *vt* to buy ▷ *vi* to go shopping

Einkaufsbummel *m* shopping trip

Einkaufstasche *f*, **Einkaufstüte** *f* shopping bag

Einkaufswagen *m* shopping cart

Einkaufszentrum *nt* shopping mall

ein|klemmen *vt* to jam; **er hat sich** (*dat*) **den Finger eingeklemmt** he got his finger caught

Einkommen (*-s, -*) *nt* income

ein|laden (*irr*) *vt* (*jdn*) to invite; (*Gegenstände*) to load; **jdn zum Essen ~** to take sb out for a meal; **ich lade dich ein** (*bezahle*) it's my treat

Einladung *f* invitation

Einlass (*-es, Einlässe*) *m* admittance; **~ ab 18 Uhr** doors open at 6 p.m.

ein|lassen (*irr*) *vr*: **sich mit jdm/auf etw** (*akk*) **~** to get involved with sb/sth

ein|leben *vr*: **sich ~** to settle down

ein|legen *vt* (*Film etc*) to put in; (*marinieren*) to marinate; **eine Pause ~** to take a break

ein|leiten *vt* to start; (*Maßnahmen*) to introduce; (*Geburt*) to induce

Einleitung *f* introduction; (*von Geburt*) induction

ein|leuchten *vi*: **jdm ~** to be (*o* become) clear to sb

einleuchtend *adj* clear

ein|loggen *vi* (*Inform*) to log on (*o* in)

ein|lösen *vt* (*Scheck*) to cash; (*Gutschein*) to redeem; (*Versprechen*) to keep

einmal *adv* once; (*früher*) before; (*in Zukunft*) some day; (*erstens*) first; **~ im Jahr** once a year; **noch ~** once more, again; **ich war schon ~ hier** I've been here before; **warst du schon ~ in London?** have you ever been to London?; **nicht ~** not even; **auf ~** suddenly; (*gleichzeitig*) at once

einmalig *adj* unique; (*einmal geschehend*) single; (*prima*) fantastic

ein|mischen *vr*: **sich ~** to interfere (*in +akk* with)

Einnahme (*-, -n*) *f* (*Geld*) takings *pl*; (*von Medizin*) taking

ein|nehmen (*irr*) *vt* (*Medizin*) to take; (*Geld*) to take in; (*Standpunkt, Raum*) to take up; **jdn für sich ~** to win sb over

ein|ordnen *vt* to put in order; (*klassifizieren*) to classify; (*Akten*) to file ▷ *vr*: **sich ~** (*Auto*) to get in lane; **sich rechts/links ~** to get into the right/left lane

ein|packen *vt* to pack (up)

ein|parken *vt, vi* to park

ein|planen *vt* to allow for

ein|prägen *vt*: **sich** (*dat*) **etw ~** to remember (*o* memorize) sth

ein|räumen *vt* (*Bücher, Geschirr*) to put away; (*Schrank*) to put things in

ein|reden *vt*: **jdm/sich etw ~** to talk sb/oneself into (believing) sth

ein|reiben (*irr*) *vt*: **sich mit etw ~** to rub sth into one's skin

ein|reichen *vt* to hand in; (*Antrag*) to submit

Einreise *f* entry

Einreisebestimmungen *pl* entry regulations *pl*

Einreiseerlaubnis *f*, **Einreisegenehmigung** *f* entry permit

ein|reisen *vi* to enter (*in ein Land* a country)

Einreisevisum *nt* entry visa

ein|renken *vt* (*Arm, Bein*) to set

ein|richten *vt* (*Wohnung*) to furnish; (*gründen*) to establish, to set up; (*arrangieren*) to arrange ▷ *vr*: **sich ~** (*in Haus*) to furnish one's home; (*sich vorbereiten*) to prepare oneself (*auf +akk* for); (*sich anpassen*) to adapt (*auf +akk* to)

Einrichtung *f* (*Wohnung*) furnishings *pl*; (*öffentliche Anstalt*) institution; (*Schwimmbad etc*) facility

eins *num* one

Eins (*-, -en*) *f* one; (*Schulnote*) ≈ A

einsam *adj* lonely

ein|sammeln *vt* to collect

Einsatz *m* (*Teil*) insert; (*Verwendung*) use; (*Spieleinsatz*) stake; (*Risiko*) risk; (*Mus*) entry

ein|schalten *vt* (*Elek*) to turn (*o* switch) on

ein|schätzen *vt* to estimate, to assess

ein|schenken *vt* to pour

ein|schiffen *vr*: **sich ~** to embark (*nach* for)

ein|schlafen (*irr*) *vi* to fall asleep, to drop off; **mir ist der Arm eingeschlafen** my arm's gone to sleep

ein|schlagen (*irr*) *vt* (*Fenster*) to smash; (*Zähne, Schädel*) to smash in; (*Weg, Richtung*) to take ▷ *vi* to hit (*in etw akk* sth, *auf jdn* sb); (*Blitz*) to strike; (*Anklang finden*) to be a success

ein|schließen (*irr*) *vt* (*jdn*) to lock in; (*Gegenstand*) to lock away; (*umgeben*) to surround; (*fig: beinhalten*) to include

einschließlich *adv* inclusive ▷ *prep* (*+gen*) including; **von Montag bis ~ Freitag** Monday through Friday

ein|schränken *vt* to limit, to restrict; *(verringern)* to cut down on ▷ *vr:* **sich ~** to cut down (on spending)

ein|schreiben *(irr) vr:* **sich ~** to register; *(Schule)* to enroll

Einschreiben *(-s, -) nt* registered letter; **etw per ~ schicken** to send sth by special delivery

ein|schüchtern *vt* to intimidate

ein|sehen *(irr) vt (verstehen)* to see; *(Fehler)* to recognize; *(Akten)* to have a look at

einseitig *adj* one-sided

ein|senden *(irr) vt* to send in

ein|setzen *vt* to put in; *(in Amt)* to appoint; *(Geld)* to bet; *(verwenden)* to use ▷ *vi (beginnen)* to set in; *(Mus)* to enter, to come in ▷ *vr:* **sich ~** to work hard; **sich für jdn/etw ~** to support sb/sth

Einsicht *f* insight; **zu der ~ kommen, dass …** to come to realize that …

ein|sperren *vt* to lock up

ein|spielen *vt (Geld)* to bring in

ein|springen *(irr) vi (aushelfen)* to step in *(für* for)

Einspruch *m* objection *(gegen* to)

einspurig *adj* single-lane

Einstand *m (Tennis)* deuce

ein|stecken *vt* to pocket; *(Elek: Stecker)* to plug in; *(Brief)* to mail; *(mitnehmen)* to take; *(hinnehmen)* to swallow

ein|steigen *(irr) vi (in Auto)* to get in; *(in Bus, Zug, Flugzeug)* to get on; *(sich beteiligen)* to get involved

ein|stellen *vt (beenden)* to stop; *(Geräte)* to adjust; *(Kamera)* to focus; *(Sender, Radio)* to tune in; *(unterstellen)* to put; *(in Firma)* to employ, to hire ▷ *vr:* **sich auf jdn/etw ~** to adapt to sb/prepare oneself for sth

Einstellung *f (von Gerät)* adjustment; *(von Kamera)* focusing; *(von Arbeiter)* hiring; *(Meinung)* attitude

ein|stürzen *vi* to collapse

eintägig *adj* one-day

ein|tauschen *vt* to exchange *(gegen* for)

eintausend *num* one *(o* a) thousand

ein|teilen *vt (in Teile)* to divide (up) *(in* +*akk* into); *(Zeit)* to organize

eintönig *adj* monotonous

Eintopf *m* stew

ein|tragen *(irr) vt (in eine Liste)* to put down, to enter ▷ *vr:* **sich ~** to put one's name down, to register

ein|treffen *(irr) vi* to happen; *(ankommen)* to arrive

ein|treten *(irr) vi (hineingehen)* to enter *(in etw akk* sth); *(in Klub, Partei)* to join *(in etw akk* sth); *(sich ereignen)* to occur; **~ für** to support

Eintritt *m* admission; **„~ frei"** 'admission free'

Eintrittskarte *f* (entrance) ticket

Eintrittspreis *m* admission charge

einverstanden *interj* okay, all right ▷ *adj:* **mit etwas ~ sein** to agree to sth, to accept sth

Einwanderer *m,* **Einwanderin** *f* immigrant

ein|wandern *vi* to immigrate

einwandfrei *adj* perfect, flawless

Einwegflasche *f* non-returnable bottle

ein|weichen *vt* to soak

ein|weihen *vt (Gebäude)* to inaugurate, to open; **jdn in etw** *(akk)* **~** to let sb in on sth

Einweihungsparty *f* housewarming party

ein|werfen *(irr) vt (Ball, Bemerkung etc)* to throw in; *(Brief)* to mail; *(Geld)* to put in, to insert; *(Fenster)* to smash

ein|wickeln *vt* to wrap up; *(fig):* **jdn ~** to take sb in

Einwohner(in) *(-s, -) m(f)* inhabitant

Einwohnermeldeamt *nt registration office for residents*

Einwurf *m (Öffnung)* slot; *(Sport)* throw-in

Einzahl *f* singular

ein|zahlen *vt* to pay in *(auf ein Konto* -to an account)

Einzel *(-s, -) nt (Tennis)* singles *sing*

Einzelbett *nt* single bed

Einzelfahrschein *m* one-way ticket

Einzelgänger(in) *m(f)* loner

Einzelhandel *m* retail trade

Einzelkind *nt* only child

einzeln *adj* individual; *(getrennt)* separate; *(einzig)* single; **~e …** several …, some …; **der/die E~e** the individual; **im E~en** in detail ▷ *adv* separately; *(verpacken, auführen)* individually; **~ angeben** to specify; **~ eintreten** to enter one by one

Einzelzimmer *nt* single room

Einzelzimmerzuschlag *m* single-room supplement

ein|ziehen *(irr) vt:* **den Kopf ~** to duck ▷ *vi (in ein Haus)* to move in

einzig *adj* only; *(einzeln)* single; *(einzigartig)* unique; **kein ~er Fehler** not a single mistake; **das E~e** the only thing; **der/die E~e** the only person ▷ *adv* only; **die ~ richtige Lösung** the only correct solution

einzigartig *adj* unique

Eis *(-es, -) nt* ice; *(Speiseeis)* ice cream

Eisbahn f ice(skating) rink
Eisbär m polar bear
Eisbecher m (ice-cream) sundae
Eisberg m iceberg
Eisbergsalat m iceberg lettuce
Eiscafé nt, **Eisdiele** f ice-cream parlor
Eisen (-s, -) nt iron
Eisenbahn f railroad
eisern adj iron
eisgekühlt adj chilled
Eishockey nt ice hockey
Eiskaffee m iced coffee
eiskalt adj ice-cold; (Temperatur) freezing
Eiskunstlauf m figure skating
eis|laufen (irr) vi to skate
Eisschokolade f iced chocolate
Eisschrank m refrigerator, ice-box
Eistee m iced tea
Eiswürfel m ice cube
Eiszapfen m icicle
eitel adj vain
Eiter (-s) m pus
Eiweiß (-es, -e) nt egg white; (Chem, Bio) protein
ekelhaft, ek(e)lig adj disgusting, revolting
ekeln vr: **sich ~** to be disgusted (vor +dat at)
EKG (-s, -s) nt (abk) = **Elektrokardiogramm** ECG
Ekzem (-s, -e) nt (Med) eczema
elastisch adj elastic
Elch (-(e)s, -e) m elk; (nordamerikanischer) moose
Elefant m elephant
elegant adj elegant
Elektriker(in) (-s, -) m(f) electrician
elektrisch adj electric
Elektrizität f electricity
Elektroauto nt electric car
Elektrogerät nt electrical appliance
Elektrogeschäft nt electrical supply; (für Haushaltsgeräte) small appliance store
Elektroherd m electric stove
Elektromotor m electric motor
Elektronik f electronics sing
elektronisch adj electronic
Elektrorasierer (-s, -) m electric razor
Element (-s, -e) nt element
elend adj miserable
Elend (-(e)s) nt misery
elf num eleven
Elf (-, -en) f (Sport) eleven
Elfenbein nt ivory
Elfmeter m (Sport) penalty (kick)
elfte(r, s) adj eleventh; siehe auch **dritte**

Ell(en)bogen m elbow
Elster (-, -n) f magpie
Eltern pl parents pl
Elternteil m parent
EM f (abk) = **Europameisterschaft** European Championship(s)
E-Mail (-, -s) f (Inform) e-mail; **jdm eine ~ schicken** to e-mail sb, to send sb an e-mail; **jdm etwas per ~ schicken** to e-mail sth to sb
E-Mail-Adresse f e-mail address
e-mailen vt to e-mail
Emoticon (-s, -s) nt emoticon
emotional adj emotional
empfahl imperf von **empfehlen**
empfand imperf von **empfinden**
Empfang (-(e)s, Empfänge) m (Rezeption; Veranstaltung) reception; (Erhalten) receipt; **in ~ nehmen** to receive
empfangen (empfing, empfangen) vt to receive
Empfänger(in) (-s, -) m(f) recipient; (Adressat) addressee ▷ m (Tech) receiver
Empfängnisverhütung f contraception
Empfangshalle f reception area
empfehlen (empfahl, empfohlen) vt to recommend
Empfehlung f recommendation
empfinden (empfand, empfunden) vt to feel
empfindlich adj (Mensch) sensitive; (Stelle) sore; (reizbar) touchy; (Material) delicate
empfing imperf von **empfangen**
empfohlen pp von **empfehlen**
empfunden pp von **empfinden**
empört adj indignant (über +akk at)
Ende (-s, -n) nt end; (Film, Roman) ending; **am ~** at the end; (schließlich) in the end; **~ Mai** at the end of May; **~ der Achtzigerjahre** in the late eighties; **sie ist ~ zwanzig** she's in her late twenties; **zu ~** over, finished
enden vi to end; **der Zug endet hier** this service (o train) terminates here
endgültig adj final; (Beweis) conclusive
Endivie f endive
endlich adv at last, finally; (am Ende) eventually
Endspiel nt final; (Endrunde) finals pl
Endstation f terminus
Endung f ending
Energie f energy; **~ sparend** energy-saving
Energiebedarf m energy requirement
Energieverbrauch m energy consumption
energisch adj (entschlossen) forceful

eng adj narrow; (Kleidung) tight; (fig: Freundschaft, Verhältnis) close; **das wird eng** (fam: zeitlich) we're running out of time, it's getting tight ▷ adv: **eng befreundet sein** to be close friends

engagieren vt to engage ▷ vr: **sich ~ to** commit oneself, to be committed (für to)

Engel (-s, -) m angel

England nt England

Engländer(in) (-s, -) m(f) Englishman/ -woman; **die ~** pl the English pl

englisch adj English; (Gastr) rare

Englisch nt English; **ins ~e übersetzen** to translate into English

Enkel (-s, -) m grandson

Enkelin f granddaughter

enorm adj enormous; (fig) tremendous

Entbindung f (Med) delivery

entdecken vt to discover

Entdeckung f discovery

Ente (-, -n) f duck

Enter-Taste f (Inform) enter (o return) key

entfernen vt to remove; (Inform) to delete ▷ vr: **sich ~ to** go away

entfernt adj distant; **15 km von X ~ 15 km** away from X; **20 km voneinander ~ 20 km** apart

Entfernung f distance; **aus der ~** from a distance

entführen vt to kidnap

Entführer(in) m(f) kidnaper

Entführung f kidnaping

entgegen prep (+dat) contrary to ▷ adv towards; **dem Wind ~** against the wind

entgegengesetzt adj (Richtung) opposite; (Meinung) opposing

entgegenkommen (irr) vi: **jdm ~ to** come to meet sb; (fig) to accommodate sb

entgegenkommend adj (Verkehr) oncoming; (fig) obliging

entgegnen vt to reply (auf +akk to)

entgehen (irr) vi: **jdm ~ to** escape sb's notice; **sich** (dat) **etw ~ lassen** to miss sth

entgleisen vi (Eisenb) to be derailed; (fig: Mensch) to misbehave

Enthaarungscreme f hair remover

enthalten (irr) vt (Behälter) to contain; (Preis) to include ▷ vr: **sich ~ to** abstain (gen from)

entkoffeiniert adj decaffeinated

entkommen (irr) vi to escape

entkorken vt to uncork

entlang prep (+akk o dat); **~ dem Fluss, den Fluss ~** along the river

entlang|gehen (irr) vi to walk along

entlassen (irr) vt (Patient) to discharge; (Arbeiter) to fire; (vorübergehend) to lay off

entlasten vt: **jdn ~** (Arbeit abnehmen) to help sb out with his/her work (o workload)

entmutigen vt to discourage

entnehmen vt to take (dat from)

entrahmt adj (Milch) skimmed

entschädigen vt to compensate

Entschädigung f compensation

entscheiden (irr) vt, vi to decide ▷ vr: **sich ~ to** decide; **sich für/gegen etw ~ to** decide on/against sth; **wir haben uns entschieden, nicht zu gehen** we decided not to go; **das entscheidet sich morgen** that'll be decided tomorrow

entscheidend adj decisive; (Frage, Problem) crucial; **~e Stimme** deciding vote

Entscheidung f decision

entschließen (irr) vr: **sich ~ to** decide (zu, für on), to make up one's mind

Entschluss m decision

entschuldigen vt to excuse ▷ vr: **sich ~ to** apologize; **sich bei jdm für etw ~ to** apologize to sb for sth ▷ vi: **entschuldige!, ~ Sie!** (vor einer Frage) excuse me!; (Verzeihung!) (I'm) sorry, excuse me!

Entschuldigung f apology; (Grund) excuse; **jdn um ~ bitten** to apologize to sb; **~!** (bei Zusammenstoß) (I'm) sorry, excuse me; (vor einer Frage) excuse me; (wenn man etw nicht verstanden hat) (I beg your) pardon?

entsetzlich adj dreadful, appalling

entsorgen vt to dispose of

entspannen vt (Körper) to relax; (Pol: Lage) to ease ▷ vr: **sich ~ to** relax; (fam) to chill out

Entspannung f relaxation

entsprechen (irr) vi (+dat) to correspond to; (Anforderungen, Wünschen etc) to comply with

entsprechend adj appropriate ▷ adv accordingly ▷ prep (+dat) according to, in accordance with

entstehen vi (Schwierigkeiten) to arise; (gebaut werden) to be built; (hergestellt werden) to be created

enttäuschen vt to disappoint

Enttäuschung f disappointment

entweder conj: **~ ... oder ...** either ... or ...; **~ oder!** take it or leave it!

entwerfen (irr) vt (Möbel, Kleider) to design; (Plan, Vertrag) to draft

entwerten *vt* to devalue; *(Fahrschein)* to stamp, to validate

Entwerter *(-s, -) m* validation *(o* validating) machine

entwickeln *vt (auch Foto)* to develop; *(Mut, Energie)* to show, to display ▷ *vr:* **sich ~** to develop

Entwicklung *f* development; *(Foto)* developing

Entwicklungshelfer(in) *(-s, -) m(f)* development worker

Entwicklungsland *nt* developing country

Entwurf *m* outline; *(Design)* design; *(Vertragsentwurf, Konzept)* draft

entzückend *adj* delightful, charming

Entzug *m* withdrawal; *(Behandlung)* detox

Entzugserscheinung *f* withdrawal symptom

entzünden *vr:* **sich ~** to catch fire; *(Med)* to become inflamed *(o* infected)

Entzündung *f (Med)* inflammation

Epidemie *(-, -n) f* epidemic

Epilepsie *(-, -n) f* epilepsy

epilieren *vt* remove body hair, depilate

Epiliergerät *nt* epilator

er *pron (Person)* he; *(Sache)* it; **er ist's** it's him; **wo ist mein Mantel? - er ist ...** where's my coat? - it's ...

Erbe *(-n, -n) m* heir ▷ *nt (-s)* inheritance; *(fig)* heritage

erben *vt* to inherit

Erbin *f* heiress

erblich *adj* hereditary

erblicken *vt* to catch sight of

erbrechen *(irr) vt* to vomit ▷ *vr:* **sich ~** to vomit

Erbrechen *nt* vomiting

Erbschaft *f* inheritance

Erbse *(-, -n) f* pea

Erdapfel *m* potato

Erdbeben *nt* earthquake

Erdbeere *f* strawberry

Erde *(-, -n) f (Planet)* earth; *(Boden)* ground; *(Bodenart)* soil, dirt

Erdgas *nt* natural gas

Erdgeschoss *nt* first floor

Erdkunde *f* geography

Erdnuss *f* peanut

Erdöl *nt* (mineral) oil

Erdrutsch *m* landslide

Erdteil *m* continent

ereignen *vr:* **sich ~** to happen, to take place

Ereignis *nt* event

erfahren *(irr) vt* to learn, to find out; *(erle-*

ben) to experience ▷ *adj* experienced

Erfahrung *f* experience

erfinden *(irr) vt* to invent

erfinderisch *adj* inventive, creative

Erfindung *f* invention

Erfolg *(-(e)s, -e) m* success; *(Folge)* result; **~ versprechend** promising; **viel ~!** good luck!

erfolglos *adj* unsuccessful

erfolgreich *adj* successful

erforderlich *adj* necessary

erforschen *vt* to explore; *(untersuchen)* investigate

erfreulich *adj* pleasing, pleasant; *(Nachricht)* good

erfreulicherweise *adv* fortunately

erfrieren *(irr) vi* to freeze to death; *(Pflanzen)* to be killed by frost

Erfrischung *f* refreshment

erfüllen *vt (Raum)* to fill; *(Bitte, Wunsch etc)* to fulfill ▷ *vr:* **sich ~** to come true

ergänzen *vt (hinzufügen)* to add; *(vervollständigen)* to complete ▷ *vr:* **sich ~** to complement one another

Ergänzung *f* completion; *(Zusatz)* supplement

ergeben *(irr) vt (Betrag)* to come to; *(zum Ergebnis haben)* to result in *(irr) vr:* **sich ~** to surrender; *(folgen)* to result *(aus* from) ▷ *adj* devoted; *(demütig)* humble

Ergebnis *nt* result

ergreifen *(irr) vt* to seize; *(Beruf)* to take up; *(Maßnahme, Gelegenheit)* to take; *(rühren)* to move

erhalten *(irr) vt (bekommen)* to receive; *(bewahren)* to preserve; **gut ~ sein** to be in good condition

erhältlich *adj* available

erheblich *adj* considerable

erhitzen *vt* to heat (up)

erhöhen *vt* to raise; *(verstärken)* to increase ▷ *vr:* **sich ~** to increase

erholen *vr:* **sich ~** to recover; *(sich ausruhen)* to rest (and recuperate)

erholsam *adj* relaxing, restful

Erholung *f* recovery; *(Entspannung)* relaxation, rest

erinnern *vt* to remind *(an +akk* of) ▷ *vr:* **sich ~** to remember *(an etw akk* sth)

Erinnerung *f* memory; *(Andenken)* souvenir; *(Mahnung)* reminder

erkälten *vr:* **sich ~** to catch a cold

erkältet *adj:* **stark ~ sein** to have a (bad) cold

Erkältung *f* cold

erkennen (*irr*) *vt* to recognize; (*sehen, verstehen*) to see; **~, dass ...** to realize that ...

erkenntlich *adj*: **sich ~ zeigen** to show one's appreciation

Erker (*-s, -*) *m* bay

erklären *vt* to explain; (*kundtun*) to declare

Erklärung *f* explanation; (*Aussage*) declaration

erkundigen *vr*: **sich ~** to inquire (*nach* about)

erlauben *vt* to allow, to permit; **jdm ~, etw zu tun** to allow (*o* permit) sb to do sth; **sich** (*dat*) **etw ~** to allow oneself sth; **~ Sie (, dass ich rauche)?** do you mind (if I smoke)?; **was ~ Sie sich?** what do you think you're doing?

Erlaubnis *f* permission

Erläuterung *f* explanation; (*zu Text*) comment

erleben *vt* to experience; (*schöne Tage etc*) to have; (*Schlimmes*) to go through; (*miterleben*) to witness; (*noch miterleben*) to live to see

Erlebnis *nt* experience

erledigen *vt* (*Angelegenheit, Aufgabe*) to take care of; (*fam: ruinieren*) to finish

erledigt *adj* (*beendet*) finished; (*gelöst*) done; (*fam: erschöpft*) beat, exhausted

erleichtert *adj* relieved

Erlös (*-es, -e*) *m* proceeds *pl*

ermahnen *vt* (*warnend*) to warn

ermäßigt *adj* reduced

Ermäßigung *f* discount

ermitteln *vt* to find out; (*Täter*) to trace ▷ *vi* (*Jur*) to investigate

ermöglichen *vt* to make possible (*dat* for)

ermorden *vt* to murder

ermüdend *adj* tiring

ermutigen *vt* to encourage

ernähren *vt* to feed; (*Familie*) to support ▷ *vr*: **sich ~** to support oneself; **sich ~ von** to live on

Ernährung *f* (*Essen*) food

Ernährungsberater(in) *m(f)* nutritionist, dietitian

erneuern *vt* to renew; (*restaurieren*) to restore; (*renovieren*) to renovate; (*auswechseln*) to replace

ernst *adj* serious ▷ *adv*: **jdn/etw ~ nehmen** take sb/sth seriously

Ernst (*-es*) *m* seriousness; **das ist mein ~** I'm absolutely serious; **im ~?** seriously?

ernsthaft *adj* serious ▷ *adv* seriously

Ernte (*-, -n*) *f* harvest

Erntedankfest *nt* Thanksgiving (Day) (*4. Donnerstag im November*)

ernten *vt* to harvest; (*Lob etc*) to earn

erobern *vt* to conquer

eröffnen *vt* to open

Eröffnung *f* opening

erogen *adj* erogenous

erotisch *adj* erotic

erpressen *vt* (*jdn*) to blackmail; (*Geld etc*) to extort

Erpressung *f* blackmail; (*von Geld*) extortion

erraten (*irr*) *vt* to guess

erregen *vt* to excite; (*sexuell*) to arouse; (*ärgern*) to annoy; (*hervorrufen*) to arouse ▷ *vr*: **sich ~** to get worked up

Erreger (*-s, -*) *m* (*Med*) germ; (*Virus*) virus

erreichbar *adj*: **~ sein** to be within reach; (*Person*) to be available; **das Stadtzentrum ist zu Fuß/mit dem Wagen leicht ~** the downtown area is within easy walking/driving distance

erreichen *vt* to reach; (*Zug etc*) to catch

Ersatz (*-es*) *m* replacement; (*auf Zeit*) substitute; (*Ausgleich*) compensation

Ersatzreifen *m* (*Auto*) spare tire

Ersatzteil *nt* spare (part)

erscheinen (*irr*) *vi* to appear; (*wirken*) to seem

erschöpft *adj* exhausted

Erschöpfung *f* exhaustion

erschrecken *vt* to frighten ▷ *vi* (**erschrak, erschrocken**) to be frightened; (*kurz alarmiert*) to be startled

erschreckend *adj* alarming

erschrocken *adj* frightened, startled

erschwinglich *adj* affordable

ersetzen *vt* to replace; (*Auslagen*) to reimburse

erst *adv* **1** first; **mach erst mal die Arbeit fertig** finish your work first; **wenn du das erst mal hinter dir hast** once you've got that behind you
2 (*nicht früher als, nur*) only; (*nicht bis*) not till; **erst gestern** only yesterday; **erst morgen** not until tomorrow; **erst als** only when, not until; **wir fahren erst später** we're not going until later; **er ist (gerade) erst angekommen** he's only just arrived
3: **wäre er doch erst zurück!** if only he were back!

erstatten vt (Kosten) to refund; **Bericht** ~ to report (über +akk on); **Anzeige gegen jdn** ~ to report sb to the police

erstaunlich adj astonishing

erstaunt adj surprised

erstbeste(r, s) adj: **das** ~ **Hotel** any old hotel; **der E~** just anyone

erste(r, s) adj first; siehe auch dritte; **zum ~n Mal** for the first time; **er wurde E~r** he came first; **auf den ~n Blick** at first sight

erstens adv first(ly), in the first place

ersticken vi (Mensch) to suffocate; **in Arbeit** ~ to be drowning in work

erstklassig adj first-class

erstmals adv for the first time

erstrecken vr: **sich** ~ to extend, to stretch (auf +akk to; über +akk over)

ertappen vt to catch

erteilen vt (Rat, Erlaubnis) to give

Ertrag (-(e)s, Erträge) m yield; (Gewinn) proceeds pl

ertragen (irr) vt (Schmerzen) to bear, to stand; (dulden) to put up with

erträglich adj bearable; (nicht zu schlecht) tolerable

ertrinken (irr) vi to drown

erwachsen adj grown-up; ~ **werden** to grow up

Erwachsene(r) mf adult, grown-up

erwähnen vt to mention

erwarten vt to expect; (warten auf) to wait for; **ich kann den Sommer kaum** ~ I can hardly wait for the summer

erwerbstätig adj employed

erwidern vt to reply; (Gruß, Besuch) to return

erwischen vt (fam) to catch (bei etw doing sth)

erwünscht adj desired; (willkommen) welcome

Erz (-es, -e) nt ore

erzählen vt to tell (jdm etw sb sth)

Erzählung f story, tale

erzeugen vt to produce; (Strom) to generate

Erzeugnis nt product

erziehen (irr) vt to raise; (geistig) to educate; (Tier) to train

Erzieher(in) (-s, -) m(f) educator; (Kindergarten) (nursery school) teacher

Erziehung f upbringing; (Bildung) education

es pron (Sache, im Nom und Akk) it; (Baby, Tier) he/she; **ich bin es** it's me; **es ist kalt** it's cold; **es gibt ...** there is .../there are ...;

ich hoffe es I hope so; **ich kann es** I can do it

Escape-Taste f (Inform) escape key

Esel (-s, -) m donkey

Espresso (-s, -) m espresso

essbar adj edible

essen (aß, gegessen) vt, vi to eat; **zu Mittag/Abend** ~ to have lunch/dinner; **was gibt's zu ~?** what's for lunch/dinner?; ~ **gehen** to eat out; **gegessen sein** (fig, fam) to be history

Essen (-s, -) nt (Mahlzeit) meal; (Nahrung) food

Essig (-s, -e) m vinegar

Esslöffel m soup spoon; (Messeinheit) tablespoon

Esszimmer nt dining room

Estland nt Estonia

Etage (-, -n) f floor, story; **in o auf der ersten** ~ on the second floor

Etagenbett nt bunk bed

Etappe (-, -n) f stage

ethnisch adj ethnic

Etikett (-(e)s, -e) nt label

etliche pron (pl) several, quite a few

etliches pron quite a lot

etwa adv (ungefähr) about; (vielleicht) perhaps; (beispielsweise) for instance

etwas pron something; (verneinend, fragend) anything; (ein wenig) a little; ~ **Neues** something/anything new; ~ **zu essen** something to eat; ~ **Salz** some salt; **wenn ich noch** ~ **tun kann ...** if I can do anything else ... ▷ adv a bit, a little; ~ **mehr** a little more

EU (-) f (abk) = **Europäische Union** EU

euch pron akk, dat von **ihr**; you, (to) you; ~ **selbst** (reflexiv) yourselves; **wo kann ich** ~ **treffen?** where can I meet you?; **sie schickt es** ~ she'll send it to you; **ein Freund von** ~ a friend of yours; **setzt** ~ **bitte** please sit down; **habt ihr** ~ **amüsiert?** did you enjoy yourselves?

euer pron (adjektivisch) your; ~ **David** (am Briefende) Yours, David ▷ pron gen von **ihr**; of you

euere(r, s) pron siehe **eure**

Eule (-, -n) f owl

eure(r, s) pron (substantivisch) yours; **das ist** ~ that's yours

euretwegen adv (wegen euch) because of you; (euch zuliebe) for your sake; (um euch) about you

Euro (-, -) m (Währung) euro

Eurocent m eurocent

Eurocity (-(s), -s) m, **Eurocityzug** m European intercity train

Europa (-s) nt Europe

Europäer(in) (-s, -) m(f) European

europäisch adj European; **E~e Union** European Union

Europameister(in) m(f) European champion; (Mannschaft) European champions pl

Europaparlament nt European Parliament

Euter (-s, -) nt udder

evangelisch adj Protestant

eventuell adj possible ▷ adv possibly, perhaps

ewig adj eternal; **er hat ~ gebraucht** it took him forever

Ewigkeit f eternity

Ex mf ex

Ex- in zW ex-, former; **Ex-frau** ex-wife; **Ex-freund** ex-boyfriend; **Ex-minister** former minister

exakt adj precise

Examen (-s, -) nt exam

Exemplar (-s, -e) nt specimen; (Buch) copy

Exil (-s, -e) nt exile

Existenz f existence; (Unterhalt) livelihood, living

existieren vi to exist

exklusiv adj exclusive

exklusive adv, prep (+gen) excluding

exotisch adj exotic

Experte (-n, -n) m, **Expertin** f expert

explodieren vi to explode

Explosion f explosion

Export (-(e)s, -e) m export

exportieren vt to export

Express (-es) m, **Expresszug** m express (train)

extra adj (inv) (fam: gesondert) separate; (zusätzlich) extra ▷ adv (gesondert) separately; (speziell) specially; (absichtlich) on purpose

extrem adj extreme ▷ adv extremely; **~ kalt** extremely cold

exzellent adj excellent

Eyeliner (-s, -) m eyeliner

F

fabelhaft *adj* fabulous, marvelous

Fabrik *f* factory

Fach (-(e)s, *Fächer*) *nt* compartment; (*Schulfach, Sachgebiet*) subject

Facharzt *m*, **Fachärztin** *f* specialist

Fachausdruck (-s, *Fachausdrücke*) *m* technical term

Fächer (-s, -) *m* fan

Fachfrau *f* specialist, expert

Fachmann (-*leute*) *m* specialist, expert

Fachwerkhaus *nt* half-timbered house

Fackel (-, -n) *f* torch

fad(e) *adj* (*Essen*) bland; (*langweilig*) dull

Faden (-s, *Fäden*) *m* thread

fähig *adj* capable (*zu, gen* of)

Fähigkeit *f* ability

Fahndung *f* search

Fahne (-, -n) *f* flag

Fahrausweis *m* ticket

Fahrbahn *f* road; (*Spur*) lane

Fähre (-, -n) *f* ferry

fahren (fuhr, gefahren) *vt* to drive; (*Rad*) to ride; (*befördern*) to drive, to take; **50 km/h ~** to drive at (*o* do) 50 kph ▷ *vi* (*sich bewegen*) to go; (*Autofahrer*) to drive; (*Schiff*) to sail; (*abfahren*) to leave; **mit dem Auto/ Zug ~** to go by car/train; **rechts ~!** keep to the right

Fahrer(in) (-s, -) *m(f)* driver

Fahrerairbag *m* driver airbag

Fahrerflucht *f*: **~ begehen** to fail to stop after an accident

Fahrersitz *m* driver's seat

Fahrgast *m* passenger

Fahrgeld *nt* fare

Fahrgemeinschaft *f* car pool

Fahrkarte *f* ticket

Fahrkartenautomat *m* ticket machine

Fahrkartenschalter *m* ticket office

fahrlässig *adj* negligent

Fahrlehrer(in) *m(f)* driving instructor

Fahrplan *m* timetable

Fahrplanauszug *m* individual timetable

fahrplanmäßig *adj* (*Eisenb*) scheduled

Fahrpreis *m* fare

Fahrpreisermäßigung *f* fare reduction

Fahrrad *nt* bicycle

Fahrradschlauch *m* bicycle tube

Fahrradschloss *nt* bicycle lock

Fahrradverleih *m* bike rental

Fahrradweg *m* bike path

Fahrschein *m* ticket

Fahrscheinautomat *m* ticket machine

Fahrscheinentwerter *m* ticket validation (*o* validating) machine

Fahrschule *f* driving school

Fahrschüler(in) *m(f)* student driver

Fahrspur *f* lane

Fahrstreifen *m* lane

Fahrstuhl *m* elevator

Fahrt (-, -en) *f* journey; (*kurz*) trip; (*Auto*) drive; **auf der ~ nach New York** on the way to New York; **nach drei Stunden ~** after traveling for three hours; **gute ~!** have a good trip!

Fahrtkosten *pl* traveling expenses *pl*

Fahrtrichtung *f* direction of travel

fahrtüchtig *f* (*Person*) able (*o* all right) to drive; (*Fahrzeug*) roadworthy

Fahrtunterbrechung *f* stop; (*fam*) pit stop

Fahrverbot *nt*: **~ erhalten/haben** to be banned from driving

Fahrzeug *nt* vehicle

Fahrzeugbrief *m* (vehicle) registration document

Fahrzeughalter(in) *m(f)* registered owner

Fahrzeugpapiere *pl* vehicle documents *pl*

fair *adj* fair

Fakultät *f* faculty

Falke (-n, -n) *m* falcon

Fall (-(e)s, *Fälle*) *m* (*Sturz*) fall; (*Sachverhalt, juristisch*) case; **auf jeden ~, auf alle Fälle** in any case; (*bestimmt*) definitely; **auf keinen ~** on no account; **für den ~, dass ...** in case ...

Falle (-, -n) *f* trap

fallen (fiel, gefallen) *vi* to fall; **etw ~ lassen** to drop sth

fällig *adj* due

falls *adv* if; (*für den Fall, dass*) in case

Fallschirm *m* parachute

Fallschirmspringen *nt* parachuting, parachute jumping

Fallschirmspringer(in) *m(f)* parachutist

falsch *adj* (*unrichtig*) wrong; (*unehrlich, unecht*) false; (*Schmuck*) fake; **~ verbunden** sorry, wrong number

fälschen *vt* to forge

Falschfahrer(in) *m(f)* wrong-way driver

Falschgeld *nt* counterfeit money

Fälschung *f* forgery, fake

Faltblatt *nt* leaflet

Falte (-, -n) *f* (*Knick*) fold; (*Haut*) wrinkle; (*Rock*) pleat; (*Bügel*) crease

falten vt to fold
faltig adj (zerknittert) creased; (Haut, Gesicht) wrinkled; (Kleider) creased
Familie f family
Familienangehörige(r) mf family member
Familienname m last name, surname
Familienstand m marital status
Fan (-s, -s) m fan
fand imperf von **finden**
fangen (fing, gefangen) vt to catch ▷ vr: **sich ~** (nicht fallen) to steady oneself; (fig) to compose oneself
Fantasie f imagination
fantastisch adj fantastic
Farbdrucker m color printer
Farbe (-, -n) f color; (zum Malen etc) paint; (für Stoff) dye
färben vt to color; (Stoff, Haar) to dye
Farbfilm m color film
farbig adj colored
Farbkopierer m color copier
farblos adj colorless
Farbstoff m dye; (für Lebensmittel) coloring
Farn (-(e)s, -e) m fern
Fasan (-(e)s, -e(n)) m pheasant
Fasching (-s, -e) m carnival, Mardi Gras
Faschingsdienstag (-s, -e) m Shrove Tuesday, Mardi Gras
Faschismus m fascism
Faser (-, -n) f fiber
Fass (-es, Fässer) nt barrel; (Öl) drum
fassen vt (ergreifen) to grasp; (enthalten) to hold; (Entschluss) to make; (verstehen) to understand; **nicht zu ~!** unbelievable! ▷ vr: **sich ~** to compose oneself
Fassung f (Umrahmung) mount; (Brille) frame; (Lampe) socket; (Wortlaut) version; (Beherrschung) composure; **jdn aus der ~ bringen** to throw sb; **die ~ verlieren** to lose one's cool
fast adv almost, nearly
fasten vi to fast
Fastenzeit f: **die ~** (christlich) Lent; (muslimisch) Ramadan
Fast Food (-s) nt fast food
Fastnacht f (Fasching) carnival
fatal adj (verhängnisvoll) disastrous; (peinlich) embarrassing
faul adj (Obst, Gemüse) rotten; (Mensch) lazy; (Ausreden) lame
faulen vi to rot
faulenzen vi to do nothing, to hang around
Faulheit f laziness
faulig adj rotten; (Geruch, Geschmack) foul

Faust (-, Fäuste) f fist
Fausthandschuh m mitten
Fax (-, -(e)) nt fax
faxen vi, vt to fax
Faxgerät nt fax machine
Faxnummer f fax number
FCKW (-, -s) nt (abk) = **Fluorchlorkohlenwasserstoff** CFC
Februar (-(s), -e) m February; siehe auch **Juni**
Fechten nt fencing
Feder (-, -n) f feather; (Schreibfeder) pen point, nib; (Tech) spring
Federball m (Ball) shuttlecock; (Spiel) badminton
Federung f suspension
Fee (-, -n) f fairy
fegen vi, vt to sweep
fehl adj: **~ am Platz** o **Ort** out of place
fehlen vi (abwesend sein) to be absent; **etw fehlt jdm** sb lacks sth; **was fehlt ihm?** what's wrong with him?; **du fehlst mir** I miss you; **es fehlt an ...** there's no...
Fehler (-s, -) m mistake, error; (Mangel, Schwäche) fault
Fehlerbeseitigung f (Inform) debugging
Fehlermeldung f (Inform) error message
Fehlzündung f (Auto) misfire
Feier (-, -n) f celebration; (Party) party
Feierabend m end of the working day; **~ haben** to finish work; **nach ~** after work
feierlich adj solemn
feiern vt, vi to celebrate, to have a party
Feiertag m holiday; **gesetzlicher ~** public holiday
feig(e) adj cowardly
Feige (-, -n) f fig
Feigling m coward
Feile (-, -n) f file
fein adj fine; (vornehm) refined; **~!** great!; **das schmeckt ~** that tastes delicious
Feind(in) (-(e)s, -e) m(f) enemy
feindlich adj hostile
Feinkost (-) f delicacies pl
Feinkostladen m gourmet shop
Feinschmecker(in) (-s, -) m(f) gourmet
Feinstaub m particulate matter
Feinwaschmittel nt laundry detergent for delicate fabrics
Feld (-(e)s, -er) nt field; (Schach) square
Feldsalat m corn salad
Feldweg m path across the fields
Felge (-, -n) f (wheel) rim
Fell (-(e)s, -e) nt fur; (von Schaf) fleece
Fels (-en, -en) m, **Felsen** (-s, -) m rock; (Klip-

pe) cliff
felsig *adj* rocky
feminin *adj* feminine
Femininum (-s, *Feminina*) *nt* (*Ling*) feminine noun
feministisch *adj* feminist
Fenchel (-s, -) *m* fennel
Fenster (-s, -) *nt* window
Fensterbrett *nt* window sill
Fensterladen *m* shutter
Fensterplatz *m* window seat
Fensterscheibe *f* window pane
Ferien *pl* vacation *sing*; ~ **haben/machen** to be/go on vacation
Ferienhaus *nt* vacation home
Ferienkurs *m* vacation course
Ferienlager *nt* vacation camp; (*für Kinder im Sommer*) summer camp
Ferienort *m* vacation resort
Ferienwohnung *f* vacation apartment
Ferkel (-s, -) *nt* piglet
fern *adj* distant, far-off; **von** ~ from a distance
Fernabfrage *f* remote-control access
Fernbedienung *f* remote control
Ferne *f* distance; **aus der** ~ from a distance
ferner *adj, adv* further; (*außerdem*) besides
Fernflug *m* long-distance flight
Ferngespräch *nt* long-distance call
ferngesteuert *adj* remote-controlled
Fernglas *nt* binoculars *pl*
Fernlicht *nt* brights *pl*, high beams *pl*
Fernsehapparat *m* TV (set)
fern|sehen (*irr*) *vi* to watch television
Fernsehen *nt* television; **im** ~ on television
Fernseher *m* TV (set)
Fernsehkanal *m* TV channel
Fernsehprogramm *nt* (*Sendung*) TV program; (*Zeitschrift*) TV guide
Fernsehserie *f* TV series *sing*
Fernsehturm *m* TV tower
Fernsehzeitschrift *f* TV guide
Fernstraße *f* major road
Ferntourismus *m* long-haul tourism
Fernverkehr *m* long-distance traffic
Ferse (-, -n) *f* heel
fertig *adj* (*bereit*) ready; (*beendet*) finished; (*gebrauchsfertig*) ready-made; ~ **machen** (*beenden*) to finish; **sich** ~ **machen** to get ready; **mit etw** ~ **werden** to be able to cope with sth; **auf die Plätze,** ~**, los!** on your mark, get set, go!
Fertiggericht *nt* ready-to-serve meal
fertig|machen *vt* (*jdn kritisieren*) to give sb

hell; (*jdn zur Verzweiflung bringen*) to drive sb crazy; (*jdn deprimieren*) to get sb down
fest *adj* firm; (*Nahrung*) solid; (*Gehalt*) regular; (*Schuhe*) sturdy; (*Schlaf*) sound
Fest (-(e)s, -e) *nt* party; (*Rel*) festival
Festbetrag *m* fixed amount
fest|binden (*irr*) *vt* to tie (*an +dat* to)
fest|halten (*irr*) *vt* to hold onto ▷ *vr*: **sich** ~ to hold on (*an +dat* to)
Festiger (-s, -) *m* setting lotion
Festival (-s, -s) *nt* festival
Festland *nt* mainland; **das europäische** ~ the (European) continent
fest|legen *vt* to set ▷ *vr*: **sich** ~ to commit oneself
festlich *adj* festive
fest|machen *vt* to fasten; (*Termin etc*) to set
fest|nehmen (*irr*) *vt* to arrest
Festnetz *nt* (*Tel*) fixed-line network
Festplatte *f* (*Inform*) hard disk
fest|setzen *vt* to fix
Festspiele *pl* festival *sing*
fest|stehen (*irr*) *vi* to be set
fest|stellen *vt* to establish; (*sagen*) to remark
Feststelltaste *f* shift lock
Festung *f* fortress
Festzelt *nt* tent, pavillion
Fete (-, -n) *f* party
fett *adj* (*dick*) fat; (*Essen etc*) greasy; (*Schrift*) bold
Fett (-(e)s, -e) *nt* fat; (*Tech*) grease
fettarm *adj* low-fat
fettig *adj* fatty; (*schmierig*) greasy
feucht *adj* damp; (*Luft*) humid
Feuchtigkeit *f* dampness; (*Luftfeuchtigkeit*) humidity
Feuchtigkeitscreme *f* moisturizing cream
Feuer (-s, -) *nt* fire; **haben Sie** ~? have you got a light?
Feueralarm *m* fire alarm
feuerfest *adj* fireproof
Feuerlöscher (-s, -) *m* fire extinguisher
Feuermelder (-s, -) *m* fire alarm
Feuertreppe *f* fire escape
Feuerwehr (-, -en) *f* fire department
Feuerwehrfrau *f* firewoman, fire fighter
Feuerwehrmann *m* fireman, fire fighter
Feuerwerk *nt* fireworks *pl*
Feuerzeug *nt* (*cigarette*) lighter
Fichte (-, -n) *f* spruce
Fieber (-s, -) *nt* temperature, fever; ~ **haben** to have a high temperature

Fieberthermometer nt thermometer
fiel imperf von **fallen**
fies adj (fam) nasty
Figur (-, -en) f figure; (im Schach) piece
Filet (-s, -s) nt fillet
filetieren vt to fillet
Filetsteak nt fillet steak
Filiale (-, -n) f (Comm) branch
Film (-(e)s, -e) m film, movie
filmen vt, vi to film
Filter (-s, -) m filter
Filterkaffee m filter coffee
filtern vt to filter
Filterpapier nt filter paper
Filz (-es, -e) m felt
Filzschreiber m, **Filzstift** m felt(-tip) pen,
  felt-tip
Finale (-s, -) nt (Sport) final
Finanzamt nt tax office
finanziell adj financial
finanzieren vt to finance
finden (**fand, gefunden**) vt to find; (mei-
  nen) to think; **ich finde nichts dabei, wenn
  ...** I don't see what's wrong if ...; **ich finde
  es gut/schlecht** I like/don't like it ▷ vr: **es
  fanden sich nur wenige Helfer** there were
  only a few helpers
fing imperf von **fangen**
Finger (-s, -) m finger
Fingerabdruck m fingerprint
Fingerhandschuh m glove
Fingernagel m fingernail
Fink (-en, -en) m finch
Finne (-n, -n) m, **Finnin** f Finn, Finnish
  man/woman
finnisch adj Finnish
Finnisch nt Finnish
Finnland nt Finland
finster adj dark; (verdächtig) dubious; (ver-
  drossen) grim; (Gedanke) dark
Finsternis f darkness
Firewall (-, -s) f (Inform) firewall
Firma (-, Firmen) f company
Fisch (-(e)s, -e) m fish; **~e** pl (Astr) Pisces
  sing
fischen vt, vi to fish
Fischer(in) (-s, -) m(f) fisherman/-woman
Fischerboot nt fishing boat
Fischgericht nt fish dish
Fischhändler(in) m(f) seafood dealer (o
  merchant)
Fischstäbchen nt fish stick
Fisole (-, -n) f green bean
fit adj fit
Fitness (-) f fitness

Fitnesscenter (-s, -) nt fitness center
Fitnesstrainer(in) m(f) fitness trainer, per-
  sonal trainer
fix adj (schnell) quick; **fix und fertig** exhaust-
  ed
fixen vi (fam) to shoot up
Fixer(in) (-s, -) m(f) (fam) junkie
FKK f (abk) = **Freikörperkultur** nudism
FKK-Strand m nudist beach
flach adj flat; (Gewässer; Teller) shallow; **~er
  Absatz** low heel
Flachbildschirm m flat screen
Fläche (-, -n) f area; (Oberfläche) surface
Flagge (-, -n) f flag
flambiert adj flambé(ed)
Flamme (-, -n) f flame
Flanell (-s) m washcloth
Flasche (-, -n) f bottle; **eine ~ sein** (fam) to
  be useless
Flaschenbier nt bottled beer
Flaschenöffner m bottle opener
Flaschenpfand nt deposit
Flaschentomate f plum tomato
flatterhaft adj fickle
flattern vi to flutter
flauschig adj fluffy
Flausen pl (fam) crazy ideas pl
Flaute (-, -n) f calm; (Comm) recession
Flechte (-, -n) f braid; (Med) scab; (Bot)
  lichen
flechten (**flocht, geflochten**) vt to braid;
  (Kranz) to bind
Fleck (-(e)s, -e) m, **Flecken** (-s, -) m spot;
  (Schmutz) stain; (Stofffleck) patch; (Makel)
  blemish
Fleckentferner (-s, -) m stain remover
fleckig adj spotted; (mit Schmutzflecken)
  stained
Fledermaus f bat
Fleisch (-(e)s) nt flesh; (Essen) meat
Fleischbrühe f meat stock
Fleischer(in) (-s, -) m(f) butcher
Fleischerei f butcher's (shop)
Fleischtomate f beefsteak tomato
fleißig adj diligent, hard-working
flennen vi (fam) to cry, to scream
flexibel adj flexible
flicken vt to mend
Flickzeug nt repair kit
Flieder (-s, -) m lilac
Fliege (-, -n) f fly; (Krawatte) bow tie
fliegen (**flog, geflogen**) vt, vi to fly
Fliese (-, -n) f tile
Fließband nt conveyor belt; (als Einrich-
  tung) production (o assembly) line

fließen (floss, geflossen) *vi* to flow

fließend *adj* (*Rede, Deutsch*) fluent; (*Übergänge*) smooth; ~ **es Wasser** running water

Flipper (-s, -) *m* pinball machine

flippern *vi* to play pinball

flippig *adj* (*fam*) eccentric

flirten *vi* to flirt

Flitterwochen *pl* honeymoon *sing*

flocht *imperf von* **flechten**

Flocke (-, -n) *f* flake

flog *imperf von* **fliegen**

Floh (-(e)s, Flöhe) *m* flea

Flohmarkt *m* flea market

Flop (-s, -s) *m* flop

Floskel (-, -n) *f* empty phrase

floss *imperf von* **fließen**

Floß (-es, Flöße) *nt* raft

Flosse (-, -n) *f* fin; (*Schwimmflosse*) flipper

Flöte (-, -n) *f* flute; (*Blockflöte*) recorder

flott *adj* lively; (*elegant*) smart; (*Naut*) afloat

Fluch (-(e)s, Flüche) *m* curse

fluchen *vi* to swear, to curse

Flucht (-, -en) *f* flight

flüchten *vi* to flee (*vor +dat* from)

flüchtig *adj*: **ich kenne ihn nur ~** I don't know him very well at all

Flüchtling *m* refugee

Flug (-(e)s, Flüge) *m* flight

Flugbegleiter(in) (-s, -) *m(f)* flight attendant

Flugblatt *nt* leaflet

Flügel (-s, -) *m* wing; (*Mus*) grand piano

Fluggast *m* (airline) passenger

Fluggesellschaft *f* airline

Flughafen *m* airport

Flugkarte *f* airline ticket

Fluglotse *m* air-traffic controller

Flugnummer *f* flight number

Flugplan *m* flight schedule

Flugplatz *m* airport; (*klein*) airfield

Flugschein *m* plane ticket

Flugschreiber *m* flight recorder, black box

Flugsteig (-s, -e) *m* gate

Flugstrecke *f* air route

Flugticket *nt* plane ticket

Flugverbindung *f* flight connection

Flugverkehr *m* air traffic

Flugzeit *f* flying time

Flugzeug *nt* airplane, plane

Flugzeugentführung *f* hijacking

Flunder (-, -n) *f* flounder

Fluor (-s) *nt* fluorine

Flur (-(e)s, -e) *m* hall

Fluss (-es, Flüsse) *m* river; (*Fließen*) flow

flüssig *adj* liquid

Flüssigkeit (-, -en) *f* liquid

Flüssigseife *f* liquid soap

flüstern *vt, vi* to whisper

Flut (-, -en) *f* (*a. fig*) flood; (*Gezeiten*) high tide

Flutlicht *nt* floodlight

Fohlen (-s, -) *nt* foal

Föhn (-(e)s, -e) *m* hair dryer; (*Wind*) foehn

föhnen *vt* to dry; (*beim Friseur*) to blow-dry

Folge (-, -n) *f* (*Reihe, Serie*) series *sing*; (*Aufeinanderfolge*) sequence; (*Fortsetzung eines Romans*) installment; (*Fortsetzung einer Fernsehserie*) episode; (*Auswirkung*) result; **etw zur ~ haben** to result in sth; **~n haben** to have consequences

folgen *vi* to follow (*jdm* sb); (*gehorchen*) to obey (*jdm* sb); **jdm ~ können** (*fig*) to be able to follow sb

folgend *adj* following

folgendermaßen *adv* as follows

folglich *adv* consequently

Folie *f* foil; (*für Projektor*) transparency

Fön® *m siehe* **Föhn**

Fondue (-s, -s) *nt* fondue

fönen *vt siehe* **föhnen**

fordern *vt* to demand

fördern *vt* to promote; (*unterstützen*) to help

Forderung *f* demand

Forelle *f* trout

Form (-, -en) *f* form; (*Gestalt*) shape; (*Gussform*) mold; (*Backform*) baking pan; **in ~ sein** to be in good form

Formalität *f* formality

Format *nt* format; **von internationalem ~** of international standing

formatieren *vt* (*Diskette*) to format; (*Text*) to edit

Formblatt *nt* form

formen *vt* to form, to shape

förmlich *adj* formal; (*buchstäblich*) real

formlos *adj* informal

Formular (-s, -e) *nt* form

formulieren *vt* to formulate

forschen *vi* to search (*nach* for); (*wissenschaftlich*) to (do) research

Forscher(in) *m(f)* researcher

Forschung *f* research

Förster(in) (-s, -) *m(f)* forester; (*für Wild*) gamekeeper

fort *adv* away; (*verschwunden*) gone

fort|bewegen *vt* to move away ▷ *vr:* **sich ~** to move

Fortbildung *f* continuing education; (*im Beruf*) further training

fort|fahren (*irr*) *vi* to go away; (*weitermachen*) to continue

fort|gehen (*irr*) *vi* to go away

fortgeschritten *adj* advanced

Fortpflanzung *f* reproduction

Fortschritt *m* progress; **~e machen** to make progress

fortschrittlich *adj* progressive

fort|setzen *vt* to continue

Fortsetzung *f* continuation; (*folgender Teil*) installment; **~ folgt** to be continued

Foto (*-s, -s*) *nt* photo ▷ (*-s, -s*) *m* (*Fotoapparat*) camera

Fotograf(in) (*-en, -en*) *m(f)* photographer

Fotografie *f* photography; (*Bild*) photograph

fotografieren *vt* to photograph ▷ *vi* to take photographs

Fotohandy *nt* camera phone

Fotokopie *f* photocopy

fotokopieren *vt* to photocopy

Foul (*-s, -s*) *nt* foul

Foyer (*-s, -s*) *nt* foyer

Fr. *f* (*abk*) **= Frau** Mrs.; (*unverheiratet, neutral*) Ms.

Fracht (*-, -en*) *f* freight; (*Naut*) cargo; (*Preis*) freight

Frachter (*-s, -*) *m* freighter

Frack (*-(e)s, Fräcke*) *m* tails *pl*

Frage (*-, -n*) *f* question; **das ist eine ~ der Zeit** that's a matter (*o* question) of time; **das kommt nicht in ~** that's out of the question

Fragebogen *m* questionnaire

fragen *vt, vi* to ask

Fragezeichen *nt* question mark

fragwürdig *adj* dubious

Franken (*-s, -*) *m* (*Schweizer Währung*) Swiss franc ▷ (*-s*) *nt* (*Land*) Franconia

frankieren *vt* to stamp; (*maschinell*) to frank

Frankreich (*-s*) *nt* France

Franzose (*-n, -n*) *m*, **Französin** *f* Frenchman/-woman; **die ~n** *pl* the French *pl*

französisch *adj* French

Französisch *nt* French

fraß *imperf von* **fressen**

Frau (*-, -en*) *f* woman; (*Ehefrau*) wife; (*Anrede*) Mrs.; (*unverheiratet, neutral*) Ms.

Frauenarzt *m*, **Frauenärztin** *f* gynecolo-

gist

Frauenbewegung *f* women's movement

frauenfeindlich *adj* misogynous

Frauenhaus *nt* women's shelter

Fräulein *nt* (*junge Dame*) young lady; (*veraltet als Anrede*) Miss

Freak (*-s, -s*) *m* (*fam*) freak

frech *adj* fresh, sassy

Frechheit *f* sassiness; **so eine ~!** what nerve!

Freeclimbing (*-s*) *nt* free climbing

frei *adj* free; (*Straße*) clear; (*Mitarbeiter*) freelance; **ein ~er Tag** a day off; **~e Arbeitsstelle** vacancy; **Zimmer ~** room(s) for rent; **im F~én** outdoors

Freibad *nt* outdoor (swimming) pool

freiberuflich *adj* freelance

freig(i)ebig *adj* generous

Freiheit *f* freedom

Freikarte *f* free ticket

frei|lassen (*irr*) *vt* to (set) free

freilich *adv* of course

Freilichtbühne *f* open-air theater

frei|machen *vr:* **sich ~** to undress

frei|nehmen (*irr*) *vt:* **sich** (*dat*) **einen Tag ~** to take a day off

Freisprechanlage *f* hands-free phone

Freistoß *m* free kick

Freitag *m* Friday; *siehe auch* **Mittwoch**

freitags *adv* on Fridays; *siehe auch* **mittwochs**

freiwillig *adj* voluntary

Freizeit *f* spare (*o* free) time

Freizeithemd *nt* sports shirt

Freizeitkleidung *f* leisure wear

Freizeitpark *m* leisure park

fremd *adj* (*nicht vertraut*) strange; (*ausländisch*) foreign; (*nicht eigen*) someone else's

Fremde(r) *mf* (*Unbekannter*) stranger; (*Ausländer*) foreigner

fremdenfeindlich *adj* anti-foreigner, xenophobic

Fremdenführer(in) *m(f)* (*tourist*) guide

Fremdenverkehr *m* tourism

Fremdenverkehrsamt *nt* tourist information office

Fremdenzimmer *nt* (*guest*) room

Fremdsprache *f* foreign language

Fremdsprachenkenntnisse *pl* knowledge *sing* of foreign languages

Fremdwort *nt* foreign word

Frequenz *f* (*Radio*) frequency

fressen (*fraß, gefressen*) *vt, vi* (*Tier*) to eat; (*Mensch*) to guzzle

Freude (-, -n) f joy, delight
freuen vt to please; **es freut mich, dass ...**
I'm pleased that ... ▷ vr: **sich ~** to be
pleased (über +akk about); **sich auf etw**
(akk) **~** to look forward to sth
Freund (-(e)s, -e) m friend; (in Beziehung)
boyfriend
Freundin f friend; (in Beziehung) girlfriend
freundlich adj friendly; (liebenswürdig)
kind
freundlicherweise adv kindly
Freundlichkeit f friendliness; (Liebenswür-
digkeit) kindness
Freundschaft f friendship
Frieden (-s, -) m peace
Friedhof m cemetery
friedlich adj peaceful
frieren (fror, gefroren) vt, vi to freeze; **ich
friere, es friert mich** I'm freezing
Frikadelle f hamburger
Frisbee® nt, **Frisbeescheibe** f frisbee®
frisch adj fresh; (lebhaft) lively; „~ gestrichen" 'wet paint'; **sich ~ machen** to fresh-
en up
Frischhaltefolie f plastic wrap
Frischkäse m cream cheese
Friseur(in) (-s, -e) m(f) hairdresser
frisieren vt: **jdn ~** to do sb's hair ▷ vr: **sich ~**
to do one's hair
Frist (-, -en) f period; (Zeitpunkt) deadline;
innerhalb einer ~ von zehn Tagen within a
ten-day period; **eine ~ einhalten** to meet a
deadline; **die ~ ist abgelaufen** the deadline has expired
fristgerecht adj, adv within the specified
time
fristlos adj: **~e Entlassung** termination
without further notice, immediate termination
Frisur f hairdo, hairstyle
frittieren vt to deep-fry
Frl. f (abk) = Fräulein Miss
froh adj happy; **~e Weihnachten!** Merry
Christmas!
fröhlich adj happy, cheerful
Fronleichnam (-(e)s) m Corpus Christi
frontal adj frontal
fror imperf von **frieren**
Frosch (-(e)s, Frösche) m frog
Frost (-(e)s, Fröste) m frost; **bei ~** in frosty
weather
Frostschutzmittel nt anti-freeze
Frottee nt terry(cloth)
Frottier(hand)tuch nt towel

Frucht (-, Früchte) f (a. fig) fruit; (Getreide)
corn
Fruchteis nt sorbet, Italian ice
Früchtetee m fruit tea
fruchtig adj fruity
Fruchtpresse f juicer
Fruchtsaft m fruit juice
Fruchtsalat m fruit salad
früh adj, adv early; **heute ~** this morning;
um fünf Uhr ~ at five (o'clock) in the
morning; **~ genug** soon enough
früher adj earlier; (ehemalig) former ▷ adv
formerly, in the past
frühestens adv at the earliest
Frühjahr nt, **Frühling** m spring
Frühlingsrolle f spring roll
Frühlingszwiebel f green onion, scallion
frühmorgens adv early in the morning
Frühstück nt breakfast
frühstücken vi to have breakfast
Frühstücksbüfett nt breakfast buffet
Frühstücksspeck m bacon
frühzeitig adj early
Frust (-s) m (fam) frustration
frustrieren vt to frustrate
Fuchs (-es, Füchse) m fox
fühlen vt, vi to feel ▷ vr: **sich ~** to feel
fuhr imperf von **fahren**
führen vt to lead; (Geschäft) to run; (Name)
to bear; (Buch) to keep ▷ vi to lead, to be
in the lead ▷ vr: **sich ~** to behave
Führerschein m driver's license
Führung f leadership; (eines Unternehmens)
management; (Mil) command; (in Muse-
um, Stadt) guided tour; **in ~ liegen** to be in
the lead
füllen vt to fill; (Gastr) to stuff ▷ vr: **sich ~**
to fill
Füller (-s, -) m, **Füllfederhalter** (-s, -) m
fountain pen
Füllung f filling
Fund (-(e)s, -e) m find
Fundbüro nt lost and found
Fundsachen pl lost and found sing
fünf num five
Fünf (-, -en) f five; (Schulnote) ≈ F
fünfhundert num five hundred
fünfmal adv five times
fünfte(r, s) adj fifth; siehe auch **dritte**
Fünftel (-s, -) nt (Bruchteil) fifth
fünfzehn num fifteen
fünfzehnte(r, s) adj fifteenth; siehe auch
dritte
fünfzig num fifty
fünfzigste(r, s) adj fiftieth

Funk (*-s*) *m* radio; **über ~** by radio
Funke (*-ns, -n*) *m* spark
funkeln *vi* to sparkle
Funkgerät *nt* radio set
Funktaxi *nt* radio taxi, radio cab
Funktion *f* function
funktionieren *vi* to work, to function
Funktionstaste *f* (*Inform*) function key
für *prep* (+*akk*) for; **was für ein ...?** what kind
    (*o* sort) of ...?; **Tag für Tag** day after day
Furcht (*-*) *f* fear
furchtbar *adj* terrible
fürchten *vt* to be afraid of, to fear ▷ *vr*: **sich**
    ~ to be afraid (*vor* +*dat* of)
fürchterlich *adj* awful
füreinander *adv* for each other
fürs *kontr von* **für das**
Fürst(in) (*-en, -en*) *m(f)* prince/princess
Fürstentum *nt* principality
fürstlich *adj* (*fig*) splendid
Furunkel (*-s, -*) *nt* boil
Fuß (*-es, Füße*) *m* foot; (*von Glas, Säule etc*)

base; (*von Möbel*) leg; **zu Fuß** on foot; **zu**
    Fuß gehen to walk
Fußball *m* soccer
Fußballmannschaft *f* soccer team
Fußballplatz *m* soccer field
Fußballspiel *nt* soccer match
Fußballspieler(in) *m(f)* soccer player
Fußboden *m* floor
Fußgänger(in) (*-s, -*) *m(f)* pedestrian
Fußgängerüberweg *m* crosswalk
Fußgängerzone *f* pedestrian zone
Fußgelenk *nt* ankle
Fußpilz *m* athlete's foot
Fußtritt *m* kick; **jdm einen ~ geben** to give
    sb a kick, to kick sb
Fußweg *m* footpath
Futon (*-s, -s*) *m* futon
Futter (*-s, -*) *nt* feed; (*Heu etc*) fodder; (*Stoff*)
    lining
füttern *vt* to feed; (*Kleidung*) to line
Futur (*-s, -e*) *nt* (*Ling*) future (tense)
Fuzzi (*-s, -s*) *m* (*fam*) guy

G

gab *imperf von* **geben**

Gabe (-, -n) *f* gift

Gabel (-, -n) *f* fork

Gabelung *f* fork

gaffen *vi* to gape

Gage (-, -n) *f* fee

gähnen *vi* to yawn

Galerie *f* gallery

Galle (-, -n) *f* gall; (*Organ*) gall bladder

Gallenstein *m* gallstone

Galopp (-s) *m* gallop

galoppieren *vi* to gallop

galt *imperf von* **gelten**

Gameboy® (-s, -s) *m* Gameboy®

Gameshow *f* game show

gammeln *vi* to loaf (*o* hang) around

Gammler(in) (-s, -) *m(f)* (lazy) bum

gang *adj:* ~ **und gäbe sein** to be quite normal

Gang (-(e)s, Gänge) *m* walk; (*im Flugzeug*) aisle; (*Essen, Ablauf*) course; (*Flur etc*) corridor; (*Durchgang*) passage; (*Auto*) gear; **den zweiten** ~ **einlegen** to shift into second (gear); **etw in** ~ **bringen** to get sth going

Gangschaltung *f* gearshift

Gangway (-, -s) *f* (*Aviat*) steps *pl*; (*Naut*) gangway

Gans (-, Gänse) *f* goose

Gänseblümchen *nt* daisy

Gänsehaut *f* goose bumps *pl*

ganz *adj* whole; (*vollständig*) complete; ~ **Europa** all of Europe; **sein** ~**es Geld** all his money; **den** ~**en Tag** all day; **die** ~**e Zeit** all the time ▷ *adv* quite; (*völlig*) completely; **es hat mir** ~ **gut gefallen** I liked it very much; ~ **schön viel** quite a lot; ~ **und gar nicht** not at all; **das ist etwas** ~ **anderes** that's a completely different matter

ganztägig *adj* all-day; (*Arbeit, Stelle*) full-time

ganztags *adv* (*arbeiten*) full time

Ganztagsschule *f* all-day school

Ganztagsstelle *f* full-time job

gar *adj* done, cooked ▷ *adv* at all; **gar nicht/nichts/keiner** not/nothing/nobody at all; **gar nicht schlecht** not bad at all

Garage (-, -n) *f* garage

Garantie *f* guarantee

garantieren *vt* to guarantee

Garderobe (-, -n) *f* (*Kleidung*) wardrobe; (*Abgabe*) cloakroom

Gardine *f* curtain

Garn (-(e)s, -e) *nt* thread

Garnele (-, -n) *f* shrimp

garnieren *vt* to decorate; (*Speisen*) to garnish

Garten (-s, Gärten) *m* garden

Gärtner(in) (-s, -) *m(f)* gardener

Gärtnerei *f* nursery; (*Gemüsegärtnerei*) truck farm

Garzeit *f* cooking time

Gas (-es, -e) *nt* gas; **Gas geben** (*Auto*) to accelerate; (*fig*) to get a move on

Gasanzünder *m* gas lighter

Gasbrenner *m* gas burner

Gasflasche *f* propane tank

Gasheizung *f* gas heating

Gasherd *m* gas stove

Gaskocher (-s, -) *m* camping stove

Gaspedal *nt* gas pedal

Gasse (-, -n) *f* alley

Gast (-es, Gäste) *m* guest; **Gäste haben** to have guests

Gastarbeiter(in) *m(f)* immigrant (*o* guest) worker

Gästebett *nt* spare bed

Gästebuch *nt* visitors' book

Gästehaus *nt* guest house

Gästezimmer *nt* guest room

gastfreundlich *adj* hospitable

Gastfreundschaft *f* hospitality

Gastgeber(in) (-s, -) *m(f)* host/hostess

Gasthaus *nt*, **Gasthof** *m* inn

Gastland *nt* host country

Gastritis (-) *f* gastritis

Gastronomie *f* (*Gewerbe*) restaurant industry

Gastspiel *nt* (*Sport*) away game

Gaststätte *f* restaurant; (*Trinklokal*) bar

Gastwirt(in) *m(f)* innkeeper, owner

Gaumen (-s, -) *m* palate

Gaze (-, -n) *f* gauze

geb. *adj* (*abk*) **= geboren** b. ▷ *adj* (*abk*) **= geborene** née; *siehe* **geboren**

Gebäck (-(e)s, -e) *nt* pastries *pl*; (*Kekse*) cookies *pl*

gebacken *pp von* **backen**

Gebärdensprache *f* sign language

Gebärmutter *f* womb

Gebäude (-s, -) *nt* building

geben (gab, gegeben) *vt, vi* to give (*jdm etw* sb sth, sth to sb); (*Karten*) to deal; **lass dir eine Quittung** ~ ask for a receipt

▷ *vt impers:* **es gibt** there is/are; (*in Zukunft*) there will be; **das gibt's nicht** I don't believe it ▷ *vr:* **sich ~** (*sich verhalten*) to behave, to act; **das gibt sich wieder** it'll sort itself out

Gebet (-(*e*)*s*, -*e*) *nt* prayer

gebeten *pp von* **bitten**

Gebiet (-(*e*)*s*, -*e*) *nt* area; (*Hoheitsgebiet*) territory; (*fig*) field

gebildet *adj* educated; (*belesen*) well-read

Gebirge (-*s*, -) *nt* mountains *pl*

gebirgig *adj* mountainous

Gebiss (-*es*, -*e*) *nt* teeth *pl*; (*künstlich*) dentures *pl*

gebissen *pp von* **beißen**

Gebissreiniger *m* denture tablets *pl*

Gebläse (-*s*, -) *nt* fan, blower

geblasen *pp von* **blasen**

geblieben *pp von* **bleiben**

gebogen *pp von* **biegen**

geboren *pp von* **gebären** ▷ *adj* born; **Andrea Jordan, ~e Christian** Andrea Jordan, née Christian

geborgen *pp von* **bergen** ▷ *adj* secure, safe

geboten *pp von* **bieten**

gebracht *pp von* **bringen**

gebrannt *pp von* **brennen**

gebraten *pp von* **braten**

gebrauchen *vt* to use

Gebrauchsanweisung *f* directions *pl* for use

gebrauchsfertig *adj* ready to use

gebraucht *adj* used; **etw ~ kaufen** to buy sth secondhand

Gebrauchtwagen *m* secondhand (*o* used) car

gebräunt *adj* tanned

gebrochen *pp von* **brechen**

Gebühr (-, -*en*) *f* charge; (*Maut*) toll; (*Honorar*) fee

Gebühreneinheit *f* (*Tel*) unit

gebührenfrei *adj* free of charge; (*Telefonnummer*) toll-free

gebührenpflichtig *adj* subject to charges; **~e Straße** toll road

gebunden *pp von* **binden**

Geburt (-, -*en*) *f* birth

gebürtig *adj:* **er ist ~er Schweizer** he is Swiss by birth

Geburtsdatum *nt* date of birth

Geburtsjahr *nt* year of birth

Geburtsname *m* birth name; (*einer Frau*) maiden name

Geburtsort *m* birthplace

Geburtstag *m* birthday; **herzlichen Glück-**

wunsch zum ~! Happy Birthday!

Geburtsurkunde *f* birth certificate

Gebüsch (-(*e*)*s*, -*e*) *nt* bushes *pl*

gedacht *pp von* **denken**

Gedächtnis *nt* memory; **im ~ behalten** to remember

Gedanke (-*ns*, -*n*) *m* thought; **sich** (*dat*) **über etw** (*akk*) **~n machen** to think about sth; (*besorgt*) to be worried about sth

Gedankenstrich *m* dash

Gedeck (-(*e*)*s*, -*e*) *nt* place setting; (*Speisenfolge*) (fixed price *o* prix fixe) menu

Gedenkstätte *f* memorial

Gedenktafel *f* commemorative plaque

Gedicht (-(*e*)*s*, -*e*) *nt* poem

Gedränge (-*s*) *nt* crush, crowd

gedrungen *pp von* **dringen**

Geduld (-) *f* patience

geduldig *adj* patient

gedurft *pp von* **dürfen**

geehrt *adj:* **Sehr ~er Herr Young** Dear Mr. Young

geeignet *adj* suitable

Gefahr (-, -*en*) *f* danger; **auf eigene ~** at one's own risk; **außer ~** out of danger

gefährden *vt* to endanger

gefahren *pp von* **fahren**

gefährlich *adj* dangerous

Gefälle (-*s*, -) *nt* gradient, slope

gefallen *pp von* **fallen** ▷ *vi* (*irr*); **jdm ~** to please sb; **er/es gefällt mir** I like him/it; **sich** (*dat*) **etw ~ lassen** to put up with sth

Gefallen (-*s*, -) *m* favor; **jdm einen ~ tun** to do sb a favor

gefälligst *adv* ..., will you!; **sei ~ still!** be quiet, will you!

gefangen *pp von* **fangen**

Gefängnis *nt* prison

Gefäß (-*es*, -*e*) *nt* (*Behälter*) container, receptacle; (*Anat, Bot*) vessel

gefasst *adj* composed, calm; **auf etw** (*akk*) **~ sein** to be prepared (*o* ready) for sth

geflochten *pp von* **flechten**

geflogen *pp von* **fliegen**

geflossen *pp von* **fließen**

Geflügel (-*s*) *nt* poultry

gefragt *adj* in demand

gefressen *pp von* **fressen**

Gefrierbeutel *m* freezer bag

gefrieren (*irr*) *vi* to freeze

Gefrierfach *nt* freezer compartment

Gefrierschrank *m* (upright) freezer

Gefriertruhe *f* (chest) freezer

gefroren *pp von* **frieren**

Gefühl (-(*e*)*s*, -*e*) *nt* feeling

gefunden pp von **finden**
gegangen pp von **gehen**
gegeben pp von **geben**
gegebenenfalls adv if need be

gegen prep +akk 1 against; **nichts gegen jdn haben** to have nothing against sb; **X gegen Y** (Sport, Jur) X versus Y; **ein Mittel gegen Schnupfen** something for colds
2 (in Richtung auf) towards; **gegen Osten** to(wards) the east; **gegen Abend** towards evening; **gegen einen Baum fahren** to drive into a tree
3 (ungefähr) around; **gegen 3 Uhr** around 3 o'clock
4 (gegenüber) towards; (ungefähr) around; **gerecht gegen alle** fair to all
5 (im Austausch für) for; **gegen bar** for cash; **gegen Quittung** against a receipt
6 (verglichen mit) compared with

Gegend (-, -en) f area; **hier in der ~** around here
gegeneinander adv against one another
Gegenfahrbahn f opposite lane
Gegenmittel nt remedy (gegen for)
Gegenrichtung f opposite direction
Gegensatz m contrast; **im ~ zu** in contrast to
gegensätzlich adj conflicting
gegenseitig adj mutual; **sich ~ helfen** to help each other
Gegenstand m object; (Thema) subject
Gegenteil nt opposite; **im ~** on the contrary
gegenteilig adj opposite, contrary
gegenüber prep (+dat) opposite; (zu jdm) to(wards); (angesichts) in the face of ▷ adv opposite
gegenüber|stehen vt to face; (Problemen) to be faced with
gegenüber|stellen vt to confront (dat with); (fig) compare (dat with)
Gegenverkehr m oncoming traffic
Gegenwart (-) f presence; (Ling) present (tense)
Gegenwind m headwind
gegessen pp von **essen**
geglichen pp von **gleichen**
geglitten pp von **gleiten**
Gegner(in) (-s, -) m(f) opponent
gegolten pp von **gelten**
gegossen pp von **gießen**

gegraben pp von **graben**
gegriffen pp von **greifen**
gehabt pp von **haben**
Gehackte(s) nt ground meat
Gehalt (-(e)s, -e) m content ▷ (-(e)s) nt (Gehälter) salary
gehalten pp von **halten**
gehangen pp von **hängen**
gehässig adj spiteful, nasty
gehauen pp von **hauen**
gehbehindert adj: **sie ist ~** she has a limited ability to walk
geheim adj secret; **etw ~ halten** to keep sth secret
Geheimnis nt secret; (rätselhaft) mystery
geheimnisvoll adj mysterious
Geheimnummer f, **Geheimzahl** f (von Kreditkarte) PIN number
geheißen pp von **heißen**
gehen (ging, gegangen) vt, vi to go; (zu Fuß) to walk; (funktionieren) to work; **über die Straße ~** to cross the street; **~ nach** (Fenster) to face ▷ vi impers: **wie geht es dir?** how are you (o things)?; **mir/ihm geht es gut** I'm/he's (doing) fine; **geht das?** is that possible?; **geht's noch?** can you still manage?; **es geht** not too bad, OK; **das geht nicht** that won't work; **es geht um ...** it's about ...
Gehirn (-(e)s, -e) nt brain
Gehirnerschütterung f concussion
gehoben pp von **heben**
geholfen pp von **helfen**
Gehör (-(e)s) nt hearing
gehorchen vi to obey (jdm sb)
gehören vi to belong (jdm to sb); **wem gehört das Buch?** whose book is this?; **gehört es dir?** is it yours? ▷ vr impers: **das gehört sich nicht** it's not done
gehörlos adj deaf
gehorsam adj obedient
Gehsteig m, **Gehweg** (-s, -e) m sidewalk
Geier (-s, -) m vulture
Geige (-, -n) f violin
geil adj horny; (fam: toll) fantastic
Geisel (-, -n) f hostage
Geist (-(e)s, -er) m spirit; (Gespenst) ghost; (Verstand) mind
Geisterbahn f tunnel of horror
Geisterfahrer(in) m(f) wrong-way driver
geizig adj stingy
gekannt pp von **kennen**
geklungen pp von **klingen**
geknickt adj (fig) dejected
gekniffen pp von **kneifen**

gekommen pp von **kommen**

gekonnt pp von **können** ▷ adj skillful

gekrochen pp von **kriechen**

Gel (-s, -s) nt gel

Gelächter (-s, -) nt laughter

geladen pp von **laden** ▷ adj loaded; (Elek) live; (fig) furious

gelähmt adj paralyzed

Gelände (-s, -) nt land, terrain; (Fabrik, Sportgelände) grounds pl; (Baugelände) site

Geländer (-s, -) nt railing; (Treppengeländer) banister

Geländewagen m off-road vehicle

gelang imperf von **gelingen**

gelassen pp von **lassen** ▷ adj calm, composed

Gelatine f gelatine

gelaufen pp von **laufen**

gelaunt adj: **gut/schlecht ~** in a good/bad mood

gelb adj yellow; (Ampel) yellow

gelblich adj yellowish

Gelbsucht f jaundice

Geld (-(e)s, -er) nt money

Geldautomat m ATM

Geldbeutel m, **Geldbörse** f wallet

Geldbuße f fine

Geldschein m bill

Geldstrafe f fine

Geldstück nt coin

Geldwechsel m exchange of money

Geldwechselautomat m, **Geldwechsler** (-s, -) m change machine

Gelee (-s, -s) nt jelly; (Süßspeise) Jell-O®

gelegen pp von **liegen** ▷ adj situated; (passend) convenient; **etw kommt jdm ~** sth is convenient for sb

Gelegenheit f opportunity; (Anlass) occasion

gelegentlich adj occasional ▷ adv occasionally; (bei Gelegenheit) some time (or other)

Gelenk (-(e)s, -e) nt joint

gelernt adj skilled

gelesen pp von **lesen**

geliehen pp von **leihen**

gelingen (gelang, gelungen) vi to succeed; **es ist mir gelungen, ihn zu erreichen** I managed to get hold of him

gelitten pp von **leiden**

gelockt adj curly

gelogen pp von **lügen**

gelten (galt, gegolten) vt (wert sein) to be worth; **jdm viel/wenig ~** to mean a lot/not

to mean much to sb ▷ vi (gültig sein) to be valid; (erlaubt sein) to be allowed; **jdm ~** (gemünzt sein auf) to be meant for (o aimed at) sb; **etw ~ lassen** to accept sth; **als etw ~** to be considered to be sth

Geltungsdauer f: **eine ~ von fünf Tagen haben** to be valid for five days

gelungen pp von **gelingen**

gemahlen pp von **mahlen**

Gemälde (-s, -) nt painting, picture

gemäß prep (+dat) in accordance with ▷ adj appropriate (dat to)

gemein adj (niederträchtig) mean, nasty; (gewöhnlich) common

Gemeinde (-, -n) f district, community; (Pfarrgemeinde) parish; (Kirchengemeinde) congregation

gemeinsam adj joint, common ▷ adv together, jointly; **das Haus gehört uns beiden ~** the house belongs to both of us

Gemeinschaft f community; **~ Unabhängiger Staaten** Commonwealth of Independent States

gemeint pp von **meinen**; **das war nicht so ~** I didn't mean it like that

gemessen pp von **messen**

gemieden pp von **meiden**

gemischt adj mixed

gemocht pp von **mögen**

Gemüse (-s, -) nt vegetables pl

Gemüsehändler(in) m(f) produce vendor

gemusst pp von **müssen**

gemustert adj patterned

gemütlich adj comfortable, cozy; (Mensch) good-natured, easy-going; **mach es dir ~** make yourself at home

genannt pp von **nennen**

genau adj exact, precise ▷ adv exactly, precisely; **~ in der Mitte** right in the middle; **es mit etw ~ nehmen** to be particular about sth; **~ genommen** strictly speaking; **ich weiß es ~** I know for certain (o for sure)

genauso adv exactly the same (way); **~ gut/ viel/viele Leute** just as well/much/many people (wie as)

genehmigen vt to approve; **sich** (dat) **etw ~** to indulge in sth

Genehmigung f approval

Generalkonsulat nt consulate general

Generation f generation

Genf (-s) nt Geneva; **~er See** Lake Geneva

Genforschung f genetic research

genial adj brilliant

Genick (-(e)s, -e) nt (back of the) neck

Genie (*-s, -s*) *nt* genius

genieren *vr:* sich ~ to feel awkward; **ich geniere mich vor ihm** I feel shy (*o* awkward) around him

genießen (**genoss, genossen**) *vt* to enjoy

Genitiv *m* genitive (case)

genmanipuliert *adj* genetically modified, GM

genommen *pp von* **nehmen**

genoss *imperf von* **genießen**

genossen *pp von* **genießen**

Gentechnik *f* genetic technology

gentechnisch *adv:* ~ **verändert** genetically modified, GM

genug *adv* enough

genügen *vi* to be enough (*jdm* for sb); **danke, das genügt** thanks, that's enough (*o* that will do)

Genuss (*-es, Genüsse*) *m* pleasure; (*Zusichnehmen*) consumption

geöffnet *adj* (*Geschäft etc*) open

Geografie *f* geography

Geologie *f* geology

Georgien (*-s*) *nt* Georgia

Gepäck (*-(e)s*) *nt* luggage, baggage

Gepäckabfertigung *f* baggage check-in

Gepäckablage *f* baggage rack

Gepäckannahme *f* (*zur Beförderung*) baggage office; (*zur Aufbewahrung*) baggage checkroom

Gepäckaufbewahrung *f* baggage checkroom

Gepäckausgabe *f* baggage office; (*am Flughafen*) baggage claim

Gepäckband *nt* baggage conveyor

Gepäckkontrolle *f* baggage check

Gepäckstück *nt* piece of luggage

Gepäckträger *m* porter; (*an Fahrrad*) rack

Gepäckversicherung *f* baggage insurance

Gepäckwagen *m* baggage car

gepfiffen *pp von* **pfeifen**

gepflegt *adj* well-groomed; (*Park*) well looked after

gequollen *pp von* **quellen**

gerade *adj* straight; (*aufrecht*) upright; **eine gerade Zahl** an even number

▷ *adv* **1** (*genau*) just, exactly; (*speziell*) especially; **gerade deshalb** that's just *o* exactly why; **das ist es ja gerade!** that's just it!; **gerade du** you especially; **warum gerade ich?** why me (of all people)?; **jetzt gerade nicht!** not now!; **gerade neben**

right next to

2 (*eben, soeben*) just; **er wollte gerade aufstehen** he was just about to get up; **gerade erst** only just; **gerade noch** (only) just

geradeaus *adv* straight ahead

gerannt *pp von* **rennen**

geraspelt *adj* grated

Gerät (*-(e)s, -e*) *nt* device, gadget; (*Werkzeug*) tool; (*Radio, Fernseher*) set; (*Zubehör*) equipment

geraten *pp von* **raten** ▷ *vi* (*irr*) to turn out; **gut/schlecht** ~ to turn out well/badly; **an jdn** ~ to come across sb; **in etw** (*akk*) ~ to get into sth

geräuchert *adj* smoked

geräumig *adj* roomy

Geräusch (*-(e)s, -e*) *nt* sound; (*unangenehm*) noise

gerecht *adj* fair; (*Strafe, Belohnung*) just; **jdm/einer Sache** ~ **werden** to do justice to sb/sth

gereizt *adj* irritable

Gericht (*-(e)s, -e*) *nt* (*Jur*) court; (*Essen*) dish

gerieben *pp von* **reiben**

gering *adj* small; (*unbedeutend*) slight; (*niedrig*) low; (*Zeit*) short

geringfügig *adj* slight, minor ▷ *adv* slightly

gerissen *pp von* **reißen**

geritten *pp von* **reiten**

gern(e) *adv* willingly, gladly; **etw** ~ **tun** to like doing sth; ~ **geschehen** you're welcome

gern|haben, gern mögen (*irr*) *vt* to like

gerochen *pp von* **riechen**

Gerste (*-, -n*) *f* barley

Gerstenkorn *nt* (*im Auge*) stye

Geruch (*-(e)s, Gerüche*) *m* smell

Gerücht (*-(e)s, -e*) *nt* rumor

gerufen *pp von* **rufen**

Gerümpel (*-s*) *nt* junk

gerungen *pp von* **ringen**

Gerüst (*-(e)s, -e*) *nt* (*auf Bau*) scaffolding; (*Gestell*) trestle; (*fig*) framework (*zu of*)

gesalzen *pp von* **salzen**

gesamt *adj* whole, entire; (*Kosten*) total; (*Werke*) complete

Gesamtschule *f* ≈ high school

gesandt *pp von* **senden**

Gesäß (*-es, -e*) *nt* bottom

geschaffen *pp von* **schaffen**

Geschäft (*-(e)s, -e*) *nt* business; (*Laden*) store; (*Geschäftsabschluss*) deal

geschäftlich *adj* commercial ▷ *adv* on business
Geschäftsfrau *f* businesswoman
Geschäftsführer(in) *m(f)* managing director; (*von Laden*) manager
Geschäftsleitung *f* executive board
Geschäftsmann *m* businessman
Geschäftsreise *f* business trip
Geschäftsstraße *f* shopping street
Geschäftszeiten *pl* business (*o* opening) hours *pl*
geschehen (**geschah, geschehen**) *vi* to happen
Geschenk (*-(e)s, -e*) *nt* present, gift
Geschenkgutschein *m* gift certificate (*o* card)
Geschenkpapier *nt* gift-wrapping paper, giftwrap
Geschichte (*-, -n*) *f* story; (*Sache*) affair; (*Hist*) history
geschickt *adj* skillful
geschieden *pp von* **scheiden** ▷ *adj* divorced
geschienen *pp von* **scheinen**
Geschirr (*-(e)s, -e*) *nt* dishes *pl*; (*zum Kochen*) pots and pans *pl*; (*von Pferd*) harness; ~ **spülen** to do (*o* wash) the dishes
Geschirrspülmaschine *f* dishwasher
Geschirrspülmittel *nt* dishwashing detergent
Geschirrtuch *nt* dish towel
geschissen *pp von* **scheißen**
geschlafen *pp von* **schlafen**
geschlagen *pp von* **schlagen**
Geschlecht (*-(e)s, -er*) *nt* sex; (*Ling*) gender
Geschlechtskrankheit *f* sexually transmitted disease, STD
Geschlechtsorgan *nt* sexual organ
Geschlechtsverkehr *m* sexual intercourse
geschlichen *pp von* **schleichen**
geschliffen *pp von* **schleifen**
geschlossen *adj* closed
Geschmack (*-(e)s, Geschmäcke*) *m* taste
geschmacklos *adj* tasteless
Geschmack(s)sache *f*: **das ist ~** that's a matter of taste
geschmackvoll *adj* tasteful
geschmissen *pp von* **schmeißen**
geschmolzen *pp von* **schmelzen**
geschnitten *pp von* **schneiden**
geschoben *pp von* **schieben**
Geschoss (*-es, -e*) *nt* (*Stockwerk*) floor
geschossen *pp von* **schießen**

Geschrei (*-s*) *nt* cries *pl*; (*fig*) fuss
geschrieben *pp von* **schreiben**
geschrie(e)n *pp von* **schreien**
geschützt *adj* protected
Geschwätz (*-es*) *nt* chatter; (*Klatsch*) gossip
geschwätzig *adj* talkative, gossipy
geschweige *adv*: ~ **denn** let alone
geschwiegen *pp von* **schweigen**
Geschwindigkeit *f* speed; (*Phys*) velocity
Geschwindigkeitsbegrenzung *f* speed limit
Geschwister *pl* siblings *pl*
geschwollen *adj* (*angeschwollen*) swollen; (*Rede*) pompous
geschwommen *pp von* **schwimmen**
geschworen *pp von* **schwören**
Geschwulst (*-, Geschwülste*) *f* growth
Geschwür (*-(e)s, -e*) *nt* ulcer
gesehen *pp von* **sehen**
gesellig *adj* sociable
Gesellschaft *f* society; (*Begleitung*) company; (*Abendgesellschaft*) party; ~ **mit beschränkter Haftung** limited corporation
gesessen *pp von* **sitzen**
Gesetz (*-es, -e*) *nt* law
gesetzlich *adj* legal; ~**er Feiertag** legal holiday
gesetzwidrig *adj* illegal
Gesicht (*-(e)s, -er*) *nt* face; (*Miene*) expression; **mach doch nicht so ein ~!** don't make such a face!
Gesichtscreme *f* face cream
Gesichtswasser *nt* toner
gesoffen *pp von* **saufen**
gesogen *pp von* **saugen**
gespannt *adj* tense; (*begierig*) eager; **ich bin ~, ob ...** I wonder if ...; **auf etw/jdn ~ sein** to look forward to sth/to seeing sb
Gespenst (*-(e)s, -er*) *nt* ghost
gesperrt *adj* closed
gesponnen *pp von* **spinnen**
Gespräch (*-(e)s, -e*) *nt* talk, conversation; (*Diskussion*) discussion; (*Anruf*) call
gesprochen *pp von* **sprechen**
gesprungen *pp von* **springen**
Gestalt (*-, -en*) *f* form, shape; (*Mensch*) figure
gestanden *pp von* **stehen, gestehen**
Gestank (*-(e)s*) *m* stench
gestatten *vt* to permit, to allow; ~ **Sie?** may I?
Geste (*-, -n*) *f* gesture
gestehen (*irr*) *vt* to confess

gestern *adv* yesterday; **~ Abend/Morgen** yesterday evening/morning

gestiegen *pp von* **steigen**

gestochen *pp von* **stechen**

gestohlen *pp von* **stehlen**

gestorben *pp von* **sterben**

gestört *adj* disturbed; *(Empfang)* poor

gestoßen *pp von* **stoßen**

gestreift *adj* striped

gestrichen *pp von* **streichen**

gestritten *pp von* **streiten**

gestunken *pp von* **stinken**

gesund *adj* healthy; **wieder ~ werden** to get better

Gesundheit *f* health; **~!** bless you!

gesundheitsschädlich *adj* bad for one's health

gesungen *pp von* **singen**

gesunken *pp von* **sinken**

getan *pp von* **tun**

getragen *pp von* **tragen**

Getränk *(-(e)s, -e) nt* drink

Getränkeautomat *m* drinks machine

Getränkekarte *f* list of drinks

Getreide *(-s, -) nt* grain

getrennt *adj* separate; **~ leben** to live apart; **~ zahlen** to pay separately

getreten *pp von* **treten**

Getriebe *(-s, -) nt (Auto)* transmission

getrieben *pp von* **treiben**

Getriebeschaden *m* transmission damage

getroffen *pp von* **treffen**

getrunken *pp von* **trinken**

Getue *nt* fuss

geübt *adj* experienced

gewachsen *pp von* **wachsen** ▷ *adj:* **jdm/ einer Sache ~ sein** to be a match for sb/up to sth

Gewähr *(-) f* guarantee; **keine ~ übernehmen für** to accept no responsibility for

Gewalt *(-, -en) f (Macht)* power; *(Kontrolle)* control; *(große Kraft)* force; *(Gewalttaten)* violence; **mit aller ~** with all one's might

gewaltig *adj* tremendous; *(Irrtum)* huge

gewandt *pp von* **wenden** ▷ *adj (flink)* nimble; *(geschickt)* skillful

gewann *imperf von* **gewinnen**

gewaschen *pp von* **waschen**

Gewebe *(-s, -) nt (Stoff)* fabric; *(Bio)* tissue

Gewehr *(-(e)s, -e) nt* rifle, gun

Geweih *(-(e)s, -e) nt* antlers *pl*

gewellt *adj (Haare)* wavy

gewendet *pp von* **wenden**

Gewerbe *(-s, -) nt* trade

Gewerbegebiet *nt* industrial park

gewerblich *adj* commercial

Gewerkschaft *f* labor union

gewesen *pp von* **sein**

Gewicht *(-(e)s, -e) nt* weight; *(fig)* importance

gewiesen *pp von* **weisen**

Gewinn *(-(e)s, -e) m* profit; *(bei Spiel)* winnings *pl*

gewinnen *(gewann, gewonnen) vt* to win; *(erwerben)* to gain; *(Kohle, Öl)* to extract ▷ *vi* to win; *(profitieren)* to gain

Gewinner(in) *(-s, -) m(f)* winner

gewiss *adj* certain ▷ *adv* certainly

Gewissen *(-s, -) nt* conscience; **ein gutes/ schlechtes ~ haben** to have a clear/bad conscience

Gewitter *(-s, -) nt* thunderstorm

gewittern *vi impers:* **es gewittert** it's thundering

gewogen *pp von* **wiegen**

gewöhnen *vt:* **jdn an etw** *(akk)* **~** to accustom sb to sth ▷ *vr:* **sich an jdn/etw ~** to get used *(o* accustomed) to sb/sth

Gewohnheit *f* habit; *(Brauch)* custom

gewöhnlich *adj* usual; *(durchschnittlich)* ordinary; *(pej)* common; **wie ~** as usual

gewohnt *adj* usual; **etw ~ sein** to be used to sth

Gewölbe *(-s, -) nt (Deckengewölbe)* vault

gewonnen *pp von* **gewinnen**

geworben *pp von* **werben**

geworden *pp von* **werden**

geworfen *pp von* **werfen**

Gewürz *(-es, -e) nt* spice

Gewürznelke *f* clove

gewürzt *adj* seasoned

gewusst *pp von* **wissen**

Gezeiten *pl* tides *pl*

gezogen *pp von* **ziehen**

gezwungen *pp von* **zwingen**

Gibraltar *(-s) nt* Gibraltar

Gicht *(-) f* gout

Giebel *(-s, -) m* gable

gierig *adj* greedy

gießen *(goss, gegossen) vt* to pour; *(Blumen)* to water; *(Metall)* to cast

Gießkanne *f* watering can

Gift *(-(e)s, -e) nt* poison

giftig *adj* poisonous

Gigabyte *nt* gigabyte

Gin *(-s, -s) m* gin

ging *imperf von* **gehen**

Gin Tonic *(-(s), -s) m* gin and tonic

Gipfel *(-s, -) m* summit, peak; *(Pol)* summit; *(fig: Höhepunkt)* height

Gips (-es, -e) m plaster; (Med) cast
Gipsbein nt: **sie hat ein ~** she's got a cast on her leg
Gipsverband m plaster cast
Giraffe (-, -n) f giraffe
Girokonto nt checking account
Gitarre (-, -n) f guitar
Gitter (-s, -) nt bars pl
glänzen vi (a. fig) to shine
glänzend adj shining; (fig) brilliant
Glas (-es, Gläser) nt glass; (Marmelade) jar; **zwei ~ Wein** two glasses of wine
Glaser(in) m(f) glazier
Glasscheibe f pane (of glass)
Glassplitter m splinter of glass
Glasur f glaze; (Gastr) icing
glatt adj smooth; (rutschig) slippery; (Lüge) downright
Glatteis nt (black) ice
Glatze (-, -n) f bald head; **er hat ein ~** he's bald; (fam: Skinhead) skinhead
glauben vt, vi to believe (an +akk in); (meinen) to think; **jdm ~** to believe sb
gleich adj equal; (identisch) same, identical; **alle Menschen sind ~** all people are the same; **es ist mir ~** it's all the same to me ▷ adv equally; (sofort) right away; (bald) in a minute; **~ groß/alt** the same size/age; **~ nach/an** right after/at
Gleichberechtigung f equal rights pl
gleichen (glich, geglichen) vi: **jdm/einer Sache ~** to be like sb/sth ▷ vr: **sich ~** to be alike
gleichfalls adv likewise; **danke ~!** thanks, and the same to you!
gleichgültig adj indifferent
gleichmäßig adj regular; (Verteilung) even, equal
gleichzeitig adj simultaneous ▷ adv at the same time
Gleis (-es, -e) nt track, rails pl; (Bahnsteig) platform
gleiten (glitt, geglitten) vi to glide; (rutschen) to slide
Gleitschirmfliegen (-s) nt paragliding
Gletscher (-s, -) m glacier
Gletscherskifahren nt glacier skiing
Gletscherspalte f crevasse
glich imperf von **gleichen**
Glied (-(e)s, -er) nt (Arm, Bein) limb; (von Kette) link; (Penis) penis
Gliedmaßen pl limbs pl
glitschig adj slippery
glitt imperf von **gleiten**
glitzern vi to glitter; (Sterne) to twinkle

Glocke (-, -n) f bell
Glockenspiel nt chimes pl
Glotze (-, -n) f (fam: TV) tube
glotzen vi (fam) to stare
Glück (-(e)s) nt luck; (Freude) happiness; **~ haben** to be lucky; **viel ~!** good luck!; **zum ~** fortunately
glücklich adj lucky; (froh) happy
glücklicherweise adv fortunately
Glückwunsch m congratulations pl; **herzlichen ~ zur bestandenen Prüfung** congratulations on passing your exam; **herzlichen ~ zum Geburtstag!** Happy Birthday
Glühbirne f light bulb
glühen vi to glow
Glühwein m mulled wine
GmbH (-, -s) f (abk) = **Gesellschaft mit beschränkter Haftung** ≈ limited liability company, LLC
Gokart (-(s), -s) m go-kart
Gold (-(e)s) nt gold
golden adj gold; (fig) golden
Goldfisch m goldfish
Goldmedaille f gold medal
Goldschmied(in) m(f) goldsmith
Golf (-(e)s, -e) m gulf; **der ~ von Biskaya** the Bay of Biscay ▷ nt (-s) golf
Golfplatz m golf course
Golfschläger m golf club
Gondel (-, -n) f gondola; (Seilbahn) cable car
gönnen vt: **ich gönne es ihm** I'm really pleased for him; **sich** (dat) **etw ~** to allow oneself sth
goss imperf von **gießen**
gotisch adj Gothic
Gott (-es, Götter) m God; (Gottheit) god
Gottesdienst m service
Göttin f goddess
Grab (-(e)s, Gräber) nt grave
graben (grub, gegraben) vt to dig
Graben (-s, Gräben) m ditch
Grabstein m gravestone
Grad (-(e)s, -e) m degree; **wir haben 30 ~ Celsius** it's 30 degrees Celsius, it's 86 degrees Fahrenheit; **bis zu einem gewissen ~** up to a certain extent
Graf (-en, -en) m count; (in Großbritannien) earl
Graffiti pl graffiti sing
Grafik (-, -en) f graph; (Kunstwerk) graphic; (Illustration) diagram
Grafikkarte f (Inform) graphics card
Grafikprogramm nt (Inform) graphics software
Gräfin (-, -nen) f countess

g

Gramm (-s) nt gram
Grammatik f grammar
Grapefruit (-, -s) f grapefruit
Graphik f siehe **Grafik**
Gras (-es, Gräser) nt grass
grässlich adj horrible
Gräte (-, -n) f (fish)bone
gratis adj, adv free (of charge)
gratulieren vi: jdm zu etw ~ to congratulate sb (on sth); **ich gratuliere!** congratulations!
grau adj gray
grauhaarig adj gray-haired
grausam adj cruel
gravierend adj (Fehler) serious
greifen (griff, gegriffen) vt to seize; **zu etw ~** (fig) to resort to sth ▷ vi (Regel etc) to have an effect (bei on)
grell adj harsh
Grenze (-, -n) f boundary; (Staat) border; (Schranke) limit
grenzen vi to border (an +akk on)
Grenzkontrolle f border control
Grenzübergang m border crossing point
Grenzverkehr m border traffic
Grieche (-n, -n) m Greek
Griechenland nt Greece
Griechin f Greek
griechisch adj Greek
Griechisch nt Greek
griesgrämig adj grumpy
Grieß (-es, -e) m (Gastr) semolina
griff imperf von **greifen**
Griff (-(e)s, -e) m grip; (Tür etc) handle
griffbereit adj handy
Grill (-s, -s) m grill; (im Freien) barbecue
Grille (-, -n) f cricket
grillen vt to grill ▷ vi to have a barbecue
Grillfest nt, **Grillfete** f barbecue
Grillkohle f charcoal
grinsen vi to grin; (höhnisch) to sneer
Grippe (-, -n) f flu
Grippeschutzimpfung f flu vaccination
grob adj coarse; (Fehler, Verstoß) gross; (Einschätzung) rough
Grönland (-s) nt Greenland
groß adj big, large; (hoch) tall; (fig) great; (Buchstabe) capital; (erwachsen) grown-up; **im G~en und Ganzen** on the whole ▷ adv greatly
großartig adj wonderful
Großbritannien (-s) nt (Great) Britain
Großbuchstabe m capital letter
Größe (-, -n) f size; (Länge) height; (fig) greatness; **welche ~ haben Sie?** what size are you (o do you wear)?

Großeltern pl grandparents pl
Großhandel m wholesale trade
Großmutter f grandmother
Großraum m: der ~ New York Greater New York
groß|schreiben (irr) vt to write with a capital letter
Großstadt f city
Großvater m grandfather
großzügig adj generous; (Planung) on a large scale
Grotte (-, -n) f grotto
grub imperf von **graben**
Grübchen nt dimple
Grube (-, -n) f pit
grüezi interj (schweizerisch) hello
Gruft (-, -en) f vault
grün adj green; ~er Salat lettuce; ~e Bohnen green beans; der ~e Punkt symbol for recyclable packaging; im ~en Bereich hunky-dory

GRÜNER PUNKT

The **grüner Punkt** is the green spot symbol which appears on packaging, indicating that the packaging should not be thrown into the normal household trash but kept separate to be recycled through the **DSD** (Duales System Deutschland) system. The recycling is financed by licenses bought by the manufacturer from the 'DSD' and the cost of this is often passed on to the consumer.

Grünanlage f park
Grund (-(e)s, Gründe) m (Ursache) reason; (Erdboden) ground; (See, Gefäß) bottom; (Grundbesitz) land, property; **aus gesundheitlichen Gründen** for health reasons; **im ~e** basically; **aus diesem ~** for this reason
gründen vt to found
Gründer(in) m(f) founder
Grundgebühr f basic charge
Grundgesetz nt (German) Constitution
gründlich adj thorough
Gründonnerstag m Maundy Thursday
grundsätzlich adj fundamental, basic; **sie kommt ~ zu spät** she's always late
Grundschule f elementary school
Grundstück nt plot; (Anwesen) estate; (Baugrundstück) lot, site
Grundwasser nt ground water
Grüne(r) mf (Pol) Green; **die ~n** the Green Party

Gruppe (-, -n) f group
Gruppenermäßigung f group discount
Gruppenreise f group tour
Gruselfilm m horror film
Gruß (-es, Grüße) m greeting; **viele Grüße** best wishes; **Grüße an** +akk regards to; **mit freundlichen Grüßen** Sincerely yours; **sag ihm einen schönen ~ von mir** give him my regards
grüßen vt to greet; **grüß deine Mutter von mir** give your mother my regards; **Julia lässt euch ~** Julia sends (you) her regards
gucken vi to look
Gulasch (-(e)s, -e) nt stew, goulash
gültig adj valid
Gummi (-s, -s) m o nt rubber
Gummiband nt rubber band
Gummibärchen pl gumdrops pl (in the shape of a bear)
Gummihandschuhe pl rubber gloves pl
Gummistiefel m rubber boot
günstig adj favorable; (Preis) good
gurgeln vi to gurgle; (im Mund) to gargle
Gurke (-, -n) f cucumber; **saure ~** gherkin
Gurt (-(e)s, -e) m belt
Gürtel (-s, -) m belt; (Geo) zone
Gürtelrose f shingles sing
GUS (-) f (akr) = Gemeinschaft Unabhängiger Staaten CIS

gut adj good; **alles Gute** all the best; **also gut** all right then
▷ adv well; **gut gehen** to work, to come off; **es geht jdm gut** sb's doing fine; **gut gemeint** well meant; **gut schmecken** to taste good; **jdm guttun** to do sb good; **gut, aber ...** OK, but ...; **(na) gut, ich komme** all right, I'll come; **gut drei Stunden** a good three hours; **das kann gut sein** that may well be; **lass es gut sein** that'll do

Gutachten (-s, -) nt report
Gutachter(in) (-s, -) m(f) expert
gutartig adj (Med) benign
Güter pl goods pl; (zum Verfrachten) freight sing
Güterbahnhof m freight depot
Güterzug m freight train
gutgläubig adj trusting
Guthaben (-s) nt (credit) balance
gutmütig adj good-natured
Gutschein m voucher
Gutschrift f credit
Gymnasium nt ≈ high school
Gymnastik f exercises pl
Gynäkologe m, **Gynäkologin** f gynecologist
Gyros (-, -) nt gyro

H

Haar (-(e)s, -e) *nt* hair; **um ein ~** nearly; **sich** (*dat*) **die ~e schneiden lassen** to have one's hair cut

Haarbürste *f* hairbrush

Haarfestiger *m* setting lotion

Haargel *nt* hair gel

haarig *adj* hairy; (*fig*) nasty

Haarschnitt *m* haircut

Haarspange *f* barrette

Haarspliss *m* split ends *pl*

Haarspray *nt* hair spray

Haartrockner (-s, -) *m* hair dryer

Haarwaschmittel *nt* shampoo

Haarwasser *nt* hair tonic

haben (hatte, gehabt) *vt, vb aux* to have; **Hunger/Angst ~** to be hungry/afraid; **Ferien ~** to be on vacation; **welches Datum ~ wir heute?** what's the date today?; **ich hätte gerne ...** I'd like ...; **hätten Sie etwas dagegen, wenn ...?** would you mind if ...?; **was hast du denn?** what's the matter (with you)?

Haben *nt* (*Comm*) credit

Habicht (-(e)s, -e) *m* hawk

Hacke (-, -n) *f* (*im Garten*) hoe; (*Ferse*) heel

hacken *vt* to chop; (*Loch*) to hack; (*Erde*) to hoe

Hacker(in) (-s, -) *m(f)* (*Inform*) hacker

Hackfleisch *nt* ground meat

Hafen (-s, Häfen) *m* harbor; (*großer*) port

Hafenstadt *f* port

Hafer (-s, -) *m* oats *pl*

Haferflocken *pl* oatmeal *sing*, rolled oats *pl*

Haft (-) *f* custody

haftbar *adj* liable, responsible

haften *vi* to stick; **~ für** to be liable (*o* responsible) for

Haftnotiz *f* sticky note, Post-it® note

Haftung *f* liability

Hagebutte (-, -n) *f* rose hip

Hagel (-s) *m* hail

hageln *vi impers* to hail

Hahn (-(e)s, Hähne) *m* rooster; (*Wasserhahn*) faucet

Hähnchen *nt* cockerel; (*Gastr*) chicken

Hai(fisch) (-(e)s, -e) *m* shark

häkeln *vi, vt* to crochet

Häkelnadel *f* crochet hook

Haken (-s, -) *m* hook; (*Zeichen*) check

halb *adj* half; **~ eins** half past twelve, twelve thirty; **eine ~e Stunde** half an hour; **~ offen** half-open

Halbfinale *nt* semifinal

halbieren *vt* to halve

Halbinsel *f* peninsula

Halbjahr *nt* half-year

halbjährlich *adj* half-yearly

Halbmond *m* (*Astr*) half-moon; (*Symbol*) crescent

Halbpension *f* half board

halbseitig *adj*: **~ gelähmt** paralyzed on one side

halbtags *adv* (*arbeiten*) part-time

halbwegs *adv* (*leidlich*) reasonably

Halbzeit *f* half; (*Pause*) half-time

half *imperf von* **helfen**

Hälfte (-, -n) *f* half

Halle (-, -n) *f* hall

Hallenbad *nt* indoor (swimming) pool

hallo *interj* hello, hi

Halogenlampe *f* halogen lamp

Halogenscheinwerfer *m* halogen headlight

Hals (-es, Hälse) *m* neck; (*Kehle*) throat

Halsband *nt* (*für Tiere*) collar

Halsentzündung *f* sore throat

Halskette *f* necklace

Hals-Nasen-Ohren-Arzt *m*, **Hals-Nasen-Ohren-Ärztin** *f* ear, nose and throat specialist

Halsschmerzen *pl* sore throat *sing*

Halstuch *nt* scarf

halt *interj* stop ▷ *adv*: **das ist ~ so** that's just the way it is

Halt (-(e)s, -e) *m* stop; (*fester*) hold; (*innerer*) stability

haltbar *adj* durable; (*Lebensmittel*) nonperishable

halten (hielt, gehalten) *vt* to keep; (*festhalten*) to hold; **~ für** to regard as; **~ von** to think of; **den Elfmeter ~** to save the penalty; **eine Rede ~** to give (*o* make) a speech ▷ *vi* to hold; (*frisch bleiben*) to keep; (*stoppen*) to stop; **zu jdm ~** to stand by sb ▷ *vr*: **sich ~** (*frisch bleiben*) to keep; (*sich behaupten*) to hold out

Haltestelle *f* stop

Halteverbot *nt*: **hier ist ~** you can't stop here

Haltung *f* (*Körper*) posture; (*fig*) attitude; (*Selbstbeherrschung*) composure; **~ bewahren** to keep one's composure

Hamburg (-s) *nt* Hamburg

Hamburger (-s, -) m (Gastr) hamburger
Hammelfleisch nt mutton
Hammer (-s, Hämmer) m hammer; (fig, fam: Fehler) blunder; **das ist der ~** (unerhört) that's outrageous
Hämorr(ho)iden pl hemorrhoids pl, piles pl
Hamster (-s, -) m hamster
Hand (-, Hände) f hand; **jdm die ~ geben** to shake hands with sb; **jdn bei der ~ nehmen** to take sb by the hand; **eine ~ voll Reis/Leute** a handful of rice/people; **zu Händen von** attention
Handarbeit f (Schulfach) handicraft; **~ sein** to be handmade
Handball m handball
Handbremse f emergency brake
Handbuch nt handbook, manual
Handcreme f hand cream
Händedruck m handshake
Handel (-s) m trade; (Geschäft) transaction
handeln vi to act; (Comm) to trade; **~ von** to be about ▷ vr impers: **sich ~ um** to be about; **es handelt sich um ...** it's about ...
Handelskammer f chamber of commerce
Handelsschule f business school
Handfeger (-s, -) m brush
Handfläche f palm
Handgelenk nt wrist
handgemacht adj handmade
Handgepäck nt carry-on bag
Händler(in) (-s, -) m(f) dealer
handlich adj handy
Handlung f act, action; (von Roman, Film) plot
Handschellen pl handcuffs pl
Handschrift f handwriting
Handschuh m glove
Handschuhfach nt glove compartment
Handtasche f handbag, purse
Handtuch nt towel
Handwerk nt trade; (Kunsthandwerk) craft
Handwerker (-s, -) m workman; (gelernt) tradesman
Handy (-s, -s) nt cell phone
Handynummer f cell phone number
Hanf (-(e)s) m hemp
Hang (-(e)s, Hänge) m (Abhang) slope; (fig) tendency
Hängebrücke f suspension bridge
Hängematte f hammock
hängen (hing, gehangen) vi to hang; **an der Wand/an der Decke ~** to hang on the wall/ from the ceiling; **an jdm ~** (fig) to be attached to sb; **~ bleiben** to get caught (an

+dat on); (fig) to get stuck ▷ vt to hang (an +akk on)
Hantel (-, -n) f dumbbell
Hardware (-, -s) f (Inform) hardware
Harfe (-, -n) f harp
harmlos adj harmless
harmonisch adj harmonious
Harn (-(e)s, -e) m urine
Harnblase f bladder
Harpune (-, -n) f harpoon
hart adj hard; (fig) harsh; **zu jdm ~ sein** to be hard on sb; **~ gekocht** (Ei) hard-boiled
hartnäckig adj stubborn
Haschee (-s, -s) nt hash
Haschisch (-) nt hashish
Hase (-n, -n) m hare
Haselnuss f hazelnut
Hasenscharte f (Med) harelip
Hass (-es) m hatred (auf, gegen +akk of), hate; **einen ~ kriegen** (fam) to see red
hassen vt to hate
hässlich adj ugly; (gemein) nasty
Hast (-) f haste, hurry
hastig adj hasty
hatte imperf von haben
Haube (-, -n) f hood; (Mütze) cap; (Auto) hood
Hauch (-(e)s, -e) m breath; (Lufthauch) breeze; (fig) trace
hauchdünn adj (Schicht, Scheibe) paper-thin
hauen (haute, gehauen) vt to hit
Haufen (-s, -) m pile; **ein ~ Geld** (viel Geld) a lot of money
häufig adj frequent ▷ adv frequently, often
Haupt- in zW main
Hauptbahnhof m central (o main) station
Hauptdarsteller(in) m(f) leading actor/ lady
Haupteingang m main entrance
Hauptgericht nt main course
Hauptgeschäftszeiten pl peak shopping hours pl
Hauptgewinn m first prize
Häuptling m chief
Hauptquartier nt headquarters pl
Hauptreisezeit f peak travel season
Hauptrolle f leading role
Hauptsache f main thing
hauptsächlich adv mainly, chiefly
Hauptsaison f high (o peak) season
Hauptsatz m main clause
Hauptschule f ≈ junior high school
Hauptspeicher m (Inform) main storage (o memory)

Hauptstadt f capital
Hauptstraße f main road; (im Stadtzentrum) main street
Hauptverkehrszeit f rush hour
Haus (-es, Häuser) nt house; **nach ~e** home; **zu ~e** at home; **jdn nach ~e bringen** to take sb home; **bei uns zu ~e** (Heimat) where we come from; (Familie) in my family; (Haus) at our place
Hausarbeit f housework
Hausaufgabe f (Schule) homework; **~n** pl homework sing
Hausbesitzer(in) (-s, -) m(f) homeowner, owner of the house; (Vermieter) landlord/-lady
Hausbesuch m home visit
Hausbewohner(in) (-s, -) m(f) occupant
Hausflur m hall
Hausfrau f housewife
hausgemacht adj homemade
Haushalt m household; (Pol) budget
Hausherr(in) m(f) host/hostess; (Vermieter) landlord/-lady
häuslich adj domestic
Hausmannskost f home(-style) cooking
Hausmeister(in) m(f) janitor
Hausnummer f house number
Hausordnung f (house) rules pl
Hausschlüssel m front-door key
Hausschuh m slipper
Haustier nt pet
Haustür f front door
Haut (-, Häute) f skin; (Tier) hide
Hautarzt m, **Hautärztin** f dermatologist
Hautausschlag m skin rash
Hautcreme f skin cream
Hautfarbe f skin color
Hautkrankheit f skin disease
Hawaii (-s) nt Hawaii
Hbf. (abk) = **Hauptbahnhof** central station
Hebamme (-, -n) f midwife
Hebel (-s, -) m lever
heben (hob, gehoben) vt to raise, to lift
Hebräisch (-) nt Hebrew
Hecht (-(e)s, -e) m pike
Heck (-(e)s, -e) nt (von Boot) stern; (von Auto) rear
Heckantrieb m rear-wheel drive
Hecke (-, -n) f hedge
Heckklappe f tailgate
Hecklicht nt tail light
Heckscheibe f rear window
Hefe (-, -n) f yeast
Heft (-(e)s, -e) nt notebook, exercise book; (Ausgabe) issue

heftig adj violent; (Kritik, Streit) fierce
Heftklammer f paper clip
Heftpflaster nt Band-Aid®
Heide (-, -n) f heath, moor
Heidekraut nt heather
Heidelbeere f blueberry
heidnisch adj (Brauch) pagan
heikel adj (Angelegenheit) awkward; (wählerisch) fussy
heil adj (Sache) in one piece, intact; (Person) unhurt
heilbar adj curable
Heilbutt (-(e)s, -e) m halibut
heilen vt to cure ▷ vi to heal
heilig adj holy
Heiligabend m Christmas Eve
Heilige(r) mf saint
Heilmittel n remedy, cure (gegen for)
Heilpraktiker(in) (-s, -) m(f) non-medical practitioner
heim adv home
Heim (-(e), -e) nt home
Heimat (-, -en) f home (town/country)
Heimatland nt home country
heim|fahren (irr) vi to drive home
Heimfahrt f trip home; **auf der ~** on the way home
heimisch adj (Bevölkerung, Brauchtum) local; (Tiere, Pflanzen) native
heim|kommen (irr) vi to come (o return) home
heimlich adj secret
Heimreise f trip home
Heimspiel nt (Sport) home game
Heimvorteil m (Sport) home advantage
Heimweg m way home
Heimweh (-s) nt homesickness; **~ haben** to be homesick
Heimwerker(in) m(f) do-it-yourselfer, DIYer
Heirat (-, -en) f marriage
heiraten vi to get married ▷ vt to marry
Heiratsantrag m proposal; **er hat ihr einen ~ gemacht** he proposed to her
heiser adj hoarse
heiß adj hot; (Diskussion) heated; **mir ist ~** I'm hot
heißen (hieß, geheißen) vi to be called; (bedeuten) to mean; **ich heiße Tom** my name is Tom; **wie ~ Sie?** what's your name?; **wie heißt sie mit Nachnamen?** what's her last name?; **wie heißt das auf Englisch?** what's that in English? ▷ vi impers: **es heißt** (man sagt) it is said; **es heißt in dem Brief ...** it says in the letter

...; **das heißt** that is
Heißluftherd *m* convection oven
heiter *adj* cheerful; *(Wetter)* bright
heizen *vt* to heat
Heizkissen *m (Med)* heating pad
Heizkörper *m* radiator
Heizöl *nt* heating oil
Heizung *f* heating
Hektar *(-s, -) nt* hectare
Hektik *(-, -en) f:* **nur keine ~!** take it easy!
hektisch *adj* hectic
Held *(-en, -en) m* hero
Heldin *f* heroine
helfen **(half, geholfen)** *vi* to help *(jdm bei etw* sb with sth); *(nützen)* to be of use; **sie weiß sich** *(dat)* **zu ~** she can manage ▷ *vi impers:* **es hilft nichts, du musst ...** it's no use, you have to ...
Helfer(in) *m(f)* helper; *(Mitarbeiter)* assistant
Helikopter-Skiing *(-s) nt* heliskiing, helicopter skiing
hell *adj* bright; *(Farbe)* light; *(Hautfarbe)* fair
hellblau *adj* light blue
hellblond *adj* ash-blond
hellgelb *adj* pale yellow
hellgrün *adj* light green
Hellseher(in) *m(f)* clairvoyant
Helm *(-(e)s, -e) m* helmet
Helmpflicht *f* compulsory wearing of helmets
Hemd *(-(e)s, -en) nt* shirt; *(Unterhemd)* undershirt
hemmen *vt* to check; *(behindern)* to hamper; **gehemmt sein** to be inhibited
Hemmung *f (psychisch)* inhibition; *(moralisch)* scruple; **sie hatte keine ~, ihn zu betrügen** she had no scruples about deceiving him
Henkel *(-s, -) m* handle
Henna *(-s) nt* henna
Henne *(-, -n) f* hen
Hepatitis *(-, Hepatitiden) f* hepatitis

her *adv* **1** *(Richtung):* **komm her zu mir** come here (to me); **von England her** from England; **von weit her** from a long way away; **her damit!** hand it over!; **wo hat er das her?** where did he get that from?; **wo bist du her?** where do you come from?
2 *(Blickpunkt):* **von der Form her** as far as the form is concerned

3 *(zeitlich):* **das ist fünf Jahre her** that was five years ago; **ich kenne ihn von früher her** I know him from before

herab *adv* down
herablassend *adj (Bemerkung)* condescending
herab|sehen *(irr) vt:* **auf jdn ~** to look down on sb
herab|setzen *vt* to reduce; *(fig)* to disparage
heran *adv:* **näher ~!** come closer
heran|kommen *(irr) vi* to approach; **~ an** *+akk* to be able to get at; *(fig)* to be able to get hold of
heran|wachsen *(irr) vi* to grow up
herauf *adv* up
herauf|beschwören *(irr) vt* to evoke; *(verursachen)* to cause
herauf|ziehen *(irr) vt* to pull up ▷ *vi* to approach; *(Sturm)* to gather
heraus *adv* out
heraus|bekommen *(irr) vt (Geheimnis)* to find out; *(Rätsel)* to solve; **ich bekomme noch zwei Euro heraus** I still have two euros in change coming
heraus|bringen *(irr) vt* to bring out
heraus|finden *(irr) vt* to find out
heraus|fordern *vt* to challenge
Herausforderung *f* challenge
heraus|geben *(irr) vt (Buch)* to edit; *(veröffentlichen)* to publish; **jdm zwei Euro ~** to give sb two euros change; **geben Sie mir bitte auf 20 Euro heraus** could you give me change for 20 euros, please?
heraus|holen *vt* to get out *(aus* of)
heraus|kommen *(irr) vi* to come out; **dabei kommt nichts heraus** nothing will come of it
heraus|stellen *vr:* **sich ~** to turn out *(als* to be)
heraus|ziehen *(irr) vt* to pull out
Herbergseltern *pl* youth hostel manager *sing*
Herbst *(-(e)s, -e) m* fall, autumn
Herd *(-(e)s, -e) m* stove
Herde *(-, -n) f* herd; *(Schafe)* flock
herein *adv* in; **~!** come in!
herein|fallen *(irr) vi:* **wir sind auf einen Betrüger hereingefallen** we were taken in by a swindler
herein|legen *vt:* **jdn ~** *(fig)* to take sb for a ride
Herfahrt *f* trip here; **auf der ~** on the way here

h

Hergang *m* course (of events); **schildern Sie mir den ~** tell me what happened

Hering *(-s, -e) m* herring

her|kommen *(irr) vi* to come; **wo kommt sie her?** where does she come from?

Heroin *(-s) nt* heroin

Herpes *(-) m (Med)* herpes

Herr *(-(e)n, -en) m (vor Namen)* Mr.; *(Mann)* gentleman; *(Adliger, Gott)* Lord; **mein ~!** sir!; **meine ~en!** gentlemen!; **Sehr geehrte Damen und ~en** Dear Sir or Madam

herrenlos *adj (Gepäckstück)* abandoned; *(Tier)* stray

Herrentoilette *f* men's room

her|richten *vt* to prepare

herrlich *adj* marvelous, splendid

Herrschaft *f* rule; *(Macht)* power; **meine ~en!** ladies and gentlemen!

herrschen *vi* to rule; *(bestehen)* to be

her|stellen *vt* to make; *(industriell)* to manufacture

Hersteller(in) *m(f)* manufacturer

Herstellung *f* production

herüber *adv* over

herum *adv* around; *(im Kreis)* round; **um etw ~** around sth; **du hast den Pulli falsch ~ an** you're wearing your sweater inside out; **anders ~** the other way around

herum|fahren *(irr) vi* to drive around

herum|führen *vt:* **jdn in der Stadt ~** to show sb around the town ▷ *vi:* **die Straße führt um das Zentrum herum** the road goes around the city center

herum|kommen *(irr) vi:* **sie ist viel in der Welt herumgekommen** she's been around the world; **um etw ~** *(vermeiden)* to get out of sth

herum|kriegen *vt* to bring *(o* talk) around

herum|treiben *(irr) vr:* **sich ~** to hang around

herunter *adv* down

heruntergekommen *adj (Gebäude, Gegend)* run-down; *(Person)* down-at-the-heels

herunter|handeln *vt* to get down

herunter|holen *vt* to bring down

herunter|kommen *(irr) vi* to come down

herunterladbar *adj (Inform)* downloadable

herunter|laden *(irr) vt (Inform)* to download

hervor *adv* out

hervor|bringen *(irr) vt* to produce; *(Wort)* to utter

hervor|heben *(irr) vt* to emphasize, to stress

hervorragend *adj* excellent

hervor|rufen *(irr) vt* to cause, to give rise to

Herz *(-ens, -en) nt* heart; *(Karten)* hearts *pl*; **von ganzem ~en** wholeheartedly; **sich** *(dat)* **etw zu ~en nehmen** to take sth to heart

Herzanfall *m* heart attack

Herzbeschwerden *pl* heart trouble *sing*

Herzfehler *m* heart defect

herzhaft *adj (Essen)* substantial; **~ lachen** to have a good laugh

Herzinfarkt *m* heart attack

Herzklopfen *(-s) nt (Med)* palpitations *pl*; **ich hatte ~ vor Aufregung** my heart was pounding (with excitement)

herzkrank *adj:* **sie ist ~** she's got a heart condition

herzlich *adj (Empfang, Mensch)* warm; **~en Glückwunsch** congratulations

Herzog(in) *(-s, Herzöge) m(f)* duke/duchess

Herzschlag *m* heartbeat; *(Herzversagen)* heart failure

Herzschrittmacher *m* pacemaker

Herzstillstand *m* cardiac arrest

Hessen *(-s) nt* Hessen

heterosexuell *adj* heterosexual

Heterosexuelle(r) *mf* heterosexual

Hetze *(-, -n) f (Eile)* rush

hetzen *vt* to rush ▷ *vr:* **sich ~** to rush

Heu *(-(e)s) nt* hay

heuer *adv* this year

heulen *vi* to howl; *(weinen)* to cry

Heuschnupfen *m* hay fever

Heuschrecke *(-, -n) f* grasshopper; *(größer)* locust

heute *adv* today; **~ Abend/früh** this evening/morning; **~ Morgen** this morning; **~ Nacht** tonight; *(letzte Nacht)* last night; **~ in acht Tagen** a week (from) today; **sie hat bis ~ nicht bezahlt** she hasn't paid to this day

heutig *adj:* **die ~e Zeitung/Generation** today's paper/generation

heutzutage *adv* nowadays

Hexe *(-, -n) f* witch

Hexenschuss *m* lumbago

hielt *imperf von* **halten**

hier *adv* here; **~ entlang** this way; **ich bin auch nicht von ~** I'm a stranger here myself

hier|bleiben *(irr) vi* to stay here

hierher *adv* here; **das gehört nicht ~** that doesn't belong here

hier|lassen *(irr) vt* to leave here

hiermit *adv* with this

hierzulande *adv* in this country

hiesig *adj* local

hieß *imperf von* **heißen**

Hi-Fi-Anlage *f* hi-fi (system)

high *adj* (*fam*) high

Highlife (*-s*) *nt* high life; **~ machen** to live it up

Hightech (*-s*) *nt* high tech

Hilfe (*-*, *-n*) *f* help; (*für Notleidende, finanziell*) aid; **~!** help!; **Erste ~ leisten** to give first aid; **um ~ bitten** to ask for help

hilflos *adj* helpless

hilfsbereit *adj* helpful

Hilfsmittel *nt* aid

Himbeere *f* raspberry

Himmel (*-s*, *-*) *m* sky; (*Rel*) heaven

Himmelfahrt *f* Ascension

Himmelsrichtung *f* direction

himmlisch *adj* heavenly

SCHLÜSSELWORT

hin *adv* 1 (*Richtung*): **hin und zurück** there and back; **hin und her** to and fro; **bis zur Mauer hin** up to the wall; **wo ist er hin?** where has he gone?; **Geld hin, Geld her** money or no money

2 (*auf ... hin*): **auf meine Bitte hin** at my request; **auf seinen Rat hin** on the basis of his advice

3: **mein Glück ist hin** my happiness is gone

hinab *adv* down

hinab|gehen (*irr*) *vi* to go down

hinauf *adv* up

hinauf|gehen (*irr*) *vi*, *vt* to go up

hinauf|steigen (*irr*) *vi* to climb (up)

hinaus *adv* out

hinaus|gehen (*irr*) *vi* to go out; **das Zimmer geht auf den See hinaus** the room looks out onto the lake; **~ über** +*akk* to exceed

hinaus|laufen (*irr*) *vi* to run out; **~ auf** +*akk* to come to, to amount to

hinaus|schieben (*irr*) *vi* to put off, to postpone

hinaus|werfen (*irr*) *vt* to throw out; (*aus Firma*) to fire

hinaus|zögern *vr*: **sich ~** to take longer than expected

Hinblick *m*: **in** *o* **im ~ auf** +*akk* with regard to; (*wegen*) in light of

hin|bringen (*irr*) *vt*: **ich bringe Sie hin** I'll take you there

hindern *vt* to prevent; **jdn daran ~, etw zu**

tun to stop (*o* prevent) sb from doing sth

Hindernis *nt* obstacle

Hinduismus *m* Hinduism

hindurch *adv* through; **das ganze Jahr ~** throughout the year, all year round; **die ganze Nacht ~** all night (long)

hinein *adv* in

hinein|gehen (*irr*) *vi* to go in; **~ in** +*akk* to go into, to enter

hinein|passen *vi* to fit in; **~ in** +*akk* to fit into

hin|fahren (*irr*) *vi* to go there ▷ *vt* to take there

Hinfahrt *f* trip (*o* way) there

hin|fallen (*irr*) *vi* to fall (down)

Hinflug *m* outbound (*o* outward) flight

hing *imperf von* **hängen**

hin|gehen (*irr*) *vi* to go there; (*Zeit*) to pass

hin|halten (*irr*) *vt* to hold out; (*warten lassen*) to put off

hinken *vi* to limp; **der Vergleich hinkt** the comparison doesn't work

hin|knien *vr*: **sich ~** to kneel down

hin|legen *vt* to put down ▷ *vr*: **sich ~** to lie down

hin|nehmen (*irr*) *vt* (*fig*) to put up with, to take

Hinreise *f* trip (*o* way) there

hin|setzen *vr*: **sich ~** to sit down

hinsichtlich *prep* (+*gen*) with regard to

hin|stellen *vt* to put (down) ▷ *vr*: **sich ~** to stand

hinten *adv* at the back; (*im Auto*) in the back; (*dahinter*) behind

hinter *prep* (+*dat o akk*) behind; (*nach*) after; **~ jdm her sein** to be after sb; **etw ~ sich** (*akk*) **bringen** to get sth over (and done) with

Hinterachse *f* rear axle

Hinterausgang *m* rear exit

Hinterbein *nt* hind leg

Hinterbliebene(r) *mf* surviving dependant

hintere(r, s) *adj* rear, back

hintereinander *adv* (*in einer Reihe*) one behind the other; (*hintereinander her*) one after the other; **drei Tage ~** three days running (*o* in a row)

Hintereingang *m* rear entrance

Hintergedanke *m* ulterior motive

hintergehen (*irr*) *vt* to deceive

Hintergrund *m* background

hinterher *adv* (*zeitlich*) afterwards; **los, ~!** come on, after him/her/them!

Hinterkopf *m* back of the head

hinterlassen *vt* to leave; **jdm eine Nachricht ~** to leave a message for sb
hinterlegen *vt* to leave (*bei* with)
Hintern (-, -) *m* (*fam*) backside, butt
Hinterradantrieb *m* (*Auto*) rear-wheel drive
Hinterteil *nt* back (part); (*Hintern*) behind
Hintertür *f* back door
hinüber *adv* over; **~ sein** (*fam: kaputt*) to be ruined; (*verdorben*) to have gone bad
hinüber|gehen (*irr*) *vi* to go over
hinunter *adv* down
hinunter|gehen (*irr*) *vi, vt* to go down
hinunter|schlucken *vt* (*a. fig*) to swallow
Hinweg *m* trip (*o* way) there
hinweg|setzen *vr*: **sich über etw** (*akk*) **~** to ignore sth
Hinweis (-es, -e) *m* (*Andeutung*) hint; (*Ratschlag*) tip; (*Anweisung*) instruction; (*Verweis*) reference
hin|weisen (*irr*) *vi*: **jdn auf etw** (*acc*) **~** to point sth out to sb; **jdn nochmal auf etw ~** to remind sb of sth
hinzu *adv* in addition
hinzu|fügen *vt* to add
hinzu|kommen (*irr*) *vi*: **zu jdm ~** to join sb; **es war kalt, hinzu kam, dass es auch noch regnete** it was cold, and on top of that it was raining
Hirn (-(e)s, -e) *nt* brain; (*Verstand*) brains *pl*
Hirnhautentzündung *f* meningitis
hirnverbrannt *adj* crazy
Hirsch (-(e)s, -e) *m* deer; (*als Speise*) venison
Hirse (-, -n) *f* millet
Hirte (-n, -n) *m* shepherd
historisch *adj* historical
Hit (-s, -s) *m* (*fig: Mus, Inform*) hit
Hitliste *f*, **Hitparade** *f* charts *pl*
Hitze (-) *f* heat
hitzebeständig *adj* heat-resistant
Hitzewelle *f* heat wave
hitzig *adj* hot-tempered; (*Debatte*) heated
Hitzschlag *m* heatstroke
HIV (-(s), -(s)) *nt* (*abk*) **= Human Immunodeficiency Virus** HIV
HIV-negativ *adj* HIV-negative
HIV-positiv *adj* HIV-positive
hob *imperf von* **heben**
Hobby (-s, -s) *nt* hobby
Hobel (-s, -) *m* plane
hoch *adj* high; (*Baum, Haus*) tall; (*Schnee*) deep; **der Zaun ist drei Meter ~** the fence is three meters high; **~ auflösend** high-resolution; **~ begabt** extremely gifted;

das ist mir zu ~ that's above my head; **~ soll sie leben!, sie lebe ~!** three cheers for her!; **4 ~ 2 ist 16** 4 squared is 16; **4 ~ 5** 4 to the power of 5
Hoch (-s, -s) *nt* (*Ruf*) cheer; (*Meteo*) high
hochachtungsvoll *adv* (*in Briefen*) Yours truly
Hochbetrieb *m*: **es herrscht ~** they/we are extremely busy
Hochdeutsch *nt* High German
Hochgebirge *nt* high mountains *pl*
Hochgeschwindigkeitszug *m* high-speed train
Hochhaus *nt* high rise
hoch|heben (*irr*) *vt* to lift (up)
hochprozentig *adj* (*Alkohol*) high-proof
Hochschule *f* college; (*Universität*) university
Hochschulreife *f*: **er hat (die) ~** he's graduated from high school
hochschwanger *adj* far along (in one's pregnancy)
Hochsommer *m* midsummer
Hochspannung *f* great tension; (*Elek*) high voltage
Hochsprung *m* high jump
höchst *adv* highly, extremely
höchste(r, s) *adj* highest; (*äußerste*) extreme
höchstens *adv* at the most
Höchstform *f* (*Sport*) top form
Höchstgeschwindigkeit *f* maximum speed
Höchstparkdauer *f* maximum stay
Hochstuhl *m* high chair
höchstwahrscheinlich *adv* very probably
Hochwasser *nt* high water; (*Überschwemmung*) flood
hochwertig *adj* high-quality
Hochzeit (-, -en) *f* wedding
Hochzeitsnacht *f* wedding night
Hochzeitsreise *f* honeymoon
Hochzeitstag *m* wedding day; (*Jahrestag*) wedding anniversary
hocken *vi* to squat, to crouch
Hocker (-s, -) *m* stool
Hockey (-s) *nt* hockey
Hoden (-s, -) *m* testicle
Hof (-(e)s, Höfe) *m* (*Hinterhof*) yard; (*Innenhof*) courtyard; (*Bauernhof*) farm; (*Königshof*) court
hoffen *vi* to hope (*auf +akk* for); **ich hoffe es** I hope so
hoffentlich *adv* hopefully; **~ nicht** I hope not

Hoffnung f hope
hoffnungslos adj hopeless
höflich adj polite
Höflichkeit f politeness
hohe(r, s) adj siehe **hoch**
Höhe (-, -n) f height; (Anhöhe) hill; (einer Summe) amount; **in einer ~ von 5000 Metern** at an altitude of 5,000 meters; (Flughöhe) altitude
Höhenangst f vertigo
Höhepunkt m (einer Reise) high point; (einer Veranstaltung) highlight; (eines Films; sexuell) climax
höher adj, adv higher
hohl adj hollow
Höhle (-, -n) f cave
holen vt to get, to fetch; (abholen) to pick up; (Atem) to catch; **die Polizei ~** to call the police; **jdn/etw ~ lassen** to send for sb/sth
Holland nt Holland
Holländer(in) (-s, -) m(f) Dutchman/-woman
holländisch adj Dutch
Hölle (-, -n) f hell
Hologramm nt hologram
holperig adj bumpy
Holunder (-s, -) m elder
Holz (-es, Hölzer) nt wood
Holzboden m wooden floor
hölzern adj wooden
holzig adj (Stängel) woody
Holzkohle f charcoal
Homebanking (-s) nt home banking, online banking
Homepage (-, -s) f home page
Hometrainer m exercise machine
Homoehe f (fam) gay marriage
homöopathisch adj homeopathic
homosexuell adj homosexual
Homosexuelle(r) mf homosexual
Honig (-s, -e) m honey
Honigmelone f honeydew melon
Honorar (-s, -e) nt fee
Hopfen (-s, -) m (Bot) hop; (beim Brauen) hops pl
hoppla interj whoops, oops
horchen vi to listen (auf +akk to); (an der Tür) to eavesdrop
hören vt, vi (passiv, mitbekommen) to hear; (zufällig) to overhear; (aufmerksam zuhören; Radio, Musik) to listen to; **ich habe schon viel von Ihnen gehört** I've heard a lot about you
Hörer m (Tel) receiver

Hörer(in) m(f) listener
Hörgerät nt hearing aid
Horizont (-(e)s, -e) m horizon; **das geht über meinen ~** that's beyond me
Hormon (-s, -e) nt hormone
Hornhaut f callus; (des Auges) cornea
Hornisse (-, -n) f hornet
Horoskop (-s, -e) nt horoscope
Hörsaal m lecture hall
Hörsturz m acute hearing loss
Hörweite f: **in/außer ~** within/out of earshot
Höschenwindel (-, -n) f diaper
Hose (-, -n) f pants pl; (Unterhose) (under)pants pl; **eine ~** a pair of pants; **kurze ~** (pair of) shorts pl
Hosenanzug m pantsuit
Hosenschlitz m fly
Hosentasche f pants pocket
Hosenträger m suspenders pl
Hospital (-s, Hospitäler) nt hospital
Hotdog (-s, -s) nt o m hot dog
Hotel (-s, -s) nt hotel; **in welchem ~ seid ihr?** which hotel are you staying at?
Hoteldirektor(in) m(f) hotel manager
Hotelkette f hotel chain
Hotelzimmer nt hotel room
Hotline (-, -s) f hot line
Hotspot m (wireless) hotspot
Hubraum m cubic capacity
hübsch adj (Mädchen, Kind, Kleid) pretty; (gutaussehend; Mann, Frau) good-looking, cute
Hubschrauber (-s, -) m helicopter
Huf (-(e)s, -e) m hoof
Hufeisen nt horseshoe
Hüfte (-, -n) f hip
Hügel (-s, -) m hill
hügelig adj hilly
Huhn (-(e)s, Hühner) nt hen; (Gastr) chicken
Hühnchen nt chicken
Hühnerauge nt corn
Hühnerbrühe f chicken broth
Hülle (-, -n) f cover; (für Ausweis) case; (Zellophan) wrapping
Hummel (-, -n) f bumblebee
Hummer (-s, -) m lobster
Hummerkrabbe f jumbo shrimp
Humor (-s) m humor; **~ haben** to have a sense of humor
humorlos adj humorless
humorvoll adj humorous
humpeln vi hobble
Hund (-(e)s, -e) m dog
Hundeleine f dog leash

hundert *num* hundred
Hundertjahrfeier *f* centennial
hundertprozentig *adj, adv* one hundred percent
hundertste(r, s) *adj* hundredth
Hündin *f* bitch
Hunger (*-s*) *m* hunger; ~ **haben/bekommen** to be/get hungry
hungern *vi* to go hungry; (*ernsthaft, dauernd*) to starve
Hupe (*-, -n*) *f* horn
hupen *vi* to beep, to blow one's horn
hüpfen *vi* to hop; (*springen*) to jump
Hürde (*-, -n*) *f* hurdle
Hure (*-, -n*) *f* whore
hurra *interj* hooray
husten *vi* to cough

Husten (*-s*) *m* cough
Hustensaft *m* cough syrup
Hut (*-(e)s, Hüte*) *m* hat
hüten *vt* to look after ▷ *vr*: **sich ~** to watch out; **sich ~, etw zu tun** to take care not to do sth; **sich ~ vor** +*dat* to beware of
Hütte (*-, -n*) *f* hut, cottage
Hüttenkäse *m* cottage cheese
Hyäne (*-, -n*) *f* hyena
Hydrant *m* hydrant
hygienisch *adj* hygienic
Hyperlink (*-s, -s*) *m* hyperlink
Hypnose (*-, -n*) *f* hypnosis
Hypnotiseur(in) *m(f)* hypnotist
hypnotisieren *vt* to hypnotize
Hypothek (*-, -en*) *f* mortgage
hysterisch *adj* hysterical

I

i. A. (*abk*) = **im Auftrag** pp

IC (*-, -s*) *m* (*abk*) = **Intercityzug** intercity (train)

ICE (*-, -s*) *m* (*abk*) = **Intercityexpresszug** *German high-speed train*

ich *pron* I; **ich bin's** it's me; **ich nicht** not me; **du und ich** you and me; **hier bin ich!** here I am!; **ich Idiot!** stupid me!

Icon (*-s, -s*) *nt* (*Inform*) icon

IC-Zuschlag *m supplement for express train service*

ideal *adj* ideal

Ideal (*-s, -e*) *nt* ideal

Idee (*-, -n*) *f* idea

identifizieren *vt* to identify ▷ *vr:* **sich mit jdm/etw ~** to identify with sb/sth

identisch *adj* identical

Idiot(in) (*-en, -en*) *m(f)* idiot

idiotisch *adj* idiotic

Idol (*-s, -e*) *nt* idol

Idylle *f* idyll

idyllisch *adj* idyllic

Igel (*-s, -*) *m* hedgehog

ignorieren *vt* to ignore

ihm *pron dat sing von* **er/es**; (to) him, (to) it; **wie geht es ihm?** how is he?; **ein Freund von ihm** a friend of his ▷ *pron dat von* **es**; (to) it

ihn *pron akk sing von* **er**; (*Person*) him; (*Sache*) it

ihnen *pron dat pl von* **sie**; (to) them; **wie geht es ~?** how are they?; **ein Freund von ~** a friend of theirs

Ihnen *pron dat sing u pl von* **Sie**; (to) you; **wie geht es ~?** how are you?; **ein Freund von ~** a friend of yours

SCHLÜSSELWORT

ihr *pron* **1** (*nom pl*) you; **ihr seid es** it's you **2** (*dat von sie*) to her; **gib es ihr** give it to her; **er steht neben ihr** he is standing beside her

▷ *possessiv pron* **1** (*sg*) her; (*bei Tieren, Dingen*) its; **ihr Mann** her husband **2** (*pl*) their; **die Bäume und ihre Blätter** the trees and their leaves

Ihr *pron von* **Sie**; (*adjektivisch*) your; **Ihr(e) XY** (*am Briefende*) Yours, XY

ihre(r, s) *pron* (*substantivisch, sing*) hers; (*pl*) theirs; **das ist ~/~r/ihr(e)s** that's hers;

(*pl*) that's theirs

Ihre(r, s) *pron* (*substantivisch*) yours; **das ist ~/~r/Ihr(e)s** that's yours

ihretwegen *adv* (*wegen ihr*) because of her; (*ihr zuliebe*) for her sake; (*um sie*) about her; (*von ihr aus*) as far as she is concerned ▷ *adv* (*wegen ihnen*) because of them; (*ihnen zuliebe*) for their sake; (*um sie*) about them; (*von ihnen aus*) as far as they are concerned

Ihretwegen *adv* (*wegen Ihnen*) because of you; (*Ihnen zuliebe*) for your sake; (*um Sie*) about you; (*von Ihnen aus*) as far as you are concerned

Ikone (*-, -n*) *f* icon

illegal *adj* illegal

Illusion *f* illusion; **sich** (*dat*) **~en machen** to delude oneself

illusorisch *adj* illusory

Illustration *f* illustration

Illustrierte (*-n, -n*) *f* (glossy) magazine

im *kontr von* **in dem**; **im Bett** in bed; **im Fernsehen** on TV; **im Radio** on the radio; **im Bus/Zug** on the bus/train; **im Januar** in January; **im Stehen** (while) standing up

Imbiss (*-es, -e*) *m* snack

Imbissbude *f*, **Imbissstube** *f* snack bar

immer *adv* always; **~ mehr** more and more; **~ wieder** again and again; **~ noch** still; **~ noch nicht** still not; **für ~** forever; **~ wenn ich ...** every time I ...; **~ schöner/trauriger** more and more beautiful/sadder and sadder; **was/wer/wo/wann auch ~** whatever/ whoever/wherever/whenever

immerhin *adv* after all

immerzu *adv* all the time

Immigrant(in) *m(f)* immigrant

Immobilien *pl* property *sing* real estate *sing*

Immobilienmakler(in) *m(f)* Realtor®

immun *adj* immune (*gegen* to)

Immunschwäche *f* immunodeficiency

Immunschwächekrankheit *f* immune deficiency syndrome

Immunsystem *nt* immune system

impfen *vt* to vaccinate; **ich muss mich gegen Pocken ~ lassen** I've got to get myself vaccinated against smallpox

Impfpass *m* vaccination card

Impfstoff *m* vaccine

Impfung *f* vaccination

imponieren *vi* to impress (*jdm* sb)

Import (*-(e)s, -e*) *m* import
importieren *vt* to import
impotent *adj* impotent
imstande *adj:* ~ **sein** to be in a position; (*fähig*) to be able

in *prep +akk* **1** (*räumlich: wohin?*) in, into; **in die Stadt** into town; **in die Schule gehen** to go to school
2 (*zeitlich*): **bis ins 20. Jahrhundert** into *o* up to the 20th century
▷ *prep +dat* **1** (*räumlich: wo?*) in; **in der Stadt** in town; **in der Schule sein** to be at school
2 (*zeitlich: wann?*): **in diesem Jahr** this year; (*in jenem Jahr*) in that year; **heute in zwei Wochen** two weeks from today

inbegriffen *adj* included
Inbusschlüssel *m* hex key
indem *conj:* **sie gewann, ~ sie mogelte** she won by cheating
Inder(in) (*-s, -*) *m(f)* Indian
Indianer(in) (*-s, -*) *m(f)* American Indian, Native American
indianisch *adj* American Indian, Native American
Indien (*-s*) *nt* India
indirekt *adj* indirect
indisch *adj* Indian
indiskret *adj* indiscreet
individuell *adj* individual
Indonesien (*-s*) *nt* Indonesia
Industrie *f* industry
Industrie- *in zW* industrial
Industriegebiet *nt* industrial area
industriell *adj* industrial
ineinander *adv* in(to) one another (*o* each other)
Infarkt (*-(e)s, -e*) *m* (*Herzinfarkt*) heart attack
Infektion *f* infection
Infektionskrankheit *f* infectious disease
infizieren *vt* to infect ▷ *vr:* **sich** ~ to be infected
Info (*-, -s*) *f* (*fam*) info
infolge *prep* (*+gen*) as a result of, owing to
infolgedessen *adv* consequently
Infomaterial *nt* info
Informatik *f* computer science
Informatiker(in) (*-s, -*) *m(f)* IT engineer
Information *f* information
Informationsschalter *m* information desk

informieren *vt* to inform; **falsch** ~ to misinform ▷ *vr:* **sich** ~ to find out (*über +akk* about)
infrage *adv:* **das kommt nicht** ~ that's out of the question; **etw** ~ **stellen** to question sth
Infrastruktur *f* infrastructure
Infusion *f* infusion
Ingenieur(in) *m(f)* engineer
Ingwer (*-s*) *m* ginger
Inhaber(in) (*-s, -*) *m(f)* owner; (*von Lizenz*) holder; (*Fin*) bearer
Inhalt (*-(e)s, -e*) *m* contents *pl*; (*eines Buchs etc*) content; (*Math*) volume; (*Flächeninhalt*) area
Inhaltsangabe *f* summary
Inhaltsverzeichnis *nt* table of contents
Initiative *f* initiative; **die** ~ **ergreifen** to take the initiative
Injektion *f* injection
inklusive *adv, prep* inclusive (*gen* of)
inkonsequent *adj* inconsistent
Inland *nt* (*Pol, Comm*) home; **im** ~ at home; (*Geo*) inland
inländisch *adj* domestic
Inlandsflug *m* domestic flight
Inlandsgespräch *nt* domestic long distance call
Inliner *pl*, **Inlineskates** *pl* (*Sport*) Rollerblades® *pl*, in-line skates *pl*
innen *adv* inside
Innenarchitekt(in) *m(f)* interior designer
Innenhof *m* (inner) courtyard
Innenminister(in) *m(f)* minister (*o* secretary) of the interior
Innenseite *f* inside
Innenspiegel *m* rearview mirror
Innenstadt *f* downtown
innere(r, s) *adj* inner; (*im Körper, inländisch*) internal
Innere(s) *nt* inside; (*Mitte*) center; (*fig*) heart
Innereien *pl* innards *pl*
innerhalb *adv, prep* (*+gen*) within; (*räumlich*) inside
innerlich *adj* internal; (*geistig*) inner
innerste(r, s) *adj* innermost
Innovation *f* innovation
innovativ *adj* innovative
inoffiziell *adj* unofficial; (*zwanglos*) informal
ins *kontr von* **in das**
Insasse (*-n, -n*) *m*, **Insassin** *f* (*Auto*) passenger; (*Anstalt*) inmate
insbesondere *adv* particularly, in particular

Inschrift *f* inscription
Insekt *(-(e)s, -en)* *nt* insect, bug
Insektenschutzmittel *nt* insect repellent
Insektenstich *m* insect bite
Insel *(-, -n)* *f* island
Inserat *nt* advertisement
insgesamt *adv* altogether, all in all
Insider(in) *(-s, -)* *m(f)* insider
insofern *adv* in that respect; *(deshalb)* (and) so ▷ *conj* if; **~ als** in so far as
Installateur(in) *m(f)* *(Klempner)* plumber; *(Elektroinstallateur)* electrician
installieren *vt* *(Inform)* to install
Instinkt *(-(e)s, -e)* *m* instinct
Institut *(-(e)s, -e)* *nt* institute
Institution *f* institution
Instrument *nt* instrument
Insulin *(-s)* *nt* insulin
Inszenierung *f* production
intakt *adj* intact
intellektuell *adj* intellectual
intelligent *adj* intelligent
Intelligenz *f* intelligence
intensiv *adj* *(gründlich)* intensive; *(Gefühl, Schmerz)* intense
Intensivkurs *m* crash course
Intensivstation *f* intensive care unit
interaktiv *adj* interactive
Intercityexpress(zug) *m* German high-speed train
Intercityzug *m* intercity (train)
Intercityzuschlag *m* supplement for express train service
interessant *adj* interesting
Interesse *(-s, -n)* *nt* interest; **~ haben an** +dat to be interested in
interessieren *vt* to interest ▷ *vr:* **sich ~ to** be interested in *(für in)*
Interface *(-, -s)* *nt* *(Inform)* interface
Internat *nt* boarding school
international *adj* international
Internet *(-s)* *nt* Internet, Net; **im ~** on the Internet; **im ~ surfen** to surf the Net
Internetanschluss *m* Internet connection
Internetauktion *f* Internet auction
Internetcafé *nt* Internet café, cybercafé
Internetfirma *f* dot-com company, Internet company
Internethandel *m* e-commerce
Internetseite *f* web page
Internetzugang *m* Internet access
interpretieren *vt* to interpret *(als* as)
Interpunktion *f* punctuation
Interview *(-s, -s)* *nt* interview
interviewen *vt* to interview

intim *adj* intimate
intolerant *adj* intolerant
investieren *vt* to invest
inwiefern *adv* in what way; *(in welchem Ausmaß)* to what extent
inwieweit *adv* to what extent
inzwischen *adv* meanwhile
Irak *(-(s))* *m:* **der ~** Iraq
Iran *(-(s))* *m:* **der ~** Iran
Ire *(-n, -n)* *m* Irishman
irgend *adv:* **~ so ein Idiot** some idiot; **wenn ~ möglich** if at all possible
irgendein *pron,* **irgendeine(r, s)** *adj* some; *(fragend, im Bedingungssatz; beliebig)* any
irgendetwas *pron* something; *(fragend, im Bedingungssatz)* anything
irgendjemand *pron* somebody; *(fragend, im Bedingungssatz)* anybody
irgendwann *adv* sometime; *(zu beliebiger Zeit)* any time
irgendwie *adv* somehow
irgendwo *adv* somewhere; *(fragend, im Bedingungssatz)* anywhere
Irin *f* Irishwoman
irisch *adj* Irish
Irland *nt* Ireland
ironisch *adj* ironic
irre *adj* crazy, mad; *(toll)* terrific
Irre(r) *mf* lunatic
irreführen *(irr)* *vt* to mislead
irremachen *vt* to confuse
irren *vi* to be mistaken; *(umherirren)* to wander ▷ *vr:* **sich ~** to be mistaken; **wenn ich mich nicht irre** if I'm not mistaken; **sich in der Nummer ~** *(Telefon)* to get the wrong number
irrsinnig *adj* mad, crazy
Irrtum *(-s, -tümer)* *m* mistake, error
irrtümlich *adj* mistaken ▷ *adv* by mistake
ISBN *(-)* *nt* *(abk)* = **industrial standard business network** ISBN *(-)* *f (abk)* = **Internationale Standard Buchnummer** ISBN
Ischias *(-)* *m* sciatica
ISDN *(-)* *nt* *(abk)* = **integrated services digital network** ISDN
Islam *(-s)* *m* Islam
islamisch *adj* Islamic
Island *nt* Iceland
Isländer(in) *(-s, -)* *m(f)* Icelander
isländisch *adj* Icelandic
Isländisch *nt* Icelandic
Isolierband *nt* duct *(o* electrical) tape
isolieren *vt* to isolate; *(Elek)* to insulate
Isomatte *f* camping *(o* exercise) mat
Israel *(-s)* *nt* Israel

Israeli (-(s), -(s)) m (-, -(s)) f Israeli
israelisch adj Israeli
IT (-) f (abk) = **Informationstechnologie** IT
Italien (-s) nt Italy

Italiener(in) (-s, -) m(f) Italian
italienisch adj Italian
Italienisch nt Italian

J

ja *adv* 1 yes; **haben Sie das gesehen? — ja** did you see it? — yes(, I did); **ich glaube ja** (yes,) I think so

2 *(fragend)* really?; **ich habe gekündigt — ja?** I've quit — you did?; **du kommst, ja?** you're coming, aren't you?

3: **sei ja vorsichtig** please be careful; **Sie wissen ja, dass ...** as you know, ...; **tu das ja nicht!** don't do that!; **ich habe es ja gewusst** I just knew it; **ja, also ...** well you see ...

Jacht *(-, -en) f* yacht
Jachthafen *m* marina
Jacke *(-, -n) f* jacket; *(Wolljacke)* cardigan
Jackett *(-s, -s o -e) nt* jacket
Jagd *(-, -en) f* hunt; *(Jagen)* hunting
jagen *vi* to hunt ▷ *vt* to hunt; *(verfolgen)* to chase
Jäger(in) *m(f)* hunter
Jaguar *(-s, -e) m* jaguar
Jahr *(-(e)s, -e) nt* year; **ein halbes ~** six months *pl;* **Anfang der neunziger ~e** in the early nineties; **mit sechzehn ~en** at (the age of) sixteen
Jahrestag *m* anniversary
Jahreszahl *f* date, year
Jahreszeit *f* season
Jahrgang *(Wein) m* year, vintage; **der ~ 1989** *(Personen)* those born in 1989
Jahrhundert *(-s, -e) nt* century
jährlich *adj* yearly, annual
Jahrmarkt *m* fair
Jahrtausend *nt* millennium
Jahrzehnt *nt* decade
jähzornig *adj* hot-tempered
Jakobsmuschel *f* scallop
Jalousie *f* (venetian) blind
Jamaika *(-s) nt* Jamaica
jämmerlich *adj* pathetic
jammern *vi* to moan, to whine
Januar *(-(s), -e) m* January; *siehe auch* **Juni**
Japan *(-s) nt* Japan
Japaner(in) *(-s, -) m(f)* Japanese
japanisch *adj* Japanese
Japanisch *nt* Japanese
jaulen *vi* to howl
jawohl *adv* yes (of course)
Jazz *(-) m* jazz

je *adv* 1 *(jemals)* ever; **hast du so was je gesehen?** did you ever see anything like it?

2 *(jeweils)* every, each; **sie zahlten je drei Euro** they paid three euros each
▷ *konj* 1: **je nach** depending on; **je nachdem** it depends; **je nachdem, ob ...** depending on whether ...

2: **je eher, desto** *o* **umso besser** the sooner the better

Jeans *(-, -) f* jeans *pl*
jede(r, s) *adj (insgesamt gesehen)* every; *(einzeln gesehen)* each; *(jede(r, s) beliebige)* any; **~s Mal** every time, each time; **~n zweiten Tag** every other day; **sie hat an ~m Finger einen Ring** she's got a ring on each finger; **~r Computer reicht aus** any computer will do; **bei ~m Wetter** in any weather ▷ *pron* everybody; *(jeder Einzelne)* each; **~r von euch/uns** each of you/us
jedenfalls *adv* in any case
jederzeit *adv* at any time
jedesmal *adv* every time
jedoch *adv* however
jemals *adv* ever
jemand *pron* somebody; *(in Frage und Verneinung)* anybody
Jemen *(-(s)) m* Yemen
jene(r, s) *adj* that, those *pl* ▷ *pron* that (one), those *pl*
jenseits *adv* on the other side ▷ *prep (+gen)* on the other side of; *(fig)* beyond
Jetlag *(-s) m* jet lag
jetzig *adj* present
jetzt *adv* now; **erst ~** only now; **~ gleich** right now; **bis ~** so far, up to now; **von ~ an** from now on
jeweils *adv:* **~ zwei zusammen** two at a time; **zu ~ fünf Euro** at five euros each
Job *(-s, -s) m* job
jobben *vi (fam)* to take a (temporary) job, to job; **~ als** to job as
Jod *(-(e)s) nt* iodine
joggen *vi* to jog
Jogging *(-s) nt* jogging
Jogginganzug *m* jogging suit, sweatsuit
Jogginghose *f* jogging pants *pl*
Jog(h)urt *(-s, -s) m o nt* yogurt
Johannisbeere *f:* **Schwarze ~** blackcur-·

rant; **Rote** ~ redcurrant
Joint (-s, -s) m (fam) joint
jonglieren vi to juggle
Jordanien (-s) nt Jordan
Journalist(in) m(f) journalist
Joystick (-s, -s) m (Inform) joystick
jubeln vi to cheer
Jubiläum (-s, Jubiläen) nt jubilee; (Jahrestag) anniversary
jucken vi to itch ▷ vt: **es juckt mich am Arm** my arm is itching; **das juckt mich nicht** (fam) I couldn't care less
Juckreiz m itch
Jude (-n, -n) m, **Jüdin** f Jew; **sie ist Jüdin** she's Jewish
jüdisch adj Jewish
Judo (-(s)) nt judo
Jugend (-) f youth
jugendfrei adj: **ein ~er Film** a G-rated film; **ein nicht ~er Film** an X-rated film
Jugendgruppe f youth group
Jugendherberge (-, -n) f youth hostel
Jugendherbergsausweis m youth hostel card
jugendlich adj youthful
Jugendliche(r) mf teen, adolescent
Jugendstil m art nouveau

Jugendzentrum nt youth center
Jugoslawien (-s) nt (Hist) Yugoslavia; **das ehemalige** ~ the former Yugoslavia
Juli (-(s), -s) m July; siehe auch **Juni**
jung adj young
Junge (-n, -n) m boy
Junge(s) (-n, -n) nt young animal; **die ~n** pl the young pl
Jungfrau f virgin; (Astr) Virgo
Junggeselle (-n, -n) m bachelor
Junggesellin f single woman
Juni (-(s), -s) m June; **im** ~ in June; **am 4.** ~ on June 4(th) (gesprochen: on the fourth of June o on June fourth); **Anfang/Mitte/Ende** ~ at the beginning/in the middle/at the end of June; **letzten/nächsten** ~ last/next June
Jupiter (-s) m Jupiter
Jura ohne Artikel (Studienfach) law; ~ **studieren** to study law
Jurist(in) m(f) lawyer
juristisch adj legal
Justiz (-) f justice
Justizminister(in) m(f) minister of justice, ≈ attorney general
Juwel (-s, -en) nt jewel
Juwelier(in) (-s, -e) m(f) jeweler

K

Kabel (-s, -) nt (*Elek*) wire; (*stark*) cable
Kabelfernsehen nt cable television
Kabeljau (-s, -e o -s) m cod
Kabine f cabin; (*im Schwimmbad*) cubicle
Kabrio (-s, -s) nt convertible
Kachel (-, -n) f tile
Kachelofen m tiled stove
Käfer (-s, -) m beetle, bug
Kaff (-s, -s) nt dump, hole
Kaffee (-s, -s) m coffee; ~ **kochen** to make some coffee
Kaffeefilter m coffee filter
Kaffeekanne f coffeepot
Kaffeeklatsch (-(e)s, -e) m chat over coffee and cakes, coffee klatch
Kaffeelöffel m coffee spoon
Kaffeemaschine f coffeemaker (o machine)
Kaffeetasse f coffee cup
Käfig (-s, -e) m cage
kahl adj (*Mensch, Kopf*) bald; (*Baum, Wand*) bare
Kahn (-(e)s, Kähne) m boat; (*Lastkahn*) barge
Kai (-s, -e o -s) m quay
Kaiser (-s, -) m emperor
Kaiserin f empress
Kaiserschnitt m (*Med*) cesarean (section)
Kajak (-s, -s) nt kayak
Kajakfahren nt kayaking
Kajal (-s) m kohl
Kajüte (-, -n) f cabin
Kakao (-s, -s) m cocoa; (*Getränk*) (hot) chocolate
Kakerlake (-, -n) f cockroach
Kaki (-) s f kaki
Kaktee (-, -n) f, **Kaktus** (-, -se) m cactus
Kalb (-(e)s, Kälber) nt calf
Kalbfleisch nt veal
Kalbsbraten m roast veal
Kalbsschnitzel nt veal cutlet; (*paniert*) escalope of veal
Kalender (-s, -) m calendar; (*Taschenkalender*) diary
Kalk (-(e)s, -e) m lime; (*in Knochen*) calcium
Kalorie f calorie
kalorienarm adj low-calorie
kalt adj cold; **mir ist es ~** I'm cold
kaltblütig adj cold-blooded
Kälte (-) f cold; (*fig*) coldness
kam imperf von **kommen**
Kambodscha (-s) nt Cambodia
Kamel (-(e)s, -e) nt camel

Kamera (-, -s) f camera
Kamerad(in) (-en, -en) m(f) friend; (*als Begleiter*) companion
Kamerafrau f, **Kameramann** m camerawoman/-man
Kamerahandy nt camera phone
Kamille (-, -n) f camomile
Kamillentee m camomile tea
Kamin (-s, -e) m (*außen*) chimney; (*innen*) fireplace
Kamm (-(e)s, Kämme) m comb; (*Berg*) ridge; (*Hahn*) crest
kämmen vr: **sich ~**, **sich** (dat) **die Haare ~** to comb one's hair
Kammermusik f chamber music
Kampf (-(e)s, Kämpfe) m fight; (*Schlacht*) battle; (*Wettbewerb*) contest; (*fig: Anstrengung*) struggle
kämpfen vi to fight (*für, um* for)
Kampfsport m martial art
Kanada (-s) nt Canada
Kanadier(in) (-s, -) m(f) Canadian
kanadisch adj Canadian
Kanal (-s, Kanäle) m (*Fluss*) canal; (*Rinne, TV*) channel; (*für Abfluss*) drain; **der ~** (*Ärmelkanal*) the (English) Channel
Kanalinseln pl Channel Islands pl
Kanalisation f sewer system
Kanarienvogel m canary
Kandidat(in) (-en, -en) m(f) candidate
Kandis(zucker) (-) m rock candy
Känguru (-s, -s) nt kangaroo
Kaninchen nt rabbit
Kanister (-s, -) m can
Kännchen nt pot; **ein ~ Kaffee/Tee** a pot of coffee/tea
Kanne (-, -n) f (*Krug*) jug; (*Kaffeekanne*) pot; (*Milchkanne*) creamer; (*Gießkanne*) watering can
kannte imperf von **kennen**
Kante (-, -n) f edge
Kantine f cafeteria
Kanton (-s, -e) m canton
Kanu (-s, -s) nt canoe
Kanzler(in) (-s, -) m(f) chancellor
Kap (-s, -s) nt cape
Kapazität f capacity; (*Fachmann*) authority
Kapelle f (*Gebäude*) chapel; (*Mus*) band
Kaper (-s, -) f caper
kapieren vt, vi (*fam*) to understand; **kapiert?** got it?
Kapital (-s, -e o -ien) nt capital

Kapitän (-s, -e) m captain
Kapitel (-s, -) nt chapter
Kappe (-, -n) f cap
Kapsel (-, -n) f capsule
kaputt adj (fam) broken; (Mensch) exhausted
kaputt|gehen (irr) vi to break; (Schuhe) to fall apart; (Firma) to go bust; (Stoff) to wear out
kaputt|machen vt to break; (jdn) to wear out
Kapuze (-, -n) f hood
Kap Verde (-s) nt Cape Verde
Karaffe (-, -n) f carafe; (mit Stöpsel) decanter
Karamell (-s) m caramel, taffy
Karaoke (-(s)) nt karaoke
Karat (-s, -e) nt karat
Karate (-s) nt karate
Kardinal (-s, Kardinäle) m cardinal
Karfreitag m Good Friday
kariert adj checked; (Papier) squared
Karies (-) f (tooth) decay; (fam) cavities pl
Karikatur f caricature
Karneval (-s, -e o -s) m carnival, Mardi Gras

Karneval is the name given to the days immediately before Lent when people gather to sing, dance, eat, drink and generally make merry before the fasting begins. **Rosenmontag**, the day before Shrove Tuesday, is the most important day of 'Karneval' on the Rhine. Most companies close for the day and allow their employees to enjoy the parades and revelry. In South Germany 'Karneval' is called **Fasching**.

Kärnten (-s) nt Carinthia
Karo (-s, -s) nt square; (Karten) diamonds pl
Karosserie f (Auto) body(work)
Karotte (-, -n) f carrot
Karpfen (-s, -) m carp
Karriere (-, -n) f career
Karte (-, -n) f card; (Landkarte) map; (Speisekarte) menu; (Eintrittskarte, Fahrkarte) ticket; **mit ~ bezahlen** to pay with (a) credit card; **~n spielen** to play cards; **die ~n mischen/geben** to shuffle/deal the cards
Kartei f card catalog
Karteikarte f index card
Kartenspiel nt card game

Kartoffel (-, -n) f potato
Kartoffelbrei m mashed potatoes pl
Kartoffelchips pl chips pl
Kartoffelpuffer m potato pancake, latke
Kartoffelpüree nt mashed potatoes pl
Kartoffelsalat m potato salad
Karton (-s, -s) m cardboard; (Schachtel) (cardboard) box
Kartusche (-, -n) f cartridge
Karussell (-s, -s) nt merry-go-round
Kaschmir (-s, e) m (Stoff) cashmere
Käse (-s, -) m cheese
Käsekuchen m cheesecake
Käseplatte f cheeseboard
Kasino (-s, -s) nt (Spielkasino) casino
Kaskoversicherung f comprehensive insurance
Kasper(l) (-s, -) m Punch; (fig) clown
Kasperl(e)theater nt (Vorstellung) puppet show; (Gebäude) puppet theater
Kasse (-, -n) f (in Geschäft) till, cash register; (im Supermarkt) checkout; (Geldkasten) cashbox; (Theater) box office; (Kino) ticket office; (Krankenkasse) health insurance company; (Sparkasse) savings bank
Kassenbon (-s, -s) m, **Kassenzettel** m receipt
Kassenzettel m receipt
Kassette f (small) box; (Tonband) cassette
Kassettenrekorder m cassette recorder
kassieren vt to take ▷ vi: **darf ich ~?** would you like to pay now?
Kassierer(in) m(f) cashier
Kastanie f chestnut
Kasten (-s, Kästen) m (Behälter) box; (Getränkekasten) crate
Kat m (abk) = **Katalysator**
Katalog (-(e)s, -e) m catalog(ue)
Katalysator m (Auto) catalytic converter; (Phys) catalyst
Katar (-s) nt Qatar
Katarr(h) (-s, -e) m catarrh
Katastrophe (-, -n) f catastrophe, disaster
Kategorie (-, -n) f category
Kater (-s, -) m tomcat; (fam: nach zu viel Alkohol) hangover
Kathedrale (-, -n) f cathedral
Katholik(in) m(f) Catholic
katholisch adj Catholic
Katze (-, -n) f cat
Kauderwelsch (-(s)) nt (unverständlich) gibberish; (Fachjargon) jargon
kauen vt, vi to chew
Kauf (-(e)s, Käufe) m purchase; (Kaufen) buying; **ein guter ~** a bargain; **etw in ~**

nehmen to put up with sth
kaufen vt to buy
Käufer(in) m(f) buyer
Kauffrau f businesswoman
Kaufhaus nt department store
Kaufmann m businessman; (im Einzelhandel) storekeeper
Kaufpreis m purchase price
Kaufvertrag m purchase agreement
Kaugummi m chewing gum
Kaulquappe (-, -n) f tadpole
kaum adv hardly, scarcely
Kaution f deposit; (Jur) bail
Kaviar m caviar
KB (-, -) nt, **Kbyte** (-, -) nt (abk) = **Kilobyte** KB
Kebab (-(s), -s) m kebab
Kegel (-s, -) m (beim Bowling) pin; (Math) cone
Kegelbahn f bowling alley
kegeln vi to play skittles; (bowlen) to bowl
Kehle (-, -n) f throat
Kehlkopf m larynx
Kehre (-, -n) f sharp bend
kehren vt (fegen) to sweep
Keilriemen m (Auto) fan belt
kein pron no, not ... any; **ich habe ~ Geld** I have no money, I don't have money; **~ Mensch** no one; **du bist ~ Kind mehr** you're not a child any more
keine(r, s) pron (Person) no one, nobody; (Sache) not ... any, none; **~r von ihnen** none of them; (bei zwei Personen/Sachen) neither of them; **ich will keins von beiden** I don't want either (of them)
keinesfalls adv on no account, under no circumstances
Keks (-es, -e) m cookie; **jdm auf den ~ gehen** (fam) to get on sb's nerves
Keller (-s, -) m cellar; (Geschoss) basement
Kellner (-s, -) m waiter
Kellnerin f waitress
Kenia (-s) nt Kenya
kennen (kannte, gekannt) vt to know; **wir ~ uns seit 1990** we've known each other since 1990; **wir ~ uns schon** we've already met; **kennst du mich noch?** do you remember me?
kennen|lernen vt to get to know; **sich ~** to get to know each other; (zum ersten Mal) to meet
Kenntnis f knowledge; **seine ~se** his knowledge
Kennwort nt (auch Inform) password
Kennzeichen nt mark, sign; (Auto) license

plate; **besondere ~** distinguishing marks
Kerl (-s, -e) m guy
Kern (-(e)s, -e) m (Obst) seed; (Pfirsich, Kirsche etc) pit; (Nuss) kernel; (Atomkern) nucleus; (fig) heart, core
Kernenergie f nuclear energy
Kernkraft f nuclear power
Kernkraftwerk nt nuclear power plant
Kerze (-, -n) f candle; (Zündkerze) plug
Ket(s)chup (-(s), -s) m o nt ketchup
Kette (-, -n) f chain; (Halskette) necklace
keuchen vi to pant
Keuchhusten m whooping cough
Keule (-, -n) f club; (Gastr) leg; (von Hähnchen a.) drumstick
Keyboard (-s, -s) nt (Mus) keyboard
Kfz nt (abk) = **Kraftfahrzeug**
Kfz-Brief m ≈ (vehicle) title
Kfz-Steuer f ≈ vehicle tax
KG (-, -s) f (abk) = **Kommanditgesellschaft** limited partnership
Kichererbse f chick pea
kichern vi to giggle
Kickboard® (-s, -s) nt micro scooter
Kicker (-s, -) m (Spiel) foosball
kidnappen vt to kidnap
Kidney-Bohne f kidney bean
Kiefer (-s, -) m jaw ▷ (-, -n) f pine
Kieferchirurg(in) m(f) oral surgeon
Kieme (-, -n) f gill
Kies (-es, -e) m gravel
Kiesel (-s, -) m, **Kieselstein** m pebble
kiffen vi (fam) to smoke pot
Kilo (-s, -(s)) nt kilo
Kilobyte nt kilobyte
Kilogramm nt kilogram
Kilometer m kilometer
Kilometerstand m ≈ mileage
Kilometerzähler m ≈ odometer
Kilowatt nt kilowatt
Kind (-(e)s, -er) nt child; **sie bekommt ein ~** she's having a baby
Kinderarzt m, **Kinderärztin** f pediatrician
Kinderbetreuung f childcare
Kinderbett nt crib
Kinderfahrkarte f child's ticket
Kindergarten m nursery school, preschool
Kindergärtner(in) m(f) nursery-school teacher
Kinderkrankheit f children's illness
Kinderkrippe f daycare center
Kinderlähmung f polio
Kindermädchen nt nanny, au pair
kindersicher adj childproof
Kindersicherung f childproof safety catch;

(an Flasche) childproof cap

Kindertagesstätte nt daycare center

Kinderteller m (im Restaurant) children's portion

Kinderwagen m baby carriage

Kinderzimmer nt children's (bed)room

Kindheit f childhood

kindisch adj childish

kindlich adj childlike

Kinn (-(e)s, -e) nt chin

Kino (-s, -s) nt movie theater; **ins ~ gehen** to go to the movies

Kiosk (-(e)s, -e) m kiosk

Kippe f (fam: Zigarettenstummel) cigarette butt

kippen vi to tip over ▷ vt to tilt; (Regierung, Minister) to topple

Kirche (-, -n) f church

Kirchturm m church tower; (mit Spitze) steeple

Kirchweih f fair

Kirmes (-, -sen) f fair

Kirsche (-, -n) f cherry

Kirschtomate f cherry tomato

Kissen (-s, -) nt cushion; (Kopfkissen) pillow

Kissenbezug m cushion cover; (für Kopfkissen) pillowcase

Kiste (-, -n) f box; (Truhe) chest

KITA (-, -s) f (abk) = **Kindertagesstätte** daycare center

kitschig adj kitschy, cheesy

kitzelig adj (a. fig) ticklish

kitzeln vt, vi to tickle

Kiwi (-, -s) f (Frucht) kiwi (fruit)

Klage (-, -n) f complaint; (Jur) lawsuit

klagen vi to complain (über +akk about, bei to)

kläglich adj wretched

Klammer (-, -n) f (in Text: rund) parenthesis; (eckig) bracket; (Büroklammer) paper clip; (Wäscheklammer) clothespin; (Zahnklammer) brace

Klammeraffe m (fam) at-sign, @

klammern vr: **sich ~** to cling (an +akk to)

Klamotten pl (fam: Kleider) clothes pl

klang imperf von klingen

Klang (-(e)s, Klänge) m sound

Klappbett nt cot, folding bed

klappen vi impers (gelingen) to work; **es hat gut geklappt** it went well

klappern vi to rattle; (Geschirr) to clatter

Klapperschlange f rattlesnake

Klappfahrad nt folding bicycle

Klappstuhl m folding chair

klar adj clear; **sich** (dat) **im K~en sein** to be clear (über +akk about); **alles ~?** everything okay?

klären vt (Flüssigkeit) to purify; (Probleme, Frage) to clarify ▷ vr: **sich ~** to clear itself up

Klarinette (-, -n) f clarinet

klar|kommen (irr) vi: **mit etw ~** to cope with something; **kommst du klar?** are you managing all right?; **mit jdm ~** to get along with sb

klar|machen vt: **jdm etw ~** to make sth clear to sb

klar|stellen vt to clarify

Klärung f (von Frage, Problem) clarification

klasse adj (inv) (fam) great, terrific

Klasse (-, -n) f class; (Schuljahr) grade; **erster ~ reisen** to travel first class; **in welche ~ gehst du?** which grade are you in?

Klassenarbeit f test

Klassenlehrer(in) m(f) class teacher

Klassenzimmer nt classroom

Klassik f (Zeit) classical period; (Musik) classical music

Klatsch (-(e)s, -e) m (Gerede) gossip

klatschen vi (schlagen) to smack; (Beifall) to applaud, to clap; (reden) to gossip

Klatschmohn m (corn) poppy

klatschnass adj soaking (wet)

Klaue (-, -n) f claw; (fam: Schrift) scrawl

klauen vt (fam) to steal

Klavier (-s, -e) nt piano

Klebeband nt adhesive tape

kleben vt to stick (an +akk to) ▷ vi (klebrig sein) to be sticky

klebrig adj sticky

Klebstoff m glue

Klebstreifen m adhesive tape

Klecks (-es, -e) m blob; (Tinte) blot

Klee (-s) m clover

Kleid (-(e)s, -er) nt (Frauenkleid) dress; **~er** pl (Kleidung) clothes pl

Kleiderbügel m coat hanger

Kleiderschrank m closet

Kleidung f clothing

klein adj small, little; (Finger) little; **mein ~er Bruder** my little (o younger) brother; **als ich noch ~ war** when I was a little boy/girl; **etw ~ schneiden** to chop sth up

Kleinanzeige f classified ad

Kleinbuchstabe m small letter

Kleinbus m minibus

Kleingeld nt change

Kleinigkeit f detail, small matter; (Zwi-

schenmahlzeit) snack
Kleinkind *nt* toddler
klein|schreiben *vt* (*mit kleinem Anfangs-buchstaben*) to lowercase, to write in lowercase letters
Kleinstadt *f* small town
Kleister (*-s, -*) *m* paste
Klempner(in) *m(f)* plumber
klettern *vi* to climb
Klettverschluss *m* Velcro® fastening
klicken *vi* (*auch Inform*) to click
Klient(in) (*-en, -en*) *m(f)* client
Klima (*-s, -s*) *nt* climate
Klimaanlage *f* air conditioning
klimatisiert *adj* air-conditioned
Klinge (*-, -n*) *f* blade
Klingel (*-, -n*) *f* bell
klingeln *vi* to ring
klingen (**klang, geklungen**) *vi* to sound
Klinik *f* clinic; (*Krankenhaus*) hospital
Klinke (*-, -n*) *f* handle
Klippe (*-, -n*) *f* cliff; (*im Meer*) reef; (*fig*) hurdle
Klischee (*-s, -s*) *nt* (*fig*) cliché
Klo (*-s, -s*) *nt* (*fam*) john
Klobrille *f* toilet seat
Klopapier *nt* toilet paper
klopfen *vt, vi* to knock; (*Herz*) to thump
Kloß (*-es, Klöße*) *m* (*im Hals*) lump; (*Gastr*) dumpling
Kloster (*-s, Klöster*) *nt* (*für Männer*) monastery; (*für Frauen*) convent
Klub (*-s, -s*) *m* club
klug *adj* clever
knabbern *vt, vi* to nibble
Knäckebrot *nt* crispbread
knacken *vt, vi* to crack
Knall (*-(e)s, -e*) *m* bang
knallen *vi* to bang
knapp *adj* (*kaum ausreichend*) scarce; (*Sieg*) narrow; **das war ~** that was close (*o* a close call); **~ bei Kasse sein** to be short of money; **~ zwei Stunden** just under two hours
Knauf (*-s, Knäufe*) *m* knob
kneifen (**kniff, gekniffen**) *vt, vi* to pinch; (*sich drücken*) to back out (*vor +dat* of)
Kneifzange *f* pincers *pl*
Kneipe (*-, -n*) *f* (*fam*) bar
Knete (*-*) *f* (*fam: Geld*) dough
kneten *vt* to knead; (*formen*) to mold
knicken *vt, vi* (*brechen*) to break; (*Papier*) to fold; **geknickt sein** (*fig*) to be downcast
Knie (*-s, -*) *nt* knee; **in die ~ gehen** to bend one's knees

Kniebeuge *f* knee bend
Kniegelenk *nt* knee joint
Kniekehle *f* back of the knee
knien *vi* to kneel
Kniescheibe *f* kneecap
Knieschoner (*-s, -*) *m*, **Knieschützer** (*-s, -*) *m* knee pad
Kniestrumpf *m* kneesock
kniff *imperf von* **kneifen**
knipsen *vt* to punch; (*Foto*) to snap ▷ *vi* (*Foto*) to take snaps
knirschen *vi* to crunch; **mit den Zähnen ~** to grind one's teeth
knitterfrei *adj* wrinkle-free, non-iron
knittern *vi* to wrinkle
Knoblauch *m* garlic
Knoblauchbrot *nt* garlic bread
Knoblauchzehe *f* clove of garlic
Knöchel (*-s, -*) *m* (*Finger*) knuckle; (*Fuß*) ankle
Knochen (*-s, -*) *m* bone
Knochenbruch *m* fracture
Knochenmark *nt* marrow
Knödel (*-s, -*) *m* dumpling
Knollensellerie *m* celeriac
Knopf (*-(e)s, Knöpfe*) *m* button
Knopfdruck *m*: **auf ~** at the touch of a button
Knopfloch *nt* buttonhole
Knospe (*-, -n*) *f* bud
knoten *vt* to knot
Knoten (*-s, -*) *m* knot; (*Med*) lump
Know-how (*-(s)*) *nt* know-how, expertise
knurren *vi* (*Hund*) to growl; (*Magen*) to rumble; (*Mensch*) to grumble
knusprig *adj* crisp; (*Keks*) crunchy
knutschen *vi* (*fam*) to smooch
k. o. *adj* (*inv*) (*Sport*) knocked out
Koalition *f* coalition
Koch (*-(e)s, Köche*) *m* cook
Kochbuch *nt* cookbook
kochen *vt, vi* to cook; (*Wasser*) to boil; (*Kaffee, Tee*) to make
Köchin *f* cook
Kochlöffel *m* wooden spoon
Kochnische *f* kitchenette
Kochplatte *f* hotplate; (*Heizplatte*) burner
Kochrezept *nt* recipe
Kochtopf *m, pot* saucepan
Kode (*-s, -s*) *m* code
Köder (*-s, -*) *m* bait
Koffein (*-s*) *nt* caffeine
koffeinfrei *adj* decaffeinated
Koffer (*-s, -*) *m* (suit)case
Kofferraum *m* (*Aut*) trunk

Kognak (*-s, -s*) *m* brandy

Kohl (*-(e)s, -e*) *m* cabbage

Kohle (*-, -n*) *f* coal; (*Holzkohle*) charcoal; (*Chem*) carbon; (*fam: Geld*) cash, dough

Kohlehydrat *nt* carbohydrate

Kohlendioxid *nt* carbon dioxide

Kohlensäure *f* (*in Getränken*) fizz; **ohne ~** still, non-carbonated; **mit ~** sparkling, carbonated

Kohletablette *f* charcoal tablet

Kohlrabi (*-(s), -(s)*) *m* kohlrabi

Koje (*-, -n*) *f* cabin; (*Bett*) bunk

Kokain (*-s*) *nt* cocaine

Kokosnuss *f* coconut

Kolben (*-s, -*) *m* (*Tech*) piston; (*Maiskolben*) cob

Kolik (*-, -en*) *f* colic

Kollaps (*-es, -e*) *m* collapse

Kollege (*-n, -n*) *m*, **Kollegin** *f* co-worker; (*Berufskollege*) colleague

Köln (*-s*) *nt* Cologne

Kölnischwasser *nt* eau de Cologne

Kolonne (*-, -n*) *f* convoy; **in ~ fahren** to drive in convoy

Kölsch (*-, -*) *nt* (*Bier*) (strong) beer (*from the Cologne region*)

Kolumbien (*-s*) *nt* Columbia

Koma (*-s, -s*) *nt* coma

Kombi (*-(s), -s*) *m* station wagon

Kombination *f* combination; (*Folgerung*) deduction; (*Hemdhose*) combinations *pl*; (*Aviat*) flying suit

kombinieren *vt* to combine ▷ *vi* to reason; (*vermuten*) to guess

Kombizange *f* (pair of) pliers *pl*

Komfort (*-s*) *m* conveniences *pl*; (*Bequemlichkeit*) comfort

Komiker(in) *m(f)* comedian, comic

komisch *adj* funny

Komma (*-s, -s*) *nt* comma

Kommanditgesellschaft *f* limited partnership

kommen (**kam, gekommen**) *vi* to come; (*näher kommen*) to approach; (*passieren*) to happen; (*gelangen, geraten*) to get; (*erscheinen*) to appear; (*in die Schule, das Gefängnis etc*) to go; **~ lassen** to send for; **zu sich ~** to come around (*o* to); **zu etw ~** (*bekommen*) to acquire sth; (*Zeit dazu finden*) to get around to sth; **wer kommt zuerst?** who's first?

kommend *adj* coming; **~e Woche** next week; **in den ~en Jahren** in the years to come

Kommentar *m* commentary; **kein ~** no comment

Kommilitone (*-n, -n*) *m*, **Kommilitonin** *f* fellow student

Kommissar(in) *m(f)* inspector

Kommode (*-, -n*) *f* chest of drawers; (*im Schlafzimmer*) dresser, bureau

Kommunikation *f* communication

Kommunion *f* (*Rel*) communion

Kommunismus *m* communism

Komödie *f* comedy

kompakt *adj* compact

Kompass (*-es, -e*) *m* compass

kompatibel *adj* compatible

kompetent *adj* competent

komplett *adj* complete

Kompliment *nt* compliment; **jdm ein ~ machen** to pay sb a compliment; **~! congratulations!**

Komplize (*-n, -n*) *m* accomplice

kompliziert *adj* complicated

Komponist(in) *m(f)* composer

Kompost (*-(e)s, -e*) *m* compost

Komposthaufen *m* compost pile

kompostierbar *adj* biodegradable

Kompott (*-(e)s, -e*) *nt* stewed fruit

Kompresse (*-, -n*) *f* compress

Kompromiss (*-es, -e*) *m* compromise

Kondensmilch *f* evaporated milk; (*süß*) condensed milk

Kondition *f* (*Leistungsfähigkeit*) condition; **sie hat eine gute ~** she's in good shape

Konditorei *f* pastry shop

Kondom (*-s, -e*) *nt* condom

Konfektionsgröße *f* size

Konferenz *f* conference

Konfession *f* religion; (*christlich*) denomination

Konfetti (*-(s)*) *nt* confetti

Konfirmation *f* (*Rel*) confirmation

Konfitüre (*-, -n*) *f* jam

Konflikt (*-(e)s, -e*) *m* conflict

konfrontieren *vt* to confront

Kongo (*-s*) *m* Congo

Kongress (*-es, -e*) *m* conference; **der ~** (*Parlament der USA*) Congress

König (*-(e)s, -e*) *m* king

Königin *f* queen

königlich *adj* royal

Königreich *nt* kingdom

Konkurrenz *f* competition

SCHLÜSSELWORT

können (*pt* **konnte**, *pp* **gekonnt** *o* (*als Hilfsverb*) **können**) *vt, vi* **1** to be able to; **ich kann es machen** I can do it, I am able to do it; **ich kann es nicht machen** I can't do it, I'm not able to do it; **ich kann nicht ...** I can't ..., I cannot ...; **ich kann nicht mehr** I can't go on

2 (*wissen, beherrschen*) to know; **können Sie Deutsch?** can you speak German?; **er kann gut Englisch** he speaks English well; **sie kann keine Mathematik** she can't do mathematics

3 (*dürfen*) to be allowed to; **kann ich gehen?** can I go?; **könnte ich ...?** could I ...?; **kann ich mit?** (*fam*) can I come with you?

4 (*möglich sein*): **Sie könnten recht haben** you may be right; **das kann sein** that's possible; **kann sein** maybe

konsequent *adj* consistent
Konsequenz *f* consequence
konservativ *adj* conservative
Konserven *pl* canned food *sing*
Konservendose *f* can
konservieren *vt* to preserve
Konservierungsmittel *nt* preservative
Konsonant *m* consonant
Konsul(in) (*-s, -n*) *m(f)* consul
Konsulat *nt* consulate
Kontakt (*-(e)s, -e*) *m* contact
kontaktarm *adj*: **er ist ~** he lacks contact with other people
kontaktfreudig *adj* sociable
Kontaktlinsen *pl* contact lenses *pl*
Kontinent *m* continent
Konto (*-s, Konten*) *nt* account
Kontoauszug *m* (bank) statement
Kontoauszugsdrucker *m* *machine that prints one's bank statement*
Kontoinhaber(in) *m(f)* account holder
Kontonummer *f* account number
Kontostand *m* balance
Kontrabass *m* double bass
Kontrast (*-(e)s, -e*) *m* contrast
Kontrolle (*-, -n*) *f* control; (*Aufsicht*) supervision
kontrollieren *vt* to control; (*nachprüfen*) to check
Konzentration *f* concentration
Konzentrationslager *nt* (*Hist*) concentration camp
konzentrieren *vt* to concentrate ▷ *vr*: **sich ~** to concentrate
Konzept (*-(e)s, -e*) *nt* rough draft; **jdn aus dem ~ bringen** to throw sb off
Konzern (*-(e)s, -e*) *m* company
Konzert (*-(e)s, -e*) *nt* concert; (*Stück*) concerto

Konzertsaal *m* concert hall
koordinieren *vt* to coordinate
Kopf (*-(e)s, Köpfe*) *m* head; **pro ~** per person; **sich den ~ zerbrechen** to rack one's brains
Kopfhörer *m* headphones *pl*
Kopfkissen *nt* pillow
Kopfsalat *m* lettuce
Kopfschmerzen *pl* headache *sing*
Kopfstütze *f* headrest
Kopftuch *nt* headscarf
kopfüber *adv* headfirst
Kopie *f* copy
kopieren *vt* (*auch Inform*) to copy
Kopierer (*-s, -*) *m*, **Kopiergerät** *nt* copier
Kopilot(in) *m(f)* co-pilot
Koralle (*-, -n*) *f* coral
Koran (*-s*) *m* (*Rel*) Koran
Korb (*-(e)s, Körbe*) *m* basket; **jdm einen ~ geben** (*fig*) to turn sb down
Kord (*-(e)s, -e*) *m* corduroy
Kordel (*-, -n*) *f* cord
Kork (*-(e)s, -e*) *m* cork
Korken (*-s, -*) *m* cork
Korkenzieher (*-s, -*) *m* corkscrew
Korn (*-(e)s, Körner*) *nt* grain
Kornblume *f* cornflower
Körper (*-s, -*) *m* body
Körperbau *m* build
Körpergeruch *m* body odor
Körpergröße *f* height
körperlich *adj* physical
Körperteil *m* part of the body
Körperverletzung *f* physical injury
korrekt *adj* correct
Korrespondent(in) *m(f)* correspondent
Korrespondenz *f* correspondence
korrigieren *vt* to correct
Kosmetik *f* cosmetics *pl*
Kosmetikkoffer *m* vanity case
Kosmetiksalon *m* beauty parlor
Kosmetiktuch *nt* paper tissue
Kost (*-*) *f* (*Nahrung*) food; (*Verpflegung*) board
kostbar *adj* precious; (*teuer*) costly, expensive
kosten *vt* to cost ▷ *vt, vi* (*versuchen*) to taste
Kosten *pl* costs *pl* cost; (*Ausgaben*) expenses *pl*; **auf ~ von** at the expense of
kostenlos *adj* free (of charge)
Kostenvoranschlag *m* estimate
köstlich *adj* (*Essen*) delicious; (*Einfall*) delightful; **sich ~ amüsieren** to have a marvelous time

k

Kostprobe f taster; (fig) sample
kostspielig adj expensive
Kostüm (-s, -e) nt costume; (Damenkostüm) suit
Kot (-(e)s) m excrement
Kotelett (-(e)s, -e o -s) nt chop, cutlet
Koteletten pl sideburns pl
Kotflügel m (Auto) wing
Krabbe (-, -n) f shrimp; (Krebs) crab
krabbeln vi to crawl
Krach (-(e)s, -s o -e) m crash; (andauernd) noise; (fam: Streit) fight
Kraft (-, Kräfte) f strength; (Pol, Phys) force; (Fähigkeit) power; (Arbeitskraft) worker; **in ~ treten** to come into effect
Kraftausdruck m swearword
Kraftfahrzeug nt motor vehicle
Kraftfahrzeugbrief m ≈ (vehicle) title
Kraftfahrzeugschein m vehicle registration document
Kraftfahrzeugsteuer f ≈ vehicle tax
Kraftfahrzeugversicherung f car insurance
kräftig adj strong; (gesund) healthy; (Farben) intense, strong
Kraftstoff m fuel
Kraftwerk nt power plant
Kragen (-s, -) m collar
Krähe (-, -n) f crow
Kralle (-, -n) f claw; (Parkkralle) Denver boot
Kram (-(e)s) m stuff
Krampf (-(e)s, Krämpfe) m cramp; (zuckend) spasm
Krampfader f varicose vein
Kran (-(e)s, Kräne) m crane
Kranich (-s, -e) m (Zool) crane
krank adj ill, sick
kränken vt to hurt
Krankengymnastik f physical therapy
Krankenhaus nt hospital
Krankenkasse f health insurance company
Krankenpfleger (-s, -) m (male) nurse
Krankenschein m health insurance certificate
Krankenschwester f nurse
Krankenversicherung f health insurance; (Unternehmen) health insurance company
Krankenwagen m ambulance
Krankheit f illness; (durch Infektion hervorgerufen) disease
Kränkung f insult
Kranz (-es, Kränze) m wreath
krass adj crass; (fam: toll) cool

kratzen vt, vi to scratch
Kratzer (-s, -) m scratch
kraulen vi (schwimmen) to do the crawl ▷ vt (streicheln) to pet
Kraut (-(e)s, Kräuter) nt plant; (Gewürz) herb; (Gemüse) cabbage
Kräuter pl herbs pl
Kräuterbutter f herb butter
Kräutertee m herbal tea
Krautsalat m coleslaw
Krawatte f tie
kreativ adj creative
Krebs (-es, -e) m (Zool) crab; (Med) cancer; (Astr) Cancer
Kredit (-(e)s, -e) m credit; **auf ~** on credit; **einen ~ aufnehmen** to take out a loan
Kreditkarte f credit card
Kreide (-, -n) f chalk
Kreis (-es, -e) m circle; (Bezirk) district
kreischen vi to shriek; (Bremsen, Säge) to screech
Kreisel (-s, -) m (Spielzeug) top; (Verkehrskreisel) traffic circle
Kreislauf m (Med) circulation; (fig: der Natur etc) cycle
Kreislaufstörungen pl (Med): **ich habe ~** I've got problems with my circulation
Kreisverkehr m traffic circle
Kren (-s) m horseradish
Kresse (-, -n) f cress
Kreuz (-es, -e) nt cross; (Anat) small of the back; (Karten) clubs pl; **mir tut das ~ weh** I've got backache
Kreuzband m cruciate ligament
kreuzen vt to cross ▷ vr: **sich ~** to cross ▷ vi (Naut) to cruise
Kreuzfahrt f cruise
Kreuzgang m cloisters pl
Kreuzotter (-, -n) f adder
Kreuzschlitzschraubenzieher m Phillips screwdriver
Kreuzschlüssel m (Auto) lug wrench
Kreuzschmerzen pl backache sing
Kreuzung f (Verkehrskreuzung) crossroads sing, intersection; (Züchtung) cross
Kreuzworträtsel nt crossword (puzzle)
kriechen (kroch, gekrochen) vi to crawl; (unauffällig) to creep; (fig, pej): **vor jdm ~** to crawl (to sb)
Krieg (-(e)s, -e) m war
kriegen vt (fam) to get; (erwischen) to catch; **sie kriegt ein Kind** she's having a baby; **ich kriege noch Geld von dir** you still owe me some money
Krimi (-s, -s) m (fam) thriller

Kriminalität f criminality
Kriminalpolizei f detective force, ≈ FBI
Kriminalroman m detective novel
kriminell adj criminal
Krippe (-, -n) f (Futterkrippe) manger; (Weihnachtskrippe) crèche; (Kinderkrippe) daycare center
Krise (-, -n) f crisis
Kristall (-s, -e) m crystal ▷ (-s) nt (Glas) crystal
Kritik f criticism; (Rezension) review
Kritiker(in) m(f) critic
kritisch adj critical
kritzeln vt, vi to scribble, to scrawl
Kroate (-n, -n) m Croat
Kroatien (-s) nt Croatia
Kroatin f Croat
kroatisch adj Croatian
Kroatisch nt Croatian
kroch imperf von **kriechen**
Krokodil (-s, -e) nt crocodile
Krokus (-, - o -se) m crocus
Krone (-, -n) f crown
Kronleuchter m chandelier
Kropf (-(e)s, Kröpfe) m (Med) goiter; (von Vogel) crop
Kröte (-, -n) f toad
Krücke (-, -n) f crutch
Krug (-(e)s, Krüge) m jug; (Bierkrug) mug
Krümel (-s, -) m crumb
krumm adj crooked
Krüppel (-s, -) m cripple
Kruste (-, -n) f crust
Kruzifix (-es, -e) nt crucifix
Kuba (-s) nt Cuba
Kübel (-s, -) m tub; (Eimer) bucket
Kubikmeter m cubic meter
Küche (-, -n) f kitchen; (Kochen) cooking
Kuchen (-s, -) m cake; (mit Teigdeckel) pie
Kuchengabel f cake fork
Küchenmaschine f food processor
Küchenpapier nt paper towel
Küchenschrank m (kitchen) cupboard
Kuckuck (-s, -e) m cuckoo
Kugel (-, -n) f ball; (Math) sphere; (Mil) bullet; (Weihnachtskugel) ornament, ball
Kugellager nt ball bearing
Kugelschreiber m (ballpoint) pen
Kugelstoßen (-s) nt shot put
Kuh (-, Kühe) f cow
kühl adj cool
Kühlakku (-s, -s) m ice pack
Kühlbox f cooler
kühlen vt to cool
Kühler (-s, -) m (Auto) radiator

Kühlerhaube f (Auto) hood
Kühlschrank m refrigerator
Kühltasche f cool bag
Kühltruhe f freezer
Kühlwasser nt (Auto) radiator water
Kuhstall m cowshed
Küken (-s, -) nt chick
Kuli (-s, -s) m (fam: Kugelschreiber) pen
Kulisse (-, -n) f scenery
Kult (-s, -e) m cult
Kultfigur f cult figure
Kultur f culture; (Lebensform) civilization
Kulturbeutel m toiletry case (o bag)
kulturell adj cultural
Kümmel (-s, -) m caraway seeds pl
Kummer (-s) m grief, sorrow
kümmern vr: **sich um jdn ~** to look after sb; **sich um etw ~** to see to sth ▷ vt to concern; **das kümmert mich nicht** that doesn't worry me
Kumpel (-s, -) m (fam) pal, buddy
Kunde (-n, -n) m customer
Kundendienst m after-sales (o customer) service
Kunden(kredit)karte f store card, charge card
Kundennummer f customer number
kündigen vi to give one's notice; (Mieter) to give notice that one is moving out; **jdm ~** to give sb his/her notice; (Vermieter) to give sb notice to move out ▷ vt to cancel; (Vertrag) to terminate; **jdm die Stellung ~** to give sb his/her notice; **jdm die Wohnung ~** to give sb notice to move out
Kündigung f (Vertrag) termination; (a. Arbeitsverhältnis) dismissal; (Abonnement) cancellation; (Frist) notice
Kündigungsfrist f period of notice
Kundin f customer
Kundschaft f customers pl
künftig adj future
Kunst (-, Künste) f art; (Können) skill
Kunstausstellung f art exhibition
Kunstgewerbe nt arts and crafts pl
Künstler(in) (-s, -) m(f) artist
künstlerisch adj artistic
künstlich adj artificial
Kunststoff m synthetic material
Kunststück nt trick
Kunstwerk nt work of art
Kupfer (-s, -) nt copper
Kuppel (-, -n) f dome
kuppeln vi (Auto) to operate the clutch
Kupplung f coupling; (Auto) clutch
Kur (-, -en) f course of treatment; (am Kur-

ort) cure

Kür (-, -en) *f* (*Sport*) free program

Kurbel (-, -n) *f* crank; (*von Rollo, Fenster*) winder

Kürbis (-*ses*, -*se*) *m* pumpkin

Kurierdienst *m* courier service

kurieren *vt* to cure

Kurort *m* health resort

Kurs (-*es*, -*e*) *m* course; (*Fin*) rate; (*Wechselkurs*) exchange rate

kursiv *adj* italic ▷ *adv* in italics

Kursleiter(in) *m(f)* instructor

Kursteilnehmer(in) *m(f)* (course) participant

Kurswagen *m* (*Eisenb*) through car

Kurve (-, -n) *f* curve; (*Straßenkurve*) bend

kurvenreich *adj* (*Straße*) winding

kurz *adj* short; (*zeitlich a.*) brief; **~ vorher/ darauf** shortly before/after; **kannst du ~ kommen?** could you come here for a minute?; **~ gesagt** in short

kurzärmelig *adj* short-sleeved

kürzen *vt* to cut short; (*in der Länge*) to shorten; (*Gehalt*) to reduce

kurzerhand *adv* on the spot

kurzfristig *adj* short-term; **das Konzert wurde ~ abgesagt** the concert was called off at the last minute

Kurzgeschichte *f* short story

kurzhaarig *adj* short-haired

kürzlich *adv* recently

Kurzparkzone *f* short-term parking zone

Kurzschluss *m* (*Elek*) short circuit

kurzsichtig *adj* nearsighted; (*Denkweise*) short-sighted

Kurztrip *m* trip, break

Kurzurlaub *m* short vacation

Kurzwelle *f* short wave

Kusine *f* cousin

Kuss (-*es*, *Küsse*) *m* kiss

küssen *vt* to kiss ▷ *vr*: **sich ~** to kiss

Küste (-, -n) *f* coast; (*Ufer*) shore

Küstenwache *f* coastguard

Kutsche (-, -n) *f* carriage; (*geschlossene*) coach

Kuvert (-*s*, -*s*) *nt* envelope

Kuvertüre (-, -n) *f* glaze

Kuwait (-*s*) *nt* Kuwait

KZ (-*s*, -*s*) *nt* (*abk*) = **Konzentrationslager** (*Hist*) concentration camp

L

Labor (*-s, -e* o *-s*) *nt* lab
Labyrinth (*-s, -e*) *nt* maze
Lache (*-, -n*) *f* (*Pfütze*) puddle; (*Blutlache, Öllache*) pool
lächeln *vi* to smile
Lächeln (*-s*) *nt* smile
lachen *vi* to laugh
lächerlich *adj* ridiculous
Lachs (*-es, -e*) *m* salmon
Lack (*-(e)s, -e*) *m* varnish; (*Farblack*) lacquer; (*an Auto*) paint
lackieren *vt* to varnish; (*Auto*) to spray
Lackschaden *m* scratch (on the paintwork)
Ladegerät *nt* (battery) charger
laden (**lud, geladen**) *vt* (*auch Inform*) to load; (*einladen*) to invite; (*Handy etc*) to charge
Laden (*-s, Läden*) *m* store; (*Fensterladen*) shutter
Ladendieb(in) *m(f)* shoplifter
Ladendiebstahl *m* shoplifting
Ladenschluss *m* closing time
Ladung *f* load; (*Naut, Aviat*) cargo; (*Jur*) summons *sing*
lag *imperf von* **liegen**
Lage (*-, -n*) *f* position, situation; (*Schicht*) layer; **in der ~ sein zu** to be in a position to
Lager (*-s, -*) *nt* camp; (*Comm*) warehouse; (*Tech*) bearing
Lagerfeuer *nt* campfire
lagern *vi* (*Dinge*) to be stored; (*Menschen*) to camp ▷ *vt* to store
Lagune *f* lagoon
lahm *adj* lame; (*langweilig*) dull
lähmen *vt* to paralyze
Lähmung *f* paralysis
Laib (*-s, -e*) *m* loaf
Laie (*-n, -n*) *m* layman
Laken (*-s, -*) *nt* sheet
Lakritze (*-, -n*) *f* licorice
Lamm (*-(e)s, Lämmer*) *nt* (*a. Lammfleisch*) lamb
Lampe (*-, -n*) *f* lamp; (*Glühbirne*) bulb
Lampenfieber *nt* stage fright
Lampenschirm *m* lampshade
Lampion (*-s, -s*) *m* Chinese lantern
Land (*-(e)s, Länder*) *nt* (*Gelände*) land; (*Nation*) country; (*Bundesland*) state, Land; **auf dem ~(e)** in the country

LAND

A **Land** (plural **Länder**) is a member state of the **BRD**. There are 16 **Länder**, namely Baden-Württemberg, Bayern, Berlin, Brandenburg, Bremen, Hamburg, Hessen, Mecklenburg-Vorpommern, Niedersachsen, Nordrhein-Westfalen, Rheinland-Pfalz, Saarland, Sachsen, Sachsen-Anhalt, Schleswig-Holstein and Thüringen. Each 'Land' has its own parliament and constitution.

Landebahn *f* runway
landen *vt, vi* to land; (*Schiff*) to dock
Länderspiel *nt* international (match)
Landesgrenze *f* national border, frontier
Landesinnere *nt* interior
landesüblich *adj* customary
Landeswährung *f* national currency
landesweit *adj* nationwide
Landhaus *nt* country house
Landkarte *f* map
Landkreis *m* administrative region, ≈ county
ländlich *adj* rural
Landschaft *f* countryside; (*schöne*) scenery; (*Kunst*) landscape
Landstraße *f* country road
Landung *f* landing
Landungsbrücke *f*, **Landungssteg** *m* gangway
Landwirt(in) *m(f)* farmer
Landwirtschaft *f* agriculture, farming
landwirtschaftlich *adj* agricultural
lang *adj* long; (*Mensch*) tall; **ein zwei Meter ~er Tisch** a table two meters long; **den ganzen Tag ~** all day long; **die Straße ~** along the street
langärmelig *adj* long-sleeved
lange *adv* (for) a long time; **ich musste ~ warten** I had to wait (for) a long time; **ich bleibe nicht ~** I won't stay long; **es ist ~ her, dass wir uns gesehen haben** it's been a long time since we saw each other
Länge (*-, -n*) *f* length; (*Geo*) longitude
langen *vi* (*fam: ausreichen*) to be enough; (*fam: fassen*) to reach (*nach* for); **mir langt's** I've had enough
Langeweile *f* boredom
langfristig *adj* long-term ▷ *adv* in the long term

Langlauf m cross-country skiing

längs prep (+gen); **die Bäume ~ der Straße** the trees along(side) the road ▷ adv: **die Streifen laufen ~ über das Hemd** the stripes run lengthways down the shirt

langsam adj slow ▷ adv slowly

Langschläfer(in) (-s, -) m(f) late sleeper (o riser)

längst adv: **das ist ~ fertig** that was finished a long time ago; **sie sollte ~ da sein** she should have been here long ago; **als sie kam, waren wir ~ weg** when she arrived we had long since left

Langstreckenflug m long-haul flight

Languste (-, -n) f crayfish, crawfish

langweilen vt to bore; **ich langweile mich** I'm bored

langweilig adj boring

Langwelle f long wave

Laos (-) nt Laos

Lappen (-s, -) m cloth, rag; (Staublappen) dustcloth

läppisch adj silly; (Summe) ridiculous

Laptop (-s, -s) m laptop

Lärche (-, -n) f larch

Lärm (-(e)s) m noise

las imperf von **lesen**

Lasche (-, -n) f flap

Laser (-s, -) m laser

Laserdrucker m laser printer

SCHLÜSSELWORT

lassen (pt **ließ**, pp **gelassen** o (als Hilfsverb) **lassen**) vt **1** (unterlassen) to stop; (momentan) to leave; **lass das (sein)!** don't (do it)!; (hör auf!) stop it!; **lass mich!** leave me alone!; **lassen wir das!** let's leave it; **er kann das Trinken nicht lassen** he can't stop drinking

2 (zurücklassen) to leave; **etw lassen, wie es ist** to leave sth (just) as it is

3 (überlassen): **jdn ins Haus lassen** to let sb into the house

▷ vi: **lass mal, ich mache das schon** leave it, I'll do it

▷ Hilfsverb **1** (veranlassen): **etw machen lassen** to have o get sth done; **sich (dat) etw schicken lassen** ≈ to have sth sent (to one)

2 (zulassen): **jdn etw wissen lassen** to let sb know sth; **das Licht brennen lassen** to leave the light on; **jdn warten lassen** to keep sb waiting; **das lässt sich machen** that can be done

3: **lass uns gehen** let's go

lässig adj casual

Last (-, -en) f load; (Bürde) burden; (Naut, Aviat) cargo

Laster (-s, -) nt vice; (fam) truck

lästern vi: **über jdn/etw ~** to make nasty remarks about sb/sth

lästig adj annoying; (Person) tiresome

Last-Minute-Angebot nt last-minute offer

Last-Minute-Flug m last-minute flight

Last-Minute-Ticket nt last-minute ticket

Lastwagen m truck

Latein (-s) nt Latin

Laterne (-, -n) f lantern; (Straßenlaterne) streetlight

Latte (-, -n) f slat; (Sport) bar

Latz (-es, Lätze) m bib

Lätzchen nt bib

Latzhose f overalls pl

lau adj (Wind, Luft) mild

Laub (-(e)s) nt foliage

Laubfrosch m tree frog

Laubsäge f fretsaw

Lauch (-(e)s, -e) m leeks pl; **eine Stange ~** a leek

Lauchzwiebel f scallion

Lauf (-(e)s, Läufe) m run; (Wettlauf) race; (Entwicklung) course; (von Gewehr) barrel

Laufbahn f career

laufen (**lief**, **gelaufen**) vi, vt to run; (gehen) to walk; (funktionieren) to work; **mir läuft die Nase** my nose is running; **was läuft im Kino?** what's playing at the movie theater?; **wie läuft's so?** how are things?

laufend adj running; (Monat, Ausgaben) current; **auf dem L~en sein/halten** to be/to keep up-to-date

Läufer (-s, -) m (Teppich) rug; (Schach) bishop

Läufer(in) m(f) (Sport) runner

Laufmasche f run

Laufwerk nt (Inform) drive

Laune (-, -n) f mood; **gute/schlechte ~ haben** to be in a good/bad mood

launisch adj moody

Laus (-, Läuse) f louse

lauschen vi to listen; (heimlich) to eavesdrop

laut adj loud ▷ adv loudly; (lesen) aloud ▷ prep (+gen o dat) according to

läuten vt, vi to ring

lauter adv (fam: nichts als) nothing but

Lautsprecher m loudspeaker

Lautstärke f loudness; (Radio, TV) volume

lauwarm adj lukewarm

Lava (-, *Laven*) *f* lava

Lavendel (-s, -) *m* lavender

Lawine *f* avalanche

LCD-Anzeige *f* LCD-display

leasen *vt* to lease

Leasing (-s) *nt* leasing

leben *vt*, *vi* to live; (*am Leben sein*) to be alive; **wie lange ~ Sie schon hier?** how long have you been living here?; **von etw ~** (*Nahrungsmittel etc*) to live on sth; (*Beruf, Beschäftigung*) to make one's living from sth

Leben (-s, -) *nt* life

lebend *adj* living

lebendig *adj* alive; (*lebhaft*) lively

lebensgefährlich *adj* very dangerous; (*Verletzung*) critical

Lebensgefährte *m*, **Lebensgefährtin** *f* partner

Lebenshaltungskosten *pl* cost *sing* of living

lebenslänglich *adj* for life; **~ bekommen** to get life (*in prison*)

Lebenslauf *m* resumé

Lebensmittel *pl* food *sing*

Lebensmittelgeschäft *nt* grocery store

Lebensmittelvergiftung *f* food poisoning

lebensnotwendig *adj* vital

Lebensretter(in) *m(f)* rescuer

Lebensstandard *m* standard of living

Lebensunterhalt *m* livelihood

Lebensversicherung *f* life insurance

Lebenszeichen *nt* sign of life

Leber (-, -n) *f* liver

Leberfleck *m* mole

Leberpastete *f* liver pâté

Lebewesen *nt* living being

lebhaft *adj* lively; (*Erinnerung, Eindruck*) vivid

Lebkuchen *m* gingerbread; **ein ~** a piece of gingerbread

leblos *adj* lifeless

Leck *nt* leak

lecken *vi* (*Loch haben*) to leak ▷ *vt*, *vi* (*schlecken*) to lick

lecker *adj* delicious, tasty

Leder (-s, -) *nt* leather

ledig *adj* single

leer *adj* empty; (*Seite*) blank; (*Batterie*) dead

leeren *vt* to empty ▷ *vr*: **sich ~** to empty

Leerlauf *m* (*Gang*) neutral

Leertaste *f* space bar

Leerung *f* emptying; (*Briefkasten*) collection

Leerzeichen *nt* blank, space

legal *adj* legal, lawful

legen *vt* to put, to place; (*Eier*) to lay ▷ *vr*: **sich ~** to lie down; (*Sturm, Begeisterung*) to die down; (*Schmerz, Gefühl*) to wear off

Legende (-, -n) *f* legend

leger *adj* casual

Lehm (-(e)s, -e) *m* loam; (*Ton*) clay

Lehne (-, -n) *f* arm(rest); (*Rückenlehne*) back(rest)

lehnen *vt* to lean ▷ *vr*: **sich ~** to lean (*an/gegen +akk* against)

Lehnstuhl *m* armchair

Lehrbuch *nt* textbook

Lehre (-, -n) *f* teaching; (*beruflich*) apprenticeship; (*moralisch*) lesson

lehren *vt* to teach

Lehrer(in) (-s, -) *m(f)* teacher

Lehrgang *m* course

Lehrling *m* apprentice

lehrreich *adj* instructive

Leib (-(e)s, -er) *m* body

Leibgericht *nt*, **Leibspeise** *f* favorite dish

Leibwächter(in) *m(f)* bodyguard

Leiche (-, -n) *f* corpse

Leichenhalle *f* mortuary

Leichenwagen *m* hearse

leicht *adj* light; (*einfach*) easy, simple; (*Erkrankung*) slight; **es sich (*dat*) ~ machen** to take the easy way out ▷ *adv* (*mühelos, schnell*) easily; (*geringfügig*) slightly

Leichtathletik *f* track and field

leicht|fallen (*irr*) *vi*: **jdm ~** to be easy for sb

leichtsinnig *adj* careless; (*stärker*) reckless

leid *adj*: **jdn/etw ~ sein** to be tired of sb/sth

Leid (-(e)s) *nt* grief, sorrow

leiden (*litt, gelitten*) *vi*, *vt* to suffer (*an, unter +dat* from); **ich kann ihn/es nicht ~** I can't stand him/it

Leiden (-s, -) *nt* suffering; (*Krankheit*) illness

Leidenschaft *f* passion

leidenschaftlich *adj* passionate

leider *adv* unfortunately; **wir müssen jetzt ~ gehen** I'm afraid we have to go now; **~ ja/nein** I'm afraid so/not

leid|tun (*irr*) *vi*: **es tut mir/ihm leid** I'm/he's sorry; **er tut mir leid** I'm sorry for him

Leihbücherei *f* lending (*o* rental) library

leihen (*lieh, geliehen*) *vt*: **jdm etw ~** to lend sb sth; **sich (*dat*) etw von jdm ~** to borrow sth from sb

Leihfrist f lending period
Leihgebühr f (für Buch) lending charge
Leihwagen m rental car
Leim (-(e)s, -e) m glue
Leine (-, -n) f cord; (für Wäsche) line; (Hundeleine) leash
Leinen (-s, -) nt linen
Leintuch nt (für Bett) sheet
Leinwand f (Kunst) canvas; (Cine) screen
leise adj quiet; (sanft) soft ▷ adv quietly
Leiste (-, -n) f ledge; (Zierleiste) strip; (Anat) groin
leisten vt (Arbeit) to do; (vollbringen) to achieve; **jdm Gesellschaft ~** to keep sb company; **sich** (dat) **etw ~** (gönnen) to treat oneself to sth; **ich kann es mir nicht ~** I can't afford it
Leistenbruch m hernia
Leistung f performance; (gute) achievement
Leitartikel m editorial
leiten vt to lead; (Firma) to run; (in eine Richtung) to direct; (Elek) to conduct
Leiter (-, -n) f ladder
Leiter(in) (-s, -) m(f) (von Geschäft) manager
Leitplanke (-, -n) f guard rail
Leitung f (Führung) direction; (Tel) line; (von Firma) management; (Wasserleitung) pipe; (Kabel) cable; **eine lange ~ haben** to be slow on the uptake
Leitungswasser nt tap water
Lektion f lesson
Lektüre (-, -n) f (Lesen) reading; (Lesestoff) reading matter
Lende (-, -n) f (Speise) loin; (vom Rind) sirloin; **die ~n** pl (Med) the lumbar region sing
lenken vt to steer; (Blick) to direct (auf +akk towards); **jds Aufmerksamkeit auf etw** (akk) **~** to draw sb's attention to sth
Lenker m (von Fahrrad, Motorrad) handlebars pl
Lenkrad nt steering wheel
Lenkradschloss nt steering lock
Lenkstange f handlebars pl
Leopard (-en, -en) m leopard
Lepra (-) f leprosy
Lerche (-, -n) f lark
lernen vt, vi to learn; (für eine Prüfung) to study, to review
lesbisch adj lesbian
Lesebuch nt reader
lesen (las, gelesen) vi, vt to read; (ernten) to pick

Leser(in) m(f) reader
Leserbrief m letter to the editor
leserlich adj legible
Lesezeichen nt bookmark
Lettland nt Latvia
letzte(r, s) adj last; (neueste) latest; (endgültig) final; **zum ~n Mal** for the last time; **am ~n Montag** last Monday; **in ~r Zeit** lately, recently
letztens adv (vor kurzem) recently
letztere(r, s) adj the latter
Leuchtanzeige f illuminated display
Leuchte (-, -n) f lamp, light
leuchten vi to shine; (Feuer, Zifferblatt) to glow
Leuchter (-s, -) m candlestick
Leuchtfarbe f fluorescent color; (Anstrichfarbe) luminous paint
Leuchtreklame f neon sign
Leuchtstoffröhre f strip (o fluorescent) light
Leuchtturm m lighthouse
leugnen vt to deny ▷ vi to deny everything
Leukämie f leukemia
Leukoplast® (-(e)s, -e) nt Band-Aid®
Leute pl people pl
Lexikon (-s, Lexika) nt encyclopedia; (Wörterbuch) dictionary
Libanon (-s) m: **der ~** Lebanon
Libelle f dragonfly
liberal adj liberal
Libyen (-s) nt Libya
Licht (-(e)s, -er) nt light
Lichtblick m ray of hope
lichtempfindlich adj sensitive to light
Lichempfindlichkeit f (Foto) speed
Lichthupe f: **die ~ betätigen** to flash one's lights
Lichtjahr nt light year
Lichtmaschine f (Auto) generator
Lichtschalter m light switch
Lichtschranke f light barrier
Lichtschutzfaktor m sun protection factor, SPF
Lichtung f clearing
Lid (-(e)s, -er) nt eyelid
Lidschatten m eye shadow
lieb adj (nett) nice; (teuer, geliebt) dear; (liebenswert) sweet; **das ist ~ von dir** that's nice of you; **L~er Herr X** Dear Mr. X
Liebe (-, -n) f love
lieben vt to love; (sexuell) to make love to
liebenswürdig adj kind
lieber adv rather; **ich möchte ~ nicht** I'd rather not; **welches ist dir ~?** which one

do you prefer?; *siehe auch* **gern, lieb**

Liebesbrief *m* love letter

Liebeskummer *m*: ~ **haben** to be lovesick

Liebespaar *nt* lovers *pl*

liebevoll *adj* loving

Liebhaber(in) (*-s, -*) *m(f)* lover

lieblich *adj* lovely; (*Wein*) sweet

Liebling *m* darling; (*Günstling*) favorite

Lieblings- *in zW* favorite

liebste(r, s) *adj* favorite

liebsten *adv*: **am ~ esse ich ...** my favorite food is ...; **am ~ würde ich bleiben** I'd real-ly like to stay

Liechtenstein (*-s*) *nt* Liechtenstein

Lied (*-(e)s, -er*) *nt* song; (*Rel*) hymn

lief *imperf von* **laufen**

Lieferant(in) *m(f)* supplier

lieferbar *adj* available

liefern *vt* to deliver; (*beschaffen*) to supply

Lieferschein *m* packing list (*o* slip)

Lieferung *f* delivery

Lieferwagen *m* delivery van

Liege (*-, -n*) *f* (*beim Arzt*) couch; (*Gartenlie-ge*) loung chair

liegen (**lag, gelegen**) *vi* to lie; (*sich befin-den*) to be; **mir liegt nichts/viel daran** it doesn't matter to me/it matters a lot to me; **woran liegt es nur, dass ...?** why is it that ...?; ~ **bleiben** (*Mensch*) to stay lying down; (*im Bett*) to stay in bed; (*Ding*) to be left (behind); ~ **lassen** (*vergessen*) to leave behind

Liegestuhl *m* deck chair

Liegestütz *m* push-up

Liegewagen *m* (*Eisenb*) sleeping car, sleep-er

lieh *imperf von* **leihen**

ließ *imperf von* **lassen**

Lift (*-(e)s, -e o -s*) *m* elevator

Liga (*-, Ligen*) *f* league, division

light *adj* (*Cola*) diet; (*fettarm*) low-fat; (*kalo-rienarm*) low-calorie; (*Zigaretten*) mild

Likör (*-s, -e*) *m* liqueur

lila *adj* (*inv*) purple

Lilie *f* lily

Limette (*-, -n*) *f* lime

Limo (*-, -s*) *f* (*fam*) soda

Limonade *f* soda; (*mit Zitronengeschmack*) lemonade

Limone (*-, -n*) *f* lime

Limousine (*-, -n*) *f* sedan; (*fam*) limo

Linde (*-, -n*) *f* linden tree

lindern *vt* to relieve, to soothe

Lineal (*-s, -e*) *nt* ruler

Linie *f* line

Linienflug *m* scheduled flight

liniert *adj* ruled, lined

Link (*-s, -s*) *m* (*Inform*) link

Linke (*-n, -n*) *f* left-hand side; (*Hand*) left hand; (*Pol*) left (wing)

linke(r, s) *adj* left; **auf der ~n Seite** on the left, on the left-hand side

links *adv* on the left; ~ **abbiegen** to turn left; ~ **von** to the left of; ~ **oben** at the top left

Linkshänder(in) (*-s, -*) *m(f)* left-hander

linksherum *adv* to the left, counterclock-wise

Linksverkehr *m* driving on the left

Linse (*-, -n*) *f* lentil; (*optisch*) lens

Lipgloss *nt* lip gloss

Lippe (*-, -n*) *f* lip

Lippenstift *m* lipstick

lispeln *vi* to lisp

List (*-, -en*) *f* cunning; (*Trick*) trick

Liste (*-, -n*) *f* list

Litauen (*-s*) *nt* Lithuania

Liter (*-s, -*) *m o nt* liter

literarisch *adj* literary

Literatur *f* literature

Litschi (*-, -s*) *f* lychee, litchi

litt *imperf von* **leiden**

live *adv* (*Radio, TV*) live

Lizenz *f* license

Lkw (*-(s), -(s)*) *m* (*abk*) = **Lastkraftwagen** truck

Lkw-Maut *f* commercial vehicle toll

Lob (*-(e)s*) *nt* praise

loben *vt* to praise

Loch (*-(e)s, Löcher*) *nt* hole

lochen *vt* to punch

Locher (*-s, -*) *m* (hole) punch

Locke (*-, -n*) *f* curl

locken *vt* (*anlocken*) to lure; (*Haare*) to curl

Lockenstab *m* curling iron

Lockenwickler (*-s, -*) *m* curler

locker *adj* (*Schraube, Zahn*) loose; (*Hal-tung*) relaxed; (*Person*) easy-going; **das schaffe ich ~** (*fam*) I'll manage it, no prob-lem

lockern *vt* to loosen ▷ *vr*: **sich ~** to loosen

lockig *adj* curly

Löffel (*-s, -*) *m* spoon; **einen ~ Mehl zugeben** add a spoonful of flour

Löffelbiskuit (*-s, -s*) *m* lady finger

log *imperf von* **lügen**

Loge (*-, -n*) *f* (*Theat*) box

logisch *adj* logical

Logo (*-s, -s*) *nt* logo

Lohn (-(e)s, Löhne) m reward; (Arbeitslohn) pay, wages pl

lohnen vr: **sich ~** to be worth it; **es lohnt sich nicht zu warten** it's no use waiting

Lohnerhöhung f pay raise

Lohnsteuer f income tax

Lokal (-(e)s, -e) nt (Gaststätte) restaurant; (Kneipe) bar

Lokomotive f locomotive

London (-s) nt London

Lorbeer (-s, -en) m laurel

Lorbeerblatt nt (Gastr) bay leaf

los adj loose; **los!** go on!; **jdn/etw los sein** to be rid of sb/sth; **was ist los?** what's the matter?, what's up?; **dort ist nichts/viel los** there's nothing/a lot going on there

Los (-es, -e) nt (Schicksal) lot, fate; (Lotterie etc) ticket

los|binden (irr) vt to untie

löschen vt (Feuer, Licht) to put out, to extinguish; (Durst) to quench; (Tonband) to erase; (Daten, Zeile) to delete

Löschtaste f delete key

lose adj loose

Lösegeld nt ransom

losen vi to draw straws

lösen vt (lockern) to loosen; (Rätsel) to solve; (Chem) to dissolve; (Fahrkarte) to buy ▷ vr: **sich ~** (abgehen) to come off; (Zucker etc) to dissolve; (Problem, Schwierigkeit) to (re)solve itself

los|fahren (irr) vi to leave

los|gehen (irr) vi to set out; (anfangen) to start

los|lassen (irr) vt to let go

löslich adj soluble

Lösung f (eines Rätsels, Problems, Flüssigkeit) solution

los|werden (irr) vt to get rid of

Lotterie f lottery

Lotto (-s) nt (state run) lottery; **~ spielen** to play the lottery

Löwe (-n, -n) m (Zool) lion; (Astr) Leo

Löwenzahn m dandelion

Luchs (-es, -e) m lynx

Lücke (-, -n) f fill-in

Lückenbüßer(in) (-s, -) m(f) fill-in

lud imperf von **laden**

Luft (-, Lüfte) f air; (Atem) breath

Luftballon m balloon

Luftblase f (air) bubble

luftdicht adj airtight

Luftdruck m (Meteo) atmospheric pressure; (in Reifen) air pressure

lüften vt to air; (Geheimnis) to reveal

Luftfahrt f aviation

Luftfeuchtigkeit f humidity

Luftfilter m air filter

Luftfracht f air freight

Luftkissenboot, Luftkissenfahrzeug nt hovercraft

Luftlinie f: **10 km ~** 10 km as the crow flies

Luftmatratze f air mattress

Luftpirat(in) m(f) hijacker

Luftpost f airmail

Luftpumpe f (bicycle) pump

Luftröhre f windpipe

Lüftung f ventilation

Luftveränderung f change of air

Luftverschmutzung f air pollution

Luftwaffe f air force

Luftzug m draft

Lüge (-, -n) f lie

lügen (log, gelogen) vi to lie

Lügner(in) (-s, -) m(f) liar

Luke (-, -n) f hatch

Lumpen (-s, -) m rag

Lunchpaket nt box lunch

Lunge (-, -n) f lungs pl

Lungenentzündung f pneumonia

Lupe (-, -n) f magnifying glass; **etw unter die ~ nehmen** (fig) to have a close look at sth

Lust (-, Lüste) f joy, delight; (Neigung) desire; **~ auf etw** (akk) **haben** to feel like sth; **~ haben, etw zu tun** to feel like doing sth

lustig adj (komisch) amusing, funny; (fröhlich) cheerful

lutschen vt to suck ▷ vi: **~ an** +dat to suck

Lutscher (-s, -) m lollipop

Luxemburg (-s) nt Luxembourg

luxuriös adj luxurious

Luxus (-) m luxury

Lymphdrüse f lymph gland

Lymphknoten m lymph node

Lyrik (-) f poetry

M

machbar *adj* feasible

machen *vt* **1** to do; (*herstellen, zubereiten*) to make; **was machst du da?** what are you doing (there)?; **das ist nicht zu machen** that can't be done; **das Radio leiser machen** to turn the radio down; **aus Holz gemacht** made of wood

2 (*verursachen, bewirken*) to make; **jdm Angst machen** to make sb afraid; **das macht die Kälte** it's the cold that does that

3 (*ausmachen*) to matter; **das macht nichts** that doesn't matter; **die Kälte macht mir nichts** I don't mind the cold

4 (*kosten, ergeben*) to be; **3 und 5 macht 8** 3 and 5 is *o* are 8; **was *o* wie viel macht das?** how much does that come to?

5: was macht die Arbeit? how's the work going?; **was macht dein Bruder?** how is your brother doing?; **das Auto machen lassen** to have the car done; **mach's gut!** take care!; (*viel Glück*) good luck!

▷ *vi*: **mach schnell!** hurry up!; **Schluss machen** to finish (off); **mach schon!** come on!; **das macht müde** it makes you tired; **in etw** (*dat*) **machen** to be *o* deal in sth

▷ *vr* to come along (nicely); **sich an etw** (*akk*) **machen** to get going *o* started on sth; **sich verständlich machen** to make o.s. understood; **sich** (*dat*) **viel aus jdm/ etw machen** to like sb/sth

Macho (*-s, -s*) *m* (*fam*) macho (type)
Macht (*-s, Mächte*) *f* power
mächtig *adj* powerful; (*fam: ungeheuer*) enormous
machtlos *adj* powerless; **da ist man ~** there's nothing you can do (about it)
Mädchen *nt* girl
Mädchenname *m* maiden name
Made (*-, -n*) *f* maggot
Magazin (*-s, -e*) *nt* magazine
Magen (*-s, -o* Mägen) *m* stomach
Magenbeschwerden *pl* stomach trouble *sing*
Magen-Darm-Infektion *f* gastroenteritis
Magengeschwür *nt* stomach ulcer
Magenschmerzen *pl* stomachache *sing*
mager *adj* (*Fleisch, Wurst*) lean; (*Person*) thin; (*Käse, Joghurt*) low-fat
Magermilch *f* skim milk
Magersucht *f* anorexia
magersüchtig *adj* anorexic
magisch *adj* magical
Magnet (*-s o -en, -en*) *m* magnet
mähen *vt, vi* to mow
mahlen (**mahlte, gemahlen**) *vt* to grind
Mahlzeit *f* meal; (*für Baby*) feeding ▷ *interj* (*guten Appetit*) enjoy your meal
Mähne (*-, -n*) *f* mane
mahnen *vt* to urge; **jdn schriftlich ~** to send sb a reminder
Mahngebühr *f* fine
Mahnung *f* warning; (*schriftlich*) reminder
Mai (*-(s), -e*) *m* May; **siehe auch Juni**
Maifeiertag *m* May Day
Maiglöckchen *nt* lily of the valley
Maikäfer *m* cockchafer
Mail (*-, -s*) *f* e-mail; **jdm eine ~ schicken** to mail sb, to e-mail sb
Mailbox *f* (*Inform*) mailbox
mailen *vi, vt* to e-mail
Mais (*-es, -e*) *m* corn, maize
Maiskolben *m* corn cob; (*Gastr*) corn on the cob
Majestät (*-, -en*) *f* majesty; (*title*) Majesty
Majonäse (*-, -n*) *f* mayonnaise
Majoran (*-s, -e*) *m* marjoram
makaber *adj* macabre
Make-up (*-s, -s*) *nt* make-up
Makler(in) (*-s, -*) *m(f)* broker; (*Immobilienmakler*) realtor
Makrele (*-, -n*) *f* mackerel
Makro (*-s, -s*) *nt* (*Inform*) macro
Makrone (*-, -n*) *f* macaroon
mal *adv* (*beim Rechnen*) times, multiplied by; (*beim Messen*) by; (*fam: einmal = früher*) once; (*einmal = zukünftig*) some day; **4 mal 3 ist 12** 4 times 3 is (*o* equals) twelve; **da habe ich mal gewohnt** I used to live there; **irgendwann mal werde ich dort hinfahren** I'll go there one day; **das ist nun mal so** well, that's just the way it is (*o* goes)
Mal (*-(e)s, -e*) *nt* (*Zeitpunkt*) time; (*Markierung*) mark; **jedes Mal** every time; **ein paar Mal** a few times; **ein einziges Mal** just once
Malaria (*-*) *f* malaria
Malaysia (*-s*) *nt* Malaysia
Malbuch *nt* coloring book

m

Malediven pl Maldives pl

malen vt, vi to paint

Maler(in) (-s, -) m(f) painter

Malerei f painting

malerisch adj picturesque

Mallorca (-s) nt Majorca, Mallorca

mal|nehmen (irr) vt to multiply (mit by)

Malta (-s) nt Malta

Malventee m mallow tea

Malz (-es) nt malt

Malzbier nt malt beer

Mama (-, -s) f mom(my)

man pron you; (förmlich) one; (jemand) someone, somebody; (die Leute) they, people pl; **wie schreibt man das?** how do you spell that?; **man hat ihr das Fahrrad gestohlen** someone stole her bike; **man sagt, dass ...** they (o people) say that ...

managen vt (fam) to manage

Manager(in) (-s, -) m(f) manager

manche(r, s) adj many a; (mit pl) a number of, some ▷ pron (einige) some; (viele) many; **~ Politiker** many politicians pl many a politician

manchmal adv sometimes

Mandant(in) m(f) client

Mandarine f mandarin, tangerine

Mandel (-, -n) f almond; **~n** (Anat) tonsils pl

Mandelentzündung f tonsillitis

Manege (-, -n) f ring

Mangel (-s, Mängel) m (Fehlen) lack; (Knappheit) shortage (an +dat of); (Fehler) defect, fault

mangelhaft adj (Ware) faulty; (Schulnote) ≈ F

Mango (-, -s) f mango

Mangold (-s) m mangel(-wurzel)

Manieren pl manners pl

Maniküre (-, -n) f manicure

manipulieren vt to manipulate

Manko (-s, -s) nt deficiency

Mann (-(e)s, Männer) m man; (Ehemann) husband

Männchen nt: **es ist ein ~** (Tier) it's a he

männlich adj masculine; (Bio) male

Mannschaft f (Sport: fig) team; (Naut, Aviat) crew

Mansarde (-, -n) f attic

Manschettenknopf m cufflink

Mantel (-s, Mäntel) m coat; (Tech) casing, jacket

Mappe (-, -n) f briefcase; (Aktenmappe) folder

Maracuja (-, -s) f passion fruit

Marathon (-s, -s) m marathon

Märchen nt fairy tale

Marder (-s, -) m marten

Margarine f margarine

Marienkäfer m ladybug

Marihuana (-s) nt marijuana

Marille (-, -n) f apricot

Marinade f marinade

Marine f navy

marinieren vt to marinate

Marionette f puppet

Mark (-(e)s) nt (Knochenmark) marrow; (Fruchtmark) pulp

Marke (-, -n) f (Warensorte) brand; (Fabrikat) make; (Briefmarke) stamp; (Essenmarke) voucher, ticket; (aus Metall etc) disk; (Messpunkt) mark

Markenartikel m branded item, brand name product

Markenzeichen nt trademark

markieren vt to mark

Markierung f marking; (Zeichen) mark

Markise (-, -n) f awning

Markt (-(e)s, Märkte) m market; **auf den ~ bringen** to launch

Markthalle f indoor market

Marktlücke f gap in the market

Marktplatz m market place

Marktwirtschaft f market economy

Marmelade f jam; (Orangenmarmelade) marmalade

Marmor (-s, -e) m marble

Marmorkuchen m marble cake

Marokko (-s) nt Morocco

Marone (-, -n) f chestnut

Mars (-) m Mars

Marsch (-(e)s, Märsche) m march

Märtyrer(in) (-s, -) m(f) martyr

März (-(es), -e) m March; siehe auch **Juni**

Marzipan (-s, -e) nt marzipan

Maschine f machine; (Motor) engine

maschinell adj mechanical, machine-

Maschinenbau m mechanical engineering

Masern pl (Med) measles sing

Maske (-, -n) f mask

Maskenball m costume ball

maskieren vr: **sich ~** (Maske aufsetzen) to put on a mask; (verkleiden) to dress up

Maskottchen nt mascot

maß imperf von **messen**

Maß (-es, -e) nt measure; (Mäßigung) moderation; (Grad) degree, extent; **Maße** (Person) measurements; (Raum) dimensions; **in gewissem/hohem Maße** to a certain/high degree; **in zunehmendem Maße**

increasingly

Mass (-, -(en)) f (Bier) liter of beer

Massage (-, -n) f massage

Masse (-, -n) f mass; (von Menschen) crowd; (Großteil) majority

massenhaft adv masses (o loads) of; **am See sind ~ Mücken** there are tons of mosquitoes at the lake

Massenkarambolage f pile-up

Massenmedien pl mass media pl

Massenproduktion f mass production

Massentourismus m mass tourism

Masseur(in) m(f) masseur/masseuse

maßgeschneidert adj (Kleidung) tailor-made

massieren vt to massage

mäßig adj moderate

massiv adj solid; (fig) massive

maßlos adj extreme

Maßnahme (-, -n) f measure, step

Maßstab m rule, measure; (fig) standard; **im ~ von 1:5** on a scale of 1:5

Mast (-(e)s, -e(n)) m mast; (Elek) pylon

Material (-s, -ien) nt material; (Arbeitsmaterial) materials pl

materialistisch adj materialistic

Materie f matter

materiell adj material

Mathe (-) f (fam) math

Mathematik f mathematics sing

Mathematiker(in) m(f) mathematician

Matinee (-, -n) f ≈ matinee

Matratze (-, -n) f mattress

Matrose (-n, -n) m sailor

Matsch (-(e)s) m mud; (Schnee) slush

matschig adj (Boden) muddy; (Schnee) slushy; (Obst) mushy

matt adj weak; (glanzlos) dull; (Foto) matt; (Schach) mate

Matte (-, -n) f mat

Matura (-) f Austrian graduation examination, ≈ High School Diploma

Mauer (-, -n) f wall

Maul (-(e)s, Mäuler) nt mouth; (fam) trap; **halt's ~!** shut your face (o trap o hole)!

Maulbeere f mulberry

Maulesel m mule

Maulkorb m muzzle

Maul- und Klauenseuche f foot-and-mouth disease

Maulwurf m mole

Maurer(in) (-s, -) m(f) mason

Mauritius (-) nt Mauritius

Maus (-, Mäuse) f mouse

Mausefalle f mousetrap

Mausklick (-s, -s) m mouse click

Mauspad (-s, -s) nt mouse pad

Maustaste f mouse key (o button)

Maut (-, -en) f toll

Mautgebühr f toll

mautpflichtig adj: **~e Straße** toll road, turnpike

Mautstelle f tollbooth, tollgate

Mautstraße f toll road, turnpike

maximal adv: **ihr habt ~ zwei Stunden Zeit** you've got two hours at (the) most; **~ vier Leute** a maximum of four people

Mayonnaise f siehe **Majonäse**

Mazedonien (-s) nt Macedonia

MB (-, -) nt, **Mbyte** (-, -) nt (abk) = **Megabyte** MB

Mechanik f mechanics sing; (Getriebe) mechanics pl

Mechaniker(in) (-s,-) m(f) mechanic

mechanisch adj mechanical

Mechanismus m mechanism

meckern vi (Ziege) to bleat; (fam: schimpfen) to moan

Mecklenburg-Vorpommern (-s) nt Mecklenburg-Western Pomerania

Medaille (-, -n) f medal

Medien pl media pl

Medikament nt medicine

Meditation f meditation

meditieren vi to meditate

medium adj (Steak) medium

Medizin (-, -en) f medicine (gegen for)

medizinisch adj medical

Meer (-(e)s, -e) nt sea; **am ~** by the sea

Meerenge f straits pl

Meeresfrüchte pl seafood sing

Meeresspiegel m sea level

Meerrettich m horseradish

Meerschweinchen nt guinea pig

Meerwasser nt seawater

Megabyte nt megabyte

Megahertz nt megahertz

Mehl (-(e)s, -e) nt flour

Mehlspeise f sweet dish made from flour, eggs and milk

mehr pron, adv more; **~ will ich nicht ausgeben** I don't want to spend any more, that's as much as I want to spend; **was willst du ~?** what more do you want? ▷ adv: **immer ~ Leute** more and more (people); **~ als fünf Minuten** more than five minutes; **je ~ ..., desto besser** the more ..., the better; **ich kann nicht ~ stehen** I can't stand any more (o longer); **es ist kein Brot ~ da** there's no bread left; **nie ~** never again

mehrdeutig adj ambiguous

mehrere pron several

mehreres pron several things

mehrfach adj multiple; (wiederholt) repeated

Mehrfachstecker m power strip, multi-outlet plug

Mehrheit f majority

mehrmals adv repeatedly

mehrsprachig adj multilingual

Mehrwegflasche f returnable bottle, deposit bottle

Mehrwertsteuer f sales tax

Mehrzahl f majority; (Plural) plural

meiden (mied, gemieden) vt to avoid

Meile (-, -n) f mile

mein pron (adjektivisch) my

meine(r, s) pron (substantivisch) mine

meinen vt, vi (glauben, der Ansicht sein) to think; (sagen) to say; (sagen wollen, beabsichtigen) to mean; **das war nicht so gemeint** I didn't mean it like that

meinetwegen adv (wegen mir) because of me; (mir zuliebe) for my sake; (von mir aus) as far as I'm concerned

Meinung f opinion; **meiner ~ nach** in my opinion

Meinungsumfrage f opinion poll

Meinungsverschiedenheit f disagreement (über +akk about)

Meise (-, -n) f titmouse; **eine ~ haben** (fam) to be crazy

Meißel (-s, -) m chisel

meist adv mostly

meiste(r, s) pron (adjektivisch) most; **die ~n Leute** most people; **die ~ Zeit** most of the time; **das ~ davon** most of it; **die ~n von ihnen** most of them; (substantivisch) most of them; **am ~n** (the) most

meistens adv mostly; (zum größten Teil) for the most part

Meister(in) (-s, -) m(f) master; (Sport) champion

Meisterschaft f championship

Meisterwerk nt masterpiece

melden vt to report ▷ vr: **sich ~ to** report (bei to); (Schule) to put one's hand up; (freiwillig) to volunteer; (auf etw, am Telefon) to answer

Meldung f announcement; (Bericht) report; (Inform) message

Melodie f tune, melody

Melone (-, -n) f melon

Memoiren pl memoirs pl

Menge (-, -n) f quantity; (Menschen) crowd;

eine ~ (große Anzahl) a lot (gen of)

Mengenrabatt m bulk discount

Meniskus (-, Menisken) m meniscus

Mensa (-, Mensen) f cafeteria

Mensch (-en, -en) m human being, man; (Person) person; **kein ~** nobody; **~!** (bewundernd) wow!; (verärgert) damn (it)!

Menschenmenge f crowd

Menschenrechte pl human rights pl

Menschenverstand m: **gesunder ~** common sense

Menschheit f humanity, mankind

menschlich adj human; (human) humane

Menstruation f menstruation

Mentalität f mentality, mindset

Menthol (-s) nt menthol

Menü (-s, -s) nt set meal; (Inform) menu

Menüleiste f (Inform) menu bar

Merkblatt nt leaflet

merken vt (bemerken) to notice; **sich** (dat) **etw ~** to remember sth

Merkmal nt feature

Merkur (-s) m Mercury

merkwürdig adj odd

Messbecher m measuring cup

Messe (-, -n) f exhibition, trade fair; (Rel) mass

Messebesucher(in) m(f) visitor to the exhibition (o trade fair)

Messegelände nt exhibition site

messen (maß, gemessen) vt to measure; (Temperatur, Puls) to take ▷ vr: **sich ~ to** compete; **sie kann sich mit ihm nicht ~** she's no match for him

Messer (-s, -) nt knife

Messgerät nt measuring device, gauge

Messing (-s) nt brass

Metall (-s, -e) nt metal

Meteorologe m, **Meteorologin** f meteorologist

Meter (-s, -) m o nt meter·

Metermaß nt tape measure

Methode (-, -n) f method

Metzger(in) (-s, -) m(f) butcher

Metzgerei f butcher shop

Mexiko (-s) nt Mexico

MEZ f (abk) = **mitteleuropäische Zeit** CET

miau interj miaow

mich pron akk von **ich**; me; **~ selbst** (reflexiv) myself; **stell dich hinter ~** stand behind me; **ich fühle ~ wohl** I feel fine

mied imperf von **meiden**

Miene (-, -n) f look, expression

mies adj (fam) lousy

Miesmuschel f mussel

Mietauto *nt siehe* **Mietwagen**

Miete (*-, -n*) *f* rent

mieten *vt* to rent; (*Auto*) to rent

Mieter(in) (*-s, -*) *m(f)* tenant

Mietshaus *nt* apartment house

Mietvertrag *m* rental agreement

Mietwagen *m* rental car; **sich** (*dat*) **einen ~ nehmen** to rent a car

Migräne (*-, -n*) *f* migraine

Migrant(in) (*-en, -en*) *m(f)* migrant (worker)

Mikrofon (*-s, -e*) *nt* microphone

Mikrowelle (*-, -n*) *f*, **Mikrowellenherd** *m* microwave (oven)

Milch (*-*) *f* milk

Milcheis *nt* ice cream (*made with milk*)

Milchglas *nt* (*dickes, trübes Glas*) frosted glass

Milchkaffee *m* (caffe) latte

Milchprodukte *pl* dairy products *pl*

Milchpulver *nt* powdered milk

Milchreis *m* rice pudding

Milchshake *m* milk shake

Milchstraße *f* Milky Way

mild *adj* mild; (*Richter*) lenient; (*freundlich*) kind

Militär (*-s*) *nt* military, army

Milliarde (*-, -n*) *f* trillion

Milligramm *nt* milligram

Milliliter *m* milliliter

Millimeter *m* millimeter

Million *f* million

Millionär(in) *m(f)* millionaire

Milz (*-, -en*) *f* spleen

Mimik *f* facial expression(s)

Minderheit *f* minority

minderjährig *adj* underage

minderwertig *adj* inferior

Minderwertigkeitskomplex *m* inferiority complex

Mindest- *in zW* minimum

mindeste(r, s) *adj* least

mindestens *adv* at least

Mindesthaltbarkeitsdatum *nt* expiration date

Mine (*-, -n*) *f* mine; (*Bleistift*) lead; (*Kugelschreiber*) refill

Mineralwasser *nt* mineral water

Minibar *f* minibar

Minigolf *nt* miniature golf

minimal *adj* minimal

Minimum (*-s, Minima*) *nt* minimum

Minirock *m* miniskirt

Minister(in) (*-s, -*) *m(f)* minister

Ministerium *nt* ministry

Ministerpräsident(in) *m(f)* (*von Bundesland*) Minister President (*Prime Minister of a Bundesland*)

minus *adv* minus

Minus (*-, -*) *nt* deficit; **im ~ sein** to be in the red; (*Konto*) to be overdrawn

Minute (*-, -n*) *f* minute

Minze (*-, -n*) *f* mint

Mio. *nt abk von* **Million(en)**; m

mir *pron dat von* **ich**; (to) me; **kannst du mir helfen?** can you help me?; **kannst du es mir erklären?** can you explain it to me?; **ich habe mir einen neuen Rechner gekauft** I bought (myself) a new computer; **ein Freund von mir** a friend of mine

Mirabelle (*-, -n*) *f* mirabelle (*small yellow plum*)

mischen *vt* to mix; (*Karten*) to shuffle

Mischmasch *m* (*fam*) hodgepodge

Mischung *f* mixture (*aus of*)

missachten *vt* to ignore

Missbrauch *m* abuse; (*falscher Gebrauch*) misuse

missbrauchen *vt* to misuse (*zu for*); (*sexuell*) to abuse

Misserfolg *m* failure

Missgeschick *nt* (*Panne*) mishap

misshandeln *vt* to mistreat, to abuse

Mission *f* mission

misslingen (**misslang, misslungen**) *vi* to fail; **der Versuch ist mir misslungen** my attempt failed

misstrauen *vt* (*+dat*) to distrust

Misstrauen (*-s*) *nt* mistrust, suspicion (*gegenüber* of)

misstrauisch *adj* distrustful; (*argwöhnisch*) suspicious

Missverständnis *nt* misunderstanding

missverstehen (*irr*) *vt* to misunderstand

Mist (*-(e)s*) *m* (*fam*) garbage; (*von Kühen*) dung; (*als Dünger*) manure

Mistel (*-, -n*) *f* mistletoe

mit *prep* (*+dat*) with; (*mittels*) by; **mit der Bahn** by train; **mit der Kreditkarte bezahlen** to pay by credit card; **mit 10 Jahren** at the age of 10; **wie wärs mit ...?** how about ...? ▷ *adv* along, too; **wollen Sie mit?** do you want to come along?

Mitarbeiter(in) *m(f)* (*Angestellter*) employee; (*an Projekt*) co-worker; (*freier*) freelancer

mit|bekommen (*irr*) *vt* (*fam: aufschnappen*) to catch; (*hören*) to hear; (*verstehen*) to get

mit|benutzen *vt* to share

m

Mitbewohner(in) *m(f)* (*im Zimmer*) room-mate; (*in Wohnung*) housemate

mit|bringen (*irr*) *vt* to bring along

Mitbringsel (*-s, -*) *nt* small present

miteinander *adv* with one another; (*gemeinsam*) together

mit|erleben *vt* to see (with one's own eyes)

Mitesser (*-s, -*) *m* blackhead

Mitfahrgelegenheit *f* ≈ ride

Mitfahrzentrale *f* *agency for arranging rides*

mit|geben (*irr*) *vt*: **jdm etw ~ to** give sb sth (to take along)

Mitgefühl *nt* sympathy

mit|gehen (*irr*) *vi* to go/come along

mitgenommen *adj* worn out, exhausted

Mitglied *nt* member

mithilfe *prep* (*+gen*); **~ von** with the help of

mit|kommen (*irr*) *vi* to come along; (*verstehen*) to follow

Mitleid *nt* pity; **~ haben mit** to feel sorry for

mit|machen *vt* to take part in ▷ *vi* to take part

mit|nehmen (*irr*) *vt* to take along; (*anstrengen*) to wear out, to exhaust

mit|schreiben (*irr*) *vi* to take notes ▷ *vt* to take down

Mitschüler(in) *m(f)* classmate

mit|spielen *vi* (*in Mannschaft*) to play; (*bei Spiel*) to join in; **in einem Film/Stück ~** to act in a film/play

Mittag *m* noontime; **gestern ~** at noontime yesterday, yesterday at lunchtime; **über ~ geschlossen** closed at lunchtime; **zu ~ essen** to have (*o* eat) lunch

Mittagessen *nt* lunch

mittags *adv* at lunchtime, at noontime

Mittagspause *f* lunch break

Mitte (*-, -n*) *f* middle; **~ Juni** in the middle of June; **sie ist ~ zwanzig** she's in her mid-twenties

mit|teilen *vt*: **jdm etw ~** to inform sb of sth

Mitteilung *f* notification

Mittel (*-s*) *nt* means *sing*; (*Maßnahme, Methode*) method; (*Med*) remedy (*gegen* for); **das ist ein gutes ~, um junge Leute zu erreichen** that's a good way to connect with young people

Mittelalter *nt* Middle Ages *pl*

mittelalterlich *adj* medieval

Mittelamerika *nt* Central America

Mitteleuropa *nt* Central Europe

Mittelfeld *nt* midfield

Mittelfinger *m* middle finger

mittelmäßig *adj* mediocre

Mittelmeer *nt* Mediterranean (Sea)

Mittelohrentzündung *f* (middle) ear infection

Mittelpunkt *m* center; **im ~ stehen** to be the center of attention

mittels *prep* (*+gen*) by means of

Mittelstreifen *m* median

Mittelstürmer(in) *m(f)* striker, center-forward

mitten *adv* in the middle; **~ auf der Straße/in der Nacht** in the middle of the street/night

Mitternacht *f* midnight

mittlere(r, s) *adj* middle; (*durchschnittlich*) average

mittlerweile *adv* meanwhile

Mittwoch (*-s, -e*) *m* Wednesday; **am ~** on Wednesday; **am ~ Morgen/Nachmittag/Abend** (on) Wednesday morning/afternoon/evening; **diesen/letzten/nächsten ~** this/last/next Wednesday; **jeden ~** every Wednesday; **~ in einer Woche** a week from Wednesday

mittwochs *adv* on Wednesdays; **~ abends** (*jeden Mittwochabend*) on Wednesday evenings

mixen *vt* to mix

Mixer (*-s, -*) *m* (*Küchengerät*) blender

MKS *f* (*abk*) = **Maul- und Klauenseuche** FMD

mobben *vt* to harass (*o* to bully) (at work)

Mobbing (*-s*) *nt* workplace bullying (*o* harassment)

Möbel (*-s, -*) *nt* piece of furniture; **die ~** *pl* the furniture *sing*

mobil *adj* mobile

Mobilfunknetz *nt* cellular network

Mobiltelefon *nt* cell phone

möblieren *vt* to furnish

mochte *imperf von* **mögen**

Mode (*-, -n*) *f* fashion

Model (*-s, -s*) *nt* model

Modell (*-s, -e*) *nt* model

Modem (*-s, -s*) *nt* (*Inform*) modem

Mode(n)schau *f* fashion show

Moderator(in) *m(f)* presenter

modern *adj* modern; (*modisch*) fashionable

Modeschmuck *m* costume jewelry

modisch *adj* fashionable

Modus (*-, Modi*) *m* (*Inform*) mode; (*fig*) way

Mofa (*-s, -s*) *nt* moped

mogeln *vi* to cheat

mögen (*pt* mochte, *pp* gemocht o (*als Hilfsverb*) mögen) *vt, vi* to like; **magst du/mögen Sie ihn?** do you like him?; **ich möchte ... I** would like ..., I'd like ...; **er möchte in die Stadt** he'd like to go into town; **ich möchte nicht, dass du ...** I don't want you to ...; **ich mag nicht mehr** I've had enough

▷ *Hilfsverb* to like to; (*wollen*) to want; **möchtest du etwas essen?** would you like something to eat?; **sie mag nicht bleiben** she doesn't want to stay; **das mag wohl sein** that may well be; **was mag das heißen?** what might that mean?; **Sie möchten zu Hause anrufen** could you please call home?

möglich *adj* possible; **so bald wie ~** as soon as possible

möglicherweise *adv* possibly

Möglichkeit *f* possibility

möglichst *adv* as ... as possible

Mohn (-(e)s, -e) *m* (*Blume*) poppy; (*Samen*) poppy seed

Möhre (-, -n) *f*, **Mohrrübe** *f* carrot

Mokka (-s, -s) *m* mocha

Moldawien (-s) *nt* Moldova

Molkerei (-, -en) *f* dairy

Moll (-) *nt* minor (key); **a~** A minor

mollig *adj* cozy; (*dicklich*) plump

Moment (-(e)s, -e) *m* moment; **im ~** at the moment; **einen ~ bitte!** just a minute!

momentan *adj* momentary ▷ *adv* at the moment

Monaco (-s) *nt* Monaco

Monarchie *f* monarchy

Monat (-(e)s, -e) *m* month; **sie ist im dritten ~** (*schwanger*) she's three months pregnant

monatlich *adj, adv* monthly; **~ 100 Euro zahlen** to pay 100 euros a month (o every month)

Monatskarte *f* monthly (commuter) pass

Mönch (-s, -e) *m* monk

Mond (-(e)s, -e) *m* moon

Mondfinsternis *f* lunar eclipse

Mongolei (-) *f*: **die ~** Mongolia

Monitor *m* (*Inform*) monitor

monoton *adj* monotonous

Monsun (-s, -e) *m* monsoon

Montag *m* Monday; *siehe auch* **Mittwoch**

montags *adv* on Mondays; *siehe auch* **mittwochs**

Montenegro (-s) *nt* Montenegro

Monteur(in) (-s, -e) *m(f)* fitter

montieren *vt* to assemble, to set up

Monument *nt* monument

Moor (-(e)s, -e) *nt* moor

Moos (-es, -e) *nt* moss

Moped (-s, -s) *nt* moped

Moral (-) *f* (*Werte*) morals *pl*; (*einer Geschichte*) moral

moralisch *adj* moral

Mord (-(e)s, -e) *m* murder

Mörder(in) (-s, -) *m(f)* murderer/murderess

morgen *adv* tomorrow; **~ früh** tomorrow morning

Morgen (-s, -) *m* morning; **am ~** in the morning

Morgenmantel *m*, **Morgenrock** *m* dressing gown

Morgenmuffel *m*: **er ist ein ~** he's not a morning person

morgens *adv* in the morning; **um 3 Uhr ~ at** 3 (o'clock) in the morning, at 3 a.m.

Morphium (-s) *nt* morphine

morsch *adj* rotten

Mosaik (-s, -e(n)) *nt* mosaic

Mosambik (-s) *nt* Mozambique

Moschee (-, -n) *f* mosque

Moskau (-s) *nt* Moscow

Moskito (-s, -s) *m* mosquito

Moskitonetz *nt* mosquito net

Moslem (-s, -s) *m*, **Moslime** (-, -n) *f* Muslim

Most (-(e)s, -e) *m* (*unfermented*) fruit juice; (*Apfelwein*) hard cider

Motel (-s, -s) *nt* motel

motivieren *vt* to motivate

Motor *m* engine; (*Elek*) motor

Motorboot *nt* motorboat

Motorenöl *nt* engine oil

Motorhaube *f* hood

Motorrad *nt* motorbike, motorcycle

Motorradfahrer(in) *m(f)* motorcyclist

Motorroller *m* (motor) scooter

Motorschaden *m* engine trouble

Motte (-, -n) *f* moth

Motto (-s, -s) *nt* motto

Mountainbike (-s, -s) *nt* mountain bike

Möwe (-, -n) *f* (sea)gull

MP3-Player (-s, -) *m* MP3 player

Mrd. *f* (*abk*) = **Milliarde(n)** bil

MS (-) *f* (*abk*) = **multiple Sklerose** MS

Mücke (-, -n) *f* gnat; (*tropische*) mosquito

Mückenstich *m* mosquito bite

müde *adj* tired

muffig *adj* (*Geruch*) musty; (*Gesicht, Mensch*) grumpy

Mühe (-, -n) f trouble, pains pl; **sich** (dat)
  große ~ geben to go to a lot of trouble
muhen vi to moo
Mühle (-, -n) f mill; (Kaffeemühle) grinder
Müll (-(e)s) m garbage
Müllabfuhr f trash (o garbage) removal
Mullbinde f gauze bandage
Müllcontainer m Dumpster®
Mülldeponie f landfill, dump
Mülleimer m garbage can
Mülltonne f garbage can
Mülltrennung f sorting and collecting
  household waste according to type of mate-
  rial
Müllverbrennungsanlage f incineration
  plant
Müllwagen m garbage truck
multikulturell adj multicultural
Multimedia- in zW multimedia
Multiple-Choice-Verfahren nt multiple
  choice
multiple Sklerose (-n, -n) f multiple sclerosis
Multiplexkino nt multiplex (cinema)
multiplizieren vt to multiply (mit by)
Mumie f mommy
Mumps (-) m mumps sing
München (-s) nt Munich
Mund (-(e)s, Münder) m mouth; **halt den ~!**
  shut up!
Mundart f dialect
Munddusche f dental water jet
münden vi to flow (in +akk into)
Mundgeruch m bad breath
mündlich adj oral
Mundschutz m mask
Mundwasser nt mouthwash
Munition f ammunition
Münster (-s, -) nt cathedral, minster
munter adj lively
Münzautomat m vending machine
Münze (-, -n) f coin
Münzeinwurf m slot
Münzrückgabe f coin return
Münztelefon nt pay phone
Münzwechsler m change machine
murmeln vt, vi to murmur, to mutter
Murmeltier nt marmot
mürrisch adj sullen, grumpy
Mus (-es, -e) nt puree
Muschel (-, -n) f mussel; (Muschelschale)
  shell
Museum (-s, Museen) nt museum
Musical (-s, -s) nt musical

Musik f music
musikalisch adj musical
Musiker(in) (-s, -) m(f) musician
Musikinstrument nt musical instrument
musizieren vi to play music
Muskat (-(e)s) m nutmeg
Muskel (-s, -n) m muscle
Muskelkater m: **~ haben** to be stiff, to have
  sore muscles
Muskelriss m torn muscle
Muskelzerrung f pulled muscle
muskulös adj muscular
Müsli (-s, -) nt muesli
Muslim(in) (-s, -s) m(f) Muslim
Muss (-) nt must

SCHLÜSSELWORT

müssen (pt musste, pp gemusst o (als
  Hilfsverb) müssen) vi **1** (Zwang) must;
  (nur im Präsens) to have to; **ich muss es
  tun** I must do it, I have to do it; **ich musste
  es tun** I had to do it; **er muss es nicht tun**
  he doesn't have to do it; **muss ich?** must
  I?, do I have to?; **wann müsst ihr zur
  Schule?** when do you have to go to
  school?; **er hat gehen müssen** he had to
  go; **muss das sein?** is that really necessary?; **ich muss mal** (fam) I have to go, I
  need the bathroom

2 (sollen): **das musst du nicht tun!** you
  oughtn't to o shouldn't do that; **Sie hätten
  ihn fragen müssen** you should have asked
  him

3: **es muss geregnet haben** it must have
  rained; **es muss nicht wahr sein** it needn't
  be true

Muster (-s, -) nt (Dessin) pattern, design;
  (Probe) sample; (Vorbild) model
mustern vt to have a close look at; **jdn ~** to
  look sb up and down
Mut (-(e)s) m courage; **jdm Mut machen** to
  encourage sb
mutig adj brave, courageous
Mutter (-, Mütter) f mother ▷ (-, -n) f (Schrau-
  benmutter) nut
Muttersprache f native language
Muttertag m Mother's Day
Mutti f mom(my)
mutwillig adj deliberate
Mütze (-, -n) f cap
Myanmar (-s) nt Myanmar

N

N (abk) = Nord N

na interj: na also!, na bitte! see?, what did I tell you?; na ja well; na und? so what?

Nabel (-s, -) m navel

nach prep +dat 1 (örtlich) to; nach Berlin to Berlin; nach links/rechts (to the) left/right; nach oben/hinten up/back

2 (zeitlich) after; einer nach dem anderen one after the other; nach Ihnen! after you!; zehn (Minuten) nach drei ten (minutes) past three

3 (gemäß) according to; nach dem Gesetz according to the law; dem Namen nach judging by his/her name; nach allem, was ich weiß as far as I know

▷ adv: ihm nach! after him!; nach und nach gradually, little by little; nach wie vor still

nach|ahmen vt to imitate

Nachbar(in) (-n, -n) m(f) neighbor

Nachbarschaft f neighborhood

nach|bestellen vt to reorder

nachdem conj after; (weil) since; je ~ (ob/wie) depending on (whether/how)

nach|denken (irr) vi to think (über +akk about)

nachdenklich adj thoughtful

nacheinander adv one after another (o the other)

Nachfolger(in) (-s, -) m(f) successor

nach|forschen vt to investigate

Nachfrage f inquiry; (Comm) demand

nach|fragen vi to inquire

nach|geben (irr) vi to give in (jdm to sb)

Nachgebühr f surcharge; (für Briefe etc) excess postage

nach|gehen (irr) vi to follow (jdm sb); (erforschen) to inquire (einer Sache dat into sth); die Uhr geht zehn Minuten nach the clock is ten minutes slow

nachher adv afterwards; bis ~! see you later!

Nachhilfe f extra help, tutoring

nach|holen vt to catch up with; (Versäumtes) to make up for

nach|kommen (irr) vi to follow; einer Verpflichtung (dat) ~ to fulfill an obligation

nach|lassen (irr) vt (Summe) to take off

▷ vi to decrease, to ease off; (schlechter werden) to deteriorate

nachlässig adj negligent, careless

nach|laufen (irr) vi to run after, to chase (jdm sb)

nach|lösen vt: eine Fahrkarte ~ to buy a ticket on the bus/train

nach|machen vt to imitate, to copy (jdm etw sth from sb); (fälschen) to counterfeit

Nachmittag m afternoon; heute ~ this afternoon; am ~ in the afternoon

nachmittags adv in the afternoon; um 3 Uhr ~ at 3 (o'clock) in the afternoon, at 3 p.m.

Nachnahme (-, -n) f cash on delivery; per ~ COD

Nachname m last name, surname

nach|prüfen vt to check

nach|rechnen vt to check

Nachricht (-, -en) f (piece of) news sing; (Mitteilung) message

Nachrichten pl news sing

Nachsaison f off-season

nach|schauen vi: jdm ~ to gaze after sb

▷ vt (prüfen) to check

nach|schicken vt to forward

nach|schlagen (irr) vt to look up

nach|sehen (irr) vt (prüfen) to check

Nachspeise f dessert

nächstbeste(r, s) adj: der ~ Zug/Job the first train/job that comes along

nächste(r, s) adj next; (nächstgelegen) nearest

Nacht (-, Nächte) f night; in der ~ during the night; (bei Nacht) at night

Nachtclub m nightclub

Nachtdienst m night duty; ~ haben (Apotheke) to be open all night

Nachteil m disadvantage

Nachtflug m night (o red-eye) flight

Nachtfrost m overnight frost

Nachthemd nt (für Damen) nightgown; (für Herren) nightshirt

Nachtigall (-, -en) f nightingale

Nachtisch m dessert

Nachtleben nt nightlife

nach|tragen (irr) vt: jdm etw ~ (übel nehmen) to hold sth against sb

nachträglich adv: alles Gute zum Geburtstag! Happy belated birthday!

nachts adv at night; um 11 Uhr ~ at 11 (o'clock) at night, at 11 p.m.; um 2 Uhr ~

at 2 (o'clock) in the morning, at 2 a.m.

Nachtschicht f night shift

Nachttarif m off-peak rate

Nachttisch m night stand (o table)

Nachtzug m night train

Nachweis (-es, -e) m proof

Nachwirkung f aftereffect

nach|zahlen vi to pay extra ▷ vt: **20 Euro ~** to pay 20 euros extra

nach|zählen vt to check

Nacken (-s, -) m (nape of the) neck

nackt adj naked; (Tatsachen) plain, bare

Nacktbadestrand m nudist beach

Nadel (-, -n) f needle; (Stecknadel) pin

Nadelstreifen pl pinstripes pl

Nagel (-s, Nägel) m nail

Nagelbürste f nailbrush

Nagelfeile f nail file

Nagellack m nail polish

Nagellackentferner (-s, -) m nail-polish remover

Nagelschere f nail scissors pl

nah(e) adj, adv (räumlich) near(by); (zeitlich) near; (Verwandte, Freunde) close

Nähe (-) f (Umgebung) vicinity; **in der ~** nearby; **in der ~ von** near

nahe|gehen (irr) vi: **jdm ~** to upset sb

nahe|legen vt: **jdm etw ~** to suggest sth to sb

nahe|liegen (irr) vi to be obvious ▷ prep (+dat) near (to), close to

nähen vt, vi to sew

nähere(r, s) adj (Erklärung, Erkundigung) more detailed; **die ~ Umgebung** the immediate area

Nähere(s) nt details pl

nähern vr: **sich ~** to approach

nahezu adv virtually, almost

nahm imperf von **nehmen**

Nähmaschine f sewing machine

nahrhaft adj nourishing, nutritious

Nahrung f food

Nahrungsmittel nt food

Naht (-, Nähte) f seam; (Med) stitches pl suture; (Tech) join

Nahverkehr m local traffic

Nahverkehrszug m local train

Nähzeug nt sewing kit

naiv adj naive

Name (-ns, -n) m name

nämlich adv that is to say, namely; (denn) since

nannte imperf von **nennen**

Napf (-(e)s, Näpfe) m bowl, dish

Narbe (-, -n) f scar

Narkose (-, -n) f anesthetic

Narzisse (-, -n) f daffodil, narcissus

naschen vt, vi to nibble

Naschkatze f (fam) nibbler; **eine ~ sein** to have a sweet tooth

Nase (-, -n) f nose

Nasenbluten (-s) nt nosebleed; **~ haben** to have a nosebleed

Nasenloch nt nostril

Nasentropfen pl nose drops pl

Nashorn nt rhinoceros

nass adj wet

Nässe (-) f wetness

nässen vi (Wunde) to weep

Nation (-, -en) f nation

national adj national

Nationalfeiertag m national holiday

Nationalhymne (-, -n) f national anthem

Nationalität f nationality

Nationalmannschaft f national team

Nationalpark m national park

Nationalspieler(in) m(f) international (player)

NATO (-) f (abk) = **North Atlantic Treaty Organization** NATO, Nato

Natur f nature

Naturkost f health food

natürlich adj natural ▷ adv naturally; (selbstverständlich) of course

Naturpark m nature reserve

naturrein adj natural, pure

Naturschutz m conservation

Naturschutzgebiet nt nature reserve

Naturwissenschaft f (natural) science

Naturwissenschaftler(in) m(f) scientist

Navigationssystem nt (Auto) navigation system

n. Chr. (abk) = **nach Christus** AD

Nebel (-s, -) m fog, mist

nebelig adj foggy, misty

Nebelscheinwerfer m foglamp

Nebelschlussleuchte f (Auto) rear foglight

neben prep (+akk o dat) next to; (außer) apart from, besides

nebenan adv next door

Nebenausgang m side exit

nebenbei adv at the same time; (außerdem) additionally; (beiläufig) incidentally

nebeneinander adv side by side

Nebeneingang m side entrance

Nebenfach nt (Univ) minor

nebenher adv (zusätzlich) besides; (gleichzeitig) at the same time; (daneben) alongside

Nebenkosten pl extra charges pl, extras pl

Nebensache *f* minor matter
nebensächlich *adj* minor
Nebensaison *f* low season
Nebenstraße *f* side street
Nebenwirkung *f* side effect
neblig *adj* foggy, misty
necken *vt* to tease
Neffe (*-n, -n*) *m* nephew
negativ *adj* negative
Negativ *nt* (*Foto*) negative
nehmen (**nahm, genommen**) *vt* to take; **wie man's nimmt** it depends on how you look at it; **den Bus/Zug ~** to take the bus/train; **jdn/etw ernst ~** to take sb/sth seriously; **etw zu sich ~** to eat sth; **jdn zu sich ~** to have sb come and live with one; **jdn an die Hand ~** to take sb by the hand
neidisch *adj* envious
neigen *vi*: **zu etw ~** to tend towards sth
Neigung *f* (*des Geländes*) slope; (*Tendenz*) inclination; (*Vorliebe*) liking
nein *adv* no
Nektarine *f* nectarine
Nelke (*-, -n*) *f* carnation; (*Gewürz*) clove
nennen (**nannte, genannt**) *vt* to name; (*mit Namen*) to call
Neonazi (*-s, -s*) *m* neo-Nazi
Nepal (*-s*) *nt* Nepal
Neptun (*-s*) *m* Neptune
Nerv (*-s, -en*) *m* nerve; **jdm auf die ~en gehen** to get on sb's nerves
nerven *vt*: **jdn ~** (*fam*) to get on sb's nerves
Nervenzusammenbruch *m* nervous breakdown
nervös *adj* nervous
Nest (*-(e)s, -er*) *nt* nest; (*pej: Ort*) dump
nett *adj* nice; (*freundlich*) kind; **sei so ~ und ... do me a favor and ...
netto *adv* net
Netz (*-es, -e*) *nt* net; (*für Einkauf*) string bag; (*System*) network; (*Stromnetz*) power
Netzanschluss *m* power connection
Netzbetreiber(in) *m(f)* (*a. Inform*) network operator
Netzgerät *nt* power pack
Netzkarte *f* commutation ticket
Netzwerk *nt* (*Inform*) network
Netzwerken *nt* (social) networking
Netzwerkkarte *f* network card
neu *adj* new; (*Sprache, Geschichte*) modern; **die neuesten Nachrichten** the latest news
Neubau *m* new building
neuerdings *adv* recently
Neueröffnung *f* (*Geschäft*) new business
Neuerung *f* innovation; (*Reform*) reform

Neugier *f* curiosity
neugierig *adj* curious (*auf +akk* about); **ich bin ~, ob ...** I wonder whether (*o if*) ...; **ich bin ~, was du dazu sagst** I'll be interested to hear what you have to say about it
Neuheit *f* novelty
Neuigkeit *f* news *sing*; **eine ~** a piece of news
Neujahr *nt* New Year; **prosit ~!** Happy New Year!
neulich *adv* recently, the other day
Neumond *m* new moon
neun *num* nine
neunhundert *num* nine hundred
neunmal *adv* nine times
neunte(r, s) *adj* ninth; *siehe auch* **dritte**
Neuntel (*-s, -*) *nt* ninth
neunzehn *num* nineteen
neunzehnte(r, s) *adj* nineteenth; *siehe auch* **dritte**
neunzig *num* ninety; **in den ~er Jahren** in the nineties
Neunzigerjahre *pl* nineties *pl*
neunzigste(r, s) *adj* ninetieth
neureich *adj* nouveau riche
Neurologe *m*, **Neurologin** *f* neurologist
Neurose (*-, -n*) *f* neurosis
neurotisch *adj* neurotic
Neuseeland *nt* New Zealand
Neustart *m* (*Inform*) restart, reboot
neutral *adj* neutral
neuwertig *adj* nearly new
Nicaragua (*-s*) *nt* Nicaragua

SCHLÜSSELWORT

nicht *adv* **1** (*Verneinung*) not; **er ist es nicht** it's not him, it isn't him; **er raucht nicht** (*gerade*) he isn't smoking; (*gewöhnlich*) he doesn't smoke; **ich kann das nicht – ich auch nicht** I can't do it – neither *o* nor can I; **es regnet nicht mehr** it's not raining any more; **nicht rostend** stainless
2 (*Bitte, Verbot*): **nicht!** don't!, no!; **nicht berühren!** do not touch!; **nicht doch!** don't!
3 (*rhetorisch*): **du bist müde, nicht (wahr)?** you're tired, aren't you?; **das ist schön, nicht (wahr)?** it's nice, isn't it?
4: **was du nicht sagst!** the things you say!

Nichte (*-, -n*) *f* niece
Nichtraucher(in) *m(f)* non-smoker
Nichtraucherabteil *nt* non-smoking compartment

Nichtraucherzone *f* non-smoking area

nichts *pron* nothing; **für ~ und wieder ~** for nothing at all; **ich habe ~ gesagt** I didn't say anything; **macht ~** never mind

Nichtschwimmer(in) *m(f)* non-swimmer

nichtssagend *adj* meaningless

nicken *vi* to nod

Nickerchen *nt* nap

nie *adv* never; **nie wieder** *o* **mehr** never again; **fast nie** hardly ever

nieder *adj* (*niedrig*) low; (*gering*) inferior ▷ *adv* down

niedergeschlagen *adj* depressed

Niederlage *f* defeat

Niederlande *pl* Netherlands *pl*

Niederländer(in) *m(f)* Dutchman/Dutchwoman

niederländisch *adj* Dutch

Niederländisch *nt* Dutch

Niederlassung *f* branch

Niederösterreich *nt* Lower Austria

Niedersachsen *nt* Lower Saxony

Niederschlag *m* (*Meteo*) precipitation; (*Regen*) rainfall

niedlich *adj* sweet, cute

niedrig *adj* low; (*Qualität*) inferior

niemals *adv* never

niemand *pron* nobody, no one; **ich habe ~en gesehen** I haven't seen anyone; **~ von ihnen** none of them

Niere (-, -n) *f* kidney

Nierenentzündung *f* kidney infection

Nierensteine *pl* kidney stones *pl*

nieseln *vi impers* to drizzle

Nieselregen *m* drizzle

niesen *vi* to sneeze

Niete (-, -n) *f* (*Los*) blank; (*Reinfall*) flop; (*pej: Mensch*) failure; (*Tech*) rivet

Nigeria (-s) *nt* Nigeria

Nikotin (-s) *nt* nicotine

Nilpferd *nt* hippopotamus

nippen *vi* to sip; **an etw** (*dat*) **~** to sip sth

nirgends *adv* nowhere

Nische (-, -n) *f* niche

Niveau (-s, -s) *nt* level; **sie hat ~** she's got class

nobel *adj* (*großzügig*) generous; (*fam: luxuriös*) classy, posh

Nobelpreis *m* Nobel Prize

SCHLÜSSELWORT

noch *adv* **1** (*weiterhin*) still; **noch nicht** not yet; **noch nie** never (yet); **noch immer** *o* **immer noch** still; **bleiben Sie doch noch** stay a bit longer

2 (*in Zukunft*) still, yet; **das kann noch passieren** that might still happen; **er wird noch kommen** he'll come (yet)

3 (*nicht später als*): **noch vor einer Woche** only a week ago; **noch am selben Tag** the very same day; **noch im 19. Jahrhundert** as late as the 19th century; **noch heute** today

4 (*zusätzlich*): **wer war noch da?** who else was there?; **noch einmal** once more, again; **noch dreimal** three more times; **noch einer** another one

5 (*bei Vergleichen*): **noch größer** even bigger; **das ist noch besser** that's better still; **und wenn es noch so schwer ist** however hard it is

6: **Geld noch und noch** heaps (and heaps) of money; **sie hat noch und noch versucht, ...** she tried again and again to ...

▷ *konj*: **weder A noch B** neither A nor B

nochmal(s) *adv* again, once more

Nominativ *m* nominative (case)

Nonne (-, -n) *f* nun

Nonstop-Flug *m* nonstop flight

Nord (-(e)s) *m* north

Nordamerika *nt* North America

Norddeutschland *nt* Northern Germany

Norden (-s) *m* north; **im ~ Deutschlands** in the north of Germany

Nordeuropa *nt* Northern Europe

Nordic Walking *nt* (*Sport*) Nordic Walking

Nordirland *nt* Northern Ireland

nordisch *adj* (*Völker, Sprache*) Nordic

Nordkorea (-s) *nt* North Korea

nördlich *adj* northern; (*Kurs, Richtung*) northerly

Nordost(en) *m* northeast

Nordpol *m* North Pole

Nordrhein-Westfalen (-s) *nt* North Rhine-Westphalia

Nordsee *f* North Sea

nordwärts *adv* north, northwards

Nordwest(en) *m* northwest

Nordwind *m* north wind

nörgeln *vi* to grumble

Norm (-, -en) *f* norm; (*Größenvorschrift*) standard

normal *adj* normal

Normalbenzin *nt* regular gas

normalerweise *adv* normally

normen *vt* to standardize

Norwegen (-s) *nt* Norway

Norweger(in) *m(f)* Norwegian

norwegisch *adj* Norwegian

Norwegisch *nt* Norwegian

Not (-, *Nöte*) *f* need; (*Armut*) poverty; (*Elend*) hardship; (*Bedrängnis*) trouble; (*Mangel*) want; (*Mühe*) trouble; (*Zwang*) necessity; **zur Not** if necessary; (*gerade noch*) just about

Notar(in) *m(f)* public notary

notariell *adj*: **~ beglaubigt** attested by a notary

Notarzt *m*, **Notärztin** *f* emergency doctor

Notarztwagen *m* emergency ambulance

Notaufnahme *f* emergency room

Notausgang *m* emergency exit

Notbremse *f* emergency brake

Notdienst *m* emergency service, after-hours service

notdürftig *adj* scanty; (*behelfsmäßig*) makeshift

Note (-, *-n*) *f* note; (*in Schule*) grade; (*Mus*) note

Notebook (-(*s*), *-s*) *nt* (*Inform*) notebook

Notfall *m* emergency

notfalls *adv* if necessary

notieren *vt* to note down

nötig *adj* necessary; **etw ~ haben** to need sth

Notiz (-, *-en*) *f* note; (*Zeitungsnotiz*) item

Notizblock *m* notepad

Notizbuch *nt* notebook

Notlage *f* crisis; (*Elend*) plight

notlanden *vi* to make a forced (*o* emergency) landing

Notlandung *f* emergency landing

Notruf *m* emergency call

Notrufnummer *f* emergency number

Notrufsäule *f* emergency telephone

notwendig *adj* necessary

Nougat (-*s*, *-s*) *m od nt* nougat

November (-(*s*), *-*) *m* November; *siehe auch* **Juni**

Nr. (*abk*) = **Nummer** No., no.

Nu *m*: **im Nu** in no time

nüchtern *adj* sober; (*Magen*) empty

Nudel (-, *-n*) *f* noodle; **~n** *pl* (*italienische*) pasta *sing*

null *num* zero; (*Tel*) zero; **~ Fehler** no mistakes; **~ Uhr** midnight

Null (-, *-en*) *f* nought, zero; (*pej: Mensch*) loser

Nulltarif *m*: **zum ~** free of charge

Numerus clausus (-) *m* restriction on the number of students allowed to study a particular subject

Nummer (-, *-n*) *f* number

nummerieren *vt* to number

Nummernschild *nt* (*Auto*) license plate

nun *adv* now; **von nun an** from now on ▷ *interj* well; **nun gut!** all right, then!; **es ist nun mal so** that's the way it is

nur *adv* only; **nicht nur ..., sondern auch ...** not only ..., but also ...; **nur Anna nicht** except Anna

Nürnberg (-*s*) *nt* Nuremberg

Nuss (-, *Nüsse*) *f* nut

Nussknacker (-*s*, *-*) *m* nutcracker

Nuss-Nougat-Creme *f* chocolate nut cream

Nutte (-, *-n*) *f* (*pej*) tart

nutz, nütze *adj*: **zu nichts ~ sein** to be useless

nutzen, nützen *vt* to use (*zu etw* for sth); **was nützt es?** what use is it? ▷ *vi* to be of use; **das nützt nicht viel** that doesn't help much; **es nützt nichts, es zu tun** it's no use (doing it)

Nutzen (-*s*, *-*) *m* usefulness; (*Gewinn*) profit

nützlich *adj* useful

Nylon (-*s*) *nt* nylon

O

o *interj* oh

O (*abk*) = **Ost** E

Oase (-, -*n*) *f* oasis

ob *conj* if, whether; **so als ob** as if; **er tut so, als ob er krank wäre** he's pretending to be sick; **und ob!** you bet!

obdachlos *adj* homeless

oben *adv* (*am oberen Ende*) at the top; (*obenauf*) on (the) top; (*im Haus*) upstairs; (*in einem Text*) above; **~ erwähnt** *o* **genannt** above-mentioned; **mit dem Gesicht nach ~** face up; **da ~** up there; **von ~ bis unten** from top to bottom; **siehe ~** see above

Ober (-*s*, -) *m* waiter

obere(r, s) *adj* upper, top

Oberfläche *f* surface

oberflächlich *adj* superficial

Obergeschoss *nt* upper floor

oberhalb *adv, prep* (+*gen*) above

Oberhemd *nt* shirt

Oberkörper *m* upper body

Oberlippe *f* upper lip

Oberösterreich *nt* Upper Austria

Oberschenkel *m* thigh

oberste(r, s) *adj* very top, topmost

Oberteil *nt* top

Oberweite *f* bust/chest measurement

obig *adj* above(-mentioned)

Objekt (-(*e*)*s*, -*e*) *nt* object

objektiv *adj* objective

Objektiv *nt* lens

obligatorisch *adj* mandatory, obligatory

Oboe (-, -*n*) *f* oboe

Observatorium *nt* observatory

Obst (-(*e*)*s*) *nt* fruit

Obstkuchen *m* fruit tart

Obstsalat *m* fruit salad

obszön *adj* obscene

obwohl *conj* although

Ochse (-*n*, -*n*) *m* ox

Ochsenschwanzsuppe *f* oxtail soup

ocker *adj* ocher

öd(e) *adj* waste; (*unbebaut*) barren; (*fig*) dull

oder *conj* or; **~ aber** or else; **er kommt doch, ~?** he's coming, isn't he?

Ofen (-*s*, **Öfen**) *m* oven; (*Heizofen*) heater; (*Kohleofen*) stove; (*Herd*) stove

offen *adj* open; (*aufrichtig*) frank; (*Stelle*) vacant ▷ *adv* frankly; **~ gesagt** to be honest

offenbar *adj* obvious

offensichtlich *adj* evident, obvious

öffentlich *adj* public

Öffentlichkeit *f* (*Leute*) public; (*einer Versammlung etc*) public nature

offiziell *adj* official

offline *adv* (*Inform*) offline

öffnen *vt* to open ▷ *vr*: **sich ~** to open

Öffner (-*s*, -) *m* opener

Öffnung *f* opening

Öffnungszeiten *pl* open hours *pl*

oft *adv* often; **schon oft** many times

öfter *adv* more often (*o* frequently)

öfters *adv* often, frequently

ohne *conj, prep* (+*akk*) without; **~ weiteres** without a second thought; (*sofort*) immediately; **~ ein Wort zu sagen** without saying a word; **~ mich** count me out

Ohnmacht (-*machten*) *f* unconsciousness; (*Hilflosigkeit*) helplessness; **in ~ fallen** to faint

ohnmächtig *adj* unconscious; **sie ist ~** she has fainted

Ohr (-(*e*)*s*, -*en*) *nt* ear; (*Gehör*) hearing

Öhr (-(*e*)*s*, -*e*) *nt* eye

Ohrenarzt *m*, **Ohrenärztin** *f* ear specialist

Ohrenschmerzen *pl* earache *sing*

Ohrentropfen *pl* ear drops *pl*

Ohrfeige *f* slap (in the face)

Ohrläppchen *nt* earlobe

Ohrringe *pl* earrings *pl*

oje *interj* oh dear

okay *interj* OK, okay

Ökoladen *m* health food store

ökologisch *adj* ecological; **~e Landwirtschaft** organic farming

ökonomisch *adj* economic; (*sparsam*) economical

Ökosystem *nt* ecosystem

Oktanzahl *f* (*bei Benzin*) octane rating

Oktober (-(*s*), -) *m* October; *siehe auch* **Juni**

OKTOBERFEST

The annual October beer festival, the **Oktoberfest**, takes place in Munich on a huge field where beer tents, roller coasters and many other amusements are set up. People sit at long wooden tables, drink beer from enormous liter beer mugs, eat soft pretzels and listen to brass bands. It is a great attraction for tourists and locals alike.

Öl (-(e)s, -e) nt oil
Ölbaum m olive tree
ölen vt to oil; (Tech) to lubricate
Ölfarbe f oil paint
Ölfilter m oil filter
Ölgemälde nt oil painting
Ölheizung f oil-fired central heating; **eine**
~ haben to heat one's home with oil
ölig adj oily
oliv adj (inv) olive-green
Olive (-, -n) f olive
Olivenöl nt olive oil
Ölmessstab m dipstick
Ölofen m oil stove
Ölpest f oil pollution
Ölsardine f sardine in oil
Ölstandanzeiger m (Auto) oil gauge
Ölteppich m oil slick
Ölwechsel m oil change
Olympiade f Olympic Games pl
olympisch adj Olympic
Oma f, **Omi** (-s, -s) f grandma, gran(ny)
Omelett (-(e)s, -s) nt, **Omelette** f omelette
Omnibus m bus
onanieren vi to masturbate
Onkel (-s, -) m uncle
online adv (Inform) online
Onlinedienst m (Inform) online service
OP (-s, -s) m (abk) = **Operationssaal** OR
Opa m, **Opi** (-s, -s) m grandpa, grandad
Open-Air-Konzert nt outdoor concert
Oper (-, -n) f opera; (Gebäude) opera house
Operation f operation
Operette f operetta
operieren vi to operate ▷ vt to operate on
Opernhaus nt opera house, opera
Opernsänger(in) m(f) opera singer
Opfer (-s, -) nt sacrifice; (Mensch) victim;
ein ~ bringen to make a sacrifice
Opium (-s) nt opium
Opposition f opposition
Optiker(in) (-s, -) m(f) optometrist
optimal adj optimal, optimum
optimistisch adj optimistic
oral adj oral
Oralverkehr m oral sex
orange adj (inv) orange
Orange (-, -n) f orange
Orangenmarmelade f marmalade
Orangensaft m orange juice
Orchester (-s, -) nt orchestra
Orchidee (-, -n) f orchid
Orden (-s, -) m (Rel) order; (Mil) decoration
ordentlich adj (anständig) respectable;

(geordnet) neat; (fam: annehmbar) not
bad; (fam: tüchtig) real ▷ adv properly
ordinär adj common, vulgar; (Witz) dirty
ordnen vt to sort out
Ordner (-s, -) m (bei Veranstaltung) steward;
(Aktenordner) file
Ordnung f order; (Geordnetsein) tidiness;
geht in ~! (that's) all right!; **mit dem Dru-**
cker ist etwas nicht in ~ there's something
wrong with the printer
Oregano (-s) m oregano
Organ (-s, -e) nt organ; (Stimme) voice
Organisation f organization
organisieren vt to organize; (fam: beschaf-
fen) to get hold of ▷ vr: **sich ~** to organize
Organismus m organism
Orgasmus m orgasm
Orgel (-, -n) f organ
Orgie f orgy
orientalisch adj oriental
orientieren vr: **sich ~** to get one's bear-
ings
Orientierung f orientation
Orientierungssinn m sense of direction
original adj original; (echt) genuine
Original (-s, -e) nt original
originell adj original; (komisch) witty
Orkan (-(e)s, -e) m hurricane
Ort (-(e)s, -e) m place; (Dorf) village; **an Ort**
und Stelle, vor Ort on the spot
Orthopäde (-n, -n) m, **Orthopädin** f ortho-
pedist
örtlich adj local
Ortschaft f village, small town
Ortsgespräch nt local call
Ortstarif m local rate
Ortszeit f local time

OSSI

Ossi is a colloquial and rather derogatory word used to describe a German
from the former **DDR**.

Ost (-(e)s) m east
Ostdeutschland nt (als Landesteil) East-
ern Germany; (Hist) East Germany
Osten (-s) m east
Osterei nt Easter egg
Osterglocke f daffodil
Osterhase m Easter bunny
Ostermontag m Easter Monday
Ostern (-, -) nt Easter; **an** o **zu ~** at Easter;
frohe ~ Happy Easter
Österreich (-s) nt Austria

Österreicher(in) (-s, -) m(f) Austrian
österreichisch adj Austrian
Ostersonntag m Easter Sunday
Osteuropa nt Eastern Europe
Ostküste f east coast
östlich adj eastern; (Kurs, Richtung) easterly
Ostsee f: **die ~** the Baltic (Sea)
Ostwind m east(erly) wind
OSZE (-) f (abk = **Organisation für Sicherheit und Zusammenarbeit in Europa**) OSCE

Otter (-s, -) m otter
out adj (fam) out
outen vt to out
oval adj oval
Overheadprojektor m overhead projector
Ozean (-s, -e) m ocean; **der Stille ~** the Pacific (Ocean)
Ozon (-s) nt ozone
Ozonbelastung f ozone level
Ozonloch nt hole in the ozone layer
Ozonschicht f ozone layer
Ozonwerte pl ozone levels pl

P

paar *adj (inv)*; **ein ~** a few; **ein ~ Mal** a few times; **ein ~ Äpfel** some apples

Paar *(-(e)s, -e) nt* pair; *(Ehepaar)* couple; **ein ~ Socken** a pair of socks

pachten *vt* to lease

Päckchen *nt* package; *(Zigaretten)* pack; *(zum Verschicken)* package, parcel

packen *vt* to pack; *(fassen)* to grasp, to seize; *(fam: schaffen)* to manage; *(fig: fesseln)* to grip

Packpapier *nt* brown paper

Packung *f* packet, pack

Packungsbeilage *f* package insert, patient information leaflet

Pädagoge *(-n, -n) m*, **Pädagogin** *f* teacher

pädagogisch *adj* educational; **~e Hochschule** teachers college

Paddel *(-s, -) nt* paddle

Paddelboot *nt* canoe

paddeln *vi* to paddle

Paket *(-(e)s, -e) nt* packet; *(Postpaket)* package, parcel; *(Inform)* package

Paketbombe *f* parcel bomb

Paketkarte *f* shipping label

Pakistan *(-s) nt* Pakistan

Palast *(-es, Paläste) m* palace

Palästina *(-s) nt* Palestine

Palästinenser(in) *(-s, -) m(f)* Palestinian

Palatschinken *pl* crepes *(pl)*

Palette *f (von Maler)* palette; *(Ladepalette)* pallet; *(Vielfalt)* range

Palme *(-, -n) f* palm (tree)

Palmsonntag *m* Palm Sunday

Pampelmuse *(-, -n) f* grapefruit

pampig *adj (fam: frech)* rude; *(a. Antwort)* smart; *(breiig)* gooey

Panda(bär) *(-s, -s) m* panda

Pandemie *(-, -n) f* pandemic

panieren *vt (Gastr)* to bread

paniert *adj* breaded

Panik *f* panic

Panne *(-, -n) f (Auto)* breakdown; *(Missgeschick)* slip

Pannendienst *m*, **Pannenhilfe** *f* roadside assistance

Pant(h)er *(-s, -) m* panther

Pantomime *(-, -n) f* mime

Panzer *(-s, -) m (Panzerung)* armor (plating); *(Mil)* tank

Papa *(-s, -s) m* dad(dy), pa

Papagei *(-s, -en) m* parrot

Papaya *(-, -s) f* papaya

Papier *(-s, -e) nt* paper; **~e** *pl (Ausweispapiere)* papers *pl*; *(Dokumente, Urkunden)* papers *pl* documents *pl*

Papiercontainer *m* recycling bin for paper

Papierformat *nt* paper size

Papiergeld *nt* paper money

Papierkorb *m* wastepaper basket; *(Inform)* recycle bin

Papiertaschentuch *nt* (paper) tissue

Papiertonne *f* recycling bin for paper

Pappbecher *m* paper cup

Pappe *(-, -n) f* cardboard

Pappkarton *m* cardboard box

Pappteller *m* paper plate

Paprika *(-s, -s) m (Gewürz)* paprika; *(Schote)* pepper

Papst *(-(e)s, Päpste) m* pope

Paradeiser *(-s, -) m* tomato

Paradies *(-es, -e) nt* paradise

Paragliding *(-s) nt* paragliding

Paragraph *(-en, -en) m* paragraph; *(Jur)* section

parallel *adj* parallel

Paranuss *f* Brazil nut

Parasit *(-en, -en) m* parasite

parat *adj* ready; **etw ~ haben** to have sth ready

Pärchen *nt* couple

Parfüm *(-s, -s o -e) nt* perfume

Parfümerie *f* perfume shop

parfümieren *vt* to scent, to perfume

Pariser *(-s, -) m (fam: Kondom)* rubber

Park *(-s, -s) m* park

Park-and-ride-System *nt* park-and-ride system

Parkbank *f* park bench

Parkdeck *nt* parking level

parken *vt, vi* to park

Parkett *(-s, -e) nt* parquet flooring; *(Theat)* parquet

Parkhaus *nt* parking garage

parkinsonsche Krankheit *f* Parkinson's disease

Parkkralle *f (Auto)* Denver boot

Parklicht *nt* parking light

Parklücke *f* parking space

Parkplatz *m (für ein Auto)* parking space; *(für mehrere Autos)* parking lot

Parkscheinautomat *m* (pay and display) ticket machine

Parkuhr *f* parking meter

Parkverbot *nt (Stelle)* no-parking zone; **hier**

ist ~ you can't park here
Parlament nt parliament
Parmesan (-s) m Parmesan (cheese)
Partei f party
Parterre (-s, -s) nt first floor
Partie f part; (Spiel) game; (Mann, Frau)
catch; **mit von der ~ sein** to be in on it
Partitur f (Mus) score
Partizip (-s, -ien) nt participle
Partner(in) (-s, -) m(f) partner
Partnerschaft f partnership; **eingetragene
~** civil partnership
Partnerstadt f sister city
Party (-, -s) f party
Partymuffel (-s, -) m party pooper
Pass (-es, Pässe) m pass; (Ausweis) passport
passabel adj reasonable
Passagier (-s, -e) m passenger
Passant(in) m(f) passer-by; **mehrere ~en
waren Zeugen des Unfalls** the accident
was witnessed by several passers-by
Passbild nt passport photo
passen vi (Größe) to fit; (Farbe, Stil) to go
(zu with); (auf Frage) to pass; **passt es dir
morgen?** does tomorrow suit you?; **das
passt mir gut** that suits me fine
passend adj suitable; (zusammenpassend)
matching; (angebracht) fitting; (Zeit) convenient; **haben Sie es nicht ~?** (Kleingeld)
do you have exact change?
passieren vi to happen
passiv adj passive
Passwort nt password
Paste (-, -n) f paste
Pastellfarbe f pastel color
Pastete (-, -n) f (warmes Gericht) pie; (Pas-
tetchen) vol-au-vent; (ohne Teig) pâté
Pastor(in) (-s, -en) m(f) pastor, minister
Pate (-n, -n) m godfather
Patenkind nt godchild
Patient(in) m(f) patient
Patin f godmother
Patrone (-, -n) f cartridge
patsch interj splat
patschnass adj soaking wet
pauschal adj (Kosten) inclusive; (Urteil)
sweeping
Pauschale (-, -n) f, **Pauschalgebühr** f flat
rate (charge)
Pauschalpreis m flat rate; (für Hotel, Reise)
all-inclusive price
Pauschalreise f package tour
Pause (-, -n) f break; (Theat) intermission;
(Kino etc: Innehalten) pause
Pavian (-s, -e) m baboon

Pavillon (-s, -s) m pavilion
Pay-TV (-s) nt pay-per-view television, pay
TV
Pazifik (-s) m Pacific (Ocean)
PC (-s, -s) m (abk) = **Personal Computer** PC
Pech (-s, -e) nt (fig) bad luck; **~ haben** to be
unlucky; **~ gehabt!** tough (luck)!
Pedal (-s, -e) nt pedal
Pediküre (-, -en) f pedicure
Peeling (-s, -s) nt (facial/body) scrub
peinlich adj (unangenehm) embarrassing,
awkward; (genau) painstaking; **es war mir
sehr ~** I was totally embarrassed
Peitsche (-, -n) f whip
Pelikan (-s, -e) m pelican
Pellkartoffeln pl potatoes pl boiled in their
skins
Pelz (-es, -e) m fur
pelzig adj (Zunge) coated, furred
pendeln vi (Zug, Bus) to shuttle; (Mensch)
to commute
Pendelverkehr m shuttle traffic; (für Pend-
ler) commuter traffic
Pendler(in) (-s, -) m(f) commuter
penetrant adj sharp; (Mensch) pushy
Penis (-, -se) m penis
Pension f (Geld) pension; (Ruhestand)
retirement; (für Gäste) guesthouse, B&B
pensioniert adj retired
Pensionsgast m guest (in a guesthouse)
Peperoni (-, -) f hot pepper, chili (pepper)
per prep (+akk) by, per; (pro) per; (bis) by
perfekt adj perfect
Pergamentpapier nt parchment paper
Periode (-, -n) f period
Perle (-, -n) f (a. fig) pearl
perplex adj dumbfounded
Person (-, -en) f person; **ein Tisch für drei
~en** a table for three
Personal (-s) nt staff, personnel; (Bedie-
nung) servants pl
Personalausweis m ID (o identification)
card
Personalien pl personal information sing
Personenschaden m injury to persons
Personenwaage f (bathroom) scale
Personenzug m passenger train
persönlich adj personal; (auf Briefen) pri-
vate ▷ adv personally; (selbst) in person
Persönlichkeit f personality
Peru (-s) nt Peru
Perücke (-, -n) f wig
pervers adj perverted
pessimistisch adj pessimistic
Pest (-) f plague

Petersilie f parsley
Petroleum (-s) nt kerosene
Pfad (-(e)s, -e) m path
Pfadfinder (-s, -) m Boy Scout
Pfadfinderin f Girl Scout, Girl Guide
Pfahl (-(e)s, Pfähle) m post, stake
Pfand (-(e)s, Pfänder) nt security; (Flaschen-pfand) deposit; (im Spiel) forfeit
Pfandflasche f returnable bottle
Pfanne (-, -n) f (frying) pan
Pfannkuchen m pancake; (dünn) crepe
Pfarrei f parish
Pfarrer(in) (-s, -) m(f) priest
Pfau (-(e)s, -en) m peacock
Pfeffer (-s, -) m pepper
Pfefferkuchen m gingerbread
Pfefferminze (-e) f peppermint
Pfefferminztee m peppermint tea
Pfeffermühle f pepper mill
pfeffern vt to put pepper on/in
Pfefferstreuer (-s, -) m pepper shaker
Pfeife (-, -n) f whistle; (für Tabak, von Orgel) pipe
pfeifen (pfiff, gepfiffen) vt, vi to whistle
Pfeil (-(e)s, -e) m arrow
Pfeiltaste f (Inform) arrow key
Pferd (-(e)s, -e) nt horse
Pferdeschwanz m (Frisur) ponytail
Pferdestall m stable
Pferdestärke f horsepower
pfiff imperf von **pfeifen**
Pfifferling m chanterelle
Pfingsten (-, -) nt Pentecost, Whitsuntide
Pfingstmontag m Whitmonday
Pfingstsonntag m Pentecost, Whitsunday
Pfirsich (-s, -e) m peach
Pflanze (-, -n) f plant
pflanzen vt to plant
Pflanzenfett nt vegetable fat
Pflaster (-s, -) nt (für Wunde) plaster, Band Aid®; (Straßenpflaster) road surface, pavement
Pflaume (-, -n) f plum
Pflege (-, -n) f care; (Krankenpflege) nurs-ing; (von Autos, Maschinen) maintenance
pflegebedürftig adj in need of care
Pflegeheim nt home for the disabled; (für ältere Leute) nursing home
pflegeleicht adj easy-care; (fig) easy to handle
pflegen vt to look after; (Kranke) to nurse; (Beziehungen) to foster; (Fingernägel, Gesicht) to take care of; (Daten) to main-tain
Pflegepersonal nt nursing staff

Pflegeversicherung f long-term care insurance
Pflicht (-, -en) f duty; (Sport) compulsory section
pflichtbewusst adj conscientious
Pflichtfach nt (Schule) mandatory subject
Pflichtversicherung f mandatory insur-ance
pflücken vt to pick
Pforte (-, -n) f gate
Pförtner(in) (-s, -) m(f) porter
Pfosten (-s, -) m post
Pfote (-, -n) f paw
pfui interj ugh
Pfund (-(e)s, -e) nt pound
pfuschen vi (fam) to be sloppy
Pfütze (-, -n) f puddle
Phantasie f siehe **Fantasie**
phantastisch adj siehe **fantastisch**
Phase (-, -n) f phase
Philippinen pl Philippines pl
Philosophie f philosophy
pH-neutral adj pH-balanced
Photo nt siehe **Foto**
pH-Wert m pH-value
Physalis (-, Physalen) f (Bot) Cape goose-berry
Physik f physics sing
physisch adj physical
Pianist(in) (-en, -en) m(f) pianist
Pickel (-s, -) m pimple; (Werkzeug) pickaxe; (Bergpickel) ice-ax
Picknick (-s, -e o -s) nt picnic; **ein ~ machen** to have a picnic
piepsen vi to chirp
piercen vt: **sich die Nase ~ lassen** to have one's nose pierced
Piercing (-s) nt (body) piercing
pieseln vi (fam) to pee
Pik (-, -) nt (Karten) spades pl
pikant adj spicy
Pilates nt (Sport) Pilates
Pilger(in) m(f) pilgrim
Pilgerfahrt f pilgrimage
Pille (-, -n) f pill; **sie nimmt die ~** she's on the pill
Pilot(in) (-en, -en) m(f) pilot
Pils (-, -) nt (Pilsner) lager
Pilz (-es, -e) m (essbar) mushroom; (giftig) toadstool; (Med) fungus
PIN (-, -s) f PIN (number)
pingelig adj (fam) fussy
Pinguin (-s, -e) m penguin
Pinie f pine
Pinienkern m pine nut

P

pink adj shocking pink
pinkeln vi (fam) to pee
Pinsel (-s, -) m (paint)brush
Pinzette f tweezers pl
Pistazie f pistachio
Piste (-, -n) f (Ski) trail, run; (Aviat) runway
Pistole (-, -n) f pistol
Pixel (-s) nt (Inform) pixel
Pizza (-, -s) f pizza
Pizzaservice m pizza delivery service
Pizzeria (-, Pizzerien) f pizzeria
Pkw (-(s), -(s)) m (abk) = **Personenkraftwagen** (passenger) car
Plakat nt poster
Plakette f (Schildchen) badge; (Aufkleber) sticker
Plan (-(e)s, Pläne) m plan; (Karte) map
planen vt to plan
Planet (-en, -en) m planet
Planetarium nt planetarium
planmäßig adj scheduled
Plan(t)schbecken nt wading pool
plan(t)schen vi to splash around
Planung f planning
Plastik f sculpture ▷ (-s) nt (Kunststoff) plastic
Plastikfolie f plastic wrap
Plastiktüte f plastic bag
Platin (-s) nt platinum
platsch interj splash
platt adj flat; (fam: überrascht) flabbergasted; (fig: geistlos) flat, boring
Platte (-, -n) f (Foto, Tech, Gastr) plate; (Steinplatte) flag; (Schallplatte) record
Plattenspieler m record player
Plattform f platform
Plattfuß m flat foot; (Reifen) flat (tire)
Platz (-es, Plätze) m place; (Sitzplatz) seat; (freier Raum) space, room; (in Stadt) square; (Sportplatz) playing field; **nehmen Sie ~** please sit down, take a seat; **ist dieser ~ frei?** is this seat taken?
Platzanweiser(in) m(f) usher/usherette
Plätzchen nt spot; (Gebäck) cookie
platzen vi to burst; (Bombe) to explode
Platzkarte f seat reservation
Platzreservierung f seat reservation
Platzverweis m: **er erhielt einen ~** he was sent off
Platzwunde f laceration, cut
plaudern vi to chat, to talk
pleite adj (fam) broke
Pleite (-, -n) f (Bankrott) bankruptcy; (fam: Reinfall) flop

Plombe (-, -n) f lead seal; (Zahnplombe) filling
plombieren vt (Zahn) to fill
plötzlich adj sudden ▷ adv suddenly, all at once
plump adj clumsy; (Hände) ungainly; (Körper) shapeless
plumps interj thud; (in Flüssigkeit) plop
Plural (-s, -e) m plural
plus adv plus; **fünf ~ sieben ist zwölf** five plus seven is twelve; **zehn Grad ~** ten degrees above zero
Plus (-, -) nt plus; (Fin) profit; (Vorteil) advantage
Plüsch (-(e)s, -e) m plush
Pluto (-) m Pluto
PLZ (abk) = **Postleitzahl** zip code
Po (-s, -s) m (fam) bottom, behind
Pocken pl smallpox sing
Podcast (-s, -s) m podcast
poetisch adj poetic
Pointe (-, -n) f punch line
Pokal (-s, -e) m goblet; (Sport) cup
pökeln vt to pickle
Pol (-s, -e) m pole
Pole (-n, -n) m Pole
Polen (-s) nt Poland
Police (-, -n) f (insurance) policy
polieren vt to polish
Polin f Pole, Polish woman
Politik f politics sing; (eine bestimmte) policy
Politiker(in) m(f) politician
politisch adj political
Politur f polish
Polizei f police pl
Polizeibeamte(r) m, **Polizeibeamtin** f police officer
polizeilich adj police; **sie wird ~ gesucht** the police are looking for her
Polizeirevier nt, **Polizeiwache** f police station
Polizeistunde f closing time
Polizeiwache f police station
Polizist(in) m(f) policeman/-woman
Pollen (-s, -) m pollen
Pollenflug (-s) m pollen count
polnisch adj Polish
Polnisch nt Polish
Polo (-s) nt polo
Polohemd nt polo shirt
Polster (-s, -) nt cushion; (Polsterung) upholstery; (in Kleidung) padding; (fig: Geld) reserves pl
Polstergarnitur f three-piece living room set

Polstermöbel *pl* upholstered furniture *sing*
polstern *vt* to upholster; (*Kleidung*) to pad
Polterabend *m party prior to a wedding, at which old crockery is smashed to bring good luck*
poltern *vi* (*Krach machen*) to crash; (*schimpfen*) to rant
Polyester (*-s, -*) *m* polyester
Polypen *pl* (*Med*) adenoids *pl*
Pommes frites *pl* French fries *pl*
Pony (*-s, -s*) *m* (*Frisur*) bangs *pl* ▷ (*-s, -s*) *nt* (*Pferd*) pony
Popcorn (*-s*) *nt* popcorn
Popmusik *f* pop (music)
populär *adj* popular
Pore (*-, -n*) *f* pore
Pornografie *f* pornography
Porree (*-s, -s*) *m* leeks *pl*; **eine Stange ~** a leek
Portemonnaie, Portmonee (*-s, -s*) *nt* wallet
Portier (*-s, -s*) *m* porter; *siehe auch* **Pförtner**
Portion *f* portion, helping
Porto (*-s, -s*) *nt* postage
Portrait, Porträt (*-s, -s*) *nt* portrait
Portugal (*-s*) *nt* Portugal
Portugiese (*-n, -n*) *m* Portuguese
Portugiesin (*-, -nen*) *f* Portuguese
portugiesisch *adj* Portuguese
Portugiesisch *nt* Portuguese
Portwein (*-s, -e*) *m* port
Porzellan (*-s, -e*) *nt* china
Posaune (*-, -n*) *f* trombone
Position *f* position
positiv *adj* positive
Post® (*-, -en*) *f* post office; (*Briefe*) mail
Postamt *nt* post office
Postanweisung *f* money order
Postbank *f German post office bank*
Postbote *m*, **-botin** *f* mailman/-woman
Posten (*-s, -*) *m* post, position; (*Comm*) item; (*auf Liste*) entry
Poster (*-s, -*) *nt* poster
Postfach *nt* post-office box, PO box
Postkarte *f* postcard
postlagernd *adv* poste restante
Postleitzahl *f* zip code
postmodern *adj* postmodern
Postsparkasse *f* post office savings bank
Poststempel *m* postmark
Postweg *m*: **auf dem ~** by mail
Potenz *f* (*Math*) power; (*eines Mannes*) potency
PR (*-, -s*) *f* (*abk*) = **Public Relations** PR

prächtig *adj* splendid
prahlen *vi* to boast, to brag
Praktikant(in) *m(f)* intern, trainee
Praktikum (*-s, Praktika*) *nt* internship
praktisch *adj* practical; **~er Arzt** general practitioner
Praline *f* chocolate
Prämie *f* (*bei Versicherung*) premium; (*Belohnung*) reward; (*von Arbeitgeber*) bonus
Präparat *nt* (*Med*) medicine; (*Bio*) preparation
Präservativ *nt* condom
Präsident(in) *m(f)* president
Praxis (*-, Praxen*) *f* practice; (*Behandlungsraum*) surgery; (*von Anwalt*) office
Praxisgebühr *f quarterly co-pay for office visits to the doctor*
präzise *adj* precise, exact
predigen *vt, vi* to preach
Predigt (*-, -en*) *f* sermon
Preis (*-es, -e*) *m* (*zu zahlen*) price; (*bei Sieg*) prize; **den ersten ~ gewinnen** to win first prize
Preisausschreiben *nt* competition
Preiselbeere *f* cranberry
preisgünstig *adj* inexpensive
Preislage *f* price range
Preisliste *f* price list
Preisschild *nt* price tag
Preisträger(in) *m(f)* prizewinner
preiswert *adj* inexpensive
Prellung *f* bruise
Premiere (*-, -n*) *f* premiere, first night
Premierminister(in) *m(f)* prime minister, premier
Prepaidhandy *nt* prepaid cell phone
Prepaidkarte *f* prepaid card
Presse (*-, -n*) *f* press
pressen *vt* to press
prickeln *vi* to tingle
Priester(in) (*-s, -*) *m(f)* priest/(woman) priest
Primel (*-, -n*) *f* primrose
primitiv *adj* primitive
Prinz (*-en, -en*) *m* prince
Prinzessin *f* princess
Prinzip (*-s, -ien*) *nt* principle; **im ~** basically; **aus ~** on principle
Priorität *f* priority
privat *adj* private
Privatfernsehen *nt* commercial television
Privatgrundstück *nt* private property
privatisieren *vt* to privatize
pro *prep* (+*akk*) per; **5 Euro pro Stück/Per-**

P

son 5 euros each/per person

Pro (-s) *nt* pro

Probe (-, -*n*) *f* test; (*Teststück*) sample; (*Theat*) rehearsal

Probefahrt *f* test drive; **eine ~ machen** to go for a test drive

Probezeit *f* trial period

probieren *vt, vi* to try; (*Wein, Speise*) to taste, to sample

Problem (-s, -e) *nt* problem

Produkt (-(*e)s, -e*) *nt* product

Produktion *f* production; (*produzierte Menge*) output

produzieren *vt* to produce

Professor(in) (-s, -*en*) *m(f)* professor

Profi (-s, -s) *m* pro

Profil (-s, -e) *nt* profile; (*von Reifen, Schuhsohle*) tread

Profit (-(*e)s, -e*) *m* profit

profitieren *vi* to profit (*von* from)

Prognose (-, -*n*) *f* prediction; (*Wetter*) forecast

Programm (-s, -e) *nt* programme; (*TV*) channel

Programmheft *nt* program

programmieren *vt* to program

Programmierer(in) (-s, -) *m(f)* programmer

Programmkino *nt* repertory cinema

Projekt (-(*e)s, -e*) *nt* project

Projektor *m* projector

Promenade (-, -*n*) *f* promenade

Promille (-(*s*), -) *nt* (blood) alcohol level; **0,8 ~ 0,08** percent

Promillegrenze *f* legal alcohol limit

prominent *adj* prominent

Prominenz *f* VIPs *pl*, prominent figures *pl*; (*fam: Stars*) the glitterati *pl*

Propeller (-s, -) *m* propeller

prosit *interj* cheers

Prospekt (-(*e)s, -e*) *m* leaflet, brochure

prost *interj* cheers

Prostituierte(r) *mf* prostitute

Protest (-(*e)s, -e*) *m* protest

Protestant(in) *m(f)* Protestant

protestantisch *adj* Protestant

protestieren *vi* to protest (*gegen* against)

Prothese (-, -*n*) *f* artificial arm/leg; (*Gebiss*) dentures *pl*

Protokoll (-s, -e) *nt* (*bei Sitzung*) minutes *pl*; (*diplomatisch: Inform*) protocol; (*bei Polizei*) statement

protzen *vi* to show off

protzig *adj* flashy

Proviant (-s, -e) *m* provisions *pl*

Provider (-s, -) *m* (*Inform*) (service) provider

Provinz (-, -*en*) *f* province

Provision *f* (*Comm*) commission

provisorisch *adj* provisional

Provisorium (-s, *Provisorien*) *nt* interim solution; (*Zahn*) temporary filling

provozieren *vt* to provoke

Prozent (-(*e)s, -e*) *nt* percent

Prozess (-es, -e) *m* (*Vorgang*) process; (*Jur*) trial; (*Rechtsfall*) (court) case

prozessieren *vi* to file suit (*mit* against)

Prozession *f* procession

Prozessor (-s, -*en*) *m* (*Inform*) processor

prüde *adj* prudish

prüfen *vt* to test; (*nachprüfen*) to check

Prüfung *f* (*Schule*) exam; (*Überprüfung*) check; **eine ~ machen** (*Schule*) to take an exam

Prügelei *f* fight

prügeln *vt* to beat ▷ *vr*: **sich ~** to fight

PS (*abk*) = **Pferdestärke** hp (*abk*) = **Postskript(um)** PS

pseudo- *präf* pseudo

Pseudokrupp (-s) *m* (*Med*) pseudocroup

Pseudonym (-s, -e) *nt* pseudonym

pst *interj* ssh

Psychiater(in) (-s, -) *m(f)* psychiatrist

psychisch *adj* psychological; (*Krankheit*) mental

Psychoanalyse *f* psychoanalysis

Psychologe (-*n*, -*n*) *m*, **Psychologin** *f* psychologist

Psychologie *f* psychology

Psychopharmaka *pl* psychoactive (*o* psychotropic) drugs *pl*

psychosomatisch *adj* psychosomatic

Psychoterror *m* psychological intimidation

Psychotherapie *f* psychotherapy

Pubertät *f* puberty

Publikum (-s) *nt* audience; (*Sport*) crowd

Pudding (-s, -e o -s) *m* pudding

Pudel (-s, -) *m* poodle

Puder (-s, -) *m* powder

Puderzucker *m* powdered sugar

Puerto Rico (-s) *nt* Puerto Rico

Pulli (-s, -s) *m*, **Pullover** (-s, -) *m* sweater, pullover

Puls (-es, -e) *m* pulse

Pulver (-s, -) *nt* powder

Pulverkaffee *m* instant coffee

Pulverschnee *m* powder snow

pummelig *adj* chubby

Pumpe (-, -*n*) *f* pump

pumpen *vt* to pump; (*fam: verleihen*) to lend; (*fam: sich ausleihen*) to borrow

Pumps *pl* pumps *pl*
Punk (*-s, -s*) *m* (*Musik, Mensch*) punk
Punkt (*-(e)s, -e*) *m* point; (*bei Muster*) dot; (*Satzzeichen*) period; **~ zwei Uhr** at two o'clock sharp
pünktlich *adj* punctual, on time
Pünktlichkeit *f* punctuality
Punsch (*-(e)s, -e*) *m* punch
Pupille (*-, -n*) *f* pupil
Puppe (*-, -n*) *f* doll
pur *adj* pure; (*völlig*) sheer; (*Whisky*) neat
Püree (*-s, -s*) *nt* puree; (*Kartoffelpüree*) mashed potatoes *pl*
Puste (*-*) *f* (*fam*) puff; **außer ~ sein** to be winded (*o* out of breath)
Pustel (*-, -n*) *f* pustule; (*Pickel*) pimple

pusten *vi* to blow; (*keuchen*) to puff
Pute (*-, -n*) *f* turkey
Putenschnitzel *nt* breaded turkey cutlet
Putsch (*-es, -e*) *m* putsch
Putz (*-es*) *m* (*Mörtel*) plaster
putzen *vt* to clean; **sich** (*dat*) **die Nase ~** to blow one's nose; **sich** (*dat*) **die Zähne ~** to brush one's teeth
Putzfrau *f* cleaning lady, maid
Putzlappen *m* cloth, **Putzmann** *m* cleaner
Putzmittel *nt* cleaning agent, cleaner
Puzzle (*-s, -s*) *nt* jigsaw (puzzle)
Pyjama (*-s, -s*) *m* pajamas *pl*
Pyramide (*-, -n*) *f* pyramid
Python (*-s, -s*) *m* python

p

Q

Quadrat *nt* square
quadratisch *adj* square
Quadratmeter *m* square meter
quaken *vi* (*Frosch*) to croak; (*Ente*) to quack
Qual (-, -en) *f* pain, agony; (*seelisch*) anguish
quälen *vt* to torment ▷ *vr*: **sich ~** to struggle; (*geistig*) to torment oneself
Quälerei *f* torture, torment
qualifizieren *vt* to qualify; (*einstufen*) to label ▷ *vr*: **sich ~** to qualify
Qualität *f* quality
Qualle (-, -n) *f* jellyfish
Qualm (-(e)s) *m* thick smoke
qualmen *vt*, *vi* to smoke
Quantität *f* quantity
Quarantäne (-, -n) *f* quarantine
Quark (-s) *m* quark; (*fam: Unsinn*) nonsense
Quartett (-s, -e) *nt* quartet; (*Kartenspiel*) ≈ Go Fish
Quartier (-s, -e) *nt* accommodation
quasi *adv* more or less

Quatsch (-es) *m* (*fam*) nonsense
quatschen *vi* (*fam*) to chat
Quecksilber *nt* mercury
Quelle (-, -n) *f* spring; (*eines Flusses*) source
quellen *vi* to pour
quer *adv* crossways, diagonally; (*rechtwinklig*) at right angles; **~ über die Straße** straight across the street
querfeldein *adv* across country
Querflöte *f* flute
Querschnitt *m* cross section
querschnittsgelähmt *adj* paraplegic
Querstraße *f* side street
quetschen *vt* to squash, to crush; (*Med*) to bruise
Quetschung *f* bruise
Queue (-s, -s) *m* (billiard) cue
quietschen *vi* to squeal; (*Tür, Bett*) to squeak; (*Bremsen*) to screech
quitt *adj* quits, even
Quitte (-, -n) *f* quince
Quittung *f* receipt
Quiz (-, -) *nt* quiz
Quote (-, -n) *f* rate; (*Comm*) quota

R

Rabatt (-(e)s, -e) m discount
Rabbi (-(s), -s) m rabbi
Rabbiner (-s, -) m rabbi
Rabe (-n, -n) m raven
Rache (-) f revenge, vengeance
Rachen (-s, -) m throat
rächen vt to avenge ▷ vr: **sich ~** to take (one's) revenge (*an +dat* on)
Rad (-(e)s, Räder) nt wheel; (*Fahrrad*) bike; **Rad fahren** to ride one's bike, to bicycle; **mit dem Rad fahren** to go by bike
Radar (-s) m o nt radar
Radarfalle f speed trap
Radarkontrolle f radar speed check
radeln vi (*fam*) to ride one's bike, to bicycle
Radfahrer(in) m(f) bicyclist, bicycler
Radfahrweg m bike path
Radicchio (-s) m (*Salatsorte*) radicchio
radieren vt to erase
Radiergummi m eraser
Radierung f (*Kunst*) etching
Radieschen nt radish
radikal adj radical
Radio (-s, -s) nt radio; **im ~** on the radio
radioaktiv adj radioactive
Radiologe (-n, -n) m, **Radiologin** f radiologist
Radiorekorder m radio cassette recorder
Radiosender m radio station
Radiowecker m clock radio
Radkappe f (*Auto*) hub cap
Radler(in) (-s, -) m(f) cyclist
Radlerhose f cycling shorts pl
Radrennen nt cycle racing; (*einzelnes Rennen*) cycle race
Radtour f bike ride; (*länger*) bicycle (o bike) tour
Radweg m bike path
raffiniert adj crafty, cunning; (*Zucker*) refined
Rafting (-s) nt white water rafting
Ragout (-s, -s) nt ragout
Rahm (-s) m cream
rahmen vt to frame
Rahmen (-s, -) m frame
Rakete (-, -n) f rocket
rammen vt to ram
Rampe (-, -n) f ramp
ramponieren vt (*fam*) to damage, to batter
Ramsch (-(e)s, -e) m junk

ran (*fam*) kontr von **heran**
Rand (-(e)s, Ränder) m edge; (*von Brille, Tasse etc*) rim; (*auf Papier*) margin; (*Schmutzrand, unter Augen*) ring; (*fig*) verge, brink
randalieren vi to (go on the) rampage
Randalierer(in) (-s, -) m(f) rowdy, troublemaker
Randstein m curb
Randstreifen m shoulder
rang imperf von **ringen**
Rang (-(e)s, Ränge) m rank; (*in Wettbewerb*) place; (*Theat*) circle
rannte imperf von **rennen**
ranzig adj rancid
Rap (-(s), -s) m (*Mus*) rap
rappen vi (*Mus*) to rap
Rapper(in) (-s, -) m(f) (*Mus*) rapper
rar adj rare, scarce
rasant adj quick, rapid
rasch adj quick
rascheln vi to rustle
rasen vi (*sich schnell bewegen*) to race; (*toben*) to go wild; **gegen einen Baum ~** to crash into a tree
Rasen (-s, -) m lawn
rasend adj (*vor Wut*) furious
Rasenmäher (-s, -) m lawnmower
Rasierapparat m razor; (*elektrischer*) shaver
Rasiercreme f shaving cream
rasieren vt to shave ▷ vr: **sich ~** to shave
Rasierer m shaver
Rasiergel nt shaving gel
Rasierklinge f razor blade
Rasiermesser nt (cutthroat) razor
Rasierpinsel m shaving brush
Rasierschaum m shaving cream
Rasierzeug nt shaving equipment
Rasse (-, -n) f race; (*Tiere*) breed
Rassismus m racism
Rassist(in) m(f) racist
rassistisch adj racist
Rast (-, -en) f rest, break; **~ machen** to take a rest (o break)
rasten vi to rest
Rastplatz m (*Auto*) rest area
Rasur f shave
Rat (-(e)s, Ratschläge) m (piece of) advice; **sie hat mir einen Rat gegeben** she gave me some advice; **um Rat fragen** to ask for advice

r

Rate (-, -n) f installment; **etw auf ~n kaufen** to buy sth on the installment plan

raten (riet, geraten) vt, vi to guess; (empfehlen) to advise (jdm sb)

Rathaus nt town hall

Ration f ration

ratlos adj at a loss, helpless

ratsam adj advisable

Rätsel (-s, -) nt puzzle; (Worträtsel) riddle; **das ist mir ein ~** it's a mystery to me

rätselhaft adj mysterious

Ratte (-, -n) f rat

rau adj rough, coarse; (Wetter) harsh

Raub (-(e)s) m robbery; (Beute) loot

rauben vt to steal; **jdm etw ~** to rob sb of sth

Räuber(in) (-s, -) m(f) robber

Raubfisch m predatory fish

Raubkopie f pirate copy

Raubmord m robbery with murder

Raubtier nt predator

Raubüberfall m mugging

Raubvogel m bird of prey

Rauch (-(e)s) m smoke; (Abgase) fumes pl

rauchen vt, vi to smoke

Raucher(in) (-s, -) m(f) smoker

Raucherabteil nt smoking compartment

Räucherlachs m smoked salmon

räuchern vt to smoke

rauchig adj smoky

Rauchmelder m smoke detector

Rauchverbot nt smoking ban; **hier ist ~** there's no smoking here

rauf (fam) kontr von **herauf**

rauh adj siehe **rau**

Rauhreif m siehe **Raureif**

Raum (-(e)s, Räume) m space; (Zimmer, Platz) room; (Gebiet) area

räumen vt to clear; (Wohnung, Platz) to vacate; (wegbringen) to shift, to move; (in Schrank etc) to put away

Raumfähre f space shuttle

Raumfahrt f space travel

Raumschiff nt spacecraft, spaceship

Raumsonde f space probe

Raumstation f space station

Raumtemperatur f room temperature

Räumungsverkauf m going-out-of-business sale, clearance sale

Raupe (-, -n) f caterpillar

Raureif m (hoar)frost

raus (fam) kontr von **heraus, hinaus**; **~!** (get) out!

Rausch (-(e)s, Räusche) m intoxication; **einen ~ haben/kriegen** (Alkohol) to be/get drunk; (Drogen) to be/get high

rauschen vi (Wasser) to rush; (Baum) to rustle; (Radio etc) to hiss

Rauschgift nt drug

Rauschgiftsüchtige(r) mf drug addict

raus|fliegen (irr) vi (fam) to be kicked out

raus|halten (irr) vr (fam): **halt du dich da raus!** you (just) keep out of it!

räuspern vr: **sich ~** to clear one's throat

raus|schmeißen (irr) vt (fam) to throw out

Razzia (-, Razzien) f raid

reagieren vi to react (auf +akk to)

Reaktion f reaction

real adj real

realisieren vt (merken) to realize; (verwirklichen) to implement

realistisch adj realistic

Realität (-, -en) f reality

Reality-TV (-s) nt reality TV

Realschule f ≈ junior high (school)

Rebe (-, -n) f vine

rebellieren vi to rebel

Rebhuhn nt partridge

rechnen vt, vi to calculate; **~ mit** to expect; (bauen auf) to count on ▷ vr: **sich ~** to pay off, to turn out to be profitable

Rechner (-s, -) m calculator; (Computer) computer

Rechnung f calculation(s); (Comm) check; **die ~, bitte!** can I have the check, please?; **das geht auf meine ~** this is on me

recht adj (richtig, passend) right; **~ haben** to be right; **jdm ~ geben** to agree with sb; **mir soll's ~ sein** it's all right by me; **mir ist es ~** I don't mind ▷ adv really, quite; (richtig) right(ly); **ich weiß nicht ~** I don't really know; **es geschieht ihm ~** it serves him right

Recht (-(e)s, -e) nt right; (Jur) law

Rechte (-n, -n) f right-hand side; (Hand) right hand; (Pol) right (wing)

rechte(r, s) adj right; **auf der ~n Seite** on the right, on the right-hand side

Rechte(s) nt right thing; **etwas/nichts ~s** something/nothing proper

Rechteck (-s, -e) nt rectangle

rechteckig adj rectangular

rechtfertigen vt to justify ▷ vr: **sich ~** to justify oneself

rechtlich adj legal

rechtmäßig adj legal, lawful

rechts adv on the right; **~ abbiegen** to turn right; **~ von** to the right of; **~ oben** at the top right

Rechtsanwalt m, **-anwältin** f lawyer
Rechtschreibung f spelling
Rechtshänder(in) (-s, -) m(f) right-hander
rechtsherum adv to the right, clockwise
rechtsradikal adj (Pol) extreme right-wing
Rechtsschutzversicherung f legal costs
insurance
Rechtsverkehr m driving on the right
rechtswidrig adj illegal
rechtwinklig adj right-angled
rechtzeitig adj timely ▷ adv in time
recyclebar adj recyclable
recyceln vt to recycle
Recycling (-s) nt recycling
Recyclingpapier nt recycled paper
Redakteur(in) m(f) editor
Redaktion f editing; (Leute) editorial staff;
(Büro) editorial office(s)
Rede (-, -n) f speech; (Gespräch) talk; **eine ~
halten** to make a speech
reden vi to talk, to speak ▷ vt to say;
(Unsinn etc) to talk
Redewendung f idiom
Redner(in) m(f) speaker
reduzieren vt to reduce
Referat (-s, -e) nt paper; **ein ~ halten** to give
a paper (über +akk on)
reflektieren vt to reflect
Reform (-, -en) f reform
Reformhaus nt health food store
reformieren vt to reform
Regal (-s, -e) nt shelf; (Möbelstück) shelves
pl
Regel (-, -n) f rule; (Med) period
regelmäßig adj regular
regeln vt to regulate, to control; (Angele-
genheit) to settle ▷ vr: **sich von selbst ~** to
sort itself out
Regelung f regulation
Regen (-s, -) m rain
Regenbogen m rainbow
Regenmantel m raincoat
Regenrinne f gutter
Regenschauer m shower
Regenschirm m umbrella
Regenwald m rainforest
Regenwurm m earthworm
Regie f direction
regieren vt, vi to govern, to rule
Regierung f government; (von Monarch)
reign
Region f region
regional adj regional
Regisseur(in) m(f) director
registrieren vt to register; (bemerken) to

notice
regnen vi impers to rain
regnerisch adj rainy
regulär adj regular
regulieren vt to regulate, to adjust
Reh (-(e)s, -e) nt deer; (Fleisch) venison
Rehabilitationszentrum nt (Med) rehabilitation center
Reibe (-, -n) f, **Reibeisen** nt grater
reiben (**rieb, gerieben**) vt to rub; (Gastr) to
grate
reibungslos adj smooth
reich adj rich
Reich (-(e)s, -e) nt empire; (eines Königs)
kingdom
reichen vi to reach; (genügen) to be enough,
to be sufficient (jdm for sb) ▷ vt to hold
out; (geben) to pass, to hand; (anbieten) to
offer
reichhaltig adj ample, rich
reichlich adj (Trinkgeld) generous; (Essen)
ample; **~ Zeit** plenty of time
Reichtum (-s, -tümer) m wealth
reif adj ripe; (Mensch, Urteil) mature
Reif (-(e)s) m (Raureif) (hoar)frost ▷ (-(e)s,
-e) m (Ring) ring, hoop
reifen vi to mature; (Obst) to ripen
Reifen (-s, -) m ring, hoop; (von Auto) tire
Reifendruck m tire pressure
Reifenpanne m flat tire
Reifenwechsel m tire change
Reihe (-, -n) f row; (von Tagen etc, fam:
Anzahl) series sing; **der ~ nach** one after
the other; **er ist an der ~** it's his turn
Reihenfolge f order, sequence
Reihenhaus nt town (o row) house
Reiher (-s, -) m heron
rein (fam) kontr von **herein, hinein** ▷ adj
pure; (sauber) clean
Reinfall m (fam) letdown
rein|fallen (irr) vi (fam): **auf etw** (akk) **~** to
fall for sth
reinigen vt to clean
Reinigung f cleaning; (Geschäft) (dry)
cleaner's
Reinigungsmittel nt cleaning agent, clean-
er
rein|legen vt: **jdn ~** to take sb for a ride
Reis (-es, -e) m rice
Reise (-, -n) f trip, journey; (auf Schiff) voy-
age
Reiseapotheke f first-aid kit
Reisebüro nt travel agency
Reisebus m tour bus
Reiseführer(in) m(f) (Mensch) tour guide;

(*Buch*) travel guide
Reisegepäck *nt* baggage
Reisegesellschaft *f* (*Veranstalter*) tour operator
Reisegruppe *f* tourist group
Reiseleiter(in) *m(f)* tour guide
reisen *vi* to travel; ~ **nach** to go to
Reisende(r) *mf* traveller
Reisepass *m* passport
Reiseroute *f* route, itinerary
Reiserücktrittversicherung *f* trip cancellation insurance
Reisescheck *m* traveler's check
Reisetasche *f* tote (bag)
Reiseveranstalter *m* tour operator
Reiseverkehr *m* holiday traffic, vacation traffic
Reiseversicherung *f* travel insurance
Reiseziel *nt* destination
Reiskocher (*-s, -*) *m* rice steamer
reißen (**riss, gerissen**) *vt, vi* to tear; (*ziehen*) to pull, to drag; (*Witz*) to crack
Reißnagel *m* thumbtack
Reißverschluss *m* zipper
Reißzwecke *f* thumbtack
reiten (**ritt, geritten**) *vt, vi* to ride
Reiter(in) *m(f)* rider
Reithose *f* riding breeches *pl*
Reitsport *m* riding
Reitstiefel *m* riding boot
Reiz (*-es, -e*) *m* stimulus; (*angenehm*) charm; (*Verlockung*) attraction
reizen *vt* to stimulate; (*unangenehm*) to annoy; (*verlocken*) to appeal to, to attract
reizend *adj* charming
Reizgas *nt* irritant gas
Reizung *f* irritation
Reklamation *f* complaint
Reklame (*-, -n*) *f* advertising; (*Einzelwerbung*) advertisement; (*im Fernsehen*) commercial
reklamieren *vi* to complain (*wegen* about)
Rekord (*-(e)s, -e*) *m* record
relativ *adj* relative ▷ *adv* relatively
relaxen *vi* to relax, to chill out
Religion *f* religion
religiös *adj* religious
Remoulade (*-, -n*) *f* tartar sauce
Renaissance *f* renaissance, revival; (*Hist*) Renaissance
Rennbahn *f* racetrack
rennen (**rannte, gerannt**) *vt, vi* to run
Rennen (*-s, -*) *nt* running; (*Wettbewerb*) race
Rennfahrer(in) *m(f)* racing driver

Rennrad *nt* racing bike
Rennwagen *m* racing car
renommiert *adj* famous, noted (*wegen, für* for)
renovieren *vt* to renovate
Renovierung *f* renovation
rentabel *adj* profitable
Rente (*-, -n*) *f* pension
Rentenversicherung *f* pension plan, ≈ Social Security (*government-run pension plan for retirees*)
Rentier *nt* reindeer
rentieren *vr*: **sich** ~ to pay, to be profitable
Rentner(in) (*-s, -*) *m(f)* retiree
Reparatur *f* repair
Reparaturwerkstatt *f* repair shop; (*Auto*) garage
reparieren *vt* to repair
Reportage *f* report
Reporter(in) (*-s, -*) *m(f)* reporter
Reptil (*-s, -ien*) *nt* reptile
Republik *f* republic
Reservat (*-s, -e*) *nt* nature reserve; (*für Ureinwohner*) reservation
Reserve (*-, -n*) *f* reserve
Reservekanister *m* spare can
Reserverad (*Auto*) spare tire
reservieren *vt* to reserve
Reservierung *f* reservation
resignieren *vi* to give up
resigniert *adj* resigned
Respekt (*-(e)s*) *m* respect
respektieren *vt* to respect
Rest (*-(e)s, -e*) *m* rest, remainder; (*Überreste*) remains *pl*; **der** ~ **ist für Sie** (*zur Bedienung*) keep the change
Restaurant (*-s, -s*) *nt* restaurant
restaurieren *vt* to restore
Restbetrag *m* balance
restlich *adj* remaining
restlos *adj* complete
Restmüll *m* non-recyclable waste
Resultat *nt* result
retten *vt* to save, to rescue
Rettich (*-s, -e*) *m* radish (*large white or red variety*)
Rettung *f* rescue; (*Hilfe*) help; (*Rettungsdienst*) ambulance service
Rettungsboot *nt* lifeboat
Rettungshubschrauber *m* rescue helicopter
Rettungsring *m* life preserver
Rettungswagen *m* ambulance
Reue (*-*) *f* remorse; (*Bedauern*) regret
reuen *vt*: **es reut ihn** he regrets it

revanchieren *vr*: **sich ~** (*sich rächen*) to get one's revenge; (*für Hilfe etc*) to return the favor

Revolution *f* revolution

Rezept (*-(e)s, -e*) *nt* (*Gastr*) recipe; (*Med*) prescription

rezeptfrei *adj* over-the-counter, non-prescription

Rezeption *f* (*im Hotel*) reception

rezeptpflichtig *adj* prescription-only

R-Gespräch *nt* collect call

Rhabarber (*-s*) *m* rhubarb

Rhein (*-s*) *m* Rhine

Rheinland-Pfalz (*-*) *nt* Rhineland-Palatinate

Rheuma (*-s*) *nt* rheumatism

Rhythmus *m* rhythm

richten *vt* (*lenken*) to direct (*auf +akk* to); (*Waffe, Kamera*) to point (*auf +akk* at); (*Brief, Anfrage*) to address (*an +akk* to); (*einstellen*) to adjust; (*instand setzen*) to repair; (*zurechtmachen*) to prepare ▷ *vr*: **sich ~ nach** (*Regel etc*) to keep to; (*Mode, Beispiel*) to follow; (*abhängen von*) to depend on

Richter(in) (*-s, -*) *m(f)* judge

Richtgeschwindigkeit *f* recommended speed

richtig *adj* right, correct; (*echt*) real, proper ▷ *adv* (*fam: sehr*) really

richtig|stellen *vt*: **etw ~** (*berichtigen*) to correct sth

Richtlinie *f* guideline

Richtung *f* direction; (*Tendenz*) tendency

Richtungstaste *f* arrow key

rieb *imperf von* **reiben**

riechen (**roch, gerochen**) *vt, vi* to smell; **nach etw ~** to smell of sth; **an etw** (*dat*) **~** to smell sth

rief *imperf von* **rufen**

Riegel (*-s, -*) *m* bolt; (*Gastr*) bar

Riemen (*-s, -*) *m* strap; (*Gürtel*) belt

Riese (*-n, -n*) *m* giant

Riesengarnele *f* jumbo shrimp

riesengroß *adj* gigantic, huge

Riesenrad *nt* big wheel

riesig *adj* enormous, huge

riet *imperf von* **raten**

Riff (*-(e)s, -e*) *nt* reef

Rind (*-(e)s, -er*) *nt* cow; (*Bulle*) bull; (*Gastr*) beef; **~er** *pl* cattle *pl*

Rinde (*-, -n*) *f* (*Baum*) bark; (*Käse*) rind; (*Brot*) crust

Rinderbraten *m* roast beef

Rinderwahn(sinn) *m* mad cow disease

Rindfleisch *nt* beef

Ring (*-(e)s, -e*) *m* ring; (*Straße*) beltway

Ringbuch *nt* ring binder

ringen (**rang, gerungen**) *vi* to wrestle

Ringer(in) *m(f)* wrestler

Ringfinger *m* ring finger

Ringkampf *m* wrestling match

ringsherum *adv* around

Rippe (*-, -n*) *f* rib

Rippenfellentzündung *f* pleurisy

Risiko (*-s, -s o Risiken*) *nt* risk; **auf eigenes ~** at one's own risk

riskant *adj* risky

riskieren *vt* to risk

riss *imperf von* **reißen**

Riss (*-es, -e*) *m* tear; (*in Mauer, Tasse etc*) crack

rissig *adj* cracked; (*Haut*) chapped

ritt *imperf von* **reiten**

Ritter (*-s, -*) *m* knight

Rivale (*-n, -n*) *m*, **Rivalin** *f* rival

Rizinusöl *nt* castor oil

Robbe (*-, -n*) *f* seal

Roboter (*-s, -*) *m* robot

robust *adj* robust

roch *imperf von* **riechen**

Rock (*-(e)s, Röcke*) *m* skirt

Rockband *f* (*Musikgruppe*) rock band

Rockmusik *f* rock (music)

Rodelbahn *f* toboggan run

rodeln *vi* to toboggan

Roggen (*-s, -*) *m* rye

Roggenbrot *nt* rye bread

roh *adj* raw; (*Mensch*) coarse, crude

Rohkost *f* raw vegetables and fruit *pl*

Rohr (*-(e)s, -e*) *nt* pipe; (*Bot*) cane; (*Schilf*) reed

Röhre (*-, -n*) *f* tube; (*Leitung*) pipe; (*Elek*) valve; (*Backröhre*) oven

Rohrzucker *m* cane sugar

Rohstoff *m* raw material

Rokoko (*-s*) *nt* rococo

Rollbrett *nt* skateboard

Rolle (*-, -n*) *f* (*etw Zusammengerolltes*) roll; (*Theat*) role

rollen *vt, vi* to roll

Roller (*-s, -*) *m* scooter

Rollerblades® *pl* Rollerblades® *pl*

Rollerskates *pl* roller skates *pl*

Rollkragenpullover *m* turtleneck sweater

Rollladen *m*, **Rollo** (*-s, -s*) *m* (roller) blinds *pl*

Rollschuh *m* roller skate

Rollstuhl *m* wheelchair

rollstuhlgerecht *adj* suitable for wheelchairs

r

Rolltreppe f escalator
Roman (-s, -e) m novel
Romantik f romance
romantisch adj romantic
römisch-katholisch adj Roman Catholic
röntgen vt to X-ray
Röntgenaufnahme f, **Röntgenbild** nt X-ray
Röntgenstrahlen pl X-rays pl
rosa adj (inv) pink
Rose (-, -n) f rose
Rosenkohl m brussels (o Brussels) sprouts pl
Rosé(wein) m rosé (wine)
rosig adj rosy
Rosine f raisin
Rosmarin (-s) m rosemary
Rosskastanie f horse chestnut
Rost (-(e)s, -e) m rust; (zum Braten) grill, gridiron
Rostbratwurst f grilled sausage
rosten vi to rust
rösten vt to roast, to grill; (Brot) to toast
rostfrei adj rustproof; (Stahl) stainless
rostig adj rusty
Rostschutz m rustproofing
rot adj red; **rot werden** to blush; **Rote Karte** red card; **Rote Bete** beet; **bei Rot über die Ampel fahren** to go through a red light; **das Rote Kreuz** the Red Cross
Röteln pl German measles sing
röten vt to redden ▷ vr: **sich ~** to redden
rothaarig adj red-haired
rotieren vi to rotate; **am R~ sein** (fam) to be rushing around like crazy
Rotkehlchen nt robin
Rotkohl m, **Rotkraut** nt red cabbage
Rotlichtviertel nt red-light district
Rotwein m red wine
Rouge (-s, -s) nt rouge
Route (-, -n) f route
Routine f experience; (Trott) routine
Rubbellos nt scratchcard
rubbeln vt to rub
Rübe (-, -n) f turnip; **Gelbe ~** carrot; **Rote ~** beet
rüber (fam) kontr von **herüber, hinüber**
rückbestätigen vt (Flug etc) to reconfirm
rücken vt, vi to move; **könntest du ein bisschen ~?** could you move over a bit?
Rücken (-s, -) m back
Rückenlehne f back(rest)
Rückenmark nt spinal cord
Rückenschmerzen pl backache sing
Rückenschwimmen (-s) nt backstroke

Rückenwind m tailwind
Rückerstattung f refund
Rückfahrkarte f round-trip ticket
Rückfahrt f return trip
Rückfall m relapse
Rückflug m return flight
Rückgabe f return
rückgängig adj: **etw ~ machen** to cancel sth
Rückgrat (-(e)s, -e) nt spine, backbone
Rückkehr (-, -en) f return
Rücklicht nt rear light
Rückreise f return trip; **auf der ~** on the way back
Rucksack m backpack
Rucksacktourist(in) m(f) backpacker
Rückschritt m step back
Rückseite f back; (hinterer Teil) rear; **siehe ~** see overleaf
Rücksicht f consideration; **~ nehmen auf** +akk to show consideration for
rücksichtslos adj inconsiderate; (Fahren) reckless; (unbarmherzig) ruthless
rücksichtsvoll adj considerate
Rücksitz m back seat
Rückspiegel m (Auto) rear-view mirror
Rückstand m: **sie sind zwei Tore im ~** they're two goals down; **im ~ sein mit** (Arbeit, Miete) to be behind with
Rücktaste f backspace key
Rückvergütung f refund
rückwärts adv backwards, back
Rückwärtsgang m (Auto) reverse (gear)
Rückweg m return trip, way back
Rückzahlung f repayment
Ruder (-s, -) nt oar; (Steuer) rudder
Ruderboot nt rowboat
rudern vt, vi to row
Ruf (-(e)s, -e) m call, cry; (Ansehen) reputation
rufen (rief, gerufen) vt, vi to call; (schreien) to cry
Rufnummer f telephone number
Ruhe (-) f rest; (Ungestörtheit) peace, quiet; (Gelassenheit, Stille) calm; (Schweigen) silence; **lass mich in ~!** leave me alone!
ruhen vi to rest
Ruhestand m retirement; **im ~ sein** to be retired
Ruhestörung f disturbance of the peace
Ruhetag m: **montags ~ haben** to be closed on Mondays
ruhig adj quiet; (bewegungslos) still; (Hand) steady; (gelassen) calm
Ruhm (-(e)s) m fame, glory

Rührei *nt* scrambled egg(s)

rühren *vt* to move; (*umrühren*) to stir ▷ *vr*:
sich ~ to move; (*sich bemerkbar machen*)
to say something

rührend *adj* touching, moving

Rührung *f* émotion

Ruine (-, -*n*) *f* ruin

ruinieren *vt* to ruin

rülpsen *vi* to burp, to belch

rum (*fam*) *kontr von* **herum**

Rum (-*s*, -*s*) *m* rum

Rumänien (-*s*) *nt* Romania

Rummel (-*s*) *m* (*Trubel*) hustle and bustle;
(*Jahrmarkt*) fair; (*Medienrummel*) hype

Rummelplatz *m* fairground

rumoren *vi*: **es rumort in meinem Bauch/
Kopf** my stomach is rumbling/my head is
spinning

Rumpf (-(*e*)*s*, *Rümpfe*) *m* (*Anat*) trunk;
(*Aviat*) fuselage; (*Naut*) hull

rümpfen *vt*: **die Nase ~** to turn one's nose
up (*über* at)

Rumpsteak *nt* rump steak

rund *adj* round ▷ *adv* (*etwa*) around; **~ um
etw** around sth

Runde (-, -*n*) *f* round; (*in Rennen*) lap

Rundfahrt *f* tour (*durch* of)

Rundfunk *m* broadcasting; (*Rundfunkan-*

stalt) broadcasting service; **im ~** on the
radio

Rundgang *m* tour (*durch* of); (*von Wäch-
ter*) round

rundlich *adj* plump

Rundreise *f* tour (*durch* of)

runter (*fam*) *kontr von* **herunter, hinunter**

runterscrollen *vt* (*Inform*) to scroll down

runzelig *adj* wrinkled

runzeln *vt*: **die Stirn ~** to frown

ruppig *adj* gruff

Rüsche (-, -*n*) *f* frill

Ruß (-*es*) *m* soot

Russe (-*n*, -*n*) *m* Russian

Rüssel (-*s*, -) *m* (*Elefant*) trunk; (*Schwein*)
snout

Russin *f* Russian

russisch *adj* Russian

Russisch *nt* Russian

Russland *nt* Russia

Rüstung *f* (*mit Waffen*) arming; (*Ritterrüs-
tung*) armor; (*Waffen*) armaments *pl*

Rutsch (-(*e*)*s*, -*e*) *m*: **guten ~ ins neue Jahr!**
Happy New Year!

Rutschbahn *f*, **Rutsche** *f* slide

rutschen *vi* to slide; (*ausrutschen*) to slip

rutschig *adj* slippery

rütteln *vt*, *vi* to shake

S

S (*abk*) = **Süd** S

s. (*abk*) = **siehe** see

S. (*abk*) = **Seite** p.

Saal (*-(e)s, Säle*) *m* hall; (*für Sitzungen*) room

Saarland *nt* Saarland

sabotieren *vt* to sabotage

Sache (*-, -n*) *f* thing; (*Angelegenheit*) affair, business; (*Frage*) matter; **bei der ~ bleiben** to keep to the point

sachkundig *adj* competent

Sachlage *f* situation

sachlich *adj* (*objektiv*) objective; (*nüchtern*) matter-of-fact; (*inhaltlich*) factual

sächlich *adj* (*Ling*) neuter

Sachschaden *m* material damage

Sachsen (*-s*) *nt* Saxony

Sachsen-Anhalt (*-s*) *nt* Saxony-Anhalt

sacht(e) *adv* softly, gently

Sachverständige(r) *mf* expert

Sack (*-(e)s, Säcke*) *m* sack; (*pej: Mensch*) bastard

Sackgasse *f* dead end

Safe (*-s, -s*) *m* safe

Safer Sex *m* safe sex

Safran (*-s, -e*) *m* saffron

Saft (*-(e)s, Säfte*) *m* juice

saftig *adj* juicy

Sage (*-, -n*) *f* legend

Säge (*-, -n*) *f* saw

Sägemehl *nt* sawdust

sagen *vt, vi* to say (*jdm* to sb), to tell (*jdm sb*); **wie sagt man ... auf Englisch?** what's ... in English?

sägen *vt, vi* to saw

sagenhaft *adj* legendary; (*fam: großartig*) fantastic

sah *imperf von* **sehen**

Sahne (*-*) *f* cream

Saison (*-, -s*) *f* season; **außerhalb der ~** out of season

Saite (*-, -n*) *f* string

Sakko (*-s, -s*) *nt* jacket

Salami (*-, -s*) *f* salami

Salat (*-(e)s, -e*) *m* salad; (*Kopfsalat*) lettuce

Salatbar *f* salad bar

Salatschüssel *f* salad bowl

Salatsoße *f* salad dressing

Salbe (*-, -n*) *f* ointment

Salbei (*-s*) *m* sage

Salmonellenvergiftung *f* salmonella (poisoning)

salopp *adj* (*Kleidung*) casual; (*Sprache*) slangy

Salsamusik *f* salsa (music)

Salto (*-s, -s*) *m* somersault

Salz (*-es, -e*) *nt* salt

salzarm *adj* low-salt

salzen (*salzte, gesalzen*) *vt* to salt

Salzgurke *f* pickle

Salzhering *m* pickled herring

salzig *adj* salty

Salzkartoffeln *pl* boiled potatoes *pl*

Salzstange *f* pretzel stick

Salzstreuer *m* salt shaker

Salzwasser *nt* salt water

Samba (*-, -s*) *f* samba

Samen (*-s, -*) *m* seed; (*Sperma*) sperm

sammeln *vt* to collect

Sammler(in) *m(f)* collector

Sammlung *f* collection; (*Ansammlung, Konzentration*) concentration

Samstag *m* Saturday; *siehe auch* **Mittwoch**

samstags *adv* on Saturdays; *siehe auch* **mittwochs**

samt *prep* (*+dat*) (along) with, together with

Samt (*-(e)s, -e*) *m* velvet

sämtliche(r, s) *adj* all (the)

Sanatorium (*-s, Sanatorien*) *nt* sanitarium

Sand (*-(e)s, -e*) *m* sand

Sandale (*-, -n*) *f* sandal

sandig *adj* sandy

Sandkasten *m* sandbox

Sandpapier *nt* sandpaper

Sandstrand *m* sandy beach

sandte *imperf von* **senden**

sanft *adj* soft, gentle

sang *imperf von* **singen**

Sänger(in) (*-s, -*) *m(f)* singer

Sangria (*-, -s*) *f* sangria

sanieren *vt* to redevelop; (*Gebäude*) to renovate; (*Betrieb*) to restore to profitability

sanitär *adj* sanitary; **~e Anlagen** *pl* sanitation

Sanitäter(in) (*-s, -*) *m(f)* paramedic

sank *imperf von* **sinken**

Sankt Gallen (*-s*) *nt* St Gallen

Saphir (*-s, -e*) *m* sapphire

Sardelle *f* anchovy

Sardine *f* sardine

Sarg (*-(e)s, Särge*) *m* coffin

saß *imperf von* **sitzen**

Satellit (*-en, -en*) *m* satellite

Satellitenfernsehen *nt* satellite TV
Satellitenschüssel *f* (*fam*) satellite dish
Satire (*-, -n*) *f* satire (*auf +akk* on)
satt *adj* full; (*Farbe*) rich, deep; ~ **sein** (*gesättigt*) to be full; ~ **machen** to be filling; **jdn/etw** ~ **sein** to be fed up with sb/ sth
Sattel (*-s, Sättel*) *m* saddle
satt|haben (*irr*) *vt*: **jdn/etw** ~ (*nicht mehr mögen*) to be fed up with sb/sth
Saturn (*-s*) *m* Saturn
Satz (*-es, Sätze*) *m* (*Ling*) sentence; (*Mus*) movement; (*Tennis*) set; (*Kaffee*) grounds *pl*; (*Comm*) rate; (*Sprung*) jump; (*Comm*) rate
Satzzeichen *nt* punctuation mark
Sau (*-, Säue*) *f* sow; (*pej: Mensch*) jerk, pig
sauber *adj* clean; (*ironisch*) fine; ~ **machen** to clean
Sauberkeit *f* cleanness; (*von Person*) cleanliness
säubern *vt* to clean
saublöd *adj* (*fam*) really stupid, dumb
Sauce (*-, -n*) *f* sauce; (*zu Braten*) gravy
Saudi-Arabien (*-s*) *nt* Saudi Arabia
sauer *adj* sour; (*Chem*) acid; (*fam: verärgert*) mad; **saurer Regen** acid rain
Sauerkirsche *f* sour cherry
Sauerkraut *nt* sauerkraut
säuerlich *adj* slightly sour
Sauermilch *f* sour milk
Sauerrahm *m* sour cream
Sauerstoff *m* oxygen
saufen (**soff**, **gesoffen**) *vt* to drink; (*fam: Mensch*) to knock back ▷ *vi* to drink; (*fam: Mensch*) to booze
saugen (**sog** *o* **saugte**, **gesogen** *o* **gesaugt**) *vt*, *vi* to suck; (*mit Staubsauger*) to vacuum
Sauger (*-s, -*) *m* (*auf Flasche*) nipple
Säugetier *nt* mammal
Säugling *m* infant, baby
Säule (*-, -n*) *f* column, pillar
Saum (*-s, Säume*) *m* hem; (*Naht*) seam
Sauna (*-, -s*) *f* sauna
Säure (*-, -n*) *f* acid
sausen *vi* (*Ohren*) to buzz; (*Wind*) to howl; (*Mensch*) to rush
Saustall *m* pigpen
Sauwetter *nt*: **was für ein** ~ (*fam*) what lousy weather
Saxophon (*-s, -e*) *nt* saxophone
S-Bahn *f* commuter train, light rail (*o* rapid transit) train
S-Bahn-Haltestelle *f*, **S-Bahnhof** *m* commuter train station, light rail (*o* radip transit) station
scannen *vt* to scan
Scanner (*-s, -*) *m* scanner
schäbig *adj* shabby
Schach (*-s, -s*) *nt* chess; (*Stellung*) check
Schachbrett *nt* chessboard
Schachfigur *f* chess piece
schachmatt *adj* checkmate
Schacht (*-(e)s, Schächte*) *m* shaft
Schachtel (*-, -n*) *f* box
schade *interj* too bad, what a shame
Schädel (*-s, -*) *m* skull
Schädelbruch *m* fractured skull
schaden *vi* to damage, to harm (*jdm* sb); **das schadet nichts** it won't do any harm
Schaden (*-s, Schäden*) *m* damage; (*Verletzung*) injury; (*Nachteil*) disadvantage; **einen** ~ **verursachen** to cause damage
Schadenersatz *m* compensation, damages *pl*
schadhaft *adj* faulty; (*beschädigt*) damaged
schädigen *vt* to damage; (*jdn*) to do harm to, to harm
schädlich *adj* harmful (*für* to)
Schadstoff *m* harmful substance
schadstoffarm *adj* low-emission
Schaf (*-(e)s, -e*) *nt* sheep
Schafbock *m* ram
Schäfer (*-s, -*) *m* shepherd
Schäferhund *m* German shepherd
Schäferin *f* shepherdess
schaffen (**schuf**, **geschaffen**) *vt* to create; (*Platz*) to make ▷ *vt* (**schaffte**, **geschafft**) (*erreichen*) to manage, to do; (*erledigen*) to finish; (*Prüfung*) to pass; (*transportieren*) to take; **jdm zu** ~ **machen** to cause sb trouble
Schaffner(in) (*-s, -*) *m(f)* conductor
Schafskäse *m* sheep's (milk) cheese
schal *adj* (*Getränk*) flat
Schal (*-s, -e* o *-s*) *m* scarf
Schälchen *nt* (small) bowl
Schale (*-, -n*) *f* skin; (*abgeschält*) peel; (*Nuss, Muschel, Ei*) shell; (*Geschirr*) bowl, dish
schälen *vt* to peel; (*Tomate, Mandel*) to skin; (*Erbsen, Eier, Nüsse*) to shell; (*Getreide*) to husk ▷ *vr*: **sich** ~ to peel
Schall (*-(e)s, -e*) *m* sound
Schalldämpfer (*-s, -*) *m* (*Auto*) muffler
Schallplatte *f* record
Schalotte (*-, -n*) *f* shallot
schalten *vt* to switch ▷ *vi* (*Auto*) to shift; (*fam: begreifen*) to catch on

S

Schalter (-s, -) m (auf Post, Bank) counter; (an Gerät) switch

Schalterhalle f main hall

Schalteröffnungszeiten pl business hours pl

Schaltfläche f (Inform) button

Schalthebel m gearshift

Schaltjahr nt leap year

Schaltknüppel m gearshift

Schaltung f gearshift

Scham (-) f shame; (Schamgefühl) modesty

schämen vr: **sich ~** to be ashamed

Schande (-) f disgrace

Schanze (-, -n) f ski jump

Schar (-, -en) f (von Vögeln) flock; (Menge) crowd; **in ~en** in droves

scharf adj (Messer, Kritik) sharp; (Essen) hot; **auf etw** (akk) **~ sein** (fam) to be into sth

Schärfe (-, -n) f sharpness; (Strenge) rigor; (Foto) focus

Scharlach (-s) m (Med) scarlet fever

Scharnier (-s, -e) nt hinge

Schaschlik (-s, -s) m o nt (shish) kebab

Schatten (-s, -) m shadow; **30 Grad im ~** 30 degrees in the shade

schattig adj shady

Schatz (-es, Schätze) m treasure; (Mensch) love

schätzen vt (abschätzen) to estimate; (Gegenstand) to value; (würdigen) to value, to esteem; (vermuten) to reckon

Schätzung f estimate; (das Schätzen) estimation; (von Wertgegenstand) valuation

schätzungsweise adv roughly, approximately

Schau (-, -en) f show; (Ausstellung) exhibition

schauen vi to look; **ich schau mal, ob ...** I'll go (and) see whether ...; **schau, dass ...** see (to it) that ...

Schauer (-s, -) m (Regen) shower; (Schreck) shudder

Schaufel (-, -n) f shovel; **~ und Besen** dustpan and brush

schaufeln vt to shovel; **Schnee ~** to clear the snow away

Schaufenster nt store window

Schaufensterbummel m window-shopping expedition

Schaukel (-, -n) f swing

schaukeln vi to rock; (mit Schaukel) to swing

Schaulustige(r) mf rubbernecker

Schaum (-(e)s, Schäume) m foam; (Seifen-

schaum) lather; (Bierschaum) froth

Schaumbad nt bubble bath

schäumen vi to foam

Schaumfestiger (-s, -) m styling mousse

Schaumgummi m foam (rubber)

Schaumwein m sparkling wine

Schauplatz m scene

Schauspiel nt spectacle; (Theat) play

Schauspieler(in) m(f) actor/actress

Scheck (-s, -s) m check

Scheckheft nt checkbook

Scheibe (-, -n) f disk; (von Brot, Käse etc) slice; (Glasscheibe) pane

Scheibenbremse f (Auto) disk brake

Scheibenwaschanlage f (Auto) windshield washer unit

Scheibenwischer (-s, -) m (Auto) windshield wiper

Scheich (-s, -s) m sheik(h)

Scheide (-, -n) f (Anat) vagina

scheiden (schied, geschieden) vt (trennen) to separate; (Ehe) to dissolve; **sich ~ lassen** to get a divorce; **sie hat sich von ihm ~ lassen** she divorced him

Scheidung f divorce

Schein (-(e)s, -e) m light; (Anschein) appearance; (Geld) bill

scheinbar adj apparent ▷ adv apparent(ly)

scheinen (schien, geschienen) vi (Sonne) to shine; (den Anschein haben) to seem

Scheinwerfer (-s, -) m floodlight; (Theat) spotlight; (Auto) headlight

Scheitel (-s, -) m part

scheitern vi to fail (an +dat because of)

Schellfisch m haddock

Schema (-s, -s o Schemata) nt scheme, plan; (Darstellung) diagram

Schenkel (-s, -) m thigh

schenken vt to give; **er hat es mir geschenkt** he gave it to me (as a present); **sich** (dat) **etw ~** (fam: weglassen) to skip sth

Scherbe (-, -n) f broken piece, fragment

Schere (-, -n) f scissors pl; (groß) shears pl; **eine ~** a pair of scissors/shears

Scherz (-es, -e) m joke

scheu adj shy

scheuen vr: **sich ~ vor** +dat to be afraid of, to shrink from ▷ vt to shun ▷ vi (Pferd) to shy

scheuern vt to scrub; **jdm eine ~** (fam) to slap sb in the face

Scheune (-, -n) f barn

scheußlich adj dreadful

Schi (-s, -er) m siehe **Ski**

Schicht (-, *-en*) *f* layer; (*in Gesellschaft*) class; (*in Fabrik etc*) shift

schick *adj* stylish, chic

schicken *vt* to send ▷ *vr:* **sich ~** (*sich beeilen*) to hurry up

Schickimicki (*-(s)*, *-s*) *m* (*fam*) trendy

Schicksal (*-s*, *-e*) *nt* fate

Schiebedach *nt* (*Auto*) sunroof

schieben (**schob, geschoben**) *vt, vi* to push; **die Schuld auf jdn ~** to put the blame on sb

Schiebetür *f* sliding door

schied *imperf von* **scheiden**

Schiedsrichter(in) *m(f)* referee; (*Tennis*) umpire; (*Schlichter*) arbitrator

schief *adj* crooked; (*Blick*) funny ▷ *adv* crooked(ly)

schief|gehen (*irr*) *vi* (*fam misslingen*) to go wrong

schielen *vi* to have cross-eyes (*o strabismus*)

schien *imperf von* **scheinen**

Schienbein *nt* shin

Schiene (-, *-n*) *f* rail; (*Med*) splint

schier *adj* pure; (*fig*) sheer ▷ *adv* nearly, almost

schießen (**schoss, geschossen**) *vt* to shoot; (*Ball*) to kick; (*Tor*) to score; (*Foto*) to take ▷ *vi* to shoot (*auf +akk* at)

Schiff (*-(e)s*, *-e*) *nt* ship; (*in Kirche*) nave

Schifffahrt *f* shipping

Schiffsreise *f* voyage

schikanieren *vt* to harass; (*Schule*) to bully

Schild (*-(e)s*, *-e*) *m* (*Schutz*) shield ▷ (*-(e)s, -er*) *nt* sign; **was steht auf dem ~?** what does the sign say?

Schilddrüse *f* thyroid gland

schildern *vt* to describe

Schildkröte *f* tortoise; (*Wasserschildkröte*) sea turtle

Schimmel (*-s*, *-*) *m* mold; (*Pferd*) white horse

schimmeln *vi* to go moldy

schimpfen *vt* to tell off ▷ *vi* (*sich beklagen*) to complain; **mit jdm ~** to tell sb off

Schimpfwort *nt* swearword

Schinken (*-s*, *-*) *m* ham

Schirm (*-(e)s*, *-e*) *m* (*Regenschirm*) umbrella; (*Sonnenschirm*) parasol, sunshade

schiss *imperf von* **scheißen**

Schlacht (-, *-en*) *f* battle

schlachten *vt* to slaughter

Schlachter(in) (*-s*, *-*) *m(f)* butcher

Schlaf (*-(e)s*) *m* sleep

Schlafanzug *m* pajamas *pl*

Schlafcouch *f* sofa bed, sleeper sofa

Schläfe (-, *-n*) *f* temple

schlafen (**schlief, geschlafen**) *vi* to sleep; **schlaf gut!** sleep well!; **hast du gut ge~?** did you sleep all right?; **er schläft noch** he's still asleep; **~ gehen** to go to bed

schlaff *adj* slack; (*kraftlos*) limp; (*erschöpft*) exhausted

Schlafgelegenheit *f* place to sleep

Schlaflosigkeit *f* sleeplessness

Schlafmittel *nt* sleeping pill

schläfrig *adj* sleepy

Schlafsaal *m* dormitory

Schlafsack *m* sleeping bag

Schlaftablette *f* sleeping pill; **er ist eine richtige ~** (*fam: langweilig*) he's such a bore

Schlafwagen *m* sleeping car, sleeper

Schlafzimmer *nt* bedroom

Schlag (*-(e)s, Schläge*) *m* blow; (*Puls*) beat; (*Elek*) shock; (*fam: Portion*) helping; (*Art*) kind, type

Schlagader *f* artery

Schlaganfall *m* (*Med*) stroke

schlagartig *adj* sudden

schlagen (**schlug, geschlagen**) *vt* to hit; (*besiegen*) to beat; (*Sahne*) to whip; **jdn zu Boden ~** to knock sb down ▷ *vi* (*Herz*) to beat; (*Uhr*) to strike; **mit dem Kopf gegen etw ~** to bang one's head against sth ▷ *vr:* **sich ~** to fight

Schläger (*-s*, *-*) *m* (*Sport*) bat; (*Tennis*) racket; (*Golf*) (golf) club; (*Hockey*) hockey stick; (*Mensch*) brawler

Schlägerei *f* fight, brawl

schlagfertig *adj* quick-witted

Schlagloch *nt* pothole

Schlagsahne *f* whipping cream; (*geschlagen*) whipped cream

Schlagzeile *f* headline

Schlagzeug *nt* drums *pl*; (*in Orchester*) percussion

Schlamm (*-(e)s, -e*) *m* mud

schlampig *adj* (*fam*) sloppy

schlang *imperf von* **schlingen**

Schlange (-, *-n*) *f* snake; (*von Menschen*) line; **~ stehen** to stand in line

Schlangenlinie *f* wavy line; **in ~n fahren** to swerve around

schlank *adj* slim

schlapp *adj* limp; (*locker*) slack

Schlappe (-, *-n*) *f* (*fam*) setback

schlau *adj* clever, smart; (*raffiniert*) crafty, cunning

S

Schlauch (-(e)s, Schläuche) m hose; (in Reifen) inner tube

Schlauchboot nt rubber dinghy

schlecht adj bad; **mir ist ~** I feel sick; **die Milch ist ~** the milk is sour (o has gone bad) ▷ adv badly; **es geht ihm ~** he's having a hard time; (gesundheitlich) he's not feeling well; (finanziell) he's pretty hard up

schlecht|machen vt: **jdn ~** (herabsetzen) to put sb down; (fam) to badmouth sb

schleichen (schlich, geschlichen) vi to creep

Schleier (-s, -) m veil

Schleife (-, -n) f (Inform, Aviat, Elek) loop; (Band) bow

schleifen vt (ziehen, schleppen) to drag ▷ vt (schliff, geschliffen) (schärfen) to grind; (Edelstein) to cut

Schleim (-(e)s, -e) m slime; (Med) mucus

Schleimer (-s, -) m (fam) creep

Schleimhaut f mucous membrane

schlendern vi to stroll

schleppen vt to drag; (Auto, Schiff) to tow; (tragen) to lug

Schlepplift m ski tow

Schleswig-Holstein (-s) nt Schleswig-Holstein

Schleuder (-, -n) f catapult; (für Wäsche) spin-dryer

schleudern vt to hurl; (Wäsche) to spin-dry ▷ vi (Auto) to skid

Schleudersitz m ejector seat

schlich imperf von schleichen

schlicht adj simple, plain

schlichten vt (Streit) to settle

schlief imperf von schlafen

schließen (schloss, geschlossen) vt, vi to close, to shut; (beenden) to close; (Freundschaft, Ehe) to enter into; (folgern) to infer (aus from) ▷ vr: **sich ~** to close, to shut

Schließfach nt locker

schließlich adv finally; (schließlich doch) after all

schliff imperf von schleifen

schlimm adj bad

schlimmer adj worse

schlimmste(r, s) adj worst

schlimmstenfalls adv at (the) worst

Schlinge (-, -n) f loop; (Med) sling

Schlips (-es, -e) m tie

Schlitten (-s, -) m sled, toboggan; (mit Pferden) sleigh

Schlittenfahren (-s) nt sledding

Schlittschuh m ice skate; **~ laufen** to ice-skate

Schlitz (-es, -e) m slit; (für Münze) slot; (an Hose) fly

schloss imperf von schließen

Schloss (-es, Schlösser) nt lock; (Burg) castle

Schlosser(in) m(f) metalsmith

Schlucht (-, -en) f gorge, ravine

schluchzen vi to sob

Schluck (-(e)s, -e) m swallow

Schluckauf (-s) m hiccups pl

schlucken vt, vi to swallow

schludern vi (fam) to do sloppy work

schlug imperf von schlagen

Schlüpfer (-s, -) m panties pl

schlürfen vt, vi to slurp

Schluss (-es, Schlüsse) m end; (Schlussfolgerung) conclusion; **am ~** at the end; **mit jdm ~ machen** to break (o split) up with sb

Schlüssel (-s, -) m (a. fig) key

Schlüsselbein nt collarbone

Schlüsselbund m bunch of keys

Schlüsseldienst m key-cutting service

Schlüsselloch nt keyhole

Schlussfolgerung f conclusion

Schlusslicht nt tail-light; (fig) tail-ender

Schlussverkauf m clearance sale

schmächtig adj frail

schmal adj narrow; (Mensch, Buch etc) slim; (karg) meager

Schmalz (-es, -e) nt dripping, lard; (fig: Sentimentalitäten) schmaltz

schmatzen vi to eat noisily

schmecken vt, vi to taste (nach of); **es schmeckt ihm** he likes it; **lass es dir ~!** bon appétit!

Schmeichelei f flattery

schmeichelhaft adj flattering

schmeicheln vi: **jdm ~** to flatter sb

schmeißen (schmiss, geschmissen) vt (fam) to chuck, to throw

schmelzen (schmolz, geschmolzen) vt, vi to melt; (Metall, Erz) to smelt

Schmelzkäse m cheese spread

Schmerz (-es, -en) m pain; (Trauer) grief; **~en haben** to be in pain; **~en im Rücken haben** to have a pain in one's back

schmerzen vt, vi to hurt

Schmerzensgeld nt compensation

schmerzhaft, schmerzlich adj painful

schmerzlos adj painless

Schmerzmittel nt painkiller

schmerzstillend adj painkilling

Schmerztablette f painkiller

Schmetterling m butterfly

Schmied(in) (-(e)s, -e) m(f) blacksmith
schmieden vt to forge; (Pläne) to make
schmieren vt to smear; (ölen) to lubricate, to grease; (bestechen) to bribe ▷ vt, vi (unsauber schreiben) to scrawl
Schmiergeld nt (fam) bribe
schmierig adj greasy
Schmierseife f soft soap
Schminke (-, -n) f make-up
schminken vr: sich ~ to put one's make-up on
schmiss imperf von **schmeißen**
schmollen vi to sulk
schmollend adj sulky
schmolz imperf von **schmelzen**
Schmuck (-(e)s, -e) m jewelry; (Verzierung) decoration
schmücken vt to decorate
schmuggeln vt, vi to smuggle
schmunzeln vi to smile
schmusen vi to (kiss and) cuddle
Schmutz (-es) m dirt, filth
schmutzig adj dirty
Schnabel (-s, Schnäbel) m beak, bill; (Ausguss) spout
Schnake (-, -n) f mosquito
Schnalle (-, -n) f buckle
Schnäppchen nt (fam) bargain
schnappen vt (fangen) to catch ▷ vi: nach Luft ~ to gasp for breath
Schnappschuss m (Foto) snap(shot)
Schnaps (-es, Schnäpse) m schnapps
schnarchen vi to snore
schnaufen vi to puff, to pant
Schnauzbart m mustache
Schnauze (-, -n) f snout, muzzle; (Ausguss) spout; (fam: Mund) trap; **die ~ voll haben** to have had enough
schnäuzen vr: sich ~ to blow one's nose
Schnecke (-, -n) f snail
Schneckenhaus nt snail's shell
Schnee (-s) m snow
Schneeball m snowball
Schneebob m snowmobile
Schneebrille f snow goggles pl
Schneeflocke f snowflake
Schneegestöber (-s, -) nt snow flurry
Schneeglöckchen nt snowdrop
Schneegrenze f snowline
Schneekanone f snowmaker, snow cannon
Schneekette f (Auto) snow chain
Schneemann m snowman
Schneepflug m snowplow
Schneeregen m sleet
Schneeschmelze f thaw

Schneesturm m snowstorm, blizzard
Schneetreiben nt blowing snow
Schneewehe f snowdrift
Schneide (-, -n) f edge; (Klinge) blade
schneiden (schnitt, geschnitten) vt to cut; **sich** (dat) **die Haare ~ lassen** to have one's hair cut ▷ vr: **sich ~** to cut oneself
Schneider(in) (-s, -) m(f) tailor; (für Damenmode) dressmaker
Schneiderin f dressmaker
Schneidezahn m incisor
schneien vi impers to snow
schnell adj quick, fast ▷ adv quickly, fast; **mach ~!** hurry up
Schnelldienst m express service
Schnellhefter m loose-leaf binder
Schnellimbiss m snack bar
Schnellkochtopf m pressure cooker
Schnellreinigung f express dry cleaning; (Geschäft) express (dry) cleaner's
Schnellstraße f expressway
Schnellzug m fast train
schneuzen vr siehe **schnäuzen**
schnitt imperf von **schneiden**
Schnitt (-(e)s, -e) m cut; (Schnittpunkt) intersection; (Querschnitt) (cross) section; (Durchschnitt) average; (eines Kleides) style
Schnitte (-, -n) f slice; (belegt) sandwich
Schnittkäse m sliced cheese
Schnittlauch m chives pl
Schnittmuster nt pattern
Schnittstelle f (Inform: fig) interface
Schnittwunde f cut, gash
Schnitzel (-s, -) nt (Papier) scrap; (Gastr) breaded cutlet
schnitzen vt to carve
Schnorchel (-s, -) m snorkel
schnorcheln vi to go snorkeling, to snorkel
schnüffeln vi to sniff
Schnuller (-s, -) m pacifier
Schnulze (-, -n) f (Film, Roman) tearjerker
Schnupfen (-s, -) m cold
schnuppern vi to sniff
Schnur (-, Schnüre) f string, cord; (Elek) lead
schnurlos adj (Telefon) cordless
Schnurrbart m mustache
schnurren vi to purr
Schnürsenkel (-s, -) m shoelace
schob imperf von **schieben**
Schock (-(e)s, -e) m shock; **unter ~ stehen** to be in a state of shock
schockieren vt to shock

s

Schokolade *f* chocolate
Schokoriegel *m* chocolate bar
Scholle (-, -n) *f* (*Fisch*) plaice; (*Eis*) ice floe

schon *adv* **1** (*bereits*) already; **er ist schon
da** he's there already, he's already there;
ist er schon da? is he there yet?; **warst du
schon einmal da?** have you ever been
there?; **ich war schon einmal da** I've been
there before; **das war schon immer so**
that has always been the case; **schon oft**
often; **hast du schon gehört?** have you
heard?
2 (*bestimmt*) all right; **du wirst schon
sehen** you'll see (all right); **das wird
schon noch gut** that'll be OK
3 (*bloß*) just; **allein schon das Gefühl ...**
just the very feeling ...; **schon der Gedanke** the very thought; **wenn ich das schon
höre** I only have to hear that
4 (*einschränkend*): **ja schon, aber ...** yes
(well), but ...
5: schon möglich possible; **schon gut!**
OK!; **du weißt schon** you know; **komm
schon!** come on!

schön *adj* beautiful; (*nett*) nice; (*Frau*)
beautiful, pretty; (*Mann*) beautiful, hand-
some; (*Wetter*) nice; **~e Grüße** best wishes;
~es Wochenende have a nice weekend
schonen *vt* (*pfleglich behandeln*) to look
after ▷ *vr*: **sich ~** to take it easy
Schönheit *f* beauty
Schonkost *f* light diet
schöpfen *vt* to scoop; (*mit Kelle*) to ladle
Schöpfkelle *f*, **Schöpflöffel** *m* ladle
Schöpfung *f* creation
Schoppen (-s, -) *m* glass (of wine)
Schorf (-(e)s, -e) *m* scab
Schorle (-, -n) *f* spritzer
Schornstein *m* chimney
Schornsteinfeger(in) (-s, -) *m(f)* chimney
sweep
schoss *imperf von* **schießen**
Schoß (-es, Schöße) *m* lap
Schotte (-n, -n) *m* Scot, Scotsman
Schottin *f* Scot, Scotswoman
schottisch *adj* Scottish, Scots
Schottland *nt* Scotland
schräg *adj* slanting; (*Dach*) sloping; (*Linie*)
diagonal; (*fam: unkonventionell*) wacky
Schrank (-(e)s, Schränke) *m* cupboard;
(*Kleiderschrank*) closet

Schranke (-, -n) *f* barrier
Schrankwand *f* wall unit
Schraube (-, -n) *f* screw
schrauben *vt* to screw
Schraubendreher (-s, -) *m* screwdriver
Schraubenschlüssel *m* wrench
Schraubenzieher (-s, -) *m* screwdriver
Schraubverschluss *m* screw top, screw
cap
Schreck (-(e)s, -e) *m*, **Schrecken** (-s, -) *m*
terror; (*Angst*) fright; **jdm einen ~ einja-
gen** to give sb a scare
schreckhaft *adj* jumpy
schrecklich *adj* terrible, horrible
Schrei (-(e)s, -e) *m* scream; (*Ruf*) shout
Schreibblock *m* writing pad
schreiben (schrieb, geschrieben) *vt, vi* to
write; (*buchstabieren*) to spell; **wie
schreibt man ...?** how do you spell ...?
Schreiben (-s, -) *nt* writing; (*Brief*) letter
Schreibfehler *m* spelling mistake
schreibgeschützt *adj* (*Diskette*) write-protected
Schreibtisch *m* desk
Schreibwaren *pl* stationery *sing*
schreien (schrie, geschrien) *vt, vi* to
scream; (*rufen*) to shout
Schreiner(in) *m(f)* cabinetmaker, carpenter
Schreinerei *f* cabinetmaker's (*o* carpenter's) workshop
schrie *imperf von* **schreien**
schrieb *imperf von* **schreiben**
Schrift (-, -en) *f* writing; (*Handschrift*) handwriting; (*Schriftart*) typeface; (*Schrifttyp*)
font
schriftlich *adj* written ▷ *adv* in writing;
würden Sie uns das bitte ~ geben? could
we have that in writing, please?
Schriftsteller(in) (-s, -) *m(f)* writer
Schritt (-(e)s, -e) *m* step; **~ für ~** step by step;
~e gegen etw unternehmen to take steps
against sth
Schrittgeschwindigkeit *f* walking speed
Schrittmacher *m* (*Med*) pacemaker
Schrott (-(e)s, -e) *m* scrap metal; (*fig*) nonsense
schrubben *vi, vt* to scrub
Schrubber (-s, -) *m* scrubbing brush
schrumpfen *vi* to shrink
Schubkarren (-s, -) *m* wheelbarrow
Schublade *f* drawer
schubsen *vt* to shove, to push
schüchtern *adj* shy
schuf *imperf von* **schaffen**

Schuh (-(e)s, -e) m shoe
Schuhcreme f shoe polish
Schuhgeschäft nt shoe store
Schuhgröße f shoe size
Schuhlöffel m shoehorn
Schulabschluss m high-school degree
schuld adj: **wer ist ~ daran?** whose fault is
it?; **er ist ~** it's his fault, he's to blame
Schuld (-) f guilt; (Verschulden) fault; **~
haben** to be to blame (an +dat for); **er hat
~** it's his fault; **sie gibt mir die ~ an dem
Unfall** she blames me for the accident
schulden vt to owe (jdm etw sb sth)
Schulden pl debts pl; **~ haben** to be in
debt; **~ machen** to run up debts; **seine ~
bezahlen** to pay off one's debts
schuldig adj guilty (an +dat of); (gebüh-
rend) due; **jdm etw ~ sein** to owe sb sth
Schule (-, -n) f school; **in der ~** at school; **in
die ~ gehen** to go to school
Schüler(in) (-s, -) m(f) student; (jüngerer)
schoolchild
Schüleraustausch m student exchange
Schulfach nt subject
Schulferien pl school vacation
schulfrei adj: **morgen ist ~** there's no school
tomorrow
Schulfreund(in) m(f) schoolmate
Schuljahr nt school year
Schulkenntnisse pl: **~ in Französisch**
high-school French
Schulklasse f class
Schulleiter(in) m(f) principal
Schulter (-, -n) f shoulder
Schulterblatt nt shoulder blade
Schulung f training; (Veranstaltung) train-
ing course
schummeln vi (fam) to cheat
Schuppe (-, -n) f (von Fisch) scale
schuppen vt to scale ▷ vr: **sich ~** to peel
Schuppen pl (im Haar) dandruff sing
Schürfwunde f scrape
Schürze (-, -n) f apron
Schuss (-es, Schüsse) m shot; **mit einem ~
Wodka** with a dash of vodka
Schüssel (-, -n) f bowl
Schuster(in) (-s, -) m(f) shoemaker
Schutt (-(e)s) m rubble
Schüttelfrost m (the) chills pl
schütteln vt to shake ▷ vr: **sich ~** to shake
schütten vt to pour; (Zucker, Kies etc) to tip
▷ vi impers to pour (down)
Schutz (-es) m protection (gegen, vor
against, from); (Unterschlupf) shelter; **jdn
in ~ nehmen** to stand up for sb

Schutzblech nt guard; (Fahrrad) fender
Schutzbrief m travel insurance document
for drivers
Schutzbrille f (safety) goggles pl
Schütze (-n, -n) m (beim Fußball) scorer;
(Astr) Sagittarius
schützen vt: **jdn gegen/vor etw ~** to protect
sb against/from sth
Schutzimpfung f inoculation, vaccination
schwach adj weak; **~e Augen** poor eyesight
sing
Schwäche (-, -n) f weakness
Schwachstelle f weak point
Schwachstrom m low-voltage current
Schwager (-s, Schwäger) m brother-in-law
Schwägerin f sister-in-law
Schwalbe (-, -n) f swallow; (beim Fußball)
dive
schwamm imperf von **schwimmen**
Schwamm (-(e)s, Schwämme) m sponge; **~
drüber!** (fam) let's forget it!
Schwan (-(e)s, Schwäne) m swan
schwanger adj pregnant; **im vierten Monat
~ sein** to be four months pregnant
Schwangerschaft f pregnancy
Schwangerschaftsabbruch m abortion
Schwangerschaftstest m pregnancy test
schwanken vi to sway; (Preise, Zahlen) to
fluctuate; (zögern) to hesitate; (taumeln)
to stagger; **ich schwanke zwischen A und
B** I can't decide between A and B
Schwanz (-es, Schwänze) m tail
Schwarm (-(e)s, Schwärme) m swarm; (fam:
angehimmelte Person) heartthrob
schwärmen vi to swarm; **~ für** to be crazy
about
schwarz adj black; **mir wurde ~ vor Augen**
everything went black
Schwarzarbeit f illegal work; **~ machen** to
work off the books
Schwarzbrot nt black bread
schwarz|fahren (irr) vi to travel without a
ticket; (ohne Führerschein) to drive without a license
Schwarzfahrer(in) m(f) fare-dodger
Schwarzmarkt m black market
schwarz|sehen (irr) vi (fam: pessimistisch
sein) to be pessimistic (für about)
Schwarzwald m Black Forest
schwarzweiß adj black and white
Schwarzwurzel f black salsify
schwatzen vi to chatter
Schwätzer(in) (-s, -) m(f) chatterbox;
(Schwafler) windbag; (Klatschmaul) gossip; **ein großer ~ sein** to be full of hot air

S

Schwebebahn f suspension railroad

schweben vi to float; (hoch) to soar

Schwede (-n, -n) m Swede

Schweden (-s) nt Sweden

Schwedin f Swede

schwedisch adj Swedish

Schwedisch nt Swedish

Schwefel (-s) m sulfur

schweigen (schwieg, geschwiegen) vi to be silent; (nicht mehr reden) to stop talking

Schweigen (-s) nt silence

Schweigepflicht f duty of confidentiality; **die ärztliche ~** medical confidentiality

Schwein (-(e)s, -e) nt pig; (fam: Glück) luck; (fam: gemeiner Mensch) swine

Schweinebraten m pork roast

Schweinefleisch nt pork

Schweinerei f mess; (Gemeinheit) dirty trick

Schweiß (-es) m sweat

schweißen vt, vi to weld

Schweiz (-) f: **die ~** Switzerland

Schweizer(in) (-s, -) m(f) Swiss

Schweizerdeutsch nt Swiss German

schweizerisch adj Swiss

Schwelle (-, -n) f doorstep; (a. fig) threshold

schwellen vi to swell (up)

Schwellung f swelling

schwer adj heavy; (schwierig) difficult, hard; (schlimm) serious, bad; **er ist ~ zu verstehen** it's difficult to understand what he's saying ▷ adv (sehr) really; (verletzt etc) seriously, badly; **etw ~ nehmen** to take sth hard

Schwerbehinderte(r) mf severely disabled person

schwer|fallen (irr) vi (Schwierigkeiten bereiten): **jdm ~** to be difficult for sb

schwerhörig adj hard of hearing

Schwert (-(e)s, -er) nt sword

Schwertlilie f iris

Schwester (-, -n) f sister; (Med) nurse

schwieg imperf von schweigen

Schwiegereltern pl parents-in-law pl

Schwiegermutter f mother-in-law

Schwiegersohn m son-in-law

Schwiegertochter f daughter-in-law

Schwiegervater m father-in-law

schwierig adj difficult, hard

Schwierigkeit f difficulty; **in ~en kommen** to get into trouble; **jdm ~en machen** to make things difficult for sb

Schwimmbad nt swimming pool

Schwimmbecken nt swimming pool

schwimmen (schwamm, geschwommen) vi to swim; (treiben) to float; (fig: unsicher sein) to be lost

Schwimmer(in) m(f) swimmer

Schwimmflosse f flipper

Schwimmflügel m water wing

Schwimmreifen m rubber ring

Schwimmweste f life jacket

Schwindel (-s) m dizziness; (Anfall) dizzy spell; (Betrug) swindle

schwindelfrei adj: **nicht ~ sein** to have a fear of heights; **~ sein** to have a head for heights

schwindlig adj dizzy; **mir ist ~** I feel dizzy

Schwips m: **einen ~ haben** to be tipsy

schwitzen vi to sweat

schwoll imperf von schwellen

schwor imperf von schwören

schwören (schwor, geschworen) vt, vi to swear; **einen Eid ~** to take an oath

schwul adj gay

schwül adj hot and humid, muggy

Schwung (-(e)s, Schwünge) m swing; (Triebkraft) momentum; (fig: Energie) energy; (fam: Menge) batch; **in ~ kommen** to get going

Schwur (-s, Schwüre) m oath

scrollen vi (Inform) to scroll

sechs num six

Sechs (-, -en) f six; (Schulnote) ≈ F

Sechserpack m six-pack

sechshundert num six hundred

sechsmal adv six times

sechste(r, s) adj sixth; siehe auch **dritte**

Sechstel (-s, -) nt sixth

sechzehn num sixteen

sechzehnte(r, s) adj sixteenth; siehe auch **dritte**

sechzig num sixty; **in den ~er Jahren** in the sixties

sechzigste(r, s) adj sixtieth

Secondhandladen m secondhand store

See (-, -n) f sea; **an der See** by the sea ▷ (-s, -n) m lake; **am See** by the lake

Seegang m waves; **hoher/schwerer/leichter ~** rough/heavy/calm seas pl

Seehund m seal

Seeigel m sea urchin

seekrank adj seasick

Seele (-, -n) f soul

Seeleute pl seamen pl sailors pl

seelisch adj mental, psychological

Seelöwe m sea lion

Seemann m sailor, seaman

Seemeile *f* nautical mile
Seemöwe *f* seagull
Seenot *f* distress (at sea)
Seepferdchen *nt* sea horse
Seerose *f* water lily
Seestern *m* starfish
Seezunge *f* sole
Segel (*-s, -*) *nt* sail
Segelboot *nt* sailboat
Segelfliegen (*-s*) *nt* gliding
Segelflugzeug *nt* glider
segeln *vt, vi* to sail
Segelschiff *nt* sailing ship
sehbehindert *adj* partially sighted
sehen (**sah, gesehen**) *vt, vi* to see; (*in bestimmte Richtung*) to look; **gut/schlecht ~** to have good/bad eyesight; **auf die Uhr ~** to look at one's watch; **kann ich das mal ~?** can I take a look at it?; **wir ~ uns morgen!** see you tomorrow!; **ich kenne sie nur vom S~** I only know her by sight
Sehenswürdigkeiten *pl* sights *pl*
Sehne (*-, -n*) *f* tendon; (*an Bogen*) string
sehnen *vr:* **sich ~** to long (*nach* for)
Sehnenscheidenentzündung *f* (*Med*) tendinitis, tendovaginitis
Sehnenzerrung *f* (*Med*) pulled tendon
Sehnsucht *f* longing
sehnsüchtig *adj* longing
sehr *adv* (*vor Adjektiv, Adverb*) very; (*mit Verben*) a lot, very much; **zu ~** too much
seicht *adj* shallow
Seide (*-, -n*) *f* silk
Seife (*-, -n*) *f* soap
Seifenoper *f* soap (opera)
Seifenschale *f* soap dish
Seil (*-(e)s, -e*) *nt* rope; (*Kabel*) cable

SCHLÜSSELWORT

sein (*pt* **war**, *pp* **gewesen**) *vi* **1** to be; **ich bin** I am; **du bist** you are; **er/sie/es ist** he/she/it is; **wir sind/ihr seid/sie sind** we/you/they are; **wir waren** we were; **wir sind gewesen** we have been

2: seien Sie nicht böse don't be angry; **sei so gut und ...** be so kind as to ...; **das wäre gut** that would *o* that'd be a good thing; **wenn ich Sie wäre** if I were *o* was you; **das wär's** that's all, that's it; **morgen bin ich in Rom** tomorrow I'll *o* I will *o* I shall be in Rome; **waren Sie mal in Rom?** have you ever been to Rome?

3: wie ist das zu verstehen? how is that to be understood?; **er ist nicht zu ersetzen**

he cannot be replaced; **mit ihr ist nicht zu reden** you can't talk to her

4: mir ist kalt I'm cold; **was ist?** what's the matter?, what is it?; **ist was?** is something the matter?; **es sei denn, dass ...** unless ...; **wie dem auch sei** be that as it may; **wie wäre es mit ...?** how *o* what about ...?; **lass das sein!** stop that!

sein *pron possessiv von* **er**; (*adjektivisch*) his ▷ *pron possessiv von* **es**; (*adjektivisch*) its; (*adjektivisch, männlich*) his; (*weiblich*) her; (*sächlich*) its; **das ist ~e Tasche** that's his bag; **jeder hat ~e Sorgen** everyone has their problems

seine(r, s) *pron possessiv von* **er**; (*substantivisch*) his ▷ *pron possessiv von* **es**; (*substantivisch*) its; (*substantivisch, männlich*) his; (*weiblich*) hers; **das ist ~r/~/~s** that's his/hers

seiner *pron gen von* **er**; of him ▷ *pron gen von* **es**; of it

seinetwegen *adv* (*wegen ihm*) because of him; (*ihm zuliebe*) for his sake; (*um ihn*) about him; (*von ihm aus*) as far as he is concerned

seit *conj* (*bei Zeitpunkt*) since; (*bei Zeitraum*) for; **er ist ~ Montag hier** he's been here since Monday; **er ist ~ einer Woche hier** he's been here for a week; **~ langem** for a long time

seitdem *adv, conj* since
Seite (*-, -n*) *f* side; (*in Buch*) page; **zur ~ gehen** to step aside
Seitenairbag *m* side-impact airbag
Seitenaufprallschutz *m* (*Auto*) side-impact protection
Seitensprung *m* affair
Seitenstechen (*-s*) *nt:* **~ haben/bekommen** to have/get a stitch (*o* cramp)
Seitenstraße *f* side street
Seitenstreifen *m* shoulder
Seitenwind *m* crosswind
seither *adv* since (then)
seitlich *adj* side
Sekretär(in) *m(f)* secretary
Sekretariat (*-s, -e*) *nt* administrative office
Sekt (*-(e)s, -e*) *m* sparkling wine; (*similar to champagne*)
Sekte (*-, -n*) *f* sect
Sekunde (*-, -n*) *f* second
Sekundenkleber (*-s, -*) *m* superglue
Sekundenschnelle *f:* **es geschah alles in ~** it was all over in a matter of seconds

S

selbst *pron* 1: **ich/er/wir selbst** I myself/he himself/we ourselves; **sie ist die Tugend selbst** she's virtue itself; **er braut sein Bier selbst** he brews his own beer; **wie geht's?** - **gut, und selbst?** how are things? - fine, and yourself?

2 (*ohne Hilfe*) alone, on my/his/one's *etc* own; **von selbst** by itself; **er kam von selbst** he came of his own accord; **selbst gemacht** home-made

▷ *adv* even; **selbst wenn** even if; **selbst Gott** even God (himself)

selbständig *adj siehe* **selbstständig**
Selbstauslöser (*-s, -*) *m* (*Foto*) self-timer
Selbstbedienung *f* self-service
Selbstbefriedigung *f* masturbation
Selbstbeherrschung *f* self-control
Selbstbeteiligung *f* (*einer Versicherung*) deductible
selbstbewusst *adj* (self-)confident
Selbstbräuner (*-s, -*) *m* self-tanning lotion
selbstgemacht *adj* homemade
selbstklebend *adj* self-adhesive
Selbstlaut *m* vowel
Selbstmord *m* suicide
Selbstmordattentat *nt* suicide bombing
Selbstmordattentäter(in) *m(f)* suicide bomber
selbstsicher *adj* self-assured
selbstständig *adj* independent; (*arbeitend*) self-employed
Selbstverpflegung *f* room without board
selbstverständlich *adj* obvious; **ich halte das für** ~ I take that for granted ▷ *adv* naturally
Selbstvertrauen *nt* self-confidence
Sellerie (*-s, -(s)*) *m* (*-, -n*) *f* (*Knollensellerie*) celeriac; (*Stangensellerie*) celery
selten *adj* rare ▷ *adv* seldom, rarely
seltsam *adj* strange; ~ **schmecken/riechen** to taste/smell strange
Semester (*-s, -*) *nt* semester
Semesterferien *pl* vacation *sing*
Semikolon (*-s, Semikola*) *nt* semicolon
Seminar (*-s, -e*) *nt* seminar
Semmel (*-, -n*) *f* roll
Semmelbrösel *pl* breadcrumbs
Senat (*-(e)s, -e*) *m* senate
senden (**sandte, gesandt**) *vt* to send ▷ *vt, vi* (*Radio, TV*) to broadcast
Sender (*-s, -*) *m* (*TV*) channel; (*Radio*) station; (*Anlage*) transmitter

Sendung *f* (*Radio, TV*) broadcasting; (*Programm*) program
Senf (*-(e)s, -e*) *m* mustard
Senior(in) *m(f)* senior citizen
Seniorenpass *m* senior citizen's discount pass
senken *vt* to lower ▷ *vr*: **sich** ~ to sink
senkrecht *adj* vertical
Sensation (*-, -en*) *f* sensation
sensibel *adj* sensitive
sentimental *adj* sentimental
separat *adj* separate
September (*-(s), -*) *m* September; *siehe auch* **Juni**
Serbien (*-s*) *nt* Serbia
Serie *f* series *sing*
seriös *adj* (*ernsthaft*) serious; (*anständig*) respectable
Serpentine *f* hairpin (bend)
Serum (*-s, Seren*) *nt* serum
Server (*-s, -*) *m* (*Inform*) server
Service (*-(s), -*) *nt* (*Geschirr*) service ▷ *m* (*-, -s*) service
servieren *vt, vi* to serve
Serviette *f* napkin
Servolenkung *f* (*Auto*) power steering
Sesam (*-s, -s*) *m* sesame seeds *pl*
Sessel (*-s, -*) *m* armchair
Sessellift *m* chairlift
Set (*-s, -s*) *m o nt* set; (*Tischset*) tablemat
setzen *vt* to put; (*Baum etc*) to plant; (*Segel*) to set ▷ *vr*: **sich** ~ to settle; (*hinsetzen*) to sit down; ~ **Sie sich doch** please sit down
Seuche (*-, -n*) *f* epidemic
seufzen *vt, vi* to sigh
Sex (*-(es)*) *m* sex
Sexismus *m* sexism
sexistisch *adj* sexist
Sextourismus *m* sex tourism
Sexualität *f* sexuality
sexuell *adj* sexual
Seychellen *pl* Seychelles *pl*
sfr (*abk*) = **Schweizer Franken** Swiss franc(s)
Shampoo (*-s, -s*) *nt* shampoo
Shareware (*-, -s*) *f* (*Inform*) shareware
Shorts *pl* shorts *pl*
Shuttlebus *m* shuttle bus

sich *pron* 1 (*akk*): **er/sie/es … sich** he/she/it … himself/herself/itself; **sie** (*pl*) /**man … sich** = they/one … themselves/oneself; **Sie … sich** you … yourself/yourselves *pl*; **sich**

wiederholen to repeat oneself/itself

2 (*dat*): **er/sie/es ... sich** he/she/it ... to himself/herself/itself; **sie** (*pl*) **... sich** ≈ they/one ... to themselves/oneself; **Sie ... sich** you ... to yourself/yourselves *pl*; **sie hat sich einen Pullover gekauft** she bought herself a sweater; **sich die Haare waschen** to wash one's hair

3 (*mit Präposition*): **haben Sie Ihren Ausweis bei sich?** do you have your ID on you?; **er hat nichts bei sich** he's got nothing on him; **sie bleiben gern unter sich** they (like to) keep to themselves

4 (*einander*) each other, one another; **sie bekämpfen sich** they fight each other *o* one another

5: **dieses Auto fährt sich gut** this car drives well; **hier sitzt es sich gut** it's good to sit here

sicher *adj* safe (*vor +dat* from); (*gewiss*) certain (*gen* of); (*zuverlässig*) reliable; (*selbstsicher*) confident; **aber ~!** of course, sure!

Sicherheit *f* safety; (*Aufgabe von Sicherheitsbeamten*: *Fin*) security; (*Gewissheit*) certainty; (*Selbstsicherheit*) confidence; **mit ~** definitely

Sicherheitsabstand *m* safe distance

Sicherheitsgurt *m* seat belt

sicherheitshalber *adv* just to be on the safe side

Sicherheitsnadel *f* safety pin

Sicherheitsvorkehrung *f* safety precaution

sicherlich *adv* certainly; (*wahrscheinlich*) probably

sichern *vt* to secure (*gegen* against); (*schützen*) to protect; (*Daten*) to back up

Sicherung *f* (*Sichern*) securing; (*Vorrichtung*) safety device; (*an Waffen*) safety catch; (*Elek*) fuse; (*Inform*) backup; **die ~ ist durchgebrannt** the fuse has blown

Sicht (-) *f* sight; (*Aussicht*) view

sichtbar *adj* visible

sichtlich *adj* evident, obvious

Sichtverhältnisse *pl* visibility *sing*

Sichtweite *f*: **in/außer ~** within/out of sight

sie *pron* (*3. Person sing*) she; (*3. Person pl*) they; (*akk von sing*) her; (*akk von pl*) them; (*für eine Sache*) it; **da ist sie ja** there she is; **da sind sie ja** there they are; **ich kenne sie** (*Frau*) I know her; (*mehrere Personen*) I know them; **sie lag gerade noch hier** (*meine Jacke, Uhr*) it was here just a minute ago; **ich hab sie gefunden** (*meine*

Jacke, Uhr) I've found it; **hast du meine Brille/Hose gesehen? - ich kann sie nirgends finden** have you seen my glasses/pants? - I can't find them anywhere

Sie *pron* (*Höflichkeitsform, Nom und Akk*) you

Sieb (-*(e)s, -e*) *nt* sieve; (*Teesieb*) strainer

sieben *num* seven

siebenhundert *num* seven hundred

siebenmal *adv* seven times

siebte(r, s) *adj* seventh; *siehe auch* **dritte**

Siebtel (-*s, -*) *nt* seventh

siebzehn *num* seventeen

siebzehnte(r, s) *adj* seventeenth; *siehe auch* **dritte**

siebzig *num* seventy; **in den ~er Jahren** in the seventies

siebzigste(r, s) *adj* seventieth

Siedlung (-, -*en*) *f* (*Wohngebiet*) housing development

Sieg (-*(e)s, -e*) *m* victory

siegen *vi* to win

Sieger(in) (-*s, -*) *m(f)* winner

Siegerehrung *f* awards ceremony

siehe *imper* see

siezen *vt* to address as 'Sie'

Signal (-*s, -e*) *nt* signal

Silbe (-, -*n*) *f* syllable

Silber (-*s*) *nt* silver

Silberhochzeit *f* silver wedding

Silbermedaille *f* silver medal

Silikon (-*s, -e*) *nt* silicone

Silvester (-*s, -*) *nt*, **Silvesterabend** *m* New Year's Eve

SILVESTER

Silvester is the German name for New Year's Eve. Although not an official holiday, most businesses shut down early and stores close at lunchtime. Most Germans celebrate in the evening and at midnight they set off fireworks and rockets; the revelry usually lasts until the early hours of the morning.

Simbabwe (-*s*) *nt* Zimbabwe

SIM-Karte *f* SIM card

simpel *adj* simple

simsen *vt, vi* (*fam*) to text

simultan *adj* simultaneous

Sinfonie (-, -*n*) *f* symphony

Sinfonieorchester *nt* symphony orchestra

Singapur (-*s*) *nt* Singapore

singen (**sang, gesungen**) *vt, vi* to sing; **richtig/falsch** ~ to sing in tune/out of tune

Single (-, -s) *f* (*CD*) single ▷ (-s, -s) *m* (*Mensch*) single

Singular *m* singular

sinken (**sank, gesunken**) *vi* to sink; (*Preise etc*) to fall, to go down

Sinn (-(e)s, -e) *m* (*Denken*) mind; (*Wahrnehmung*) sense; (*Bedeutung*) sense, meaning; ~ **machen** to make sense; **das hat keinen** ~ it's no use

sinnlich *adj* sensuous; (*erotisch*) sensual; (*Wahrnehmung*) sensory

sinnlos *adj* (*unsinnig*) stupid; (*Verhalten*) senseless; (*zwecklos*) pointless; (*bedeutungslos*) meaningless

sinnvoll *adj* meaningful; (*vernünftig*) sensible

Sirup (-s, -e) *m* syrup

Sitte (-, -n) *f* custom

Situation *f* situation

Sitz (-es, -e) *m* seat

sitzen (**saß, gesessen**) *vi* to sit; (*Bemerkung, Schlag*) to strike home; (*Gelerntes*) to have sunk in; **der Rock sitzt gut** the skirt is a good fit; ~ **bleiben** (*Schule*) to have to repeat a year

Sitzgelegenheit *f* place to sit down

Sitzplatz *m* seat

Sitzung *f* meeting

Sizilien (-s) *nt* Sicily

Skandal (-s, -e) *m* scandal

Skandinavien (-s) *nt* Scandinavia

Skateboard (-s, -s) *nt* skateboard

skateboarden *vi* to skateboard

Skelett (-s, -e) *nt* skeleton

skeptisch *adj* skeptical

Ski (-s, -er) *m* ski; **Ski laufen** *o* **fahren** to ski

Skianzug *m* ski suit

Skibrille *f* ski goggles *pl*

Skifahren (-s) *nt* skiing

Skigebiet (-s, -e) *nt* ski area

Skihose *f* ski pants *pl*

Skikurs *m* ski course

Skilanglauf *m* cross-country skiing

Skiläufer(in) *m(f)* skier

Skilehrer(in) *m(f)* ski instructor

Skilift *m* ski-lift

Skinhead (-s, -s) *m* skinhead

Skipiste *f* ski run

Skischanze (-, -n) *f* ski jump

Skischuh *m* ski boot

Skischule *f* ski school

Skispringen (-s, -n) *nt* ski jumping

Skistiefel (-s, -) *m* ski boot

Skistock *m* ski pole

Skiträger *m* ski rack

Skiurlaub *m* skiing vacation

Skizze (-, -n) *f* sketch

Skonto (-s, -s) *m o nt* discount

Skorpion (-s, -e) *m* (*Zool*) scorpion; (*Astr*) Scorpio

Skulptur (-, -en) *f* sculpture

S-Kurve *f* double bend

Slalom (-s, -s) *m* slalom

Slip (-s, -s) *m* (pair of) briefs *pl*

Slipeinlage *f* panty liner

Slowakei (-) *f* Slovakia

slowakisch *adj* Slovakian; **S~e Republik** Slovak Republic

Slowakisch *nt* Slovakian

Slowenien (-s) *nt* Slovenia

slowenisch *adj* Slovenian

Slowenisch *nt* Slovenian

Smiley (-s, -s) *m* smiley

Smog (-s) *m* smog

Smogalarm *m* smog alert

Smoking (-s, -s) *m* tuxedo

SMS *nt* (*abk*) = **Short Message Service** ▷ *f* (*Nachricht*) text message; **ich schicke dir eine SMS** I'll text you, I'll send you a text (message)

Snowboard (-s, -s) *nt* snowboard

snowboarden *vi* to snowboard

Snowboardfahren (-s) *nt* snowboarding

Snowboardfahrer(in) *m(f)* snowboarder

SCHLÜSSELWORT

so *adv* **1** (*so sehr*) so; **so groß/schön** *etc* so big/nice *etc*; **so groß/schön wie ...** as big/nice as ...; **so viel (wie)** as much as; **rede nicht so viel** don't talk so much; **so weit sein** to be ready; **so weit wie** *o* **als möglich** as far as possible; **ich bin so weit zufrieden** by and large I'm quite satisfied; **so wenig (wie)** as little (as); **das hat ihn so geärgert, dass ...** that annoyed him so much that ...; **so einer wie ich** somebody like me; **na so was!** well, well!

2 (*auf diese Weise*) like this; **mach es nicht so** don't do it like that; **so oder so** in one way or the other; **und so weiter** and so on; **... oder so was** ... or something like that; **das ist gut so** that's fine

3 (*fam: umsonst*): **ich habe es so bekommen** I got it for nothing

▷ *konj*: **sodass** so that; **so wie es jetzt ist** as things are at the moment

▷ *excl*: **so?** really?; **so, das wär's** so, that's it then

s. o. (*abk*) = **siehe oben** see above
sobald *conj* as soon as
Socke (-, -n) *f* sock
Sodbrennen (-s) *nt* heartburn
Sofa (-s, -s) *nt* sofa
sofern *conj* if, provided (that)
soff *imperf von* **saufen**
sofort *adv* immediately, at once
Sofortbildkamera *f* instant camera
Softeis *nt* soft ice-cream
Software (-, -s) *f* software
sog *imperf von* **saugen**
sogar *adv* even; **kalt, ~ sehr kalt** cold, in fact very cold
sogenannt *adj* so-called
Sohle (-, -n) *f* sole
Sohn (-(e)s, Söhne) *m* son
Soja (-, Sojen) *f* soy
Sojasprossen *pl* bean sprouts *pl*
solang(e) *conj* as long as
Solarium *nt* solarium
Solarzelle *f* solar cell
solche(r, s) *pron* such; **eine ~ Frau, solch eine Frau** such a woman, a woman like that; **~ Sachen** things like that, such things; **ich habe ~ Kopfschmerzen** I've got such a headache; **ich habe ~n Hunger** I'm so hungry
Soldat(in) (-en, -en) *m(f)* soldier
solid(e) *adj* solid; (*Leben, Mensch*) respectable
solidarisch *adj* showing solidarity; **sich ~ erklären mit** to declare one's solidarity with
Soll (-(s), -(s)) *nt* (*Fin*) debit; (*Arbeitsmenge*) quota, target

SCHLÜSSELWORT

sollen (*pt* **sollte**, *pp* **gesollt** *o* (*als Hilfsverb*) **sollen**) *Hilfsverb* **1** (*Pflicht, Befehl*) to be supposed to; **du hättest nicht gehen sollen** you shouldn't have gone; **soll ich?** should I?; **soll ich dir helfen?** should I help you?, would you like me to help you?; **sag ihm, er soll warten** tell him to wait; **was soll ich machen?** what should I do?
2 (*Vermutung*): **sie soll verheiratet sein** she's said to be married; **was soll das heißen?** what's that supposed to mean?; **man sollte glauben, dass ...** you would think that ...; **sollte das passieren, ...** if that

should happen ...
▷ *vt, vi*: **was soll das?** what's all this?; **das sollst du nicht** you shouldn't do that; **was soll's?** what the hell!

Solo (-s, -) *nt* solo
Sommer (-s, -) *m* summer
Sommerfahrplan *m* summer timetable
Sommerferien *pl* summer vacation *sing*
sommerlich *adj* summery; (*Sommer-*) summer
Sommerreifen *m* normal tire
Sommersprossen *pl* freckles *pl*
Sommerzeit *f* summertime; (*Uhrzeit*) daylight saving time
Sonderangebot *nt* special offer
sonderbar *adj* strange, odd
Sondermarke *f* special stamp
Sondermaschine *f* special plane
Sondermüll *m* hazardous waste
sondern *conj* but; **nicht nur ..., ~ auch** not only ..., but also
Sonderpreis *m* special price
Sonderschule *f* special ed(ucation) school
Sonderzeichen *nt* (*Inform*) special character
Sonderzug *m* special train
Song (-s, -s) *m* song
Sonnabend *m* Saturday; *siehe auch* **Mittwoch**
sonnabends *adv* on Saturdays; **~ morgens** on Saturday mornings; *siehe auch* **mittwochs**
Sonne (-, -n) *f* sun
sonnen *vr*: **sich ~** to sunbathe
Sonnenallergie *f* sun allergy
Sonnenaufgang *m* sunrise
Sonnenblume *f* sunflower
Sonnenblumenkern *m* sunflower seed
Sonnenbrand *m* sunburn
Sonnenbrille *f* sunglasses *pl*, shades *pl*
Sonnencreme *f* sun cream
Sonnendach *nt* (*an Haus*) awning; (*Auto*) sunroof
Sonnendeck *nt* sun deck
Sonnenmilch *f* suntan lotion
Sonnenöl *nt* suntan oil
Sonnenschein *m* sunshine
Sonnenschirm *m* parasol, sunshade
Sonnenschutzcreme *f* sunscreen
Sonnenstich *m* sunstroke
Sonnenstudio *nt* solarium
Sonnenuhr *f* sundial
Sonnenuntergang *m* sunset
sonnig *adj* sunny

Sonntag *m* Sunday; *siehe auch* **Mittwoch**

sonntags *adv* on Sundays; *siehe auch* **mittwochs**

sonst *adv, conj* (*außerdem*) else; (*andernfalls*) otherwise, (or) else; (*mit Pron, in Fragen*) else; (*normalerweise*) normally, usually; ~ **noch etwas?** anything else?; ~ **nichts** nothing else

soft *conj* whenever

Sopran (*-s, -e*) *m* soprano

Sorge (*-, -n*) *f* worry; (*Fürsorge*) care; **sich** (*dat*) **um jdn ~n machen** to be worried about sb

sorgen *vi*: **für jdn ~** to look after sb; **für etw ~** to take care of sth, to see to sth ▷ *vr*: **sich ~** to worry (*um* about)

sorgfältig *adj* careful

sortieren *vt* to sort (out)

Sortiment *nt* assortment

sosehr *conj* however much

Soße (*-, -n*) *f* sauce; (*zu Braten*) gravy

Soundkarte *f* (*Inform*) sound card

Souvenir (*-s, -s*) *nt* souvenir

soviel *conj* as far as

soweit *conj* as far as

sowie *conj* (*wie auch*) as well as; (*sobald*) as soon as

sowohl *conj*: ~ ... **als** *o* **wie auch** both ... and

sozial *adj* social; ~**er Wohnungsbau** public-sector housing (program)

Sozialhilfe *f* welfare (aid)

Sozialismus *m* socialism

Sozialkunde *f* social studies *pl*

Sozialversicherung *f* social security

Sozialwohnung *f* state-subsidized apartment

Soziologie *f* sociology

sozusagen *adv* so to speak

Spachtel (*-s, -*) *m* spatula

Spag(h)etti *pl* spaghetti *sing*

Spalte (*-, -n*) *f* crack; (*Gletscher*) crevasse; (*in Text*) column

spalten *vt* to split ▷ *vr*: **sich ~** to split

Spam (*-s, -s*) *nt* (*Inform*) spam

Spange (*-, -n*) *f* clasp; (*Haarspange*) barrette

Spanien (*-s*) *nt* Spain

Spanier(in) (*-s, -*) *m(f)* Spaniard

spanisch *adj* Spanish

Spanisch *nt* Spanish

spann *imperf von* **spinnen**

spannen *vt* (*straffen*) to tighten; (*befestigen*) to brace ▷ *vi* to be tight

spannend *adj* exciting, gripping

Spannung *f* tension; (*Elek*) voltage; (*fig*) suspense

Sparbuch *nt* savings book; (*Konto*) savings account

sparen *vt, vi* to save

Spargel (*-s, -*) *m* asparagus

Spargelsuppe *f* asparagus soup

Sparkasse *f* savings bank

Sparkonto (*-s*) *nt* savings account

spärlich *adj* meager; (*Bekleidung*) scanty

sparsam *adj* economical

Sparschwein *nt* piggy bank

Spaß (*-es, Späße*) *m* joke; (*Freude*) fun; **es macht mir ~** I enjoy it, it's (great) fun; **viel ~!** have fun!

spät *adj, adv* late; **zu ~ kommen** to be late

Spaten (*-s, -*) *m* spade

später *adj, adv* later

spätestens *adv* at the latest

Spätlese *f* late vintage (wine)

Spätvorstellung *f* late-night performance

Spatz (*-en, -en*) *m* sparrow

spazieren *vi* to stroll, to walk; ~ **gehen** to go for a walk

Spaziergang *m* walk

Specht (*-(e)s, -e*) *m* woodpecker

Speck (*-(e)s, -e*) *m* bacon fat; (*durchwachsen*) bacon

Speiche (*-, -n*) *f* spoke

Speichel (*-s*) *m* saliva

Speicher (*-s, -*) *m* storehouse; (*Dachboden*) attic; (*Inform*) memory

speichern *vt* (*Inform*) to store; (*sichern*) to save

Speise (*-, -n*) *f* food; (*Gericht*) dish

Speisekarte *f* menu

Speiseröhre *f* esophagus

Speisesaal *m* dining hall

Speisewagen *m* dining car

Spende (*-, -n*) *f* donation

spenden *vt* to donate, to give

spendieren *vt*: **jdm etw ~** to treat sb to sth

Sperre (*-, -n*) *f* barrier; (*Verbot*) ban

sperren *vt* to block; (*Sport*) to suspend; (*verbieten*) to ban

Sperrgepäck *m* bulky baggage

Sperrmüll *m* bulky trash

Sperrstunde *f* closing time

Sperrung *f* closing

Spesen *pl* expenses *pl*

spezialisieren *vr*: **sich ~** to specialize (*auf +akk* in)

Spezialist(in) *m(f)* specialist

Spezialität *f* specialty

speziell *adj* special ▷ *adv* especially

Spiegel (-s, -) m mirror
Spiegelei nt egg sunny-side up
spiegelglatt adj very slippery
Spiegelreflexkamera f SLR (o reflex) camera
Spiel (-(e)s, -e) nt game; (Tätigkeit) play(ing); (Karten) pack, deck; (Tech) (free) play
Spielautomat m (ohne Geldgewinn) gaming machine; (mit Geldgewinn) slot machine
spielen vt, vi to play; (um Geld) to gamble; (Theat) to perform, to. act; **Klavier ~** to play the piano
spielend adv easily
Spieler(in) (-s, -) m(f) player; (um Geld) gambler
Spielfeld nt (für Fußball, Hockey) field; (für Basketball) court
Spielfilm m feature film
Spielkasino nt casino
Spielplatz m playground
Spielraum m room to maneuver
Spielregel f rule; **sich an die ~n halten** to stick to the rules
Spielsachen pl toys pl
Spielzeug nt toys pl; (einzelnes) toy
Spieß (-es, -e) m spear; (Bratspieß) spit
Spießer(in) (-s, -) m(f) square, stuffy type
spießig adj square, uncool
Spikes pl (Sport) spikes pl; (Auto) studs pl
Spinat (-(e)s, -e) m spinach
Spinne (-, -n) f spider
spinnen (spann, gesponnen) vt, vi to spin; (fam: Unsinn reden) to talk nonsense; (verrückt sein) to be crazy; **du spinnst!** you must be crazy!
Spinnwebe (-, -n) f cobweb
Spion(in) (-s, -e) m(f) spy
spionieren vi to spy; (fig) to snoop around
Spirale (-, -n) f spiral; (Med) IUD
Spirituosen pl spirits pl, liquor sing
Spiritus (-, -se) m rubbing alcohol
spitz adj (Nase, Kinn) pointed; (Bleistift, Messer) sharp; (Winkel) acute
Spitze (-, -n) f point; (von Finger, Nase) tip; (Bemerkung) taunt, dig; (erster Platz) lead; (Gewebe) lace
Spitzer (-s, -) m pencil sharpener
Spitzname m nickname
Spliss (-) m split ends pl
sponsern vt to sponsor
Sponsor(in) (-s, -en) m(f) sponsor
spontan adj spontaneous
Sport (-(e)s, -e) m sport; **~ treiben** to do sports

Sportanlage f sports facilities pl; (für Veranstaltungen) sports complex
Sportart f sport
Sportbekleidung f sportswear
Sportgeschäft nt sports store
Sporthalle f gymnasium, gym
Sportlehrer(in) (-s, -) m(f) sports instructor; (Schule) PE teacher
Sportler(in) (-s, -) m(f) sportsman/-woman
sportlich adj sporting; (Mensch) sporty
Sportplatz m playing field
Sporttauchen nt (skin-)diving; (mit Gerät) scuba-diving
Sportverein m sports club
Sportwagen m sports car
sprach imperf von sprechen
Sprache (-, -n) f language; (Sprechen) speech
Sprachenschule f language school
Sprachführer m phrasebook
Sprachkenntnisse pl knowledge sing of languages; **gute englische ~ haben** to have a good knowledge of English
Sprachkurs m language course
Sprachunterricht m language teaching
sprang imperf von springen
Spray (-s, -s) m o nt spray
Sprechanlage f intercom
sprechen (sprach, gesprochen) vt, vi to speak (jdn, mit jdm to sb); (sich unterhalten) to talk (mit to, über, von about); **~ Sie Deutsch?** do you speak German?; **kann ich bitte mit David ~?** (am Telefon) can I speak to David, please?
Sprecher(in) m(f) speaker; (Ansager) announcer
Sprechstunde f consultation; (Anwalt etc) office hours pl; (Arzt) consultation hours pl
Sprechzimmer nt consulting room
Sprengstoff m explosive
Sprichwort nt proverb
Springbrunnen m fountain
springen (sprang, gesprungen) vi to jump; (Glas) to crack; (mit Kopfsprung) to dive
Sprit (-(e)s, -e) m (fam: Benzin) gas
Spritze (-, -n) f (Gegenstand) syringe; (Injektion) injection; (fam) shot; (an Schlauch) nozzle
spritzen vt to spray; (Med) to inject ▷ vi to splash; (Med) to give injections (o shots)
Spruch (-(e)s, Sprüche) m saying
Sprudel (-s, -) m sparkling mineral water; (süßer) soda
sprudeln vi to bubble

Sprühdose f aerosol (can)

sprühen vt, vi to spray; (fig) to sparkle

Sprühregen m drizzle

Sprung (-(e)s, Sprünge) m jump; (Riss) crack

Sprungbrett nt springboard

Sprungschanze f ski jump

Sprungturm m diving platform

Spucke (-) f spit

spucken vt, vi to spit; (fam: sich erbrechen) to throw up

Spucktüte f sick bag

spuken vi (Geist) to walk; **hier spukt es** this place is haunted

Spülbecken nt sink

Spule (-, -n) f spool; (Elek) coil

Spüle (-, -n) f sink

spülen vt, vi to rinse; (Geschirr) to wash up; (Toilette) to flush

Spülmaschine f dishwasher

Spülmittel nt dishwashing detergent

Spültuch nt dishcloth

Spülung f (von WC) flush

Spur (-, -en) f trace; (Fußspur, Radspur) track; (Fährte) trail; (Fahrspur) lane; **die ~ wechseln** to change lanes pl

spüren vt to feel; (merken) to notice

Spürhund m scenthound

Squash (-) nt squash

Squashschläger m squash racket

Sri Lanka (-s) nt Sri Lanka

Staat (-(e)s, -en) m state

staatlich adj state(-); (vom Staat betrieben) state-run

Staatsangehörigkeit f nationality

Staatsanwalt m, **-anwältin** f district attorney

Staatsbürger(in) m(f) citizen

Staatsbürgerschaft f nationality; **doppelte ~** dual nationality

Staatsexamen nt final exam taken by trainee teachers, medical and law students

Stab (-(e)s, Stäbe) m rod; (Gitter) bar

Stäbchen nt (Essstäbchen) chopstick

Stabhochsprung m pole vault

stabil adj stable; (Möbel) sturdy

stach imperf von stechen

Stachel (-s, -n) m spike; (von Tier) spine; (von Insekten) stinger

Stachelbeere f gooseberry

Stacheldraht m barbed wire

stachelig adj prickly

Stadion (-s, Stadien) nt stadium

Stadt (-, Städte) f town; (groß) city; **in der ~** in town

Stadtautobahn f urban expressway

Stadtbummel (-s, -) m: **einen ~ machen** to go around town

Stadtführer m (Heft) city guide

Stadtführung f city sightseeing tour

Stadthalle f municipal hall

städtisch adj municipal

Stadtmauer f city wall(s)

Stadtmitte f town/city center, downtown

Stadtplan m (street) map

Stadtrand m outskirts pl

Stadtrundfahrt f city tour

Stadtteil m, **Stadtviertel** nt district, part of town

Stadtzentrum nt town/city center, downtown

stahl imperf von stehlen

Stahl (-(e)s, Stähle) m steel

Stall (-(e)s, Ställe) m stable; (Kaninchen) hutch; (Schweine) pigpen; (Hühner) henhouse

Stamm (-(e)s, Stämme) m (Baum) trunk; (von Menschen) tribe

stammen vi: **~ aus** to come from

Stammgast m regular (guest)

Stammkunde m, **Stammkundin** f regular (customer)

Stammtisch m table reserved for regulars

stampfen vt, vi to stamp; (mit Werkzeug) to pound; (stapfen) to tramp

stand imperf von stehen

Stand (-(e)s, Stände) m (Wasser, Benzin) level; (Stehen) standing position; (Zustand) state; (Spielstand) score; (auf Messe etc) stand; (Klasse) class; **im ~e sein** to be in a position; (fähig) to be able

Stand-by-Betrieb m stand-by

Stand-by-Ticket nt stand-by ticket

Ständer (-s, -) m (Gestell) stand; (fam: Erektion) hard-on

ständig adj permanent; (ununterbrochen) constant, continual

Standlicht nt parking lights pl

Standort m position

Standpunkt m standpoint

Standspur f (Auto) shoulder

Stange (-, -n) f stick; (Stab) pole; (Metall) bar; (Zigaretten) carton

Stangenbohne f string bean

Stangenbrot nt baguette

Stangensellerie m celery

stank imperf von stinken

Stapel (-s, -) m pile

Star (-(e)s, -e) m (Vogel) starling; (Med) cataract ▷ (-s, -s) m (in Film etc) star

starb *imperf von* **sterben**

stark *adj* strong; (*heftig, groß*) heavy; (*Maßangabe*) thick

Stärke (-, -n) *f* strength; (*Dicke*) thickness; (*Wäschestärke, Speisestärke*) starch

stärken *vt* to strengthen; (*Wäsche*) to starch

Starkstrom *m* high-voltage current

Stärkung *f* strengthening; (*Essen*) refreshment

starr *adj* stiff; (*unnachgiebig*) rigid; (*Blick*) staring

starren *vi* to stare

Start (-(e)s, -e) *m* start; (*Aviat*) takeoff

Startautomatik *f* automatic choke

Startbahn *f* runway

starten *vt, vi* to start; (*Aviat*) to take off

Starthilfekabel *nt* jumper cables *pl*

Startmenü *nt* (*Inform*) start menu

Station *f* (*Haltestelle*) stop; (*Bahnhof*) station; (*im Krankenhaus*) ward

stationär *adj* stationary; **~e Behandlung** inpatient treatment; **jdn ~ behandeln** to treat sb as an in-patient

Statistik *f* statistics *pl*

Stativ *nt* tripod

statt *conj, prep* (+*gen o dat*) instead of; **~ zu arbeiten** instead of working

statt|finden (*irr*) *vi* to take place

Statue (-, -n) *f* statue

Statusleiste *f*, **Statuszeile** *f* (*Inform*) status bar

Stau (-(e)s, -e) *m* (*im Verkehr*) (traffic) jam; **im ~ stehen** to be stuck in a traffic jam

Staub (-(e)s) *m* dust; **~ wischen** to dust

staubig *adj* dusty

staubsaugen *vt, vi* to vacuum

Staubsauger *m* vacuum cleaner

Staubtuch *nt* dust cloth

Staudamm *m* dam

staunen *vi* to be astonished (*über* +*akk* at)

Stausee *m* reservoir

Stauung *f* (*von Wasser*) damming-up; (*von Blut, Verkehr*) congestion

Stauwarnung *f* traffic report

Std. (*abk*) = **Stunde** h

Steak (-s, -s) *nt* steak

stechen (**stach, gestochen**) *vt, vi* (*mit Nadel etc*) to prick; (*mit Messer*) to stab; (*mit Finger*) to poke; (*Biene*) to sting; (*Mücke*) to bite; (*Sonne*) to burn; (*Kartenspiel*) to trump

Stechen (-s, -) *nt* sharp pain, stabbing pain

Stechmücke *f* mosquito

Steckdose *f* socket

stecken *vt* to put; (*Nadel*) to stick; (*beim Nähen*) to pin ▷ *vi* (*festsitzen*) to be stuck; (*Nadeln*) to be (sticking); **der Schlüssel steckt** the key is in the door

Stecker (-s, -) *m* plug

Steckrübe *f* rutabaga

Steg (-s, -e) *m* (foot)bridge

stehen (**stand, gestanden**) *vi* to stand (*zu* by); (*sich befinden*) to be; (*stillstehen*) to have stopped; **was steht im Brief?** what does it say in the letter?; **jdm gut ~** to suit sb; **~ bleiben** (*Uhr*) to stop; **~ lassen** to leave ▷ *vi impers:* **wie steht's?** (*Sport*) what's the score?

stehlen (**stahl, gestohlen**) *vt* to steal

Stehplatz *m* (*im Konzert etc*) standing-room (-only) ticket

Steiermark (-) *f* Styria

steif *adj* stiff

steigen (**stieg, gestiegen**) *vi* (*Preise, Temperatur*) to rise; (*klettern*) to climb; **~ in/auf** +*akk* to get in/on

steigern *vt* to increase ▷ *vr:* **sich ~** to increase

Steigung *f* incline, gradient

steil *adj* steep

Steilhang *m* steep slope

Steilküste *f* steep coast

Stein (-(e)s, -e) *m* stone

Steinbock *m* (*Zool*) ibex; (*Astr*) Capricorn

steinig *adj* stony

Steinschlag *m* falling rocks *pl*

Stelle (-, -n) *f* place, spot; (*Arbeit*) position, job; (*Amt*) office; **ich an deiner ~** if I were you; **auf der ~** on the spot, immediately

stellen *vt* to put; (*Uhr etc*) to set (*auf* +*akk* to); (*zur Verfügung stellen*) to provide ▷ *vr:* **sich ~** (*bei Polizei*) to give oneself up; **sich schlafend ~** to pretend to be asleep

Stellenangebot *nt* job offer, vacancy

stellenweise *adv* in places

Stellenwert *m* (*fig*) status; **einen hohen ~ haben** to play an important role

Stellplatz *m* parking space

Stellung *f* position; **zu etw ~ nehmen** to comment on sth

Stellvertreter(in) *m(f)* representative; (*amtlich*) deputy; (*von Arzt*) locum tenens

Stempel (-s, -) *m* stamp

stempeln *vt* to stamp; (*Briefmarke*) to cancel

sterben (**starb, gestorben**) *vi* to die

Stereoanlage *f* stereo (system)

steril *adj* sterile

sterilisieren *vt* to sterilize

Stern (-(e)s, -e) *m* star; **ein Hotel mit vier ~en** a four-star hotel

Sternbild *nt* constellation; (*Sternzeichen*) star sign, sign of the zodiac

Sternfrucht *f* star fruit

Sternschnuppe (-, -n) *f* shooting star

Sternwarte (-e, -n) *f* observatory

Sternzeichen *nt* star sign, sign of the zodiac; **welches ~ bist du?** what's your sign?

stets *adv* always

Steuer (-s, -) *nt* (*Auto*) steering wheel ▷ (-, -n) *f* tax

Steuerberater(in) *m(f)* tax adviser

Steuerbord *nt* starboard

Steuererklärung *f* tax declaration

steuerfrei *adj* tax-free; (*Waren*) duty-free

Steuerknüppel *m* control column; (*Aviat, Inform*) joystick

steuern *vt, vi* to steer; (*Flugzeug*) to pilot; (*Entwicklung, Tonstärke: Inform*) to control

steuerpflichtig *adj* taxable

Steuerung *f* (*Auto*) steering; (*Vorrichtung*) controls *pl*; (*Aviat*) piloting; (*fig*) control

Steuerungstaste *f* (*Inform*) control key

Stich (-(e)s, -e) *m* (*von Insekt*) sting; (*von Mücke*) bite; (*durch Messer*) stab; (*beim Nähen*) stitch; (*Färbung*) tinge; (*Kartenspiel*) trick; (*Kunst*) engraving

sticken *vt, vi* to embroider

Sticker (-s, -) *m* sticker

Stickerei *f* embroidery

stickig *adj* stuffy

Stiefbruder *m* stepbrother

Stiefel (-s, -) *m* boot

Stiefmutter *f* stepmother

Stiefmütterchen *nt* pansy

Stiefschwester *f* stepsister

Stiefsohn *m* stepson

Stieftochter *f* stepdaughter

Stiefvater *m* stepfather

stieg *imperf von* **steigen**

Stiege (-, -n) *f* steps *pl*, stairs *pl*

Stiel (-(e)s, -e) *m* handle; (*Bot*) stalk; **ein Eis am ~** an ice-cream bar

Stier (-(e)s, -e) *m* (*Zool*) bull; (*Astr*) Taurus

Stierkampf *m* bullfight

stieß *imperf von* **stoßen**

Stift (-(e)s, -e) *m* (*aus Holz*) peg; (*Nagel*) tack; (*zum Schreiben*) pen; (*Farbstift*) colored pencil; (*Bleistift*) pencil

Stil (-s, -e) *m* style

still *adj* quiet; (*unbewegt*) still

stillen *vt* (*Säugling*) to breast-feed

still|halten (*irr*) *vi* to keep still

still|stehen (*irr*) *vi* to stand still

Stimme (-, -n) *f* voice; (*bei Wahl*) vote

stimmen *vi* to be right; **stimmt!** that's right!; **hier stimmt was nicht** there's something wrong here; **stimmt so!** (*beim Bezahlen*) keep the change!

Stimmung *f* mood; (*Atmosphäre*) atmosphere

Stinkefinger *m* (*fam*): **jdm den ~ zeigen** to give sb the finger

stinken (**stank, gestunken**) *vi* to stink (*nach of*)

Stipendium *nt* scholarship; (*als Unterstützung*) grant

Stirn (-, -en) *f* forehead

Stirnhöhle *f* sinus

Stock (-(e)s, Stöcke) *m* stick; (*Bot*) stock ▷ (*Stockwerke*) *m* floor, story

Stockbett *nt* bunk bed

Stöckelschuhe *pl* high heels *pl*

Stockwerk *nt* floor; **im ersten ~** on the second floor

Stoff (-(e)s, -e) *m* (*Gewebe*) material; (*Materie*) matter; (*von Buch etc*) subject (matter); (*fam: Rauschgift*) stuff

stöhnen *vi* to groan (*vor* with)

stolpern *vi* to stumble, to trip

stolz *adj* proud

stopp *interj* hold it; (*Moment mal!*) hang on a minute

stoppen *vt, vi* to stop; (*mit Uhr*) to time

Stoppschild *nt* stop sign

Stoppuhr *f* stopwatch

Stöpsel (-s, -) *m* plug; (*für Flaschen*) stopper

Storch (-(e)s, Störche) *m* stork

stören *vt* to disturb; (*behindern*) to interfere with; **darf ich dich kurz ~?** can I trouble you for a minute?; **stört es dich, wenn ...?** do you mind if ...?

stornieren *vt* to cancel

Stornogebühr *f* cancellation fee

Störung *f* disturbance; (*in der Leitung*) fault

Stoß (-es, Stöße) *m* (*Schub*) push; (*Schlag*) blow; (*mit Fuß*) kick; (*Haufen*) pile

Stoßdämpfer (-s, -) *m* shock absorber

stoßen (**stieß, gestoßen**) *vt* (*mit Druck*) to shove, to push; (*mit Schlag*) to knock; (*mit Fuß*) to kick; (*anstoßen*) to bump; (*zerkleinern*) to pulverize ▷ *vr*: **sich ~** to bang oneself; **sich ~ an** +*dat* (*fig*) to take exception to

Stoßstange *f* (*Auto*) bumper

stottern *vt, vi* to stutter
Str. *abk von* **Straße;** St, Rd
Strafe (-, -n) *f* punishment; (*Sport*) penalty; (*Gefängnisstrafe*) sentence; (*Geldstrafe*) fine
strafen *vt* to punish
Straftat *f* (criminal) offense
Strafzettel *m* ticket
Strahl (-s, -en) *m* ray, beam; (*Wasser*) jet
strahlen *vi* to radiate; (*fig*) to beam
Strähne (-, -n) *f* strand; (*weiß*) streak; (*a. gefärbt*) highlight
Strand (-(e)s, Strände) *m* beach; **am ~** on the beach
Strandcafé *nt* beach café
Strandkorb *m* wicker beach chair with a hood
Strandpromenade *f* boardwalk
strapazieren *vt* (*Material*) to be hard on; (*Mensch, Kräfte*) to be a strain on
Straße (-, -n) *f* road; (*in der Stadt*) street
Straßenarbeiten *pl* roadwork *sing*
Straßenbahn *f* streetcar
Straßencafé *nt* sidewalk café
Straßenfest *nt* street party
Straßenglätte *f* slippery roads *pl*
Straßenkarte *f* road map
Straßenrand *m*: **am ~** at the roadside
Straßenschild *nt* street sign
Straßensperre *f* roadblock
Straßenverhältnisse *pl* road conditions *pl*
Strategie (-, -n) *f* strategy
Strauch (-(e)s, Sträucher) *m* bush, shrub
Strauchtomate *f* vine-ripened tomato
Strauß (-es, Sträuße) *m* bunch; (*als Geschenk*) bouquet ▷ (*Strauße*) *m* (*Vogel*) ostrich
Strecke (-, -n) *f* route; (*Entfernung*) distance; (*Eisenb*) line
strecken *vt* to stretch ▷ *vr*: **sich ~** to stretch
streckenweise *adv* (*teilweise*) in parts; (*zeitweise*) at times
Streich (-(e)s, -e) *m* trick, prank
streicheln *vt* to stroke, to pet
streichen (**strich, gestrichen**) *vt* (*anmalen*) to paint; (*berühren*) to stroke; (*auftragen*) to spread; (*durchstreichen*) to delete; (*nicht genehmigen*) to cancel
Streichholz *nt* match
Streichholzschachtel *f* matchbox
Streichkäse *m* cheese spread
Streifen (-s, -) *m* (*Linie*) stripe; (*Stück*) strip; (*Film*) movie
Streifenwagen *m* squad car

Streik (-(e)s, -s) *m* strike
streiken *vi* to be on strike
Streit (-(e)s, -e) *m* argument (*um, wegen* about, over)
streiten (**stritt, gestritten**) *vi* to argue (*um, wegen* about, over) ▷ *vr*: **sich ~** to argue (*um, wegen* about, over)
streng *adj* (*Blick*) severe; (*Lehrer*) strict; (*Geruch*) sharp
Stress (-es) *m* stress
stressen *vt* to stress (out)
stressig *adj* (*fam*) stressful
Stretching (-s) *nt* (*Sport*) stretching exercises *pl*
streuen *vt* to scatter; **die Straßen ~** to sand the roads; (*mit Salz*) to put salt down on the roads
Streufahrzeug *nt* sander
strich *imperf von* **streichen**
Strich (-(e)s, -e) *m* (*Linie*) line
Stricher *m* (*fam*: *Strichjunge*) boy prostitute
Stricherin *f* (*fam*: *Strichmädchen*) hooker
Strichkode (-s, -s) *m* bar code
Strichpunkt *m* semicolon
Strick (-(e)s, -e) *m* rope
stricken *vt, vi* to knit
Strickjacke *f* cardigan
Stricknadel *f* knitting needle
String (-s, -s) *m*, **Stringtanga** *m* G-string
Stripper(in) *m(f)* stripper
Striptease (-) *m* striptease
stritt *imperf von* **streiten**
Stroh (-(e)s) *nt* straw
Strohdach *nt* thatched roof
Strohhalm *m* (drinking) straw
Strom (-(e)s, Ströme) *m* river; (*fig*) stream; (*Elek*) current
Stromanschluss *m* connection
Stromausfall *m* power failure
strömen *vi* to stream, to pour
Strömung *f* current
Stromverbrauch *m* power consumption
Stromzähler *m* electricity meter
Strophe (-, -n) *f* verse
Strudel (-s, -) *m* (*in Fluss*) whirlpool; (*Gebäck*) strudel
Struktur *f* structure; (*von Material*) texture
Strumpf (-(e)s, Strümpfe) *m* (*Damenstrumpf*) stocking; (*Socke*) sock
Strumpfhose *f* pantyhose
Stück (-(e)s, -e) *nt* piece; (*von Zucker*) lump; (*etwas*) bit; (*Zucker*) lump; (*Theat*) play; **ein ~ Käse** a piece of cheese
Student(in) *m(f)* student

S

Studentenausweis *m* student ID
Studentenwohnheim *nt* dormitory
Studienabschluss *m* college degree
Studienfahrt *f* study trip
Studienplatz *m*: **sich um einen ~ bewerben** to apply to college; **einen ~ bekommen** to be admited into college
studieren *vt, vi* to go to college, to study
Studium *nt* studies *pl*; **während seines ~s** while he is/was at college
Stufe (-, -n) *f* step; (*Entwicklungsstufe*) stage
Stuhl (*-(e)s, Stühle*) *m* chair
stumm *adj* silent; (*Med*) dumb
stumpf *adj* blunt; (*teilnahmslos, glanzlos*) dull
stumpfsinnig *adj* dull
Stunde (-, -n) *f* hour; (*Unterricht*) lesson; **eine halbe ~** half an hour
Stundenkilometer *m*: **80 ~** 80 kilometers an hour
stundenlang *adv* for hours
Stundenlohn *m* hourly wage
Stundenplan *m* timetable
stündlich *adj* hourly
Stuntman (*-s, Stuntmen*) *m* stuntman
Stuntwoman (-, *Stuntwomen*) *f* stuntwoman
stur *adj* stubborn; (*stärker*) pigheaded
Sturm (*-(e)s, Stürme*) *m* (wind)storm
stürmen *vi* (*Wind*) to blow hard; (*rennen*) to storm
Stürmer(in) *m(f)* striker, forward
Sturmflut *f* storm tide
stürmisch *adj* stormy; (*fig*) tempestuous; (*Zeit*) turbulent; (*Liebhaber*) passionate; (*Beifall, Begrüßung*) tumultuous
Sturmwarnung *f* gale warning
Sturz (*-es, Stürze*) *m* fall; (*Pol*) overthrow
stürzen *vt* (*werfen*) to hurl; (*Pol*) to overthrow; (*umkehren*) to overturn ▷ *vi* to fall; (*rennen*) to dash
Sturzhelm *m* crash helmet
Stute (-, -n) *f* mare
Stütze (-, -n) *f* support; (*Hilfe*) help; (*fam: Arbeitslosenunterstützung*) welfare
stützen *vt* to support; (*Ellbogen*) to prop
stutzig *adj* perplexed, puzzled; (*misstrauisch*) suspicious
Styropor® (*-s*) *nt* styrofoam
subjektiv *adj* subjective
Substanz (-, -en) *f* substance
subtrahieren *vt* to subtract
Subvention *f* subsidy
subventionieren *vt* to subsidize

Suche *f* search (*nach* for); **auf der ~ nach etw sein** to be looking for sth
suchen *vt* to look for; (*Inform*) to search ▷ *vi* to look, to search (*nach* for)
Suchmaschine *f* (*Inform*) search engine
Sucht (-, *Süchte*) *f* mania; (*Med*) addiction
süchtig *adj* addicted
Süchtige(r) *mf* addict
Süd south
Südafrika *nt* South Africa
Südamerika *nt* South America
Süddeutschland *nt* Southern Germany
Süden (*-s*) *m* south; **im ~ Deutschlands** in the south of Germany
Südeuropa *nt* Southern Europe
Südkorea (*-s*) *nt* South Korea
südlich *adj* southern; (*Kurs, Richtung*) southerly; **Verkehr in ~er Richtung** southbound traffic
Südost(en) *m* southeast
Südpol *m* South Pole
Südstaaten *pl* (*der USA*) the South *sing*
südwärts *adv* south, southwards
Südwest(en) *m* southwest
Südwind *m* southerly (*o* southern) wind
Sülze (-, -n) *f* meat aspic
Summe (-, -n) *f* sum; (*Gesamtsumme*) total
summen *vi, vt* to hum; (*Insekt*) to buzz
Sumpf (*-(e)s, Sümpfe*) *m* marsh; (*subtropischer*) swamp
sumpfig *adj* marshy
Sünde (-, -n) *f* sin
super *adj* (*fam*) super, great
Super (*-s*) *nt* (*Benzin*) premium
Supermarkt *m* supermarket
Suppe (-, -n) *f* soup
Suppengrün *nt* bunch of herbs and vegetables for flavoring soup
Suppenlöffel *m* soup spoon
Suppenschüssel *f* soup tureen
Suppentasse *f* soup cup
Suppenteller *m* soup plate
Suppenwürfel *m* bouillon cube
Surfbrett *nt* surfboard
surfen *vi* to surf; **im Internet ~** to surf the Internet
Surfer(in) (*-s, -*) *m(f)* surfer
Surrealismus *m* surrealism
Sushi (*-s, -s*) *nt* sushi
süß *adj* sweet
süßen *vt* to sweeten
Süßigkeit *f* (*Bonbon etc*) candy
Süßkartoffel *f* yam
süßsauer *adj* sweet-and-sour
Süßspeise *f* dessert

Süßstoff *m* sweetener
Süßwasser *nt* fresh water
Sweatshirt (*-s, -s*) *nt* sweatshirt
Swimmingpool (*-s, -s*) *m* (swimming) pool
Sylvester *nt siehe* **Silvester**
Symbol (*-s, -e*) *nt* symbol
Symbolleiste *f* (*Inform*) toolbar
Symmetrie (*-, -n*) *f* symmetry
symmetrisch *adj* symmetrical
sympathisch *adj* nice; **jdn ~ finden** to like sb
Symphonie (*-, -n*) *f* symphony

Symptom (*-s, -e*) *nt* symptom (*für* of)
Synagoge (*-, -n*) *f* synagogue
synchronisiert *adj* (*Film*) dubbed
Synchronstimme *f* dubbing voice
Synthetik (*-, -en*) *f* synthetic (fiber)
synthetisch *adj* synthetic
Syrien (*-s*) *nt* Syria
System (*-s, -e*) *nt* system
systematisch *adj* systematic
Systemsteuerung *f* (*Inform*) control panel
Szene (*-, -n*) *f* scene

S

T

Tabak (-s, -e) m tobacco
Tabelle f table
Tablett (-s, -e) nt tray
Tablette f tablet, pill
Tabulator m tabulator, tab
Tacho(meter) (-s, -) m (Auto) speedometer
Tafel (-, -n) f (auch Math) table; (Anschlagtafel) board; (Wandtafel) blackboard; (Schiefertafel) slate; (Gedenktafel) plaque; **eine ~ Schokolade** a bar of chocolate
Tafelwasser nt table water
Tafelwein m table wine
Tag (-(e)s, -e) m day; (Tageslicht) daylight; **guten Tag!** good morning/afternoon!; **am Tag** during the day; **sie hat ihre Tage** she's having her period; **eines Tages** one day; **Tag der Arbeit** Labor Day
Tagebuch nt diary
tagelang adj for days (on end)
Tagesanbruch m daybreak
Tagesausflug m day trip
Tagescreme f day cream
Tagesdecke f bedspread
Tagesgericht nt dish of the day
Tageskarte f (Fahrkarte) day ticket; **die ~** (Speisekarte) today's specials
Tageslicht nt daylight
Tagesordnung f agenda
Tagestour f day trip
Tageszeitung f daily newspaper
täglich adj, adv daily
tags(über) adv during the day
Tagung f conference
Tai Chi (-) nt tai chi
Taille (-, -n) f waist
Taiwan (-s) nt Taiwan
Takt (-(e)s, -e) m (Taktgefühl) tact; (Mus) time
Taktik (-, -en) f tactics pl
taktlos adj tactless
taktvoll adj tactful
Tal (-(e)s, Täler) nt valley
Talent (-(e)s, -e) nt talent
talentiert adj talented
Talkmaster(in) (-s, -) m(f) talk-show host
Talkshow (-, -s) f talkshow
Tampon (-s, -s) m tampon
Tandem (-s, -s) nt tandem (bicycle)
Tang (-s, -e) m seaweed
Tanga (-s, -s) m thong
Tank (-s, -s) m tank
Tankanzeige f fuel gauge

Tankdeckel m fuel cap
tanken vi to get some gas; (Aviat) to refuel
Tanker (-s, -) m (oil) tanker
Tankstelle f gas station
Tankwart(in) (-s, -e) m(f) gas station attendant
Tanne (-, -n) f fir
Tannenzapfen m fir cone
Tansania (-s) nt Tanzania
Tante (-, -n) f aunt
Tante-Emma-Laden m mom-and-pop store
Tanz (-es, Tänze) m dance
tanzen vt, vi to dance
Tänzer(in) m(f) dancer
Tanzfläche f dance floor
Tanzkurs m dance class
Tanziehrer(in) m(f) dance instructor
Tanzstunde f dance lesson
Tapete (-, -n) f wallpaper
tapezieren vt, vi to wallpaper
Tarantel (-, -n) f tarantula
Tarif (-s, -e) m table of fares/charges; (für Gehälter) pay scale
Tasche (-, -n) f bag; (Hosentasche) pocket; (Handtasche) purse
Taschen- in zW pocket
Taschenbuch nt paperback
Taschendieb(in) m(f) pickpocket
Taschengeld nt spending money; (für Kinder) allowance
Taschenlampe f flashlight
Taschenmesser nt penknife
Taschenrechner m pocket calculator
Taschentuch nt tissue; (aus Stoff) handkerchief
Tasse (-, -n) f cup; **eine ~ Kaffee** a cup of coffee
Tastatur f keyboard
Taste (-, -n) f button; (von Klavier, Computer) key
Tastenkombination f (Inform) shortcut
tat imperf von tun
Tat (-, -en) f action
Tatar (-s, -s) nt steak tartare
Täter(in) (-s, -) m(f) culprit
tätig adj active; **in einer Firma ~ sein** to work for a firm
Tätigkeit f activity; (Beruf) occupation
tätowieren vt to tattoo
Tätowierung f tattoo (an +dat on)
Tatsache f fact

tatsächlich *adj* actual ▷ *adv* really
Tau (*-(e)s, -e*) *nt* (*Seil*) rope ▷ (*-(e)s*) *m* dew
taub *adj* deaf; (*Füße etc*) numb (*vor Kälte* with cold)
Taube (*-, -n*) *f* pigeon; (*Turteltaube, fig: Friedenssymbol*) dove
taubstumm *adj* deaf-and-dumb
Taubstumme(r) *mf* deaf-mute
tauchen *vt* to dip ▷ *vi* to dive; (*Naut*) to submerge
Tauchen (*-s*) *nt* diving
Taucher(in) (*-s, -*) *m(f)* diver
Taucheranzug *m* diving (*o wet*) suit
Taucherbrille *f* diving goggles *pl*
Tauchermaske *f* diving mask
Tauchkurs *m* diving course
Tauchsieder (*-s, -*) *m* immersion heater
tauen *vi impers* to thaw
Taufe (*-, -n*) *f* baptism
taufen *vt* to baptize; (*nennen*) to christen
taugen *vi* to be suitable (*für* for); **nichts ~** to be no good
Tausch (*-(e)s, -e*) *m* exchange
tauschen *vt* to exchange, to swap
täuschen *vt* to deceive ▷ *vi* to be deceptive ▷ *vr*: **sich ~** to be wrong
täuschend *adj* deceptive
Täuschung *f* deception; (*optisch*) illusion
tausend *num* a thousand; **vier~** four thousand; **~ Dank!** thanks a lot!
tausendmal *adv* a thousand times
tausendste(r, s) *adj* thousandth
Tausendstel (*-s, -*) *nt* (*Bruchteil*) thousandth
Taxi *nt* taxi
Taxifahrer(in) *m(f)* taxi driver
Taxistand *m* taxi stand
Team (*-s, -s*) *nt* team
Teamarbeit *f* teamwork
teamfähig *adj* able to work in a team
Technik *f* technology; (*angewandte*) engineering; (*Methode*) technique
Techniker(in) (*-s, -*) *m(f)* engineer; (*Sport, Mus*) technician
technisch *adj* technical
Techno (*-s*) *m* (*Mus*) techno
Teddybär *m* teddy bear
TEE *abk* (= *Trans-Europ-Express*) Trans-Europe-Express
Tee (*-s, -s*) *m* tea
Teebeutel *m* teabag
Teekanne *f* teapot
Teelöffel *m* teaspoon
Teer (*-(e)s, -e*) *m* tar
Teesieb *nt* tea strainer

Teetasse *f* teacup
Teich (*-(e)s, -e*) *m* pond
Teig (*-(e)s, -e*) *m* dough
Teigwaren *pl* pasta *sing*
Teil (*-(e)s, -e*) *m* part; (*Anteil*) share; **zum ~** partly ▷ *nt* (*-(e)s, -e*) part; (*Bestandteil*) component
teilen *vt* to divide; (*mit jdm*) to share (*mit* with); **20 durch 4 ~** to divide 20 by 4 ▷ *vr*: **sich ~** to divide
Teilkaskoversicherung *f* comprehensive auto insurance without collision
teilmöbliert *adj* partly furnished
Teilnahme (*-, -n*) *f* participation (*an +dat* in)
teil|nehmen (*irr*) *vi* to take part (*an +dat* in)
Teilnehmer(in) (*-s, -*) *m(f)* participant
teils *adv* partly
teilweise *adv* partially, in part
Teilzeit *f*: **~ arbeiten** to work part-time
Teint (*-s, -s*) *m* complexion
Tel. *abk von* **Telefon**; tel.
Telefon (*-s, -e*) *nt* telephone
Telefonanruf *m*, **Telefonat** *nt* (tele)phone call
Telefonanschluss *m* telephone connection
Telefonauskunft *f* directory assistance
Telefonbuch *nt* phonebook, telephone directory
Telefongebühren *pl* telephone charges *pl*
Telefongespräch *nt* telephone conversation
telefonieren *vi*: **ich telefoniere gerade mit ...** I'm on the phone (to ...)
telefonisch *adj* telephone; (*Benachrichtigung*) by telephone
Telefonkarte *f* phonecard
Telefonnummer *f* (tele)phone number
Telefonrechnung *f* phone bill
Telefonverbindung *f* telephone connection
Telefonzelle *f* phone booth
Telefonzentrale *f* switchboard; **über die ~** through the switchboard
Telegramm *nt* telegram
Teleobjektiv *nt* telephoto lens
Teleshopping (*-s*) *nt* home shopping
Teleskop (*-s, -e*) *nt* telescope
Teller (*-s, -*) *m* plate
Tempel (*-s, -*) *m* temple
Temperament *nt* temperament; (*Schwung*) liveliness
temperamentvoll *adj* lively

Temperatur f temperature; **bei ~en von 30 Grad** at temperatures of 30 degrees; **~ haben** to have a temperature; **~ bei jdm messen** to take sb's temperature

Tempo (-s, -s) nt (Geschwindigkeit) speed

Tempolimit (-s, -s) nt speed limit

Tempotaschentuch® nt (Papiertaschentuch) (paper) tissue, = Kleenex®

Tendenz f tendency; (Absicht) intention

Tennis (-) nt tennis

Tennisball m tennis ball

Tennisplatz m tennis court

Tennisschläger m tennis racket

Tennisspieler(in) m(f) tennis player

Tenor (-s, Tenöre) m tenor

Teppich (-s, -e) m rug

Teppichboden m (wall-to-wall) carpet

Termin (-s, -e) m (Zeitpunkt) date; (Frist) deadline; (Arzttermin etc) appointment

Terminal (-s, -s) nt (Inform, Aviat) terminal

Terminkalender m appointment book

Terminplaner m (in Buchform) daily planner, personal organizer; (Taschencomputer) personal digital assistant, PDA

Terpentin (-s, -e) nt turpentine, turps sing

Terrasse (-, -n) f terrace; (hinter einem Haus) patio

Terror (-s) m terror

Terroranschlag m terrorist attack

terrorisieren vt to terrorize

Terrorismus m terrorism

Terrorist(in) m(f) terrorist

Tesafilm® m ≈ Scotch tape®

Test (-s, -s) m test

Testament nt will; **das Alte/Neue ~** the Old/New Testament

testen vt to test

Testergebnis nt test results pl

Tetanus (-) m tetanus

Tetanusimpfung f tetanus shot (o vaccine)

teuer adj expensive

Teufel (-s, -) m devil; **was/wo zum ~** what/where the devil

Teufelskreis m vicious circle

Text (-(e)s, -e) m text; (Liedertext) words pl, lyrics pl

Textmarker (-s, -) m highlighter

Textverarbeitung f word processing

Textverarbeitungsprogramm nt word processing program

Thailand nt Thailand

Theater (-s, -) nt theater; (fam) fuss; **ins ~ gehen** to go to the theater

Theaterkasse f box office

Theaterstück nt (stage) play

Theatervorstellung f (stage) performance

Theke (-, -n) f (Schanktisch) bar; (Ladentisch) counter

Thema (-s, Themen) nt subject, topic; **kein ~!** no problem!

Themse (-) f Thames

Theologie f theology

theoretisch adj theoretical; **~ stimmt das** that's right in theory

Theorie f theory

Therapeut(in) m(f) therapist

Therapie f therapy; **eine ~ machen** to undergo therapy

Thermalbad nt thermal bath; (Ort) thermal spa

Thermometer (-s, -) nt thermometer

Thermosflasche® f thermos (bottle)

Thermoskanne® f thermos (bottle)

Thermostat (-(e)s, -e) m thermostat

These (-, -n) f theory

Thron (-(e)s, -e) m throne

Thunfisch m tuna

Thüringen (-s) nt Thuringia

Thymian (-s, -e) m thyme

Tick (-(e)s, -s) m tic; (Eigenart) quirk; (Fimmel) craze

ticken vi to tick; **er tickt nicht ganz richtig** he's off his rocker

Ticket (-s, -s) nt (plane) ticket

tief adj deep; (Ausschnitt, Ton, Sonne) low; **zwei Meter ~** two meters deep

Tief (-s, -s) nt (Meteo) low; (seelisch) depression

Tiefdruck m (Meteo) low pressure

Tiefe (-, -n) f depth

Tiefgarage f underground garage

tiefgekühlt adj frozen

Tiefkühlfach nt freezer compartment

Tiefkühlkost f frozen food

Tiefkühltruhe f (chest) freezer

Tiefpunkt m low

Tier (-(e)s, -e) nt animal

Tierarzt m, **Tierärztin** f veterinarian, vet

Tiergarten m zoo

Tierhandlung f pet store

Tierheim nt animal shelter

tierisch adj animal ▷ adv (fam) really; **~ ernst** deadly serious; **ich hatte ~ Angst** I was scared to death

Tierkreiszeichen nt sign of the zodiac

Tierpark m zoo

Tierquälerei f cruelty to animals

Tierschützer(in) (-s, -) m(f) animal rights activist

Tierversuch m animal experiment

Tiger (*-s*, *-*) *m* tiger
timen *vt* to time
Timing (*-s*) *nt* timing
Tinte (*-*, *-n*) *f* ink
Tintenfisch *m* cuttlefish; (*klein*) squid; (*achtarmig*) octopus
Tintenfischringe *pl* calamari *pl*
Tintenstrahldrucker *m* ink-jet printer
Tipp (*-s*, *-s*) *m* tip
tippen *vt*, *vi* to tap; (*fam: schreiben*) to type; (*fam: raten*) to guess
Tirol (*-s*) *nt* Tyrol
Tisch (*-(e)s*, *-e*) *m* table
Tischdecke *f* tablecloth
Tischlerei *f* carpenter's (*o* cabinetmaker's) workshop; (*Arbeit*) carpentry, cabinet-making
Tischtennis *nt* table tennis
Tischtennisschläger *m* table-tennis paddle
Titel (*-s*, *-*) *m* title
Titelbild *nt* cover picture
Toast (*-(e)s*, *-s*) *m* toast
toasten *vt* to toast
Toaster (*-s*, *-*) *m* toaster
Tochter (*-*, *Töchter*) *f* daughter
Tod (*-(e)s*, *-e*) *m* death
Todesopfer *nt* casualty
Todesstrafe *f* death penalty
todkrank *adj* terminally ill; (*sehr krank*) seriously ill
tödlich *adj* deadly, fatal; **er ist ~ verunglückt** he was killed in an accident
todmüde *adj* (*fam*) dead tired
todsicher *adj* (*fam*) dead certain
Tofu (*-(s)*) *m* tofu, bean curd
Toilette *f* toilet, restroom
Toilettenpapier *nt* toilet paper
toi, toi, toi *interj* good luck
tolerant *adj* tolerant (*gegen* of)
toll *adj* mad; (*Treiben*) wild; (*fam: großartig*) great
Tollkirsche *f* belladonna
Tollwut *f* rabies *sing*
Tomate (*-*, *-n*) *f* tomato
Tomatenmark *nt* tomato paste
Tomatensaft *m* tomato juice
Tombola (*-*, *-s*) *f* raffle
Ton (*-(e)s*, *-e*) *m* (*Erde*) clay ▷ (*Töne*) *m* (*Laut*) sound; (*Mus*) note; (*Redeweise*) tone; (*Farbton, Nuance*) shade
Tonband *nt* tape
Tonbandgerät *nt* tape recorder
tönen *vi* to sound ▷ *vt* to shade; (*Haare*) to tint

Toner (*-s*, *-*) *m* toner
Tonerkassette *f* toner cartridge
Tonne (*-*, *-n*) *f* (*Fass*) barrel; (*Gewicht*) ton, metric ton
Tontechniker(in) *m(f)* sound engineer
Tönung *f* hue; (*für Haar*) rinse
Top (*-s*, *-s*) *nt* top
Topf (*-(e)s*, *Töpfe*) *m* pot
Töpfer(in) (*-s*, *-*) *m(f)* potter
Töpferei *f* pottery; (*Gegenstand*) piece of pottery
Tor (*-(e)s*, *-e*) *nt* gate; (*Sport*) goal; **ein Tor schießen** to score a goal
Torhüter(in) *m(f)* goalkeeper, goalie
torkeln *vi* to stagger
Tornado (*-s*, *-s*) *m* tornado
Torschütze *m*, **Torschützin** *f* (goal)scorer
Torte (*-*, *-n*) *f* cake; (*Obsttorte*) tart; (*Sahnetorte*) torte
Torwart(in) (*-s*, *-e*) *m(f)* goalkeeper, goalie
tot *adj* dead; **toter Winkel** blind spot
total *adj* total, complete
Totalschaden *m* complete write-off; **das Auto hat einen ~** the car is totaled
Tote(r) *mf* dead man/woman; (*Leiche*) corpse
töten *vt*, *vi* to kill
Totenkopf *m* skull
tot|lachen *vr*: **sich ~** to almost die laughing
Toto (*-s*, *-s*) *m* o *nt* (*Sport*) pool
tot|schlagen (*irr*) *vt* to beat to death; **die Zeit ~** to kill time
Touchscreen (*-s*, *-s*) *m* touch screen
Tour (*-*, *-en*) *f* trip; (*Rundfahrt*) tour; **eine ~ nach York machen** to go on a trip to York
Tourenski *m* touring ski
Tourismus *m* tourism
Tourist(in) *m(f)* tourist
Touristenklasse *f* tourist class
touristisch *adj* tourist; (*pej*) touristy
Tournee (*-*, *-n*) *f* tour
traben *vi* to trot
Tracht (*-*, *-en*) *f* (*Kleidung*) traditional costume
Trackball (*-s*, *-s*) *m* (*Inform*) trackball
Tradition *f* tradition
traditionell *adj* traditional
traf *imperf von* **treffen**
Tragbahre (*-*, *-n*) *f* stretcher
tragbar *adj* portable
träge *adj* sluggish, slow
tragen (**trug**, **getragen**) *vt* to carry; (*Kleidung, Brille, Haare*) to wear; (*Namen, Früchte*) to bear

Träger (-s, -) m (an Kleidung) strap; (Hosenträger) suspenders pl; (in der Architektur) beam; (Stahlträger, Eisenträger) girder
Tragfläche f wing
Tragflügelboot nt hydrofoil
tragisch adj tragic
Tragödie f tragedy
Trainer(in) (-s, -) m(f) trainer, coach
trainieren vt, vi to train; (jdn a.) to coach; (Übung) to practice
Training (-s, -s) nt training; (Sport) practice
Trainingsanzug m sweatsuit
Traktor m tractor
Trambahn f streetcar
trampen vi to hitchhike
Tramper(in) m(f) hitchhiker
Träne (-, -n) f tear
tränen vi to water
Tränengas nt teargas
trank imperf von trinken
Transfusion f transfusion
Transitverkehr m transit traffic
Transitvisum nt transit visa
Transplantation f transplant; (Hauttransplantation) graft
Transport (-(e)s, -e) m transport
transportieren vt to transport
Transportmittel nt means sing of transport
Transportunternehmen nt trucking firm
Transvestit (-en, -en) m transvestite
trat imperf von treten
Traube (-, -n) f (einzelne Beere) grape; (ganze Frucht) bunch of grapes
Traubensaft m grape juice
Traubenzucker m glucose
trauen vi: jdm/einer Sache ~ to trust sb/sth; ich traute meinen Ohren nicht I couldn't believe my ears ▷ vr: sich ~ to dare ▷ vt to marry; sich ~ lassen to get married
Trauer (-) f sorrow; (für Verstorbenen) mourning
Traum (-(e)s, Träume) m dream
träumen vt, vi to dream (von of, about)
traumhaft adj dreamlike; (fig) wonderful
traurig adj sad (über +akk about)
Trauschein m marriage certificate
Trauung f wedding ceremony
Trauzeuge m, **Trauzeugin** f witness (at wedding ceremony), ≈ best man/maid of honor
Travellerscheck m traveler's check
treffen (traf, getroffen) vr: sich ~ to meet ▷ vt, vi to hit; (Bemerkung) to hurt; (begegnen) to meet; (Entscheidung) to make;

(Maßnahmen) to take
Treffen (-s, -) nt meeting
Treffer (-s, -) m (Tor) goal
Treffpunkt m meeting place
treiben (trieb, getrieben) vt to drive; (Sport) to do ▷ vi (im Wasser) to drift; (Pflanzen) to sprout; (Tee, Kaffee) to be diuretic
Treiber (-s, -) m (Inform) driver
Treibgas nt propellant
Treibhaus nt greenhouse
Treibstoff m fuel
trennen vt to separate; (teilen) to divide ▷ vr: sich ~ to separate; sich von jdm ~ to leave sb; sich von etw ~ to part with sth
Trennung f separation
Treppe (-, -n) f stairs pl; (im Freien) steps pl
Treppengeländer nt banister
Treppenhaus nt stairway, stairwell
Tresen (-s, -) m (in Kneipe) bar; (in Laden) counter
Tresor (-s, -e) m safe
Tretboot nt pedal boat
treten (trat, getreten) vi to step; mit jdm in Verbindung ~ to get in contact with sb ▷ vt to kick; (niedertreten) to tread
treu adj (gegenüber Partner) faithful; (Kunde, Fan) loyal
Treue (-) f (eheliche) faithfulness; (von Kunde, Fan) loyalty
Triathlon (-s, -s) m triathlon
Tribüne (-, -n) f stand; (Rednertribüne) platform
Trick (-s, -e o -s) m trick
Trickfilm m cartoon
trieb imperf von treiben
Trieb (-(e)s, -e) m urge; (Instinkt) drive; (Neigung) inclination; (an Baum etc) shoot
Triebwerk nt engine
Trikot (-s, -s) nt shirt, jersey
Trimm-Dich-Pfad m fitness trail
trinkbar adj drinkable
trinken (trank, getrunken) vt, vi to drink; einen ~ gehen to go out for a drink
Trinkgeld nt tip
Trinkhalm m (drinking) straw
Trinkwasser nt drinking water
Trio (-s, -s) nt trio
Tripper (-s, -) m gonorrhoea
Tritt (-(e)s, -e) m (Schritt) step; (Fußtritt) kick
Trittbrett nt running board
Triumph (-(e)s, -e) m triumph
triumphieren vi to triumph (über +akk over)
trivial adj trivial

trocken *adj* dry
Trockenhaube *f* hair-dryer
Trockenheit *f* dryness
trocken|legen *vt* (*Baby*) to change
trocknen *vt, vi* to dry
Trockner (*-s, -*) *m* dryer
Trödel (*-s*) *m* (*fam*) junk
Trödelmarkt *m* flea market
trödeln *vi* (*fam*) to dawdle
Trommel (*-, -n*) *f* drum
Trommelfell *nt* eardrum
trommeln *vt, vi* to drum
Trompete (*-, -n*) *f* trumpet
Tropen *pl* tropics *pl*
Tropf (*-(e)s, -e*) *m* (*Med*) drip; **am ~ hängen** to be on a drip
tröpfeln *vi* to drip; **es tröpfelt** it's drizzling
tropfen *vt, vi* to drip
Tropfen (*-s, -*) *m* drop
tropfenweise *adv* drop by drop
tropfnass *adj* dripping wet
Tropfsteinhöhle *f* stalactite cave
tropisch *adj* tropical
Trost (*-es*) *m* consolation, comfort
trösten *vt* to console, to comfort
trostlos *adj* bleak; (*Verhältnisse*) miserable
Trostpreis *m* consolation prize
Trottoir (*-s, -s*) *nt* sidewalk
trotz *prep* (+*gen o dat*) in spite of
Trotz (*-es*) *m* defiance
trotzdem *adv* nevertheless ▷ *conj* although
trotzig *adj* defiant
trüb *adj* dull; (*Flüssigkeit, Glas*) cloudy; (*fig*) gloomy
Trüffel (*-, -n*) *f* truffle
trug *imperf von* **tragen**
trügerisch *adj* deceptive
Truhe (*-, -n*) *f* chest
Trümmer *pl* wreckage *sing*; (*Bautrümmer*) ruins *pl*
Trumpf (*-(e)s, Trümpfe*) *m* trump
Trunkenheit *f* intoxication; **~ am Steuer** drunk driving
Truthahn *m* turkey
Tscheche (*-n, -n*) *m*, **Tschechin** *f* Czech
Tschechien (*-s*) *nt* Czech Republic
tschechisch *adj* Czech; **T~e Republik** Czech Republic
Tschechisch *nt* Czech
Tschetschenien (*-s*) *nt* Chechnya
tschüs(s) *interj* bye
T-Shirt (*-s, -s*) *nt* T-shirt
Tube (*-, -n*) *f* tube
Tuberkulose (*-, -n*) *f* tuberculosis, TB
Tuch (*-(e)s, Tücher*) *nt* cloth; (*Halstuch*)

scarf; (*Kopftuch*) headscarf
tüchtig *adj* competent; (*fleißig*) hard-working; (*fam: kräftig*) good
Tugend (*-, -en*) *f* virtue
tugendhaft *adj* virtuous
Tulpe (*-, -n*) *f* tulip
Tumor (*-s, -en*) *m* tumor
tun (**tat, getan**) *vt* (*machen*) to do; (*legen*) to put; **was tust du da?** what are you doing?; **das tut man nicht** you shouldn't do that; **jdm etw tun** (*antun*) to do sth to sb; **das tut es auch** that'll do ▷ *vi* to act; **so tun, als ob** to act as if ▷ *vr impers*: **es tut sich etwas/viel** something/a lot is happening
Tuner (*-s, -*) *m* tuner
Tunesien (*-s*) *nt* Tunisia
Tunfisch *m siehe* **Thunfisch** tuna
Tunnel (*-s, -s o -*) *m* tunnel
Tunte (*-, -n*) *f* (*pej, fam*) fairy
tupfen *vt, vi* to dab; (*mit Farbe*) to dot
Tupfen (*-s, -*) *m* dot
Tür (*-, -en*) *f* door; **vor/an der Tür** at the door; **an die Tür gehen** to answer the door
Türke (*-n, -n*) *m* Turk
Türkei (*-*) *f*: **die ~** Turkey
Türkin *f* Turk
Türkis (*-es, -e*) *m* turquoise
türkisch *adj* Turkish
Türkisch *nt* Turkish
Turm (*-(e)s, Türme*) *m* tower; (*spitzer Kirchturm*) steeple; (*Sprungturm*) diving platform; (*Schach*) rook, castle
turnen *vi* to do gymnastics
Turnen (*-s*) *nt* gymnastics *sing*; (*Schule*) physical education, PE
Turner(in) *m(f)* gymnast
Turnhalle *f* gym(nasium)
Turnhose *f* gym shorts *pl*
Turnier (*-s, -e*) *nt* tournament
Turnschuh *m* sneaker
Türschild *nt* doorplate
Türschloss *nt* lock
tuscheln *vt, vi* to whisper
Tussi (*-, -s*) *f* (*pej, fam*) chick
Tüte (*-, -n*) *f* bag
TÜV (*-s, -s*) *m* (*akr*) = **Technischer Überwachungsverein** ≈ vehicle inspection

TÜV

The **TÜV** is the organization responsible for checking the safety of machinery, particularly vehicles. Cars over

three years old have to be examined
every two years for their safety and for
their exhaust emissions. **TÜV** is also
the name given to the test itself.

TÜV-Plakette *f sticker attached to a vehicle's
license plate, indicating that it has passed
the 'TÜV',* ≈ inspection sticker

Tweed (*-s, -s*) *m* tweed
Typ (*-s, -en*) *m* type; (*Auto*) model; (*Mann*)
guy
Typhus (*-*) *m* typhoid
typisch *adj* typical (*für* of); **ein ~er Fehler** a
common mistake; **~ Marcus!** that's just
like Marcus!; **~ amerikanisch!** that's so
American!

U

u. (*abk*) = **und**

u. a. (*abk*) = **und andere(s)** and others; = **unter anderem, unter anderen** among other things

u. A. w. g. (*abk*) = **um Antwort wird gebeten** RSVP

U-Bahn *f* subway

übel *adj* bad; (*moralisch*) wicked; **mir ist ~** I feel sick; **diese Bemerkung hat er mir ~ genommen** he took offense at my remark

Übelkeit *f* nausea

üben *vt, vi* to practice

SCHLÜSSELWORT

über *prep* +*dat* **1** (*räumlich*) over, above; **zwei Grad über null** two degrees above zero

2 (*zeitlich*) over; **über der Arbeit einschlafen** to fall asleep over one's work

▷ *prep* +*akk* **1** (*räumlich*) over; (*hoch über auch*) above; (*quer über auch*) across

2 (*zeitlich*) over; **über Weihnachten** over Christmas; **über kurz oder lang** sooner or later

3 (*mit Zahlen*): **Kinder über 12 Jahren** children over 12, children 12 and over; **ein Scheck über 200 Euro** a check for 200 euros

4 (*auf dem Wege*) via; **nach Köln über Aachen** to Cologne via Aachen; **ich habe es über die Auskunft erfahren** I found out from information

5 (*betreffend*) about; **ein Buch über ... a** book about *o* on ...; **über jdn/etw lachen** to laugh about *o* at sb/sth

6: Macht über jdn haben to have power over sb; **sie liebt ihn über alles** she loves him more than anything

▷ *adv* over; **über und über** over and over; **den ganzen Tag über** all day long; **jdm in etw** (*dat*) **über sein** to be superior to sb in sth

überall *adv* everywhere

überanstrengen *vr*: **sich ~** to overexert oneself

überbacken *adj*: **mit Käse ~** au gratin

überbelichten *vt* (*Foto*) to overexpose

überbieten (*irr*) *vt* to outbid; (*übertreffen*) to surpass; (*Rekord*) to break

Überbleibsel (*-s, -*) *nt* remnant

Überblick *m* overview; (*fig: in Darstellung*) survey; (*Fähigkeit zu verstehen*) grasp (*über* +*akk* of)

überbuchen *vt* to overbook

Überbuchung *f* overbooking

überdurchschnittlich *adj* above average

übereinander *adv* on top of each other; (*sprechen etc*) about each other

überein|stimmen *vi* to agree (*mit* with)

überempfindlich *adj* hypersensitive

überfahren (*irr*) *vt* (*Auto*) to run over

Überfahrt *f* crossing

Überfall *m* (*Banküberfall*) robbery; (*Mil*) raid; (*auf jdn*) assault

überfallen (*irr*) *vt* to attack; (*Bank*) to rob

überfällig *adj* overdue

überfliegen (*irr*) *vt* to fly over; (*Buch*) to skim through

Überfluss *m* overabundance, excess (*an* +*dat* of)

überflüssig *adj* superfluous

überfordern *vt* to demand too much of; (*Kräfte*) to overtax; **da bin ich überfordert** (*bei Antwort*) you've got me there

Überführung *f* (*Brücke*) overpass

überfüllt *adj* overcrowded

Übergabe *f* handover

Übergang *m* crossing; (*Wandel, Überleitung*) transition

Übergangslösung *f* temporary solution, stopgap

übergeben (*irr*) *vt* to hand over ▷ *vr*: **sich ~** to throw up, to vomit

Übergepäck *nt* excess baggage

Übergewicht *nt* excess weight; **10 Kilo ~ haben** to be (10 kilos) overweight

überglücklich *adj* overjoyed; (*fam*) over the moon

Übergröße *f* plus size, outsize

überhaupt *adv* at all; (*im Allgemeinen*) in general; (*besonders*) especially; **was willst du ~?** what is it you want?

überheblich *adj* arrogant

überholen *vt* to pass; (*Tech*) to overhaul

Überholspur *f* passing lane

überholt *adj* outdated

Überholverbot *nt* no passing; **hier herrscht ~** you can't pass here

überhören *vt* to miss, to fail to catch; (*absichtlich*) to ignore

überladen (*irr*) *vt* to overload ▷ *adj* (*fig*) cluttered

u

überlassen (*irr*) *vt*: **jdm etw ~** to leave sth to sb

über|laufen (*irr*) *vi* (*Flüssigkeit*) to overflow

überleben *vt, vi* to survive

Überlebende(r) *mf* survivor

überlegen *vt* to consider; **sich** (*dat*) **etw ~** to think about sth; **er hat es sich** (*dat*) **anders überlegt** he's changed his mind ▷ *adj* superior (*dat* to)

Überlegung *f* consideration

überm *kontr von* über dem

übermäßig *adj* excessive

übermorgen *adv* the day after tomorrow

übernächste(r, s) *adj*: **~ Woche** the week after next

übernachten *vi* to spend the night (*bei jdm* at sb's place)

übernächtigt *adj* bleary-eyed, very tired

Übernachtung *f* overnight stay; **~ mit Frühstück** bed and breakfast

übernehmen (*irr*) *vt* to take on; (*Amt, Geschäft*) to take over ▷ *vr*: **sich ~** to take on too much

überprüfen *vt* to check

Überprüfung *f* check; (*Überprüfen*) checking

überqueren *vt* to cross

überraschen *vt* to surprise

Überraschung *f* surprise

überreden (*irr*) *vt* to persuade; **er hat mich überredet** he talked me into it

überreichen *vt* to hand over

übers *kontr von* über das

überschätzen *vt* to overestimate

überschlagen (*irr*) *vt* (*berechnen*) to estimate; (*auslassen: Seite*) to skip ▷ *vr*: **sich ~** to somersault; (*Auto*) to overturn; (*Stimme*) to crack

überschneiden (*irr*) *vr*: **sich ~** (*Linien etc*) to intersect; (*Termine*) to overlap

Überschrift *f* heading

Überschwemmung *f* flood

Übersee *f*: **nach/in ~** overseas

übersehen (*irr*) *vt* (*Gelände*) to look (out) over; (*nicht beachten*) to overlook

übersetzen *vt* to translate (*aus* from, *in* +*akk* into)

Übersetzer(in) (*-s, -*) *m(f)* translator

Übersetzung *f* translation

Übersicht *f* overall view; (*Darstellung*) survey

übersichtlich *adj* clear

überstehen (*irr*) *vt* (*durchstehen*) to get over; (*Winter etc*) to get through

Überstunden *pl* overtime *sing*

überstürzt *adj* hasty

überteuert *adj* overpriced

übertragbar *adj* transferable; (*Med*) infectious

übertragen (*irr*) *vt* to transfer (*auf* +*akk* to); (*Radio*) to broadcast; (*Krankheit*) to transmit ▷ *vr* to spread (*auf* +*akk* to) ▷ *adj* figurative

Übertragung *f* (*Radio*) broadcast; (*von Daten*) transmission

übertreffen (*irr*) *vt* to surpass

übertreiben (*irr*) *vt, vi* to exaggerate, to overdo

Übertreibung *f* exaggeration

übertrieben *adj* exaggerated, overdone

überwachen *vt* to supervise; (*Verdächtigen*) to keep under surveillance

überwand *imperf von* überwinden

überweisen (*irr*) *vt* to transfer; (*Patienten*) to refer (*an* +*akk* to)

Überweisung *f* transfer; (*von Patienten*) referral

überwiegend *adv* mainly

überwinden (**überwand, überwunden**) *vt* to overcome ▷ *vr*: **sich ~** to make an effort, to force oneself

überwunden *pp von* überwinden

Überzelt *nt* (rain) fly

überzeugen *vt* to convince

Überzeugung *f* conviction

überziehen (*irr*) *vt* (*bedecken*) to cover; (*Jacke etc*) to put on; (*Konto*) to overdraw; **die Betten frisch ~** to change the sheets

üblich *adj* usual

übrig *adj* remaining; **ist noch Saft ~?** is there any juice left?; **die Ü~en** *pl* the rest *pl*; **im Ü~en** besides; **~ bleiben** to be left (over); **mir blieb nichts anderes ~, als zu gehen** I had no other choice but to go

übrigens *adv* besides; (*nebenbei bemerkt*) by the way

übrig|haben (*irr*) *vt*: **für jdn etwas ~** (*fam*: *jdn mögen*) to have a soft spot for sb

Übung *f* practice; (*im Sport, Aufgabe etc*) exercise

Ufer (*-s, -*) *nt* (*Fluss*) bank; (*Meer, See*) shore; **am ~** on the bank/shore

Ufo (*-(s), -s*) *nt* (*akr*) = **unbekanntes Flugobjekt** UFO

Uhr (*-, -en*) *f* clock; (*am Arm*) watch; **wie viel Uhr ist es?** what time is it?; **1 Uhr** 1 o'clock; **20 Uhr** 8 o'clock, 8 p.m.

Uhrzeigersinn *m*: **im ~** clockwise; **gegen den ~** counterclockwise

Uhrzeit f time (of day)
Ukraine (-) f: **die ~** the Ukraine
UKW (abk) = **Ultrakurzwelle** VHF
Ulme (-, -n) f elm
Ultrakurzwelle f very high frequency
Ultraschallaufnahme f (Med) scan

SCHLÜSSELWORT

um prep +akk 1 (um herum) around; **um Weihnachten** around Christmas; **er schlug um sich** he was throwing punches left and right
2 (mit Zeitangabe) at; **um acht (Uhr)** at eight (o'clock)
3 (mit Größenangabe) by; **etw um 4 cm kürzen** to shorten sth by 4 cm; **um 10% teurer** 10% more expensive; **um vieles besser** better by far; **um so besser** so much the better
4: **der Kampf um den Titel** the battle for the title; **um Geld spielen** to play for money; **Stunde um Stunde** hour after hour; **Auge um Auge** an eye for an eye
▷ prep +gen: **um ... willen** for the sake of ...; **um Gottes willen** for goodness' o; (stärker) God's sake
▷ konj: **um ... zu** (in order) to ...; **zu klug, um zu ...** too clever to ...; siehe **umso**
▷ adv 1 (ungefähr) about; **um (die) 30 Leute** about o around 30 people
2 (vorbei): **die zwei Stunden sind um** the two hours are up

umarmen vt to hug; (romantisch) to embrace
Umbau m rebuilding; (zu etwas) conversion (zu into)
um|bauen vt to rebuild; (zu etwas) to convert (zu into)
um|blättern vt, vi to turn over
um|bringen (irr) vt to kill
um|buchen vi to change (o rebook) one's reservation/flight
um|drehen vt to turn (around); (obere Seite nach unten) to turn over ▷ vr: **sich ~** to turn (around)
Umdrehung f turn; (Phys, Auto) revolution
um|fahren (irr) vt to knock down
um|fallen (irr) vi to fall over
Umfang m (Ausmaß) extent; (von Buch) size; (Reichweite) range; (Math) circumference
umfangreich adj extensive
Umfeld nt environment

Umfrage f survey
Umgang m company; (mit jdm) dealings pl
umgänglich adj sociable
Umgangssprache f colloquial language, slang
Umgebung f surroundings pl; (Milieu) environment; (Personen) people around one
umgehen (irr) vi (Gerücht) to go around; **~ können mit** (know how to) handle (irr) vt to avoid; (Schwierigkeit, Verbot) to get around
um|gehen (irr) vi: **mit etw ~** to handle sth
Umgehungsstraße f bypass
umgekehrt adj reverse; (gegenteilig) opposite ▷ adv the other way around; **und ~** and vice versa
um|hören vr: **sich ~** to ask around
um|kehren vi to turn back ▷ vt to reverse; (Kleidungsstück) to turn inside out
um|kippen vt to tip over ▷ vi to overturn; (fig) to change one's mind; (fam: ohnmächtig werden) to pass out
Umkleidekabine f dressing room
Umkleideraum m changing room
Umkreis m neighborhood; **im ~ von** within a radius of
um|leiten vt to divert
Umleitung f diversion
um|rechnen vt to convert (in +akk into)
Umrechnung f conversion
Umrechnungskurs m rate of exchange
Umriss m outline
um|rühren vi, vt to stir
ums kontr von **um das**
Umsatz m turnover
um|schalten vi to switch (auf +akk to)
Umschlag m cover; (Buch) jacket; (Med) compress; (Brief) envelope
Umschulung f retraining
um|sehen (irr) vr: **sich ~** to look around; (suchen) to look out (nach for)
umso adv all the; **~ mehr** all the more; **~ besser** so much the better
umsonst adv (vergeblich) in vain; (gratis) for free
Umstand m circumstance; **Umstände** pl (fig) fuss; **in anderen Umständen sein** to be pregnant; **jdm Umstände machen** to cause sb a lot of trouble; **machen Sie bitte keine Umstände** please, don't put yourself out; **unter diesen/keinen Umständen** under these/no circumstances; **unter Umständen** possibly

u

umständlich *adj* (*Methode*) complicated; (*Ausdrucksweise*) long-winded; (*Mensch*) ponderous

Umstandsmode *f* maternity wear

um|steigen (*irr*) *vi* to change (trains/buses)

um|stellen *vt* (*an anderen Ort*) to change around; (*Tech*) to convert ▷ *vr*: **sich ~** to adapt (*auf +akk* to)

Umstellung *f* change; (*Umgewöhnung*) adjustment; (*Tech*) conversion

Umtausch *m* exchange

um|tauschen *vt* to exchange; (*Währung*) to change

Umweg *m* detour

Umwelt *f* environment

Umweltbelastung *f* ecological damage

umweltbewusst *adj* environmentally aware

umweltfreundlich *adj* environmentally friendly

Umweltpapier *nt* recycled paper

umweltschädlich *adj* harmful to the environment

Umweltschutz *m* environmental protection

Umweltschützer(in) (*-s, -*) *m(f)* environmentalist

Umweltverschmutzung *f* pollution

umweltverträglich *adj* environment-friendly

um|werfen (*irr*) *vt* to knock over; (*fig: ändern*) to upset; (*fig, fam: jdn*) to flabbergast

um|ziehen (*irr*) *vt* to change ▷ *vr*: **sich ~** to change ▷ *vi* to move (house)

Umzug *m* (*Straßenumzug*) parade; (*Wohnungsumzug*) move

unabhängig *adj* independent

Unabhängigkeitstag *m* Independence Day, Fourth of July

unabsichtlich *adv* unintentionally

unangenehm *adj* unpleasant

Unannehmlichkeit *f* inconvenience; **~en** *pl* trouble *sing*

unanständig *adj* indecent

unappetitlich *adj* (*Essen*) unappetizing; (*abstoßend*) off-putting

unbeabsichtigt *adj* unintentional

unbedeutend *adj* insignificant, unimportant; (*Fehler*) slight

unbedingt *adj* unconditional ▷ *adv* absolutely

unbefriedigend *adj* unsatisfactory

unbegrenzt *adj* unlimited

unbekannt *adj* unknown

unbeliebt *adj* unpopular

unbemerkt *adj* unnoticed

unbequem *adj* (*Stuhl, Mensch*) uncomfortable; (*Regelung*) inconvenient

unbeständig *adj* (*Wetter*) unsettled; (*Lage*) unstable; (*Mensch*) unreliable

unbestimmt *adj* indefinite

unbeteiligt *adj* (*nicht dazugehörig*) uninvolved; (*innerlich nicht berührt*) indifferent, unconcerned

unbewacht *adj* unguarded

unbewusst *adj* unconscious

unbezahlt *adj* unpaid

unbrauchbar *adj* useless

und *conj* and; **und so weiter** and so on; **na und?** so what?

undankbar *adj* (*Person*) ungrateful; (*Aufgabe*) thankless

undenkbar *adj* inconceivable

undeutlich *adj* indistinct

undicht *adj* leaky

uneben *adj* uneven

unecht *adj* (*Schmuck etc*) fake

unehelich *adj* (*Kind*) illegitimate

unendlich *adj* endless; (*Math*) infinite

unentbehrlich *adj* indispensable

unentgeltlich *adj* free (of charge)

unentschieden *adj* undecided; **~ enden** (*Sport*) to end in a tie

unerfreulich *adj* unpleasant

unerhört *adj* unheard-of; (*Bitte*) outrageous

unerlässlich *adj* indispensable

unerträglich *adj* unbearable

unerwartet *adj* unexpected

unerwünscht *adj* unwelcome; (*Eigenschaften*) undesirable

unfähig *adj* incompetent; **~ sein, etw zu tun** to be incapable of doing sth

unfair *adj* unfair

Unfall *m* accident

Unfallbericht *m* accident report

Unfallflucht *f* failure to stop after an accident

Unfallhergang *m*: **den ~ schildern** to give details of the accident

Unfallstation *f* trauma unit

Unfallstelle *f* scene of the accident

Unfallversicherung *f* accident insurance

unfreundlich *adj* unfriendly

Ungarn (*-s*) *nt* Hungary

Ungeduld *f* impatience

ungeduldig *adj* impatient

ungeeignet *adj* unsuitable

ungefähr *adj* approximate ▷ *adv* approximately; **~ 10 Kilometer** about 10 kilometers; **wann ~?** about what time?; **wo ~?** whereabouts?

ungefährlich *adj* harmless; (*sicher*) safe

ungeheuer *adj* huge ▷ *adv* (*fam*) enormously

Ungeheuer (*-s, -*) *nt* monster

ungehorsam *adj* disobedient (*gegenüber* to)

ungelegen *adj* inconvenient

ungemütlich *adj* unpleasant; (*Mensch*) disagreeable

ungenießbar *adj* inedible; (*Getränk*) undrinkable

ungenügend *adj* unsatisfactory; (*Schulnote*) ≈ F

ungepflegt *adj* (*Garten*) untended; (*Aussehen*) unkempt; (*Hände*) neglected

ungerade *adj* odd

ungerecht *adj* unjust

ungerechtfertigt *adj* unjustified

Ungerechtigkeit *f* injustice, unfairness

ungern *adv* reluctantly

ungeschickt *adj* clumsy

ungeschminkt *adj* without make-up

ungesund *adj* unhealthy

ungewiss *adj* uncertain

ungewöhnlich *adj* unusual

Ungeziefer (*-s*) *nt* pests *pl*, vermin *pl*

ungezogen *adj* ill-mannered

ungezwungen *adj* relaxed

ungiftig *adj* non-toxic

unglaublich *adj* incredible

Unglück (*-(e)s, -e*) *nt* (*Unheil*) misfortune; (*Pech*) bad luck; (*Unglücksfall*) disaster; (*Verkehrsunglück*) accident; **das bringt ~** that's unlucky

unglücklich *adj* unhappy; (*erfolglos*) unlucky; (*unerfreulich*) unfortunate

unglücklicherweise *adv* unfortunately

ungültig *adj* invalid

ungünstig *adj* inconvenient

unheilbar *adj* incurable; **~ krank sein** to be terminally ill

unheimlich *adj* eerie ▷ *adv* (*fam*) incredibly

unhöflich *adj* impolite

uni *adj* plain

Uni (*-, -s*) *f* (*fam*) college, university

Uniform (*-, -en*) *f* uniform

Universität *f* university

Unkenntnis *f* ignorance

unklar *adj* unclear

Unkosten *pl* expenses *pl*

Unkostenbeitrag *m* contribution (towards expenses)

Unkraut *nt* weeds *pl*; (*Unkrautart*) weed

unlogisch *adj* illogical

unmissverständlich *adj* unambiguous

unmittelbar *adj* immediate; **~ darauf** immediately afterwards

unmöbliert *adj* unfurnished

unmöglich *adj* impossible

unnahbar *adj* unapproachable

unnötig *adj* unnecessary

UNO (*-*) *f* (*akr*) = United Nations Organization UN

unordentlich *adj* messy

Unordnung *f* disorder; (*fam*) mess

unpassend *adj* inappropriate; (*Zeit*) inconvenient

unpersönlich *adj* impersonal

unpraktisch *adj* impractical

Unrecht *nt* wrong; **zu ~** wrongly; **im ~ sein** to be wrong

unrecht *adj* wrong; **~ haben** to be wrong

unregelmäßig *adj* irregular

unreif *adj* unripe, green; (*Mensch*) immature

unruhig *adj* restless; **~ schlafen** to have a bad night

uns *pron akk, dat von* **wir**; us, (to) us; **uns selbst** (*reflexiv*) ourselves; **sehen Sie uns?** can you see us?; **er schickte es uns** he sent it to us; **lasst uns in Ruhe** leave us alone; **ein Freund von uns** a friend of ours; **wir haben uns hingesetzt** we sat down; **wir haben uns amüsiert** we enjoyed ourselves; **wir mögen uns** we like each other

unscharf *adj* (*Foto*) blurred, out of focus

unscheinbar *adj* insignificant; (*Aussehen*) nondescript

unschlüssig *adj* undecided

unschuldig *adj* innocent

unser *pron* (*adjektivisch*) our ▷ *pron gen von* **wir**; of us

unsere(r, s) *pron* (*substantivisch*) ours

unseretwegen *adv* (*wegen uns*) because of us; (*uns zuliebe*) for our sake; (*um uns*) about us; (*von uns aus*) as far as we are concerned

unseriös *adj* dubious

unsicher *adj* (*ungewiss*) uncertain; (*Person, Job*) insecure

Unsinn *m* nonsense

unsterblich *adj* immortal; **~ verliebt** madly in love

unsympathisch *adj* unpleasant; **er ist mir**

u

~ I don't like him

unten *adv* below; (*im Haus*) downstairs; (*an der Treppe etc*) at the bottom; **nach ~** down

unter *prep +dat* **1** (*räumlich, mit Zahlen*) under; (*drunter*) underneath, below; **unter 18 Jahren** under 18 years
2 (*zwischen*) among(st); **sie waren unter sich** they were by themselves; **einer unter ihnen** one of them; **unter anderem** among other things
▷ *prep +akk* under, below

Unterarm *m* forearm
unterbelichtet *adj* (*Foto*) underexposed
Unterbewusstsein *nt* subconscious
unterbrechen (*irr*) *vt* to interrupt
Unterbrechung *f* interruption; **ohne ~** nonstop
unterdrücken *vt* to suppress; (*Leute*) to oppress
unterdurchschnittlich *adj* below average
untere(r, s) *adj* lower
untereinander *adv* (*räumlich*) one below the other; (*gegenseitig*) each other; (*miteinander*) among themselves/yourselves/ourselves
Unterführung *f* underpass
unter|gehen (*irr*) *vi* to go down; (*Sonne*) to set; (*Volk*) to perish; (*Welt*) to come to an end; (*im Lärm*) to be drowned out
Untergeschoss *nt* basement
Untergewicht *nt*: **drei Kilo ~ haben** to be three kilos underweight
Untergrund *m* foundation; (*Pol*) underground
Untergrundbahn *f* subway
unterhalb *adv, prep* (*+gen*) below; **~ von** below
Unterhalt *m* maintenance; (*für Exehemann o -ehefrau*) alimony; (*für Kinder*) child support
unterhalten (*irr*) *vt* to maintain; (*belustigen*) to entertain ▷ *vr*: **sich ~** to talk; (*sich belustigen*) to enjoy oneself
Unterhaltung *f* (*Belustigung*) entertainment; (*Gespräch*) talk, conversation
Unterhemd *nt* undershirt
Unterhose *f* underpants *pl*; (*fig*) underwear *sing*
unterirdisch *adj* underground
Unterkiefer *m* lower jaw

Unterkunft (-, -*künfte*) *f* accommodation
Unterlage *f* (*Beleg*) document; (*Schreibunterlage*) pad
unterlassen (*irr*) *vt*: **es ~, etw zu tun** (*versäumen*) to fail to do sth; (*bleiben lassen*) to refrain from doing sth
unterlegen *adj* inferior (*dat* to); (*besiegt*) defeated
Unterleib *m* abdomen
Unterlippe *f* lower lip
Untermiete *f*: **zur ~ wohnen** to sublet a place
Untermieter(in) *m(f)* subtenant
unternehmen (*irr*) *vt* (*Reise*) to go on; (*Versuch*) to make; **etwas ~** to do something (*gegen* about)
Unternehmen (-*s*, -) *nt* undertaking; (*Comm*) company
Unternehmensberater(in) (-*s*, -) *m(f)* management consultant
Unternehmer(in) (-*s*, -) *m(f)* entrepreneur
Unterricht (-(*e*)*s*, -*e*) *m* lessons *pl*
unterrichten *vt* to teach
unterschätzen *vt* to underestimate
unterscheiden (*irr*) *vt* to distinguish (*von* from, *zwischen +dat* between) ▷ *vr*: **sich ~** to differ (*von* from)
Unterschenkel *m* lower leg
Unterschied (-(*e*)*s*, -*e*) *m* difference; **im ~ zu dir** unlike you
unterschiedlich *adj* different
unterschreiben (*irr*) *vt* to sign
Unterschrift *f* signature
Untersetzer (-*s*, -) *m* table mat; (*für Gläser*) coaster
unterste(r, s) *adj* lowest, bottom
unter|stellen *vr*: **sich ~** to take shelter
unterstellen *vt* (*rangmäßig*) to subordinate (*dat* to); (*fig*) to impute (*jdm etw* sth to sb)
unterstreichen (*irr*) *vt* (*a. fig*) to underline
Unterstrich *m* (*Inform*) underscore
unterstützen *vt* to support
Unterstützung *f* support
untersuchen *vt* (*Med*) to examine; (*Polizei*) to investigate
Untersuchung *f* examination; (*polizeiliche*) investigation
untertags *adv* during the day
Untertasse *f* saucer
Unterteil *nt* lower part, bottom
Untertitel *m* subtitle
untervermieten *vt* to sublet
Unterwäsche *f* underwear
unterwegs *adv* on the way

unterzeichnen vt to sign
untreu adj unfaithful
untröstlich adj inconsolable
unüberlegt adj ill-considered ▷ adv without thinking
unüblich adj unusual
unverantwortlich adj irresponsible; (unentschuldbar) inexcusable
unverbindlich adj not binding; (Antwort) noncommittal ▷ adv (Comm) without obligation
unverbleit adj unleaded
unverheiratet adj unmarried, single
unvermeidlich adj unavoidable
unvernünftig adj silly
unverschämt adj impudent
unverständlich adj incomprehensible
unverträglich adj (Person) argumentative; (Essen) indigestible
unverwüstlich adj indestructible; (Mensch) irrepressible
unverzeihlich adj unforgivable
unverzüglich adj immediate
unvollständig adj incomplete
unvorsichtig adj careless
unwahrscheinlich adj improbable, unlikely ▷ adv (fam) incredibly
Unwetter nt thunderstorm
unwichtig adj unimportant
unwiderstehlich adj irresistible
unwillkürlich adj involuntary ▷ adv instinctively; **ich musste ~ lachen** I couldn't help laughing
unwohl adj unwell, ill
unzählig adj innumerable, countless
unzerbrechlich adj unbreakable
unzertrennlich adj inseparable
unzufrieden adj dissatisfied
unzugänglich adj inaccessible
unzumutbar adj unacceptable
unzusammenhängend adj disconnected; (Äußerung) incoherent
unzutreffend adj inapplicable; (unwahr) incorrect
unzuverlässig adj unreliable
Update (-s, -s) nt (Inform) update
üppig adj (Essen) lavish; (Vegetation) lush
uralt adj ancient, very old
Uran (-s) nt uranium
Uranus (-) m Uranus
Uraufführung f premiere
Urenkel m great-grandson
Urenkelin f great-granddaughter
Urgroßeltern pl great-grandparents pl
Urgroßmutter f great-grandmother
Urgroßvater m great-grandfather
Urheber(in) (-s, -) m(f) originator; (Autor) author
Urin (-s, -e) m urine
Urinprobe f urine sample
Urkunde (-, -n) f document
Urlaub (-(e)s, -e) m vacation; **im ~** on vacation; **in ~ fahren** to go on vacation
Urlauber(in) (-s, -) m(f) vacationer
urlaubsreif adj ready for a vacation
Urlaubszeit f vacation time
Urne (-, -n) f urn
Urologe m, **Urologin** f urologist
Ursache f cause (für of); **keine ~!** not at all!; (bei Entschuldigung) that's all right!
Ursprung m origin; (von Fluss) source
ursprünglich adj original ▷ adv originally
Ursprungsland adj country of origin
Urteil (-s, -e) nt (Meinung) opinion; (Jur) verdict; (Strafmaß) sentence
urteilen vi to judge
Uruguay (-s) nt Uruguay
Urwald m jungle
USA pl USA sing
User(in) (-s, -) m(f) (Inform) user
usw. (abk) = **und so weiter** etc
Utensilien pl utensils pl

u

V

vage *adj* vague

Vagina (-, *Vaginen*) *f* vagina

Valentinstag *m* St Valentine's Day

Vandalismus *m* vandalism

Vanille (-) *f* vanilla

variieren *vt, vi* to vary

Vase (-, -n) *f* vase

Vaseline (-) *f* Vaseline®

Vater (-s, *Väter*) *m* father

väterlich *adj* paternal

Vaterschaft *f* fatherhood; (*Jur*) paternity

Vatertag *m* Father's Day

Vaterunser *nt*: **das ~ beten** (to say) the Lord's Prayer

V-Ausschnitt *m* V-neck

v. Chr. (*abk*) = **vor Christus** BC

Veganer(in) (-s, -) *m(f)* vegan

Vegetarier(in) (-s, -) *m(f)* vegetarian

vegetarisch *adj* vegetarian

Veilchen *nt* violet

Velo (-s, -s) *nt* (*schweizerisch*) bicycle

Vene (-, -n) *f* vein

Venedig (-s) *nt* Venice

Venezuela (-s) *nt* Venezuela

Ventil (-s, -e) *nt* valve

Ventilator *m* ventilator

Venus (-) *f* Venus

Venusmuschel *f* clam

verabreden *vt* to arrange ▷ *vr*: **sich ~ to** arrange to meet (*mit jdm* sb); **ich bin schon verabredet** I'm already meeting someone

Verabredung *f* arrangement; (*Termin*) appointment; (*zum Ausgehen*) date

verabschieden *vt* (*Gäste*) to say goodbye to; (*Gesetz*) to pass ▷ *vr*: **sich ~ to say** goodbye

verachten *vt* to despise

verächtlich *adj* contemptuous; (*verachtenswert*) contemptible

Verachtung *f* contempt

verallgemeinern *vt* to generalize

Veranda (-, *Veranden*) *f* veranda, porch

veränderlich *adj* changeable

verändern *vt* to change ▷ *vr*: **sich ~ to** change

Veränderung *f* change

veranlassen *vt* to cause

veranstalten *vt* to organize

Veranstalter(in) (-s, -) *m(f)* organizer

Veranstaltung *f* event

Veranstaltungsort *m* venue

verantworten *vt* to take responsibility for ▷ *vr*: **sich für etw ~ to** answer for sth

verantwortlich *adj* responsible (*für* for)

Verantwortung *f* responsibility (*für* for)

verärgern *vt* to annoy

verarschen *vt* (*fam*) to mess around with; (*boshaft*) to make a fool out of

Verb (-s, -en) *nt* verb

Verband *m* (*Med*) bandage; (*Bund*) association

Verband(s)kasten *m* first-aid kit

Verband(s)zeug *nt* dressing material

verbergen (*irr*) *vt* to hide (*vor* +*dat* from) ▷ *vr*: **sich ~ to** hide (*vor* +*dat* from)

verbessern *vt* to improve; (*berichtigen*) to correct ▷ *vr*: **sich ~ to** improve; (*berichtigen*) to correct oneself

Verbesserung *f* improvement; (*Berichtigung*) correction

verbiegen (*irr*) *vi* to bend ▷ *vr*: **sich ~ to** bend

verbieten (*irr*) *vt* to forbid; **jdm ~, etw zu tun** to forbid sb to do sth

verbinden (*irr*) *vt* to connect; (*kombinieren*) to combine; (*Med*) to bandage; **können Sie mich mit ... ~?** (*Tel*) can you put me through to ...?; **ich verbinde** (*Tel*) I'm putting you through ▷ *vr* (*Chem*): **sich ~ to** combine

verbindlich *adj* binding; (*freundlich*) friendly

Verbindung *f* connection

verbleit *adj* leaded

verblüffen *vt* to amaze

verblühen *vi* to fade

verborgen *adj* hidden

Verbot (-(e)s, -e) *nt* ban (*für, von* on)

verboten *adj* forbidden; **es ist ~** it's not allowed; **es ist ~, hier zu parken** you're not allowed to park here; **Rauchen ~** no smoking

verbrannt *adj* burnt

Verbrauch (-(e)s) *m* consumption

verbrauchen *vt* to use up

Verbraucher(in) (-s, -) *m(f)* consumer

Verbrechen (-s, -) *nt* crime

Verbrecher(in) (-s, -) *m(f)* criminal

verbreiten *vt* to spread ▷ *vr*: **sich ~ to** spread

verbrennen (*irr*) *vt* to burn

Verbrennung *f* burning; (*in Motor*) combustion

verbringen (*irr*) *vt* to spend

verbunden *adj*: **falsch ~** sorry, wrong number

Verdacht (*-(e)s*) *m* suspicion

verdächtig *adj* suspicious

verdächtigen *vt* to suspect

verdammt *interj* (*fam*) damn

verdanken *vt*: **jdm etw ~** to owe sth to sb

verdarb *imperf von* **verderben**

verdauen *vt* (*a. fig*) to digest

verdaulich *adj* digestible; **das ist schwer ~** that is hard to digest

Verdauung *f* digestion

Verdeck (*-(e)s, -e*) *nt* top

verderben (**verdarb, verdorben**) *vt* to spoil; (*schädigen*) to ruin; (*moralisch*) to corrupt; **es sich** (*dat*) **mit jdm ~** to get onto sb's bad side; **ich habe mir den Magen verdorben** I've got an upset stomach ▷ *vi* (*Lebensmittel*) to go bad

verdienen *vt* to earn; (*moralisch*) to deserve

Verdienst (*-(e)s, -e*) *m* earnings *pl* ▷ (*-(e)s, -e*) *nt* merit; (*Leistung*) service (*um* to)

verdoppeln *vt* to double

verdorben *pp von* **verderben** ▷ *adj* spoiled; (*geschädigt*) ruined; (*moralisch*) corrupt

verdrehen *vt* to twist; (*Augen*) to roll; **jdm den Kopf ~** (*fig*) to turn sb's head

verdünnen *vt* to dilute

verdunsten *vi* to evaporate

verdursten *vi* to die of thirst

verehren *vt* to admire; (*Rel*) to worship

Verehrer(in) (*-s, -*) *m(f)* admirer

Verein (*-(e)s, -e*) *m* association; (*Klub*) club

vereinbar *adj* compatible

vereinbaren *vt* to arrange

Vereinbarung *f* agreement, arrangement

vereinigen *vt* to unite ▷ *vr*: **sich ~** to unite

Vereinigtes Königreich *nt* United Kingdom

Vereinigte Staaten (von Amerika) *pl* United States *sing* (of America)

Vereinigung *f* union; (*Verein*) association

Vereinte Nationen *pl* United Nations *pl*

vereisen *vi* (*Straße*) to freeze over; (*Fenster*) to ice up ▷ *vt* (*Med*) to freeze

vererben *vt*: **jdm etw ~** to leave sth to sb; (*Bio*) to pass sth on to sb ▷ *vr*: **sich ~** to be hereditary

vererblich *adj* hereditary

verfahren (*irr*) *vi* to proceed ▷ *vr*: **sich ~** to get lost

Verfahren (*-s, -*) *nt* procedure; (*Tech*) method; (*Jur*) proceedings *pl*

verfallen (*irr*) *vi* to decline; (*Haus*) to be falling apart; (*Fin*) to lapse; (*Fahrkarte etc*) to expire; **~ in** +*akk* to lapse into

Verfallsdatum *nt* (*auch von Lebensmitteln*) expiration date

verfärben *vr*: **sich ~** to change color; (*Wäsche*) to discolor

Verfasser(in) (*-s, -*) *m(f)* author, writer

Verfassung *f* (*gesundheitlich*) condition; (*Pol*) constitution

verfaulen *vi* to rot

verfehlen *vt* to miss

verfeinern *vt* to refine

Verfilmung *f* film (*o* screen) version

verfluchen *vt* to curse

verfolgen *vt* to pursue; (*Pol*) to persecute

verfügbar *adj* available

verfügen *vi*: **über etw** (*akk*) **~** to have sth available

Verfügung *f* order; **jdm zur ~ stehen** to be available for (*o* to) sb; **jdm etw zur ~ stellen** to make sth available for (*o* to) sb

verführen *vt* to tempt; (*sexuell*) to seduce

verführerisch *adj* seductive

vergangen *adj* past; **~e Woche** last week

Vergangenheit *f* past

Vergaser (*-s, -*) *m* (*Auto*) carburetor

vergaß *imperf von* **vergessen**

vergeben (*irr*) *vt* to forgive (*jdm etw* sb for sth); (*weggeben*) to award, to allocate

vergebens *adv* in vain

vergeblich *adv* in vain ▷ *adj* vain, futile

vergehen (*irr*) *vi* to pass ▷ *vr*: **sich an jdm ~** to sexually assault sb

Vergehen (*-s, -*) *nt* offense

Vergeltung *f* retaliation

vergessen (**vergaß, vergessen**) *vt* to forget

vergesslich *adj* forgetful

vergeuden *vt* to squander, to waste

vergewaltigen *vt* to rape

Vergewaltigung *f* rape

vergewissern *vr*: **sich ~** to make sure

vergiften *vt* to poison

Vergiftung *f* poisoning

Vergissmeinnicht (*-(e)s, -e*) *nt* forget-me-not

Vergleich (*-(e)s, -e*) *m* comparison; (*Jur*) settlement; **im ~ zu** compared to (*o* with)

vergleichen (*irr*) *vt* to compare (*mit* to, with)

Vergnügen (*-s, -*) *nt* pleasure; **viel ~!** enjoy yourself!

vergnügt *adj* cheerful

Vergnügungspark *m* amusement park

vergoldet adj gold-plated

vergriffen adj (Buch) out of print; (Ware) out of stock

vergrößern vt to enlarge; (Menge) to increase; (mit Lupe) to magnify

Vergrößerung f enlargement; (Menge) increase; (mit Lupe) magnification

Vergrößerungsglas nt magnifying glass

verh. adj (abk) = **verheiratet** married

verhaften vt to arrest

verhalten (irr) vr: **sich ~** (sich benehmen) to behave; (Sache) to be

Verhalten (-s) nt behavior

Verhältnis nt relationship (zu with); (Math) ratio; **~se** pl circumstances pl, conditions pl; **im ~ von 1 zu 2** in a ratio of 1 to 2

verhältnismäßig adj relative ▷ adv relatively

verhandeln vi to negotiate (über etw akk sth)

Verhandlung f negotiation

verheimlichen vt to keep secret (jdm from sb)

verheiratet adj married

verhindern vt to prevent; **sie ist verhindert** she can't make it

Verhör (-(e)s, -e) nt interrogation; (gerichtlich) examination

verhören vt to interrogate; (bei Gericht) to examine ▷ vr: **sich ~** to mishear

verhungern vi to starve to death

verhüten vt to prevent

Verhütung f prevention; (mit Pille, Kondom etc) contraception

Verhütungsmittel nt contraceptive

verirren vr: **sich ~** to get lost

Verkauf m sale

verkaufen vt to sell; **zu ~** for sale

Verkäufer(in) m(f) seller; (beruflich) salesperson; (in Laden) sales clerk

verkäuflich adj for sale

Verkehr (-s, -e) m traffic; (Sex) intercourse; (Umlauf) circulation

verkehren vi (Bus etc) to run; **~ in** to frequent; **~ mit** to associate (o mix) with

Verkehrsampel f traffic light

Verkehrsamt nt tourist information office

verkehrsfrei adj traffic-free

Verkehrsfunk m travel news sing

Verkehrsinsel f traffic island

Verkehrsmeldung f traffic report

Verkehrsmittel nt means sing of transportation; **öffentliche ~** pl public transportation sing

Verkehrsschild nt traffic sign

Verkehrstote(r) mf road casualty; **die Zahl der ~n** the number of deaths on the road

Verkehrsunfall m traffic accident

Verkehrszeichen nt traffic sign

verkehrt adj wrong; (verkehrt herum) the wrong way around; (Pullover etc) inside out; **du machst es ~** you're doing it wrong

verklagen vt to take to court, to sue

verkleiden vt to dress up (als as) ▷ vr: **sich ~** to dress up (als as); (um unerkannt zu bleiben) to disguise oneself

Verkleidung f (Karneval) costume; (um nicht erkannt zu werden) disguise

verkleinern vt to reduce; (Zimmer, Gebiet etc) to make smaller

verkneifen (irr) vt: **sich** (dat) **etw ~** (Lachen) to stifle sth; (Schmerz) to hide sth; (sich versagen) to do without sth

verkommen (irr) vi to deteriorate; (Mensch) to go downhill ▷ adj (Haus) dilapidated; (moralisch) depraved

verkraften vt to cope with

verkratzt adj scratched

verkühlen vr: **sich ~** to get a chill

verkürzen vt to shorten

Verlag (-(e)s, -e) m publishing company

verlangen vt (fordern) to demand; (wollen) to want; (Preis) to ask; (Qualifikation) to require; (erwarten) to ask (von of); (fragen nach) to ask for; (Pass etc) to ask to see; **~ Sie Herrn X** ask for Mr. X ▷ vi: **~ nach** to ask for

verlängern vt to extend; (Pass, Erlaubnis) to renew

Verlängerung f extension; (Sport) overtime; (von Pass, Erlaubnis) renewal

Verlängerungsschnur f extension cable

Verlängerungswoche f extra week

verlassen (irr) vt to leave (irr) vr: **sich ~** to rely (auf +akk on) ▷ adj desolate; (Mensch) abandoned

verlässlich adj reliable

Verlauf m course

verlaufen (irr) vi (Weg, Grenze) to run (entlang along); (zeitlich) to pass; (Farben) to run ▷ vr: **sich ~** to get lost; (Menschenmenge) to disperse

verlegen vt to move; (verlieren) to mislay; (Buch) to publish ▷ adj embarrassed

Verlegenheit f embarrassment; (Situation) difficulty

Verleih (-(e)s, -e) m (Firma) rental company

verleihen (irr) vt to lend; (vermieten) to rent (out); (Preis, Medaille) to award

verleiten vt: jdn dazu ~, etw zu tun to lure (o entice) sb to do sth

verlernen vt to forget

verletzen vt to injure; (fig) to hurt

Verletzte(r) mf injured person

Verletzung f injury; (Verstoß) violation

verlieben vr: sich ~ to fall in love (in jdn with sb)

verliebt adj in love

verlieren (verlor, verloren) vt, vi to lose

verloben vr: sich ~ to get engaged (mit to)

Verlobte(r) mf fiancé/fiancée

Verlobung f engagement

verlor imperf von verlieren

verloren pp von verlieren ▷ adj lost; (Eier) poached; ~ gehen to go missing

verlosen vt to raffle

Verlosung f raffle

Verlust (-(e)s, -e) m loss

vermehren vt to multiply; (Menge) to increase ▷ vr: sich ~ to multiply; (Menge) to increase

vermeiden (irr) vt to avoid

vermeintlich adj supposed

vermieten vt (auch Auto) to rent (out)

Vermieter(in) m(f) landlord/-lady

vermischen vt to mix ▷ vr: sich ~ to mix

vermissen vt to miss

vermisst adj missing; jdn als ~ melden to report sb missing

Vermittlung f (bei Streit) mediation; (Herbeiführung) arranging; (Stelle) agency

Vermögen (-s, -) nt fortune

vermuten vt to suppose; (argwöhnen) to suspect

vermutlich adj probable ▷ adv probably

Vermutung f supposition; (Verdacht) suspicion

vernachlässigen vt to neglect

vernichten vt to destroy

vernichtend adj (fig) crushing; (Blick) withering; (Kritik) scathing

Vernunft (-) f reason; ich kann ihn nicht zur ~ bringen I can't make him see reason

vernünftig adj sensible; (Preis) reasonable

veröffentlichen vt to publish

verordnen vt (Med) to prescribe

Verordnung f order; (Med) prescription

verpachten vt to lease (out) (an +akk to)

verpacken vt to pack; (einwickeln) to wrap up

Verpackung f packaging

Verpackungskosten pl packing charges pl

verpassen vt to miss

verpflegen vt to feed

Verpflegung f feeding; (Kost) food; (in Hotel) board

verpflichten vt to oblige; (anstellen) to engage ▷ vr: sich ~ to commit oneself (etw zu tun to doing sth)

verprügeln vt to beat up

verraten (irr) vt to betray; (Geheimnis) to divulge; aber nicht ~! but don't tell anyone! ▷ vr: sich ~ to give oneself away

verrechnen vt: ~ mit to set off against ▷ vr: sich ~ to miscalculate

Verrechnungsscheck m check for deposit only

verregnet adj rainy

verreisen vi to go away (nach to); sie ist geschäftlich verreist she's away on business

verrenken vt to contort; (Med) to dislocate; sich (dat) den Knöchel ~ to sprain (o twist) one's ankle

verringern vt to reduce

verrostet adj rusty

verrückt adj crazy, insane; es macht mich ~ it's driving me crazy

versagen vi to fail

Versagen (-s) nt failure

Versager(in) (-s, -) m(f) failure

versalzen (irr) vt to put too much salt in/on

versammeln vt to assemble, to gather ▷ vr: sich ~ to assemble, to gather

Versammlung f meeting

Versand (-(e)s) m dispatch; (Abteilung) shipping department

Versandhaus nt mail-order company

versäumen vt to miss; (unterlassen) to neglect; ~, etw zu tun to fail to do sth

verschätzen vr: sich ~ to miscalculate

verschenken vt to give away; (Chance) to waste

verschicken vt to send off

verschieben vt (irr) (auf später) to postpone, to put off; (an anderen Ort) to move

verschieden adj (unterschiedlich) different; (mehrere) various; sie sind ~ groß they are of different sizes; V~e pl various people/things pl; V~es various things pl

verschimmelt adj moldy

verschlafen (irr) vt to sleep through; (fig) to miss ▷ vi to oversleep

verschlechtern vr: sich ~ to deteriorate, to get worse

Verschlechterung f deterioration

Verschleiß (-es) m wear and tear

verschließbar adj lockable

verschließen (*irr*) *vt* to close; (*mit Schlüssel*) to lock

verschlimmern *vt* to make worse ▷ *vr*: **sich ~** to get worse

verschlossen *adj* locked; (*fig*) reserved

verschlucken *vt* to swallow ▷ *vr*: **sich ~** to choke (*an +dat* on)

Verschluss *m* lock; (*von Kleid*) fastener; (*Foto*) shutter; (*Stöpsel*) stopper

verschmutzen *vt* to get dirty; (*Umwelt*) to pollute

verschnaufen *vi*: **ich muss mal ~** I need to get my breath back

verschneit *adj* snow-covered

verschnupft *adj*: **~ sein** to have a cold; (*fam: beleidigt*) to be peeved

verschonen *vt* to spare (*jdn mit etw* sb sth)

verschreiben (*irr*) *vt* (*Med*) to prescribe

verschreibungspflichtig *adj* available only on prescription

verschwand *imperf von* **verschwinden**

verschweigen (*irr*) *vt* to keep secret; **jdm etw ~** to keep sth from sb

verschwenden *vt* to waste

Verschwendung *f* waste

verschwiegen *adj* discreet; (*Ort*) secluded

verschwinden (**verschwand, verschwunden**) *vi* to disappear, to vanish; **verschwinde!** get lost!

verschwunden *pp von* **verschwinden**

Versehen (*-s, -*) *nt*: **aus ~** by mistake

versehentlich *adv* by mistake

versenden (*irr*) *vt* to send off

versessen *adj*: **~ auf +akk** crazy about

versetzen *vt* to transfer; (*verpfänden*) to pawn; (*fam: bei Verabredung*) to stand up ▷ *vr*: **sich in jdn** *o* **jds Lage ~** to put oneself in sb's place

verseuchen *vt* to contaminate

versichern *vt* to insure; (*bestätigen*) to assure; **versichert sein** to be insured

Versichertenkarte *f* health-insurance card

Versicherung *f* insurance

Versicherungskarte *f*: **grüne ~** insurance document for driving abroad

Versicherungspolice *f* insurance policy

versilbert *adj* silver-plated

versinken (*irr*) *vi* to sink

Version *f* version

versöhnen *vt* to reconcile ▷ *vr*: **sich ~** to become reconciled; (*fam*) to make up (with each other)

versorgen *vt* to provide, to supply (*mit* with); (*Familie*) to look after ▷ *vr*: **sich ~** to look after oneself

Versorgung *f* provision; (*Unterhalt*) maintenance; (*für Alter etc*) benefit

verspäten *vr*: **sich ~** to be late

verspätet *adj* late

Verspätung *f* delay; **eine Stunde ~ haben** to be (an hour) late

versprechen (*irr*) *vt* to promise ▷ *vr*: **ich habe mich versprochen** I didn't mean to say that

Verstand *m* mind; (*Vernunft*) (common) sense; **den ~ verlieren** to lose one's mind

verständigen *vt* to inform ▷ *vr*: **sich ~** to communicate; (*sich einigen*) to come to an understanding

Verständigung *f* communication

verständlich *adj* understandable

Verständnis *nt* understanding (*für* of); (*Mitgefühl*) sympathy

verständnisvoll *adj* understanding

verstauchen *vt* to sprain

verstaucht *pp von* **verstauchen**; sprained

Versteck (*-(e)s, -e*) *nt* hiding place; **~ spielen** to play hide-and-seek

verstecken *vt* to hide (*vor +dat* from) ▷ *vr*: **sich ~** to hide (*vor +dat* from)

verstehen (*irr*) *vt* to understand; **falsch ~** to misunderstand ▷ *vr*: **sich ~** to get along (*mit* with)

Versteigerung *f* auction

verstellbar *adj* adjustable

verstellen *vt* to move; (*Uhr*) to adjust; (*versperren*) to block; (*Stimme, Handschrift*) to disguise ▷ *vr*: **sich ~** to pretend, to put on an act

verstopfen *vt* to block up; (*Med*) to constipate

Verstopfung *f* obstruction; (*Med*) constipation

Verstoß *m* infringement, violation (*gegen* of)

Versuch (*-(e)s, -e*) *m* attempt; (*wissenschaftlich*) experiment

versuchen *vt* to try

vertauschen *vt* to exchange; (*versehentlich*) to mix up

verteidigen *vt* to defend

Verteidiger(in) (*-s, -*) *m(f)* (*Sport*) defender; (*Jur*) defense counsel

Verteidigung *f* defense

verteilen *vt* to distribute

Vertrag (*-(e)s, Verträge*) *m* contract; (*Pol*) treaty

vertragen (*irr*) *vt* to stand, to bear ▷ *vr*: **sich ~** to get along (with each other); (*sich* *aussöhnen*) to make up (with each other)

verträglich *adj* (*Mensch*) good-natured; (*Speisen*) digestible

vertrauen *vi*: jdm/einer Sache ~ to trust sb/ sth

Vertrauen (*-s*) *nt* trust (*in +akk* in, *zu* in); **ich habe kein ~ zu ihm** I don't trust him; **ich hab's ihm im ~ gesagt** I told him in confidence

vertraulich *adj* (*geheim*) confidential

vertraut *adj*: **sich mit etw ~ machen** to familiarize oneself with sth

vertreten (*irr*) *vt* to represent; (*Ansicht*) to hold

Vertreter(in) (*-s, -*) *m(f)* representative

Vertrieb (*-(e)s, -e*) *m* (*Abteilung*) sales department

vertrocknen *vi* to dry up

vertun (*irr*) *vr*: **sich ~** to make a mistake

vertuschen *vt* to cover up

verunglücken *vi* to have an accident; **tödlich ~** to be killed in an accident

verunsichern *vt* to make uneasy

verursachen *vt* to cause

verurteilen *vt* to condemn

vervielfältigen *vt* to make copies of

verwählen *vr*: **sich ~** to dial the wrong number

verwalten *vt* to manage; (*behördlich*) to administer

Verwalter(in) (*-s, -*) *m(f)* manager; (*Vermögensverwalter*) trustee

Verwaltung *f* management; (*amtlich*) administration

verwandt *adj* related (*mit* to)

Verwandte(r) *mf* relative, relation

Verwandtschaft *f* relationship; (*Menschen*) relatives *pl*

verwarnen *vt* to warn; (*Sport*) to caution

verwechseln *vt* to confuse (*mit* with); (*halten für*) to mistake (*mit* for)

verweigern *vt* to refuse

verwenden *vt* to use; (*Zeit*) to spend; **Mühe auf etw** (*akk*) ~ to take trouble over sth

Verwendung *f* use

verwirklichen *vt* to realize; **sich selbst ~** to fulfill oneself

verwirren *vt* to confuse

Verwirrung *f* confusion

verwitwet *adj* widowed

verwöhnen *vt* to spoil

verwunderlich *adj* surprising

Verwunderung *f* astonishment

verwüsten *vt* to devastate

verzählen *vr*: **sich ~** to miscount

verzehren *vt* to consume

Verzeichnis *nt* (*Liste*) list; (*Katalog*) catalogue; (*in Buch*) index; (*Inform*) directory

verzeihen (**verzieh, verziehen**) *vt, vi* to forgive (*jdm etw* sb for sth); ~ **Sie bitte, ...** (*vor Frage etc*) excuse me, ...; ~ **Sie die Störung** sorry to disturb you

Verzeihung *f*: **~!** sorry!; **~, ...** (*vor Frage etc*) excuse me, ...; **jdn um ~ bitten** to apologize (to sb)

verzichten *vi*: **auf etw** (*akk*) ~ to do without sth; (*aufgeben*) to give sth up

verzieh *imperf von* **verzeihen**

verziehen *pp von* **verzeihen**

verziehen (*irr*) *vt* (*Kind*) to spoil; **das Gesicht ~** to make a face ▷ *vr*: **sich ~** to go out of shape; (*Gesicht*) to contort; (*verschwinden*) to disappear

verzieren *vt* to decorate

verzögern *vt* to delay ▷ *vr*: **sich ~** to be delayed

Verzögerung *f* delay

verzweifeln *vi* to despair (*an +dat* of)

verzweifelt *adj* desperate

Verzweiflung *f* despair

Veterinär(in) (*-s, -e*) *m(f)* veterinarian

Vetter (*-s, -n*) *m* cousin

vgl. (*abk*) = **vergleiche** cf

Viagra® (*-s*) *nt* Viagra®

Vibrator (*-s, -en*) *m* vibrator

vibrieren *vi* to vibrate

Video (*-s, -s*) *nt* video; **auf ~ aufnehmen** to video

Videoclip (*-s, -s*) *m* video clip

Videofilm *m* video

Videogerät *nt* video (recorder)

Videokamera *f* video camera

Videokassette *f* video (cassette)

Videorekorder *m* video recorder

Videospiel *nt* video game

Videothek (*-, -en*) *f* video library

Vieh (*-(e)s*) *nt* cattle

viel *pron* a lot (of), lots of; ~ **Arbeit** a lot of work, lots of work; **~e Leute** a lot of people, lots of people, many people; **zu ~** too much; **zu ~e** too many; **sehr ~** a great deal of; **sehr ~e** a great many; **ziemlich ~/~e** quite a lot of; **nicht ~** not much, not a lot of; **nicht ~e** not many, not a lot of ▷ *pron* a lot; **sie sagt nicht ~** she doesn't say a lot; **nicht ~** not much, not a lot of; **nicht ~e** not many, not a lot of; **gibt es ~?** is there much?, is there a lot?; **gibt es ~e?** are there many?, are there a lot? ▷ *adv* a lot; **er geht ~ ins Kino** he goes to the movies a

V

lot; **sehr ~** a great deal; **ziemlich ~** quite a lot; **~ besser** much better; **~ teurer** much more expensive; **~ zu ~** far too much

vielleicht adv maybe, perhaps; **~ ist sie krank** maybe she's sick, she might be sick; **weißt du ~, wo er ist?** do you know where he is (by any chance)?

vielmal(s) adv many times; **danke ~s** many thanks

vielmehr adv rather

vielseitig adj very varied; (Mensch, Gerät) versatile

vier num four; **auf allen ~en** on all fours; **unter ~ Augen** in private, privately

Vier (-, -en) f four; (Schulnote) ≈ D

Vierbettzimmer nt room for four (people)

Viereck (-(e)s, -e) nt quadrilateral; (Quadrat) square

viereckig adj four-sided; (quadratisch) square

vierfach adj: **die ~e Menge** four times the amount

vierhundert num four hundred

viermal adv four times

vierspurig adj four-lane

viert adv: **wir sind zu ~** there are four of us

vierte(r, s) adj fourth; siehe auch **dritte**

Viertel (-s, -) nt (Stadtviertel) quarter, district; (Bruchteil) quarter; (Viertelliter) quarter-liter; (Uhrzeit) quarter; **~ vor/nach drei** a quarter to/past three; **viertel drei** a quarter past two; **drei viertel drei** a quarter to three

Viertelfinale nt quarter-final

vierteljährlich adj quarterly

Viertelstunde f quarter of an hour

vierzehn num fourteen; **in ~ Tagen** in two weeks

vierzehntägig adj two-week, biweekly

vierzehnte(r, s) adj fourteenth; siehe auch **dritte**

vierzig num forty

vierzigste(r, s) adj fortieth

Vietnam (-s) nt Vietnam

Vignette f (Autobahnvignette) freeway permit

Villa (-, Villen) f villa

violett adj purple

Violine f violin

Virus (-, Viren) m o nt virus

Visitenkarte f card

Visum (-s, Visa o Visen) nt visa

Vitamin (-s, -e) nt vitamin

Vitrine (-, -n) f (glass) cabinet; (Schaukasten) display case

Vogel (-s, Vögel) m bird

Vogelgrippe f bird flu, avian flu

Voicemail (-, -s) f voice mail

Vokal (-s, -e) m vowel

Volk (-(e)s, Völker) nt people pl; (Nation) nation

Volksfest nt festival; (Jahrmarkt) fair

Volkshochschule f adult education center

Volkslied nt folk song

Volksmusik f folk music

volkstümlich adj (einfach und beliebt) popular; (herkömmlich) traditional; (Kunst) folk

voll adj full (von of)

Vollbart m beard

Vollbremsung f: **eine ~ machen** to slam on the brakes

vollends adv completely

Volleyball m volleyball

Vollgas nt: **mit ~** at full throttle; **~ geben** to step on it

völlig adj complete ⊳ adv completely

volljährig adj of age

Vollkaskoversicherung f comprehensive insurance with collision

vollklimatisiert adj fully air-conditioned

vollkommen adj perfect; **~er Unsinn** complete nonsense ⊳ adv completely

Vollkornbrot nt whole wheat bread

voll|machen vt to fill (up)

Vollmacht (-, -en) f authority; (Urkunde) power of attorney

Vollmilch f whole milk

Vollmilchschokolade f milk chocolate

Vollmond m full moon

Vollnarkose f general anesthetic

Vollpension f full board

vollständig adj complete

voll|tanken vi to fill up

Volltreffer m direct hit

Vollwertkost f wholefood

vollzählig adj complete

Volt (-, -) nt volt

Volumen (-s, -) nt volume

vom kontr von **von dem**; (räumlich, zeitlich, Ursache) from; **ich kenne sie nur vom Sehen** I only know her by sight

von prep +dat **1** (Ausgangspunkt) from; **von ... bis** from ... to; **von morgens bis abends** from morning till night; **von ... nach ...** from ... to ...; **von ... an** from ...; **von ...**

aus from ...; **von dort aus** from there; **etw von sich aus tun** to do sth of one's own accord; **von mir aus** (*fam*) if you like, I don't mind; **von wo/wann ...?** where/when ... from?

2 (*Ursache, im Passiv*) by; **ein Gedicht von Schiller** a poem by Schiller; **von etw müde** tired from sth

3 (*als Genitiv*) of; **ein Freund von mir** a friend of mine; **nett von dir** nice of you; **jeweils zwei von zehn** two out of every ten

4 (*über*) about; **er erzählte vom Urlaub** he talked about his vacation

5: **von wegen!** (*fam*) no way!

voneinander *adv* from each other

vor *prep +dat* **1** (*räumlich*) in front of; **vor der Kirche links abbiegen** turn left before the church

2 (*zeitlich*) before; **ich war vor ihm da** I was there before him; **vor zwei Tagen** two days ago; **5 (Minuten) vor 4** 5 (minutes) to 4; **vor Kurzem** a little while ago

3 (*Ursache*) with; **vor Wut/Liebe** with rage/love; **vor Hunger sterben** to die of hunger; **vor lauter Arbeit** because of work

4: **vor allem, vor allen Dingen** most of all
▷ *prep +akk* (*räumlich*) in front of
▷ *adv*: **vor und zurück** back and forth

voran|gehen (*irr*) *vi* to go ahead; **einer Sache** (*dat*) **~** to precede sth
voran|kommen (*irr*) *vi* to make progress
Vorarlberg (*-s*) *nt* Vorarlberg
voraus *adv* ahead; **im V~** in advance
voraus|fahren (*irr*) *vi* to drive on ahead
vorausgesetzt *conj* provided (that)
Voraussage *f* prediction; (*Wetter*) forecast
voraus|sagen *vt* to predict
voraus|sehen (*irr*) *vt* to foresee
voraus|sein (*irr*) *vi*: **jdm ~** to be ahead of sb
voraus|setzen *vt* to assume
Voraussetzung *f* requirement, prerequisite
voraussichtlich *adj* expected ▷ *adv* probably
voraus|zahlen *vt* to pay in advance
Vorbehalt (*-(e)s, -e*) *m* reservation
vor|behalten (*irr*) *vt*: **sich/jdm etw ~** to reserve sth (for oneself)/for sb

vorbei *adv* past, over, finished
vorbei|bringen (*irr*) *vt* to drop by (*o* in)
vorbei|fahren (*irr*) *vi* to drive past
vorbei|gehen (*irr*) *vi* to pass by, to go past; (*verstreichen, aufhören*) to pass
vorbei|kommen (*irr*) *vi* to drop by
vorbei|lassen (*irr*) *vt*: **kannst du die Leute ~?** would you let these people pass?; **lässt du mich bitte mal vorbei?** can I get past, please?
vorbei|reden *vi*: **aneinander ~** to talk at cross purposes, to talk past each other
vor|bereiten *vt* to prepare ▷ *vr*: **sich ~** to get ready (*auf +akk , für* for)
Vorbereitung *f* preparation
vor|bestellen *vt* to book in advance; (*Essen*) to order in advance
Vorbestellung *f* booking, reservation
vor|beugen *vi* to prevent (*dat* sth)
vorbeugend *adj* preventive
Vorbeugung *f* prevention
Vorbild *nt* (role) model
vorbildlich *adj* model, ideal
Vorderachse *f* front axle
vordere(r, s) *adj* front
Vordergrund *m* foreground
Vorderradantrieb *m* (*Auto*) front-wheel drive
Vorderseite *f* front
Vordersitz *m* front seat
Vorderteil *m o nt* front (part)
Vordruck *m* form
voreilig *adj* hasty, rash; **~e Schlüsse ziehen** to jump to conclusions
voreingenommen *adj* biased
vor|enthalten (*irr*) *vt*: **jdm etw ~** to withhold sth from sb
vorerst *adv* for the moment
vor|fahren (*irr*) *vi* (*vorausfahren*) to drive on ahead; **vor das Haus ~** to drive up to the house; **fahren Sie bis zur Ampel vor** drive as far as the traffic lights
Vorfahrt *f* (*Auto*) right of way; **~ achten** yield
Vorfahrtsschild *nt* yield sign
Vorfahrtsstraße *f* main (*o* major) road
Vorfall *m* incident
vor|führen *vt* to demonstrate; (*Film*) to show; (*Theaterstück, Trick*) to perform
Vorgänger(in) *m(f)* predecessor
vor|gehen (*irr*) *vi* (*vorausgehen*) to go on ahead; (*nach vorn*) to go forward; (*handeln*) to act, to proceed; (*Uhr*) to be fast; (*Vorrang haben*) to take precedence; (*passieren*) to go on

Vorgehen (*-s*) *nt* procedure

Vorgesetzte(r) *mf* superior

vorgestern *adv* the day before yesterday

vor|haben (*irr*) *vt* to plan; **hast du schon was vor?** do you have any plans?; **ich habe vor, nach Rom zu fahren** I'm planning to go to Rome

vor|halten (*irr*) *vt*: **jdm etw ~** to accuse sb of sth

Vorhand *f* forehand

vorhanden *adj* existing; (*erhältlich*) available

Vorhang *m* curtain

Vorhaut *f* foreskin

vorher *adv* before; **zwei Tage ~** two days before; **~ essen wir** we'll eat first

Vorhersage *f* forecast

vorher|sehen (*irr*) *vt* to foresee

vorhin *adv* just now, a moment ago

Vorkenntnisse *pl* previous knowledge *sing*

vor|kommen (*irr*) *vi* (*nach vorne kommen*) to come forward; (*geschehen*) to happen; (*sich finden*) to occur; (*scheinen*) to seem (to be); **sich** (*dat*) **dumm ~** to feel stupid

Vorlage *f* model

vor|lassen (*irr*) *vt*: **jdn ~** to let sb go first

vorläufig *adj* temporary

vor|lesen (*irr*) *vt* to read out

Vorlesung *f* lecture

vorletzte(r, s) *adj* second to last; **am ~n Samstag** (on) the Saturday before last

Vorliebe *f* preference

vor|machen *vt*: **kannst du es mir ~?** can you show me how to do it?; **jdm etwas ~** (*fig: täuschen*) to fool sb

vor|merken *vt* to note down; (*Plätze*) to book

Vormittag *m* morning; **am ~** in the morning; **heute ~** this morning

vormittags *adv* in the morning; **um 9 Uhr ~** at 9 (o'clock) in the morning, at 9 a.m.

vorn(e) *adv* in front; **von ~ anfangen** to start at the beginning; **nach ~** to the front; **weiter ~** further up; **von ~ bis hinten** from beginning to end

Vorname *m* first name; **wie heißt du mit ~n?** what's your first name?

vornehm *adj* (*von Rang*) distinguished; (*Benehmen*) refined; (*fein, elegant*) elegant

vor|nehmen (*irr*) *vt*: **sich** (*dat*) **etw ~** to start on sth; **sich** (*dat*) **~, etw zu tun** (*beschließen*) to decide to do sth

vornherein *adv*: **von ~** from the start

Vorort *m* suburb

vorrangig *adj* primary

Vorrat *m* stock, supply

vorrätig *adj* in stock

Vorrecht *nt* privilege

Vorruhestand *m* early retirement

Vorsaison *f* early season

Vorsatz *m* intention; (*Jur*) intent

vorsätzlich *adj* intentional; (*Jur*) premeditated

Vorschau *f* preview; (*Film*) trailer

Vorschlag *m* suggestion, proposal

vorschlagen (*irr*) *vt* to suggest, to propose; **ich schlage vor, dass wir gehen** I suggest we go

vor|schreiben (*irr*) *vt* (*befehlen*) to stipulate; **jdm etw ~** to dictate sth to sb

Vorschrift *f* regulation, rule; (*Anweisung*) instruction

vorschriftsmäßig *adj* correct

Vorschule *f* nursery school, pre-school

Vorsicht *f* care; **~!** look out!; (*Schild*) caution; **~ Stufe!** watch your step!

vorsichtig *adj* careful

vorsichtshalber *adv* just in case

Vorsorge *f* precaution; (*Vorbeugung*) prevention

Vorsorgeuntersuchung *f* checkup

vorsorglich *adv* as a precaution

Vorspann (*-(e)s, -e*) *m* credits *pl*

Vorspeise *f* appetizer

Vorsprung *m* projection; (*Abstand*) lead

vor|stellen *vt* (*bekannt machen*) to introduce; (*Uhr*) to put forward; (*vor etw*) to put in front; **sich** (*dat*) **etw ~** to imagine sth

Vorstellung *f* (*Bekanntmachen*) introduction; (*Theat*) performance; (*Gedanke*) idea

Vorstellungsgespräch *nt* interview

vor|täuschen *vt* to feign

Vorteil *m* advantage (*gegenüber* over); **die Vor- und Nachteile** the pros and cons

vorteilhaft *adj* advantageous

Vortrag (*-(e)s, Vorträge*) *m* talk (*über +akk* on); (*akademisch*) lecture; **einen ~ halten** to give a talk

vorüber *adv* over

vorüber|gehen (*irr*) *vi* to pass

vorübergehend *adj* temporary ▷ *adv* temporarily, for the time being

Vorurteil *nt* prejudice

Vorverkauf *m* advance booking

vor|verlegen *vt* to bring forward

Vorwahl *f* (*Tel*) area code

Vorwand (*-(e)s, Vorwände*) *m* pretext,

excuse; **unter dem ~, dass** with the excuse that
vorwärts *adv* forward
vorwärts|gehen (*irr*) *vi* (*fig*) to progress
vorweg *adv* in advance
vorweg|nehmen (*irr*) *vt* to anticipate
Vorweihnachtszeit *f* pre-Christmas period
vor|werfen (*irr*) *vt*: **jdm etw ~** to accuse sb of sth
vorwiegend *adv* mainly
Vorwort *nt* preface
Vorwurf *m* reproach; **sich** (*dat*) **Vorwürfe**

machen to reproach oneself; **jdm Vorwürfe machen** to accuse sb
vorwurfsvoll *adj* reproachful
vor|zeigen *vt* to show
vorzeitig *adj* premature, early
vor|ziehen (*irr*) *vt* (*lieber haben*) to prefer
Vorzug *m* preference; (*gute Eigenschaft*) merit; (*Vorteil*) advantage
vorzüglich *adj* excellent
vulgär *adj* vulgar
Vulkan (*-s, -e*) *m* volcano
Vulkanausbruch *m* volcanic eruption

V

W

W (*abk*) = **West** W

Waage (-, -n) *f* scale; (*Astr*) Libra

waagerecht *adj* horizontal

wach *adj* awake; **~ werden** to wake up

Wache (-, -n) *f* guard

Wachs (-es, -e) *nt* wax

wachsen (**wuchs, gewachsen**) *vi* to grow

wachsen *vt* (*Skier*) to wax

Wachstum *nt* growth

Wachtel (-, -n) *f* quail

Wächter(in) (-s, -) *m(f)* guard; (*auf Parkplatz*) attendant

wackelig *adj* wobbly; (*fig*) shaky

Wackelkontakt *m* loose connection

wackeln *vi* (*Stuhl*) to be wobbly; (*Zahn, Schraube*) to be loose; **mit dem Kopf ~** to bob one's head (up and down)

Wade (-, -n) *f* (*Anat*) calf

Waffe (-, -n) *f* weapon

Waffel (-, -n) *f* waffle; (*Keks, Eiswaffel*) wafer

wagen *vt* to risk; **es ~, etw zu tun** to dare to do sth

Wagen (-s, -) *m* (*Auto, Eisenb*) car

Wagenheber (-s, -) *m* jack

Wagentyp *m* make and model

Wahl (-, -en) *f* choice; (*Pol*) election

wählen *vt* to choose; (*Tel*) to dial; (*Pol*) to vote for; (*durch Wahl ermitteln*) to elect ▷ *vi* to choose; (*Tel*) to dial; (*Pol*) to vote

Wähler(in) (-s, -) *m(f)* voter

wählerisch *adj* choosy

Wahlkampf *m* election campaign

wahllos *adv* at random

Wahlwiederholung *f* redial

Wahnsinn *m* madness; **~!** amazing!

wahnsinnig *adj* insane, crazy ▷ *adv* (*fam*) incredibly

wahr *adj* true; **das darf doch nicht ~ sein!** I don't believe it!; **nicht ~?** that's right, isn't it?

während *prep* (+*gen*) during ▷ *conj* while

währenddessen *adv* meanwhile, in the meantime

Wahrheit *f* truth

wahrnehmbar *adj* noticeable, perceptible

wahr|nehmen (*irr*) *vt* to perceive

Wahrsager(in) (-s, -) *m(f)* fortune-teller

wahrscheinlich *adj* probable, likely ▷ *adv* probably; **ich komme ~ zu spät** I'll probably be late

Wahrscheinlichkeit *f* probability

Währung *f* currency

Wahrzeichen *nt* symbol

Waise (-, -n) *f* orphan

Wal (-(e)s, -e) *m* whale

Wald (-(e)s, **Wälder**) *m* wood; (*groß*) forest

Waldbrand *m* forest fire

Waldsterben (-s) *nt* forest dieback

Wales (-) *nt* Wales

Waliser(in) *m(f)* Welshman/Welshwoman

walisisch *adj* Welsh

Walisisch *nt* Welsh

Walkie-Talkie (-(s), -s) *nt* walkie-talkie

Walkman® (-s, -s) *m* Walkman®

Wall (-(e)s, **Wälle**) *m* embankment

Wallfahrt *f* pilgrimage

Wallfahrtsort *m* place of pilgrimage

Walnuss *f* walnut

Walross (-es, -e) *nt* walrus

wälzen *vt* to roll; (*Bücher*) to pore over; (*Probleme*) to deliberate on ▷ *vr*: **sich ~** to wallow; (*vor Schmerzen*) to roll around; (*im Bett*) to toss and turn

Walzer (-s, -) *m* waltz

Wand (-, **Wände**) *f* wall; (*Trennwand*) partition; (*Bergwand*) (rock) face

Wandel (-s) *m* change

wandeln *vt* to change ▷ *vr*: **sich ~** to change

Wanderer (-s, -) *m*, **Wanderin** *f* hiker

Wanderkarte *f* hiking map

wandern *vi* to hike; (*Blick*) to wander; (*Gedanken*) to stray

Wanderschuh *m* walking shoe

Wanderstiefel *m* hiking boot

Wanderung *f* hike; **eine ~ machen** to go on a hike

Wanderweg *m* walking (*o* hiking) trail

Wandleuchte *f* wall lamp

Wandmalerei *f* mural

Wandschrank *m* built-in closet

wandte *imperf von* **wenden**

Wange (-, -n) *f* cheek

wann *adv* when; **seit ~ ist sie da?** how long has she been here?; **bis ~ bleibt ihr?** how long are you staying?

Wanne (-, -n) *f* (bath) tub

Wappen (-s, -) *nt* coat of arms

war *imperf von* **sein**

warb *imperf von* **werben**

Ware (-, -n) *f* product; **~n** goods *pl*

Warenhaus *nt* department store

Warenprobe *f* sample

Warenzeichen *nt* trademark

warf *imperf von* **werfen**

warm *adj* warm; (*Essen*) hot; **~ laufen** to warm up; **mir ist es zu ~** I'm too warm

Wärme (*-, -n*) *f* warmth

wärmen *vt* to warm; (*Essen*) to warm (*o to heat*) up ▷ *vi* (*Kleidung, Sonne*) to be warm ▷ *vr:* **sich ~** to warm up; (*gegenseitig*) to keep each other warm

Wärmflasche *f* hot-water bottle

Warmstart *m* (*Inform*) warm start

warnen *vt* to warn (*vor +dat* about, of)

Warnung *f* warning

Warteliste *f* waiting list

warten *vi* to wait (*auf +akk* for); **warte mal!** wait (*o hang on*) a minute! ▷ *vt* (*Tech*) to service

Wärter(in) *m(f)* attendant

Wartesaal *m*, **Wartezimmer** *nt* waiting room

Wartung *f* service; (*das Warten*) servicing

warum *adv* why

Warze (*-, -n*) *f* wart

was *pron* what; (*fam: etwas*) something; **was kostet das?** what does it cost? how much is it?; **was für ein Auto ist das?** what kind of car is that?; **was für eine Farbe/Größe?** what color/size?; **was?** (*fam: wie bitte?*) what?; **was ist/gibt's?** what is it? what's up?; **du weißt, was ich meine** you know what I mean; **was auch immer** whatever; **soll ich dir was mitbringen?** do you want me to bring you anything?; **alles, was er hat** everything he's got

Waschanlage *f* (*Auto*) car wash

waschbar *adj* washable

Waschbär *m* raccoon

Waschbecken *nt* washbasin

Wäsche (*-, -n*) *f* washing; (*schmutzig*) laundry; (*Bettwäsche*) linen; (*Unterwäsche*) underwear; **in der ~** in the wash

Wäscheklammer *f* clothespin

Wäscheleine *f* clothesline

waschen (**wusch, gewaschen**) *vt, vi* to wash; **W~ und Legen** shampoo and set ▷ *vr:* **sich ~** to (have a) wash; **sich** (*dat*) **die Haare ~** to wash one's hair

Wäscherei *f* laundry

Wäscheständer *m* clothes horse

Wäschetrockner *m* (tumble) dryer

Waschgelegenheit *f* washing facilities *pl*

Waschlappen *m* washcloth

Waschmaschine *f* washing machine

Waschmittel *nt*, **Waschpulver** *nt* laundry detergent

Waschraum *m* washroom

Waschsalon (*-s, -s*) *m* laundromat

Waschstraße *f* car wash

Wasser (*-s, -*) *nt* water; **fließendes ~** running water

Wasserball *m* (*Sport*) water polo

Wasserbob *m* jet ski

wasserdicht *adj* watertight; (*Uhr etc*) waterproof

Wasserfall *m* waterfall

Wasserfarbe *f* watercolor

wasserfest *adj* watertight, waterproof

Wasserhahn *m* faucet

wässerig *adj* watery

Wasserkessel (*-s, -*) *m* electric kettle

Wasserkocher (*-s, -*) *m* electric kettle

Wasserleitung *f* water pipe

wasserlöslich *adj* water-soluble

Wassermann *m* (*Astr*) Aquarius

Wassermelone *f* watermelon

Wasserrutschbahn *f* water slide

Wasserschaden *m* water damage

wasserscheu *adj* scared of water

Wasserski *nt* water-skiing

Wasserspiegel *m* surface of the water; (*Wasserstand*) water level

Wassersport *m* water sports *pl*

wasserundurchlässig *adj* watertight, waterproof

Wasserverbrauch *m* water consumption

Wasserversorgung *f* water supply

Wasserwaage *f* (spirit) level

Wasserwerk *nt* waterworks *pl*

waten *vi* to wade

Watt (*-(e)s, -en*) *nt* (*Geo*) mud flats *pl* ▷ (*-s, -*) *nt* (*Elek*) watt

Watte (*-, -n*) *f* cotton ball

Wattepad (*-s, -s*) *m* cotton pad

Wattestäbchen *nt* cotton bud, Q-tip®

WC (*-s, -s*) *nt* restroom, bathroom

WC-Reiniger *m* toilet cleaner

Web (*-s*) *nt* (*Inform*) Web

Webseite *f* (*Inform*) Web page

Wechsel (*-s, -*) *m* change; (*Spielerwechsel: Sport*) substitution

Wechselgeld *nt* change

wechselhaft *adj* (*Wetter*) variable

Wechseljahre *pl* menopause *sing*

Wechselkurs *m* exchange rate

wechseln *vt* to change; (*Blicke*) to exchange; **Geld ~** to change some money; (*in Kleingeld*) to get some change; **Euro in Dollar ~** to change euros into dollars ▷ *vi* to change; **kannst du ~?** can you change this?

Wechselstrom *m* alternating current, AC
Weckdienst *m* wake-up call service
wecken *vt* to wake (up)
Wecker (-*s*, -) *m* alarm clock
Weckruf *m* wake-up call
wedeln *vi* (*Ski*) to wedel; **mit etw ~** to wave sth; **mit dem Schwanz ~** to wag its tail; **der Hund wedelte mit dem Schwanz** the dog wagged its tail
weder *conj*: **~ ..., noch ...** neither ... nor ...
weg *adv* (*entfernt, verreist*) away; (*los, ab*) off; **er war schon weg** he had already left (*o gone*); **Hände weg!** hands off!; **weit weg** a long way away (*o off*)
Weg (-(*e*)*s*, -*e*) *m* way; (*Pfad*) path; (*Route*) route; **jdn nach dem Weg fragen** to ask sb the way; **auf dem Weg sein** to be on the way
weg|bleiben (*irr*) *vi* to stay away
weg|bringen (*irr*) *vt* to take away
wegen *prep* (+*gen o dat*) because of
weg|fahren (*irr*) *vi* to drive away; (*abfahren*) to leave; (*in Urlaub*) to go away
Wegfahrsperre *f* (*Auto*) immobilizer
weg|gehen (*irr*) *vi* to go away
weg|kommen (*irr*) *vi* to get away; (*fig*): **gut/schlecht ~** to come off well/badly
weg|lassen (*irr*) *vt* to leave out
weg|laufen (*irr*) *vi* to run away
weg|legen *vt* to put aside
weg|machen *vt* (*fam*) to get rid of
weg|müssen (*irr*) *vi*: **ich muss weg** I've got to go
weg|nehmen (*irr*) *vt* to take away
weg|räumen *vt* to clear away
weg|rennen (*irr*) *vi* to run away
weg|schicken *vt* to send away
weg|schmeißen (*irr*) *vt* to throw away
weg|sehen (*irr*) *vi* to look away
weg|tun (*irr*) *vt* to put away
Wegweiser (-*s*, -) *m* signpost
weg|werfen (*irr*) *vt* to throw away
weg|wischen *vt* to wipe off
weg|ziehen (*irr*) *vi* to move (away)
weh *adj* sore; *siehe auch* **wehtun**
wehen *vt, vi* to blow; (*Fahne*) to flutter
Wehen *pl* contractions *pl*
Wehrdienst *m* military service
wehren *vr*: **sich ~** to defend oneself
weh|tun (*irr*) *vi* to hurt; **jdm/sich ~** to hurt sb/oneself
Weibchen *nt*: **es ist ein ~** (*Tier*) it's a she
weiblich *adj* feminine; (*Bio*) female
weich *adj* soft; **~ gekocht** (*Ei*) soft-boiled
Weichkäse *m* soft cheese; (*Streichkäse*)

cheese spread
weichlich *adj* soft; (*körperlich*) weak
Weichspüler (-*s*, -) *m* (*für Wäsche*) (fabric) softener
Weide (-, -*n*) *f* (*Baum*) willow; (*Grasfläche*) meadow
weigern *vr*: **sich ~** to refuse
Weigerung *f* refusal
Weiher (-*s*, -) *m* pond
Weihnachten (-, -) *nt* Christmas
Weihnachtsabend *m* Christmas Eve
Weihnachtsbaum *m* Christmas tree
Weihnachtsfeier *f* Christmas party
Weihnachtsferien *pl* Christmas vacation *sing*
Weihnachtsgeld *nt* Christmas bonus
Weihnachtsgeschenk *nt* Christmas present
Weihnachtskarte *f* Christmas card
Weihnachtslied *nt* Christmas carol
Weihnachtsmann *m* Father Christmas, Santa (Claus)

WEIHNACHTSMARKT

The **Weihnachtsmarkt** is a market held in most large towns in Germany during the weeks prior to Christmas. People visit it to buy presents, toys and Christmas decorations, and to enjoy the festive atmosphere. Food and drink associated with the Christmas festivities can also be enjoyed there, for example, gingerbread and mulled wine.

Weihnachtsstern *m* (*Bot*) poinsettia
Weihnachtstag *m*: **erster ~** Christmas Day
Weihnachtszeit *f* Christmas season
weil *conj* because
Weile (-) *f* while, short time; **es kann noch eine ~ dauern** it could take some time
Wein (-(*e*)*s*, -*e*) *m* wine; (*Pflanze*) vine
Weinbeere *f* grape
Weinberg *m* vineyard
Weinbergschnecke *f* snail
Weinbrand *m* brandy
weinen *vt, vi* to cry
Weinglas *nt* wine glass
Weinkarte *f* wine list
Weinkeller *m* wine cellar
Weinlese (-, -*n*) *f* vintage
Weinprobe *f* wine tasting
Weintraube *f* grape
weise *adj* wise

Weise (-, -n) f manner, way; **auf diese Art und ~** this way

weisen (wies, gewiesen) vt to show

Weisheit f wisdom

Weisheitszahn m wisdom tooth

weiß adj white

Weißbier nt ≈ wheat beer

Weißbrot nt white bread

weißhaarig adj white-haired

Weißkohl m, **Weißkraut** nt (white) cabbage

Weißwein m white wine

weit adj wide; (Begriff) broad; (Reise, Wurf) long; (Kleid) loose; **wie ~ ist es ...?** how far is it ...?; **so ~ sein** to be ready ▷ adv far; **~ verbreitet** widespread; **~ gereist** widely traveled; **~ offen** wide open; **das geht zu ~** that's going too far, that's pushing it

weiter adj wider; (weiter weg) farther (away); (zusätzlich) further; **~e Informationen** further information sing ▷ adv further; **~!** go on!; (weitergehen!) keep moving!; **~ nichts/niemand** nothing/nobody else; **und so ~** and so on

weiter|arbeiten vi to continue (on) working

Weiterbildung f continuing education

weiter|empfehlen (irr) vt to recommend

weiter|erzählen vt: **nicht ~!** don't tell anyone

weiter|fahren (irr) vi to go on (nach to, bis as far as)

weiter|geben (irr) vt to pass on

weiter|gehen (irr) vi to go on

weiter|helfen (irr) vi: **jdm ~** to help sb

weiterhin adv: **etw ~ tun** to go on doing sth

weiter|machen vt, vi to continue

weiter|reisen vi to continue one's trip

weitgehend adj considerable ▷ adv largely

weitsichtig adj long-sighted; (fig) farsighted

Weitsprung m long jump

Weitwinkelobjektiv nt (Foto) wide-angle lens

Weizen (-s, -) m wheat

Weizenbier nt ≈ wheat beer

welche(r, s) interrogativ pron which; **welcher von beiden?** which (one) of the two?; **welchen hast du genommen?** which (one) did you take?; **welche eine ...!** what a ...!; **welche Freude!** what joy!

▷ indef pron some; (in Fragen) any; **ich habe welche** I have some; **haben Sie welche?** do you have any?

▷ relativ pron (bei Menschen) who; (bei Sachen) which, that; **welche(r, s) auch immer** whoever/whichever/whatever

welk adj withered

welken vi to wither

Welle (-, -n) f wave

Wellengang m waves pl; **starker ~** heavy seas pl

Wellenlänge f (a. fig) wavelength

Wellenreiten nt surfing

Wellensittich (-s, -e) m budgerigar, ≈ parakeet

wellig adj wavy

Wellness f wellness

Welpe (-n, -n) m puppy

Welt (-, -en) f world; **auf der ~** in the world; **auf die ~ kommen** to be born

Weltall nt universe

weltbekannt, weltberühmt adj world-famous

Weltkrieg m world war

Weltmacht f world power

Weltmeister(in) m(f) world champion

Weltmeisterschaft f world championship; (im Fußball) World Cup

Weltraum m space

Weltreise f trip around the world

Weltrekord m world record

Weltstadt f metropolis

weltweit adj worldwide, global

wem pron dat von **wer**; who ... to, (to) whom; **wem hast du's gegeben?** who did you give it to?; **wem gehört es?** who does it belong to?, whose is it?; **wem auch immer es gehört** whoever it belongs to

wen pron akk von **wer**; who, whom; **wen hast du besucht?** who did you visit?; **wen möchten Sie sprechen?** who would you like to speak to?

Wende (-, -n) f turning point; (Veränderung) change; **die ~** (Hist) the fall of the Berlin Wall

Wendekreis m (Auto) turning circle

Wendeltreppe f spiral staircase

wenden (wendete o wandte, gewendet o gewandt) vt, vi to turn (around); (um 180°) to make a U-turn; **sich an jdn ~** to turn to sb; **bitte ~!** please turn over, PTO ▷ vr: **sich ~** to turn; **sich an jdn ~** to turn to sb

wenig pron, adv little; **~e** pl few; **nur ein klein ~** (just) a little (bit); **ein ~ Zucker** a little bit of sugar, a little sugar; **wir haben ~ Zeit** we haven't got much time; **zu ~** too little; *pl* too few; **nur ~ wissen** to only know a little, to not know much ▷ *adv:* **er spricht ~** he doesn't talk much; **~ bekannt** little known

wenige *pron (pl)* few *pl*
wenigste(r, s) *adj* least
wenigstens *adv* at least

SCHLÜSSELWORT

wenn *konj* 1 *(falls, bei Wünschen)* if; **wenn auch ..., selbst wenn ...** even if ...; **wenn ich doch ...** if only I ...
2 *(zeitlich)* when; **immer wenn** whenever

wennschon *adv:* **na ~** so what?
wer *pron* who; **wer war das?** who was that?; **wer von euch?** which (one) of you? ▷ *pron* anybody who, anyone who; **wer das glaubt, ist dumm** anyone who believes that is stupid; **wer auch immer** whoever ▷ *pron* somebody, someone; *(in Fragen)* anybody, anyone; **ist da wer?** is (there) anybody there?

Werbefernsehen *nt* TV commercials *pl*
Werbegeschenk *nt* promotional gift
werben *(warb, geworben)* *vt* to win; *(Mitglied)* to recruit ▷ *vi* to advertise
Werbespot *(-s, -s)* *m* commercial
Werbung *f* advertising

SCHLÜSSELWORT

werden *(pt* wurde, *pp* geworden *o (bei Passiv)* worden) *vi* to become; **was ist aus ihm/aus der Sache geworden?** what became of him/it?; **es ist nichts/gut geworden** it came to nothing/turned out well; **es wird Nacht/Tag** it's getting dark/light; **mir wird kalt** I'm getting cold; **mir wird schlecht** I feel sick *o* nauseous; **Erster werden** to come *o* be first; **das muss anders werden** that'll have to change; **rot/zu Eis werden** to turn red/to ice; **was willst du (mal) werden?** what do you want to be?; **die Fotos sind gut geworden** the pictures turned out nicely
▷ *als Hilfsverb* 1 *(bei Futur):* **er wird es tun** he will *o* he'll do it; **er wird das nicht tun** he will not *o* he won't do it; **es wird gleich regnen** it's going to rain
2 *(bei Konjunktiv):* **ich würde ...** I would ...; **er würde gern ...** he would *o* he'd like

to ...; **ich würde lieber ...** I would *o* I'd rather ...
3 *(bei Vermutung):* **sie wird in der Küche sein** she will be in the kitchen
4 *(bei Passiv):* **gebraucht werden** to be used; **er ist erschossen worden** he has *o* he's been shot; **mir wurde gesagt, dass ...** I was told that ...

werfen *(warf, geworfen)* *vt* to throw
Werft *(-, -en)* *f* shipyard, dockyard
Werk *(-(e)s, -e)* *nt (Kunstwerk, Buch etc)* work; *(Fabrik)* factory; *(Mechanismus)* works *pl*
Werkstatt *(-, -stätten)* *f* workshop; *(Auto)* garage
Werktag *m* workday, weekday
werktags *adv* on weekdays, during the week
Werkzeug *nt* tool
Werkzeugkasten *m* toolbox
wert *adj* worth; **es ist etwa 50 Euro ~** it's worth about 50 euros; **das ist nichts ~** it's worthless
Wert *(-(e)s, -e)* *m* worth; *(Zahlenwert: Fin)* value; **~ legen auf** +*akk* to attach importance to; **es hat doch keinen ~** *(Sinn)* it's pointless
Wertangabe *f* declaration of value
Wertbrief *m* insured letter
Wertgegenstand *m* valuable object
wertlos *adj* worthless
Wertmarke *f* token
Wertpapiere *pl* securities *pl*
Wertsachen *pl* valuables *pl*
Wertstoff *m* recyclable waste
wertvoll *adj* valuable
Wesen *(-s, -)* *nt* being; *(Natur, Charakter)* nature
wesentlich *adj* significant; *(beträchtlich)* considerable ▷ *adv* considerably
weshalb *adv* why
Wespe *(-, -n)* *f* yellow jacket, wasp
Wespenstich *m* yellow jacket sting
wessen *pron gen von* **wer**; whose

WESSI

A **Wessi** is a colloquial and often derogatory word used to describe a German from the former West Germany. The expression 'Besserwessi' is used by East Germans to refer to a West German who acts like a know-it-all.

West (-s) m west

Westdeutschland nt (als Landesteil) Western Germany; (Hist) West Germany

Weste (-, -n) f vest; (Wollweste) cardigan

Westen (-s) m west; **im ~ Kanadas** in western Canada; **der Wilde ~** the Wild West

Westeuropa nt Western Europe

Westküste f West Coast

westlich adj western; (Kurs, Richtung) westerly

Westwind m west(erly) wind

weswegen adv why

Wettbewerb m competition

Wettbüro nt betting office

Wette (-, -n) f bet; **eine ~ abschließen** to make a bet; **die ~ gilt!** you're on!

wetten vt, vi to bet (auf +akk on); **ich habe mit ihm gewettet, dass ...** I bet him that ...; **ich wette mit dir um 50 Euro** I'll bet you 50 euros; **~, dass?** wanna bet?

Wetter (-s, -) nt weather

Wetterbericht m, **Wettervorhersage** f weather forecast

Wetterkarte f weather map

Wetterlage f weather situation

Wettervorhersage f weather forecast

Wettkampf m contest

Wettlauf m race

Wettrennen nt race

WG (-, -s) f (abk) = **Wohngemeinschaft**

Whirlpool® (-s, -s) m Jacuzzi®

Whisky (-s, -s) m (schottisch) whisky or whiskey

wichtig adj important

wickeln vt (Schnur) to wind (um around); (Schal, Decke) to wrap (um around); **ein Baby ~** to change a baby's diaper

Wickelraum m baby-changing room

Wickeltisch m baby-changing table

Widder (-s, -) m (Zool) ram; (Astr) Aries sing

wider prep (+akk) against

widerlich adj disgusting

widerrufen (irr) vt to withdraw; (Auftrag, Befehl etc) to cancel

widersprechen (irr) vi to contradict (jdm sb)

Widerspruch m contradiction

Widerstand m resistance

widerstandsfähig adj resistant (gegen to)

widerwärtig adj disgusting

widerwillig adj unwilling, reluctant

widmen vt to dedicate ▷ vr: **sich jdm/etw ~** to devote oneself to sb/sth

Widmung f dedication

wie adv how; **wie groß/schnell?** how big/fast?; **wie wär's?** how about it?; **wie ist er?** what's he like?; **wie gut du das kannst!** you're very good at it; **wie bitte?** pardon?; (entrüstet) I beg your pardon!; **und wie!** and how!; **wie viel** how much; **wie viele Menschen** how many people; **wie weit** to what extent

▷ konj **1** (bei Vergleichen): **so schön wie ...** as beautiful as ...; **wie ich schon sagte** as I said; **wie du** like you; **singen wie ein ...** to sing like a ...; **wie (zum Beispiel)** such as (for example)

2 (zeitlich): **wie er das hörte, ging er** when he heard that he left; **er hörte, wie der Regen fiel** he heard the rain falling

wieder adv again; **~ ein e ...** another ...; **~ erkennen** to recognize; **etw ~ gutmachen** to make up for sth; **~ verwerten** to recycle

wieder|bekommen (irr) vt to get back

wiederbeschreibbar adj (CD, DVD) rewritable

wiederholen vt to repeat

Wiederholung f repetition

Wiederhören nt (Tel): **auf ~** goodbye

wieder|kommen (irr) vi to come back

wieder|sehen (irr) vt to see again; (wieder treffen) to meet again

Wiedersehen (-s) nt reunion; **auf ~!** goodbye!

Wiedervereinigung f reunification

Wiege (-, -n) f cradle

wiegen (wog, gewogen) vt, vi (Gewicht) to weigh

Wien (-s) nt Vienna

wies imperf von **weisen**

Wiese (-, -n) f meadow

Wiesel (-s, -) nt weasel

wieso adv why

wievielmal adv how often

wievielte(r, s) adj: **zum ~n Mal?** how many times?; **den W~n haben wir heute?** what's the date today?; **am W~n hast du Geburtstag?** which day is your birthday?

wieweit conj to what extent

Wi-Fi nt Wi-Fi

wild adj wild

Wild (-(e)s) nt game

wildfremd adj (fam): **ein ~er Mensch** a complete (o total) stranger

Wildleder nt suede

Wildpark *m* game park
Wildschwein *nt* (wild) boar
Wildwasserfahren (*-s*) *nt* white-water rafting
Wille (*-ns, -n*) *m* will
willen *prep* (+*gen*): **um ... ~** for the sake of ...; **um Himmels ~!** (*vorwurfsvoll*) for heaven's sake!; (*betroffen*) goodness me
willkommen *adj* welcome; **jdn ~ heißen** to welcome sb
Wimper (*-, -n*) *f* eyelash
Wimperntusche *f* mascara
Wind (*-(e)s, -e*) *m* wind
Windel (*-, -n*) *f* diaper
windgeschützt *adj* sheltered from the wind
windig *adj* windy; (*fig*) dubious
Windjacke *f* windbreaker
Windmühle *f* windmill
Windpark *m* wind farm
Windpocken *pl* chickenpox *sing*
Windschutzscheibe *f* (*Auto*) windshield
Windstärke *f* wind force
Windsurfen (*-s*) *nt* windsurfing
Windsurfer(in) *m(f)* windsurfer
Winkel (*-s, -*) *m* (*Math*) angle; (*Gerät*) set square; (*in Raum*) corner; **im rechten ~ zu** at right angles to
winken *vt, vi* to wave
Winter (*-s, -*) *m* winter
Winterausrüstung *f* (*Auto*) winter equipment
Winterfahrplan *m* winter timetable
winterlich *adj* wintry
Wintermantel *m* winter coat
Winterreifen *m* winter tire
Winterschlussverkauf *m* winter sales *pl*
Wintersport *m* winter sports *pl*
Winterzeit *f* (*Uhrzeit*) standard time
winzig *adj* tiny
wir *pron* we; **wir selbst** we ourselves; **wir alle** all of us; **wir drei** the three of us; **wir sind's** it's us; **wir nicht** not us
Wirbel (*-s, -*) *m* whirl; (*Trubel*) hubbub, hustle and bustle; (*Aufsehen*) fuss; (*Anat*) vertebra
Wirbelsäule *f* spine
wirken *vi* to be effective; (*erfolgreich sein*) to work; (*scheinen*) to seem
wirklich *adj* real
Wirklichkeit *f* reality
wirksam *adj* effective
Wirkung *f* effect
wirr *adj* confused
Wirrwarr (*-s*) *m* confusion

Wirsing (*-s*) *m* savoy cabbage
Wirt (*-(e)s, -e*) *m* landlord
Wirtin *f* landlady
Wirtschaft *f* (*Comm*) economy; (*Gaststätte*) bar
wirtschaftlich *adj* (*Pol, Comm*) economic; (*sparsam*) economical
Wirtshaus *nt* bar
wischen *vt, vi* to wipe
Wischer (*-s, -*) *m* wiper
wissen (**wusste, gewusst**) *vt* to know; **weißt du schon, ...?** did you know ...?; **woher weißt du das?** how do you know that?; **das musst du selbst ~** that's up to you
Wissen (*-s*) *nt* knowledge
Wissenschaft *f* science
Wissenschaftler(in) (*-s, -*) *m(f)* scientist; (*Geisteswissenschaftler*) academic
wissenschaftlich *adj* scientific; (*geisteswissenschaftlich*) academic
Witwe (*-, -n*) *f* widow
Witwer (*-s, -*) *m* widower
Witz (*-(e)s, -e*) *m* joke; **mach keine ~e!** you're kidding!; **das soll wohl ein ~ sein** you've got to be joking
witzig *adj* funny
wo *adv* where; **zu einer Zeit, wo ...** at a time when ...; **überall, wo ich hingehe** wherever I go ▷ *conj*: **jetzt, wo du da bist** now that you're here; **wo ich dich gerade spreche** while I'm talking to you
woanders *adv* somewhere else
wobei *adv*: **~ mir einfällt ...** which reminds me ...
Woche (*-, -n*) *f* week; **während** *o* **unter der ~** during the week; **einmal die ~** once a week
Wochenende *nt* weekend; **am ~** on the weekend; **wir fahren übers ~ weg** we're going away for the weekend
Wochenendhaus *nt* weekend cottage
Wochenendtrip *m* weekend trip
Wochenendurlaub *m* weekend getaway
Wochenkarte *f* weekly pass
wochenlang *adv* for weeks (on end)
Wochenmarkt *m* farmer's market
Wochentag *m* weekday
wöchentlich *adj, adv* weekly
Wodka (*-s, -s*) *m* vodka
wodurch *adv*: **~ unterscheiden sie sich?** what's the difference between them?; **~ hast du es gemerkt?** how did you notice?
wofür *adv* (*relativ*) for which; (*Frage*) what ... for; **~ brauchst du das?** what do you need that for?

wog *imperf von* **wiegen**
woher *adv* where ... from
wohin *adv* where ... to

wohl *adv* 1: **wohl oder übel** whether one likes it or not
2 (*wahrscheinlich*) probably; (*gewiss*) certainly; (*vielleicht*) perhaps; **sie ist wohl zu Hause** she's probably at home; **das ist doch wohl nicht dein Ernst!** surely you can't be serious!; **das mag wohl sein** that may well be; **ob das wohl stimmt?** I wonder if that's true; **er weiß das sehr wohl** he knows that perfectly well

Wohl (*-(e)s*) *nt*: **zum ~!** cheers!
wohlbehalten *adv* safe and sound
wohl|fühlen *vr*: **sich ~** (*zufrieden*) to feel happy; (*gesundheitlich*) to feel well
Wohlstand *m* prosperity, affluence
wohl|tun (*irr*) *vi*: **jdm ~** to do sb good
Wohlwollen *nt* goodwill
Wohnblock *m* apartment building; (*mit mehreren Gebäuden*) apartment complex
wohnen *vi* to live
Wohngemeinschaft *f* shared apartment; **ich wohne in einer ~** I share an apartment
wohnhaft *adj* resident
Wohnküche *f* eat-in kitchen
Wohnmobil (*-s, -e*) *nt* camper, RV
Wohnort *m* place of residence
Wohnsitz *m* place of residence
Wohnung *f* apartment
Wohnungstür *f* front door
Wohnwagen *m* travel trailer
Wohnzimmer *nt* living room
Wolf (*-(e)s, Wölfe*) *m* wolf
Wolke (*-, -n*) *f* cloud
Wolkenkratzer *m* skyscraper
wolkenlos *adj* cloudless
wolkig *adj* cloudy
Wolldecke *f* wool blanket
Wolle (*-, -n*) *f* wool

wollen (*pt* **wollte**, *pp* **gewollt** *o* (*als Hilfsverb*) **wollen**) *vt*, *vi* to want; **ich will nach Hause** I want to go home; **er will nicht** he doesn't want it; **er wollte das nicht** he didn't want it; **wenn du willst** if you like; **ich will, dass du mir zuhörst** I want you to

listen to me
▷ *Hilfsverb*: **er will ein Haus kaufen** he wants to buy a house; **ich wollte, ich wäre ...** I wish I were ...; **etw gerade tun wollen** to be going to do sth

Wolljacke *f* cardigan
womit *adv* what ... with; **~ habe ich das verdient?** what have I done to deserve that?
womöglich *adv* possibly
woran *adv*: **~ denkst du?** what are you thinking of?; **~ ist er gestorben?** what did he die of?; **~ sieht man das?** how can you tell?
worauf *adv*: **~ wartest du?** what are you waiting for?
woraus *adv*: **~ ist das gemacht?** what is it made of?
Workshop (*-s, -s*) *m* workshop
World Wide Web *nt* World Wide Web
Wort (*-(e) s, Wörter*) *nt* (*Vokabel*) word ▷ (*-(e)s, -e*) *nt* (*Äußerung*) word; **mit anderen ~en** in other words; **jdn beim ~ nehmen** to take sb at his/her word
Wörterbuch *nt* dictionary
wörtlich *adj* literal
worüber *adv*: **~ redet sie?** what is she talking about?
worum *adv*: **~ gehts?** what is it about?
worunter *adv*: **~ leidet er?** what is he suffering from?
wovon *adv* (*relativ*) from which; **~ redest du?** what are you talking about?
wozu *adv* (*relativ*) to/for which; (*interrogativ*) what ... for/to; (*warum*) why; **~?** what for?; **~ brauchst du das?** what do you need it for?; **~ soll das gut sein?** what's it for?; **~ hast du Lust?** what do you feel like doing?
Wrack (*-(e)s, -s*) *nt* wreck
Wucher (*-s*) *m* profiteering; **das ist ~!** that's highway robbery!
wuchs *imperf von* **wachsen**
wühlen *vi* to rummage; (*Tier*) to root; (*Maulwurf*) to burrow
Wühltisch *m* bargain counter
wund *adj* sore
Wunde (*-, -n*) *f* wound
Wunder (*-s, -*) *nt* miracle; **es ist kein ~** it's no wonder
wunderbar *adj* wonderful, marvelous
Wunderkerze *f* sparkler
Wundermittel *nt* miracle cure
wundern *vr*: **sich ~** to be surprised (*über +akk* at) ▷ *vt* to surprise

W

wunderschön *adj* beautiful
wundervoll *adj* wonderful
Wundsalbe *f* antiseptic ointment
Wundstarrkrampf *m* tetanus
Wunsch (*-(e)s, Wünsche*) *m* wish (*nach* for)
wünschen *vt* to wish; **sich** (*dat*) **etw ~** to want sth; **ich wünsche dir alles Gute** I wish you all the best
wünschenswert *adj* desirable
wurde *imperf von* **werden**
Wurf (*-s, Würfe*) *m* throw; (*Zool*) litter
Würfel (*-s, -*) *m* dice; (*Math*) cube
würfeln *vi* to throw (the dice); (*Würfel spielen*) to play dice ▷ *vt* (*Zahl*) to throw; (*Gastr*) to dice
Würfelzucker *m* sugar cubes *pl*
Wurm (*-(e)s, Würmer*) *m* worm
Wurst (*-, Würste*) *f* sausage; **das ist mir ~**

(*fam*) I couldn't care less
Würstchen *nt* frankfurter
Würze (*-, -n*) *f* seasoning, spice
Wurzel (*-, -n*) *f* root
Wurzelbehandlung *f* root canal (work)
würzen *vt* to season, to spice
würzig *adj* spicy
wusch *imperf von* **waschen**
wusste *imperf von* **wissen**
wüst *adj* (*unordentlich*) chaotic; (*ausschweifend*) wild; (*öde*) desolate; (*fam: heftig*) terrible
Wüste (*-, -n*) *f* desert
Wut (*-*) *f* rage, fury; **ich habe eine Wut auf ihn** I'm really mad at him
wütend *adj* furious
WWW (*-*) *nt* (*abk*) = **World Wide Web** WWW

X

X-Beine *pl* knock-knees *pl*
x-beinig *adj* knock-kneed
x-beliebig *adj*: **ein ~es Buch** any book (you like)
x-mal *adv* umpteen times
Xylophon (*-s, -e*) *nt* xylophone

Y

Yoga (-(s)) *m o nt* yoga

Yuppie (-s, -s) *m* (-, -s) *f* yuppie

Z

zackig *adj* (*Linie etc*) jagged; (*fam: Tempo*) brisk

zaghaft *adj* timid

zäh *adj* tough; (*Flüssigkeit*) thick

Zahl (-, -en) *f* number

zahlbar *adj* payable

zahlen *vt, vi* to pay; **~ bitte!** could I have the check please?; **bar ~** to pay cash

zählen *vt, vi* to count (*auf +akk* on); **~ zu** to be one of

Zahlenschloss *nt* combination lock

Zähler (-s, -) *m* (*Gerät*) counter; (*für Strom, Wasser*) meter

zahlreich *adj* numerous

Zahlung *f* payment

Zahlungsanweisung *f* money order

Zahlungsbedingungen *pl* terms *pl* of payment

zahm *adj* tame

zähmen *vt* to tame

Zahn (-(e)s, Zähne) *m* tooth

Zahnarzt *m*, **Zahnärztin** *f* dentist

Zahnbürste *f* toothbrush

Zahncreme *f* toothpaste

Zahnersatz *m* dentures *pl*

Zahnfleisch *nt* gums *pl*

Zahnfleischbluten *nt* bleeding gums *pl*

Zahnfüllung *f* filling

Zahnklammer *f* brace

Zahnpasta *f*, **Zahnpaste** *f* toothpaste

Zahnradbahn *f* rack railroad

Zahnschmerzen *pl* toothache *sing*

Zahnseide *f* dental floss

Zahnspange *f* braces *pl*

Zahnstocher (-s, -) *m* toothpick

Zange (-, -n) *f* pliers *pl*; (*Zuckerzange*) tongs *pl*; (*Beißzange: Zool*) pincers *pl*; (*Med*) forceps *pl*

zanken *vi* to quarrel ▷ *vr:* **sich ~** to quarrel

Zäpfchen *nt* (*Anat*) uvula; (*Med*) suppository

zapfen *vt* (*Bier*) to draw

Zapfsäule *f* gas pump

zappeln *vi* to wriggle; (*unruhig sein*) to fidget

zappen *vi* to zap, to channel-hop

zart *adj* (*weich, leise*) soft; (*Braten etc*) tender; (*fein, schwächlich*) delicate

zartbitter *adj* (*Schokolade*) dark, bittersweet

zärtlich *adj* tender, affectionate

Zärtlichkeit *f* tenderness; **~en** *pl* hugs and kisses *pl*

Zauber (-s, -) *m* magic; (*Bann*) spell

Zauberei *f* magic

Zauberer (-s, -) *m* magician, sorcerer; (*Künstler*) magician

Zauberformel *f* (magic) spell

zauberhaft *adj* enchanting

Zauberin *f* sorceress

Zauberkünstler(in) *m(f)* magician, conjuror

Zaubermittel *nt* magic potion; (*fig*) cure-all; (*gegen Krankheit*) miracle cure

zaubern *vi* to do magic; (*Künstler*) to do magic tricks

Zauberspruch *m* (magic) spell

Zaun (-(e)s, Zäune) *m* fence

z. B. (*abk*) = **zum Beispiel** e.g., eg

ZDF *nt* (= *Zweites Deutsches Fernsehen*) second German television channel

Zebra (-s, -s) *nt* zebra

Zebrastreifen *m* crosswalk

Zecke (-, -n) *f* tick

Zehe (-, -n) *f* toe; (*Knoblauch*) clove

Zehennagel *m* toenail

Zehenspitze *f* tip of one's toes; **auf den ~n** on one's tiptoes

zehn *num* ten

Zehnerkarte *f* ticket valid for ten rides

Zehnkampf *m* decathlon

Zehnkämpfer(in) *m(f)* decathlete

zehnmal *adv* ten times

zehntausend *num* ten thousand

zehnte(r, s) *adj* tenth; *siehe auch* **dritte**

Zehntel (-s, -) *nt* (*Bruchteil*) tenth

Zehntelsekunde *f* tenth of a second

Zeichen (-s, -) *nt* sign; (*Schriftzeichen*) character

Zeichenblock *m* sketch pad

Zeichenerklärung *f* key

Zeichensetzung *f* punctuation

Zeichensprache *f* sign language

Zeichentrickfilm *m* cartoon

zeichnen *vt, vi* to draw

Zeichnung *f* drawing

Zeigefinger *m* index finger

zeigen *vt* to show; **sie zeigte uns die Stadt** she showed us around the town; **zeig mal!** let me see! ▷ *vi* to point (*auf +akk* to, at) ▷ *vr:* **sich ~** to show oneself; **es wird sich ~** time will tell

Zeiger (-s, -) *m* pointer; (*Uhr*) hand

Zeile (-, -n) *f* line

Z

Zeit (-, -en) f time; **ich habe keine ~** I haven't got time; **lass dir ~ take your time; das hat ~ there's no rush; von ~ zu ~** from time to time

Zeitansage f (Tel) correct time

Zeitarbeit f temporary work

zeitgenössisch adj contemporary, modern

zeitgleich adj simultaneous ▷ adv at exactly the same time

zeitig adj early

Zeitkarte f commutation ticket

zeitlich adj (Reihenfolge) chronological; **es passt ~ nicht** it isn't a convenient time; **ich schaff es ~ nicht** I'm not going to make it

Zeitlupe f slow motion

Zeitplan m schedule

Zeitpunkt m point in time

Zeitraum m period (of time)

Zeitschrift f magazine; (wissenschaftliche) journal, periodical

Zeitung f newspaper; **es steht in der ~** it's in the paper(s)

Zeitungsanzeige f newspaper advertisement

Zeitungsartikel m newspaper article

Zeitungskiosk m, **Zeitungsstand** m newsstand

Zeitunterschied m time difference

Zeitverschiebung f time difference

Zeitvertreib (-(e)s, -e) m: **zum ~** to pass the time

zeitweise adv occasionally

Zeitzone f time zone

Zelle (-, -n) f cell

Zellophan® (-s) nt cellophane, plastic wrap

Zelt (-(e)s, -e) nt tent

zelten vi to camp, to go camping

Zeltplatz m campground, campsite

Zement (-(e)s, -e) m cement

Zentimeter m o nt centimeter

Zentner (-s, -) m (metric) hundredweight; (in Deutschland) fifty kilos; (in Österreich und der Schweiz) one hundred kilos

zentral adj central

Zentrale (-, -n) f central office; (Tel) switchboard, exchange

Zentralheizung f central heating

Zentrum (-s, Zentren) nt center

zerbrechen (irr) vt, vi to break

zerbrechlich adj fragile

Zeremonie (-, -n) f ceremony

zergehen (irr) vi to dissolve; (schmelzen) to melt

zerkleinern vt to cut up; (zerhacken) to chop (up)

zerkratzen vt to scratch (up)

zerlegen vt to take apart; (Gerät, Maschine) to dismantle; (Fleisch) to carve

zerquetschen vt to squash

zerreißen (irr) vt to tear apart (o to pieces) ▷ vi to tear

zerren vt to drag; **sich** (dat) **einen Muskel ~** to pull a muscle ▷ vi to tug (an +dat at)

Zerrung f (Med) pulled muscle

zerschlagen (irr) vt to smash ▷ vr: **sich ~** to come to nothing

zerschneiden (irr) vt to cut up

zerstören vt to destroy

Zerstörung f destruction

zerstreuen vt to scatter; (Menge) to disperse; (Zweifel etc) to dispel ▷ vr: **sich ~** (Menge) to disperse

zerstreut adj scattered; (Mensch) absent-minded; (kurzfristig) distracted

zerteilen vt to split up

Zertifikat (-(e)s, -e) nt certificate

Zettel (-s, -) m piece of paper; (Notizzettel) note

Zeug (-(e)s, -e) nt (fam) stuff; (Ausrüstung) gear; **dummes ~** nonsense

Zeuge (-n, -n) m, **Zeugin** f witness

Zeugnis nt certificate; (Schule) report card; (Referenz) reference

z. H(d). (abk) = **zu Händen von** attn

zickig adj (fam) touchy; (vulg) bitchy

Zickzack (-(e)s, -e) m: **im ~ fahren** to zigzag (across the road)

Ziege (-, -n) f goat

Ziegel (-s, -) m brick; (Dach) tile

Ziegenkäse m goat's cheese

Ziegenpeter m mumps

ziehen (zog, gezogen) vt to draw; (zerren) to pull; (Spielfigur) to move; (züchten) to raise; (Pflanzen) to grow ▷ vi (zerren) to pull; (sich bewegen) to move; (Rauch, Wolke etc) to drift; **den Tee ~ lassen** to let the tea steep ▷ vi impers: **es zieht** there's a draft ▷ vr: **sich ~** (Treffen, Rede) to drag on

Ziel (-(e)s, -e) nt (Reise) destination; (Sport) finish; (Absicht) goal, aim

zielen vi to aim (auf +akk at)

Zielgruppe f target group

ziellos adj aimless

Zielscheibe f target

ziemlich adj considerable; **ein ~es Durcheinander** quite a mess; **mit ~er Sicherheit** with some certainty ▷ adv rather, quite; ~

viel quite a lot

zierlich *adj* dainty; (*Frau*) petite

Ziffer (-, -*n*) *f* figure; **arabische/römische ~n** *pl* Arabic/Roman numerals *pl*

Zifferblatt *nt* dial, face

zig *adj* (*fam*) umpteen

Zigarette *f* cigarette

Zigarettenautomat *m* cigarette machine

Zigarettenpapier *nt* cigarette paper

Zigarettenschachtel *f* cigarette pack

Zigarettenstummel *m* cigarette butt

Zigarillo (-*s*, -*s*) *m* cigarillo

Zigarre (-, -*n*) *f* cigar

Zigeuner(in) (-*s*, -) *m(f)* gipsy

Zimmer (-*s*, -) *nt* room; **haben Sie ein ~ für zwei Personen?** do you have a room for two?

Zimmerlautstärke *f* reasonable volume

Zimmermädchen *nt* chambermaid

Zimmermann *m* carpenter

Zimmerpflanze *f* house plant

Zimmerschlüssel *m* room key

Zimmerservice *m* room service

Zimmervermittlung *f* rental agency

Zimt (-(*e*)*s*, -*e*) *m* cinnamon

Zimtstange *f* cinnamon stick

Zink (-(*e*)*s*) *nt* zinc

Zinn (-(*e*)*s*) *nt* (*Element*) tin; (*legiertes*) pewter

Zinsen *pl* interest *sing*

Zipfel (-*s*, -) *m* corner; (*spitz*) tip; (*Hemd*) tail; (*Wurst*) end

Zipfelmütze *f* pointed hat

zirka *adv* about, approximately

Zirkel (-*s*, -) *m* (*Math*) (pair of) compasses *pl*

Zirkus (-, -*se*) *m* circus

zischen *vi* to hiss

Zitat (-(*e*)*s*, -*e*) *nt* quotation (*aus* from)

zitieren *vt* to quote

Zitronat (-(*e*)*s*) *nt* candied lemon peel

Zitrone (-, -*n*) *f* lemon

Zitronenlimonade *f* lemonade

Zitronensaft *m* lemon juice

zittern *vi* to tremble (*vor* +*dat* with)

zivil *adj* civilian; (*Preis*) reasonable

Zivil (-*s*) *nt* plain clothes *pl*; (*Mil*) civilian clothes *pl*

Zivildienst *m* community service (*for conscientious objectors*)

zocken *vi* (*fam*) to gamble

Zoff (-*s*) *m* (*fam*) trouble

zog *imperf von* **ziehen**

zögerlich *adj* hesitant

zögern *vi* to hesitate

Zoll (-(*e*)*s*, *Zölle*) *m* customs *pl*; (*Abgabe*) duty

Zollabfertigung *f* customs clearance

Zollamt *nt* customs office

Zollbeamte(r) *m*, **-beamtin** *f* customs official

Zollerklärung *f* customs declaration

zollfrei *adj* duty-free

Zollgebühren *pl* customs duties *pl*

Zollkontrolle *f* customs check

Zöllner(in) *m(f)* customs officer

zollpflichtig *adj* liable to duty

Zombie (-*s*, -*s*) *m* zombie

Zone (-, -*n*) *f* zone

Zoo (-*s*, -*s*) *m* zoo

Zoom (-*s*, -*s*) *nt* zoom (shot); (*Objektiv*) zoom (lens)

Zopf (-(*e*)*s*, *Zöpfe*) *m* braid

Zorn (-(*e*)*s*) *m* anger

zornig *adj* angry (*über etw akk* about sth, *auf jdn* with sb)

SCHLÜSSELWORT

zu *prep* +*dat* **1** (*örtlich*) to; **zum Bahnhof/ Arzt gehen** to go to the station/doctor; **zur Schule/Kirche gehen** to go to school/ church; **sollen wir zu euch gehen?** shall we go to your place?; **sie sah zu ihm hin** she looked towards him; **zum Fenster herein** through the window; **zu meiner Linken** to *o* on my left

2 (*zeitlich*) at; **zu Ostern** at Easter; **bis zum 1. Mai** until May 1st; (*nicht später als*) by May 1st; **zu meiner Zeit** in my time

3 (*Zusatz*) with; **Wein zum Essen trinken** to drink wine with one's meal; **sich zu jdm setzen** to sit down beside sb; **setz dich doch zu uns** (come and) sit with us; **Anmerkungen zu etw** notes on sth

4 (*Zweck*) for; **Wasser zum Waschen** water for washing; **Papier zum Schreiben** paper to write on; **etw zum Geburtstag bekommen** to get sth for one's birthday

5 (*Veränderung*) into; **zu etw werden** to turn into sth; **jdn zu etw machen** to make sb (into) sth; **zu Asche verbrennen** to burn to ashes

6 (*mit Zahlen*): **3 zu 2** (*Sport*) 3-2; **das Stück zu fünf Euro** at five euros each; **zum ersten Mal** for the first time

7: **zu meiner Freude** to my joy; **zum Glück** luckily; **zu Fuß** on foot; **es ist zum Weinen** it's enough to make you cry

▷ *konj* to; **etw zu essen** sth to eat; **um bes-**

ser sehen zu können in order to see better; **ohne es zu wissen** without knowing
it; **noch zu bezahlende Rechnungen** bills
that are still to be paid, outstanding bills
▷ *adv* 1 (*allzu*) too; **zu sehr** too much; **zu
viel** too much; **zu wenig** too little
2 (*örtlich*) toward(s); **er kam auf mich zu**
he came up to me
3 (*geschlossen*) shut, closed; **die Geschäfte
haben zu** the stores are closed; **„auf/zu"**
(*Wasserhahn etc*) "on/off"
4 (*fam: los*): **nur zu!** just keep on!; **mach
zu!** hurry up!

zuallererst *adv* first of all
zuallerletzt *adv* last of all
Zubehör (-(e)s, -e) *nt* accessories *pl*
zu|bereiten *vt* to prepare
Zubereitung *f* preparation
zu|binden (*irr*) *vt* to tie up; (*Schuhe*) to tie
Zucchini *pl* zucchini
züchten *vt* (*Tiere*) to breed; (*Pflanzen*) to
grow
zucken *vi* to jerk; (*krampfhaft*) to twitch;
(*Strahl etc*) to flicker; **mit den Schultern ~**
to shrug (one's shoulders)
Zucker (-s, -) *m* sugar; (*Med*) diabetes *sing*
Zuckerdose *f* sugar bowl
zuckerkrank *adj* diabetic
Zuckerrohr *nt* sugar cane
Zuckerrübe *f* sugar beet
Zuckerwatte *f* cotton candy
zu|decken *vt* to cover up
zu|drehen *vt* to turn off
zueinander *adv* to one other; (*mit Verb*)
together
zueinander|halten (*irr*) *vi* to stick togeth-
er
zuerst *adv* first; (*zu Anfang*) at first; **~ einmal** first of all
Zufahrt *f* access; (*Einfahrt*) drive(way)
Zufahrtsstraße *f* access road; (*Autobahn*)
ramp
Zufall *m* chance; (*Ereignis*) coincidence;
durch ~ by accident; **so ein ~!** what a coincidence!
zufällig *adj* chance ▷ *adv* by chance; **weißt
du ~, ob ...?** do you happen to know
whether ...?
zufrieden *adj* content(ed); (*befriedigt*) satisfied; **lass sie ~** leave her alone (*o* in
peace)
zufrieden|geben (*irr*) *vr*: **sich mit etw ~** to
settle for sth
Zufriedenheit *f* contentment; (*Befriedigt-*

sein) satisfaction
zufrieden|stellen *vt*: **sie ist schwer zufrie-
denzustellen** she is hard to please
zu|fügen *vt* to add (*dat* to); **jdm Schaden/
Schmerzen ~** to cause sb harm/pain
Zug (-(e)s, Züge) *m* (*Eisenb*) train; (*Luft*)
draft; (*Ziehen*) pull; (*Gesichtszug*) feature;
(*Schach*) move; (*Charakterzug*) trait; (*an
Zigarette*) puff, drag; (*Schluck*) gulp
Zugabe *f* extra; (*in Konzert etc*) encore
Zugabteil *nt* train compartment
Zugang *m* access; **„kein ~!"** 'do not enter!'
Zugauskunft *f* (*Stelle*) train information
office/desk
Zugbegleiter(in) *m(f)* conductor
zu|geben (*irr*) *vt* (*zugestehen*) to admit
zugegeben *adv* admittedly
zu|gehen (*irr*) *vi* (*schließen*) to shut; **auf
jdn/etw ~** to walk towards sb/sth; **dem
Ende ~** to be coming to a close ▷ *vi impers*
(*sich ereignen*) to happen; **es ging lustig
zu** we/they had a lot of fun; **dort geht es
streng zu** it's strict there
Zügel (-s, -) *m* rein
Zugführer(in) *m(f)* conductor
zugig *adj* drafty
zügig *adj* speedy
zugleich *adv* (*zur gleichen Zeit*) at the same
time; (*ebenso*) both
Zugluft *f* draft
Zugpersonal *nt* train staff
zu|greifen (*irr*) *vi* (*fig*) to seize the opportu-
nity; (*beim Essen*) to help oneself; **~ auf
+akk** (*Inform*) to access
Zugrestauraunt *nt* diner
Zugriffsberechtigung *f* (*Inform*) access
right
zugrunde *adv*: **~ gehen** to perish; **~ gehen
an** +*dat* (*sterben*) to die of
Zugschaffner(in) *m(f)* conductor
Zugunglück *nt* train crash
zugunsten *prep* (+*gen o dat*) in favor of
Zugverbindung *f* train connection
zu|haben (*irr*) *vi* to be closed
zu|halten (*irr*) *vt*: **sich** (*dat*) **die Nase ~** to
hold one's nose; **sich** (*dat*) **die Ohren ~** to
hold one's hands over one's ears; **die Tür ~**
to hold the door shut
Zuhause (-s) *nt* home
zu|hören *vi* to listen (*dat* to)
Zuhörer(in) *m(f)* listener
zu|kleben *vt* to seal
zu|kommen (*irr*) *vi* to come up (*auf +akk*
to); **jdm etw ~ lassen** to give/send sb sth;
etw auf sich (*akk*) **~ lassen** to take sth as

it comes

zu|kriegen *vt*: **ich krieg den Koffer nicht zu** I can't shut the case

Zukunft (-, *Zukünfte*) *f* future

zukünftig *adj* future ▷ *adv* in future

zu|lassen (*irr*) *vt* (*hereinlassen*) to admit; (*erlauben*) to permit; (*Auto*) to register; (*fam: nicht öffnen*) to keep shut

zulässig *adj* permissible, permitted

zuletzt *adv* finally, at last

zuliebe *adv*: **jdm ~** for sb's sake

zum *kontr von* **zu dem**; **zum dritten Mal** for the third time; **zum Scherz** as a joke; **zum Trinken** for drinking

zu|machen *vt* to shut; (*Kleidung*) to button (*o* zip) up ▷ *vi* to shut

zumindest *adv* at least

zu|muten *vt*: **jdm etw ~** to expect sth of sb ▷ *vr*: **sich** (*dat*) **zu viel ~** to overdo things

zunächst *adv* first of all; **~ einmal** to start with

Zunahme (-, *-n*) *f* increase

Zuname *m* surname, last name

zünden *vt*, *vi* (*Auto*) to ignite, to fire

Zündkabel *f* (*Auto*) ignition cable

Zündkerze *f* (*Auto*) spark plug

Zündschloss *nt* ignition lock

Zündung *f* ignition

zu|nehmen (*irr*) *vi* to increase; (*Mensch*) to put on weight ▷ *vt*: **fünf Kilo ~** to gain five kilos

Zunge (-, *-n*) *f* tongue

Zungenkuss *m* French kiss

zunichte|machen *vt* (*zerstören*) to ruin

zunutze *adv*: **sich** (*dat*) **etw ~ machen** to make use of sth

zu|parken *vt* to block

zur *kontr von* **zu der**

zurecht|finden (*irr*) *vr*: **sich ~** to find one's way around

zurecht|kommen (*irr*) *vi* to cope (**mit etw** with sth)

zurecht|machen *vt* to prepare ▷ *vr*: **sich ~** to get ready

Zürich (*-s*) *nt* Zurich

zurück *adv* back

zurück|bekommen (*irr*) *vt* to get back

zurück|blicken *vi* to look back (**auf** +*akk* at)

zurück|bringen (*irr*) *vt* (*hierhin*) to bring back; (*woandershin*) to take back

zurück|erstatten *vt* to refund

zurück|fahren (*irr*) *vi* to go back

zurück|geben (*irr*) *vt* to give back; (*antworten*) to answer

zurück|gehen (*irr*) *vi* to go back; (*zeitlich*) to date back (**auf** +*akk* to)

zurück|halten (*irr*) *vt* to hold back; (*hindern*) to prevent ▷ *vr*: **sich ~** to hold back

zurückhaltend *adj* reserved

zurück|holen *vt* to get (*o* bring) back

zurück|kommen (*irr*) *vi* to come back; **auf etw** (*akk*) **~** to return (*o* get back) to sth

zurück|lassen (*irr*) *vt* to leave behind

zurück|legen (*irr*) *vt* to put back; (*Geld*) to set aside; (*reservieren*) to keep back; (*Strecke*) to cover

zurück|nehmen (*irr*) *vt* to take back

zurück|rufen (*irr*) *vt* to call back

zurück|schicken *vt* to send back

zurück|stellen *vt* to put back

zurück|treten (*irr*) *vi* to step back; (*von Amt*) to step down

zurück|verlangen *vt*: **etw ~** to ask for sth back

zurück|zahlen *vt* to pay back

zurzeit *adv* at present

Zusage *f* promise; (*Annahme*) acceptance

zu|sagen *vt* to promise ▷ *vi* to accept; **jdm ~** (*gefallen*) to appeal to sb

zusammen *adv* together

Zusammenarbeit *f* collaboration

zusammen|arbeiten *vi* to work together

zusammen|brechen (*irr*) *vi* to collapse; (*psychisch*) to break down

Zusammenbruch *m* collapse; (*psychischer*) breakdown

zusammen|fassen *vt* to summarize; (*vereinigen*) to unite

zusammenfassend *adj* summarizing ▷ *adv* to summarize

Zusammenfassung *f* summary

zusammen|gehören *vi* to belong together

zusammen|halten (*irr*) *vi* to stick together

Zusammenhang *m* connection; **im/aus dem ~** in/out of context

zusammen|hängen (*irr*) *vi* to be connected

zusammenhängend *adj* coherent

zusammenhang(s)los *adj* incoherent

zusammen|klappen *vi*, *vt* to fold up

zusammen|knüllen *vt* to screw up

zusammen|kommen (*irr*) *vi* to meet; (*sich ereignen*) to happen together

zusammen|legen *vt* to fold up ▷ *vi* (*Geld sammeln*) to chip (*o* pitch) in

zusammen|nehmen (*irr*) *vt* to summon up; **alles zusammengenommen** all in all ▷ *vr*: **sich ~** to pull oneself together; (*fam*) to

z

get a grip, to get one's act together

zusammen|passen vi to go together; (*Personen*) to fit together

zusammen|rechnen vt to add up

Zusammensein (*-s*) nt get-together

zusammen|setzen vt to put together ▷ vr: **sich ~ aus** to be composed of

Zusammensetzung f composition

Zusammenstoß m crash, collision

zusammen|stoßen (*irr*) vi to crash (*mit* into)

zusammen|zählen vt to add up

zusammen|ziehen (*irr*) vi (*in Wohnung etc*) to move in together

Zusatz m addition

zusätzlich adj additional ▷ adv in addition

zu|schauen vi to watch

Zuschauer(in) (*-s, -*) m(f) spectator; **die ~** pl (*Theat*) the audience *sing*

Zuschauertribüne f stand

zu|schicken vt to send

Zuschlag m extra charge; (*Fahrkarte*) supplement

zuschlagpflichtig adj subject to an extra charge; (*Eisenb*) subject to a supplement

zu|schließen (*irr*) vt to lock up

zu|sehen (*irr*) vi to watch (*jdm* sb); **~, dass** (*dafür sorgen*) to make sure that

zu|sichern vt: **jdm etw ~** to assure sb of sth

Zustand m state, condition; **sie bekommt Zustände, wenn sie das sieht** (*fam*) she'll have a fit if she sees that

zustande adv: **~ bringen** to bring about; **~ kommen** to come about

zuständig adj (*Behörde*) relevant; **~ für** responsible for

Zustellung f delivery

zu|stimmen vi to agree (*einer Sache dat* to sth, *jdm* with sb)

Zustimmung f approval

zu|stoßen (*irr*) vi (*fig*) to happen (*jdm* to sb)

Zutaten pl ingredients pl

zu|trauen vt: **jdm etw ~** to think sb is capable of sth; **das hätte ich ihm nie zugetraut** I'd never have thought he was capable of it; **ich würde es ihr ~** (*etw Negatives*) I wouldn't put it past her

Zutrauen (*-s*) nt confidence (*zu* in)

zutraulich adj trusting; (*Tier*) friendly

zu|treffen (*irr*) vi to be correct; **~ auf** +*akk* to apply to; **Z~des bitte streichen** please delete as applicable

Zutritt m entry; (*Zugang*) access; **~ verboten!** do not enter!

zuverlässig adj reliable

Zuverlässigkeit f reliability

Zuversicht f confidence

zuversichtlich adj confident

zuvor adv before; (*zunächst*) first

zuvor|kommen (*irr*) vi: **jdm ~** to beat sb to it

zuvorkommend adj obliging

Zuwachs (*-es, Zuwächse*) m increase, growth; (*fam: Baby*) addition to the family

zuwider adv: **es ist mir ~** I hate (*o detest*) it

zu|winken vi: **jdm ~** to wave to sb

zuzüglich prep (+*gen*) plus

zwang imperf von **zwingen**

Zwang (*-(e)s, Zwänge*) m (*innerer*) compulsion; (*Gewalt*) force

zwängen vt to squeeze (*in* +*akk* into) ▷ vr: **sich ~** to squeeze (*in* +*akk* into)

zwanglos adj informal

zwanzig num twenty

zwanzigste(r, s) adj twentieth; *siehe auch* **dritte**

zwar adv: **und ~ ...** (*genauer*) ..., to be precise; **das ist ~ schön, aber ...** it is nice, but ...; **ich kenne ihn ~, aber ...** I know him all right, but ...

Zweck (*-(e)s, -e*) m purpose

zwecklos adj pointless

zwei num two

Zwei (*-, -en*) f two; (*Schulnote*) ≈ B

Zweibettzimmer nt double room

zweideutig adj ambiguous; (*unanständig*) suggestive

zweifach adj, adv double

Zweifel (*-s, -*) m doubt

zweifellos adv undoubtedly

zweifeln vi to doubt (*an etw dat* sth)

Zweifelsfall m: **im ~** in case of doubt

Zweig (*-(e)s, -e*) m branch

Zweigstelle f branch

zweihundert num two hundred

zweimal adv twice

zweisprachig adj bilingual

zweispurig adj (*Auto*) two-lane

zweit adv: **wir sind zu ~** there are two of us

zweite(r, s) adj second; *siehe auch* **dritte**; **eine ~ Portion** a second helping

zweitens adv secondly; (*bei Aufzählungen*) second

zweitgrößte(r, s) adj second largest

Zweitschlüssel m spare key

Zwerchfell nt diaphragm

Zwerg(in) (*-(e)s, -e*) m(f) dwarf

Zwetschge (-, -n) *f* plum
zwicken *vt* to pinch
Zwieback (-*(e)s*, -e) *m* zwieback, rusk
Zwiebel (-, -n) *f* onion; (*von Blume*) bulb
Zwiebelsuppe *f* onion soup
Zwilling (-*s*, -e) *m* twin; **~e** *pl* (*Astr*) Gemini *sing*
zwingen (**zwang, gezwungen**) *vt* to force
zwinkern *vi* to blink; (*absichtlich*) to wink
zwischen *prep* (+*akk o dat*) between
Zwischenablage *f* (*Inform*) clipboard
zwischendurch *adv* in between
Zwischenfall *m* incident

Zwischenlandung *f* stopover
zwischenmenschlich *adj* interpersonal
Zwischenraum *m* space
Zwischenstopp (-*s*, -*s*) *m* stopover
Zwischensumme *f* subtotal
Zwischenzeit *f*: **in der ~** in the meantime
zwitschern *vt, vi* to twitter, to chirp
zwölf *num* twelve
zwölfte(r, s) *adj* twelfth; *siehe auch* **dritte**
Zylinder (-*s*, -) *m* cylinder; (*Hut*) top hat
zynisch *adj* cynical
Zypern (-*s*) *nt* Cyprus
Zyste (-, -n) *f* cyst

z

English–German
Dictionary

A

a [ə, STRONG eɪ] (*before vowel or silent h:* **an**) *indef art* **1** ein, eine; **a woman** eine Frau; **a book** ein Buch; **an eagle** ein Adler; **she's a doctor** sie ist Ärztin

2 (*instead of the number "one"*) ein, eine; **a year ago** vor einem Jahr; **a hundred/thousand** *etc* **dollars** (ein) hundert/(ein) tausend *etc* Dollar

3 (*in expressing ratios, prices etc*) pro; **3 a day/week** 3 pro Tag/Woche, 3 am Tag/in der Woche; **10 km an hour** 10 km pro Stunde/in der Stunde

aback [əˈbæk] *adv:* **taken ~** erstaunt

abandon [əˈbændən] *vt* (*desert*) verlassen; (*give up*) aufgeben

abbey [ˈæbɪ] *n* Abtei *f*

abbreviate [əˈbriːvɪeɪt] *vt* abkürzen

abbreviation [əˈbriːvɪeɪʃⁿn] *n* Abkürzung *f*

ABC [eɪ biː siː] *n* (*a. fig*) Abc *nt*

abdicate [ˈæbdɪkeɪt] *vi* (*king*) abdanken

abdication [æbdɪˈkeɪʃⁿn] *n* Abdankung *f*

abdomen [ˈæbdoʊmən] *n* Unterleib *m*

ability [əˈbɪlɪtɪ] *n* Fähigkeit *f*

able [eɪbⁿl] *adj* fähig; **to be ~ to do sth** etw tun können

abnormal [æbˈnɔːrmⁿl] *adj* anormal

aboard [əˈbɔːrd] *adv, prep* an Bord +*gen*

abolish [əˈbɒlɪʃ] *vt* abschaffen

aborigine [æbəˈrɪdʒɪnɪ] *n* Ureinwohner(in) *m(f)* (Australiens)

abort [əˈbɔːrt] *vt* (*Med: fetus*) abtreiben; (*Space: mission*) abbrechen

abortion [əˈbɔːrʃⁿn] *n* Abtreibung *f*

about [əˈbaʊt] *adv* **1** (*approximately*) etwa, ungefähr; **about a hundred/thousand** *etc* etwa hundert/tausend *etc*; **at about 2 o'clock** etwa um 2 Uhr; **I've just about finished** ich bin gerade fertig

2 (*referring to place*) herum, umher; **to leave things lying about** Sachen herumliegen lassen; **to run/walk** *etc* **about** herumrennen/gehen *etc*

3: **to be about to do sth** im Begriff sein, etw zu tun; **he was about to go to bed** er wollte gerade ins Bett gehen

▷ *prep* **1** (*relating to*) über +*akk*; **a book**
about London ein Buch über London; **what is it about?** worum geht es?; (*book etc*) wovon handelt es?; **we talked about it** wir haben darüber geredet; **what** *o* **how about doing this?** wollen wir das machen?

2 (*referring to place*) um (... herum); **to walk about the town** in der Stadt herumgehen; **her clothes were scattered about the room** ihre Kleider waren über das ganze Zimmer verstreut

above [əˈbʌv] *adv* oben; **children aged 8 and ~** Kinder ab 8 Jahren; **on the floor ~** ein Stockwerk höher ▷ *prep* über; **~ 40 degrees** über 40 Grad; **~ all** vor allem ▷ *adj* obig

abroad [əˈbrɔːd] *adv* im Ausland; **to go ~** ins Ausland gehen

abrupt [əˈbrʌpt] *adj* (*sudden*) plötzlich, abrupt

abscess [ˈæbsɛs] *n* Geschwür *nt*

absence [ˈæbsⁿns] *n* Abwesenheit *f*

absent [ˈæbsⁿnt] *adj* abwesend; **to be ~** fehlen

absentminded [æbsⁿntˈmaɪndɪd] *adj* zerstreut

absolute [ˈæbsəluːt] *adj* absolut; (*power*) unumschränkt; (*rubbish*) vollkommen, total

absolutely [æbsəˈluːtlɪ] *adv* absolut; (*true, stupid*) vollkommen; **~!** genau!; **you're ~ right** du hast/Sie haben völlig recht

absorb [əbˈsɔːrb, -zɔːrb] *vt* absorbieren; (*fig: information*) in sich aufnehmen

absorbed [əbˈsɔːrbd, -zɔːrbd] *adj:* **~ in sth** etw vertieft

absorbent [əbˈsɔːrbənt, -zɔːrbənt] *adj* absorbierend; **~ cotton** Watte *f*

absorbing [əbˈsɔːrbɪŋ, -zɔːrbɪŋ] *adj* (*fig*) faszinierend, fesselnd

abstain [æbˈsteɪn] *vi:* **to ~ from voting** sich (der Stimme) enthalten

abstract [ˈæbstrækt] *adj* abstrakt

absurd [əbˈsɜːrd, -zɜːrd] *adj* absurd

abundance [əˈbʌndəns] *n* Reichtum *m* (*of* an +*dat*)

abuse [*n* əˈbjuːs, *vb* əˈbjuːz] *n* (*rude language*) Beschimpfungen *pl*; (*mistreatment*) Missbrauch *m* ▷ *vt* (*misuse*) missbrauchen

abusive [əˈbjuːsɪv] *adj* beleidigend

AC [eɪ siː] *abbr* = **alternating current** Wechselstrom *m*; = **air conditioning** Klimaanlage
a/c (*abbr*) = **account** Kto.
academic [ækədɛmɪk] *n* Wissenschaftler(in) *m(f)* ▷ *adj* akademisch, wissenschaftlich
accelerate [æksɛlərɛɪt] *vi* (*car etc*) beschleunigen; (*driver*) Gas geben
acceleration [æksɛlərɛɪʃn] *n* Beschleunigung *f*
accelerator [æksɛlərɛɪtər] *n* Gas(pedal) *nt*
accent [æksɛnt] *n* Akzent *m*
accept [æksɛpt] *vt* annehmen; (*agree to*) akzeptieren; (*responsibility*) übernehmen
acceptable [æksɛptəbᵊl] *adj* annehmbar
access [æksɛs] *n* Zugang *m*; (*Inform*) Zugriff *m*
accessible [æksɛsɪbᵊl] *adj* (leicht) zugänglich/erreichbar; (*place*) (leicht) erreichbar
accessory [æksɛsəri] *n* Zubehörteil *nt*
access road *n* Zufahrtsstraße *f*
accident [æksɪdənt] *n* Unfall *m*; **by ~** zufällig
accidental [æksɪdɛntᵊl] *adj* unbeabsichtigt; (*meeting*) zufällig; (*death*) durch Unfall; **~ damage** Unfallschaden *m*
accident-prone [æksɪdəntprəʊn] *adj* vom Pech verfolgt
acclimatize [əklaɪmətaɪz] *vt*: **to ~ oneself** sich gewöhnen (*to an* +*akk*)
accommodate [əkɒmədeɪt] *vt* unterbringen
accommodation(s) [əkɒmədeɪʃn(z)] *n* Unterkunft *f*
accompany [əkʌmpəni] *vt* begleiten
accomplish [əkʌmplɪʃ] *vt* erreichen
accord [əkɔːd] *n*: **of one's own ~** freiwillig
according to [əkɔːdɪŋ tu] *prep* nach, laut +*dat*
account [əkaʊnt] *n* (*in bank etc*) Konto *nt*; (*narrative*) Bericht *m*; **on ~ of** wegen; **on no ~** auf keinen Fall; **to take into ~** berücksichtigen, in Betracht ziehen
accountant [əkaʊntənt] *n* Buchhalter(in) *m(f)*
account for *vt* (*explain*) erklären; (*expenditure*) Rechenschaft ablegen für
account number *n* Kontonummer *f*
accumulate [əkjuːmjəleɪt] *vt* ansammeln ▷ *vi* sich ansammeln
accuracy [ækjərəsi] *n* Genauigkeit *f*
accurate [ækjərɪt] *adj* genau
accusation [ækjuːzeɪʃn] *n* Anklage *f*, Beschuldigung *f*

accusative [əkjuːzətɪv] *n* Akkusativ *m*
accuse [əkjuːz] *vt* beschuldigen; (*Jur*) anklagen (*of* wegen +*gen*); **~ sb of doing sth** jdn beschuldigen, etw getan zu haben
accused [əkjuːzd] *n* (*Jur*) Angeklagte(r) *mf*
accustom [əkʌstəm] *vt* gewöhnen (*to an* +*akk*)
accustomed [əkʌstəmd] *adj* gewohnt; **to get ~ to sth** sich an etw *akk* gewöhnen
ace [eɪs] *n* Ass *nt* ▷ *adj* Star-
ache [eɪk] *n* Schmerz *m* ▷ *vi* wehtun
achieve [ətʃiːv] *vt* erreichen
achievement [ətʃiːvmənt] *n* Leistung *f*
acid [æsɪd] *n* Säure *f* ▷ *adj* sauer; **~ rain** saurer Regen
acknowledge [əknɒlɪdʒ] *vt* (*recognize*) anerkennen; (*admit*) zugeben; (*receipt of letter etc*) bestätigen
acknowledgement [əknɒlɪdʒmənt] *n* Anerkennung *f*; (*of letter*) Empfangsbestätigung *f*
acne [ækni] *n* Akne *f*
acorn [eɪkɔːn] *n* Eichel *f*
acoustic [əkuːstɪk] *adj* akustisch
acoustics [əkuːstɪks] *npl* Akustik *f*
acquaintance [əkweɪntəns] *n* (*person*) Bekannte(r) *mf*
acquire [əkwaɪər] *vt* erwerben, sich aneignen
acquisition [ækwɪzɪʃn] *n* (*of skills etc*) Erwerb *m*; (*object*) Anschaffung *f*
acrobat [ækrəbæt] *n* Akrobat(in) *m(f)*
across [əkrɒs] *prep* über +*akk*; **he lives ~ the street** er wohnt auf der anderen Seite der Straße ▷ *adv* hinüber, herüber; **100m ~** 100m breit
act [ækt] *n* (*deed*) Tat *f*; (*Jur: law*) Gesetz *nt*; (*Theat*) Akt *m*; (*fig: pretence*) Schau *f*; **it's all an act** es ist alles nur Theater; **to be in the act of doing sth** gerade dabei sein, etw zu tun ▷ *vi* (*take action*) handeln; (*behave*) sich verhalten; (*Theat*) spielen; **to act as** (*person*) fungieren als; (*thing*) dienen als ▷ *vt* (*a part*) spielen
action [ækʃn] *n* (*of play, novel etc*) Handlung *f*; (*in film etc*) Action *f*; (*Mil*) Kampf *m*; **to take ~** etwas unternehmen; **out of ~** (*machine*) außer Betrieb; **to put a plan into ~** einen Plan in die Tat umsetzen
activate [æktɪveɪt] *vt* aktivieren
active [æktɪv] *adj* aktiv; (*child*) lebhaft
activity [æktɪvɪti] *n* Aktivität *f*; (*occupation*) Beschäftigung *f*; (*organized event*)

Veranstaltung f

actor [ǽktər] n Schauspieler(in) m(f)

actress [ǽktrɪs] n Schauspielerin f

actual [ǽktʃuəl] adj wirklich

actually [ǽktʃuəli] adv eigentlich; (said in surprise) tatsächlich

acupuncture [ǽkyʊpʌŋktʃər] n Akupunktur f

acute [əkyút] adj (pain) akut; (sense of smell) fein; (Math: angle) spitz

AD [eɪ dí] (abbr) = **Anno Domini** nach Christi, n. Chr.

ad [ǽd] see **advertisement**

adapt [ədǽpt] vi sich anpassen (to +dat) ▷ vt anpassen (to +dat); (rewrite) bearbeiten (for für)

adaptable [ədǽptəbᵊl] adj anpassungsfähig

adaptation [ædæpteɪʃᵊn] n (of book etc) Bearbeitung f

adapter [ədǽptər] n (Elec) Zwischenstecker m, Adapter m

add [ǽd] vt (ingredient) hinzufügen; (numbers) addieren

addict [ǽdɪkt] n Süchtige(r) mf

addicted [ədíktɪd] adj: ~ **to alcohol/drugs** alkohol-/drogensüchtig

addition [ədíʃᵊn] n Zusatz m; (to bill) Aufschlag m; (Math) Addition f; **in ~** außerdem, zusätzlich (to zu)

additional [ədíʃənᵊl] adj zusätzlich, weiter

additive [ǽdɪtɪv] n Zusatz m

add-on n Zusatzgerät nt

address [n ǽdrɛs, vb ədrɛ́s] n Adresse f ▷ vt (letter) adressieren; (person) anreden

add up vi (make sense) stimmen ▷ vt (numbers) addieren

adequate [ǽdɪkwɪt] adj (appropriate) angemessen; (sufficient) ausreichend; (time) genügend

adhesive [ædhíːsɪv] n Klebstoff m

adhesive tape n Klebstreifen m

adjacent [ədʒéɪsᵊnt] adj benachbart

adjective [ǽdʒɪktɪv] n Adjektiv nt

adjoining [ədʒɔ́ɪnɪŋ] adj benachbart, Neben-

adjust [ədʒʌ́st] vt einstellen; (put right also) richtig stellen; (speed, flow) regulieren; (in position) verstellen ▷ vi sich anpassen (to +dat)

adjustable [ədʒʌ́stəbᵊl] adj verstellbar

administration [ædmɪnɪstreɪʃᵊn] n Verwaltung f; (Pol) Regierung f

admirable [ǽdmɪrəbᵊl] adj bewundernswert

admiration [ædmɪreɪʃᵊn] n Bewunderung f

admire [ədmáɪər] vt bewundern

admission [ædmíʃᵊn] n (entrance) Zutritt m; (to university etc) Zulassung f; (fee) Eintritt m; (confession) Eingeständnis nt

admission charge, admission fee n Eintrittspreis m

admit [ædmít] vt (let in) hereinlassen (to in +akk); (to university etc) zulassen; (confess) zugeben, gestehen; **to be ~ted to hospital** ins Krankenhaus eingeliefert werden

adolescent [ædəlɛ́sᵊnt] n Jugendliche(r) mf

adopt [ədɑ́pt] vt (child) adoptieren; (idea) übernehmen

adoption [ədɑ́pʃᵊn] n (of child) Adoption f; (of idea) Übernahme f

adorable [ədɔ́rəbᵊl] adj entzückend

adore [ədɔ́r] vt anbeten; (person) über alles lieben, vergöttern

adult [ədʌ́lt] adj (person) erwachsen; (film etc) für Erwachsene ▷ n Erwachsene(r) mf

adultery [ədʌ́ltəri] n Ehebruch m

advance [ædvǽns] n (money) Vorschuss m; (progress) Fortschritt m; **in ~** im Voraus; **to book in ~** vorbestellen ▷ vi (move forward) vorrücken ▷ vt (money) vorschießen

advanced [ædvǽnst] adj (modern) fortschrittlich; (course, study) für Fortgeschrittene

advantage [ædvǽntɪdʒ, -væn-] n Vorteil m; **to take ~ of** (exploit) ausnutzen; (profit from) Nutzen ziehen aus; **it's to your ~** es ist in deinem/Ihrem Interesse

adventure [ædvɛ́ntʃər] n Abenteuer nt

adventurous [ædvɛ́ntʃərəs] adj (person) abenteuerlustig

adverb [ǽdvɜrb] n Adverb nt

adverse [ǽdvɜrs] adj (conditions etc) ungünstig; (effect, comment etc) negativ

advertise [ǽdvərtaɪz] vt werben für; (in newspaper) inserieren; (job) ausschreiben ▷ vi Reklame machen; (in newspaper) annoncieren (for für)

advertisement [ædvərtáɪzmənt] n Werbung f; (announcement) Anzeige f

advertising [ǽdvərtaɪzɪŋ] n Werbung f

advice [ædváɪs] n Rat(schlag) m; **word o piece of ~** Ratschlag m; **take my ~** hör auf mich

advisable [ædváɪzəbᵊl] adj ratsam

advise [ædvaɪz] vt raten (*sb* jdm); **to ~ sb to do sth/not to do sth** jdm zuraten/abraten, etw zu tun

Aegean [ɪdʒiən] *n*: **the ~ Sea** die Ägäis

aerial [ɛərɪəl] *n* Antenne *f* ▷ *adj* Luft-

aerobatics [ɛərəbætɪks] *npl* Kunstfliegen *nt*

aerobics [ɛəroʊbɪks] *nsing* Aerobic *nt*

affair [əfɛər] *n* (*matter, business*) Sache *f*, Angelegenheit *f*; (*scandal*) Affäre *f*; (*love affair*) Verhältnis *nt*

affect [əfɛkt] vt (*influence*) (ein)wirken auf +*akk*; (*health, organ*) angreifen; (*move deeply*) berühren; (*concern*) betreffen

affection [əfɛkʃⁿn] *n* Zuneigung *f*

affectionate [əfɛkʃənɪt] *adj* liebevoll

affluent [æfluənt] *adj* wohlhabend

afford [əfɔrd] vt sich leisten; **I can't ~ it** ich kann es mir nicht leisten

affordable [əfɔrdəbⁿl] *adj* erschwinglich

Afghanistan [æfgænɪstæn] *n* Afghanistan *nt*

aforementioned [əfɔrmɛnʃⁿnd] *adj* oben genannt

afraid [əfreɪd] *adj*: **to be ~** Angst haben (*of* vor +*dat*); **to be ~ that ...** fürchten, dass ...; **I'm ~ I don't know** das weiß ich leider nicht

Africa [æfrɪkə] *n* Afrika *nt*

African [æfrɪkən] *adj* afrikanisch ▷ *n* Afrikaner(in) *m(f)*

African American, Afro-American [æfrou-] *n* Afroamerikaner(in) *m(f)*

after [æftər] *prep* nach; **ten ~ five** zehn nach fünf; **to be ~ sb/sth** (*following, seeking*) hinter jdm/etw her sein; **~ all** schließlich; (*in spite of everything*) (schließlich) doch ▷ *conj* nachdem ▷ *adv*: **soon ~** bald danach

aftercare [æftərkɛər] *n* Nachbehandlung *f*

aftereffect [æftərɪfɛkt] *n* Nachwirkung *f*

afternoon [æftərnun] *n* Nachmittag *m*; **~, good ~** guten Tag!; **in the ~** nachmittags

aftershave (lotion) [æftərʃeɪv (louʃⁿn)] *n* Rasierwasser *nt*

afterwards [æftərwərdz] *adv* nachher; (*after that*) danach

again [əgɛn, əgeɪn] *adv* wieder; (*one more time*) noch einmal; **not ~!** (nicht) schon wieder; **~ and ~** immer wieder; **the same ~ please** das Gleiche noch mal bitte

against [əgɛnst, əgeɪnst] *prep* gegen; **~ my will** wider Willen; **~ the law** unrechtmäßig, illegal

age [eɪdʒ] *n* Alter *nt*; (*period of history*) Zeitalter *nt*; **at the age of four** im Alter von vier (Jahren); **what age is she?, what is her age?** wie alt ist sie?; **to come of age** volljährig werden; **under age** minderjährig ▷ *vi* altern, alt werden

aged [eɪdʒd, eɪdʒɪd] *adj*: **~ thirty** dreißig Jahre alt; **a son ~ twenty** ein zwanzigjähriger Sohn ▷ *adj* (*elderly*) betagt

age group *n* Altersgruppe *f*

ageism [eɪdʒɪzəm] *n* Diskriminierung *f* aufgrund des Alters

age limit *n* Altersgrenze *f*

agency [eɪdʒənsi] *n* Agentur *f*

agenda [ədʒɛndə] *n* Tagesordnung *f*

agent [eɪdʒənt] *n* (*Comm*) Vertreter(in) *m(f)*; (*for writer, actor etc*) Agent(in) *m(f)*

aggression [əgrɛʃⁿn] *n* Aggression *f*

aggressive [əgrɛsɪv] *adj* aggressiv

agitated [ædʒɪteɪtɪd] *adj* aufgeregt; **to get ~** sich aufregen

ago [əgoʊ] *adv*: **two days ago** heute vor zwei Tagen; **not long ago** (erst) vor Kurzem

agonize [ægənaɪz] *vi* sich den Kopf zerbrechen (*over* über *dat*)

agonizing [ægənaɪzɪŋ] *adj* qualvoll

agony [ægəni] *n* Qual *f*

agree [əgri] vt (*date, price etc*) vereinbaren; **to ~ to do sth** sich bereit erklären, etw zu tun; **to ~ that ...** sich *dat* einig sein, dass ...; (*decide*) beschließen, dass ...; (*admit*) zugeben, dass ... ▷ *vi* (*have same opinion, correspond*) übereinstimmen (*with* mit); (*consent*) zustimmen; (*come to an agreement*) sich einigen (*about, on* auf +*akk*); (*food*): **not to ~ with sb** jdm nicht bekommen

agreement [əgrimənt] *n* (*agreeing*) Übereinstimmung *f*; (*contract*) Abkommen *nt*, Vereinbarung *f*

agricultural [ægrɪkʌltʃərəl] *adj* landwirtschaftlich, Landwirtschafts-

agriculture [ægrɪkʌltʃər] *n* Landwirtschaft *f*

ahead [əhɛd] *adv*: **to be ~** führen, vorne liegen; **~ of** vor +*dat*; **to be ~ of sb** (*person*) jdm voraus sein; (*thing*) vor jdm liegen; **to be 3 meters ~** 3 Meter Vorsprung haben

aid [eɪd] *n* Hilfe *f*; **in aid of** zugunsten +*gen*; **with the aid of** mithilfe +*gen* ▷ *vt* helfen +*dat*; (*support*) unterstützen

AIDS [eɪdz] *n* (*acr*) = **acquired immune deficiency syndrome** Aids *nt*

aim [eɪm] vt (*gun, camera*) richten (*at* auf +*akk*) ▷ *vi*: **to aim at** (*with gun etc*) zielen

auf +*akk*; (*fig*) abzielen auf +*akk*; **to aim to
do sth** beabsichtigen, etw zu tun ▷ *n* Ziel
nt

air [ɛər] *n* Luft *f*; **in the open air** im Freien;
(*Radio, TV*): **to be on the air** (*programme*)
auf Sendung sein; (*station*) senden ▷ *vt*
lüften

airbag [ɛərbæg] *n* (*Auto*) Airbag *m*

air-conditioned [ɛərkəndɪ̈ʂᵊnd] *adj* mit
Klimaanlage

air-conditioning [ɛərkəndɪ̈ʂᵊnɪŋ] *n* Klimaanlage *f*

aircraft [ɛərkræft] *n* Flugzeug *nt*

airfield [ɛərfild] *n* Flugplatz *m*

air force *n* Luftwaffe *f*

airgun [ɛərgʌn] *n* Luftgewehr *nt*

airline [ɛərlaɪn] *n* Fluggesellschaft *f*

airmail [ɛərmeɪl] *n* Luftpost *f*; **by ~** mit
Luftpost

airplane [ɛərpleɪn] *n* Flugzeug *nt*

air pollution *n* Luftverschmutzung *f*

airport [ɛərpɔrt] *n* Flughafen *m*

airsick [ɛərsɪk] *adj* luftkrank

airsick(ness) bag *n* Spucktüte *f*

airtight [ɛərtaɪt] *adj* luftdicht

air-traffic controller [ɛərtræfɪk kəntroʊlər]
n Fluglotse *m*, Fluglotsin *f*

airy [ɛəri] *adj* luftig; (*manner*) lässig

aisle [aɪl] *n* Gang *m*; (*in church*) Seiten-
schiff *nt*; **~ seat** Sitz *m* am Gang

ajar [ədʒɑr] *adj* (*door*) angelehnt

alarm [əlɑrm] *n* (*warning*) Alarm *m*; (*bell
etc*) Alarmanlage *f* ▷ *vt* beunruhigen

alarm clock *n* Wecker *m*

alarmed [əlɑrmd] *adj* (*protected*) alarmge-
sichert

alarming [əlɑrmɪŋ] *adj* beunruhigend

Albania [ælbeɪniə] *n* Albanien *nt*

Albanian [ælbeɪniən] *adj* albanisch ▷ *n*
(*person*) Albaner(in) *m(f)*; (*language*)
Albanisch *nt*

album [ælbəm] *n* Album *nt*

alcohol [ælkəhɔl] *n* Alkohol *m*

alcohol-free *adj* alkoholfrei

alcoholic [ælkəhɔlɪk] *adj* (*drink*) alkoholisch ▷ *n* Alkoholiker(in) *m(f)*

alcoholism [ælkəhɒlɪzəm] *n* Alkoholis-
mus *m*

ale [eɪl] *n* Ale *nt* (*helles englisches Bier*)

alert [ələrt] *adj* wachsam ▷ *n* Alarm *m* ▷ *vt*
warnen (*to* vor +*dat*)

algebra [ældʒɪbrə] *n* Algebra *f*

Algeria [ældʒɪəriə] *n* Algerien *nt*

alibi [ælɪbaɪ] *n* Alibi *nt*

alien [eɪliən] *n* (*foreigner*) Ausländer(in)

m(f); (*from space*) Außerirdische(r) *mf*

align [əlaɪn] *vt* ausrichten (*with* auf +*akk*)

alike [əlaɪk] *adj, adv* gleich; (*similar*) ähnlich

alive [əlaɪv] *adj* lebendig; **to keep sth ~** etw
am Leben erhalten; **he's still ~** er lebt
noch

KEYWORD

all [ɔl] *adj* alle(r, s); **all day/night** den ganzen Tag/die ganze Nacht; **all men are equal**
alle Menschen sind gleich; **all five came**
alle fünf kamen; **all the books/food** die
ganzen Bücher/das ganze Essen; **all the
time** die ganze Zeit (über); **all his life** sein
ganzes Leben (lang)

▷ *pron* **1** alles; **I ate it all, I ate all of it** ich
habe alles gegessen; **all of us/the boys
went** wir gingen alle/alle Jungen gingen;
we all sat down wir setzten uns alle

2 (*in phrases*): **above all** vor allem; **after all**
schließlich; **at all: not at all** (*in answer to
question*) überhaupt nicht; (*in answer to
thanks*) gern geschehen; **I'm not at all
tired** ich bin überhaupt nicht müde; **anything at all will do** es ist egal, welche(r, s);
all in all alles in allem

▷ *adv* ganz; **all alone** ganz allein; **it's not
as hard as all that** so schwer ist es nun
auch wieder nicht; **all the more/the better**
umso mehr/besser; **all but fast; the score
is 2 all** es steht 2 zu 2

allegation [æligeɪ̈ʂᵊn] *n* Behauptung *f*

alleged [əlɛdʒd] *adj* angeblich

allergic [ələrdʒɪk] *adj* allergisch (*to* gegen)

allergy [ælərdʒi] *n* Allergie *f*

alleviate [əlivieɪt] *vt* (*pain*) lindern

alley [æli] *n* (*enge*) Gasse; (*passage*) Durchgang *m*; (*bowling*) Bahn *f*

alliance [əlaɪəns] *n* Bündnis *nt*

alligator [æligeɪtər] *n* Alligator *m*

all-night *adj* (*café, cinema*) die ganze Nacht
geöffnet

allocate [æləkeɪt] *vt* zuweisen, zuteilen (*to*
dat)

allotment [əlɒtmənt] *n* (*plot*) Schrebergar-
ten *m*

allow [əlaʊ] *vt* (*permit*) erlauben (*sb* jdm);
(*grant*) bewilligen; (*time*) einplanen

allow for *vt* berücksichtigen; (*cost etc*) ein-
kalkulieren

all right *adj* okay, in Ordnung; **I'm ~** mir
geht's gut ▷ *adv* (*satisfactorily*) ganz gut

▷ *interj* okay

all-time *adj* (*record, high*) aller Zeiten

allusion [əluːʒⁿn] *n* Anspielung *f* (*to* auf +*akk*)

ally [ælaɪ] *n* Verbündete(r) *mf*; (*Hist*) Alliierte(r) *mf*

almond [ɑmənd, æm-, ælm-] *n* Mandel *f*

almost [ɔlmoʊst] *adv* fast

alone [əloʊn] *adj, adv* allein

along [əlɔŋ] *prep* entlang +*akk*; ~ **the river** den Fluss entlang; (*position*) am Fluss entlang ▷ *adv* (*onward*) weiter; ~ **with** zusammen mit; **all** ~ die ganze Zeit, von Anfang an

alongside [əlɔŋsaɪd] *prep* neben +*dat* ▷ *adv* (*walk*) nebenher

aloud [əlaʊd] *adv* laut

alphabet [ælfəbet, -bɪt] *n* Alphabet *nt*

alpine [ælpaɪn] *adj* alpin

Alps [ælps] *npl*: **the ~** die Alpen

already [ɔlrɛdi] *adv* schon, bereits

Alsace [ælsæs] *n* Elsass *nt*

Alsatian [ælseɪʃⁿn] *adj* elsässisch ▷ *n* Elsässer(in) *m(f)*

also [ɔlsoʊ] *adv* auch

altar [ɔltər] *n* Altar *m*

alter [ɔltər] *vt* ändern

alteration [ɔltəreɪʃⁿn] *n* Änderung *f*; ~**s** (*to building*) Umbau *m*

alternate (*vb* ɔltərneɪt, *adj,* ɔltɜrnɪt) *adj* abwechselnd ▷ *vi* abwechseln (*with* mit)

alternating current [ɔltərˈneɪtɪŋ kɜrənt] *n* Wechselstrom *m*

alternative [ɔltɜrnətɪv] *adj* Alternativ- ▷ *n* Alternative *f*

although [ɔlðoʊ] *conj* obwohl

altitude [æltɪtud] *n* Höhe *f*

altogether [ɔltəgɛðər] *adv* (*in total*) insgesamt; (*entirely*) ganz und gar

aluminum [əluːmɪnəm] *n* Aluminium *nt*

always [ɔlweɪz] *adv* immer

am [əm, STRONG æm] *present of* **be**; bin

am, a.m. (*abbr*) = **ante meridiem** vormittags, vorm.

amateur [æmətʃɜr, -tʃʊər] *n* Amateur(in) *m(f)* ▷ *adj* Amateur-; (*theater, choir*) Laien-

amaze [əmeɪz] *vt* erstaunen

amazed [əmeɪzd] *adj* erstaunt (*at* über +*akk*)

amazing [əmeɪzɪŋ] *adj* erstaunlich

Amazon [æməzɒn, -zən] *n*: ~ **river** Amazonas *m*

ambassador [æmbæsədər] *n* Botschafter *m*

amber [æmbər] *n* Bernstein *m*

ambiguity [æmbɪgyuːɪti] *n* Zweideutigkeit *f*

ambiguous [æmbɪgyuəs] *adj* zweideutig

ambition [æmbɪʃⁿn] *n* Ambition *f*; (*ambitious nature*) Ehrgeiz *m*

ambitious [æmbɪʃəs] *adj* ehrgeizig

ambulance [æmbyələns] *n* Krankenwagen *m*

amend [əmɛnd] *vt* (*law etc*) ändern

America [əmɛrɪkə] *n* Amerika *nt*

American [əmɛrɪkən] *adj* amerikanisch ▷ *n* Amerikaner(in) *m(f)*; **native ~** Indianer(in) *m(f)*

amiable [eɪmiəbⁿl] *adj* liebenswürdig

amicable [æmɪkəbⁿl] *adj* freundlich; (*relations*) freundschaftlich; (*Jur: settlement*) gütlich

amnesia [æmniːʒə] *n* Gedächtnisverlust *m*

among(st) [əmʌŋ(st)] *prep* unter +*dat*

amount [əmaʊnt] *n* (*quantity*) Menge *f*; (*of money*) Betrag *m*; **a large/small ~ of ...** ziemlich viel/wenig ... ▷ *vi*: **to ~ to** (*total*) sich belaufen auf +*akk*

amp [æmp], **ampere** *n* Ampere *nt*

amplifier [æmplɪfaɪər] *n* Verstärker *m*

amputate [æmpyuteɪt] *vt* amputieren

Amtrak® [æmtræk] *n* amerikanische Eisenbahngesellschaft

amuse [əmyuz] *vt* amüsieren; (*entertain*) unterhalten

amused [əmyuzd] *adj*: **I'm not ~** das finde ich gar nicht lustig

amusement [əmyuzmənt] *n* (*enjoyment*) Vergnügen *nt*; (*recreation*) Unterhaltung *f*

amusement park *n* Vergnügungspark *m*

amusing [əmyuzɪŋ] *adj* amüsant

an [ən, STRONG æn] *art* ein(e)

analysis [ənælɪsɪs] *n* Analyse *f*

analyze [ænəlaɪz] *vt* analysieren

anatomy [ənætəmi] *n* Anatomie *f*; (*structure*) Körperbau *m*

ancestor [ænsɛstər] *n* Vorfahr *m*

anchor [æŋkər] *n* Anker *m* ▷ *vt* verankern

anchorage [æŋkərɪdʒ] *n* Ankerplatz *m*

anchovy [æntʃoʊvi] *n* Sardelle *f*

ancient [eɪnʃənt] *adj* alt; (*fam: person, clothes etc*) uralt

and [ənd, STRONG ænd] *conj* und

Andorra [ændɔrə] *n* Andorra *nt*

anemic [əniːmɪk] *adj* blutarm

anesthetic [ænɪsθɛtɪk] *n* Narkose *f*; (*substance*) Narkosemittel *nt*

angel [eɪndʒⁿl] *n* Engel *m*

anger [æŋgər] *n* Zorn *m* ▷ *vt* ärgern

angina [ændʒaɪnə], **angina pectoris** n Angina Pectoris f

angle [æŋgºl] n Winkel m; (fig) Standpunkt m

angler [æŋglər] n Angler(in) m(f)

angling [æŋglɪŋ] n Angeln nt

angry [æŋgri] adj verärgert; (stronger) zornig; **to be ~ with sb** auf jdn böse sein

angular [æŋgyʊlər] adj eckig; (face) kantig

animal [ænɪmºl] n Tier nt

animal rights npl Tierrechte pl

animated [ænɪmeɪtɪd] adj lebhaft; **~ film** Zeichentrickfilm m

aniseed [ænɪsɪd] n Anis m

ankle [æŋkºl] n (Fuß)knöchel m

annex [ænɛks] n Anbau m

anniversary [ænɪvɜrsəri] n Jahrestag m

announce [ənaʊns] vt bekannt geben; (officially) bekannt machen; (on radio, TV etc) ansagen

announcement [ənaʊnsmənt] n Bekanntgabe f; (official) Bekanntmachung f; (Radio, TV) Ansage f

announcer [ənaʊnsər] n (Radio, TV) Ansager(in) m(f)

annoy [ənɔɪ] vt ärgern

annoyance [ənɔɪəns] n Ärger m

annoyed [ənɔɪd] adj ärgerlich; **to be ~ with sb about sth** sich über jdn (über etw) ärgern

annoying [ənɔɪɪŋ] adj ärgerlich; (person) lästig, nervig

annual [ænyuəl] adj jährlich ▷ n Jahrbuch nt

anonymous [ənɒnɪməs] adj anonym

anorak [ænəræk] n Anorak m

anorexia [ænərɛksiə] n Magersucht f

anorexic [ænərɛksɪk] adj magersüchtig

another [ənʌðər] adj, pron (different) ein(e) andere(r, s); (additional) noch eine(r, s); **let me put it ~ way** lass es mich anders sagen

answer [ænsər] n Antwort f (to auf +akk); (solution) Lösung f +gen ▷ vi antworten; (on phone) sich melden ▷ vt (person) antworten +dat; (letter, question) beantworten; (telephone) gehen an +akk, abnehmen; (door) öffnen

answer back vi widersprechen

answering machine [ænsərɪŋ məʃɪn] n Anrufbeantworter m

ant [ænt] n Ameise f

Antarctic [æntɑrktɪk] n Antarktis f

Antarctic Circle n südlicher Polarkreis

antelope [æntºloʊp] n Antilope f

antenna [æntɛnə] (pl **antennae**) n (Zool) Fühler m; (Radio) Antenne f

anti- [ænti, -taɪ] pref Anti-, anti-

antibiotic [æntibaɪptɪk, -taɪ-] n Antibiotikum nt

anticipate [æntɪsɪpeɪt] vt (expect: trouble, question) erwarten, rechnen mit

anticipation [æntɪsɪpeɪʃºn] n Erwartung f

anticlimax [æntiklaɪmæks, æntaɪ-] n Enttäuschung f

antidote [æntidoʊt] n Gegenmittel nt

antifreeze [æntifriz, æntaɪ-] n Frostschutzmittel nt

Antipodes [æntɪpədiz] npl Australien und Neuseeland

antiquarian [æntɪkwɛəriən] adj: **~ bookshop** Antiquariat nt

antique [æntik] n Antiquität f ▷ adj antik

antique shop n Antiquitätengeschäft nt

anti-Semitism [æntisɛmɪtɪzəm, æntaɪ-] n Antisemitismus m

antiseptic [æntəsɛptɪk] n Antiseptikum nt ▷ adj antiseptisch

antisocial [æntisoʊʃºl, æntaɪ-] adj (person) ungesellig; (behavior) unsozial, asozial

antivirus [æntivaɪrəs] adj (Inform) Antiviren-

antivirus software n Antivirensoftware f

antlers [æntlərz] npl Geweih nt

anxiety [æŋzaɪɪti] n Sorge f (about um)

anxious [æŋkʃəs] adj besorgt (about um); (apprehensive) ängstlich

KEYWORD

any [ɛni] adj **1** (in questions etc): **have you any butter?** haben Sie (etwas) Butter?; **have you any children?** haben Sie Kinder?; **if there are any tickets left** falls noch Karten da sind

2 (with negative): **I haven't any money/books** ich habe kein Geld/keine Bücher

3 (no matter which) jede(r, s)(beliebige); **any color (at all)** jede beliebige Farbe; **choose any book you like** nehmen Sie ein beliebiges Buch

4 (in phrases): **in any case** in jedem Fall; **any day now** jeden Tag; **at any moment** jeden Moment; **at any rate** auf jeden Fall ▷ pron **1** (in questions etc): **have you got any?** haben Sie welche?; **can any of you sing?** kann (irgend)einer von euch singen?

2 (*with negative*): **I haven't any (of them)** ich habe keinen/keines (davon)
3 (*no matter which one(s)*: #); **take any of those books (you like)** nehmen Sie irgendeines dieser Bücher
▷ *adv* **1** (*in questions etc*): **do you want any more soup/sandwiches?** möchten Sie noch Suppe/Brote?; **are you feeling any better?** fühlen Sie sich etwas besser?
2 (*with negative*): **I can't hear him any more** ich kann ihn nicht mehr hören

anybody [ɛnibɒdi, -bʌdi] *pron* (*whoever one likes*) irgendjemand; (*everyone*) jeder; (*in question*) jemand
anyhow [ɛnihaʊ] *adv*: **I don't want to talk about it, not now ~** ich möchte nicht darüber sprechen, jedenfalls nicht jetzt; **they asked me not to go, but I went ~** sie baten mich, nicht hinzugehen, aber ich bin trotzdem hingegangen
anyone [ɛniwʌn] *pron* (*whoever one likes*) irgendjemand; (*everyone*) jeder; (*in question*) jemand; **isn't there ~ you can ask?** gibt es denn niemanden, den du fragen kannst/den Sie fragen können?
anyplace [ɛnipleɪs] *adv* irgendwo; (*direction*) irgendwohin; (*everywhere*) überall

KEYWORD

anything [ɛnɪθɪŋ] *pron* **1** (*in questions etc*) (irgend)etwas; **can you see anything?** können Sie etwas sehen?
2 (*with negative*): **I can't see anything** ich kann nichts sehen
3 (*no matter what*): **you can say anything you like** Sie können sagen, was Sie wollen; **anything will do** irgendetwas (wird genügen), irgendeine(r, s) (wird genügen); **he'll eat anything** er isst alles

anytime [ɛnitaɪm] *adv* jederzeit
anyway [ɛniweɪ] *adv*: **I didn't want to go there ~** ich wollte da sowieso nicht hingehen; **thanks ~** trotzdem danke; **~, as I was saying, ...** jedenfalls, wie ich schon sagte, ...
anywhere [ɛniwɛər] *adv* irgendwo; (*direction*) irgendwohin; (*everywhere*) überall
apart [əpɑrt] *adv* auseinander; **~ from** außer; **live ~** getrennt leben
apartment [əpɑrtmənt] *n* Wohnung *f*
apartment building *n* Wohnblock *m*
ape [eɪp] *n* (Menschen)affe *m*

aperitif [æpɛrɪtɪf] *n* Aperitif *m*
aperture [æpərtʃər] *n* Öffnung *f*; (*Foto*) Blende *f*
apologize [əpɒlədʒaɪz] *vi* sich entschuldigen
apology [əpɒlədʒi] *n* Entschuldigung *f*
apostrophe [əpɒstrəfi] *n* Apostroph *m*
appalled [əpɔld] *adj* entsetzt (*at* über +*akk*)
appalling [əpɔlɪŋ] *adj* entsetzlich
apparatus [æpərætəs, -rei-] *n* Apparat *m*; (*piece of apparatus*) Gerät *nt*
apparent [əpærənt] *adj* (*obvious*) offensichtlich (*to* für); (*seeming*) scheinbar
apparently [əpærəntli] *adv* anscheinend
appeal [əpil] *vi* (dringend) bitten (*for* um, *to* +*akk*); (*Jur*) Berufung einlegen; **to ~ to sb** (*be attractive*) jdm zusagen ▷ *n* Aufruf *m* (*to an* +*akk*); (*Jur*) Berufung *f*; (*attraction*) Reiz *m*
appealing [əpilɪŋ] *adj* ansprechend, attraktiv
appear [əpɪər] *vi* erscheinen; (*Theat*) auftreten; (*seem*) scheinen
appearance [əpɪərəns] *n* Erscheinen *nt*; (*Theat*) Auftritt *m*; (*look*) Aussehen *nt*
appendicitis [əpɛndɪsaɪtɪs] *n* Blinddarmentzündung *f*
appendix [əpɛndɪks] *n* Blinddarm *m*; (*to book*) Anhang *m*
appetite [æpɪtaɪt] *n* Appetit *m*; (*fig*: *desire*) Verlangen *nt*; (*sexual*) Lust *f*
appetizer [æpɪtaɪzər] *n* (*first course*) Vorspeise *f*
appetizing [æpɪtaɪzɪŋ] *adj* appetitlich, appetitanregend
applause [əplɔz] *n* Beifall *m*, Applaus *m*
apple [æpᵊl] *n* Apfel *m*
apple crumble *n* mit Streuseln bestreutes Apfeldessert
apple juice *n* Apfelsaft *m*
apple pie *n* gedeckter Apfelkuchen *m*
apple sauce *n* Apfelmus *nt*
apple tart *n* Apfelkuchen *m*
apple tree *n* Apfelbaum *m*
appliance [əplaɪəns] *n* Gerät *nt*
applicable [æplɪkəbᵊl, əplɪkə-] *adj* anwendbar; (*on forms*) zutreffend
applicant [æplɪkənt] *n* Bewerber(in) *m(f)*
application [æplɪkeɪʃᵊn] *n* (*request*) Antrag *m* (*for* auf +*akk*); (*for job*) Bewerbung *f* (*for* um)
application form *n* Anmeldeformular *nt*
apply [əplaɪ] *vi* (*be relevant*) zutreffen (*to* auf +*akk*); (*for job etc*) sich bewerben (*for*

um) ▷ vt (cream, paint etc) auftragen; (put into practice) anwenden; (brakes) betätigen

appoint [əpɔɪnt] vt (to post) ernennen

appointment [əpɔɪntmənt] n Verabredung f; (at doctor, hairdresser etc, in business) Termin m; **by ~** nach Vereinbarung

appreciate [əpriːʃieɪt] vt (value) zu schätzen wissen; (understand) einsehen; **to be much ~d** richtig gewürdigt werden ▷ vi (increase in value) im Wert steigen

appreciation [əpriːʃieɪʃᵊn] n (esteem) Anerkennung f, Würdigung f; (of person also) Wertschätzung f

apprehensive [æprɪhɛnsɪv] adj ängstlich

apprentice [əprɛntɪs] n Lehrling m

approach [əprəʊtʃ] vi sich nähern ▷ vt (place) sich nähern +dat; (person) herantreten an +akk; (problem) angehen

appropriate [əprəʊpriːɪt] adj passend; (to occasion) angemessen; (remark) treffend

appropriately [əprəʊpriːɪtli] adv passend; (expressed) treffend

approval [əpruːvᵊl] n (show of satisfaction) Anerkennung f; (permission) Zustimmung f (of zu)

approve [əpruːv] vt billigen ▷ vi: **to ~ of sth/sb** etw billigen/von jdm etwas halten; **I don't ~** ich missbillige das

approximate [əprɒksɪmət] adj ungefähr

approximately [əprɒksɪmətli] adv ungefähr, circa

apricot [eɪprɪkɒt] n Aprikose f

April [eɪprɪl] n April m; see also **September**

apron [eɪprən] n Schürze f

aptitude [æptɪtud] n Begabung f

aquarium [əkwɛəriəm] n Aquarium nt

Aquarius [əkwɛəriəs] n (Astr) Wassermann m

Arab [ærəb] n Araber(in) m(f); (horse) Araber m

Arabian [əreɪbiən] adj arabisch

Arabic [ærəbɪk] n (language) Arabisch nt ▷ adj arabisch

arbitrary [ɑrbɪtrɛri] adj willkürlich

arcade [ɑrkeɪd] n Arkade f; (shopping arcade) Einkaufspassage f

arch [ɑrtʃ] n Bogen m

archaic [ɑrkeɪɪk] adj veraltet

archbishop [ɑrtʃbɪʃəp] n Erzbischof m

archaeologist [ɑrkiɒlədʒɪst] n Archäologe m, Archäologin f

archaeology [ɑrkiɒlədʒi] n Archäologie f

archery [ɑrtʃəri] n Bogenschießen nt

architect [ɑrkɪtɛkt] n Architekt(in) m(f)

architecture [ɑrkɪtɛktʃər] n Architektur f

archive(s) [ɑrkaɪv(z)] n(pl) Archiv nt

archway [ɑrtʃweɪ] n Torbogen m

Arctic [ɑrktɪk] n Arktis f

Arctic Circle n nördlicher Polarkreis

are [ər, STRONG ɑr] present of **be**

area [ɛəriə] n (region, district) Gebiet nt, Gegend f; (amount of space) Fläche f; (part of building etc) Bereich m, Zone f; (fig: field) Bereich m; **the London ~** der Londoner Raum

area code n Vorwahl f

aren't [ɑrnt, ɑrənt] contr of **are not**

Argentina [ɑrdʒəntiːnə] n Argentinien nt

argue [ɑrgyu] vi streiten (about, over über +akk); **to ~ that ...** behaupten, dass ...; **to ~ for/against ...** sprechen für/gegen ...

argument [ɑrgyəmənt] n (reasons) Argument nt; (quarrel) Streit m; **to have an ~** sich streiten

Aries [ɛəriz] nsing (Astr) Widder m

arise [əraɪz] (arose, arisen) vi sich ergeben, entstehen; (problem, question, wind) aufkommen

aristocracy [ærɪstɒkrəsi] n (class) Adel m

aristocrat [ærɪstəkræt, ərɪst-] n Adlige(r) mf

aristocratic [ərɪstəkrætɪk] adj aristokratisch, adlig

arm [ɑrm] n Arm m; (sleeve) Ärmel m; (of armchair) Armlehne f ▷ vt bewaffnen

armchair [ɑrmtʃɛər] n Lehnstuhl m

armed [ɑrmd] adj bewaffnet

armpit [ɑrmpɪt] n Achselhöhle f

arms [ɑrmz] npl Waffen pl

army [ɑrmi] n Armee f, Heer nt

aroma [ərəʊmə] n Duft m, Aroma nt

aromatherapy [ərəʊməθɛrəpi] n Aromatherapie f

arose [ərəʊz] pt of **arise**

around [əraʊnd] adv herum, umher; (present) hier (irgendwo); (approximately) ungefähr; (with time) gegen; **he's ~ somewhere** er ist hier irgendwo in der Nähe; **all ~** (on all sides) rundherum; **the long way ~** der längere Weg; **I'll be ~ at 8** ich werde um acht Uhr da sein; **the other way ~** umgekehrt ▷ prep (surrounding) um ... (herum); (about in in ... herum; ~ **about** (approximately) ungefähr; ~ **the corner** um die Ecke; **to go ~ the world** um die Welt reisen; **she lives ~ here** sie wohnt hier in der Gegend

arr. (abbr) = **arrival, arrives** Ank.

arrange [əreɪndʒ] vt (put in order) (an)ordnen; (*alphabetically*) ordnen; (*artistically*) arrangieren; (*agree to: meeting etc*) vereinbaren, festsetzen; (*holidays*) festlegen; (*organize*) planen; **to ~ that ...** es so einrichten, dass ...; **we ~d to meet at eight o'clock** wir haben uns für acht Uhr verabredet; **it's all ~d** es ist alles arrangiert

arrangement [əˈreɪndʒmənt] *n* (*layout*) Anordnung *f*; (*agreement*) Vereinbarung *f*, Plan *m*; **to make ~s** Vorbereitungen treffen

arrest [əˈrɛst] *vt* (*person*) verhaften ▷ *n* Verhaftung *f*; **under ~** verhaftet

arrival [əˈraɪvˀl] *n* Ankunft *f*; **new ~** (*person*) Neuankömmling *m*

arrivals *n* (*airport*) Ankunftshalle *f*

arrive [əˈraɪv] *vi* ankommen (*at* bei, in +*dat*); **to ~ at a solution** eine Lösung finden

arrogant [ˈærəgənt] *adj* arrogant

arrow [ˈærəʊ] *n* Pfeil *m*

art [ɑːt] *n* Kunst *f*; **the arts** *pl* Geisteswissenschaften *pl*

artery [ˈɑːtəri] *n* Schlagader *f*, Arterie *f*

art gallery *n* Kunstgalerie *f*, Kunstmuseum *nt*

arthritis [ɑːˈθraɪtɪs] *n* Arthritis *f*

artichoke [ˈɑːtɪtʃəʊk] *n* Artischocke *f*

article [ˈɑːtɪkˀl] *n* Artikel *m*; (*object*) Gegenstand *m*

artificial [ɑːtɪˈfɪʃˀl] *adj* künstlich, Kunst-; (*smile etc*) gekünstelt

artist [ˈɑːtɪst] *n* Künstler(in) *m(f)*

artistic [ɑːˈtɪstɪk] *adj* künstlerisch

KEYWORD

as [əz, STRONG æz] *conj* **1** (*referring to time*) als; **as the years went by** mit den Jahren; **he came in as I was leaving** als er hereinkam, ging ich gerade; **as from tomorrow** ab morgen

2 (*in comparisons*): **as big as** so groß wie; **twice as big as** zweimal so groß wie; **as much/many as** so viel/so viele wie; **as soon as** sobald

3 (*since, because*) da; **he left early as he had to be home by 10** er ging früher, da er um 10 zu Hause sein musste

4 (*referring to manner, way*) wie; **do as you wish** mach was du willst; **as she said** wie sie sagte

5 (*concerning*): **as for** *o* **to that** was das betrifft *o* angeht

6: as if *o* **though** als ob

▷ *prep* als; **he works as a driver** er arbeitet als Fahrer; **he gave it to me as a present** er hat es mir als Geschenk gegeben; *see also* **long; such; well**

ASAP [eɪ ɛs eɪ piː] (*acr*) = **as soon as possible** möglichst bald

ascertain [æsəˈteɪn] *vt* feststellen

ash [æʃ] *n* (*dust*) Asche *f*; (*tree*) Esche *f*

ashamed [əˈʃeɪmd] *adj* beschämt; **to be ~ of sb/sth** sich (für jdn/etw) schämen

ashore [əˈʃɔː] *adv* an Land

ashtray [ˈæʃtreɪ] *n* Aschenbecher *m*

Asia [ˈeɪʒə] *n* Asien *nt*

Asian [ˈeɪʒˀn] *adj* asiatisch ▷ *n* Asiat(in) *m(f)*

aside [əˈsaɪd] *adv* beiseite, zur Seite; **~ from** außer

ask [æsk, ɑːsk] *vt, vi* fragen; (*question*) stellen; (*request*) bitten um; (*invite*) einladen; **to ask sb the way** jdn nach dem Weg fragen; **to ask sb to do sth** jdn darum bitten, etw zu tun

ask for *vt* bitten um

asleep [əˈsliːp] *adj, adv*: **to be ~** schlafen; **to fall ~** einschlafen

asparagus [əˈspærəgəs] *n* Spargel *m*

aspect [ˈæspɛkt] *n* Aspekt *m*

aspirin [ˈæspərɪn, -prɪn] *n* Aspirin® *nt*

ass [æs] *n* (*a. fig*) Esel *m*

assassinate [əˈsæsɪneɪt] *vt* ermorden

assassination [əsæsɪˈneɪʃˀn] *n* Ermordung *f*; **~ attempt** Attentat *nt*

assault [əˈsɔːlt] *n* Angriff *m*; (*Jur*) Körperverletzung *f* ▷ *vt* überfallen, herfallen über +*akk*

assemble [əˈsɛmbˀl] *vt* (*parts*) zusammensetzen; (*people*) zusammenrufen ▷ *vi* sich versammeln

assembly [əˈsɛmbli] *n* (*of people*) Versammlung *f*; (*putting together*) Zusammensetzen *nt*

assembly hall *n* Aula *f*

assert [əˈsɜːt] *vt* behaupten

assertion [əˈsɜːʃˀn] *n* Behauptung *f*

assess [əˈsɛs] *vt* einschätzen

assessment [əˈsɛsmənt] *n* Einschätzung *f*

asset [ˈæsɛt] *n* Vermögenswert *m*; (*fig*) Vorteil *m*; **~s** *pl* Vermögen *nt*

assign [əˈsaɪn] *vt* zuweisen

assignment [əˈsaɪnmənt] *n* Aufgabe *f*; (*mission*) Auftrag *m*

assist [əˈsɪst] *vt* helfen +*dat*

assistance [əˈsɪstəns] *n* Hilfe *f*

assistant [əˈsɪstənt] *n* Assistent(in) *m(f)*,

Mitarbeiter(in) *m(f)*; (*in shop*) Verkäufer(in) *m(f)*

assistant referee *n* (*Sport*) Schiedsrichterassistent(in) *m(f)*

associate [əsəʊʃɪeɪt, -sɪeɪt] *vt* verbinden (*with* mit)

association [əsəʊʃɪeɪʃᵊn, -sɪeɪ-] *n* (*organization*) Verband *m*, Vereinigung *f*; **in ~ with** ... in Zusammenarbeit mit ...

assorted [əsɔːtɪd] *adj* gemischt

assortment [əsɔːtmənt] *n* Auswahl *f* (*of* an +*dat*); (*of sweets*) Mischung *f*

assume [əsuːm] *vt* annehmen (*that* ... dass ...); (*role, responsibility*) übernehmen

assumption [əsʌmpʃᵊn] *n* Annahme *f*

assurance [əʃʊərəns] *n* Versicherung *f*; (*confidence*) Zuversicht *f*

assure [əʃʊər] *vt* (*say confidently*) versichern +*dat*; **to ~ sb of sth** jdm etw zusichern; **to be ~d of sth** einer Sache sicher sein

asterisk [æstərɪsk] *n* Sternchen *nt*

asthma [æzmə] *n* Asthma *nt*

astonish [əstɒnɪʃ] *vt* erstaunen

astonished [əstɒnɪʃt] *adj* erstaunt (*at* über)

astonishing [əstɒnɪʃɪŋ] *adj* erstaunlich

astonishment [əstɒnɪʃmənt] *n* Erstaunen *nt*

astound [əstaʊnd] *vt* sehr erstaunen

astounding [əstaʊndɪŋ] *adj* erstaunlich

astray [əstreɪ] *adv*: **to go ~** (*letter etc*) verloren gehen; (*person*) vom Weg abkommen; **to lead ~** irreführen, verführen

astrology [əstrɒlədʒɪ] *n* Astrologie *f*

astronaut [æstrənɔːt] *n* Astronaut(in) *m(f)*

astronomy [əstrɒnəmɪ] *n* Astronomie *f*

asylum [əsaɪləm] *n* (*home*) Anstalt *f*; (*political asylum*) Asyl *nt*

asylum seeker [əsaɪləm siːkər] *n* Asylbewerber(in) *m(f)*

KEYWORD

at [ət, STRONG æt] *prep* **1** (*referring to position, direction*) an +*dat*, bei +*dat*; (*with place*) in +*dat*; **at the top** an der Spitze; **at home** zu Hause, zuhause (*österreichisch, schweizerisch*); **at school** in der Schule; **at the baker's** beim Bäcker; **to look at sth** auf etw *akk* blicken; **to throw sth at sb** etw nach jdm werfen

2 (*referring to time*): **at 4 o'clock** um 4 Uhr; **at night** bei Nacht; **at Christmas** zu Weihnachten; **at times** manchmal

3 (*referring to rates, speed etc*): **at $1 a kilo** zu $1 pro Kilo; **two at a time** zwei auf einmal; **at 50 km/h** mit 50 km/h

4 (*referring to manner*): **at a stroke** mit einem Schlag; **at peace** in Frieden

5 (*referring to activity*): **to be at work** bei der Arbeit sein; **to play at being cowboys** Cowboy spielen; **to be good at sth** gut in etw *dat* sein

6 (*referring to cause*): **shocked/surprised/annoyed at sth** schockiert/überrascht/verärgert über etw *akk*; **I went at his suggestion** ich ging auf seinen Vorschlag hin

7 (@ *symbol*) At-Zeichen *nt*

ate [eɪt] *pt of* **eat**

athlete [æθliːt] *n* Athlet(in) *m(f)*; (*track and field*) Leichtathlet(in) *m(f)*; (*sportsman*) Sportler(in) *m(f)*; **~'s foot** Fußpilz *m*

athletic [æθlɛtɪk] *adj* sportlich; (*build*) athletisch

Atlantic [ətlæntɪk] *n*: **the ~ Ocean** der Atlantik

atlas [ætləs] *n* Atlas *m*

ATM [eɪ tiː ɛm] (*abbr*) = **automated teller machine** Geldautomat *m*

atmosphere [ætməsfɪər] *n* Atmosphäre *f*; (*fig*) Stimmung *f*

atom [ætəm] *n* Atom *nt*

atomic [ətɒmɪk] *adj* Atom-; **~ energy** Atomenergie *f*; **~ power** Atomkraft *f*

atom(ic) bomb *n* Atombombe *f*

atrocious [ətrəʊʃəs] *adj* grauenhaft

atrocity [ətrɒsɪtɪ] *n* Grausamkeit *f*; (*deed*) Gräueltat *f*

attach [ətætʃ] *vt* befestigen, anheften (*to* an +*dat*); **to ~ importance to sth** Wert auf etw *akk* legen; **to be ~ed to sb/sth** an jdm/ etw hängen; **to ~ a file to an email** eine Datei an eine E-Mail anhängen

attachment [ətætʃmənt] *n* (*affection*) Zuneigung *f*; (*Inform*) Attachment *nt*, Anhang *m*, Anlage *f*

attack [ətæk] *vt, vi* angreifen ▷ *n* Angriff *+akk* (*on* auf *m*); (*Med*) Anfall *m*

attempt [ətɛmpt] *n* Versuch *m*; **to make an ~ to do sth** versuchen, etw zu tun ▷ *vt* versuchen

attend [ətɛnd] *vt* (*go to*) teilnehmen an +*dat*; (*lectures, school*) besuchen ▷ *vi* (*be present*) anwesend sein

attendance [ətɛndəns] *n* (*presence*) Anwesenheit *f*; (*people present*) Teilnehmerzahl *f*

attendant [ətɛndənt] *n* (*in car park etc*)

Wächter(in) *m(f)*; (*in museum*) Aufseher(in) *m(f)*

attend to *vt* sich kümmern um; (*customer*) bedienen

attention [ətɛnʃⁿn] *n* Aufmerksamkeit *f*; **your ~ please** Achtung!; **to pay ~ to** etw beachten; **to pay ~ to sb** (*listen*) jdm aufmerksam zuhören; **for the ~ of ...** zu Händen von ...

attentive [ətɛntɪv] *adj* aufmerksam

attic [ætɪk] *n* Dachboden *m*; (*lived in*) Mansarde *f*

attitude [ætɪtud] *n* (*mental*) Einstellung *f* (*to, towards* zu); (*more general, physical*) Haltung *f*

attorney [ətɜrni] *n* (*lawyer*) Rechtsanwalt *m*, Rechtsanwältin *f*

attract [ətrækt] *vt* anziehen; (*attention*) erregen; **to be ~ed to** *o* by sb sich zu jdm hingezogen fühlen

attraction [ətrækʃⁿn] *n* Anziehungskraft *f*; (*thing*) Attraktion *f*

attractive [ətræktɪv] *adj* attraktiv; (*thing, idea*) reizvoll

auction [ɔkʃⁿn] *n* Versteigerung *f*, Auktion *f* ▷ *vt* versteigern

audible [ɔdɪbⁿl] *adj* hörbar

audience [ɔdiəns] *n* Publikum *nt*; (*Radio*) Zuhörer *pl*; (*TV*) Zuschauer *pl*

audio [ɔdiou] *adj* Ton-

audition [ɔdɪʃⁿn] *n* Probe *f* ▷ *vi* (*Theat*) vorspielen, vorsingen

auditorium [ɔdɪtɔriəm] *n* Zuschauerraum *m*

Aug (*abbr*) = **August**

August [ɔgəst] *n* August *m*; *see also* **September**

aunt [ænt, ɑnt] *n* Tante *f*

au pair [ou pɛər] *n* Aupairmädchen *nt*, Aupairjunge *m*

Australia [ɒstreɪlyə] *n* Australien *nt*

Australian [ɒstreɪlyən] *adj* australisch ▷ *n* Australier(in) *m(f)*

Austria [ɒstriə] *n* Österreich *nt*

Austrian [ɔstriən] *adj* österreichisch ▷ *n* Österreicher(in) *m(f)*

authentic [ɔθɛntɪk] *adj* echt; (*signature*) authentisch

authenticity [ɔθɛntɪsiti] *n* Echtheit *f*

author [ɔθər] *n* Autor(in) *m(f)*; (*of report etc*) Verfasser(in) *m(f)*

authority [əθɔriti] *n* (*power, expert*) Autorität *f*; **an ~ on sth** eine Autorität auf dem Gebiet einer Sache; **the authorities** *pl* die Behörden *pl*

authorize [ɔθəraɪz] *vt* (*permit*) genehmi-

gen; **to be ~d to do sth** offiziell berechtigt sein, etw zu tun

auto [ɔtou] (*pl* **-s**) *n* Auto *nt*

autobiography [ɔtəbaɪɒgrəfi] *n* Autobiographie *f*

autograph [ɔtəgræf] *n* Autogramm *nt*

automatic [ɔtəmætɪk] *adj* automatisch; **~ gear shift** Automatikschaltung *f* ▷ *n* (*car*) Automatikwagen *m*

automobile [ɔtəməbil] *n* Auto(mobil) *nt*

auto racing *n* Autorennsport *m*

auto show *n* Automobilausstellung *f*

Auto Train® *n* Autoreisezug *m*

autumn [ɔtəm] *n* Herbst *m*

auxiliary [ɔgzɪlyəri, -zɪləri] *adj* Hilfs-; **~ verb** Hilfsverb *nt* ▷ *n* Hilfskraft *f*

availability [əveɪləbɪliti] *n* (*of product*) Lieferbarkeit *f*; (*of resources*) Verfügbarkeit *f*

available [əveɪləbⁿl] *adj* erhältlich; (*existing*) vorhanden; (*product*) lieferbar; (*person*) erreichbar; **to be/make ~ to sb** jdm zur Verfügung stehen/stellen; **they're only ~ in black** es gibt sie nur in Schwarz, sie sind nur in Schwarz erhältlich

avalanche [ævəlæntʃ] *n* Lawine *f*

Ave (*abbr*) = **avenue**

avenue [ævɪnyu, -nu] *n* Allee *f*

average [ævərɪdʒ, ævrɪdʒ] *n* Durchschnitt *m*; **on ~** im Durchschnitt ▷ *adj* durchschnittlich; **~ speed** Durchschnittsgeschwindigkeit *f*; **of ~ height** von mittlerer Größe

avian flu [eɪviən flu] *n* Vogelgrippe *f*

aviation [eɪviɛʃⁿn] *n* Luftfahrt *f*

avocado [ævəkɑdou] (*pl* **-s**) *n* Avocado *f*

avoid [əvɔɪd] *vt* vermeiden; **to ~ sb** jdm aus dem Weg gehen

avoidable [əvɔɪdəbⁿl] *adj* vermeidbar

awake [əweɪk] (**awoke, awoken**) *vi* aufwachen ▷ *adj* wach

award [əwɔrd] *n* (*prize*) Preis *m*; (*for bravery etc*) Auszeichnung *f* ▷ *vt* zuerkennen (*to sb* jdm); (*present*) verleihen (*to sb* jdm)

aware [əwɛər] *adj* bewusst; **to be ~ of sth** sich *dat* einer Sache *gen* bewusst sein; **I was not ~ that ...** es war mir nicht klar, dass ...

away [əweɪ] *adv* weg; **to look ~** wegsehen; **he's ~** er ist nicht da; (*on a trip*) er ist verreist; (*from school, work*) er fehlt; (*Sport*): **they are playing ~** sie spielen auswärts; (*with distance*): **three miles ~** drei Meilen (von hier) entfernt; **to work ~** drauflos arbeiten

awful [ɔ́fəl] *adj* schrecklich, furchtbar
awfully [ɔ́fli] *adv* furchtbar
awkward [ɔ́kwərd] *adj* (*clumsy*) unge-schickt; (*embarrassing*) peinlich; (*difficult*) schwierig

awning [ɔ́nɪŋ] *n* Markise *f*
awoke [əwóuk] *pt of* **awake**
awoken [əwóukən] *pp of* **awake**
ax [æks] *n* Axt *f*
axle [ǽksᵊl] *n* (*Tech*) Achse *f*

B

BA [biː eɪ] (abbr) = **Bachelor of Arts**
babe [beɪb] n (fam) Baby nt; (fam: affectionate) Schatz m, Kleine(r) mf
baby [beɪbi] n Baby nt; (of animal) Junge(s) nt; (fam: affectionate) Schatz m, Kleine(r) mf; **to have a ~** ein Kind bekommen; **it's your ~** (fam: responsibility) das ist dein Bier
baby carriage [beɪbi kærɪdʒ] n Kinderwagen m
baby food n Babynahrung f
babyish [beɪbiɪʃ] adj kindisch
baby shower n Party für die werdende Mutter
babysit [beɪbɪsɪt] (irr) vi babysitten
babysitter [beɪbɪsɪtər] n Babysitter(in) m(f)
bachelor [bætʃələr] n Junggeselle m; **B~ of Arts/Science** erster akademischer Grad, ≈ Magister/Diplom
bachelorette [bætʃələrɛt] n Junggesellin f
bachelorette party [bætʃələrɛt pɑrti] n Junggesellinnenabschied
bachelor party n Junggesellenabschied
back [bæk] n (of person, animal) Rücken m; (of house, coin etc) Rückseite f; (of chair) Rückenlehne f; (of car) Rücksitz m; (of train) Ende nt; (Sport: defender) Verteidiger(in) m(f); **at the ~ of ...**, **in ~ of ...** (inside) hinten in ...; (outside) hinter ...; **~ to front** verkehrt herum ▷ vt (support) unterstützen; (car) rückwärtsfahren ▷ vi (go backwards) rückwärtsgehen, rückwärtsfahren ▷ adj Hinter-; **~ wheel** Hinterrad nt ▷ adv zurück; **they're ~** sie sind wieder da
backache [bækeɪk] n Rückenschmerzen pl
back away vi sich zurückziehen
backbone [bækboʊn] n Rückgrat nt
backdate [bækdeɪt] vt zurückdatieren
backdoor [bækdɔr] n Hintertür f
back down vi nachgeben
backfire [bækfaɪər] vi (plan) fehlschlagen; (Auto) fehlzünden
background [bækgraʊnd] n Hintergrund m
backhand [bækhænd] n (Sport) Rückhand f
backlog [bæklɔg] n (of work) Rückstand m
backpack [bækpæk] n Rucksack m

backpacker [bækpækər] n Rucksacktourist(in) m(f)
backpacking [bækpækɪŋ] n Rucksacktourismus m
backseat [bæksit] n Rücksitz m
backside [bæksaɪd] n (fam) Po m
back street n Seitensträßchen nt
backstroke [bækstroʊk] n Rückenschwimmen nt
back up vi (car etc) zurücksetzen ▷ vt (support) unterstützen; (Inform) sichern; (car) zurückfahren
backup [bækʌp] n (support) Unterstützung f; **~ copy** (Inform) Sicherungskopie f
backward [bækwərd] adj (child) zurückgeblieben; (region) rückständig; **~ movement** Rückwärtsbewegung f
backwards [bækwərdz] adv rückwärts
backyard [bækyɑrd] n Hinterhof m
bacon [beɪkən] n Frühstücksspeck m
bacteria [bæktɪəriə] npl Bakterien pl
bad [bæd] (worse, worst) adj schlecht, schlimm; (smell) übel; **I have a bad back** mir tut der Rücken weh; **I'm bad at math/sports** ich bin schlecht in Mathe/Sport; **to go bad** schlecht werden, verderben
badge [bædʒ] n Abzeichen nt
badger [bædʒər] n Dachs m
badly [bædli] adv schlecht; **~ wounded** schwer verwundet; **to need sth** ~ etw dringend brauchen
bad-tempered [bædtɛmpərd] adj schlecht gelaunt
bag [bæg] n (small) Tüte f; (larger) Beutel m; (handbag) Tasche f; **my bags** (luggage) mein Gepäck
baggage [bægɪdʒ] n Gepäck nt
baggage allowance [bægɪdʒ əlaʊəns] n Freigepäck nt
baggage claim n Gepäckrückgabe f
baggy [bægi] adj (zu) weit; (trousers, suit) ausgebeult
bag lady n Stadtstreicherin f
bagpipes [bægpaɪps] npl Dudelsack m
Bahamas [bəhɑmˈɛz] npl: **the ~** die Bahamas pl
bail [beɪl] n (money) Kaution f
bait [beɪt] n Köder m
bake [beɪk] vt, vi backen
baker [beɪkər] n Bäcker(in) m(f)
bakery [beɪkəri, beɪkri] n Bäckerei f
baking powder [beɪkɪŋ paʊdər] n Back-

pulver *nt*

balance [bǽləns] *n* (*equilibrium*) Gleichgewicht *nt* ▷ *vt* (*make up for*) ausgleichen

balanced [bǽlənst] *adj* ausgeglichen

balance sheet *n* Bilanz *f*

balcony [bǽlkəni] *n* Balkon *m*

bald [bɔld] *adj* kahl; **to be ~** eine Glatze haben

Balkans [bɔlkˈnz] *npl:* **the ~** der Balkan, die Balkanländer *pl*

ball [bɔl] *n* Ball *m*; **to have a ~** (*fam*) sich prima amüsieren

ballet [bǽleɪ] *n* Ballett *nt*

ballet dancer *n* Balletttänzer(in) *m(f)*

balloon [bəlún] *n* (Luft)ballon *m*

ballot box *n* (geheime) Abstimmung

ballot box *n* Wahlurne *f*

ballpoint (pen) [bɔlpɔɪnt (pɛn)] *n* Kugelschreiber *m*

ballroom [bɔlrum] *n* Tanzsaal *m*

Baltic [bɔltɪk] *adj:* **~ Sea** Ostsee *f*; **the ~ States** die baltischen Staaten

Baltics *n:* **the ~** das Baltikum

bamboo [bæmbú] *n* Bambus *m*

bamboo shoots *npl* Bambussprossen *pl*

ban [bæn] *n* Verbot *nt* ▷ *vt* verbieten

banana [bənǽnə] *n* Banane *f*; **he's ~s** (*fam*) er ist völlig durchgeknallt

banana split *n* Bananensplit *nt*

band [bænd] *n* (*group*) Gruppe *f*; (*of criminals*) Bande *f*; (*Mus*) Kapelle *f*; (*pop, rock etc*) Band *f*; (*strip*) Band *nt*

bandage [bǽndɪdʒ] *n* Verband *m*; (*elastic*) Bandage *f* ▷ *vt* verbinden

B & B [bi ən bi] (*abbr*) = **bed and breakfast**

bang [bæŋ] *n* (*noise*) Knall *m*; (*blow*) Schlag *m* ▷ *vt, vi* knallen; (*door*) zuschlagen, zuknallen

bangs [bæŋz] *npl* (*of hair*) Pony *m*

banish [bǽnɪʃ] *vt* verbannen

banister(s) [bǽnɪstər(z)] *n* (Treppen)geländer *nt*

bank [bæŋk] *n* (*Fin*) Bank *f*; (*of river etc*) Ufer *nt*

bank account *n* Bankkonto *nt*

bank balance *n* Kontostand *m*

bank card *n* Bankkarte *f*

bank manager *n* Filialleiter(in) *m(f)*

banknote [bǽŋknout] *n* Banknote *f*

bankrupt [bǽŋkrʌpt] *vt* ruinieren; **to go ~** Pleite gehen

bank statement *n* Kontoauszug *m*

baptism [bǽptɪzəm] *n* Taufe *f*

baptize [bæptaɪz] *vt* taufen

bar [bɑr] *n* (*for drinks*) Bar *f*; (*less fancy*) Lokal *nt*; (*rod*) Stange *f*; (*of chocolate etc*) Riegel *m*, Tafel *f*; (*of soap*) Stück *nt*; (*counter*) Theke *f* ▷ *prep* außer; **bar none** ohne Ausnahme

barbecue [bɑrbɪkyu] *n* (*device*) Grill *m*; (*party*) Barbecue *nt*, Grillfete *f*; **to have a ~** grillen

barbed wire [bɑrbd waɪər] *n* Stacheldraht *m*

barber [bɑrbər] *n* (Herren)friseur *m*

bar code *n* Strichkode *m*

bare [bɛər] *adj* nackt; **~ patch** kahle Stelle

barefoot [bɛərfut] *adj, adv* barfuß

bareheaded [bɛərhɛdɪd] *adj, adv* ohne Kopfbedeckung

barely [bɛərli] *adv* kaum; (*with age*) knapp

bargain [bɑrgɪn] *n* (*cheap offer*) günstiges Angebot, Schnäppchen *nt*; (*transaction*) Geschäft *nt*; **a ~** das ist aber günstig! ▷ *vi* (ver)handeln

barge [bɑrdʒ] *n* (*for freight*) Lastkahn *m*; (*unpowered*) Schleppkahn *m*

bark [bɑrk] *n* (*of tree*) Rinde *f*; (*of dog*) Bellen *nt* ▷ *vi* (*dog*) bellen

barley [bɑrli] *n* Gerste *f*

barn [bɑrn] *n* Scheune *f*

barometer [bərɒmɪtər] *n* Barometer *nt*

baroque [bərouk] *adj* barock, Barock-

barracks [bǽrəks] *npl* Kaserne *f*

barrel [bǽrəl] *n* Fass *nt*

barrel organ *n* Drehorgel *f*

barricade [bǽrɪkeɪd] *n* Barrikade *f*

barrier [bǽriər] *n* (*obstruction*) Absperrung *f*, Barriere *f*; (*across road etc*) Schranke *f*

bartender [bɑrtɛndər] *n* Barkeeper(in) *m(f)*

base [beɪs] *n* Basis *f*; (*of lamp, pillar etc*) Fuß *m*; (*Mil*) Stützpunkt *m* ▷ *vt* gründen (*on* auf +*akk*); **to be ~d on sth** auf etw *dat* basieren

baseball [beɪsbɔl] *n* Baseball *m*

baseball cap *n* Baseballmütze *f*

basement [beɪsmənt] *n* Kellergeschoss *nt*

bash [bæʃ] *n* (*fam*) Schlag *m*; (*party*) Party *f* ▷ *vt* hauen

basic [beɪsɪk] *adj* einfach; (*fundamental*) Grund-; (*importance, difference*) grundlegend; (*in principle*) grundsätzlich; **the accommodation is very ~** die Unterkunft ist sehr bescheiden

basically [beɪsɪkli] *adv* im Grunde

basics [beɪsɪks] *npl:* **the ~** das Wesentliche

basil [beɪzˀl] *n* Basilikum *nt*

basin [beɪsˀn] *n* (*for washing, valley*)

(Wasch)becken nt

basis [beɪsɪs] n Basis f; **on the ~ of** aufgrund +gen; **on a monthly ~** monatlich

basket [baskɪt, bæs-] n Korb m

basketball [baskɪtbɔl, bæs-] n Basketball m

Basque [bæsk] n (person) Baske m, Baskin f; (language) Baskisch nt ▷ adj baskisch

bass¹ [beɪs] n (Mus) Bass m; ▷ adj (Mus) Bass-

bass² [bæs] (Zool) Barsch m

bat [bæt] n (Zool) Fledermaus f; (Sport: baseball) Schlagholz nt; (:table tennis) Schläger m

batch [bætʃ] n Schwung m; (fam: of letters, books etc) Stoß m

bath [bɑːθ] n Bad nt; (tub) Badewanne f; **to have a ~** baden ▷ vt (child etc) baden

bathing suit [beɪðɪŋ suːt] n Badeanzug m

bath mat [bæθmæt] n Badevorleger m

bathrobe [bæθroub] n Bademantel m

bathroom [bæθrum] n Bad(ezimmer) nt

baths [bæðz] npl (Schwimm)bad nt

bath towel n Badetuch nt

bathtub [bæθtʌb] n Badewanne f

baton [bətɒn] n (Mus) Taktstock m; (police) Schlagstock m

batter [bætər] n Teig m ▷ vt heftig schlagen

battered [bætərd] adj übel zugerichtet; (hat, car) verbeult; (wife, baby) misshandelt

battery [bætəri] n (Elec) Batterie f

battery charger [bætəri tʃɑrdʒˑr] n Ladegerät nt

battle [bætᵊl] n Schlacht f; (fig) Kampf m (for um +akk

battlefield [bætᵊlfild] n Schlachtfeld nt

battlements [bætᵊlmənts] npl Zinnen pl

bay [beɪ] n (of sea) Bucht f; (on house) Erker m; (tree) Lorbeerbaum m

bay leaf n Lorbeerblatt nt

bay window n Erkerfenster nt

BC [biː siː] (abbr) (= before Christ) vor Christi Geburt, v. Chr.

KEYWORD

be [bi, STRONG biː] (pt was, were, pp been) vb aux 1 (with present participle: forming continuous tenses): **what are you doing?** was machst du (gerade)?; **it is raining** es regnet; **I've been waiting for you for hours** ich warte schon seit Stunden auf dich

2 (with pp: forming passives): **to be killed** getötet werden; **the thief was nowhere to be seen** der Dieb war nirgendwo zu sehen

3 (in tag questions): **it was fun, wasn't it?** es hat Spaß gemacht, nicht wahr?

4 (+to +infin): **the house is to be sold** das Haus soll verkauft werden; **he's not to open it** er darf es nicht öffnen

▷ vb +complement 1 (usu) sein; **I'm tired** ich bin müde; **I'm hot/cold** mir ist heiß/kalt; **he's a doctor** er ist Arzt; **2 and 2 are 4** 2 und 2 ist o sind 4; **she's tall/pretty** sie ist groß/hübsch; **be careful/quiet** sei vorsichtig/ruhig

2 (of health): **how are you?** wie geht es dir?; **he's very ill** er ist sehr krank; **I'm fine now** jetzt geht es mir gut

3 (of age): **how old are you?** wie alt bist du?; **I'm sixteen (years old)** ich bin sechzehn (Jahre alt)

4 (cost): **how much was the meal?** was o wie viel hat das Essen gekostet?; **that'll be $5.75, please** das macht $5.75, bitte

▷ vi 1 (exist, occur etc) sein; **is there a God?** gibt es einen Gott?; **be that as it may** wie dem auch sei; **so be it** also gut

2 (referring to place) sein; **I won't be here tomorrow** ich werde morgen nicht hier sein

3 (referring to movement): **where have you been?** wo bist du gewesen?; **I've been in the garden** ich war im Garten

▷ impers vb 1 (referring to time, distance, weather) sein; **it's 5 o'clock** es ist 5 Uhr; **it's 10 km to the village** es sind 10 km bis zum Dorf; **it's too hot/cold** es ist zu heiß/kalt

2 (emphatic): **it's me** ich bin's; **it's the mailman** es ist der Briefträger

beach [biːtʃ] n Strand m

beachwear [biːtʃwɛər] n Strandkleidung f

bead [biːd] n (of glass, wood etc) Perle f; (drop) Tropfen m

beak [biːk] n Schnabel m

beam [biːm] (of wood etc) Balken m; (of light) Strahl m ▷ vi (smile etc) strahlen

bean [biːn] n Bohne f

bear [bɛər] (bore, borne) vt (carry) tragen; (tolerate) ertragen ▷ n Bär m

bearable [bɛərəbᵊl] adj erträglich

beard [bɪərd] n Bart m

beast [biːst] n Tier nt; (brutal person) Bestie f; (disliked person) Biest nt

beat [biːt] (beat, beaten) vt schlagen; (as

punishment) prügeln; **to ~ sb at tennis** jdn im Tennis schlagen ▷ *n* (*of heart, drum etc*) Schlag *m*; (*Mus*) Takt *m*; (*type of music*) Beat *m*

beaten [biːtⁿn] *pp of* **beat**; **off the ~ track** abgelegen

beat up *vt* zusammenschlagen

beautiful [byuːtɪfəl] *adj* schön; (*splendid*) herrlich

beauty [byuːti] *n* Schönheit *f*

beaver [biːvər] *n* Biber *m*

became [bɪkeɪm] *pt of* **become**

because [bɪkɔːz, bɪkʌz] *adv, conj* weil ▷ *prep*: ~ **of** wegen +*gen o dat*

become [bɪkʌm] (**became, become**) *vt* werden; **what's ~ of him?** was ist aus ihm geworden?

bed [bɛd] *n* Bett *nt*; (*in garden*) Beet *nt*

bed and breakfast *n* Übernachtung *f* mit Frühstück

bedclothes [bɛdklouz, -klouðz] *npl* Bettwäsche *f*

bedding [bɛdɪŋ] *n* Bettzeug *nt*

bed linens *npl* Bettwäsche *f*

bedroom [bɛdrum] *n* Schlafzimmer *nt*

bedspread [bɛdsprɛd] *n* Tagesdecke *f*

bedtime [bɛdtaɪm] *n* Schlafenszeit *f*

bee [biː] *n* Biene *f*

beech [biːtʃ] *n* Buche *f*

beef [biːf] *n* Rindfleisch *nt*

beehive [biːhaɪv] *n* Bienenstock *m*

been [bɪn] *pp of* **be**

beer [bɪər] *n* Bier *nt*

beet [biːt] *n* Rote Bete

beetle [biːtⁿl] *n* Käfer *m*

before [bɪfɔr] *prep* vor; **the year ~ last** vorletztes Jahr; **the day ~ yesterday** vorgestern ▷ *conj* bevor ▷ *adv* (*of time*) vorher; **have you been there ~?** waren Sie/warst du schon einmal dort?

beforehand [bɪfɔrhænd] *adv* vorher

beg [bɛg] *vt*: **to beg sb to do sth** jdn inständig bitten, etw zu tun ▷ *vi* (*beggar*) betteln (*for* um +*akk*)

began [bɪgæn] *pt of* **begin**

beggar [bɛgər] *n* Bettler(in) *m(f)*

begin [bɪgɪn] (**began, begun**) *vt, vi* anfangen, beginnen; **to ~ to do sth** anfangen, etw zu tun

beginner [bɪgɪnər] *n* Anfänger(in) *m(f)*

beginning [bɪgɪnɪŋ] *n* Anfang *m*

begun [bɪgʌn] *pp of* **begin**

behalf [bɪhæf] *n*: **on ~ of, in ~ of** im Namen/Auftrag von; **on my ~** für mich

behave [bɪheɪv] *vi* sich benehmen; **~ yourself!** benimm dich!

behavior [bɪheɪvyər] *n* Benehmen *nt*

behind [bɪhaɪnd] *prep* hinter; **to be ~ time** Verspätung haben ▷ *adv* hinten; **to be ~ with one's work** mit seiner Arbeit im Rückstand sein ▷ *n* (*fam*) Hinterteil *nt*

beige [beɪʒ] *adj* beige

being [biːɪŋ] *n* (*existence*) Dasein *nt*; (*person*) Wesen *nt*

Belarus [bɛlərus] *n* Weißrussland *nt*

belch [bɛltʃ] *n* Rülpser *m* ▷ *vi* rülpsen

belfry [bɛlfri] *n* Glockenturm *m*

Belgian [bɛldʒⁿn] *adj* belgisch ▷ *n* Belgier(in) *m(f)*

Belgium [bɛldʒəm] *n* Belgien *nt*

belief [bɪlif] *n* Glaube *m* (*in an* +*akk*); (*conviction*) Überzeugung *f*; **it's my ~ that ...** ich bin der Überzeugung, dass ...

believe [bɪliv] *vt* glauben

believe in *vi* glauben an +*akk*

believer [bɪlivər] *n* (*Rel*) Gläubige(r) *mf*

bell [bɛl] *n* (*church*) Glocke *f*; (*bicycle, door*) Klingel *f*

bellboy [bɛlbɔɪ] *n* Page *m*

bellows [bɛlouz] *npl* (*for fire*) Blasebalg *m*

belly [bɛli] *n* Bauch *m*

bellyache [bɛlieɪk] *n* Bauchweh *nt* ▷ *vi* (*fam*) meckern

belly button *n* (*fam*) Bauchnabel *m*

belly flop *n* (*fam*) Bauchklatscher *m*

belong [bɪlɔŋ] *vi* gehören (*to sb* jdm); (*to club*) angehören +*dat*

belongings [bɪlɔŋɪŋz] *npl* Habe *f*

below [bɪlou] *prep* unter ▷ *adv* unten

belt [bɛlt] *n* (*round waist*) Gürtel *m*; (*safety belt*) Gurt *m*; **below the ~** unter die Gürtellinie ▷ *vt* (*fam: go fast*) rasen, düsen

beltway [bɛltweɪ] *n* Umgehungsstraße *f*

bench [bɛntʃ] *n* Bank *f*

bend [bɛnd] *n* Biegung *f*; (*in road*) Kurve *f* ▷ *vt* (**bent, bent**) (*curve*) biegen; (*head, arm*) beugen ▷ *vi* sich biegen; (*person*) sich beugen

beneath [bɪniθ] *prep* unter ▷ *adv* darunter

beneficial [bɛnɪfɪʃⁿl] *adj* gut, nützlich (*to* für)

benefit [bɛnɪfɪt] *n* (*advantage*) Vorteil *m*; (*profit*) Nutzen *m*; **for your/his ~** deinetwegen/seinetwegen; **unemployment ~** Arbeitslosengeld *nt* ▷ *vt* guttun +*dat* ▷ *vi* Nutzen ziehen (*from* aus)

benign [bɪnaɪn] *adj* (*person*) gütig; (*climate*) mild; (*Med*) gutartig

bent [bɛnt] *pt, pp of* **bend** ▷ *adj* krumm; (*fam*) korrupt

beret [bəreɪ] n Baskenmütze f

Bermuda [bɜrmjudə] n: **the ~s** pl die Bermudas pl ▷ adj: **~ shorts** pl Bermudashorts pl; **the ~ triangle** das Bermudadreieck

berry [bɛri] n Beere f

berth [bɜrθ] n (for ship) Ankerplatz m; (in ship) Koje f; (in train) Bett nt ▷ vt am Kai festmachen ▷ vi anlegen

beside [bɪsaɪd] prep neben; **~ the sea/lake** am Meer/See

besides [bɪsaɪdz] prep außer ▷ adv außerdem

besiege [bɪsidʒ] vt belagern

best [bɛst] adj beste(r, s); **my ~ friend** mein bester o engster Freund; **the ~ thing to do would be to ...** das Beste wäre zu ...; (on food packaging): **~ before ...** mindestens haltbar bis ... ▷ n der/die/das Beste; **all the ~** alles Gute; **to make the ~ of it** das Beste daraus machen ▷ adv am besten; **I like this ~** das mag ich am liebsten

best man (pl **-men**) n Trauzeuge m

best seller [bɛstsɛlər] n Bestseller m

bet [bɛt] (**bet, bet**) vt, vi wetten (on auf +akk); **I bet him $5 that ...** ich habe mit ihm um 5 Dollar gewettet, dass ...; **you bet** (fam) und ob!; **I bet he'll be late** er kommt mit Sicherheit zu spät ▷ n Wette f

betray [bɪtreɪ] vt verraten

betrayal [bɪtreɪəl] n Verrat m

better [bɛtər] adj, adv besser; **to get ~** (in health) sich erholen, wieder gesund werden; (improve) sich verbessern; **I'm much ~ today** es geht mir heute viel besser; **you'd ~ go** du solltest/Sie sollten lieber gehen; **a change for the ~** eine Wendung zum Guten

betting [bɛtɪŋ] n Wetten nt

between [bɪtwin] prep zwischen; (among) unter; **~ you and me, ...** unter uns gesagt, ... ▷ adv: **in ~** dazwischen

beverage [bɛvərɪdʒ] n (formal) Getränk nt

beware [bɪwɛər] vt: **to ~ of sth** sich vor etw +dat hüten; **"~ of the dog"** „Vorsicht, bissiger Hund!"

bewildered [bɪwɪldərd] adj verwirrt

beyond [bɪyɒnd] prep (place) jenseits +gen; (time) über ... hinaus; (out of reach) außerhalb +gen; **it's ~ me** da habe ich keine Ahnung, da bin ich überfragt ▷ adv darüber hinaus

bias [baɪəs] n (prejudice) Vorurteil nt, Voreingenommenheit f

biased [baɪəst] adj voreingenommen

bib [bɪb] n Latz m

Bible [baɪbəl] n Bibel f

bicycle [baɪsɪkəl] n Fahrrad nt

bid [bɪd] (**bid, bid**) vt (offer) bieten ▷ n (attempt) Versuch m; (offer) Gebot nt

big [bɪg] adj groß; **it's no big deal** (fam) es ist nichts Besonderes

big-headed [bɪghɛdɪd] adj eingebildet

bike [baɪk] n (fam) Rad nt

bike lane n Radweg m

bikini [bɪkini] n Bikini m

bilingual [baɪlɪŋgwəl] adj zweisprachig

bill [bɪl] n (account) Rechnung f; (banknote) Banknote f; (Pol) Gesetzentwurf m; (Zool) Schnabel m

billfold [bɪlfoʊld] n Brieftasche f

bind [baɪnd] (**bound, bound**) vt binden; (bind together) zusammenbinden; (wound) verbinden

binding [baɪndɪŋ] n (ski) Bindung f; (book) Einband m

binge [bɪndʒ] n (fam: drinking) Sauferei f; **to go on a ~** auf Sauftour gehen

bingo [bɪŋgoʊ] n Bingo nt

binoculars [bɪnɒkyələrz] npl Fernglas nt

biodegradable [baɪoʊdɪgreɪdəbəl] adj biologisch abbaubar

biography [baɪɒgrəfi] n Biografie f

biological [baɪəlɒdʒɪkəl] adj biologisch

biology [baɪɒlədʒi] n Biologie f

birch [bɜrtʃ] n Birke f

bird [bɜrd] n Vogel m

bird flu n Vogelgrippe f

birdwatcher [bɜrdwɒtʃər] n Vogelbeobachter(in) m(f)

birth [bɜrθ] n Geburt f

birth certificate n Geburtsurkunde f

birth control n Geburtenkontrolle f

birthday [bɜrθdeɪ, -di] n Geburtstag m; **happy ~** herzlichen Glückwunsch zum Geburtstag

birthday card n Geburtstagskarte f

birthday party n Geburtstagsfeier f

birthplace [bɜrθpleɪs] n Geburtsort m

bisexual [baɪsɛkʃuəl] adj bisexuell

bishop [bɪʃəp] n Bischof m; (in chess) Läufer m

bit [bɪt] pt of **bite** ▷ n (piece) Stück(chen) nt; (Inform) Bit nt; **a bit of ...** (small amount) ein bisschen ...; **a bit tired** etwas müde; **bit by bit** allmählich; (time): **for a bit** ein Weilchen; **quite a bit** (a lot) ganz schön viel

bitch [bɪtʃ] n (dog) Hündin f

bitchy [bɪtʃi] adj gemein, zickig

bite [baɪt] (**bit, bitten**) vt, vi beißen ▷ n Biss m; (mouthful) Bissen m; (insect) Stich m;

to have a ~ eine Kleinigkeit essen

bitten [bɪtˀn] *pp of* **bite**

bitter [bɪtər] *adj* bitter; (*memory etc*) schmerzlich

bizarre [bɪzɑr] *adj* bizarr

black [blæk] *adj* schwarz

blackberry [blækbɛri] *n* Brombeere *f*

blackbird [blækbɜrd] *n* Amsel *f*

blackboard [blækbɔrd] *n* (Wand)tafel *f*

black box *n* (*Aviat*) Flugschreiber *m*

black eye *n* blaues Auge

blackmail [blækmeɪl] *n* Erpressung *f* ▷ *vt* erpressen

black market *n* Schwarzmarkt *m*

blackout [blækaʊt] *n* (*Med*) Ohnmacht *f*; **to have a ~** ohnmächtig werden

Black Sea *n*: **the ~** das Schwarze Meer

blacksmith [blæksmɪθ] *n* Schmied(in) *m(f)*

black tie *n* Abendanzug *m*, Smoking *m*; **is it ~?** ist o besteht da Smokingzwang?

blacktop [blæktɒp] *n* (*Aviat*) Rollfeld *nt*

bladder [blædər] *n* Blase *f*

blade [bleɪd] *n* (*of knife*) Klinge *f*; (*of propeller*) Blatt *nt*; (*of grass*) Halm *m*

blame [bleɪm] *n* Schuld *f* ▷ *vt*: **to ~ sth on sb** jdm die Schuld an etw *dat* geben; **he is to ~** er ist daran schuld

bland [blænd] *adj* (*taste*) fade; (*comment*) nichtssagend

blank [blæŋk] *adj* (*page, space*) leer, unbeschrieben; (*look*) ausdruckslos; **~ cheque** Blankoscheck *m*

blanket [blæŋkɪt] *n* (Woll)decke *f*

blast [blæst] *n* (*of wind*) Windstoß *m*; (*of explosion*) Druckwelle *f* ▷ *vt* (*blow up*) sprengen; **~!** (*fam*) Mist!, verdammt!

blatant [bleɪtˀnt] *adj* (*undisguised*) offen; (*obvious*) offensichtlich

blaze [bleɪz] *vi* lodern; (*sun*) brennen ▷ *n* (*building*) Brand *m*; (*other fire*) Feuer *nt*; **a ~ of color** eine Farbenpracht

blazer [bleɪzər] *n* Blazer *m*

bleach [blitʃ] *n* Bleichmittel *nt* ▷ *vt* bleichen

bleak [blik] *adj* öde, düster; (*future*) trostlos

bleary [blɪəri] *adj* (*eyes*) trübe, verschlafen

bleed [blid] (**bled, bled**) *vi* bluten

blend [blɛnd] *n* Mischung *f* ▷ *vt* mischen ▷ *vi* sich mischen

blender [blɛndər] *n* Mixer *m*

bless [blɛs] *vt* segnen; **~ you!** Gesundheit!

blessing [blɛsɪŋ] *n* Segen *m*

blew [blu] *pt of* **blow**

blind [blaɪnd] *adj* blind; (*corner*) unübersichtlich; **to turn a ~ eye to sth** bei etw ein Auge zudrücken ▷ *n* (*for window*) Rollo *nt* ▷ *vt* blenden

blind alley *n* Sackgasse *f*

blind spot *n* (*Auto*) toter Winkel; (*fig*) schwacher Punkt

blink [blɪŋk] *vi* blinzeln; (*light*) blinken

bliss [blɪs] *n* (Glück)seligkeit *f*

blister [blɪstər] *n* Blase *f*

blizzard [blɪzərd] *n* Schneesturm *m*

bloated [bloʊtɪd] *adj* aufgedunsen

block [blɒk] *n* (*of wood, stone, ice*) Block *m*, Klotz *m*; (*of buildings*) Häuserblock ▷ *vt* (*road etc*) blockieren; (*pipe, nose*) verstopfen

blockage [blɒkɪdʒ] *n* Verstopfung *f*

blockbuster [blɒkbʌstər] *n* Knüller *m*

block letters *npl* Blockschrift *f*

blog [blɒg] *n* (*Inform*) Blog *nt*, Weblog *m* ▷ *vi* bloggen

blond(e) *adj* blond ▷ *n* (*person*) Blondine *f*, blonder Typ

blood [blʌd] *n* Blut *nt*

blood count *n* Blutbild *nt*

blood donor *n* Blutspender(in) *m(f)*

blood group *n* Blutgruppe *f*

blood orange *n* Blutorange *f*

blood poisoning [blʌd pɔɪzˀnɪŋ] *n* Blutvergiftung *f*

blood pressure *n* Blutdruck *m*

blood sample *n* Blutprobe *f*

bloodthirsty [blʌdθɜrsti] *adj* blutrünstig

bloody [blʌdi] *adj* blutig

bloom [blum] *n* Blüte *f* ▷ *vi* blühen

blossom [blɒsəm] *n* Blüte *f* ▷ *vi* blühen

blot [blɒt] *n* (*of ink*) Klecks *m*; (*fig*) Fleck *m*

blouse [blaʊs] *n* Bluse *f*

blow [bloʊ] *n* Schlag *m* ▷ *vi, vt* (**blew, blown**) (*wind*) wehen, blasen; (*person: trumpet etc*) blasen; **to ~ one's nose** sich *dat* die Nase putzen

blow-dry *vt* föhnen

blown [bloʊn] *pp of* **blow**

blow out *vt* (*candle etc*) ausblasen

blowout [bloʊaʊt] *n* (*Auto*) geplatzter Reifen

blow up *vi* explodieren ▷ *vt* sprengen; (*balloon, tyre*) aufblasen; (*Foto: enlarge*) vergrößern

blue [blu] *adj* blau; (*fam: unhappy*) trübsinnig, niedergeschlagen; (*film*) pornografisch; (*joke*) anzüglich; (*language*) derb

bluebell [blubɛl] *n* Glockenblume *f*

blueberry [bluɛri] *n* Blaubeere *f*

blue cheese *n* Blauschimmelkäse *m*

blues [bluz] *npl*: **the ~** (*Mus*) der Blues; **to have the ~** (*fam*) niedergeschlagen sein

blunder [blʌndər] *n* Schnitzer *m*

blunt [blʌnt] *adj* (*knife*) stumpf; (*fig*) unverblümt

bluntly [blʌntli] *adv* geradeheraus

blurred [blɜrd] *adj* verschwommen, unklar

blush [blʌʃ] *vi* erröten

board [bɔrd] *n* (*of wood*) Brett *nt*; (*committee*) Ausschuss *m*; (*of firm*) Vorstand *m*; **room and ~** Unterkunft und Verpflegung; **on ~** an Bord ▷ *vt* (*train, bus*) einsteigen in +*akk*; (*ship*) an Bord +*gen* gehen

board game *n* Brettspiel *nt*

boarding pass [bɔrdɪŋ pæs] *n* Bordkarte *f*, Einsteigekarte *f*

boarding school [bɔrdɪŋ skul] *n* Internat *nt*

board meeting *n* Vorstandssitzung *f*

boardroom [bɔrdrum] *n* Sitzungssaal *m* (des Vorstands)

boast [boust] *vi* prahlen (*about* mit) ▷ *n* Prahlerei *f*

boat [bout] *n* Boot *nt*; (*ship*) Schiff *nt*

boatman [boutmən] *n* (*hirer*) Bootsverleiher *m*

bodily [bɒdili] *adj* körperlich ▷ *adv* (*forcibly*) gewaltsam

body [bɒdi] *n* Körper *m*; (*dead*) Leiche *f*; (*of car*) Karosserie *f*

bodybuilding [bɒdibɪldɪŋ] *n* Bodybuilding *nt*

bodyguard [bɒdigɑrd] *n* Leibwächter *m*; (*group*) Leibwache *f*

body jewelry *n* Intimschmuck *m*

body odor *n* Körpergeruch *m*

body piercing *n* Piercing *nt*

bodywork [bɒdiwɜrk] *n* Karosserie *f*

boil [bɔɪl] *vt, vi* kochen ▷ *n* (*Med*) Geschwür *nt*

boiler [bɔɪlər] *n* Boiler *m*

boiling [bɔɪlɪŋ] *adj* (*water etc*) kochend (heiß); **I was ~** (*hot*) mir war fürchterlich heiß; (*with rage*) ich kochte vor Wut

boiling point *n* Siedepunkt *m*

bold [bould] *adj* kühn, mutig; (*colors*) kräftig; (*type*) fett

Bolivia [bəlɪviə] *n* Bolivien *nt*

bolt [boult] *n* (*lock*) Riegel *m*; (*screw*) Bolzen *m* ▷ *vt* verriegeln

bomb [bɒm] *n* Bombe *f* ▷ *vt* bombardieren

bond [bɒnd] *n* (*link*) Bindung *f*; (*Fin*) Obligation *f*

bone [boun] *n* Knochen *m*; (*of fish*) Gräte *f*

boner [bounər] *n* (*fam*) Schnitzer *m*

bonfire [bɒnfaɪər] *n* Feuer *nt* (im Freien)

bonnet [bɒnɪt] *n* (*for baby*) Häubchen *nt*

bonus [bounəs] *n* Bonus *m*, Prämie *f*

boo [bu] *vt* auspfeifen, ausbuhen ▷ *vi* buhen ▷ *n* Buhruf *m*

book [buk] *n* Buch *nt*; (*of tickets, stamps*) Heft *nt* ▷ *vt* (*ticket etc*) bestellen; (*hotel, flight etc*) buchen; (*Sports*) verwarnen; **fully ~ed (up)** ausgebucht; (*performance*) ausverkauft

bookcase [bukkeɪs] *n* Bücherregal *nt*

booking [bukɪŋ] *n* Buchung *f*

bookkeeping *n* Buchhaltung *f*

booklet [buklɪt] *n* Broschüre *f*

bookmark [bukmɑrk] *n* (*a. Inform*) Lesezeichen *nt*

bookshelf [bukʃelf] *n* Bücherbord *nt*; **bookshelves** Bücherregal *nt*

bookstore [bukstɔr] *n* Buchhandlung *f*

boom [bum] *n* (*of business*) Boom *m*; (*noise*) Dröhnen *nt* ▷ *vi* (*business*) boomen; (*fam*) florieren; (*voice etc*) dröhnen

boomerang [buməræŋ] *n* Bumerang *m*

boost [bust] *n* Auftrieb *m* ▷ *vt* (*production, sales*) ankurbeln; (*power, profits etc*) steigern

booster [bustər] *n* (*Med*) Wiederholungsimpfung *f*

boot [but] *n* Stiefel *m* ▷ *vt* (*Inform*) laden, booten

booth [buθ] *n* (*at fair etc*) Bude *f*; (*at trade fair etc*) Stand *m*

booze [buz] (*fam*) *n* Alkohol *m* ▷ *vi* saufen

border [bɔrdər] *n* Grenze *f*; (*edge*) Rand *m*

borderline [bɔrdərlaɪn] *n* Grenze *f*

bore [bɔr] *pt of* **bear** ▷ *vt* (*hole etc*) bohren; (*person*) langweilen ▷ *n* (*person*) Langweiler(in) *m(f)*, langweiliger Mensch; (*thing*) langweilige Sache

bored [bɔrd] *adj*: **to be ~** sich langweilen

boredom [bɔrdəm] *n* Langeweile *f*

boring [bɔrɪŋ] *adj* langweilig

born [bɔrn] *adj*: **he was ~ in London** er ist in London geboren

borne [bɔrn] *pp of* **bear**

borough [bɜrou] *n* Stadtbezirk *m*

borrow [bɒrou] *vt* borgen

Bosnia [bæzniə] *n* Bosnien-Herzegowina *nt*

boss [bɒs] *n* Chef(in) *m(f)*, Boss *m*

bossy [bɒsi] *adj* herrisch

botanical [bətænɪkəl] *adj* botanisch; **~ garden(s)** botanischer Garten

both [bouθ] *adj* beide; ~ **the books** beide Bücher ▷ *pron* (*people*) beide; ~ (**of**) **the boys** die beiden Jungs; **I like** ~ **of them** ich mag sie (alle) beide ▷ *adv*: ~ **X and Y** sowohl X als auch Y

bother [boðər] *vt* ärgern, belästigen; **it doesn't** ~ **me** das stört mich nicht; **he can't be** ~**ed with details** mit Details gibt er sich nicht ab; **I'm not** ~**ed** das ist mir egal ▷ *vi* sich kümmern (*about* um); **don't** ~ (**das ist**) **nicht nötig, lass es!** ▷ *n* (*trouble*) Mühe *f*; (*annoyance*) Ärger *m*

bottle [botͦl] *n* Flasche *f* ▷ *vt* (*in Flaschen*) abfüllen

bottled [botͦld] *adj* in Flaschen; ~ **beer** Flaschenbier *nt*

bottleneck [botͦlnɛk] *n* (*fig*) Engpass *m*

bottle opener [botͦl oupənər] *n* Flaschenöffner *m*

bottom [botəm] *n* (*of container*) Boden *m*; (*underside*) Unterseite *f*; (*fam: of person*) Po *m*; **at the** ~ **of the sea/table/page** auf dem Meeresgrund/am Tabellenende/ unten auf der Seite ▷ *adj* unterste(r, s); **to be** ~ **of the class/league** Klassenletzte(r)/ Tabellenletzte(r) sein

bought [bot] *pt, pp of* **buy**

bouillon cube [buljɒn-] *n* Brühwurfel *m*

bounce [bauns] *vi* (*ball*) springen, aufprallen; (*cheque*) platzen; **to** ~ **up and down** (*person*) herumhüpfen

bouncy [baunsi] *adj* (*ball*) gut springend; (*person*) munter

bound [baund] *pt, pp of* **bind** ▷ *adj* (*tied up*) gebunden; (*obliged*) verpflichtet; **to be** ~ **to do sth** (*sure to*) etw bestimmt tun (werden); (*have to*) etw tun müssen; **it's** ~ **to happen** es muss so kommen; **to be** ~ **for ...** auf dem Weg nach ... sein

boundary [baundəri] *n* Grenze *f*

bouquet [boukeɪ, bu-] *n* (*flowers*) Strauß *m*; (*of wine*) Blume *f*

boutique [butik] *n* Boutique *f*

bow [bau] *n* (*ribbon*) Schleife *f*; (*instrument, weapon*) Bogen *m* ▷ *vi* sich verbeugen ▷ *n* (*with head*) Verbeugung *f*; (*of ship*) Bug *m*

bowels [bauəlz] *npl* Darm *m*

bowl [boul] *n* (*basin*) Schüssel *f*; (*shallow*) Schale *f*; (*for animal*) Napf *m*

bowler [boulər] *n* (*hat*) Melone *f*

bowling [boulɪŋ] *n* Kegeln *nt*

bowling alley *n* Kegelbahn *f*

bow tie [bou taɪ] *n* Fliege *f*

box [bɒks] *n* Schachtel *f*; (*cardboard*) Kar-

ton *m*; (*bigger*) Kasten *m*; (*space on form*) Kästchen *nt*; (*Theat*) Loge *f*

boxer [bɒksər] *n* Boxer(in) *m(f)*

boxers *npl* Boxershorts *pl*

boxing [bɒksɪŋ] *n* (*Sport*) Boxen *nt*

boxing gloves *npl* Boxhandschuhe *pl*

boxing ring *n* Boxring *m*

box lunch *n* Lunchpaket *nt*

box number *n* Chiffre *f*

box office *n* (*cinema, theater*) Kasse *f*

boy [bɔɪ] *n* Junge *m*

boycott [bɔɪkɒt] *n* Boykott *m* ▷ *vt* boykottieren

boyfriend [bɔɪfrɛnd] *n* (*fester*) Freund *m*

Boy Scout *n* Pfadfinder *m*

bra [brɑ] *n* BH *m*

brace [breɪs] *n* (*on teeth*) Spange *f*

bracelet [breɪslɪt] *n* Armband *nt*

bracket [brækɪt] *n* (*in text*) Klammer *f*; (*Tech*) Träger *m* ▷ *vt* einklammern

brag [bræg] *vi* angeben

braid [breɪd] *n* Zopf *m* ▷ *vt* flechten

Braille [breɪl] *n* Blindenschrift *f*

brain [breɪn] *n* (*Anat*) Gehirn *nt*; (*mind*) Verstand *m*; ~**s** *pl* (*intelligence*) Grips *m*

brainstorm [breɪnstɔrm] *n* Geistesblitz *m*

brainy [breɪni] *adj* schlau, clever

braise [breɪz] *vt* schmoren

brake [breɪk] *n* Bremse *f* ▷ *vi* bremsen

brake fluid *n* Bremsflüssigkeit *f*

brake light *n* Bremslicht *nt*

brake pedal *n* Bremspedal *nt*

branch [bræntʃ] *n* (*of tree*) Ast *m*; (*of family, subject*) Zweig *m*; (*of firm*) Filiale *f*, Zweigstelle *f*

branch off *vi* (*road*) abzweigen

brand [brænd] *n* (*Comm*) Marke *f*

brand-new *adj* (*funkel*)nagelneu

brandy [brændi] *n* Weinbrand *m*

brass [bræs] *n* Messing *nt*

brass band *n* Blaskapelle *f*

brat [bræt] *n* (*pej, fam*) Gör *nt*

brave [breɪv] *adj* tapfer, mutig

bravery [breɪvəri] *n* Mut *m*

brawl [brɔl] *n* Schlägerei *f*

brawny [brɔni] *adj* muskulös

Brazil [brəzɪl] *n* Brasilien *nt*

Brazilian [brəzɪliən] *adj* brasilianisch ▷ *n* Brasilianer(in) *m(f)*

brazil nut *n* Paranuss *f*

bread [brɛd] *n* Brot *nt*

breadcrumbs [brɛdkrʌmz] *npl* Brotkrumen *pl*; (*Gastr*) Paniermehl *nt*

breaded [brɛdɪd] *adj* paniert

breadknife [brɛdnaɪf] *n* Brotmesser *nt*

breadth [brɛtθ] n Breite f

break [breɪk] n (fracture) Bruch m; (rest) Pause f; (short holiday) Kurzurlaub m; **give me a ~** gib mir eine Chance, hör auf damit! ▷vt (**broke, broken**) (fracture) brechen; (in pieces) zerbrechen; (toy, device) kaputt machen; (promise) nicht halten; (silence) brechen; (law) verletzen; (journey) unterbrechen; (news) mitteilen (to sb jdm); **I broke my leg** ich habe mir das Bein gebrochen; **he broke it to her gently** er hat es ihr schonend beigebracht ▷ vi (come apart) (auseinander)brechen; (in pieces) zerbrechen; (toy, device) kaputtgehen; (person) zusammenbrechen; (day, dawn) anbrechen; (news) bekannt werden

breakable [breɪkəbᵊl] adj zerbrechlich

breakage [breɪkɪdʒ] n Bruch m

break down vi (car) eine Panne haben; (machine) versagen; (person) zusammenbrechen

breakdown [breɪkdaʊn] n (of car) Panne f; (of machine) Störung f; (of person, relations, system) Zusammenbruch m

breakfast [brɛkfəst] n Frühstück nt; **to have ~** frühstücken

breakfast cereal n Cornflakes, Müsli etc

break in vi (burglar) einbrechen

break-in n Einbruch m

break into vt einbrechen in +akk

break off vi, vt abbrechen

break out vi ausbrechen; **to ~ in a rash** einen Ausschlag bekommen

break up vi aufbrechen; (meeting, organization) sich auflösen; (marriage) in die Brüche gehen; (couple) sich trennen; **school breaks up on Friday** am Freitag beginnen die Ferien ▷ vt aufbrechen; (marriage) zerstören; (meeting) auflösen

breakup [breɪkʌp] n (of meeting, organization) Auflösung f; (of marriage) Zerrüttung f

breast [brɛst] n Brust f

breastfeed [brɛstfid] vt stillen

breaststroke [brɛststroʊk, brɛsstroʊk] n Brustschwimmen nt

breath [brɛθ] n Atem m; **out of ~** außer Atem

Breathalyzer® [brɛθəlaɪzər] n Promillemesser m

breathe [briθ] vt, vi atmen

breathe in vt, vi einatmen

breathe out vt, vi ausatmen

breathless [brɛθlɪs] adj atemlos

breathtaking [brɛθteɪkɪŋ] adj atemberaubend

bred [brɛd] pt, pp of **breed**

breed [brid] n (race) Rasse f ▷ vi (**bred, bred**) sich vermehren ▷ vt züchten

breeder [bridər] n Züchter(in) m(f); (fam) Hetero m

breeding [bridɪŋ] n (of animals) Züchtung f; (of person) (gute) Erziehung

breeze [briz] n Brise f

brevity [brɛvɪti] n Kürze f

brew [bru] vt (beer) brauen; (tea) kochen

brewery [bruəri] n Brauerei f

bribe [braɪb] n Bestechungsgeld nt ▷ vt bestechen

bribery [braɪbəri] n Bestechung f

brick [brɪk] n Backstein m

bricklayer [brɪkleɪər] n Maurer(in) m(f)

bridal shower n Party für die zukünftige Braut

bride [braɪd] n Braut f

bridegroom [braɪdgrum] n Bräutigam m

bridesmaid [braɪdzmeɪd] n Brautjungfer f

bridge [brɪdʒ] n Brücke f; (cards) Bridge nt

brief [brif] adj kurz ▷ vt instruieren (on über +akk)

briefcase [brifkeɪs] n Aktentasche f

briefs npl Slip m

bright [braɪt] adj hell; (color) leuchtend; (cheerful) heiter; (intelligent) intelligent; (idea) glänzend

brilliant [brɪliənt] adj (sunshine, color) strahlend; (person) brillant; (idea) glänzend

brim [brɪm] n Rand m

bring [brɪŋ] (**brought, brought**) vt bringen; (with one) mitbringen

bring about vt herbeiführen, bewirken

bring back vt zurückbringen; (memories) wecken

bring down vt (reduce) senken; (government etc) zu Fall bringen

bring in vt hereinbringen; (introduce) einführen

bring out vt herausbringen

bring up vt (child) aufziehen; (question) zur Sprache bringen

brisk [brɪsk] adj (trade) lebhaft; (wind) frisch

bristle [brɪsᵊl] n Borste f

Brit [brɪt] n (fam) Brite m, Britin f

Britain [brɪt ᵊn] n Großbritannien nt

British [brɪtɪʃ] adj britisch; **the ~ Isles** pl die Britischen Inseln pl ▷ npl: **the ~** die Briten pl

brittle [brɪtᵊl] *adj* spröde
broad [brɔd] *adj* breit; *(accent)* stark; **in ~ daylight** am helllichten Tag ▷ *n (fam)* Frau *f*
broadcast [brɔdkæst] *n* Sendung *f (irr) vt, vi* senden; *(event)* übertragen
broaden [brɔdᵊn] *vt:* **to ~ the mind** den Horizont erweitern
broad-minded [brɔdmaɪndɪd] *adj* tolerant
broccoli [brɒkəli] *n* Brokkoli *pl*
brochure [brouʃʊr] *n* Prospekt *m*, Broschüre *f*
broke [brouk] *pt of* **break**
broken [broukən] *pp of* **break**
brokenhearted [broukənhɑrtɪd] *adj* untröstlich
broker [broukər] *n* Makler(in) *m(f)*
bronchitis [brɒŋkaɪtɪs] *n* Bronchitis *f*
bronze [brɒnz] *n* Bronze *f*
brooch [broutʃ] *n* Brosche *f*
broom [brum] *n* Besen *m*
Bros. *(abbr)* = **brothers** Gebr.
broth [brɔθ] *n* Fleischbrühe *f*
brothel [brɒθᵊl] *n* Bordell *nt*
brother [brʌðər] *n* Bruder *m;* **~s** *pl (Comm)* Gebrüder *pl*
brother-in-law [brʌðərɪnlɔ] *(pl* **brothers-in-law)** *n* Schwager *m*
brought [brɔt] *pt, pp of* **bring**
brow [brau] *n (eyebrow)* (Augen)braue *f,* *(forehead)* Stirn *f*
brown [braun] *adj* braun
brownie [brauni] *n (Gastr)* Brownie *m*
brown paper *n* Packpapier *nt*
brown rice *n* Naturreis *m*
brown sugar *n* brauner Zucker
browse [brauz] *vi (in book)* blättern; *(in shop)* schmökern, herumschauen
browser [brauzər] *n (Inform)* Browser *m*
bruise [bruz] *n* blauer Fleck ▷ *vt:* **to ~ one's arm** sich *dat* einen blauen Fleck (am Arm) holen
brunette [brunɛt] *n* Brünette *f*
brush [brʌʃ] *n* Bürste *f;* *(for sweeping)* Handbesen *m;* *(for painting)* Pinsel *m* ▷ *vt* bürsten; *(sweep)* fegen; **to ~ one's teeth** sich *dat* die Zähne putzen
brush up *vt (French etc)* auffrischen
Brussels sprouts [brʌsᵊlz sprauts] *npl* Rosenkohl *m,* Kohlsprossen *pl*
brutal [brutᵊl] *adj* brutal
brutality [brutælɪti] *n* Brutalität *f*
BS [bi ɛs] *(abbr)* = **Bachelor of Science**
BSE [bi ɛs i] *(abbr)* = **bovine spongiform**

encephalopathy BSE *f*
bubble [bʌbᵊl] *n* Blase *f*
bubble bath *n* Schaumbad *nt,* Badeschaum *m*
bubbly [bʌbli] *adj* sprudelnd; *(person)* temperamentvoll ▷ *n (fam)* Schampus *m*
buck [bʌk] *n (animal)* Bock *m;* *(fam)* Dollar *m*
bucket [bʌkɪt] *n* Eimer *m*
buckle [bʌkᵊl] *n* Schnalle *f* ▷ *vi (Tech)* sich verbiegen ▷ *vt* zuschnallen
bud [bʌd] *n* Knospe *f*
Buddhism [budɪzəm, bud-] *n* Buddhismus *m*
Buddhist [budɪst, bud-] *adj* buddhistisch ▷ *n* Buddhist(in) *m(f)*
buddy [bʌdi] *n (fam)* Kumpel *m*
budget [bʌdʒɪt] *n* Budget *nt* ▷ *adj* preisgünstig; **~ airline** Billigflieger *m*
budgie [bʌdʒi] *n (fam)* Wellensittich *m*
buff [bʌf] *adj* muskulös; **in the ~** nackt ▷ *n (enthusiast)* Fan *m*
buffalo [bʌfəlou] *(pl* **-es)** *n* Büffel *m*
buffer [bʌfər] *n (a. Inform)* Puffer *m*
buffet [bʌfɪt] *n (food)* (kaltes) Büfett *nt*
bug [bʌg] *n (Inform)* Bug *m,* Programmfehler *m;* *(listening device)* Wanze *f;* *(insect)* Insekt *nt;* *(fam: illness)* Infektion *f* ▷ *vt (fam)* nerven
buggy [bʌgi] *n* *(for baby)* Buggy® *m;* *(pram)* Kinderwagen *m*
build [bɪld] *(built, built) vt* bauen
builder [bɪldər] *n* Bauunternehmer(in) *m(f)*
building [bɪldɪŋ] *n* Gebäude *nt*
building site *n* Baustelle *f*
build up *vt* aufbauen
built [bɪlt] *pt, pp of* **build**
built-in *adj (cabinet)* Einbau-, eingebaut
bulb [bʌlb] *n (Bot)* (Blumen)zwiebel *f;* *(Elec)* Glühbirne *f*
Bulgaria [bʌlgɛəriə] *n* Bulgarien *nt*
Bulgarian [bʌlgɛəriən] *adj* bulgarisch ▷ *n (person)* Bulgare *m,* Bulgarin *f;* *(language)* Bulgarisch *nt*
bulimia [bulɪmiə, -lɪm-] *n* Bulimie *f*
bulk [bʌlk] *n (size)* Größe *f;* *(greater part)* Großteil *m (of +gen);* **in ~** en gros
bulky [bʌlki] *adj (goods)* sperrig; *(person)* stämmig
bull [bʊl] *n* Stier *m*
bulldog [bʊldɒg] *n* Bulldogge *f*
bulldoze [bʊldouz] *vt* planieren
bulldozer [bʊldouzər] *n* Planierraupe *f*

bullet [bʊlɪt] *n* Kugel *f*

bulletin [bʊlɪtɪn] *n* Bulletin *nt*; (*announcement*) Bekanntmachung *f*; (*Med*) Krankenbericht *m*

bulletin board *n* (*Inform*) schwarzes Brett

bullfight [bʊlfaɪt] *n* Stierkampf *m*

bully [bʊli] *n* Tyrann *m*

bum [bʌm] *n* (*vagrant*) Penner *m*; (*worthless person*) Rumtreiber *m*

bumblebee [bʌmbªlbi] *n* Hummel *f*

bump [bʌmp] *n* (*fam: swelling*) Beule *f*; (*in road*) Unebenheit *f*; (*blow*) Stoß *m* ▷ *vt* stoßen; **to ~ one's head** sich *dat* den Kopf anschlagen (*on an +dat*)

bumper [bʌmpər] *n* (*Auto*) Stoßstange *f* ▷ *adj* (*crop etc*) Rekord-

bump into *vt* stoßen gegen; (*fam: meet*) (zufällig) begegnen +*dat*

bumpy [bʌmpi] *adj* holp(e)rig

bun [bʌn] *n* süßes Brötchen

bunch [bʌntʃ] *n* (*of flowers*) Strauß *m*; (*fam: of people*) Haufen *m*; **~ of keys** Schlüsselbund *m*; **~ of grapes** Weintraube *f*

bundle [bʌndªl] *n* Bündel *nt*

bungalow [bʌŋɡəloʊ] *n* Bungalow *m*

bungee jumping [bʌndʒi dʒʌmpɪŋ] *n* Bungeejumping *nt*

bunk [bʌŋk] *n* Koje *f*

bunk bed(s) [bʌŋk bɛd(z)] *n(pl)* Etagenbett *nt*

bunker [bʌŋkər] *n* (*Mil*) Bunker *m*

bunny [bʌni] *n* Häschen *nt*

buoy [bʊi] *n* Boje *f*

buoyant [bɔɪənt] *adj* (*floating*) schwimmend

burden [bɜrdªn] *n* Last *f*

bureau [byʊəroʊ] *n* Büro *nt*; (*government department*) Amt *nt*

bureaucracy [byʊrɒkrəsi] *n* Bürokratie *f*

bureaucratic [byʊərəkrætɪk] *adj* bürokratisch

burger [bɜrɡər] *n* Hamburger *m*

burglar [bɜrɡlər] *n* Einbrecher(in) *m(f)*

burglar alarm *n* Alarmanlage *f*

burglarize [bɜrɡləraɪz] *vt* einbrechen in +*akk*

burglary [bɜrɡləri] *n* Einbruch *m*

burial [bɛriəl] *n* Beerdigung *f*

burn [bɜrn] (**burned** *o* **burnt**, **burned** *o* **burnt**) *vt* verbrennen; (*food, slightly*) anbrennen; **to ~ one's hand** sich *dat* die Hand verbrennen ▷ *vi* brennen ▷ *n* (*injury*) Brandwunde *f*; (*on material*) verbrannte Stelle

burn down *vt, vi* abbrennen

burner [bɜrnər] *n* (*of stove*) Kochfeld *nt*

burp [bɜrp] *vi* rülpsen ▷ *vt* (*baby*) aufstoßen lassen

burst [bɜrst] (**burst, burst**) *vt* platzen lassen ▷ *vi* platzen; **to ~ into tears** in Tränen ausbrechen

bury [bɛri] *vt* begraben; (*in grave*) beerdigen; (*hide*) vergraben

bus [bʌs] *n* Bus *m*

bus driver *n* Busfahrer(in) *m(f)*

bush [bʊʃ] *n* Busch *m*

business [bɪznɪs] *n* Geschäft *nt*; (*enterprise*) Unternehmen *nt*; (*concern, affair*) Sache *f*; (*study*) Betriebswirtschaftslehre *f*; **I'm here on ~** ich bin geschäftlich hier; **it's none of your ~** das geht dich nichts an

business card *n* Visitenkarte *f*

business class *n* (*Aviat*) Businessclass *f*

business hours *npl* Geschäftsstunden *pl*

businessman [bɪznɪsmæn] (*pl* **-men**) *n* Geschäftsmann *m*

businesswoman [bɪznɪswʊmən] (*pl* **-women**) *n* Geschäftsfrau *f*

bus service *n* Busverbindung *f*

bus shelter *n* Wartehäuschen *nt*

bus station *n* Busbahnhof *m*

bus stop *n* Bushaltestelle *f*

bust [bʌst] *n* Büste *f* ▷ *adj* (*broken*) kaputt; **to go ~** Pleite gehen

busy [bɪzi] *adj* beschäftigt; (*street, place*) belebt; (*telephone*) besetzt; **~ signal** Besetztzeichen *nt*

KEYWORD

but [bət, STRONG bʌt] *conj* **1** (*yet*) aber; **not X but Y** nicht X sondern Y

2 (*however*): **I'd love to come, but I'm busy** ich würde gern kommen, bin aber beschäftigt

3 (*showing disagreement, surprise etc*): **but that's fantastic!** (aber) das ist ja fantastisch!

▷ *prep* (*apart from, except*): **nothing but trouble** nichts als Ärger; **no one but him can do it** niemand außer ihm kann es machen; **but for you/your help** ohne dich/deine Hilfe; **anything but that** alles, nur das nicht

▷ *adv* (*just, only*): **she's but a child** sie ist noch ein Kind; **had I but known** wenn ich es nur gewusst hätte; **I can but try** ich kann es immerhin versuchen; **all but finished** so gut wie fertig

butcher [bʊtʃər] n Fleischer(in) m(f), Metzger(in) m(f)

butler [bʌtlər] n Butler m

butt [bʌt] (fam) n Hintern m

butter [bʌtər] n Butter f ▷ vt buttern

buttercup [bʌtərkʌp] n Butterblume f

butterfly [bʌtərflaɪ] n Schmetterling m

button [bʌtⁿn] n Knopf m; (badge) Button m ▷ vt zuknöpfen

buttonhole [bʌtⁿnhoʊl] n Knopfloch nt

buy [baɪ] n Kauf m ▷ vt (**bought, bought**) kaufen (from von); **he bought me a ring** er hat mir einen Ring gekauft

buyer [baɪər] n Käufer(in) m(f)

buzz [bʌz] n Summen nt; **to give sb a ~** (fam) jdn anrufen ▷ vi summen

buzzer [bʌzər] n Summer m

buzz word n (fam) Modewort nt

by [baɪ] prep **1** (referring to cause, agent) von, durch; **killed by lightning** vom Blitz getötet; **a painting by Picasso** ein Gemälde von Picasso

2 (referring to method, manner): **by bus/car/train** mit dem Bus/Auto/Zug; **to pay by check** per Scheck bezahlen; **by moonlight** bei Mondschein; **by saving hard, he ...** indem er eisern sparte, ... er ...

3 (via, through) über +akk; **he came in by the back door** er kam durch die Hintertür herein

4 (close to, past) bei, an +dat; **a holiday by the sea** ein Urlaub am Meer; **she rushed by me** sie eilte an mir vorbei

5 (not later than): **by 4 o'clock** bis 4 Uhr; **by this time tomorrow** morgen um diese Zeit; **by the time I got here it was too late** als ich hier ankam, war es zu spät

6 (during): **by day** bei Tag

7 (amount): **by the kilo/meter** kiloweise/meterweise; **paid by the hour** stundenweise bezahlt

8 (Math, measure): **to divide by 3** durch 3 teilen; **to multiply by 3** mit 3 malnehmen; **a room 3 meters by 4** ein Zimmer 3 mal 4 Meter; **it's broader by a meter** es ist (um) einem Meter breiter

9 (according to) nach; **it's all right by me** von mir aus gern

10: (**all**) **by oneself** etc ganz allein

11: by the way übrigens

▷ adv **1** see go; pass etc

2: by and by irgendwann; (with past tenses) nach einiger Zeit; **by and large** (on the whole) im Großen und Ganzen

bye-bye [baɪbaɪ] interj (fam) Wiedersehen, tschüss

bypass [baɪpæs] n Umgehungsstraße f; (Med) Bypass m

byproduct [baɪprɒdʌkt] n Nebenprodukt nt

bystander [baɪstændər] n Zuschauer(in) m(f)

byte [baɪt] n Byte nt

C

C [siː] (*abbr*) = **Celsius** C

c (*abbr*) = **circa** ca

cab [kæb] *n* Taxi *nt*

cabbage [kæbɪdʒ] *n* Kohl *m*

cabin [kæbɪn] *n* (*Naut*) Kajüte *f*; (*Aviat*) Passagierraum *m*; (*wooden house*) Hütte *f*

cabin crew *n* Flugbegleitpersonal *nt*

cabin cruiser [kæbɪn kruːzər] *n* Kajütboot *nt*

cabinet [kæbɪnɪt] *n* Schrank *m*; (*for display*) Vitrine *f*; (*Pol*) Kabinett *nt*

cable [keɪbˈl] *n* (*Elec*) Kabel *nt*

cable car *n* Seilbahn *f*

cable television *n* Kabelfernsehen *nt*

cactus [kæktəs] *n* Kaktus *m*

CAD [kæd] (*abbr*) = **computer-aided design** CAD *nt*

café [kæfeɪ] *n* Café *nt*

cafeteria [kæfɪtɪəriə] *n* Cafeteria *f*

caffeine [kæfiːn] *n* Koffein *nt*

cage [keɪdʒ] *n* Käfig *m*

Cairo [kaɪrou] *n* Kairo *nt*

cake [keɪk] *n* Kuchen *m*

calamity [kəlæmɪti] *n* Katastrophe *f*

calculate [kælkyəleɪt] *vt* berechnen; (*estimate*) kalkulieren

calculating [kælkyəleɪtɪŋ] *adj* berechnend

calculation [kælkyəleɪʃˈn] *n* Berechnung *f*; (*estimate*) Kalkulation *f*

calculator [kælkyəleɪtər] *n* Taschenrechner *m*

calendar [kælɪndər] *n* Kalender *m*

calf [kæf] (*pl* **calves**) *n* Kalb *nt*; (*Anat*) Wade *f*

California [kælɪfɔːrnjə] *n* Kalifornien *nt*

call [kɔl] *vt* rufen; (*name, describe as*) nennen; (*Tel*) anrufen; (*Inform, Aviat*) aufrufen; **what's this ~ed?** wie heißt das?; **that's what I ~ service** das nenne ich guten Service ▷ *vi* (*shout*) rufen (*for help* um Hilfe); (*visit*) vorbeikommen; **to ~ on sb** bei jdm vorbeigehen ▷ *n* (*shout*) Ruf *m*; (*Tel*) Anruf; (*Inform, Aviat*) Aufruf *m*; **to make a ~** telefonieren; **to give sb a ~** jdn anrufen; **to be on ~** Bereitschaftsdienst haben

call back *vt, vi* zurückrufen

call center *n* Callcenter *nt*

caller [kɔlər] *n* Besucher(in) *m(f)*; (*Tel*) Anrufer(in) *m(f)*

call for *vt* (*come to pick up*) abholen; (*demand, require*) verlangen

call-in *n* Rundfunkprogramm, bei dem Hörer anrufen können

call off *vt* absagen

calm [kɑm] *n* Stille *f*; (*of person*) Ruhe *f*; (*of sea*) Flaute *f* ▷ *vt* beruhigen ▷ *adj* ruhig

calm down *vi* sich beruhigen

calorie [kæləri] *n* Kalorie *f*

calves [kɑvz] *pl of* **calf**

Cambodia [kæmboudiə] *n* Kambodscha *nt*

camcorder [kæmkɔrdər] *n* Camcorder *m*

came [keɪm] *pt of* **come**

camel [kæmˈl] *n* Kamel *nt*

camera [kæmrə] *n* Fotoapparat *m*, Kamera *f*

camera phone *n* Fotohandy *nt*

camomile [kæməmaɪl] *n* Kamille *f*

camouflage [kæməflɑʒ] *n* Tarnung *f*

camp [kæmp] *n* Lager *nt*; (*camping place*) Zeltplatz *m* ▷ *vi* zelten, campen ▷ *adj* (*fam*) theatralisch, tuntig

campaign [kæmpeɪn] *n* Kampagne *f*; (*Pol*) Wahlkampf *m* ▷ *vi* sich einsetzen (*for/against* für/gegen)

camper [kæmpər] *n* (*person*) Camper(in) *m(f)*; (*van*) Wohnmobil *nt*

camping [kæmpɪŋ] *n* Zelten *nt*, Camping *nt*

campsite [kæmpsaɪt] *n* Zeltplatz *m*, Campingplatz *m*

campus [kæmpəs] *n* (*of university*) Universitätsgelände *nt*, Campus *m*

KEYWORD

can [kən, STRONG kæn] (*negative* **cannot, can't,** *conditional* **could**) *vb aux* **1** (*be able to, know how to*) können; **I can see you tomorrow, if you like** ich könnte Sie morgen sehen, wenn Sie wollen; **I can swim** ich kann schwimmen; **can you speak German?** sprechen Sie Deutsch?

2 (*may*) können, dürfen; **could I have a word with you?** könnte ich Sie kurz sprechen?

Canada [kænədə] *n* Kanada *nt*

Canadian [kəneɪdiən] *adj* kanadisch ▷ *n* Kanadier(in) *m(f)*

canal [kənæl] *n* Kanal *m*

canary [kənɛəri] *n* Kanarienvogel *m*

cancel [kænsᵊl] *vt* (*plans*) aufgeben; (*meeting, event*) absagen; (*Comm: order etc*) stornieren; (*contract*) kündigen; (*Inform*) löschen; (*Aviat flight*) streichen; **to be ~ed** (*event, train, bus*) ausfallen

cancellation [kænsəleɪʃᵊn] *n* Absage *f*; (*Comm*) Stornierung *f*; (*Aviat*) gestrichener Flug

Cancer [kænsər] *n* (*Astr*) Krebs *m*

cancer [kænsər] *n* (*Med*) Krebs *m*

candid [kændɪd] *adj* (*person, conversation*) offen

candidate [kændɪdeɪt] *n* (*for post*) Bewerber(in) *m(f)*; (*Pol*) Kandidat(in) *m(f)*

candle [kændᵊl] *n* Kerze *f*

candlelight [kændᵊllaɪt] *n* Kerzenlicht *nt*

candlestick [kændᵊlstɪk] *n* Kerzenhalter *m*

candy [kændi] *n* Bonbon *nt*; (*quantity*) Süßigkeiten *pl*

candy apple *n* kandierter Apfel

cane [keɪn] *n* Rohr *nt*; (*stick*) Stock *m*

cannabis [kænəbɪs] *n* Cannabis *m*

canned [kænd] *adj* Dosen-

cannot [kænɒt, kənɒt] *contr of* **can not**

canny [kæni] *adj* (*shrewd*) schlau

canoe [kənuː] *n* Kanu *nt*

canoeing [kənuːɪŋ] *n* Kanufahren *nt*

can opener [kæn oupᵊnˈɛr] *n* Dosenöffner *m*

canopy [kænəpi] *n* Baldachin *m*; (*awning*) Markise *f*; (*over entrance*) Vordach *nt*

can't [kænt] *contr of* **can not**

canteen [kæntiːn] *n* (*cafeteria*) Kantine *f*

canvas [kænvəs] *n* (*for sails, shoes*) Segeltuch *nt*; (*for tent*) Zeltstoff *m*; (*for painting*) Leinwand *f*

canvass [kænvəs] *vi* um Stimmen werben (*for* für)

canyon [kænyən] *n* Felsenschlucht *f*

canyoneering [kænyənɪərɪŋ] *n* Canyoning *nt*

cap [kæp] *n* Mütze *f*; (*lid*) Verschluss *m*, Deckel *m*

capability [keɪpəbɪliti] *n* Fähigkeit *f*

capable [keɪpəbᵊl] *adj* fähig; **to be ~ of sth** zu etw fähig (*o* imstande) sein; **to be ~ of doing sth** etw tun können

capacity [kəpæsɪti] *n* (*of building, container*) Fassungsvermögen *nt*; (*ability*) Fähigkeit *f*; (*function*): **in his ~ as ...** in seiner Eigenschaft als ...

cape [keɪp] *n* (*garment*) Cape *nt*, Umhang *m*; (*Geo*) Kap *nt*

caper [keɪpər] *n* (*for cooking*) Kaper *f*

capital [kæpɪtᵊl] *n* (*Fin*) Kapital *nt*; (*letter*) Großbuchstabe *m*; **~ city** Hauptstadt *f*

capitalism [kæpɪtˈlɪzəm] *n* Kapitalismus *m*

capital punishment *n* die Todesstrafe

Capricorn [kæprɪkɔrn] *n* (*Astr*) Steinbock *m*

capsize [kæpsaɪz] *vi* kentern

capsule [kæpsᵊl] *n* Kapsel *f*

captain [kæptɪn] *n* Kapitän *m*; (*army*) Hauptmann *m*

caption [kæpʃᵊn] *n* Bildunterschrift *f*

captive [kæptɪv] *n* Gefangene(r) *mf*

capture [kæptʃər] *vt* (*person*) fassen, gefangen nehmen; (*town etc*) einnehmen; (*Inform: data*) erfassen ▷ *n* Gefangennahme *f*; (*Inform*) Erfassung *f*

car [kɑr] *n* Auto *nt*; (*Rail*) Wagen *m*

carafe [kəræf] *n* Karaffe *f*

caramel [kærəmɛl, -məl, kɑrməl] *n* Karamelle *f*

caraway (seed) [kɪrəweɪ (sid)] *n* Kümmel *m*

carbohydrate [kɑrbouhaɪdreɪt] *n* Kohle(n)hydrat *nt*

car bomb *n* Autobombe *f*

carbon [kɑrbən] *n* Kohlenstoff *m*

carbon footprint *n* ökologischer Fußabdruck

carburetor [kɑrbəreɪtər] *n* Vergaser *m*

card [kɑrd] *n* Karte *f*; (*material*) Pappe *f*

cardboard [kɑrdbɔrd] *n* Pappe *f*; **~ box** Karton *m*; (*smaller*) Pappschachtel *f*

card catalog *n* Kartei *f*

card game *n* Kartenspiel *nt*

cardigan [kɑrdɪgən] *n* Strickjacke *f*

care [kɛər] *n* (*worry*) Sorge *f*; (*carefulness*) Sorgfalt *f*; (*looking after things, people*) Pflege *f*; **with ~** sorgfältig; (*cautiously*) vorsichtig; **to take ~** (*watch out*) vorsichtig sein; (*in address*): **~ of** bei; **to take ~ of** sorgen für, sich kümmern um ▷ *vi*: **I don't ~** es ist mir egal; **to ~ about sth** Wert auf etw *akk* legen; **he ~s about her** sie liegt ihm am Herzen

career [kərɪər] *n* Karriere *f*, Laufbahn *f*

career woman (*pl* **-women**) *n* Karrierefrau *f*

care for *vt* (*look after*) sorgen für, sich kümmern um; (*like*) mögen

carefree [kɛərfri] *adj* sorgenfrei

careful [kɛərfəl] *adj*, **carefully** *adv* sorgfältig; (*cautious, cautiously*) vorsichtig

caregiver [kɛərgɪvər] *n* Betreuer(in) *m(f)*,

Pfleger(in) m(f)

careless [kɛərlɪs] adj, **carelessly** adv
nachlässig; (driving etc) leichtsinnig;
(remark) unvorsichtig

car ferry n Autofähre f

cargo [kɑrgoʊ] (pl -(e)s) n Ladung f

Caribbean [kærəbiən, kərɪbiən] n Kari-
bik f ▷ adj karibisch

caring [kɛərɪŋ] adj mitfühlend; (parent,
partner) liebevoll; (looking after sb) für-
sorglich

car insurance n Kraftfahrzeugversicherung f

carnation [kɑrneɪʃᵊn] n Nelke f

carnival [kɑrnɪvᵊl] n Volksfest nt, Jahrmarkt m; (before Lent) Karneval m

carol [kærəl] n Weihnachtslied nt

carp [kɑrp] n (fish) Karpfen m

carpenter [kɑrpɪntər] n Zimmermann m

carpet [kɑrpɪt] n Teppich m; (wall-to-wall)
Teppichboden m

carpool [kɑrpul] n Fahrgemeinschaft f;
(vehicles) Fuhrpark m ▷ vi eine Fahrgemeinschaft bilden

car rental [kɑr rɛntᵊl] n Autovermietung f

carriage [kærɪdʒ] n (horse-drawn) Kutsche
f; (transport) Beförderung f

carrier [kæriər] n (Comm) Spediteur(in)
m(f)

carrot [kærət] n Karotte f

carry [kæri] vt tragen; (in vehicle) befördern; (have on one) bei sich haben

carryall [kæriɔl] n Reisetasche f

carry on vi (continue) weitermachen; (fam:
make a scene) ein Theater machen ▷ vt
(continue) fortführen; **to ~ working** weiter
arbeiten

carry-on luggage n Handgepäck nt

carry out vt (orders, plan) ausführen, durchführen

carsick [kɑrsɪk] adj: **he gets ~** ihm wird
beim Autofahren übel

cart [kɑrt] n Wagen m, Karren m; (shopping
trolley) Einkaufswagen m

carton [kɑrtᵊn] n (Papp)karton m; (of cigarettes) Stange f

cartoon [kɑrtun] n Cartoon m o nt; (one
drawing) Karikatur f; (film) (Zeichen)
trickfilm m

cartridge [kɑrtrɪdʒ] n (for film) Kassette f;
(for gun, pen, printer) Patrone f; (for copier)
Kartusche f

carve [kɑrv] vt, vi (wood) schnitzen; (stone)
meißeln; (meat) schneiden, tranchieren

carving [kɑrvɪŋ] n (in wood) Schnitzerei f;

(in stone) Skulptur f; (Ski) Carving nt

car wash n Autowaschanlage f

case [keɪs] n (crate) Kiste f; (box) Schachtel
f; (for jewels) Schatulle f; (for spectacles)
Etui nt; (Jur: matter) Fall m; **in ~** falls; **in
that ~** in dem Fall; **in ~ of fire** bei Brand;
it's a ~ of … es handelt sich hier um …

cash [kæʃ] n Bargeld nt; **in ~** bar; **~ on
delivery** per Nachnahme ▷ vt (check) einlösen

cashier [kæʃɪər] n Kassierer(in) m(f)

cashmere [kæʒmɪər] n Kaschmirwolle f

cash payment n Barzahlung f

casing [keɪsɪŋ] n Gehäuse nt

casino [kəsinoʊ] (pl -s) n Kasino nt

cask [kæsk] n Fass nt

casserole [kæsəroʊl] n Kasserole f; (food)
Schmortopf m

cassette [kəsɛt] n Kassette f

cassette recorder [kəsɛt rɪkɔrdər] n Kassettenrekorder m

cast [kæst] (cast, cast) vt (throw) werfen;
(Theat, Cine) besetzen; (roles) verteilen
▷ n (Theat, Cine) Besetzung f; (Med) Gipsverband m

castle [kæsᵊl] n Burg f

cast off vi (Naut) losmachen

castrate [kæstreɪt] vt kastrieren

casual [kæʒuəl] adj (arrangement, remark)
beiläufig; (attitude, manner) (nach)lässig,
zwanglos; (dress) leger; (work, earnings)
Gelegenheits-; (look, glance) flüchtig; **~
wear** Freizeitkleidung f; **~ sex** Gelegen-
heitssex m

casually [kæʒuəli] adv (remark, say) beiläufig; (meet) zwanglos; (dressed) leger

casualty [kæʒuəlti] n Verletzte(r) mf;
(dead) Tote(r) mf

cat [kæt] n Katze f; (male) Kater m

catalog [kætᵊlɒg] n Katalog m ▷ vt katalo-
gisieren

cataract [kætərækt] n Wasserfall m; (Med)
grauer Star

catarrh [kətɑr] n Katarr(h) m

catastrophe [kətæstrəfi] n Katastrophe f

catch [kætʃ] n (fish etc) Fang m ▷ vt
(caught, caught) fangen; (thief) fassen;
(train, bus etc) nehmen; (not miss) erreichen; **to ~ a cold** sich erkälten; **to ~ fire**
Feuer fangen; **I didn't ~ that** das habe ich
nicht verstanden

catching [kætʃɪŋ] adj ansteckend

catch on vi (become popular) Anklang finden

catch up vt, vi: **to ~ with sb** jdn einholen; **to**

~ on sth etw nachholen

category [kætɪgɔri] n Kategorie f

cater [keɪtər] vi die Speisen und Getränke liefern (for für)

catering [keɪtərɪŋ] n Versorgung f mit Speisen und Getränken, Gastronomie f

caterpillar [kætərpɪlər] n Raupe f

cathedral [kəθidrəl] n Kathedrale f, Dom m

Catholic [kæθlɪk] adj katholisch, Katholik(in) m(f)

catsup [kætsəp] n Ketchup n o m

cattle [kæt⁰l] npl Vieh nt

caught [kɔt] pt, pp of **catch**

cauliflower [kɔlɪflaʊər] n Blumenkohl m

cause [kɔz] n (origin) Ursache f (of für); (reason) Grund m (for zu); (purpose) Sache f; **for a good ~** für wohltätige Zwecke; **no ~ for alarm/complaint** kein Grund zur Aufregung/Klage ▷ vt verursachen

causeway [kɔzweɪ] n Damm m

caution [kɔʃⁿn] n Vorsicht f; (Jur, Sport) Verwarnung f ▷ vt (ver)warnen

cautious [kɔʃəs] adj vorsichtig

cave [keɪv] n Höhle f

cave in vi einstürzen

cavity [kævɪti] n Hohlraum m; (in tooth) Loch nt

cayenne (pepper) [keɪɛn (pɛpər)] n Cayennepfeffer m

CCTV [si si ti vi] (abbr) = **closed circuit television** Videoüberwachungsanlage f

CD [si di] (abbr) = **Compact Disc** CD f

CD player n CD-Spieler m

CD-ROM [si di rɒm] (abbr) = **Compact Disc Read Only Memory** CD-ROM f

cease [sis] vi aufhören ▷ vt beenden; **to ~ doing sth** aufhören, etw zu tun

cease-fire [sisfaɪər] n Waffenstillstand m

ceiling [silɪŋ] n Decke f

celebrate [sɛlɪbreɪt] vt, vi feiern

celebrated [sɛlɪbreɪtɪd] adj gefeiert

celebration [sɛlɪbreɪʃⁿn] n Feier f

celebrity [sɪlɛbrɪti] n Berühmtheit f, Star m

celeriac [sələgæriæk] n (Knollen)sellerie m o f

celery [sɛləri] n (Stangen)sellerie m o f

cell [sɛl] n Zelle f; see **cell phone**

cellar [sɛlər] n Keller m

cello [tʃɛloʊ] (pl **-s**) n Cello nt

cell phone [sɛlfoʊn], **cellular phone** n Mobiltelefon nt, Handy nt

Celt [kɛlt, sɛlt] n Kelte m, Keltin f

Celtic [kɛltɪk, sɛl-] adj keltisch ▷ n (lan-

guage) Keltisch nt

cement [sɪmɛnt] n Zement m

cemetery [sɛmətɛri] n Friedhof m

censorship [sɛnsərʃɪp] n Zensur f

cent [sɛnt] n (of dollar, euro etc) Cent m

center [sɛntər] n Mitte f; (building, of city) Zentrum nt ▷ vt zentrieren

centiliter [sɛntɪlitər] n Zentiliter m

centimeter [sɛntɪmitər] n Zentimeter m

central [sɛntrəl] adj zentral

Central America n Mittelamerika nt

Central Europe n Mitteleuropa nt

central heating n Zentralheizung f

centralize [sɛntrəlaɪz] vt zentralisieren

century [sɛntʃəri] n Jahrhundert nt

ceramic [sɪræmɪk] adj keramisch

cereal [sɪəriəl] n (any grain) Getreide nt; (breakfast cereal) Frühstücksflocken pl

ceremony [sɛrɪmoʊni] n Feier f, Zeremonie f

certain [sɜrtⁿn] adj sicher (of +gen); (particular) bestimmt; **for ~** mit Sicherheit

certainly [sɜrtⁿnli] adv sicher; (without doubt) bestimmt; **~!** aber sicher!; **~ not!** ganz bestimmt nicht!

certificate [sərtɪfɪkɪt] n Bescheinigung f; (in school, of qualification) Zeugnis nt

certify [sɜrtɪfaɪ] vt, vi bescheinigen

Cesarean [sɪzɛəriən] adj: **~ section** Kaiserschnitt m

CFC [si ɛf si] (abbr) = **chlorofluorocarbon** FCKW nt

chain [tʃeɪn] n Kette f ▷ vt: **to ~ up** anketten

chain reaction n Kettenreaktion f

chain store n Kettenladen m

chair [tʃɛər] n Stuhl m; (university) Lehrstuhl m; (armchair) Sessel m; (chairperson) Vorsitzende(r) mf

chairlift [tʃɛərlɪft] n Sessellift m

chairman [tʃɛərmən] (pl **-men**) n Vorsitzende(r) m; (of firm) Präsident m

chairperson [tʃɛərpɜrsⁿn] n Vorsitzende(r) mf; (of firm) Präsident(in) m(f)

chairwoman [tʃɛərwʊmən] (pl **-women**) n Vorsitzende f; (of firm) Präsidentin f

chalet [ʃæleɪ] n (in mountains) Berghütte f; (holiday dwelling) Ferienhäuschen nt

chalk [tʃɔk] n Kreide f

challenge [tʃælɪndʒ] n Herausforderung f ▷ vt (person) herausfordern; (statement) bestreiten

chambermaid [tʃeɪmbərmeɪd] n Zimmermädchen nt

chamois n (for cleaning windows) Fensterleder *nt*

champagne [ʃæmpeɪn] *n* Champagner *m*

champion [tʃæmpiən] *n* (*Sport*) Meister(in) *m(f)*

championship [tʃæmpiənʃɪp] *n* Meisterschaft *f*

chance [tʃæns] *n* (*fate*) Zufall *m*; (*possibility*) Möglichkeit *f*; (*opportunity*) Gelegenheit *f*; (*risk*) Risiko *nt*; **by ~** zufällig; **he doesn't stand a ~ of winning** er hat keinerlei Chance(, zu gewinnen)

chancellor [tʃænsələr, -slər] *n* Kanzler(in) *m(f)*

chandelier [ʃændˈlɪər] *n* Kronleuchter *m*

change [tʃeɪndʒ] *vt* verändern; (*alter*) ändern; (*money, wheel, diaper*) wechseln; (*exchange*) (um)tauschen; **to ~ one's clothes** sich umziehen; **to ~ trains** umsteigen; **to ~ gear** (*Auto*) schalten ▷ *vi* sich ändern; (*esp outwardly*) sich verändern; (*get changed*) sich umziehen ▷ *n* Veränderung *f*; (*alteration*) Änderung *f*; (*money*) Wechselgeld *nt*; (*coins*) Kleingeld *nt*; **for a ~** zur Abwechslung; **can you give me ~ for $10?** können Sie mir auf 10 Dollar herausgeben?

changeable [tʃeɪndʒəbᵊl] *adj* (*weather*) veränderlich, wechselhaft

change machine *n* Geldwechsler *m*

change over *vi* sich umstellen (*to auf +akk*)

changing room [tʃeɪndʒɪŋ rum] *n* Umkleideraum *m*

channel [tʃænᵊl] *n* Kanal *m*; (*Radio, TV*) Kanal *m*, Sender *m*; **the English C~** der Ärmelkanal; **the C~ Islands** die Kanalinseln; **the C~ Tunnel** der Kanaltunnel

channel-surfing [tʃænᵊlsɜrfɪŋ] *n* Zappen *nt*

chaos [keɪɒs] *n* Chaos *nt*

chaotic [keɪɒtɪk] *adj* chaotisch

chapel [tʃæpᵊl] *n* Kapelle *f*

chapped [tʃæpt] *adj* (*lips*) aufgesprungen

chapter [tʃæptər] *n* Kapitel *nt*

character [kærɪktər] *n* Charakter *m*, Wesen *nt*; (*in a play, novel etc*) Figur *f*; (*Typo*) Zeichen *nt*; **he's a real ~** er ist ein echtes Original

characteristic [kærɪktərɪstɪk] *n* typisches Merkmal

charcoal [tʃɑrkoʊl] *n* Holzkohle *f*

charge [tʃɑrdʒ] *n* (*cost*) Gebühr *f*; (*Jur*) Anklage *f*; **free of ~** gratis, kostenlos; **to be in ~ of** verantwortlich sein für ▷ *vt* (*money*) verlangen; (*Jur*) anklagen; (*battery*) laden

charge card *n* Kundenkreditkarte *f*

charity [tʃærɪti] *n* (*institution*) wohltätige Organisation *f*; **a collection for ~** eine Sammlung für wohltätige Zwecke

charm [tʃɑrm] *n* Charme *m* ▷ *vt* bezaubern

charming [tʃɑrmɪŋ] *adj* reizend, charmant

chart [tʃɑrt] *n* Diagramm *nt*; (*map*) Karte *f*; **the ~s** *pl* die Charts, die Hitliste

charter [tʃɑrtər] *n* Urkunde *f* ▷ *vt* (*Naut, Aviat*) chartern

chase [tʃeɪs] *vt* jagen, verfolgen ▷ *n* Verfolgungsjagd *f*; (*hunt*) Jagd *f*

chassis [tʃæsi, ʃæsi] *n* (*Auto*) Fahrgestell *nt*

chat [tʃæt] *vi* plaudern; (*Inform*) chatten ▷ *n* Plauderei *f*; (*Inform*) Chat *m*

chat room *n* (*Inform*) Chatroom *m*

chatty [tʃæti] *adj* geschwätzig

chauffeur [ʃoʊfər, ʃoʊfɜr] *n* Chauffeur(in) *m(f)*, Fahrer(in) *m(f)*

cheap [tʃip] *adj* billig; (*of poor quality*) minderwertig

cheat [tʃit] *vt, vi* betrügen; (*in school, game*) mogeln

Chechen [tʃɛtʃɛn] *adj* tschetschenisch ▷ *n* Tschetschene *m*, Tschetschenin *f*

Chechnya [tʃɛtʃniə] *n* Tschetschenien *nt*

check [tʃɛk] *vt* (*examine*) überprüfen (*for auf +akk*); (*Tech: adjustment etc*) kontrollieren; (*tick*) abhaken; (*Aviat: luggage*) einchecken; (*coat*) abgeben ▷ *n* (*examination, restraint*) Kontrolle *f*; (*Fin*) Scheck *m*; (*restaurant bill*) Rechnung *f*; (*pattern*) Karo(muster) *nt*

checkered [tʃɛkərd] *adj* kariert

checkers [tʃɛkˉrz] *nsing* Damespiel *nt*

check in *vt, vi* (*Aviat*) einchecken; (*in hotel*) sich anmelden

check-in [tʃɛkɪn] *n* (*airport*) Check-in *m*; (*hotel*) Anmeldung *f*

check-in desk *n* Abfertigungsschalter *m*

checking account [tʃɛkɪŋ əkaʊnt] *n* Scheckkonto *nt*, Girokonto *nt*

checklist [tʃɛklɪst] *n* Kontrollliste *f*

check out *vi* sich abmelden, auschecken

checkout [tʃɛkaʊt] *n* (*supermarket*) Kasse *f*

checkout time *n* (*hotel*) Abreise(zeit) *f*

checkpoint [tʃɛkpɔɪnt] *n* Kontrollpunkt *m*

checkroom [tʃɛkrum] *n* Gepäckaufbewahrung *f*; (*for coats*) Garderobe *f*

check up *vi* nachprüfen; **to ~ on sb** Nachforschungen über jdn anstellen

checkup [tʃɛkʌp] *n* (*Med*) (ärztliche)

Untersuchung

cheddar [tʃɛdər] *n* Cheddarkäse *m*

cheek [tʃik] *n* Backe *f*, Wange *f*; (*insolence*) Frechheit *f*

cheekbone [tʃikboʊn] *n* Backenknochen *m*

cheeky [tʃiki] *adj* frech

cheer [tʃɪər] *n* Beifallsruf *m* ▷ *vt* zujubeln +*dat* ▷ *vi* jubeln

cheerful [tʃɪərfəl] *adj* fröhlich

cheer up *vt* aufmuntern ▷ *vi* fröhlicher werden; ~! Kopf hoch!

cheese [tʃiz] *n* Käse *m*

cheeseboard [tʃizbɔrd] *n* Käsebrett *nt*; (*as course*) (gemischte) Käseplatte

cheesecake [tʃizkeɪk] *n* Käsekuchen *m*

chef [ʃɛf] *n* Koch *m*; (*in charge of kitchen*) Küchenchef(in) *m(f)*

chemical [kɛmɪkəl] *adj* chemisch, Chemikalie *f*

chemist [kɛmɪst] *n* (*industrial chemist*) Chemiker(in) *m(f)*

chemistry [kɛmɪstri] *n* Chemie *f*

cherish [tʃɛrɪʃ] *vt* (*look after*) liebevoll sorgen für; (*hope*) hegen; (*memory*) bewahren

cherry [tʃɛri] *n* Kirsche *f*

cherry tomato (*pl* **-es**) *n* Kirschtomate *f*

chess [tʃɛs] *n* Schach *nt*

chessboard [tʃɛsbɔrd] *n* Schachbrett *nt*

chest [tʃɛst] *n* Brust *f*; (*box*) Kiste *f*; ~ **of drawers** Kommode *f*

chestnut [tʃɛsnʌt, -nət] *n* Kastanie *f*

chew [tʃu] *vt, vi* kauen

chewing gum [tʃuɪn gʌm] *n* Kaugummi *m*

chick [tʃɪk] *n* Küken *nt*

chicken [tʃɪkɪn] *n* Huhn *nt*; (*food: roast*) Hähnchen *nt*; (*coward*) Feigling *m*

chicken breast *n* Hühnerbrust *f*

chickenpox [tʃɪkɪnpɒks] *n* Windpocken *pl*

chickpea [tʃɪkpi] *n* Kichererbse *f*

chief [tʃif] *n* (*of department etc*) Leiter(in) *m(f)*; (*boss*) Chef(in) *m(f)*; (*of tribe*) Häuptling *m* ▷ *adj* Haupt-

chiefly [tʃifli] *adv* hauptsächlich

child [tʃaɪld] (*pl* **children**) *n* Kind *nt*

child abuse *n* Kindesmisshandlung *f*

childbirth [tʃaɪldbɜrθ] *n* Geburt *f*, Entbindung *f*

childhood [tʃaɪldhʊd] *n* Kindheit *f*

childish [tʃaɪldɪʃ] *adj* kindisch

childproof [tʃaɪldpruf] *adj* kindersicher

children [tʃɪldrən] *pl of* **child**

child safety lock *n* Kindersicherung *f*

Chile [tʃɪli] *n* Chile *nt*

chill [tʃɪl] *n* Kühle *f*; (*Med*) Erkältung *f* ▷ *vt* (*wine*) kühlen

chilled [tʃɪld] *adj* gekühlt

chilli [tʃɪli] *n* Pepperoni *pl*; (*spice*) Chili *m*

chilli con carne [tʃɪli kɒn kɑni] *n* Chili con carne *nt*

chill out *vi* (*fam*) chillen, relaxen

chilly [tʃɪli] *adj* kühl, frostig

chimney [tʃɪmni] *n* Schornstein *m*

chimney sweep *n* Schornsteinfeger(in) *m(f)*

chimpanzee [tʃɪmpænzi] *n* Schimpanse *m*

chin [tʃɪn] *n* Kinn *nt*

China [tʃaɪnə] *n* China *nt*

china [tʃaɪnə] *n* Porzellan *nt*

Chinese [tʃaɪniz] *adj* chinesisch ▷ *n* (*person*) Chinese *m*, Chinesin *f*; (*language*) Chinesisch *nt*

Chinese cabbage *npl* Chinakohl *m*

chip [tʃɪp] *n* (*of wood etc*) Splitter *m*; (*damage*) angeschlagene Stelle; (*Inform*) Chip *m*; (*potato chips*) Kartoffelchips *pl* ▷ *vt* anschlagen, beschädigen

chiropodist [kɪrɒpədɪst] *n* Fußpfleger(in) *m(f)*

chirp [tʃɜrp] *vi* zwitschern

chisel [tʃɪzəl] *n* Meißel *m*

chitchat [tʃɪttʃæt] *n* Gerede *nt*

chives [tʃaɪvz] *npl* Schnittlauch *m*

chlorine [klɔrin] *n* Chlor *nt*

chocoholic [tʃɒkəhɔlɪk], **chocaholic** *n* Schokoladenfreak *m*

chocolate [tʃɔkəlɪt, tʃɔklɪt] *n* Schokolade *f*; (*chocolate-covered candy*) Praline *f*; **a bar of ~** eine Tafel Schokolade; **a box of ~s** eine Schachtel Pralinen

chocolate cake *n* Schokoladenkuchen *m*

chocolate sauce *n* Schokoladensoße *f*

choice [tʃɔɪs] *n* Wahl *f*; (*selection*) Auswahl *f* ▷ *adj* auserlesen; (*product*) Qualitäts-

choir [kwaɪər] *n* Chor *m*

choke [tʃoʊk] *vi* sich verschlucken; (*Sport*) die Nerven verlieren ▷ *vt* erdrosseln ▷ *n* (*Auto*) Choke *m*

cholera [kɒlərə] *n* Cholera *f*

cholesterol [kəlɛstərɒl] *n* Cholesterin *nt*

choose [tʃuz] (**chose, chosen**) *vt* wählen; (*pick out*) sich aussuchen; **there are three to ~ from** es stehen drei zur Auswahl

chop [tʃɒp] *vt* (*zer*)hacken; (*meat etc*) klein schneiden ▷ *n* (*meat*) Kotelett *nt*; **to get the ~** gefeuert werden

chopper [tʃɒpər] *n* Hackbeil *nt*; (*fam: helicopter*) Hubschrauber *m*

chopsticks [tʃɒpstɪks] *npl* Essstäbchen *pl*

chorus [kɔrəs] n Chor m; (in song) Refrain m

chose [tʃouz], **chosen** pt, pp of **choose**

chowder [tʃaudər] n dicke Suppe mit Meeresfrüchten

christen [krɪsⁿn] vt taufen

christening [krɪstⁿnɪŋ] n Taufe f

Christian [krɪstʃən] adj christlich ▷ n Christ(in) m(f)

Christmas [krɪsməs] n Weihnachten pl

Christmas bonus n Weihnachtsgeld nt

Christmas card n Weihnachtskarte f

Christmas carol n Weihnachtslied nt

Christmas Day n der erste Weihnachtstag

Christmas Eve [krɪsməs iv] n Heiligabend m

Christmas tree n Weihnachtsbaum m

chronic [krɒnɪk] adj (Med, fig) chronisch; (fam: very bad) miserabel

chrysanthemum [krɪsænθəməm] n Chrysantheme f

chubby [tʃʌbi] adj (child) pummelig; (adult) rundlich

chuck [tʃʌk] vt (fam) schmeißen

chuck in vt (fam: job) hinschmeißen

chuck out vt (fam) rausschmeißen

chunk [tʃʌŋk] n Klumpen m; (of bread) Brocken m; (of meat) Batzen m

chunky [tʃʌŋki] adj (person) stämmig

church [tʃɜrtʃ] n Kirche f

churchyard [tʃɜrtʃyɑrd] n Kirchhof m

chute [ʃut] n Rutsche f

chutney [tʃʌtni] n Chutney m

CIA [si aɪ eɪ] (abbr) = **Central Intelligence Agency** CIA f

cider [saɪdər] n ≈ Apfelmost m

cigar [sɪgɑr] n Zigarre f

cigarette [sɪgərɛt] n Zigarette f

cinnamon [sɪnəmən] n Zimt m

circle [sɜrkⁿl] n Kreis m ▷ vi kreisen

circuit [sɜrkɪt] n Rundfahrt f; (on foot) Rundgang m; (for racing) Rennstrecke f; (Elec) Stromkreis m

circular [sɜrkyələr] adj (kreis)rund, kreisförmig ▷ n Rundschreiben nt

circulation [sɜrkyəleɪʃⁿn] n (of blood) Kreislauf m; (of newspaper) Auflage f

circumstances [sɜrkəmstæns] npl (facts) Umstände pl; (financial condition) Verhältnisse pl; **in/under the ~** unter den Umständen; **under no ~** auf keinen Fall

circus [sɜrkəs] n Zirkus m

cistern [sɪstərn] n Zisterne f

citizen [sɪtɪzⁿn] n Bürger(in) m(f); (of nation) Staatsangehörige(r) mf

citizenship [sɪtɪzⁿnʃɪp] n Staatsangehörigkeit f

city [sɪti] n Stadt f; (large) Großstadt f

civil [sɪvⁿl] adj (of town) Bürger-; (of state) staatsbürgerlich; (not military) zivil

civil ceremony n standesamtliche Hochzeit

civil engineering n Hoch- und Tiefbau m, Bauingenieurwesen nt

civilian [sɪvɪlyən] n Zivilist(in) m(f)

civilization [sɪvɪlɪzeɪʃⁿn] n Zivilisation f, Kultur f

civilized [sɪvɪlaɪzd] adj zivilisiert, kultiviert

civil partnership n eingetragene Partnerschaft

civil rights npl Bürgerrechte pl

civil servant n (Staats)beamte(r) m, (Staats)beamtin f

civil service n Staatsdienst m

civil war n Bürgerkrieg m

CJD [si dʒeɪ di] (abbr) = **Creutzfeld-Jakob disease** Creutzfeld-Jakob-Krankheit f

cl [si: ɛl or the full out version at centiliter] (abbr) = **centilitre(s)** cl

claim [kleɪm] vt beanspruchen; (apply for) beantragen; (demand) fordern; (assert) behaupten (that dass) ▷ n (demand) Forderung f (for für); (right) Anspruch m (to auf +akk); **for damages** Schadenersatzforderung f; **to make** o **put in a ~** (insurance) Ansprüche geltend machen

claimant [kleɪmənt] n Antragsteller(in) m(f)

clam [klæm] n Venusmuschel f

clam chowder [klæm tʃaudər] n dicke Muschelsuppe (mit Sellerie, Zwiebeln etc)

clap [klæp] vi (Beifall) klatschen

claret [klærɪt] n roter Bordeaux(wein)

clarify [klærɪfaɪ] vt klären

clarinet [klærɪnɛt] n Klarinette f

clarity [klærɪti] n Klarheit f

clash [klæʃ] vi (physically) zusammenstoßen (with mit); (argue) sich auseinandersetzen (with mit); (fig: colors) sich beißen ▷ n Zusammenstoß m; (argument) Auseinandersetzung f

clasp [klæsp] n (on belt) Schnalle f

class [klæs] n Klasse f ▷ vt einordnen, einstufen

classic [klæsɪk] adj (mistake, example etc) klassisch ▷ n Klassiker m

classical [klæsɪkⁿl] adj (music, ballet etc) klassisch

classification [klæsɪfɪkeɪʃⁿn] n Klassifizie-

rung f
classify [klǽsıfaı] vt klassifizieren; **classified advertisement** Kleinanzeige f
classroom [klǽsrum] n Klassenzimmer nt
classy [klǽsı] adj (fam) nobel, exklusiv
clatter [klǽtər] vi klappern
clause [klɔz] n (Ling) Satz m; (Jur) Klausel f
claw [klɔ] n Kralle f
clay [kleı] n Lehm m; (for pottery) Ton m
clean [klin] adj sauber; ~ **driving record** Führerschein ohne Strafpunkte ▷ vt sauber machen; (carpet etc) reinigen; (window, shoes, vegetables) putzen; (wound) säubern
cleaner [klinər] n (person) Putzmann m, Putzfrau f; (substance) Putzmittel nt; ~'s (firm) Reinigung f
cleanse [klɛnz] vt reinigen; (wound) säubern
cleanser [klɛnzər] n Reinigungsmittel nt
clean up vt sauber machen ▷ vi aufräumen
clear [klıər] adj klar; (distinct) deutlich; (conscience) rein; (free, road etc) frei; **to be ~ about sth** sich über etw im Klaren sein ▷ adv: **to stand ~** zurücktreten ▷ vt (road, room etc) räumen; (table) abräumen; (Jur: find innocent) freisprechen (of von) ▷ vi (fog, mist) sich verziehen; (weather) aufklaren
clearance sale [klıərəns-] n Räumungsverkauf m
clear away vt wegräumen; (dishes) abräumen
clearing [klıərıŋ] n Lichtung f
clearly [klıərlı] adv klar; (speak, remember) deutlich; (obviously) eindeutig
clear off vi (fam) abhauen
clear up vi (tidy up) aufräumen; (weather) sich aufklären ▷ vt (room) aufräumen; (litter) wegräumen; (matter) klären
clench [klɛntʃ] vt (fist) ballen; (teeth) zusammenbeißen
clergyman [klɜrdʒımən] (pl -men) n Geistliche(r) m
clergywoman [klɜrdʒıwʊmən] (pl -women) n Geistliche f
clerk [klɜrk] n (in office) Büroangestellte(r) mf; (salesperson) Verkäufer(in) m(f)
clever [klɛvər] adj schlau, klug; (idea) clever
cliché [klíʃeı] n Klischee nt
click [klık] n Klicken nt; (Inform) Maus-

klick m ▷ vi klicken; **to ~ on sth** (Inform) etw anklicken; **it ~ed** (fam) ich hab's/er hat's etc geschnallt, es hat gefunkt, es hat Klick gemacht; **they ~ed** sie haben sich gleich verstanden
click on vt (Inform) anklicken
client [klaıənt] n Kunde m, Kundin f; (Jur) Mandant(in) m(f)
cliff [klıf] n Klippe f
climate [klaımıt] n Klima nt
climax [klaımæks] n Höhepunkt m
climb [klaım] vi (person) klettern; (aircraft, sun) steigen; (road) ansteigen ▷ vt (mountain) besteigen; (tree etc) klettern auf +akk ▷ n Aufstieg m
climber [klaımər] n (mountaineer) Bergsteiger(in) m(f)
climbing [klaımıŋ] n Klettern nt, Bergsteigen nt
cling [klıŋ] (**clung, clung**) vi sich klammern (to an +akk)
clinic [klınık] n Klinik f
clinical [klınıkəl] adj klinisch
clip [klıp] n Klammer f ▷ vt (fix) anklemmen (to an +akk); (fingernails) schneiden
clipboard [klıpbɔrd] n Klemmbrett nt
clippers [klıpərz] npl Schere f; (for nails) Zwicker m
cloak [kloʊk] n Umhang m
clock [klɒk] n Uhr f; (Auto fam) Tacho m; **round the ~** rund um die Uhr
clockwise [klɒkwaız] adv im Uhrzeigersinn
clog [klɒg] n Holzschuh m ▷ vt verstopfen
cloister [klɔıstər] n Kreuzgang m
clone [kloʊn] n Klon m ▷ vt klonen
close [kloʊs adj, adv kloʊz, vb, n] adj nahe (to +dat); (friend, contact) eng; (resemblance) groß; ~ **to the beach** in der Nähe des Strandes; ~ **win** knapper Sieg; **on ~r examination** bei näherer o genauerer Untersuchung ▷ adv dicht; **he lives ~ by** er wohnt ganz in der Nähe ▷ vt schließen; (road) sperren; (discussion, matter) abschließen ▷ vi schließen ▷ n Ende nt
closed [kloʊzd] adj (road) gesperrt; (shop etc) geschlossen
closed circuit television n Videoüberwachungsanlage f
close down vi schließen; (factory) stillgelegt werden ▷ vt (shop) schließen; (factory) stilllegen
closely [kloʊslı] adv (related) eng, nah; (packed, follow) dicht; (attentively) genau
closet [klɒzıt] n Schrank m

close-up [kloʊs ʌp] *n* Nahaufnahme *f*

closing [kloʊzɪŋ] *adj*: ~ **date** letzter Termin; (*for competition*) Einsendeschluss *m*; ~ **time** (*of shop*) Ladenschluss *m*

closure [kloʊzər] *n* Schließung *f*, Abschluss *m*; **to look for** ~ mit etw abschließen wollen

clot [klɒt]: **blood** ~ Blutgerinnsel *nt*; (*fam: idiot*) Trottel *m vi* (*blood*) gerinnen

cloth [klɒθ] *n* (*material*) Tuch *nt*; (*for cleaning*) Lappen *m*

clothe [kloʊð] *vt* kleiden

clothes [kloʊz, kloʊðz] *npl* Kleider *pl*, Kleidung *f*

clothesline [kloʊzlaɪn, kloʊðz-] *n* Wäscheleine *f*

clothespin [kloʊzpɪn, kloʊðz-] *n* Wäscheklammer *f*

clothing [kloʊðɪŋ] *n* Kleidung *f*

clotted [clɒtɪd] *adj*: ~ **cream** dicke Sahne (*aus erhitzter Milch*)

cloud [klaʊd] *n* Wolke *f*

cloudy [klaʊdi] *adj* (*sky*) bewölkt; (*liquid*) trüb

clove [kloʊv] *n* Gewürznelke *f*; ~ **of garlic** Knoblauchzehe *f*

clover [kloʊvər] *n* Klee *m*

cloverleaf [kloʊvərlif] (*pl* -**leaves**) *n* Kleeblatt *nt*

clown [klaʊn] *n* Clown *m*

club [klʌb] *n* (*weapon*) Knüppel *m*; (*society*) Klub *m*, Verein *m*; (*nightclub*) Disko *f*; (*golf club*) Golfschläger *m*; ~**s** (*Cards*) Kreuz *nt*

clubbing [klʌbɪŋ] *n*: **to go** ~ in die Disko gehen

clue [klu] *n* Anhaltspunkt *m*, Hinweis *m*; **he hasn't a** ~ er hat keine Ahnung

clumsy [klʌmzi] *adj* unbeholfen, ungeschickt

clung [klʌŋ] *pt, pp of* **cling**

clutch [klʌtʃ] *n* (*Auto*) Kupplung *f* ▷ *vt* umklammern; (*book etc*) an sich *akk* klammern

cm [si; ɛm or the full out version at centimeter] (*abbr*) = **centimetre(s)** cm

Co (*abbr*) = **company** Co

c/o (*abbr*) = **care of** bei

coach [koʊtʃ] *n* (*Rail*) (Personen)wagen *m*; (*Sport: trainer*) Trainer(in) *m(f)* ▷ *vt* Nachhilfeunterricht geben +*dat*; (*Sport*) trainieren

coach (class) *n* (*Aviat*) Economyclass *f*

coal [koʊl] *n* Kohle *f*

coalition [koʊəlɪʃⁿn] *n* (*Pol*) Koalition *f*

coal mine *n* Kohlenbergwerk *nt*

coal miner *n* Bergarbeiter *m*

coast [koʊst] *n* Küste *f*

coast guard *n* Küstenwache *f*

coastline [koʊstlaɪn] *n* Küste *f*

coat [koʊt] *n* Mantel *m*; (*jacket*) Jacke *f*; (*on animals*) Fell *nt*, Pelz *m*; (*of paint*) Schicht *f*; ~ **of arms** Wappen *nt*

coat hanger *n* Kleiderbügel *m*

coating [koʊtɪŋ] *n* Überzug *m*; (*layer*) Schicht *f*

cobblestone *n* Kopfstein *m*; (*surface*) Kopfsteinpflaster *nt*

cobweb [kɒbwɛb] *n* Spinnennetz *nt*

cocaine [koʊkeɪn] *n* Kokain *nt*

cock [kɒk] *n* Hahn *m*

cockerel [kɒkərəl, kɒkrəl] *n* junger Hahn

cockle [kɒkⁿl] *n* Herzmuschel *f*

cockpit [kɒkpɪt] *n* (*in plane, race car*) Cockpit *nt*

cockroach [kɒkroʊtʃ] *n* Kakerlake *f*

cocktail [kɒkteɪl] *n* Cocktail *m*

cocky [kɒki] *adj* großspurig, von sich selbst überzeugt

cocoa [koʊkoʊ] *n* Kakao *m*

coconut [koʊkənʌt] *n* Kokosnuss *f*

COD [si; oʊ di] (*abbr*) = **cash on delivery** per Nachnahme

cod [kɒd] *n* Kabeljau *m*

code [koʊd] *n* Kode *m*

coeducational [koʊɛdʒʊkeɪʃⁿl] *adj* (*school*) gemischt

coffee [kɔfi] *n* Kaffee *m*

coffee bar *n* Café *nt*

coffee break *n* Kaffeepause *f*

coffeemaker [kɔfimeɪkər] *n* Kaffeemaschine *f*

coffeepot [kɔfipɒt] *n* Kaffeekanne *f*

coffee shop *n* Café *nt*

coffee table *n* Couchtisch *m*

coffin [kɔfɪn] *n* Sarg *m*

coil [kɔɪl] *n* Rolle *f*; (*Elec*) Spule *f*; (*Med*) Spirale *f*

coin [kɔɪn] *n* Münze *f*

coincide [koʊɪnsaɪd] *vi* (*happen together*) zusammenfallen (*with* mit)

coincidence [koʊɪnsɪdəns] *n* Zufall *m*

coke [koʊk] *n* Koks *m*; **Coke®** Cola *f*

cola [koʊlə] *n* Cola *f*

cold [koʊld] *adj* kalt; **I'm** ~ mir ist kalt, ich friere ▷ *n* Kälte *f*; (*illness*) Erkältung *f*, Schnupfen *m*; **to catch a** ~ sich erkälten

cold sore *n* Herpes *m*

cold turkey *n* (*fam*) Totalentzug *m*; (*symptoms*) Entzugserscheinungen *pl*

coleslaw [koʊlslɔ] n Krautsalat m

collaborate [kəlæbəreɪt] vi zusammenarbeiten (with mit)

collaboration [kəlæbəreɪʃⁿn] n Zusammenarbeit f; (of one party) Mitarbeit f

collapse [kəlæps] vi zusammenbrechen; (building etc) einstürzen ▷ n Zusammenbruch m; (of building) Einsturz m

collapsible [kəlæpsɪbⁿl] adj zusammenklappbar, Klapp-

collar [kɒlər] n Kragen m; (for dog, cat) Halsband nt

collarbone [kɒlərboʊn] n Schlüsselbein nt

colleague [kɒliɡ] n Kollege m, Kollegin f

collect [kəlɛkt] vt sammeln; (fetch) abholen ▷ vi sich sammeln

collect call n R-Gespräch nt

collected [kəlɛktɪd] adj (works) gesammelt; (person) gefasst

collection [kəlɛkʃⁿn] n Sammlung f; (Rel) Kollekte f; (from postbox) Leerung f

collector [kəlɛktər] n Sammler(in) m(f)

college [kɒlɪdʒ] n (residential) College nt; (specialist) Fachhochschule f; (vocational) Berufsschule f; (university) Universität f; **to go to ~** studieren

collide [kəlaɪd] vi zusammenstoßen

collision [kəlɪʒⁿn] n Zusammenstoß m

colloquial [kəloʊkwiəl] adj umgangssprachlich

Cologne [kəloʊn] n Köln nt

colon [koʊlən] n (punctuation mark) Doppelpunkt m

colonial [kəloʊniəl] adj Kolonial-

colonize [kɒlənaɪz] vt kolonisieren

colony [kɒləni] n Kolonie f

color [kʌlər] n Farbe f; (of skin) Hautfarbe f ▷ vt anmalen; (bias) färben

color-blind adj farbenblind

colored [kʌlərd] adj farbig; (biased) gefärbt

color film n Farbfilm m

colorful [kʌlərfəl] adj (lit, fig) bunt; (life, past) bewegt

coloring [kʌlərɪŋ] n (in food etc) Farbstoff m; (complexion) Gesichtsfarbe f

colorless [kʌlərlɪs] adj (lit, fig) farblos

column [kɒləm] n Säule f; (of print) Spalte f

comb [koʊm] n Kamm m ▷ vt kämmen; **to ~ one's hair** sich kämmen

combination [kɒmbɪneɪʃⁿn] n Kombination f; (mixture) Mischung f (of aus)

combine [kəmbaɪn] vt verbinden (with mit); (two things) kombinieren

come [kʌm] (**came, come**) vi kommen; (arrive) ankommen; (on list, in order) stehen; (with adjective: become) werden; **~ and see us** besuchen Sie uns mal; **coming!** ich komm ja schon!; **to ~ first/second** erster/zweiter werden; **to ~ true** wahr werden; **to ~ loose** sich lockern; **the years to ~** die kommenden Jahre; **there's one more to ~** es kommt noch eins/noch einer; **how ~ ...?** (fam) wie kommt es, dass ...?; **~ to think of it** (fam) wo es mir gerade einfällt

come across vt (find) stoßen auf +akk

come around vi (visit) vorbeikommen; (regain consciousness) wieder zu sich kommen

come back vi zurückkommen; **I'll ~ to that** ich komme darauf zurück

comedian [kəmidiən] n Komiker(in) m(f)

come down vi herunterkommen; (rain, snow, price) fallen

comedown [kʌmdaʊn] n Abstieg m

comedy [kɒmədi] n Komödie f, Comedy f

come from vt (result) kommen von; **where do you ~?** wo kommen Sie her?; **I ~ London** ich komme aus London

come in vi hereinkommen; (arrive) ankommen; (in race): **to ~ fourth** Vierter werden

come off vi (button, handle etc) abgehen; (succeed) gelingen; **to ~ well/badly** gut/schlecht wegkommen

come on vi (progress) vorankommen; **~!** komm!; (hurry) beeil dich!; (encouraging) los!

come out vi herauskommen; (photo) was werden; (homosexual) sich outen

come to vi (regain consciousness) wieder zu sich kommen ▷ vt (sum) sich belaufen auf +akk; **when it comes to ...** wenn es um ... geht

come up vi hochkommen; (sun, moon) aufgehen; **to ~ for discussion** zur Sprache kommen

come up to vt (approach) zukommen auf +akk; (water) reichen bis zu; (expectations) entsprechen +dat

come up with vt (idea) haben; (solution, answer) kommen auf +akk; **to ~ a suggestion** einen Vorschlag machen

comfort [kʌmfərt] n Komfort m; (consolation) Trost m ▷ vt trösten

comfortable [kʌmftəbⁿl, -fərtəbⁿl] adj bequem; (income) ausreichend; (temperature, life) angenehm

comforter [kʌmfərtər] n Federbett nt,

Daunendecke f

comforting [kʌmfərtɪŋ] adj tröstlich

comic [kɒmɪk] n (magazine) Comic(heft) nt; (comedian) Komiker(in) m(f) ▷ adj komisch

coming [kʌmɪŋ] adj kommend; (event) bevorstehend

comma [kɒmə] n Komma nt

command [kəmænd] n Befehl m; (control) Führung f; (Mil) Kommando nt ▷ vt befehlen +dat

commemorate [kəmɛməreɪt] vt gedenken +gen

commemoration [kəmɛməreɪʃən] n: in ~ of in Gedenken an +akk

comment [kɒmɛnt] n (remark) Bemerkung f; (note) Anmerkung f; (official) Kommentar m (on zu); **no** ~ kein Kommentar ▷ vi sich äußern (on zu)

commentary [kɒmənteri] n Kommentar m (on zu); (TV, Sport) Livereportage f

commentator [kɒmənteɪtər] n Kommentator(in) m(f); (TV, Sport) Reporter(in) m(f)

commerce [kɒmɜrs] n Handel m

commercial [kəmɜrʃəl] adj kommerziell; (training) kaufmännisch; ~ **break** Werbepause f; ~ **vehicle** Lieferwagen m ▷ n (TV) Werbespot m

commission [kəmɪʃən] n Auftrag m; (fee) Provision f; (reporting body) Kommission f ▷ vt beauftragen

commit [kəmɪt] vt (crime) begehen ▷ vr: to ~ **oneself** (undertake) sich verpflichten (to zu)

commitment [kəmɪtmənt] n Verpflichtung f; (Pol) Engagement nt

committee [kəmɪti] n Ausschuss m, Komitee nt

commodity [kəmɒdɪti] n Ware f

common [kɒmən] adj (experience) allgemein, alltäglich; (shared) gemeinsam; (widespread, frequent) häufig; (pej) gewöhnlich, ordinär; **to have sth in ~** etw gemein haben ▷ n

commonly [kɒmənli] adv häufig, allgemein

commonplace [kɒmənpleɪs] adj alltäglich; (pej) banal

common room n Gemeinschaftsraum m

common sense n gesunder Menschenverstand

Commonwealth [kɒmənwɛlθ] n Commonwealth nt; ~ **of Independent States** Gemeinschaft f Unabhängiger Staaten

communal [kəmjunəl] adj gemeinsam; (of a community) Gemeinschafts-, Gemeinde-

communicate [kəmjunɪkeɪt] vi kommunizieren (with mit)

communication [kəmjunɪkeɪʃən] n Kommunikation f, Verständigung f

communications satellite n Nachrichtensatellit m

communications technology n Nachrichtentechnik f

communicative [kəmjunɪkeɪtɪv, -kətɪv] adj gesprächig

communion [kəmjunyən] n: **Holy C~** Heiliges Abendmahl; (Catholic) Kommunion f

communism [kɒmyənɪzəm] n Kommunismus m

communist [kɒmyənɪst] adj kommunistisch ▷ n Kommunist(in) m(f)

community [kəmjunɪti] n Gemeinschaft f

community center n Gemeindezentrum nt

community service n (Jur) Sozialdienst m

commutation ticket [kɒmjəteɪʃn-] n Zeitkarte f

commute [kəmjut] vi pendeln

commuter [kəmjutər] n Pendler(in) m(f)

compact [adj; kəmpækt, n kɒmpækt] adj kompakt ▷ n (for makeup) Puderdose f; (car) ≈ Mittelklassewagen m

compact camera n Kompaktkamera f

compact disc n Compact Disc f, CD f

companion [kəmpænyən] n Begleiter(in) m(f)

company [kʌmpəni] n Gesellschaft f; (Comm) Firma f; **to keep sb ~** jdm Gesellschaft leisten

company car n Firmenauto nt

comparable [kɒmpərəbəl] adj vergleichbar (with, to mit)

comparative [kəmpærətɪv] adj relativ ▷ n (Ling) Komparativ m

comparatively [kəmpærətɪvli] adv verhältnismäßig

compare [kəmpɛɑr] vt vergleichen (with, to mit); ~**d with** o to im Vergleich zu; **beyond** ~ unvergleichlich

comparison [kəmpærɪsən] n Vergleich m; **in** ~ **with** im Vergleich mit (o zu)

compartment [kəmpɑrtmənt] n (Rail) Abteil nt; (in desk etc) Fach nt

compass [kʌmpəs] n Kompass m; ~**es** pl Zirkel m

compassion [kəmpæʃən] n Mitgefühl nt

compatible [kəmpætɪbəl] adj vereinbar

(*with* mit); (*Inform*) kompatibel; **we're not ~** wir passen nicht zueinander

compensate [kɒmpənseit] *vt* (*person*) entschädigen (*for* für) ▷ *vi:* **to ~ for sth** Ersatz für etw leisten; (*make up for*) etw ausgleichen

compensation [kɒmpənseiʃⁿn] *n* Entschädigung *f*; (*money*) Schadenersatz *m*; (*Jur*) Abfindung *f*

compete [kəmpiːt] *vi* konkurrieren (*for* um); (*Sport*) kämpfen (*for* um); (*take part*) teilnehmen (*in* an +*dat*)

competence [kɒmpitəns] *n* Fähigkeit *f*; (*Jur*) Zuständigkeit *f*

competent [kɒmpitənt] *adj* fähig; (*Jur*) zuständig

competition [kɒmpitiʃⁿn] *n* (*contest*) Wettbewerb *m*; (*Comm*) Konkurrenz *f* (*for* um)

competitive [kəmpɛtitiv] *adj* (*firm, price, product*) konkurrenzfähig

competitor [kəmpɛtitər] *n* (*Comm*) Konkurrent(in)*m(f)*; (*Sport*)Teilnehmer(in) *m(f)*

complain [kəmplein] *vi* klagen; (*formally*) sich beschweren (*about* über +*akk*)

complaint [kəmpleint] *n* Klage *f*, Beanstandung *f*; (*formal*) Beschwerde *f*; (*Med*) Leiden *nt*

complement [kɒmplimɛnt] *vt* ergänzen

complete [kəmpliːt] *adj* vollständig; (*finished*) fertig; (*failure, disaster*) total; (*happiness*) vollkommen ▷ *vt* vervollständigen; (*finish*) beenden; (*form*) ausfüllen

completely [kəmpliːtli] *adv* völlig; **not ~ ...** nicht ganz ...

complex [kɒmplɛks] *adj* komplex; (*task, theory etc*) kompliziert ▷ *n* Komplex *m*

complexion [kəmplɛkʃⁿn] *n* Gesichtsfarbe *f*, Teint *m*

complicated [kɒmplikeitid] *adj* kompliziert

complication [kɒmplikeiʃⁿn] *n* Komplikation *f*

compliment [kɒmplimənt] *n* Kompliment *nt*

complimentary [kɒmplimɛntəri, -mɛntri] *adj* lobend; (*free of charge*) Gratis-; **~ ticket** Freikarte *f*

comply [kəmplai] *vi:* **to ~ with the regulations** den Vorschriften entsprechen

component [kəmpounənt] *n* Bestandteil *m*

compose [kəmpouz] *vt* (*music*) komponieren; **to ~ oneself** sich zusammennehmen

composed [kəmpouzd] *adj* gefasst; **to be ~**

of bestehen aus

composer [kəmpouzər] *n* Komponist(in) *m(f)*

composition [kɒmpəziʃⁿn] *n* (*of a group*) Zusammensetzung *f*; (*Mus*) Komposition *f*

comprehend [kɒmprihɛnd] *vt* verstehen

comprehension [kɒmprihɛnʃⁿn] *n* Verständnis *nt*

comprehensive [kɒmprihɛnsiv] *adj* umfassend; **~ school** Gesamtschule *f*

compress [kəmprɛs] *vt* komprimieren

comprise [kəmpraiz] *vt* umfassen, bestehen aus

compromise [kɒmprəmaiz] *n* Kompromiss *m* ▷ *vi* einen Kompromiss schließen

compulsory [kəmpʌlsəri] *adj* obligatorisch; **~ subject** Pflichtfach *nt*

computer [kəmpjuːtər] *n* Computer *m*

computer-aided [kəmpjuːtəreidid] *adj* computergestützt

computer-controlled [kəmpjuːtərkəntrould] *adj* rechnergesteuert

computer game *n* Computerspiel *nt*

computer-literate [kəmpjuːtərlitərit] *adj:* **to be ~** mit dem Computer umgehen können

computer scientist *n* Informatiker(in) *m(f)*

computing [kəmpjuːtin] *n* (*subject*) Informatik *f*

con [kɒn] (*fam*) *n* Schwindel *m* ▷ *vt* betrügen (*out of* um)

conceal [kənsiːl] *vt* verbergen (*from* vor +*dat*)

conceivable [kənsiːvəbⁿl] *adj* denkbar, vorstellbar

conceive [kənsiːv] *vt* (*imagine*) sich vorstellen; (*child*) empfangen

concentrate [kɒnsⁿntreit] *vi* sich konzentrieren (*on* auf +*akk*)

concentration [kɒnsⁿntreiʃⁿn] *n* Konzentration *f*

concept [kɒnsept] *n* Begriff *m*

concern [kənsɜrn] *n* (*affair*) Angelegenheit *f*; (*worry*) Sorge *f*; (*Comm: firm*) Unternehmen *nt*; **it's not my ~** das geht mich nichts an; **there's no cause for ~** kein Grund zur Beunruhigung ▷ *vt* (*affect*) angehen; (*have connection with*) betreffen; (*be about*) handeln von; **those ~ed** die Betroffenen; **as far as I'm ~ed** was mich betrifft

concerned [kənsɜrnd] *adj* (*anxious*) besorgt

concerning [kənsɜrnin] *prep* bezüglich,

hinsichtlich +*gen*

concert [kɒnsərt] *n* Konzert *nt*; **~ hall** Konzertsaal *m*

concession [kənsɛʃⁿ] *n* Zugeständnis *nt*; (*reduction*) Ermäßigung *f*

concise [kənsaɪs] *adj* knapp gefasst, prägnant

conclude [kənklud] *vt* (*end*) beenden, (ab)schließen; (*infer*) folgern (*from* aus); **to ~ that** ... zu dem Schluss kommen, dass ...

conclusion [kənkluʒⁿ] *n* Schluss *m*, Schlussfolgerung *f*

concrete [kɒnkrit] *n* Beton *m* ▷ *adj* konkret

concussion [kənkʌʃⁿ] *n* Gehirnerschütterung *f*

condemn [kəndɛm] *vt* verdammen; (*esp. Jur*) verurteilen

condensed milk [kəndɛnst mɪlk] *n* Kondensmilch *f*, Dosenmilch *f*

condition [kəndɪʃⁿ] *n* (*state*) Zustand *m*; (*requirement*) Bedingung *f*; **on ~ that** ... unter der Bedingung, dass ...; **~s** *pl* (*circumstances, weather*) Verhältnisse *pl*

conditional [kəndɪʃənˀl] *adj* bedingt; (*Ling*) Konditional-

conditioner [kəndɪʃənər] *n* Weichspüler *m*; (*for hair*) Pflegespülung *f*, Haarspülung *f*

condo [kɒndoʊ] (*pl* **-s**) *n see* **condominium**

condolences [kəndoʊlənsɪz] *npl* Beileid *nt*

condom [kɒndəm] *n* Kondom *nt*

condominium [kɒndəmɪniəm] *n* (*apartment*) Eigentumswohnung *f*

conduct [*vb* kənd∆kt, *n* kɒnd∆kt] *n* (*behavior*) Verhalten *nt* ▷ *vt* führen, leiten; (*orchestra*) dirigieren

conductor [kənd∆ktər] *n* (*of orchestra*) Dirigent(in) *m(f)*; (*on train*) Zugführer(in) *m(f)*

cone [koʊn] *n* Kegel *m*; (*for ice cream*) Waffeltüte *f*; (*fir cone*) (Tannen)zapfen *m*

conference [kɒnfərəns, -frəns] *n* Konferenz *f*

confess [kənfɛs] *vt, vi*: **to ~ that** ... gestehen, dass ...

confession [kənfɛʃⁿ] *n* Geständnis *nt*; (*Rel*) Beichte *f*

confetti [kənfɛti] *n* Konfetti *nt*

confidence [kɒnfɪdəns] *n* Vertrauen *nt* (*in* zu); (*assurance*) Selbstvertrauen *nt*

confident [kɒnfɪdənt] *adj* (*sure*) zuversichtlich (*that* ... dass ...), überzeugt (*of*

von); (*self-assured*) selbstsicher

confidential [kɒnfɪdɛnʃˀl] *adj* vertraulich

confine [kənfaɪn] *vt* beschränken (*to* auf +*akk*)

confirm [kənfɜrm] *vt* bestätigen

confirmation [kɒnfərmeɪʃⁿ] *n* Bestätigung *f*; (*Rel*) Konfirmation *f*

confirmed [kənfɜrmd] *adj* überzeugt; (*bachelor*) eingefleischt

confiscate [kɒnfɪskeɪt] *vt* beschlagnahmen, konfiszieren

conflict [kɒnflɪkt] *n* Konflikt *m*

confuse [kənfyuz] *vt* verwirren; (*sth with sth*) verwechseln (*with* mit); (*several things*) durcheinanderbringen

confused [kənfyuzd] *adj* (*person*) konfus, verwirrt; (*account*) verworren

confusing [kənfyuzɪŋ] *adj* verwirrend

confusion [kənfyuʒⁿ] *n* Verwirrung *f*; (*of two things*) Verwechslung *f*; (*muddle*) Chaos *nt*

congested [kəndʒɛstɪd] *adj* verstopft; (*overcrowded*) überfüllt

congestion [kəndʒɛstʃⁿ] *n* Stau *m*

congratulate [kəngrætʃəleɪt] *vt* gratulieren (*on* zu)

congratulations [kəngrætʃəleɪʃⁿnz] *npl* Glückwünsche *pl*; **~!** gratuliere!, herzlichen Glückwunsch!

congregation [kɒngrigeɪʃⁿ] *n* (*Rel*) Gemeinde *f*

congress [kɒŋgrɪs] *n* Kongress *m*; **C~** der Kongress

CONGRESS

Die Legislative der USA heißt Congress. Sie besteht aus zwei Kammern, dem Senat und dem Repräsentantenhaus. Jeder Bundesstaat wird im Senat durch zwei Senatoren und im Repräsentantenhaus, das aus 435 Abgeordneten besteht, proportional zu seiner Bevölkerung vertreten. Gesetzesentwürfe stehen in beiden Kammern zur Debatte. Danach werden beide Fassungen durch einen Vermittlungsausschuss abgeglichen.

Ein Veto vom Präsidenten kann durch eine Zweidrittelmehrheit in beiden Kammern zurückgewiesen werden.

congressman [kɒŋgrɪsmən] (*pl* **-men**), **congresswoman** (*pl* **-women**) *n* Mitglied *nt* des Repräsentantenhauses

conifer [kɒnɪfər] *n* Nadelbaum *m*

conjunction [kəndʒʌŋkʃᵊn] *n* (*Ling*) Konjunktion *f*; **in ~ with** in Verbindung mit

conk out [kɒŋk aut] *vi* (*fam: appliance, car*) den Geist aufgeben, streiken; (*person: die*) ins Gras beißen

connect [kənɛkt] *vt* verbinden (*with, to* mit); (*Elec, Tech: appliance etc*) anschließen (*to* an +*akk*) ▷ *vi* (*train, plane*) Anschluss haben (*with* an +*akk*); **~ing flight** Anschlussflug *m*; **~ing train** Anschlusszug *m*

connection [kənɛkʃᵊn] *n* Verbindung *f*; (*link*) Zusammenhang *m*; (*for train, plane, electrical appliance*) Anschluss *m* (*with, to* an +*akk*); (*business etc*) Beziehung *f*; **in ~ with** in Zusammenhang mit; **bad ~** (*Tel*) schlechte Verbindung; (*Elec*) Wackelkontakt *m*

connector [kənɛktər] *n* (*Inform: computer*) Stecker *m*

conscience [kɒnʃns] *n* Gewissen *nt*

conscientious [kɒnʃiɛnʃəs] *adj* gewissenhaft

conscious [kɒnʃəs] *adj* (*act*) bewusst; (*Med*) bei Bewusstsein; **to be ~** bei Bewusstsein sein

consciousness [kɒnʃəsnɪs] *n* Bewusstsein *nt*

consecutive [kənsɛkyətɪv] *adj* aufeinanderfolgend

consent [kənsɛnt] *n* Zustimmung *f* ▷ *vi* zustimmen (*to dat*)

consequence [kɒnsɪkwɛns, -kwəns] *n* Folge *f*, Konsequenz *f*

consequently [kɒnsɪkwɛntli, -kwəntli] *adv* folglich, deshalb

conservation [kɒnsərveɪʃᵊn] *n* Erhaltung *f*; (*nature conservation*) Naturschutz *m*

conservation area *n* Naturschutzgebiet *nt*

conservative [kənsɜrvətɪv], (*Pol*) **Conservative** *adj* konservativ

conservatory [kənsɜrvətɔri] *n* (*greenhouse*) Gewächshaus *nt*; (*room*) Wintergarten *m*

consider [kənsɪdər] *vt* (*reflect on*) nachdenken über, sich überlegen; (*take into account*) in Betracht ziehen; (*regard*) halten für; **he is ~ed to be ...** er gilt als ...

considerable [kənsɪdərəbᵊl] *adj* beträchtlich

considerate [kənsɪdərɪt] *adj* aufmerksam, rücksichtsvoll

consideration [kənsɪdəreɪʃᵊn] *n* (*thought-fulness*) Rücksicht *f*; (*thought*) Überlegung *f*; **to take sth into ~** etw in Betracht ziehen

considering [kənsɪdərɪŋ] *prep* in Anbetracht +*gen* ▷ *conj* da

consist [kənsɪst] *vi*: **to ~ of ...** bestehen aus ...

consistent [kənsɪstənt] *adj* (*behavior, process etc*) konsequent; (*statements*) übereinstimmend; (*argument*) folgerichtig; (*performance, results*) beständig

consolation [kɒnsəleɪʃᵊn] *n* Trost *m*

console [kənsoul] *vt* trösten

consolidate [kənsɒlɪdeɪt] *vt* festigen

consonant [kɒnsənənt] *n* Konsonant *m*

conspicuous [kənspɪkyuəs] *adj* auffällig, auffallend

conspiracy [kənspɪrəsi] *n* Komplott *nt*

conspire [kənspaɪər] *vi* sich verschwören (*against* gegen)

Constance [kɒnstəns] *n* Konstanz *nt*; **Lake ~** der Bodensee

constant [kɒnstənt] *adj* (*continual*) ständig, dauernd; (*unchanging: temperature etc*) gleichbleibend

constantly [kɒnstəntli] *adv* dauernd

consternation [kɒnstərneɪʃᵊn] *n* (*dismay*) Bestürzung *f*

constituency [kənstɪtʃuənsi] *n* Wahlkreis *m*

constitution [kɒnstɪtuːʃᵊn] *n* Verfassung *f*; (*of person*) Konstitution *f*

construct [kənstrʌkt] *vt* bauen

construction [kənstrʌkʃᵊn] *n* (*process, result*) Bau *m*; (*method*) Bauweise *f*; **under ~** im Bau befindlich

construction site *n* Baustelle *f*

construction worker *n* Bauarbeiter(in) *m(f)*

consulate [kɒnsəlɪt] *n* Konsulat *nt*

consult [kənsʌlt] *vt* um Rat fragen; (*doctor*) konsultieren; (*book*) nachschlagen in +*dat*

consultant [kənsʌltənt] *n* (*Med*) Facharzt *m*, Fachärztin *f*

consultation [kɒnsəlteɪʃᵊn] *n* Beratung *f*; (*Med*) Konsultation *f*; **~ room** Besprechungsraum, Sprechzimmer

consume [kənsuːm] *vt* verbrauchen; (*food*) konsumieren

consumer [kənsuːmər] *n* Verbraucher(in) *m(f)*

consumer-friendly *adj* verbraucherfreundlich

contact [kɒntækt] *n* (*touch*) Berührung *f*;

(*communication*) Kontakt *m*; (*person*) Kontaktperson *f*; **to be/keep in ~ with sb** (mit jdm) in Kontakt sein/bleiben ▷ *vt* sich in Verbindung setzen mit

contact lenses *npl* Kontaktlinsen *pl*

contagious [kənteɪdʒəs] *adj* ansteckend

contain [kənteɪn] *vt* enthalten

container [kənteɪnər] *n* Behälter *m*; (*for transport*) Container *m*

contaminate [kəntæmɪneɪt] *vt* verunreinigen; (*chemically*) verseuchen; **~d by radiation** strahlenverseucht, verstrahlt

contamination [kəntæmɪneɪʃən] *n* Verunreinigung *f*; (*by radiation*) Verseuchung *f*

contemporary [kəntempərəri] *adj* zeitgenössisch

contempt [kəntempt] *n* Verachtung *f*

contemptuous [kəntemptʃuəs] *adj* verächtlich; **to be ~** voller Verachtung sein (*of* für)

content [kəntent] *adj* zufrieden

content(s) [kəntent(s)] *npl* Inhalt *m*

contest [*n* kəntest, *vb* kəntest] *n* (Wett)kampf *m* (*for* um); (*competition*) Wettbewerb *m* ▷ *vt* kämpfen um +*akk*; (*dispute*) bestreiten

contestant [kəntestənt] *n* Teilnehmer(in) *m(f)*

context [kəntekst] *n* Zusammenhang *m*; **out of ~** aus dem Zusammenhang gerissen

continent [kəntɪnənt] *n* Kontinent *m*, Festland *nt*

continental [kəntɪnentəl] *adj* kontinental; **~ breakfast** *kleines Frühstück mit Brötchen und Marmelade, Kaffee oder Tee*

continual [kəntɪnyuəl] *adj* (*endless*) ununterbrochen; (*constant*) dauernd, ständig

continually [kəntɪnyuəli] *adv* dauernd; (*again and again*) immer wieder

continuation [kəntɪnyueɪʃən] *n* Fortsetzung *f*

continue [kəntɪnyu] *vi* weitermachen (*with* mit); (*esp talking*) fortfahren (*with* mit); (*travelling*) weiterfahren; (*state, conditions*) fortdauern, anhalten ▷ *vt* fortsetzen; **to be ~d** Fortsetzung folgt

continuous [kəntɪnyuəs] *adj* (*endless*) ununterbrochen; (*constant*) ständig

contraceptive [kəntrəseptɪv] *n* Verhütungsmittel *nt*

contract [kəntrækt] *n* Vertrag *m*

contradict [kəntrədɪkt] *vt* widersprechen +*dat*

contradiction [kəntrədɪkʃən] *n* Widerspruch *m*

contrary [kəntreri] *n* Gegenteil *nt*; **on the ~** im Gegenteil ▷ *adj*: **~ to** entgegen +*dat*

contrast [*n* kəntræst, *vb* kəntræst] *n* Kontrast *m*, Gegensatz *m*; **in ~ to** im Gegensatz zu ▷ *vt* entgegensetzen

contribute [kəntrɪbyut] *vt*, *vi* beitragen (*to* zu); (*money*) spenden (*to* für)

contribution [kəntrɪbyuʃən] *n* Beitrag *m*

control [kəntroʊl] *vt* (*master*) beherrschen; (*temper etc*) im Griff haben; (*esp Tech*) steuern; **to ~ oneself** sich beherrschen ▷ *n* Kontrolle *f*; (*mastery*) Beherrschung *f*; (*esp Tech*) Steuerung *f*; **~s** *pl* (*knobs, switches etc*) Bedienungselemente *pl*; (*collectively*) Steuerung *f*; **to be out of ~** außer Kontrolle sein

control panel *n* Schalttafel *f*

controversial [kəntrəvɜrʃəl] *adj* umstritten

convalesce [kɒnvəles] *vi* gesund werden

convalescence [kɒnvələsəns] *n* Genesung *f*

convenience [kənviːnjəns] *n* (*quality, thing*) Annehmlichkeit *f*; **at your ~** wann es Ihnen passt; **with all modern ~s** mit allem Komfort

convenience food *n* Fertiggericht *nt*

convenient [kənviːnjənt] *adj* günstig, passend

convent [kɒnvent, -vənt] *n* Kloster *nt*

convention [kənvenʃən] *n* (*custom*) Konvention *f*; (*meeting*) Konferenz *f*; **the Geneva C~** die Genfer Konvention

conventional [kənvenʃənəl] *adj* herkömmlich, konventionell

conversation [kɒnvərseɪʃən] *n* Gespräch *nt*, Unterhaltung *f*

conversion [kənvɜrʒən] *n* Umwandlung *f* (*into* in +*akk*); (*of building*) Umbau *m* (*into* zu); (*calculation*) Umrechnung *f*

conversion table *n* Umrechnungstabelle *f*

convert [kənvɜrt] *vt* umwandeln; (*person*) bekehren; (*Inform*) konvertieren; **to ~ into Euros** in Euro umrechnen

convertible [kənvɜrtɪbəl] *n* (*Auto*) Kabrio *nt* ▷ *adj* umwandelbar

convey [kənveɪ] *vt* (*carry*) befördern; (*feelings*) vermitteln

conveyor belt [kənveɪər belt] *n* Förderband *nt*, Fließband *nt*

convict [*vb* kənvɪkt, *n* kɒnvɪkt] *vt* verurteilen (*of* wegen) ▷ *n* Strafgefangene(r) *mf*

conviction [kənvɪkʃən] *n* (*Jur*) Verurtei-

lung f; (strong belief) Überzeugung f
convince [kənvɪns] vt überzeugen (of von)
convincing [kənvɪnsɪŋ] adj überzeugend
cook [kʊk] vt, vi kochen ▷ n Koch m, Köchin f
cookbook [kʊkbʊk] n Kochbuch nt
cooker [kʊkər] n Herd m
cookery [kʊkəri] n Kochkunst f; ~ **book** Kochbuch nt
cookie [kʊki] n Keks m
cooking [kʊkɪŋ] n Kochen nt; (style of cooking) Küche f
cool [kul] adj kühl, gelassen; (fam: brilliant) cool, stark ▷ vt, vi (ab)kühlen; ~ **it** reg dich ab! ▷ n: **to keep/lose one's ~** (fam) ruhig bleiben/durchdrehen
cool down vi abkühlen; (calm down) sich beruhigen
cooperate [koʊɒpəreɪt] vi zusammenarbeiten, kooperieren
cooperation [koʊɒpəreɪʃən] n Zusammenarbeit f, Kooperation f
cooperative [koʊɒpərətɪv] adj hilfsbereit ▷ n Genossenschaft f
coordinate [koʊɔrdəneɪt] vt koordinieren
cop [kɒp] n (fam: policeman) Bulle m
cope [koʊp] vi zurechtkommen, fertig werden (with mit)
Copenhagen [koʊpˈnheɪgən] n Kopenhagen nt
copier [kɒpiər] n Kopierer m
copper [kɒpər] n Kupfer nt; (fam: coin) Kupfermünze f; ~**s** Kleingeld nt
copy [kɒpi] n Kopie f; (of book) Exemplar nt ▷ vt kopieren; (imitate) nachahmen
copyright [kɒpiraɪt] n Urheberrecht nt
coral [kɔrəl] n Koralle f
cord [kɔrd] n Schnur f; (material) Kordsamt m
cordless [kɔrdlɪs] adj (phone) schnurlos
core [kɔr] n (a. fig) Kern m; (of apple, pear) Kerngehäuse nt
core business n Kerngeschäft nt
cork [kɔrk] n (material) Kork m; (stopper) Korken m
corkscrew [kɔrkskru] n Korkenzieher m
corn [kɔrn] n Getreide nt, Korn nt; (maize) Mais m; (on foot) Hühnerauge nt; ~ **on the cob** (gekochter) Maiskolben
corned beef [kɔrnd bif] n Cornedbeef nt
corner [kɔrnər] n Ecke f; (on road) Kurve f; (Sport) Eckstoß m ▷ vt in die Enge treiben
corner store n Laden m an der Ecke

cornflakes [kɔrnfleɪks] npl Cornflakes pl
Cornish [kɔrnɪʃ] adj kornisch; ~ **pasty** mit Fleisch und Kartoffeln gefüllte Pastete
Cornwall [kɔrnwɔl] n Cornwall nt
coronation [kɔrəneɪʃən] n Krönung f
corporation [kɔrpəreɪʃən] n (Comm) Aktiengesellschaft f
corpse [kɔrps] n Leiche f
correct [kərɛkt] adj (accurate) richtig; (proper) korrekt ▷ vt korrigieren, verbessern
correction [kərɛkʃən] n (esp written) Korrektur f
correspond [kɔrɪspɒnd] vi entsprechen (to dat); (two things) übereinstimmen; (exchange letters) korrespondieren
corresponding [kɔrɪspɒndɪŋ] adj entsprechend
corridor [kɔrɪdər, -dɔr] n (in building) Flur m; (in train) Gang m
corrupt [kərʌpt] adj korrupt
cosmetic [kɒzmɛtɪk] adj kosmetisch
cosmetics npl Kosmetika pl
cosmetic surgeon n Schönheitschirurg(in) m(f)
cosmetic surgery n Schönheitschirurgie f
cosmopolitan [kɒzməpɒlɪtən] adj international; (attitude) weltoffen
cost [kɔst] n (cost, cost) vt kosten ▷ n Kosten pl; **at all ~s, at any ~** um jeden Preis; ~ **of living** Lebenshaltungskosten pl
costly [kɔstli] adj kostspielig
costume [kɒstum] n (Theat) Kostüm nt
cot [kɒt] n Campingliege f
cottage [kɒtɪdʒ] n kleines Haus; (country cottage) Landhäuschen nt
cottage cheese n Hüttenkäse m
cotton [kɒtˈn] n Baumwolle f
cotton ball n Watte f
cotton candy n Zuckerwatte f
couch [kaʊtʃ] n Couch f; (sofa) Sofa nt
cough [kɔf] vi husten ▷ n Husten m
cough syrup [kɔf sɪrʌp] n Hustensaft m
could [kəd, STRONG kʊd] pt of **can**; konnte ▷ conditional könnte; ~ **you come earlier?** könntest du/könnten Sie früher kommen?
couldn't [kʊdˈnt] contr of **could not**
council [kaʊnsˈl] n (Pol) Rat m; (local council) Gemeinderat m; (town council) Stadtrat m
councillor [kaʊnsələr] n Gemeinderat m, Gemeinderätin f
count [kaʊnt] vt, vi zählen; (include) mitrechnen ▷ n Zählung f; (noble) Graf m

counter [kaʊntər] n (in shop) Ladentisch m; (in café) Theke f; (in bank, post office) Schalter m

counterattack [kaʊntərətæk] n Gegenangriff m ▷ vi zurückschlagen

counterclockwise [kaʊntərklɒkwaɪz] adv entgegen dem Uhrzeigersinn

counterpart [kaʊntərpart] n Gegenstück nt (of zu)

countess [kaʊntɪs] n Gräfin f

countless [kaʊntlɪs] adj zahllos, unzählig

count on vt (rely on) sich verlassen auf +akk; (expect) rechnen mit

country [kʌntri] n Land nt; **in the ~** auf dem Land(e); **in this ~** hierzulande

country cousin n (fam) Landei nt

country house n Landhaus nt

countryman [kʌntrɪmən] n (compatriot) Landsmann m

country music n Countrymusic f

country road n Landstraße f

countryside [kʌntrisaɪd] n Landschaft f; (rural area) Land nt

county [kaʊnti] n Verwaltungsbezirk m

couple [kʌpᵊl] n Paar nt; **a ~ of** ein paar

coupon [kuːpɒn, kyuː-] n (voucher) Gutschein m

courage [kʌrɪdʒ] n Mut m

courageous [kəreɪdʒəs] adj mutig

courier [kʊəriər, kər-] n (for tourists) Reiseleiter(in) m(f); (messenger) Kurier m

course [kɔrs] n (of study) Kurs m; (for race) Strecke f; (Naut, Aviat) Kurs m; (at university) Studiengang m; (in meal) Gang m; **of ~** natürlich; **in the ~ of** während

court [kɔrt] n (Sport) Platz m; (Jur) Gericht nt

courteous [kɜrtiəs] adj höflich

courtesy [kɜrtisi] n Höflichkeit f; **~ bus** (gebührenfreier) Zubringerbus

courthouse [kɔrthaʊs] n Gerichtsgebäude nt

court order n Gerichtsbeschluss m

courtroom [kɔrtrum] n Gerichtssaal m

courtyard [kɔrtyard] n Hof m

cousin [kʌzᵊn] n (male) Cousin m; (female) Cousine f

cover [kʌvər] vt bedecken (in, with mit); (distance) zurücklegen; (loan, costs) decken ▷ n (for bed etc) Decke f; (of cushion) Bezug m; (lid) Deckel m; (of book) Umschlag m; **insurance ~** Versicherungsschutz m

coverage [kʌvərɪdʒ] n Berichterstattung f

(of über +akk)

cover charge n Kosten pl für ein Gedeck

covering [kʌvərɪŋ] n Decke f

cover letter n Begleitbrief m

cover story n (newspaper) Titelgeschichte f

cover up vt zudecken; (error etc) vertuschen

cow [kaʊ] n Kuh f

coward [kaʊərd] n Feigling m

cowardly [kaʊərdli] adj feig(e)

cowboy [kaʊbɔɪ] n Cowboy m

coy [kɔɪ] adj gespielt schüchtern, kokett

cozy [koʊzi] adj gemütlich

CPU [si pi yu] (abbr) **= central processing unit** Zentraleinheit f

crab [kræb] n Krabbe f

crabby [kræbi] adj mürrisch, reizbar

crack [kræk] n Riss m; (in pottery, glass) Sprung m; (drug) Crack nt; **to have a ~ at sth** etw ausprobieren ▷ vi (pottery, glass) einen Sprung bekommen; (wood, ice etc) einen Riss bekommen; **to get ~ing** (fam) loslegen ▷ vt (bone) anbrechen; (nut, code) knacken

cracker [krækər] n Kräcker m

crackers [krækərz] adj (fam) verrückt, bekloppt; **he's ~** er hat nicht alle Tassen im Schrank

crackle [krækᵊl] vi knistern; (telephone, radio) knacken

crackling [kræklɪŋ] n (Gastr) Kruste f (des Schweinebratens)

cradle [kreɪdᵊl] n Wiege f

craft [kræft] n Handwerk nt; (art) Kunsthandwerk nt; (Naut) Boot nt

craftsman [kræftsmən] (pl -men) n Handwerker m

craftsmanship [kræftsmənʃɪp] n Handwerkskunst f; (ability) handwerkliches Können

crafty [kræfti] adj schlau

cram [kræm] vt stopfen (into in +akk); **to be ~med with ...** mit ... vollgestopft sein ▷ vi (revise for exam) pauken (for für)

cramp [kræmp] n Krampf m

cranberry [krænberi] n Preiselbeere f

crane [kreɪn] n (machine) Kran m; (bird) Kranich m

crash [kræʃ] vi einen Unfall haben; (two vehicles) zusammenstoßen; (plane, computer) abstürzen; (economy) zusammenbrechen; **to ~ into sth** gegen etw knallen ▷ vt einen Unfall haben mit ▷ n (car) Unfall m; (train) Unglück nt; (collision) Zusammenstoß m; (Aviat, Inform) Absturz m; (noise) Krachen nt

crash course n Intensivkurs m

crash helmet n Sturzhelm m

crash landing n Bruchlandung f

crate [kreɪt] n Kiste f; (of beer) Kasten m

crater [kreɪtər] n Krater m

craving [kreɪvɪŋ] n starkes Verlangen, Bedürfnis nt

crawl [krɔl] vi kriechen; (baby) krabbeln ▷ n (swimming) Kraul m

crayfish [kreɪfɪʃ] n Languste f

crayon [kreɪɒn] n Buntstift m

crazy [kreɪzi] adj verrückt (about nach)

cream [krim] n (from milk) Sahne f, Rahm m; (polish, cosmetic) Creme f ▷ adj cremefarben

cream cheese n Frischkäse m

creamer [krimər] n Kaffeeweißer m

creamy [krimi] adj sahnig

crease [kris] n Falte f ▷ vt falten; (untidy) zerknittern

create [krieɪt] vt schaffen; (cause) verursachen

creative [krieɪtɪv] adj schöpferisch; (person) kreativ

creature [kritʃər] n Geschöpf nt

credibility [krɛdɪbɪlɪti] n Glaubwürdigkeit f

credible [krɛdɪbʰl] adj (person) glaubwürdig

credit [krɛdɪt] n (Fin: amount allowed) Kredit m; (amount possessed) Guthaben nt; (recognition) Anerkennung f; ~s (of film) Abspann m

credit card n Kreditkarte f

credit crunch [krɛdɪt krʌntʃ] n Kreditklemme f

creep [krip] (crept, crept) vi kriechen

creeps [krips] n: he gives me the ~ er ist mir nicht ganz geheuer

creepy [kripi] adj (frightening) gruselig, unheimlich

crept [krɛpt] pt, pp of creep

cress [krɛs] n Kresse f

crest [krɛst] n Kamm m; (coat of arms) Wappen nt

crew [kru] n Besatzung f, Mannschaft f

crib [krɪb] n Kinderbett nt

cricket [krɪkɪt] n (insect) Grille f; (game) Kricket m

crime [kraɪm] n Verbrechen nt

criminal [krɪmɪnʰl] n Verbrecher(in) m(f) ▷ adj kriminell, strafbar

cripple [krɪpʰl] n Krüppel m ▷ vt verkrüp-

peln, lähmen

crisis [kraɪsɪs] (pl crises) n Krise f

crisp [krɪsp] adj knusprig

crispbread [krɪspbrɛd] n Knäckebrot nt

criterion [kraɪtɪəriən] n Kriterium nt

critic [krɪtɪk] n Kritiker(in) m(f)

critical [krɪtɪkʰl] adj kritisch

critically [krɪtɪkli] adv kritisch; ~ ill/injured schwer krank/verletzt

criticism [krɪtɪsɪzəm] n Kritik f

criticize [krɪtɪsaɪz] vt kritisieren

Croat [krouæt] n Kroate m, Kroatin f

Croatia [kroueɪʃə] n Kroatien nt

Croatian [kroueɪʃən] adj kroatisch

crockery [krɒkəri] n Geschirr nt

crocodile [krɒkədaɪl] n Krokodil nt

crocus [kroukəs] n Krokus m

crop [krɒp] n (harvest) Ernte f

crops npl Getreide nt

crop up vi auftauchen

croquette [kroukɛt] n Krokette f

cross [krɔs] n Kreuz nt; to mark sth with a ~ etw ankreuzen ▷ vt (road, river etc) überqueren; (legs) übereinanderschlagen; it ~ed my mind es fiel mir ein; to ~ one's fingers die Daumen drücken ▷ adj ärgerlich, böse

crossbar [krɔsbar] n (of bicycle) Stange f; (Sport) Querlatte f

cross-country [krɔskʌntri] adj: ~ running Geländelauf m; ~ skiing Langlauf m

cross-examination n Kreuzverhör nt

cross-eyed [krɔsaɪd] adj: to be ~ schielen

crossing [krɔsɪŋ] n (crossroads) (Straßen)kreuzung f; (for pedestrians) Fußgängerüberweg m; (on ship) Überfahrt f

cross out vt durchstreichen

crossroads [krɔsroudz] nsing o pl Straßenkreuzung f

cross section n Querschnitt m

crosswalk [krɔswɔk] n Fußgängerüberweg m

crossword (puzzle) [krɔswɜrd (pʌzʰl)] n Kreuzworträtsel nt

crouch [krautʃ] vi hocken

crouton [krutɒn] n Croûton m

crow [krou] n Krähe f

crowbar [kroubar] n Brecheisen nt

crowd [kraud] n Menge f ▷ vi sich drängen (into in +akk; round um)

crowded [kraudɪd] adj überfüllt

crown [kraun] n Krone f ▷ vt krönen; (fam): and to ~ it all ... und als Krönung ...

crucial [kruʃʰl] adj entscheidend

crude [kruːd] *adj* primitiv; (*humor, behavior*) derb, ordinär ▷ *n*: ~ **oil** Rohöl *nt*

cruel [kruəl] *adj* grausam (*to* zu, gegen); (*unfeeling*) gefühllos

cruelty [kruəlti] *n* Grausamkeit *f*; ~ **to animals** Tierquälerei *f*

cruise [kruːz] *n* Kreuzfahrt *f* ▷ *vi* (*ship*) kreuzen; (*car*) mit Reisegeschwindigkeit fahren

cruise liner *n* Kreuzfahrtschiff *nt*

cruise missile *n* Marschflugkörper *m*

cruising speed [kruːzɪɪn spiːd] *n* Reisegeschwindigkeit *f*

crumb [krʌm] *n* Krume *f*

crumble [krʌmbᵊl] *vt, vi* zerbröckeln ▷ *n* mit Streuseln überbackenes Kompott

crumple [krʌmpᵊl] *vt* zerknittern

crusade [kruseɪd] *n* Kreuzzug *m*

crush [krʌʃ] *vt* zerdrücken; (*finger etc*) quetschen; (*spices, stone*) zerstoßen ▷ *n*: **to have a ~ on sb** in jdn verknallt sein

crushing [krʌʃɪŋ] *adj* (*defeat, remark*) vernichtend

crust [krʌst] *n* Kruste *f*

crusty [krʌsti] *adj* knusprig

crutch [krʌtʃ] *n* Krücke *f*

cry [kraɪ] *vi* (*call*) rufen; (*scream*) schreien; (*weep*) weinen ▷ *n* (*call*) Ruf *m*; (*louder*) Schrei *m*

crypt [krɪpt] *n* Krypta *f*

crystal [krɪstᵊl] *n* Kristall *m*

cu (*abbr*) = **see you** (*SMS, email*) bis bald

Cuba [kyuːbə] *n* Kuba *nt*

cube [kyuːb] *n* Würfel *m*

cubic [kyuːbɪk] *adj* Kubik-

cubicle [kyuːbɪkᵊl] *n* Kabine *f*

cuckoo [kuku, kuku] *n* Kuckuck *m*

cucumber [kyuːkʌmbər] *n* Salatgurke *f*

cuddle [kʌdᵊl] *vt* in den Arm nehmen; (*amorously*) schmusen mit ▷ *n* Liebkosung *f*, Umarmung *f*; **to have a ~** schmusen

cuddly [kʌdli] *adj* verschmust

cuff [kʌf] *n* Manschette *f*; (*pant cuff*) Aufschlag *m*; **off the ~** aus dem Stegreif

cuff link [kʌflɪŋk] *n* Manschettenknopf *m*

cuisine [kwiziːn] *n* Kochkunst *f*, Küche *f*

culprit [kʌlprɪt] *n* Schuldige(r) *mf*; (*fig*) Übeltäter(in) *m(f)*

cult [kʌlt] *n* Kult *m*

cultivate [kʌltɪveɪt] *vt* (*Agr: land*) bebauen; (*crop*) anbauen

cultivated [kʌltɪveɪtd] *adj* (*person*) kultiviert, gebildet

cultural [kʌltʃərəl] *adj* kulturell, Kultur-

culture [kʌltʃər] *n* Kultur *f*

cultured [kʌltʃərd] *adj* gebildet, kultiviert

cumbersome [kʌmbərsəm] *adj* (*object*) unhandlich

cumin [kʌmɪn, kumɪn] *n* Kreuzkümmel *m*

cunning [kʌnɪŋ] *adj* schlau; (*person a.*) gerissen

cup [kʌp] *n* Tasse *f*; (*prize*) Pokal *m*; **it's not his cup of tea** das ist nicht sein Fall

cupboard [kʌbərd] *n* Schrank *m*

cupola [kyuːpələ] *n* Kuppel *f*

curable [kyuərəbᵊl] *adj* heilbar

curb [kɜrb] *n* Randstein *m*

curd [kɜrd] *n* ≈ Quark *m*

cure [kyuər] *n* Heilmittel *nt* (*for* gegen); (*process*) Heilung *f* ▷ *vt* heilen; (*Gastr*) pökeln; (*smoke*) räuchern

curious [kyuəriəs] *adj* neugierig; (*strange*) seltsam

curl [kɜrl] *n* Locke *f* ▷ *vi* sich kräuseln

curly [kɜrli] *adj* lockig

currant [kɜrənt] *n* (*dried*) Korinthe *f*; (*red, black*) Johannisbeere *f*

currency [kɜrənsi] *n* Währung *f*; **foreign ~** Devisen *pl*

current [kɜrənt] *n* (*in water*) Strömung *f*; (*electric current*) Strom *m* ▷ *adj* (*issue, affairs*) aktuell, gegenwärtig; (*expression*) gängig

currently [kɜrəntli] *adv* zur Zeit

curriculum [kərɪkyələm] *n* Lehrplan *m*

curry [kɜri] *n* Currygericht *nt*

curry powder *n* Curry(pulver) *nt*

curse [kɜrs] *vi* (*swear*) fluchen (*at* auf +*akk*) ▷ *n* Fluch *m*

cursor [kɜrsər] *n* (*Inform*) Cursor *m*

curt [kɜrt] *adj* schroff, kurz angebunden

curtain [kɜrtᵊn] *n* Vorhang *m*; **it was ~s for Benny** für Benny war alles vorbei

curve [kɜrv] *n* Kurve *f* ▷ *vi* einen Bogen machen

curved [kɜrvd] *adj* gebogen

cushion [kuʃᵊn] *n* Kissen *nt*

custard [kʌstərd] *n* dicke Vanillesoße, die warm oder kalt zu vielen englischen Nachspeisen gegessen wird

custom [kʌstəm] *n* Brauch *m*; (*habit*) Gewohnheit *f*

customary [kʌstəmɛri] *adj* üblich

custom-built *adj* nach Kundenangaben gefertigt

customer [kʌstəmər] *n* Kunde *m*, Kundin *f*

customer service *n* Kundendienst *m*

customs [kʌstəmz] *npl* (*organization, location*) Zoll *m*; **to pass through ~** durch den

Zoll gehen
customs officer n Zollbeamte(r) m, Zoll-
beamtin f
cut [kʌt] (**cut, cut**) vt schneiden; (*cake*)
anschneiden; (*wages, benefits*) kürzen;
(*prices*) heruntersetzen; **I cut my finger** ich
habe mir in den Finger geschnitten ▷ n
Schnitt m; (*wound*) Schnittwunde f;
(*reduction*) Kürzung f (*in gen*); **price/tax
cut** Preissenkung/Steuersenkung f; **to be
a cut above the rest** eine Klasse besser als
die anderen sein
cut back vt (*workforce etc*) reduzieren
cutback [kʌtbæk] n Kürzung f
cut down vt (*tree*) fällen; **to ~ on sth** etwas
einschränken
cute [kyut] adj putzig, niedlich; (*shrewd*)
clever
cut in vi (*Auto*) scharf einscheren; **to ~ on
sb** jdn schneiden
cutlet [kʌtlɪt] n (*pork*) Kotelett nt; (*veal*)
Schnitzel nt
cut off vt abschneiden; (*gas, electricity*)
abdrehen, abstellen; (*Tel*): **I was ~** ich

wurde unterbrochen
cut-rate [kʌtreɪt] adj verbilligt
cutting [kʌtɪŋ] n (*from paper*) Ausschnitt
m; (*of plant*) Ableger m ▷ adj (*comment*)
verletzend
cwt (*abbr*) = **hundredweight** = Zentner, Ztr.
cybercafé [saɪbərkæfeɪ] n Internetcafé nt
cyberspace [saɪbərspeɪs] n Cyberspace m
cycle [saɪkˀl] n Fahrrad nt ▷ vi Rad fahren
cycling [saɪklɪŋ] n Radfahren nt
cyclist [saɪklɪst] n Radfahrer(in) m(f)
cylinder [sɪlɪndər] n Zylinder m
cynical [sɪnɪkˀl] adj zynisch
cypress [saɪprɪs] n Zypresse f
Cypriot [sɪprɪət] adj zypriotisch ▷ n Zyprio-
te m, Zypriotin f
Cyprus [saɪprəs] n Zypern nt
czar [zɑr] n Zar m
czarina [zɑrinə] n Zarin f
Czech [tʃɛk] adj tschechisch ▷ n (*person*)
Tscheche m, Tschechin f; (*language*)
Tschechisch nt
Czech Republic [tʃɛk rɪpʌblɪk] n Tschechi-
sche Republik, Tschechien nt

D

dab [dæb] *vt* (*wound, nose etc*) betupfen (*with* mit)

dachshund [dɑksʊnt] *n* Dackel *m*

dad(dy) [dæd(i)] *n* Papa *m*, Vati *m*

daddy-longlegs [dædilɔŋlegz] *n sing* Weberknecht *m*

daffodil [dæfədıl] *n* Osterglocke *f*

dahlia [dælyə, dɑl-] *n* Dahlie *f*

daily [deıli] *adj, adv* täglich ▷ *n* (*paper*) Tageszeitung *f*

dairy [dɛəri] *n* (*on farm*) Molkerei *f*

dairy products *npl* Milchprodukte *pl*

daisy [deızi] *n* Gänseblümchen *nt*

dam [dæm] *n* Staudamm *m* ▷ *vt* stauen

damage [dæmıdʒ] *n* Schaden *m*; **~s** *pl* (*Jur*) Schadenersatz *m* ▷ *vt* beschädigen; (*reputation, health*) schädigen, schaden +*dat*

damn [dæm] *adj* (*fam*) verdammt ▷ *vt* (*condemn*) verurteilen; **~ it!** verflucht! ▷ *n*: **he doesn't give a ~** es ist ihm völlig egal

damp [dæmp] *adj* feucht ▷ *n* Feuchtigkeit *f*

dampen [dæmpən] *vt* befeuchten

dance [dæns] *n* Tanz *m*; (*event*) Tanzveranstaltung *f* ▷ *vi* tanzen

dance floor *n* Tanzfläche *f*

dancer [dænsər] *n* Tänzer(in) *m(f)*

dancing [dænsıŋ] *n* Tanzen *nt*

dandelion [dændılaıən] *n* Löwenzahn *m*

dandruff [dændrəf] *n* Schuppen *pl*

Dane [deın] *n* Däne *m*, Dänin *f*

danger [deındʒər] *n* Gefahr *f*; **~** (*sign*) Achtung!; **to be in ~** in Gefahr sein

dangerous [deındʒərəs, deındʒrəs] *adj* gefährlich

Danish [deınıʃ] *adj* dänisch ▷ *n* (*language*) Dänisch *nt*; **the ~** *pl* die Dänen

Danish pastry *n* Plundergebäck *nt*

Danube [dænjub] *n* Donau *f*

dare [dɛər] *vi*: **to ~ to do sth** es wagen, etw zu tun; **I didn't ~ ask** ich traute mich nicht, zu fragen; **how ~ you** was fällt dir ein!

daring [dɛərıŋ] *adj* (*person*) mutig; (*film, clothes etc*) gewagt

dark [dɑrk] *adj* dunkel; (*gloomy*) düster, trübe; (*sinister*) finster; **~ chocolate** Bitterschokolade *f*; **~ green/blue** dunkelgrün/dunkelblau ▷ *n* Dunkelheit *f*; **in the ~** im Dunkeln

dark glasses *npl* Sonnenbrille *f*

darkness [dɑrknıs] *n* Dunkelheit *nt*

darling [dɑrlıŋ] *n* Schatz *m*; (*also favorite*) Liebling *m*

darts [dɑrts] *nsing* (*game*) Darts *nt*

dash [dæʃ] *vi* stürzen, rennen ▷ *vt*: **to ~ hopes** Hoffnungen zerstören ▷ *n* (*in text*) Gedankenstrich *m*; (*of liquid*) Schuss *m*

dashboard [dæʃbɔrd] *n* Armaturenbrett *nt*

data [deıtə, dætə] *npl* Daten *pl*

data bank, database *n* Datenbank *f*

data capture *n* Datenerfassung *f*

data processing *n* Datenverarbeitung *f*

data protection *n* Datenschutz *m*

date [deıt] *n* Datum *nt*; (*for meeting, delivery etc*) Termin *m*; (*with person*) Verabredung *f*; (*with girlfriend/boyfriend etc*) Date *nt*; (*fruit*) Dattel *f*; **what's the ~ today?** der Wievielte ist heute?; **out of ~** *adj* veraltet; **up to ~** (*news*) aktuell; (*fashion*) zeitgemäß ▷ *vt* (*letter etc*) datieren; (*person*) gehen mit

dated [deıtıd] *adj* altmodisch

date of birth *n* Geburtsdatum *nt*

dating service *n* Partnervermittlung *f*

dative [deıtıv] *n* Dativ *m*

daughter [dɔtər] *n* Tochter *f*

daughter-in-law [dɔtərınlɔ] *n* (*pl* **daughters-in-law**) *n* Schwiegertochter *f*

dawn [dɔn] *n* Morgendämmerung *f* ▷ *vi* dämmern; **it ~ed on me** mir ging ein Licht auf

day [deı] *n* Tag *m*; **one day** eines Tages; **by day** bei Tage; **day after day, day by day** Tag für Tag; **the day after/before** am Tag danach/zuvor; **the day before yesterday** vorgestern; **the day after tomorrow** übermorgen; **these days** heutzutage; **in those days** damals; **let's call it a day** Schluss für heute!

daybreak [deıbreık] *n* Tagesanbruch *m*

day-care center *n* Kita *f* (*Kindertagesstätte*)

daydream [deıdrim] *n* Tagtraum *m* ▷ *vi* (*mit offenen Augen*) träumen

daylight [deılaıt] *n* Tageslicht *nt*; **in ~** bei Tage

daytime [deıtaım] *n*: **in the ~** bei Tage, tagsüber

day trip *n* Tagesausflug *m*

dazed [deızd] *adj* benommen

dazzle [dæzᵊl] *vt* blenden

dazzling [dæzlıŋ] *adj* blendend, glänzend

dead [dɛd] *adj* tot; (*limb*) abgestorben

▷ *adv* genau; *(fam)* total, völlig; **~ tired** todmüde; **~ slow** *(sign)* Schritt fahren

dead end *n* Sackgasse *f*

deadline [dɛdlaɪn] *n* Termin *m*; *(period)* Frist *f*; **~ for applications** Anmeldeschluss *m*

deadly [dɛdli] *adj* tödlich ▷ *adv*: **~ dull** todlangweilig

deaf [dɛf] *adj* taub

deafen [dɛfən] *vt* taub machen

deafening [dɛfənɪŋ] *adj* ohrenbetäubend

deal [diːl] **(dealt, dealt)** *vt, vi (cards)* geben, austeilen ▷ *n (business deal)* Geschäft *nt*; *(agreement)* Abmachung *f*; **it's a ~** abgemacht!; **a good/great ~ of** ziemlich/sehr viel

dealer [diːlər] *n (Comm)* Händler(in) *m(f)*; *(drugs)* Dealer(in) *m(f)*

deal in *vt* handeln mit

dealings [diːlɪŋz] *npl (Comm)* Geschäfte *pl*

dealt [dɛlt] *pt, pp of* **deal**

deal with *vt (matter)* sich beschäftigen mit; *(book, film)* behandeln; *(successfully: person, problem)* fertig werden mit; *(matter)* erledigen

dear [dɪər] *adj* lieb, teuer; **D~ Sir or Madam** Sehr geehrte Damen und Herren; **D~ David** Lieber David ▷ *n* Schatz *m*; *(as address)* mein Schatz, Liebling

dearly [dɪərli] *adv (love)* (heiß und) innig; *(pay)* teuer

death [dɛθ] *n* Tod *m*; *(of project, hopes)* Ende *nt*; *(in accident etc)* Todesfall *m*, Todesopfer *nt*

death certificate *n* Totenschein *m*

death penalty *n* Todesstrafe *f*

death toll *n* Zahl *f* der Todesopfer

death trap *n* Todesfalle *f*

debatable [dɪbeɪtəbˀl] *adj* fraglich; *(question)* strittig

debate [dɪbeɪt] *n* Debatte *f* ▷ *vt* debattieren

debauched [dɪbɔtʃt] *adj* ausschweifend

debit [dɛbɪt] *n* Soll *nt* ▷ *vt (account)* belasten

debit card *n* Geldkarte *f*

debris [dɛɪbriː] *n* Trümmer *pl*

debt [dɛt] *n* Schuld *f*; **to be in ~** verschuldet sein

debug [diːbʌg] *vt (Inform)* Fehler beseitigen in +*dat*

decade [dɛkeɪd] *n* Jahrzehnt *nt*

decadent [dɛkədənt] *adj* dekadent

decaff [diːkæf] *n (fam)* koffeinfreier Kaffee

decaffeinated [diːkæfɪneɪtɪd, -kæfiə-] *adj* koffeinfrei

decanter [dɪkæntər] *n* Dekanter *m*, Karaffe *f*

decay [dɪkeɪ] *n* Verfall *m*; *(rotting)* Verwesung *f*; *(of tooth)* Karies *f* ▷ *vi* verfallen; *(rot)* verwesen; *(wood)* vermodern; *(teeth)* faulen; *(leaves)* verrotten

deceased [dɪsiːst] *n*: **the ~** der/die Verstorbene

deceit [dɪsiːt] *n* Betrug *m*

deceive [dɪsiːv] *vt* täuschen

December [dɪsɛmbər] *n* Dezember *m*; *see also* **September**

decent [diːsˀnt] *adj* anständig

deception [dɪsɛpʃˀn] *n* Betrug *m*

deceptive [dɪsɛptɪv] *adj* täuschend, irreführend

decide [dɪsaɪd] *vt (question)* entscheiden; *(body of people)* beschließen; **I can't ~ what to do** ich kann mich nicht entscheiden, was ich tun soll ▷ *vi* sich entscheiden; **to ~ on sth** *(in favor of sth)* sich für etw entscheiden, sich zu etw entschließen

decided [dɪsaɪdɪd] *adj* entschieden; *(clear)* deutlich

decidedly [dɪsaɪdɪdli] *adv* entschieden

decimal [dɛsɪmˀl] *adj* Dezimal-

decimal system *n* Dezimalsystem *nt*

decipher [dɪsaɪfər] *vt* entziffern

decision [dɪsɪʒˀn] *n* Entscheidung *f* *(on über +akk)*; *(of committee, jury etc)* Beschluss *m*; **to make a ~** eine Entscheidung treffen

decisive [dɪsaɪsɪv] *adj* entscheidend; *(person)* entscheidungsfreudig

deck [dɛk] *n (Naut)* Deck *nt*; *(of cards)* Blatt *nt*

deckchair [dɛktʃɛər] *n* Liegestuhl *m*

declaration [dɛkləreɪʃˀn] *n* Erklärung *f*

declare [dɪklɛər] *vt* erklären; *(state)* behaupten *(that* dass); *(at customs)*: **have you anything to ~?** haben Sie etwas zu verzollen?

decline [dɪklaɪn] *n* Rückgang *m* ▷ *vt (invitation, offer)* ablehnen ▷ *vi (become less)* sinken, abnehmen; *(health)* sich verschlechtern

decode [diːkoʊd] *vt* entschlüsseln

decompose [diːkəmpoʊz] *vi* sich zersetzen

decontaminate [diːkəntæmɪneɪt] *vt* entgiften; *(from radioactivity)* entseuchen

decorate [dɛkəreɪt] *vt* (aus)schmücken; *(wallpaper)* tapezieren; *(paint)* anstreichen

decoration [dɛkəreɪʃˀn] n Schmuck m; (process) Schmücken nt; (wallpapering) Tapezieren nt; (painting) Anstreichen nt; **Christmas ~s** Weihnachtsschmuck m

decorator [dɛkəreɪtər] n Maler(in) m(f)

decrease [vb dɪkriːs, n dɪkriːs] n Abnahme f ▷ vi abnehmen

dedicate [dɛdɪkeɪt] vt widmen (to sb jdm)

dedicated [dɛdɪkeɪtɪd] adj (person) engagiert

dedication [dɛdɪkeɪʃˀn] n Widmung f; (commitment) Hingabe f, Engagement nt

deduce [dɪdjuːs] vt folgern, schließen (from aus, that dass)

deduct [dɪdʌkt] vt abziehen (from von)

deduction [dɪdʌkʃˀn] n (of money) Abzug m; (conclusion) (Schluss)folgerung f

deed [diːd] n Tat f

deep [diːp] adj tief

deepen [diːpən] vt vertiefen

deep-freeze n Tiefkühltruhe f; (upright) Gefrierschrank m

deep-fry vt frittieren

deer [dɪər] n Reh nt; (with stag) Hirsch m

defeat [dɪfiːt] n Niederlage f; **to admit ~** sich geschlagen geben ▷ vt besiegen

defect [diːfɛkt] n Defekt m, Fehler m

defective [dɪfɛktɪv] adj fehlerhaft

defend [dɪfɛnd] vt verteidigen

defendant [dɪfɛndənt] n (Jur) Angeklagte(r) mf

defender [dɪfɛndər] n (Sport) Verteidiger(in) m(f)

defense [dɪfɛns] n Verteidigung f

defensive [dɪfɛnsɪv] adj defensiv

deficiency [dɪfɪʃˀnsi] n Mangel m

deficient [dɪfɪʃˀnt] adj mangelhaft

deficit [dɛfəsɪt] n Defizit nt

define [dɪfaɪn] vt (word) definieren; (duties, powers) bestimmen

definite [dɛfɪnɪt] adj (clear) klar, eindeutig; (certain) sicher; **it's ~** es steht fest

definitely [dɛfɪnɪtli] adv bestimmt

definition [dɛfɪnɪʃˀn] n Definition f; (Foto) Schärfe f

defogger [diːfɒgər] n Defroster m

defrost [diːfrɒst] vt (refrigerator) abtauen; (food) auftauen

degrading [dɪgreɪdɪŋ] adj erniedrigend

degree [dɪgriː] n Grad m; (at university) akademischer Grad; **a certain/high ~ of** ein gewisses/hohes Maß an +dat; **to a certain ~** einigermaßen; **I have a ~ in chemistry** = ich habe einen Abschluss in Chemie

dehydrated [diːhaɪdreɪtɪd] adj (food)

getrocknet, Trocken-; (person) ausgetrocknet

de-ice [diːaɪs] vt enteisen

delay [dɪleɪ] vt (postpone) verschieben, aufschieben; **to be ~ed** (event) sich verzögern; **the train/flight was ~ed** der Zug/die Maschine hatte Verspätung ▷ vi warten; (hesitate) zögern ▷ n Verzögerung f; (of train etc) Verspätung f; **without ~** unverzüglich

delayed [dɪleɪd] adj (train etc) verspätet

delegate [n dɛlɪgɪt, vb dɛlɪgeɪt] n Delegierte(r) mf ▷ vt delegieren

delegation [dɛlɪgeɪʃˀn] n Abordnung f; (foreign) Delegation f

delete [dɪliːt] vt (aus)streichen; (Inform) löschen

deletion [dɪliːʃˀn] n Streichung f; (Inform) Löschung f

deli [dɛli] n (fam) Feinkostgeschäft nt

deliberate [dɪlɪbərɪt] adj (intentional) absichtlich

deliberately [dɪlɪbərɪtli] adv mit Absicht, extra

delicate [dɛlɪkɪt] adj (fine) fein; (fragile) zart; (a. Med) empfindlich; (situation) heikel

delicatessen [dɛlɪkətɛsˀn] nsing Feinkostgeschäft nt

delicious [dɪlɪʃəs] adj köstlich, lecker

delight [dɪlaɪt] n Freude f ▷ vt entzücken

delighted [dɪlaɪtɪd] adj sehr erfreut (with über +akk)

delightful [dɪlaɪtfəl] adj entzückend; (weather, meal etc) herrlich

deliver [dɪlɪvər] vt (goods) liefern (to sb jdm); (letter, parcel) zustellen; (speech) halten; (baby) entbinden

delivery [dɪlɪvəri] n Lieferung f; (of letter, parcel) Zustellung f; (of baby) Entbindung f

delude [dɪluːd] vt täuschen; **don't ~ yourself** mach dir nichts vor

delusion [dɪluːʒˀn] n Irrglaube m

deluxe [dəlʌks] adj Luxus-

demand [dɪmænd] vt verlangen (from von); (time, patience etc) erfordern ▷ n (request) Forderung f, Verlangen nt (for nach); (Comm: for goods) Nachfrage f; **on ~** auf Wunsch; **very much in ~** sehr gefragt

demanding [dɪmændɪŋ] adj anspruchsvoll

demented [dɪmɛntɪd] adj wahnsinnig

demo [dɛmoʊ] (pl -s) n (fam) Demo f

democracy [dɪmɒkrəsi] n Demokratie f

Democrat [dɛməkræt] (*Pol*) Demokrat(in) *m(f)*

democrat [dɛməkræt]

democratic [dɛməkrætɪk] *adj* demokratisch; **the D~ Party** (*Pol*) die Demokratische Partei

demolish [dɪmɒlɪʃ] *vt* abreißen; (*fig*) zerstören

demolition [dɛməlɪʃⁿn] *n* Abbruch *m*

demonstrate [dɛmənstreɪt] *vt, vi* demonstrieren, beweisen

demonstration [dɛmənstreɪʃⁿn] *n* Demonstration *f*

demoralize [dɪmɔrəlaɪz] *vt* demoralisieren

denial [dɪnaɪəl] *n* Leugnung *f*; (*official denial*) Dementi *nt*

denim [dɛnɪm] *n* Jeansstoff *m*

denim jacket *n* Jeansjacke *f*

denims [dɛnɪmz] *npl* Bluejeans *pl*

Denmark [dɛnmɑrk] *n* Dänemark *nt*

denomination [dɪnɒmɪneɪʃⁿn] *n* (*Rel*) Konfession *f*; (*Comm*) Nennwert *m*

dense [dɛns] *adj* dicht; (*fam: stupid*) schwer von Begriff

density [dɛnsɪti] *n* Dichte *f*

dent [dɛnt] *n* Beule *f*, Delle *f* ▷ *vt* einbeulen

dental [dɛntⁿl] *adj* Zahn-; **~ care** Zahnpflege *f*; **~ floss** Zahnseide *f*

dentist [dɛntɪst] *n* Zahnarzt *m*, Zahnärztin

dentures [dɛntʃərz] *npl* Zahnprothese *f*; (*full*) Gebiss *nt*

Denver boot *n* Parkkralle *f*

Denver boot [dɛnvər bʊt] *n* Parkkralle *f*

deny [dɪnaɪ] *vt* leugnen, bestreiten; (*refuse*) ablehnen

deodorant [dioʊdərənt] *n* Deo(dorant) *nt*

depart [dɪpɑrt] *vi* abreisen; (*bus, train*) abfahren (*for* nach, *from* von); (*plane*) abfliegen (*for* nach, *from* von)

department [dɪpɑrtmənt] *n* Abteilung *f*; (*at university*) Institut *nt*; (*Pol: ministry*) Ministerium *nt*

department store *n* Kaufhaus *nt*

departure [dɪpɑrtʃər] *n* (*of person*) Weggang *m*; (*on journey*) Abreise *f* (*for* nach); (*of train etc*) Abfahrt *f* (*for* nach); (*of plane*) Abflug *m* (*for* nach)

departure lounge *n* (*Aviat*) Abflughalle *f*

departure time *n* Abfahrtzeit *f*; (*Aviat*) Abflugzeit *f*

depend [dɪpɛnd] *vi*: **it ~s** es kommt darauf an (*whether, if* ob)

dependable [dɪpɛndəbⁿl] *adj* zuverlässig

dependence [dɪpɛndəns] *n* Abhängigkeit *f* (*on* von)

dependent [dɪpɛndənt] *adj* abhängig (*on* von)

depend on *vt* (*thing*) abhängen von; (*person: rely on*) sich verlassen auf +*akk*; (*person, area etc*) angewiesen sein auf +*akk*; **it ~s on the weather** es kommt auf das Wetter an

deport [dɪpɔrt] *vt* ausweisen, abschieben

deportation [dɪpɔrteɪʃⁿn] *n* Abschiebung *f*

deposit [dɪpɒzɪt] *n* (*down payment*) Anzahlung *f*; (*security*) Kaution *f*; (*for bottle*) Pfand *nt*; (*to bank account*) Einzahlung *f*; (*in river etc*) Ablagerung *f* ▷ *vt* (*put down*) abstellen, absetzen; (*to bank account*) einzahlen; (*sth valuable*) deponieren

depot [dipoʊ] *n* Depot *nt*

depreciate [dɪpriʃieɪt] *vi* an Wert verlieren

depress [dɪprɛs] *vt* (*in mood*) deprimieren

depressed [dɪprɛst] *adj* (*person*) niedergeschlagen, deprimiert; **~ area** Notstandsgebiet *nt*

depressing [dɪprɛsɪŋ] *adj* deprimierend

depression [dɪprɛʃⁿn] *n* (*mood*) Depression *f*; (*Meteo*) Tief *nt*

deprive [dɪpraɪv] *vt*: **to ~ sb of sth** jdn einer Sache berauben

deprived [dɪpraɪvd] *adj* (*child*) (sozial) benachteiligt

dept. (*abbr*) = **department** Abt.

depth [dɛpθ] *n* Tiefe *f*

deputy [dɛpyəti] *adj* stellvertretend, Vize- ▷ *n* Stellvertreter(in) *m(f)*; (*Pol*) Abgeordnete(r) *mf*

derail [dɪreɪl] *vt* entgleisen lassen; **to be ~ed** entgleisen

deranged [dɪreɪndʒd] *adj* geistesgestört

derivation [dɛrɪveɪʃⁿn] *n* Ableitung *f*

derive [dɪraɪv] *vt* ableiten (*from* von), abstammen (*from* von)

dermatitis [dɜrmətaɪtɪs] *n* Hautentzündung *f*

derogatory [dɪrɒgətɔri] *adj* abfällig

descend [dɪsɛnd] *vt, vi* hinabsteigen, hinuntergehen; (*person*): **to ~ o** be **~ed from** abstammen von

descendant [dɪsɛndənt] *n* Nachkomme *m*

descent [dɪsɛnt] *n* (*coming down*) Abstieg *m*; (*origin*) Abstammung *f*

describe [dɪskraɪb] *vt* beschreiben

description [dɪskrɪpʃⁿn] *n* Beschreibung *f*

desert [*n* dɛzⁿrt, *vb* dɪzɜrt] *n* Wüste *f* ▷ *vt* verlassen; (*abandon*) im Stich lassen

deserted [dɪzɜ:tɪd] *adj* verlassen; (*empty*) menschenleer

deserve [dɪzɜːv] *vt* verdienen

design [dɪzaɪn] *n* (*plan*) Entwurf *m*; (*of vehicle, machine*) Konstruktion *f*; (*of object*) Design *nt*; (*planning*) Gestaltung *f* ▷ *vt* entwerfen; (*machine etc*) konstruieren; **~ed for sb/sth** (*intended*) für jdn/etw konzipiert

designate [dɛzɪgneɪt] *vt* bestimmen

designer [dɪzaɪnər] *n* Designer(in) *m(f)*; (*Tech*) Konstrukteur(in) *m(f)*

designer drug *n* Designerdroge *f*

desirable [dɪzaɪərəbˀl] *n* wünschenswert; (*person*) begehrenswert

desire [dɪzaɪər] *n* Wunsch *m* (*for* nach); (*esp sexual*) Begierde *f* (*for* nach) ▷ *vt* wünschen; (*ask for*) verlangen; **if ~d** auf Wunsch

desk [dɛsk] *n* Schreibtisch *m*; (*reception desk*) Empfang *m*; (*at airport etc*) Schalter *m*

desktop publishing [dɛsktɒp pʌblɪʃɪŋ] *n* Desktoppublishing *nt*

desolate [dɛsəlɪt] *adj* trostlos

despair [dɪspɛər] *n* Verzweiflung *f* (*at* über +*akk*) ▷ *vi* verzweifeln (*of* an +*dat*)

desperate [dɛspərɪt] *adj* verzweifelt; (*situation*) hoffnungslos; **to be ~ for sth** etw dringend brauchen, unbedingt wollen

desperation [dɛspəreɪʃˀn] *n* Verzweiflung *f*

despicable [dɪspɪkəbˀl] *adj* verachtenswert

despise [dɪspaɪz] *vt* verachten

despite [dɪspaɪt] *prep* trotz +*gen*

dessert [dɪzɜːt] *n* Nachtisch *m*

dessert spoon *n* Dessertlöffel *m*

destination [dɛstɪneɪʃˀn] *n* (*of person*) (Reise)ziel *nt*; (*of goods*) Bestimmungsort *m*

destiny [dɛstɪni] *n* Schicksal *nt*

destroy [dɪstrɔɪ] *vt* zerstören; (*completely*) vernichten

destruction [dɪstrʌkʃˀn] *n* Zerstörung *f*; (*complete*) Vernichtung *f*

destructive [dɪstrʌktɪv] *adj* zerstörerisch; (*esp fig*) destruktiv

detach [dɪtætʃ] *vt* abnehmen; (*from form etc*) abtrennen; (*free*) lösen (*from* von)

detachable [dɪtætʃəbˀl] *adj* abnehmbar; (*from form etc*) abtrennbar

detached [dɪtætʃt] *adj* (*attitude*) distanziert, objektiv; **~ house** Einzelhaus *nt*

detail [diːteɪl] *n* Einzelheit *f*, Detail *nt*; **fur-**ther **~s from ...** Näheres erfahren Sie bei ...; **to go into ~** ins Detail gehen; **in ~** ausführlich

detailed [diːteɪld] *adj* detailliert, ausführlich

detain [dɪteɪn] *vt* aufhalten; (*police*) in Haft nehmen

detect [dɪtɛkt] *vt* entdecken; (*notice*) wahrnehmen

detective [dɪtɛktɪv] *n* Detektiv(in) *m(f)*

detective story *n* Krimi *m*

detention [dɪtɛnʃˀn] *n* Haft *f*; (*Sch*) Nachsitzen *nt*

deter [dɪtɜː] *vt* abschrecken (*from* von)

detergent [dɪtɜːdʒˀnt] *n* Reinigungsmittel *nt*; (*soap powder*) Waschmittel *nt*

deteriorate [dɪtɪərɪəreɪt] *vi* sich verschlechtern

determination [dɪtɜːmɪneɪʃˀn] *n* Entschlossenheit *f*

determine [dɪtɜːmɪn] *vt* bestimmen

determined [dɪtɜːmɪnd] *adj* (*fest*) entschlossen

deterrent [dɪtɜːrənt] *n* Abschreckungsmittel *nt*

detest [dɪtɛst] *vt* verabscheuen

detestable [dɪtɛstəbˀl] *adj* abscheulich

detour [diːtʊər] *n* Umweg *m*; (*of traffic*) Umleitung *f*

deuce [djuːs] *n* (*Tennis*) Einstand *m*

devalue [diːvæljuː] *vt* abwerten

devastate [dɛvəsteɪt] *vt* verwüsten

devastating [dɛvəsteɪtɪŋ] *adj* verheerend

develop [dɪvɛləp] *vt* entwickeln; (*illness*) bekommen ▷ *vi* sich entwickeln

developing country [dɪvɛləpɪŋ kʌntri] *n* Entwicklungsland *nt*

development [dɪvɛləpmənt] *n* Entwicklung *f*; (*of land*) Erschließung *f*

device [dɪvaɪs] *n* Vorrichtung *f*, Gerät *nt*

devil [dɛvˀl] *n* Teufel *m*

devilish [dɛvəlɪʃ, dɛvlɪʃ] *adj* teuflisch

devote [dɪvəʊt] *vt* widmen (*to* dat)

devoted [dɪvəʊtɪd] *adj* liebend; (*servant etc*) treu ergeben

devotion [dɪvəʊʃˀn] *n* Hingabe *f*

devour [dɪvaʊər] *vt* verschlingen

dew [djuː] *n* Tau *m*

diabetes [daɪəbiːtɪs, -tiːz] *n* Diabetes *m*, Zuckerkrankheit *f*

diabetic [daɪəbɛtɪk] *adj* zuckerkrank, für Diabetiker *m* ▷ *n* Diabetiker(in) *m(f)*

diagnosis [daɪəgnəʊsɪs] (*pl* **diagnoses**) *n* Diagnose *f*

diagonal [daɪægən*l*, -ægnˀl] *adj* diagonal

diagram [daɪəgræm] *n* Diagramm *nt*

dial [daɪəl] *n* Skala *f*; (*of clock*) Zifferblatt *nt* ▷ *vt* (*Tel*) wählen

dialect [daɪəlɛkt] *n* Dialekt *m*

dialog [daɪəlɔːɡ] *n* Dialog *m*

dial tone *n* Amtszeichen *nt*

dialysis [daɪælɪsɪs] *n* (*Med*) Dialyse *f*

diameter [daɪæmɪtər] *n* Durchmesser *m*

diamond [daɪmənd, daɪə-] *n* Diamant *m*; (*Cards*) Karo *nt*

diaper [daɪpər, daɪə-] *n* Windel *f*

diarrhea [daɪəriə] *n* Durchfall *m*

diary [daɪəri] *n* (Taschen)kalender *m*; (*account*) Tagebuch *nt*

dice [daɪs] *npl* Würfel *pl*

diced [daɪst] *adj* in Würfel geschnitten

dictate [dɪkteɪt, dɪkteɪt] *vt* diktieren

dictation [dɪkteɪʃⁿn] *n* Diktat *nt*

dictator [dɪkteɪtər] *n* Diktator(in) *m(f)*

dictatorship [dɪkteɪtərʃɪp] *n* Diktatur *f*

dictionary [dɪkʃənɛri] *n* Wörterbuch *nt*

did [dɪd] *pt of* **do**

didn't [dɪdⁿnt] *contr of* **did not**

die [daɪ] *vi* sterben (*of* an +*dat*); (*plant, animal*) eingehen; (*engine*) absterben; **to be dying to do sth** darauf brennen, etw zu tun; **I'm dying for a drink** ich brauche unbedingt was zu trinken

die away *vi* schwächer werden; (*wind*) sich legen

die down *vi* nachlassen

die out *vi* aussterben

diesel [diːzⁿl] *n* (*fuel, car*) Diesel *m*; **~ engine** Dieselmotor *m*

diet [daɪɪt] *n* Kost *f*; (*special food*) Diät *f* ▷ *vi* eine Diät machen

differ [dɪfər] *vi* (*be different*) sich unterscheiden; (*disagree*) anderer Meinung sein

difference [dɪfərəns, dɪfrəns] *n* Unterschied *m*; **it makes no ~ to me** es ist (mir) egal; **it makes a big ~** es macht viel aus

different [dɪfərənt, dɪfrənt] *adj* andere(r, s); (*with pl*) verschieden; **to be quite ~** ganz anders sein (*from* als); (*two people, things*) völlig verschieden sein; **a ~ person** ein anderer Mensch

differentiate [dɪfərɛnʃieɪt] *vt, vi* unterscheiden

differently [dɪfərəntli, dɪfrəntli] *adv* anders (*from* als); (*from one another*) unterschiedlich

difficult [dɪfɪkʌlt, -kəlt] *adj* schwierig; **I find it ~** es fällt mir schwer

difficulty [dɪfɪkʌlti, -kəlti] *n* Schwierigkeit

f; **with ~** nur schwer; **to have ~ in doing sth** etw nur mit Mühe machen können

dig [dɪg] (**dug, dug**) *vt, vi* (*hole*) graben

digest [dɪdʒɛst] *vt* (*a. fig*) verdauen

digestible [daɪdʒɛstɪbⁿl] *adj* verdaulich

digestion [daɪdʒɛstʃən] *n* Verdauung *f*

dig in *vi* (*fam: to food*) reinhauen; **~!** greif(t) zu!

digit [dɪdʒɪt] *n* Ziffer *f*

digital [dɪdʒɪtⁿl] *adj* digital; **~ computer** Digitalrechner *m*; **~ watch/clock** Digitaluhr *f*

digital camera *n* Digitalkamera *f*

digital television, digital TV *n* Digitalfernsehen *nt*

dignified [dɪgnɪfaɪd] *adj* würdevoll

dignity [dɪgnɪti] *n* Würde *f*

dig up *vt* ausgraben

dilapidated [dɪlæpɪdeɪtɪd] *adj* baufällig

dilemma [dɪlɛmə] *n* Dilemma *nt*

dill [dɪl] *n* Dill *m*

dilute [daɪluːt] *vt* verdünnen

dim [dɪm] *adj* (*light*) schwach; (*outline*) undeutlich; (*stupid*) schwer von Begriff ▷ *vt* verdunkeln; (*Auto*) abblenden; **dimmed headlights** Abblendlicht *nt*

dime [daɪm] *n* Zehncentstück *nt*

dimension [dɪmɛnʃⁿn, daɪ-] *n* Dimension *f*; **~s** *pl* Maße *pl*

diminish [dɪmɪnɪʃ] *vt* verringern ▷ *vi* sich verringern

dimple [dɪmpⁿl] *n* Grübchen *nt*

dine [daɪn] *vi* speisen

dine out *vi* außer Haus essen

diner [daɪnər] *n* Gast *m*; (*Rail*) Speisewagen *m*, Speiselokal *nt*

dinghy [dɪŋi] *n* Ding(h)i *nt*; (*inflatable*) Schlauchboot *nt*

dingy [dɪndʒi] *adj* düster; (*dirty*) schmuddelig

dining car [daɪnɪŋ kar] *n* Speisewagen *m*

dining room [daɪnɪŋ rum] *n* Esszimmer *nt*; (*in hotel*) Speiseraum *m*

dining table [daɪnɪŋ teɪbⁿl] *n* Esstisch *m*

dinner [dɪnər] *n* Abendessen *nt*; (*lunch*) Mittagessen *nt*; (*public*) Diner *nt*; **to be at ~** beim Essen sein; **to have ~** zu Abend/Mittag essen

dinner party *n* Abendgesellschaft *f* mit Essen

dinnertime [dɪnərtaɪm] *n* Essenszeit *f*

dinosaur [daɪnəsɔr] *n* Dinosaurier *m*

dip [dɪp] *vt* tauchen (*in* in +*akk*) ▷ *n* (*in ground*) Bodensenke *f*; (*sauce*) Dip *m*

diploma [dɪploʊmə] *n* Diplom *nt*

diplomat [dɪpləmæt] *n* Diplomat(in) *m(f)*
diplomatic [dɪpləmætɪk] *adj* diplomatisch
dipstick [dɪpstɪk] *n* Ölmessstab *m*
direct [dɪrɛkt, daɪ-] *adj* direkt; (*cause, consequence*) unmittelbar; (*transaction*) Abbuchung *f* im Lastschriftverfahren; ~ **train** durchgehender Zug ▷ *vt* (*aim, send*) richten (*at, to* an +*akk*); (*film*) die Regie führen bei; (*traffic*) regeln
direct current *n* (*Elec*) Gleichstrom *m*
direction [dɪrɛkʃ°n, daɪ-] *n* (*course*) Richtung *f*; (*Cine*) Regie *f*; **in the ~ of** ... in Richtung ...; **~s** *pl* (*to a place*) Wegbeschreibung *f*
directly [dɪrɛktli, daɪ-] *adv* direkt; (*at once*) sofort
director [dɪrɛktər, daɪ-] *n* Direktor(in) *m(f)*, Leiter(in) *m(f)*; (*of film*) Regisseur(in) *m(f)*
directory [dɪrɛktəri, daɪ-] *n* Adressbuch *nt*; (*Tel*) Telefonbuch *nt*; ~ **assistance** (*Tel*) Auskunft *f*
dirt [dɜrt] *n* Schmutz *m*, Dreck *m*
dirt cheap *adj* spottbillig
dirt road *n* unbefestigte Straße
dirty [dɜrti] *adj* schmutzig
disability [dɪsəbɪliti] *n* Behinderung *f*
disabled [dɪseɪb°ld] *adj* behindert, Behinderten- ▷ *npl*: **the ~** die Behinderten
disadvantage [dɪsədvæntɪdʒ] *n* Nachteil *m*; **at a ~** benachteiligt
disadvantageous [dɪsædvənteɪdʒəs] *adj* unvorteilhaft, ungünstig
disagree [dɪsəgri] *vi* anderer Meinung sein; (*two people*) sich nicht einig sein; (*two reports etc*) nicht übereinstimmen; **to ~ with sb** mit jdm nicht übereinstimmen; (*food*) jdm nicht bekommen
disagreeable [dɪsəgriəb°l] *adj* unangenehm; (*person*) unsympathisch
disagreement [dɪsəgrimənt] *n* Meinungsverschiedenheit *f*
disappear [dɪsəpɪər] *vi* verschwinden
disappearance [dɪsəpɪərəns] *n* Verschwinden *nt*
disappoint [dɪsəpɔɪnt] *vt* enttäuschen
disappointing [dɪsəpɔɪntɪŋ] *adj* enttäuschend
disappointment [dɪsəpɔɪntmənt] *n* Enttäuschung *f*
disapproval [dɪsəpruv°l] *n* Missbilligung *f*
disapprove [dɪsəpruv] *vi* missbilligen (*of akk*)
disarm [dɪsɑrm] *vt* entwaffnen ▷ *vi* (*Pol*) abrüsten

disarmament [dɪsɑrməmənt] *n* Abrüstung *f*
disarming [dɪsɑrmɪŋ] *adj* (*smile, look*) gewinnend
disaster [dɪzæstər] *n* Katastrophe *f*
disastrous [dɪzæstrəs] *adj* katastrophal
disbelief [dɪsbɪlif] *n* Ungläubigkeit *f*
discharge [*n* dɪstʃɑrdʒ *vb* dɪstʃɑrdʒ,] *n* (*Med*) Ausfluss *m* ▷ *vt* (*person*) entlassen; (*emit*) ausstoßen; (*Med*) ausscheiden
discipline [dɪsɪplɪn] *n* Disziplin *f*
disclose [dɪsklouz] *vt* bekannt geben; (*secret*) enthüllen
disco [dɪskoʊ] (*pl* **-s**) *n* Disko *f*, Diskomusik *f*
discomfort [dɪskʌmfərt] *n* (*slight pain*) leichte Schmerzen *pl*; (*unease*) Unbehagen *nt*
disconnect [dɪskənɛkt] *vt* (*electricity, gas, phone*) abstellen; (*unplug*): **to ~ the TV from the plug** den Stecker des Fernsehers herausziehen; (*Tel*): **I've been ~ed** das Gespräch ist unterbrochen worden
discontent [dɪskəntɛnt] *n* Unzufriedenheit *f*
discontented [dɪskəntɛntɪd] *adj* unzufrieden
discontinue [dɪskəntɪnyu] *vt* einstellen; (*product*) auslaufen lassen
discount [dɪskaʊnt] *n* Rabatt *m*
discover [dɪskʌvər] *vt* entdecken
discovery [dɪskʌvəri] *n* Entdeckung *f*
discredit [dɪskrɛdɪt] *vt* in Verruf bringen ▷ *n* Misskredit *m*
discreet [dɪskrit] *adj* diskret
discrepancy [dɪskrɛpənsi] *n* Unstimmigkeit *f*, Diskrepanz *f*
discriminate [dɪskrɪmɪneɪt] *vi* unterscheiden; **to ~ against sb** jdn diskriminieren
discrimination [dɪskrɪmɪneɪʃ°n] *n* (*different treatment*) Diskriminierung *f*
discus [dɪskəs] *n* Diskus *m*
discuss [dɪskʌs] *vt* diskutieren, besprechen
discussion [dɪskʌʃ°n] *n* Diskussion *f*
disease [dɪziz] *n* Krankheit *f*
disembark [dɪsɪmbɑrk] *vi* von Bord gehen
disentangle [dɪsɪntæŋg°l] *vt* entwirren
disgrace [dɪsgreɪs] *n* Schande *f* ▷ *vt* Schande machen +*dat*; (*family etc*) Schande bringen über +*akk*; (*less strong*) blamieren
disgraceful [dɪsgreɪsfəl] *adj* skandalös
disguise [dɪsgaɪz] *vt* verkleiden; (*voice*) verstellen ▷ *n* Verkleidung *f*; **in ~** verkleidet

disgust [dɪsgʌst] *n* Abscheu *m*; *(physical)* Ekel *m* ▷ *vt* anekeln, anwidern

disgusting [dɪsgʌstɪŋ] *adj* widerlich; *(physically)* ekelhaft

dish [dɪʃ] *n* Schüssel *f*; *(food)* Gericht *nt*; **~es** *pl (crockery)* Geschirr *nt*; **to do/wash the ~es** abwaschen

dishcloth [dɪʃklɔθ] *n (for washing)* Spültuch *nt*; *(for drying)* Geschirrtuch *nt*

dishearten [dɪshɑrtᵊn] *vt* entmutigen; **don't be ~ed** lass den Kopf nicht hängen!

dishonest [dɪsɒnɪst] *adj* unehrlich

dishonor [dɪsɒnər] *n* Schande *f*

dish towel *n* Geschirrtuch *nt*

dishwasher [dɪʃwɒʃər] *n* Geschirrspülmaschine *f*

disillusioned [dɪsɪluːʒᵊnd] *adj* desillusioniert

disinfect [dɪsɪnfɛkt] *vt* desinfizieren

disinfectant [dɪsɪnfɛktənt] *n* Desinfektionsmittel *nt*

disintegrate [dɪsɪntɪgreɪt] *vi* zerfallen; *(group)* sich auflösen

disjointed [dɪsdʒɔɪntɪd] *adj* unzusammenhängend

disk [dɪsk] *n* Scheibe *f*, CD *f*; *(Anat)* Bandscheibe *f*; *(Inform: floppy)* Diskette *f*

disk drive *n* Diskettenlaufwerk *nt*

diskette [dɪskɛt] *n* Diskette *f*

disk jockey *n* Diskjockey *m*

dislike [dɪslaɪk] *n* Abneigung *f* ▷ *vt* nicht mögen; **to ~ doing sth** etw ungern tun

dislocate [dɪsloʊkeɪt, dɪsloʊkeɪt] *vt (Med)* verrenken, ausrenken

dismal [dɪzmᵊl] *adj* trostlos

dismantle [dɪsmæntᵊl] *vt* auseinandernehmen; *(machine)* demontieren

dismay [dɪsmeɪ] *n* Bestürzung *f*

dismayed [dɪsmeɪd] *adj* bestürzt

dismiss [dɪsmɪs] *vt (employee)* entlassen

dismissal [dɪsmɪsᵊl] *n* Entlassung *f*

disobedience [dɪsəbiːdiəns] *n* Ungehorsam *m*

disobedient [dɪsəbiːdiənt] *adj* ungehorsam

disobey [dɪsəbeɪ] *vt* nicht gehorchen +*dat*

disorder [dɪsɔrdər] *n (mess)* Unordnung *f*; *(riot)* Aufruhr *m*; *(Med)* Störung *f*, Leiden *nt*

disorganized [dɪsɔrgənaɪzd] *adj* chaotisch

disparaging [dɪspærɪdʒɪŋ] *adj* geringschätzig

dispatch [dɪspætʃ] *vt* abschicken, abfertigen

dispensable [dɪspɛnsəbᵊl] *adj* entbehrlich

dispense [dɪspɛns] *vt* verteilen

dispenser [dɪspɛnsər] *n* Automat *m*

dispense with *vt* verzichten auf +*akk*

disperse [dɪspɜrs] *vi* sich zerstreuen

display [dɪspleɪ] *n (exhibition)* Ausstellung *f*, Show *f*; *(of goods)* Auslage *f*; *(Tech)* Anzeige *f*, Display *nt* ▷ *vt* zeigen; *(goods)* ausstellen

disposable [dɪspoʊzəbᵊl] *adj (container, razor etc)* Wegwerf-; **~ nappy** Wegwerfwindel *f*

disposal [dɪspoʊzᵊl] *n* Loswerden *nt*; *(of waste)* Beseitigung *f*; **to be at sb's ~** jdm zur Verfügung stehen; **to have at one's ~** verfügen über

dispose of [dɪspoʊz əv] *vt* loswerden; *(waste etc)* beseitigen

dispute [dɪspyut] *n* Streit *m*; *(industrial)* Auseinandersetzung *f* ▷ *vt* bestreiten

disqualification [dɪskwɒlɪfɪkeɪʃᵊn] *n* Disqualifikation *f*

disqualify [dɪskwɒlɪfaɪ] *vt* disqualifizieren

disregard [dɪsrɪgɑrd] *vt* nicht beachten

disreputable [dɪsrɛpyətəbᵊl] *adj* verrufen

disrespect [dɪsrɪspɛkt] *n* Respektlosigkeit *f*

disrupt [dɪsrʌpt] *vt* stören; *(interrupt)* unterbrechen

disruption [dɪsrʌpʃᵊn] *n* Störung *f*; *(interruption)* Unterbrechung *f*

dissatisfied [dɪssætɪsfaɪd] *adj* unzufrieden

dissent [dɪsɛnt] *n* Widerspruch *m*

dissolve [dɪzɒlv] *vt* auflösen ▷ *vi* sich auflösen

dissuade [dɪsweɪd] *vt (davon abbringen)*: **to ~ sb from doing sth** jdn davon abbringen, etw zu tun

distance [dɪstəns] *n* Entfernung *f*; **in the/from a ~** in/aus der Ferne

distant [dɪstənt] *adj (a. in time)* fern; *(relative etc)* entfernt; *(person)* distanziert

distaste [dɪsteɪst] *n* Abneigung *f (for gegen)*

distill [dɪstɪl] *vt* destillieren

distillery [dɪstɪləri] *n* Brennerei *f*

distinct [dɪstɪŋkt] *adj* verschieden; *(clear)* klar, deutlich

distinction [dɪstɪŋkʃᵊn] *n (difference)* Unterschied *m*; *(in exam etc)* Auszeichnung *f*

distinctive [dɪstɪŋktɪv] *adj* unverkennbar

distinctly [dɪstɪŋktli] *adv* deutlich

distinguish [dɪstɪŋgwɪʃ] *vt* unterscheiden (*sth from sth* etw von etw)

distort [dɪstɔːt] *vt* verzerren; (*truth*) verdrehen

distract [dɪstrækt] *vt* ablenken

distraction [dɪstrækʃən] *n* Ablenkung *f*; (*diversion*) Zerstreuung *f*

distress [dɪstrɛs] *n* (*need, danger*) Not *f*; (*suffering*) Leiden *nt*; (*mental*) Qual *f*; (*worry*) Kummer *m* ▷ *vt* mitnehmen, erschüttern

distressed area *n* Notstandsgebiet *nt*

distress signal *n* Notsignal *nt*

distribute [dɪstrɪbjuːt] *vt* verteilen; (*Comm: goods*) vertreiben

distribution [dɪstrɪbjuːʃən] *n* Verteilung *f*; (*Comm: of goods*) Vertrieb *m*

distributor [dɪstrɪbjətər] *n* (*Auto*) Verteiler *m*; (*Comm*) Händler(in) *m(f)*

district [dɪstrɪkt] *n* Gegend *f*; (*administrative*) Bezirk *m*

district attorney *n* Staatsanwalt *m*, Staatsanwältin *f*

distrust [dɪstrʌst] *vt* misstrauen +*dat* ▷ *n* Misstrauen *nt*

disturb [dɪstɜːb] *vt* stören; (*worry*) beunruhigen

disturbance [dɪstɜːbəns] *n* Störung *f*

disturbing [dɪstɜːbɪŋ] *adj* beunruhigend

ditch [dɪtʃ] *n* Graben *m* ▷ *vt* (*fam: person*) den Laufpass geben +*dat*; (*plan etc*) verwerfen

ditto [dɪtoʊ] *n* dito, ebenfalls

dive [daɪv] *n* (*into water*) Kopfsprung *m*; (*Aviat*) Sturzflug *m*; (*fam*) zwielichtiges Lokal ▷ *vi* (*under water*) tauchen

diver [daɪvər] *n* Taucher(in) *m(f)*

diverse [daɪvɜːs] *adj* verschieden

diversion [daɪvɜːʒən] *n* (*of traffic*) Umleitung *f*; (*distraction*) Ablenkung *f*

divert [daɪvɜːt, daɪ-] *vt* ablenken; (*traffic*) umleiten

divide [dɪvaɪd] *vt* teilen; (*in several parts, between people*) aufteilen ▷ *vi* sich teilen

dividend [dɪvɪdɛnd] *n* Dividende *f*

divine [dɪvaɪn] *adj* göttlich

diving [daɪvɪŋ] *n* (*Sport*)tauchen *nt*; (*jumping in*) Springen *nt*; (*Sport: from board*) Kunstspringen *nt*

diving board *n* Sprungbrett *nt*

diving mask *n* Tauchmaske *f*

division [dɪvɪʒən] *n* Teilung *f*; (*Math*) Division *f*; (*department*) Abteilung *f*; (*Sport*) Liga *f*

divorce [dɪvɔːs] *n* Scheidung *f* ▷ *vt* sich

scheiden lassen von

divorced [dɪvɔːrst] *adj* geschieden; **to get ~** sich scheiden lassen

divorcee [dɪvɔːrseɪ, -siː] *n* Geschiedene(r) *mf*

DIY [diː aɪ waɪ] (*abbr*) = **do-it-yourself**

dizzy [dɪzi] *adj* schwindlig

DJ [diː dʒeɪ] (*abbr*) = **disk jockey** Diskjockey *m*, DJ *m*

DNA [diː en eɪ] (*abbr*) = **desoxyribonucleic acid** DNS *f*

KEYWORD

do [də, STRONG duː] (*pt* **did**, *pp* **done**) *n* (*inf: party etc*) Fete *f*

▷ *vb aux* **1** (*in negative constructions and questions*): **I don't understand** ich verstehe nicht; **didn't you know?** wusstest du das nicht?; **what do you think?** was meinen Sie?

2 (*for emphasis, in polite phrases*): **she does seem rather tired** sie scheint wirklich sehr müde zu sein; **do sit down/help yourself** setzen Sie sich doch hin/greifen Sie doch zu

3 (*used to avoid repeating vb*): **she swims better than I do** sie schwimmt besser als ich; **she lives in New York - so do I** sie wohnt in New York - ich auch

4 (*in tag questions*): **you like him, don't you?** du magst/Sie mögen ihn doch, oder?

▷ *vt* **1** (*carry out, perform etc*) tun, machen; **what are you doing tonight?** was machst du/machen Sie heute Abend?; **I've got nothing to do** ich habe nichts zu tun; **to do one's hair/nails** sich die Haare/Nägel machen

2 (*car etc*) fahren

▷ *vi* **1** (*act, behave*): **do as I do** mach es wie ich

2 (*get on, fare*): **he's doing well/badly at school** er ist gut/schlecht in der Schule; **how do you do?** guten Tag

3 (*be suitable*) gehen; (*be sufficient*) reichen; **to make do (with)** auskommen mit

do away with *vt* (*kill*) umbringen; (*abolish: law etc*) abschaffen

dock [dɒk] *n* Dock *nt*; (*Jur*) Anklagebank *f*

dockyard [dɒkjɑːd] *n* Werft *f*

doctor [dɒktər] *n* Arzt *m*, Ärztin *f*; (*in title, also academic*) Doktor *m*

document [dɒkjəmənt] *n* Dokument *nt*

documentary [dɒkyəmɛntəri, -tri] *n* Dokumentarfilm *m*

documentation [dɒkyəmɛnteɪʃⁿn] *n* Dokumentation *f*

doddery [dɒdəri] *adj* tatterig

dodgy [dɒdʒi] *adj* nicht ganz in Ordnung; *(dishonest, unreliable)* zwielichtig; **he has a ~ stomach** er hat sich den Magen verdorben

dog [dɔg] *n* Hund *m*

dog food *n* Hundefutter *nt*

doggie bag [dɔgi bæg] *n* Tüte oder Box, in der Essensreste aus dem Restaurant mit nach Hause genommen werden können

do-it-yourself [duɪtyɔrsɛlf] *n* Heimwerken *nt*, Do-it-yourself *nt* ▷ *adj* Heimwerker-

do-it-yourselfer [duɪtyɔrsɛlfər] *n* Bastler(in) *m(f)*, Heimwerker(in) *m(f)*

doll [dɒl] *n* Puppe *f*

dollar [dɒlər] *n* Dollar *m*

dolphin [dɒlfɪn] *n* Delphin *m*

domain [doumeɪn] *n* Domäne *f*; *(Inform)* Domain *f*

dome [doum] *n* Kuppel *f*

domestic [dəmɛstɪk] *adj* häuslich; *(within country)* Innen-, Binnen-

domestic animal *n* Haustier *nt*

domesticated [dəmɛstɪkeɪtɪd] *adj (person)* häuslich; *(animal)* zahm

domestic flight *n* Inlandsflug *m*

domicile [dɒmɪsaɪl] *n* (ständiger) Wohnsitz

dominant [dɒmɪnənt] *adj* dominierend, vorherrschend

dominate [dɒmɪneɪt] *vt* beherrschen

dominoes [dɒmənouz] *npl* Domino(spiel) *nt*

donate [douneɪt] *vt* spenden

donation [douneɪʃⁿn] *n* Spende *f*

done [dʌn] *pp of* **do** ▷ *adj (cooked)* gar; **well ~** durchgebraten

donkey [dɒŋki] *n* Esel *m*

donor [dounər] *n* Spender(in) *m(f)*

don't [dount] *contr of* **do not**

doom [dum] *n* Schicksal *nt*; *(downfall)* Verderben *nt*

door [dɔr] *n* Tür *f*

doorbell [dɔrbɛl] *n* Türklingel *f*

door handle *n* Türklinke *f*

doorknob [dɔrnɒb] *n* Türknauf *m*

doormat [dɔrmæt] *n* Fußabtreter *m*

door phone *n* Türsprechanlage *f*

doorstep [dɔrstɛp] *n* Türstufe *f*; **right on our ~** direkt vor unserer Haustür

dope [doup] *(Sport) n (for athlete)* Auf-putschmittel *nt* ▷ *vt* dopen

dormitory [dɔrmɪtɔri] *n* Schlafsaal *m*, Studentenwohnheim *nt*

dosage [dousɪdʒ] *n* Dosierung *f*

dose [dous] *n* Dosis *f* ▷ *vt* dosieren

dot [dɒt] *n* Punkt *m*; **on the dot** auf die Minute genau, pünktlich

dotcom [dɒtkɒm] *n*: **~ company** Internetfirma *f*, Dotcom-Unternehmen *nt*

dote on [dout ɒn] *vt* abgöttisch lieben

dotted line [dɒtɪd laɪn] *n* punktierte Linie

double [dʌbⁿl] *adj, adv* doppelt; **~ the quantity** die zweifache Menge, doppelt so viel ▷ *vt* verdoppeln ▷ *n (person)* Doppelgänger(in) *m(f)*; *(Cine)* Double *nt*

double bass [dʌbⁿl beɪs] *n* Kontrabass *m*

double bed *n* Doppelbett *nt*

double-click *vt (Inform)* doppelklicken

double-decker *n* Doppeldecker *m*

double glazing [dʌbⁿl gleɪzɪŋ] *n* Doppelverglasung *f*

double-park *vi* in zweiter Reihe parken

double room *n* Doppelzimmer *nt*

doubles [dʌbⁿlz] *npl (Sport: also match)* Doppel *nt*

doubt [daut] *n* Zweifel *m*; **no ~** ohne Zweifel, zweifellos, wahrscheinlich; **to have one's ~s** Bedenken haben ▷ *vt* bezweifeln; *(statement, word)* anzweifeln; **I ~ it** das bezweifle ich

doubtful [dautfəl] *adj* zweifelhaft, zweifelnd; **it is ~ whether ...** es ist fraglich, ob ...

doubtless [dautlɪs] *adv* ohne Zweifel, sicherlich

dough [dou] *n* Teig *m*

doughnut [dounʌt, -nət] *n* Donut *m*, rundes Hefegebäck

do up *vt (fasten)* zumachen; *(parcel)* verschnüren; *(renovate: room, house)* renovieren

dove [dʌv] *n* Taube *f*

do with *vt (need)* brauchen; *(be connected)* zu tun haben mit; **I could ~ a drink** ich könnte einen Drink gebrauchen

do without *vt, vi* auskommen ohne; **I can ~ your comments** auf deine Kommentare kann ich verzichten

down [daun] *n* Daunen *pl*; *(fluff)* Flaum *m* ▷ *adv* unten; *(motion)* nach unten; *(towards speaker)* herunter; *(away from speaker)* hinunter; **~ here/there** hier/dort unten; *(downstairs)*: **they came ~ for breakfast** sie kamen zum Frühstück herunter; *(southwards)*: **he came ~ from Alaska** er kam von Alaska herunter ▷ *prep*

d

(*towards speaker*) herunter; (*away from speaker*) hinunter; **to drive ~ the hill/road** den Berg/die Straße hinunter fahren; (*along*): **to walk ~ the street** die Straße entlang gehen; **he's ~ at the store** (*fam*) er ist einkaufen ▷ *vt* (*fam: drink*) runterkippen ▷ *adj* niedergeschlagen, deprimiert

down-and-out *adj* heruntergekommen ▷ *n* Obdachlose(r) *mf*, Penner(in) *m(f)*

downcast [daʊnkæst] *adj* niedergeschlagen

downfall [daʊnfɔl] *n* Sturz *m*

down-hearted [daʊnhɑrtɪd] *adj* entmutigt

downhill [daʊnhɪl] *adv* bergab; **he's going ~** (*fig*) mit ihm geht es bergab

download [daʊnloʊd] *vt* downloaden, herunterladen

downloadable [daʊnloʊdəbˈl] *adj* herunterladbar

down payment *n* Anzahlung *f*

downpour [daʊnpɔr] *n* Platzregen *m*

downs *npl* Hügelland *nt*

downscale [daʊnskeɪl] *adj* für den Massenmarkt

downsize [daʊnsaɪz] *vt* (*business*) verkleinern ▷ *vi* sich verkleinern

downspout [daʊnspaʊt] *n* Abflussrohr *nt*

Down's syndrome [daʊnz sɪndroʊm] *n* (*Med*) Downsyndrom *nt*

downstairs [daʊnstɛərz] *adv* unten; (*motion*) nach unten

downstream [daʊnstrim] *adv* flussabwärts

downtime [daʊntaɪm] *n* Ausfallzeit *f*

downtown [daʊntaʊn] *adv* (*be, work etc*) in der Innenstadt; (*go*) in die Innenstadt ▷ *adj* in der Innenstadt; **~ Chicago** die Innenstadt von Chicago

down under *adv* (*fam: in/to Australia*) in/ nach Australien; (*in/to New Zealand*) in/ nach Neuseeland

downwards [daʊnwərdz] *adv*, *adj* nach unten; (*movement, trend*) Abwärts-

doze [doʊz] *vi* dösen ▷ *n* Nickerchen *nt*

dozen [dʌzˀn] *n* Dutzend *nt*; **two ~ eggs** zwei Dutzend Eier; **~s of times** x-mal

DP [di pi] (*abbr*) = **data processing** DV *f*

drab [dræb] *adj* trist; (*color*) düster

draft [dræft] *n* (*outline*) Entwurf *m*; (*of air*) (Luft)zug *m*; (*Mil*) Einberufung *f*; **there's a ~** es zieht; **on ~** (*beer*) vom Fass

drafty [dræfti] *adj* zugig

drag [dræg] *vt* schleppen ▷ *n* (*fam*): **to be a ~** (*boring*) stinklangweilig sein; (*labori-*

ous) ein ziemlicher Schlauch sein

drag on *vi* sich in die Länge ziehen

dragon [drægən] *n* Drache *m*

dragonfly [drægənflaɪ] *n* Libelle *f*

drain [dreɪn] *n* Abfluss *m* ▷ *vt* (*water, oil*) ablassen; (*vegetables etc*) abgießen; (*land*) entwässern, trockenlegen ▷ *vi* (*of water*) abfließen

drama [drɑmə, dræmə] *n* (*a. fig*) Drama *nt*

dramatic [drəmætɪk] *adj* dramatisch

drank [dræŋk] *pt of* **drink**

drapes [dreɪps] *npl* Vorhänge *pl*

drastic [dræstɪk] *adj* drastisch

draw [drɔ] (**drew, drawn**) *vt* (*pull*) ziehen; (*crowd*) anlocken, anziehen; (*picture*) zeichnen ▷ *vi* (*Sport*) unentschieden spielen ▷ *n* (*Sport*) Unentschieden *nt*; (*attraction*) Attraktion *f*; (*for lottery*) Ziehung *f*

drawback [drɔbæk] *n* Nachteil *m*

drawbridge [drɔbrɪdʒ] *n* Zugbrücke *f*

drawer [drɔr] *n* Schublade *f*

drawing [drɔɪŋ] *n* Zeichnung *f*

drawn [drɔn] *pp of* **draw**

draw out *vt* herausziehen; (*money*) abheben

draw up *vt* (*formulate*) entwerfen; (*list*) erstellen ▷ *vi* (*car*) anhalten

dread [drɛd] *n* Furcht *f* (*of* vor +*dat*) ▷ *vt* sich fürchten vor +*dat*

dreadful [drɛdfəl] *adj* furchtbar

dreadlocks [drɛdlɒks] *npl* Rastalocken *pl*

dream [drim] (**dreamed** *o* **dreamt, dreamed** *o* **dreamt**) *vt*, *vi* träumen (*about* von) ▷ *n* Traum *m*

dreamt [drɛmt] *pt*, *pp of* **dream**

dreary [drɪəri] *adj* (*weather, place*) trostlos; (*book etc*) langweilig

drench [drɛntʃ] *vt* durchnässen

dress [drɛs] *n* Kleidung *f*; (*garment*) Kleid *nt* ▷ *vt* anziehen; (*Med: wound*) verbinden; **to get ~ed** sich anziehen

dress circle *n* (*Theat*) erster Rang

dresser [drɛsər] *n* Anrichte *f*; (*dressing table*) Frisier)kommode *f*

dressing [drɛsɪŋ] *n* (*Gastr*) Dressing *nt*, Soße *f*; (*Med*) Verband *m*

dressing room *n* (*Theat*) Künstlergarderobe *f*

dressing table *n* Frisierkommode *f*

dress rehearsal *n* (*Theat*) Generalprobe *f*

dress up *vi* sich fein machen; (*in costume*) sich verkleiden (*as* als)

drew [dru] *pt of* **draw**

dried [draɪd] *adj* getrocknet; (*milk, flowers*)

Trocken-; **~ fruit** Dörrobst *nt*

drier [draɪər] *n see* **dryer**

drift [drɪft] *vi* treiben ▷ *n* (*of snow*) Verwehung *f*; (*fig*) Tendenz *f*; **if you get my ~** wenn du mich richtig verstehst/wenn Sie mich richtig verstehen

drill [drɪl] *n* Bohrer *m* ▷ *vt*, *vi* bohren

drink [drɪŋk] (**drank, drunk**) *vt*, *vi* trinken ▷ *n* Getränk *nt*; (*alcoholic*) Drink *m*

drinking water [drɪŋkɪŋ wɔtər] *n* Trinkwasser *nt*

drip [drɪp] *n* Tropfen *m* ▷ *vi* tropfen

drip-dry [drɪpdraɪ] *adj* bügelfrei

dripping [drɪpɪŋ] *n* Bratenfett *nt* ▷ *adj*: **~ wet** tropfnass

drive [draɪv] (**drove, driven**) *vt* (*car, person in car*) fahren; (*force: person, animal*) treiben; (*Tech*) antreiben; **to ~ sb crazy** jdn verrückt machen ▷ *vi* fahren ▷ *n* Fahrt *f*; (*entrance*) Einfahrt *f*, Auffahrt *f*; (*Inform*) Laufwerk *nt*; **to go for a ~** spazieren fahren

drive away, drive off *vi* wegfahren ▷ *vt* vertreiben

drive-in *adj* Drive-in-; **~ movie** Autokino *nt*

driven [drɪvⁿn] *pp of* **drive**

driver [draɪvər] *n* Fahrer(in) *m(f)*; (*Inform*) Treiber *m*; **~'s seat** Fahrersitz *m*

driver's license *n* Führerschein *m*

driving [draɪvɪŋ] *n* (Auto)fahren *nt*; **he likes ~** er fährt gern Auto

driving lesson *n* Fahrstunde *f*

driving school *n* Fahrschule *f*

driving test *n* Fahrprüfung *f*

drizzle [drɪzᵊl] *n* Nieselregen *m* ▷ *vi* nieseln

drop [drɒp] *n* (*of liquid*) Tropfen *m*; (*fall in price etc*) Rückgang *m* ▷ *vt* (*a. fig: give up*) fallen lassen ▷ *vi* (*fall*) herunterfallen; (*figures, temperature*) sinken, zurückgehen

drop by, drop in *vi* vorbeikommen

drop off *vi* (*to sleep*) einnicken

drop out *vi* (*withdraw*) aussteigen; (*university*) das Studium abbrechen

dropout [drɒpaʊt] *n* Aussteiger(in) *m(f)*

drought [draʊt] *n* Dürre *f*

drove [droʊv] *pt of* **drive**

drown [draʊn] *vi* ertrinken ▷ *vt* ertränken

drowsy [draʊzi] *adj* schläfrig

drug [drʌg] *n* (*Med*) Medikament *nt*, Arznei *f*; (*addictive*) Droge *f*; (*narcotic*) Rauschgift *nt*; **to be on ~s** drogensüchtig sein ▷ *vt* (mit Medikamenten) betäuben

drug addict *n* Rauschgiftsüchtige(r) *mf*

drug dealer *n* Drogenhändler(in) *m(f)*

druggist [drʌgɪst] *n* Drogist(in) *m(f)*

drugstore [drʌgstɔr] *n* Drogerie *f*

drum [drʌm] *n* Trommel *f*; **~s** *pl* Schlagzeug *nt*

drummer [drʌmər] *n* Schlagzeuger(in) *m(f)*

drunk [drʌŋk] *pp of* **drink** ▷ *adj* betrunken; **to get ~** sich betrinken ▷ *n* Betrunkene(r) *mf*; (*alcoholic*) Trinker(in) *m(f)*

drunk driving *n* Trunkenheit *f* am Steuer

drunken [drʌŋkən] *adj* betrunken, besoffen

dry [draɪ] *adj* trocken ▷ *vt* trocknen; (*dishes, oneself, one's hands etc*) abtrocknen ▷ *vi* trocknen, trocken werden

dry-clean [draɪklin] *vt* chemisch reinigen

dry cleaning *n* chemische Reinigung

dryer [draɪər] *n* Wäschetrockner *m*; (*for hair*) Föhn *m*; (*over head*) Trockenhaube *f*

dry out *vi* trocknen

dry up *vi* austrocknen

DTP [di ti pi] (*abbr*) = desktop publishing DTP *nt*

dual [duəl] *adj* doppelt; **~ nationality** doppelte Staatsangehörigkeit

dubbed [dʌbd] *adj* (*film*) synchronisiert

dubious [dubiəs] *adj* zweifelhaft

duchess [dʌtʃɪs] *n* Herzogin *f*

duck [dʌk] *n* Ente *f*

dude [dud] *n* (*fam*) Typ *m*; **a cool ~** ein cooler Typ

due [du] *adj* (*time*) fällig; (*fitting*) angemessen; **in due course** zu gegebener Zeit; **due to** infolge +*gen*, wegen +*gen* ▷ *adv*: **due south/north** *etc* direkt nach Norden/Süden *etc*

dug [dʌg] *pt*, *pp of* **dig**

duke [duk] *n* Herzog *m*

dull [dʌl] *adj* (*color, light, weather*) trübe; (*boring*) langweilig

duly [duli] *adv* ordnungsgemäß; (*as expected*) wie erwartet

dumb [dʌm] *adj* stumm; (*fam: stupid*) doof, blöde

dumbbell [dʌmbɛl] *n* Hantel *f*

dummy [dʌmi] *n* (*sham*) Attrappe *f*; (*in shop*) Schaufensterpuppe *f*; (*fam: person*) Dummkopf *m* ▷ *adj* unecht, Schein-; **~ run** Testlauf *m*

dump [dʌmp] *n* Abfallhaufen *m*; (*fam: place*) Kaff *nt* ▷ *vt* (*lit, fig*) abladen; (*fam*): **he ~ed her** er hat mir ihr Schluss gemacht

dumpling [dʌmplɪŋ] *n* Kloß *m*, Knödel *m*

dune [dun] *n* Düne *f*

dung [dʌŋ] *n* Dung *m*; (*manure*) Mist *m*
dungeon [dʌndʒᵊn] *n* Kerker *m*
duplex [duːplɛks] *n* zweistöckige Wohnung,
   Doppelhaushälfte *f*
duplicate [*n* duːplɪkɪt, *vb* duːplɪkeɪt] *n*
   Duplikat *nt* ▷ *vt* (*make copies of*) kopieren;
   (*repeat*) wiederholen
durable [dʊərəbᵊl] *adj* haltbar
duration [dʊəreɪʃᵊn] *n* Dauer *f*
during [dʊərɪŋ] *prep* (*time*) während +*gen*
dusk [dʌsk] *n* Abenddämmerung *f*
dust [dʌst] *n* Staub *m* ▷ *vt* abstauben
duster [dʌstər] *n* Staubtuch *nt*
dust jacket *n* Schutzumschlag *m*
dustpan [dʌstpæn] *n* Kehrschaufel *f*
dusty [dʌsti] *adj* staubig
Dutch [dʌtʃ] *adj* holländisch ▷ *n* (*language*)
   Holländisch *nt*; **the ~** *pl* die Holländer
Dutchman [dʌtʃmən] (*pl* -**men**) *n* Holländer *m*

Dutchwoman [dʌtˉwʊmən] (*pl* -**women**) *n*
   Holländerin *f*
duty [duːti] *n* Pflicht *f*; (*task*) Aufgabe *f*;
   (*tax*) Zoll *m*; **on/off ~** im Dienst/nicht im
   Dienst; **to be on ~** Dienst haben
duty-free *adj* zollfrei; **~ shop** Dutyfreeshop *m*
DVD [diː viː diː] *n* (*abbr*) = **digital versatile
   disk** DVD *f*
DVD player *n* DVD-Player *m*
DVD recorder *n* DVD-Rekorder *m*
dwelling [dwɛlɪŋ] *n* Wohnung *f*
dwindle [dwɪndᵊl] *vi* schwinden
dye [daɪ] *n* Farbstoff *m* ▷ *vt* färben
dynamic [daɪnæmɪk] *adj* dynamisch
dynamo [daɪnəmoʊ] *n* Dynamo *m*
dyslexia [dɪslɛksiə] *n* Legasthenie *f*
dyslexic [dɪslɛksɪk] *adj* legasthenisch; **to
   be ~** Legastheniker(in) sein

E

E [i] (*abbr*) (*Geo*) = **east** O ▷ (*abbr*) (*drug*) = **ecstasy** Ecstasy *nt*

each [itʃ] *adj* jeder/jede/jedes ▷ *pron* jeder/jede/jedes; **I'll have one of** ~ ich nehme von jedem eins; **they** ~ **have a car** jeder von ihnen hat ein Auto; ~ **other** einander, sich; **for/against** ~ **other** füreinander/gegeneinander ▷ *adv* je; **they cost 10 euros** ~ sie kosten je 10 Euro, sie kosten 10 Euro das Stück

eager [igər] *adj* eifrig; **to be** ~ **to do sth** darauf brennen, etw zu tun

eagle [igˀl] *n* Adler *m*

ear [ɪər] *n* Ohr *nt*

earache [ɪəreɪk] *n* Ohrenschmerzen *pl*

eardrum [ɪərdrʌm] *n* Trommelfell *nt*

earl [ɜrl] *n* Graf *m*

early [ɜrli] *adj, adv* früh; **to be 10 minutes** ~ 10 Minuten zu früh kommen; **at the earliest** frühestens; **in** ~ **June/2008** Anfang Juni/2008; ~ **retirement** vorzeitiger Ruhestand; ~ **warning system** Frühwarnsystem *nt*

earn [ɜrn] *vt* verdienen

earnest [ɜrnɪst] *adj* ernst; **in** ~ im Ernst

earnings [ɜrnɪŋz] *npl* Verdienst *m*, Einkommen *nt*

earplug [ɪərplʌg] *n* Ohrenstöpsel *m*, Ohropax® *nt*

earring [ɪərɪŋ] *n* Ohrring *m*

earth [ɜrθ] *n* Erde *f*; **what on** ~ ...? was in aller Welt ...? ▷ *vt* erden

earthenware [ɜrθˀnweər] *n* Tonwaren *pl*

earthquake [ɜrθkweɪk] *n* Erdbeben *nt*

earwig [ɪərwɪg] *n* Ohrwurm *m*

ease [iz] *vt* (*pain*) lindern; (*burden*) erleichtern ▷ *n* (*easiness*) Leichtigkeit *f*; **to feel at** ~ sich wohlfühlen; **to feel ill at** ~ sich nicht wohlfühlen

easily [izɪli] *adv* leicht; **he is** ~ **the best** er ist mit Abstand der Beste

east [ist] *n* Osten *m*; **to the** ~ **of** östlich von ▷ *adv* (*go, face*) nach Osten ▷ *adj* Ost-; ~ **wind** Ostwind *m*

eastbound [istbaʊnd] *adj* (in) Richtung Osten

Easter [istər] *n* Ostern *nt*; **at** ~ zu Ostern

Easter egg *n* Osterei *nt*

eastern [istərn] *adj* Ost-, östlich; **E~ Europe** Osteuropa *nt*

Easter Sunday *n* Ostersonntag *m*

East Germany *n* Ostdeutschland *nt*; **former**

~ die ehemalige DDR, die neuen Bundesländer

eastwards [istwərdz] *adv* nach Osten

easy [izi] *adj* leicht; (*task, solution*) einfach; (*life*) bequem; (*manner*) ungezwungen

easy-going [izigoʊɪŋ] *adj* gelassen

eat [it] (**ate, eaten**) *vt* essen; (*animal*) fressen

eaten [itˀn] *pp of* **eat**

eat out *vi* zum Essen ausgehen

eat up *vt* aufessen; (*animal*) auffressen

eavesdrop [ivzdrɒp] *vi* (heimlich) lauschen; **to** ~ **on sb** jdn belauschen

eccentric [ɪksɛntrɪk] *adj* exzentrisch

echo [ɛkoʊ] (*pl* **-es**) *n* Echo *nt* ▷ *vi* widerhallen

ecological [ɛkəlɒdʒɪkˀl, ik-] *adj* ökologisch; ~ **disaster** Umweltkatastrophe *f*

ecology [ɪkɒlədʒi] *n* Ökologie *f*

economic [ɛkənɒmɪk, ik-] *adj* wirtschaftlich, Wirtschafts-; ~ **aid** Wirtschaftshilfe *f*

economical [ɛkənɒmɪkˀl, ik-] *adj* wirtschaftlich; (*person*) sparsam

economics [ɛkənɒmɪks, ik-] *nsing o pl* Wirtschaftswissenschaft *f*

economist [ɪkɒnəmɪst] *n* Wirtschaftswissenschaftler(in) *m(f)*

economize [ɪkɒnəmaɪz] *vi* sparen (**on** an +*dat*)

economy [ɪkɒnəmi] *n* (*of state*) Wirtschaft *f*; (*thrift*) Sparsamkeit *f*

economy class *n* (*Aviat*) Economyclass *f*

ecstasy [ɛkstəsi] *n* Ekstase *f*; (*drug*) Ecstasy *f*

eczema [ɛksəmə, ɛgzə-, ɪgzi-] *n* Ekzem *nt*

edge [ɛdʒ] *n* Rand *m*; (*of knife*) Schneide *f*; **on** ~ nervös

edgy [ɛdʒi] *adj* nervös

edible [ɛdɪbˀl] *adj* essbar

Edinburgh [ɛdɪnbɹoʊ] *n* Edinburg *nt*

edit [ɛdɪt] *vt* (*series, newspaper etc*) herausgeben; (*text*) redigieren; (*film*) schneiden; (*Inform*) editieren

edition [ɪdɪʃˀn] *n* Ausgabe *f*

editor [ɛdɪtər] *n* Redakteur(in) *m(f)*; (*of series etc*) Herausgeber(in) *m(f)*

editorial [ɛdɪtɔriˀl] *adj* Redaktions- ▷ *n* Leitartikel *m*

educate [ɛdʒʊkeɪt] *vt* (*child*) erziehen; (*at school, university*) ausbilden; (*public*) aufklären

educated [ɛdʒʊkeɪtɪd] *adj* gebildet
education [ɛdʒʊkeɪʃⁿn] *n* Erziehung *f*; *(studies, training)* Ausbildung *f*; *(subject of study)* Pädagogik *f*; *(system)* Schulwesen *nt*; *(knowledge)* Bildung *f*
educational [ɛdʒʊkeɪʃənl] *adj* pädagogisch; *(instructive)* lehrreich; ~ **television** Schulfernsehen *nt*
eel [il] *n* Aal *m*
eerie [ɪəri] *adj* unheimlich
effect [ɪfɛkt] *n* Wirkung *f* *(on* auf *+akk)*; **to come into** ~ in Kraft treten
effective [ɪfɛktɪv] *adj* wirksam, effektiv
effeminate [ɪfɛmɪnɪt] *adj (of man)* tuntig
efficiency [ɪfɪʃⁿnsi] *n* Leistungsfähigkeit *f*; *(of method)* Wirksamkeit *f*
efficient [ɪfɪʃⁿnt] *adj (Tech)* leistungsfähig; *(method)* wirksam, effizient
effort [ɛfərt] *n* Anstrengung *f*; *(attempt)* Versuch *m*; **to make an** ~ sich anstrengen
effortless [ɛfərtlɪs] *adj* mühelos
e.g. [i dʒi] *(abbr)* = **exempli gratia (for example)** z. B.
egg [ɛg] *n* Ei *nt*
eggcup [ɛgkʌp] *n* Eierbecher *m*
eggplant [ɛgplænt] *n* Aubergine *f*
eggshell [ɛgʃɛl] *n* Eierschale *f*
ego [igoʊ, ɛgoʊ] *(pl* -**s**) *n* Ich *nt*; *(self-esteem)* Selbstbewusstsein *nt*
ego(t)ist [igoʊ(t)ɪst] *n* Egozentriker(in) *m(f)*
Egypt [idʒɪpt] *n* Ägypten *nt*
Egyptian [idʒɪpʃⁿn] *adj* ägyptisch ▷ *n* Ägypter(in) *m(f)*
eight [eɪt] *num* acht; **at the age of** ~ im Alter von acht Jahren; **it's** ~ **o'clock** es ist acht Uhr ▷ *n (a. bus etc)* Acht *f*; *(boat)* Achter *m*
eighteen [eɪtin] *num* achtzehn ▷ *n* Achtzehn *f*; *see also* **eight**
eighteenth [eɪtinθ] *adj* achtzehnte(r, s); *see also* **eight**
eighth [eɪtθ] *adj* achte(r, s); **June** ~ der achte Juni ▷ *n (fraction)*-Achtel *nt*; **an** ~ **of a liter** ein Achtelliter
eightieth [eɪtiəθ] *adj* achtzigste(r, s); *see also* **eighth**
eighty [eɪti] *num* achtzig ▷ *n* Achtzig *f*; *see also* **eight**
Eire [ɛrə] *n* die Republik Irland
either [iðər, aɪðər] *conj*: ~ ... **or** entweder ... oder ▷ *pron*: ~ **of the two** eine(r, s) von beiden ▷ *adj*: **on** ~ **side** auf beiden Seiten ▷ *adv*: **I won't go** ~ ich gehe auch nicht
eject [idʒɛkt] *vt* ausstoßen; *(person)* vertreiben

elaborate [*adj* ɪlæbərɪt, *vb* ɪlæbəreɪt] *adj* *(complex)* kompliziert; *(plan)* ausgeklügelt; *(decoration)* kunstvoll ▷ *vi*: **could you** ~ **on that?** könntest du/könnten Sie mehr darüber sagen?
elastic [ɪlæstɪk] *adj* elastisch; ~ **band** Gummiband *nt*
elbow [ɛlboʊ] *n* Ellbogen *m*; **to give sb the** ~ *(fam)* jdm den Laufpass geben
elder [ɛldər] *adj (of two)* älter ▷ *n* Ältere(r) *mf*; *(Bot)* Holunder *m*
elderly [ɛldərli] *adj* ältere(r, s) ▷ *n*: **the** ~ die älteren Leute
eldest [ɛldɪst] *adj* älteste(r, s)
elect [ɪlɛkt] *vt* wählen; **he was** ~**ed chairman** er wurde zum Vorsitzenden gewählt
election [ɪlɛkʃⁿn] *n* Wahl *f*
election campaign *n* Wahlkampf *m*
electioneering [ɪlɛkʃənɪərɪŋ] *n* Wahlpropaganda *f*
electorate [ɪlɛktərɪt] *n* Wähler *pl*
electric [ɪlɛktrɪk] *adj* elektrisch; *(car, motor, razor etc)* Elektro-; ~ **blanket** Heizdecke *f*; ~ **cooker** Elektroherd *m*; ~ **current** elektrischer Strom; ~ **shock** Stromschlag *m*
electrical [ɪlɛktrɪkⁿl] *adj* elektrisch; ~ **goods/appliances** Elektrogeräte
electrician [ɪlɛktrɪʃⁿn, ilɛk-] *n* Elektriker(in) *m(f)*
electricity [ɪlɛktrɪsɪti, ilɛk-] *n* Elektrizität *f*
electrocute [ɪlɛktrəkyut] *vt* durch einen Stromschlag töten
electronic [ɪlɛktrɒnɪk, i-] *adj* elektronisch
elegance [ɛlɪgəns] *n* Eleganz *f*
elegant [ɛlɪgənt] *adj* elegant
element [ɛlɪmənt] *n* Element *nt*; **an** ~ **of truth** ein Körnchen Wahrheit
elementary [ɛlɪmɛntəri, -tri] *adj* einfach; *(basic)* grundlegend; ~ **stage** Anfangsstadium *nt*; ~ **school** Grundschule *f*; ~ **maths/French** Grundkenntnisse in Mathematik/Französisch
elephant [ɛlɪfənt] *n* Elefant *m*
elevator [ɛlɪveɪtər] *n* Fahrstuhl *m*
eleven [ɪlɛvⁿn] *num* elf ▷ *n (team, bus etc)* Elf *f*; *see* **eight**
eleventh [ɪlɛvⁿnθ] *adj* elfte(r, s) ▷ *n (fraction)* Elftel *nt*; *see* **eighth**
eligible [ɛlɪdʒɪbⁿl] *adj* infrage kommend; *(for grant etc)* berechtigt; ~ **for a pension/competition** pensions-/teilnahmeberechtigt; ~ **bachelor** begehrter Junggeselle
eliminate [ɪlɪmɪneɪt] *vt* ausschließen *(from*

aus), ausschalten; (*problem etc*) beseitigen

elimination [ɪlɪmɪneɪʃ°n] *n* Ausschluss *m* (*from* aus); (*of problem etc*) Beseitigung *f*

elm [ɛlm] *n* Ulme *f*

elope [ɪloʊp] *vi* durchbrennen (*with sb* mit jdm)

eloquent [ɛləkwənt] *adj* redegewandt

else [ɛls] *adv*: **anybody/anything ~** (*in addition*) sonst (noch) jemand/etwas; (*other*) ein anderer/etwas anderes; **somebody ~** jemand anders; **everyone ~** alle anderen; **or ~** sonst

elsewhere [ɛlsweər] *adv* anderswo, woanders; (*direction*) woandershin

ELT [i ɛl ti] (*abbr*) = **English Language Teaching**

e-mail [imeɪl] *vi, vt* mailen (*sth to sb* jdm etw) ▷ *n* E-Mail *f*

e-mail address *n* E-Mail-Adresse *f*

emancipated [ɪmænsɪpeɪtɪd] *adj* emanzipiert

embankment [ɪmbæŋkmənt] *n* Böschung *f*; (*for railway*) Bahndamm *m*

embargo [ɪmbɑrgoʊ] (*pl* **-es**) *n* Embargo *nt*

embark [ɪmbɑrk] *vi* an Bord gehen

embarrass [ɪmbærəs] *vt* in Verlegenheit bringen

embarrassed [ɪmbærəst] *adj* verlegen

embarrassing [ɪmbærəsɪŋ] *adj* peinlich

embassy [ɛmbəsi] *n* Botschaft *f*

embrace [ɪmbreɪs] *vt* umarmen ▷ *n* Umarmung *f*

embroider [ɪmbrɔɪdər] *vt* besticken

embroidery [ɪmbrɔɪdəri] *n* Stickerei *f*

embryo [ɛmbrioʊ] (*pl* **-s**) *n* Embryo *m*

emerald [ɛmərəld, ɛmrəld] *n* Smaragd *m*

emerge [ɪmɜrdʒ] *vi* auftauchen; **it ~d that** ... es stellte sich heraus, dass ...

emergency [ɪmɜrdʒ°nsi] *n* Notfall *m* ▷ *adj* Not-; **~ brake** Handbremse *f*; **~ exit** Notausgang *m*; **~ landing** Notlandung *f*; **~ room** Unfallstation *f*; **~ service** Notdienst *m*; **~ stop** Vollbremsung *f*

emigrate [ɛmɪgreɪt] *vi* auswandern

emit [ɪmɪt] *vt* ausstoßen; (*heat*) abgeben

emoticon [ɪmoʊtɪkɒn] *n* (*Inform*) Emoticon *nt*

emotion [ɪmoʊʃ°n] *n* Emotion *f*, Gefühl *nt*

emotional [ɪmoʊʃən°l] *adj* (*person*) emotional; (*experience, moment, scene*) ergreifend

emperor [ɛmpərər] *n* Kaiser *m*

emphasis [ɛmfəsɪs] *n* Betonung *f*

emphasize [ɛmfəsaɪz] *vt* betonen

emphatic [ɪmfætɪk] *adj*, **emphatically** *adv* nachdrücklich

empire [ɛmpaɪər] *n* Reich *nt*

employ [ɪmplɔɪ] *vt* beschäftigen; (*hire*) anstellen; (*use*) anwenden

employee [ɪmplɔɪi] *n* Angestellte(r) *mf*

employer [ɪmplɔɪər] *n* Arbeitgeber(in) *m(f)*

employment [ɪmplɔɪmənt] *n* Beschäftigung *f*; (*position*) Stellung *f*

employment agency *n* Stellenvermittlung *f*

empress [ɛmprɪs] *n* Kaiserin *f*

empty [ɛmpti] *adj* leer ▷ *vt* (*contents*) leeren; (*container*) ausleeren

enable [ɪneɪb°l] *vt*: **to ~ sb to do sth** es jdm ermöglichen, etw zu tun

enamel [ɪnæm°l] *n* Email *nt*; (*of teeth*) Zahnschmelz *m*

enchanting [ɪntʃæntɪn] *adj* bezaubernd

enclose [ɪnkloʊz] *vt* einschließen; (*in letter*) beilegen (*in, with dat*)

enclosure [ɪnkloʊʒər] *n* (*for animals*) Gehege *nt*; (*in letter*) Anlage *f*

encore [ɒŋkɔr, -kɔr] *n* Zugabe *f*

encounter [ɪnkaʊntər] *n* Begegnung *f* ▷ *vt* (*person*) begegnen +*dat*; (*difficulties*) stoßen auf +*akk*

encourage [ɪnkɜrɪdʒ] *vt* ermutigen

encouragement [ɪnkɜrɪdʒmənt] *n* Ermutigung *f*

encyclopedia [ɪnsaɪkləpidiə] *n* Lexikon *nt*, Enzyklopädie *f*

end [ɛnd] *n* Ende *nt*; (*of film, play etc*) Schluss *m*; (*purpose*) Zweck *m*; **at the end of May** Ende Mai; **in the end** schließlich; **to come to an end** zu Ende gehen ▷ *vt* beenden ▷ *vi* enden

endanger [ɪndeɪndʒər] *vt* gefährden; **~ed species** vom Aussterben bedrohte Art

endeavor [ɪndɛvər] *n* Bemühung *f* ▷ *vt* sich bemühen (*to do sth* etw zu tun)

ending [ɛndɪn] *n* (*of book*) Ausgang *m*; (*last part*) Schluss *m*; (*of word*) Endung *f*

endive [ɛndaɪv] *n* Chicorée *f*

endless [ɛndlɪs] *adj* endlos; (*possibilities*) unendlich

end up *vi* enden

endurance [ɪndʊrəns] *n* Ausdauer *f*

endure [ɪndʊər] *vt* ertragen

enemy [ɛnəmi] *n* Feind(in) *m(f)* ▷ *adj* feindlich

energetic [ɛnərdʒɛtɪk] *adj* energiegeladen; (*active*) aktiv energy [ɛnərdʒi] n Energie f

enforce [ɪnfɔrs] vt durchsetzen; (obedience) erzwingen

engage [ɪngeɪdʒ] vt (employ) einstellen; (singer, performer) engagieren

engaged [ɪngeɪdʒd] adj verlobt; (toilet, telephone line) besetzt; to get ~ sich verloben (to mit)

engagement [ɪngeɪdʒmənt] n (to marry) Verlobung f; ~ ring Verlobungsring m

engaging [ɪngeɪdʒɪŋ] adj gewinnend

engine [ɛndʒɪn] n (Auto) Motor m; (Rail) Lokomotive f; ~ failure (Auto) Motorschaden m; ~ trouble (Auto) Defekt m am Motor

engineer [ɛndʒɪnɪər] n Ingenieur(in) m(f); (Rail) Lokomotivführer(in) m(f)

engineering [ɛndʒɪnɪərɪŋ] n Technik f; (mechanical engineering) Maschinenbau m; (subject) Ingenieurwesen nt

engine immobilizer n (Auto) Wegfahrsperre f

England [ɪŋglənd] n England nt

English [ɪŋglɪʃ] adj englisch; he's ~ er ist Engländer; the ~ Channel der Ärmelkanal ▷ n (language) Englisch nt; in ~ auf Englisch; to translate into ~ ins Englische übersetzen; (people): the ~ pl die Engländer

Englishman [ɪŋglɪʃmən] (pl -men) n Engländer m

Englishwoman [ɪŋglɪʃwʊmən] (pl -women) n Engländerin f

engrave [ɪngreɪv] vt eingravieren

engraving [ɪngreɪvɪŋ] n Stich m

engrossed [ɪngroʊst] adj vertieft (in sth in etw akk)

enigma [ɪnɪgmə] n Rätsel nt

enjoy [ɪndʒɔɪ] vt genießen; I ~ reading ich lese gern; he ~s teasing her es macht ihm Spaß, sie aufzuziehen; did you ~ the movie? hat dir der Film gefallen?

enjoyable [ɪndʒɔɪəbəl] adj angenehm; (entertaining) unterhaltsam

enjoyment [ɪndʒɔɪmənt] n Vergnügen nt; (stronger) Freude f (of an +dat)

enlarge [ɪnlɑrdʒ] vt vergrößern; (expand) erweitern

enlargement [ɪnlɑrdʒmənt] n Vergrößerung f

enormous [ɪnɔrməs] adj, enormously adv riesig, ungeheuer

enough [ɪnʌf] adj genug; that's ~ das reicht!; (stop it) Schluss damit!; I've had ~ das hat mir gereicht; (to eat) ich bin satt

▷ adv genug, genügend

enquire [ɪnkwaɪər] see inquire

enquiry [ɪnkwaɪəri] see inquiry

enroll [ɪnroʊl] vi sich einschreiben; (for course, school) sich anmelden

enrollment n Einschreibung f; Anmeldung f

ensure [ɪnʃʊər] vt sicherstellen

enter [ɛntər] vt eintreten in +akk, betreten; (drive into) einfahren in +akk; (country) einreisen in +akk; (in list) eintragen; (Inform) eingeben; (race, contest) teilnehmen an +dat ▷ vi (towards speaker) hereinkommen; (away from speaker) hineingehen

enterprise [ɛntərpraɪz] n (Comm) Unternehmen nt

entertain [ɛntərteɪn] vt (guest) bewirten; (amuse) unterhalten

entertaining [ɛntərteɪnɪŋ] adj unterhaltsam

entertainment [ɛntərteɪnmənt] n (amusement) Unterhaltung f

enthusiasm [ɪnθuziæzəm] n Begeisterung f

enthusiastic [ɪnθuziæstɪk] adj begeistert (about von)

entice [ɪntaɪs] vt locken; (lead astray) verleiten

entire [ɪntaɪər] adj, entirely adv ganz

entitle [ɪntaɪtəl] vt (qualify) berechtigen (to zu); (name) betiteln

entrance [ɛntrəns] n Eingang m; (for vehicles) Einfahrt f; (entering) Eintritt m; (Theat) Auftritt m

entrance exam n Aufnahmeprüfung f

entrance fee n Eintrittsgeld nt

entrust [ɪntrʌst] vt: to ~ sb with sth jdm etw anvertrauen

entry [ɛntri] n (way in) Eingang m; (entering) Eintritt m; (in vehicle) Einfahrt f; (into country) Einreise f; (admission) Zutritt m; (in diary, accounts) Eintrag m; 'no ~' „Eintritt verboten"; (for vehicles) „Einfahrt verboten"

envelope [ɛnvəloʊp, ɒn-] n (Brief)umschlag m

enviable [ɛnviəbəl] adj beneidenswert

envious [ɛnviəs] adj neidisch

environment [ɪnvaɪrənmənt, -vaɪərn-] n Umgebung f; (ecology) Umwelt f

environmental [ɪnvaɪrənmɛntəl, -vaɪərn-] adj Umwelt-; ~ pollution Umweltverschmutzung f

environmentalist [ɪnvaɪrənmɛntəlɪst,

-vaɪərn-] n Umweltschützer(in) m(f)
envy [ɛnvi] n Neid m (of auf +akk) ▷ vt beneiden (sb sth jdn um etw)
epic [ɛpɪk] n Epos nt; (film) Monumentalfilm m
epidemic [ɛpɪdɛmɪk] n Epidemie f
epilepsy [ɛpɪlɛpsi] n Epilepsie f
epileptic [ɛpɪlɛptɪk] adj epileptisch
episode [ɛpɪsoʊd] n Episode f; (TV) Folge f
epoch [ɛpək] n Zeitalter nt, Epoche f
equal [ikwəl] adj gleich (to +dat) ▷ n Gleichgestellte(r) mf ▷ vt gleichen; (match) gleichkommen +dat; **two times two ~s four** zwei mal zwei ist gleich vier
equality [ɪkwɒlɪti] n Gleichheit f; (equal rights) Gleichberechtigung f
equalize [ikwəlaɪz] vi (Sport) ausgleichen
equalizer [ikwəlaɪzər] n (Sport) Ausgleichstreffer m
equally [ikwəli] adv gleich; (on the other hand) andererseits
equation [ɪkweɪʒ³n] n (Math) Gleichung f
equator [ɪkweɪtər] n Äquator m
equilibrium [ikwɪlɪbriəm] n Gleichgewicht nt
equip [ɪkwɪp] vt ausrüsten; (kitchen) ausstatten
equipment [ɪkwɪpmənt] n Ausrüstung f; (for kitchen) Ausstattung f; **electrical ~** Elektrogeräte pl
equivalent [ɪkwɪvələnt] adj gleichwertig (to dat); (corresponding) entsprechend (to dat) ▷ n Äquivalent nt; (amount) gleiche Menge; (in money) Gegenwert m
era [ɪərə] n Ära f, Zeitalter nt
erase [ɪreɪs] vt ausradieren; (tape, disk) löschen
eraser [ɪreɪsər] n Radiergummi m
erect [ɪrɛkt] adj aufrecht ▷ vt (building, monument) errichten; (tent) aufstellen
erection [ɪrɛkˀⁿ] n Errichtung f; (Anat) Erektion f
erode [ɪroʊd] vt zerfressen; (land) auswaschen; (rights, power) aushöhlen
erosion [ɪroʊʒˀⁿ] n Erosion f
erotic [ɪrɒtɪk] adj erotisch
err [ɜr, ɛr] vi sich irren
errand [ɛrənd] n Besorgung f
erratic [ɪrætɪk] adj (behavior) unberechenbar; (bus link etc) unregelmäßig; (performance) unbeständig
error [ɛrər] n Fehler m; **in ~** irrtümlicherweise
error message n (Inform) Fehlermeldung f

erupt [ɪrʌpt] vi ausbrechen
escalator [ɛskəleɪtər] n Rolltreppe f
escalope [ɪskɒləp, ɛskəloʊp] n Schnitzel nt
escape [ɪskeɪp] n Flucht f; (from prison etc) Ausbruch m; **to have a narrow ~** gerade noch davonkommen; **there's no ~** (fig) es gibt keinen Ausweg ▷ vt (pursuers) entkommen +dat; (punishment etc) entgehen +dat ▷ vi (from pursuers) entkommen (from dat); (from prison etc) ausbrechen (from dat); (leak: gas) ausströmen; (water) auslaufen
escort [n ɛskɔrt, vb ɪskɔrt] n (companion) Begleiter(in) m(f); (guard) Eskorte f ▷ vt (lady) begleiten
especially [ɪspɛˀli] adv besonders
espionage [ɛspiənɑʒ] n Spionage f
essay [ɛseɪ] n Aufsatz m; (literary) Essay m
essential [ɪsɛnʃˀl] adj (necessary) unentbehrlich, unverzichtbar; (basic) wesentlich ▷ n: **the ~s** pl das Wesentliche
essentially [ɪsɛnʃəli] adv im Wesentlichen
establish [ɪstæblɪʃ] vt (set up) gründen; (introduce) einführen; (relations) aufnehmen; (prove) nachweisen; **to ~ that ...** feststellen, dass ...
establishment [ɪstæblɪʃmənt] n Institution f; (business) Unternehmen nt
estate [ɪsteɪt] n Gut nt; (of deceased) Nachlass m; (housing estate) Siedlung f; (country house) Landsitz m
estimate [n ɛstɪmɪt, vb ɛstɪmeɪt] n Schätzung f; (Comm: of price) Kostenvoranschlag m ▷ vt schätzen
Estonia [ɛstoʊniə] n Estland nt
Estonian [ɛstoʊniən] adj estnisch ▷ n (person) Este m, Estin f; (language) Estnisch nt
estuary [ɛstʃuɛri] n Mündung f
etching [ɛtʃɪŋ] n Radierung f
eternal [ɪtɜrnˀl] adj, **eternally** adv ewig
eternity [ɪtɜrnɪti] n Ewigkeit f
ethical [ɛθɪkˀl] adj ethisch
ethics [ɛθɪks] npl Ethik f
Ethiopia [iθioupiə] n Äthiopien nt
ethnic [ɛθnɪk] adj ethnisch; (clothes etc) landesüblich; **~ minority** ethnische Minderheit
e-ticket [itɪkɪt] n E-Ticket nt
EU [i yu] (abbr) = **European Union** EU f
euphemism [yuˀfəmɪzəm] n Euphemismus m
euro [yuərou] (pl **-s**) n (Fin) Euro m; **~ sym-**

bol Eurozeichen *nt*
Europe [ˈjʊərəp] *n* Europa *nt*
European [jʊərəpiən] *adj* europäisch; ~
Parliament Europäisches Parlament; ~
Union Europäische Union ▷ *n* Europäer(in)
m(f)
evacuate [ɪvækjuɛɪt] *vt* (*place*) räumen;
(*people*) evakuieren
evade [ɪveɪd] *vt* ausweichen +*dat*; (*pursuers*) sich entziehen +*dat*
evaluate [ɪvæljuɛɪt] *vt* auswerten
evaporate [ɪvæpəreɪt] *vi* verdampfen; (*fig*)
verschwinden; ~**d milk** Kondensmilch *f*
even [ˈiːvⁿn] *adj* (*flat*) eben; (*regular*) gleichmäßig; (*equal*) gleich; (*number*) gerade;
the score is ~ es steht unentschieden
▷ *adv* sogar; ~ **you** selbst (*o* sogar) du/Sie;
~ **if** selbst wenn, wenn auch; ~ **though**
obwohl; **not** ~ nicht einmal; ~ **better** noch
besser
evening [ˈiːvnɪŋ] *n* Abend *m*; **in the** ~
abends, am Abend; **this** ~ heute Abend
evening class *n* Abendkurs *m*
evening dress *n* (*generally*) Abendklei-
dung *f*; (*woman's*) Abendkleid *nt*
evenly [ˈiːvⁿnli] *adv* gleichmäßig
even out *vi* (*prices*) sich einpendeln
event [ɪvɛnt] *n* Ereignis *nt*; (*organized*) Veranstaltung *f*; (*Sport: discipline*) Disziplin *f*;
in the ~ **of** im Falle +*gen*
eventful [ɪvɛntfəl] *adj* ereignisreich
eventual [ɪvɛntʃuəl] *adj* (*final*) letztend-
lich
eventually [ɪvɛntʃuəli] *adv* (*at last*) am
Ende; (*given time*) schließlich
ever [ˈɛvər] *adv* (*at any time*) je(mals); **don't**
~ **do that again** tu das ja nie wieder; **he's**
the best ~ er ist der Beste, den es je gegeben hat; **have you** ~ **been to the States?**
bist du schon einmal in den Staaten gewesen?; **for** ~ (für) immer; **for** ~ **and** ~ auf
immer und ewig; ~ **so ...** (*fam*) äußerst ...;
~ **so drunk** ganz schön betrunken
every [ˈɛvri] *adj* jeder/jede/jedes; ~ **day**
jeden Tag; ~ **other day** jeden zweiten Tag;
~ **five days** alle fünf Tage; **I have** ~ **reason**
to believe that ... ich habe allen Grund
anzunehmen, dass ...
everybody [ˈɛvrɪbɒdi, -bʌdi] *pron* jeder,
alle *pl*
everyday [ˈɛvrɪdeɪ] *adj* (*commonplace*) alltäglich; (*clothes, language etc*) Alltags-
everyone [ˈɛvrɪwʌn] *pron* jeder, alle *pl*
everything [ˈɛvrɪθɪŋ] *pron* alles
everywhere [ˈɛvrɪwɛər] *adv* überall; (*with*

direction) überallhin
evidence [ˈɛvɪdəns] *n* Beweise *pl*; (*single*
piece) Beweis *m*; (*testimony*) Aussage *f*;
(*signs*) Spuren *pl*
evident [ˈɛvɪdənt] *adj*, **evidently** *adv* offensichtlich
evil [ˈiːvⁿl] *adj* böse ▷ *n* Böse(s) *nt*; **an** ~ **ein**
Übel
evolution [iːvəluːʃⁿn, ɛv-] *n* Entwicklung *f*;
(*of life*) Evolution *f*
evolve [ɪvɒlv] *vi* sich entwickeln
ex [ɛks] *n* (*fam*) Verflossene(r) *mf*, Ex *mf*
ex- [ɛks-] *pref* Ex-, ehemalig; **ex-boyfriend**
Exfreund *m*; **ex-wife** frühere Frau, Exfrau
f
exact [ɪgzækt] *adj* genau
exactly [ɪgzæktli] *adv* genau; **not** ~ **fast**
nicht gerade schnell
exaggerate [ɪgzædʒəreɪt] *vt, vi* übertreiben
exaggerated [ɪgzædʒəreɪtɪd] *adj* übertrieben
exaggeration [ɪgzædʒəreɪʃⁿn] *n* Übertreibung *f*
exam [ɪgzæm] *n* Prüfung *f*
examination [ɪgzæmɪneɪʃⁿn] *n* (*Med etc*)
Untersuchung *f*; (*Prüfung f*; (*at university*)
Examen *nt*; (*at customs etc*) Kontrolle *f*
examine [ɪgzæmɪn] *vt* untersuchen (*for*
auf +*akk*); (*check*) kontrollieren, prüfen
examiner [ɪgzæmɪnər] *n* Prüfer(in) *m(f)*
example [ɪgzæmpⁿl] *n* Beispiel *nt* (*of* für
+*akk*); **for** ~ zum Beispiel
excavation [ɛkskəveɪʃⁿn] *n* Ausgrabung *f*
exceed [ɪksiːd] *vt* überschreiten, übertreffen
exceedingly [ɪksiːdɪŋli] *adv* äußerst
excel [ɪksɛl] *vt* übertreffen; **he** ~**led him-**
self er hat sich selbst übertroffen ▷ *vi* sich
auszeichnen (*in* in +*dat* at bei)
excellent [ˈɛksələnt] *adj*, **excellently** *adv*
ausgezeichnet
except [ɪksɛpt] *prep*: ~ außer +*dat*; ~ **for**
abgesehen von ▷ *vt* ausnehmen
exception [ɪksɛpʃⁿn] *n* Ausnahme *f*
exceptional [ɪksɛpʃənⁿl] *adj*, **exceptional-**
ly *adv* außergewöhnlich
excess [ɪksɛs] *n* Übermaß *nt* (*of* an +*dat*)
excess baggage *n* Übergepäck *nt*
excesses *npl* Exzesse *pl*; (*drink, sex*) Aus-
schweifungen *pl*
excessive [ɪksɛsɪv] *adj*, **excessively** *adv*
übermäßig
excess weight *n* Übergewicht *nt*
exchange [ɪkstʃeɪndʒ] *n* Austausch *m* (*for*

gegen); (*of bought items*) Umtausch *m* (*for gegen*); (*Fin*) Wechsel *m*; (*Tel*) Vermittlung *f*, Zentrale *f* ▷ *vt* austauschen; (*goods*) tauschen; (*bought items*) umtauschen (*for gegen*); (*money, blows*) wechseln

exchange rate *n* Wechselkurs *m*

excite [ɪksaɪt] *vt* erregen

excited [ɪksaɪtɪd] *adj* aufgeregt; **to get ~** sich aufregen

exciting [ɪksaɪtɪŋ] *adj* aufregend; (*book, film*) spannend

exclamation [ɛkskləmeɪʃ°n] *n* Ausruf *m*

exclamation point [ɛkskləmeɪʃ°n pɔɪnt] *n* Ausrufezeichen *nt*

exclude [ɪksklud] *vt* ausschließen

exclusion [ɪkskluʒ°n] *n* Ausschluss *m*

exclusive [ɪksklusɪv] *adj* (*select*) exklusiv; (*sole*) ausschließlich

exclusively [ɪksklusɪvli] *adv* ausschließlich

excrement [ɛkskrɪmənt] *n* Kot *m*, Exkremente *pl*

excruciating [ɪkskruʃieɪtɪŋ] *adj* fürchterlich, entsetzlich

excursion [ɪkskɜrʒ°n] *n* Ausflug *m*

excusable [ɪkskyuzəb°l] *adj* entschuldbar

excuse [*vb* ɪkskyuz, *n* ɪkskyus] *vt* entschuldigen; **~ me** Entschuldigung!; **to ~ sb for sth** jdm etw verzeihen; **to ~ sb from sth** jdn von etw befreien ▷ *n* Entschuldigung *f*, Ausrede *f*

execute [ɛksɪkyut] *vt* (*carry out*) ausführen; (*kill*) hinrichten

execution [ɛksɪkyuʃ°n] *n* (*killing*) Hinrichtung *f*; (*carrying out*) Ausführung *f*

executive [ɪgzɛkyətɪv] *n* (*Comm*) leitender Angestellter, leitende Angestellte

exemplary [ɪgzɛmpləri] *adj* beispielhaft

exempt [ɪgzɛmpt] *adj* befreit (*from* von) ▷ *vt* befreien

exercise [ɛksərsaɪz] *n* (*in school, sports*) Übung *f*; (*movement*) Bewegung *f*; **to get more ~** mehr Sport treiben

exercise bike *n* Heimtrainer *m*

exercise book *n* Heft *nt*

exert [ɪgzɜrt] *vt* (*influence*) ausüben

exhaust [ɪgzɔst] *n* (*fumes*) Abgase *pl*; (*Auto*): **~ (pipe)** Auspuff *m*

exhausted [ɪgzɔstɪd] *adj* erschöpft

exhausting [ɪgzɔstɪŋ] *adj* anstrengend

exhibit [ɪgzɪbɪt] *n* (*in exhibition*) Ausstellungsstück *nt*

exhibition [ɛksɪbɪʃ°n] *n* Ausstellung *f*

exhibitionist [ɛksɪbɪʃənɪst] *n* Selbstdarsteller(in) *m(f)*

exhibitor [ɪgzɪbɪtər] *n* Aussteller(in) *m(f)*

exhilarating [ɪgzɪləreɪtɪŋ] *adj* belebend, erregend

exile [ɛksaɪl, ɛgz-] *n* Exil *nt*; (*person*) Verbannte(r) *mf* ▷ *vt* verbannen

exist [ɪgzɪst] *vi* existieren; (*live*) leben (*on* von)

existence [ɪgzɪstəns] *n* Existenz *f*; **to come into ~** entstehen

existing [ɪgzɪstɪŋ] *adj* bestehend

exit [ɛgzɪt, ɛksɪt] *n* Ausgang *m*; (*for vehicles*) Ausfahrt *f*

exit poll *n* Umfrage direkt nach dem Wahlgang

exorbitant [ɪgzɔrbɪtənt] *adj* astronomisch

exotic [ɪgzɒtɪk] *adj* exotisch

expand [ɪkspænd] *vt* ausdehnen, erweitern ▷ *vi* sich ausdehnen

expansion [ɪkspænʃ°n] *n* Expansion *f*, Erweiterung *f*

expect [ɪkspɛkt] *vt* erwarten; (*suppose*) annehmen; **he ~s me to do it** er erwartet, dass ich es mache; **I ~ it'll rain** es wird wohl regnen; **I ~ so** ich denke schon ▷ *vi*: **she's ~ing** sie bekommt ein Kind

expedition [ɛkspɪdɪʃ°n] *n* Expedition *f*

expenditure [ɪkspɛndɪtʃər] *n* Ausgaben *pl*

expense [ɪkspɛns] *n* Kosten *pl*; (*single cost*) Ausgabe *f*; **business~s** *pl* Spesen *pl*; **at sb's ~** auf jds Kosten

expensive [ɪkspɛnsɪv] *adj* teuer

experience [ɪkspɪəriəns] *n* Erfahrung *f*; (*particular incident*) Erlebnis *nt*; **by/from ~** aus Erfahrung ▷ *vt* erfahren, erleben; (*hardship*) durchmachen

experienced [ɪkspɪəriənst] *adj* erfahren

experiment [*n* ɪkspɛrɪmənt, *vb* ɪkspɛrɪmɛnt] *n* Versuch *m*, Experiment *nt* ▷ *vi* experimentieren

expert [ɛkspɜrt] *n* Experte *m*, Expertin *f*; (*professional*) Fachmann *m*, Fachfrau *f*; (*Jur*) Sachverständige(r) *mf* ▷ *adj* fachmännisch, Fach-

expertise [ɛkspɜrtiz] *n* Sachkenntnis *f*

expire [ɪkspaɪər] *vi* (*end*) ablaufen

explain [ɪkspleɪn] *vt* erklären (*sth to sb* jdm etw)

explanation [ɛkspləneɪʃ°n] *n* Erklärung *f*

explicit [ɪksplɪsɪt] *adj* ausdrücklich, eindeutig

explode [ɪksploud] *vi* explodieren

exploit [ɪksplɔɪt] *vt* ausbeuten

explore [ɪksplɔr] *vt* erforschen

explosion [ɪksplouʒ°n] *n* Explosion *f*

explosive [ɪksplousɪv] *adj* explosiv ▷ *n*

Sprengstoff *m*

export [*vb* ɪksˈpɔrt, *n* ˈɛkspɔrt] *vt, vi* exportieren ▷ *n*, *adj* Export *m* ▷ *adj* (*trade*) Export-

expose [ɪksˈpouz] *vt* (*to danger etc*) aussetzen (*to dat*); (*uncover*) freilegen; (*imposter*) entlarven

exposed [ɪksˈpouzd] *adj* (*position*) ungeschützt

exposure [ɪksˈpouʒər] *n* (*Med*) Unterkühlung *f*; (*Foto: time*) Belichtung(szeit) *f*; **24 ~s** 24 Aufnahmen

express [ɪksˈprɛs] *adj* (*speedy*) Express-, Schnell-; **~ delivery** Eilzustellung *f* ▷ *n* (*Rail*) Schnellzug *m* ▷ *vt* ausdrücken ▷ *vr*: **to ~ oneself** sich ausdrücken

expression [ɪksˈprɛʃ⁰n] *n* (*phrase*) Ausdruck *m*; (*look*) Gesichtsausdruck *m*

expressive [ɪksˈprɛsɪv] *adj* ausdrucksvoll

expressway [ɪksˈprɛsweɪ] *n* Schnellstraße *f*

extend [ɪksˈtɛnd] *vt* (*arms*) ausstrecken; (*lengthen*) verlängern; (*building*) vergrößern, ausbauen; (*business, limits*) erweitern

extension [ɪksˈtɛnʃ⁰n] *n* (*lengthening*) Verlängerung *f*; (*of building*) Anbau *m*; (*Tel*) Anschluss *m*; (*of business, limits*) Erweiterung *f*

extensive [ɪksˈtɛnsɪv] *adj* (*knowledge*) umfangreich; (*use*) häufig

extent [ɪksˈtɛnt] *n* (*length*) Länge *f*; (*size*) Ausdehnung *f*; (*scope*) Umfang *m*, Ausmaß *nt*; **to a certain/large ~** in gewissem/hohem Maße

exterior [ɪksˈtɪərɪər] *n* Äußere(s) *nt*

external [ɪksˈtɜrnⁿl] *adj* äußere(r, s), Außen-

externally [ɪksˈtɜrnⁿlɪ] *adv* äußerlich

extinct [ɪksˈtɪŋkt] *adj* (*species*) ausgestorben

extinguish [ɪksˈtɪŋgwɪʃ] *vt* löschen

extinguisher [ɪksˈtɪŋgwɪʃər] *n* Löschgerät *nt*

extra [ˈɛkstrə] *adj* zusätzlich; **~ charge** Zuschlag *m*; **~ time** (*Sport*) Verlängerung *f* ▷ *adv* besonders; **~ large** (*clothing*) übergroß ▷ *npl*: **~s** zusätzliche Kosten *pl*; (*food*) Beilagen *pl*; (*accessories*) Zubehör *nt*; (*for car etc*) Extras *pl*

extract [*vb* ɪksˈtrækt, *n* ˈɛkstrækt] *vt* herausziehen (*from* aus); (*tooth*) ziehen ▷ *n* (*from book etc*) Auszug *m*

extraordinary [ɪksˈtrɔrdⁿɛri] *adj* außerordentlich; (*unusual*) ungewöhnlich; (*amazing*) erstaunlich

extreme [ɪksˈtrim] *adj* äußerste(r, s); (*drastic*) extrem ▷ *n* Extrem *nt*

extremely [ɪksˈtrimli] *adv* äußerst, höchst

extreme sports *npl* Extremsportarten *pl*

extremist [ɪksˈtrimɪst] *adj* extremistisch ▷ *n* Extremist *m*

extricate [ˈɛkstrɪkeɪt] *vt* befreien (*from* aus)

extrovert [ˈɛkstrəvɜrt] *adj* extrovertiert

exuberance [ɪgˈzubərəns] *n* Überschwang *m*

exuberant [ɪgˈzubərənt] *adj* überschwänglich

exultation [ˌɛgzʌlˈteɪʃ⁰n] *n* Jubel *m*

eye [aɪ] *n* Auge *nt*; **to keep an eye on sb/sth** auf jdn/etw aufpassen ▷ *vt* mustern

eyebrow [ˈaɪbrau] *n* Augenbraue *f*

eyelash [ˈaɪlæʃ] *n* Wimper *f*

eyelid [ˈaɪlɪd] *n* Augenlid *nt*

eyeliner [ˈaɪlaɪnər] *n* Eyeliner *m*

eye-opener [ˈaɪoupənər] *n*: **that was an ~** das hat mir die Augen geöffnet

eye shadow *n* Lidschatten *m*

eyesight [ˈaɪsaɪt] *n* Sehkraft *f*

eyesore [ˈaɪsɔr] *n* Schandfleck *m*

eyewitness *n* Augenzeuge *m*, Augenzeugin *f*

F

fabric [ˈfæbrɪk] *n* Stoff *m*

fabulous [ˈfæbyələs] *adj* sagenhaft

façade [fəˈsɑːd] *n (a. fig)* Fassade *f*

face [feɪs] *n* Gesicht *nt; (of clock)* Zifferblatt *nt; (of mountain)* Wand *f;* **in the ~ of** trotz *+gen;* **to be ~ to ~** *(people)* einander gegenüberstehen ▷ *vt, vi (person)* gegenüberstehen *+dat; (at table)* gegenübersitzen *+dat;* **to ~ north** *(room)* nach Norden gehen; **to ~ up to the facts** den Tatsachen ins Auge sehen; **to be ~d with sth** mit etw konfrontiert sein

face lift *n* Gesichtsstraffung *f; (fig)* Verschönerung *f*

face powder *n* Gesichtspuder *m*

facet [ˈfæsɪt] *n (fig)* Aspekt *m*

face value *n* Nennwert *m*

facial [ˈfeɪʃl] *adj* Gesichts- ▷ *n (fam)* (kosmetische) Gesichtsbehandlung

facilitate [fəˈsɪlɪteɪt] *vt* erleichtern

facility [fəˈsɪlɪtɪ] *n (building etc to be used)* Einrichtung *f,* Möglichkeit *f; (installation)* Anlage *f; (skill)* Gewandtheit *f*

fact [fækt] *n* Tatsache *f;* **as a matter of ~, in ~** eigentlich, tatsächlich

factor [ˈfæktər] *n* Faktor *m*

factory [ˈfæktərɪ, -trɪ] *n* Fabrik *f*

factory outlet *n* Fabrikverkauf *m*

factual [ˈfæktʃuəl] *adj* sachlich

faculty [ˈfækˀltɪ] *n* Fähigkeit *f; (at university)* Fakultät *f; (teaching staff)* Lehrkörper *m*

fade [feɪd] *vi (a. fig)* verblassen

faded [ˈfeɪdɪd] *adj* verblasst, verblichen

Fahrenheit [ˈfærənhaɪt] *n* Fahrenheit

fail [feɪl] *vt (exam)* nicht bestehen ▷ *vi* versagen; *(plan, marriage)* scheitern; *(student)* durchfallen; *(eyesight)* nachlassen; **words ~ me** ich bin sprachlos

failing [ˈfeɪlɪŋ] *n* Schwäche *f*

failure [ˈfeɪlyər] *n (person)* Versager(in) *m(f); (act, a. Tech)* Versagen *nt; (of engine etc)* Ausfall *m; (of plan, marriage)* Scheitern *nt*

faint [feɪnt] *adj* schwach; *(sound)* leise; *(fam):* **I haven't the ~est idea** ich habe keinen blassen Schimmer ▷ *vi* ohnmächtig werden *(with* vor *+dat)*

faintness [ˈfeɪntnɪs] *n (Med)* Schwächegefühl *nt*

fair [fɛər] *adj (hair)* (dunkel)blond; *(skin)* hell; *(just)* gerecht, fair; *(reasonable)* ganz ordentlich; *(in school)* befriedigend; *(weather)* schön; *(wind)* günstig; **a ~ number/amount of** ziemlich viele/viel ▷ *adv:* **to play ~** fair spielen; *(fig)* fair sein; **~ enough** in Ordnung! ▷ *n (funfair)* Jahrmarkt *m; (Comm)* Messe *f*

fair-haired [fɛərˈhɛərd] *adj* (dunkel)blond

fairly [ˈfɛərlɪ] *adv (honestly)* fair; *(rather)* ziemlich

fairy [ˈfɛərɪ] *n* Fee *f*

fairy tale *n* Märchen *nt*

faith [feɪθ] *n (trust)* Vertrauen *nt (in sb* zu jdm); *(Rel)* Glaube *m*

faithful [ˈfeɪθfəl] *adj,* **faithfully** *adv* treu; **Yours ~ly** Hochachtungsvoll

fake [feɪk] *n (thing)* Fälschung *f* ▷ *adj* vorgetäuscht ▷ *vt* fälschen

falcon [ˈfɔlkən, ˈfælk-] *n* Falke *m*

fall [fɔl] (**fell, fallen**) *vi* fallen; *(from a height, badly)* stürzen; **to ~ ill** krank werden; **to ~ asleep** einschlafen; **to ~ in love** sich verlieben ▷ *n* Fall *m; (accident, fig: of regime)* Sturz *m; (decrease)* Sinken *nt (in +gen);* (*autumn)* Herbst *m*

fall apart *vi* auseinanderfallen

fall behind *vi* zurückbleiben; *(with work, rent)* in Rückstand geraten

fall down *vi (person)* hinfallen

fallen [ˈfɔlən] *pp of* **fall**

fall off *vi* herunterfallen; *(decrease)* zurückgehen

fall out *vi* herausfallen; *(quarrel)* sich streiten

fallout [ˈfɔlaʊt] *n* radioaktiver Niederschlag, Fall-out *m*

fall over *vi* hinfallen

fall through *vi (plan etc)* ins Wasser fallen

false [fɔls] *adj* falsch; *(artificial)* künstlich

false alarm *n* blinder Alarm

false start *n (Sport)* Fehlstart *m*

false teeth *npl* (künstliches) Gebiss

fame [feɪm] *n* Ruhm *m*

familiar [fəˈmɪlyər] *adj* vertraut, bekannt; **to be ~ with** vertraut sein mit, gut kennen

familiarity [fəmɪlɪˈærɪtɪ] *n* Vertrautheit *f*

family [ˈfæmɪlɪ, ˈfæmlɪ] *n* Familie *f; (including relations)* Verwandtschaft *f*

family man *n* Familienvater *m*

family name *n* Familienname *m,* Nachname *m*

family practitioner [fæmɪlɪ prækˈtɪʃˀnər] *n*

Allgemeinarzt *m*, Allgemeinärztin *f*

famine [fæmɪn] *n* Hungersnot *f*

famished [fæmɪʃt] *adj* ausgehungert

famous [feɪməs] *adj* berühmt

fan [fæn] *n* (*handheld*) Fächer *m*; (*Elec*) Ventilator *m*; (*admirer*) Fan *m*

fanatic [fənætɪk] *n* Fanatiker(in) *m(f)*

fancy [fænsi] *adj* (*elaborate*) kunstvoll; (*unusual*) ausgefallen ▷ *vt* (*like*) gernhaben; **he fancies her** er steht auf sie; **~ that** stell dir vor!, so was!

fancy dress *n* Kostüm *nt*, Verkleidung *f*

fan mail *n* Fanpost *f*

fantastic [fæntæstɪk] *adj* (*a. fam*) fantastisch; **that's ~** (*fam*) das ist ja toll!

fantasy [fæntəsi] *n* Fantasie *f*

far [fɑr] (*further o* farther, furthest *o* farthest) *adj* weit; **the far end of the room** das andere Ende des Zimmers; **the Far East** der Ferne Osten ▷ *adv* weit; **far better** viel besser; **by far the best** bei weitem der/die/das Beste; **as far as ...** bis zum *o* zur ...; (*with place name*) bis nach ...; **as far as I'm concerned** was mich betrifft, von mir aus; **so far** soweit, bisher

faraway [fɑrəweɪ] *adj* weit entfernt; (*look*) verträumt

fare [fɛər] *n* Fahrpreis *m*; (*money*) Fahrgeld *nt*

farm [fɑrm] *n* Bauernhof *m*, Farm *f*

farmer [fɑrmər] *n* Bauer *m*, Bäuerin *f*, Landwirt(in) *m(f)*

farmhouse [fɑrmhaʊs] *n* Bauernhaus *nt*

farming [fɑrmɪŋ] *n* Landwirtschaft *f*

farmland [fɑrmlænd] *n* Ackerland *nt*

farmyard [fɑrmyɑrd] *n* Hof *m*

far-reaching [fɑrriːtʃɪŋ] *adj* weit reichend

farsighted [fɑrsaɪtɪd] *adj* weitsichtig; (*fig*) weitblickend

farther [fɑrðər] *adj, adv comparative of* **far**; *see* **further**

farthest [fɑrðɪst] *adj, adv superlative of* **far**; *see* **furthest**

fascinating [fæsɪneɪtɪŋ] *adj* faszinierend

fascination [fæsɪneɪʃ°n] *n* Faszination *f*

fascism [fæʃɪzəm] *n* Faschismus *m*

fascist [fæʃɪst] *adj* faschistisch, Faschist(in) *m(f)*

fashion [fæʃ°n] *n* (*clothes*) Mode *f*; (*manner*) Art (und Weise) *f*; **to be in ~** (in) Mode sein; **out of ~** unmodisch

fashionable [fæʃənəb°l] *adj*, **fashionably** *adv* (*clothes, person*) modisch; (*author, pub etc*) in Mode

fast [fæst] *adj* schnell; **to be ~** (*clock*) vorge-

hen ▷ *adv* schnell; (*firmly*) fest; **to be ~ asleep** fest schlafen ▷ *n* Fasten *nt* ▷ *vi* fasten

fastback [fæstbæk] *n* (*Auto*) Fließheck *nt*

fasten [fæs°n] *vt* (*attach*) befestigen (*to* an *+dat*); (*do up*) zumachen; **~ your seatbelts** bitte anschnallen

fastener [fæsənər], **fastening** *n* Verschluss *m*

fast food *n* Fast Food *nt*

fast-forward *n* (*for tape*) Schnellvorlauf *m*

fast lane *n* Überholspur *f*

fat [fæt] *adj* dick; (*meat*) fett ▷ *n* Fett *nt*

fatal [feɪt°l] *adj* tödlich

fate [feɪt] *n* Schicksal *nt*

fat-free *adj* (*food*) fettfrei

father [fɑðər] *n* Vater *m*; (*priest*) Pfarrer *m* ▷ *vt* (*child*) zeugen

father-in-law [fɑðərɪnlɔ] (*pl* **fathers-in-law**) *n* Schwiegervater *m*

fatigue [fətiːg] *n* Ermüdung *f*

fattening [fæt°nɪŋ] *adj*: **to be ~** dick machen

fatty [fæti] *adj* (*food*) fettig

faucet [fɔsɪt] *n* Wasserhahn *m*

fault [fɔlt] *n* Fehler *m*; (*Tech*) Defekt *m*; (*Elec*) Störung *f*; (*blame*) Schuld *f*; **it's your ~** du bist daran schuld

faulty [fɔlti] *adj* fehlerhaft; (*Tech*) defekt

favor [feɪvər] *n* (*approval*) Gunst *f*; (*kindness*) Gefallen *m*; **in ~ of** für; **I'm in ~ of going** ich bin dafür(, dass wir gehen); **to do sb a ~** jdm einen Gefallen tun ▷ *vt* (*prefer*) vorziehen

favorable [feɪvərəb°l] *adj* günstig (*to, for* für)

favorite [feɪvərɪt, feɪvrɪt] *n* Liebling *m*, Favorit(in) *m(f)* ▷ *adj* Lieblings-

fax [fæks] *vt* faxen ▷ *n* Fax *nt*

fax number *n* Faxnummer *f*

faze [feɪz] *vt* (*fam*) aus der Fassung bringen

FBI [ɛf bi aɪ] (*abbr*) = **Federal Bureau of Investigation** FBI *nt*

fear [fɪər] *n* Angst *f* (*of* vor *+dat*) ▷ *vt* befürchten

fearful [fɪərfəl] *adj* (*timid*) ängstlich, furchtsam; (*terrible*) fürchterlich

fearless [fɪərlɪs] *adj* furchtlos

feasible [fiːzəb°l] *adj* machbar

feast [fiːst] *n* Festessen *nt*

feather [fɛðər] *n* Feder *f*

feature [fiːtʃər] *n* (*facial*) (Gesichts)zug *m*; (*characteristic*) Merkmal *nt*; (*of car etc*) Ausstattungsmerkmal *nt*; (*in the press*,

Cine) Feature *nt* ▷ *vt* bringen, (als Besonderheit) zeigen

feature film *n* Spielfilm *m*

February [fɛbyuɛri, fɛbru-] *n* Februar *m*; *see also* **September**

fed [fɛd] *pt, pp of* **feed**

federal [fɛdərəl] *adj* Bundes-; **the F~ Republic of Germany** die Bundesrepublik Deutschland

fed-up *adj*: **to be ~ with sth** etw satthaben; **I'm ~** ich habe die Nase voll

fee [fi] *n* Gebühr *f*; (*of doctor, lawyer*) Honorar *nt*

feeble [fib°l] *adj* schwach

feed [fid] (**fed, fed**) *vt* (*baby, animal*) füttern; (*support*) ernähren ▷ *n* (*for baby*) Mahlzeit *f*; (*for animals*) Futter *nt*; (*Inform: paper feed*) Zufuhr *f*

feedback [fidbæk] *n* (*information*) Feedback *nt*

feed in *vt* (*information*) eingeben

feel [fil] (**felt, felt**) *vt* (*sense*) fühlen; (*pain*) empfinden; (*touch*) anfassen; (*think*) meinen ▷ *vi* (*person*) sich fühlen; **I ~ cold** mir ist kalt; **do you ~ like a walk?** hast du Lust, spazieren zu gehen?

feeling [filɪŋ] *n* Gefühl *nt*

feet [fit] *pl of* **foot**

fell [fɛl] *pt of* **fall** ▷ *vt* (*tree*) fällen

fellow [fɛlou] *n* Kerl *m*, Typ *m*; **~ citizen** Mitbürger(in) *m(f)*; **~ countryman** Landsmann *m*; **~ worker** Mitarbeiter(in) *m(f)*

felt [fɛlt] *pt, pp of* **feel** ▷ *n* Filz *m*

felt tip, felt-tip pen *n* Filzstift *m*

female [fimeɪl] *n* (*of animals*) Weibchen *nt* ▷ *adj* weiblich; **~ doctor** Ärztin *f*

feminine [fɛmɪnɪn] *adj* weiblich

feminist [fɛmɪnɪst] *n* Feminist(in) *m(f)* ▷ *adj* feministisch

fence [fɛns] *n* Zaun *m*

fencing [fɛnsɪŋ] *n* (*Sport*) Fechten *nt*

fender [fɛndər] *n* (*Auto*) Kotflügel *m*

fennel [fɛn°l] *n* Fenchel *m*

fern [fɜrn] *n* Farn *m*

ferocious [fərouʃəs] *adj* wild

ferry [fɛri] *n* Fähre *f* ▷ *vt* übersetzen

fertile [fɜrt°l] *adj* fruchtbar

fertility [fɜrtɪliti] *n* Fruchtbarkeit *f*

fertilize [fɜrt°laɪz] *vt* (*Bio*) befruchten; (*Agr: land*) düngen

fertilizer [fɜrt°laɪzər] *n* Dünger *m*

festival [fɛstɪv°l] *n* (*Rel*) Fest *nt*; (*Art, Mus*) Festspiele *pl*; (*pop music*) Festival *nt*

festive [fɛstɪv] *adj* festlich

festivities [fɛstɪvɪtiz] *n* Feierlichkeiten *pl*

fetch [fɛtʃ] *vt* holen; (*collect*) abholen; (*in sale, money*) einbringen

fetching [fɛtʃɪŋ] *adj* reizend

fetish [fɛtɪʃ] *n* Fetisch *m*

fetus [fitəs] *n* Fötus *m*

fever [fivər] *n* Fieber *nt*

feverish [fivərɪʃ] *adj* (*Med*) fiebrig; (*fig*) fieberhaft

few [fyu] *adj, pron* (*pl*) wenige *pl*; **a few** *pl* ein paar

fewer [fyuər] *adj* weniger

fewest [fyuɪst] *adj* wenigste(r, s)

fiancé [fiɑnseɪ] *n* Verlobte(r) *m*

fiancée [fiɑnseɪ] *n* Verlobte *f*

fiasco [fiæskou] (*pl* **-es**) *n* Fiasko *nt*

fiber [faɪbər], **fiber** *n* Faser *f*; (*material*) Faserstoff *m*

fickle [fɪk°l] *adj* unbeständig

fiction [fɪkʃ°n] *n* (*novels*) Prosaliteratur *f*

fictional [fɪkʃən°l], **fictitious** [fɪktɪʃəs] *adj* erfunden

fiddle [fɪd°l] *n* Geige *f*; (*trick*) Betrug *m* ▷ *vt* (*accounts, results*) frisieren

fiddle with *vt* herumfingern an +*dat*

fidelity [fɪdɛliti] *n* Treue *f*

fidget [fɪdʒɪt] *vi* zappeln

fidgety [fɪdʒɪti] *adj* zappelig

field [fild] *n* Feld *nt*; (*grass-covered*) Wiese *f*; (*fig: of work*) (Arbeits)gebiet *nt*

fierce [fiərs] *adj* heftig; (*animal, appearance*) wild; (*criticism, competition*) scharf

fifteen [fiftin] *num* fünfzehn ▷ *n* Fünfzehn *f*; *see also* **eight**

fifteenth [fiftinθ] *adj* fünfzehnte(r, s); *see also* **eighth**

fifth [fɪfθ] *adj* fünfte(r, s) ▷ *n* (*fraction*) Fünftel *nt*; *see also* **eighth**

fiftieth [fɪftiəθ] *adj* fünfzigste(r, s); *see also* **eighth**

fifty [fɪfti] *num* fünfzig ▷ *n* Fünfzig *f*; *see also* **eight**

fig [fɪg] *n* Feige *f*

fight [faɪt] (**fought, fought**) *vi* kämpfen (*with, against* gegen, *for, over* um) ▷ *vt* (*person*) kämpfen mit; (*fig: disease, fire etc*) bekämpfen ▷ *n* Kampf *m*; (*brawl*) Schlägerei *f*; (*argument*) Streit *m*

fight back *vi* zurückschlagen

fighter [faɪtər] *n* Kämpfer(in) *m(f)*

fight off *vt* abwehren

figurative [fɪgyərətɪv] *adj* übertragen

figure [fɪgyər] *n* (*person*) Gestalt *f*; (*of person*) Figur *f*; (*number*) Zahl *f*, Ziffer *f*; (*amount*) Betrag *m*; **a four-~ sum** eine vierstellige Summe ▷ *vt* (*think*) glauben

▷ *vi (appear)* erscheinen

figure out *vt (work out)* herausbekommen; **I can't figure him out** ich werde aus ihm nicht schlau

figure skating *n* Eiskunstlauf *m*

file [faɪl] *n (tool)* Feile *f*; *(dossier)* Akte *f*; *(Inform)* Datei *f*; *(folder)* Aktenordner *m*; **on ~** in den Akten ▷ *vt (metal, nails)* feilen; *(papers)* ablegen *(under* unter) ▷ *vi:* **to ~ in/out** hintereinander hereinkommen/hinausgehen

filing cabinet [faɪlɪŋ kæbɪnɪt] *n* Aktenschrank *m*

fill [fɪl] *vt* füllen; *(tooth)* plombieren; *(post)* besetzen

fillet [fɪleɪ] *n* Filet *nt*

fill in *vt (hole)* auffüllen; *(form)* ausfüllen; *(tell)* informieren *(on* über)

filling [fɪlɪŋ] *n (Gastr)* Füllung *f*; *(for tooth)* Plombe *f*

fill out *vt (form)* ausfüllen

fill up *vi (Auto)* volltanken

film [fɪlm] *n* Film *m* ▷ *vt (scene)* filmen

film studio *n* Filmstudio *nt*

filter [fɪltər] *n* Filter *m*; *(traffic lane)* Abbiegespur *f* ▷ *vt* filtern

filth [fɪlθ] *n* Dreck *m*

filthy [fɪlθi] *adj* dreckig

fin [fɪn] *n* Flosse *f*

final [faɪnᵊl] *adj* letzte(r, s); *(stage, round)* End-; *(decision, version)* endgültig; **~ score** Schlussstand *m* ▷ *n (Sport)* Endspiel *nt*; *(competition)* Finale *nt*; **~s** *pl* Abschlussexamen *nt*

finalize [faɪnᵊlaɪz] *vt* die endgültige Form geben *+dat*

finally [faɪnᵊli] *adv (lastly)* zuletzt; *(eventually)* schließlich, endlich

finance [faɪnæns, fɪnæns] *n* Finanzwesen *nt*; **~s** *pl* Finanzen *pl* ▷ *vt* finanzieren

financial [faɪnænᵊl, fɪn-] *adj* finanziell; *(adviser, crisis, policy etc)* Finanz-

find [faɪnd] **(found, found)** *vt* finden; **he was found dead** er wurde tot aufgefunden; **I ~ myself in difficulties** ich befinde mich in Schwierigkeiten; **she ~s it difficult/easy** es fällt ihr schwer/leicht

findings [faɪndɪŋz] *npl (Jur)* Ermittlungsergebnis *nt*; *(of report, Med)* Befund *m*

find out *vt* herausfinden

fine [faɪn] *adj (thin)* dünn, fein; *(good)* gut; *(splendid)* herrlich; *(clothes)* elegant; *(weather)* schön; **I'm ~** es geht mir gut; **that's ~** das ist OK ▷ *adv (well)* gut ▷ *n (Jur)* Geldstrafe *f* ▷ *vt (Jur)* mit einer Geldstrafe belegen

fine arts *npl:* **the ~** die schönen Künste *pl*

finely [faɪnli] *adv (cut)* dünn; *(ground)* fein

finger [fɪŋgər] *n* Finger *m* ▷ *vt* herumfingern an *+dat*

fingernail [fɪŋgərneɪl] *n* Fingernagel *m*

fingerprint [fɪŋgərprɪnt] *n* Fingerabdruck *m*

fingertip [fɪŋgərtɪp] *n* Fingerspitze *f*

finicky [fɪnɪki] *adj (person)* pingelig; *(work)* knifflig

finish [fɪnɪʃ] *n* Ende *nt*; *(Sport)* Finish *nt*; *(line)* Ziel *nt*; *(of product)* Verarbeitung *f* ▷ *vt* beenden; *(book etc)* zu Ende lesen; *(food)* aufessen; *(drink)* austrinken ▷ *vi* zu Ende gehen; *(song, story)* enden; *(person)* fertig sein; *(stop)* aufhören; **have you ~ed?** bist du fertig?; **to ~ first/second** *(Sport)* als erster/zweiter durchs Ziel gehen

finish line *n* Ziellinie *f*

Finland [fɪnlənd] *n* Finnland *nt*

Finn [fɪn] *n* Finne *m*, Finnin *f*

Finnish [fɪnɪʃ] *adj* finnisch ▷ *n (language)* Finnisch *nt*

fir [fɜr] *n* Tanne *f*

fire [faɪər] *n* Feuer *nt*; *(house etc)* Brand *m*; **to set ~ to sth** etw in Brand stecken; **to be on ~** brennen ▷ *vt (bullets, rockets)* abfeuern; *(fam: dismiss)* feuern ▷ *vi (Auto: engine)* zünden; **to ~ at sb** auf jdn schießen

fire alarm *n* Feuermelder *m*

fire department *n* Feuerwehr *f*

fire engine *n* Feuerwehrauto *nt*

fire escape *n* Feuerleiter *f*

fire extinguisher *n* Feuerlöscher *m*

firefighter [faɪərfaɪtər] *n* Feuerwehrmann *m*, Feuerwehrfrau *f*

fireman [faɪərmən] *n* Feuerwehrmann *m*

fireplace [faɪərpleɪs] *n* (offener) Kamin

fireproof [faɪərpruf] *adj* feuerfest

fire station *n* Feuerwache *f*

firewood [faɪərwʊd] *n* Brennholz *nt*

fireworks [faɪərwɜrks] *npl* Feuerwerk *nt*

firm [fɜrm] *adj* fest; *(person):* **to be ~** entschlossen auftreten ▷ *n* Firma *f*

first [fɜrst] *adj* erste(r, s) ▷ *adv (at first)* zuerst; *(firstly)* erstens; *(arrive, finish)* als erste(r); *(happen)* zum ersten Mal; **~ of all** zuallererst ▷ *n (person)* Erste(r) *mf*; *(Auto: gear)* erster Gang; **at ~** zuerst, anfangs

first aid *n* erste Hilfe

first-class *adj* erstklassig; *(compartment,*

ticket) erster Klasse ▷ *adv* (*travel*) erster Klasse

first floor *n* Erdgeschoss *nt*

first lady *n* Frau *f* des Präsidenten

firstly [fɜrstli] *adv* erstens

first name *n* Vorname *m*

first night *n* (*Theat*) Premiere *f*

first-rate [fɜrstreɪt] *adj* erstklassig

fir tree *n* Tannenbaum *m*

fish [fɪʃ] *n* Fisch *m* ▷ *vi* fischen; (*with rod*) angeln; **to go ~ing** fischen/angeln gehen

fish cake *n* Fischfrikadelle *f*

fish farm *n* Fischzucht *f*

fishing [fɪʃɪŋ] *n* Fischen *nt*; (*with rod*) Angeln *nt*; (*as industry*) Fischerei *f*

fishing boat *n* Fischerboot *nt*

fishing line *n* Angelschnur *f*

fishing rod *n* Angelrute *f*

fishing village *n* Fischerdorf *nt*

fish stick *n* Fischstäbchen *nt*

fish tank *n* Aquarium *nt*

fishy [fɪʃi] *adj* (*fam: suspicious*) faul

fist [fɪst] *n* Faust *f*

fit [fɪt] *adj* (*Med*) gesund; (*Sport*) in Form, fit; (*suitable*) geeignet; **to keep fit** sich in Form halten ▷ *vt* passen +*dat*; (*attach*) anbringen (*to* an +*dat*); (*install*) einbauen (*in* in +*akk*) ▷ *vi* passen; (*in space, gap*) hineinpassen ▷ *n* (*of clothes*) Sitz *m*; (*Med*) Anfall *m*; **it's a good fit** es passt gut

fit in *vt* (*accommodate*) unterbringen; (*find time for*) einschieben ▷ *vi* (*in space*) hineinpassen; (*plans, ideas*) passen; **he doesn't ~ here** er passt nicht hierher; **to ~ with sb's plans** sich mit jds Plänen vereinbaren lassen

fitness [fɪtnɪs] *n* (*Med*) Gesundheit *f*; (*Sport*) Fitness *f*

fitness trainer *n* (*Sport*) Fitnesstrainer(in) *m(f)*

fitting [fɪtɪŋ] *adj* passend ▷ *n* (*of dress*) Anprobe *f*; **~s** *pl* Ausstattung *f*

five [faɪv] *num* fünf ▷ *n* Fünf *f*; *see also* **eight**

fix [fɪks] *vt* befestigen (*to* an +*dat*); (*settle*) festsetzen; (*place, time*) ausmachen; (*repair*) reparieren

fixer [fɪksər] *n* (*drug addict*) Fixer(in) *m(f)*

fixture [fɪkstʃər] *n* (*Sport*) Veranstaltung *f*; (*match*) Spiel *nt*; (*in building*) Installationsteil *nt*; **~s (and fittings)** *pl* Ausstattung *f*

fizzy [fɪzi] *adj* sprudelnd

flabbergasted [flæbərgæstɪd] *adj* (*fam*) platt

flabby [flæbi] *adj* (*fat*) wabbelig

flag [flæg] *n* Fahne *f*

flagstone [flægstoʊn] *n* Steinplatte *f*

flake [fleɪk] *n* Flocke *f* ▷ *vi*: **to ~ off** abblättern

flamboyant [flæmbɔɪənt] *adj* extravagant

flame [fleɪm] *n* Flamme *f*; (*person*): **an old ~** eine alte Liebe

flan [flæn, flɑn] *n* (*fruit flan*) Obstkuchen *m*

flap [flæp] *n* Klappe *f*; (*fam*): **to be in a ~** rotieren ▷ *vt* (*wings*) schlagen mit ▷ *vi* flattern

flared [flɛərd] *adj* (*pants*) mit Schlag

flared pants *npl* Schlaghose *f*

flash [flæʃ] *n* Blitz *m*; (*news flash*) Kurzmeldung *f*; (*Foto*) Blitzlicht *nt*; **in a ~** im Nu ▷ *vt*: **to ~ one's (head)lights** die Lichthupe betätigen ▷ *vi* aufblinken; (*brightly*) aufblitzen

flashback [flæʃbæk] *n* Rückblende *f*, Flashback *m*

flash camera *n* Blitzgerät *nt*

flashlight [flæʃlaɪt] *n* (*Photo*) Blitzlicht *nt*; (*torch*) Taschenlampe *f*

flashy [flæʃi] *adj* grell, schrill; (*pej*) protzig

flat [flæt] *adj* flach; (*surface*) eben; (*drink*) abgestanden; (*tyre*) platt; (*battery*) leer; (*refusal*) glatt ▷ *n* (*Auto*) Reifenpanne *f*

flat screen *n* (*Inform*) Flachbildschirm *m*

flatten [flætn] *vt* platt machen, einebnen

flatter [flætər] *vt* schmeicheln +*dat*

flattering [flætərɪŋ] *adj* schmeichelhaft

flatware [flætwɛər] *n* Besteck *nt*

flavor [fleɪvər]' *n* Geschmack *m* ▷ *vt* Geschmack geben +*dat*; (*with spices*) würzen

flavoring [fleɪvərɪŋ] *n* Aroma *nt*

flaw [flɔ] *n* Fehler *m*

flawless [flɔlɪs] *adj* fehlerlos; (*complexion*) makellos

flea [fliː] *n* Floh *m*

fled [flɛd] *pt, pp* of **flee**

flee [fliː] (**fled, fled**) *vi* fliehen

fleece [fliːs] *n* (*of sheep*) Vlies *nt*; (*soft material*) Fleece *m*; (*jacket*) Fleecejacke *f*

fleet [fliːt] *n* Flotte *f*

Flemish [flɛmɪʃ] *adj* flämisch ▷ *n* (*language*) Flämisch *nt*

flesh [flɛʃ] *n* Fleisch *nt*

flew [fluː] *pt* of **fly**

flexibility [flɛksɪbɪlɪti] *n* Biegsamkeit *f*; (*fig*) Flexibilität *f*

flexible [flɛksɪbᵊl] *adj* biegsam; (*plans, person*) flexibel

flextime *n* gleitende Arbeitszeit, Gleitzeit *f*

flicker [flɪkər] *vi* flackern; (*TV*) flimmern

flies [flaɪz] *n pl see* **fly**

flight [flaɪt] *n* Flug *m*; (*escape*) Flucht *f*; **~ of stairs** Treppe *f*

flight attendant [flaɪt ətɛndənt] *n* Flugbegleiter(in) *m(f)*

flight recorder *n* Flugschreiber *m*

flimsy [flɪmzi] *adj* leicht gebaut, nicht stabil; (*thin*) hauchdünn; (*excuse*) fadenscheinig

fling [flɪŋ] (**flung, flung**) *vt* schleudern ▷ *n*: **to have a ~** eine (kurze) Affäre haben

flip [flɪp] *vt* schnippen; **to ~ a coin** eine Münze werfen

flipchart [flɪptʃɑrt] *n* Flipchart *nt*

flipper [flɪpər] *n* Flosse *f*

flip through *vt* (*book*) durchblättern

flirt [flɜrt] *vi* flirten

float [floʊt] *n* (*for fishing*) Schwimmer *m*; (*in procession*) Festwagen *m*; (*money*) Wechselgeld *nt* ▷ *vi* schwimmen; (*in air*) schweben

flock [flɒk] *n* (*of sheep: Rel*) Herde *f*; (*of birds*) Schwarm *m*; (*of people*) Schar *f*

flog [flɒg] *vt* auspeitschen

flood [flʌd] *n* Hochwasser *nt*, Überschwemmung *f*; (*fig*) Flut *f* ▷ *vt* überschwemmen

floodlight [flʌdlaɪt] *n* Flutlicht *nt*

floodlit [flʌdlɪt] *adj* (*building*) angestrahlt

floor [flɔr] *n* Fußboden *m*; (*storey*) Stock *m*; **first ~** Erdgeschoss *nt*; **second ~** erster Stock

floorboard [flɔrbɔrd] *n* Diele *f*

flop [flɒp] *n* (*fam: failure*) Reinfall *m*, Flop *m* ▷ *vi* misslingen, floppen

floppy disk [flɒpi dɪsk] *n* Diskette *f*

Florence [flɔrⁱəns] *n* Florenz *nt*

florist [flɔrɪst] *n* Blumenhändler(in) *m(f)*

florist's (shop) *n* Blumengeschäft *m(f)*

flounder [flaʊndər] *n* (*fish*) Flunder *f*

flour [flaʊər] *n* Mehl *nt*

flourish [flɜrɪʃ] *vi* gedeihen; (*business*) gut laufen; (*boom*) florieren ▷ *vt* (*wave about*) schwenken

flourishing [flɜrɪʃɪŋ] *adj* blühend

flow [floʊ] *n* Fluss *m*; **to go with the ~** mit dem Strom schwimmen ▷ *vi* fließen

flower [flaʊər] *n* Blume *f* ▷ *vi* blühen

flower bed *n* Blumenbeet *nt*

flowerpot [flaʊərpɒt] *n* Blumentopf *m*

flown [floʊn] *pp of* **fly**

flu [flu] *n* (*fam*) Grippe *f*

fluent [fluənt] *adj* (*Italian etc*) fließend; **to be ~ in German** fließend Deutsch sprechen

fluid [fluɪd] *n* Flüssigkeit *f* ▷ *adj* flüssig

flung [flʌŋ] *pt, pp of* **fling**

fluorescent [flʊrɛsⁿnt] *adj* fluoreszierend, Leucht-

flush [flʌʃ] *n* (*lavatory*) Wasserspülung *f*; (*blush*) Röte *f* ▷ *vi* (*lavatory*) spülen

flute [flut] *n* Flöte *f*

fly [flaɪ] (**flew, flown**) *vt, vi* fliegen; **how time flies** wie die Zeit vergeht! ▷ *n* (*insect*) Fliege *f*; **fly/flies** *pl* (*on trousers*) Hosenschlitz *m*

fly-drive *n* Urlaub *m* mit Flug und Mietwagen

FM [ɛf ɛm] (*abbr*) **= frequency modulation** ≈ UKW

FO [ɛf oʊ] (*abbr*) **= Foreign Office** ≈ AA *nt*

foal [foʊl] *n* Fohlen *nt*

foam [foʊm] *n* Schaum *m* ▷ *vi* schäumen

fob off [fɒb ɔf] *vt*: **to fob sb off with sth** jdm etw andrehen

focus [foʊkəs] *n* Brennpunkt *m*; **in/out of ~** (*photo*) scharf/unscharf; (*camera*) scharf/unscharf eingestellt ▷ *vt* (*camera*) scharf stellen ▷ *vi* sich konzentrieren (*on* auf +*akk*)

fog [fɒg] *n* Nebel *m*

foggy [fɒgi] *adj* neblig

fog light *n* (*Auto: at rear*) Nebelschlussleuchte *f*

foil [fɔɪl] *vt* vereiteln ▷ *n* Folie *f*

fold [foʊld] *vt* falten ▷ *vi* (*fam: business*) eingehen ▷ *n* Falte *f*

folder [foʊldər] *n* (*portfolio*) Aktenmappe *f*; (*pamphlet*) Broschüre *f*; (*Inform*) Ordner *m*

folding [foʊldɪŋ] *adj* zusammenklappbar; (*bicycle, chair*) Klapp-

fold up *vt* (*map etc*) zusammenfalten; (*chair etc*) zusammenklappen ▷ *vi* (*fam: business*) eingehen

folk [foʊk] *n* Leute *pl*; (*Mus*) Folk *m*; **my ~s** *pl* (*fam*) meine Leute ▷ *adj* Volks-

follow [fɒloʊ] *vt* folgen +*dat*; (*pursue*) verfolgen; (*understand*) folgen können +*dat*; (*career, news etc*) verfolgen; **as ~s** wie folgt ▷ *vi* folgen; (*result*) sich ergeben (*from* aus)

follower [fɒloʊər] *n* Anhänger(in) *m(f)*

following [fɒloʊɪŋ] *adj* folgend; **the ~ day** am (darauf)folgenden Tag ▷ *prep* nach

follow up *vt* (*request, rumor*) nachgehen +*dat*, weiter verfolgen

follow-up *n* (*event, book etc*) Fortsetzung *f*

fond [fɒnd] *adj*: **to be ~ of** gernhaben
fondly [fɒndli] *adv* (*with love*) liebevoll
fondness [fɒndnɪs] *n* Vorliebe *f*; (*for people*) Zuneigung *f*
fondue [fɒndu] *n* Fondue *nt*
font [fɒnt] *n* Taufbecken *nt*; (*Typo*) Schriftart *f*
food [fud] *n* Essen *nt*, Lebensmittel *pl*; (*for animals*) Futter *nt*; (*groceries*) Lebensmittel *pl*
food poisoning [fud pɔɪzⁿnɪŋ] *n* Lebensmittelvergiftung *f*
food processor [fud prɒsɛsər] *n* Küchenmaschine *f*
foodstuff [fudstʌf] *n* Lebensmittel *nt*
fool [ful] *n* Idiot *m*, Narr *m*; **to make a ~ of oneself** sich blamieren ▷ *vt* (*deceive*) hereinlegen ▷ *vi*: **to ~ around** herumalbern; (*waste time*) herumtrödeln
foolish [fulɪʃ] *adj* dumm
foolproof [fulpruf] *adj* idiotensicher
foot [fut] (*pl* **feet**) *n* Fuß *m*; (*measure*) Fuß *m* (30,48 cm); **on ~** zu Fuß ▷ *vt* (*bill*) bezahlen
foot-and-mouth disease [futⁿnmauθ dɪzɪz] *n* Maul- und Klauenseuche *f*
footbridge [futbrɪdʒ] *n* Fußgängerbrücke *f*
footing [futɪŋ] *n* (*hold*) Halt *m*
footlights [futlaɪts] *npl* Rampenlicht *nt*
footnote [futnoʊt] *n* Fußnote *f*
footpath [futpæθ] *n* Fußweg *m*
footprint [futprɪnt] *n* Fußabdruck *m*
footwear [futwɛər] *n* Schuhwerk *nt*

KEYWORD

for [fər, STRONG fɔr] *prep* **1** für; **is this for me?** ist das für mich?; **the train for London** der Zug nach London; **he went for the paper** er ging die Zeitung holen; **give it to me – what for?** gib es mir – warum?
2 (*because of*) wegen; **for this reason** aus diesem Grunde
3 (*referring to distance*): **there is road construction for 5 mi** die Baustelle ist 5 mi lang; **we walked for miles** wir sind meilenweit gegangen
4 (*referring to time*) seit; (*with future sense*) für; **he was away for 2 years** er war zwei Jahre lang weg
5 (+*infin clauses*): **it is not for me to decide** das kann ich nicht entscheiden; **for this to be possible ...** damit dies möglich wird/wurde ...
6 (*in spite of*) trotz +*gen o* (*inf*) *dat*; **for all**

his complaints obwohl er sich ständig beschwert
▷ *conj* denn

forbade [fərbæd, -beɪd] *pt of* **forbid**
forbid [fərbɪd, fɔr-] (**forbade, forbidden**) *vt* verbieten
force [fɔrs] *n* Kraft *f*; (*compulsion*) Zwang *m*, Gewalt *f*; **to come into ~** in Kraft treten; **the F~s** *pl* die Streitkräfte ▷ *vt* zwingen
forced [fɔrst] *adj* (*smile*) gezwungen; **~ landing** Notlandung *f*
forceful [fɔrsfəl] *adj* kraftvoll
forceps [fɔrsɛps] *npl* Zange *f*
forearm [fɔrɑrm] *n* Unterarm *m*
forecast [fɔrkæst] *vt* voraussagen; (*weather*) vorhersagen ▷ *n* Vorhersage *f*
forefinger [fɔrfɪŋgər] *n* Zeigefinger *m*
foreground [fɔrgraʊnd] *n* Vordergrund *m*
forehand [fɔrhænd] *n* (*Sport*) Vorhand *f*
forehead [fɔrhɛd, fɔrɪd] *n* Stirn *f*
foreign [fɔrɪn] *adj* ausländisch
foreigner [fɔrɪnər] *n* Ausländer(in) *m(f)*
foreign exchange *n* Devisen *pl*
foreign language *n* Fremdsprache *f*
foreign minister *n* Außenminister(in) *m(f)*
foreign policy *n* Außenpolitik *f*
foremost [fɔrmoʊst] *adj* erste(r, s); (*leading*) führend
forerunner [fɔrrʌnər] *n* Vorläufer(in) *m(f)*
foresee [fɔrsi] (*irr*) *vt* vorhersehen
foreseeable [fɔrsiəbⁿl] *adj* absehbar
forest [fɔrɪst] *n* Wald *m*
forestry [fɔrɪstri] *n* Forstwirtschaft *f*
forever [fɔrɛvər, fər-] *adv* für immer
forgave [fərgeɪv] *pt of* **forgive**
forge [fɔrdʒ] *n* Schmiede *f* ▷ *vt* schmieden; (*fake*) fälschen
forger [fɔrdʒər] *n* Fälscher(in) *m(f)*
forgery [fɔrdʒəri] *n* Fälschung *f*
forget [fərgɛt] (**forgot, forgotten**) *vt, vi* vergessen; **to ~ about sth** etw vergessen
forgetful [fərgɛtfəl] *adj* vergesslich
forgetfulness [fərgɛtfəlnɪs] *n* Vergesslichkeit *f*
forget-me-not *n* Vergissmeinnicht *nt*
forgive [fərgɪv] (**forgave, forgiven**) (*irr*) *vt* verzeihen; **to ~ sb for sth** jdm etw verzeihen
forgot [fərgɒt] *pt of* **forget**
forgotten [fərgɒtⁿn] *pp of* **forget**
fork [fɔrk] *n* Gabel *f*; (*in road*) Gabelung *f* ▷ *vi* (*road*) sich gabeln
form [fɔrm] *n* (*shape*) Form *f*, Klasse *f*; (*document*) Formular *nt*; (*person*): **to be in**

good ~ in Form sein ▷ *vt* bilden
formal [fɔrmᵊl] *adj* förmlich, formell
formality [fɔrmælɪti] *n* Formalität *f*
format [fɔrmæt] *n* Format *nt* ▷ *vt* (*Inform*) formatieren
former [fɔrmər] *adj* frühere(r, s); (*opposite of latter*) erstere(r, s)
formerly [fɔrmərli] *adv* früher
formidable [fɔrmɪdəbᵊl, fərmɪd-] *adj* gewaltig; (*opponent*) stark
formula [fɔrmyələ] *n* Formel *f*
formulate [fɔrmyəleɪt] *vt* formulieren
forth [fɔrθ] *adv*: **and so** ~ und so weiter
forthcoming [fɔrθkʌmɪŋ] *adj* kommend, bevorstehend
fortieth [fɔrtiəθ] *adj* vierzigste(r, s); *see also* **eighth**
fortify [fɔrtɪfaɪ] *vt* verstärken; (*for protection*) befestigen
fortnight [fɔrtnaɪt] *n* vierzehn Tage *pl*
fortress [fɔrtrɪs] *n* Festung *f*
fortunate [fɔrtʃənɪt] *adj* glücklich; **I was** ~ ich hatte Glück
fortunately [fɔrtʃənɪtli] *adv* zum Glück
fortune [fɔrtʃən] *n* (*money*) Vermögen *nt*; **good** ~ Glück *nt*
fortune-teller [fɔrtʃᵊntɛlᵊr] *n* Wahrsager(in) *m(f)*
forty [fɔrti] *num* vierzig ▷ *n* Vierzig *f*; *see also* **eight**
forward [fɔrwərd] *adv* vorwärts ▷ *n* (*Sport*) Stürmer(in) *m(f)* ▷ *vt* (*send on*) nachsenden; (*Inform*) weiterleiten
forwards [fɔrwərdz] *adv* vorwärts
foster child [fɔstər-] *n* Pflegekind *nt*
foster parents *npl* Pflegeeltern *pl*
fought [fɔt] *pt, pp of* **fight**
foul [faʊl] *adj* (*weather*) schlecht; (*smell*) übel ▷ *n* (*Sport*) Foul *nt*
found [faʊnd] *pt, pp of* **find** ▷ *vt* (*establish*) gründen
foundations [faʊndeɪʃnz] *npl* Fundament *nt*
fountain [faʊntɪn] *n* Springbrunnen *m*
fountain pen *n* Füller *m*
four [fɔr] *num* vier ▷ *n* Vier *f*; *see also* **eight**
fourteen [fɔrtin] *num* vierzehn ▷ *n* Vierzehn *f*; *see also* **eight**
fourteenth [fɔrtinθ] *adj* vierzehnte(r, s); *see also* **eighth**
fourth [fɔrθ] *adj* vierte(r, s); *see also* **eighth**
four-wheel drive *n* Allradantrieb *m*; (*car*) Geländewagen *m*
fowl [faʊl] *n* Geflügel *nt*
fox [fɒks] *n* (*a. fig*) Fuchs *m*

fraction [frækʃ°n] *n* (*Math*) Bruch *m*; (*part*) Bruchteil *m*
fracture [fræktʃər] *n* (*Med*) Bruch *m* ▷ *vt* brechen
fragile [frædʒᵊl] *adj* zerbrechlich
fragment [frægmənt] *n* Bruchstück *nt*
fragrance [freɪgrəns] *n* Duft *m*
fragrant [freɪgrənt] *adj* duftend
frail [freɪl] *adj* gebrechlich
frame [freɪm] *n* Rahmen *m*; (*of spectacles*) Gestell *nt*; ~ **of mind** Verfassung *f* ▷ *vt* einrahmen; **to** ~ **sb** (*fam: incriminate*) jdm etwas anhängen
framework [freɪmwɜrk] *n* Rahmen *m*, Struktur *f*
France [fræns] *n* Frankreich *nt*
frank [fræŋk] *adj* offen
frankfurter [fræŋkfɜrtər] *n* (Frankfurter) Würstchen *nt*
frankly [fræŋkli] *adv* offen gesagt; **quite** ~ ganz ehrlich
frankness [fræŋknɪs] *n* Offenheit *f*
frantic [fræntɪk] *adj* (*activity*) hektisch; (*effort*) verzweifelt; ~ **with worry** außer sich vor Sorge
fraud [frɔd] *n* (*trickery*) Betrug *m*; (*person*) Schwindler(in) *m(f)*
freak [frik] *n* Anomalie *f*; (*animal, person*) Missgeburt *f*; (*fam: fan*) Fan *m*, Freak *m* ▷ *adj* (*conditions*) außergewöhnlich, seltsam
freak out [frik aʊt] *vi* (*fam*) ausflippen
freckle [frɛkᵊl] *n* Sommersprosse *f*
free [fri] *adj, adv* frei; (*without payment*) gratis, kostenlos; **for** ~ umsonst ▷ *vt* befreien
freebie [fribi] *n* (*fam*) Werbegeschenk *nt*; **it was a** ~ es war gratis
freedom [fridəm] *n* Freiheit *f*
free kick *n* (*Sport*) Freistoß *m*
freelance [frilæns] *adj* freiberuflich tätig; (*artist*) freischaffend ▷ *n* Freiberufler(in) *m(f)*
free-range *adj* (*hen*) frei laufend; ~ **eggs** *pl* Freilandeier *pl*
freeway [friweɪ] *n* (gebührenfreie) Autobahn
freeze [friz] (**froze, frozen**) *vi* (*feel cold*) frieren; (*of lake etc*) zufrieren; (*water etc*) gefrieren ▷ *vt* einfrieren
freezer [frizər] *n* Tiefkühltruhe *f*; (*in fridge*) Gefrierfach *nt*
freezing [frizɪŋ] *adj* eiskalt; **I'm** ~ mir ist eiskalt
freezing point *n* Gefrierpunkt *m*

freight [freɪt] n (goods) Fracht f; (money charged) Frachtgebühr f
freight car n Güterwagen m
freight train n Güterzug m
French [frentʃ] adj französisch ▷ n (language) Französisch nt; **the ~** pl die Franzosen
French bread n Baguette f
French dressing n Vinaigrette f
french fries npl Pommes frites pl
French kiss n Zungenkuss m
Frenchman [frentʃmən] (pl -men) n Franzose m
French toast n in Ei und Milch getunktes gebratenes Brot
French window(s) n(pl) Balkontür f, Terrassentür f
Frenchwoman [frentʃwumən] (pl -women) n Französin f
frequency [friːkwənsi] n Häufigkeit f; (Phys) Frequenz f
frequent [friːkwənt] adj häufig
frequently [friːkwəntli] adv häufig
fresco [freskoʊ] (pl -es) n Fresko nt
fresh [freʃ] adj frisch; (new) neu
freshen [freʃn] vi: **to ~ up** (person) sich frisch machen
freshman [freʃmən] (pl -men) n Erstsemester nt
freshwater fish [freʃwɔtər fɪʃ] n Süßwasserfisch m
Fri (abbr) = **Friday** Fr
friction [frɪkʃn] n (a. fig) Reibung f
friction tape n Isolierband nt
Friday [fraɪdeɪ, -di] n Freitag m; see also **Tuesday**
fridge [frɪdʒ] n (fam) Kühlschrank m
fried [fraɪd] adj gebraten; **~ potatoes** Bratkartoffeln pl; **~ egg** Spiegelei nt; **~ rice** gebratener Reis
friend [frend] n Freund(in) m(f); (less close) Bekannte(r) mf; **to make ~s with sb** sich mit jdm anfreunden; **we're good ~s** wir sind gut befreundet
friendly [frendli] adj freundlich; **to be ~ with sb** mit jdm befreundet sein ▷ n (Sport) Freundschaftsspiel nt
friendship [frendʃɪp] n Freundschaft f
fright [fraɪt] n Schrecken m
frighten [fraɪtᵊn] vt erschrecken; **to be ~ed** Angst haben
frightening [fraɪtᵊnɪŋ] adj beängstigend
frill [frɪl] n Rüsche f; **~s** (fam) Schnickschnack
fringe [frɪndʒ] n (edge) Rand m; (on shawl etc) Fransen pl
frivolous [frɪvələs] adj leichtsinnig; (remark) frivol
frizzy [frɪzi] adj kraus
frog [frɔg] n Frosch m

KEYWORD

from [frəm, STRONG fram] prep 1 (indicating starting place) von; (indicating origin etc) aus +dat; **a letter/telephone call from my sister** ein Brief/Anruf von meiner Schwester; **where do you come from?** woher kommen Sie?; **to drink from the bottle** aus der Flasche trinken
2 (indicating time) von ... an; (past) seit; **from one o'clock to** o until o **till two** von ein Uhr bis zwei; **from January (on)** ab Januar
3 (indicating distance) von ... (entfernt)
4 (indicating price, number etc) ab +dat; **from $10 to $10; there were from 20 to 30 people there** es waren zwischen 20 und 30 Leute da
5 (indicating difference): **he can't tell red from green** er kann nicht zwischen Rot und Grün unterscheiden; **to be different from sb/sth** anders sein als jd/etw
6 (because of, based on): **from what he says** aus dem, was er sagt; **weak from hunger** schwach vor Hunger

front [frʌnt] n Vorderseite f; (of house) Fassade f; (in war, of weather) Front f; (at seaside) Promenade f; **in ~, at the ~** vorne; **in ~ of** vor; **up ~** (in advance) vorher, im Voraus ▷ adj vordere(r, s), Vorder-; (first) vorderste(r, s); **~ door** Haustür f; **~ page** Titelseite f; **~ seat** Vordersitz m; **~ wheel** Vorderrad nt
frontier [frʌntɪər, frɒn-] n Grenze f
front-wheel drive n (Auto) Frontantrieb m
frost [frɔst] n Frost m; (white frost) Reif m
frosting [frɔstɪŋ] n Zuckerguss m
frosty [frɔsti] adj frostig
froth [frɔθ] n Schaum m
frothy [frɔθi] adj schaumig
frown [fraʊn] vi die Stirn runzeln
froze [froʊz] pt of **freeze**
frozen [froʊzᵊn] pp of **freeze** ▷ adj (food) tiefgekühlt, Tiefkühl-
fruit [fruːt] n (as collective, a. type) Obst nt; (single fruit, a. fig) Frucht f
fruit salad n Obstsalat m
frustrated [frʌstreɪtɪd] adj frustriert

frustration [frʌstreɪʃⁿn] *n* Frustration *f*, Frust *m*

fry [fraɪ] *vt* braten

frying pan [fraɪɪŋ pæn] *n* Bratpfanne *f*

fuchsia [fyuʃə] *n* Fuchsie *f*

fudge [fʌdʒ] *n weiche Karamellsüßigkeit*

fuel [fyuəl] *n* Kraftstoff *m*; (*for heating*) Brennstoff *m*

fuel consumption [fyuəl kənsʌmʃⁿn] *n* Kraftstoffverbrauch *m*

fuel gauge *n* Benzinuhr *f*

fuel oil *n* Gasöl *nt*

fuel rod *n* Brennstab *m*

fuel tank *n* Tank *m*; (*for oil*) Öltank *m*

fugitive [fyudʒɪtɪv] *n* Flüchtling *m*

fulfill [fʊlfɪl] *vt* erfüllen

full [fʊl] *adj* voll; (*person: satisfied*) satt; (*member, employment*) Voll(zeit)-; (*complete*) vollständig; **~ of ...** voller ... *gen*

full moon *n* Vollmond *m*

full-time *adj*: **~ job** Ganztagsarbeit *f*

fully [fʊli] *adv* völlig; (*recover*) voll und ganz; (*discuss*) ausführlich

fumble [fʌmbⁿl] *vi* herumfummeln (*with, at* an +*dat*)

fumes [fyumz] *npl* Dämpfe *pl*; (*of car*) Abgase *pl*

fun [fʌn] *n* Spaß *m*; **for fun** zum Spaß; **it's fun** es macht Spaß; **to make fun of** sich lustig machen über +*akk*

function [fʌŋkʃⁿn] *n* Funktion *f*; (*event*) Feier *f*; (*reception*) Empfang *m* ▷ *vi* funktionieren

function key *n* (*Inform*) Funktionstaste *f*

fund [fʌnd] *n* Fonds *m*; **~s** *pl* Geldmittel *pl*

fundamental [fʌndəmɛntⁿl] *adj* grundlegend

fundamentally [fʌndəmɛntⁿli] *adv* im Grunde

funding [fʌndɪŋ] *n* finanzielle Unterstützung

funeral [fyunərəl] *n* Beerdigung *f*

fungus [fʌŋgəs] (*pl* **fungi** *o* **funguses**) *n* Pilz *m*

funicular [fyunɪkyələr] *n* Seilbahn *f*

funnel [fʌnⁿl] *n* Trichter *m*; (*of steamer*) Schornstein *m*

funny [fʌni] *adj* (*amusing*) komisch, lustig; (*strange*) seltsam

fur [fɜr] *n* Pelz *m*; (*of animal*) Fell *nt*

furious [fyuəriəs] *adj* wütend (*with sb* auf jdn)

furnished [fɜrnɪʃt] *adj* möbliert

furniture [fɜrnɪtʃər] *n* Möbel *pl*; **piece of ~** Möbelstück *nt*

further [fɜrðər] *comparative of* **far** ▷ *adj* weitere(r, s); **~ education** Weiterbildung *f*; **until ~ notice** bis auf weiteres ▷ *adv* weiter

furthest [fɜrðɪst] *superlative of* **far** ▷ *adj* am weitesten entfernt ▷ *adv* am weitesten

fury [fyuəri] *n* Wut *f*

fuse [fyuz] *n* (*Elec*) Sicherung *f* ▷ *vi* (*Elec*) durchbrennen

fuse box *n* Sicherungskasten *m*

fuss [fʌs] *n* Theater *nt*; **to make a ~** (ein) Theater machen

fussy [fʌsi] *adj* (*difficult*) schwierig, kompliziert; (*attentive to detail*) pingelig

future [fyutʃər] *adj* künftig ▷ *n* Zukunft *f*

fuze [fyuz] *see* **fuse**

fuzzy [fʌzi] *adj* (*indistinct*) verschwommen; (*hair*) kraus

G

gable [geɪbᵊl] n Giebel m
gadget [gædʒɪt] n Vorrichtung f, Gerät nt
Gaelic [geɪlɪk, gælɪk] adj gälisch ▷ n (language) Gälisch nt
gain [geɪn] vt (obtain, win) gewinnen; (advantage, respect) sich verschaffen; (wealth) erwerben; (weight) zunehmen ▷ vi (improve) gewinnen (in an +dat); (clock) vorgehen ▷ n Gewinn m (in an +dat)
gale [geɪl] n Sturm m
gall bladder [gɔɪl-] n Gallenblase f
gallery [gæləri] n Galerie f, Museum nt
gallon [gælən] n Gallone f (3,79 l)
gallop [gæləp] n Galopp m ▷ vi galoppieren
gallstone [gɔlstoʊn] n Gallenstein m
Gambia [gæmbiə] n Gambia nt
gamble [gæmbᵊl] vi um Geld spielen, wetten ▷ n: it's a ~ es ist riskant
gambling [gæmblɪŋ] n Glücksspiel nt
game [geɪm] n Spiel nt; (animals) Wild nt; a ~ of chess eine Partie Schach; ~s (in school) Sport m
game show n (TV) Gameshow f
gang [gæŋ] n (of criminals, youths) Bande f, Gang f, Clique f ▷ vt: to ~ up on sich verschwören gegen
gangster [gæŋstər] n Gangster m
gangway [gæŋweɪ] n (for ship) Gangway f
gap [gæp] n (hole) Lücke f; (in time) Pause f; (in age) Unterschied m
gape [geɪp] vi (mit offenem Mund) starren
garage [gərɑʒ] n Garage f; (for repair) (Auto)werkstatt f; (for fuel) Tankstelle f
garbage [gɑrbɪdʒ] n Müll m; (fam: nonsense) Quatsch m
garbage can n Mülleimer m; (outside) Mülltonne f
garbage collector n Müllmann m
garbage truck n Müllwagen m
garden [gɑrdᵊn] n Garten m; public ~s Park m
garden center n Gartencenter nt
gardener [gɑrdənər] n Gärtner(in) m(f)
gardening [gɑrdənɪŋ] n Gartenarbeit f
gargle [gɑrgᵊl] vi gurgeln
gargoyle [gɑrgɔɪl] n Wasserspeier m
garlic [gɑrlɪk] n Knoblauch m
garlic bread n Knoblauchbrot nt
garlic butter n Knoblauchbutter f
gas [gæs] n Gas nt; (petroleum) Benzin nt;

to step on the gas Gas geben
gas cylinder n Gasflasche f
gas fire n Gasofen m
gasket [gæskɪt] n Dichtung f
gas lighter n (for cigarettes) Gasfeuerzeug nt
gas mask n Gasmaske f
gas meter n Gaszähler m
gasoline [gæsəlin] n Benzin nt
gasp [gæsp] vi keuchen; (in surprise) nach Luft schnappen
gas pedal n Gaspedal nt
gas pump n Zapfsäule f
gas station n Tankstelle f
gas tank n Benzintank m
gastric [gæstrɪk] adj Magen-; ~ flu Magen-Darm-Grippe f; ~ ulcer Magengeschwür nt
gate [geɪt] n Tor nt; (barrier) Schranke f; (Aviat) Gate nt, Flugsteig m
gateau [gætoʊ] (pl gateaux) n Torte f
gateway [geɪtweɪ] n Tor nt
gather [gæðər] vt (collect) sammeln; to ~ speed beschleunigen ▷ vi (assemble) sich versammeln; (understand) schließen (from aus)
gathering [gæðərɪŋ] n Versammlung f
gauge [geɪdʒ] n Meßgerät nt
gauze [gɔz] n Gaze f; (for bandages) Mull m
gave [geɪv] pt of give
gay [geɪ] adj (homosexual) schwul; gay marriage Homoehe (fam) f
gaze [geɪz] n Blick m ▷ vi starren
gear [gɪər] n (Auto) Gang m; (equipment) Ausrüstung f; (clothes) Klamotten pl; to change ~ schalten
gearbox [gɪərbɒks] n Getriebe nt
gear shift n Gangschaltung f
geese [gis] pl of goose
gel [dʒɛl] n Gel nt ▷ vi gelieren; they really gelled sie verstanden sich auf Anhieb
gem [dʒɛm] n Edelstein m; (fig) Juwel nt
Gemini [dʒɛmɪni] nsing (Astr) Zwillinge pl
gender [dʒɛndər] n Geschlecht nt
gene [dʒin] n Gen nt
general [dʒɛnᵊrəl] adj allgemein; ~ knowledge Allgemeinbildung f; ~ election Parlamentswahlen pl
generalize [dʒɛnᵊrəlaɪz] vi verallgemeinern
generally [dʒɛnᵊrəli] adv im Allgemeinen

generation [dʒɛnəreɪʃⁿn] n Generation f
generation gap n Generationsunterschied m
generator [dʒɛnəreɪtər] n Generator m
generosity [dʒɛnərɒsɪti] n Großzügigkeit f
generous [dʒɛnərəs] adj großzügig; (portion) reichlich
genetic [dʒɪnɛtɪk] adj genetisch; ~ **research** Genforschung f; ~ **technology** Gentechnik f
genetically modified [dʒɪnɛtɪkli mɒdɪfaɪd] adj gentechnisch verändert, genmanipuliert; see also **GM**
Geneva [dʒəniːvə] n Genf nt; **Lake ~** der Genfer See
genitals [dʒɛnɪtⁿlz] npl Geschlechtsteile pl
genitive [dʒɛnɪtɪv] n Genitiv m
genius [dʒiːnyəs] n Genie nt
gentle [dʒɛntⁿl] adj sanft; (touch) zart
gentleman [dʒɛntⁿlmən] (pl **-men**) n Herr m; (polite man) Gentleman m
genuine [dʒɛnyuɪn] adj echt
geographical [dʒiəgræfɪkⁿl] adj geografisch
geography [dʒiɒgrəfi] n Geografie f; (at school) Erdkunde f
geological [dʒiəlɒdʒɪkⁿl] adj geologisch
geology [dʒiɒlədʒi] n Geologie f
geometry [dʒiɒmɪtri] n Geometrie f
geranium [dʒɪreɪniəm] n Geranie f
gerbil [dʒɜːbɪl] n (Zool) Wüstenrennmaus f
germ [dʒɜːm] n Keim m; (Med) Bazillus m
German [dʒɜːmən] adj deutsch; **she's ~** sie ist Deutsche; ~ **shepherd** Deutscher Schäferhund ▷ n (person) Deutsche(r) mf; (language) Deutsch nt; **in ~** auf Deutsch
German measles n sing Röteln pl
Germany [dʒɜːməni] n Deutschland nt
gesture [dʒɛstʃər] n Geste f

KEYWORD

get [gɛt] (pt, pp **got**, pp **gotten**) vi 1 (become, be) werden; **to get old/tired** alt/müde werden; **to get married** heiraten
2 (go) (an)kommen, gehen
3 (begin): **to get to know sb** jdn kennenlernen; **let's get going** o **started!** fangen wir an!
4 (modal vb aux): **you've got to do it** du musst/Sie müssen es tun
▷ vt 1: **to get sth done** (do) etw machen; (have done) etw machen lassen; **to get sth going** o **to go** etw in Gang bringen o

bekommen; **to get sb to do sth** jdn dazu bringen, etw zu tun
2 (obtain: money, permission, results) erhalten; (find: job, appartment) finden; (fetch: person, object) holen; **to get sth for sb** jdm etw besorgen; **get me Mr Jones, please** (Tel) verbinde/verbinden Sie mich bitte mit Mr Jones; **get a life!** (annoyed) mach dich mal locker!, reg dich bloß ab!
3 (receive: present, letter) bekommen, kriegen; (acquire: reputation etc) erwerben
4 (catch) bekommen, kriegen; (hit: target etc) treffen, erwischen; **get him!** (to dog) fass!
5 (take, move) bringen; **to get sth to sb** jdm etw bringen
6 (understand) verstehen; (hear) mitbekommen; **I've got it!** ich hab's!
7 (have, possess): **to have got sth** etw haben

get across vi: **to ~ sth** über etw akk kommen ▷ vt: **to get sth across** (communicate) etw klarmachen
get along vi (people) (gut) zurecht-/auskommen (with) mit; (depart) sich akk auf den Weg machen
get around vi herumkommen um ▷ vt (fig: person) herumkriegen
get at vt (reach) herankommen an +akk; (facts) herausbekommen; **what are you getting at?** worauf wollen Sie hinaus?, was meinst du damit?; **to ~ sb** (nag) an jdm herumnörgeln
get away vi (leave) sich akk davonmachen, wegkommen; (escape): **to ~ from sth** von etw dat entkommen; **to ~ with sth** mit etw davonkommen
getaway [gɛtəweɪ] n Flucht f
get back vi (return) zurückkommen; (Tel): **to ~ to sb** jdn zurückrufen ▷ vt zurückbekommen
get by vi (pass) vorbeikommen; (manage) zurecht-/auskommen (on) mit
get down vi (her)untergehen; **to ~ to** in Angriff nehmen; (find time to do) kommen zu ▷ vt (depress) fertigmachen; **it gets me down** (fam) es macht mich fertig; **to get sth down** (write) etw aufschreiben
get in vi (train) ankommen; (arrive home) heimkommen
get into vt (enter) hinein-/hereinkommen in +akk; (car, train etc) einsteigen in +akk; (clothes) anziehen; (rage, panic etc) geraten in +akk; **to ~ trouble** in Schwierigkei-

ten kommen

get off vi (from train etc) aussteigen; (from horse etc) absteigen; (fam: be enthusiastic): **to ~ on sth** auf etw abfahren ▷ vt (nail, sticker) los-/abbekommen; (clothes) ausziehen

get on vi (progress) vorankommen; (be friends) auskommen; (age) alt werden; (onto train etc) einsteigen; (onto horse etc) aufsteigen ▷ vt etw +akk vorantreiben, mit etw akk loslegen

get out vi (of house) herauskommen; (of vehicle) aussteigen; ~! raus! ▷ vt (take out) herausholen; (stain, nail) herausbekommen

get out of vi (duty etc) herumkommen um

get over vi (illness) sich akk erholen von; (surprise) verkraften; (news) fassen; (loss) sich abfinden mit

get through vi (Tel) durchkommen (to) zu

get together vi zusammenkommen

get-together n Treffen nt

get up vi aufstehen ▷ vt hinaufbringen; (go up) hinaufgehen; (organize) auf die Beine stellen

get up to vi (reach) erreichen; (prank etc) anstellen

Ghana [gɑnə] n Ghana nt

gherkin [gɜrkɪn] n Gewürzgurke f

ghetto [gɛtoʊ] n (pl -es) n Ghetto nt

ghost [goʊst] n Gespenst nt; (of person) Geist m

giant [dʒaɪənt] n Riese m ▷ adj riesig

giblets [dʒɪblɪts] npl Geflügelinnereien pl

Gibraltar [dʒɪbrɔltər] n Gibraltar nt

giddy [gɪdi] adj schwindlig

gift [gɪft] n Geschenk nt; (talent) Begabung f

gifted [gɪftɪd] adj begabt

giftwrap [gɪftræp] vt als Geschenk verpacken

gigantic [dʒaɪgæntɪk] adj riesig

giggle [gɪgᵊl] vi kichern ▷ n Gekicher nt

gill [gɪl] n (of fish) Kieme f

gimmick [gɪmɪk] n (for sales, publicity) Gag m

gin [dʒɪn] n Gin m

ginger [dʒɪndʒər] n Ingwer m ▷ adj (color) kupferrot; (cat) rötlichgelb

ginger ale n Gingerale nt

ginger beer n Ingwerlimonade f

gingerbread [dʒɪndʒərbrɛd] n Lebkuchen m (mit Ingwergeschmack)

ginger(-haired) [dʒɪndʒər(hɛərd)] adj rotblond

gingerly [dʒɪndʒərli] adv (move) vorsichtig

gipsy [dʒɪpsi] n Zigeuner(in) m(f)

giraffe [dʒɪræf] n Giraffe f

girl [gɜrl] n Mädchen nt

girlfriend [gɜrlfrɛnd] n (feste) Freundin f

Girl Scout n Pfadfinderin f

gist [dʒɪst] n: **to get the ~ of it** das Wesentliche verstehen

give [gɪv] (gave, given) vt geben; (as present) schenken (to sb jdm); (state: name etc) angeben; (speech) halten; (blood) spenden; **to ~ sb sth** jdm etw geben/ schenken ▷ vi (yield) nachgeben

give away vt (give free) verschenken; (secret) verraten

give back vt zurückgeben

give in vi aufgeben

given [gɪvᵊn] pp of give ▷ adj (fixed) festgesetzt; (certain) bestimmt; **~ name** Vorname m ▷ conj: **~ that ...** angesichts der Tatsache, dass ...

give up vt, vi aufgeben

give way vi (collapse, yield) nachgeben; (traffic) die Vorfahrt beachten

glacier [gleɪʃər] n Gletscher m

glad [glæd] adj froh (about über); **I was ~ to hear that ...** es hat mich gefreut, dass ...

gladly [glædli] adv gerne

glance [glæns] n Blick m ▷ vi einen Blick werfen (at auf +akk)

gland [glænd] n Drüse f

glare [glɛər] n grelles Licht; (stare) stechender Blick ▷ vi (angrily): **to ~ at sb** jdn böse anstarren

glaring [glɛərɪŋ] adj (mistake) krass

glass [glɑs, glæs] n Glas nt; **~es** pl Brille f

glen [glɛn] n (SCOT) (enges) Bergtal nt

glide [glaɪd] vi gleiten; (hover) schweben

glider [glaɪdər] n Segelflugzeug nt

gliding [glaɪdɪŋ] n Segelfliegen nt

glimmer [glɪmər] n (of hope) Schimmer m

glimpse [glɪmps] n flüchtiger Blick

glitter [glɪtər] vi glitzern; (eyes) funkeln

glitzy [glɪtsi] adj (fam) glanzvoll, Schickimicki-

global [gloʊbᵊl] adj global, Welt-; **~ warming** die Erwärmung der Erdatmosphäre

globe [gloʊb] n (sphere) Kugel f; (world) Erdball m; (map) Globus m

gloomily [glumɪli], **gloomy** [glumɪ] adv, adj düster

glorious [glɔriəs] adj (victory, past) ruhmreich; (weather, day) herrlich

glory [glɔːri] *n* Herrlichkeit *f*
gloss [glɔs] *n* (*shine*) Glanz *m*
glossary [glɔsəri] *n* Glossar *nt*
glossy [glɔsi] *adj* (*surface*) glänzend ▷ *n* (*magazine*) Hochglanzmagazin *nt*
glove [glʌv] *n* Handschuh *m*
glove compartment *n* Handschuhfach *nt*
glow [gloʊ] *vi* glühen
glucose [gluːkoʊs] *n* Traubenzucker *m*
glue [gluː] *n* Klebstoff *m* ▷ *vt* kleben
glutton [glʌtⁿn] *n* Vielfraß *m*; **a ~ for punishment** (*fam*) Masochist *m*
GM [dʒiː ɛm] (*abbr*) = **genetically modified** Gen-; **GM foods** gentechnisch veränderte Lebensmittel
GMT [dʒiː ɛm tiː] (*abbr*) = **Greenwich Mean Time** WEZ *f*
go [goʊ] (**went, gone**) *vi* gehen; (*in vehicle, travel*) fahren; (*plane*) fliegen; (*road*) führen (*to* nach); (*depart: train, bus*) (ab)fahren; (*person*) (fort)gehen; (*disappear*) verschwinden; (*time*) vergehen; (*function*) gehen, funktionieren; (*machine, engine*) laufen; (*fit, suit*) passen (*with* zu); (*fail*) nachlassen; **I have to go to the doctor/to New York** ich muss zum Arzt/nach New York; **to go shopping** einkaufen gehen; **to go for a walk/swim** spazieren/schwimmen gehen; **has he gone yet?** ist er schon weg?; **the wine goes in the cabinet** der Wein kommt in den Schrank; **to get sth going** etw in Gang setzen; **to keep going** weitermachen; (*machine etc*) weiterlaufen; **how's the job going?** was macht der Job?; **his memory/eyesight is going** sein Gedächtnis lässt nach/seine Augen werden schwach; **to go deaf/mad/gray** taub/verrückt/grau werden ▷ *vb aux:* **to be going to do sth** etw tun werden; **I was going to do it** ich wollte es tun ▷ *n* (*pl* **-es**) (*attempt*) Versuch *m*; **can I have another go?** darf ich noch mal (probieren)?; **it's my go** ich bin dran; **in one go** auf einen Schlag; (*drink*) in einem Zug
go after *vt* nachlaufen +*dat*; (*in vehicle*) nachfahren +*dat*
go ahead *vi* (*in front*) vorausgehen; (*start*) anfangen
go-ahead *adj* (*progressive*) fortschrittlich ▷ *n* grünes Licht
goal [goʊl] *n* (*aim*) Ziel *nt*; (*Sport*) Tor *nt*
goalie [goʊli], **goalkeeper** *n* Torwart *m*, Torfrau *f*
goalpost [goʊlpoʊst] *n* Torpfosten *m*
goat [goʊt] *n* Ziege *f*

go away *vi* weggehen; (*on holiday, business*) verreisen
go back *vi* (*return*) zurückgehen; **we ~ a long way** (*fam*) wir kennen uns schon ewig
go by *vi* vorbeigehen; (*vehicle*) vorbeifahren; (*years, time*) vergehen ▷ *vt* (*judge by*) gehen nach
god [gɒd] *n* Gott *m*; **thank God** Gott sei Dank
godchild [gɒdtʃaɪld] *n* (*pl* **-children**) *n* Patenkind *nt*
goddaughter [gɒddɔːtər] *n* Patentochter *f*
goddess [gɒdɪs] *n* Göttin *f*
godfather [gɒdfaðər] *n* Pate *m*
godmother [gɒdmʌðər] *n* Patin *f*
go down *vi* (*sun, ship*) untergehen; (*flood, temperature*) zurückgehen; (*price*) sinken; **to ~ well/badly** gut/schlecht ankommen
godson [gɒdsʌn] *n* Patensohn *m*
goggles [gɒgⁿlz] *npl* Schutzbrille *f*; (*for skiing*) Skibrille *f*; (*for diving*) Taucherbrille *f*
go in *vi* hineingehen
going [goʊɪŋ] *adj* (*rate*) üblich
goings-on [goʊɪŋzɒn] *npl* Vorgänge *pl*
go into *vt* (*enter*) hineingehen in +*akk*; (*crash*) fahren gegen, hineinfahren in +*akk*; **to ~ teaching/politics/the army** Lehrer werden/in die Politik gehen/zum Militär gehen
go-kart [goʊkɑrt] *n* Gokart *m*
gold [goʊld] *n* Gold *nt*
golden [goʊldⁿn] *adj* golden
goldfish [goʊldfɪʃ] *n* Goldfisch *m*
gold-plated [goʊldpleɪtɪd] *adj* vergoldet
golf [gɒlf] *n* Golf *nt*
golf ball *n* Golfball *m*
golf club *n* Golfschläger *m*; (*association*) Golfklub *m*
golf course *n* Golfplatz *m*
golfer [gɒlfər] *n* Golfspieler(in) *m(f)*
gone [gɒn] *pp of* **go**; **he's ~** er ist weg ▷ *prep:* **just ~ three** kurz nach drei
good [gʊd] *n* (*benefit*) Wohl *nt*; (*morally good things*) Gute(s) *nt*; **for the ~ of** zum Wohle +*gen*; **it's for your own ~** es ist zu deinem/Ihrem Besten *o* Vorteil; **it's no ~** (*doing sth*) es hat keinen Sinn *o* Zweck; (*thing*) es taugt nichts; **for ~** für immer ▷ *adj* (**better, best**) gut; (*suitable*) passend; (*thorough*) gründlich; (*well-behaved*) brav; (*kind*) nett, lieb; **to be ~ at sports/math** gut in Sport/Mathe sein; **to be no ~ at sports/math** schlecht in Sport/Mathe sein;

it's ~ **for you** es tut dir gut; **this is ~ for colds** das ist gut gegen Erkältungen; **too ~ to be true** zu schön, um wahr zu sein; **this is just not ~ enough** so geht das nicht; **a ~ three hours** gute drei Stunden; **~ morning/evening** guten Morgen/Abend; **~ night** gute Nacht; **to have a ~ time** sich gut amüsieren

goodbye [gʊdbaɪ] *interj* auf Wiedersehen

Good Friday *n* Karfreitag *m*

good-looking [gʊdlʊkɪŋ] *adj* gut aussehend

goods [gʊdz] *npl* Waren *pl*, Güter *pl*

goodwill [gʊdwɪl] *n* Wohlwollen *nt*

go off *vi* (*depart*) weggehen; (*in vehicle*) wegfahren; (*lights*) ausgehen; (*milk etc*) sauer werden; (*gun, bomb, alarm*) losgehen ▷ *vt* (*dislike*) nicht mehr mögen

go on *vi* (*continue*) weitergehen; (*lights*) angehen; **to ~ with** *o* **doing sth** etw weitermachen

goose [gus] (*pl* **geese**) *n* Gans *f* ▷ *vt* (*fam*): **to ~ sb** jdn in den Arsch kneifen

gooseberry [gʊsberɪ] *n* Stachelbeere *f*

goose bumps [gʊsbʌmps] *n*, **goose pimples** *npl* Gänsehaut *f*

go out *vi* (*leave house*) hinausgehen; (*fire, light, person socially*) ausgehen; **to ~ for a meal** essen gehen

gorge [gɔrdʒ] *n* Schlucht *f*

gorgeous [gɔrdʒəs] *adj* wunderschön; **he's ~** er sieht toll aus

gorilla [gərɪlə] *n* Gorilla *m*

gossip [gɒsɪp] *n* (*talk*) Klatsch *m*; (*person*) Klatschtante *f* ▷ *vi* klatschen, tratschen

got [gɒt] *pt, pp of* **get**

gotten [gɒtʰn] *pp of* **get**

go up *vi* (*temperature, price*) steigen; (*lift*) hochfahren

govern [gʌvərn] *vt* regieren; (*province etc*) verwalten

government [gʌvərnmənt] *n* Regierung *f*

governor [gʌvərnər] *n* Gouverneur(in) *m(f)*

govt (*abbr*) = **government** Regierung *f*

go without *vt* verzichten auf +*akk*; (*food, sleep*) auskommen ohne

gown [gaʊn] *n* Abendkleid *nt*; (*academic*) Robe *f*

GP [dʒi pi] (*abbr*) = **General Practitioner** Allgemeinarzt *m*, Allgemeinärztin *f*

GPS [dʒi pi ɛs] *n* (*abbr*) = **global positioning system** GPS *nt*

grab [græb] *vt* packen; (*person*) schnappen

grace [greɪs] *n* Anmut *f*; (*prayer*) Tischgebet *nt*; **5 days' ~** 5 Tage Aufschub

graceful [greɪsfəl] *adj* anmutig

grade [greɪd] *n* Niveau *nt*; (*of goods*) Güteklasse *f*; (*mark*) Note *f*; (*year*) Klasse *f*; **to make the ~** es schaffen

grade crossing *n* Bahnübergang *m*

grade school *n* Grundschule *f*

gradient [greɪdiənt] *n* (*upward*) Steigung *f*; (*downward*) Gefälle *nt*

gradual [grædʒuəl] *adj*, **gradually** *adv* allmählich

graduate [*n* grædʒuɪt, *vb* grædʒueɪt] *n* Uniabsolvent(in) *m(f)*, Hochschulabsolvent(in) *m(f)* ▷ *vi* einen akademischen Grad erwerben

graduate student *n* jd, der seine Studien nach dem ersten akademischen Grad weiterführt

grain [greɪn] *n* (*cereals*) Getreide *nt*; (*of corn, sand*) Korn *nt*; (*in wood*) Maserung *f*

gram [græm] *n* Gramm *nt*

grammar [græmər] *n* Grammatik *f*

gran [græn] *n* (*fam*) Oma *f*

grand [grænd] *adj* (*pej*) hochnäsig; (*posh*) vornehm ▷ *n* (*fam*) 1000 Dollar bzw. 1000 Pfund

granddad [grændæd] *n* (*fam*) Opa *m*

granddaughter [grændɔtər] *n* Enkelin *f*

grandfather [grænfɑðər] *n* Großvater *m*

grandma [grænmɑ] *n* (*fam*) Oma *f*

grandmother [grænmʌðər] *n* Großmutter *f*

grandpa [grænpɑ] *n* (*fam*) Opa *m*

grandparents [grænpeərənts] *npl* Großeltern *pl*

grandson [grænsʌn] *n* Enkel *m*

grandstand [grændstænd] *n* (*Sport*) Tribüne *f*

granny [grænɪ] *n* (*fam*) Oma *f*

grant [grænt] *vt* gewähren (*sb sth* jdm etw); **to take sb/sth for ~ed** jdn/etw als selbstverständlich hinnehmen ▷ *n* Subvention *f*, finanzielle Unterstützung *f*; (*for university*) Stipendium *nt*

grape [greɪp] *n* Weintraube *f*

grapefruit [greɪpfrut] *n* Grapefruit *f*

grape juice *n* Traubensaft *m*

graph [græf] *n* Diagramm *nt*

graphic [græfɪk] *adj* grafisch; (*description*) anschaulich

grasp [græsp] *vt* ergreifen; (*understand*) begreifen

grass [græs] *n* Gras *nt*; (*lawn*) Rasen *m*

grasshopper [græshɒpər] *n* Heuschrecke *f*

grate [greɪt] *n* Feuerrost *m* ▷ *vi* kratzen ▷ *vt* (*cheese*) reiben

grateful [greɪtfəl] *adj*, **gratefully** *adv* dankbar

grater [greɪtər] *n* Reibe *f*

gratifying [grætɪfaɪɪŋ] *adj* erfreulich

gratitude [grætɪtud] *n* Dankbarkeit *f*

grave [greɪv] *n* Grab *nt* ▷ *adj* ernst; (*mistake*) schwer

gravel [græv°l] *n* Kies *m*

graveyard [greɪvyɑrd] *n* Friedhof *m*

gravity [grævɪti] *n* Schwerkraft *f*; (*seriousness*) Ernst *m*

gravy [greɪvi] *n* Bratensoße *f*

gray [greɪ] *adj* grau

gray-haired [greɪ(heərd)] *adj* grauhaarig

graze [greɪz] *vi* (*animals*) grasen ▷ *vt* (*touch*) streifen; (*Med*) abschürfen ▷ *n* (*Med*) Abschürfung *f*

grease [gris] *n* (*fat*) Fett *nt*; (*lubricant*) Schmiere *f* ▷ *vt* einfetten; (*Tech*) schmieren

greasy [grisi, -zi] *adj* fettig; (*hands, tools*) schmierig; (*fam: person*) schleimig

great [greɪt] *adj* groß; (*fam: good*) großartig, super; **a ~ deal of** viel

Great Britain [greɪt brɪt°n] *n* Großbritannien *nt*

great-grandfather *n* Urgroßvater *m*

great-grandmother *n* Urgroßmutter *f*

greatly [greɪtli] *adv* sehr; **~ disappointed** zutiefst enttäuscht

Greece [gris] *n* Griechenland *nt*

greed [grid] *n* Gier *f* (*for* nach); (*for food*) Gefräßigkeit *f*

greedy [gridi] *adj* gierig; (*for food*) gefräßig

Greek [grik] *adj* griechisch ▷ *n* (*person*) Grieche *m*, Griechin *f*; (*language*) Griechisch *nt*; **it's all ~ to me** ich verstehe nur Bahnhof

green [grin] *adj* grün; **~ with envy** grün/gelb vor Neid ▷ *n* (*color; for golf*) Grün *nt*; (*village green*) Dorfwiese *f*; **~s** (*vegetables*) grünes Gemüse; **the G~s, the G~ Party** (*Pol*) die Grünen

green bean *n* grüne Bohne

green card *n* (*work permit*) Arbeitserlaubnis *f*

greenhouse [grinhaʊs] *n* Gewächshaus *nt*; **~ effect** Treibhauseffekt *m*

Greenland [grinlənd] *n* Grönland *nt*

green onion *n* Frühlingszwiebel *f*

green pepper *n* grüner Paprika

green salad *n* grüner Salat

Greenwich Mean Time [grɛnɪtʃ min taɪm] *n* westeuropäische Zeit

greet [grit] *vt* grüßen

greeting [gritɪŋ] *n* Gruß *m*

grew [gru] *pt of* **grow**

greyhound [greɪhaʊnd] *n* Windhund *m*

grid [grɪd] *n* Gitter *nt*

gridlock [grɪdlɒk] *n* Verkehrsinfarkt *m*

gridlocked [grɪdlɒkt] *adj* (*roads*) völlig verstopft; (*talks*) festgefahren

grief [grif] *n* Kummer *m*; (*over loss*) Trauer *f*

grievance [griv°ns] *n* Beschwerde *f*

grieve [griv] *vi* trauern (*for* um)

grill [grɪl] *n* (*on cooker*) Grill *m* ▷ *vt* grillen

grim [grɪm] *adj* (*face, humour*) grimmig; (*situation, prospects*) trostlos

grin [grɪn] *n* Grinsen *nt* ▷ *vi* grinsen

grind [graɪnd] (**ground, ground**) *vt* mahlen; (*sharpen*) schleifen; (*meat*) durchdrehen, hacken

grip [grɪp] *n* Griff *m*; **get a ~** nimm dich zusammen!; **to get to ~s with sth** etw in den Griff bekommen ▷ *vt* packen

gripping [grɪpɪŋ] *adj* (*exciting*) spannend

groan [groʊn] *vi* stöhnen (*with* vor +*dat*)

grocer [groʊsər] *n* Lebensmittelhändler(in) *m(f)*; (*for fruit and vegetables*) Obst- und Gemüsehändler(in) *m(f)*

groceries [groʊs°riz] *npl* Lebensmittel *pl*

groin [grɔɪn] *n* (*Anat*) Leiste *f*

groin pull *n* (*Med*) Leistenbruch *m*

groom [grum] *n* Bräutigam *m* ▷ *vt*: **well ~ed** gepflegt

grope [groʊp] *vi* tasten ▷ *vt* (*sexually harrass*) befummeln

gross [groʊs] *adj* (*coarse*) derb; (*extreme: negligence, error*) grob; (*disgusting*) ekelhaft; (*Comm*) brutto; **~ national product** Bruttosozialprodukt *nt*; **~ salary** Bruttogehalt *nt*

ground [graʊnd] *pt, pp of* **grind** ▷ *n* Boden *m*, Erde *f*; (*Sport*) Platz *m*; **~s** *pl* (*around house*) (Garten)anlagen *pl*; (*reasons*) Gründe *pl*; (*of coffee*) Satz *m*; **on the ~s of** aufgrund von

ground meat *n* Hackfleisch *nt*

group [grup] *n* Gruppe *f* ▷ *vt* gruppieren

grouse [graʊs] (*pl* -) *n* (*bird*) Schottisches Moorhuhn; (*complaint*) Nörgelei *f*

grow [groʊ] (**grew, grown**) *vi* wachsen; (*increase*) zunehmen (*in* an); (*become*) werden; **to ~ old** alt werden; **to ~ into** sich entwickeln zu ... ▷ *vt* (*crop, plant*) ziehen; (*commercially*) anbauen; **I'm ~ing a**

beard ich lasse mir einen Bart wachsen
growing [grəʊɪŋ] *adj* wachsend; **a ~ number of people** immer mehr Leute
growl [graʊl] *vi* knurren
grown [grəʊn] *pp of* **grow**
grown-up *adj* erwachsen ▷ *n* Erwachsene(r) *mf*
growth [grəʊθ] *n* Wachstum *nt*; (*increase*) Zunahme *f*; (*Med*) Wucherung *f*
grow up *vi* aufwachsen; (*mature*) erwachsen werden
grubby [grʌbi] *adj* schmuddelig
grudge [grʌdʒ] *n* Abneigung *f* (*against* gegen) ▷ *vt*: **to ~ sb sth** jdm etw nicht gönnen
grueling [gruəlɪŋ] *adj* aufreibend; (*pace*) mörderisch
gruesome [grusəm] *adj* grausig
grumble [grʌmbˀl] *vi* murren (*about* über +*akk*)
grumpy [grʌmpi] *adj* (*fam*) mürrisch, grantig
grunt [grʌnt] *vi* grunzen
G-string [dʒi strɪŋ] *n* String *m*, Stringtanga *m*
guarantee [gærənti] *n* Garantie *f* (*of* für); **it's still under ~** es ist noch Garantie darauf ▷ *vt* garantieren
guard [gard] *n* (*sentry*) Wache *f*; (*in prison*) Wärter(in) *m(f)* ▷ *vt* bewachen; **a closely ~ed secret** ein streng gehütetes Geheimnis
guardian [gardiən] *n* Vormund *m*; **~ angel** Schutzengel *m*
guardrail *n* Leitplanke *f*
guess [gɛs] *n* Vermutung *f*; (*estimate*) Schätzung *f*; **have a ~ rate** mal! ▷ *vt, vi* raten; (*estimate*) schätzen; **I ~ you're right** du hast wohl recht; **I ~ so** ich glaube schon
guest [gɛst] *n* Gast *m*; **be my ~** nur zu!
guest room *n* Gästezimmer *nt*
guidance [gaɪdˀns] *n* (*direction*) Leitung *f*; (*advice*) Rat *m*; (*counseling*) Beratung *f*; **for your ~** zu Ihrer Orientierung
guide [gaɪd] *n* (*person*) Führer(in) *m(f)*;

(*tour*) Reiseleiter(in) *m(f)*; (*book*) Führer *m* ▷ *vt* führen
guidebook [gaɪdbʊk] *n* Reiseführer *m*
guided tour [gaɪdɪd tʊər] *n* Führung *f* (*of* durch)
guidelines [gaɪdlaɪnz] *npl* Richtlinien *pl*
guilt [gɪlt] *n* Schuld *f*
guilty [gɪlti] *adj* schuldig (*of gen*); (*look*) schuldbewusst; **to have a ~ conscience** ein schlechtes Gewissen haben
guinea pig [gɪni-] *n* Meerschweinchen *nt*; (*person*) Versuchskaninchen *nt*
guitar [gɪtar] *n* Gitarre *f*
gulf [gʌlf] *n* Golf *m*; (*gap*) Kluft *f*
Gulf States *npl* Golfstaaten *pl*
gull [gʌl] *n* Möwe *f*
gullible [gʌlɪbˀl] *adj* leichtgläubig
gulp [gʌlp] *n* (kräftiger) Schluck ▷ *vi* schlucken
gum [gʌm] *n* (*around teeth, usu pl*) Zahnfleisch *nt*; (*chewing gum*) Kaugummi *m*
gun [gʌn] *n* Schusswaffe *f*; (*rifle*) Gewehr *nt*; (*pistol*) Pistole *f*
gunfire [gʌnfaɪr] *n* Schüsse *pl*, Geschützfeuer *nt*
gunpowder [gʌnpaʊdər] *n* Schießpulver *nt*
gunshot [gʌnʃɒt] *n* Schuss *m*
gush [gʌʃ] *vi* (heraus)strömen (*from* aus)
gut [gʌt] *n* Darm *m*; **guts** *pl* (*intestines*) Eingeweide; (*courage*) Mumm *m*
gutter [gʌtər] *n* (*for roof*) Dachrinne *f*; (*in street*) Rinnstein *m*, Gosse *f*
guy [gaɪ] *n* (*man*) Typ *m*, Kerl *m*; **guys** *pl* Leute *pl*
gym [dʒɪm] *n* Turnhalle *f*; (*for working out*) Fitnesscenter *nt*
gymnasium [dʒɪmneɪziəm] *n* Turnhalle *f*
gymnastics [dʒɪmnæstɪks] *nsing* Turnen *nt*
gynecologist [gaɪnɪkɒlədʒɪst] *n* Frauenarzt *m*, Frauenärztin *f*, Gynäkologe *m*, Gynäkologin *f*
gynecology [gaɪnɪkɒlədʒi] *n* Gynäkologie *f*, Frauenheilkunde *f*
gypsy [dʒɪpsi] *n* Zigeuner(in) *m(f)*

g

H

habit [ˈhæbɪt] *n* Gewohnheit *f*
habitual [həˈbɪtʃuəl] *adj* gewohnt; (*drinker, liar*) gewohnheitsmäßig
hack [hæk] *vt* hacken
hacker [ˈhækər] *n* (*Inform*) Hacker(in) *m(f)*
had [hæd] *pt, pp of* **have**
haddock [ˈhædək] *n* Schellfisch *m*
hadn't [ˈhædⁿt] *contr of* **had not**
haggis [ˈhægɪs] *n* (*SCOT*) mit gehackten Schafsinnereien und Haferschrot gefüllter Schafsmagen
Hague [heɪg] *n*: **the ~** Den Haag
hail [heɪl] *n* Hagel *m* ▷ *vi* hageln ▷ *vt*: **to ~ sb as sth** jdn als etw feiern
hailstone [ˈheɪlstoun] *n* Hagelkorn *nt*
hailstorm [ˈheɪlstɔːrm] *n* Hagelschauer *m*
hair [hɛər] *n* Haar *nt*, Haare *pl*; **to do one's ~** sich frisieren; **to get one's ~ cut** sich *dat* die Haare schneiden lassen
hairbrush [ˈhɛərbrʌʃ] *n* Haarbürste *f*
haircut [ˈhɛərkʌt] *n* Haarschnitt *m*; **to have a ~** sich *dat* die Haare schneiden lassen
hairdo [ˈhɛərduː] (*pl* **-s**) *n* Frisur *f*
hairdresser [ˈhɛərdrɛsər] *n* Friseur *m*, Friseuse *f*
hairdryer [ˈhɛərdraɪər] *n* Haartrockner *m*; (*hand-held*) Fön® *m*; (*over head*) Trockenhaube *f*
hair gel *n* Haargel *nt*
hairpin [ˈhɛərpɪn] *n* Haarnadel *f*
hair remover [hɛər rɪmuːvər] *n* Enthaarungsmittel *nt*
hair spray *n* Haarspray *nt*
hair style *n* Frisur *f*
hairy [ˈhɛəri] *adj* haarig, behaart; (*fam: dangerous*) brenzlig
hake [heɪk] *n* Seehecht *m*
half [hæf] (*pl* **halves**) *n* Hälfte *f*; (*Sport: of game*) Halbzeit *f*; **to cut in ~** halbieren ▷ *adj* halb; **three and a ~ pounds** dreieinhalb Pfund; **~ an hour, a ~ hour** eine halbe Stunde; **one and a ~** eineinhalb, anderthalb ▷ *adv* halb, zur Hälfte; **~ past three** halb vier; **at ~ past** um halb; **~ asleep** fast eingeschlafen; **she's ~ German** sie ist zur Hälfte Deutsche; **~ as big as** halb so groß (wie)
half-hearted [hæfˈhɑːrtɪd] *adj* halbherzig
half-hour *n* halbe Stunde
half moon *n* Halbmond *m*
half pint *n* ≈ Viertelliter *m o nt*

half price *n*: **at ~** zum halben Preis
half-time *n* Halbzeit *f*
halfway [ˈhæfweɪ] *adv* auf halbem Wege
halfwit [ˈhæfwɪt] *n* (*fam*) Trottel *m*
halibut [ˈhælɪbət] *n* Heilbutt *m*
hall [hɔːl] *n* (*building*) Halle *f*; (*for audience*) Saal *m*; (*entrance hall*) Flur *m*; (*large*) Diele *f*
hallmark [ˈhɔːlmɑːrk] *n* Stempel *m*; (*fig*) Kennzeichen *nt*
hallo [hæˈlou] *interj* hallo
Halloween [hæləˈwiːn] *n* Halloween *nt* (*Tag vor Allerheiligen, an dem sich Kinder verkleiden und von Tür zu Tür gehen*)

HALLOWEEN

Hallow∋en ist der 31. Oktober, der Vorabend von Allerheiligen, und nach altem Glauben der Abend, an dem man Geister und Hexen sehen kann. In Großbritannien und vor allem in den USA feiern die Kinder Hallowe'en, indem sie sich verkleiden und mit selbst gemachten Laternen aus Kürbissen von Tür zu Tür ziehen.

halo [ˈheɪlou] (*pl* **-es**) *n* (*of saint*) Heiligenschein *m*
halt [hɔːlt] *n* Pause *f*, Halt *m*; **to come to a ~** zum Stillstand kommen ▷ *vt, vi* anhalten
halve [hæv] *vt* halbieren
ham [hæm] *n* Schinken *m*; **ham and eggs** Schinken mit Spiegelei
hamburger [ˈhæmbɜːrgər] *n* (*Gastr*) Hamburger *m*
hammer [ˈhæmər] *n* Hammer *m* ▷ *vt, vi* hämmern
hammock [ˈhæmək] *n* Hängematte *f*
hamper [ˈhæmpər] *vt* behindern ▷ *n* (*as gift*) Geschenkkorb *m*; (*for picnic*) Picknickkorb *m*
hamster [ˈhæmstər] *n* Hamster *m*
hand [hænd] *n* Hand *f*; (*of clock, instrument*) Zeiger *m*; (*in card game*) Blatt *nt*; **to be made by ~** Handarbeit sein; **~s up!** Hände hoch!; (*at school*) meldet euch!; **~s off!** Finger weg!; **on the one ~ ..., on the other ~ ...** einerseits ..., andererseits ...; **to give sb a ~** jdm helfen (*with* bei); **it's in his ~s** er hat es in der Hand; **to be in good ~s** gut aufgehoben sein; **to get out of ~**

außer Kontrolle geraten ▷ *vt* (*pass*) reichen (*to sb* jdm)

handbook [hændbʊk] *n* Handbuch *nt*

handcuffs [hændkʌfs] *npl* Handschellen *pl*

hand down *vt* (*tradition*) überliefern; (*heirloom*) vererben

handful [hændfʊl] *n* Handvoll *f*

handheld PC [hændhɛld piːsiː] *n* Handheld *m*

handicap [hændikæp] *n* Behinderung *f*, Handikap *nt* ▷ *vt* benachteiligen

handicapped [hændikæpt] *adj* behindert; **the ~** die Behinderten

handicraft [hændikræft] *n* Kunsthandwerk *nt*

hand in *vt* einreichen; (*at school, university etc*) abgeben

handkerchief [hæŋkətʃif] *n* Taschentuch *nt*

handle [hænd⁰l] *n* Griff *m*; (*of door*) Klinke *f*; (*of cup etc*) Henkel *m*; (*for winding*) Kurbel *f* ▷ *vt* (*touch*) anfassen; (*deal with: matter*) sich befassen mit; (*people, machine etc*) umgehen mit; (*situation, problem*) fertig werden mit

handlebars [hænd⁰lbɑːz] *npl* Lenkstange *f*

hand luggage *n* Handgepäck *nt*

handmade [hændmeɪd] *adj* handgefertigt; **to be ~** Handarbeit sein

hand out *vt* verteilen

handout [hændaʊt] *n* (*sheet*) Handout *nt*, Thesenpapier *nt*

hand over *vt* übergeben

handset [hændsɛt] *n* Hörer *m*; **please replace the ~** bitte legen Sie auf

hands-free phone [hændzfriː fəʊn] *n* Freisprechanlage *f*

handshake [hændʃeɪk] *n* Händedruck *m*

handsome [hænsəm] *adj* (*man*) gut aussehend

hands-on [hændzɒn] *adj* praxisorientiert; **~ experience** praktische Erfahrung

handwriting [hændraɪtɪŋ] *n* Handschrift *f*

handy [hændi] *adj* (*useful*) praktisch

hang [hæŋ] (**hung, hung**) *vt* (auf)hängen; (*execute:* **hanged, hanged**) hängen; **to ~ sth on sth** etw an etw *akk* hängen ▷ *vi* hängen ▷ *n*: **he's got the ~ of it** er hat den Dreh raus

hangar [hæŋər] *n* Flugzeughalle *f*

hanger [hæŋər] *n* Kleiderbügel *m*

hang glider *n* (Flug)drachen *m*; (*person*) Drachenflieger(in) *m(f)*

hang gliding *n* Drachenfliegen *nt*

hang on *vi* sich festhalten (*to* an +*dat*); (*fam: wait*) warten; **to ~ to sth** etw behalten

hangover [hæŋəʊvər] *n* (*bad head*) Kater *m*; (*relic*) Überbleibsel *nt*

hang up *vi* (*Tel*) auflegen ▷ *vt* aufhängen

hankie [hæŋki] *n* (*fam*) Taschentuch *nt*

happen [hæpən] *vi* geschehen; (*sth strange, unpleasant*) passieren; **if anything should ~ to me** wenn mir etwas passieren sollte; **it won't ~ again** es wird nicht wieder vorkommen; **I ~ed to be passing** ich kam zufällig vorbei

happening [hæpənɪŋ] *n* Ereignis *nt*, Happening *nt*

happily [hæpɪli] *adv* fröhlich, glücklich; (*luckily*) glücklicherweise

happiness [hæpɪnɪs] *n* Glück *nt*

happy [hæpi] *adj* glücklich; (*satisfied*): **with sth** mit etw zufrieden; (*willing*): **to be ~ to do sth** etw gerne tun; **H~ New Year** ein glückliches Neues Jahr!; **H~ Birthday** herzlichen Glückwunsch zum Geburtstag!

happy hour *n* Happy Hour *f* (*Zeit, in der man in Bars Getränke zu günstigeren Preisen bekommt*)

harass [hərəs, hærəs] *vt* (ständig) belästigen

harassment [hərəsmənt, hærəs-] *n* Belästigung *f*; (*at work*) Mobbing *nt*; **sexual ~** sexuelle Belästigung

harbor [hɑːbər] *n* Hafen *m*

hard [hɑːd] *adj* hart; (*difficult*) schwer, schwierig; (*harsh*) hart(herzig); **don't be ~ on him** sei nicht zu streng zu ihm; **it's ~ to believe** es ist kaum zu glauben ▷ *adv* (*work*) schwer; (*run*) schnell; (*rain, snow*) stark; **to try ~/-er** sich *dat* große/mehr Mühe geben

hardback [hɑːdbæk] *n* gebundene Ausgabe

hard-boiled [hɑːdbɔɪld] *adj* (*egg*) hart gekocht

hard copy *n* (*Inform*) Ausdruck *m*

hard disk *n* (*Inform*) Festplatte *f*

harden [hɑːd⁰n] *vt* härten ▷ *vi* hart werden

hardened [hɑːd⁰nd] *adj* (*person*) abgehärtet (*to* gegen)

hard-hearted [hɑːdhɑːtɪd] *adj* hartherzig

hardliner [hɑːdlaɪnər] *n* Hardliner(in) *m(f)*

hardly [hɑːdli] *adv* kaum; **~ ever** fast nie

h

hardship [hɑːdʃɪp] n Not f

hardware [hɑːdwɛr] n (Inform) Hardware f; (Comm) Haushalts- und Eisenwaren pl

hard-working [hɑːdwɜːkɪŋ] adj fleißig, tüchtig

hare [hɛər] n Hase m

harm [hɑːm] n Schaden m; (bodily) Verletzung f; **it wouldn't do any ~** es würde nicht schaden ▷ vt schaden +dat; (person) verletzen

harmful [hɑːmfəl] adj schädlich

harmless [hɑːmlɪs] adj harmlos

harp [hɑːp] n Harfe f

harsh [hɑːʃ] adj (climate, voice) rau; (light, sound) grell; (severe) hart, streng

harvest [hɑːvɪst] n Ernte f; (time) Erntezeit f ▷ vt ernten

has [hæz] present of **have**

hash [hæʃ] n (Gastr) Haschee nt; (fam: hashish) Haschisch nt; **to make a ~ of sth** etw vermasseln

hash browns npl ≈ Kartoffelpuffer/Rösti mit Zwiebeln pl

hasn't [hæzˀnt] contr of **has not**

hassle [hæsˀl] n Ärger m; (fuss) Theater nt; **no ~** kein Problem ▷ vt bedrängen

haste [heɪst] n Eile f

hastily [heɪstɪli] adv, **hasty** adj hastig; (rash) vorschnell

hat [hæt] n Hut m

hatch [hætʃ] n (Naut) Luke f; (in house) Durchreiche f

hatchback [hætʃbæk] n (car) Wagen m mit Hecktür

hate [heɪt] vt hassen; **I ~ doing this** ich mache das sehr ungern ▷ n Hass m (of auf +akk)

haul [hɔːl] vt ziehen, schleppen ▷ n (booty) Beute f

haunted [hɔːntɪd] adj: **a ~ house** ein Haus, in dem es spukt

KEYWORD

have [həv, STRONG hæv] (pt, pp **had**) vb aux
1 haben; (esp with vbs of motion) sein; **to have arrived/slept** angekommen sein/geschlafen haben; **to have been** gewesen sein; **having eaten** o **when he had eaten, he left** nachdem er gegessen hatte, ging er

2 (in tag questions): **you've done it, haven't you?** du hast/Sie haben es doch gemacht, oder nicht?

3 (in short answers and questions): **you've made a mistake – so I have/no I haven't** du hast/Sie haben einen Fehler gemacht – ja, stimmt/nein; **we haven't paid – yes we have!** wir haben nicht bezahlt – doch!; **I've been there before, have you?** ich war schon einmal da, du/Sie auch?

▷ modal vb aux (be obliged: #): **to have (got) to do sth** etw tun müssen; **you haven't to tell her** du darfst es ihr nicht erzählen

▷ vt **1** (possess) haben; **he has (got) blue eyes** er hat blaue Augen; **I have (got) an idea** ich habe eine Idee

2 (referring to meals etc): **to have breakfast/a cigarette** frühstücken/eine Zigarette rauchen

3 (receive, obtain etc) haben; **may I have your address?** kann ich deine/Ihre Adresse haben?; **to have a baby** ein Kind bekommen

4 (maintain, allow): **he will have it that he is right** er besteht darauf, dass er recht hat; **I won't have it** das lasse ich mir nicht bieten

5: **to have sth done** etw machen lassen; **to have sb do sth** jdn etw machen lassen; **he soon had them all laughing** er brachte sie alle zum Lachen

6 (experience, suffer): **she had her bag stolen** man hat ihr die Tasche gestohlen; **he had his arm broken** er hat sich den Arm gebrochen

7 (+noun: take, hold etc): **to have a walk/rest** spazieren gehen/sich ausruhen; **to have a meeting/party** eine Besprechung/Party haben

have on vt (be wearing) anhaben; (have arranged) vorhaben

have out vt: **to have it out with sb** (settle problem) etw mit jdm bereden

Hawaii [həwɑɪi] n Hawaii nt

hawk [hɔːk] n Habicht m

hay [heɪ] n Heu nt

hay fever n Heuschnupfen m

hazard [hæzərd] n Gefahr f; (risk) Risiko nt

hazardous [hæzərdəs] adj gefährlich; **~ waste** Sondermüll m

haze [heɪz] n Dunst m

hazelnut [heɪzˀlnʌt] n Haselnuss f

hazy [heɪzi] adj (misty) dunstig; (vague) verschwommen

he [hi, STRONG hiː] pron er

head [hɛd] n Kopf m; (leader) Leiter(in)

m(f); *(at school)* Schulleiter(in) *m(f)*; **~ of state** Staatsoberhaupt *nt*; **at the ~ of** an der Spitze von; *(tossing coin)*: **~s or tails?** Kopf oder Zahl? ▷ *adj (leading)* Ober- ▷ *vt* anführen; *(organization)* leiten

headache [hɛdeɪk] *n* Kopfschmerzen *pl*, Kopfweh *nt*

header [hɛdər] *n (football)* Kopfball *m*; *(dive)* Kopfsprung *m*

headfirst [hɛdfɜrst] *adj* kopfüber

head for *vt* zusteuern auf +*akk*; **he's heading for trouble** er wird Ärger bekommen

headhunt [hɛdhʌnt] *vt (Comm)* abwerben

heading [hɛdɪŋ] *n* Überschrift *f*

headlight [hɛdlaɪt] *n*, **headlamp** *n* Scheinwerfer *m*

headline [hɛdlaɪn] *n* Schlagzeile *f*

headmaster [hɛdmæstər] *n* Schulleiter *m*

headmistress [hɛdmɪstrɪs] *n* Schulleiterin *f*

head-on collision *adj* Frontalzusammenstoß *m*

headphones [hɛdfoʊnz] *npl* Kopfhörer *m*

headquarters [hɛdkwɔrtərz] *npl (of firm)* Zentrale *f*

headrest [hɛdrɛst], **head restraint** *n* Kopfstütze *f*

headscarf [hɛdskɑrf] *(pl -scarves)* *n* Kopftuch *nt*

heal [hil] *vt, vi* heilen

health [hɛlθ] *n* Gesundheit *f*; **good/bad for one's ~** gesund/ungesund; **your ~!** zum Wohl!; **~ and beauty** Wellness

health-care system *n* Gesundheitswesen *nt*

health club *n* Fitnesscenter *nt*

health food *n* Reformkost *f*; **~ store** Bioladen *m*

health insurance *n* Krankenversicherung *f*

healthy [hɛlθi] *adj* gesund

heap [hip] *n* Haufen *m*; **~s of** *(fam)* jede Menge ▷ *vt, vi* häufen

hear [hɪər] **(heard, heard)** *vt, vi* hören; **to ~ about sth** von etw erfahren; **I've ~d of it/him** ich habe schon davon/von ihm gehört

hearing [hɪərɪŋ] *n* Gehör *nt*; *(Jur)* Verhandlung *f*

hearing aid *n* Hörgerät *nt*

hearsay [hɪərseɪ] *n*: **from ~** vom Hörensagen

heart [hɑrt] *n* Herz *nt*; **to lose/take ~** den Mut verlieren/Mut fassen; **to learn by ~** auswendig lernen; *(cards)*: **~s** Herz *nt*; **queen of ~s** Herzdame *f*

heart attack *n* Herzanfall *m*

heartbeat [hɑrtbit] *n* Herzschlag *m*

heartbreaking [hɑrtbreɪkɪŋ] *adj* herzzerreißend

heartbroken [hɑrtbroʊkən] *adj* todunglücklich, untröstlich

heartburn [hɑrtbɜrn] *n* Sodbrennen *nt*

heart failure *n* Herzversagen *nt*

heartfelt [hɑrtfɛlt] *adj* tief empfunden

heartless [hɑrtlɪs] *adj* herzlos

heartthrob [hɑrtθrɒb] *n (fam)* Schwarm *m*

heart-to-heart *n* offene Aussprache

hearty [hɑrti] *adj (meal, appetite)* herzhaft; *(welcome)* herzlich

heat [hit] *n* Hitze *f*; *(pleasant)* Wärme *f*; *(temperature)* Temperatur *f*; *(Sport)* Vorlauf *m* ▷ *vt (house, room)* heizen

heated [hitɪd] *adj* beheizt; *(fig)* hitzig

heater [hitər] *n* Heizofen *m*; *(Auto)* Heizung *f*

heather [hɛðər] *n* Heidekraut *nt*

heating [hitɪŋ] *n* Heizung *f*

heat resistant *adj* hitzebeständig

heat up *vi* warm werden ▷ *vt* aufwärmen

heat wave [hitweɪv] *n* Hitzewelle *f*

heaven [hɛvən] *n* Himmel *m*

heavenly [hɛvənli] *adj* himmlisch

heavily [hɛvɪli] *adv (rain, drink etc)* stark

heavy [hɛvi] *adj* schwer; *(rain, traffic, smoker etc)* stark

Hebrew [hibru] *adj* hebräisch ▷ *n (language)* Hebräisch *nt*

hectic [hɛktɪk] *adj* hektisch

he'd [hid, STRONG hid] *contr of* **he had**; **he would**

hedge [hɛdʒ] *n* Hecke *f*

hedgehog [hɛdʒhɔg] *n* Igel *m*

heel [hil] *n (Anat)* Ferse *f*; *(of shoe)* Absatz *m*

hefty [hɛfti] *adj* schwer; *(person)* stämmig; *(fine, amount)* saftig

height [haɪt] *n* Höhe *f*; *(of person)* Größe *f*

heir [ɛər] *n* Erbe *m*

heiress [ɛərɪs] *n* Erbin *f*

held [hɛld] *pt, pp of* **hold**

helicopter [hɛlikɒptər] *n* Hubschrauber *m*

heliport [hɛlipɔrt] *n* Hubschrauberlandeplatz *m*

hell [hɛl] *n* Hölle *f*; **go to ~** scher dich zum Teufel ▷ *interj* verdammt; **that's a ~ of a lot of money** das ist verdammt viel Geld

he'll [hil, hil] *contr of* **he will**; **he shall**

hello [hɛloʊ] *interj* hallo

helmet [hɛlmɪt] *n* Helm *m*

help [hɛlp] *n* Hilfe *f* ▷ *vt, vi* helfen +*dat* (*with* bei); **to ~ sb to do sth** jdm helfen, etw zu tun; **can I ~?** kann ich (Ihnen) behilflich sein?; **I couldn't ~ laughing** ich musste einfach lachen; **I can't ~ it** ich kann nichts dafür; **~ yourself** bedienen Sie sich

helpful [hɛlpfʊl] *adj* (*person*) hilfsbereit; (*useful*) nützlich

helping [hɛlpɪŋ] *n* Portion *f*

helpless [hɛlpləs] *adj* hilflos

hem [hɛm] *n* Saum *m*

hemophiliac [himəfɪliæk] *n* Bluter *m*

hemorrhage [hɛmərɪdʒ] *n* Blutung *f* ▷ *vi* bluten

hemorrhoids [hɛmərɔɪdz] *npl* Hämorrhoiden *pl*

hen [hɛn] *n* Henne *f*

hence [hɛns] *adv* (*reason*) daher

henpecked [hɛnpɛkt] *adj:* **to be ~** unter dem Pantoffel stehen

hepatitis [hɛpətaɪtɪs] *n* Hepatitis *f*

her [hər, STRONG hɜr] *adj* ihr; **she's hurt her leg** sie hat sich *dat* das Bein verletzt ▷ *pron* (*direct object*) sie; (*indirect object*) ihr; **do you know her?** kennst du sie?; **can you help her?** kannst du ihr helfen?; **it's her** sie ist's

herb [ɜrb] *n* Kraut *nt*

herbal medicine [ɜrbᵊl mɛdɪsɪn] *n* Pflanzenheilkunde *f*

herbal tea [ɜrbᵊl ti] *n* Kräutertee *m*

herd [hɜrd] *n* Herde *f*

herd instinct *n* Herdentrieb *m*

here [hɪər] *adv* hier; (*to this place*) hierher; **come ~** komm her; **I won't be here for lunch** ich bin zum Mittagessen nicht da; **~ and there** hier und da, da und dort

hereditary [hɪrɛdɪteri] *adj* erblich

hereditary disease *n* Erbkrankheit *f*

heritage [hɛrɪtɪdʒ] *n* Erbe *nt*

hernia [hɜrniə] *n* Leistenbruch *m*, Eingeweidebruch *m*

hero [hɪərou] *n* (*pl* **-es**) *n* Held *m*

heroin [hɛrouɪn] *n* Heroin *nt*

heroine [hɛrouɪn] *n* Heldin *f*

heroism [hɛrouɪzəm] *n* Heldentum *nt*

herring [hɛrɪŋ] *n* Hering *m*

hers [hɜrz] *pron* ihre(r, s); **this is ~** das gehört ihr; **a friend of ~** ein Freund von ihr

herself [hərsɛlf] *pron* (*reflexive*) sich; **she's bought ~ a flat** sie hat sich eine Wohnung gekauft; **she needs it for ~** sie braucht es für sich (selbst); (*emphatic*): **she did it ~**

sie hat es selbst gemacht; **all by ~** allein

he's [hiz, STRONG hiz] *contr of* **he is; he has**

hesitant [hɛzɪtᵊnt] *adj* zögernd

hesitate [hɛzɪteɪt] *vi* zögern; **don't ~ to ask** fragen Sie ruhig

hesitation [hɛzɪteɪʃᵊn] *n* Zögern *nt*; **without ~** ohne zu zögern

heterosexual [hɛtərousɛkʃuəl] *adj* heterosexuell ▷ *n* Heterosexuelle(r) *mf*

hi [haɪ] *interj* hi, hallo

hiccup [hɪkʌp] *n* Schluckauf *m*; (*minor problem*) Problemchen *nt*; **to have the ~s** Schluckauf haben

hid [hɪd] *pt of* **hide**

hidden [hɪdᵊn] *pp of* **hide**

hide [haɪd] (**hid, hidden**) *vt* verstecken (*from* vor +*dat*); (*feelings, truth*) verbergen; (*cover*) verdecken ▷ *vi* sich verstecken (*from* vor +*dat*)

hideous [hɪdiəs] *adj* scheußlich

hiding [haɪdɪŋ] *n* (*beating*) Tracht *f* Prügel; (*concealment*): **to be in ~** sich versteckt halten

hiding place *n* Versteck *nt*

hi-fi [haɪ faɪ] *n* Hi-Fi *nt*; (*system*) Hi-Fi-Anlage *f*

high [haɪ] *adj* hoch; (*wind*) stark; (*living*) im großen Stil; (*on drugs*) high ▷ *adv* hoch ▷ *n* (*Meteo*) Hoch *nt*

high beam *n* (*Auto*) Fernlicht *nt*

highchair [haɪtʃeər] *n* Hochstuhl *m*

higher [haɪər] *adj* höher

higher education [haɪər ɛdʒukeɪʃᵊn] *n* Hochschulbildung *f*

high-flier [haɪ flaɪər] *n* Hochbegabte(r) (*m*)*f*

high heels *npl* Stöckelschuhe *pl*

high jump *n* Hochsprung *m*

Highlands [haɪləndz] *npl* (schottisches) Hochland *nt*

highlight [haɪlaɪt] *n* (*in hair*) Strähnchen *nt*; (*fig*) Höhepunkt *m* ▷ *vt* (*with pen*) hervorheben

highlighter [haɪlaɪtər] *n* Textmarker *m*

highly [haɪli] *adj* hoch, sehr; **~ paid** hoch bezahlt; **I think ~ of him** ich habe eine hohe Meinung von ihm

high-performance *adj* Hochleistungs-

high-rise *n* Hochhaus *nt*

high school *n* Highschool *f*, ≈ Gymnasium *nt*

high-speed *adj* Schnell-; **~ train** Hochgeschwindigkeitszug *m*

high-tech [haɪtɛk] *adj* Hightech- ▷ *n* High-

tech nt
high tide n Flut f
highway [haɪweɪ] n ≈ Autobahn f
hijack [haɪdʒæk] vt entführen, hijacken
hijacker [haɪdʒækər] n Entführer(in) m(f), Hijacker m
hike [haɪk] vi wandern ▷ n Wanderung f
hiker [haɪkər] n Wanderer m, Wanderin f
hiking [haɪkɪŋ] n Wandern nt
hilarious [hɪlɛərɪəs] adj zum Schreien komisch
hill [hɪl] n Hügel m; (higher) Berg m
hilly [hɪli] adj hügelig
him [hɪm] pron (direct object) ihn; (indirect object) ihm; **do you know him?** kennst du ihn?; **can you help him?** kannst du ihm helfen?; **it's him** er ist's; **him too** er auch
himself [hɪmsɛlf] pron (reflexive) sich; **he's bought ~ a car** er hat sich ein Auto gekauft; **he needs it for ~** er braucht es für sich (selbst); (emphatic): **he did it ~** er hat es selbst gemacht; **all by ~** allein
hinder [hɪndər] vt behindern
hindrance [hɪndrəns] n Behinderung f
Hindu [hɪndu] adj hinduistisch ▷ n Hindu m
Hinduism [hɪnduɪzəm] n Hinduismus m
hinge [hɪndʒ] n Scharnier nt; (on door) Angel f
hint [hɪnt] n Wink m, Andeutung f; (trace) Spur f ▷ vi andeuten (at akk)
hip [hɪp] n Hüfte f
hippopotamus [hɪpəpptəməs] n Nilpferd nt
hire [haɪər] vt (worker) anstellen ▷ n Miete f; **for ~** (taxi) frei
his [hɪz] adj sein; **he's hurt his leg** er hat sich dat das Bein verletzt ▷ pron seine(r, s); **it's his** es gehört ihm; **a friend of his** ein Freund von ihm
historic [hɪstɒrɪk] adj (significant) historisch
historical [hɪstɒrɪkəl] adj (monument etc) historisch; (studies etc) geschichtlich
history [hɪstəri, -tri] n Geschichte f
hit [hɪt] n (blow) Schlag m; (on target) Treffer m; (successful film, CD etc) Hit m ▷ vt (hit, hit) schlagen; (bullet, stone etc) treffen; **the car hit the tree** das Auto fuhr gegen einen Baum; **to hit one's head on sth** sich dat den Kopf an etw dat stoßen
hit-and-run adj: **~ accident** Unfall m mit Fahrerflucht
hitch [hɪtʃ] vt (pull up) hochziehen ▷ n Schwierigkeit f; **without a ~** reibungslos

hitchhike [hɪtʃhaɪk] vi trampen
hitchhiker [hɪtʃhaɪkər] n Tramper(in) m(f)
hitchhiking [hɪtʃhaɪkɪŋ] n Trampen nt
hit (up)on vt stoßen auf +akk
HIV [eɪtʃ aɪ vi] (abbr) = human immunodeficiency virus HIV nt; **HIV positive/negative** HIV-positiv/negativ
hive [haɪv] n Bienenstock m
HM [eɪtʃ ɛm] (abbr) = His/Her Majesty
HMS [eɪtʃ ɛm ɛs] (abbr) = His/Her Majesty's Ship
hoarse [hɔrs] adj heiser
hoax [hoʊks] n Streich m, Jux m; (false alarm) blinder Alarm
hobble [hɒbəl] vi humpeln
hobby [hɒbi] n Hobby nt
hobo [hoʊboʊ] (pl -es) n Penner(in) m(f)
hockey [hɒki] n Hockey nt
hold [hoʊld] (held, held) vt halten; (contain) enthalten; (be able to contain) fassen; (post, office) innehaben; (value) behalten; (meeting) abhalten; (person as prisoner) gefangen halten; **to ~ one's breath** den Atem anhalten; **to ~ hands** Händchen halten; **~ the line** (Tel) bleiben Sie am Apparat ▷ vi halten; (weather) sich halten ▷ n (grasp) Halt m; (of ship, aircraft) Laderaum m
hold back vt zurückhalten; (keep secret) verheimlichen
holder [hoʊldər] n (person) Inhaber(in) m(f)
hold on vi sich festhalten; (wait) warten; (Tel) dranbleiben; **to ~ to sth** etw festhalten
hold out vt ausstrecken; (offer) hinhalten; (offer) bieten ▷ vi durchhalten
hold up vt hochhalten; (support) stützen; (delay) aufhalten
holdup [hoʊldʌp] n (in traffic) Stau m; (robbery) Überfall m
hole [hoʊl] n Loch nt; (of fox, rabbit) Bau m; **~ in the wall** (cash dispenser) Geldautomat m
Holland [hɒlənd] n Holland nt
hollow [hɒloʊ] adj hohl; (words) leer ▷ n Vertiefung f
holly [hɒli] n Stechpalme f
holy [hoʊli] adj heilig
Holy Week n Karwoche f
home [hoʊm] n Zuhause nt; (area, country) Heimat f; (institution) Heim nt; **at ~** zu Hause; **to make oneself at ~** es sich dat bequem machen; **away from ~** verreist ▷ adv: **to go ~** nach Hause gehen/fahren

home address n Heimatadresse f
home country n Heimatland nt
home game n (Sport) Heimspiel nt
homeless [houmlıs] adj obdachlos
homemade [hoummeıd] adj selbst
gemacht
home movie n Amateurfilm m
homeopathic [houmioupæθık] adj homöopathisch
home page n (Inform) Homepage f
homesick [houmsık] adj: to be ~ Heimweh haben
hometown [houmtaun] n Heimatstadt f
homework [houmwɜrk] n Hausaufgaben
pl
homey [houmi] adj häuslich; (ugly)
unscheinbar
homicide [hɒmısaıd, houmı-] n Totschlag
m
homosexual [houmousɛkʃuəl] adj homosexuell ▷ n Homosexuelle(r) mf
Honduras [hɒnduərəs] n Honduras nt
honest [ɒnıst] adj ehrlich
honesty [ɒnısti] n Ehrlichkeit f
honey [hʌni] n Honig m
honeycomb [hʌnıkoum] n Honigwabe f
honeydew melon [hʌnıdu mɛlən] n
Honigmelone f
honeymoon [hʌnımun] n Flitterwochen
pl
Hong Kong [hɒŋ kɒŋ] n Hongkong nt
honor [ɒnər] vt ehren; (check) einlösen;
(contract) einhalten ▷ n Ehre f; **in ~ of** zu
Ehren von
honorable [ɒnrəbᵊl] adj ehrenhaft
honorary [ɒnəreri] adj (member, title etc)
Ehren-, ehrenamtlich
hood [hud] n Kapuze f; (Auto) Verdeck nt;
(Auto) Kühlerhaube f
hoof [huf, huf] (pl hooves) n Huf m
hook [huk] n Haken m
hooked [hukt] adj (keen) besessen (on
von); (drugs) abhängig sein (on von)
hooligan [hulıgən] n Hooligan m
hoot [hut] vi (Auto) hupen
hop [hɒp] vi hüpfen ▷ n (Bot) Hopfen m
hope [houp] vi, vt hoffen (for auf +akk); **I ~
so/~ not** hoffentlich/hoffentlich nicht; **I ~
that we'll meet** ich hoffe, dass wir uns
sehen werden ▷ n Hoffnung f; **there's no ~**
es ist aussichtslos
hopeful [houpfəl] adj hoffnungsvoll
hopefully [houpfəli] adv (full of hope) hoffnungsvoll; (I hope so) hoffentlich
hopeless [houplıs] adj hoffnungslos;

(incompetent) miserabel
horizon [həraız°n] n Horizont m
horizontal [hɒrızɒntᵊl] adj horizontal
hormone [hɔrmoun] n Hormon nt
horn [hɔrn] n Horn nt; (Auto) Hupe f
hornet [hɔrnıt] n Hornisse f
horny [hɔrni] adj (fam) geil
horoscope [hɔrəskoup] n Horoskop nt
horrible [hɔribᵊl, hɒr-] adj, **horribly** adv
schrecklich
horrid [hɔrıd, hɒr-] adj, **horridly** adv
abscheulich
horrify [hɔrıfaı, hɒr-] vt entsetzen
horror [hɔrər, hɒr-] n Entsetzen nt; **~s**
(things) Schrecken pl
hors d'oeuvre [ɔrdɜrv] n Vorspeise f
horse [hɔrs] n Pferd nt
horse chestnut n Rosskastanie f
horsepower [hɔrspauər] n Pferdestärke f,
PS nt
horse racing n Pferderennen nt
horseradish [hɔrsrædıʃ] n Meerrettich m
horse riding n Reiten nt
horseshoe [hɔrsʃu] n Hufeisen nt
horticulture [hɔrtıkʌltʃər] n Gartenbau m
hose [houz], **hosepipe** n Schlauch m
hospitable [hɒspıtəbᵊl, hɒspıt-] adj gastfreundlich
hospital [hɒspıtᵊl] n Krankenhaus nt
hospitality [hɒspıtælıti] n Gastfreundschaft f
host [houst] n Gastgeber m; (TV: of show)
Moderator(in) m(f), Talkmaster(in) m(f)
▷ vt (party) geben; (TV: show) moderie-
ren
hostage [hɒstıdʒ] n Geisel f
hostel [hɒstᵊl] n Wohnheim nt; (youth hostel) Jugendherberge f
hostess [houstıs] n (of a party) Gastgebe-
rin f
hostile [hɒstᵊl] adj feindlich
hostility [hɒstılıti] n Feindseligkeit f
hot [hɒt] adj heiß; (drink, food, water)
warm; (spiced) scharf; **I'm feeling hot** mir
ist heiß
hot cross bun n Rosinenbrötchen mit einem
Kreuz darauf, hauptsächlich zu Ostern
gegessen
hot dog n Hotdog nt
hotel [houtɛl] n Hotel nt; (small hotel) Pension f
hotel room n Hotelzimmer nt
hothouse [hɒthaus] n Treibhaus nt
hotline [hɒtlaın] n Hotline f
hotplate [hɒtpleıt] n Kochplatte f

hotspot [hɒtspɒt] *n* (*Inform*) Hotspot *m*
hot-water bottle *n* Wärmflasche *f*
hour [auər] *n* Stunde *f*; **to wait for ~s** stundenlang warten; **~s** *pl* (*of shops etc*) Geschäftszeiten *pl*
hourly [auərli] *adj* stündlich
house [*n* haus, *vb* hauz] (*pl* **houses**) *n* Haus *nt*; **at my ~** bei mir (zu Hause); **to my ~** zu mir (nach Hause); **on the ~** auf Kosten des Hauses ▷ *vt* unterbringen
houseboat [hausbout] *n* Hausboot *nt*
household [haushould] *n* Haushalt *m*; **~ appliance** Haushaltsgerät *nt*
housekeeping [hauskipɪŋ] *n* Haushaltung *f*; (*money*) Haushaltsgeld *nt*
housewarming (party) [hauswɔrmɪŋ (pɑrti)] *n* Einzugsparty *f*
housewife [hauswaɪf] (*pl* -**wives**) *n* Hausfrau *f*
house wine *n* Hauswein *m*
housework [hauswɜrk] *n* Hausarbeit *f*
housing [hauzɪŋ] *n* (*houses*) Wohnungen *pl*; (*house building*) Wohnungsbau *m*
housing development *n* Wohnsiedlung *f*
hover [hʌvər] *vi* schweben
hovercraft [hʌvərkræft] *n* Luftkissenboot *nt*
how [hau] *adv* wie; **how many** wie viele; **how much** wie viel; **how are you?** wie geht es Ihnen?; **how are things?** wie geht's?; **how's work?** was macht die Arbeit?; **how about ...?** wie wäre es mit ...?
however [hauɛvər] *conj* (*but*) jedoch, aber ▷ *adv* (*no matter how*) wie ... auch; **~ much it costs** wie viel es auch kostet; **~ you do it** wie man es auch macht
howl [haul] *vi* heulen
howler [haulər] *n* (*fam*) grober Schnitzer
hp [eɪtʃ pi] (*abbr*) = **horsepower** PS
HQ [eɪtʃ kyu] (*abbr*) = **headquarters**
hubcap [hʌbkæp] *n* Radkappe *f*
hug [hʌg] *vt* umarmen ▷ *n* Umarmung *f*
huge [hyudʒ] *adj* riesig
hum [hʌm] *vi, vt* summen
human [hyumən] *adj* menschlich; **~ rights** Menschenrechte *pl* ▷ *n*: **~ being** Mensch *m*
humanitarian [hyumænɪtɛəriən] *adj* humanitär
humanity [hyumænɪti] *n* Menschheit *f*; (*kindliness*) Menschlichkeit *f*; **humanities** Geisteswissenschaften *pl*
humble [hʌmbəl] *adj* demütig; (*modest*) bescheiden

humid [hyumɪd] *adj* feucht
humidity [hyumɪdɪti] *n* (Luft)feuchtigkeit *f*
humiliate [hyumɪlieɪt] *vt* demütigen
humiliation [hyumɪlieɪʃⁿn] *n* Erniedrigung *f*, Demütigung *f*
humor [hyumər] *n* Humor *m*; **sense of ~** Sinn *m* für Humor
humorous [hyumərəs] *adj* humorvoll; (*story*) lustig, witzig
hump [hʌmp] *n* Buckel *m*
hunch [hʌntʃ] *n* Gefühl *nt*, Ahnung *f* ▷ *vt* (*back*) krümmen
hunchback [hʌntʃbæk] *n* Bucklige(r) *mf*
hundred [hʌndrɪd] *num*: **one ~, a ~** (ein) hundert; **a ~ and one** hundert(und)eins; **two ~** zweihundert
hundredth [hʌndrɪdθ] *adj* hundertste(r, s) ▷ *n* (*fraction*) Hundertstel *nt*
hundredweight [hʌndrɪdweɪt] *n* Zentner *m* (*50,8 kg*)
hung [hʌŋ] *pt, pp of* **hang**
Hungarian [hʌŋgɛəriən] *adj* ungarisch ▷ *n* (*person*) Ungar(in) *m(f)*; (*language*) Ungarisch *nt*
Hungary [hʌŋgəri] *n* Ungarn *nt*
hunger [hʌŋgər] *n* Hunger *m*
hungry [hʌŋgri] *adj* hungrig; **to be ~** Hunger haben
hunk [hʌŋk] *n* (*fam*) gut gebauter Mann
hunky [hʌŋki] *adj* (*fam*) gut gebaut
hunt [hʌnt] *n* Jagd *f*; (*search*) Suche *f* (*for* nach) ▷ *vt, vi* jagen; (*search*) suchen (*for* nach)
hunting [hʌntɪŋ] *n* Jagen *nt*, Jagd *f*
hurdle [hɜrdⁿl] *n* (*a. fig*) Hürde *f*; **the 400m ~s** der 400m-Hürdenlauf
hurl [hɜrl] *vt* schleudern
hurricane [hɜrɪkeɪn, hʌr-] *n* Orkan *m*
hurried [hɜrid, hʌr-] *adj* eilig
hurry [hɜri, hʌr-] *n* Eile *f*; **to be in a ~** es eilig haben; **there's no ~** es eilt nicht ▷ *vi* sich beeilen; **~ up** mach schnell! ▷ *vt* antreiben
hurt [hɜrt] (**hurt, hurt**) *vt* wehtun +*dat*; (*wound: person, feelings*) verletzen; **I've ~ my arm** ich habe mir am Arm wehgetan ▷ *vi* wehtun; **my arm ~s** mir tut der Arm weh
husband [hʌzbənd] *n* Ehemann *m*
husky [hʌski] *adj* rau ▷ *n* Schlittenhund *m*
hut [hʌt] *n* Hütte *f*
hyacinth [haɪəsɪnθ] *n* Hyazinthe *f*
hybrid [haɪbrɪd] *n* Kreuzung *f*
hydroelectric [haɪdrouɪlɛktrɪk] *adj*: **~**

power station Wasserkraftwerk *nt*
hydrofoil [haɪdrəfɔɪl] *n* Tragflächenboot *nt*
hydrogen [haɪdrədʒⁿn] *n* Wasserstoff *m*
hygiene [haɪdʒin] *n* Hygiene *f*
hygienic [haɪdʒɛnɪk] *adj* hygienisch
hymn [hɪm] *n* Kirchenlied *nt*
hyperlink [haɪpərlɪŋk] *n* Hyperlink *m*
hypersensitive [haɪpərsɛnsɪtɪv] *adj* überempfindlich
hyphen [haɪfⁿn] *n* Bindestrich *m*
hypnosis [hɪpnoʊsɪs] *n* Hypnose *f*
hypnotize [hɪpnətaɪz] *vt* hypnotisieren

hypochondriac [haɪpəkɒndriæk] *n*
eingebildete(r) Kranke(r), eingebildete
Kranke
hypocrisy [hɪpɒkrɪsi] *n* Heuchelei *f*
hypocrite [hɪpəkrɪt] *n* Heuchler(in) *m(f)*
hypodermic [haɪpədɜrmɪk] *adj, n:* ~ **needle** Spritze *f*
hypothetical [haɪpəθɛtɪkⁿl] *adj* hypothe-
tisch
hysteria [hɪstɛriə] *n* Hysterie *f*
hysterical [hɪstɛrɪkⁿl] *adj* hysterisch;
(amusing) zum Totlachen

I

I [aɪ] *pron* ich

ice [aɪs] *n* Eis *nt* ▷ *vt* (*cake*) glasieren

iceberg [aɪsbɜrg] *n* Eisberg *m*

iceberg lettuce *n* Eisbergsalat *m*

icebox [aɪsbɒks] *see* **refrigerator**

ice-cold *adj* eiskalt

ice cream *n* Eis *nt*

ice cube *n* Eiswürfel *m*

iced [aɪst] *adj* eisgekühlt; (*coffee, tea*) Eis-; (*cake*) glasiert

ice hockey *n* Eishockey *nt*

Iceland [aɪslənd] *n* Island *nt*

Icelander [aɪslændər] *n* Isländer(in) *m(f)*

Icelandic [aɪslændɪk] *adj* isländisch ▷ *n* (*language*) Isländisch *nt*

ice rink *n* Kunsteisbahn *f*

ice skating *n* Schlittschuhlaufen *nt*

icing [aɪsɪŋ] *n* (*on cake*) Zuckerguss *m*

icon [aɪkɒn] *n* Ikone *f*; (*Inform*) Icon *nt*, Programmsymbol *nt*

icy [aɪsi] *adj* (*slippery*) vereist; (*cold*) eisig

ID [aɪ di] (*abbr*) = **identification** Ausweis *m*

I'd [aɪd] *contr of* **I would; I had**

ID card [aɪ di kard] *n* Personalausweis *m*

idea [aɪdiə] *n* Idee *f*; **I've no ~** (ich habe) keine Ahnung; **that's my ~ of …** so stelle ich mir … vor

ideal [aɪdiəl] *n* Ideal *nt* ▷ *adj* ideal

ideally [aɪdiəli] *adv* ideal; (*before statement*) idealerweise

identical [aɪdɛntɪkʰl] *adj* identisch; **~ twins** eineiige Zwillinge

identify [aɪdɛntɪfaɪ] *vt* identifizieren

identity [aɪdɛntiti] *n* Identität *f*

idiom [ɪdiəm] *n* Redewendung *f*

idiomatic [ɪdiəmætɪk] *adj* idiomatisch

idiot [ɪdiət] *n* Idiot(in) *m(f)*

idle [aɪdʰl] *adj* (*doing nothing*) untätig; (*worker*) unbeschäftigt; (*machines*) außer Betrieb; (*lazy*) faul; (*promise, threat*) leer

idol [aɪdʰl] *n* Idol *nt*

idolize [aɪdəlaɪz] *vt* vergöttern

idyllic [aɪdɪlɪk] *adj* idyllisch

i.e. [aɪ i] (*abbr*) = **id est** d.h.

KEYWORD

if [ɪf] *conj* **1** wenn; (*in case also*) falls; **if I were you** wenn ich Sie wäre

2 (*although*): **(even) if** (selbst *o* auch) wenn

3 (*whether*) ob

4: **if so/not** wenn ja/nicht; **if only …** wenn … doch nur …; **if only I could** wenn ich doch nur könnte; *see also* **as**

ignition [ɪgnɪʃʰn] *n* Zündung *f*

ignorance [ɪgnərəns] *n* Unwissenheit *f*

ignorant [ɪgnərənt] *adj* unwissend

ignore [ɪgnɔr] *vt* ignorieren, nicht beachten

I'll [aɪl] *contr of* **I will; I shall**

ill [ɪl] *adj* krank; **ill at ease** unbehaglich

illegal [ɪligʰl] *adj* illegal

illegitimate [ɪlɪdʒɪtɪmɪt] *adj* unzulässig; (*child*) unehelich

illiterate [ɪlɪtərɪt] *adj*: **to be ~** Analphabet(in) sein

illness [ɪlnɪs] *n* Krankheit *f*

illuminate [ɪluminɛit] *vt* beleuchten

illuminating [ɪluminɛitɪŋ] *adj* (*remark*) aufschlussreich

illusion [ɪluʒʰn] *n* Illusion *f*; **to be under the ~ that …** sich einbilden, dass …

illustrate [ɪləstreit] *vt* illustrieren

illustration [ɪləstreiʃʰn] *n* Abbildung *f*, Bild *nt*

I'm [aɪm] *contr of* **I am**

image [ɪmɪdʒ] *n* Bild *nt*; (*public image*) Image *nt*

imaginable [ɪmædʒɪnəbʰl] *adj* denkbar

imaginary [ɪmædʒɪnɛri] *adj* eingebildet; **~ world** Fantasiewelt *f*

imagination [ɪmædʒɪnɛiʃʰn] *n* Fantasie *f*; (*mistaken*) Einbildung *f*

imaginative [ɪmædʒɪnətɪv] *adj* fantasievoll

imagine [ɪmædʒɪn] *vt* sich vorstellen; (*wrongly*) sich einbilden; **~!** stell dir vor!

imbecile [ɪmbɪsʰl] *n* Trottel *m*

imitate [ɪmɪteit] *vt* nachahmen, nachmachen

imitation [ɪmɪteiʃʰn] *n* Nachahmung *f* ▷ *adj* imitiert, Kunst-

immaculate [ɪmækyʊlɪt] *adj* tadellos; (*spotless*) makellos

immature [ɪmətʃʊər, -tʊər] *adj* unreif

immediate [ɪmidiɪt] *adj* unmittelbar; (*instant*) sofortig; (*reply*) umgehend

immediately [ɪmidiɪtli] *adv* sofort

immense [ɪmɛns] *adj*, **immensely** *adv* riesig, enorm

immigrant [ɪmɪgrənt] *n* Einwanderer *m*, Einwanderin *f*

immigration [ˌɪmɪˈgreɪʃ°n] *n* Einwanderung *f*; *(facility)* Einwanderungskontrolle *f*
immobilize [ɪˈmoʊbɪlaɪz] *vt* lähmen
immobilizer [ɪˈmoʊbɪlaɪzər] *n* *(Auto)* Wegfahrsperre *f*
immoral [ɪˈmɒr°l] *adj* unmoralisch
immortal [ɪˈmɔrt°l] *adj* unsterblich
immune [ɪˈmjuːn] *adj* *(Med)* immun *(from, to* gegen)
immune system *n* Immunsystem *nt*
impact [ˈɪmpækt] *n* Aufprall *m*; *(effect)* Auswirkung *f* *(on* auf *+akk)*
impatience [ɪmˈpeɪʃns] *n* Ungeduld *f*
impatient [ɪmˈpeɪʃ°nt] *adj*, **impatiently** *adv* ungeduldig
impeccable [ɪmˈpekəb°l] *adj* tadellos
impede [ɪmˈpiːd] *vt* behindern
imperative [ɪmˈperətɪv] *adj* unbedingt erforderlich ▷ *n* *(Ling)* Imperativ *m*
imperfect [ɪmˈpɜrfɪkt] *adj* unvollkommen; *(goods)* fehlerhaft ▷ *n* *(Ling)* Imperfekt *nt*
imperfection [ɪmpərˈfekʃ°n] *n* Unvollkommenheit *f*; *(fault)* Fehler *m*
imperial [ɪmˈpɪəriəl] *adj* kaiserlich, Reichs-
imperialism [ɪmˈpɪəriəlɪzəm] *n* Imperialismus *m*
impertinence [ɪmˈpɜrt°nəns] *n* Unverschämtheit *f*, Zumutung *f*
impertinent [ɪmˈpɜrt°nənt] *adj* unverschämt
implant [ˈɪmplænt] *n* *(Med)* Implantat *nt*
implausible [ɪmˈplɔːzɪb°l] *adj* unglaubwürdig
implement [*n* ˈɪmplɪmənt, *vb* ˈɪmplɪment] *n* Werkzeug *nt*, Gerät *nt* ▷ *vt* durchführen
implication [ɪmplɪˈkeɪʃ°n] *n* Folge *f*, Auswirkung *f*; *(logical)* Schlussfolgerung *f*
implicit [ɪmˈplɪsɪt] *adj* implizit, unausgesprochen
imply [ɪmˈplaɪ] *vt* *(indicate)* andeuten; *(mean)* bedeuten; **are you ~ing that ...** wollen Sie damit sagen, dass ...
impolite [ɪmpəˈlaɪt] *adj* unhöflich
import [*vb* ɪmˈpɔrt, *n* ˈɪmpɔrt] *vt* einführen, importieren ▷ *n* Einfuhr *f*, Import *m*
importance [ɪmˈpɔrt°ns] *n* Bedeutung *f*; **of no ~** unwichtig
important [ɪmˈpɔrt°nt] *adj* wichtig *(to sb* für jdn); *(significant)* bedeutend; *(influential)* einflussreich
impose [ɪmˈpoʊz] *vt* *(conditions)* auferlegen *(on* dat); *(penalty, sanctions)* verhängen *(on* gegen)
imposing [ɪmˈpoʊzɪŋ] *adj* eindrucksvoll, imposant

impossible [ɪmˈpɒsɪb°l] *adj* unmöglich
impotence [ˈɪmpətəns] *n* Machtlosigkeit *f*; *(sexual)* Impotenz *f*
impotent [ˈɪmpətənt] *adj* machtlos; *(sexually)* impotent
impractical [ɪmˈpræktɪk°l] *adj* unpraktisch; *(plan)* undurchführbar
impress [ɪmˈpres] *vt* beeindrucken
impression [ɪmˈpreʃ°n] *n* Eindruck *m*
impressive [ɪmˈpresɪv] *adj* eindrucksvoll
imprison [ɪmˈprɪz°n] *vt* inhaftieren
imprisonment [ɪmˈprɪz°nmənt] *n* Inhaftierung *f*
improbability [ɪmprɒbəˈbɪliti] *n* Unwahrscheinlichkeit *f*
improbable [ɪmˈprɒbəb°l] *adj* unwahrscheinlich
improper [ɪmˈprɒpər] *adj* *(indecent)* unanständig; *(use)* unsachgemäß
improve [ɪmˈpruːv] *vt* verbessern ▷ *vi* sich verbessern, besser werden; *(patient)* Fortschritte machen
improvement [ɪmˈpruːvmənt] *n* Verbesserung *f* *(in* on gegenüber); *(in appearance)* Verschönerung *f*
improvise [ˈɪmprəvaɪz] *vt*, *vi* improvisieren
impulse [ˈɪmpʌls] *n* Impuls *m*
impulsive [ɪmˈpʌlsɪv] *adj* impulsiv

KEYWORD

in [*prep* ɪn, *adv* ɪn] *prep* **1** *(indicating place, position)* in *+dat*; *(with motion)* in *+akk*; **in here/there** hier/dort; **in London** in London; **in the United States** in den Vereinigten Staaten
2 *(indicating time: during)* in *+dat*; **in summer** im Sommer; **in 1988** (im Jahre) 1988; **in the afternoon** nachmittags, am Nachmittag
3 *(indicating time: in the space of)* innerhalb von; **I'll see you in 2 weeks** *o* **in 2 weeks' time** ich sehe dich/Sie in zwei Wochen
4 *(indicating manner, circumstances, state etc)* in *+dat*; **in the sun/rain** in der Sonne/im Regen; **in English/French** auf Englisch/Französisch; **in a loud/soft voice** mit lauter/leiser Stimme
5 *(with numbers)*: **they lined up in twos** sie stellten sich in Zweierreihe auf
6 *(referring to people, works)*: **the disease is common in children** die Krankheit ist bei Kindern häufig; **in Dickens** bei

Dickens; **we have a loyal friend in him** er ist uns ein treuer Freund

7 (*indicating profession etc*): **to be in teaching/the army** Lehrer, Lehrerin/beim Militär sein; **to be in publishing** im Verlagswesen arbeiten

8 (*with present participle*): **in saying this, I … wenn ich das sage, … ich; in accepting this view, he … weil er diese Meinung akzeptierte, … er**

▷ *adv*: **to be in** (*person: at home, work*) da sein; (*train, ship, plane*) angekommen sein; (*in fashion*) in sein; **to ask sb in** jdn hereinbitten; **to run/limp** *etc* **in** hereingerannt/-gehumpelt *etc* kommen

▷ *n*: **the ins and outs** (*of proposal, situation etc*) die Feinheiten

inability [ɪnəbɪlɪti] *n* Unfähigkeit *f*

inaccessible [ɪnəksɛsɪbəl] *adj* (*a. fig*) unzugänglich

inaccurate [ɪnækyərɪt] *adj* ungenau

inadequate [ɪnædɪkwɪt] *adj* unzulänglich

inapplicable [ɪnæplɪkəbəl] *adj* unzutreffend

inappropriate [ɪnəprouprɪɪt] *adj* unpassend; (*clothing*) ungeeignet; (*remark*) unangebracht

inborn [ɪnbɔrn] *adj* angeboren

incapable [ɪnkeɪpəbəl] *adj* unfähig (*of* zu); **to be ~ of doing sth** nicht imstande sein, etw zu tun

incense [ɪnsɛns] *n* Weihrauch *m*

incentive [ɪnsɛntɪv] *n* Anreiz *m*

incessant [ɪnsɛsənt] *adj*, **incessantly** *adv* unaufhörlich

incest [ɪnsɛst] *n* Inzest *m*

inch [ɪntʃ] *n* Zoll *m* (*2,54 cm*)

incident [ɪnsɪdənt] *n* Vorfall *m*; (*disturbance*) Zwischenfall *m*

incidentally [ɪnsɪdɛntli] *adv* nebenbei bemerkt, übrigens

inclination [ɪnklɪneɪʃən] *n* Neigung *f*

inclined [ɪnklaɪnd] *adj*: **to be ~ to do sth** dazu neigen, etw zu tun

include [ɪnkluːd] *vt* einschließen; (*on list, in group*) aufnehmen

including [ɪnkluːdɪŋ] *prep* einschließlich +*gen*; **not ~ service** Bedienung nicht inbegriffen

inclusive [ɪnkluːsɪv] *adj* einschließlich (*of* +*gen*); (*price*) Pauschal-

incoherent [ɪnkouhɪərənt] *adj* zusammenhanglos

income [ɪnkʌm] *n* Einkommen *nt*; (*from business*) Einkünfte *pl*

income tax *n* Einkommensteuer *f*; (*on wages, salary*) Lohnsteuer *f*

incoming [ɪnkʌmɪŋ] *adj* ankommend; (*mail*) eingehend

incompatible [ɪnkəmpætɪbəl] *adj* unvereinbar; (*people*) unverträglich; (*Inform*) nicht kompatibel

incompetent [ɪnkɒmpɪtənt] *adj* unfähig

incomplete [ɪnkəmpliːt] *adj* unvollständig

incomprehensible [ɪnkɒmprɪhɛnsɪbəl] *adj* unverständlich

inconceivable [ɪnkənsiːvəbəl] *adj* unvorstellbar

inconsiderate [ɪnkənsɪdərɪt] *adj* rücksichtslos

inconsistency [ɪnkənsɪstənsi] *n* Inkonsequenz *f*; (*contradictory*) Widersprüchlichkeit *f*

inconsistent [ɪnkənsɪstənt] *adj* inkonsequent; (*contradictory*) widersprüchlich; (*work*) unbeständig

inconvenience [ɪnkənviːnyəns] *n* Unannehmlichkeit *f*; (*trouble*) Umstände *pl*

inconvenient [ɪnkənviːnyənt] *adj* ungünstig, unbequem; (*time*): **it's ~ for me** es kommt mir ungelegen; **if it's not too ~ for you** wenn es dir/Ihnen passt

incorporate [ɪnkɔrpəreɪt] *vt* aufnehmen (*into* in +*akk*); (*include*) enthalten

incorrect [ɪnkərɛkt] *adj* falsch; (*improper*) inkorrekt

increase [*n* ɪnkriːs, *vb* ɪnkriːs] *n* Zunahme *f* (*in an* +*dat*; *amount, speed*) Erhöhung *f* (*in* +*gen*) ▷ *vt* (*price, taxes, salary, speed etc*) erhöhen; (*wealth*) vermehren; (*number*) vergrößern; (*business*) erweitern ▷ *vi* zunehmen (*in an* +*dat*); (*prices*) steigen; (*in size*) größer werden; (*in number*) sich vermehren

increasingly [ɪnkriːsɪŋli] *adv* zunehmend

incredible [ɪnkrɛdɪbəl] *adj*, **incredibly** *adv* unglaublich; (*very good*) fantastisch

incredulous [ɪnkrɛdʒələs] *adj* ungläubig, skeptisch

incriminate [ɪnkrɪmɪneɪt] *vt* belasten

incubator [ɪnkyəbeɪtər, ɪŋ] *n* Brutkasten *m*

incurable [ɪnkyuərəbəl] *adj* unheilbar

indecent [ɪndiːsənt] *adj* unanständig

indecisive [ɪndɪsaɪsɪv] *adj* (*person*) unentschlossen; (*result*) nicht entscheidend

indeed [ɪndiːd] *adv* tatsächlich; (*as answer*) allerdings; **very hot ~** wirklich sehr heiß

indefinite [ɪndɛfɪnɪt] *adj* unbestimmt

indefinitely [ɪndɛfɪnɪtli] *adv* endlos; *(postpone)* auf unbestimmte Zeit
independence [ɪndɪpɛndəns] *n* Unabhängigkeit *f*

INDEPENDENCE DAY

Der **Independence Day**, der 4. Juli, ist in den USA ein gesetzlicher Feiertag zum Gedenken an die Unabhängigkeitserklärung am 4. Juli 1776, mit der die 13 amerikanischen Kolonien ihre Freiheit und Unabhängigkeit von Großbritannien erklärten.

independent [ɪndɪpɛndənt] *adj* unabhängig *(of* von); *(person)* selbstständig
indescribable [ɪndɪskraɪbəbˀl] *adj* unbeschreiblich
index [ɪndɛks] *n* Index *m*, Verzeichnis *nt*
index finger *n* Zeigefinger *m*
India [ɪndiə] *n* Indien *nt*
Indian [ɪndiən] *adj* indisch; *(Native American)* indianisch ⊳ *n* Inder(in) *m(f)*; *(Native American)* Indianer(in) *m(f)*
Indian Ocean *n* Indischer Ozean
Indian summer *n* Spätsommer *m*, Altweibersommer *m*
indicate [ɪndɪkeɪt] *vt (show)* zeigen; *(instrument)* anzeigen; *(suggest)* hinweisen auf *+akk* ⊳ *vi (Auto)* blinken
indication [ɪndɪkeɪʃˀn] *n (sign)* Anzeichen *nt (of* für)
indicator [ɪndɪkeɪtər] *n (Auto)* Blinker *m*
indifferent [ɪndɪfərənt] *adj (not caring)* gleichgültig *(to, towards* gegenüber); *(mediocre)* mittelmäßig
indigestible [ɪndɪdʒɛstɪbˀl, -daɪ-] *adj* unverdaulich
indigestion [ɪndɪdʒɛstʃˀn, -daɪ-] *n* Verdauungsstörung *f*
indignity [ɪndɪgnɪti] *n* Demütigung *f*
indirect [ɪndaɪrɛkt, -dɪr-] *adj*, **indirectly** *adv* indirekt
indiscreet [ɪndɪskriːt] *adj* indiskret
indispensable [ɪndɪspɛnsəbˀl] *adj* unentbehrlich
indisposed [ɪndɪspəʊzd] *adj* unwohl
indisputable [ɪndɪspjuːtəbˀl] *adj* unbestreitbar; *(evidence)* unanfechtbar
individual [ɪndɪvɪdʒuˀl] *n* Einzelne(r) *mf* ⊳ *adj* einzeln; *(distinctive)* eigen, individuell; ~ **case** Einzelfall *m*
individually [ɪndɪvɪdʒuˀli] *adv (separately)* einzeln

Indonesia [ɪndəniːʒə] *n* Indonesien *nt*
indoor [ɪndɔːr] *adj (shoes)* Haus-; *(plant, games)* Zimmer-; *(Sport: football, championship, record etc)* Hallen-
indoors [ɪndɔːrz] *adv* drinnen, im Haus
indulge [ɪndʌldʒ] *vi:* **to ~ in sth** sich *dat* etw gönnen
indulgence [ɪndʌldʒˀns] *n* Nachsicht *f*; *(enjoyment)* (übermäßiger) Genuss; *(luxury)* Luxus *m*
indulgent [ɪndʌldʒˀnt] *adj* nachsichtig *(with* gegenüber)
industrial [ɪndʌstriəl] *adj* Industrie-, industriell; ~ **estate** Industriegebiet *nt*
industry [ɪndəstri] *n* Industrie *f*
inedible [ɪnɛdɪbˀl] *adj* nicht essbar, ungenießbar
ineffective [ɪnɪfɛktɪv] *adj* unwirksam, wirkungslos
inefficient [ɪnɪfɪʃˀnt] *adj* unwirksam; *(use, machine)* unwirtschaftlich; *(method etc)* unrationell
ineligible [ɪnɛlɪdʒəbˀl] *adj* nicht berechtigt *(for* zu)
inequality [ɪnɪkwɒlɪti] *n* Ungleichheit *f*
inevitable [ɪnɛvɪtəbˀl] *adj* unvermeidlich
inevitably [ɪnɛvɪtəbli] *adv* zwangsläufig
inexcusable [ɪnɪkskjuːzəbˀl] *adj* unverzeihlich; **that's ~** das kann man nicht verzeihen
inexpensive [ɪnɪkspɛnsɪv] *adj* preisgünstig
inexperience [ɪnɪkspɪəriəns] *n* Unerfahrenheit *f*
inexperienced [ɪnɪkspɪəriənst] *adj* unerfahren
inexplicable [ɪnɛksplɪkəbˀl, ɪnɪksplɪk-] *adj* unerklärlich
infallible [ɪnfælɪbˀl] *adj* unfehlbar
infamous [ɪnfəməs] *adj (person)* berüchtigt *(for* wegen); *(deed)* niederträchtig
infancy [ɪnfənsi] *n* frühe Kindheit
infant [ɪnfənt] *n* Säugling *m*; *(small child)* Kleinkind *nt*
infatuated [ɪnfætʃueɪtɪd] *adj* vernarrt *(with* in *+akk)*, verknallt *(with* in *+akk)*
infect [ɪnfɛkt] *vt (person)* anstecken; *(wound)* infizieren
infection [ɪnfɛkʃˀn] *n* Infektion *f*
infectious [ɪnfɛkʃəs] *adj* ansteckend
inferior [ɪnfɪəriər] *adj (in quality)* minderwertig; *(in rank)* untergeordnet
inferiority [ɪnfɪəriɒrɪti] *n* Minderwertigkeit *f*; ~ **complex** Minderwertigkeitskomplex *m*

infertile [ɪnfɜrtᵊl] *adj* unfruchtbar

infidelity [ɪnfɪdɛlɪti] *n* Untreue *f*

infinite [ɪnfɪnɪt] *adj* unendlich

infinitive [ɪnfɪnɪtɪv] *n* (*Ling*) Infinitiv *m*

infinity [ɪnfɪnɪti] *n* Unendlichkeit *f*

infirmary [ɪnfɜrməri] *n* Krankenhaus *nt*

inflame [ɪnfleɪm] *vt* (*Med*) entzünden

inflammation [ɪnfləmeɪʃᵊn] *n* (*Med*) Entzündung *f*

inflatable [ɪnfleɪtəbᵊl] *adj* aufblasbar; **~ dinghy** Schlauchboot *nt*

inflate [ɪnfleɪt] *vt* aufpumpen; (*by blowing*) aufblasen; (*prices*) hochtreiben

inflation [ɪnfleɪʃᵊn] *n* Inflation *f*

inflexible [ɪnflɛksɪbᵊl] *adj* unflexibel

inflict [ɪnflɪkt] *vt:* **to ~ sth on sb** jdm etw zufügen; (*punishment*) jdm etw auferlegen; (*wound*) jdm etw beibringen

in-flight *adj* (*catering, magazine*) Bord-; **~ entertainment** Bordprogramm *nt*

influence [ɪnfluəns] *n* Einfluss *m* (*on* auf +*akk*) ▷ *vt* beeinflussen

influential [ɪnfluɛnʃᵊl] *adj* einflussreich

influenza [ɪnfluɛnzə] *n* Grippe *f*

inform [ɪnfɔrm] *vt* informieren (*of, about* über +*akk*); **to keep sb ~ed** jdn auf dem Laufenden halten

informal [ɪnfɔrmᵊl] *adj* zwanglos, ungezwungen

information [ɪnfərmeɪʃᵊn] *n* Auskunft *f*, Informationen *pl*; **for your ~** zu deiner/ Ihrer Information; **further ~** weitere Informationen, Weiteres

information desk *n* Auskunftsschalter *m*

information technology *n* Informationstechnik *f*

informative [ɪnfɔrmətɪv] *adj* aufschlussreich

infrared [ɪnfrərɛd] *adj* infrarot

infrastructure [ɪnfrəstrʌktʃər] *n* Infrastruktur *f*

infuriate [ɪnfyʊərieɪt] *vt* wütend machen

infuriating [ɪnfyʊərieɪtɪŋ] *adj* äußerst ärgerlich

infusion [ɪnfyuʒᵊn] *n* (*herbal tea*) Aufguss *m*; (*Med*) Infusion *f*

ingenious [ɪndʒinyəs] *adj* (*person*) erfinderisch; (*device*) raffiniert; (*idea*) genial

ingredient [ɪngridiənt] *n* (*Gastr*) Zutat *f*

inhabit [ɪnhæbɪt] *vt* bewohnen

inhabitant [ɪnhæbɪtənt] *n* Einwohner(in) *m(f)*

inhale [ɪnheɪl] *vt* einatmen; (*cigarettes, Med*) inhalieren

inhaler [ɪnheɪlər] *n* Inhalationsgerät *nt*

inherit [ɪnhɛrɪt] *vt* erben

inheritance [ɪnhɛrɪtᵊns] *n* Erbe *nt*

inhibited [ɪnhɪbɪtɪd] *adj* gehemmt

inhibition [ɪnɪbɪʃᵊn] *n* Hemmung *f*

in-house *adj* intern

inhuman [ɪnhyumən] *adj* unmenschlich

initial [ɪnɪʃᵊl] *adj* anfänglich; **~ stage** Anfangsstadium *nt* ▷ *vt* mit Initialen unterschreiben

initially [ɪnɪʃəli] *adv* anfangs

initials *npl* Initialen *pl*

initiative [ɪnɪʃiətɪv, -ʃətɪv] *n* Initiative *f*

inject [ɪndʒɛkt] *vt* (*drug etc*) einspritzen; **to ~ sb with sth** jdm etw (ein)spritzen

injection [ɪndʒɛkʃᵊn] *n* Spritze *f*, Injektion *f*

injure [ɪndʒər] *vt* verletzen; **to ~ one's leg** sich *dat* das Bein verletzen

injury [ɪndʒəri] *n* Verletzung *f*

injustice [ɪndʒʌstɪs] *n* Ungerechtigkeit *f*

ink [ɪŋk] *n* Tinte *f*

ink-jet printer [ɪŋkdʒɛt prɪntər] *n* Tintenstrahldrucker *m*

inland [*adj* ɪnlənd, *adv* ɪnlænd] *adj* Binnen- ▷ *adv* landeinwärts

in-laws [ɪnlɔz] *npl* (*fam*) Schwiegereltern *pl*

inline skates [ɪnlaɪn skeɪts] *npl* Inlineskates *pl*, Inliner *pl*

inmate [ɪnmeɪt] *n* Insasse *m*

inn [ɪn] *n* Gasthaus *nt*

innate [ɪneɪt] *adj* angeboren

inner [ɪnər] *adj* innere(r, s); **~ city** Innenstadt *f*

innocence [ɪnəsəns] *n* Unschuld *f*

innocent [ɪnəsənt] *adj* unschuldig

innovation [ɪnəveɪʃᵊn] *n* Neuerung *f*

innumerable [ɪnumərəbᵊl] *adj* unzählig

inoculate [ɪnɒkyəleɪt] *vt* impfen (*against* gegen)

inoculation [ɪnɒkyəleɪʃᵊn] *n* Impfung *f*

inpatient [ɪnpeɪʃənt] *n* stationärer Patient, stationäre Patientin

input [ɪnpʊt] *n* (*contribution*) Beitrag *m*; (*Inform*) Eingabe *f*

inquest [ɪnkwɛst] *n* gerichtliche Untersuchung (einer Todesursache)

inquire [ɪnkwaɪər] *vi* sich erkundigen (*about* nach)

inquiry [ɪnkwaɪəri, ɪŋkwɪri] *n* (*question*) Anfrage *f*; (*for information*) Erkundigung *f* (*about* über +*akk*); (*investigation*) Untersuchung *f*

insane [ɪnseɪn] *adj* wahnsinnig; (*Med*) geisteskrank

insanity [ɪnsænɪti] *n* Wahnsinn *m*

insatiable [ɪnseɪʃəbᵊl, -ʃiə-] *adj* unersättlich

inscription [ɪnskrɪpʃᵊn] *n (on stone etc)* Inschrift *f*

insect [ɪnsɛkt] *n* Insekt *nt*

insecticide [ɪnsɛktɪsaɪd] *n* Insektenbekämpfungsmittel *nt*

insect repellent [ɪnsɛkt rɪpɛlənt] *n* Insektenschutzmittel *nt*

insecure [ɪnsɪkyʊər] *adj (person)* unsicher; *(shelves)* instabil

insensitive [ɪnsɛnsɪtɪv] *adj* unempfindlich *(to* gegen); *(unfeeling)* gefühllos

insensitivity [ɪnsɛnsɪtɪvɪti] *n* Unempfindlichkeit *f (to* gegen); *(unfeeling nature)* Gefühllosigkeit *f*

inseparable [ɪnsɛpərəbᵊl] *adj* unzertrennlich

insert [*vb* ɪnsɜrt, *n* ɪnsɜrt] *vt* einfügen; *(coin)* einwerfen; *(key etc)* hineinstecken ▷ *n (in magazine)* Beilage *f*

insertion [ɪnsɜrʃᵊn] *n (in text)* Einfügen *nt*

inside [ɪnsaɪd] *n:* the ~ das Innere; *(surface)* die Innenseite; **from the** ~ von innen ▷ *adj* innere(r, s), Innen-; ~ **lane** *(Auto)* Innenspur *f; (Sport)* Innenbahn *f* ▷ *adv (place)* innen; *(direction)* hinein; **to go** ~ hineingehen ▷ *prep (place)* in +*dat; (into)* in +*akk* ... hinein; *(time, within)* innerhalb +*gen*

inside out *adv* verkehrt herum; *(know)* in- und auswendig

insider [ɪnsaɪdər] *n* Eingeweihte(r) *mf,* Insider(in) *m(f)*

insight [ɪnsaɪt] *n* Einblick *m (into* in +*akk)*

insignificant [ɪnsɪgnɪfɪkənt] *adj* unbedeutend

insincere [ɪnsɪnsɪər] *adj* unaufrichtig, falsch

insinuate [ɪnsɪnyueɪt] *vt* andeuten

insinuation [ɪnsɪnyueɪʃᵊn] *n* Andeutung *f*

insist [ɪnsɪst] *vi* darauf bestehen; **to** ~ **on sth** auf etw *dat* bestehen

insistent [ɪnsɪstənt] *adj* hartnäckig

insoluble [ɪnsɒlyəbᵊl] *adj* unlösbar

insomnia [ɪnsɒmniə] *n* Schlaflosigkeit *f*

inspect [ɪnspɛkt] *vt* prüfen, kontrollieren

inspection [ɪnspɛkʃᵊn] *n* Prüfung *f; (check)* Kontrolle *f*

inspector [ɪnspɛktər] *n (police inspector)* Inspektor(in) *m(f); (senior)* Kommissar(in) *m(f); (on bus etc)* Kontrolleur(in) *m(f)*

inspiration [ɪnspɪreɪʃᵊn] *n* Inspiration *f*

inspire [ɪnspaɪər] *vt (respect)* einflößen *(in*

dat); (person) inspirieren

install [ɪnstɔl] *vt (software)* installieren; *(furnishings)* einbauen

installment [ɪnstɔlmənt] *n* Rate *f; (of story)* Folge *f;* **to pay in** ~**s** auf Raten zahlen

installment plan *n* Ratenkauf *m*

instance [ɪnstəns] *n (of discrimination)* Fall *m; (example)* Beispiel *nt (of* für +*akk)* **for** ~ zum Beispiel

instant [ɪnstənt] *n* Augenblick *m* ▷ *adj* sofortig

instant coffee *n* löslicher Kaffee *m*

instantly [ɪnstᵊntli] *adv* sofort

instant replay *n (Sport, TV)* Wiederholung *f*

instead [ɪnstɛd] *adv* stattdessen

instead of *prep* (an)statt +*gen;* ~ **me** an meiner Stelle; ~ **of going** (an)statt zu gehen

instinct [ɪnstɪŋkt] *n* Instinkt *m*

instinctive [ɪnstɪŋktɪv] *adj,* **instinctively** *adv* instinktiv

institute [ɪnstɪtut] *n* Institut *nt*

institution [ɪnstɪtuʃᵊn] *n (organisation)* Institution *f,* Einrichtung *f; (home)* Anstalt *f*

instruct [ɪnstrʌkt] *vt* anweisen

instruction [ɪnstrʌkʃᵊn] *n (teaching)* Unterricht *m; (command)* Anweisung *f;* ~**s for use** Gebrauchsanweisung *f*

instructor [ɪnstrʌktər] *n* Lehrer(in) *m(f),* Dozent(in) *m(f)*

instrument [ɪnstrəmənt] *n* Instrument *nt*

instrument panel *n* Armaturenbrett *nt*

insufficient [ɪnsəfɪʃᵊnt] *adj* ungenügend

insulate [ɪnsəleɪt] *vt (Elec)* isolieren

insulation [ɪnsəleɪʃᵊn] *n* Isolierung *f*

insulin [ɪnsəlɪn] *n* Insulin *nt*

insult [*n* ɪnsʌlt, *vb* ɪnsʌlt] *n* Beleidigung *f* ▷ *vt* beleidigen

insulting [ɪnsʌltɪŋ] *adj* beleidigend

insurance [ɪnʃʊərəns] *n* Versicherung *f;* ~ **company** Versicherungsgesellschaft *f;* ~ **policy** Versicherungspolice *f*

insure [ɪnʃʊər] *vt* versichern *(against* gegen)

intact [ɪntækt] *adj* intakt

intake [ɪnteɪk] *n* Aufnahme *f*

integrate [ɪntɪgreɪt] *vt* integrieren *(into* in +*akk)*

integration [ɪntɪgreɪʃᵊn] *n* Integration *f*

integrity [ɪntɛgrɪti] *n* Integrität *f,* Ehrlichkeit *f*

intellect [ɪntɪlɛkt] *n* Intellekt *m*

intellectual [ɪntɪlɛktʃuəl] *adj* intellektuell; *(interests etc)* geistig

intelligence [ɪntɛlɪdʒ³ns] n (*understanding*) Intelligenz f

intelligent [ɪntɛlɪdʒ³nt] adj intelligent

intend [ɪntɛnd] vt beabsichtigen; **to ~ to do sth** vorhaben, etw zu tun

intense [ɪntɛns] adj intensiv; (*pressure*) enorm; (*competition*) heftig

intensity [ɪntɛnsɪti] n Intensität f

intensive [ɪntɛnsɪv] adj intensiv

intensive care unit n Intensivstation f

intensive course n Intensivkurs m

intent [ɪntɛnt] adj: **to be ~ on doing sth** fest entschlossen sein, etw zu tun

intention [ɪntɛnʃ³n] n Absicht f

intentional [ɪntɛnʃən³l] adj, **intentionally** adv absichtlich

interact [ɪntərækt] vi aufeinander einwirken

interaction [ɪntəræk³ʃ³n] n Interaktion f, Wechselwirkung f

interactive [ɪntəræktɪv] adj interaktiv

interchange [ɪntərtʃeɪndʒ] n (*of highways*) Autobahnkreuz nt

interchangeable [ɪntərtʃeɪndʒəb³l] adj austauschbar

intercom [ɪntərkɒm] n (Gegen)sprechanlage f

intercourse [ɪntərkɔrs] n (*sexual*) Geschlechtsverkehr m

interest [ɪntrɪst, -tərɪst] n Interesse nt; (*Fin: on money*) Zinsen pl; (*Comm: share*) Anteil m; **to be of ~** von Interesse sein (*to* für) ▷ vt interessieren

interested [ɪntərɛstɪd, -trɪstɪd] adj interessiert (*in* an +dat); **to be ~ed in** sich interessieren für; **are you ~ in coming?** hast du Lust, mitzukommen?

interest-free adj zinsfrei

interesting [ɪntərɛstɪŋ, -trɪstɪŋ] adj interessant

interest rate n Zinssatz m

interface [ɪntərfeɪs] n (*Inform*) Schnittstelle f

interfere [ɪntərfɪər] vi (*meddle*) sich einmischen (*with, in* in +akk)

interference [ɪntərfɪərəns] n Einmischung f; (*TV, Radio*) Störung f

interior [ɪntɪərɪər] adj Innen- ▷ n Innere(s) nt; (*of car*) Innenraum m; (*of house*) Innenausstattung f

intermediate [ɪntərmiːdiːɪt] adj Zwischen-; **~ stage** Zwischenstadium nt

intermission [ɪntərmɪʃ³n] n (*space, time*) Abstand m; (*theater etc*) Pause f

intern [ɪntɜrn] n Assistent(in) m(f)

internal [ɪntɜrn³l] adj innere(r, s); (*flight*) Inlands-; **~ revenue** Finanzamt nt

internally [ɪntɜrn³li] adv innen; (*in body*) innerlich

international [ɪntərnæʃən³l] adj international; **~ match** Länderspiel nt; **~ flight** Auslandsflug m ▷ n (*Sport: player*) Nationalspieler(in) m(f)

internet [ɪntərnɛt] n (*Inform*) Internet nt

internet access n Internetzugang m

internet auction n Internetauktion f

internet banking n Onlinebanking nt

internet café n Internetcafé nt

internet connection n Internetanschluss m

internet provider n Internetprovider m

interpret [ɪntɜrprɪt] vi, vt (*translate*) dolmetschen; (*explain*) interpretieren

interpretation [ɪntɜrprɪteɪʃ³n] n Interpretation f

interpreter [ɪntɜrprɪtər] n Dolmetscher(in) m(f)

interrogate [ɪntɛrəgeɪt] vt verhören

interrogation [ɪntɛrəgeɪʃ³n] n Verhör nt

interrupt [ɪntərʌpt] vt unterbrechen

interruption [ɪntərʌpʃ³n] n Unterbrechung f

intersection [ɪntərsɛkʃ³n] n (*of roads*) Kreuzung f

interstate [ɪntərsteɪt] n zwischenstaatlich; **~ highway** ≈ Bundesautobahn f

intervene [ɪntərviːn] vi eingreifen (*in* in)

intervention [ɪntərvɛnʃ³n] n Eingreifen nt; (*Pol*) Intervention f

interview [ɪntərvjuː] n Interview nt; (*for job*) Vorstellungsgespräch nt ▷ vt interviewen; (*job applicant*) ein Vorstellungsgespräch führen mit

interviewer [ɪntərvjuːər] n Interviewer(in) m(f)

intestine [ɪntɛstɪn] n Darm m; **~s** pl Eingeweide pl

intimate [ɪntɪmɪt] adj (*friends*) vertraut, eng; (*atmosphere*) gemütlich; (*sexually*) intim

intimidate [ɪntɪmɪdeɪt] vt einschüchtern

intimidation [ɪntɪmɪdeɪʃ³n] n Einschüchterung f

into [ɪntu] prep in +akk; (*crash*) gegen; **to change ~ sth** (*turn into*) zu etw werden; (*put on*) sich dat etw anziehen; **to translate ~ French** ins Französische übersetzen; **to be ~ sth** (*fam*) auf etw akk stehen

intolerable [ɪntɒlərəb³l] adj unerträglich

intolerant [ɪntɒlərənt] adj intolerant

intoxicated [ɪntɒksɪkeɪtɪd] *adj* betrunken; (*fig*) berauscht

intricate [ɪntrɪkət] *adj* kompliziert

intrigue [ɪntriːg] *vt* faszinieren

intriguing [ɪntriːgɪŋ] *adj* faszinierend, fesselnd

introduce [ɪntrədjuːs] *vt* (*person*) vorstellen (*to sb* jdm); (*sth new*) einführen (*to in* +*akk*)

introduction [ɪntrədʌkʃ°n] *n* Einführung *f* (*to in* +*akk*); (*to book*) Einleitung *f* (*to* zu); (*to person*) Vorstellung *f*

introvert [ɪntrəvɜːt] *n* Introvertierte(r) *mf*

intuition [ɪntjuːɪʃ°n] *n* Intuition *f*

invade [ɪnveɪd] *vt* einfallen in +*akk*

invalid [*n* ɪnvəlɪd, *adj* ɪnvælɪd] *n* Kranke(r) *mf*; (*disabled*) Invalide *m* ▷ *adj* (*not valid*) ungültig

invaluable [ɪnvæljuəb°l] *adj* äußerst wertvoll, unschätzbar

invariably [ɪnveəriəbli] *adv* ständig; (*every time*) jedes Mal, ohne Ausnahme

invasion [ɪnveɪʒ°n] *n* Invasion *f* (*of in* +*akk*), Einfall *m* (*of in* +*akk*)

invent [ɪnvent] *vt* erfinden

invention [ɪnvenʃ°n] *n* Erfindung *f*

inventor [ɪnventər] *n* Erfinder(in) *m(f)*

invest [ɪnvest] *vt, vi* investieren (*in in* +*akk*)

investigate [ɪnvestɪgeɪt] *vt* untersuchen

investigation [ɪnvestɪgeɪʃ°n] *n* Untersuchung *f* (*into* +*gen*)

investment [ɪnvestmənt] *n* Investition *f*; **it's a good ~** es ist eine gute Anlage; (*it'll be useful*) es macht sich bezahlt

invigorating [ɪnvɪgəreɪtɪŋ] *adj* erfrischend, belebend; (*tonic*) stärkend

invisible [ɪnvɪzɪb°l] *adj* unsichtbar

invitation [ɪnvɪteɪʃ°n] *n* Einladung *f*

invite [ɪnvaɪt] *vt* einladen

invoice [ɪnvɔɪs] *n* (*bill*) Rechnung *f*

involuntary [ɪnvɒlənteri] *adj* unbeabsichtigt

involve [ɪnvɒlv] *vt* verwickeln (*in sth* in etw *akk*); (*entail*) zur Folge haben; **to be ~d in sth** (*participate in*) in etw *dat* beteiligt sein; **I'm not ~d** (*affected*) ich bin nicht betroffen

inward [ɪnwərd] *adj* innere(r, s)

inwardly [ɪnwərdli] *adv* innerlich

inwards [ɪnwərdz] *adv* nach innen

iodine [aɪədaɪn] *n* Jod *nt*

IOU [aɪ oʊ juː] (*abbr*) = **I owe you** Schuldschein *m*

iPod® [aɪpɒd] *n* iPod® *m*

IQ [aɪ kyuː] (*abbr*) = **intelligence quotient** IQ *m*

Iran [ɪræn] *n* der Iran

Iraq [ɪræk] *n* der Irak

Ireland [aɪrlənd] *n* Irland *nt*

iris [aɪrɪs] *n* (*flower*) Schwertlilie *f*; (*of eye*) Iris *f*

Irish [aɪrɪʃ] *adj* irisch; **~ coffee** Irish Coffee *m*; **~ Sea** die Irische See ▷ *n* (*language*) Irisch *nt*; **the ~** *pl* die Iren *pl*

Irishman [aɪrɪʃmən] (*pl* **-men**) *n* Ire *m*

Irishwoman [aɪrɪʃwʊmən] (*pl* **-women**) *n* Irin *f*

iron [aɪərn] *n* Eisen *nt*; (*for ironing*) Bügeleisen *nt* ▷ *adj* eisern ▷ *vt* bügeln

ironic [aɪrɒnɪk] *adj* ironisch

ironing board *n* Bügelbrett *nt*

irony [aɪrəni, aɪər-] *n* Ironie *f*

irrational [ɪræʃ°l] *adj* irrational

irregular [ɪregyələr] *adj* unregelmäßig; (*shape*) ungleichmäßig

irrelevant [ɪreləvnt] *adj* belanglos, irrelevant

irreplaceable [ɪrɪpleɪsəb°l] *adj* unersetzlich

irresistible [ɪrɪzɪstɪb°l] *adj* unwiderstehlich

irrespective of [ɪrɪspektɪv əv] *prep* ungeachtet +*gen*

irresponsible [ɪrɪspɒnsɪb°l] *adj* verantwortungslos

irretrievable [ɪrɪtriːvəb°l] *adv* unwiederbringlich; (*loss*) unersetzlich

irritable [ɪrɪtəb°l] *adj* reizbar

irritate [ɪrɪteɪt] *vt* (*annoy*) ärgern; (*deliberately*) reizen

irritation [ɪrɪteɪʃ°n] *n* (*anger*) Ärger *m*; (*Med*) Reizung *f*

IRS [aɪ ɑːr es] (*abbr*) = **Internal Revenue Service** Finanzamt *nt*

is [ɪz] *present of* **be**; ist

Islam [ɪslɑːm] *n* Islam *m*

Islamic [ɪslæmɪk, -lɑ-] *adj* islamisch

island [aɪlənd] *n* Insel *f*

Isle [aɪl] *n* (*in names*): **the ~ of Man** die Insel Man; **the ~ of Wight** die Insel Wight; **the British ~s** die Britischen Inseln

isn't [ɪz°nt] *contr of* **is not**

isolate [aɪsəleɪt] *vt* isolieren

isolated [aɪsəleɪtɪd] *adj* (*remote*) abgelegen; (*cut off*) abgeschnitten (*from von*); **an ~ case** ein Einzelfall

isolation [aɪsəleɪʃ°n] *n* Isolierung *f*

Israel [ɪzriəl] *n* Israel *nt*

Israeli [ɪzreɪli] *adj* israelisch ▷ *n* Israeli *m o f*

issue [ɪʃu] *n* (*matter*) Frage *f*; (*problem*) Problem *nt*; (*subject*) Thema *nt*; (*of newspaper etc*) Ausgabe *f*; **that's not the ~** darum geht es nicht ▷ *vt* ausgeben; (*document*) ausstellen; (*orders*) erteilen; (*book*) herausgeben

IT [aɪ tiː] (*abbr*) = **information technology** IT *f*

KEYWORD

it [ɪt] *pron* **1** (*specific: subject*) er/sie/es; (*direct object*) ihn/sie/es; (*indirect object*) ihm/ihr/ihm; **about/from/in/of it** darüber/davon/darin/davon
2 (*impers*) es; **it's raining** es regnet; **it's Friday tomorrow** morgen ist Freitag; **who is it? – it's me** wer ist da? – ich (bin's)

Italian [ɪtælɪən] *adj* italienisch ▷ *n* Italiener(in) *m(f)*; (*language*) Italienisch *nt*

italic [ɪtælɪk] *adj* kursiv ▷ *npl*: **in ~s** kursiv

Italy [ɪtəli] *n* Italien *nt*

itch [ɪtʃ] *n* Juckreiz *m*; **I have an ~** mich juckt es ▷ *vi* jucken; **he is ~ing to ...** es juckt ihn, zu ...

itchy [ɪtʃi] *adj* juckend

it'd [ɪtəd] *contr of* **it would; it had**

item [aɪtəm] *n* (*article*) Gegenstand *m*; (*in catalogue*) Artikel *m*; (*on list, in accounts*) Posten *m*; (*on agenda*) Punkt *m*; (*in show, program*) Nummer *f*; (*in news*) Bericht *m*; (*TV: radio*) Meldung *f*

itinerary [aɪtɪnərəri] *n* Reiseroute *f*

it'll [ɪtᵊl] *contr of* **it will; it shall**

its [ɪts] *pron* sein; (*feminine form*) ihr

it's [ɪts] *contr of* **it is; it has**

itself [ɪtsɛlf] *pron* (*reflexive*) sich; (*emphatic*): **the house ~** das Haus selbst *o* an sich; **by ~** allein; **the door closes by ~** die Tür schließt sich von selbst

I've [aɪv] *contr of* **I have**

ivory [aɪvəri] *n* Elfenbein *nt*

ivy [aɪvi] *n* Efeu *m*

J

jab [dʒæb] *vt* (*needle, knife*) stechen (*into* in +*akk*) ▷ *n* (*fam*) Spritze *f*

jack [dʒæk] *n* (*Auto*) Wagenheber *m*; (*Cards*) Bube *m*

jacket [dʒækɪt] *n* Jacke *f*; (*of man's suit*) Jackett *nt*; (*of book*) Schutzumschlag *m*

jackknife [dʒæknaɪf] (*pl* **jackknives**) *n* Klappmesser *nt* ▷ *vi* (*truck*) sich quer stellen

jackpot [dʒækpɒt] *n* Jackpot *m*

jack up *vt* (*car etc*) aufbocken

Jacuzzi® [dʒakuzi] *n* (*bath*) Whirlpool® *m*

jail [dʒeɪl] *n* Gefängnis *nt* ▷ *vt* einsperren

jam [dʒæm] *n* Konfitüre *f*, Marmelade *f*; (*traffic jam*) Stau *m* ▷ *vt* (*street*) verstopfen; (*machine*) blockieren; **to be jammed** (*stuck*) klemmen; **to jam on the brakes** eine Vollbremsung machen

Jamaica [dʒəmeɪkə] *n* Jamaika *nt*

jam-packed [dʒæmpækt] *adj* proppenvoll

Jan (*abbr*) = **January** Jan

janitor [dʒænɪtər] *n* Hausmeister(in) *m(f)*

January [dʒænyuɛri] *n* Januar *m*

Japan [dʒəpæn] *n* Japan *nt*

Japanese [dʒæpəniz] *adj* japanisch ▷ *n* (*person*) Japaner(in) *m(f)*; (*language*) Japanisch *nt*

jar [dʒɑr] *n* Glas *nt*

jaundice [dʒɔndɪs] *n* Gelbsucht *f*

javelin [dʒævlɪn] *n* Speer *m*; (*Sport*) Speerwerfen *nt*

jaw [dʒɔ] *n* Kiefer *m*

jazz [dʒæz] *n* Jazz *m*

jealous [dʒɛləs] *adj* eifersüchtig (*of* auf +*akk*); **don't make me ~** mach mich nicht neidisch

jealousy [dʒɛləsi] *n* Eifersucht *f*

jeans [dʒinz] *npl* Jeans *pl*

Jeep® [dʒip] *n* Jeep® *m*

Jell-O® [dʒɛloʊ] *n* (*dessert*) Götterspeise *f*

jelly [dʒɛli] *n* Gelee *nt*; (*jam*) Marmelade *f*

jellyfish [dʒɛlifɪʃ] *n* Qualle *f*

jeopardize [dʒɛpərdaɪz] *vt* gefährden

jerk [dʒɜrk] *n* Ruck *m*; (*fam: idiot*) Trottel *m* ▷ *vt* ruckartig bewegen ▷ *vi* (*rope*) rucken; (*muscles*) zucken

Jerusalem [dʒərusələm] *n* Jerusalem *nt*

jet [dʒɛt] *n* (*of water etc*) Strahl *m*; (*nozzle*) Düse *f*; (*aircraft*) Düsenflugzeug *nt*

jetlag [dʒɛtlæg] *n* Jetlag *m* (*Müdigkeit nach langem Flug*)

Jew [dʒu] *n* Jude *m*, Jüdin *f*

jewel [dʒuəl] *n* Edelstein *m*; (*esp fig*) Juwel *nt*

jeweler [dʒuələr] *n* Juwelier(in) *m(f)*

jewelry [dʒuəlri] *n* Schmuck *m*

Jewish [dʒuɪʃ] *adj* jüdisch; **she's ~** sie ist Jüdin

jigsaw (puzzle) [dʒɪgsɔ-] *n* Puzzle *nt*

jilt [dʒɪlt] *vt* den Laufpass geben +*dat*

jingle [dʒɪŋgəl] *n* (*advert*) Jingle *m*; (*verse*) Reim *m*

jitters [dʒɪtərz] *npl* (*fam*): **to have the ~** Bammel haben

jittery [dʒɪtəri] *adj* (*fam*) ganz nervös

job [dʒɒb] *n* (*piece of work*) Arbeit *f*; (*task*) Aufgabe *f*; (*occupation*) Stellung *f*, Job *m*; **what's your job?** was machen Sie beruflich?

job hunting *n*: **to go ~** auf Arbeitssuche gehen

jobless [dʒɒblɪs] *adj* arbeitslos

jobseeker [dʒɒbsikər] *n* Arbeitsuchende(r) *mf*

jockey [dʒɒki] *n* Jockey *m*

jog [dʒɒg] *vt* (*person*) anstoßen ▷ *vi* (*run*) joggen

jogging [dʒɒgɪŋ] *n* Jogging *nt*; **to go ~** joggen gehen

john [dʒɒn] *n* (*fam*) Klo *nt*

join [dʒɔɪn] *vt* (*put together*) verbinden (*to* mit); (*club etc*) beitreten +*dat*; **to ~ sb** sich jdm anschließen; (*sit with*) sich zu jdm setzen ▷ *vi* (*unite*) sich vereinigen; (*rivers*) zusammenfließen ▷ *n* Verbindungsstelle *f*; (*seam*) Naht *f*

join in *vi, vt* mitmachen (*sth* bei etw)

joint [dʒɔɪnt] *n* (*of bones*) Gelenk *nt*; (*in pipe etc*) Verbindungsstelle *f*; (*of meat*) Braten *m*; (*of marijuana*) Joint *m* ▷ *adj* gemeinsam

joint account *n* Gemeinschaftskonto *nt*

jointly [dʒɔɪntli] *adv* gemeinsam

joke [dʒoʊk] *n* Witz *m*; (*prank*) Streich *m*; **for a ~** zum Spaß; **it's no ~** das ist nicht zum Lachen ▷ *vi* Witze machen; **you must be joking** das ist ja wohl nicht dein Ernst!

jolly [dʒɒli] *adj* lustig, vergnügt

Jordan [dʒɔrdən] *n* (*country*) Jordanien *nt*; (*river*) Jordan *m*

jot down [dʒɒt daʊn] *vt* sich notieren

journal [dʒɜrnəl] *n* (*diary*) Tagebuch *nt*;

(*magazine*) Zeitschrift *f*

journalism [dʒɜːnəlɪzəm] *n* Journalismus *m*

journalist [dʒɜːnəlɪst] *n* Journalist(in) *m(f)*

journey [dʒɜːni] *n* Reise *f*; (*esp on stage, by car, train*) Fahrt *f*

joy [dʒɔɪ] *n* Freude *f* (*at* über +*akk*)

joystick [dʒɔɪstɪk] *n* (*Inform*) Joystick *m*; (*Aviat*) Steuerknüppel *m*

judge [dʒʌdʒ] *n* Richter(in) *m(f)*; (*Sport*) Punktrichter(in) *m(f)* ▷ *vt* beurteilen (*by* nach); **as far as I can ~** meinem Urteil nach ▷ *vi* urteilen (*by* nach)

judgment [dʒʌdʒmənt] *n* (*Jur*) Urteil *nt*; (*opinion*) Ansicht *f*; **an error of ~** Fehleinschätzung *f*

judo [dʒuːdoʊ] *n* Judo *nt*

jug [dʒʌg] *n* Krug *m*

juggle [dʒʌgəl] *vi* (*lit, fig*) jonglieren (*with* mit)

juice [dʒuːs] *n* Saft *m*

juicy [dʒuːsi] *adj* saftig; (*story, scandal*) pikant

July [dʒʊlaɪ] *n* Juli *m*; *see also* **September**

jumble [dʒʌmbəl] *n* Durcheinander *nt* ▷ *vt*: **to ~ up** durcheinanderwerfen; (*facts*) durcheinanderbringen

jumbo [dʒʌmboʊ] *adj* (*sausage etc*) Riesen-

jumbo jet *n* Jumbojet *m*

jump [dʒʌmp] *vi* springen; (*nervously*) zusammenzucken; **to ~ to conclusions** voreilige Schlüsse ziehen; **to ~ from one thing to another** dauernd das Thema wechseln ▷ *vt* (*a. fig: omit*) überspringen; **to ~ the lights** bei Rot über die Kreuzung fahren; **to ~ the line** sich vordrängen ▷ *n* Sprung *m*; (*for horses*) Hindernis *nt*

jumper [dʒʌmpər] *n* (*dress*) Trägerkleid *nt*; (*person, horse*) Springer(in) *m(f)*

jumper cable *n* Starthilfekabel *nt*

June [dʒuːn] *n* Juni *m*; *see also* **September**

jungle [dʒʌŋgəl] *n* Dschungel *m*

jungle gym *n* Klettergerüst *nt*

junior [dʒuːniər] *adj* (*younger*) jünger; (*lower position*) untergeordnet (*to sb* jdm) ▷ *n*: **she's two years my ~** sie ist zwei Jahre jünger als ich

junior high (school) *n* ≈ Mittelschule *f*

junk [dʒʌŋk] *n* (*trash*) Plunder *m*

junk food *n* Nahrungsmittel *pl* mit geringem Nährwert, Junkfood *nt*

junkie [dʒʌŋki] *n* (*fam*) Junkie *m*, Fixer(in) *m(f)*; (*fig: fan*) Freak *m*

junk mail *n* Reklame *f*; (*Inform*) Junkmail *f*

jury [dʒʊəri] *n* Geschworene *pl*; (*in competition*) Jury *f*

just [dʒʌst] *adj* gerecht ▷ *adv* (*recently*) gerade; (*exactly*) genau; **~ as expected** genau wie erwartet; **~ as nice** genauso nett; (*barely*): **~ in time** gerade noch rechtzeitig; (*immediately*): **~ before/after ...** gleich vor/nach ...; (*small distance*): **~ around the corner** gleich um die Ecke; (*a little*): **~ over an hour** etwas mehr als eine Stunde; (*only*): **~ the two of us** nur wir beide; **~ a moment** Moment mal; (*absolutely, simply*): **it was ~ fantastic** es war einfach klasse; **~ about** so etwa; (*more or less*) mehr oder weniger; **~ about ready** fast fertig

justice [dʒʌstɪs] *n* Gerechtigkeit *f*

justifiable [dʒʌstɪfaɪəbəl] *adj* berechtigt

justifiably [dʒʌstɪfaɪəbli] *adv* zu Recht

justify [dʒʌstɪfaɪ] *vt* rechtfertigen

jut [dʒʌt] *vi*: **to jut out** herausragen

juvenile [dʒuːvənəl, -naɪl] *n, adj* Jugend-, jugendlich ▷ *n* Jugendliche(r) *mf*

K

K [keɪ] (*abbr*) = **kilobyte** KB

k [keɪ] (*abbr*) = **thousand; 15k** 15 000

kangaroo [kæŋgəɾu] *n* Känguru *nt*

karaoke [kæɾiouki] *n* Karaoke *nt*

karate [kəɾɑti] *n* Karate *nt*

kart [kɑrt] *n* Gokart *m*

kayak [kaɪæk] *n* Kajak *m o nt*

kayaking [kaɪækɪŋ] *n* Kajakfahren *nt*

Kazakhstan [kæzəkstæn] *n* Kasachstan *nt*

kebab [kəbɑb] *n* (*shish kebab*) Schaschlik *nt o m*

keel [kil] *n* (*Naut*) Kiel *m*

keel over *vi* (*boat*) kentern; (*person*) umkippen

keen [kin] *adj* begeistert (*on* von); (*hardworking*) eifrig; (*mind, wind*) scharf; (*interest, feeling*) stark; **to be ~ on sb** von jdm angetan sein; **she's ~ on riding** sie reitet gern; **to be ~ to do sth** darauf erpicht sein, etw zu tun

keep [kip] (**kept, kept**) *vt* (*retain*) behalten; (*secret*) für sich behalten; (*observe*) einhalten; (*promise*) halten; (*run: shop, diary, accounts*) führen; (*animals*) halten; (*support, family etc*) versorgen; (*store*) aufbewahren; **to ~ sb waiting** jdn warten lassen; **to ~ sb from doing sth** jdn davon abhalten, etw zu tun; **to ~ sth clean/secret** etw sauber/geheim halten; **'~ clear'** „(bitte) frei halten"; **~ this to yourself** behalten Sie das für sich ▷ *vi* (*food*) sich halten; (*remain, with adj*) bleiben; **~ quiet** sei ruhig!; **to ~ left** links fahren; **to ~ doing sth** (*repeatedly*) etw immer wieder tun; **~ at it** mach weiter so!; **it ~s happening** es passiert immer wieder ▷ *n* (*livelihood*) Unterhalt *m*

keeper [kipər] *n* (*museum etc*) Aufseher(in) *m(f)*; (*goalkeeper*) Torwart *m*; (*zoo keeper*) Tierpfleger(in) *m(f)*

keep off *vt* (*person, animal*) fernhalten; **'~ the grass'** „Betreten des Rasens verboten"

keep on *vi* weitermachen; (*walking*) weitergehen; (*in car*) weiterfahren; **to ~ doing sth** (*persistently*) etw immer wieder tun ▷ *vt* (*coat etc*) anbehalten

keep out *vt* nicht hereinlassen ▷ *vi* draußen bleiben; **'~'** „Eintritt verboten"

keep to *vt* (*road, path*) bleiben auf +*dat*; (*plan etc*) sich halten an +*akk*; **to ~ the point** bei der Sache bleiben

keep up *vi* Schritt halten (*with* mit) ▷ *vt* (*maintain*) aufrechterhalten; (*speed*) halten; **to ~ appearances** den Schein wahren; **keep it up!** (*fam*) weiter so!

kennel [kɛnˀl] *n* Hundehütte *f*

kennels *n* Hundepension *f*

Kenya [kɛnyə] *n* Kenia *nt*

kept [kɛpt] *pt, pp of* **keep**

kerosene [kɛɾəsin] *n* Petroleum *nt*

ketchup [kɛtʃəp, kætʃ-] *n* Ketchup *nt o m*

key [ki] *n* Schlüssel *m*; (*of piano, computer*) Taste *f*; (*Mus*) Tonart *f*; (*for map etc*) Zeichenerklärung *f* ▷ *vt*: **to key in** (*Inform*) eingeben ▷ *adj* entscheidend

keyboard [kibɔrd] *n* (*piano, computer*) Tastatur *f*

keyhole [kihoul] *n* Schlüsselloch *nt*

keypad [kipæd] *n* (*Inform*) Nummernblock *m*

key ring *n* Schlüsselring *m*

kick [kɪk] *n* Tritt *m*; (*Sport*) Stoß *m*; **I get a ~ out of it** (*fam*) es turnt mich an ▷ *vt, vi* treten

kickoff [kɪkɔf] *n* (*Sport*) Anstoß *m*

kick out *vt* (*fam*) rausschmeißen (*of* aus)

kid [kɪd] *n* (*child*) Kind *nt* ▷ *vt* (*tease*) auf den Arm nehmen ▷ *vi* Witze machen; **you're kidding** das ist doch nicht dein Ernst!; **no kidding** aber echt!

kidnap [kɪdnæp] *vt* entführen

kidnaping *n* Entführung *f*

kidnapper [kɪdnæpər] *n* Entführer(in) *m(f)*

kidney [kɪdni] *n* Niere *f*

kill [kɪl] *vt* töten; (*esp intentionally*) umbringen; (*weeds*) vernichten

killer [kɪlər] *n* Mörder(in) *m(f)*

kilo [kilou] (*pl* **-s**) *n* Kilo *nt*

kilobyte [kɪləbaɪt] *n* Kilobyte *nt*

kilogram [kɪləgræm] *n* Kilogramm *nt*

kilometer [kɪləmitər, kɪlɒmitər] *n* Kilometer *m*; **~s per hour** Stundenkilometer *pl*

kilowatt [kɪləwɒt] *n* Kilowatt *nt*

kilt [kɪlt] *n* Schottenrock *m*

kind [kaɪnd] *adj* nett, freundlich (*to* zu) ▷ *n* Art *f*; (*of coffee, cheese etc*) Sorte *f*; **what ~ of ...?** was für ein(e) ...?; **this ~ of ...** so ein(e) ...; **~ of** (+ *adj*) irgendwie

kindergarten [kɪndərgɑrtˀn] *n* Kindergarten *m*

kindly [kaɪndli] *adj* nett, freundlich ▷ *adv*

liebenswürdigerweise

kindness [kaɪndnɪs] n Freundlichkeit f

king [kɪŋ] n König m

kingdom [kɪŋdəm] n Königreich nt

kingfisher [kɪŋfɪʃər] n Eisvogel m

king-size [kɪŋsaɪz] adj im Großformat; (bed) extra groß

kipper [kɪpər] n Räucherhering m

kiss [kɪs] n Kuss m; **~ of life** Mund-zu-Mund-Beatmung f ▷ vt küssen

kit [kɪt] n (for building sth) Bausatz m

kitchen [kɪtʃən] n Küche f

kitchen foil n Alufolie f

kitchen scales n Küchenwaage f

kitchenware [kɪtʃənwɛər] n Küchenge-schirr nt

kite [kaɪt] n Drachen m

kitten [kɪtən] n Kätzchen nt

kiwi [kiwi] n (fruit) Kiwi f

km (abbr) = **kilometers** km

knack [næk] n Dreh m, Trick m; **to get/have got the ~** den Dreh herauskriegen/heraushaben

knee [niː] n Knie nt

kneecap [niːkæp] n Kniescheibe f

knee-jerk [niːdʒɜːk] adj (reaction) reflexar-tig

kneel [niːl] (knelt o kneeled, knelt o kneeled) vi knien; (action, kneel down) sich hinknien

knelt [nɛlt] pt, pp of **kneel**

knew [njuː] pt of **know**

knife [naɪf] (pl knives) n Messer nt

knight [naɪt] n Ritter m; (in chess) Pferd nt, Springer m

knit [nɪt] vt, vi stricken

knitting [nɪtɪŋ] n (piece of work) Strickar-beit f; (activity) Stricken nt

knitting needle n Stricknadel f

knitwear [nɪtwɛər] n Strickwaren pl

knob [nɒb] n (on door) Knauf m; (on radio etc) Knopf m

knock [nɒk] vt (with hammer etc) schla-gen; (accidentally) stoßen; **to ~ one's head** sich dat den Kopf anschlagen ▷ vi klopfen (on, at an +akk) ▷ n (blow) Schlag m; (on

door) Klopfen nt; **there was a ~ at the door** es hat geklopft

knock down vt (object) umstoßen; (person) niederschlagen; (with car) anfahren; (building) abreißen

knocker [nɒkər] n Türklopfer m

knock out vt (stun) bewusstlos schlagen; (boxer) k.o. schlagen

knock over vt umstoßen; (with car) anfah-ren

knot [nɒt] n Knoten m

know [noʊ] (knew, known) vt, vi wissen; (be acquainted with: people, places) ken-nen; (recognize) erkennen; (language) kön-nen; **I'll let you ~** ich sage dir Bescheid; **I ~ some French** ich kann etwas Französisch; **to get to ~ sb** jdn kennenlernen; **to be ~n as** bekannt sein als

know about vt Bescheid wissen über +akk; (subject) sich auskennen in +dat; (cars, horses etc) sich auskennen mit

know-how [noʊhaʊ] n Kenntnis f, Know-how nt

knowing [noʊɪŋ] adj wissend; (look, smile) vielsagend

know-it-all [noʊɪtɔːl] n (fam) Klugscheißer m

knowledge [nɒlɪdʒ] n Wissen nt; (of a sub-ject) Kenntnisse pl; **to the best of my ~** meines Wissens

known [noʊn] pp of **know**

know of vt kennen; **not that I ~** nicht dass ich wüsste

knuckle [nʌkəl] n (Finger)knöchel m; (Gastr) Hachse f

knuckle down vi sich an die Arbeit machen

Koran [kɔrɑːn] n Koran m

Korea [kəriːə] n Korea nt

Kosovo [kɔsəvoʊ] n der Kosovo

kph [keɪ piː eɪtʃ] (abbr) = **kilometers per hour** km/h

Kremlin [krɛmlɪn] n: **the ~** der Kreml

Kurd [kɜːd] n Kurde m, Kurdin f

Kurdish [kɜːdɪʃ] adj kurdisch

Kuwait [kʊweɪt] n Kuwait nt

L

LA [ɛl eɪ] (*abbr*) = Los Angeles

lab [læb] *n* (*fam*) Labor *nt*

label [leɪbʲl] *n* Etikett *nt*; (*tied*) Anhänger *m*; (*adhesive*) Aufkleber *m*; (*record label*) Label *nt* ▷ *vt* etikettieren; (*pej*) abstempeln

labor [leɪbər] *n* Arbeit *f*; (*Med*) Wehen *pl*; **to be in ~** Wehen haben ▷ *adj* (*Pol*) Labour-; **~ Party** Labour Party *f*

laboratory [læbrətɔri] *n* Labor *nt*

LABOR DAY

Der **Labor Day** ist in den USA und Kanada der Name für den Tag der Arbeit. Er wird dort als gesetzlicher Feiertag am ersten Montag im September begangen.

laborer [leɪbərər] *n* Arbeiter(in) *m(f)*

laborious [ləbɔriəs] *adj* mühsam

labor union *n* Gewerkschaft *f*

lace [leɪs] *n* (*fabric*) Spitze *f*; (*of shoe*) Schnürsenkel *m* ▷ *vt*: **to ~ up** zuschnüren

lace-up [leɪsʌp] *n* Schnürschuh *m*

lack [læk] *vt*, *vi*: **to be ~ing** fehlen; **sb ~s o is ~ing in sth** es fehlt jdm an etw *dat*; **we ~ the time** uns fehlt die Zeit ▷ *n* Mangel *m* (*of an +dat*)

lacquer [lækər] *n* Lack *m*

lad [læd] *n* Junge *m*

ladder [lædər] *n* Leiter *f*; (*in pantyhose*) Laufmasche *f*

laden [leɪdʲn] *adj* beladen (*with* mit)

ladies' room [leɪdiz rum] *n* Damentoilette *f*

lady [leɪdi] *n* Dame *f*; (*as title*) Lady *f*

ladybug [leɪdibʌg] *n* Marienkäfer *m*

lag [læg] *vi*: **to lag behind** zurückliegen ▷ *vt* (*pipes*) isolieren

lager [lagər] *n* helles Bier; **~ lout** betrunkener Rowdy

lagging [lægɪŋ] *n* Isolierung *f*

laid [leɪd] *pt*, *pp* of **lay**

laid-back [leɪdbæk] *adj* (*fam*) cool, gelassen

lain [leɪn] *pp* of **lie**

lake [leɪk] *n* See *m*; **the L~ District** Seengebiet im Nordwesten Englands

lamb [læm] *n* Lamm *nt*; (*meat*) Lammfleisch *nt*

lamb chop *n* Lammkotelett *nt*

lame [leɪm] *adj* lahm; (*excuse*) faul; (*argument*) schwach

lament [ləmɛnt] *n* Klage *f* ▷ *vt* beklagen

laminated [læmɪneɪtɪd] *adj* beschichtet

lamp [læmp] *n* Lampe *f*; (*in street*) Laterne *f*; (*in car*) Licht *nt*, Scheinwerfer *m*

lamppost [læmppoʊst] *n* Laternenpfahl *m*

lampshade [læmpʃeɪd] *n* Lampenschirm *m*

land [lænd] *n* Land *nt* ▷ *vi* (*from ship*) an Land gehen; (*Aviat*) landen ▷ *vt* (*passengers*) absetzen; (*goods*) abladen; (*plane*) landen

landing [lændɪŋ] *n* Landung *f*; (*on stairs*) Treppenabsatz *m*

landing gear *n* Fahrgestell *nt*

landing strip *n* Landebahn *f*

landlady [lændleɪdi] *n* Hauswirtin *f*, Vermieterin *f*

landlord [lændlɔrd] *n* (*of house*) Hauswirt *m*, Vermieter *m*; (*of pub*) Gastwirt *m*

landmark [lændmɑrk] *n* Wahrzeichen *nt*; (*event*) Meilenstein *m*

landowner [lændoʊnər] *n* Grundbesitzer(in) *m(f)*

landscape [lændskeɪp] *n* Landschaft *f*; (*format*) Querformat *nt*

landslide [lændslaɪd] *n* (*Geo*) Erdrutsch *m*

lane [leɪn] *n* (*in country*) enge Landstraße, Weg *m*; (*in town*) Gasse *f*; (*of highway*) Spur *f*; (*Sport*) Bahn *f*

language [læŋgwɪdʒ] *n* Sprache *f*; (*style*) Ausdrucksweise *f*

lantern [læntərn] *n* Laterne *f*

lap [læp] *n* Schoß *m*; (*in race*) Runde *f* ▷ *vt* (*in race*) überholen

lapse [læps] *n* (*mistake*) Irrtum *m*; (*moral*) Fehltritt *m* ▷ *vi* ablaufen

laptop [læptɒp] *n* Laptop *m*

large [lɑrdʒ] *adj* groß; **by and ~** im Großen und Ganzen

largely [lɑrdʒli] *adv* zum größten Teil

large-scale [lɑrdʒskeɪl] *adj* groß angelegt, Groß-

lark [lɑrk] *n* (*bird*) Lerche *f*

laryngitis [lærɪndʒaɪtɪs] *n* Kehlkopfentzündung *f*

larynx [lærɪŋks] *n* Kehlkopf *m*

laser [leɪzər] *n* Laser *m*

laser printer *n* Laserdrucker *m*

lash [læʃ] *vt* peitschen

lash out *vi* (*with fists*) um sich schlagen

lass [læs] *n* Mädchen *nt*

last [læst] *adj* letzte(r, s); **the ~ but one** der/die/das vorletzte; **~ night** gestern Abend; **~ but not least** nicht zuletzt ▷ *adv* zuletzt; (*last time*) das letzte Mal; **at ~** endlich ▷ *n* (*person*) Letzte(r) *mf*; (*thing*) Letzte(s) *nt*; **he was the ~ to leave** er ging als Letzter ▷ *vi* (*continue*) dauern; (*remain in good condition*) durchhalten; (*remain good*) sich halten; (*money*) ausreichen

lasting [læstɪŋ] *adj* dauerhaft; (*impression*) nachhaltig

lastly [læstli] *adv* schließlich

last-minute [læstmɪnɪt] *adj* in letzter Minute

last name *n* Nachname *m*

late [leɪt] *adj* spät; (*after proper time*) zu spät; (*train etc*) verspätet; (*dead*) verstorben; **to be ~** zu spät kommen; (*train etc*) Verspätung haben ▷ *adv* spät; (*after proper time*) zu spät

lately [leɪtli] *adv* in letzter Zeit

later [leɪtər] *adj, adv* später; **see you ~** bis später

latest [leɪtɪst] *adj* späteste(r, s); (*most recent*) neueste(r, s) ▷ *n*: **the ~** (*news*) das Neueste; **at the ~** spätestens

Latin [lætɪn, -t³n] *n* Latein *nt* ▷ *adj* lateinisch

Latin America *n* Lateinamerika *nt*

Latin American *adj* lateinamerikanisch ▷ *n* Lateinamerikaner(in) *m(f)*

latter [lætər] *adj* (*second of two*) letztere(r, s); (*last: part, years*) letzte(r, s), später

Latvia [lætviə] *n* Lettland *nt*

Latvian [lætviən] *adj* lettisch ▷ *n* (*person*) Lette *m*, Lettin *f*; (*language*) Lettisch *nt*

laugh [læf] *n* Lachen *nt*; **for a ~** aus Spaß ▷ *vi* lachen (*at, about* über +*akk*); **to ~ at sb** sich über jdn lustig machen; **it's no ~ing matter** es ist nicht zum Lachen

laughter [læftər] *n* Gelächter *nt*

launch [lɔːntʃ] *n* (*launching: of ship*) Stapellauf *m*; (*of rocket*) Abschuss *m*; (*of product*) Markteinführung *f*; (*with hype*) Lancierung *f*; (*event*) Eröffnungsfeier *f* ▷ *vt* (*ship*) vom Stapel lassen; (*rocket*) abschießen; (*product*) einführen; (*with hype*) lancieren; (*project*) in Gang setzen

launder [lɔːndər] *vt* waschen und bügeln; (*fig: money*) waschen

laundromat [lɔːndrəmæt] *n* Waschsalon *m*

laundry [lɔːndri] *n* (*place*) Wäscherei *f*; (*clothes*) Wäsche *f*

lavatory [lævətɔri] *n* Toilette *f*

lavender [lævɪndər] *n* Lavendel *m*

lavish [lævɪʃ] *adj* verschwenderisch; (*furnishings etc*) üppig; (*gift*) großzügig

law [lɔ] *n* Gesetz *nt*; (*system*) Recht *nt*; (*for study*) Jura; (*of sport*) Regel *f*; **against the law** gesetzwidrig

law-abiding [lɔːəbaɪdɪŋ] *adj* gesetzestreu

lawful [lɔːfəl] *adj* rechtmäßig

lawn [lɔn] *n* Rasen *m*

lawn mower [lɔnmoʊər] *n* Rasenmäher *m*

lawsuit [lɔːsut] *n* Prozess *m*

lawyer [lɔɪər, lɔjər] *n* Rechtsanwalt *m*, Rechtsanwältin *f*

laxative [læksətɪv] *n* Abführmittel *nt*

lay [leɪ] *pt of* **lie** ▷ *vt* (**laid, laid**) legen; (*table*) decken; (*egg*) legen ▷ *adj* Laien-

layabout [leɪəbaʊt] *n* Faulenzer(in) *m(f)*

lay down *vt* hinlegen

layer [leɪər] *n* Schicht *f*

layman [leɪmən] *n* Laie *m*

lay off *vt* (*workers*) (vorübergehend) entlassen; (*stop attacking*) in Ruhe lassen

lay on *vt* (*paint*) auftragen

layout [leɪaʊt] *n* Gestaltung *f*; (*of book etc*) Lay-out *nt*

laze [leɪz] *vi* faulenzen

laziness [leɪzinɪs] *n* Faulheit *f*

lazy [leɪzi] *adj* faul; (*day, time*) gemütlich

lb (*abbr*) = **pound** Pfd.

lead [liːd] *n* Blei *nt* ▷ *vt*, (**led, led**) führen; (*group etc*) leiten; **to ~ the way** vorangehen; **this is ~ing us nowhere** das bringt uns nicht weiter ▷ *n* (*race*) Führung *f*; (*distance, time ahead*) Vorsprung *m* (*over* vor +*dat*); (*of police*) Spur *f*; (*Theat*) Hauptrolle *f*; (*dog's*) Leine *f*; (*Elec: flex*) Leitung *f*

lead astray *vt* irreführen

lead away *vt* wegführen

lead back *vi* zurückführen

leaded [lɛdɪd] *adj* (*petrol*) verbleit

leader [liːdər] *n* Führer(in) *m(f)*; (*of party*) Vorsitzende(r) *mf*; (*of project, expedition*) Leiter(in) *m(f)*; (*Sport: in race*) der/die Erste; (*in league*) Tabellenführer *m*

leadership [liːdərʃip] *n* Führung *f*

lead-free [lɛd friː] *adj* (*petrol*) bleifrei

leading [liːdɪŋ] *adj* führend, wichtig

lead on *vt* anführen

lead to *vt* (*street*) hinführen nach; (*result in*) führen zu

lead up to *vt* (*drive*) führen zu

leaf [liːf] *n* (*pl* **leaves**) Blatt *nt*

leaflet [liːflɪt] *n* Prospekt *m*; (*pamphlet*) Flugblatt *nt*; (*with instructions*) Merkblatt *nt*

league [liːɡ] n Bund m; (*Sport*) Liga f
leak [liːk] n (*gap*) undichte Stelle; (*escape*) Leck nt ▷ vi (*pipe etc*) undicht sein; (*liquid etc*) auslaufen
leaky [liːki] adj undicht
lean [liːn] adj (*meat*) mager; (*face*) schmal; (*person*) drahtig ▷ vi (**leant** o **leaned, leant** o **leaned**) (*not vertical*) sich neigen; (*rest*): **to ~ against sth** sich an etw *akk* lehnen; (*support oneself*): **to ~ on sth** sich auf etw *akk* stützen ▷ vt lehnen (*on, against* an +*akk*)
lean back vi sich zurücklehnen
lean forward vi sich vorbeugen
lean over vi sich hinüberbeugen
lean towards vt tendieren zu
leap [liːp] n Sprung m ▷ vi (**leapt** o **leaped, leapt** o **leaped**) springen
leapt [lɛpt] pt, pp of **leap**
leap year n Schaltjahr nt
learn [lɜːrn] (**learnt, learned**) vt, vi lernen; (*find out*) erfahren; **to ~ how to swim** schwimmen lernen
learned [lɜːrnɪd] adj gelehrt
learner [lɜːrnər] n Anfänger(in) m(f)
lease [liːs] n (*of land, premises etc*) Pacht f; (*contract*) Pachtvertrag m; (*of house, car etc*) Miete f; (*contract*) Mietvertrag m ▷ vt pachten; (*house, car etc*) mieten
leasing [liːsɪŋ] n Leasing nt
least [liːst] adj wenigste(r, s); (*slightest*) geringste(r, s) ▷ adv am wenigsten; ~ **expensive** billigste(r, s) ▷ n: **the ~** das Mindeste; **not in the ~** nicht im geringsten; **at ~** wenigstens; (*with number*) mindestens
leather [lɛðər] n Leder nt ▷ adj ledern, Leder-
leave [liːv] n (*time off*) Urlaub m; **on ~** auf Urlaub; **to take one's ~** Abschied nehmen (*of* von) ▷ vt (**left, left**) (*place, person*) verlassen; (*not remove, not change*) lassen; (*leave behind: message, scar etc*) hinterlassen; (*forget*) hinter sich lassen; (*after death*) hinterlassen (*to sb* jdm); (*entrust*) überlassen (*to sb* jdm); **to be left** (*remain*) übrig bleiben; ~ **me alone** lass mich in Ruhe!; **don't ~ it to the last minute** warte nicht bis zur letzten Minute ▷ vi (*weg*) gehen, (weg)fahren; (*on journey*) abreisen; (*bus, train*) abfahren (*for* nach)
leave behind vt zurücklassen; (*scar etc*) hinterlassen; (*forget*) hinter sich lassen
leave out vt auslassen; (*person*) ausschließen (*of* von)

leaves [liːvz] pl of **leaf**
Lebanon [lɛbənɒn] n: **the ~** der Libanon
lecture [lɛktʃər] n Vortrag m; (*at university*) Vorlesung f; **to give a ~** einen Vortrag/eine Vorlesung halten
lecturer [lɛktʃərər] n Dozent(in) m(f)
LED [ɛl o diː] (*abbr*) = **light-emitting diode** Leuchtdiode f
led [lɛd] pt, pp of **lead**
ledge [lɛdʒ] n Leiste f; (*window ledge*) Sims m o nt
leek [liːk] n Lauch m
left [lɛft] pt, pp of **leave** ▷ adj linke(r, s) ▷ adv (*position*) links; (*movement*) nach links ▷ n (*side*) linke Seite; **the L~** (*Pol*) die Linke; **on/to the ~** links (*of* von); **move/fall to the ~** nach links rücken/fallen
left-hand [lɛfthænd] adj linke(r, s); ~ **bend** Linkskurve f; ~ **drive** Linkssteuerung f
left-handed [lɛfthændɪd] adj linkshändig
left-hand side n linke Seite
leftovers [lɛftoʊvərz] npl Reste pl
left wing [lɛft wɪŋ] n linker Flügel
left-wing [lɛftwɪŋ] adj (*Pol*) linksgerichtet
leg [lɛɡ] n Bein nt; (*of meat*) Keule f
legacy [lɛɡəsi] n Erbe nt, Erbschaft f
legal [liːɡəl] adj Rechts-, rechtlich; (*allowed*) legal; (*limit, age*) gesetzlich; ~ **aid** Rechtshilfe f
legalize [liːɡəlaɪz] vt legalisieren
legally [liːɡəli] adv legal
legend [lɛdʒənd] n Legende f
legible [lɛdʒɪbəl] adj, **legibly** adv leserlich
legislation [lɛdʒɪsleɪʃən] n Gesetze pl
legitimate [lɪdʒɪtɪmɪt] adj rechtmäßig, legitim
legroom [lɛɡrʊm] n Beinfreiheit f
leisure [liːʒər, lɛʒ-] n (*time*) Freizeit f ▷ adj Freizeit-
leisurely [liːʒərli, lɛʒ-] adj gemächlich
lemon [lɛmən] n Zitrone f
lemonade [lɛməneɪd] n Limonade f
lemon curd n Brotaufstrich aus Zitronen, Butter, Eiern und Zucker
lemon juice n Zitronensaft m
lend [lɛnd] (**lent, lent**) vt leihen; **to ~ sb sth** jdm etw leihen; **to sb ~ a hand** (jdm) behilflich sein
length [lɛŋθ] n Länge f; **4 metres in ~** 4 Meter lang; **what ~ is it?** wie lange ist es?; **for any ~ of time** für längere Zeit; **at ~** (*lengthily*) ausführlich
lengthen [lɛŋθən] vt verlängern
lengthy [lɛŋθi] adj sehr lange; (*dragging*) langwierig

lenient [liːniənt, liːnyənt] *adj* nachsichtig
lens [lɛnz] *n* Linse *f*; (*Foto*) Objektiv *nt*
Lent [lɛnt] *n* Fastenzeit *f*
lent [lɛnt] *pt, pp of* lend
lentil [lɛntɪl, -tᵊl] *n* (*Bot*) Linse *f*
Leo [liːou] (*pl* **-s**) *n* (*Astr*) Löwe *m*
leopard [lɛpərd] *n* Leopard *m*
lesbian [lɛzbiən] *adj* lesbisch ▷ *n* Lesbe *f*
less [lɛs] *adj, adv, n* weniger; **~ and ~** immer weniger; (*less often*) immer seltener
lessen [lɛsᵊn] *vi* abnehmen, nachlassen ▷ *vt* verringern; (*pain*) lindern
lesser [lɛsər] *adj* geringer; (*amount*) kleiner
lesson [lɛsᵊn] *n* (*at school*) Stunde *f*; (*unit of study*) Lektion *f*; (*fig*) Lehre *f*; (*Rel*) Lesung *f*; **~s start at 9** der Unterricht beginnt um 9
let [lɛt] (**let, let**) *vt* lassen; (*lease*) vermieten; **to let sb have sth** jdm etw geben; **let's go** gehen wir; **to let go of sth** (etw) loslassen
let down *vt* herunterlassen; (*fail to help*) im Stich lassen; (*disappoint*) enttäuschen
lethal [liːθᵊl] *adj* tödlich
let in *vt* hereinlassen
let off *vt* (*bomb*) hochgehen lassen; (*person*) laufen lassen
let out *vt* hinauslassen; (*secret*) verraten; (*scream etc*) ausstoßen
let's [lɛts] (*contr*) = let us
letter [lɛtər] *n* (*of alphabet*) Buchstabe *m*; (*message*) Brief *m*; (*official letter*) Schreiben *nt*
letter bomb *n* Briefbombe *f*
lettuce [lɛtɪs] *n* Kopfsalat *m*
let up *vi* nachlassen; (*stop*) aufhören
leukemia [luːkiːmiə] *n* Leukämie *f*
level [lɛvᵊl] *adj* (*horizontal*) waagerecht; (*ground*) eben; (*two things, two runners*) auf selber Höhe; **to be ~ with sb/sth** mit jdm/etw auf gleicher Höhe sein ▷ *adv* (*run etc*) auf gleicher Höhe, gleich auf; (*in game*) ausgleichen ▷ *n* (*altitude*) Höhe *f*; (*standard*) Niveau *nt*; (*amount, degree*) Grad *m*; **to be on a ~ with** auf gleicher Höhe sein mit ▷ *vt* (*ground*) einebnen
levelheaded [lɛvᵊlhɛdɪd] *adj* vernünftig
lever [livər, lɛv-] *n* Hebel *m*; (*fig*) Druckmittel *nt*
liability [laɪəbɪlɪti] *n* Haftung *f*; (*burden*) Belastung *f*; (*obligation*) Verpflichtung *f*
liable [laɪəbᵊl] *adj*: **to be ~ for sth** (*responsible*) für etw haften; **~ for tax** steuerpflichtig
liar [laɪər] *n* Lügner(in) *m(f)*

liberal [lɪbərəl, lɪbrəl] *adj* (*generous*) großzügig; (*broad-minded*) liberal
liberate [lɪbəreɪt] *vt* befreien
liberation [lɪbəreɪ∫ᵊn] *n* Befreiung *f*
Liberia [laɪbɪriə] *n* Liberia *nt*
liberty [lɪbərti] *n* Freiheit *f*
Libra [liːbrə] *n* (*Astr*) Waage *f*
library [laɪbrɛri] *n* Bibliothek *f*; (*lending library*) Bücherei *f*; (*public library*) Leihbücherei *f*
Libya [lɪbiə] *n* Libyen *nt*
lice [laɪs] *pl of* louse
license [laɪsᵊns] *n* (*permit*) Genehmigung *f*; (*Comm*) Lizenz *f*; (*driver's license*) Führerschein *m* ▷ *vt* genehmigen
licensed [laɪsᵊnst] *adj* (*restaurant etc*) mit Schankerlaubnis
license number *n* (*Auto*) (polizeiliches) Kennzeichen
license plate *n* (*Auto*) Nummernschild *nt*
lick [lɪk] *vt* lecken ▷ *n* Lecken *nt*
licorice [lɪkərɪ∫, -ɪs] *n* Lakritze *f*
lid [lɪd] *n* Deckel *m*; (*eyelid*) Lid *nt*
lie [laɪ] *n* Lüge *f*; **lie detector** Lügendetektor *m* ▷ *vi* lügen; **to lie to sb** jdn belügen ▷ *vi* (**lay, lain**) (*rest, be situated*) liegen; (*lie down*) sich legen; (*snow*) liegen bleiben; **to be lying third** an dritter Stelle liegen
lie around *vi* herumliegen
Liechtenstein [lɪktənstaɪn] *n* Liechtenstein *nt*
lie down *vi* sich hinlegen
life [laɪf] (*pl* **lives**) *n* Leben *nt*; **to get ~** lebenslänglich bekommen; **there isn't much ~ here** hier ist nicht viel los; **how many lives were lost?** wie viele sind ums Leben gekommen?
lifeboat [laɪfbout] *n* Rettungsboot *nt*
lifeguard [laɪfgard] *n* Bademeister(in) *m(f)*, Rettungsschwimmer(in) *m(f)*
life insurance *n* Lebensversicherung *f*
life jacket *n* Schwimmweste *f*
lifeless [laɪflɪs] *adj* (*dead*) leblos
lifelong [laɪflɔŋ] *adj* lebenslang
life preserver [laɪf prɪzɜrvər] *n* Rettungsring *m*
lifesaving [laɪfseɪvɪŋ] *adj* lebensrettend
life-size(d) [laɪfsaɪz(d)] *adj* in Lebensgröße
life span *n* Lebensspanne *f*
lifestyle [laɪfstaɪl] *n* Lebensstil *m*
lifetime [laɪftaɪm] *n* Lebenszeit *f*
lift [lɪft] *vt* (hoch)heben; (*ban*) aufheben ▷ *n* Aufzug *m*, Lift *m*; **to give sb a ~** jdn im Auto mitnehmen

liftoff [lɪftɔf] n Start m
lift up vt hochheben
ligament [lɪgəmənt] n Band nt
light [laɪt] (lit o lighted, lit o lighted) vt beleuchten; (fire, cigarette) anzünden ▷ n Licht nt; (lamp) Lampe f; **~s** pl (Auto) Beleuchtung f; (traffic lights) Ampel f; **in the ~ of** angesichts +gen ▷ adj (bright) hell; (not heavy, easy) leicht; (punishment) milde; (taxes) niedrig; **~ blue/green** hellblau/hellgrün
light bulb n Glühbirne f
lighten [laɪtⁿn] vi hell werden ▷ vt (give light to) erhellen; (make less heavy) leichter machen; (fig) erleichtern
lighter [laɪtər] n (cigarette lighter) Feuerzeug nt
lighthearted [laɪthɑrtɪd] adj unbeschwert
lighthouse [laɪthaʊs] n Leuchtturm m
lighting [laɪtɪŋ] n Beleuchtung f
lightly [laɪtlɪ] adv leicht
light meter n (Foto) Belichtungsmesser m
lightning [laɪtnɪŋ] n Blitz m
light up vt (illuminate) beleuchten ▷ vi (a. eyes) aufleuchten
lightweight [laɪtweɪt] adj leicht
like [laɪk, laɪk] vt mögen, gernhaben; **he ~s** swimming er schwimmt gern; **would you ~ ...?** hättest du/hätten Sie gern ...?; **I'd ~ to go home** ich möchte nach Hause (gehen); **I don't ~ the movie** der Film gefällt mir nicht ▷ prep wie; **what's it/he ~?** wie ist es/er?; **he looks ~ you** er sieht dir/Ihnen ähnlich; **~ that/this** so
likeable [laɪkəbⁿl] adj sympathisch
likelihood [laɪklɪhʊd] n Wahrscheinlichkeit f
likely [laɪklɪ] adj wahrscheinlich; **the bus is ~ to be late** der Bus wird wahrscheinlich Verspätung haben; **he's not at all ~ to come** (höchst)wahrscheinlich kommt er nicht
like-minded [laɪkmaɪndɪd] adj gleichgesinnt
likewise [laɪkwaɪz] adv ebenfalls; **to do ~** das Gleiche tun
liking [laɪkɪŋ] n (for person) Zuneigung f; (for type, things) Vorliebe f (for für)
lilac [laɪlɑk, -læk, -lək] n Flieder m ▷ adj fliederfarben
lily [lɪlɪ] n Lilie f; **~ of the valley** Maiglöckchen nt
limb [lɪm] n Glied nt
limbo [lɪmboʊ] n: **in ~** (plans) auf Eis gelegt

lime [laɪm] n (tree) Linde f; (fruit) Limone f; (substance) Kalk m
lime juice n Limonensaft m
limelight [laɪmlaɪt] n (fig) Rampenlicht nt
limerick [lɪmərɪk] n Limerick m (fünfzeiliges komisches Gedicht)
limestone [laɪmstoʊn] n Kalkstein m
limit [lɪmɪt] n Grenze f; (for pollution etc) Grenzwert m; **there's a ~ to that** dem sind Grenzen gesetzt; **to be over the ~** (speed) das Tempolimit überschreiten; (alcohol consumption) fahruntüchtig sein; **that's the ~** jetzt reicht's!, das ist die Höhe! ▷ vt beschränken (to auf +akk); (freedom, spending) einschränken
limitation [lɪmɪteɪʃⁿn] n Beschränkung f; (of freedom, spending) Einschränkung f
limited [lɪmɪtɪd] adj begrenzt; **~ liability company** Gesellschaft f mit beschränkter Haftung, GmbH f; **public ~ company** Aktiengesellschaft f
limousine [lɪməzin] n Limousine f
limp [lɪmp] vi hinken ▷ adj schlaff
line [laɪn] n Linie f; (written) Zeile f; (rope) Leine f; (on face) Falte f; (row) Reihe f; (queue) Schlange f; (Rail) Bahnlinie f; (between A and B) Strecke f; (Tel) Leitung f; (range of items) Kollektion f; **hold the ~** bleiben Sie am Apparat; **to stand in ~** Schlange stehen; **in ~ with** in Übereinstimmung mit; **something along those ~s** etwas in dieser Art; **drop me a ~** schreib mir ein paar Zeilen; **~s** (Theat) Text m ▷ vt (clothes) füttern; (streets) säumen
lined [laɪnd] adj (paper) liniert; (face) faltig
linen [lɪnɪn] n Leinen nt; (sheets etc) Wäsche f
liner [laɪnər] n Überseedampfer m, Passagierschiff nt
line up vi sich aufstellen; (form queue) sich anstellen
linger [lɪŋgər] vi verweilen; (smell) nicht weggehen
lingerie [lɑnʒəreɪ, læn-] n Damenunterwäsche f
lining [laɪnɪŋ] n (of clothes) Futter nt; (brake lining) Bremsbelag m
link [lɪŋk] n (connection) Verbindung f; (of chain) Glied nt; (relationship) Beziehung f (with zu); (between events) Zusammenhang m; (internet) Link m ▷ vt verbinden
lion [laɪən] n Löwe m
lioness [laɪənɪs] n Löwin f
lip [lɪp] n Lippe f

lipstick [lɪpstɪk] n Lippenstift m

liqueur [lɪkɜr, -kyuər] n Likör m

liquid [lɪkwɪd] n Flüssigkeit f ▷ adj flüssig

liquidate [lɪkwɪdeɪt] vt liquidieren

liquor [lɪkər] n Spirituosen pl

liquor store n Wein- und Spirituosenhandlung f

Lisbon [lɪzbən] n Lissabon nt

lisp [lɪsp] vt, vi lispeln

list [lɪst] n Liste f ▷ vi (ship) Schlagseite haben ▷ vt auflisten, aufzählen

listen [lɪsˀn] vi zuhören, horchen (for sth auf etw akk)

listener [lɪsˀnər, lɪsnər] n Zuhörer(in) m(f); (to radio) Hörer(in) m(f)

listen to vt (person) zuhören +dat; (radio) hören; (advice) hören auf

lit [lɪt] pt, pp of light

liter [lɪtər] n Liter m

literacy [lɪtərəsi] n Fähigkeit f zu lesen und zu schreiben

literal [lɪtərəl] adj (translation, meaning) wörtlich; (actual) buchstäblich

literally [lɪtərəli] adv (translate, take sth) wörtlich; (really) buchstäblich, wirklich

literary [lɪtəreri] adj literarisch; (critic, journal etc) Literatur-; (language) gehoben

literature [lɪtərətʃər, -tʃur] n Literatur f; (brochures etc) Informationsmaterial nt

Lithuania [lɪθyueɪniə] n Litauen nt

Lithuanian [lɪθyueɪniən] adj litauisch ▷ n (person) Litauer(in) m(f); (language) Litauisch nt

litter [lɪtər] n Abfälle pl; (of animals) Wurf m ▷ vt: to be ~ed with übersät sein mit

little [lɪtˀl] adj (smaller, smallest) klein; (in quantity) wenig; a ~ while ago vor kurzer Zeit ▷ adv, n (fewer, fewest) wenig; a ~ ein bisschen, ein wenig; as ~ as possible so wenig wie möglich; for as ~ as $5 ab nur 5 Dollar; I see very ~ of them ich sehe sie sehr selten; ~ by ~ nach und nach

little finger n kleiner Finger

live [laɪv] adj lebendig; (Elec) geladen, unter Strom; (TV, Radio: event) live; ~ broadcast Direktübertragung f ▷ vi [lɪv] leben; (not die) überleben; (dwell) wohnen; you ~ and learn man lernt nie aus ▷ vt [lɪv] (life) führen; to ~ a life of luxury im Luxus leben

liveliness [laɪvlinɪs] n Lebhaftigkeit f

lively [laɪvli] adj lebhaft

live on vi weiterleben ▷ vt: to ~ sth von etw leben; (feed) sich von etw ernähren; to

earn enough to ~ genug verdienen, um davon zu leben

liver [lɪvər] n Leber f

lives [laɪvz] pl of life

livestock [laɪvstɒk] n Vieh nt

live together vi zusammenleben

live up to vt (reputation) gerecht werden +dat; (expectations) entsprechen +dat

live with vt (parents etc) wohnen bei; (partner) zusammenleben mit; (difficulty): you'll just have to ~ it du musst dich/Sie müssen sich eben damit abfinden

living [lɪvɪŋ] n Lebensunterhalt m; what do you do for a ~? was machen Sie beruflich? ▷ adj lebend

living room n Wohnzimmer nt

lizard [lɪzərd] n Eidechse f

llama [lɑmə] n (Zool) Lama nt

load [loud] n Last f; (cargo) Ladung f; (Tech: fig) Belastung f; ~s of (fam) massenhaft; it was a ~ of garbage (fam) es war grottenschlecht ▷ vt (vehicle) beladen; (Inform) laden; (film) einlegen

loaf [louf] (pl loaves) n: a ~ of bread ein (Laib) Brot (m)nt

loan [loun] n (item lent) Leihgabe f; (Fin) Darlehen nt; on ~ geliehen ▷ vt leihen (to sb jdm)

loathe [louð] vt verabscheuen

loaves [louvz] pl of loaf

lobby [lɒbi] n Vorhalle f; (Pol) Lobby f

lobster [lɒbstər] n Hummer m

local [loukˀl] adj (traffic, time etc) Orts-; (radio, news, paper) Lokal-; (government, authority) Kommunal-; (anaesthetic) örtlich; ~ call (Tel) Ortsgespräch nt; ~ elections Kommunalwahlen pl; ~ time Ortszeit f; ~ train Nahverkehrszug m; the ~ stores die Geschäfte am Ort ▷ n (pub) Stammlokal nt; the ~s pl die Ortsansässigen pl

locally [loukˀli] adv örtlich, am Ort

locate [loukeɪt] vt (find) ausfindig machen; (position) legen; (establish) errichten; to be ~d sich befinden (in, at in +dat)

location [loukeɪˀn] n (position) Lage f; (Cine) Drehort m

loch [lɒx, lɒk] n (SCOT) See m

lock [lɒk] n Schloss nt; (Naut) Schleuse f; (of hair) Locke f ▷ vt (door etc) abschließen ▷ vi (door etc) sich abschließen lassen; (wheels) blockieren

locker [lɒkər] n Schließfach nt

locker room n Umkleideraum m

lock in vt einschließen, einsperren

lock out vt aussperren

locksmith [lɒksmɪθ] *n* Schlosser(in) *m(f)*

lock up *vt* (*house*) abschließen; (*person*) einsperren

locust [loukəst] *n* Heuschrecke *f*

lodge [lɒdʒ] *n* (*small house*) Pförtnerhaus *nt*; (*porter's lodge*) Pförtnerloge *f* ▷ *vi* in Untermiete wohnen (*with* bei); (*get stuck*) stecken bleiben

lodger [lɒdʒər] *n* Untermieter(in) *m(f)*

lodging [lɒdʒɪŋ] *n* Unterkunft *f*

loft [lɒft] *n* Dachboden *m*

log [lɒg] *n* Klotz *m*; (*Naut*) Log *nt*; **to keep a log of sth** über etw Buch führen

logic [lɒdʒɪk] *n* Logik *f*

logical [lɒdʒɪkᵊl] *adj* logisch

log in *vi* (*Inform*) sich einloggen

login [lɒgɪn] *n* (*Inform*) Log-in *nt*, Anmeldung *f*

logo [lougou] (*pl* -s) *n* Logo *nt*

log off *vi* (*Inform*) sich ausloggen

log on *vi* (*Inform*) sich einloggen

log out *vi* (*Inform*) sich ausloggen

loin [lɔɪn] *n* Lende *f*

loiter [lɔɪtər] *vi* sich herumtreiben

lollipop [lɒlipɒp] *n* Lutscher *m*

London [lʌndən] *n* London *nt*

Londoner [lʌndənər] *n* Londoner(in) *m(f)*

loneliness [lounlinɪs] *n* Einsamkeit *f*

lonely [lounli], **lonesome** [lounsəm] *adj* einsam

long [lɒŋ] *adj* lang; (*distance*) weit; **it's a way** es ist weit (*to* nach); **for a ~ time** lange; **how ~ is the movie?** wie lange dauert der Film?; **in the ~ run** auf die Dauer ▷ *adv* lange; **not for ~** nicht lange; **~ ago** vor langer Zeit; **before ~** bald; **all day ~** den ganzen Tag; **no ~er** nicht mehr; **as ~ as** solange ▷ *vi* sich sehnen (*for* nach); (*be waiting*) sehnsüchtig warten (*for* auf)

long-distance call [lɒŋdɪstəns kɔl] *n* Ferngespräch *nt*

long-haul flight [lɒŋhɔl flaɪt] *n* Langstreckenflug *m*

longing [lɒŋɪŋ] *n* Sehnsucht *f* (*for* nach)

longingly [lɒŋɪŋli] *adv* sehnsüchtig

longitude [lɒndʒɪtud] *n* Länge *f*

long jump *n* Weitsprung *m*

long-range [lɒŋreɪndʒ] *adj* Langstrecken-, Fern-; **~ missile** Langstreckenrakete *f*

longshoreman [lɒŋʃɔrmən] *n* Hafenarbeiter *m*

long-standing [lɒŋstændɪŋ] *adj* alt, langjährig

long-term [lɒŋtɜrm] *adj* langfristig; (*parking, effect etc*) Langzeit-; **~ unemployment** Langzeitarbeitslosigkeit *f*

long wave *n* Langwelle *f*

look [lʊk] *n* Blick *m*; (*appearance*): **~s** *pl* Aussehen *nt*; **I'll have a ~** ich schau mal nach; **to have a ~ at sth** sich *dat* etw ansehen; **can I have a ~?** darf ich mal sehen? ▷ *vi* schauen, gucken; (*with prep*) sehen; (*search*) nachsehen; (*appear*) aussehen; **I'm just ~ing** ich schaue nur; **it ~s like rain** es sieht nach Regen aus ▷ *vt*: **~ what you've done** sieh dir mal an, was du da angestellt hast; (*appear*): **he ~s his age** man sieht ihm sein Alter an; **to ~ one's best** sehr vorteilhaft aussehen

look after *vt* (*care for*) sorgen für; (*keep an eye on*) aufpassen auf +*akk*

look at *vt* ansehen, anschauen

look back *vi* sich umsehen; (*fig*) zurückblicken

look down on *vt* (*fig*) herabsehen auf +*akk*

look for *vt* suchen

look forward to *vt* sich freuen auf +*akk*

look into *vt* (*investigate*) untersuchen

look out *vi* hinaussehen (*of the window* zum Fenster); (*watch out*) Ausschau halten (*for* nach); (*be careful*) aufpassen, Acht geben (*for* auf +*akk*); **~!** Vorsicht!

look up *vi* aufsehen ▷ *vt* (*word etc*) nachschlagen

look up to *vt* aufsehen zu

loony [luni] *adj* (*fam*) bekloppt

loop [lup] *n* Schleife *f*

loose [lus] *adj* locker; (*knot, button*) lose

loosen [lusᵊn] *vt* lockern; (*knot*) lösen

loot [lut] *n* Beute *f*

lopsided [lɒpsaɪdɪd] *adj* schief

lord [lɔrd] *n* (*ruler*) Herr *m*; (*BRIT: title*) Lord *m*; **the L~ God** Gott der Herr

lose [luz] (*lost, lost*) *vt* verlieren; (*chance*) verpassen; **to ~ weight** abnehmen; **to ~ one's life** umkommen ▷ *vi* verlieren; (*clock, watch*) nachgehen

loser [luzər] *n* Verlierer(in) *m(f)*

loss [lɒs] *n* Verlust *m*

lost [lɒst] *pt, pp of* **lose**; **we're ~** wir haben uns verlaufen ▷ *adj* verloren

lost and found *n* Fundbüro *nt*

lot [lɒt] *n* (*fam: batch*) Menge *f*, Haufen *m*, Stoß *m*; **this is the first lot** das ist die erste Ladung; **a lot** viel(e); **a lot of money** viel Geld; **lots of people** viele Leute; **the whole lot** alles; (*people*) alle; **parking lot** Parkplatz *m*

lotion [louʃᵊn] *n* Lotion *f*

lottery [lɒtəri] n Lotterie f
loud [laʊd] adj laut; (color) schreiend
loudspeaker [laʊdspiːkər] n Lautsprecher m; (of stereo) Box f
lounge [laʊndʒ] n Wohnzimmer nt; (in hotel) Aufenthaltsraum m; (at airport) Warteraum m ▷ vi sich herumlümmeln
louse [laʊs] (pl lice) n Laus f
lousy [laʊzi] adj (fam) lausig
lout [laʊt] n Rüpel m
lovable [lʌvəbəl] adj liebenswert
love [lʌv] n Liebe f (of zu); (person, address) Liebling m, Schatz m; (Sport) null; **to be in ~** verliebt sein (with sb in jdn); **to fall in ~** sich verlieben (with sb in jdn); **to make ~** (sexually) sich lieben; **to make ~ to** o **with sb** mit jdm schlafen; (in letter): **he sends his ~** er lässt grüßen; **give her my ~** grüße sie von mir; **~, Tom** liebe Grüße, Tom ▷ vt (person) lieben; (activity) sehr gerne mögen; **to ~ to do sth** etw für sein Leben gerne tun; **I'd ~ a cup of tea** ich hätte liebend gern eine Tasse Tee
love affair n (Liebes)verhältnis nt
love letter n Liebesbrief m
love life n Liebesleben nt
lovely [lʌvli] adj schön, wunderschön; (charming) reizend; **we had a ~ time** es war sehr schön
lover [lʌvər] n Liebhaber(in) m(f)
loving [lʌvɪŋ] adj liebevoll
low [loʊ] adj niedrig; (rank) niedere(r, s); (level, note, neckline) tief; (intelligence, density) gering; (quality, standard) schlecht; (not loud) leise; (depressed) niedergeschlagen; **we're low on gas** wir haben kaum noch Benzin ▷ n (Meteo) Tief nt
low-calorie [loʊkæləri] adj kalorienarm
low-cut [loʊkʌt] adj (dress) tief ausgeschnitten
low-emission [loʊɪmɪʃən] adj schadstoffarm
lower [loʊər] adj niedriger; (storey, class etc) untere(r, s) ▷ vt herunterlassen; (eyes, price) senken; (pressure) verringern
low-fat [loʊfæt] adj fettarm
low tide n Ebbe f
loyal [lɔɪəl] adj treu

loyalty [lɔɪəlti] n Treue f
lozenge [lɒzɪndʒ] n Pastille f
Ltd (abbr) = **limited** = GmbH f
lubricant [luːbrɪkənt] n Schmiermittel nt, Gleitmittel nt
luck [lʌk] n Glück nt; **bad ~** Pech nt
luckily [lʌkɪli] adv glücklicherweise, zum Glück
lucky [lʌki] adj (number, day etc) Glücks-; **to be ~** Glück haben; **~ coincidence** glücklicher Zufall
ludicrous [luːdɪkrəs] adj grotesk
luggage [lʌgɪdʒ] n Gepäck nt
luggage compartment n Gepäckraum m
luggage rack n Gepäcknetz nt
lukewarm [luːkwɔːrm] adj lauwarm
lullaby [lʌləbaɪ] n Schlaflied nt
lumbago [lʌmbeɪgoʊ] n Hexenschuss m
luminous [luːmɪnəs] adj leuchtend
lump [lʌmp] n Klumpen m; (Med) Schwellung f; (in breast) Knoten m; (of sugar) Stück nt
lump sum n Pauschalsumme f
lumpy [lʌmpi] adj klumpig
lunacy [luːnəsi] n Wahnsinn m
lunatic [luːnətɪk] adj wahnsinnig ▷ n Wahnsinnige(r) mf
lunch [lʌntʃ], **luncheon** [lʌntʃən] n Mittagessen nt; **to have ~** zu Mittag essen
lunch break, lunch hour n Mittagspause f
lunchtime [lʌntʃtaɪm] n Mittagszeit f
lung [lʌŋ] n Lunge f
lurch [lɜːrtʃ] n: **to leave sb in the ~** jdn im Stich lassen
lurid [lʊərɪd] adj (color) grell; (details) widerlich
lurk [lɜːrk] vi lauern
lust [lʌst] n (sinnliche) Begierde (for nach)
Luxembourg [lʌksəmbɜːrg] n Luxemburg nt
Luxembourger [lʌksᵊmbɜːrgər] n Luxemburger(in) m(f)
luxurious [lʌgʒʊəriəs] adj luxuriös, Luxus-
luxury [lʌkʃəri, lʌgʒə-] n (a. luxuries pl) Luxus m; **~ goods** Luxusgüter pl
lynx [lɪŋks] n Luchs m
lyrics [lɪrɪks] npl (words for song) Liedtext m

M

M [ɛm] (*abbr*) (*size*) = **medium** M

m (*abbr*) = **meter** m

MA [ɛm eɪ] (*abbr*) = **Master of Arts** Magister Artium *m*

ma [mɑ] *n* (*fam*) Mutti *f*

macaroon [mækərun] *n* Makrone *f*

Macedonia [mæsɪdəʊniə] *n* Mazedonien *nt*

machine [məʃiːn] *n* Maschine *f*

machine gun *n* Maschinengewehr *nt*

machinery [məʃiːnəri] *n* Maschinen *pl*; (*fig*) Apparat *m*

machine washable *adj* waschmaschinenfest

mackerel [mækərəl, mækrəl] *n* Makrele *f*

macro [mækrəʊ] (*pl* **-s**) *n* (*Inform*) Makro *nt*

mad [mæd] *adj* wahnsinnig, verrückt; (*dog*) tollwütig; (*angry*) wütend, sauer (*at* auf +*akk*); (*fam*): **mad about** (*fond of*) verrückt nach; **to work like mad** wie verrückt arbeiten; **are you mad?** spinnst du/spinnen Sie?

madam [mædəm] *n* gnädige Frau

mad cow disease *n* Rinderwahnsinn *m*

maddening [mæd°nɪŋ] *adj* zum Verrücktwerden

made [meɪd] *pt*, *pp of* **make**

made-to-measure *adj* nach Maß; **~ suit** Maßanzug *m*

madly [mædli] *adv* wie verrückt; (*with adj*) wahnsinnig

madman [mædmæn, -mən] (*pl* **-men**) *n* Verrückte(r) *m*

madness [mædnɪs] *n* Wahnsinn *m*

madwoman [mædwʊmən] (*pl* **-women**) *n* Verrückte *f*

magazine [mægəziːn, -zɪn] *n* Zeitschrift *f*

maggot [mægət] *n* Made *f*

magic [mædʒɪk] *n* Magie *f*; (*activity*) Zauberei *f*; (*fig: effect*) Zauber *m*; **as if by ~** wie durch Zauberei ▷ *adj* Zauber-; (*powers*) magisch

magician [mədʒɪʃ°n] *n* Zauberer *m*, Zaub(r)erin *f*

magnet [mægnɪt] *n* Magnet *m*

magnetic [mægnɛtɪk] *adj* magnetisch

magnetism [mægnɪtɪzəm] *n* (*fig*) Anziehungskraft *f*

magnificent [mægnɪfɪsənt] *adj*, **magnificently** *adv* herrlich, großartig

magnify [mægnɪfaɪ] *vt* vergrößern

magnifying glass [mægnɪfaɪɪŋ glɑs] *n* Vergrößerungsglas *nt*, Lupe *f*

magpie [mægpaɪ] *n* Elster *f*

maid [meɪd] *n* Dienstmädchen *nt*

maiden name [meɪd°n neɪm] *n* Mädchenname *m*

maiden voyage [meɪd°n vɔɪɪdʒ] *n* Jungfernfahrt *f*

mail [meɪl] *n* Post *f*; (*email*) Mail *f* ▷ *vt* (*post*) aufgeben; (*send*) mit der Post schicken (*to* an +*akk*)

mailbox [meɪlbɒks] *n* Briefkasten *m*; (*Inform*) Mailbox *f*

mailing list [meɪlɪŋ lɪst] *n* Adressenliste *f*

mailman [meɪlmæn] *n* (*pl* **-men**) Briefträger *m*

mail order *n* Bestellung *f* per Post

mail order company *n* Versandhaus *nt*

main [meɪn] *adj* Haupt-; **~ course** Hauptgericht *nt*; **the ~ thing** die Hauptsache ▷ *n* (*pipe*) Hauptleitung *f*

mainframe [meɪnfreɪm] *n* Großrechner *m*

mainland [meɪnlænd] *n* Festland *nt*

mainly [meɪnli] *adv* hauptsächlich

main road *n* Hauptverkehrsstraße *f*

main street *n* Hauptstraße *f*

maintain [meɪnteɪn] *vt* (*keep up*) aufrechterhalten; (*machine, roads*) instand halten; (*service*) warten; (*claim*) behaupten

maintenance [meɪntɪnəns] *n* Instandhaltung *f*, (*Tech*) Wartung *f*

maize [meɪz] *n* Mais *m*

majestic [mədʒɛstɪk] *adj* majestätisch

majesty [mædʒɪsti] *n* Majestät *f*; **Your/His/Her M~** Eure/Seine/Ihre Majestät

major [meɪdʒər] *adj* (*bigger*) größer; (*important*) bedeutend; **~ part** Großteil *m*; (*role*) wichtige Rolle; **~ road** Hauptverkehrsstraße *f*; (*Mus*): **A ~** A-Dur *nt* ▷ *vi*: **to ~ in sth** etw als Hauptfach studieren

Majorca [məjɔrkə] *n* Mallorca *nt*

majority [mədʒɔrɪti] *n* Mehrheit *f*; **to be in the ~** in der Mehrzahl sein

make [meɪk] *n* Marke *f* ▷ *vt* (**made, made**) machen; (*manufacture*) herstellen; (*clothes*) anfertigen; (*dress*) nähen; (*soup*) zubereiten; (*bread, cake*) backen; (*tea, coffee*) kochen; (*speech*) halten; (*earn*) verdienen; (*decision*) treffen; **it's made of gold** es ist aus Gold; **to ~ sb do sth** jdn dazu bringen, etw zu tun; (*force*) jdn zwingen, etw zu tun; **she made us wait** sie ließ uns warten; **what ~s you think that?** wie kommen Sie darauf?; **it ~s the room look smaller** es lässt den Raum kleiner wirken; **to ~ it to the airport** (*reach*) den Flughafen erreichen; (*in time*) es zum Flughafen schaffen; **he never really made it** er hat es nie zu etwas gebracht; **she didn't ~ it through the night** sie hat die Nacht nicht überlebt; (*calculate*): **I ~ it $5/a quarter to six** nach meiner Rechnung kommt es auf 5 Dollar/nach meiner Uhr ist es dreiviertel sechs; **he's just made for this job** er ist für diese Arbeit wie geschaffen

make-believe *adj* Fantasie-

make for *vt* zusteuern auf +*akk*

make of *vt* (*think of*) halten von; **I couldn't ~ anything of it** ich wurde daraus nicht schlau

make off *vi* sich davonmachen (*with* mit)

make out *vi* zurechtkommen ▷ *vt* (*check*) ausstellen; (*list*) aufstellen; (*understand*) verstehen; (*discern*) ausmachen; **to ~ that ...** es so hinstellen, als ob ...

makeover [meɪkoʊvər] *n* gründliche Veränderung, Verschönerung *f*

maker [meɪkər] *n* (*Comm*) Hersteller(in) *m(f)*

makeshift [meɪkʃɪft] *adj* behelfsmäßig

make up *vt* (*team etc*) bilden; (*face*) schminken; (*invent: story etc*) erfinden; **to ~ one's mind** sich entscheiden; **to make (it) up with sb** sich mit jdm aussöhnen ▷ *vi* sich versöhnen

makeup *n* Make-up *nt*, Schminke *f*

make up for *vt* ausgleichen; (*time*) aufholen

making [meɪkɪŋ] *n* Herstellung *f*

maladjusted [mælədʒʌstɪd] *adj* verhaltensgestört

malaria [məlɛəriə] *n* Malaria *f*

Malaysia [məleɪʒə] *n* Malaysia *nt*

male [meɪl] *n* Mann *m*; (*animal*) Männchen *nt* ▷ *adj* männlich; **~ chauvinist** Chauvi *m*, Macho *m*; **~ nurse** Krankenpfleger *m*

malfunction [mælfʌŋkʃ⁰n] *vi* nicht richtig funktionieren ▷ *n* Defekt *m*

malice [mælɪs] *n* Bosheit *f*

malicious [məlɪʃəs] *adj* boshaft; (*behavior, action*) böswillig; (*damage*) mutwillig

malignant [məlɪgnənt] *adj* bösartig

mall [mɔl] *n* Einkaufszentrum *nt*

malnutrition [mælnutrɪʃ⁰n] *n* Unterernährung *f*

malt [mɔlt] *n* Malz *nt*

Malta [mɔltə] *n* Malta *nt*

Maltese [mɒltiz] *adj* maltesisch ▷ *n* (*person*) Malteser(in) *m(f)*; (*language*) Maltesisch *nt*

maltreat [mæltrit] *vt* schlecht behandeln; (*violently*) misshandeln

mammal [mæm⁰l] *n* Säugetier *nt*

mammoth [mæməθ] *adj* Mammut-, Riesen-

man [mæn] (*pl* **men**) *n* (*male*) Mann *m*; (*human race*) der Mensch, die Menschen *pl*; (*in chess*) Figur *f* ▷ *vt* besetzen

manage [mænɪdʒ] *vi* zurechtkommen; **can you ~?** schaffst du es?; **to ~ without sth** ohne etw auskommen, auf etw verzichten können ▷ *vt* (*control*) leiten; (*musician, sportsman*) managen; (*cope with*) fertig werden mit; (*task, portion, climb etc*) schaffen; **to ~ to do sth** es schaffen, etw zu tun

manageable [mænɪdʒəb⁰l] *adj* (*object*) handlich; (*task*) zu bewältigen

management [mænɪdʒmənt] *n* Leitung *f*; (*directors*) Direktion *f*; (*subject*) Management *nt*, Betriebswirtschaft *f*

management consultant *n* Unternehmensberater(in) *m(f)*

manager [mænɪdʒər] *n* Geschäftsführer(in) *m(f)*; (*departmental manager*) Abteilungsleiter(in) *m(f)*; (*of branch, bank*) Filialleiter(in) *m(f)*; (*of musician, sportsman*) Manager(in) *m(f)*

managing director [mænɪdʒɪŋ dɪrɛktər] *n* Geschäftsführer(in) *m(f)*

mane [meɪn] *n* Mähne *f*

maneuver [mənuvər] *n* Manöver *nt* ▷ *vt, vi* manövrieren

mango [mæŋgoʊ] (*pl* **-es**) *n* Mango *f*

man-hour *n* Arbeitsstunde *f*

manhunt [mænhʌnt] *n* Fahndung *f*

mania [meɪniə] *n* Manie *f*

maniac [meɪniæk] *n* Wahnsinnige(r) *mf*; (*fan*) Fanatiker(in) *m(f)*

manicure [mænɪkyʊər] *n* Maniküre *f*

manipulate [mənɪpyəleɪt] *vt* manipulieren

mankind [mænkaɪnd] *n* Menschheit *f*

manly [mænli] *adj* männlich

man-made *adj* (*product*) künstlich

manner [mænər] *n* Art *f*; **in this ~** auf diese Art und Weise; **~s** *pl* Manieren *pl*

manor [mænər] *n*: **~ house** Herrenhaus *nt*

manpower [mænpaʊər] *n* Arbeitskräfte *pl*

mansion [mænʃ⁰n] *n* Villa *f*; (*of old family*) Herrenhaus *nt*

manslaughter [mænslɔtər] *n* Totschlag *m*

mantelpiece [mæntᵊlpis] *n* Kaminsims *m*

manual [mænyuəl] *adj* manuell, Hand- ▷ *n* Handbuch *nt*

manufacture [mænyəfæktʃər] *vt* herstellen ▷ *n* Herstellung *f*

manufacturer [mænyəfæktʃərər] *n* Hersteller *m*

manure [mənuər] *n* Dung *m*; (*esp artificial*) Dünger *m*

many [mɛni] (**more, most**) *adj, pron* viele; **~ times** oft; **not ~ people** nicht viele Leute; **too ~ problems** zu viele Probleme

map [mæp] *n* Landkarte *f*; (*of town*) Stadtplan *m*

maple [meɪpᵊl] *n* Ahorn *m*

marathon [mærəθɒn] *n* Marathon *m*

marble [mɑrbᵊl] *n* Marmor *m*; (*for playing*) Murmel *f*

March [mɑrtʃ] *n* März *m*; *see also* **September**

march [mɑrtʃ] *vi* marschieren ▷ *n* Marsch *m*; (*protest*) Demonstration *f*

mare [mɛər] *n* Stute *f*

margarine [mɑrdʒərɪn] *n* Margarine *f*

margin [mɑrdʒɪn] *n* Rand *m*; (*extra amount*) Spielraum *m*; (*Comm*) Gewinnspanne *f*

marginal [mɑrdʒɪnᵊl] *adj* (*difference etc*) geringfügig

marijuana [mærɪwɑnə] *n* Marihuana *nt*

marine [mərin] *adj* Meeres-

marital [mærɪtᵊl] *adj* ehelich; **~ status** Familienstand *m*

maritime [mærɪtaɪm] *adj* See-

marjoram [mɑrdʒərəm] *n* Majoran *m*

mark [mɑrk] *n* (*spot*) Fleck *m*; (*at school*) Note *f*; (*sign*) Zeichen *nt* ▷ *vt* (*make mark*) Flecken machen auf +*akk*; (*indicate*) markieren; (*schoolwork*) benoten, korrigieren; Flecken machen auf +*akk*

markedly [mɑrkɪdli] *adv* merklich; (*with comp adj*) wesentlich

marker [mɑrkər] *n* (*in book*) Lesezeichen *nt*; (*pen*) Marker *m*

market [mɑrkɪt] *n* Markt *m*; (*stock market*) Börse *f* ▷ *vt* (*Comm: new product*) auf den Markt bringen; (*goods*) vertreiben

marketing [mɑrkɪtɪŋ] *n* Marketing *nt*

market leader *n* Marktführer *m*

marketplace [mɑrkɪtpleɪs] *n* Marktplatz *m*

market research *n* Marktforschung *f*

marmalade [mɑrməleɪd] *n* Orangenmarmelade *f*

maroon [mərun] *adj* rötlich braun

marquee [mɑrki] *n* großes Zelt

marriage [mærɪdʒ] *n* Ehe *f*; (*wedding*) Heirat *f* (*to* mit)

married [mærid] *adj* (*person*) verheiratet

marrow [mæroʊ] *n* (*bone marrow*) Knochenmark *nt*; (*vegetable*) Kürbis *m*

marry [mæri] *vt* heiraten; (*join*) trauen; (*take as husband, wife*) heiraten ▷ *vi*: **to ~/ to get married** heiraten

marsh [mɑrʃ] *n* Marsch *f*, Sumpf *m*

marshal [mɑrʃᵊl] *n* (*at rally etc*) Ordner *m*; (*police*) Bezirkspolizeichef *m*

martial arts [mɑrʃᵊl ɑrts] *npl* Kampfsportarten *pl*

martyr [mɑrtər] *n* Märtyrer(in) *m(f)*

marvel [mɑrvᵊl] *n* Wunder *nt* ▷ *vi* staunen (*at* über +*akk*)

marvelous [mɑrvələs] *adj* wunderbar

marzipan [mɑrzipæn] *n* Marzipan *nt o m*

mascara [mæskærə] *n* Wimperntusche *f*

mascot [mæskɒt] *n* Maskottchen *nt*

masculine [mæskyəlɪn] *adj* männlich

mashed [mæʃt] *adj*: **~ potatoes** *pl* Kartoffelbrei *m*, Kartoffelpüree *nt*

mask [mæsk] *n* (*auch Inform*) Maske *f*; **diving ~** Tauchmaske *f* ▷ *vt* (*feelings*) verbergen

masochist [mæsəkɪst] *n* Masochist(in) *m(f)*

mason [meɪsᵊn] *n* (*stonemason*) Steinmetz(in) *m(f)*

masonry [meɪsənri] *n* Mauerwerk *nt*

mass [mæs] *n* Masse *f*; (*of people*) Menge *f*; (*Rel*) Messe *f*; **~es of** massenhaft

massacre [mæsəkər] *n* Blutbad *nt*

massage [məsɑʒ] *n* Massage *f* ▷ *vt* massieren

massive [mæsɪv] *adj* (*powerful*) gewaltig; (*very large*) riesig

mass media *npl* Massenmedien *pl*

mass-produce *vt* in Massenproduktion herstellen

mass production *n* Massenproduktion *f*

master [mæstər] *n* Herr *m*; (*of dog*) Besitzer *m*, Herrchen *nt*; (*teacher*) Lehrer *m*; (*artist*) Meister *m* ▷ *vt* meistern; (*language etc*) beherrschen

masterly [mæstərli] *adj* meisterhaft

masterpiece [mæstərpis] *n* Meisterwerk *nt*

masturbate [mæstərbeɪt] *vi* masturbieren

mat [mæt] *n* Matte *f*; (*for table*) Untersetzer *m*

match [mætʃ] *n* Streichholz *nt*; (*Sport*)

Wettkampf *m*; (*ball games*) Spiel *nt*; (*tennis*) Match *nt* ▷ *vt* (*be like, suit*) passen zu; (*equal*) gleichkommen +*dat* ▷ *vi* zusammenpassen

matchbox [mætʃbɒks] *n* Streichholzschachtel *f*

matching [mætʃɪŋ] *adj* (*one item*) passend; (*two items*) zusammenpassend

mate [meɪt] *n* (*of animal*) Weibchen *nt*/Männchen *nt* ▷ *vi* sich paaren

material [mətɪəriəl] *n* Material *nt*; (*for book etc, cloth*) Stoff *m*

materialistic [mətɪəriəlɪstɪk] *adj* materialistisch

materialize [mətɪəriəlaɪz] *vi* zustande kommen; (*hope*) wahr werden

maternal [mətɜrnəl] *adj* mütterlich

maternity [mətɜrnɪti] *adj*: ~ **dress** Umstandskleid *nt*; ~ **leave** Elternzeit *f* (der Mutter); ~ **ward** Entbindungsstation *f*

math [mæθ] *n* (*fam*) Mathe *f*

mathematical [mæθəmætɪkəl] *adj* mathematisch

mathematics [mæθəmætɪks] *nsing* Mathematik *f*

matinée [mætⁿeɪ] *n* Nachmittagsvorstellung *f*

matter [mætər] *n* (*substance*) Materie *f*; (*affair*) Sache *f*; **a personal ~** eine persönliche Angelegenheit; **a ~ of taste** eine Frage des Geschmacks; **no ~ how/what** egal wie/was; **what's the ~?** was ist los?; **as a ~ of fact** eigentlich; **a ~ of time** eine Frage der Zeit ▷ *vi* darauf ankommen, wichtig sein; **it doesn't ~** es macht nichts

matter-of-fact *adj* sachlich, nüchtern

mattress [mætrɪs] *n* Matratze *f*

mature [mətʊər, -tʊər, -tʃʊər] *adj* reif ▷ *vi* reif werden

maturity [mətʊərɪti, -tʊər-, -tʃʊər-] *n* Reife *f*

maximum [mæksɪməm] *adj* Höchst-, höchste(r, s); ~ **speed** Höchstgeschwindigkeit *f* ▷ *n* Maximum *nt*

May [meɪ] *n* Mai *m*; *see also* **September**

may [meɪ] (**might**) *vb aux* (*be possible*) können; (*have permission*) dürfen; **it may rain** es könnte regnen; **may I smoke?** darf ich rauchen?; **it may not happen** es passiert vielleicht gar nicht; **we may as well go** wir können ruhig gehen

maybe [meɪbi] *adv* vielleicht

May Day *n* der erste Mai

mayo [meɪoʊ] (*fam*), **mayonnaise** [meɪə-

neiz] *n* Mayo *f*, Mayonnaise *f*, Majonäse *f*

mayor [meɪər, mɛər] *n* Bürgermeister *m*

maze [meɪz] *n* Irrgarten *m*; (*fig*) Wirrwarr *nt*

MB [ɛm bi] (*abbr*) = **megabyte** MB *nt*

KEYWORD

me [mi, STRONG miː] *pron* **1** (*direct*) mich; **it's me** ich bin's

2 (*indirect*) mir; **give them to me** gib sie mir

3 (*after prep*: +*akk*) mich; (+*dat*) mir; **with/without me** mit mir/ohne mich

meadow [mɛdoʊ] *n* Wiese *f*

meal [miːl] *n* Essen *nt*, Mahlzeit *f*; **to go out for a ~** essen gehen

mealtime *n* Essenszeit *f*

mean [miːn] (**meant, meant**) *vt* (*signify*) bedeuten; (*have in mind*) meinen; (*intend*) vorhaben; **I ~ it** ich meine das ernst; **what do you ~ by that?** was willst du damit sagen?; **to ~ to do sth** etw tun wollen; **it was ~t for you** es war für dich bestimmt (*o* gedacht); **it was ~t to be a joke** es sollte ein Witz sein ▷ *vi*: **he ~s well** er meint es gut ▷ *adj* (*stingy*) geizig; (*spiteful*) gemein (*to zu*)

meaning [miːnɪŋ] *n* Bedeutung *f*; (*of life, poem*) Sinn *m*

meaningful [miːnɪŋfəl] *adj* sinnvoll

meaningless [miːnɪŋlɪs] *adj* (*text*) ohne Sinn

means [miːnz] (*pl* **means**) *n* Mittel *nt*; (*pl*: *funds*) Mittel *pl*; **by ~ of** durch, mittels; **by all ~** selbstverständlich; **by no ~** keineswegs; ~ **of transport** Beförderungsmittel

meant [mɛnt] *pt, pp of* **mean**

meantime [miːntaɪm] *adv*: **in the ~** inzwischen

meanwhile [miːnwaɪl] *adv* inzwischen

measles [miːzəlz] *nsing* Masern *pl*; **German ~** Röteln *pl*

measure [mɛʒər] *vt, vi* messen ▷ *n* (*unit, device for measuring*) Maß *nt*; (*step*) Maßnahme *f*; **to take ~s** Maßnahmen ergreifen

measurement [mɛʒərmənt] *n* (*amount measured*) Maß *nt*

meat [miːt] *n* Fleisch *nt*

meatball [miːtbɔl] *n* Fleischbällchen *nt*

mechanic [mɪkænɪk] *n* Mechaniker(in) *m(f)*

mechanical [mɪkænɪkəl] *adj* mechanisch

m

mechanics *nsing* Mechanik *f*

mechanism [mɛkənɪzəm] *n* Mechanismus *m*

medal [mɛdᵊl] *n* Medaille *f*; *(decoration)* Orden *m*

medalist [mɛdᵊlɪst] *n* Medaillengewinner(in) *m(f)*

media [miːdiə] *npl* Medien *pl*

median strip [miːdiən strɪp] *n* Mittelstreifen *m*

mediate [miːdieɪt] *vi* vermitteln

medical [mɛdɪkᵊl] *adj* medizinisch; *(treatment etc)* ärztlich; **~ student** Medizinstudent(in) *m(f)* ▷ *n* Untersuchung *f*

Medicare [mɛdɪkɛər] *n* Krankenkasse *f* für ältere Leute

medication [mɛdɪkeɪʃᵊn] *n* Medikamente *pl*; **to be on ~** Medikamente nehmen

medicinal [mədɪsənᵊl] *adj* Heil-; **~ herbs** Heilkräuter *pl*

medicine [mɛdɪsɪn] *n* Arznei *f*; *(science)* Medizin *f*

medieval [miːdiiːvᵊl, mɪdiːvᵊl] *adj* mittelalterlich

mediocre [miːdioʊkər] *adj* mittelmäßig

meditate [mɛdɪteɪt] *vi* meditieren; *(fig)* nachdenken *(on* über *+akk)*

Mediterranean [mɛdɪtəreɪniən] *n (sea)* Mittelmeer *nt*; *(region)* Mittelmeerraum *m*

medium [miːdiəm] *adj (quality, size)* mittlere(r, s); *(steak)* halbdurch; **~ dry** *(wine)* halbtrocken; **~ sized** mittelgroß; **~ wave** Mittelwelle *f* ▷ *n (pl* **media**) Medium *nt*; *(means)* Mittel *nt*

meet [miːt] **(met, met)** *vt* treffen; *(by arrangement)* sich treffen mit; *(difficulties)* stoßen auf *+akk*; *(get to know)* kennenlernen; *(requirement, demand)* gerecht werden *+dat*; *(deadline)* einhalten; **pleased to ~ you** sehr angenehm!; **to ~ sb at the station** jdn vom Bahnhof abholen ▷ *vi* sich treffen; *(become acquainted)* sich kennenlernen; **we've met before** wir kennen uns schon

meeting [miːtɪŋ] *n* Treffen *nt*; *(business meeting)* Besprechung *f*; *(of committee)* Sitzung *f*; *(assembly)* Versammlung *f*

meeting place, meeting point *n* Treffpunkt *m*

meet up *vt* sich treffen *(with* mit)

meet with *vt (group)* zusammenkommen mit; *(difficulties, resistance etc)* stoßen auf *+akk*

megabyte [mɛgəbaɪt] *n* Megabyte *nt*

melody [mɛlədi] *n* Melodie *f*

melon [mɛlən] *n* Melone *f*

melt [mɛlt] *vt, vi* schmelzen

member [mɛmbər] *n* Mitglied *nt*; *(of tribe, species)* Angehörige(r) *mf*; **~ of Congress** Mitglied *nt* des Repräsentantenhauses

membership [mɛmbərʃɪp] *n* Mitgliedschaft *f*

membership card *n* Mitgliedskarte *f*

memento [mɪmɛntoʊ] *(pl* **-es**) *n* Andenken *nt (of* an *+akk)*

memo [mɛmoʊ] *(pl* **-s**) *n* Mitteilung *f*, Memo *nt*

memo pad *n* Notizblock *m*

memorable [mɛmərəbᵊl] *adj* unvergesslich

memorial [mɪmɔːriəl] *n* Denkmal *nt (to* für)

memorize [mɛməraɪz] *vt* sich einprägen, auswendig lernen

memory [mɛməri] *n* Gedächtnis *nt*; *(Inform: of computer)* Speicher *m*; *(sth recalled)* Erinnerung *f*; **in ~ of** zur Erinnerung an *+akk*

Memory stick® *n (Inform)* Memorystick® *m*

men [mɛn] *pl of* **man**

menace [mɛnɪs] *n* Bedrohung *f*; *(danger)* Gefahr *f*

mend [mɛnd] *vt* reparieren; *(clothes)* flicken ▷ *n*: **to be on the ~** auf dem Wege der Besserung sein

meningitis [mɛnɪndʒaɪtɪs] *n* Hirnhautentzündung *f*

menopause [mɛnəpɔːz] *n* Wechseljahre *pl*

mental [mɛntᵊl] *adj* geistig

mentality [mɛntæliti] *n* Mentalität *f*

mentally [mɛntᵊli] *adv* geistig; **~ handicapped** geistig behindert; **~ ill** geisteskrank

mention [mɛnʃᵊn] *n* Erwähnung *f* ▷ *vt* erwähnen *(to sb* jdm gegenüber); **don't ~ it** bitte sehr, gern geschehen

menu [mɛnyu] *n* Speisekarte *f*; *(Inform)* Menü *nt*

merchandise [mɜːrtʃəndaɪz, -daɪs] *n* Handelsware *f*

merchant [mɜːrtʃənt] *adj* Handels- ▷ *n* Einzelhändler(in) *m(f)*

merciful [mɜːrsɪfəl] *adj* gnädig

mercifully [mɜːrsɪfəli] *adv* glücklicherweise

mercury [mɜːrkyəri] *n* Quecksilber *nt*

mercy [mɜːrsi] *n* Gnade *f*

mere [mɪər] *adj* bloß

merely [mɪərli] *adv* bloß, lediglich

merge [mɜrdʒ] *vi* verschmelzen; *(Auto)* sich einfädeln; *(Comm)* fusionieren

merger [mɜrdʒər] *n (Comm)* Fusion *f*

meringue [məræŋ] *n* Baiser *nt*

merit [mɛrɪt] *n* Verdienst *nt*; *(advantage)* Vorzug *m*

merry [mɛri] *adj* fröhlich; *(fam: tipsy)* angeheitert; **M~ Christmas** Fröhliche Weihnachten!

merry-go-round *n* Karussell *nt*

mess [mɛs] *n* Unordnung *f*; *(muddle)* Durcheinander *nt*; *(dirty)* Schweinerei *f*; *(trouble)* Schwierigkeiten *pl*; **in a ~** *(muddled)* durcheinander; *(untidy)* unordentlich; *(fig: person)* in der Klemme; **to make a ~ of sth** etw verpfuschen; **to look a ~** unmöglich aussehen

message [mɛsɪdʒ] *n* Mitteilung *f*, Nachricht *f*; *(meaning)* Botschaft *f*; **can I give him a ~?** kann ich ihm etwas ausrichten?; **please leave a ~** *(on answering machine)* bitte hinterlassen Sie eine Nachricht; **I get the ~** ich hab's verstanden

messenger [mɛsɪndʒər] *n* Bote *m*

mess up *vt* verpfuschen; *(make untidy)* in Unordnung bringen; *(dirty)* schmutzig machen

messy [mɛsi] *adj (untidy)* unordentlich; *(situation etc)* verfahren

met [mɛt] *pt, pp of* **meet**

metal [mɛtᵊl] *n* Metall *nt*

metallic [mətælɪk] *adj* metallisch

meteorology [mitiərɒlədʒi] *n* Meteorologie *f*

meter [mitər] *n* Zähler *m*; *(parking meter)* Parkuhr *f*, Meter *m o nt*

method [mɛθəd] *n* Methode *f*

methodical [məθɒdɪkᵊl] *adj* methodisch

meticulous [mətɪkyələs] *adj (peinlich)* genau

metric [mɛtrɪk] *adj* metrisch; **~ system** Dezimalsystem *nt*

Mexico [mɛksɪkoʊ] *n* Mexiko *nt*

mice [maɪs] *pl of* **mouse**

microchip [maɪkroʊtʃɪp] *n (Inform)* Mikrochip *m*

microphone [maɪkrəfoʊn] *n* Mikrofon *nt*

microscope [maɪkrəskoʊp] *n* Mikroskop *nt*

microwave (oven) [maɪkroʊweɪv (ʌvᵊn)] *n* Mikrowelle(nherd) *f(m)*

mid [mɪd] *adj:* **in mid January** Mitte Januar; **he's in his mid forties** er ist Mitte vierzig

midday [mɪddeɪ] *n* Mittag *m*; **at ~** mittags

middle [mɪdᵊl] *n* Mitte *f*; *(waist)* Taille *f*; **in the ~ of** mitten in +*dat*; **to be in the ~ of doing sth** gerade dabei sein, etw zu tun ▷ *adj* mittlere(r, s), Mittel-; **the ~ one** der/die/das Mittlere

middle-aged [mɪdᵊleɪdʒd] *adj* mittleren Alters

Middle Ages *npl:* **the ~** das Mittelalter

middle-class *adj* mittelständisch; *(bourgeois)* bürgerlich

middle classes *npl:* **the ~** der Mittelstand

Middle East *n:* **the ~** der Nahe Osten

middle name *n* zweiter Vorname

midnight [mɪdnaɪt] *n* Mitternacht *f*

midst [mɪdst] *n:* **in the ~ of** mitten in +*dat*

midsummer [mɪdsʌmər] *n* Hochsommer *m*; **M~'s Day** Sommersonnenwende *f*

midway [mɪdweɪ] *adv* auf halbem Wege; **~ through the film** nach der Hälfte des Films

midweek [mɪdwik] *adj, adv* in der Mitte der Woche

midwife [mɪdwaɪf] *(pl* **-wives***) n* Hebamme *f*

midwinter [mɪdwɪntər] *n* tiefster Winter

might [maɪt] *pt of* **may**; *(possibility)* könnte; *(permission)* dürfte; *(would)* würde; **they ~ still come** sie könnten noch kommen; **he ~ have let me know** er hätte mir doch Bescheid sagen können; **I thought she ~ change her mind** ich dachte schon, sie würde sich anders entscheiden ▷ *n* Macht *f*, Kraft *f*

mighty [maɪti] *adj* gewaltig; *(powerful)* mächtig

migraine [maɪgreɪn] *n* Migräne *f*

migrant [maɪgrənt] *n (bird)* Zugvogel *m*; **~ worker** Gastarbeiter(in) *m(f)*, Migrant(in) *m(f)*

migrate [maɪgreɪt] *vi* abwandern; *(birds)* nach Süden ziehen

mike [maɪk] *n (fam)* Mikro *nt*

Milan [mɪlæn] *n* Mailand *nt*

mild [maɪld] *adj* mild; *(person)* sanft

mildly [maɪldli] *adv:* **to put it ~** gelinde gesagt

mildness [maɪldnɪs] *n* Milde *f*

mile [maɪl] *n* Meile *f* (= *1,609 km*); **for ~s and ~s** ≈ kilometerweit; **~s per hour** Meilen pro Stunde; **~s better** als hundertmal besser als

mileage [maɪlɪdʒ] *n* Meilen *pl*, Meilenzahl *f*

milestone [maɪlstoʊn] *n (a. fig)* Meilenstein *m*

m

militant [mɪlɪtənt] *adj* militant
military [mɪlɪtri] *adj* Militär-, militärisch
milk [mɪlk] *n* Milch *f* ▷ *vt* melken
milk chocolate *n* Vollmilchschokolade *f*
milkman [mɪlkmæn] (*pl* **-men**) *n* Milchmann *m*
milk shake *n* Milkshake *m*, Milchmixgetränk *nt*
mill [mɪl] *n* Mühle *f*; (*factory*) Fabrik *f*
millennium [mɪlɛnɪəm] *n* Jahrtausend *nt*
milligram [mɪlɪɡræm] *n* Milligramm *nt*
milliliter [mɪlɪlitər] *n* Milliliter *m*
millimeter [mɪlɪmitər] *n* Millimeter *m*
million [mɪlyən] *n* Million *f*; **five ~** fünf Millionen; **~s of people** Millionen von Menschen
millionaire [mɪlyənɛər] *n* Millionär(in) *m(f)*
mime [maɪm] *n* Pantomime *f* ▷ *vt, vi* mimen
mimic [mɪmɪk] *n* Imitator(in) *m(f)* ▷ *vt, vi* nachahmen
mimicry [mɪmɪkri] *n* Nachahmung *f*
mind [maɪnd] *n* (*intellect*) Verstand *m*; (*also person*) Geist *m*; **out of sight, out of ~** aus den Augen, aus dem Sinn; **he is out of his ~** er ist nicht bei Verstand; **to keep sth in ~** etw im Auge behalten; **do you have sth in ~?** denken Sie an etwas Besonderes?; **I've a lot on my ~** mich beschäftigt so vieles im Moment; **to change one's ~** es sich *dat* anders überlegen ▷ *vt* (*look after*) aufpassen auf +*akk*; (*object to*) etwas haben gegen; **~ you,** ... allerdings ...; **I wouldn't ~** ... ich hätte nichts gegen ...; **'~ the step'** „Vorsicht Stufe!" ▷ *vi* etwas dagegen haben; **do you ~ if I** ... macht es Ihnen etwas aus, wenn ich ...; **I don't ~** es ist mir egal, meinetwegen; **never ~** macht nichts
mine [maɪn] *pron* meine(r, s); **this is ~** das gehört mir; **a friend of ~** ein Freund von mir ▷ *n* (*coalmine*) Bergwerk *nt*; (*Mil*) Mine *f*
miner [maɪnər] *n* Bergarbeiter(in) *m(f)*
mineral [mɪnərəl] *n* Mineral *nt*
mineral water [mɪnərəl wɔtər] *n* Mineralwasser *nt*
mingle [mɪŋɡ°l] *vi* sich mischen (*with* unter +*akk*)
miniature [mɪnɪətʃər, -tʃʊər] *adj* Miniatur-
minibar [mɪnibar] *n* Minibar *f*
minibus [mɪnibʌs] *n* Kleinbus *m*
minimal [mɪnɪm°l] *adj* minimal
minimize [mɪnɪmaɪz] *vt* auf ein Minimum

reduzieren
minimum [mɪnɪməm] *n* Minimum *nt* ▷ *adj* Mindest-
mining [maɪnɪŋ] *n* Bergbau *m*
miniskirt [mɪniskɜrt] *n* Minirock *m*
minister [mɪnɪstər] *n* (*Pol*) Minister(in) *m(f)*; (*Rel*) Pastor(in) *m(f)*, Pfarrer(in) *m(f)*
ministry [mɪnɪstri] *n* (*Pol*) Ministerium *nt*
minor [maɪnər] *adj* kleiner; (*insignificant*) unbedeutend; (*operation, offense*) harmlos; **~ road** Nebenstraße *f*; (*Mus*): **A ~** a-Moll *nt* ▷ *n* (*under 18*) Minderjährige(r) *mf*
minority [mɪnɔrɪti, maɪ-] *n* Minderheit *f*
mint [mɪnt] *n* Minze *f*; (*sweet*) Pfefferminz (bonbon) *nt*
mint sauce *n* Minzsoße *f*
minus [maɪnəs] *prep* minus; (*without*) ohne
minute [mɪnɪt] *adj* winzig; **in ~ detail** genauestens ▷ *n* Minute *f*; **just a ~** Moment mal!; **any ~** jeden Augenblick; **~s** *pl* (*of meeting*) Protokoll *nt*
miracle [mɪrək°l] *n* Wunder *nt*
miraculous [mɪrækyələs] *adj* unglaublich
mirage [mɪrɑʒ] *n* Fata Morgana *f*, Luftspiegelung *f*
mirror [mɪrər] *n* Spiegel *m*
misbehave [mɪsbɪheɪv] *vi* sich schlecht benehmen
miscalculation [mɪskælkyəleɪʃ°n] *n* Fehlkalkulation *f*; (*misjudgement*) Fehleinschätzung *f*
miscarriage [mɪskærɪdʒ, -kær-] *n* (*Med*) Fehlgeburt *f*
miscellaneous [mɪsəleɪniəs] *adj* verschieden
mischief [mɪstʃɪf] *n* Unfug *m*
mischievous [mɪstʃɪvəs] *adj* (*person*) durchtrieben; (*glance*) verschmitzt
misconception [mɪskənsɛpʃ°n] *n* falsche Vorstellung
misconduct [mɪskɒndʌkt] *n* Vergehen *nt*
miser [maɪzər] *n* Geizhals *m*
miserable [mɪzərəb°l] *adj* (*person*) todunglücklich; (*conditions, life*) elend; (*pay, weather*) miserabel
miserly [maɪzərli] *adj* geizig
misery [mɪzəri] *n* Elend *nt*; (*suffering*) Qualen *pl*
misfit [mɪsfɪt] *n* Außenseiter(in) *m(f)*
misfortune [mɪsfɔrtʃən] *n* Pech *nt*
misguided [mɪsɡaɪdɪd] *adj* irrig; (*optimism*) unangebracht

misinform [mɪsɪnfɔːrm] *vt* falsch informieren

misinterpret [mɪsɪntɜːrprɪt] *vt* falsch auslegen

misjudge [mɪsdʒʌdʒ] *vt* falsch beurteilen

mislay [mɪsleɪ] (*irr*) *vt* verlegen

mislead [mɪsliːd] (*irr*) *vt* irreführen

misleading [mɪsliːdɪŋ] *adj* irreführend

misprint [mɪsprɪnt] *n* Druckfehler *m*

mispronounce [mɪsprənauns] *vt* falsch aussprechen

Miss [mɪs] *n* (*unmarried woman*) Fräulein *nt*

miss [mɪs] *vt* (*fail to hit, catch*) verfehlen; (*not notice, hear*) nicht mitbekommen; (*be too late for*) verpassen; (*chance*) versäumen; (*regret the absence of*) vermissen; **I ~ you** du fehlst mir ▷ *vi* nicht treffen; (*shooting*) danebenschießen; (*ball, shot etc*) danebengehen

missile [mɪsəl] *n* Geschoss *nt*; (*rocket*) Rakete *f*

missing [mɪsɪŋ] *adj* (*person*) vermisst; (*thing*) fehlend; **to be/go ~** vermisst werden, fehlen

mission [mɪʃən] *n* (*Pol, Mil, Rel*) Auftrag *m*, Mission *f*

missionary [mɪʃəneri] *n* Missionar(in) *m(f)*

mist [mɪst] *n* (*feiner*) Nebel *m*; (*haze*) Dunst *m*

mistake [mɪsteɪk] *n* Fehler *m*; **by ~ aus Versehen** ▷ *irr vt* (**mistook, mistaken**) (*misunderstand*) falsch verstehen; (*mix up*) verwechseln (*for* mit); **there's no mistaking ... ...** ist unverkennbar; (*meaning*) ... ist unmissverständlich

mistaken [mɪsteɪkən] *adj* (*idea, identity*) falsch; **to be ~** sich irren, falschliegen

mistletoe [mɪsəltou] *n* Mistel *f*

mistreat [mɪstriːt] *vt* schlecht behandeln

mistress [mɪstrɪs] *n* (*lover*) Geliebte *f*

mistrust [mɪstrʌst] *n* Misstrauen *nt* (*of* gegen) ▷ *vt* misstrauen +*dat*

misty [mɪsti] *adj* neblig; (*hazy*) dunstig

misunderstand [mɪsʌndərstænd] (*irr*) *vt*, *vi* falsch verstehen

misunderstanding [mɪsʌndərstændɪŋ] *n* Missverständnis *nt*; (*disagreement*) Differenz *f*

mitten [mɪtən] *n* Fausthandschuh *m*

mix [mɪks] *n* (*mixture*) Mischung *f* ▷ *vt* mischen; (*blend*) vermischen (*with* mit); (*drinks, music*) mixen; **to mix business with pleasure** das Angenehme mit dem

Nützlichen verbinden ▷ *vi* (*liquids*) sich vermischen lassen

mixed [mɪkst] *adj* gemischt; **a ~ bunch** eine bunt gemischte Truppe; **~ grill** Mixed Grill *m*; **~ vegetables** Mischgemüse *nt*

mixer [mɪksər] *n* (*for food*) Mixer *m*

mixture [mɪkstʃər] *n* Mischung *f*; (*Med*) Saft *m*

mix up *vt* (*mix*) zusammenmischen; (*confuse*) verwechseln (*with* mit)

mix-up *n* Durcheinander *nt*, Missverständnis *nt*

ml (*abbr*) = **milliliter** ml

mm (*abbr*) = **millimeter** mm

moan [moun] *n* Stöhnen *nt*; (*complaint*) Gejammer *nt* ▷ *vi* stöhnen; (*complain*) jammern, meckern (*about* über +*akk*)

mobile [moubəl] *adj* beweglich; (*on wheels*) fahrbar ▷ *n* (*phone*) Handy *nt*

mobility [moubɪliti] *n* Beweglichkeit *f*

mock [mɒk] *vt* verspotten ▷ *adj* Schein-

mockery [mɒkəri] *n* Spott *m*

mode [moud] *n* Art *f*; (*Inform*) Modus *m*

model [mɒdəl] *n* Modell *nt*; (*example*) Vorbild *nt*; (*fashion model*) Model *nt* ▷ *adj* (*miniature*) Modell-; (*perfect*) Muster- ▷ *vt* (*make*) formen ▷ *vi*: **she ~s for Versace** sie arbeitet als Model bei Versace

modem [moudəm, -dɛm] *n* Modem *nt*

moderate [*adj, n* mɒdərɪt, *vb* mɒdəreɪt] *adj* mäßig; (*views, politics*) gemäßigt; (*income, success*) mittelmäßig ▷ *n* (*Pol*) Gemäßigte(r) *mf* ▷ *vt* mäßigen

moderation [mɒdəreɪʃən] *n* Mäßigung *f*; **in ~** mit Maßen

modern [mɒdərn] *adj* modern; **~ history** neuere Geschichte; **~ Greek** Neugriechisch *nt*

modernize [mɒdərnaɪz] *vt* modernisieren

modest [mɒdɪst] *adj* bescheiden

modesty [mɒdɪsti] *n* Bescheidenheit *f*

modification [mɒdɪfɪkeɪʃən] *n* Abänderung *f*

modify [mɒdɪfaɪ] *vt* abändern

moist [mɔɪst] *adj* feucht

moisten [mɔɪsən] *vt* befeuchten

moisture [mɔɪstʃər] *n* Feuchtigkeit *f*

moisturizer [mɔɪstʃəraɪzər] *n* Feuchtigkeitscreme *f*

molar [moulər] *n* Backenzahn *m*

mold [mould] *n* Form *f*; (*mildew*) Schimmel *m* ▷ *vt* (*a. fig*) formen

moldy [mouldi] *adj* schimmelig

mole [moul] *n* (*spot*) Leberfleck *m*; (*animal*) Maulwurf *m*

m

molecule [mɒlɪkyul] n Molekül nt
molest [məlɛst] vt belästigen
molt [moult] vi sich mausern, haaren
molten [moultªn] adj geschmolzen
mom [mɒm] n (fam: mother) Mutti f, Mami f
moment [moumənt] n Moment m, Augenblick m; **just a ~** Moment mal!; **at o for the ~** im Augenblick; **in a ~** gleich
momentous [moumɛntəs] adj bedeutsam
mommy [mɒmi] n (fam: mother) Mutti f, Mami f
Monaco [mɒnəkou] n Monaco nt
monarchy [mɒnərki] n Monarchie f
monastery [mɒnəstɛri] n (for monks) Kloster nt
Monday [mʌndeɪ, -di] n Montag m; see also **Tuesday**
monetary [mɒnɪtɛri] adj (reform, policy, union) Währungs-; **~ unit** Geldeinheit f
money [mʌni] n Geld nt; **to get one's ~'s worth** auf seine Kosten kommen
money order n Postanweisung f
mongrel [mʌŋgrəl, mɒŋ-] n Promenadenmischung f
monitor [mɒnɪtər] n (screen) Monitor m ▷ vt (progress etc) überwachen; (broadcasts) abhören
monk [mʌŋk] n Mönch m
monkey [mʌŋki] n Affe m; **~ business** Unfug m
mononucleosis [mɒnounukliousɪs] n Drüsenfieber nt
monopolize [mənɒpəlaɪz] vt monopolisieren; (fig: person, thing) in Beschlag nehmen
monopoly [mənɒpəli] n Monopol nt
monotonous [mənɒtªnəs] adj eintönig, monoton
monsoon [mɒnsun] n Monsun m
monster [mɒnstər] n (animal, thing) Monstrum nt ▷ adj Riesen-
monstrosity [mɒnstrɒsɪti] n Monstrosität f; (thing) Ungetüm nt
Montenegro [mɒntɪnigrou] n Montenegro nt
month [mʌnθ] n Monat m
monthly [mʌnθli] adj monatlich; (ticket, salary) Monats- ▷ adv monatlich ▷ n (magazine) Monats(zeit)schrift f
monty [mɒnti] n: **to go the full ~** (fam: strip) alle Hüllen fallen lassen; (go the whole hog) aufs Ganze gehen
monument [mɒnyəmənt] n Denkmal nt (to für)

monumental [mɒnyəmɛntªl] adj (huge) gewaltig
mood [mud] n (of person) Laune f; (a. general) Stimmung f; **to be in a good/bad ~** gute/schlechte Laune haben, gut/schlecht drauf sein; **to be in the ~ for sth** zu etw aufgelegt sein; **I'm not in the ~** ich fühle mich nicht danach
moody [mudi] adj launisch
moon [mun] n Mond m; **to be over the ~** (fam) überglücklich sein
moonlight [munlaɪt] n Mondlicht nt ▷ vi schwarzarbeiten
moonlit [munlɪt] adj (night, landscape) mondhell
moor [muər] n Moor nt ▷ vt, vi festmachen
moorings [muərɪŋz] npl Liegeplatz m
moorland [muərlænd] n Moorland nt, Heideland nt
moose [mus] (pl -) n Elch m
mop [mɒp] n Mopp m
mope [moup] vi Trübsal blasen
moped [mouped] n Moped nt
mop up vt aufwischen
moral [mɒrªl] adj moralisch; (values) sittlich ▷ n Moral f; **~s** pl Moral f
morale [məræl] n Stimmung f, Moral f
morality [məræliti] n Moral f, Ethik f
morbid [mɔrbɪd] adj krankhaft

KEYWORD

more [mɔr] adj (greater in number etc) mehr; (additional) noch mehr; **do you want (some) more tea?** möchtest du/möchten Sie noch etwas Tee?; **I have no o I don't have any more money** ich habe kein Geld mehr
▷ pron (greater amount) mehr; (further o additional amount) noch mehr; **is there any more?** gibt es noch mehr?; (left over) ist noch etwas da?; **there's no more** es ist nichts mehr da
▷ adv mehr; **more dangerous/easily etc (than)** gefährlicher/einfacher etc (als); **more and more** immer mehr; **more and more excited** immer aufgeregter; **more or less** mehr oder weniger; **more than ever** mehr denn je; **more beautiful than ever** schöner denn je

moreover [mɔrouvər] adv außerdem
morgue [mɔrg] n Leichenschauhaus nt

morning [mɔːnɪŋ] n Morgen m; **in the ~** am Morgen, morgens; (*tomorrow*) morgen früh; **this ~** heute morgen ▷ adj Morgen-; (*early*) Früh-; (*walk etc*) morgendlich

morning-after pill n die Pille danach

morning sickness n Schwangerschaftsübelkeit f

Morocco [mərɒkou] n Marokko nt

moron [mɔːrɒn] n Idiot(in) m(f)

morphine [mɔːfiːn] n Morphium nt

morsel [mɔːrsˀl] n Bissen m

mortal [mɔːrtˀl] adj sterblich; (*wound*) tödlich ▷ n Sterbliche(r) mf

mortality [mɔːrtælɪti] n (*death rate*) Sterblichkeitsziffer f

mortally [mɔːrtˀli] adv tödlich

mortgage [mɔːrgɪdʒ] n Hypothek f ▷ vt mit einer Hypothek belasten

mortified [mɔːrtɪfaɪd] adj: **I was ~** es war mir schrecklich peinlich

mortuary [mɔːrtʃueri] n Leichenhalle f

mosaic [mouzeɪɪk] n Mosaik nt

Moscow [mɒskau] n Moskau nt

Moslem [mɒzləm, muːzlɪm] adj, n see **Muslim**

mosque [mɒsk] n Moschee f

mosquito [məskiːtou] (*pl* **-es**) n (*Stech*)mücke f; (*tropical*) Moskito m; **~ net** Moskitonetz nt

moss [mɔːs] n Moos nt

most [moust] adj meiste pl, die meisten; **in ~ cases** in den meisten Fällen ▷ adv (*with verbs*) am meisten; (*with adj*) …ste; (*with adv*) am …sten; (*very*) äußerst, höchst; **he ate the ~** er hat am meisten gegessen; **the ~ beautiful/interesting** der/die/das schönste/interessanteste; **~ interesting!** hochinteressant! ▷ n das meiste, der größte Teil; (*people*) die meisten; **~ of the money/players** das meiste Geld/die meisten Spieler; **for the ~ part** zum größten Teil; **five at the ~** höchstens fünf; **to make the ~ of sth** etw voll ausnützen

mostly [moustli] adv (*most of the time*) meistens; (*mainly*) hauptsächlich; (*for the most part*) größtenteils

motel [moutel] n Motel nt

moth [mɔːθ] n Nachtfalter m; (*wool-eating*) Motte f

mothball [mɔːθbɔːl] n Mottenkugel f

mother [mʌðər] n Mutter f ▷ vt bemuttern

mother-in-law [mʌðərɪnlɔː] (*pl* **mothers-in-law**) n Schwiegermutter f

mother-to-be (*pl* **mothers-to-be**) n werdende Mutter

motif [moutiːf] n Motiv nt

motion [mouʃˀn] n Bewegung f; (*in meeting*) Antrag m

motionless [mouʃˀnlɪs] adj bewegungslos

motivate [moutɪveɪt] vt motivieren

motive [moutɪv] n Motiv nt

motor [moutər] n Motor m; (*fam: car*) Auto nt ▷ adj Motor-

motorbike [moutərbaɪk] n Motorrad nt

motorboat [moutərbout] n Motorboot nt

motorcycle [moutərsaɪkˀl] n Motorrad nt

motorist [moutərɪst] n Autofahrer(in) m(f)

motor oil n Motorenöl nt

motor scooter n Motorroller m

motor vehicle n Kraftfahrzeug nt

motto [mɒtou] (*pl* **-es**) n Motto nt

mount [maunt] vt (*horse*) steigen auf +akk; (*exhibition etc*) organisieren; (*painting*) mit einem Passepartout versehen ▷ vi: **to ~ up** (an)steigen ▷ n Passepartout nt

mountain [mauntˀn] n Berg m

mountain bike n Mountainbike nt

mountaineer [mauntˀnɪər] n Bergsteiger(in) m(f)

mountaineering [mauntˀnɪərɪŋ] n Bergsteigen nt

mountainous [mauntˀnəs] adj bergig

mountainside [mauntˀnsaɪd] n Berghang m

mourn [mɔːrn] vt betrauern ▷ vi trauern (*for* um)

mourner [mɔːrnər] n Trauernde(r) mf

mournful [mɔːrnfəl] adj trauervoll

mourning [mɔːrnɪŋ] n Trauer f; **to be in ~** trauern (*for* um)

mouse [maus] (*pl* **mice**) n (*a. Inform*) Maus f

mouse pad n Mauspad nt

mouse trap n Mausefalle f

mousse [muːs] n (*Gastr*) Creme f; (*styling mousse*) Schaumfestiger m

mouth [mauθ] n Mund m; (*of animal*) Maul nt; (*of cave*) Eingang m; (*of bottle etc*) Öffnung f; (*of river*) Mündung f; **to keep one's ~ shut** (*fam*) den Mund halten

mouthful [mauθfʊl] n (*of drink*) Schluck m; (*of food*) Bissen m

mouthwash [mauθwɒʃ] n Mundwasser nt

mouthwatering [mauθwɔːtˀrɪŋ] adj appetitlich, lecker

move [muːv] n (*movement*) Bewegung f; (*in game*) Zug m; (*step*) Schritt m; **to make a ~** (*in game*) ziehen; (*leave*) sich auf den Weg machen; **to get a ~ on with sth** sich (mit etw) beeilen ▷ vt bewegen; (*object*) rücken; (car) wegfahren; (transport: goods) befördern; (people) transportieren; (in job) versetzen; (emotionally) bewegen, rühren; **I can't ~ it** (stuck, too heavy) ich bringe es nicht von der Stelle; (relocate) umziehen ▷ vi sich bewegen; (change place) gehen; (vehicle, ship) fahren; (relocate) umziehen; (in game) ziehen

move away vi weggehen; (move town) wegziehen

move in vi (to house) einziehen

movement [muːvmənt] n Bewegung f

move off vi losfahren

move on vi weitergehen; (vehicle) weiterfahren

move out vi ausziehen

move up vi (in queue etc) aufrücken

movie [muːvi] n Film m; **the ~s** das Kino

movie star n Filmstar m

movie studio n Filmstudio nt

movie theater n Kino nt

moving [muːvɪŋ] adj (emotionally) ergreifend, berührend

mow [moʊ] (**mowed, mown** o **mowed**) vt mähen

mower [moʊər] n (lawnmower) Rasenmäher m

mown [moʊn] pp of **mow**

Mozambique [moʊzəmbiːk] n Mosambik nt

mph (abbr) = **miles per hour** Meilen pro Stunde

MP3 player [ɛm pi θriː pleɪər] n MP3-Player m

Mr. [mɪstər] n (written form of address) Herr

Mrs. [mɪsɪz] n (written form of address) Frau

MS [ɛm ɛs] n (abbr) (= multiple sclerosis) MS f

Ms. [mɪz] n (written form of address for any woman, married or unmarried) Frau

Mt (abbr) = **Mount** Berg m

much [mʌtʃ] (**more, most**) adj viel; **we haven't got ~ time** wir haben nicht viel Zeit; **how ~ money?** wie viel Geld? ▷ adv viel; (with verb) sehr; **~ better** viel besser; **I like it very ~** es gefällt mir sehr gut; **I don't like it ~** ich mag es nicht besonders; **thank you very ~** danke sehr; **I thought as ~** das habe ich mir gedacht; **~ as I like him** so sehr ich ihn mag; **we don't see them ~** wir sehen sie nicht sehr oft; **~ the same** fast gleich ▷ n viel; **as ~ as you want** so viel du willst; **he's not ~ of a cook** er ist

kein großer Koch

muck [mʌk] n (fam) Dreck m

mucky [mʌki] adj dreckig

mucus [myuːkəs] n Schleim m

mud [mʌd] n Schlamm m

muddle [mʌdʰl] n Durcheinander nt; **to be in a ~** ganz durcheinander sein ▷ vt: **to ~ up** durcheinanderbringen

muddled [mʌdʰld] adj konfus

muddy [mʌdi] adj schlammig; (shoes) schmutzig

mudguard [mʌdgɑrd] n Schutzblech nt

muesli [myuːzli] n Müsli nt

muffin [mʌfɪn] n Muffin m

muffle [mʌfʰl] vt (sound) dämpfen

muffler [mʌflər] n Schalldämpfer m

mug [mʌg] n (cup) Becher m; (fam: fool) Trottel m ▷ vt (attack and rob) überfallen

mugging [mʌgɪŋ] n Raubüberfall m

muggy [mʌgi] adj (weather) schwül

mule [myuːl] n Maulesel m

mulled [mʌld] adj: **~ wine** Glühwein m

mull over [mʌl oʊvər] vt nachdenken über +akk

multicolored [mʌltɪkʌlərd] adj bunt

multicultural [mʌltɪkʌltʃərəl] adj multikulturell

multilingual [mʌltɪlɪŋgwʰl] adj mehrsprachig

multinational [mʌltɪnæʃənʰl] n (company) Multi m

multiple [mʌltɪpʰl] n Vielfache(s) nt ▷ adj mehrfach; (several) mehrere

multiple-choice (method) [mʌltɪpʰltʃɔɪs (mɛθəd)] n Multiple-Choice-Verfahren nt

multiple sclerosis [mʌltɪpʰl skləroʊsɪs] n Multiple Sklerose f

multiplex [mʌltɪplɛks] adj, n: **~ (cinema)** Multiplexkino nt

multiplication [mʌltɪplɪkeɪʃʰn] n Multiplikation f

multiply [mʌltɪplaɪ] vt multiplizieren (by mit) ▷ vi sich vermehren

multi-purpose [mʌltɪpɜrpəs] adj Mehrzweck-

multitasking [mʌltɪtæskɪŋ] n (Inform) Multitasking nt

mumble [mʌmbʰl] vt, vi murmeln

mummy [mʌmi] n (dead body) Mumie f

mumps [mʌmps] nsing Mumps m

munch [mʌntʃ] vt, vi mampfen

Munich [myuːnɪk] n München nt

municipal [myuːnɪsɪpʰl] adj städtisch

mural [myʊərəl] n Wandgemälde nt

murder [mɜrdər] n Mord m; **the traffic was**

~ der Verkehr war die Hölle ▷ *vt* ermorden

murderer [mɜrdərər] *n* Mörder(in) *m(f)*

murky [mɜrki] *adj* düster; (*water*) trüb

murmur [mɜrmər] *vt, vi* murmeln

muscle [mʌsəl] *n* Muskel *m*

muscular [mʌskyələr] *adj* (*strong*) muskulös; (*cramp, pain etc*) Muskel-

museum [myuziəm] *n* Museum *nt*

mushroom [mʌʃrum] *n* (essbarer) Pilz; (*button mushroom*) Champignon *m* ▷ *vi* (*fig*) emporschießen

mushy [mʌʃi] *adj* breiig; ~ **peas** Erbsenmus *nt*

music [myuzɪk] *n* Musik *f*; (*printed*) Noten *pl*

musical [myuzɪkəl] *adj* (*sound*) melodisch; (*person*) musikalisch; ~ **instrument** Musikinstrument *nt* ▷ *n* (*show*) Musical *nt*

musically [myuzɪkli] *adv* musikalisch

musician [myuzɪʃən] *n* Musiker(in) *m(f)*

Muslim [mʌzlɪm, mʊs-] *adj* moslemisch ▷ *n* Moslem *m*, Muslime *f*

mussel [mʌsəl] *n* Miesmuschel *f*

must [məst, STRONG mʌst] (**had to, had to**) *vb aux* (*need to*) müssen; (*in negation*) dürfen; **I ~n't forget that** ich darf das nicht vergessen; (*certainty*): **he ~ be there by now** er ist inzwischen bestimmt schon da; (*assumption*): **I ~ have lost it** ich habe es wohl verloren; **~ you?** muss das sein? ▷ *n* Muss *nt*

mustache [mʌstæʃ] *n* Schnurrbart *m*

mustard [mʌstərd] *n* Senf *m*; **to cut the ~** es bringen

mustn't [mʌsᵊnt] *contr of* **must not**

mute [myut] *adj* stumm

mutter [mʌtər] *vt, vi* murmeln

mutton [mʌtᵊn] *n* Hammelfleisch *nt*

mutual [myutʃuəl] *adj* gegenseitig; **by ~ consent** in gegenseitigem Einvernehmen

my [maɪ] *adj* mein; **I've hurt my leg** ich habe mir das Bein verletzt

Myanmar [maɪænmɑr] *n* Myanmar *nt*

myself [maɪsɛlf] *pron* (*reflexive*) mich *akk*, mir *dat*; **I've hurt ~** ich habe mich verletzt; **I've bought ~ a car** ich habe mir ein Auto gekauft; **I need it for ~** ich brauche es für mich (selbst); (*emphatic*): **I did it ~** ich habe es selbst gemacht; **all by ~** allein

mysterious [mɪstɪəriəs] *adj* geheimnisvoll, mysteriös; (*inexplicable*) rätselhaft

mystery [mɪstəri, mɪstri] *n* Geheimnis *nt*; (*puzzle*) Rätsel *nt*; **it's a ~ to me** es ist mir schleierhaft

mystify [mɪstɪfaɪ] *vt* verblüffen

myth [mɪθ] *n* Mythos *m*; (*fig: untrue story*) Märchen *nt*

mythical [mɪθɪkᵊl] *adj* mythisch; (*fig: untrue*) erfunden

mythology [mɪθɒlədʒi] *n* Mythologie *f*

m

N

N [ɛn] *(abbr)* = **north** N

nag [næg] *vt, vi* herumnörgeln *(sb* an jdm)

nagging [ˈnægɪŋ] *n* Nörgelei *f*

nail [neɪl] *n* Nagel *m* ▷ *vt* nageln *(to* an)

nailbrush [ˈneɪlbrʌʃ] *n* Nagelbürste *f*

nail clippers [neɪl ˈklɪpərz] *npl* Nagelknipser *m*

nail down *vt* festnageln

nail file *n* Nagelfeile *f*

nail polish *n* Nagellack *m*

nail-polish remover *n* Nagellackentferner *m*

nail scissors *npl* Nagelschere *f*

naive [naɪˈiːv] *adj* naiv

naked [ˈneɪkɪd] *adj* nackt

name [neɪm] *n* Name *m;* **his ~ is ...** er heißt ...; **what's your ~?** wie heißen Sie?; *(reputation):* **to have a good/bad ~** einen guten/ schlechten Ruf haben ▷ *vt* nennen *(after* nach); *(sth new)* benennen; *(nominate)* ernennen *(as* als/zu); **a boy ~d ...** ein Junge namens ...

namely [ˈneɪmli] *adv* nämlich

nameplate *n* Namensschild *nt*

nan bread [næn brɛd] *n (warm serviertes) indisches Fladenbrot*

nanny [ˈnæni] *n* Kindermädchen *nt*

nap [næp] *n:* **to have/take a nap** ein Nickerchen machen

napkin [ˈnæpkɪn] *n (at table)* Serviette *f*

Naples [ˈneɪpᵊlz] *n* Neapel *nt*

narcotic [nɑːrkˈɒtɪk] *n* Rauschgift *nt*

narrate [ˈnæreɪt] *vt* erzählen

narration [nəreɪˈʃᵊn], **narrative** [ˈnærətɪv] *n* Erzählung *f*

narrator [ˈnæreɪtər] *n* Erzähler(in) *m(f)*

narrow [ˈnærou] *adj* eng, schmal; *(victory, majority)* knapp; **to have a ~ escape** mit knapper Not davonkommen ▷ *vi* sich verengen

narrow down *vt* einschränken *(to sth* auf etw *akk)*

narrow-minded [ˈnæroumaɪndɪd] *adj* engstirnig

nasty [ˈnæsti] *adj* ekelhaft; *(person)* fies; *(remark)* gehässig; *(accident, wound etc)* schlimm

nation [neɪˈʃᵊn] *n* Nation *f*

national [ˈnæʃᵊnᵊl] *adj* national; **~ anthem** Nationalhymne *f;* **~ park** Nationalpark *m;* **~ service** Wehrdienst *m;* **~ socialism** *(Hist)* Nationalsozialismus *m* ▷ *n* Staatsbürger(in) *m(f)*

nationality [næʃənˈæliti] *n* Staatsangehörigkeit *f,* Nationalität *f*

nationalize [ˈnæʃᵊnᵊlaɪz] *vt* verstaatlichen

nationwide [neɪˈʃᵊnwaɪd] *adj, adv* landesweit

native [ˈneɪtɪv] *adj* einheimisch; *(inborn)* angeboren, natürlich; **N~ American** Indianer(in) *m(f);* **~ country** Heimatland *nt;* **a ~ German** ein gebürtiger Deutscher, eine gebürtige Deutsche; **~ language** Muttersprache *f;* **~ speaker** Muttersprachler(in) *m(f)* ▷ *n* Einheimische(r) *mf; (in colonial context)* Eingeborene(r) *mf*

nativity play [nətˈɪviti pleɪ] *n* Krippenspiel *nt*

NATO [ˈneɪtou] *(acr)* = **North Atlantic Treaty Organization** Nato *f*

natural [ˈnætʃərᵊl, ˈnætʃrᵊl] *adj* natürlich; *(law, science, forces etc)* Natur-; *(inborn)* angeboren; **~ gas** Erdgas *nt;* **~ resources** Bodenschätze *pl*

naturally [ˈnætʃərᵊli, ˈnætʃrᵊli] *adv* natürlich; *(by nature)* von Natur aus; **it comes ~ to her** es fällt ihr leicht

nature [ˈneɪtʃər] *n* Natur *f; (type)* Art *f;* **it is not in my ~** es entspricht nicht meiner Art; **by ~** von Natur aus

nature reserve *n* Naturschutzgebiet *nt*

naughty [ˈnɔːti] *adj (child)* ungezogen; *(cheeky)* frech

nausea [ˈnɔːziə, -ʒə, -siə, -ʃə] *n* Übelkeit *f*

nautical [ˈnɔːtɪkᵊl] *adj* nautisch; **~ mile** Seemeile *f*

nave [neɪv] *n* Hauptschiff *nt*

navel [ˈneɪvᵊl] *n* Nabel *m*

navigate [ˈnævɪgeɪt] *vi* navigieren; *(in car)* lotsen, dirigieren

navigation [nævɪgeɪˈʃᵊn] *n* Navigation *f; (in car)* Lotsen *nt*

navy [ˈneɪvi] *n* Marine *f;* **~ blue** Marineblau *nt*

Nazi [ˈnɑːtsi] *n* Nazi *m*

NB [ɛn ˈbiː] *(abbr)* = **nota bene** NB

NE *(abbr)* = **northeast** NO

near [nɪər] *adj* nahe; **in the ~ future** in nächster Zukunft; **that was a ~ miss** *o* **thing** das war knapp; *(with price):* **... or ~est offer** Verhandlungsbasis ... ▷ *adv* in der Nähe; **so ~** so nahe; **to come ~er** näher kommen; *(event)* näher rücken ▷ *prep:* **~ to** *(space)* nahe an +*dat; (vicinity)* in der

Nähe +*gen*; ~ **the sea** nahe am Meer; ~ **the station** in der Nähe des Bahnhofs, in Bahnhofsnähe

nearby [nɪərbaɪ] *adj* nahe gelegen ▷ *adv* in der Nähe

nearly [nɪərli] *adv* fast

nearsighted [nɪərsaɪtɪd] *adj* kurzsichtig

neat [nit] *adj* ordentlich; (*work, writing*) sauber; (*undiluted*) pur

necessarily [nɛsɪsɛərɪli] *adv* notwendigerweise; **not** ~ nicht unbedingt

necessary [nɛsɪsɛri] *adj* notwendig, nötig; **it's** ~ **to ...** man muss ...; **it's not** ~ **for him to come** er braucht nicht mitzukommen

necessity [nɪsɛsɪti] *n* Notwendigkeit *f*; **the bare necessities** das absolut Notwendigste; **there is no** ~ **to ...** man braucht nicht (zu) ..., man muss nicht ...

neck [nɛk] *n* Hals *m*; (*size*) Halsweite *f*; **back of the** ~ Nacken *m*

necklace [nɛklɪs] *n* Halskette *f*

necktie [nɛktaɪ] *n* Krawatte *f*

nectarine [nɛktərin] *n* Nektarine *f*

née [neɪ] *adj* geborene

need [nid] *n* (*requirement*) Bedürfnis *nt* (*for* für); (*necessity*) Notwendigkeit *f*; (*poverty*) Not *f*; **to be in** ~ **of sth** etw brauchen; **if** ~**(s) be** wenn nötig; **there is no** ~ **to ...** man braucht nicht (zu) ..., man muss nicht ... ▷ *vt* brauchen; **I** ~ **to speak to you** ich muss mit dir reden; **you** ~**n't go** du brauchst nicht (zu) gehen, du musst nicht gehen

needle [nidᵊl] *n* Nadel *f*

needless [nidlɪs] *adj*, **needlessly** *adv* unnötig; ~ **to say** selbstverständlich

needy [nidi] *adj* bedürftig

negative [nɛgətɪv] *n* (*Ling*) Verneinung *f*; (*Foto*) Negativ *nt* ▷ *adj* negativ; (*answer*) verneinend

neglect [nɪglɛkt] *n* Vernachlässigung *f* ▷ *vt* vernachlässigen; **to** ~ **to do sth** es versäumen, etw zu tun

negligence [nɛglɪdʒᵊns] *n* Nachlässigkeit *f*

negligent [nɛglɪdʒᵊnt] *adj* nachlässig

negligible [nɛglɪdʒɪbᵊl] *adj* unbedeutend; (*amount*) geringfügig

negotiate [nɪgoʊʃieɪt] *vi* verhandeln

negotiation [nɪgoʊʃieɪʃᵊn] *n* Verhandlung *f*

neigh [neɪ] *vi* (*horse*) wiehern

neighbor [neɪbər] *n* Nachbar(in) *m(f)*

neighborhood [neɪbərhʊd] *n* Nachbarschaft *f*

neighboring [neɪbərɪŋ] *adj* benachbart

neither [niðər, naɪ-] *adj, pron* keine(r, s) von beiden; ~ **of you/us** keiner von euch/uns beiden ▷ *adv*: ~ **...** nor **...** weder ... noch ... ▷ *conj*: **I'm not going** - ~ **am I** ich gehe nicht - ich auch nicht

neon [niɒn] *n* Neon *nt*; ~ **sign** (*advertisement*) Leuchtreklame *f*

nephew [nɛfyu] *n* Neffe *m*

nerd [nɜrd] *n* (*fam*) Schwachkopf *m*; **he's a real computer** ~ er ist ein totaler Computerfreak

nerve [nɜrv] *n* Nerv *m*; **he gets on my** ~**s** er geht mir auf die Nerven; (*courage*): **to keep/lose one's** ~ die Nerven behalten/verlieren; (*cheek*): **to have the** ~ **to do sth** die Frechheit besitzen, etw zu tun

nerve-racking [nɜrvrækɪŋ] *adj* nervenaufreibend

nervous [nɜrvəs] *adj* (*apprehensive*) ängstlich; (*on edge*) nervös

nervous breakdown *n* Nervenzusammenbruch *m*

nest [nɛst] *n* Nest *nt* ▷ *vi* nisten

net [nɛt] *n* Netz *nt*; **the Net** (*internet*) das Internet; **on the net** im Netz ▷ *adj* (*price, weight*) Netto-; **net profit** Reingewinn *m*

Netherlands [nɛðərləndz] *npl*: **the** ~ die Niederlande *pl*

nettle [nɛtᵊl] *n* Nessel *f*

network [nɛtwɜrk] *n* Netz *nt*; (*TV, Radio*) Sendenetz *nt*; (*Inform*) Netzwerk *nt*

networking [nɛtwɜrkɪŋ] *n* Networking *nt* (*das Knüpfen und Pflegen von Kontakten, die dem beruflichen Fortkommen dienen*)

neurosis [nʊəroʊsɪs] *n* Neurose *f*

neurotic [nʊərɒtɪk] *adj* neurotisch

neuter [nutər] *adj* (*Bio*) geschlechtslos; (*Ling*) sächlich

neutral [nutrəl] *adj* neutral ▷ *n* (*gear in car*) Leerlauf *m*

never [nɛvər] *adv* nie(mals); ~ **before** noch nie; ~ **mind** macht nichts!

never-ending *adj* endlos

nevertheless [nɛvərðəlɛs] *adv* trotzdem

new [nu] *adj* neu; **this is all new to me** das ist für mich noch ungewohnt

newcomer [nukʌmər] *n* Neuankömmling *m*; (*in job, subject*) Neuling *m*

New England *n* Neuengland *nt*

Newfoundland [nufəndlænd] *n* Neufundland *nt*

newly [nuli] *adv* neu; ~ **made** (*cake*) frisch gebacken

newlyweds *npl* Frischvermählte *pl*

new moon *n* Neumond *m*

news [nuz] *nsing* (*item of news*) Nachricht *f*; (*Radio, TV*) Nachrichten *pl*; **good ~** ein erfreuliche Nachricht; **what's the ~?** was gibt's Neues?; **have you heard the ~?** hast du das Neueste gehört?; **that's ~ to me** das ist mir neu

news bulletin *n* Nachrichtensendung *f*

news dealer *n* Zeitungshändler(in) *m(f)*

news flash *n* Kurzmeldung *f*

newsgroup [nuzgrup] *n* (*Inform*) Diskussionsforum *nt*, Newsgroup *f*

newsletter [nuzlɛtər] *n* Mitteilungsblatt *nt*

newspaper [nuzpeɪpər, nus-] *n* Zeitung *f*

New Year *n* das neue Jahr; **Happy ~** (ein) frohes Neues Jahr!; (*toast*) Prosit Neujahr!; **~'s Day** Neujahr *nt*, Neujahrstag *m*; **~'s Eve** Silvesterabend *m*; **~'s resolution** *guter Vorsatz fürs neue Jahr*

New York [nu yɔrk] *n* New York *nt*

New Zealand [nu zilənd] *n* Neuseeland *nt* ▷ *adj* neuseeländisch

New Zealander [nu ziləndər] *n* Neuseeländer(in) *m(f)*

next [nɛkst] *adj* nächste(r, s); **the week after ~** übernächste Woche; **~ time I see him** wenn ich ihn das nächste Mal sehe; **you're ~** du bist jetzt dran ▷ *adv* als Nächstes; (*then*) dann, darauf; **~ to** neben +*dat*; **~ to last** vorletzte(r, s); **~ to impossible** nahezu unmöglich; **the ~ best thing** das Nächstbeste; **~ door** nebenan

Niagara Falls [naɪægərə] *npl* Niagarafälle *pl*

nibble [nɪbªl] *vt* knabbern an +*dat*

nibbles *npl* Knabberzeug *nt*

Nicaragua [nɪkərɑgwə] *n* Nicaragua *nt*

nice [naɪs] *adj* nett, sympathisch; (*taste, food, drink*) gut; (*weather*) schön; **~ and ...** schön ...; **be ~ to him** sei nett zu ihm; **have a ~ day** schönen Tag noch!

nicely [naɪsli] *adv* nett; (*well*) gut; **that'll do ~** das genügt vollauf

nickel [nɪkªl] *n* (*Chem*) Nickel *nt*; (*coin*) Nickel *m*

nickname [nɪkneɪm] *n* Spitzname *m*

nicotine [nɪkitin] *n* Nikotin *nt*

nicotine patch *n* Nikotinpflaster *nt*

niece [nis] *n* Nichte *f*

Nigeria [naɪdʒiriə] *n* Nigeria *nt*

night [naɪt] *n* Nacht *f*; (*before bed*) Abend *m*; **good ~** gute Nacht!; **at o by ~** nachts; **to have an early ~** früh schlafen gehen

nightcap [naɪtkæp] *n* Schlummertrunk *m*

nightclub [naɪtklʌb] *n* Nachtklub *m*

nightgown [naɪtgaʊn] *n* Nachthemd *nt*

nightie [naɪti] *n* (*fam*) Nachthemd *nt*

nightingale [naɪtªngeɪl] *n* Nachtigall *f*

night life *n* Nachtleben *nt*

nightly [naɪtli] *adv* (*every evening*) jeden Abend; (*every night*) jede Nacht

nightmare [naɪtmɛər] *n* Albtraum *m*

nighttime [naɪttaɪm] *n* Nacht *f*; **at ~** nachts

nil [nɪl] *n* (*Sport*) null

Nile [naɪl] *n* Nil *m*

nine [naɪn] *num* neun; **~ times out of ten** so gut wie immer ▷ *n* (*a. bus etc*) Neun *f*; *see also* **eight**

nineteen [naɪntin] *num* neunzehn ▷ *n* (*a. bus etc*) Neunzehn *f*; *see also* **eight**

nineteenth [naɪntinθ] *adj* neunzehnte(r, s); *see also* **eighth**

ninetieth [naɪntiiθ] *adj* neunzigste(r, s); *see also* **eighth**

ninety [naɪnti] *num* neunzig ▷ *n* Neunzig *f*; *see also* **eight**

ninth [naɪnθ] *adj* neunte(r, s) ▷ *n* (*fraction*) Neuntel *nt*; *see also* **eighth**

nipple [nɪpªl] *n* Brustwarze *f*

nitrogen [naɪtrədʒən] *n* Stickstoff *m*

KEYWORD

no [noʊ] (*pl* **noes**) *adv* (*opposite of yes*) nein; **to answer no** (*to question*) mit Nein antworten; (*to request*) Nein *o* nein sagen; **no thank you** nein, danke
▷ *adj* (*not any*) kein(e); **I have no money/time** ich habe kein Geld/keine Zeit; **'no smoking'** „Rauchen verboten"
▷ *n* Nein *nt*; (*no vote*) Neinstimme *f*

nobility [noʊbɪliti] *n* Adel *m*

noble [noʊbªl] *adj* (*rank*) adlig; (*quality*) edel ▷ *n* Adlige(r) *mf*

nobody [noʊbɒdi, -bʌdi] *pron* niemand; (*emphatic*) keiner; **~ knows** keiner weiß es; **~ else** sonst niemand, kein anderer ▷ *n* Niemand *m*

nod [nɒd] *vi, vt* nicken

nod off *vi* einnicken

noise [nɔɪz] *n* (*loud*) Lärm *m*; (*sound*) Geräusch *nt*

noisy [nɔɪzi] *adj* laut; (*crowd*) lärmend

nominate [nɒmɪneɪt] *vt* (*in election*) aufstellen; (*appoint*) ernennen

nominative [nɒmɪnətɪv] *n* (*Ling*) Nominativ *m*

nominee [nɒmɪni] *n* Kandidat(in) *m(f)*

non- [nɒn-] *pref* Nicht-; (*with adj*) nicht-, un-

nonalcoholic [nɒnælkəhɔlɪk] *adj* alkoholfrei

none [nʌn] *pron* keine(r, s); **~ of them** keiner von ihnen; **~ of it is any use** nichts
davon ist brauchbar; **there are ~ left** es
sind keine mehr da; (*with comparative*):
to be ~ the wiser auch nicht schlauer sein;
I was ~ the worse for it es hat mir nichts
geschadet

nonentity [nɒnɛntɪtɪ] *n* Null *f*

nonetheless [nʌnðəlɛs] *adv* nichtsdesto-
weniger, dennoch

nonevent [nɒnɪvɛnt] *n* Reinfall *m*

nonexistent [nɒnɪgzɪstənt] *adj* nicht vorhanden

nonfiction [nɒnfɪkʃ°n] *n* Sachbücher *pl*

non-iron [nɒnaɪərn] *adj* bügelfrei

non-polluting [nɒnpəlutɪŋ] *adj* schad-
stofffrei

nonresident [nɒnrɛzɪdənt] *n*: 'open to ~s'
„auch für Nichthotelgäste"

nonreturnable [nɒnrɪtɜːnəb°l] *adj*: **~ bottle** Einwegflasche *f*

nonsense [nɒnsɛns, -səns] *n* Unsinn *m*;
don't talk ~ red keinen Unsinn

nonsmoker [nɒnsmoʊkər] *n*
Nichtraucher(in) *m(f)*

nonsmoking [nɒnsmoʊkɪŋ] *adj* Nichtrau-
cher-; **~ area** Nichtraucherbereich *m*

nonstop [nɒnstɒp] *adj* (*train*) durchgehend; (*flight*) Nonstop- ▷ *adv* (*talk*) ununterbrochen; (*travel*) ohne Unterbrechung;
(*fly*) ohne Zwischenlandung

nonviolent [nɒnvaɪələnt] *adj* gewaltfrei

noodles [nudlz] *npl* Nudeln *pl*

noon [nun] *n* Mittag *m*; **at ~** um 12 Uhr
mittags

no one *pron* niemand; (*emphatic*) keiner; **~
else** sonst niemand, kein anderer

nor [nɔr] *conj*: **neither ... nor ...** weder ...
noch ...; **I don't smoke, nor does he** ich
rauche nicht, er auch nicht

norm [nɔrm] *n* Norm *f*

normal [nɔrm°l] *adj* normal; **to get back to
~** sich wieder normalisieren

normally [nɔrməlɪ] *adv* (*usually*) normalerweise

north [nɔrθ] *n* Norden *m*; **to the ~ of** nördlich von ▷ *adv* (*go, face*) nach Norden ▷ *adj*
Nord-; **~ wind** Nordwind *m*

North America *n* Nordamerika *nt*

northbound [nɔrθbaʊnd] *adj* (in) Richtung Norden

northeast [nɔrθist] *n* Nordosten *m*; **to the
~ of** nordöstlich von ▷ *adv* (*go, face*) nach

Nordosten ▷ *adj* Nordost-

northern [nɔrðərn] *adj* nördlich; **~ France**
Nordfrankreich *nt*

Northern Ireland *n* Nordirland *nt*

North Pole *n* Nordpol *m*

North Sea *n* Nordsee *f*

northwards [nɔrθwərdz] *adv* nach Norden

northwest [nɔrθwɛst] *n* Nordwesten *m*; **to
the ~ of** nordwestlich von ▷ *adv* (*go, face*)
nach Nordwesten ▷ *adj* Nordwest-

Norway [nɔrweɪ] *n* Norwegen *nt*

Norwegian [nɔrwidʒ°n] *adj* norwegisch
▷ *n* (*person*) Norweger(in) *m(f)*; (*language*)
Norwegisch *nt*

nos. (*abbr*) **= numbers** Nr.

nose [noʊz] *n* Nase *f*

nose around *vi* herumschnüffeln

nosebleed [noʊzblid] *n* Nasenbluten *nt*

nosedive [noʊzdaɪv] *n* Sturzflug *m*; **to
take a ~** abstürzen

nosey [noʊzɪ] *see* **nosy**

nostalgia [nɒstældʒə] *n* Nostalgie *f* (*for*
nach)

nostalgic [nɒstældʒɪk] *adj* nostalgisch

nostril [nɒstrɪl] *n* Nasenloch *nt*

nosy [noʊzɪ] *adj* neugierig

not [nɒt] *adv* nicht; **~ a** kein; **not one of
them** kein einziger von ihnen; **he is not an
expert** er ist kein Experte; **I told him not
to do it** ich sagte ihm, er solle es nicht tun;
not at all überhaupt nicht, keineswegs;
(*don't mention it*) gern geschehen; **not yet**
noch nicht

notable [noʊtəb°l] *adj* bemerkenswert

note [noʊt] *n* (*written*) Notiz *f*; (*short letter*)
paar Zeilen *pl*; (*on scrap of paper*) Zettel
m; (*comment in book etc*) Anmerkung *f*;
(*banknote*) Schein *m*; (*Mus: sign*) Note *f*;
(*sound*) Ton *m*; **to make a ~ of sth** sich *dat*
etw notieren; **~s** (*of lecture etc*) Aufzeich-
nungen *pl*; **to take ~s** sich *dat* Notizen
machen (*of* über +*akk*) ▷ *vt* (*notice*) bemerken (*that* dass); (*write down*) notieren

notebook [noʊtbʊk] *n* Notizbuch *nt*;
(*Inform*) Notebook *nt*

notepad [noʊtpæd] *n* Notizblock *m*

notepaper [noʊtpeɪpər] *n* Briefpapier *nt*

nothing [nʌθɪŋ] *n* nichts; **~ but ...** lauter ...;
for ~ umsonst; **he thinks ~ of it** er macht
sich nichts daraus

notice [noʊtɪs] *n* (*announcement*) Bekanntmachung *f*; (*on bulletin board*) Anschlag
m; (*attention*) Beachtung *f*; (*advance warning*) Ankündigung *f*; (*to leave apartment,
job etc*) Kündigung *f*; **at short ~** kurzfris-

tig; **until further ~** bis auf weiteres; **to give sb ~** jdm kündigen; **to hand in one's ~** kündigen; **to take no ~ of sth** etw (nicht) beachten; **take no ~** kümmere dich nicht darum! ▷ *vt* bemerken

noticeable [nֿoʊtɪsəbᵊl] *adj* erkennbar; (*visible*) sichtbar; **to be ~** auffallen

notification [nֿoʊtɪfɪkeɪʃᵊn] *n* Benachrichtigung *f* (*of* von)

notify [nֿoʊtɪfaɪ] *vt* benachrichtigen (*of* von)

notion [nֿoʊʃᵊn] *n* Idee *f*

notorious [noʊtɔֿriəs] *adj* berüchtigt

noun [nֿaʊn] *n* Substantiv *nt*

nourish [nɜֿrɪʃ] *vt* nähren

nourishing [nɜֿrɪʃɪŋ] *adj* nahrhaft

nourishment [nɜֿrɪʃmənt] *n* Nahrung *f*

novel [nֿɒvᵊl] *n* Roman *m* ▷ *adj* neuartig

novelist [nֿɒvəlɪst] *n* Schriftsteller(in) *m(f)*

novelty [nֿɒvᵊlti] *n* Neuheit *f*

November [noʊvɛֿmbər] *n* November *m*; *see also* **September**

novice [nֿɒvɪs] *n* Neuling *m*

now [nֿaʊ] *adv* (*at the moment*) jetzt; (*introductory phrase*) also; **right now** jetzt gleich; **just now** gerade; **by now** inzwischen; **from now on** ab jetzt; **now and again** o **then** ab und zu

nowadays [nֿaʊədeɪz] *adv* heutzutage

nowhere [nֿoʊwɛər] *adv* nirgends; **we're getting ~** wir kommen nicht weiter; **~ near** noch lange nicht

nozzle [nֿɒzᵊl] *n* Düse *f*

nuclear [nֿukliər] *adj* (*energy etc*) Kern-; **~ power station** Kernkraftwerk *nt*

nuclear waste *n* Atommüll *m*

nude [nֿud] *adj* nackt ▷ *n* (*person*) Nackte(r) *mf*; (*painting etc*) Akt *m*

nude beach *n* FKK-Strand *m*

nudge [nֿʌdʒ] *vt* stupsen

nudist [nֿudɪst] *n* Nudist(in) *m(f)*, FKK-Anhänger(in) *m(f)*

nuisance [nֿusᵊns] *n* Ärgernis *nt*; (*person*) Plage *f*; **what a ~** wie ärgerlich!

nuke [nֿuk] (*fam*) *n* (*bomb*) Atombombe *f* ▷ *vt* eine Atombombe werfen auf +*akk*

numb [nֿʌm] *adj* taub, gefühllos ▷ *vt* betäuben

number [nֿʌmbər] *n* Nummer *f*; (*Math*) Zahl *f*; (*quantity*) (An)zahl *f*; **in small/large ~s** in kleinen/großen Mengen; **a ~ of times** mehrmals ▷ *vt* (*give a number to*) nummerieren; (*count*) zählen (*among* zu); **his days are ~ed** seine Tage sind gezählt

numeral [nֿumərəl] *n* Ziffer *f*

numerical [numɛֿrɪkᵊl] *adj* numerisch; (*superiority*) zahlenmäßig

numerous [nֿumərəs] *adj* zahlreich

nun [nֿʌn] *n* Nonne *f*

Nuremberg [nֿurəmbɜrg] *n* Nürnberg *nt*

nurse [nֿɜrs] *n* Krankenschwester *f*; (*male nurse*) Krankenpfleger *m* ▷ *vt* (*patient*) pflegen; (*baby*) stillen

nursery [nֿɜrsəri] *n* Kinderzimmer *nt*; (*for plants*) Gärtnerei *f*; (*tree*) Baumschule *f*

nursery rhyme *n* Kinderreim *m*

nursery school *n* Kindergarten *m*; **~ teacher** Kindergärtner(in) *m(f)*, Erzieher(in) *m(f)*

nursing [nֿɜrsɪŋ] *n* (*profession*) Krankenpflege *f*; **~ home** Privatklinik *f*

nut [nֿʌt] *n* Nuss *f*; (*Tech: for bolt*) Mutter *f*

nutcase [nֿʌtkeɪs] *n* (*fam*) Spinner(in) *m(f)*

nutcracker [nֿʌtkrækər] *n*, **nutcrackers** *npl* Nussknacker *m*

nutmeg [nֿʌtmɛg] *n* Muskat *m*, Muskatnuss *f*

nutrient [nֿutriənt] *n* Nährstoff *m*

nutrition [nutrɪֿʃᵊn] *n* Ernährung *f*

nutritious [nutrɪֿʃəs] *adj* nahrhaft

nuts [nֿʌts] (*fam*) *adj* verrückt; **to be ~ about sth** nach etw verrückt sein ▷ *npl* (*testicles*) Eier *pl*

nutshell [nֿʌtʃɛl] *n* Nussschale *f*; **in a ~** kurz gesagt

nutty [nֿʌti] *adj* (*fam*) verrückt

NW (*abbr*) = **northwest** NW

nylon [nֿaɪlɒn] *n* Nylon® *nt* ▷ *adj* Nylon-

O

O [ou] *n* (*Tel*) Null *f*

oak [ouk] *n* Eiche *f* ▷ *adj* Eichen-

oar [ɔr] *n* Ruder *nt*

oasis [oueɪsɪs] (*pl* **oases**) *n* Oase *f*

oath [ouθ] *n* (*statement*) Eid *m*

oatmeal [outmil] *n* Haferbrei *m*

oats [outs] *npl* Hafer *m*; (*Gastr*) Haferflocken *pl*

obedience [oubidiəns] *n* Gehorsam *m*

obedient [oubidiənt] *adj* gehorsam

obey [oubeɪ] *vt, vi* gehorchen +*dat*

object [*n* ɒbdʒɪkt, *vb* əbdʒɛkt] *n* Gegenstand *m*; (*abstract*) Objekt *nt*; (*purpose*) Ziel *nt* ▷ *vi* dagegen sein; (*raise objection*) Einwände erheben (*to* gegen); (*morally*) Anstoß nehmen (*to* an +*dat*); **do you ~ to my smoking?** haben Sie etwas dagegen, wenn ich rauche?

objection [əbdʒɛkʃⁿn] *n* Einwand *m*

objective [əbdʒɛktɪv] *n* Ziel *nt* ▷ *adj* objektiv

objectivity [ɒbdʒɛktɪvɪti] *n* Objektivität *f*

obligation [ɒblɪgeɪʃⁿn] *n* (*duty*) Pflicht *f*; (*commitment*) Verpflichtung *f*; **no ~** unverbindlich

obligatory [əblɪgətɔri] *adj* obligatorisch

oblige [əblaɪdʒ] *vt*: **to ~ sb to do sth** jdn (dazu) zwingen, etw zu tun; **he felt ~d to accept the offer** er fühlte sich verpflichtet, das Angebot anzunehmen

oblique [oublik] *adj* schräg; (*angle*) schief

oboe [oubou] *n* Oboe *f*

obscene [əbsin] *adj* obszön

obscure [əbskyuər] *adj* unklar; (*unknown*) unbekannt

observant [əbzɜrvⁿnt] *adj* aufmerksam

observation [ɒbzərveɪʃⁿn] *n* (*watching*) Beobachtung *f*; (*remark*) Bemerkung *f*

observe [əbzɜrv] *vt* (*notice*) bemerken; (*watch*) beobachten; (*customs*) einhalten

obsessed [əbsɛst] *adj* besessen (*with an idea etc* von einem Gedanken *etc*)

obsession [əbsɛʃⁿn] *n* Manie *f*

obsolete [ɒbsəlit] *adj* veraltet

obstacle [ɒbstək⁰l] *n* Hindernis *nt* (*to* für); **to be an ~ to sth** einer Sache im Weg stehen

obstinate [ɒbstɪnɪt] *adj* hartnäckig

obstruct [əbstrʌkt] *vt* versperren; (*pipe*) verstopfen; (*hinder*) behindern, aufhalten

obstruction [əbstrʌkʃⁿn] *n* Blockierung *f*; (*of pipe*) Verstopfung *f*; (*obstacle*) Hindernis *nt*

obtain [əbteɪn] *vt* erhalten

obtainable [əbteɪnəb⁰l] *adj* erhältlich

obvious [ɒbviəs] *adj* offensichtlich; **it was ~ to me that ...** es war mir klar, dass ...

obviously [ɒbviəsli] *adj* offensichtlich

occasion [əkeɪʒⁿn] *n* Gelegenheit *f*; (*special event*) (großes) Ereignis *nt*; **on the ~ of** anlässlich +*gen*; **special ~** besonderer Anlass

occasional [əkeɪʒən⁰l] *adj*, **occasionally** *adv* gelegentlich

occupant [ɒkyəpənt] *n* (*of house*) Bewohner(in) *m(f)*; (*of vehicle*) Insasse *m*, Insassin *f*

occupation [ɒkyəpeɪʃⁿn] *n* Beruf *m*; (*pastime*) Beschäftigung *f*; (*of country etc*) Besetzung *f*

occupied [ɒkyəpaɪd] *adj* (*country, seat, toilet*) besetzt; (*person*) beschäftigt; **to keep sb/oneself ~** jdn/sich beschäftigen

occupy [ɒkyəpaɪ] *vt* (*country*) besetzen; (*time*) beanspruchen; (*mind, person*) beschäftigen

occur [əkɜr] *vi* vorkommen; **~ to sb** jdm einfallen

occurrence [əkɜrəns] *n* (*event*) Ereignis *nt*; (*presence*) Vorkommen *nt*

ocean [ouʃⁿn] *n* Ozean *m*; (*sea*) Meer *nt*

o'clock [əklɒk] *adv*: **5 ~ 5 Uhr**; **at 10 ~** um 10 Uhr

octagon [ɒktəgɒn] *n* Achteck *nt*

October [ɒktoubər] *n* Oktober *m*; *see also* **September**

octopus [ɒktəpəs] *n* Tintenfisch *m*

odd [ɒd] *adj* (*strange*) sonderbar; (*not even*) ungerade; (*one missing*) einzeln; **to be the odd one out** nicht dazugehören; **odd jobs** Gelegenheitsarbeiten *pl*

odds [ɒdz] *npl* Chancen *pl*; **against all ~** entgegen allen Erwartungen; **~ and ends** (*fam*) Kleinkram *pl*

odometer [oudɒmɪtər] *n* (*Auto*) Meilenzähler *m*, ≈ Kilometerzähler *m*

odor [oudər] *n* Geruch *m*

KEYWORD

of [əv, STRONG ʌv] *prep* 1 von +*dat*, ≈ use of gen; **the history of Germany** die Geschichte Deutschlands; **a friend of ours** ein Freund von uns; **a boy of 10** ein 10-jähriger Junge; **that was kind of you** das war

sehr freundlich von Ihnen
2 (*expressing quantity, amount, dates etc*):
a pound of flour ein Pfund Mehl; **how
much of this do you need?** wie viel brauchen Sie (davon)?; **there were 3 of them**
(*people*) sie waren zu dritt; (*objects*) es gab
3 (davon); **a cup of tea/vase of flowers**
eine Tasse Tee/Vase mit Blumen; **the 5th
of July** der 5 Juli
3 (*from, out of*) aus; **a bridge made of
wood** eine Holzbrücke, eine Brücke aus
Holz

off [*prep* ɔf, *adv* ɔf] *adv* (*away*) weg, fort;
(*free*) frei; (*switch*) ausgeschaltet; (*milk*)
sauer; **a mile off** eine Meile entfernt; **I'll
be off now** ich gehe jetzt; **to have the day/
Monday off** heute/Montag freihaben; **the
lights are off** die Lichter sind aus; **the
concert is off** das Konzert fällt aus; **I got
10 % off** ich habe 10 % Nachlass bekommen ▷ *prep* (*away from*) von; **to jump/fall
off the roof** vom Dach springen/fallen; **to
get off the bus** aus dem Bus aussteigen;
he's off work er hat frei; **to take $20 off
the price** den Preis um 20 Dollar herabsetzen

offend [əfɛnd] *vt* kränken; (*eye, ear*) beleidigen

offender [əfɛndər] *n* Straffällige(r) *mf*

offense [əfɛns] *n* (*crime*) Straftat *f*; (*minor*)
Vergehen *nt*; (*to feelings*) Kränkung *f*; **to
cause/take ~** Anstoß erregen/nehmen

offensive [əfɛnsɪv] *adj* anstößig; (*insulting*) beleidigend; (*smell*) übel, abstoßend
▷ *n* (*Mil*) Offensive *f*

offer [ɔfər] *n* Angebot *nt*; **on ~** (*Comm*) im
Angebot ▷ *vt* anbieten (*to sb* jdm); (*money,
a chance etc*) bieten

offhand [ɔfhænd] *adj* lässig ▷ *adv* (*say*) auf
Anhieb

office [ɔfɪs] *n* Büro *nt*; (*position*) Amt *nt*;
doctor's ~ Arztpraxis *f*

office building *n* Bürogebäude *nt*

office hours *npl* Dienstzeit *f*; (*notice*)
Geschäftszeiten *pl*

officer [ɔfɪsər] *n* (*Mil*) Offizier(in) *m(f)*;
(*official*) Polizeibeamte(r) *m*, Polizeibeamtin *f*

office worker *n* Büroangestellte(r) *mf*

official [əfɪʃl] *adj* offiziell; (*report etc*) amtlich; **~ language** Amtssprache *f* ▷ *n*
Beamte(r) *m*, Beamtin *f*, Repräsentant(in)
m(f)

off-line [ɔflaɪn] *adj* (*Inform*) offline

off-peak *adj* außerhalb der Stoßzeiten;
(*rate, ticket*) verbilligt

off-putting [ɔfpʊtɪŋ] *adj* abstoßend, ent-
mutigend, irritierend

off-season *adj* außerhalb der Saison

offshore [ɔfʃɔr] *adj* küstennah, Küsten-;
(*oil rig*) im Meer

offside [ɔfsaɪd] *n* (*Sport*) Abseits *nt*

often [ɔfᵊn] *adv* oft; **every so ~** von Zeit zu
Zeit

oil [ɔɪl] *n* Öl *nt* ▷ *vt* ölen

oil level *n* Ölstand *m*

oil painting *n* Ölgemälde *nt*

oil rig *n* (Öl)bohrinsel *f*

oil slick *n* Ölteppich *m*

oil tanker *n* Öltanker *m*; (*truck*) Tankwagen
m

oily [ɔɪli] *adj* ölig; (*skin, hair*) fettig

ointment [ɔɪntmənt] *n* Salbe *f*

OK, okay [ou keɪ] *adj* (*fam*) okay, in Ordnung; **that's OK by** *o* **with me** das ist mir
recht

old [ould] *adj* alt

old age *n* Alter *nt*; **~ pension** Rente *f*; **~
pensioner** Rentner(in) *m(f)*

old-fashioned [ouldfæʃn] *adj* altmodisch

olive [ɒlɪv] *n* Olive *f*

olive oil *n* Olivenöl *nt*

Olympic [əlɪmpɪk] *adj* olympisch; **the ~
Games, the ~s** *pl* die Olympischen Spiele
pl, die Olympiade

omelette [ɒmlɪt] *n* Omelett *nt*

omission [oumɪʃn] *n* Auslassung *f*

omit [oumɪt] *vt* auslassen

KEYWORD

on [ɒn] *prep* **1** (*indicating position*) auf +*dat*;
(*with vb of motion*) auf +*akk*; (*on vertical
surface, part of body*) an +*dat/akk*; **it's on
the table** es ist auf dem Tisch; **she put the
book on the table** sie legte das Buch auf
den Tisch; **on the left** links
2 (*indicating means, method, condition
etc*): **on foot** (*go, be*) zu Fuß; **on the train/
plane** (*go*) mit dem Zug/Flugzeug; (*be*) im
Zug/Flugzeug; **on the telephone/televi-
sion** am Telefon/im Fernsehen; **to be on
drugs** Drogen nehmen; **to be on vacation/
business** im Urlaub/auf Geschäftsreise
sein
3 (*referring to time*): **on Friday** (am) Freitag; **on Fridays** freitags; **on June 20th** am
20. Juni; **on arrival he ...** als er ankam, ...
er ...

4 (*about, concerning*) über +*akk*
▷ *adv* **1** (*referring to dress*) an; **she put her boots/hat on** sie zog ihre Stiefel an/setzte ihren Hut auf
2 (*further, continuously*) weiter; **to walk on** weitergehen
▷ *adj* (*functioning, in operation: machine, TV, light*) an; (*tap*) aufgedreht; (*brakes*) angezogen; **is the meeting still on?** findet die Versammlung noch statt?; **there's a good movie on** es läuft ein guter Film

once [wʌns] *adv* (*one time, in the past*) einmal; **at ~** sofort; (*at the same time*) gleichzeitig; **~ more** noch einmal; **for ~** ausnahmsweise (einmal); **~ in a while** ab und zu mal ▷ *conj* wenn ... einmal; **~ you've got used to it** sobald Sie sich daran gewöhnt haben
oncoming [ɒnkʌmɪŋ] *adj* entgegenkommend; **~ traffic** Gegenverkehr *m*

KEYWORD

one [wʌn] *num* eins; (*with noun, referring back to noun*) ein/eine/ein; **it is one** (*o'clock*) es ist eins, es ist ein Uhr; **one hundred and fifty** einhundertfünfzig
▷ *adj* **1** (*sole*) einzige(r, s); **the one book which** das einzige Buch, welches
2 (*same*) derselbe/dieselbe/dasselbe; **they came in the one car** sie kamen alle in dem einen Auto
3 (*indef*): **one day I discovered ...** eines Tages bemerkte ich ...
▷ *pron* **1** eine(r, s); **do you have a red one?** haben Sie einen roten/eine rote/ein rotes?; **this one** diese(r, s); **that one** der/die/das; **which one?** welche(r, s)?; **one by one** einzeln
2: **one another** einander; **do you two ever see one another?** seht ihr beide euch manchmal?
3 (*impers*) man; **one never knows** man kann nie wissen; **to cut one's finger** sich in den Finger schneiden

one-piece *adj* einteilig
oneself [wʌnsɛlf] *pron* (*reflexive*) sich
one-time *adj* einmalig ▷ *n*: **a one-off** etwas Einmaliges
one-way *adj*: **~ street** Einbahnstraße *f*; **~ ticket** einfache Fahrkarte
onion [ʌnjən] *n* Zwiebel *f*
online *adj* (*Inform*) online; **~ banking** Homebanking *nt*

only [əunli] *adv* nur; (*with time*) erst; **~ yesterday** erst gestern; **he's ~ four** er ist erst vier; **~ just arrived** gerade erst angekommen ▷ *adj* einzige(r, s); **~ child** Einzelkind *nt*
onside [ɒnsaɪd] *adv* (*Sport*) nicht im Abseits
onto [ɒntu] *prep* auf +*akk*; (*vertical surface*) an +*akk*; **to be ~ sb** jdm auf die Schliche gekommen sein
onwards [ɒnwədz] *adv* voran, vorwärts; **from today ~** von heute an, ab heute
open [əupən] *adj* offen; **in the ~ air** im Freien; **to the public** für die Öffentlichkeit zugänglich; **the store is ~ all day** das Geschäft hat den ganzen Tag offen ▷ *vt* öffnen, aufmachen; (*meeting, account, new building*) eröffnen; (*road*) dem Verkehr übergeben ▷ *vi* (*door, window etc*) aufgehen, sich öffnen; (*shop, bank*) öffnen, aufmachen; (*begin*) anfangen (*with* mit)
open-air *adj* Freiluft-
open floorplan *adj*: **~ office** Großraumbüro *nt*
open house *n* Tag *m* der offenen Tür
opening [əupənɪŋ] *n* Öffnung *f*; (*beginning*) Anfang *m*; (*official, of exhibition etc*) Eröffnung *f*; (*opportunity*) Möglichkeit *f*; **~ times** Öffnungszeiten *pl*
openly [əupənli] *adv* offen
open-minded [əupənmaɪndɪd] *adj* aufgeschlossen
opera [ɒpərə, ɒprə] *n* Oper *f*
opera glasses *npl* Opernglas *nt*
opera house *n* Oper *f*, Opernhaus *nt*
opera singer *n* Opernsänger(in) *m(f)*
operate [ɒpəreɪt] *vt* (*machine*) bedienen; (*brakes, lights*) betätigen ▷ *vi* (*machine*) laufen; (*bus etc*) verkehren (*between* zwischen); **to ~ on sb** (*Med*) (jdn) operieren
operating room [ɒpəreɪtɪŋ ruːm] *n* Operationssaal *m*
operation [ɒpəreɪʃⁿn] *n* (*of machine*) Bedienung *f*; (*functioning*) Funktionieren *nt*; (*Med*) Operation *f* (*on* an +*dat*); (*undertaking*) Unternehmen *nt*; **in ~** (*machine*) in Betrieb; **to have an ~** operiert werden (*for* wegen)
operator [ɒpəreɪtər] *n*: **to phone the ~** die Vermittlung anrufen
opinion [əpɪnjən] *n* Meinung *f* (*on* zu); **in my ~** meiner Meinung nach
opponent [əpəunənt] *n* Gegner(in) *m(f)*

opportunity [ɔpərtuːnɪti] *n* Gelegenheit *f*
oppose [əpouz] *vt* sich widersetzen +*dat*;
  (*idea*) ablehnen
opposed [əpouzd] *adj*: **to be ~ to sth** gegen
  etw sein; **as ~ to** im Gegensatz zu
opposing [əpouzɪn] *adj* (*team*) gegnerisch;
  (*points of view*) entgegengesetzt
opposite [ppəzɪt] *adj* (*house*) gegenüber-
  liegend; (*direction*) entgegengesetzt; **the ~
  sex** das andere Geschlecht ▷ *adv* gegenüber ▷ *prep* gegenüber +*dat*; **~ me** mir
  gegenüber ▷ *n* Gegenteil *nt*
opposition [ppəzɪʃⁿn] *n* Widerstand *m* (*to*
  gegen); (*Pol*) Opposition *f*
oppress [əprɛs] *vt* unterdrücken
oppressive [əprɛsɪv] *adj* (*heat*) drückend
opt [ppt] *vi*: **to opt for sth** sich für etw entscheiden; **to opt to do sth** sich entscheiden, etw zu tun
optimist [pptɪmɪst] *n* Optimist(in) *m(f)*
optimistic [pptɪmɪstɪk] *adj* optimistisch
option [ppʃⁿn] *n* Möglichkeit *f*; (*Comm*)
  Option *f*; **to have no ~** keine Wahl haben
optional [ppʃənⁿl] *adj* freiwillig; **~ extras**
  (*Auto*) Extras *pl*
optometrist [pptɒmətrɪst] *n* Optiker(in)
  m(f)
or [ər, STRONG ɔr] *conj* oder; (*otherwise*)
  sonst; (*after neg*) noch; **hurry up, or else
  we'll be late** beeil dich, sonst kommen wir
  zu spät
oral [ɔrəl] *adj* mündlich ▷ *n* (*exam*)
  Mündliche(s) *nt*
oral surgeon *n* Kieferchirurg(in) *m(f)*
orange [ɔrɪndʒ] *n* Orange *f* ▷ *adj* orangefar-
  ben
orange juice *n* Orangensaft *m*
orbit [ɔrbɪt] *n* Umlaufbahn *f*; **to be out of ~**
  (*fam*) nicht zu erreichen sein ▷ *vt* umkrei-
  sen
orchard [ɔrtʃərd] *n* Obstgarten *m*
orchestra [ɔrkɪstrə] *n* Orchester *nt*; (*Theat*)
  Parkett *nt*
orchid [ɔrkɪd] *n* Orchidee *f*
ordeal [ɔrdil] *n* Tortur *f*; (*emotional*) Qual *f*
order [ɔrdər] *n* (*sequence*) Reihenfolge *f*;
  (*good arrangement*) Ordnung *f*; (*command*)
  Befehl *m*; (*Jur*) Anordnung *f*; (*condition*)
  Zustand *m*; (*Comm*) Bestellung *f*; **out of ~**
  (*not functioning*) außer Betrieb; (*unsuitable*) nicht angebracht; **in ~** (*items*) richtig
  geordnet; (*all right*) in Ordnung; **in ~ to do
  sth** um etw zu tun ▷ *vt* (*arrange*) ordnen;
  (*command*) befehlen; **to ~ sb to do sth**
  jdm befehlen, etw zu tun; (*food, product*)

bestellen
order form *n* Bestellschein *m*
ordinary [ɔrdⁿnɛri] *adj* gewöhnlich, normal; (*average*) durchschnittlich
ore [ɔr] *n* Erz *nt*
organ [ɔrgən] *n* (*Mus*) Orgel *f*; (*Anat*)
  Organ *nt*
organic [ɔrgænɪk] *adj* organisch; (*farming,
  vegetables*) Bio-, Öko-; **~ farmer** Biobauer
  m, Biobäuerin *f*; **~ food** Biokost *f*
organization [ɔrgənɪzeɪʃⁿn] *n* Organisation *f*; (*arrangement*) Ordnung *f*
organize [ɔrgənaɪz] *vt* organisieren
organizer [ɔrgənaɪzər] *n* (elektronisches)
  Notizbuch
orgasm [ɔrgæzəm] *n* Orgasmus *m*
orgy [ɔrdʒi] *n* Orgie *f*
oriental [ɔriɛntⁿl] *adj* orientalisch
orientation [ɔriənteɪʃⁿn] *n* Orientierung *f*
origin [ɔrɪdʒɪn] *n* Ursprung *m*; (*of person*)
  Herkunft *f*
original [ərɪdʒɪnⁿl] *adj* (*first*) ursprünglich;
  (*painting*) original; (*idea*) originell ▷ *n*
  Original *nt*
originality [ərɪdʒɪnælɪti] *n* Originalität *f*
originally [ərɪdʒɪnⁿli] *adv* ursprünglich
Orkneys [ɔrkniz] *npl*, **Orkney Islands** *npl*
  Orkneyinseln *pl*
ornament [ɔrnəmənt] *n* Schmuckgegen-
  stand *m*
ornamental [ɔrnəmɛntⁿl] *adj* dekorativ
orphan [ɔrfən] *n* Waise *f*, Waisenkind *nt*
orphanage [ɔrfənɪdʒ] *n* Waisenhaus *nt*
orthodox [ɔrθədɒks] *adj* orthodox
orthopedic [ɔrθəpiːdɪk] *adj* orthopädisch
ostentatious [ɒstenteɪʃəs] *adj* protzig
ostrich [ɒstrɪtʃ] *n* (*Zool*) Strauß *m*
other [ʌðər] *adj, pron* andere(r, s); **any ~
  questions?** sonst noch Fragen?; **the ~ day**
  neulich; **every ~ day** jeden zweiten Tag;
  any person ~ than him alle außer ihm;
  someone/something or ~ irgendjemand/
  irgendetwas
otherwise [ʌðərwaɪz] *adv* sonst; (*differently*) anders
otter [ɒtər] *n* Otter *m*
ought [ɔt] *vb aux* (*obligation*) sollte; (*probability*) dürfte; (*stronger*) müsste; **you ~ to
  do that** du solltest/Sie sollten das tun; **he
  ~ to win** er müsste gewinnen; **that ~ to do**
  das müsste (*o* dürfte) reichen
ounce [auns] *n* Unze *f* (*28,35 g*)
our [auər] *adj* unser
ours [auərz] *pron* unsere(r, s); **this is ~** das
  gehört uns; **a friend of ~** ein Freund von

uns

ourselves [auərsɛlvz] *pron (reflexive)* uns;
we enjoyed ~ wir haben uns amüsiert;
we've got the house to ~ wir haben das
Haus für uns; *(emphatic):* **we did it ~** wir
haben es selbst gemacht; **all by ~** allein

out [aut] *adv* hinaus/heraus; *(not indoors)*
draußen; *(not at home)* nicht zu Hause;
(not alight) aus; *(unconscious)* bewusstlos;
(published) herausgekommen; *(results)*
bekannt gegeben; **have you been out yet?**
warst du/waren Sie schon draußen?; **I was
out when they called** ich war nicht da, als
sie vorbeikamen; **to be out and about**
unterwegs sein; **the sun is out** die Sonne
scheint; **the fire is out** das Feuer ist ausge-
gangen; *(wrong):* **they're out to get him** sie
sind hinter ihm her ▷ *vt (fam)* outen

outage [autɪdʒ] *n* Stromausfall *m*

outback [autbæk] *n (in Australia):* **the ~**
das Hinterland

outboard [autbɔrd] *adj:* **~ motor** Außenbordmotor *m*

outbreak [autbreɪk] *n* Ausbruch *m*

outburst [autbɜrst] *n* Ausbruch *m*

outcome [autkʌm] *n* Ergebnis *nt*

outcry [autkraɪ] *n (public protest)* Protest-
welle *f (against gegen)*

outdo [autdu] *(irr) vt* übertreffen

outdoor [autdɔr] *adj* Außen-; *(Sport)* im
Freien; **~ swimming pool** Freibad *nt*

outdoors [autdɔrz] *adv* draußen, im Frei-
en

outer [autər] *adj* äußere(r, s)

outer space *n* Weltraum *m*

outfit [autfɪt] *n* Ausrüstung *f; (clothes)* Kleidung *f*

outgoing [autɡouɪŋ] *adj* kontaktfreudig

outgrow [autɡrou] *(irr) vt (clothes)* heraus-
wachsen aus

outing [autɪŋ] *n* Ausflug *m*

outlet [autlet, -lɪt] *n* Auslass *m*, Abfluss *m*,
Steckdose *f; (shop)* Verkaufsstelle *f*

outline [autlaɪn] *n* Umriss *m; (summary)*
Abriss *m*

outlive [autlɪv] *vt* überleben

outlook [autluk] *n* Aussicht(en) *f(pl); (prospects)* Aussichten *pl; (attitude)* Einstellung *f (on zu)*

outnumber [autnʌmbər] *vt* zahlenmäßig
überlegen sein *+dat;* **~ed** zahlenmäßig
unterlegen

out of *prep (motion, motive, origin)* aus;
(position, away from) außerhalb *+gen;* **~
danger/sight/breath** außer Gefahr/Sicht/

Atem; **made ~ wood** aus Holz gemacht;
we are ~ bread wir haben kein Brot mehr

out-of-date *adj* veraltet

out-of-the-way *adj* abgelegen

outpatient [autpeɪʃənt] *n* ambulanter Patient, ambulante Patientin

output [autput] *n* Produktion *f; (of engine)*
Leistung *f; (Inform)* Ausgabe *f*

outrage [autreɪdʒ] *n (great anger)* Empö-
rung *f (at über); (wicked deed)* Schandtat *f;
(crime)* Verbrechen *nt; (indecency)* Skandal *m*

outrageous [autreɪdʒəs] *adj* unerhört;
(clothes, behavior etc) unmöglich, schrill

outright [*adv* autraɪt, *adj* autraɪt] *adv
(killed)* sofort ▷ *adj* total; *(denial)* völlig;
(winner) unbestritten

outside [autsaɪd] *n* Außenseite *f;* **on the ~**
außen ▷ *adj* äußere(r, s), Außen-; *(chance)*
sehr gering ▷ *adv* außen; **to go ~** nach
draußen gehen ▷ *prep* außerhalb *+gen*

outsider [autsaɪdər] *n* Außenseiter(in)
m(f)

outskirts [autskɜrts] *npl (of town)* Stadtrand *m*

outstanding [autstændɪŋ] *adj* hervorragend; *(debts etc)* ausstehend

outward [autwərd] *adj* äußere(r, s); **~ journey** Hinfahrt *f*

outwardly [autwərdli] *adv* nach außen
hin

outwards [autwərdz] *adv* nach außen

oval [ouvᵊl] *adj* oval

ovary [ouvəri] *n* Eierstock *m*

ovation [ouveɪʃᵊn] *n* Ovation *f*, Applaus *m*

oven [ʌvᵊn] *n* Backofen *m*

oven glove *n* Topfhandschuh *m*

ovenproof [ʌvᵊnpruf] *adj* feuerfest

oven-ready *adj* bratfertig

over [ouvər] *prep (position)* über *+dat;
(motion)* über *+akk;* **they spent a long
time ~ it** sie haben lange dazu gebraucht;
from all ~ America aus ganz Amerika; **~
$20** mehr als 20 Dollar; **~ the phone/radio**
am Telefon/im Radio; **to talk ~ a glass of
wine** sich bei einem Glas Wein unterhalten; **~ and above this** darüber hinaus; **~
the summer** während des Sommers ▷ *adv
(across)* hinüber/herüber; *(finished)* vorbei; *(match, play etc)* zu Ende; *(left)* übrig;
(more) mehr; **~ there/in England** da drü-
ben/drüben in England; **~ to you** du bist/
Sie sind dran; **it's all ~ between us** es ist
aus zwischen uns; **~ and ~ again** immer
wieder; **to start all ~ again** noch einmal

o

von vorn anfangen; **children of 8 and ~** Kinder ab 8 Jahren

over- [ouvər-] *pref* über-

overall [ouvərɔl] *adj (situation)* allgemein; *(length)* Gesamt-; **~ majority** absolute Mehrheit ▷ *adv* insgesamt

overboard [ouvərbɔrd] *adv* über Bord

overbooked [ouvərbukt] *adj* überbucht

overbooking [ouvərbukɪŋ] *n* Überbuchung *f*

overcharge [ouvərtʃɑrdʒ] *vt* zu viel verlangen von

overcoat [ouvərkout] *n* Wintermantel *m*

overcome [ouvərkʌm] *(irr) vt* überwinden; **~ by sleep/emotion** von Schlaf/Rührung übermannt; **we shall ~** wir werden siegen

overcooked [ouvərkukt] *adj* verkocht; *(meat)* zu lange gebraten

overcrowded [ouvərkraudɪd] *adj* überfüllt

overdo [ouvərdu] *(irr) vt* übertreiben

overdone [ouvərdʌn] *adj* übertrieben; *(food)* zu lange gekocht; *(meat)* zu lange gebraten

overdose [ouvərdous] *n* Überdosis *f*

overdraft [ouvərdræft] *n* Kontoüberziehung *f*

overdrawn [ouvərdrɔn] *adj* überzogen

overdue [ouvərdu] *adj* überfällig

overestimate [ouvərɛstɪmeɪt] *vt* überschätzen

overexpose [ouvərɪkspouz] *vt (Foto)* überbelichten

overflow [ouvərflou] *vi* überlaufen

overhead [*adj, n* ouvərhɛd, *adv* ouvərhɛd] *adj (Aviat):* **~ compartment** Gepäckfach *nt;* **~ projector** Overheadprojektor *m;* **~ railway** Hochbahn *f* ▷ *n (Comm)* allgemeine Geschäftskosten *pl* ▷ *adv* oben

overhear [ouvərhɪər] *(irr) vt* zufällig mit anhören

overheat [ouvərhit] *vi (engine)* heiß laufen

overjoyed [ouvərdʒɔɪd] *adj* überglücklich *(at* über*)*

overland [ouvərlænd] *adj* Überland- ▷ *adv (travel)* über Land

overlap [ouvərlæp] *vi (dates etc)* sich überschneiden; *(objects)* sich teilweise decken

overload [ouvərloud] *vt* überladen

overlook [ouvərluk] *vt (view from above)* überblicken; *(not notice)* übersehen; *(pardon)* hinwegsehen über *+akk*

overnight [ouvərnaɪt] *adj (journey, train)* Nacht-; **~ bag** Reisetasche *f;* **~ stay** Übernachtung *f* ▷ *adv* über Nacht

overpass [ouvərpæs] *n* Überführung *f,* Straßenüberführung *f,* Eisenbahnüberführung *f*

overpay [ouvərpeɪ] *vt* überbezahlen

overrule [ouvərrul] *vt* verwerfen; *(decision)* aufheben

overseas [ouvərsiz] *adj* Übersee-; ausländisch; *(fam)* Auslands- ▷ *adv (go)* nach Übersee; *(live, work)* in Übersee

oversee [ouvərsi] *(irr) vt* beaufsichtigen

overshadow [ouvərʃædou] *vt* überschatten

overshoot [ouvərʃut] *(irr) vt (runway)* hinausschießen über *+akk; (turning)* vorbeifahren *+dat*

oversight [ouvərsaɪt] *n* Versehen *nt*

oversimplify [ouvərsɪmplɪfaɪ] *vt* zu sehr vereinfachen

oversleep [ouvərslip] *(irr) vi* verschlafen

overtake [ouvərteɪk] *(irr) vt, vi* überholen

overtime [ouvərtaɪm] *n* Überstunden *pl*

overturn [ouvərtɜrn] *vt, vi* umkippen

overweight [ouvərweɪt] *adj:* **to be ~** Übergewicht haben

overwhelm [ouvərwɛlm] *vt* überwältigen

overwhelming [ouvərwɛlmɪŋ] *adj* überwältigend

overwork [ouvərwɜrk] *n* Überarbeitung *f* ▷ *vi* sich überarbeiten

overworked [ouvərwɜrkt] *adj* überarbeitet

owe [ou] *vt* schulden; **to owe sth to sb** *(money)* jdm etw schulden; *(favor etc)* jdm etw verdanken; **how much do I owe you?** was bin ich dir/Ihnen schuldig?

owl [aul] *n* Eule *f*

own [oun] *vt* besitzen ▷ *adj* eigen; **on one's own** allein; **he has an apartment of his own** er hat eine eigene Wohnung

owner [ounər] *n* Besitzer(in) *m(f); (of business)* Inhaber(in) *m(f)*

ownership [ounərʃɪp] *n* Besitz *m;* **under new ~** unter neuer Leitung

own up *vi:* **to ~ to sth** etw zugeben

ox [ɒks] *(pl oxen) n* Ochse *m*

oxtail [ɒksteɪl] *n* Ochsenschwanz *m;* **~ soup** Ochsenschwanzsuppe *f*

oxygen [ɒksɪdʒən] *n* Sauerstoff *m*

oyster [ɔɪstər] *n* Auster *f*

Oz [ɒz] *n (fam)* Australien *nt*

oz *(abbr)* **= ounces** Unzen *pl*

ozone [ouzoun] *n* Ozon *nt;* **~ layer** Ozonschicht *f*

P

p (*abbr*) = **page** S. ▷ (*abbr*) = **penny, pence**
p.a. (*abbr*) = **per annum**
pace [peɪs] *n* (*speed*) Tempo *nt*; (*step*)
Schritt *m*
pacemaker [peɪsmeɪkər] *n* (*Med*) Schrittmacher *m*
Pacific [pəsɪfɪk] *n*: **the ~ Ocean** der Pazifik
Pacific Standard Time *n* pazifische Zeit
pacifier [pæsɪfaɪər] *n* (*for baby*) Schnuller
m
pack [pæk] *n* (*of cards*) Spiel *nt*; (*of cigarettes*) Schachtel *f*; (*gang*) Bande *f*; (*backpack*) Rucksack *m* ▷ *vt* (*case*) packen;
(*clothes*) einpacken ▷ *vi* (*for holiday*)
packen
package [pækɪdʒ] *n* (*a. Inform, fig*) Paket
nt
package deal *n* Pauschalangebot *nt*
packaging [pækɪdʒɪŋ] *n* (*material*) Verpackung *f*
packet [pækɪt] *n* Päckchen *nt*
pad [pæd] *n* (*of paper*) Schreibblock *m*;
(*padding*) Polster *nt*
padded envelope [pædɪð ɛnvəloʊp] *n*
wattierter Umschlag
padding [pædɪŋ] *n* (*material*) Polsterung *f*
paddle [pædᵊl] *n* (*for boat*) Paddel *nt* ▷ *vi*
(*in boat*) paddeln
padlock [pædlɒk] *n* Vorhängeschloss *nt*
page [peɪdʒ] *n* (*of book etc*) Seite *f*
pager [peɪdʒər] *n* Piepser *m*
paid [peɪd] *pt, pp of* **pay** ▷ *adj* bezahlt
pain [peɪn] *n* Schmerz *m*; **to be in ~** Schmerzen haben; **she's a real ~** sie nervt
painful [peɪnfəl] *adj* (*physically*) schmerzhaft; (*embarrassing*) peinlich
painkiller [peɪnkɪlər] *n* schmerzstillendes
Mittel
painstaking [peɪnzteɪkɪŋ, peɪnsteɪ-] *adj*
sorgfältig
paint [peɪnt] *n* Farbe *f* ▷ *vt* anstreichen;
(*picture*) malen
paintbrush [peɪntbrʌʃ] *n* Pinsel *m*
painter [peɪntər] *n* Maler(in) *m(f)*
painting [peɪntɪŋ] *n* (*picture*) Bild *nt*,
Gemälde *nt*
pair [peər] *n* Paar *nt*; **a ~ of shoes** ein Paar
Schuhe; **a ~ of scissors** eine Schere; **a ~ of
pants** eine Hose
pajamas [pədʒɑməz] *npl* Schlafanzug *m*
Pakistan [pækɪstæn] *n* Pakistan *nt*

pal [pæl] *n* (*fam*) Kumpel *m*
palace [pælɪs] *n* Palast *m*
pale [peɪl] *adj* (*face*) blass, bleich; (*color*)
hell
palm [pɑm] (*of hand*) Handfläche *f*; **~ tree**
Palme *f*
palmtop (computer) [pɑmtɒp (kəmpyuɾər)]
n Palmtop(computer) *m*
pamper [pæmpər] *vt* verhätscheln
pan [pæn] *n* (*saucepan*) Topf *m*; (*frying
pan*) Pfanne *f*
pancake [pænkeɪk] *n* Pfannkuchen *m*
panda [pændə] *n* Panda *m*
pandemic [pændɛmɪk] *n* Pandemie *f*
panel [pænᵊl] *n* (*of wood*) Tafel *f*; (*in discussion*) Diskussionsteilnehmer *pl*; (*in jury*)
Jurymitglieder *pl*
panic [pænɪk] *n* Panik *f* ▷ *vi* in Panik geraten
panicky [pæniki] *adj* panisch
pansy [pænzi] *n* (*flower*) Stiefmütterchen
nt
panties [pæntiz] *npl* (Damen)slip *m*; (*fam*)
Schlüpfer *m*
pants [pænts] *npl* Hose *f*
pants suit *n* Hosenanzug *m*
pantyhose [pæntihoʊz] *npl* Strumpfhose
f
panty-liner [pæntilaɪnər] *n* Slipeinlage *f*
paper [peɪpər] *n* Papier *nt*; (*newspaper*)
Zeitung *f*; (*exam*) Klausur *f*; (*for reading at
conference*) Referat *nt*; **~s** *pl* (*identity
papers*) Papiere *pl*; **~ bag** Papiertüte *f*; **~
cup** Pappbecher *m* ▷ *vt* (*wall*) tapezieren
paperback [peɪpərbæk] *n* Taschenbuch *nt*
paper clip *n* Büroklammer *f*
paper feed *n* (*of printer*) Papiereinzug *m*
paper route *n*: **to do a ~** Zeitungen austra-
gen
paperwork [peɪpərwɜrk] *n* Schreibarbeit *f*
parachute [pærəʃut] *n* Fallschirm *m* ▷ *vi*
abspringen
parade [pəreɪd] *n* (*procession*) Umzug *m*;
(*Mil*) Parade *f* ▷ *vi* vorbeimarschieren
paradise [pærədaɪs] *n* Paradies *nt*
paragliding [pærəglaɪdɪŋ] *n* Gleitschirmfliegen *nt*
paragraph [pærəgræf] *n* Absatz *m*
parallel [pærəlɛl] *adj* parallel ▷ *n* (*Math,
fig*) Parallele *f*
paralyze [pærəlaɪz] *vt* lähmen; (*fig*) lahm-
legen

paranoid [pǽrənɔɪd] *adj* paranoid
paraphrase [pǽrəfreɪz] *vt* umschreiben; (*sth spoken*) anders ausdrücken
parasailing [pǽrəseɪlɪŋ] *n* Parasailing *nt*
parasol [pǽrəsɔl] *n* Sonnenschirm *m*
parcel [pɑrsˀl] *n* Paket *nt*
pardon [pɑrdˀn] *n* (*Jur*) Begnadigung *f*; ~ **me/I beg your** ~ verzeih/verzeihen Sie bitte; (*objection*) aber ich bitte dich/Sie; **I beg your ~?/~ me?** wie bitte?
parent [pɛǝrənt, pǽr-] *n* Elternteil *m*; ~**s** *pl* Eltern *pl*; ~**s-in-law** *pl* Schwiegereltern *pl*
parental [pərɛntˀl] *adj* elterlich, Eltern-
parish [pǽrɪʃ] *n* Gemeinde *f*
park [pɑrk] *n* Park *m* ▷ *vt*, *vi* parken
parking [pɑrkɪŋ] *n* Parken *nt*; '**no ~**' „Parken verboten"
parking brake *n* Handbremse *f*
parking garage *n* Parkhaus *nt*
parking lights *npl* Standlicht *nt*
parking lot *n* Parkplatz *m*
parking meter *n* Parkuhr *f*
parking place, parking space *n* Parkplatz *m*
parking ticket *n* Strafzettel *m*
parliament [pɑrləmənt] *n* Parlament *nt*
parrot [pǽrət] *n* Papagei *m*
parsley [pɑrsli] *n* Petersilie *f*
parsnip [pɑrsnɪp] *n* Pastinake *f* (*längliches, weißes Wurzelgemüse*)
part [pɑrt] *n* Teil *m*; (*of machine*) Teil *nt*; (*Theat*) Rolle *f*; (*in hair*) Scheitel *m*; **to take** ~ teilnehmen (*in* an +*dat*); **for the most** ~ zum größten Teil ▷ *adj* Teil- ▷ *vt* (*separate*) trennen; (*hair*) scheiteln ▷ *vi* (*people*) sich trennen
partial [pɑrʃˀl] *adj* (*incomplete*) teilweise, Teil-
participant [pɑrtɪsɪpənt] *n* Teilnehmer(in) *m(f)*
participate [pɑrtɪsɪpeɪt] *vi* teilnehmen (*in* an +*dat*)
particular [pərtɪkyələr] *adj* (*specific*) bestimmt; (*exact*) genau; (*fussy*) eigen; **in** ~ insbesondere ▷ *n*: ~**s** *pl* (*details*) Einzelheiten *pl*; (*about person*) Personalien *pl*
particularly [pərtɪkyələrli] *adv* besonders
parting [pɑrtɪŋ] *n* (*farewell*) Abschied *m*
partly [pɑrtli] *adv* teilweise
partner [pɑrtnər] *n* Partner(in) *m(f)*
partnership [pɑrtnərʃɪp] *n* Partnerschaft *f*
partridge [pɑrtrɪdʒ] *n* Rebhuhn *nt*
part-time *adj* Teilzeit- ▷ *adv*: **to work** ~ Teilzeit arbeiten

party [pɑrti] *n* (*celebration*) Party *f*; (*Pol, Jur*) Partei *f*; (*group*) Gruppe *f* ▷ *vi* feiern
pass [pǽs] *vt* (*on foot*) vorbeigehen an +*dat*; (*in car etc*) vorbeifahren an +*dat*; (*time*) verbringen; (*exam*) bestehen; (*law*) verabschieden; **to ~ sth to sb, to ~ sb sth** jdm etw reichen; **to ~ the ball to sb** jdm den Ball zuspielen ▷ *vi* (*on foot*) vorbeigehen; (*in car etc*) vorbeifahren; (*years*) vergehen; (*in exam*) bestehen ▷ *n* (*document*) Ausweis *m*; (*Sport*) Pass *m*
passage [pǽsɪdʒ] *n* (*corridor*) Gang *m*; (*in book, music*) Passage *f*
passageway [pǽsɪdʒweɪ] *n* Durchgang *m*
pass away *vi* (*die*) verscheiden
pass by *vi* (*on foot*) vorbeigehen; (*in car etc*) vorbeifahren ▷ *vt* (*on foot*) vorbeigehen an +*dat*; (*in car etc*) vorbeifahren an +*dat*
passenger [pǽsɪndʒər] *n* Passagier(in) *m(f)*; (*on bus*) Fahrgast *m*; (*on train*) Reisende(r) *mf*; (*in car*) Mitfahrer(in) *m(f)*
passer-by [pǽsərbaɪ] (*pl* **passers-by**) *n* Passant(in) *m(f)*
passion [pǽʃˀn] *n* Leidenschaft *f*
passionate [pǽʃənɪt] *adj* leidenschaftlich
passion fruit *n* Passionsfrucht *f*
passive [pǽsɪv] *adj* passiv; ~ **smoking** Passivrauchen *nt* ▷ *n*: ~ **voice** (*Ling*) Passiv *nt*
pass on *vt* weitergeben (*to* an +*akk*); (*disease*) übertragen (*to* auf +*akk*)
pass out *vi* (*faint*) ohnmächtig werden
passport [pǽspɔrt] *n* (*Reise*)pass *m*
password [pǽswɜrd] *n* (*Inform*) Passwort *nt*
past [pǽst] *n* Vergangenheit *f* ▷ *adv* (*by*) vorbei; **it's five** ~ es ist fünf nach ▷ *adj* (*years*) vergangen; (*president etc*) ehemalig; **in the** ~ **two months** in den letzten zwei Monaten ▷ *prep* (*telling time*) nach; **half** ~ **10** halb 11; **to go** ~ **sth** an etw *dat* vorbeigehen/-fahren
pasta [pɑstə] *n* Nudeln *pl*
paste [peɪst] *vt* (*stick*) kleben; (*Inform*) einfügen ▷ *n* (*glue*) Kleister *m*
pastime [pǽstaɪm] *n* Zeitvertreib *m*
pastry [peɪstri] *n* Teig *m*; (*cake*) Stückchen *nt*
patch [pǽtʃ] *n* (*area*) Fleck *m*; (*for mending*) Flicken ▷ *vt* flicken
patchy [pǽtʃi] *adj* (*uneven*) ungleichmäßig
pâté [pɑteɪ] *n* Pastete *f*
paternal [pətɜrnˀl] *adj* väterlich; ~ **grandmother** Großmutter *f* väterlicherseits

paternity leave [pətɜːrnɪti liv] n Elternzeit f (des Vaters)

path [pæθ] n (a. Inform) Pfad m; (a. fig) Weg m

pathetic [pəθɛtɪk] adj (bad) kläglich, erbärmlich; **it's ~** es ist zum Heulen

patience [peɪʃᵊns] n Geduld f

patient [peɪʃᵊnt] adj geduldig ▷ n Patient(in) m(f)

patio [pætiou] n Terrasse f

patriotic [peɪtriɒtɪk] adj patriotisch

patrolman [pətroulmən] (pl -**men**) n Streifenpolizist m

patron [peɪtrən] n (sponsor) Förderer m, Förderin f; (in shop) Kunde m, Kundin f

patronize [peɪtrənaɪz] vt (treat condescendingly) von oben herab behandeln

patronizing [peɪtrənaɪzɪŋ] adj (attitude) herablassend

pattern [pætərn] n Muster nt

pause [pɔz] n Pause f ▷ vi (speaker) innehalten

pavement [peɪvmənt] Pflaster nt

pay [peɪ] (paid, paid) vt bezahlen; **he paid me $20 for it** er hat (mir) 20 Dollar dafür gezahlt; **to pay attention** Acht geben (to auf +akk); **to pay sb a visit** jdn besuchen ▷ vi zahlen; (be profitable) sich bezahlt machen; **to pay for sth** etw bezahlen ▷ n Bezahlung f, Lohn m

payable [peɪəbᵊl] adj zahlbar; (due) fällig

pay back vt (money) zurückzahlen

payday [peɪdeɪ] n Zahltag m

payee [peɪi] n Zahlungsempfänger(in) m(f)

pay in vt (into account) einzahlen

payment [peɪmənt] n Bezahlung f; (money) Zahlung f

pay-per-view adj Pay-per-View-

pay phone n Münzfernsprecher m

pay TV n Pay-TV nt

PC [pi si] abbr = **personal computer** PC m ▷ (abbr) = **politically correct** politisch korrekt

PDA [pi di eɪ] (abbr) = **personal digital assistant** PDA m

PE [pi i] (abbr) = **physical education**; (school) Sport m

pea [pi] n Erbse f

peace [pis] n Frieden m

peaceful [pisfəl] adj friedlich

peach [pitʃ] n Pfirsich m

peacock [pikɒk] n Pfau m

peak [pik] n (of mountain) Gipfel m; (fig) Höhepunkt m

peak period n Stoßzeit f; (season) Hochsaison

peanut [pinʌt, -nət] n Erdnuss f

peanut butter n Erdnussbutter f

pear [pɛər] n Birne f

pearl [pɜrl] n Perle f

pebble [pɛbᵊl] n Kiesel m

pecan [pikɑn, -kæn] n Pekannuss

peck [pɛk] vt, vi picken

peculiar [pɪkjulyər] adj (odd) seltsam; **~ to** charakteristisch für

peculiarity [pɪkjuliærɪti] n (singular quality) Besonderheit f; (strangeness) Eigenartigkeit f

pedal [pɛdᵊl] n Pedal nt

pedestrian [pɪdɛstriən] n Fußgänger(in) m(f)

pee [pi] vi (fam) pinkeln

peel [pil] n Schale f ▷ vt schälen ▷ vi (paint etc) abblättern; (skin etc) sich schälen

peer [pɪər] n Gleichaltrige(r) mf ▷ vi starren

peg [pɛg] n (for coat etc) Haken m; (for tent) Hering m; **clothes peg** (Wäsche)klammer f

pelvis [pɛlvɪs] n Becken nt

pen [pɛn] n (ballpoint) Kuli m, Kugelschreiber; (fountain pen) Füller m

penalize [pinəlaɪz] vt (punish) bestrafen

penalty [pɛnᵊlti] n (punishment) Strafe f; (in soccer) Elfmeter m

pence [pɛns] (pl) (Brit) of penny

pencil [pɛnsᵊl] n Bleistift m

pencil sharpener n (Bleistift)spitzer m

penetrate [pɛnɪtreɪt] vt durchdringen; (enter into) eindringen in +akk

penguin [pɛŋgwɪn] n Pinguin m

penicillin [pɛnɪsɪlɪn] n Penizillin nt

peninsula [pənɪnsələ, -nɪnsyə-] n Halbinsel f

penis [pinɪs] n Penis m

penknife [pɛnnaɪf] (pl **penknives**) n Taschenmesser nt

penny [pɛni] (pl **pence** o **pennies**) n (Brit) Penny m, Centstück nt

pension [pɛnʃᵊn] n Rente f; (for civil servants, executives etc) Pension f

pensioner [pɛnʃənər] n Rentner(in) m(f)

pension plan n Rentenversicherung f

penultimate [pɪnʌltɪmɪt] adj vorletzte(r, s)

people [pipᵊl] npl (persons) Leute pl; (von Staat) Volk nt; (inhabitants) Bevölkerung f

pepper [pɛpər] n Pfeffer m; (vegetable)

Paprika *m*

peppermint [pɛpərmɪnt] *n* (*sweet*) Pfefferminz *nt*

per [pər, STRONG pɜr] *prep* pro; **per annum** pro Jahr; **percent** Prozent *nt*

percentage [pərsɛntɪdʒ] *n* Prozentsatz *m*

perceptible [pərsɛptɪbªl] *adj* wahrnehmbar

percolator [pɜrkəleɪtər] *n* Kaffeemaschine *f*

percussion [pərkʌʃªn] *n* (*Mus*) Schlagzeug *nt*

perfect [*adj* pɜrfɪkt, *vb* pərfɛkt] *adj* perfekt; (*utter*) völlig ▷ *vt* vervollkommnen

perfectly [pɜrfɪktli] *adv* perfekt; (*utterly*) völlig

perform [pərfɔrm] *vt* (*task*) ausführen; (*play*) aufführen; (*Med: operation*) durchführen ▷ *vi* (*Theat*) auftreten

performance [pərfɔrməns] *n* (*show*) Vorstellung *f*; (*efficiency*) Leistung *f*

perfume [pɜrfyum, pərfyum] *n* Duft *m*; (*substance*) Parfüm *nt*

perhaps [pərhæps, præps] *adv* vielleicht

period [pɪərɪəd] *n* (*length of time*) Zeit *f*; (*in history*) Zeitalter *nt*; (*school*) Stunde *f*; (*Med*) Periode *f*; (*full stop*) Punkt *m*; **for a ~ of three years** für einen Zeitraum von drei Jahren

periodical [pɪərɪɒdɪkəl] *n* Zeitschrift *f*

peripheral [pərɪfərəl] *n* (*Inform*) Peripheriegerät *nt*

perjury [pɜrdʒəri] *n* Meineid *m*

perm [pɜrm] *n* Dauerwelle *f*

permanent [pɜrmənənt] *adj*, **permanently** *adv* ständig

permission [pərmɪʃªn] *n* Erlaubnis *f*

permit [*n* pɜrmɪt, *vb* pərmɪt] *n* Genehmigung *f* ▷ *vt* erlauben, zulassen; **to ~ sb to do sth** jdm erlauben, etw zu tun

persecute [pɜrsɪkyut] *vt* verfolgen

perseverance [pɜrsɪvɪərəns] *n* Ausdauer *f*

persist [pərsɪst] *vi* (*in belief etc*) bleiben (*in* bei); (*rain, smell*) andauern

persistent [pərsɪstənt] *adj* beharrlich

person [pɜrsªn] *n* Mensch *m*; (*in official context*) Person *f*; **in ~** persönlich

personal [pɜrsənªl] *adj* persönlich; (*private*) privat

personal exemption [pɜrsənªl ɪgzɛmpʃªn] *n* (*from tax*) Steuerfreibetrag *m*

personality [pɜrsənælɪti] *n* Persönlichkeit *f*

personal organizer *n* Organizer *m*

personnel [pɜrsənɛl] *n* Personal *nt*

perspective [pərspɛktɪv] *n* Perspektive *f*

persuade [pərsweɪd] *vt* überreden; (*convince*) überzeugen

persuasive [pərsweɪsɪv] *adj* überzeugend

perverse [pərvɜrs] *adj* eigensinnig, abwegig

pervert [*n* pɜrvɜrt, *vb* pərvɜrt] *n* Perverse(r) *mf* ▷ *vt* (*morally*) verderben

perverted [pərvɜrtɪd] *adj* pervers

pessimist [pɛsɪmɪst] *n* Pessimist(in) *m(f)*

pessimistic [pɛsɪmɪstɪk] *adj* pessimistisch

pest [pɛst] *n* (*insect*) Schädling *m*; (*fig: person*) Nervensäge *f*; (*thing*) Plage *f*

pester [pɛstər] *vt* plagen

pesticide [pɛstɪsaɪd] *n* Schädlingsbekämpfungsmittel *nt*

pet [pɛt] *n* (*animal*) Haustier *nt*; (*person*) Liebling *m*

petal [pɛtªl] *n* Blütenblatt *nt*

petition [pətɪʃªn] *n* Petition *f*

pharmacy [fɑrməsi] *n* (*shop*) Apotheke *f*; (*science*) Pharmazie *f*

phase [feɪz] *n* Phase *f*

PhD [pi eɪtʃ di] (*abbr*) = **Doctor of Philosophy** Dr. phil; (*dissertation*) Doktorarbeit *f*; **to do one's PhD** promovieren

pheasant [fɛzªnt] *n* Fasan *m*

phenomenon [fɪnɒmɪnɒn] (*pl* **phenomena**) *n* Phänomen *nt*

Philippines [fɪlɪpinz] *npl* Philippinen *pl*

philosophical [fɪləspfɪkªl] *adj* philosophisch; (*fig*) gelassen

philosophy [fɪlɒsəfi] *n* Philosophie *f*

phone [foʊn] *n* Telefon *nt* ▷ *vt*, *vi* anrufen

phone bill *n* Telefonrechnung *f*

phone book *n* Telefonbuch *nt*

phone booth *n* Telefonzelle *f*

phone call *n* Telefonanruf *m*

phonecard [foʊnkɑrd] *n* Telefonkarte *f*

phone number *n* Telefonnummer *f*

photo [foʊtoʊ] (*pl* **-s**) *n* Foto *nt*

photo booth *n* Fotoautomat *m*

photocopier [foʊtəkɒpiər] *n* Kopiergerät *nt*

photocopy [foʊtəkɒpi] *n* Fotokopie *f* ▷ *vt* fotokopieren

photograph [foʊtəgræf] *n* Fotografie *f*, Aufnahme *f* ▷ *vt* fotografieren

photographer [fətɒgrəfər] *n* Fotograf(in) *m(f)*

photography [fətɒgrəfi] *n* Fotografie *f*

phrase [freɪz] *n* (*expression*) Redewendung *f*, Ausdruck *m*

phrase book *n* Sprachführer *m*

physical [ˈfɪzɪkᵊl] *adj* (*bodily*) körperlich, physisch ▷ *n* ärztliche Untersuchung

physically [ˈfɪzɪkᵊli] *adv* (*bodily*) körperlich, physisch; **~ handicapped** körperbehindert

physical therapy *n* Physiotherapie *f*

physics [ˈfɪzɪks] *nsing* Physik *f*

physique [fɪˈziːk] *n* Körperbau *m*

piano [piˈænoʊ, pyˈænoʊ] (*pl* **-s**) *n* Klavier *nt*

pick [pɪk] *vt* (*flowers, fruit*) pflücken; (*choose*) auswählen; (*team*) aufstellen

pickle [ˈpɪkᵊl] *n* (*food*) (Mixed) Pickles *pl* ▷ *vt* einlegen

pick out *vt* auswählen

pickpocket [ˈpɪkpɒkɪt] *n* Taschendieb(in) *m(f)*

pick up *vt* (*lift up*) aufheben; (*collect*) abholen; (*learn*) lernen

picnic [ˈpɪknɪk] *n* Picknick *nt*

picture [ˈpɪktʃər] *n* Bild *nt* ▷ *vt* (*visualize*) sich vorstellen

picture book *n* Bilderbuch *nt*

picturesque [pɪktʃəˈrɛsk] *adj* malerisch

pie [paɪ] *n* (*meat*) Pastete *f*; (*fruit*) Kuchen *m*

piece [piːs] *n* Stück *nt*; (*part*) Teil *nt*; (*in chess*) Figur *f*; (*in draughts*) Stein *m*; **a ~ of cake** ein Stück Kuchen; **to fall to ~s** auseinanderfallen

pier [pɪər] *n* Pier *m*

pierce [pɪərs] *vt* durchstechen, durchbohren; (*cold, sound*) durchdringen

pierced [pɪərst] *adj* (*part of body*) gepierct

piercing [ˈpɪərsɪn] *adj* durchdringend

pig [pɪg] *n* Schwein *nt*

pigeon [ˈpɪdʒɪn] *n* Taube *f*

pigeonhole [ˈpɪdʒɪnhoʊl] *n* (*compartment*) Ablegefach *nt*

piggy [ˈpɪgi] *adj* (*fam*) verfressen

pigheaded [ˈpɪgˈhɛdɪd] *adj* dickköpfig

piglet [ˈpɪglɪt] *n* Ferkel *nt*

pigpen [ˈpɪgpɛn] *n* Schweinestall *m*

pigtail [ˈpɪgteɪl] *n* Zopf *m*

pile [paɪl] *n* (*heap*) Haufen *m*; (*one on top of another*) Stapel *m*

piles *npl* Hämorr(ho)iden *pl*

pile up *vi* (*accumulate*) sich anhäufen

pileup [ˈpaɪlʌp] *n* (*Auto*) Massenkarambolage *f*

pilgrim [ˈpɪlgrɪm] *n* Pilger(in) *m(f)*

pill [pɪl] *n* Tablette *f*; **the ~** die (Antibaby)pille; **to be on the ~** die Pille nehmen

pillar [ˈpɪlər] *n* Pfeiler *m*

pillow [ˈpɪloʊ] *n* (Kopf)kissen *nt*

pillowcase [ˈpɪloʊkeɪs] *n* (Kopf)kissenbezug *m*

pilot [ˈpaɪlət] *n* (*Aviat*) Pilot(in) *m(f)*

pimple [ˈpɪmpᵊl] *n* Pickel *m*

PIN [pɪn] (*acr*) = **personal identification number** PIN *f*, Geheimzahl *f*

pin [pɪn] *n* (*for fixing*) Nadel *f*; (*in sewing*) Stecknadel *f*; (*Tech*) Stift *m*; **I've got pins and needles in my leg** mein Bein ist mir eingeschlafen ▷ *vt* (*fix with pin*) heften (*to an +akk*)

pinch [pɪntʃ] *n* (*of salt*) Prise *f* ▷ *vt* zwicken; (*fam: steal*) klauen ▷ *vi* (*shoe*) drücken

pine [paɪn] *n* Kiefer *f*

pineapple [ˈpaɪnæpᵊl] *n* Ananas *f*

pink [pɪŋk] *adj* rosa

pinstripe(d) [ˈpɪnstraɪp(t)] *adj* Nadelstreifen-

pint [paɪnt] *n* Pint *nt* (*0,473l*)

pious [ˈpaɪəs] *adj* fromm

pipe [paɪp] *n* (*for smoking*) Pfeife *f*; (*for water, gas*) Rohrleitung *f*

pirate [ˈpaɪrɪt] *n* Pirat(in) *m(f)*

pirated copy [ˈpaɪrɪtɪd ˈkɒpɪ] *n* Raubkopie *f*

Pisces [ˈpaɪsiːz] *nsing* (*Astr*) Fische *pl*; **she's a ~** sie ist Fisch

pissed [pɪst] *adj* (*fam: annoyed*) stocksauer

pistachio [pɪstæʃioʊ] (*pl* **-s**) *n* Pistazie *f*

piste [piːst] *n* (*Ski*) Piste *f*

pistol [ˈpɪstᵊl] *n* Pistole *f*

pit [pɪt] *n* (*hole*) Grube *f*; (*coalmine*) Zeche *f*; **the pits** (*motor racing*) die Box; **to be the pits** (*fam*) grottenschlecht sein

pitch [pɪtʃ] *n* (*Sport*) Spielfeld *nt*; (*Mus: of instrument*) Tonlage *f*; (*of voice*) Stimmlage *f* ▷ *vt* (*tent*) aufschlagen; (*throw*) werfen

pitch-black [ˈpɪtʃˈblæk] *adj* pechschwarz

pitcher [ˈpɪtʃər] *n* (*jug*) Krug *m*

pitiful [ˈpɪtɪfəl] *adj* (*contemptible*) jämmerlich

pitta bread [ˈpɪtə brɛd] *n* Pittabrot *nt*

pity [ˈpɪti] *n* Mitleid *nt*; **what a ~** wie schade; **it's a ~** es ist schade ▷ *vt* Mitleid haben mit

pizza [ˈpiːtsə] *n* Pizza *f*

place [pleɪs] *nm* (*spot, in text*) Stelle *f*; (*town etc*) Ort; (*house*) Haus *nt*; (*position, seat, on course*) Platz *m*; **~ of birth** Geburtsort *m*; **at my ~** bei mir; **in third ~** auf dem dritten Platz; **to three decimal ~s** bis auf drei Stellen nach dem Komma; **out of ~** nicht an der richtigen Stelle; (*fig: remark*)

unangebracht; **in ~ of** anstelle von; **in the
first ~** (firstly) erstens; (immediately)
gleich; (in any case) überhaupt ▷ vt (put)
stellen, setzen; (lay flat) legen; (advertisement) setzen (in in +akk); (Comm: order)
aufgeben

place mat n Set nt

plague [pleɪg] n Pest f

plaice [pleɪs] n Scholle f

plain [pleɪn] adj (clear) klar, deutlich; (simple) einfach; (not beautiful) unattraktiv;
(yoghurt) Natur- ▷ n Ebene f

plainly [pleɪnli] adv (frankly) offen; (simply) einfach; (obviously) eindeutig

plan [plæn] n Plan m; (for essay etc) Konzept nt ▷ vt planen; **to ~ to do sth, to ~ on
doing sth** vorhaben, etw zu tun ▷ vi planen

plane [pleɪn] n (aircraft) Flugzeug nt; (tool)
Hobel m

planet [plænɪt] n Planet m

plank [plæŋk] n Brett nt

plant [plænt] n Pflanze f; (equipment)
Maschinen pl; (factory) Werk nt ▷ vt (tree
etc) pflanzen

plantation [plænteɪʃ°n] n Plantage f

plaque [plæk] n Gedenktafel f; (on teeth)
Zahnbelag m

plaster [plæstər] n (on wall) Verputz m

plastered [plæstərd] adj (fam) besoffen; **to
get absolutely ~** sich besaufen

plastic [plæstɪk] n Kunststoff m; **to pay
with ~** mit Kreditkarte bezahlen ▷ adj
Plastik-

plastic bag n Plastiktüte f

plastic surgery n plastische Chirurgie f

plate [pleɪt] n (for food) Teller m; (flat sheet)
Platte f; (plaque) Schild nt

platform [plætfɔrm] n (Rail) Bahnsteig m;
(at meeting) Podium nt

platinum [plætɪnəm, plætnəm] n Platin
nt

play [pleɪ] n Spiel nt; (Theat) (Theater)
stück nt ▷ vt spielen; (another player or
team) spielen gegen; **to ~ the piano** Klavier spielen; **to ~ a part in** (fig) eine Rolle
spielen bei ▷ vi spielen

playacting [pleɪæktɪŋ] n Schauspielerei f

play at vt: **what are you ~ing at?** was soll
das?

play back vt abspielen

playback [pleɪbæk] n Wiedergabe f

play down vt herunterspielen

player [pleɪər] n Spieler(in) m(f)

playful [pleɪfəl] adj (person) verspielt;

(remark) scherzhaft

playground [pleɪgraʊnd] n Spielplatz m;
(in school) Schulhof m

playgroup [pleɪgrup] n Spielgruppe f

playing card [pleɪɪŋ kɑrd] n Spielkarte f

playing field [pleɪɪŋ fild] n Sportplatz m

playmate [pleɪmeɪt] n Spielkamerad(in)
m(f)

playwright [pleɪraɪt] n Dramatiker(in)
m(f)

plea [pli] n Bitte f (for um)

plead [plid] vi dringend bitten (with sb
jdn); (Jur): **to ~ guilty** sich schuldig beken-
nen

pleasant [plɛzᵊnt] adj, **pleasantly** adv
angenehm

please [pliz] adv bitte; **more tea? - yes, ~
noch Tee? - ja, bitte ▷ vt (be agreeable to)
gefallen +dat; **~ yourself** wie du willst/Sie
wollen

pleased [plizd] adj zufrieden; (glad)
erfreut; **~ to meet you** freut mich, angenehm

pleasing [plizɪŋ] adj erfreulich

pleasure [plɛʒər] n Vergnügen nt, Freude f;
it's a ~ gern geschehen

pledge [plɛdʒ] n (promise) Versprechen nt
▷ vt (promise) versprechen

plenty [plɛnti] n: **~ of** eine Menge, viel(e);
to be ~ genug sein, reichen; **I've got ~** ich
habe mehr als genug ▷ adv (fam) ganz
schön

pliable [plaɪəb°l] adj biegsam

pliers [plaɪərz] npl (Kombi)zange f

plot [plɒt] n (of story) Handlung f; (conspiracy) Komplott nt; (of land) Stück nt Land,
Grundstück nt ▷ vi ein Komplott schmieden

plow [plaʊ] n Pflug m ▷ vt, vi (Agr) pflü-
gen

pluck [plʌk] vt (eyebrows, guitar) zupfen;
(chicken) rupfen

pluck up vt: **to ~ one's courage** Mut aufbringen

plug [plʌg] n (for sink, bath) Stöpsel m;
(Elec) Stecker m; (Auto) (Zünd)kerze f;
(fam: publicity) Schleichwerbung f ▷ vt
(fam: advertise) Reklame machen für

plug in vt anschließen

plum [plʌm] n Pflaume f ▷ adj (fam: job etc)
Super-

plumber [plʌmər] n Klempner(in) m(f)

plumbing [plʌmɪŋ] n (fittings) Leitungen
pl; (craft) Installieren nt

plump [plʌmp] adj rundlich

plunge [plʌndʒ] *vt* (*knife*) stoßen; (*into water*) tauchen ▷ *vi* stürzen; (*into water*) tauchen

plunk [plʌŋk] *vt*: **to ~ sth down** etw hinknallen

plural [pluərəl] *n* Plural *m*

plus [plʌs] *prep* plus; (*as well as*) und ▷ *adj* Plus-; **20 ~** mehr als 20 ▷ *n* (*fig*) Plus *nt*

plush toy Plüschtier *nt*

plywood [plaɪwʊd] *n* Sperrholz *nt*

pm [piː ɛm] (*abbr*) = **post meridiem**; **at 3 pm** um 3 Uhr nachmittags; **at 8 pm** um 8 Uhr abends

pneumonia [nuːmoʊnyə, -moʊniə] *n* Lungenentzündung *f*

poached [poʊtʃt] *adj* (*egg*) pochiert, verloren

PO Box [piː oʊ bɒks] (*abbr*) = **post office box** Postfach *nt*

pocket [pɒkɪt] *n* Tasche *f* ▷ *vt* (*put in pocket*) einstecken

pocketbook [pɒkɪtbʊk] *n* (*wallet*) Brieftasche *f*

pocket calculator *n* Taschenrechner *m*

pocket money *n* Taschengeld *nt*

poem [poʊəm] *n* Gedicht *nt*

poet [poʊɪt] *n* Dichter(in) *m(f)*

poetic [poʊɛtɪk] *adj* poetisch

poetry [poʊɪtri] *n* (*art*) Dichtung *f*; (*poems*) Gedichte *pl*

point [pɔɪnt] *n* Punkt *m*; (*spot*) Stelle *f*; (*sharp tip*) Spitze *f*; (*moment*) Zeitpunkt *m*; (*purpose*) Zweck *m*; (*idea*) Argument *nt*; (*decimal*) Dezimalstelle *f*; **~s** *pl* (*Rail*) Weiche *f*; **~ of view** Standpunkt *m*; **three ~ two** drei Komma zwei; **at some ~** irgendwann (mal); **to get to the ~** zur Sache kommen; **there's no ~** es hat keinen Sinn; **I was on the ~ of leaving** ich wollte gerade gehen ▷ *vt* (*gun etc*) richten (*at* auf +*akk*); **to ~ one's finger at** mit dem Finger zeigen auf +*akk* ▷ *vi* (*with finger etc*) zeigen (*at, to* auf +*akk*)

pointed [pɔɪntɪd] *adj* spitz; (*question*) gezielt

pointer [pɔɪntər] *n* (*on dial*) Zeiger *m*; (*tip*) Hinweis *m*

pointless [pɔɪntlɪs] *adj* sinnlos

point out *vt* (*indicate*) aufzeigen; (*mention*) hinweisen auf +*akk*

poison [pɔɪzⁿn] *n* Gift *nt* ▷ *vt* vergiften

poisonous [pɔɪzⁿnəs] *adj* giftig

poke [poʊk] *vt* (*with stick, finger*) stoßen, stupsen; (*put*) stecken

Poland [poʊlənd] *n* Polen *nt*

polar [poʊlər] *adj* Polar-, polar; **~ bear** Eisbär *m*

Pole [poʊl] *n* Pole *m*, Polin *f*

pole [poʊl] *n* Stange *f*; (*Geo, Elec*) Pol *m*

pole vault [poʊl vɔlt] *n* Stabhochsprung *m*

police [pəlis] *n* Polizei *f*

police car *n* Polizeiwagen *m*

policeman [pəlismən] (*pl* **-men**) *n* Polizist *m*

police station *n* (Polizei)wache *f*

policewoman [pəliswʊmən] (*pl* **-women**) *n* Polizistin *f*

policy [pɒlɪsi] *n* (*plan*) Politik *f*; (*principle*) Grundsatz *m*; (*insurance policy*) (Versicherungs)police *f*

polio [poʊliou] *n* Kinderlähmung *f*

Polish [poʊlɪʃ] *adj* polnisch ▷ *n* Polnisch *nt*

polish [pɒlɪʃ] *n* (*for furniture*) Politur *f*; (*for floor*) Wachs *nt*; (*for shoes*) Creme *f*; (*shine*) Glanz *m*; (*fig*) Schliff *m* ▷ *vt* polieren; (*shoes*) putzen; (*fig*) den letzten Schliff geben +*dat*

polite [pəlaɪt] *adj* höflich

politeness [pəlaɪtnɪs] *n* Höflichkeit *f*

political [pəlɪtɪkⁿl] *adj* politisch

politically [pəlɪtɪkⁿli] *adv* politisch; **~ correct** politisch korrekt

politician [pɒlɪtɪʃⁿn] *n* Politiker(in) *m(f)*

politics [pɒlɪtɪks] *nsing o pl* Politik *f*

poll [poʊl] *n* (*election*) Wahl *f*; (*opinion poll*) Umfrage *f*

pollen [pɒlən] *n* Pollen *m*, Blütenstaub *m*

pollen count *n* Pollenflug *m*

polling station [poʊlɪŋ steɪʃⁿn] *n* Wahllokal *nt*

pollute [pəlut] *vt* verschmutzen

pollution [pəluʃⁿn] *n* Verschmutzung *f*

pompous [pɒmpəs] *adj* aufgeblasen; (*language*) geschwollen

pond [pɒnd] *n* Teich *m*

pony [poʊni] *n* Pony *nt*

ponytail [poʊniteɪl] *n* Pferdeschwanz *m*

poodle [pudⁿl] *n* Pudel *m*

pool [pul] *n* (*swimming pool*) Schwimmbad *nt*; (*private*) Swimmingpool *m*; (*of spilled liquid, blood*) Lache *f*; (*game*) Poolbillard *nt* ▷ *vt* (*money etc*) zusammenlegen

poor [pʊər] *adj* arm; (*not good*) schlecht ▷ *npl*: **the ~** die Armen *pl*

poorly [pʊərli] *adv* (*badly*) schlecht

pop [pɒp] *n* (*music*) Pop *m*; (*noise*) Knall *m* ▷ *vt* (*put*) stecken; (*balloon*) platzen lassen ▷ *vi* (*balloon*) platzen; (*cork*) knallen; **to pop in** (*person*) vorbeischauen

pop concert *n* Popkonzert *nt*

P

popcorn [pɒpkɔrn] n Popcorn nt
Pope [poup] n Papst m
pop group n Popgruppe f
pop music n Popmusik f
poppy [pɒpi] n Mohn m
Popsicle® [pɒpsɪkºl] n Eis nt am Stiel
pop star n Popstar m
popular [pɒpyələr] adj (well-liked) beliebt (with bei); (widespread) weit verbreitet
population [pɒpyəleɪʃºn] n Bevölkerung f; (of town) Einwohner pl
porcelain [pɔrsəlin, pɔrslin] n Porzellan nt
porch [pɔrtʃ] n Vorbau m; (verandah) Veranda f
porcupine [pɔrkyəpaɪn] n Stachelschwein nt
pork [pɔrk] n Schweinefleisch nt
pork chop n Schweinekotelett nt
porn [pɔrn] n Porno m
pornographic [pɔrnəgræfɪk] adj pornografisch
pornography [pɔrnɒgrəfi] n Pornografie f
port [pɔrt] n (harbor) Hafen m; (town) Hafenstadt f; (Naut: left side) Backbord nt; (wine) Portwein m; (Inform) Anschluss m
portable [pɔrtəbºl] adj tragbar; (radio) Koffer-
portal [pɔrtºl] n (Inform) Portal nt
porter [pɔrtər] n Pförtner(in) m(f); (for luggage) Gepäckträger m
porthole [pɔrthoul] n Bullauge nt
portion [pɔrʃºn] n Teil m; (of food) Portion f
portrait [pɔrtrɪt, -treɪt] n Porträt nt
portray [pɔrtreɪ] vt darstellen
Portugal [pɔrtʃʊgºl] n Portugal nt
Portuguese [pɔrtʃʊgiz] adj portugiesisch ▷ n Portugiese m, Portugiesin f; (language) Portugiesisch nt
pose [pouz] n Haltung f ▷ vi posieren ▷ vt (threat, problem) darstellen
posh [pɒʃ] adj (fam) piekfein
position [pəzɪʃºn] n Stellung f; (place) Position f, Lage f; (job) Stelle f; (opinion) Standpunkt m; **to be in a ~ to do sth** in der Lage sein, etw zu tun; **in third ~** auf dem dritten Platz ▷ vt aufstellen; (Inform: cursor) positionieren
positive [pɒzɪtɪv] adj positiv; (convinced) sicher
possess [pəzɛs] vt besitzen
possession [pəzɛʃºn] n: **~s** pl Besitz m
possessive [pəzɛsɪv] adj (person) besitzergreifend

possibility [pɒsɪbɪliti] n Möglichkeit f
possible [pɒsɪbºl] adj möglich; **if ~** wenn möglich; **as big/soon as ~** so groß/bald wie möglich
possibly [pɒsɪbli] adv (perhaps) vielleicht; **I've done all I ~ can** ich habe mein Möglichstes getan
post [poust] n (mail) Post f; (pole) Pfosten m; (job) Stelle f ▷ vt (letters) aufgeben; **to keep sb ~ed** jdn auf dem Laufenden halten
postage [poustɪdʒ] n Porto nt; **~ and handling** Porto und Verpackung
postal [poustºl] adj Post-
postcard [poustkard] n Postkarte f
poster [poustər] n Plakat nt, Poster nt
postmark [poustmark] n Poststempel m
postmortem [poustmɔrtəm] n Autopsie f
post office n Post® f
postpone [poustpoun, pouspoun] vt verschieben (till auf +akk)
posture [pɒstʃər] n Haltung f
pot [pɒt] n Topf m; (teapot, coffee pot) Kanne f; (fam: marijuana) Pot m ▷ vt (plant) eintopfen
potato [pəteɪtou] (pl -es) n Kartoffel f
potato chips npl Kartoffelchips pl
potato peeler [pəteɪtou pilər] n Kartoffelschäler m
potent [poutºnt] adj stark
potential [pətɛnʃºl] adj potenziell ▷ n Potenzial nt
potentially [pətɛnʃºli] adv potenziell
pothole [pɒthoul] n Höhle f; (in road) Schlagloch nt
pottery [pɒtəri] n (objects) Töpferwaren pl
potty [pɒti] n Töpfchen nt
poultry [poultri] n Geflügel nt
pounce [pauns] vi: **to ~ on** sich stürzen auf +akk
pound [paund] n (money) Pfund nt; (weight) Pfund nt (0,454 kg); **a ~ of cherries** ein Pfund Kirschen
pour [pɔr] vt (liquid) gießen; (rice, sugar etc) schütten; **to ~ sb sth** (drink) jdm etw eingießen
pouring [pɔrɪŋ] adj (rain) strömend
poverty [pɒvərti] n Armut f
powder [paudər] n Pulver nt; (cosmetic) Puder m
powdered milk n Milchpulver nt
powder room n Damentoilette f
power [pauər] n Macht f; (ability) Fähigkeit f; (strength) Stärke f; (Elec) Strom m; **to be in ~** an der Macht sein ▷ vt betrei-

ben, antreiben

powerful [pauərfəl] *adj (politician etc)*
mächtig; *(engine, government)* stark;
(argument) durchschlagend

powerless [pauərlıs] *adj* machtlos

power station *n* Kraftwerk *nt*

PR [pi ɑr] *(abbr)* = **public relations** ▷ *(abbr)*
= **proportional representation**

practical [præktıkªl] *adj*, **practically** *adv*
praktisch

practice [præktıs] *n (training)* Übung *f*;
(custom) Gewohnheit *f*; *(doctor's, lawyer's)*
Praxis *f*; **in ~** *(in reality)* in der Praxis; **out
of ~** außer Übung; **to put sth into ~** etw in
die Praxis umsetzen ▷ *vt (instrument,
movement)* üben; *(profession)* ausüben
▷ *vi* üben; *(doctor, lawyer)* praktizieren

Prague [prɑg] *n* Prag *nt*

praise [preız] *n* Lob *nt* ▷ *vt* loben

pray [preı] *vi* beten; **to ~ for sth** *(fig)* stark
auf etw *akk* hoffen

prayer [preər] *n* Gebet *nt*

pre- [pri-] *pref* vor-, prä-

preach [pritʃ] *vi* predigen

prearrange [priərreındʒ] *vt* im Voraus vereinbaren

precaution [prıkɔʃªn] *n* Vorsichtsmaßnah-
me *f*

precede [prısid] *vt* vorausgehen +*dat*

preceding [prısidıŋ] *adj* vorhergehend

precinct [prisıŋkt] *n (district)* Bezirk *m*

precious [preʃəs] *adj* kostbar; **~ stone**
Edelstein *m*

précis [preısi] *n* Zusammenfassung *f*

precise [prısaıs] *adj*, **precisely** *adv* genau

precondition [prikəndıʃªn] *n* Vorbedin-
gung *f*

predecessor [predısesər] *n* Vorgänger(in)
m(f)

predicament [prıdıkəmənt] *n* missliche
Lage

predict [prıdıkt] *vt* voraussagen

predictable [prıdıktəbªl] *adj* vorherseh-
bar; *(person)* berechenbar

predominant [prıdpmınənt] *adj* vorherrschend

predominantly [prıdpmınıtli] *adv* überwiegend

preface [prefıs] *n* Vorwort *nt*

prefer [prıfər] *vt* vorziehen *(to dat)*, lieber
mögen *(to* als); **to ~ to do sth** etw lieber
tun

preferably [prefərəbli, prefrə-, prıfɜrə-]
adv vorzugsweise, am liebsten

preference [prefərəns] *n (liking)* Vorliebe *f*

preferential [prefərenʃªl] *adj*: **to get ~ treatment** bevorzugt behandelt werden

prefix [prifıks] *n (Tel)* Vorwahl *f*

pregnancy [pregnənsi] *n* Schwangerschaft
f

pregnant [pregnənt] *adj* schwanger; **two
months ~** im zweiten Monat schwanger

prejudice [predʒədıs] *n* Vorurteil *nt*

prejudiced [predʒədıst] *adj (person)* voreingenommen

preliminary [prılımıneri] *adj (measures)*
vorbereitend; *(results)* vorläufig; *(remarks)*
einleitend

premature [primətʃuər] *adj* vorzeitig;
(hasty) voreilig

premiere [prımjər, primyɜər] *n* Premiere
f

premises [premısız] *npl (offices)* Räum-
lichkeiten *pl*; *(of factory, school)* Gelände
nt

premium-rate [primiəmreıt] *adj (Tel)* zum
Höchsttarif

preoccupied [priɒkyəpaıd] *adj*: **to be ~
with sth** mit etw sehr beschäftigt sein

prepaid [pripeıd] *adj* vorausbezahlt; *(envelope)* frankiert

preparation [prepəreıʃªn] *n* Vorbereitung *f*

prepare [prıpeər] *vt* vorbereiten *(for* auf
+*akk*); *(food)* zubereiten; **to be ~d to do
sth** bereit sein, etw zu tun ▷ *vi* sich vorbereiten *(for* auf +*akk*)

prerequisite [prirekwızıt] *n* Voraussetzung *f*

prescribe [prıskraıb] *vt* vorschreiben;
(Med) verschreiben

prescription [prıskrıpʃªn] *n* Rezept *nt*

presence [prezªns] *n* Gegenwart *f*

present [prezªnt] *adj (in attendance)* anwesend *(at* bei); *(current)* gegenwärtig; **~
tense** Gegenwart *f*, Präsens *nt* ▷ *n* Gegenwart *f*; *(gift)* Geschenk *nt*; **at ~** zurzeit ▷ *vt
(TV, Radio)* präsentieren; *(problem)* darstellen; *(report etc)* vorlegen; **to ~ sb with
sth** jdm etw überreichen

present-day *adj* heutig

presently [prezªntli] *adv* bald; *(at present)*
zurzeit

preservative [prızɜrvətıv] *n* Konservierungsmittel *nt*

preserve [prızɜrv] *vt* erhalten; *(food)* ein-
machen, konservieren

president [prezıdənt] *n* Präsident(in) *m(f)*

presidential [prezıdenʃªl] *adj* Präsiden-
ten-; *(election)* Präsidentschafts-

press [pres] *n (newspapers, machine)* Pres-

P

se f ▷ vt (*push*) drücken; **to ~ a button** auf einen Knopf drücken ▷ vi (*push*) drücken

pressing [prɛsɪŋ] *adj* dringend

pressure [prɛʃər] *n* Druck *m*; **to be under ~** unter Druck stehen; **to put ~ on sb** jdn unter Druck setzen

pressure cooker *n* Schnellkochtopf *m*

pressurize [prɛʃəraɪz] *vt* (*person*) unter Druck setzen

presumably [prɪzuːməbli] *adv* vermutlich

presume [prɪzuːm] *vt*, *vi* annehmen

presumptuous [prɪzʌmptʃuəs] *adj* anmaßend

presuppose [priːsəpouz] *vt* voraussetzen

pretend [prɪtɛnd] *vt*: **to ~ that** so tun als ob; **to ~ to do sth** vorgeben, etw zu tun ▷ vi: **she's ~ing** sie tut nur so

pretentious [prɪtɛnʃəs] *adj* anmaßend; (*person*) wichtigtuerisch

pretty [prɪti] *adj* hübsch ▷ *adv* ziemlich

prevent [prɪvɛnt] *vt* verhindern; **to ~ sb from doing sth** jdn daran hindern, etw zu tun

preview [priːvyu] *n* (*Cine*) Voraufführung *f*; (*trailer*) Vorschau *f*

previous [priːviəs] *adj*, **previously** *adv* früher

prey [preɪ] *n* Beute *f*

price [praɪs] *n* Preis *m* ▷ *vt*: **it's ~d at $10** es ist mit 10 Dollar ausgezeichnet

priceless [praɪsləs] *adj* unbezahlbar

price list *n* Preisliste *f*

price tag *n* Preisschild *nt*

prick [prɪk] *n* Stich *m* ▷ *vt* stechen in +*akk*; **to ~ one's finger** sich *dat* in den Finger stechen

prickly [prɪkli] *adj* stachelig

pride [praɪd] *n* Stolz *m*; (*arrogance*) Hochmut *m* ▷ *vt*: **to ~ oneself on sth** auf etw *akk* stolz sein

priest [priːst] *n* Priester *m*

primarily [praɪmɛˈrɪli] *adv* vorwiegend

primary [praɪmɛri, -məri] *adj* Haupt-; **~ education** Grundschulausbildung *f*; **~ school** Grundschule *f*

prime [praɪm] *adj* Haupt-; (*excellent*) erstklassig ▷ *n*: **in one's ~** in den besten Jahren

prime minister *n* Premierminister(in) *m(f)*

prime time *n* (*TV*) Hauptsendezeit *f*

primitive [prɪmɪtɪv] *adj* primitiv

primrose [prɪmrouz] *n* Schlüsselblume *f*

prince [prɪns] *n* Prinz *m*; (*ruler*) Fürst *m*

princess [prɪnsɪs, -sɛs] *n* Prinzessin *f*, Fürstin *f*

principal [prɪnsɪpᵊl] *adj* Haupt-, wichtigste(r, s) ▷ *n* (*school*) Rektor(in) *m(f)*

principle [prɪnsɪpᵊl] *n* Prinzip *nt*; **in ~** im Prinzip; **on ~** aus Prinzip

print [prɪnt] *n* (*picture*) Druck *m*; (*Foto*) Abzug *m*; (*made by feet, fingers*) Abdruck *m*; **out of ~** vergriffen ▷ *vt* drucken; (*photo*) abziehen; (*write in block letters*) in Druckschrift schreiben

printed matter *n* Drucksache *f*

printer [prɪntər] *n* Drucker *m*

print out *vt* (*Inform*) ausdrucken

printout [prɪntaʊt] *n* (*Inform*) Ausdruck *m*

prior [praɪər] *adj* früher; **a ~ engagement** eine vorher getroffene Verabredung; **~ to sth** vor etw *dat*; **~ to going abroad, she had ... bevor** sie ins Ausland ging, hatte sie ...

priority [praɪɒriti] *n* (*thing having precedence*) Priorität *f*

prison [prɪzᵊn] *n* Gefängnis *nt*

prisoner [prɪzənər] *n* Gefangene(r) *mf*; **~ of war** Kriegsgefangene(r) *mf*

privacy [praɪvəsi] *n* Privatleben *nt*

private [praɪvɪt] *adj* privat; (*confidential*) vertraulich ▷ *n* einfacher Soldat; **in ~** privat

privately [praɪvɪtli] *adv* privat; (*confidentially*) vertraulich

privatize [praɪvətaɪz] *vt* privatisieren

privilege [prɪvɪlɪdʒ, prɪvlɪdʒ] *n* Privileg *nt*

privileged [prɪvɪlɪdʒd, prɪvlɪdʒd] *adj* privilegiert

prize [praɪz] *n* Preis *m*

prize money *n* Preisgeld *nt*

prizewinner [praɪzwɪnər] *n* Gewinner(in) *m(f)*

prizewinning [praɪzwɪnɪŋ] *adj* preisgekrönt

pro [proʊ] (*pl* **-s**) *n* (*professional*) Profi *m*; **the pros and cons** *pl* das Für und Wider

pro- [proʊ-] *pref* pro-

probability [prɒbəbɪlɪti] *n* Wahrscheinlichkeit *f*

probable [prɒbəbᵊl] *adj*, **probably** *adv* wahrscheinlich

probation [proʊbeɪʃᵊn] *n* Probezeit *f*; (*Jur*) Bewährung *f*

probe [proʊb] *n* (*investigation*) Untersuchung *f* ▷ *vt* untersuchen

problem [prɒbləm] *n* Problem *nt*; **no ~!** kein Problem!

procedure [prəsiːdʒər] *n* Verfahren *nt*

proceed [prəsiːd] *vi* (*continue*) fortfahren;

(*set about sth*) vorgehen ▷ *vt*: **to ~ to do sth** anfangen, etw zu tun

proceedings [prəsiːdɪŋz] *npl* (*Jur*) Verfahren *nt*

proceeds [prɒsiːdz] *npl* Erlös *m*

process [prɒsɛs] *n* Prozess *m*, Vorgang *m*; (*method*) Verfahren *nt* ▷ *vt* (*application etc*) bearbeiten; (*food, data*) verarbeiten; (*film*) entwickeln

procession [prəsɛʃᵊn] *n* Umzug *m*

processor [prɒsɛsər] *n* (*Inform*) Prozessor *m*; (*Gastr*) Küchenmaschine *f*

produce [*n* proʊdʊs, *vb* prədʊs] *n* (*Agr*) Produkte *pl*, Erzeugnisse *pl* ▷ *vt* (*manufacture*) herstellen, produzieren; (*on farm*) erzeugen; (*film, play, record*) produzieren; (*cause*) hervorrufen; (*evidence, results*) liefern

producer [prədʊsər] *n* (*manufacturer*) Hersteller(in) *m(f)*; (*of film, play, record*) Produzent(in) *m(f)*

product [prɒdʌkt] *n* Produkt *nt*, Erzeugnis *nt*

production [prədʌkʃᵊn] *n* Produktion *f*; (*Theat*) Inszenierung *f*

productive [prədʌktɪv] *adj* produktiv; (*land*) ertragreich

prof [prɒf] *n* (*fam*) Prof *m*

profession [prəfɛʃᵊn] *n* Beruf *m*

professional [prəfɛʃənᵊl] *n* Profi *m* ▷ *adj* beruflich; (*expert*) fachlich; (*sportsman, actor etc*) Berufs-

professor [prəfɛsər] *n* Professor(in) *m(f)*; (*lecturer*) Dozent(in) *m(f)*

proficient [prəfɪʃᵊnt] *adj* kompetent (*in* in +*dat*)

profile [proʊfaɪl] *n* Profil *nt*; **to keep a low ~** sich rarmachen

profit [prɒfɪt] *n* Gewinn *m* ▷ *vi* profitieren (*by, from* von)

profitable [prɒfɪtəbᵊl] *adj* rentabel

profound [prəfaʊnd] *adj* tief; (*idea, thinker*) tiefgründig; (*knowledge*) profund

program [proʊgræm, -grəm] *n* Programm *nt*; (*Inform*) Programm *nt*; (*TV, Radio*) Sendung *f* ▷ *vt* (*Inform*) programmieren

programmer [proʊgræmər] *n* Programmierer(in) *m(f)*

programing [proʊgræmɪŋ] *n* (*Inform*) Programmieren *nt*; **~ language** Programmiersprache *f*

progress [*n* prɒgrɛs, *vb* prəgrɛs] *n* Fortschritt *m*; **to make ~** Fortschritte machen ▷ *vi* (*work, illness etc*) fortschreiten; (*improve*) Fortschritte machen

progressive [prəgrɛsɪv] *adj* (*person, policy*) fortschrittlich

progressively [prəgrɛsɪvli] *adv* zunehmend

prohibit [proʊhɪbɪt] *vt* verbieten

project [prɒdʒɛkt] *n* Projekt *nt*

projector [prədʒɛktər] *n* Projektor *m*

prolong [prəlɒŋ] *vt* verlängern

prom [prɒm] *n* (*dance*) Ball für die Schüler und Studenten von Highschools oder Colleges

prominent [prɒmɪnənt] *adj* (*politician, actor etc*) prominent; (*easily seen*) auffallend

promiscuous [prəmɪskyuəs] *adj* promisk

promise [prɒmɪs] *n* Versprechen *nt* ▷ *vt* versprechen; **to ~ sb sth** jdm etw versprechen; **to ~ to do sth** versprechen, etw zu tun ▷ *vi* versprechen

promising [prɒmɪsɪŋ] *adj* vielversprechend

promote [prəmoʊt] *vt* (*in rank*) befördern; (*help on*) fördern; (*Comm*) werben für

promotion [prəmoʊʃᵊn] *n* (*in rank*) Beförderung *f*; (*Comm*) Werbung *f* (*of* für)

prompt [prɒmpt] *adj* prompt; (*punctual*) pünktlich ▷ *adv*: **at two o'clock ~** Punkt zwei Uhr ▷ *vt* (*Theat: actor*) soufflieren +*dat*

prone [proʊn] *adj*: **to be ~ to sth** zu etw neigen

pronounce [prənaʊns] *vt* (*word*) aussprechen

pronounced [prənaʊnst] *adj* ausgeprägt

pronunciation [prənʌnsieɪʃᵊn] *n* Aussprache *f*

proof [pruːf] *n* Beweis *m*; (*of alcohol*) Alkoholgehalt *m*

prop [prɒp] *n* Stütze *f*; (*Theat*) Requisit *nt* ▷ *vt*: **to ~ sth against sth** etw gegen etw lehnen

proper [prɒpər] *adj* richtig; (*morally correct*) anständig

property [prɒpərti] *n* (*possession*) Eigentum *nt*; (*house*) Haus *nt*; (*land*) Grundbesitz *m*; (*characteristic*) Eigenschaft *f*

proportion [prəpɔrʃᵊn] *n* Verhältnis *nt*; (*share*) Teil *m*; **~s** *pl* (*size*) Proportionen *pl*; **in ~ to** im Verhältnis zu

proportional [prəpɔrʃənᵊl] *adj* proportional; **~ representation** Verhältniswahlrecht *nt*

proposal [prəpoʊzᵊl] *n* Vorschlag *m*; **~ of marriage** (Heirats)antrag *m*

propose [prəpoʊz] *vt* vorschlagen ▷ *vi*

(*offer marriage*) einen Heiratsantrag machen (*to sb* jdm)

proprietor [prəpraɪətər] *n* Besitzer(in) *m(f)*; (*of bar, hotel*) Inhaber(in) *m(f)*

prop up *vt* stützen; (*fig*) unterstützen

prose [prouz] *n* Prosa *f*

prosecute [prɒsɪkyut] *vt* verfolgen (*for* wegen)

prospect [prɒspɛkt] *n* Aussicht *f*

prosperity [prɒspɛriti] *n* Wohlstand *m*

prosperous [prɒspərəs] *adj* wohlhabend; (*business*) gut gehend

prostitute [prɒstɪtut] *n* Prostituierte(r) *mf*

protect [prətɛkt] *vt* schützen (*from, against* vor +*dat* gegen)

protection [prətɛkʃᵊn] *n* Schutz *m* (*from, against* vor +*dat* gegen)

protective [prətɛktɪv] *adj* beschützend; (*clothing etc*) Schutz-

protein [proutin] *n* Protein *nt*, Eiweiß *nt*

protest [*n* proutest, *vb* prətɛst] *n* Protest *m*; (*demonstration*) Protestkundgebung *f* ▷ *vi* protestieren (*against* gegen); (*demonstrate*) demonstrieren

Protestant [prɒtɪstənt] *adj* protestantisch ▷ *n* Protestant(in) *m(f)*

proud [praud] *adj*, **proudly** *adv* stolz (*of* auf +*akk*)

prove [pruv] *vt* beweisen; (*turn out to be*) sich erweisen als

proverb [prɒvɜrb] *n* Sprichwort *nt*

provide [prəvaɪd] *vt* zur Verfügung stellen; (*drinks, music etc*) sorgen für; (*person*) versorgen (*with* mit)

provided [prəvaɪdɪd] *conj*: ~ **that** vorausgesetzt, dass

provide for *vt* (*family etc*) sorgen für

provider [prəvaɪdər] *n* (*Inform*) Provider *m*

provision [prəvɪʒᵊn] *n* (*condition*) Bestimmung *f*; ~**s** *pl* (*food*) Proviant *m*

provisional [prəvɪʒənᵊl] *adj*, **provisionally** *adv* provisorisch

provoke [prəvouk] *vt* provozieren; (*cause*) hervorrufen

proximity [prɒksɪmɪti] *n* Nähe *f*

prudent [prudᵊnt] *adj* klug; (*person*) umsichtig

prudish [prudɪʃ] *adj* prüde

prune [prun] *n* Backpflaume *f* ▷ *vt* (*tree etc*) zurechtstutzen

PS [pi ɛs] (*abbr*) = **postscript** PS *nt*

psalm [sɑm] *n* Psalm *m*

pseudo [sudou] *adj* pseudo-, Pseudo-

pseudonym [sudənɪm] *n* Pseudonym *nt*

PST [pi ɛs ti] (*abbr*) = **Pacific Standard Time**

psychiatric [saɪkiætrɪk] *adj* psychiatrisch; (*illness*) psychisch

psychiatrist [sɪkaɪətrɪst] *n* Psychiater(in) *m(f)*

psychiatry [sɪkaɪətri] *n* Psychiatrie *f*

psychic [saɪkɪk] *adj* übersinnlich; **I'm not ~** ich kann keine Gedanken lesen

psychoanalysis [saɪkouənælɪsɪs] *n* Psychoanalyse *f*

psychoanalyst [saɪkouænᵊlɪst] *n* Psychoanalytiker(in) *m(f)*

psychological [saɪkəlɒdʒɪkᵊl] *adj* psychologisch

psychology [saɪkɒlədʒi] *n* Psychologie *f*

psychopath [saɪkəpæθ] *n* Psychopath(in) *m(f)*

pt (*abbr*) = **pint**

pto (*abbr*) = **please turn over** b.w.

puberty [pyubərti] *n* Pubertät *f*

public [pʌblɪk] *n*: **the general ~** die (breite) Öffentlichkeit; **in ~** in der Öffentlichkeit ▷ *adj* öffentlich; (*relating to the State*) Staats-; ~ **holiday** gesetzlicher Feiertag; ~ **opinion** die öffentliche Meinung; ~ **relations** *pl* Öffentlichkeitsarbeit *f*, Public Relations *pl*

publication [pʌblɪkeɪʃᵊn] *n* Veröffentlichung *f*

publicity [pʌblɪsiti] *n* Publicity *f*; (*advertisements*) Werbung *f*

publish [pʌblɪʃ] *vt* veröffentlichen

publisher [pʌblɪʃər] *n* Verleger(in) *m(f)*; (*company*) Verlag *m*

publishing [pʌblɪʃɪŋ] *n* Verlagswesen *nt*

pudding [pudɪŋ] *n* (*course*) Nachtisch *m*

puddle [pʌdᵊl] *n* Pfütze *f*

puff [pʌf] *vi* (*pant*) schnaufen

puffin [pʌfɪn] *n* Papageientaucher *m*

puff pastry *n* Blätterteig *m*

pull [pul] *n* Ziehen *nt*; **to give sth a ~** an etw *dat* ziehen ▷ *vt* (*cart, tooth*) ziehen; (*rope, handle*) ziehen an +*dat*; (*fam: date*) abschleppen; **to ~ a muscle** sich *dat* einen Muskel zerren; **to ~ sb's leg** jdn auf den Arm nehmen ▷ *vi* ziehen

pull apart *vt* (*separate*) auseinanderziehen

pull down *vt* (*blind*) herunterziehen; (*house*) abreißen

pull in *vi* hineinfahren; (*stop*) anhalten

pull off *vt* (*deal etc*) zuwege bringen; (*clothes*) ausziehen

pull on *vt* (*clothes*) anziehen

pull out *vi* (*car from lane*) ausscheren; (*train*) abfahren; (*withdraw*) aussteigen (*of aus*) ▷ *vt* herausziehen; (*tooth*) ziehen; (*troops*) abziehen

pullover [pʊloʊvər] *n* Pullover *m*

pull up *vt* (*raise*) hochziehen; (*chair*) heranziehen ▷ *vi* anhalten

pulp [pʌlp] *n* Brei *m*; (*of fruit*) Fruchtfleisch *nt*

pulpit [pʊlpɪt, pʌl-] *n* Kanzel *f*

pulse [pʌls] *n* Puls *m*

pump [pʌmp] *n* Pumpe *f*; (*in gas station*) Zapfsäule *f*

pumpkin [pʌmpkɪn] *n* Kürbis *m*

pump up *vt* (*tire etc*) aufpumpen

pun [pʌn] *n* Wortspiel *nt*

punch [pʌntʃ] *n* (*blow*) (Faust)schlag *m*; (*tool*) Locher *m*; (*hot drink*) Punsch *m*; (*cold drink*) Bowle *f* ▷ *vt* (*strike*) schlagen; (*ticket, paper*) lochen

punctual [pʌŋktʃuəl] *adj*, **punctually** *adv* pünktlich

punctuation [pʌŋktʃueɪʃᵊn] *n* Interpunktion *f*

punctuation mark *n* Satzeichen *nt*

puncture [pʌŋktʃər] *n* (*flat tire*) Reifenpanne *f*

punish [pʌnɪʃ] *vt* bestrafen

punishment [pʌnɪʃmənt] *n* Strafe *f*; (*action*) Bestrafung *f*

pupil [pyuːpɪl] *n* (*school*) Schüler(in) *m(f)*

puppet [pʌpɪt] *n* Marionette *f*

puppy [pʌpi] *n* junger Hund

purchase [pɜrtʃɪs] *n* Kauf *m* ▷ *vt* kaufen

pure [pyʊər] *adj* rein; (*clean*) sauber; (*utter*) pur

purely [pyʊərli] *adv* rein

purify [pyʊərɪfaɪ] *vt* reinigen

purity [pyʊərɪti] *n* Reinheit *f*

purple [pɜrpᵊl] *adj* violett

purpose [pɜrpəs] *n* Zweck *m*; (*of person*) Absicht *f*; **on ~** absichtlich

purr [pɜr] *vi* (*cat*) schnurren

purse [pɜrs] *n* (*handbag*) Handtasche *f*

pursue [pərsuː] *vt* (*person, car*) verfolgen; (*hobby, studies*) nachgehen +*dat*

pursuit [pərsuːt] *n* (*chase*) Verfolgung *f*; (*occupation*) Beschäftigung *f*; (*hobby*) Hobby *nt*

pus [pʌs] *n* Eiter *m*

push [pʊʃ] *n* Stoß *m* ▷ *vt* (*person*) stoßen; (*car, chair etc*) schieben; (*button*) drücken; (*drugs*) dealen ▷ *vi* (*in crowd*) drängeln

pushcart [pʊʃkɑrt] *n* (*cart*) Schubkarren *m*

pusher [pʊʃər] *n* (*of drugs*) Dealer(in) *m(f)*

push in *vi* (*in line*) sich vordrängeln

push off *vi* (*fam: leave*) abhauen

push on *vi* (*with job*) weitermachen

push up *vt* (*prices*) hochtreiben

push-up *n* Liegestütz *m*

pushy [pʊʃi] *adj* (*fam*) aufdringlich, penetrant

put [pʊt] (*put, put*) *vt* tun; (*upright*) stellen; (*flat*) legen; (*express*) ausdrücken; (*write*) schreiben; **he put his hand in his pocket** er steckte die Hand in die Tasche; **he put his hand on her shoulder** er legte ihr die Hand auf die Schulter; **to put money into one's account** Geld auf sein Konto einzahlen

put aside *vt* (*money*) zurücklegen

put away *vt* (*tidy up*) wegräumen

put back *vt* zurücklegen; (*clock*) zurückstellen

put down *vt* (*in writing*) aufschreiben; (*rebellion*) niederschlagen; **to put the phone down** (den Hörer) auflegen; **to put one's name down for sth** sich für etw eintragen

put forward *vt* (*idea*) vorbringen; (*name*) vorschlagen; (*clock*) vorstellen

put in *vt* (*install*) einbauen; (*submit*) einreichen

put off *vt* (*switch off*) ausschalten; (*postpone*) verschieben; **to put sb off doing sth** jdn davon abbringen, etw zu tun

put on *vt* (*switch on*) anmachen; (*clothes*) anziehen; (*hat, glasses*) aufsetzen; (*makeup, CD*) auflegen; (*play*) aufführen; **to put the kettle on** Wasser aufsetzen; **to put weight on** zunehmen

put out *vt* (*hand, foot*) ausstrecken; (*light, cigarette*) ausmachen

putt [pʌt] *vt, vi* (*Sport*) putten

put up *vt* (*hand*) hochheben; (*picture*) aufhängen; (*tent*) aufstellen; (*building*) errichten; (*price*) erhöhen; (*person*) unterbringen; **to ~ with** sich abfinden mit; **I won't ~ with it** das lasse ich mir nicht gefallen

puzzle [pʌzᵊl] *n* Rätsel *nt*; (*toy*) Geduldsspiel *nt*; **jigsaw ~** Puzzle *nt* ▷ *vt* vor ein Rätsel stellen; **it ~s me** es ist mir ein Rätsel

puzzling [pʌzᵊlɪŋ] *adj* rätselhaft

pylon [paɪlɒn] *n* Mast *m*

pyramid [pɪrəmɪd] *n* Pyramide *f*

Q

quack [kwæk] *vi* quaken

quaint [kweɪnt] *adj* (*idea, tradition*) kurios; (*picturesque*) malerisch

qualification [kwɒlɪfɪkeɪʃⁿn] *n* (*for job*) Qualifikation *f*; (*from school, university*) Abschluss *m*

qualified [kwɒlɪfaɪd] *adj* (*for job*) qualifiziert

qualify [kwɒlɪfaɪ] *vt* (*limit*) einschränken; **to be qualified to do sth** berechtigt sein, etw zu tun ▷ *vi* (*finish training*) seine Ausbildung abschließen; (*contest etc*) sich qualifizieren

quality [kwɒlɪti] *n* Qualität *f*; (*characteristic*) Eigenschaft *f*

quantity [kwɒntɪti] *n* Menge *f*, Quantität *f*

quarantine [kwɒrəntin] *n* Quarantäne *f*

quarrel [kwɒrəl] *n* Streit *m* ▷ *vi* sich streiten

quarter [kwɔrtər] *n* Viertel *nt*; (*of year*) Vierteljahr *nt*; (*coin*) Vierteldollar *m*; **a ~ of an hour** eine Viertelstunde; **~ of/after three** Viertel vor/nach drei ▷ *vt* vierteln

quarter final *n* Viertelfinale *nt*

quarters *npl* (*Mil*) Quartier *nt*

quartet [kwɔrtɛt] *n* Quartett *nt*

quay [ki] *n* Kai *m*

queasy [kwizi] *adj*: **I feel ~** mir ist übel

queen [kwin] *n* Königin *f*; (*in cards, chess*) Dame *f*

queer [kwɪər] *adj* (*strange*) seltsam, sonderbar

quench [kwɛntʃ] *vt* (*thirst*) löschen

query [kwɪəri] *n* Frage *f* ▷ *vt* infrage stellen; (*bill*) reklamieren

question [kwɛstʃⁿn] *n* Frage *f*; **that's out of the ~** das kommt nicht infrage ▷ *vt* (*person*) befragen; (*suspect*) verhören; (*express doubt about*) bezweifeln

questionable [kwɛstʃənəbˡl] *adj* zweifelhaft; (*improper*) fragwürdig

question mark *n* Fragezeichen *nt*

questionnaire [kwɛstʃənɛər] *n* Fragebogen *m*

quibble [kwɪbˡl] *vi* kleinlich sein; (*argue*) streiten

quiche [kiʃ] *n* Quiche

quick [kwɪk] *adj* schnell; (*short*) kurz; **be ~** mach schnell!

quickly [kwɪkli] *adv* schnell

quiet [kwaɪət] *adj* (*not noisy*) leise; (*peaceful, calm*) still, ruhig; **be ~** sei still!; **to keep ~ about sth** über etw *akk* nichts sagen ▷ *n* Stille *f*, Ruhe *f*

quiet down *vi* sich beruhigen ▷ *vt* beruhigen

quietly [kwaɪətli] *adv* leise; (*calmly*) ruhig

quit [kwɪt] (*quit, quit*) *vt* (*leave*) verlassen; (*job*) aufgeben; **to ~ doing sth** aufhören, etw zu tun ▷ *vi* aufhören; (*resign*) kündigen

quite [kwaɪt] *adv* (*fairly*) ziemlich; (*completely*) ganz, völlig; **I don't ~ understand** ich verstehe das nicht ganz; **~ a few** ziemlich viele; **~ so** richtig!

quits *adj*: **to be ~ with sb** mit jdm quitt sein

quiver [kwɪvər] *vi* zittern

quiz [kwɪz] *n* (*competition*) Quiz *nt*

quota [kwoʊtə] *n* Anteil *m*; (*Comm, Pol*) Quote *f*

quotation [kwoʊteɪʃⁿn] *n* Zitat *nt*; (*price*) Kostenvoranschlag *m*

quotation marks *npl* Anführungszeichen *pl*

quote [kwoʊt] *vt* (*text, author*) zitieren; (*price*) nennen ▷ *n* Zitat *nt*; (*price*) Kostenvoranschlag *m*; **in ~s** in Anführungszeichen

R

rabbi [ræbaɪ] *n* Rabbiner *m*

rabbit [ræbɪt] *n* Kaninchen *nt*

rabies [reɪbiz] *nsing* Tollwut *f*

raccoon [rækun] *n* Waschbär *m*

race [reɪs] *n* (*competition*) Rennen *nt*; (*people*) Rasse *f* ▷ *vt* um die Wette laufen/fahren ▷ *vi* (*rush*) rennen

racehorse [reɪshɔrs] *n* Rennpferd *nt*

racetrack [reɪstræk] *n* Rennbahn *f*

racial [reɪʃˀl] *adj* Rassen-; **~ discrimination** Rassendiskriminierung *f*

racing [reɪsɪŋ] *n*: **horse ~** Pferderennen *nt*; **motor ~** Autorennen *nt*

racing car *n* Rennwagen *m*

racism [reɪsɪzəm] *n* Rassismus *m*

racist [reɪsɪst] *n* Rassist(in) *m(f)* ▷ *adj* rassistisch

rack [ræk] *n* Ständer *m*, Gestell *nt* ▷ *vt*: **to ~ one's brains** sich *dat* den Kopf zerbrechen

racket [rækɪt] *n* (*Sport*) Schläger *m*; (*noise*) Krach *m*

radar [reɪdər] *n* Radar *nt o m*

radar trap *n* Radarfalle *f*

radiation [reɪdieɪʃˀn] *n* (*radioactive*) Strahlung *f*

radiator [reɪdieɪtər] *n* Heizkörper *m*; (*Auto*) Kühler *m*

radical [rædɪkˀl] *adj* radikal

radio [reɪdiou] (*pl* **-s**) *n* Rundfunk *m*, Radio *nt*

radioactivity [reɪdiouæktɪvɪti] *n* Radioaktivität *f*

radio alarm clock *n* Radiowecker *m*

radio station *n* Rundfunkstation *f*

radiotherapy [reɪdiouθɛrəpi] *n* Strahlenbehandlung *f*

radish [rædɪʃ] *n* Radieschen *nt*

radius [reɪdiəs] *n* Radius *m*; **within a five-mile ~** im Umkreis von fünf Meilen (*of* um)

raffle [ræfˀl] *n* Tombola *f*

raffle ticket *n* Los *nt*

raft [ræft] *n* Floß *nt*

rag [ræg] *n* Lumpen *m*; (*for cleaning*) Lappen *m*

rage [reɪdʒ] *n* Wut *f*; **to be all the ~** der letzte Schrei sein ▷ *vi* toben; (*disease*) wüten

raid [reɪd] *n* Überfall *m* (*on* auf +*akk*); (*by police*) Razzia *f* (*on* gegen) ▷ *vt* (*bank etc*) überfallen; (*by police*) eine Razzia machen in +*dat*

rail [reɪl] *n* (*on stairs, balcony etc*) Geländer *nt*; (*of ship*) Reling *f*; (*Rail*) Schiene *f*

railing [reɪlɪŋ] *n* Geländer *nt*; **~s** *pl* (*fence*) Zaun *m*

railroad [reɪlroud] *n* Eisenbahn *f*

railroad crossing *n* (schienengleicher) Bahnübergang *m*

railroad station *n* Bahnhof *m*

rain [reɪn] *n* Regen *m* ▷ *vi* regnen; **it's ~ing** es regnet

rainbow [reɪnbou] *n* Regenbogen *m*

raincoat [reɪnkout] *n* Regenmantel *m*

rainfall [reɪnfɔl] *n* Niederschlag *m*

rainfly *n* Überzelt *nt*

rain forest *n* Regenwald *m*

rainy [reɪni] *adj* regnerisch

raise [reɪz] *n* (*of wages/salary*) Gehalts-/Lohnerhöhung *f* ▷ *vt* (*lift*) hochheben; (*increase*) erhöhen; (*family*) großziehen; (*livestock*) züchten; (*money*) aufbringen; (*objection*) erheben; **to ~ one's voice** (*in anger*) laut werden

raisin [reɪzˀn] *n* Rosine *f*

rally [ræli] *n* (*Pol*) Kundgebung *f*; (*Auto*) Rallye *f*; (*Tennis*) Ballwechsel *m*

RAM [ræm] (*acr*) = **random access memory** RAM *m*

ramble [ræmbˀl] *n* Wanderung *f* ▷ *vi* (*walk*) wandern; (*talk*) schwafeln

ramp [ræmp] *n* Rampe *f*

ran [ræn] *pt of* **run**

ranch [ræntʃ] *n* Ranch *f*

rancid [rænsɪd] *adj* ranzig

random [rændəm] *adj* willkürlich ▷ *n*: **at ~** (*choose*) willkürlich; (*fire*) ziellos

rang [ræŋ] *pt of* **ring**

range [reɪndʒ] *n* (*selection*) Auswahl *f* (*of* an +*dat*); (*Comm*) Sortiment *nt* (*of* an +*dat*); (*of missile, telescope*) Reichweite *f*; (*of mountains*) Kette *f*; **in this price ~** in dieser Preisklasse ▷ *vi*: **to ~ from … to …** gehen von … bis …; (*temperature, sizes, prices*) liegen zwischen … und …

rank [ræŋk] *n* (*Mil*) Rang *m*; (*social position*) Stand *m* ▷ *vt* einstufen

ransom [rænsəm] *n* Lösegeld *nt*

rap [ræp] *n* (*Mus*) Rap *m*

rape [reɪp] *n* Vergewaltigung *f* ▷ *vt* vergewaltigen

rapid [ræpɪd] *adj*, **rapidly** *adv* schnell

rapist [reɪpɪst] *n* Vergewaltiger *m*

rare [rɛər] *adj* selten, rar; (*especially good*)

vortrefflich; (*steak*) blutig

rarely [ˈrɛərli] *adv* selten

rarity [ˈrɛərɪti] *n* Seltenheit *f*

rash [ræʃ] *adj* unbesonnen ▷ *n* (*Med*) (Haut)
ausschlag *m*

raspberry [ˈrɑːzbɛri] *n* Himbeere *f*

rat [ræt] *n* Ratte *f*; (*pej: person*) Schwein *nt*

rate [reɪt] *n* (*proportion, frequency*) Rate *f*;
(*speed*) Tempo *nt*; ~ **of exchange** (Wechsel)kurs *m*; ~ **of inflation** Inflationsrate *f*;
~ **of interest** Zinssatz *m*; **at any** ~ auf jeden
Fall ▷ *vt* (*evaluate*) einschätzen (*as* als)

rather [ˈrɑːðər] *adv* (*in preference*) lieber;
(*fairly*) ziemlich; **I'd** ~ **stay here** ich würde
lieber hierbleiben; **I'd** ~ **not** lieber nicht;
or ~ (*more accurately*) vielmehr

ratio [ˈreɪʃəʊ, -ʃiəʊ] (*pl* -**s**) *n* Verhältnis *nt*

rational [ˈræʃənˀl] *adj* rational

rationalize [ˈræʃnˀlaɪz] *vt* rationalisieren

rattle [ˈrætˀl] *n* (*toy*) Rassel *f* ▷ *vt* (*keys,
coins*) klimpern mit; (*person*) durcheinanderbringen ▷ *vi* (*window*) klappern; (*bot-
tles*) klirren

rattle off *vt* herunterrasseln

rattlesnake [ˈrætˀlsneɪk] *n* Klapperschlange *f*

rave [reɪv] *vi* (*talk wildly*) fantasieren;
(*rage*) toben; (*enthuse*) schwärmen (*about*
von)

raven [ˈreɪvˀn] *n* Rabe *m*

raving [ˈreɪvɪŋ] *adv*: ~ **mad** total verrückt

ravishing [ˈrævɪʃɪŋ] *adj* hinreißend

raw [rɔː] *adj* (*food*) roh; (*skin*) wund; (*climate*) rau

ray [reɪ] *n* (*of light*) Strahl *m*; **ray of hope**
Hoffnungsschimmer *m*

razor [ˈreɪzər] *n* Rasierapparat *m*

razor blade *n* Rasierklinge *f*

Rd *n* (*abbr*) = **road** Str.

re [riː] *prep* (*Comm*) betreffs +*gen*

reach [riːtʃ] *n*: **within/out of sb's** ~ in/außer
(jds) Reichweite; **within easy** ~ **of the
shops** nicht weit von den Geschäften ▷ *vt*
(*arrive at, contact*) erreichen; (*come down/
up as far as*) reichen bis zu; (*contact*): **can
you** ~ **it?** kommst du/kommen Sie dran?

reach for *vt* greifen nach

reach out *vi* die Hand ausstrecken; **to** ~ **for**
greifen nach

react [riˈækt] *vi* reagieren (*to* auf +*akk*)

reaction [riˈækʃˀn] *n* Reaktion *f* (*to* auf
+*akk*)

reactor [riˈæktər] *n* Reaktor *m*

read [riːd] (**read, read**) *vt* lesen; (*meter*)
ablesen; **to** ~ **sth to sb** jdm etw vorlesen
▷ *vi* lesen; **to** ~ **to sb** jdm vorlesen; **it** ~**s
well** es liest sich gut; **it** ~**s as follows** es
lautet folgendermaßen

readable [ˈriːdəbˀl] *adj* (*book*) lesenswert;
(*handwriting*) lesbar

reader [ˈriːdər] *n* Leser(in) *m(f)*

readership [ˈriːdərʃɪp] *n* Leserschaft *f*

readily [ˈrɛdɪli] *adv* (*willingly*) bereitwillig;
~ **available** leicht erhältlich

reading [ˈriːdɪŋ] *n* (*action*) Lesen *nt*; (*from
meter*) Zählerstand *m*

reading glasses *npl* Lesebrille *f*

reading lamp *n* Leselampe *f*

reading list *n* Leseliste *f*

reading matter *n* Lektüre *f*

readjust [riːədˈʒʌst] *vt* (*mechanism etc*) neu
einstellen ▷ *vi* sich wieder anpassen (*to*
an +*akk*)

read out *vt* vorlesen

read through *vt* durchlesen

read up on *vt* nachlesen über +*akk*

ready [ˈrɛdi] *adj* fertig, bereit; **to be** ~ **to do
sth** (*willing*) bereit sein, etw zu tun; **are
you** ~ **to go?** bist du so weit?; **to get sth** ~
etw fertig machen; **to get oneself** ~ sich
fertig machen

ready cash *n* Bargeld *nt*

ready-made *adj* (*product*) Fertig-; (*clothes*)
Konfektions-; ~ **meal** Fertiggericht *nt*

real [rɪəl] *adj* wirklich; (*actual*) eigentlich;
(*genuine*) echt; (*idiot etc*) richtig ▷ *adv*
(*fam*) echt; **for** ~ echt; **this time it's for** ~
diesmal ist es ernst; **get** ~ sei realistisch!

real estate *n* Immobilien *pl*

realistic [rɪəˈlɪstɪk] *adj*, **realistically** *adv*
realistisch

reality [riˈælɪti] *n* Wirklichkeit *f*; **in** ~ in
Wirklichkeit

reality TV *n* Reality-TV *nt*

realization [rɪəlaɪˈzeɪʃˀn] *n* (*awareness*)
Erkenntnis *f*

realize [ˈrɪəlaɪz] *vt* (*understand*) begreifen;
(*plan, idea*) realisieren; **I** ~**d that ...** mir
wurde klar, dass ...

really [ˈrɪəli] *adv* wirklich

real time *n* (*Inform*): **in** ~ in Echtzeit

Realtor® *n* Grundstücksmakler(in) *m(f)*

reappear [riːəˈpɪər] *vi* wieder erscheinen

rear [rɪər] *adj* hintere(r, s), Hinter- ▷ *n* (*of
building, vehicle*) hinterer Teil; **at the** ~ **of**
hinter +*dat*; (*inside*) hinten in +*dat*

rearm [riːˈɑːrm] *vi* wieder aufrüsten

rearrange [riːəˈreɪndʒ] *vt* (*furniture, system*)
umstellen; (*meeting*) verlegen (*for* auf
+*akk*)

rearview mirror [rɪərvyu mɪrər] n Rückspiegel m

rear window n (Auto) Heckscheibe f

reason [riz²n] n (cause) Grund m (for für); (ability to think) Verstand m; (common sense) Vernunft f; **for some ~** aus irgendeinem Grund ▷ vi: **to ~ with sb** mit jdm vernünftig reden

reasonable [rizənəb²l] adj (person, price) vernünftig; (offer) akzeptabel; (chance) reell; (food, weather) ganz gut

reasonably [rizənəbli] adv vernünftig; (fairly) ziemlich

reassure [rɪəʃʊər] vt beruhigen; **she ~d me that ...** sie versicherte mir, dass ...

rebel [n rɛbəl, vb rɪbɛl] n Rebell(in) m(f) ▷ vi rebellieren

rebellion [rɪbɛlyən] n Aufstand m

reboot [ributt] vt, vi (Inform) rebooten

rebound [rɪbaʊnd] vi (ball etc) zurückprallen

rebuild [ribɪld] (irr) vt wieder aufbauen

recall [rɪkɔl] vt (remember) sich erinnern an +akk; (call back) zurückrufen

recap [rikæp] vt, vi rekapitulieren

receipt [rɪsit] n (document) Quittung f; (receiving) Empfang m; **~s** pl (money) Einnahmen pl

receive [rɪsiv] vt (news etc) erhalten, bekommen; (visitor) empfangen

receiver [rɪsivər] n (Tel) Hörer m; (Radio) Empfänger m

recent [ris²nt] adj (event) vor Kurzem stattgefunden; (photo) neueste(r,s); (invention) neu; **in ~ years** in den letzten Jahren

recently [ris²ntli] adv vor Kurzem; (in the last few days or weeks) in letzter Zeit

reception [rɪsɛpʃ²n] n Empfang m

receptionist [rɪsɛpʃənɪst] n (in hotel) Empfangschef m, Empfangsdame f; (woman in firm) Empfangsdame f; (Med) Sprechstundenhilfe f

recess [risɛs, rɪsɛs] n (in wall) Nische f; (in school) Pause f

recession [rɪsɛʃ²n] n Rezession f

recharge [ritʃɑrdʒ] vt (battery) aufladen

rechargeable [ritʃɑrdʒəb²l] adj wiederaufladbar

recipe [rɛsɪpi] n Rezept nt (for für)

recipient [rɪsɪpiənt] n Empfänger(in) m(f)

reciprocal [rɪsɪprək²l] adj gegenseitig

recite [rɪsaɪt] vt vortragen; (details) aufzählen

reckless [rɛklɪs] adj leichtsinnig; (driving)

gefährlich

reckon [rɛkən] vt (calculate) schätzen; (think) glauben ▷ vi: **to ~ with/on** rechnen mit

reclaim [rɪkleɪm] vt (baggage) abholen; (expenses, tax) zurückverlangen

recline [rɪklaɪn] vi (person) sich zurücklehnen

recliner [rɪklaɪnər] n Liegesitz m

recognition [rɛkəgnɪʃ²n] n (acknowledgement) Anerkennung f; **in ~ of** in Anerkennung +gen

recognize [rɛkəgnaɪz] vt erkennen; (approve officially) anerkennen

recommend [rɛkəmɛnd] vt empfehlen

recommendation [rɛkəmɛndeɪʃ²n] n Empfehlung f

reconfirm [rikənfɜrm] vt (flight etc) rückbestätigen

reconsider [rikənsɪdər] vt noch einmal überdenken ▷ vi es sich dat noch einmal überlegen

reconstruct [rikənstrʌkt] vt wieder aufbauen; (crime) rekonstruieren

record [adj rɛkərd, vb rɪkɔrd] n (Mus) (Schall)platte f; (best performance) Rekord m; **~s** pl (files) Akten pl; **to keep a ~ of** Buch führen über +akk ▷ adj (time etc) Rekord- ▷ vt (write down) aufzeichnen; (on tape etc) aufnehmen; **~ed message** Ansage f

recorder [rɪkɔrdər] n (Mus) Blockflöte f; **cassette ~** (Kassetten)rekorder m

recording [rɪkɔrdɪŋ] n (on tape etc) Aufnahme f

record player n Plattenspieler m

recover [rɪkʌvər] vt (money, item) zurückbekommen; (appetite, strength) wiedergewinnen ▷ vi sich erholen

recreation [rɛkrieɪʃən] n Erholung f

recreational [rɛkrieɪʃən²l] adj Freizeit-; **~ vehicle** Wohnmobil nt

recruit [rɪkrut] n (Mil) Rekrut(in) m(f); (in firm, organization) neues Mitglied ▷ vt (Mil) rekrutieren; (members) anwerben; (staff) einstellen

recruitment agency [rɪkrutmənt eɪdʒənsi] n Personalagentur f

rectangle [rɛktæŋg²l] n Rechteck nt

rectangular [rɛktæŋgyələr] adj rechteckig

rectify [rɛktɪfaɪ] vt berichtigen

recuperate [rɪkupəreɪt] vi sich erholen

recyclable [risaɪkləb²l] adj recycelbar, wiederverwertbar

recycle [risaɪk²l] vt recyceln, wiederverwerten; **~d paper** Recyclingpapier *nt*

recycling [riːsaɪkᵊlɪŋ] *n* Recycling *nt*, Wiederverwertung *f*

red [rɛd] *adj* rot ▷ *n*: **in the red** in den roten Zahlen

red cabbage *n* Rotkohl *m*

Red Cross *n* Rotes Kreuz

red currant *n* (rote) Johannisbeere

redeem [riːdiːm] *vt* (*Comm*) einlösen

red-handed [rɛdhændɪd] *adj*: **to catch sb ~** jdn auf frischer Tat ertappen

redhead [rɛdhɛd] *n* Rothaarige(r) *mf*

redial [riːdaɪəl] *vt, vi* nochmals wählen

redirect [riːdɪrɛkt, -daɪ-] *vt* (*traffic*) umleiten; (*forward*) nachsenden

red light *n* (*traffic signal*) rotes Licht; **to go through the ~** bei Rot über die Ampel fahren

red meat *n* Rind-, Lamm-, Rehfleisch

redo [riːduː] (*irr*) *vt* nochmals machen

reduce [rɪdjuːs] *vt* reduzieren (*to* auf *+akk by* um)

reduction [rɪdʌkʃᵊn] *n* Reduzierung *f*; (*in price*) Ermäßigung *f*

redundant [rɪdʌndənt] *adj* überflüssig; **to be made ~** entlassen werden

red wine *n* Rotwein *m*

reef [riːf] *n* Riff *nt*

reel [riːl] *n* Spule *f*; (*on fishing rod*) Rolle *f*

reel off *vt* herunterrasseln

ref [rɛf] *n* (*fam: referee*) Schiri *m*

refectory [rɪfɛktərɪ] *n* (*at college*) Mensa *f*

refer [rɪfɜːr] *vt*: **to ~ sb to sb/sth** jdn an jdn/ etw verweisen; **to ~ sth to sb** (*query, problem*) etw an jdn weiterleiten ▷ *vi*: **to ~ to** (*mention, allude to*) sich beziehen auf *+akk*; (*book*) nachschlagen in *+dat*

referee [rɛfəriː] *n* Schiedsrichter(in) *m(f)*; (*in boxing*) Ringrichter *m*

reference [rɛfərəns, rɛfrəns] *n* (*allusion*) Anspielung *f* (*to* auf *+akk*); (*for job*) Referenz *f*; (*in book*) Verweis *m*; **~ number** (*in document*) Aktenzeichen *nt*; **with ~ to** mit Bezug auf *+akk*

reference book *n* Nachschlagewerk *nt*

referendum [rɛfərɛndəm] (*pl* **referenda**) *n* Referendum *nt*

refill [*vb* riːfɪl, *n* riːfɪl] *vt* nachfüllen ▷ *n* (*for ballpoint pen*) Ersatzmine *f*

refine [rɪfaɪn] *vt* (*purify*) raffinieren; (*improve*) verfeinern

refined [rɪfaɪnd] *adj* (*genteel*) fein

reflect [rɪflɛkt] *vt* reflektieren; (*fig*) widerspiegeln ▷ *vi* nachdenken (*on* über *+akk*)

reflection [rɪflɛkʃᵊn] *n* (*image*) Spiegelbild

nt; (*thought*) Überlegung *f*; **on ~** nach reiflicher Überlegung

reflex [riːflɛks] *n* Reflex *m*

reform [rɪfɔːrm] *n* Reform *f* ▷ *vt* reformieren; (*person*) bessern

refrain [rɪfreɪn] *vi*: **to ~ from doing sth** es unterlassen, etw zu tun

refresh [rɪfrɛʃ] *vt* erfrischen

refresher course [rɪfrɛʃər kɔːrs] *n* Auffrischungskurs *m*

refreshing [rɪfrɛʃɪŋ] *adj* erfrischend

refreshments [rɪfrɛʃmənts] *npl* Erfrischungen *pl*

refrigerator [rɪfrɪdʒəreɪtər] *n* Kühlschrank *m*

refuel [riːfjuːəl] *vt, vi* auftanken

refugee [rɛfjudʒiː] *n* Flüchtling *m*

refund [*n* riːfʌnd, *vb* rɪfʌnd] *n* (*of money*) Rückerstattung *f*; **to get a ~ on sth** sein Geld (für etw) zurückbekommen ▷ *vt* zurückerstatten

refusal [rɪfjuːzᵊl] *n* (*to do sth*) Weigerung *f*

refuse [*n* rɛfjuːs, *vb* rɪfjuːz] *n* Müll *m*, Abfall *m* ▷ *vt* ablehnen; **to ~ sb sth** jdm etw verweigern; **to ~ to do sth** sich weigern, etw zu tun ▷ *vi* sich weigern

regain [rɪgeɪn] *vt* wiedergewinnen, wiedererlangen; **to ~ consciousness** wieder zu Bewusstsein kommen

regard [rɪgɑːrd] *n*: **with ~ to** in Bezug auf *+akk*; **in this ~** in dieser Hinsicht; **~s** (*at end of letter*) mit freundlichen Grüßen; **give my ~s to ...** viele Grüße an ... *+akk* ▷ *vt*: **to ~ sb/sth as sth** jdn/etw als etw betrachten; **as ~s ...** was ... betrifft

regarding [rɪgɑːrdɪŋ] *prep* bezüglich *+gen*

regardless [rɪgɑːrdlɪs] *adj*: **~ of** ohne Rücksicht auf *+akk* ▷ *adv* trotzdem; **to carry on ~** einfach weitermachen

regime [rəʒiːm, reɪ-] *n* (*Pol*) Regime *nt*

region [riːdʒᵊn] *n* (*of country*) Region *f*, Gebiet *nt*; **in the ~ of** (*about*) ungefähr

regional [riːdʒənᵊl] *adj* regional

register [rɛdʒɪstər] *n* Register *nt*; (*school*) Namensliste *f* ▷ *vt* (*with an authority*) registrieren lassen; (*birth, death, vehicle*) anmelden ▷ *vi* (*at hotel, for course*) sich anmelden; (*at university*) sich einschreiben

registered [rɛdʒɪstərd] *adj* eingetragen; (*letter*) eingeschrieben; **by ~ post** per Einschreiben

registration [rɛdʒɪstreɪʃᵊn] *n* (*for course*) Anmeldung *f*; (*at university*) Einschreibung *f*; (*Auto: number*) (polizeiliches)

Kennzeichen

registration form n Anmeldeformular nt

regret [rɪgrɛt] n Bedauern nt ▷ vt bedauern

regrettable [rɪgrɛtəbᵊl] adj bedauerlich

regular [rɛgyələr] adj regelmäßig; (size) normal ▷ n (client) Stammkunde m, Stammkundin f; (in bar) Stammgast m; (gas) Normalbenzin nt

regularly [rɛgyələrli] adv regelmäßig

regulate [rɛgyəleɪt] vt regulieren; (using rules) regeln

regulation [rɛgyəleɪʃᵊn] n (rule) Vorschrift f

rehabilitation [riˌhəbɪlɪteɪʃᵊn] n Rehabilitation f

rehearsal [rɪhɜrsᵊl] n Probe f

rehearse [rɪhɜrs] vt, vi proben

reign [reɪn] n Herrschaft f ▷ vi herrschen (over über +akk)

reimburse [riɪmbɜrs] vt (person) entschädigen; (expenses) zurückerstatten

reindeer [reɪndɪər] n Rentier nt

reinforce [riɪnfɔrs] vt verstärken

reinstate [riɪnsteɪt] vt (employee) wieder einstellen; (passage in text) wieder aufnehmen

reject [vb rɪdʒɛkt, n rɪdʒɛkt] n (Comm) Ausschussartikel m ▷ vt ablehnen

rejection [rɪdʒɛkʃᵊn] n Ablehnung f

relapse [rɪlæps] n Rückfall m

relate [rɪleɪt] vt (story) erzählen; (connect) in Verbindung bringen (to mit) ▷ vi: to ~ to (refer) sich beziehen auf +akk

related [rɪleɪtɪd] adj verwandt (to mit)

relation [rɪleɪʃᵊn] n (relative) Verwandte(r) mf; (connection) Beziehung f; ~s pl (dealings) Beziehungen pl

relationship [rɪleɪʃᵊnʃɪp] n (connection) Beziehung f; (between people) Verhältnis nt

relative [rɛlətɪv] n Verwandte(r) mf ▷ adj relativ

relatively [rɛlətɪvli] adv relativ, verhältnismäßig

relax [rɪlæks] vi sich entspannen; ~! reg dich nicht auf! ▷ vt (grip, conditions) lockern

relaxation [riˌlækseɪʃᵊn] n (rest) Entspannung f

relaxed [rɪlækst] adj entspannt

relaxing [rɪlæksɪŋ] adj entspannend

release [rɪliːs] n (from prison) Entlassung f; **new/recent ~** (film, CD) Neuerscheinung f ▷ vt (animal, hostage) freilassen; (prisoner) entlassen; (handbrake) lösen; (news) veröffentlichen; (film, CD) herausbringen

relent [rɪlɛnt] vi nachgeben

relentless [rɪlɛntlɪs] adj, **relentlessly** adv (merciless) erbarmungslos; (neverending) unaufhörlich

relevance [rɛləvᵊns] n Relevanz f (to für)

relevant [rɛləvᵊnt] adj relevant (to für)

reliable [rɪlaɪəbᵊl] adj, **reliably** adv zuverlässig

reliant [rɪlaɪənt] adj: ~ **on** abhängig von

relic [rɛlɪk] n (from past) Relikt nt

relief [rɪliːf] n (from anxiety, pain) Erleichterung f; (assistance) Hilfe f

relieve [rɪliːv] vt (pain) lindern; (boredom) überwinden; (take over from) ablösen; **I'm ~d** ich bin erleichtert

religion [rɪlɪdʒᵊn] n Religion f

religious [rɪlɪdʒəs] adj religiös

relish [rɛlɪʃ] n (for food) würzige Soße ▷ vt (enjoy) genießen; **I don't ~ the thought of it** der Gedanke behagt mir gar nicht

reluctant [rɪlʌktənt] adj widerwillig; **to be ~ to do sth** etw nur ungern tun

reluctantly [rɪlʌktəntli] adv widerwillig

rely on [rɪlaɪ ɒn] vt sich verlassen auf +akk; (depend on) abhängig sein von

remain [rɪmeɪn] vi bleiben; (be left over) übrig bleiben

remainder [rɪmeɪndər] n (a. Math) Rest m

remaining [rɪmeɪnɪŋ] adj übrig

remains npl Überreste pl

remark [rɪmɑrk] n Bemerkung f ▷ vt: **to ~ that** bemerken, dass ▷ vi: **to ~ on sth** über etw akk eine Bemerkung machen

remarkable [rɪmɑrkəbᵊl] adj, **remarkably** adv bemerkenswert

remarry [riˌmæri] vi wieder heiraten

remedy [rɛmədi] n Mittel nt (for gegen) ▷ vt abhelfen +dat

remember [rɪmɛmbər] vt sich erinnern an +akk; **to ~ to do sth** daran denken, etw zu tun; **I ~ seeing her** ich erinnere mich daran, sie gesehen zu haben; **I must ~ that** das muss ich mir merken ▷ vi sich erinnern

remind [rɪmaɪnd] vt: **to ~ sb of/about sb/ sth** jdn an jdn/etw erinnern; **to ~ sb to do sth** jdn daran erinnern, etw zu tun; **that ~s me ...** dabei fällt mir ein ...

reminder [rɪmaɪndər] n (to pay) Mahnung f

reminisce [rɛmɪnɪs] vi in Erinnerungen schwelgen (about an +akk)

reminiscent [rɛmɪnɪsənt] adj: **to be ~ of**

r

erinnern an +*akk*

remittance [rɪmɪtᵊns] *n* Überweisung *f* (*to* an +*akk*)

remnant [rɛmnənt] *n* Rest *m*

remote [rɪmout] *adj* (*place*) abgelegen; (*slight*) gering ▷ *n* (*TV*) Fernbedienung *f*

remote control *n* Fernsteuerung *f*; (*device*) Fernbedienung *f*

removal [rɪmuːvᵊl] *n* Entfernung *f*

remove [rɪmuːv] *vt* entfernen; (*lid*) abnehmen; (*clothes*) ausziehen; (*doubt, suspicion*) zerstreuen

rename [riːneɪm] *vt* umbenennen

renew [rɪnjuː] *vt* erneuern; (*license, passport, library book*) verlängern lassen

renewable [rɪnjuːəbᵊl] *adj* (*energy*) erneuerbar

renounce [rɪnauns] *vt* verzichten auf +*akk*; (*faith, opinion*) abschwören +*dat*

renovate [rɛnəveɪt] *vt* renovieren

renowned [rɪnaund] *adj* berühmt (*for* für)

rent [rɛnt] *n* Miete *f*; **for ~** zu vermieten ▷ *vt* (*as hirer, tenant*) mieten; (*as owner*) vermieten; **~ed car** Mietwagen *m*

rental [rɛntᵊl] *n* Miete *f*; (*for car, TV etc*) Leihgebühr *f* ▷ *adj* Miet-

rent out *vt* vermieten

reorganize [riːɔːrɡənaɪz] *vt* umorganisieren

rep [rɛp] *n* (*Comm*) Vertreter(in) *m(f)*

repair [rɪpɛər] *n* Reparatur *f* ▷ *vt* reparieren; (*damage*) wiedergutmachen

repair kit *n* Flickzeug *nt*

repay [rɪpeɪ] *vt* (*irr*) (*money*) zurückzahlen; **to ~ sb for sth** (*fig*) sich bei jdm für etw revanchieren

repeat [rɪpiːt] *n* (*Radio, TV*) Wiederholung *f* ▷ *vt* wiederholen

repetition [rɛpɪtɪʃᵊn] *n* Wiederholung *f*

repetitive [rɪpɛtɪtɪv] *adj* sich wiederholend

rephrase [riːfreɪz] *vt* anders formulieren

replace [rɪpleɪs] *vt* ersetzen (*with* durch); (*put back*) zurückstellen, zurücklegen

replacement [rɪpleɪsmənt] *n* (*thing, person*) Ersatz *m*; (*temporarily in job*) Vertretung *f*

replacement part *n* Ersatzteil *nt*

replay [*n* riːpleɪ, *vb* riːpleɪ] *n*: **instant ~** Wiederholung *f* ▷ *vt* (*game*) wiederholen

replica [rɛplɪkə] *n* Kopie *f*

reply [rɪplaɪ] *n* Antwort *f* ▷ *vi* antworten; **to ~ to sb/sth** jdm/auf etw *akk* antworten ▷ *vt*: **to ~ that** antworten, dass

report [rɪpɔrt] *n* Bericht *m*; (*school*) Zeug-

nis *nt* ▷ *vt* (*tell*) berichten; (*give information against*) melden; (*to police*) anzeigen ▷ *vi* (*present oneself*) sich melden; **to ~ sick** sich krankmelden

report card *n* (*school*) Zeugnis *nt*

reporter [rɪpɔrtər] *n* Reporter(in) *m(f)*

represent [rɛprɪzɛnt] *vt* darstellen; (*speak for*) vertreten

representation [rɛprɪzɛnteɪʃᵊn] *n* (*picture etc*) Darstellung *f*

representative [rɛprɪzɛntətɪv] *n* Vertreter(in) *m(f)*; (*Pol*) Abgeordnete(r) *mf* ▷ *adj* repräsentativ (*of* für)

reprimand [rɛprɪmænd] *n* Tadel *m* ▷ *vt* tadeln

reprint [riːprɪnt] *n* Nachdruck *m*

reproduce [riːprədjuːs] *vt* (*copy*) reproduzieren ▷ *vi* (*Bio*) sich fortpflanzen

reproduction [riːprədʌkʃᵊn] *n* (*copy*) Reproduktion *f*; (*Bio*) Fortpflanzung *f*

reptile [rɛptaɪl, -tɪl] *n* Reptil *nt*

republic [rɪpʌblɪk] *n* Republik *f*

republican [rɪpʌblɪkən] *adj* republikanisch ▷ *n* Republikaner(in) *m(f)*

repulsive [rɪpʌlsɪv] *adj* abstoßend

reputable [rɛpyətəbᵊl] *adj* seriös

reputation [rɛpyəteɪʃᵊn] *n* Ruf *m*; **he has a ~ for being difficult** er hat den Ruf, schwierig zu sein

request [rɪkwɛst] *n* Bitte *f* (*for* um); **on ~** auf Wunsch ▷ *vt* bitten um; **to ~ sb to do sth** jdn bitten, etw zu tun

require [rɪkwaɪər] *vt* (*need*) brauchen; (*desire*) verlangen; **what qualifications are ~d?** welche Qualifikationen sind erforderlich?

required [rɪkwaɪərd] *adj* erforderlich

requirement [rɪkwaɪərmənt] *n* (*condition*) Anforderung *f*; (*need*) Bedingung *f*

rerun [riːrʌn] *n* Wiederholung *f*

rescue [rɛskyu] *n* Rettung *f*; **to come to sb's ~** jdm zu Hilfe kommen ▷ *vt* retten

rescue party *n* Rettungsmannschaft *f*

research [rɪsɜrtʃ, riːsɜrtʃ] *n* Forschung *f* ▷ *vi* forschen (*into* über +*akk*) ▷ *vt* erforschen

researcher [rɪsɜrtʃər, riːsɜrtʃər] *n* Forscher(in) *m(f)*

resemblance [rɪzɛmbləns] *n* Ähnlichkeit *f* (*to* mit)

resemble [rɪzɛmbᵊl] *vt* ähneln +*dat*

resent [rɪzɛnt] *vt* übel nehmen

reservation [rɛzərveɪʃᵊn] *n* (*booking*) Reservierung *f*; (*doubt*) Vorbehalt *m*; **I have a ~** (*in hotel, restaurant*) ich habe reserviert

reserve [rɪzɜːrv] n (*store*) Vorrat m (*of an* +*dat*); (*manner*) Zurückhaltung f; (*Sport*) Reservespieler(in) m(f); (*game reserve*) Naturschutzgebiet nt ▷ vt (*book in advance*) reservieren

reserved [rɪzɜːrvd] adj reserviert

reservoir [rɛzərvwɑr] n (*for water*) Reservoir nt

reside [rɪzaɪd] vi wohnen

residence [rɛzɪdəns] n Wohnsitz m; (*living*) Aufenthalt m; ~ **permit** Aufenthaltsgenehmigung f; ~ **hall** Studentenwohnheim nt

resident [rɛzɪdənt] n (*in house*) Bewohner(in) m(f); (*in town, area*) Einwohner(in) m(f)

resign [rɪzaɪn] vt (*post*) zurücktreten von; (*job*) kündigen ▷ vi (*from post*) zurücktreten; (*from job*) kündigen

resignation [rɛzɪɡneɪʃ°n] n (*from post*) Rücktritt m; (*from job*) Kündigung f

resigned [rɪzaɪnd] adj resigniert; **he is ~ to it** er hat sich damit abgefunden

resist [rɪzɪst] vt widerstehen +*dat*

resistance [rɪzɪstəns] n Widerstand m (*to* gegen)

resolution [rɛzəluːʃ°n] n (*intention*) Vorsatz m; (*decision*) Beschluss m

resolve [rɪzɒlv] vt (*problem*) lösen

resort [rɪzɔrt] n (*holiday resort*) Urlaubsort m; (*health resort*) Kurort m; **as a last ~** als letzter Ausweg ▷ vi: **to ~ to** greifen zu; (*violence*) anwenden

resources [rɪsɔrsɪz] npl (*money*) (Geld)mittel pl; (*mineral resources*) Bodenschätze pl

respect [rɪspɛkt] n Respekt m (*for* vor +*dat*); (*consideration*) Rücksicht f (*for* auf +*akk*); **with ~ to** in Bezug auf +*akk*; **in this ~** in dieser Hinsicht; **with all due ~** bei allem Respekt ▷ vt respektieren

respectable [rɪspɛktəb°l] adj (*person, family*) angesehen; (*district*) anständig; (*achievement, result*) beachtlich

respected [rɪspɛktɪd] adj angesehen

respective [rɪspɛktɪv] adj jeweilig

respectively [rɪspɛktɪvli] adv: **5 % and 10 % ~** 5 % beziehungsweise 10 %

respiratory [rɛspərətɔri] adj: ~ **problems** o **trouble** Atembeschwerden pl

respond [rɪspɒnd] vi antworten (*to* auf +*akk*); (*react*) reagieren (*to* auf +*akk*); (*to treatment*) ansprechen (*to* auf +*akk*)

response [rɪspɒns] n Antwort f; (*reaction*) Reaktion f; **in ~ to** als Antwort auf +*akk*

responsibility [rɪspɒnsɪbɪliti] n Verantwortung f; **that's her ~** dafür ist sie verantwortlich

responsible [rɪspɒnsɪb°l] adj verantwortlich (*for* für); (*trustworthy*) verantwortungsbewusst; (*job*) verantwortungsvoll

rest [rɛst] n (*relaxation*) Ruhe f; (*break*) Pause f; (*remainder*) Rest m; **to have a ~** sich ausruhen; (*break*) Pause machen; **the ~ of the wine/the people** der Rest des Weins/der Leute ▷ vi (*relax*) sich ausruhen; (*lean*) lehnen (*on, against* an +*dat* gegen)

restaurant [rɛstərənt, -tərɑnt, -trɑnt] n Restaurant nt

restful [rɛstfəl] adj (*holiday etc*) erholsam, ruhig

restless [rɛstlɪs] adj unruhig

restore [rɪstɔr] vt (*painting, building*) restaurieren; (*order*) wiederherstellen; (*give back*) zurückgeben

restrain [rɪstreɪn] vt (*person, feelings*) zurückhalten; **to ~ oneself** sich beherrschen

restrict [rɪstrɪkt] vt beschränken (*to* auf +*akk*)

restricted [rɪstrɪktɪd] adj beschränkt

restriction [rɪstrɪkʃ°n] n Einschränkung f (*on* +*gen*)

restroom n Toilette f

rest stop, rest area n Parkbucht f; (*bigger*) Parkplatz m

result [rɪzʌlt] n Ergebnis nt; (*consequence*) Folge f; **as a ~ of** infolge +*gen* ▷ vi: **to ~ in** führen zu; **to ~ from** sich ergeben aus

resume [rɪzuːm] vt (*work, negotiations*) wieder aufnehmen; (*journey*) fortsetzen

résumé [rɛzəmeɪ] n Zusammenfassung f; (*curriculum vitae*) Lebenslauf m

resuscitate [rɪsʌsɪteɪt] vt wiederbeleben

retail [riteɪl] adv im Einzelhandel

retain [rɪteɪn] vt behalten; (*heat*) halten

rethink [riθɪŋk] (*irr*) vt noch einmal überdenken

retire [rɪtaɪər] vi (*from work*) in den Ruhestand treten; (*withdraw*) sich zurückziehen

retired [rɪtaɪərd] adj (*person*) pensioniert

retirement [rɪtaɪərmənt] n (*time of life*) Ruhestand m

retirement age n Rentenalter nt

retirement home n Altersheim nt

retrace [ritreɪs] vt zurückverfolgen

retrain [ritreɪn] vi sich umschulen lassen

retreat [rɪtriːt] n (*Mil*) Rückzug m (*from*

r

aus); (*refuge*) Zufluchtsort *m* ▷ *vi* (*Mil*) sich zurückziehen; (*step back*) zurückweichen

retrieve [rɪtriv] *vt* (*recover*) wiederbekommen; (*rescue*) retten; (*data*) abrufen

retrospect [rɛtrəspɛkt] *n*: **in ~** rückblickend

retrospective [rɛtrəspɛktɪv] *adj* rückblickend; (*pay rise*) rückwirkend

return [rɪtɜrn] *n* (*going back*) Rückkehr *f*; (*giving back*) Rückgabe *f*; (*profit*) Gewinn *m*; (*Tennis*) Return *m*; **in ~** als Gegenleistung (*for* für); **many happy ~s of the day** herzlichen Glückwunsch zum Geburtstag! ▷ *vi* (*person*) zurückkehren; (*doubts, symptoms*) wieder auftreten; **to ~ to school/ work** wieder in die Schule/die Arbeit gehen ▷ *vt* (*give back*) zurückgeben; **I ~ed his call** ich habe ihn zurückgerufen

returnable [rɪtɜrnəbˀl] *adj* (*bottle*) Pfand-

return flight *n* (*both ways*) Hin- und Rückflug *m*

return key *n* (*Inform*) Eingabetaste *f*

reunification [riyunɪfɪkeɪʃˀn] *n* Wiedervereinigung *f*

reunion [riyunɪən] *n* (*party*) Treffen *nt*

reunite [riyunaɪt] *vt* wieder vereinigen

reusable [riyuzəbˀl] *adj* wiederverwendbar

reveal [rɪvil] *vt* (*make known*) enthüllen; (*secret*) verraten; (*show*) zeigen

revealing [rɪvilɪŋ] *adj* aufschlussreich; (*dress*) freizügig

revenge [rɪvɛndʒ] *n* Rache *f*; (*in game*) Revanche *f*; **to take ~ on sb for sth** sich an jdm (für etw) rächen

revenue [rɛvənyu] *n* Einnahmen *pl*

reverse [rɪvɜrs] *n* (*back*) Rückseite *f*; (*opposite*) Gegenteil *nt*; (*Auto*): **~ gear** Rückwärtsgang *m* ▷ *adj*: **in ~ order** in umgekehrter Reihenfolge ▷ *vt* (*order*) umkehren; (*decision*) umstoßen; (*car*) zurücksetzen ▷ *vi* (*Auto*) rückwärtsfahren

review [rɪvyu] *n* (*of book, film etc*) Rezension *f*, Kritik *f*; **to be under ~** überprüft werden ▷ *vt* (*book, film etc*) rezensieren; (*re-examine*) überprüfen

revise [rɪvaɪz] *vt* revidieren; (*text*) überarbeiten

revision [rɪvɪʒˀn] *n* (*of text*) Überarbeitung *f*

revitalize [rivaɪtˀlaɪz] *vt* neu beleben

revive [rɪvaɪv] *vt* (*person*) wiederbeleben; (*tradition, interest*) wieder aufleben lassen ▷ *vi* (*regain consciousness*) wieder zu

sich kommen

revolt [rɪvoʊlt] *n* Aufstand *m*

revolting [rɪvoʊltɪŋ] *adj* widerlich

revolution [rɛvəluʃˀn] *n* (*Pol: fig*) Revolution *f*; (*turn*) Umdrehung *f*

revolutionary [rɛvəluʃənɛri] *adj* revolutionär ▷ *n* Revolutionär(in) *m(f)*

revolve [rɪvɒlv] *vi* sich drehen (*around* um)

revolver [rɪvɒlvər] *n* Revolver *m*

revolving door [rɪvɒlvɪŋ dɔr] *n* Drehtür *f*

reward [rɪwɔrd] *n* Belohnung *f* ▷ *vt* belohnen

rewarding [rɪwɔrdɪŋ] *adj* lohnend

rewind [riwaɪnd] (*irr*) *vt* (*tape*) zurückspulen

rewritable [riraɪtəbˀl] *adj* (*CD; DVD*) wiederbeschreibbar

rewrite [riraɪt] (*irr*) *vt* (*write again; recast*) umschreiben

rheumatism [rumətɪzəm] *n* Rheuma *nt*

Rhine [raɪn] *n* Rhein *m*

rhinoceros [raɪnɒsərəs] *n* Nashorn *nt*

Rhodes [roʊdz] *n* Rhodos *nt*

rhubarb [rubɑrb] *n* Rhabarber *m*

rhyme [raɪm] *n* Reim *m* ▷ *vi* sich reimen (*with* auf +*akk*)

rhythm [rɪðəm] *n* Rhythmus *m*

rib [rɪb] *n* Rippe *f*

ribbon [rɪbən] *n* Band *nt*

rice [raɪs] *n* Reis *m*

rice pudding *n* Milchreis *m*

rich [rɪtʃ] *adj* reich; (*food*) schwer ▷ *npl*: **the ~** die Reichen *pl*

rickety [rɪkɪti] *adj* wackelig

rid [rɪd] (*rid, rid*) *vt*: **to get rid of sb/sth** jdn/ etw loswerden

ridden [rɪdˀn] *pp of* **ride**

riddle [rɪdˀl] *n* Rätsel *nt*

ride [raɪd] (*rode, ridden*) *vt* (*horse*) reiten; (*bicycle*) fahren ▷ *vi* (*on horse*) reiten; (*on bike*) fahren ▷ *n* (*in vehicle, on bike*) Fahrt *f*; (*on horse*) (Aus)ritt *m*; **to go for a ~** (*in car, on bike*) spazieren fahren; (*on horse*) reiten gehen; **to take sb for a ~** (*fam*) jdn verarschen

rider [raɪdər] *n* (*on horse*) Reiter(in) *m(f)*; (*on bike*) Fahrer(in) *m(f)*

ridiculous [rɪdɪkyələs] *adj* lächerlich; **don't be ~** red keinen Unsinn!

riding [raɪdɪŋ] *n* Reiten *nt*; **to go ~** reiten gehen ▷ *adj* Reit-

rifle [raɪfˀl] *n* Gewehr *nt*

rig [rɪg] *n*: **oil rig** Bohrinsel *f* ▷ *vt* (*election etc*) manipulieren

right [raɪt] *adj (correct, just)* richtig; *(opposite of left)* rechte(r, s); *(clothes, job etc)* passend; **to be ~** *(person)* recht haben; *(clock)* richtig gehen; **that's ~** das stimmt! ▷ *n* Recht *nt (to* auf *+akk)*; *(side)* rechte Seite; **the R~** *(Pol)* die Rechte; **to take a ~** *(Auto)* rechts abbiegen; **on the ~** rechts *(of* von); **to the ~** nach rechts; *(on the right)* rechts *(of* von) ▷ *adv (towards the right)* nach rechts; *(directly)* direkt; *(exactly)* genau; **to turn ~** *(Auto)* rechts abbiegen; **~ away** sofort; **~ now** im Moment; *(immediately)* sofort

right angle *n* rechter Winkel

right-handed [raɪthændɪd] *adj*: **he is ~** er ist Rechtshänder

right-hand side *n* rechte Seite; **on the ~** auf der rechten Seite

rightly [raɪtlɪ] *adv* zu Recht

right of way *n*: **to have the ~** *(Auto)* Vorfahrt haben

right wing *n (Pol, Sport)* rechter Flügel

right-wing *adj* Rechts-; **~ extremist** Rechtsradikale(r) *mf*

rigid [rɪdʒɪd] *adj (stiff)* starr; *(strict)* streng

rigorous [rɪgərəs] *adj*, **rigorously** *adv* streng

rim [rɪm] *n (of cup etc)* Rand *m*; *(of wheel)* Felge *f*

rind [raɪnd] *n (of cheese)* Rinde *f*; *(of bacon)* Schwarte *f*; *(of fruit)* Schale *f*

ring [rɪŋ] *(rang, rung) vt, vi (bell)* läuten; *(Tel)* anrufen ▷ *n (on finger, in boxing)* Ring *m*; *(circle)* Kreis *m*; *(at circus)* Manege *f*; **to give sb a ~** *(Tel)* jdn anrufen

ring binder [rɪŋ baɪndər] *n* Ringbuch *nt*

ringleader [rɪŋliːdər] *n* Anführer(in) *m(f)*

ringtone [rɪŋtoʊn] *n* Klingelton *m*

rink [rɪŋk] *n (ice rink)* Eisbahn *f*; *(for roller-skating)* Rollschuhbahn *f*

rinse [rɪns] *vt* spülen

riot [raɪət] *n* Aufruhr *m*

rip [rɪp] *n* Riss *m* ▷ *vt* zerreißen; **to rip sth open** etw aufreißen ▷ *vi* reißen

ripe [raɪp] *adj (fruit)* reif

ripen [raɪpən] *vi* reifen

rip off *vt (fam: person)* übers Ohr hauen

rip-off [rɪpɔf] *n*: **that's a ~** *(fam: too expensive)* das ist Wucher

rip up *vt* zerreißen

rise [raɪz] *(rose, risen) vi (from sitting, lying)* aufstehen; *(sun)* aufgehen; *(prices, temperature)* steigen; *(ground)* ansteigen; *(in revolt)* sich erheben ▷ *n (increase)* Anstieg *m (in +gen)*; *(pay rise)* Gehaltser-

höhung *f*; *(to power, fame)* Aufstieg *m (to* zu); *(slope)* Steigung *f*

risen [rɪzˀn] *pp of* **rise**

risk [rɪsk] *n* Risiko *nt* ▷ *vt* riskieren; **to ~ doing sth** es riskieren, etw zu tun

risky [rɪskɪ] *adj* riskant

risotto [rɪsɔtoʊ, -sɔtoʊ] *(pl* **-s)** *n* Risotto *nt*

ritual [rɪtʃuəl] *n* Ritual *nt* ▷ *adj* rituell

rival [raɪvˀl] *n* Rivale *m*, Rivalin *f (for* um); *(Comm)* Konkurrent(in) *m(f)*

rivalry [raɪvˀlrɪ] *n* Rivalität *f*; *(Comm, Sport)* Konkurrenz *f*

river [rɪvər] *n* Fluss *m*; **the Hudson R~** der Hudson

riverside [rɪvərsaɪd] *n* Flussufer *nt* ▷ *adj* am Flussufer

road [roʊd] *n* Straße *f*; *(fig)* Weg *m*; **on the ~** *(travelling)* unterwegs, mit dem Auto/ Bus *etc* fahren

roadblock [roʊdblɒk] *n* Straßensperre *f*

roadmap [roʊdmæp] *n* Straßenkarte *f*

road rage *n aggressives Verhalten im Straßenverkehr*

roadside [roʊdsaɪd] *n*: **at** *o* **by the ~** am Straßenrand

road sign *n* Verkehrsschild *nt*

roadworthy [roʊdwɜrðɪ] *adj* fahrtüchtig

roar [rɔr] *n (of person, lion)* Brüllen *nt*; *(von Verkehr)* Donnern *nt* ▷ *vi (person, lion)* brüllen *(with* vor *+dat)*

roast [roʊst] *n* Braten *m* ▷ *adj*: **~ beef** Rinderbraten *m*; **~ chicken** Brathähnchen *nt*; **~ pork** Schweinebraten *m*; **~ potatoes** *pl* im Backofen gebratene Kartoffeln ▷ *vt (meat)* braten

rob [rɒb] *vt* bestehlen; *(bank, shop)* ausrauben

robber [rɒbər] *n* Räuber(in) *m(f)*

robbery [rɒbərɪ] *n* Raub *m*

robe [roʊb] *n (bathrobe)* Morgenrock *m*; *(of judge, priest etc)* Robe *f*, Talar *m*

robin [rɒbɪn] *n* Rotkehlchen *nt*

robot [roʊbət, -bɒt] *n* Roboter *m*

robust [roʊbʌst, roʊbʌst] *adj* robust; *(defence)* stark

rock [rɒk] *n (substance)* Stein *m*; *(boulder)* Felsbrocken *m*; *(Mus)* Rock *m*; **on the ~s** *(drink)* mit Eis; *(marriage)* gescheitert ▷ *vt, vi (swing)* schaukeln; *(dance)* rocken

rock climbing *n* Klettern *nt*; **to go ~** klettern gehen

rocket [rɒkɪt] *n* Rakete *f*; *(in salad)* Rucola *m*

rocking chair [rɒkɪŋ tʃɛər] *n* Schaukelstuhl *m*

rocky [rɒki] *adj* (*landscape*) felsig; (*path*) steinig

rod [rɒd] *n* (*bar*) Stange *f*; (*fishing rod*) Rute *f*

rode [rəʊd] *pt of* **ride**

rogue [rəʊg] *n* Schurke *m*, Gauner *m*

role [rəʊl] *n* Rolle *f*

role model *n* Vorbild *nt*

roll [rəʊl] *n* (*of film, paper etc*) Rolle *f*; (*bread roll*) Brötchen *nt* ▷ *vt* (*move by rolling*) rollen; (*cigarette*) drehen ▷ *vi* (*move by rolling*) rollen; (*ship*) schlingern; (*camera*) laufen

roller [rəʊlər] *n* (*hair roller*) (Locken)wickler *m*

Rollerblades® [rəʊlərbleɪdz] *npl* Inlineskates *pl*

rollerblading [rəʊlərbleɪdɪŋ] *n* Inlineskaten *nt*

roller coaster *n* Achterbahn *f*

roller skates *npl* Rollschuhe *pl*

roller-skating [rəʊlərskeɪtɪŋ] *n* Rollschuhlaufen *nt*

rolling pin [rəʊlɪŋ pɪn] *n* Nudelholz *nt*

roll-on (deodorant) [rəʊlɒn (diəʊdərənt)] *n* Deoroller *m*

roll out *vt* (*pastry*) ausrollen

roll over *vi* (*person*) sich umdrehen

roll up *vi* (*fam: arrive*) antanzen ▷ *vt* (*carpet*) aufrollen; **to roll one's sleeves up** die Ärmel hochkrempeln

ROM [rɒm] (*acr*) = **read only memory** ROM *m*

Roman [rəʊmən] *adj* römisch ▷ *n* Römer(in) *m(f)*

Roman Catholic *adj* römisch-katholisch ▷ *n* Katholik(in) *m(f)*

romance [rəʊmæns, rəʊmæns] *n* Romantik *f*; (*love affair*) Romanze *f*

Romania [rəʊmeɪnɪə] *n* Rumänien *nt*

Romanian [rəʊmeɪnɪən] *adj* rumänisch ▷ *n* Rumäne *m*, Rumänin *f*; (*language*) Rumänisch *nt*

romantic [rəʊmæntɪk] *adj* romantisch

roof [ruːf] *n* Dach *nt*

roof rack *n* Dachgepäckträger *m*

rook [rʊk] *n* (*in chess*) Turm *m*

room [ruːm] *n* Zimmer *nt*, Raum *m*; (*large, for gatherings etc*) Saal *m*; (*space*) Platz *m*; (*fig*) Spielraum *m*; **to make ~ for** Platz machen für

roommate [ruːmmeɪt] *n* Zimmergenosse *m*, Zimmergenossin *f*, Mitbewohner(in) *m(f)*

room service *n* Zimmerservice *m*

roomy [ruːmi] *adj* geräumig; (*garment*) weit

root [ruːt] *n* Wurzel *f*

root out *vt* (*eradicate*) ausrotten

root vegetable *n* Wurzelgemüse *nt*

rope [rəʊp] *n* Seil *nt*; **to know the ~s** (*fam*) sich auskennen

rose [rəʊz] *pt of* **rise** ▷ *n* Rose *f*

rosé [rəʊzeɪ] *n* Rosé(wein) *m*

rot [rɒt] *vi* verfaulen

rotate [rəʊteɪt] *vt* (*turn*) rotieren lassen ▷ *vi* rotieren

rotation [rəʊteɪʃən] *n* (*turning*) Rotation *f*; **in ~** abwechselnd

rotten [rɒtən] *adj* (*decayed*) faul; (*mean*) gemein; (*unpleasant*) scheußlich; (*ill*) elend

rough [rʌf] *adj* (*not smooth*) rau; (*path*) uneben; (*coarse, violent*) grob; (*crossing*) stürmisch; (*without comforts*) hart; (*unfinished, makeshift*) grob; (*approximate*) ungefähr; **~ draft** Rohentwurf *m*; **I have a ~ idea** ich habe eine ungefähre Vorstellung ▷ *adv*: **to sleep ~** im Freien schlafen ▷ *vt*: **to ~ it** primitiv leben ▷ *n*: **to write sth in ~** etw ins Unreine schreiben

roughly [rʌfli] *adv* grob; (*approximately*) ungefähr

round [raʊnd] *adj* rund ▷ *adv, prep, n* Runde *f*; **it's my ~** (*of drinks*) die Runde geht auf mich ▷ *vt* (*corner*) biegen um

roundabout [raʊndəbaʊt] *adj* umständlich

round off *vt* abrunden

round-the-clock *adj* rund um die Uhr

round trip *n* Rundreise *f*

round-trip ticket *n* Rückfahrkarte *f*; (*for plane*) Rückflugticket *nt*

round up *vt* (*number, price*) aufrunden

rouse [raʊz] *vt* (*from sleep*) wecken

route [ruːt, raʊt] *n* Route *f*; (*bus, plane etc service*) Linie *f*; (*fig*) Weg *m*

routine [ruːtiːn] *n* Routine *f* ▷ *adj* Routine-

row[1] [rəʊ] *n* (*line*) Reihe *f*; **three times in a row** dreimal hintereinander ▷ *vt, vi* (*boat*) rudern

row[2] [raʊ] *n* (*noise*) Krach *m*; (*dispute*) Streit *m*

rowboat [rəʊbəʊt] *n* Ruderboot *nt*

row house *n* Reihenhaus *nt*

rowing [rəʊɪŋ] *n* Rudern *nt*

rowing machine *n* Rudergerät *nt*

royal [rɔɪəl] *adj* königlich

royalty [rɔɪəlti] *n* (*family*) Mitglieder *pl*

der königlichen Familie; **royalties** *pl* (*from book, music*) Tantiemen *pl*

RSVP [ɑr ɛs vi pi] (*abbr*) = **répondez s'il vous plaît** u. A. w. g.

rub [rʌb] *vt* reiben

rubber [rʌbər] *n* Gummi *m*; (*fam: contraceptive*) Gummi *m*

rubber band *n* Gummiband *nt*

rubber stamp *n* Stempel *m*

rubbish [rʌbɪʃ] *n* Abfall *m*; (*nonsense*) Quatsch *m*; (*poor-quality thing*) Mist *m*; **don't talk ~** red keinen Unsinn!

rubble [rʌbªl] *n* Schutt *m*

rub in *vt* einmassieren

ruby [rubi] *n* (*stone*) Rubin *m*

rude [rud] *adj* (*impolite*) unhöflich; (*indecent*) unanständig

rug [rʌg] *n* Teppich *m*; (*next to bed*) Bettvorleger *m*; (*for knees*) Wolldecke *f*

rugby [rʌgbi] *n* Rugby *nt*

rugged [rʌgɪd] *adj* (*coastline*) zerklüftet; (*features*) markant

ruin [ruɪn] *n* Ruine *f*; (*financial, social*) Ruin *m* ▷ *vt* ruinieren

rule [rul] *n* Regel *f*; (*governing*) Herrschaft *f*; **as a ~** in der Regel ▷ *vt, vi* (*govern*) regieren; (*decide*) entscheiden

ruler [rulər] *n* Lineal *nt*; (*person*) Herrscher(in) *m(f)*

rum [rʌm] *n* Rum *m*

rumble [rʌmbªl] *vi* (*stomach*) knurren; (*train, truck*) rumpeln

rummage [rʌmɪdʒ] *vi:* **to ~ around** herumstöbern

rumor [rumər] *n* Gerücht *nt*

run [rʌn] (**ran, run**) *vt* (*race, distance*) laufen; (*machine, engine, computer program, water*) laufen lassen; (*manage*) leiten, führen; (*car*) unterhalten; **I ran her home** ich habe sie nach Hause gefahren ▷ *vi* laufen; (*move quickly*) rennen; (*bus, train*) fahren; (*path etc*) verlaufen; (*machine, engine, computer program*) laufen; (*flow*) fließen; (*colors, make-up*) verlaufen; **to run for President** für die Präsidentschaft kandidieren; **to be running low** knapp werden; **my nose is running** mir läuft die Nase; **it runs in the family** es liegt in der Familie ▷ *n* (*on foot*) Lauf *m*; (*in car*) Spazierfahrt *f*; (*series*) Reihe *f*; (*sudden demand*) Ansturm *m* (*on* auf +*akk*); (*in tights*) Lauf-

masche *f*; (*in baseball*) Lauf *m*; **to go for a run** laufen gehen; (*in car*) eine Spazierfahrt machen; **in the long run** auf die Dauer; **on the run** auf der Flucht (*from* vor +*dat*)

run away *vi* weglaufen

run down *vt* (*with car*) umfahren; (*criticize*) heruntermachen; **to be ~** (*tired*) abgespannt sein

rung [rʌŋ] *pp of* **ring**

run into *vt* (*meet*) zufällig treffen; (*problem*) stoßen auf +*akk*

runner [rʌnər] *n* (*athlete*) Läufer(in) *m(f)*

running [rʌnɪŋ] *n* (*Sport*) Laufen *nt*; (*management*) Leitung *f*, Führung *f* ▷ *adj* (*water*) fließend; **~ costs** Betriebskosten *pl*; (*for car*) Unterhaltskosten *pl*; **3 days ~** 3 Tage hintereinander

runny [rʌni] *adj* (*food*) flüssig; (*nose*) laufend

run off *vi* weglaufen

run out *vi* (*person*) hinausrennen; (*liquid*) auslaufen; (*lease, time*) ablaufen; (*money, supplies*) ausgehen; **he ran ~ of money** ihm ging das Geld aus

run over *vt* (*with car*) überfahren

run up *vt* (*debt, bill*) machen

runway [rʌnweɪ] *n* Start- und Landebahn *f*

rural [ruərəl] *adj* ländlich

rush [rʌʃ] *n* Eile *f*; (*for tickets etc*) Ansturm *m* (*for* auf +*akk*); **to be in a ~** es eilig haben; **there's no ~** es eilt nicht ▷ *vt* (*do too quickly*) hastig machen; (*meal*) hastig essen; **to ~ sb to the hospital** jdn auf den schnellsten Weg ins Krankenhaus bringen; **don't ~ me** dräng mich nicht ▷ *vi* (*hurry*) eilen; **don't ~** lass dir Zeit

rush hour *n* Hauptverkehrszeit *f*

rusk [rʌsk] *n* Zwieback *m*

Russia [rʌʃə] *n* Russland *nt*

Russian [rʌʃªn] *adj* russisch ▷ *n* Russe *m*, Russin *f*; (*language*) Russisch *nt*

rust [rʌst] *n* Rost *m* ▷ *vi* rosten

rustproof [rʌstpruf] *adj* rostfrei

rusty [rʌsti] *adj* rostig

rutabaga [rutəbeɪgə] *n* Steckrübe *f*

ruthless [ruθlɪs] *adj* rücksichtslos; (*treatment, criticism*) schonungslos

rye [raɪ] *n* Roggen *m*

rye bread *n* Roggenbrot *nt*

S

S [ɛs] (*abbr*) = **south** S
sabotage [sæbətaʒ] *vt* sabotieren
sachet [sæʃeɪ] *n* Päckchen *nt*
sack [sæk] *n* (*bag*) Sack *m*; **to get the ~**
(*fam*) rausgeschmissen werden ▷ *vt* (*fam*)
rausschmeißen
sacred [seɪkrɪd] *adj* heilig
sacrifice [sækrɪfaɪs] *n* Opfer *nt* ▷ *vt*
opfern
sad [sæd] *adj* traurig
saddle [sædᵊl] *n* Sattel *m*
sadistic [sədɪstɪk] *adj* sadistisch
sadly [sædli] *adv* (*unfortunately*) leider
safari [səfɑri] *n* Safari
safe [seɪf] *adj* (*free from danger*) sicher; (*out
of danger*) in Sicherheit; (*careful*) vorsichtig; **have a ~ journey** gute Fahrt! ▷ *n* Safe
m
safeguard [seɪfgɑrd] *n* Schutz *m* ▷ *vt*
schützen (*against* vor +*dat*)
safely [seɪfli] *adv* sicher; (*arrive*) wohlbehalten; (*drive*) vorsichtig
safety [seɪfti] *n* Sicherheit *f*
safety belt *n* Sicherheitsgurt *m*
safety pin *n* Sicherheitsnadel *f*
Sagittarius [sædʒɪtɛɑriəs] *n* (*Astr*) Schütze
m
Sahara [səhærə] *n*: **the ~ Desert** die
(Wüste) Sahara
said [sɛd] *pt*, *pp* of **say**
sail [seɪl] *n* Segel *nt*; **to set ~** losfahren (*for*
nach) ▷ *vi* (*in yacht*) segeln; (*on ship*) mit
dem Schiff fahren; (*ship*) auslaufen (*for*
nach) ▷ *vt* (*yacht*) segeln mit; (*ship*) steuern
sailboat [seɪlboʊt] *n* Segelboot *nt*
sailing [seɪlɪŋ] *n*: **to go ~** segeln gehen
sailor [seɪlər] *n* Seemann *m*; (*in navy*) Matrose *m*
saint [seɪnt] *n* Heilige(r) *mf*
sake [seɪk] *n*: **for the ~ of** um +*gen* ... willen; **for your ~** deinetwegen, dir zuliebe
salad [sæləd] *n* Salat *m*
salad dressing *n* Salatsoße *f*
salary [sæləri] *n* Gehalt *nt*
sale [seɪl] *n* Verkauf *m*; (*at reduced prices*)
Ausverkauf *m*; **the ~s** *pl* (*in summer, winter*) der Schlussverkauf; **for ~** zu verkaufen
sales clerk *n* Verkäufer(in) *m(f)*
salesman [seɪlzmən] (*pl* **-men**) *n* Verkäu-
fer *m*; (*rep*) Vertreter *m*

sales rep *n* Vertreter(in) *m(f)*
sales tax *n* Verkaufssteuer *f*
saleswoman [seɪlzwʊmən] (*pl* **-women**) *n*
Verkäuferin *f*; (*rep*) Vertreterin *f*
salmon [sæmən] *n* Lachs *m*
saloon [səlun] *n* (*ship's lounge*) Salon *m*;
(*bar*) Kneipe *f*
salt [sɔlt] *n* Salz *nt* ▷ *vt* (*flavor*) salzen;
(*roads*) mit Salz streuen
salt shaker [sɔlt ʃeɪkər] *n* Salzstreuer *m*
salty [sɔlti] *adj* salzig
salvage [sælvɪdʒ] *vt* bergen (*from* aus);
(*fig*) retten
same [seɪm] *adj*: **the ~** (*similar*) der/die/das
gleiche, die gleichen *pl*; (*identical*) der-/
die-/dasselbe, dieselben *pl*; **they live in the
~ house** sie wohnen im selben Haus
▷ *pron*: **the ~** (*similar*) der/die/das Gleiche,
die Gleichen *pl*; (*identical*) der-/die-/das-
selbe, dieselben *pl*; **all the ~** trotzdem; **the
~ to you** gleichfalls; **it's all the ~ to me** es
ist mir egal ▷ *adv*: **the ~** gleich; **they look
the ~** sie sehen gleich aus
sample [sæmpᵊl] *n* Probe *f*; (*of fabric*) Muster *nt* ▷ *vt* probieren
sanctions [sæŋkʃᵊnz] *npl* (*Pol*) Sanktionen
pl
sanctuary [sæŋktʃuɛri] *n* (*refuge*) Zuflucht
f; (*for animals*) Schutzgebiet *nt*
sand [sænd] *n* Sand *m*
sandal [sændᵊl] *n* Sandale *f*
sandpaper [sændpeɪpər] *n* Sandpapier *nt*
▷ *vt* schmirgeln
sand trap *n* (*Golf*) Bunker *m*
sandwich [sænwɪtʃ, sænd-] *n* Sandwich
nt
sandy [sændi] *adj* (*full of sand*) sandig; **~
beach** Sandstrand *m*
sane [seɪn] *adj* geistig gesund, normal;
(*sensible*) vernünftig
sang [sæŋ] *pt* of **sing**
sanitary [sænɪteri] *adj* hygienisch
sanitary napkin [sænɪteri næpkɪn] *n*
Damenbinde *f*
sank [sæŋk] *pt* of **sink**
Santa (Claus) [sæntə (klɔz)] *n* der Weihnachtsmann
sarcastic [sɑrkæstɪk] *adj* sarkastisch
sardine [sɑrdin] *n* Sardine *f*
Sardinia [sɑrdɪniə] *n* Sardinien *nt*
sari [sɑri] *n* Sari *m* (*von indischen Frauen
getragenes Gewand*)

Sat (*abbr*) = **Saturday** Sa.

sat [sæt] *pt, pp* of **sit**

satellite [sætᵊlaɪt] *n* Satellit *m*

satellite dish *n* Satellitenschüssel *f*

satellite TV *n* Satellitenfernsehen *nt*

satin [sætᵊn] *n* Satin *m*

satisfaction [sætɪsfækʃᵊn] *n* (*contentment*) Zufriedenheit *f*; **is that to your ~?** bist du/ sind Sie damit zufrieden?

satisfactory [sætɪsfæktəri] *adj* zufriedenstellend

satisfied [sætɪsfaɪd] *adj* zufrieden (*with* mit)

satisfy [sætɪsfaɪ] *vt* zufriedenstellen; (*convince*) überzeugen; (*conditions*) erfüllen; (*need, demand*) befriedigen

satisfying [sætɪsfaɪɪŋ] *adj* befriedigend

Saturday [sætərdeɪ, -di] *n* Samstag *m*, Sonnabend *m*; *see also* **Tuesday**

sauce [sɔs] *n* Soße *f*

saucepan [sɔspæn] *n* Kochtopf *m*

saucer [sɔsər] *n* Untertasse *f*

saucy [sɔsi] *adj* frech

Saudi Arabia [saʊdi əreɪbiə] *n* Saudi-Arabien *nt*

sauna [sɔnə] *n* Sauna *f*

sausage [sɔsɪdʒ] *n* Wurst *f*

savage [sævɪdʒ] *adj* (*person, attack*) brutal; (*animal*) wild

save [seɪv] *vt* (*rescue*) retten (*from* vor +*dat*); (*money, time, electricity etc*) sparen; (*strength*) schonen; (*Inform*) speichern; **to ~ sb's life** jdm das Leben retten ▷ *vi* sparen ▷ *n* (*in soccer*) Parade *f*

save up *vi* sparen (*for auf* +*akk*)

saving [seɪvɪŋ] *n* (*of money*) Sparen *nt*; **~s** *pl* Ersparnisse *pl*; **~s account** Sparkonto *nt*

savory [seɪvəri] *adj* (*not sweet*) pikant

saw [sɔ] (**sawed, sawn**) *vt, vi* sägen ▷ *n* (*tool*) Säge *f pt* of **see**

sawdust [sɔdʌst] *n* Sägemehl *nt*

saxophone [sæksəfoʊn] *n* Saxophon *nt*

say [seɪ] (**said, said**) *vt* sagen (*to sb* jdm); (*prayer*) sprechen; **what does the letter say?** was steht im Brief?; **the rules say that ...** in den Regeln heißt es, dass ...; **he's said to be rich** er soll reich sein ▷ *n*: **to have a say in sth** bei etw ein Mitspracherecht haben ▷ *adv* zum Beispiel

saying [seɪɪŋ] *n* Sprichwort *nt*

scab [skæb] *n* (*on cut*) Schorf *m*

scaffolding [skæfəldɪŋ] *n* (Bau)gerüst *nt*

scale [skeɪl] *n* (*of map etc*) Maßstab *m*; (*on thermometer etc*) Skala *f*; (*of pay*) Tarifsys-

tem *nt*; (*Mus*) Tonleiter *f*; (*of fish, snake*) Schuppe *f*; **to ~** maßstabsgerecht; **on a large/small ~** in großem/kleinem Umfang

scales *npl* (*for weighing*) Waage *f*

scalp [skælp] *n* Kopfhaut *f*

scan [skæn] *vt* (*examine*) genau prüfen; (*read quickly*) überfliegen; (*Inform*) scannen ▷ *n* (*Med*) Ultraschall *m*

scandal [skændᵊl] *n* Skandal *m*

scandalous [skændᵊləs] *adj* skandalös

scandal sheets *npl* Skandalpresse *f*

Scandinavia [skændɪneɪviə] *n* Skandinavien *nt*

Scandinavian [skændɪneɪviən] *adj* skandinavisch ▷ *n* Skandinavier(in) *m(f)*

scan in *vt* (*Inform*) einscannen

scanner [skænər] *n* Scanner *m*

scapegoat [skeɪpgoʊt] *n* Sündenbock *m*

scar [skɑr] *n* Narbe *f*

scarce [skɛərs] *adj* selten; (*in short supply*) knapp

scarcely [skɛərsli] *adv* kaum

scare [skɛər] *n* (*general alarm*) Panik *f* ▷ *vt* erschrecken; **to be ~d** Angst haben (*of* vor +*dat*)

scarf [skɑrf] (*pl* **scarves**) *n* Schal *m*; (*on head*) Kopftuch *nt*

scarlet [skɑrlɪt] *adj* scharlachrot

scarlet fever *n* Scharlach *m*

scary [skɛəri] *adj* (*film, story*) gruselig

scatter [skætər] *vt* verstreuen; (*seed, gravel*) streuen; (*disperse*) auseinandertreiben

scene [sin] *n* (*location*) Ort *m*; (*division of play: Theat*) Szene *f*; (*view*) Anblick *m*; **to make a ~** eine Szene machen

scenery [sinəri] *n* (*landscape*) Landschaft *f*; (*Theat*) Kulissen *pl*

scenic [sinɪk] *adj* (*landscape*) malerisch; **~ route** landschaftlich schöne Strecke

scent [sɛnt] *n* (*perfume*) Parfüm *nt*; (*smell*) Duft *m*

schedule [skɛdʒul, -uəl] *n* (*plan*) Programm *nt*; (*of work*) Zeitplan *m*; (*list*) Liste *f*; (*of trains, buses, air traffic*) Fahr-, Flugplan *m*; **on ~** planmäßig; **to be behind ~ with sth** mit etw in Verzug sein ▷ *vt*: **the meeting is ~d for next Monday** die Besprechung ist für nächsten Montag angesetzt

scheduled [skɛdʒuld, -uəld] *adj* (*departure, arrival*) planmäßig; **~ flight** Linienflug *m*

scheme [skim] *n* (*plan*) Plan *m*; (*project*) Projekt *nt*; (*dishonest*) Intrige *f* ▷ *vi* intrigieren

schizophrenic [skɪtsəfrɛnɪk] *adj* schizo-

phren
scholar [skɒlər] *n* Gelehrte(r) *mf*
scholarship [skɒlərʃıp] *n* (*grant*) Stipendium *nt*
school [skul] *n* Schule *f*; (*university department*) Fachbereich *m*; (*university*) Universität *f*
school bag *n* Schultasche *f*
schoolbook [skulbʊk] *n* Schulbuch *nt*
schoolboy [skulbɔı] *n* Schüler *m*
school bus *n* Schulbus *m*
schoolgirl [skulgɜrl] *n* Schülerin *f*
schoolteacher [skultitʃər] *n* Lehrer(in) *m(f)*
schoolwork [skulwɜrk] *n* Schularbeiten *pl*
sciatica [saıætıkə] *n* Ischias *m*
science [saıəns] *n* Wissenschaft *f*; (*natural science*) Naturwissenschaft *f*
science fiction *n* Sciencefiction *f*
scientific [saıəntıfık] *adj* wissenschaftlich
scientist [saıəntıst] *n* Wissenschaftler(in) *m(f)*; (*in natural sciences*) Naturwissenschaftler(in) *m(f)*
scissors [sızərz] *npl* Schere *f*
scone [skoun, skɒn] *n* kleines süßes Hefebrötchen mit oder ohne Rosinen, das mit Butter oder Dickrahm und Marmelade gegessen wird
scoop [skup] *n* (*exclusive story*) Exklusivbericht *m*; **a ~ of ice-cream** eine Kugel Eis ▷ *vt*: **to ~ up** schaufeln
scooter [skutər] *n* (Motor)roller *m*; (*toy*) (Tret)roller *m*
scope [skoup] *n* Umfang *m*; (*opportunity*) Möglichkeit *f*
score [skɔr] *n* (*Sport*) Spielstand *m*; (*final result*) Spielergebnis *nt*; (*in quiz etc*) Punktestand *m*; (*Mus*) Partitur *f*; **to keep the ~** mitzählen ▷ *vt* (*goal*) schießen; (*points*) punkten ▷ *vi* (*keep score*) mitzählen
scoreboard [skɔrbɔrd] *n* Anzeigetafel *f*
scorn [skɔrn] *n* Verachtung *f*
scornful [skɔrnfəl] *adj* verächtlich
Scorpio [skɔrpiou] (*pl* **-s**) *n* (*Astr*) Skorpion *m*
scorpion [skɔrpiən] *n* Skorpion *m*
Scot [skɒt] *n* Schotte *m*, Schottin *f*
Scotch [skɒtʃ] *n* (*whisky*) schottischer Whisky, Scotch *m*
Scotch® tape *n* Tesafilm® *m*
Scotland [skɒtlənd] *n* Schottland *nt*
Scotsman [skɒtsmən] (*pl* **-men**) *n* Schotte *m*

Scotswoman [skɒtswʊmən] (*pl* **-women**) *n* Schottin *f*
Scottish [skɒtıʃ] *adj* schottisch
scout [skaʊt] *n* (*boy scout*) Pfadfinder *m*
scowl [skaʊl] *vi* finster blicken
scrambled eggs [skræmbᵊld egz] *npl* Rührei *nt*
scrap [skræp] *n* (*bit*) Stückchen *nt*, Fetzen *m*; (*metal*) Schrott *m* ▷ *vt* (*car*) verschrotten; (*plan*) verwerfen
scrapbook [skræpbʊk] *n* Sammelalbum *nt*
scrape [skreıp] *n* (*scratch*) Kratzer *m* ▷ *vt* (*car*) schrammen; (*wall*) streifen; **to ~ one's knee** sich das Knie schürfen
scrape through *vi* (*exam*) mit knapper Not bestehen
scrap heap *n* Schrotthaufen *m*
scrap metal *n* Schrott *m*
scrap paper *n* Schmierpapier *nt*
scratch [skrætʃ] *n* (*mark*) Kratzer *m*; **to start from ~** von vorne anfangen ▷ *vt* kratzen; (*car*) zerkratzen; **to ~ one's arm** sich am Arm kratzen ▷ *vi* kratzen; (*scratch oneself*) sich kratzen
scream [skrim] *n* Schrei *m* ▷ *vi* schreien (*with* vor +*dat*); **to ~ at sb** jdn anschreien
screen [skrin] *n* (*TV*, *Inform*) Bildschirm *m*; (*Cine*) Leinwand *f* ▷ *vt* (*protect*) abschirmen; (*hide*) verdecken; (*film*) zeigen; (*applicants*, *luggage*) überprüfen
screenplay [skrinpleı] *n* Drehbuch *nt*
screensaver [skrinseıvər] *n* (*Inform*) Bildschirmschoner *m*
screw [skru] *n* Schraube *f* ▷ *vt*: **to ~ sth to sth** etw an etw *akk* schrauben; **to ~ off/on** (*lid*) ab-/aufschrauben
screwdriver [skrudraıvər] *n* Schraubenzieher *m*
screw top *n* Schraubverschluss *m*
screw up *vt* (*paper*) zusammenknüllen; (*make a mess of*) vermasseln
scribble [skrıbᵊl] *vt*, *vi* kritzeln
script [skrıpt] *n* (*of play*) Text *m*; (*of film*) Drehbuch *nt*; (*style of writing*) Schrift *f*
scroll bar [skroul bɑr] *n* (*Inform*) Scrollbar *f*
scroll down [skroul daʊn] *vi* (*Inform*) runterscrollen
scroll up [skroul ʌp] *vi* (*Inform*) raufscrollen
scrub [skrʌb] *vt* schrubben
scrub brush *n* Scheuerbürste *f*
scruffy [skrʌfi] *adj* vergammelt
scrupulous [skrupyələs] *adj*, **scrupu-**

lously adv gewissenhaft; (painstaking) peinlich genau

scuba diving [skuːbə daɪvɪŋ] n Sporttauchen nt

sculptor [skʌlptər] n Bildhauer(in) m(f)

sculpture [skʌlptʃər] n (Art) Bildhauerei f; (statue) Skulptur f

sea [siː] n Meer nt, See f

seafood [siːfuːd] n Meeresfrüchte pl

seagull [siːgʌl] n Möwe f

seal [siːl] n (animal) Robbe f; (stamp, impression) Siegel nt; (Tech) Verschluss m; (ring etc) Dichtung f ▷ vt versiegeln; (envelope) zukleben

seam [siːm] n Naht f

search [sɜːtʃ] n Suche f (for nach); **to do a ~ for** (Inform) suchen nach; **in ~ of** auf der Suche nach ▷ vi suchen (for nach) ▷ vt durchsuchen

search engine n (Inform) Suchmaschine f

seashell [siːʃɛl] n Muschel f

seashore [siːʃɔr] n Strand m

seasick [siːsɪk] adj seekrank

seaside [siːsaɪd] n: **at the ~** am Meer; **to go to the ~** ans Meer fahren

seaside resort n Seebad nt

season [siːzᵊn] n Jahreszeit f; (Comm) Saison f; **high/low ~** Hoch-/Nebensaison f ▷ vt (flavor) würzen

seasoning [siːzənɪŋ] n Gewürz nt

seat [siːt] n (place) Platz m; (chair) Sitz m; **take a ~** setzen Sie sich ▷ vt: **the hall ~s 300** der Saal hat 300 Sitzplätze; **please be ~ed** bitte setzen Sie sich; **to remain ~ed** sitzen bleiben

seat belt n Sicherheitsgurt m

seaweed [siːwiːd] n Seetang m

secluded [sɪkluːdɪd] adj abgelegen

second [sɛkənd] adj zweite(r, s); **June ~** der zweite Juni ▷ adv (in second position) an zweiter Stelle; (secondly) zweitens; **he came ~** er ist Zweiter geworden ▷ n (of time) Sekunde f; (moment) Augenblick m; **~ gear** der zweite Gang; (second helping) zweite Portion; **just a ~!** (einen) Augenblick!

secondary [sɛkəndɛri] adj (less important) zweitrangig; **~ education** höhere Schulbildung f; **~ school** weiterführende Schule

second-class adj (ticket) zweiter Klasse ▷ adv (travel) zweiter Klasse

second-hand adj, adv gebraucht; (information) aus zweiter Hand

secondly [sɛkəndli] adv zweitens

second-rate [sɛkəndreɪt] adj (pej) zweit-

klassig

secret [siːkrɪt] n Geheimnis nt ▷ adj geheim; (admirer) heimlich

secretary [sɛkrɪtɛri] n Sekretär(in) m(f); (minister) Minister(in) m(f)

Secretary of State n Außenminister(in) m(f)

secretary's office n Sekretariat nt

secretive [siːkrətɪv, sɪkriːt-] adj (person) geheimnistuerisch

secretly [siːkrɪtli] adv heimlich

sect [sɛkt] n Sekte f

section [sɛkʃᵊn] n (part) Teil m; (of document) Abschnitt m; (department) Abteilung f

secure [sɪkyuər] adj (safe) sicher (from vor +dat); (firmly fixed) fest ▷ vt (make firm) befestigen; (window, door) fest verschließen

securely [sɪkyuərli] adv fest; (safely) sicher

security [sɪkyuəriti] n Sicherheit f

sedative [sɛdətɪv] n Beruhigungsmittel nt

seduce [sɪduːs] vt verführen

seductive [sɪdʌktɪv] adj verführerisch; (offer) verlockend

see [siː] (saw, seen) vt sehen; (understand) verstehen; (check) nachsehen; (accompany) bringen; (visit) besuchen; (talk to) sprechen; **to see the doctor** zum Arzt gehen; **to see sb home** jdn nach Hause begleiten; **I saw him swimming** ich habe ihn schwimmen sehen; **see you!** tschüs!; **see you on Friday** bis Freitag! ▷ vi sehen; (understand) verstehen; (check) nachsehen; **you see** siehst du!; **we'll see** mal sehen

see about vt (attend to) sich kümmern um

seed [siːd] n (of plant) Samen m; (in fruit) Kern m

seedless [siːdlɪs] adj kernlos

seedy [siːdi] adj zwielichtig

Seeing-eye® dog n Blindenhund m

seek [siːk] (sought, sought) vt suchen; (fame) streben nach; **to ~ sb's advice** jdn um Rat fragen

seem [siːm] vi scheinen; **he ~s to be honest** er scheint ehrlich zu sein; **it ~s to me that ...** es scheint mir, dass ...

seen [siːn] pp of **see**

see off vt (say goodbye to) verabschieden

see out vt (show out) zur Tür bringen

seesaw [siːsɔ] n Wippe f

see through vt: **to see sth through** etw zu Ende bringen; **to ~ sb/sth** jdn/etw durchschauen

see-through *adj* durchsichtig

see to *vt* sich kümmern um; ~ **it that ...** sieh zu, dass ...

segment [sɛgmənt] *n* Teil *m*

seize [siz] *vt* packen; (*confiscate*) beschlagnahmen; (*opportunity, power*) ergreifen

seldom [sɛldəm] *adv* selten

select [sɪlɛkt] *adj* (*exclusive*) exklusiv ▷ *vt* auswählen

selection [sɪlɛkʃən] *n* Auswahl *f* (*of* an +*dat*)

selective [sɪlɛktɪv] *adj* (*choosy*) wählerisch

self [sɛlf] (*pl* **selves**) *n* Selbst *nt*, Ich *nt*; **he's his old ~ again** er ist wieder ganz der Alte

self-addressed stamped envelope *n* frankierter Rückumschlag

self-adhesive [sɛlfædhisɪv] *adj* selbstklebend

self-assured [sɛlfəʃʊərd] *n* selbstsicher

self-catering [sɛlfkeɪtərɪŋ] *adj* für Selbstversorger

self-centered [sɛlfsɛntərd] *adj* egozentrisch

self-confidence [sɛlfkɒnfɪdəns] *n* Selbstbewusstsein *nt*

self-confident [sɛlfkɒnfɪdənt] *adj* selbstbewusst

self-conscious [sɛlfkɒnʃəs] *adj* befangen, verklemmt

self-contained [sɛlfkənteɪnd] *adj* (*apartment*) separat

self-control [sɛlfkəntroʊl] *n* Selbstbeherrschung *f*

self-defense [sɛlfdɪfɛns] *n* Selbstverteidigung *f*

self-employed [sɛlfɪmplɔɪd] *adj* selbstständig

self-evident [sɛlfɛvɪdənt], *adj* offensichtlich

selfish [sɛlfɪʃ] *adj*, **selfishly** *adv* egoistisch, selbstsüchtig

selfless [sɛlflɪs] *adj*, **selflessly** *adv* selbstlos

self-pity [sɛlfpɪt] *n* Selbstmitleid *nt*

self-portrait [sɛlfpɔrtrɪt] *n* Selbstporträt *nt*

self-respect [sɛlfrɪspɛkt] *n* Selbstachtung *f*

self-service [sɛlfsɜrvɪs] *n* Selbstbedienung *f* ▷ *adj* Selbstbedienungs-

sell [sɛl] (**sold, sold**) *vt* verkaufen; **to ~ sb sth, to ~ sth to sb** jdm etw verkaufen; **do you ~ postcards?** haben Sie Postkarten?

▷ *vi* (*product*) sich verkaufen

sell-by date *n* Haltbarkeitsdatum *nt*

sell out *vt*: **to be sold out** ausverkauft sein

semester [sɪmɛstər] *n* Semester *nt*

semicircle [sɛmisɜrkəl, sɛmaɪ-] *n* Halbkreis *m*

semicolon [sɛmikoʊlən] *n* Semikolon *nt*

semifinal [sɛmifaɪnəl, sɛmaɪ-] *n* Halbfinale *nt*

seminar [sɛmɪnɑr] *n* Seminar *nt*

senate [sɛnɪt] *n* Senat *m*

senator [sɛnɪtər] *n* Senator(in) *m(f)*

send [sɛnd] (**sent, sent**) *vt* schicken; **to ~ sb sth, to ~ sth to sb** jdm etw schicken; ~ **her my best wishes** grüße sie von mir

send away *vt* wegschicken ▷ *vi*: **to ~ for** anfordern

send back *vt* zurückschicken

sender [sɛndər] *n* Absender(in) *m(f)*

send for *vt* (*person*) holen lassen; (*by post*) anfordern

send off *vt* (*by post*) abschicken

send out *vt* (*invitations etc*) verschicken ▷ *vi*: **to ~ for sth** etw holen lassen

senior [sinyər] *adj* (*older*) älter; (*high-ranking*) höher; (*pupils*) älter; **he is ~ to me** er ist mir übergeordnet ▷ *n*: **he's eight years my ~** er ist acht Jahre älter als ich

senior citizen *n* Senior(in) *m(f)*

sensation [sɛnseɪʃən] *n* Gefühl *nt*; (*excitement, person, thing*) Sensation *f*

sensational [sɛnseɪʃənəl] *adj* sensationell

sense [sɛns] *n* (*faculty, meaning*) Sinn *m*; (*feeling*) Gefühl *nt*; (*understanding*) Verstand *m*; ~ **of smell/taste** Geruchs-/Geschmackssinn *m*; **to have a ~ of humor** Humor haben; **to make ~** (*sentence etc*) einen Sinn ergeben; (*be sensible*) Sinn machen; **in a ~** gewissermaßen ▷ *vt* spüren

senseless [sɛnslɪs] *adj* (*stupid*) sinnlos

sensible [sɛnsɪbəl] *adj*, **sensibly** *adv* vernünftig

sensitive [sɛnsɪtɪv] *adj* empfindlich (*to* gegen); (*easily hurt*) sensibel; (*subject*) heikel

sensual [sɛnʃuəl] *adj* sinnlich

sensuous [sɛnʃuəs] *adj* sinnlich

sent [sɛnt] *pt, pp of* **send**

sentence [sɛntəns] *n* (*Ling*) Satz *m*; (*Jur*) Strafe *f* ▷ *vt* verurteilen (*to* zu)

sentiment [sɛntɪmənt] *n* (*sentimentality*) Sentimentalität *f*; (*opinion*) Ansicht *f*

sentimental [sɛntɪmɛntəl] *adj* sentimental

separate [*adj* sɛpərɪt, *vb* sɛpəreɪt] *adj* getrennt, separat; (*individual*) einzeln ▷ *vt* trennen (*from* von); **they are ~d** (*couple*) sie leben getrennt ▷ *vi* sich trennen

separately [sɛpərɪtli] *adv* getrennt; (*singly*) einzeln

September [sɛptɛmbər] *n* September *m*; **in ~** im September; **on ~ 2nd** am 2. September; **at the beginning/in the middle/at the end of ~** Anfang/Mitte/Ende September; **last/next ~** letzten/nächsten September

septic [sɛptɪk] *adj* vereitert

sequel [siːkwᵊl] *n* (*to film, book*) Fortsetzung *f* (*to* von)

sequence [siːkwəns] *n* (*order*) Reihenfolge *f*

Serbia [sɜrbiə] *n* Serbien *nt*

sergeant [sɑrdʒᵊnt] *n* Polizeimeister(in) *m(f)*; (*Mil*) Feldwebel(in) *m(f)*

serial [sɪəriəl] *n* (*TV*) Serie *f*; (*in newspaper etc*) Fortsetzungsroman *m* ▷ *adj* (*Inform*) seriell; **~ number** Seriennummer *f*

series [sɪəriːz] *nsing* Reihe *f*; (*TV, Radio*) Serie *f*

serious [sɪəriəs] *adj* ernst; (*injury, illness, mistake*) schwer; (*discussion*) ernsthaft; **are you ~?** ist das dein Ernst?

seriously [sɪəriəsli] *adv* ernsthaft; (*hurt*) schwer; **~?** im Ernst?; **to take sb ~** jdn ernst nehmen

sermon [sɜrmən] *n* (*Rel*) Predigt *f*

servant [sɜrvᵊnt] *n* Diener(in) *m(f)*

serve [sɜrv] *vt* (*customer*) bedienen; (*food*) servieren; (*one's country etc*) dienen +*dat*; (*sentence*) verbüßen; **I'm being ~d** ich werde schon bedient; **it ~s him right** es geschieht ihm recht ▷ *vi* dienen (*as* als), aufschlagen ▷ *n* Aufschlag *m*

server [sɜrvər] *n* (*Inform*) Server *m*

service [sɜrvɪs] *n* (*in store, hotel*) Bedienung *f*; (*activity, amenity*) Dienstleistung *f*; (*set of dishes*) Service *nt*; (*Auto*) Inspektion *f*; (*Tech*) Wartung *f*; (*Rel*) Gottesdienst *m*, Aufschlag *m*; **train/bus ~** Zug-/Busverbindung *f*; **'~ not included'** „Bedienung nicht inbegriffen" ▷ *vt* (*Auto, Tech*) warten

service charge *n* Bedienung *f*

service provider *n* (*Inform*) Provider *m*

service station *n* Tankstelle *f*

session [sɛʃᵊn] *n* (*of court, assembly*) Sitzung *f*

set [sɛt] (**set, set**) *vt* (*place*) stellen; (*lay flat*) legen; (*arrange*) anordnen; (*table*) decken; (*trap, record*) aufstellen; (*time, price*) festsetzen; (*watch, alarm*) stellen (*for* auf +*akk*); **to set sb a task** jdm eine Aufgabe stellen; **to set free** freilassen; **to set a good example** ein gutes Beispiel geben; **the novel is set in London** der Roman spielt in London ▷ *vi* (*sun*) untergehen; (*become hard*) fest werden; (*bone*) zusammenwachsen ▷ *n* (*collection of things*) Satz *m*; (*of silverware, furniture*) Garnitur *f*; (*group of people*) Kreis *m*; (*Radio, TV*) Apparat *m*, Satz *m*; (*Theat*) Bühnenbild *nt*; (*Cine*) (Film)kulisse *f* ▷ *adj* (*agreed, prescribed*) festgelegt; (*ready*) bereit; **set meal** Menü *nt*

set aside *vt* (*money*) beiseitelegen; (*time*) einplanen

setback [sɛtbæk] *n* Rückschlag *m*

set off *vi* aufbrechen (*for* nach) ▷ *vt* (*alarm*) auslösen; (*enhance*) hervorheben

set out *vi* aufbrechen (*for* nach) ▷ *vt* (*chairs, chess pieces etc*) aufstellen; (*state*) darlegen; **to ~ to do sth** (*intend*) beabsichtigen, etw zu tun

settee [sɛtiː] *n* Sofa *nt*, Couch *f*

setting [sɛtɪŋ] *n* (*of novel, film*) Schauplatz *m*; (*surroundings*) Umgebung *f*

settle [sɛtᵊl] *vt* (*bill, debt*) begleichen; (*dispute*) beilegen; (*question*) klären; (*stomach*) beruhigen ▷ *vi*: **to ~ down** (*feel at home*) sich einleben; (*calm down*) sich beruhigen

settle in *vi* (*in place*) sich einleben; (*in job*) sich eingewöhnen

settlement [sɛtᵊlmənt] *n* (*of bill, debt*) Begleichung *f*; (*colony*) Siedlung *f*; **to reach a ~** sich einigen

settle up *vi* (be)zahlen; **to ~ with sb** mit jdm abrechnen

set up *vt* (*firm, organization*) gründen; (*stall, tent, camera*) aufbauen; (*meeting*) vereinbaren ▷ *vi*: **to ~ as a doctor** sich als Arzt niederlassen

setup [sɛtʌp] *n* (*organization*) Organisation *f*; (*situation*) Situation *f*

seven [sɛvᵊn] *num* sieben ▷ *n* Sieben *f*; *see also* **eight**

seventeen [sɛvᵊntiːn] *num* siebzehn ▷ *n* Siebzehn *f*; *see also* **eight**

seventeenth [sɛvᵊntiːnθ] *adj* siebzehnte(r, s); *see also* **eighth**

seventh [sɛvᵊnθ] *adj* siebte(r, s) ▷ *n* (*fraction*) Siebtel *nt*; *see also* **eighth**

seventieth [sɛvᵊntiəθ] *adj* siebzigste(r, s); *see also* **eighth**

seventy [sɛvˀnti] *num* siebzig; **~one** ein-undsiebzig ▷ *n* Siebzig *f*; **to be in one's seventies** in den Siebzigern sein; *see also* **eight**

several [sɛvrəl] *adj, pron* mehrere

severe [sɪvɪər] *adj* (*strict*) streng; (*serious*) schwer; (*pain*) stark; (*winter*) hart

severely [sɪvɪərli] *adv* (*harshly*) hart; (*seriously*) schwer

sew [soʊ] (**sewed, sewn**) *vt, vi* nähen

sewage [suːdʒ] *n* Abwasser *nt*

sewer [suːər] *n* Abwasserkanal *m*

sewing [soʊɪŋ] *n* Nähen *nt*

sewing machine *n* Nähmaschine *f*

sewn [soʊn] *pp of* **sew**

sex [sɛks] *n* Sex *m*; (*gender*) Geschlecht *nt*; **to have sex** Sex haben (*with* mit)

sexism [sɛksɪzəm] *n* Sexismus *m*

sexist [sɛksɪst] *adj* sexistisch ▷ *n* Sexist(in) *m(f)*

sex life *n* Sex(ual)leben *nt*

sexual [sɛkʃuəl] *adj* sexuell; **~ discrimination/harassment** sexuelle Diskriminierung/Belästigung; **~intercourse** Geschlechtsverkehr *m*

sexuality [sɛkʃuˈæliti] *n* Sexualität *f*

sexually [sɛkʃuəli] *adv* sexuell

sexy [sɛksi] *adj* sexy, geil

Seychelles [seɪʃɛlz] *npl* Seychellen *pl*

shabby [ʃæbi] *adj* schäbig

shack [ʃæk] *n* Hütte *f*

shade [ʃeɪd] *n* (*shadow*) Schatten *m*; (*for lamp*) (Lampen)schirm *m*; (*color*) Farbton *m*; **~s** (*sunglasses*) Sonnenbrille *f* ▷ *vt* (*from sun*) abschirmen; (*in drawing*) schattieren

shadow [ʃædoʊ] *n* Schatten *m*

shady [ʃeɪdi] *adj* schattig; (*fig*) zwielichtig

shake [ʃeɪk] (**shook, shaken**) *vt* schütteln; (*shock*) erschüttern; **to ~ hands with sb** jdm die Hand geben; **to ~ one's head** den Kopf schütteln ▷ *vi* (*tremble*) zittern; (*building, ground*) schwanken

shaken [ʃeɪkən] *pp of* **shake**

shake off *vt* abschütteln

shaky [ʃeɪki] *adj* (*trembling*) zittrig; (*table, chair, position*) wackelig; (*weak*) unsicher

shall [ʃəl, STRONG ʃæl] (**should**) *vb aux* werden; (*in questions*) sollen; **I ~ do my best** ich werde mein Bestes tun; **~ I come too?** soll ich mitkommen?; **where ~ we go?** wo gehen wir hin?

shallow [ʃæloʊ] *adj* (*a. fig*) seicht; (*person*) oberflächlich

shame [ʃeɪm] *n* (*feeling of shame*) Scham *f*; (*disgrace*) Schande *f*; **what a ~!** wie schade!; **~ on you!** schäm dich/schämen Sie sich!; **it's a ~ that ...** schade, dass ...

shampoo [ʃæmpuː] *n* Shampoo *nt*; **to have a ~ and set** sich die Haare waschen und legen lassen ▷ *vt* (*hair*) waschen; (*carpet*) schamponieren

shape [ʃeɪp] *n* Form *f*; (*unidentified figure*) Gestalt *f*; **in the ~ of** in Form +*gen*; **to be in good ~** (*in health*) in guter Verfassung sein; **to take ~** (*plan, idea*) Gestalt annehmen ▷ *vt* (*clay, person*) formen

-shaped [-ʃeɪpt] *suf* -förmig

shapeless [ʃeɪplɪs] *adj* formlos

share [ʃɛər] *n* Anteil *m* (*in, of* an *m*); (*Fin*) Aktie *f* ▷ *vt, vi* teilen

shareholder [ʃɛərhoʊldər] *n* Aktionär(in) *m(f)*

shark [ʃɑrk] *n* (*Zool*) Haifisch *m*

sharp [ʃɑrp] *adj* scharf; (*pin*) spitz; (*person*) scharfsinnig; (*pain*) heftig; (*increase, fall*) abrupt; (*Mus*) Cis/Dis *nt* ▷ *adv*: **at 2 o'clock** ~ Punkt 2 Uhr

sharpen [ʃɑrpən] *vt* (*knife*) schärfen; (*pencil*) spitzen

sharpener [ʃɑrpənər] *n* (*pencil sharpener*) Spitzer *m*

shatter [ʃætər] *vt* zerschmettern; (*fig*) zerstören ▷ *vi* zerspringen

shave [ʃeɪv] (**shaved, shaved** *o* **shaven**) *vt* rasieren ▷ *vi* sich rasieren ▷ *n* Rasur *f*; **that was a close ~** (*fig*) das war knapp

shaven [ʃeɪvˀn] *pp of* **shave** ▷ *adj* (*head*) kahl geschoren

shave off *vt*: **to shave one's beard off** sich den Bart abrasieren

shaver [ʃeɪvər] *n* (*Elec*) Rasierapparat *m*

shaving brush [ʃeɪvɪŋ brʌʃ] *n* Rasierpinsel *m*

shaving cream [ʃeɪvɪŋ kriːm] *n* Rasierschaum *m*

shawl [ʃɔl] *n* Tuch *nt*

she [ʃɪ, STRONG ʃiː] *pron* sie

shed [ʃɛd] (**shed, shed**) *n* Schuppen *m* ▷ *vt* (*tears, blood*) vergießen; (*hair, leaves*) verlieren

she'd [ʃid, ʃɪd] *contr of* **she had; she would**

sheep [ʃip] (*pl* -) *n* Schaf *nt*

sheepdog [ʃipdɒg] *n* Schäferhund *m*

sheepskin [ʃipskɪn] *n* Schaffell *nt*

sheer [ʃɪər] *adj* (*madness*) rein; (*steep*) steil; **by ~ chance** rein zufällig

sheet [ʃit] *n* (*on bed*) Betttuch *nt*; (*of paper*) Blatt *nt*; (*of metal*) Platte *f*; (*of glass*) Scheibe *f*; **a ~ of paper** ein Blatt Papier

shelf [ʃɛlf] (*pl* **shelves**) *n* Bücherbord *nt*, Regal *nt*; **shelves** *pl* (*item of furniture*) Regal *nt*

shell [ʃɛl] *n* (*of egg, nut*) Schale *f*; (*seashell*) Muschel *f* ▷ *vt* (*peas, nuts*) schälen

she'll [ʃiːl, ʃɪl] *contr of* **she will; she shall**

shellfish [ʃɛlfɪʃ] *n* (*as food*) Meeresfrüchte *pl*

shelter [ʃɛltər] *n* (*protection*) Schutz *m*; (*accommodation*) Unterkunft *f*; (*bus shelter*) Wartehäuschen *nt* ▷ *vt* schützen (*from* vor +*dat*) ▷ *vi* sich unterstellen

sheltered [ʃɛltərd] *adj* (*spot*) geschützt; (*life*) behütet

shelve [ʃɛlv] *vt* (*fig*) aufschieben

shelves [ʃɛlvz] *pl of* **shelf**

shepherd [ʃɛpərd] *n* Schäfer *m*

shepherd's pie *n* Hackfleischauflauf mit Decke aus Kartoffelpüree

sherry [ʃɛri] *n* Sherry *m*

she's [ʃiːz, ʃɪz] *contr of* **she is; she has**

shield [ʃiːld] *n* Schild *m*; (*fig*) Schutz *m* ▷ *vt* schützen (*from* vor +*dat*)

shift [ʃɪft] *n* (*change*) Veränderung *f*; (*period at work, workers*) Schicht *f*; (*on keyboard*) Umschalttaste *f* ▷ *vt* (*furniture etc*) verrücken; (*stain*) entfernen; **to ~ gear(s)** (*Auto*) schalten ▷ *vi* (*move*) sich bewegen; (*move up*) rutschen

shift key *n* Umschalttaste *f*

shin [ʃɪn] *n* Schienbein *nt*

shine [ʃaɪn] (**shone, shone**) *vi* (*be shiny*) glänzen; (*sun*) scheinen; (*lamp*) leuchten ▷ *vt* (*polish*) polieren ▷ *n* Glanz *m*

shingles [ʃɪŋgəlz] *nsing* (*Med*) Gürtelrose *f*

shiny [ʃaɪni] *adj* glänzend

ship [ʃɪp] *n* Schiff *nt* ▷ *vt* (*send*) versenden; (*by ship*) verschiffen

shipment [ʃɪpmənt] *n* (*goods*) Sendung *f*; (*sent by ship*) Ladung *f*

shipwreck [ʃɪprɛk] *n* Schiffbruch *m*

shipyard [ʃɪpyɑrd] *n* Werft *f*

shirt [ʃɜrt] *n* Hemd *nt*

shiver [ʃɪvər] *vi* zittern (*with* vor +*dat*)

shock [ʃɒk] *n* (*mental, emotional*) Schock *m*; **to be in ~** unter Schock stehen; **to get a ~** (*Elec*) einen Schlag bekommen ▷ *vt* schockieren

shock absorber [ʃɒk əbsɔrbər] *n* Stoßdämpfer *m*

shocked [ʃɒkt] *adj* schockiert (*by* über +*akk*)

shocking [ʃɒkɪŋ] *adj* schockierend; (*awful*) furchtbar

shoe [ʃuː] *n* Schuh *m*

shoehorn [ʃuːhɔrn] *n* Schuhlöffel *m*

shoelace [ʃuːleɪs] *n* Schnürsenkel *m*

shoe polish *n* Schuhcreme *f*

shone [ʃoʊn] *pt, pp of* **shine**

shook [ʃʊk] *pt of* **shake**

shoot [ʃuːt] (**shot, shot**) *vt* (*wound*) anschießen; (*kill*) erschießen; (*Cine*) drehen; (*fam: heroin*) drücken ▷ *vi* (*with gun, move quickly*) schießen; **to ~ at sb** auf jdn schießen ▷ *n* (*of plant*) Trieb *m*

shooting [ʃuːtɪŋ] *n* (*exchange of gunfire*) Schießerei *f*; (*killing*) Erschießung *f*

shop [ʃɒp] *n* (*store*) Geschäft *nt*, Laden *m* ▷ *vi* einkaufen

shoplifting [ʃɒplɪftɪŋ] *n* Ladendiebstahl *m*

shopper [ʃɒpər] *n* Käufer(in) *m(f)*

shopping [ʃɒpɪŋ] *n* (*activity*) Einkaufen *nt*; (*goods*) Einkäufe *pl*; **to do the ~** einkaufen; **we are**; **to go ~** einkaufen gehen

shopping bag *n* Einkaufstasche *f*

shopping cart *n* Einkaufswagen *m*

shopping center *n* Einkaufszentrum *nt*

shopping list *n* Einkaufszettel *m*

shore [ʃɔr] *n* Ufer *nt*; **on ~** an Land

short [ʃɔrt] *adj* kurz; (*person*) klein; **to be ~ of money** knapp bei Kasse sein; **to be ~ of time** wenig Zeit haben; **~ of breath** kurzatmig; **to cut ~** (*holiday*) abbrechen; **we are two ~** wir haben zwei zu wenig; **it's ~ for ...** das ist die Kurzform von ... ▷ *n* (*drink, Elec*) Kurze(r) *m*

shortage [ʃɔrtɪdʒ] *n* Knappheit *f* (*of* an +*dat*)

shortbread [ʃɔrtbrɛd] *n* Buttergebäck *nt*

short circuit [ʃɔrt sɜrkɪt] *n* Kurzschluss *m*

shortcoming [ʃɔrtkʌmɪŋ] *n* Unzulänglichkeit *f*; (*of person*) Fehler *m*

shortcut [ʃɔrtkʌt] *n* (*quicker route*) Abkürzung *f*; (*Inform*) Shortcut *m*

shorten [ʃɔrtᵊn] *vt* kürzen; (*in time*) verkürzen

shorthand [ʃɔrthænd] *n* Stenografie *f*

shortlist [ʃɔrtlɪst] *n*: **to be on the ~** in der engeren Wahl sein

short-lived [ʃɔrtlɪvd] *adj* kurzlebig

shortly [ʃɔrtli] *adv* bald

shorts *npl* Shorts *pl*

short-sighted [ʃɔrtsaɪtɪd] *adj* (*a. fig*) kurzsichtig

short-sleeved [ʃɔrtsliːvd] *adj* kurzärmelig

short story *n* Kurzgeschichte *f*

short-term *adj* kurzfristig

short wave *n* Kurzwelle *f*

shot [ʃɒt] *pt, pp of* **shoot** ▷ *n* (*from gun, in soccer*) Schuss *m*; (*Foto, Cine*) Aufnahme *f*;

S

(*injection*) Spritze *f*; (*of alcohol*) Schuss *m*

should [ʃəd, STRONG ʃʊd] *pt of* **shall** ▷ *vb aux*: I ~ go now ich sollte jetzt gehen; **what ~ I do?** was soll ich tun?; **you ~n't have said that** das hättest du/hätten Sie nicht sagen sollen; **that ~ be enough** das müsste reichen

shoulder [ʃəʊldər] *n* Schulter *f*

shouldn't [ʃʊdᵊnt] *contr of* **should not**

should've [ʃʊdəv] *contr of* **should have**

shout [ʃaʊt] *n* Schrei *m*; (*call*) Ruf *m* ▷ *vt* rufen; (*order*) brüllen ▷ *vi* schreien; **to ~ at** anschreien; **to ~ for help** um Hilfe rufen

shove [ʃʌv] *vt* (*person*) schubsen; (*car, table etc*) schieben ▷ *vi* (*in crowd*) drängeln

shovel [ʃʌvᵊl] *n* Schaufel *f* ▷ *vt* schaufeln

show [ʃəʊ] (**showed, shown**) *vt* zeigen; **to ~ sb sth, to ~ sth to sb** jdm etw zeigen; **to ~ sb in** jdn hereinführen; **to ~ sb out** jdn zur Tür bringen ▷ *n* (*Cine, Theat*) Vorstellung *f*; (*TV*) Show *f*; (*exhibition*) Ausstellung *f*

shower [ʃaʊər] *n* Dusche *f*; (*rain*) Schauer *m*; **to have** *o* **take a ~** duschen ▷ *vi* (*wash*) duschen

shower gel *n* Duschgel *nt*

showing [ʃəʊɪŋ] *n* (*Cine*) Vorstellung *f*

shown [ʃəʊn] *pp of* **show**

show off *vi* (*pej*) angeben

showroom [ʃəʊruːm] *n* Ausstellungsraum *m*

show up *vi* (*arrive*) auftauchen

shrank [ʃræŋk] *pt of* **shrink**

shred [ʃrɛd] *n* (*of paper, fabric*) Fetzen *m* ▷ *vt* (*in shredder*) (im Reißwolf) zerkleinern

shredder [ʃrɛdər] *n* (*for paper*) Reißwolf *m*

shrimp [ʃrɪmp] *n* Garnele *f*, Krabbe *f*

shrink [ʃrɪŋk] (**shrank, shrunk**) *vi* schrumpfen; (*clothes*) eingehen

shrivel [ʃrɪvᵊl] *vi*: **to ~ up** schrumpfen; (*skin*) runzlig werden; (*plant*) welken

Shrove Tuesday [ʃrəʊv tuːzdeɪ] *n* Fastnachtsdienstag *m*

shrub [ʃrʌb] *n* Busch *m*, Strauch *m*

shrug [ʃrʌg] *vt, vi*: **to ~ one's shoulders** die Achseln zucken

shrunk [ʃrʌŋk] *pp of* **shrink**

shudder [ʃʌdər] *vi* schaudern; (*ground, building*) beben

shuffle [ʃʌfᵊl] *vt, vi* mischen

shut [ʃʌt] (**shut, shut**) *vt* zumachen, schließen; **~ your face!** (*fam*) halt den Mund! ▷ *vi* schließen ▷ *adj* geschlossen; **we're ~** wir haben geschlossen

shut down *vt* schließen; (*computer*) aus-

schalten ▷ *vi* schließen; (*computer*) sich ausschalten

shut in *vt* einschließen

shut out *vt* (*lock out*) aussperren; **to shut oneself out** sich aussperren

shutter [ʃʌtər] *n* (*on window*) (Fenster)laden *m*

shutter release *n* Auslöser *m*

shutter speed *n* Belichtungszeit *f*

shuttle bus [ʃʌtᵊl bʌs] *n* Shuttlebus *m*

shuttlecock [ʃʌtᵊlkɒk] *n* Federball *m*

shuttle service [ʃʌtᵊl sɜːvɪs] *n* Pendelverkehr *m*

shut up *vt* (*lock up*) abschließen; (*silence*) zum Schweigen bringen ▷ *vi* (*keep quiet*) den Mund halten; **~!** halt den Mund!

shy [ʃaɪ] *adj* schüchtern; (*animal*) scheu

Siberia [saɪbɪriə] *n* Sibirien *nt*

Sicily [sɪsəli] *n* Sizilien *nt*

sick [sɪk] *adj* krank; (*joke*) makaber; **to be off** ~ wegen Krankheit fehlen; **I feel ~** mir ist schlecht; **to be ~ of sb/sth** jdn/etw satthaben; **it makes me ~** (*fig*) es ekelt mich an

sick leave *n*: **to be on ~** krankgeschrieben sein

sickness [sɪknɪs] *n* Krankheit *f*

side [saɪd] *n* Seite *f*; (*of road*) Rand *m*; (*of mountain*) Hang *m*; (*Sport*) Mannschaft *f*; **by my ~** neben mir; **~ by ~** nebeneinander ▷ *adj* (*door, entrance*) Seiten-

sideboard [saɪdbɔːd] *n* Anrichte *f*

sideburns [saɪdbɜːnz] *npl* Koteletten *pl*

side dish *n* Beilage *f*

side effect *n* Nebenwirkung *f*

side order *n* Beilage *f*

side road *n* Nebenstraße *f*

side street *n* Seitenstraße *f*

sidewalk [saɪdwɔːk] *n* Bürgersteig *m*

sideways [saɪdweɪz] *adv* seitwärts

sieve [sɪv] *n* Sieb *nt*

sift [sɪft] *vt* (*flour etc*) sieben

sigh [saɪ] *vi* seufzen

sight [saɪt] *n* (*power of seeing*) Sehvermögen *nt*; (*view, thing seen*) Anblick *m*; **~s** *pl* (*of city etc*) Sehenswürdigkeiten *pl*; **to have bad ~** schlecht sehen; **to lose ~ of** aus den Augen verlieren; **out of ~** außer Sicht

sightseeing [saɪtsiːɪŋ] *n*: **to go ~** Sehenswürdigkeiten besichtigen; **~ tour** Rundfahrt *f*

sign [saɪn] *n* Zeichen *nt*; (*notice, road sign*) Schild *nt* ▷ *vt* unterschreiben ▷ *vi* unterschreiben; **to ~ for sth** den Empfang einer

Sache *gen* bestätigen; **to ~ in/out** sich ein-/austragen

signal [sɪgnəl] *n* Signal *nt* ▷ *vi* (*car driver*) blinken

signature [sɪgnətʃər, -tʃʊər] *n* Unterschrift *f*

significant [sɪgnɪfɪkənt] *adj* (*important*) bedeutend, wichtig; (*meaning sth*) bedeutsam

significantly [sɪgnɪfɪkəntli] *adv* (*considerably*) bedeutend

sign language *n* Zeichensprache *f*

signpost [saɪnpoʊst] *n* Wegweiser *m*

sign up *vi* (*for course*) sich einschreiben; (*Mil*) sich verpflichten

silence [saɪləns] *n* Stille *f*; (*of person*) Schweigen *nt*; **~!** Ruhe! ▷ *vt* zum Schweigen bringen

silent [saɪlənt] *adj* still; (*taciturn*) schweigsam; **she remained ~** sie schwieg

silk [sɪlk] *n* Seide *f* ▷ *adj* Seiden-

silly [sɪli] *adj* dumm, albern; **don't do anything ~** mach keine Dummheiten; **the ~ season** das Sommerloch

silver [sɪlvər] *n* Silber *nt*; (*coins*) Silbermünzen *pl* ▷ *adj* Silber-, silbern

silver-plated [sɪlvərpleɪtɪd] *adj* versilbert

silverware [sɪlvərweər] *n* Besteck *nt*

silver wedding anniversary *n* silberne Hochzeit

SIM card [sɪm kɑrd] *n* (*Tel*) SIM-Karte *f*

similar [sɪmɪlər] *adj* ähnlich (*to dat*)

similarity [sɪmɪlærɪti] *n* Ähnlichkeit *f* (*to* mit)

similarly [sɪmɪlərli] *adv* (*equally*) ebenso

simple [sɪmpᵊl] *adj* einfach; (*unsophisticated*) schlicht

simplify [sɪmplɪfaɪ] *vt* vereinfachen

simply [sɪmpli] *adv* einfach; (*merely*) bloß; (*dress*) schlicht

simulate [sɪmjəleɪt] *vt* simulieren

simultaneous [saɪməlt␣eɪniəs] *adj*, **simultaneously** *adv* gleichzeitig

sin [sɪn] *n* Sünde *f* ▷ *vi* sündigen

since [sɪns] *adv* seitdem; (*in the meantime*) inzwischen ▷ *prep* seit +*dat*; **ever ~ 1995** schon seit 1995 ▷ *conj* (*time*) seit, seitdem; (*because*) da, weil; **ever ~ I've known her** seit ich sie kenne; **it's been ages ~ I've seen him** ich habe ihn seit Langem nicht mehr gesehen

sincere [sɪnsɪər] *adj* aufrichtig

sincerely [sɪnsɪərli] *adv* aufrichtig; **Yours ~** mit freundlichen Grüßen

sing [sɪŋ] (**sang, sung**) *vt, vi* singen

Singapore [sɪŋgəpɔr] *n* Singapur *nt*

singer [sɪŋər] *n* Sänger(in) *m(f)*

single [sɪŋgᵊl] *adj* (*one only*) einzig; (*not double*) einfach; (*unmarried*) ledig ▷ *n* (*Mus*) Single *f*

single-handed [sɪŋgᵊlhændɪd], **single-handedly** *adv* im Alleingang

single out *vt* (*choose*) auswählen

single parent *n* Alleinerziehende(r) *mf*

single-parent family *n* Einelternfamilie *f*

singular [sɪŋgjələr] *n* Singular *m*

sinister [sɪnɪstər] *adj* unheimlich

sink [sɪŋk] (**sank, sunk**) *vt* (*ship*) versenken ▷ *vi* sinken ▷ *n* Spülbecken *nt*; (*in bathroom*) Waschbecken *nt*

sip [sɪp] *vt* nippen an +*dat*

sir [sɜr] *n*: **yes, sir** ja(, mein Herr); **can I help you, sir?** kann ich Ihnen helfen?; **Sir James** (*title*) Sir James

sissy *n* (*fam*) Weichling *m*

sister [sɪstər] *n* Schwester *f*

sister-in-law [sɪstərɪnlɔ] (*pl* **sisters-in-law**) *n* Schwägerin *f*

sit [sɪt] (**sat, sat**) *vi* (*be sitting*) sitzen; (*sit down*) sich setzen; (*committee, court*) tagen

sitcom [sɪtkɒm] *n* Situationskomödie *f*

sit down *vi* sich hinsetzen

site [saɪt] *n* Platz *m*; (*building site*) Baustelle *f*; (*website*) Site *f*

sitting [sɪtɪŋ] *n* (*meeting, for portrait*) Sitzung *f*

sitting room *n* Wohnzimmer *nt*

situated [sɪtʃueɪtɪd] *adj*: **to be ~** liegen

situation [sɪtʃueɪʃ°n] *n* (*circumstances*) Situation *f*, Lage *f*; (*job*) Stelle *f*

sit up *vi* (*from lying position*) sich aufsetzen

six [sɪks] *num* sechs ▷ *n* Sechs *f*; *see also* **eight**

sixpack [sɪkspæk] *n* (*of beer etc*) Sechserpack *nt*

sixteen [sɪkstin] *num* sechzehn ▷ *n* Sechzehn *f*; *see also* **eight**

sixteenth [sɪkstinθ] *adj* sechzehnte(r, s); *see also* **eighth**

sixth [sɪksθ] *adj* sechste(r, s) ▷ *n* (*fraction*) Sechstel *nt*; *see also* **eighth**

sixtieth [sɪkstiəθ] *adj* sechzigste(r, s); *see also* **eighth**

sixty [sɪksti] *num* sechzig; **~-one** einundsechzig ▷ *n* Sechzig *f*; **to be in one's sixties** in den Sechzigern sein; *see also* **eight**

size [saɪz] *n* Größe *f*; **what ~ are you?** welche Größe hast du/haben Sie?; **a ~ too big**

eine Nummer zu groß

sizzle [sɪzˀl] vi (Gastr) brutzeln

skate [skeɪt] n Schlittschuh m; (roller skate) Rollschuh m ▷ vi Schlittschuh laufen; (roller-skate) Rollschuh laufen

skateboard [skeɪtbɔrd] n Skateboard nt

skating [skeɪtɪŋ] n Eislauf m; (roller-skating) Rollschuhlauf m

skating rink n Eisbahn f; (for roller-skating) Rollschuhbahn f

skeleton [skɛlɪtˀn] n (a. fig) Skelett nt

skeptical [skɛptɪkˀl] n, adj skeptisch

sketch [skɛtʃ] n Skizze f; (Theat) Sketch m ▷ vt skizzieren

sketchbook [skɛtʃbʊk] n Skizzenbuch nt

ski [ski] n Ski m ▷ vi Ski laufen

ski boot n Skistiefel m

skid [skɪd] vi (Auto) schleudern

skier [skiər] n Skiläufer(in) m(f)

skiing [skiɪŋ] n Skilaufen nt; **to go ~** Ski laufen gehen; **~ holiday** Skiurlaub m

skiing instructor n Skilehrer(in) m(f)

ski-lift [skilɪft] n Skilift m

skill [skɪl] n Geschick nt; (acquired technique) Fertigkeit f

skilled [skɪld] adj geschickt (at, in in +dat); (worker) Fach-; (work) fachmännisch

skillful [skɪlfəl] adj, **skillfully** adv geschickt

skim [skɪm] vt: **to ~ off** (fat etc) abschöpfen; **to ~ through** (read) überfliegen

skim milk n Magermilch f

skin [skɪn] n Haut f; (fur) Fell nt; (peel) Schale f

skin diving n Sporttauchen nt

skinny [skɪni] adj dünn

skip [skɪp] vi hüpfen; (with rope) seilspringen ▷ vt (miss out) überspringen; (meal) ausfallen lassen; (school, lesson) schwänzen

ski pants npl Skihose f

ski pass n Skipass m

ski pole n Skistock m

ski resort n Skiort m

skirt [skɜrt] n Rock m

ski run n (Ski)abfahrt f

ski tow n Schlepplift m

skull [skʌl] n Schädel m

sky [skaɪ] n Himmel m

skydiving [skaɪdaɪvɪŋ] n Fallschirmspringen nt

skylight [skaɪlaɪt] n Dachfenster nt

skyscraper [skaɪskreɪpər] n Wolkenkratzer m

slam [slæm] vt (door) zuschlagen

slam on vt: **to slam the brakes on** voll auf die Bremse treten

slander [slændər] n Verleumdung f ▷ vt verleumden

slang [slæŋ] n Slang m

slap [slæp] n Klaps m; (across face) Ohrfeige f ▷ vt schlagen; **to ~ sb's face** jdn ohrfeigen

slash [slæʃ] n (punctuation mark) Schrägstrich m ▷ vt (face, tire) aufschlitzen; (prices) stark herabsetzen

slate [sleɪt] n (rock) Schiefer m; (roof slate) Schieferplatte f

slaughter [slɔtər] vt (animals) schlachten; (people) abschlachten

Slav [slav] adj slawisch ▷ n Slawe m, Slawin f

slave [sleɪv] n Sklave m, Sklavin f

slave away vi schuften

slave driver [sleɪv draɪvər] n (fam) Sklaventreiber(in) m(f)

slavery [sleɪvəri, sleɪvri] n Sklaverei f

sleaze [sliz] n (corruption) Korruption f

sleazy [slizi] adj (bar, district) zwielichtig

sled [slɛd] n Schlitten m

sleep [slip] (**slept, slept**) vi schlafen; **to ~ with sb** mit jdm schlafen ▷ n Schlaf m; **to put to ~** (animal) einschläfern

sleeper [slipər] n (train car) Schlafwagen m

sleep in vi (lie in) ausschlafen

sleeping bag [slipɪŋ bæg] n Schlafsack m

sleeping car [slipɪŋ kɑr] n Schlafwagen m

sleeping pill [slipɪŋ pɪl] n Schlaftablette f

sleepless [sliplɪs] adj schlaflos

sleepover [slipoʊvər] n Übernachtung f (bei Freunden etc)

sleepy [slipi] adj schläfrig; (place) verschlafen

sleet [slit] n Schneeregen m

sleeve [sliv] n Ärmel m

sleeveless [slivlɪs] adj ärmellos

sleigh [sleɪ] n (Pferde)schlitten m

slender [slɛndər] adj schlank; (fig) gering

slept [slɛpt] pt, pp of sleep

slice [slaɪs] n Scheibe f; (of cake, pizza) Stück nt ▷ vt: **to ~ up** in Scheiben schneiden

sliced bread [slaɪst brɛd] n geschnittenes Brot

slid [slɪd] pt, pp of slide

slide [slaɪd] (**slid, slid**) vt gleiten lassen; (push) schieben ▷ vi gleiten; (slip) rutschen ▷ n (Foto) Dia nt; (in playground)

Rutschbahn f

slight [slaɪt] adj leicht; (problem, difference) klein; **not in the ~est** nicht im Geringsten

slightly [slaɪtli] adv etwas; (injured) leicht

slim [slɪm] adj (person) schlank; (book) dünn; (chance, hope) gering ▷ vi abnehmen

slime [slaɪm] n Schleim m

slimy [slaɪmi] adj schleimig

sling [slɪŋ] (**slung, slung**) vt werfen ▷ n (for arm) Schlinge f

slip [slɪp] n (mistake) Flüchtigkeitsfehler m; ~ **of paper** Zettel m ▷ vt (put) stecken; **to ~ on/off** (garment) an-/ausziehen; **it ~ped my mind** ich habe es vergessen ▷ vi (lose balance) (aus)rutschen

slip away vi (leave) sich wegstehlen

slipper [slɪpər] n Hausschuh m

slippery [slɪpəri] adj (path, road) glatt; (soap, fish) glitschig

slit [slɪt] (**slit, slit**) vt aufschlitzen ▷ n Schlitz m

slope [sloʊp] n Neigung f; (side of hill) Hang m ▷ vi (be sloping) schräg sein

sloping [sloʊpɪŋ] adj (floor, roof) schräg

sloppy [slɒpi] adj (careless) schlampig; (sentimental) rührselig

slot [slɒt] n (opening) Schlitz m; (Inform) Steckplatz m; **we have a ~ free at 2** (free time) um 2 ist noch ein Termin frei

slot machine [slɒt məʃin] n Automat m; (for gambling) Spielautomat m

Slovak [sloʊvæk] adj slowakisch ▷ n (person) Slowake m, Slowakin f; (language) Slowakisch nt

Slovakia [sloʊvækiə] n Slowakei f

Slovene [sloʊvin], **Slovenian** [sloʊviniən] adj slowenisch ▷ n (person) Slowene m, Slowenin f; (language) Slowenisch nt

Slovenia [sloʊviniə] n Slowenien nt

slow [sloʊ] adj langsam; (business) flau; **to be ~** (clock) nachgehen; (stupid) begriffsstutzig sein

slow down vi langsamer werden; (when driving/walking) langsamer fahren/gehen

slowly [sloʊli] adv langsam

slow motion n: **in ~** in Zeitlupe

slug [slʌg] n (Zool) Nacktschnecke f

slum [slʌm] n Slum m

slump [slʌmp] n Rückgang m (in an +dat) ▷ vi (onto chair etc) sich fallen lassen; (prices) stürzen

slung [slʌŋ] pt, pp of **sling**

slur [slɜr] n (insult) Verleumdung f

slurred [slɜrd] adj undeutlich

slush [slʌʃ] n (snow) Schneematsch m

slushy [slʌʃi] adj matschig; (fig) schmalzig

slut [slʌt] n (pej) Schlampe f

smack [smæk] n Klaps m ▷ vt: **to ~ sb** jdm einen Klaps geben ▷ vi: **to ~ of** riechen nach

small [smɔl] adj klein

small change n Kleingeld nt

small letters npl: **in ~** in Kleinbuchstaben

smallpox [smɔlpɒks] n Pocken pl

small print n: **the ~** das Kleingedruckte

small-scale adj (map) in kleinem Maßstab

small talk n Konversation f, Smalltalk m

smart [smɑrt] adj (elegant) schick; (clever) clever

smartass [smɑrtæs] n (fam) Klugscheißer(in) m(f)

smart card n Chipkarte f

smartly [smɑrtli] adv (dressed) schick

smartphone [smɑrtfoʊn] n (Tel) Smartphone nt

smash [smæʃ] n (car crash) Zusammenstoß m; (Tennis) Schmetterball m ▷ vt (break) zerschlagen; (fig: record) brechen, deutlich übertreffen ▷ vi (break) zerbrechen; **to ~ into** (car) krachen gegen

smear [smɪər] n (mark) Fleck m; (Med) Abstrich m; (fig) Verleumdung f ▷ vt (spread) schmieren; (make dirty) beschmieren; (fig) verleumden

smell [smɛl] (**smelled** o **smelt, smelled** o **smelt**) vt riechen ▷ vi riechen (of nach); (unpleasantly) stinken ▷ n Geruch m; (unpleasant) Gestank m

smelly [smɛli] adj übel riechend

smelt [smɛlt] pt, pp of **smell**

smile [smaɪl] n Lächeln nt ▷ vi lächeln; **to ~ at sb** jdn anlächeln

smock [smɒk] n Kittel m

smog [smɒg] n Smog m

smoke [smoʊk] n Rauch m ▷ vt rauchen; (food) räuchern ▷ vi rauchen

smoke alarm n Rauchmelder m

smoked [smoʊkt] adj (food) geräuchert

smoke-free adj (zone, building) rauchfrei

smoker [smoʊkər] n Raucher(in) m(f)

smoking [smoʊkɪŋ] n Rauchen nt; 'no ~' „Rauchen verboten"

smooth [smuð] adj glatt; (flight, crossing) ruhig; (movement) geschmeidig; (without problems) reibungslos; (pej: person) aalglatt ▷ vt (hair, dress) glatt streichen; (surface) glätten

smoothly [smuðli] adv reibungslos; **to run ~** (engine) ruhig laufen

smudge [smʌdʒ] *vt* (*writing, lipstick*) verschmieren

smug [smʌg] *adj* selbstgefällig

smuggle [smʌgⁿl] *vt* schmuggeln; **to ~ in/out** herein-/herausschmuggeln

smutty [smʌti] *adj* (*obscene*) schmutzig

snack [snæk] *n* Imbiss *m*; **to have a ~** eine Kleinigkeit essen

snack bar *n* Imbissstube *f*

snail [sneɪl] *n* Schnecke *f*

snail mail *n* (*fam*) Schneckenpost *f*

snake [sneɪk] *n* Schlange *f*

snap [snæp] *n* (*photo*) Schnappschuss *m* ▷ *adj* (*decision*) spontan ▷ *vt* (*break*) zerbrechen; (*rope*) zerreißen ▷ *vi* (*break*) brechen; (*rope*) reißen ▷ (*bite*) schnappen (*at* nach)

snap fastener *n* Druckknopf *m*

snap off *vt* (*break*) abbrechen

snapshot [snæpʃɒt] *n* Schnappschuss *m*

snatch [snætʃ] *vt* (*grab*) schnappen

sneak [snik] *vi* (*move*) schleichen

sneakers [snikərz] *npl* Turnschuhe *pl*

sneeze [sniz] *vi* niesen

sniff [snɪf] *vi* schniefen; (*smell*) schnüffeln (*at* an +*dat*) ▷ *vt* schnuppern an +*dat*; (*glue*) schnüffeln

snob [snɒb] *n* Snob *m*

snobbish [snɒbɪʃ] *adj* versnobt

snooker [snukər] *n* Snooker *nt*

snoop [snup] *vi*: **to ~ around** (herum)schnüffeln

snooze [snuz] *n, vi*: **to have a ~** ein Nickerchen machen

snore [snɔr] *vi* schnarchen

snorkel [snɔrkⁿl] *n* Schnorchel *m*

snorkeling [snɔrkⁿlɪŋ] *n* Schnorcheln *nt*; **to go ~** schnorcheln gehen

snout [snaʊt] *n* Schnauze *f*

snow [snoʊ] *n* Schnee *m* ▷ *vi* schneien

snowball [snoʊbɔl] *n* Schneeball *m*

snowboard [snoʊbɔrd] *n* Snowboard *nt*

snowboarding [snoʊbɔrdɪŋ] *n* Snowboarding *nt*

snowdrift [snoʊdrɪft] *n* Schneewehe *f*

snowdrop [snoʊdrɒp] *n* Schneeglöckchen *nt*

snowflake [snoʊfleɪk] *n* Schneeflocke *f*

snowman [snoʊmæn] (*pl* **-men**) *n* Schneemann *m*

snowplow [snoʊplaʊ] *n* Schneepflug *m*

snowstorm [snoʊstɔrm] *n* Schneesturm *m*

snowy [snoʊi] *adj* (*region*) schneereich; (*landscape*) verschneit

snug [snʌg] *adj* (*person, place*) gemütlich

snuggle up [snʌgⁿl ʌp] *vi*: **to ~ to sb** sich an jdn ankuscheln

KEYWORD

so [soʊ] *adv* **1** (*thus*) so; (*likewise*) auch; **so saying he walked away** indem er das sagte, ging er; **if so** wenn ja; **I didn't do it – you did so!** ich hab das nicht gemacht – hast du wohl!; **so do I, so am I** *etc* ich auch; **so it is!** tatsächlich!; **I hope/think so** hoffentlich/ich glaube schon; **so far** bis jetzt

2 (*in comparisons etc: to such a degree*) so; **so quickly/big (that)** so schnell/groß, dass; **I'm so glad to see you** ich freue mich so, dich/Sie zu sehen

3: **so many** so viele; **so much work** so viel Arbeit; **I love you so much** ich liebe dich so sehr

4 (*phrases*): **10 or so** etwa 10; **so long!** (*inf: goodbye*) tschüss!

▷ *conj* **1** (*expressing purpose*): **so as to ...** um ... zu; **so (that)** damit

2 (*expressing result*) also; **so I was right after all** ich hatte also doch recht; **so you see ...** wie du siehst/Sie sehen ...

soak [soʊk] *vt* durchnässen; (*leave in liquid*) einweichen; **I'm ~ed** ich bin klatschnass

soaking [soʊkɪŋ] *adj*: **~ wet** klatschnass

soap [soʊp] *n* Seife *f*

soap (opera) *n* Seifenoper *f*

soap powder *n* Waschpulver *nt*

sob [sɒb] *vi* schluchzen

sober [soʊbər] *adj* nüchtern

sober up *vi* nüchtern werden

so-called [soʊkɔld] *adj* sogenannt

soccer [sɒkər] *n* Fußball *m*

soccer player [sɒkər pleɪər] *n* Fußballspieler(in) *m(f)*

sociable [soʊʃəbⁿl] *adj* gesellig

social [soʊʃⁿl] *adj* sozial; (*sociable*) gesellig

socialist [soʊʃəlɪst] *adj* sozialistisch ▷ *n* Sozialist(in) *m(f)*

socialize [soʊʃəlaɪz] *vi* unter die Leute gehen

social networking [soʊʃⁿl nɛtwɜrkɪŋ] *n* Netzwerken *nt*

social security *n* Sozialversicherung *f*

society [səsaɪti] *n* Gesellschaft *f*; (*club*) Verein *m*

sock [sɒk] *n* Socke *f*

socket [sɒkɪt] *n* (*Elec*) Steckdose *f*

soda [sˈoʊdə] n (soda water) Soda f; (pop) Limo f

soda water n Sodawasser nt

sofa [sˈoʊfə] n Sofa nt

sofa bed n Schlafcouch f

soft [sˈɒft] adj weich; (quiet) leise; (lighting) gedämpft; (kind) gutmütig; (weak) nachgiebig; ~ **drink** alkoholfreies Getränk

softly [sˈɒftli] adv sanft; (quietly) leise

software [sˈɒftwɛər] n (Inform) Software f

soil [sˈɔɪl] n Erde f; (ground) Boden m

solar [sˈoʊlər] adj Sonnen-, Solar-

solarium [səlˈɛəriəm, soʊ-] n Solarium nt

sold [sˈoʊld] pt, pp of **sell**

soldier [sˈoʊldʒər] n Soldat(in) m(f)

sole [sˈoʊl] n Sohle f; (fish) Seezunge f ▷ vt besohlen ▷ adj einzig; (owner, responsibility) alleinig

solely [sˈoʊlli] adv nur

solemn [sˈɒləm] adj feierlich; (person) ernst

solid [sˈɒlɪd] adj (hard) fest; (gold, oak etc) massiv; (solidly built) solide; (meal) kräftig; **three hours ~** drei volle Stunden

solitary [sˈɒlɪtəri] adj einsam; (single) einzeln

solitude [sˈɒlɪtud] n Einsamkeit f

solo [sˈoʊloʊ] n (Mus) Solo nt

soluble [sˈɒljəbəl] adj löslich

solution [səlˈuʃᵊn] n Lösung f (to +gen)

solve [sˈɒlv] vt lösen

somber [sˈɒmbər] adj düster

KEYWORD

some [səm, STRONG sˈʌm] adj 1 (a certain amount o number of) einige; (a few) ein paar; (with singular nouns) etwas; **some tea/cookies** etwas Tee/ein paar Kekse; **I've got some money, but not much** ich habe ein bisschen Geld, aber nicht viel

2 (certain: in contrasts) manche(r, s); **some people say that ...** manche Leute sagen, dass ...

3 (unspecified) irgendein(e); **some woman was asking for you** da hat eine Frau nach dir/Ihnen gefragt; **some day** eines Tages; **some day next week** irgendwann nächste Woche

▷ pron 1 (a certain number) einige; **have you got some?** hast du/haben Sie welche?

2 (a certain amount) etwas; **I've read some of the book** ich habe das Buch teilweise gelesen

▷ adv: **some 10 people** etwa 10 Leute

somebody [sˈʌmbɑdi, -bʌdi] pron jemand; ~ **or other** irgendjemand; ~ **else** jemand anders

someday [sˈʌmdeɪ] adv irgendwann

somehow [sˈʌmhaʊ] adv irgendwie

someone [sˈʌmwʌn] pron see **somebody**

someplace [sˈʌmpleɪs] adv see **somewhere**

something [sˈʌmθɪŋ] pron etwas; ~ **or other** irgendetwas; ~ **else** etwas anderes; ~ **nice** etwas Nettes; **would you like ~ to drink?** möchtest du/möchten Sie etwas trinken? ▷ adv: **like 20** ungefähr 20

sometime [sˈʌmtaɪm] adv irgendwann

sometimes [sˈʌmtaɪmz] adv manchmal

somewhat [sˈʌmwʌt, -wɒt] adv ein wenig

somewhere [sˈʌmwɛər] adv irgendwo; (to a place) irgendwohin; ~ **else** irgendwo anders; (to another place) irgendwo anders hin

son [sˈʌn] n Sohn m

song [sˈɒŋ] n Lied nt, Song m

son-in-law [sˈʌnɪnlɔ] (pl **sons-in-law**) n Schwiegersohn m

soon [sˈun] adv bald; (early) früh; **too ~** zu früh; **as ~ as I ...** sobald ich ...; **as ~ as possible** so bald wie möglich

sooner [sˈunər] adv (time) früher; (for preference) lieber

soot [sˈut, sˈʌt] n Ruß m

soothe [sˈuð] vt beruhigen; (pain) lindern

sophisticated [səfˈɪstɪkeɪtɪd] adj (person) kultiviert; (machine) hoch entwickelt; (plan) ausgeklügelt

sophomore [sˈɒfəmɔr] n College-Student(in) m(f) im zweiten Jahr

soppy [sˈɒpi] adj (fam) rührselig

soprano [səprˈænoʊ, -prˈɑn-] n Sopran m

sore [sˈɔr] adj: **to be ~** wehtun; **to have a ~ throat** Halsschmerzen haben ▷ n wunde Stelle

sorrow [sˈɒroʊ] n Kummer m

sorry [sˈɒri] adj (sight, figure) traurig; **(I'm) ~** (excusing) Entschuldigung!; **I'm ~** (regretful) es tut mir leid; ~? wie bitte?; **I feel ~ for him** er tut mir leid

sort [sˈɔrt] n Art f; **what ~ of film is it?** was für ein Film ist das?; **a ~ of** eine Art +gen; **all ~s of things** alles Mögliche ▷ adv: ~ **of** (fam) irgendwie ▷ vt sortieren; **everything's ~ed** (dealt with) alles ist geregelt

sort out vt (classify etc) sortieren; (problems) lösen

sought [sˈɔt] pt, pp of **seek**

soul [soul] *n* Seele *f*; (*music*) Soul *m*
sound [saund] *adj* (*healthy*) gesund; (*safe*)
sicher; (*sensible*) vernünftig; (*theory*)
stichhaltig; (*thrashing*) tüchtig ▷ *n* (*noise*)
Geräusch *nt*; (*Mus*) Klang *m*; (*TV*) Ton *m*
▷ *vt*: **to ~ the alarm** Alarm schlagen; **to ~
one's horn** hupen ▷ *vi* (*seem*) klingen (*like
wie*)
soundcard [saundkard] *n* (*Inform*) Soundkarte *f*
sound effects *npl* Klangeffekte *pl*
soundproof [saundpruf] *adj* schalldicht
soundtrack [saundtræk] *n* (*of film*) Film-
musik *f*, Soundtrack *m*
soup [sup] *n* Suppe *f*
sour [sauər] *adj* sauer; (*fig*) mürrisch
source [sɔrs] *n* Quelle *f*; (*fig*) Ursprung *m*
sour cream *n* saure Sahne
south [sauθ] *n* Süden *m*; **to the ~ of** südlich
von ▷ *adv* (*go, face*) nach Süden ▷ *adj* Süd-
South Africa *n* Südafrika *nt*
South African *adj* südafrikanisch ▷ *n*
Südafrikaner(in) *m(f)*
South America *n* Südamerika *nt*
South American *adj* südamerikanisch ▷ *n*
Südamerikaner(in) *m(f)*
southbound [sauθbaund] *adj* (in) Richtung Süden
southern [sʌðərn] *adj* Süd-, südlich; **~
Europe** Südeuropa *nt*
southwards [sauθwərdz] *adv* nach Süden
souvenir [suvənɪər] *n* Andenken *nt* (*of* an
+*akk*)
sow [sou] (**sowed, sown** *o* **sowed**) *vt* (*a. fig*)
säen; (*field*) besäen ▷ *n* (*pig*) Sau *f*
soy bean [sɔɪ bin] *n* Sojabohne *f*
soy sauce [sɔɪ sɔs] *n* Sojasoße *f*
spa [spa] *n* (*place*) Kurort *m*
space [speɪs] *n* (*room*) Platz *m*, Raum *m*;
(*outer space*) Weltraum *m*; (*gap*) Zwischenraum *m*; (*for parking*) Lücke *f*
space bar *n* Leertaste *f*
spacecraft [speɪskræft] (*pl* **-**) *n* Raumschiff *nt*
space heater *n* Heizlüfter *m*
spaceship *n* Raumschiff *nt*
space shuttle [speɪs ʃʌtˀl] *n* Raumfähre *f*
spacing [speɪsɪn] *n* (*in text*) Zeilenabstand
m; **double ~** zweizeiliger Abstand
spacious [speɪʃəs] *adj* geräumig
spade [speɪd] *n* Spaten *m*; **~s** Pik *nt*
spaghetti [spəgɛti] *nsing* Spaghetti *pl*
Spain [speɪn] *n* Spanien *nt*
spam [spæm] *n* (*Inform*) Spam *m*
Spaniard [spænyərd] *n* Spanier(in) *m(f)*

Spanish [spænɪʃ] *adj* spanisch ▷ *n* (*language*) Spanisch *nt*
spare [spɛər] *adj* (*as replacement*) Ersatz-; **~
part** Ersatzteil *nt*; **~ room** Gästezimmer
nt; **~ time** Freizeit *f*; **~ tire** Ersatzreifen *m*
▷ *n* (*spare part*) Ersatzteil *nt* ▷ *vt* (*lives,
feelings*) verschonen; **can you ~ me a
moment?** hättest du/hätten Sie einen
Moment Zeit?
spark [spark] *n* Funke *m*
sparkle [sparkˀl] *vi* funkeln
sparkling wine [sparkˀlɪn waɪn] *n*
Schaumwein *m*, Sekt *m*
spark plug [spark plʌg] *n* Zündkerze *f*
sparrow [spærou] *n* Spatz *m*
sparse [spars] *adj* spärlich
sparsely *adv*: **~ populated** dünn besiedelt
spasm [spæzəm] *n* (*Med*) Krampf *m*
spat [spæt] *pt, pp of* **spit**
speak [spik] (**spoke, spoken**) *vt* sprechen;
can you ~ French? sprechen Sie Französisch?; **to ~ one's mind** seine Meinung
sagen ▷ *vi* sprechen (*to* mit, zu); (*make
speech*) reden; **~ing** (*Tel*) am Apparat; **so
to ~** sozusagen; **~ for yourself!** das meinst
auch nur du!
speaker [spikər] *n* Sprecher(in) *m(f)*; (*public speaker*) Redner(in) *m(f)*; (*loudspeaker*)
Lautsprecher *m*, Box *f*
speak up *vi* (*louder*) lauter sprechen
special [spɛʃˀl] *adj* besondere(r, s), speziell
▷ *n* (*on menu*) Tagesgericht *nt*; (*TV, Radio*)
Sondersendung *f*
special delivery *n* Eilzustellung *f*
special effects *npl* Spezialeffekte *pl*
specialist [spɛʃəlɪst] *n* Spezialist(in) *m(f)*;
(*Tech*) Fachmann *m*, Fachfrau *f*; (*Med*)
Facharzt *m*, Fachärztin *f*
specialize [spɛʃəlaɪz] *vi* sich spezialisieren
(*in* auf +*akk*)
specially [spɛʃəli] *adv* besonders; (*specifi-
cally*) extra
special offer *n* Sonderangebot *nt*
specialty [spɛʃˀlti] *n* Spezialität *f*
species [spiʃiz] *nsing* Art *f*
specific [spɪsɪfɪk] *adj* spezifisch; (*precise*)
genau
specify [spɛsɪfaɪ] *vt* genau angeben
specimen [spɛsɪmɪn] *n* (*sample*) Probe *f*;
(*example*) Exemplar *nt*
specs [spɛks] *npl* (*fam*) Brille *f*
spectacle [spɛktəkˀl] *n* Schauspiel *nt*
spectacles *npl* Brille *f*
spectacular [spɛktækyələr] *adj* spektaku-
lär

spectator [spɛkteɪtər] *n* Zuschauer(in) *m(f)*

sped [spɛd] *pt, pp of* **speed**

speech [spitʃ] *n* (*address*) Rede *f;* (*faculty*) Sprache *f;* **to make a ~** eine Rede halten

speechless [spitʃlɪs] *adj* sprachlos (*with* vor +*dat*)

speed [spid] (**sped** *o* **speeded, sped** *o* **speeded**) *vi* rasen; (*exceed speed limit*) zu schnell fahren ▷ *n* Geschwindigkeit *f;* (*of film*) Lichtempfindlichkeit *f*

speedboat [spidbout] *n* Rennboot *nt*

speed bump *n* Bodenschwelle *f*

speed limit *n* Geschwindigkeitsbegrenzung *f*

speedometer [spidɒmɪtər] *n* Tachometer *m*

speed trap *n* Radarfalle *f*

speed up *vt* beschleunigen ▷ *vi* schneller werden/fahren; (*drive faster*) schneller fahren

speedy [spidi] *adj* schnell

spell [spɛl] (**spelled** *o* **spelt, spelled** *o* **spelt**) *vt* buchstabieren; **how do you ~ ...?** wie schreibt man ...? ▷ *n* (*period*) Weile *f;* (*enchantment*) Zauber *m;* **a cold/hot ~** (*weather*) ein Kälteeinbruch/eine Hitzewelle

spell-checker *n* (*Inform*) Rechtschreibprüfung *f*

spelling [spɛlɪŋ] *n* Rechtschreibung *f;* (*of a word*) Schreibweise *f;* **~ mistake** Schreibfehler *m*

spelt [spɛlt] *pt, pp of* **spell**

spend [spɛnd] (**spent, spent**) *vt* (*money*) ausgeben (on für); (*time*) verbringen

spending money [spɛndɪŋ mʌni] *n* Taschengeld *nt*

spent [spɛnt] *pt, pp of* **spend**

sperm [spɜrm] *n* Sperma *nt*

SPF *abbr* = **sun protection factor**

sphere [sfɪər] *n* (*globe*) Kugel *f;* (*fig*) Sphäre *f*

spice [spaɪs] *n* Gewürz *nt;* (*fig*) Würze *f* ▷ *vt* würzen

spicy [spaɪsi] *adj* würzig; (*fig*) pikant

spider [spaɪdər] *n* Spinne *f*

spike [spaɪk] *n* (*on railing etc*) Spitze *f;* (*on shoe, tire*) Spike *m*

spill [spɪl] (**spilled** *o* **spilt, spilled** *o* **spilt**) *vt* verschütten

spin [spɪn] (**spun, spun**) *vi* (*turn*) sich drehen; (*washing*) schleudern; **my head is ~ning** mir dreht sich alles ▷ *vt* (*turn*) drehen; (*coin*) hochwerfen ▷ *n* (*turn*) Drehung *f*

spinach [spɪnɪtʃ] *n* Spinat *m*

spin doctor *n* Spindoktor *m* (*Verantwortlicher für die schönrednerische Öffentlichkeitsarbeit besonders von Politikern*)

spin-dry [spɪndraɪ] *vt* schleudern

spin-dryer *n* Wäscheschleuder *f*

spine [spaɪn] *n* (*of animal, plant*) Stachel *m;* (*of book*) Rücken *m*

spiral [spaɪrəl] *n* Spirale *f* ▷ *adj* spiralförmig

spiral staircase *n* Wendeltreppe *f*

spire [spaɪər] *n* Turmspitze *f*

spirit [spɪrɪt] *n* (*essence, soul*) Geist *m;* (*humor, mood*) Stimmung *f;* (*courage*) Mut *m;* (*verve*) Elan *m;* **~s** *pl* (*drinks*) Spirituosen *pl*

spiritual [spɪrɪtʃuəl] *adj* geistig; (*Rel*) geistlich

spit [spɪt] (**spat, spat**) *vi* spucken ▷ *n* (*for roasting*) (Brat)spieß *m;* (*saliva*) Spucke *f*

spite [spaɪt] *n* Boshaftigkeit *f;* **in ~ of** trotz +*gen*

spiteful [spaɪtfəl] *adj* boshaft

spit out *vt* ausspucken

spitting image [spɪtɪŋ ɪmɪdʒ] *n:* **he's the ~ of you** er ist dir/Ihnen wie aus dem Gesicht geschnitten

splash [splæʃ] *vt* (*person, object*) bespritzen ▷ *vi* (*liquid*) spritzen; (*play in water*) planschen

splendid [splɛndɪd] *adj* herrlich

splinter [splɪntər] *n* Splitter *m*

split [splɪt] (**split, split**) *vt* (*stone, wood*) spalten; (*share*) teilen ▷ *vi* (*stone, wood*) sich spalten; (*seam*) platzen ▷ *n* (*in stone, wood*) Spalt *m;* (*in clothing*) Riss *m;* (*fig*) Spaltung *f*

split ends *npl* (Haar)spliss *m*

splitting [splɪtɪŋ] *adj* (*headache*) rasend

split up *vi* (*couple*) sich trennen ▷ *vt* (*divide up*) aufteilen

spoil [spɔɪl] (**spoiled** *o* **spoilt, spoiled** *o* **spoilt**) *vt* verderben; (*child*) verwöhnen ▷ *vi* (*food*) verderben

spoilt [spɔɪlt] *pt, pp of* **spoil**

spoke [spouk] *pt of* **speak** ▷ *n* Speiche *f*

spoken [spoukən] *pp of* **speak**

spokesperson [spoukspɜrsⁿn] (*pl* **-people**) *n* Sprecher(in) *m(f)*

sponge [spʌndʒ] *n* (*for washing*) Schwamm *m*

sponge cake *n* Biskuitkuchen *m*

sponsor [spɒnsər] *n* (*of event, program*) Sponsor(in) *m(f)* ▷ *vt* unterstützen; (*event, program*) sponsern

S

spontaneous [spɒnˈteɪnɪəs] *adj*, **spontaneously** *adv* spontan

spool [spuːl] *n* Spule *f*

spoon [spuːn] *n* Löffel *m*

sport [spɔːt] *n* Sport *m*

sports car *n* Sportwagen *m*

sports club *n* Sportverein *m*

sportsman [ˈspɔːtsmən] (*pl* **-men**) *n* Sportler *m*

sportswear [ˈspɔːtsweər] *n* Sportkleidung *f*

sportswoman [ˈspɔːtswʊmən] (*pl* **-women**) *n* Sportlerin *f*

sporty [ˈspɔːtɪ] *adj* sportlich

spot [spɒt] *n* (*dot*) Punkt *m*; (*of paint, blood etc*) Fleck *m*; (*place*) Stelle *f*; **on the ~** vor Ort; (*at once*) auf der Stelle ▷ *vt* (*notice*) entdecken; (*difference*) erkennen

spotless [ˈspɒtlɪs] *adj* (*clean*) blitzsauber

spotlight [ˈspɒtlaɪt] *n* (*lamp*) Scheinwerfer *m*

spouse [spaʊs] *n* Gatte *m*, Gattin *f*

spout [spaʊt] *n* Schnabel *m*

sprain [spreɪn] *n* Verstauchung *f* ▷ *vt*: **to ~ one's ankle** sich den Knöchel verstauchen

sprang [spræŋ] *pt of* **spring**

spray [spreɪ] *n* (*liquid in can*) Spray *nt* o *m*; (*spray (can)*) Spraydose *f* ▷ *vt* (*plant, insects*) besprühen; (*car*) spritzen

spread [spred] *vt* (*spread, spread*) (*open out*) ausbreiten; (*news, disease*) verbreiten; (*butter, jam*) streichen; (*bread, surface*) bestreichen ▷ *vi* (*news, disease, fire*) sich verbreiten ▷ *n* (*of disease, religion etc*) Verbreitung *f*; (*for bread*) Aufstrich *m*

spreadsheet [ˈspredʃit] *n* (*Inform*) Tabellenkalkulation *f*

spring [sprɪŋ] (**sprang, sprung**) *vi* (*leap*) springen ▷ *n* (*season*) Frühling *m*; (*coil*) Feder *f*; (*water*) Quelle *f*

springboard [ˈsprɪŋbɔːd] *n* Sprungbrett *nt*

springy [ˈsprɪŋɪ] *adj* (*mattress*) federnd

sprinkle [ˈsprɪŋkᵊl] *vt* streuen; (*liquid*) (be)träufeln; **to ~ sth with sth** etw mit etw bestreuen; (*with liquid*) etw mit etw besprengen

sprinkler [ˈsprɪŋklər] *n* (*for lawn*) Rasensprenger *m*; (*for fire*) Sprinkler *m*

sprint [sprɪnt] *vi* rennen; (*Sport*) sprinten

sprout [spraʊt] *n* (*of plant*) Trieb *m*; (*from seed*) Keim *m*; (**Brussels**) **~s** *pl* Rosenkohl *m* ▷ *vi* sprießen

sprung [sprʌŋ] *pp of* **spring**

spun [spʌn] *pt, pp of* **spin**

spy [spaɪ] *n* Spion(in) *m(f)* ▷ *vi* spionieren; **to spy on sb** jdm nachspionieren ▷ *vt* erspähen

squad [skwɒd] *n* (*Sport*) Kader *m*; (*police squad*) Kommando *nt*

squad car *n* Streifenwagen *m*

square [skweər] *n* (*shape*) Quadrat *nt*; (*open space*) Platz *m*; (*on chessboard etc*) Feld *nt* ▷ *adj* (*in shape*) quadratisch; **2 ~ meters** 2 Quadratmeter; **2 meters ~** 2 Meter im Quadrat ▷ *vt*: **3 ~d** 3 hoch 2

square root *n* Quadratwurzel *f*

squash [skwɒʃ] *n* (*drink*) Fruchtsaftgetränk *nt*; (*Sport*) Squash *nt*; (*vegetable*) Kürbis *m* ▷ *vt* zerquetschen

squat [skwɒt] *vi* (*be crouching*) hocken; **to ~ down** sich (hin)hocken

squeak [skwiːk] *vi* (*door, shoes etc*) quietschen; (*animal*) quieken

squeal [skwiːl] *vi* (*person*) kreischen (*with* vor +*dat*)

squeeze [skwiːz] *vt* drücken; (*orange*) auspressen ▷ *vi*: **to ~ into the car** sich in den Wagen hineinzwängen

squid [skwɪd] *n* Tintenfisch *m*

squint [skwɪnt] *vi* schielen; (*in bright light*) blinzeln

squirrel [ˈskwɜrəl] *n* Eichhörnchen *nt*

squirt [skwɜrt] *vt, vi* (*liquid*) spritzen

Sri Lanka [sriː ˈlæŋkə] *n* Sri Lanka *nt*

St (*abbr*) = **saint** St. ▷ (*abbr*) = **street** Str.

stab [stæb] *vt* (*person*) einstechen auf +*akk*; (*to death*) erstechen

stabbing [ˈstæbɪŋ] *adj* (*pain*) stechend

stabilize [ˈsteɪbɪlaɪz] *vt* stabilisieren ▷ *vi* sich stabilisieren

stable [ˈsteɪbᵊl] *n* Stall *m* ▷ *adj* stabil

stack [stæk] *n* (*pile*) Stapel *m* ▷ *vt*: **to ~ up** (auf)stapeln

stadium [ˈsteɪdɪəm] *n* Stadion *nt*

staff [stæf] *n* (*personnel*) Personal *nt*; (*teachers*) Lehrkräfte *pl*

stag [stæg] *n* Hirsch *m*

stage [steɪdʒ] *n* (*Theat*) Bühne *f*; (*of project, life etc*) Stadium *nt*; (*of journey*) Etappe *f*; **at this ~** zu diesem Zeitpunkt ▷ *vt* (*Theat*) aufführen, inszenieren; (*demonstration*) veranstalten

stagger [ˈstægər] *vi* wanken ▷ *vt* (*amaze*) verblüffen

staggering [ˈstægərɪŋ] *adj* (*amazing*) umwerfend; (*amount, price*) schwindelerregend

stagnate [stægˈneɪt] *vi* (*fig*) stagnieren

stain [steɪn] *n* Fleck *m*

stained-glass window [ˈsteɪndglɑs ˈwɪndoʊ] n Buntglasfenster nt

stainless steel [ˈsteɪnlɪs stiːl] n rostfreier Stahl

stain remover [ˈsteɪn rɪmuːvər] n Fleck(en)entferner m

stair [stɛər] n (Treppen)stufe f; **~s** pl Treppe f

staircase [ˈstɛərkeɪs] n Treppe f

stake [steɪk] n (post) Pfahl m; (in betting) Einsatz m; (Fin) Anteil m (in an +dat); **to be at ~** auf dem Spiel stehen

stale [steɪl] adj (bread) alt; (beer) schal

stalk [stɔːk] n Stiel m ⊳ vt (wild animal) sich anpirschen an +akk; (person) nachstellen +dat

stall [stɔːl] n (in market) (Verkaufs)stand m; (in stable) Box f; **~s** pl (Theat) Parkett nt ⊳ vt (engine) abwürgen ⊳ vi (driver) den Motor abwürgen; (car) stehen bleiben; (delay) Zeit schinden

stamina [ˈstæmɪnə] n Durchhaltevermögen nt

stammer [ˈstæmər] vi, vt stottern

stamp [stæmp] n (postage stamp) Briefmarke f; (for document) Stempel m ⊳ vt (passport etc) stempeln; (mail) frankieren

stand [stænd] (stood, stood) vi stehen; (as candidate) kandidieren ⊳ vt (place) stellen; (endure) aushalten; **I can't ~ her** ich kann sie nicht ausstehen ⊳ n (stall) Stand m; (seats in stadium) Tribüne f; (for coats, bicycles) Ständer m; (for small objects) Gestell nt

standard [ˈstændərd] n (norm) Norm f; **~ of living** Lebensstandard m ⊳ adj Standard-

standardize [ˈstændərdaɪz] vt vereinheitlichen

stand around vi herumstehen

stand by vi (be ready) sich bereithalten; (be inactive) danebenstehen ⊳ vt (fig: person) halten zu; (decision, promise) stehen zu

standby n (thing in reserve) Reserve f; **on ~** in Bereitschaft ⊳ adj (flight, ticket) Standby-

stand for vt (represent) stehen für; (tolerate) hinnehmen

stand in for vt einspringen für

standing order [ˈstændɪŋ ɔːrdər] n (at bank) Dauerauftrag m

stand out vi (be noticeable) auffallen

standpoint [ˈstændpɔɪnt] n Standpunkt m

standstill [ˈstændstɪl] n Stillstand m; **to come to a ~** stehen bleiben; (fig) zum Erliegen kommen

stand up vi (get up) aufstehen ⊳ vt (girlfriend, boyfriend) versetzen

stand up for vt sich einsetzen für

stand up to vt: **to ~ sb** jdm die Stirn bieten

stank [stæŋk] pt of **stink**

staple [ˈsteɪpəl] n (for paper) Heftklammer f ⊳ vt heften (to an +akk)

stapler [ˈsteɪplər] n Hefter m

star [stɑːr] n Stern m; (person) Star m ⊳ vt: **the film ~s Brad Pitt** der Film zeigt Brad Pitt in der Hauptrolle ⊳ vi die Hauptrolle spielen

starch [stɑːrtʃ] n Stärke f

stare [stɛər] vi starren; **to ~ at** anstarren

starfish [ˈstɑːrfɪʃ] n Seestern m

star sign n Sternzeichen nt

start [stɑːrt] n (beginning) Anfang m, Beginn m; (Sport) Start m; (lead) Vorsprung m; **from the ~** von Anfang an ⊳ vt anfangen; (car, engine) starten; (business, family) gründen; **to ~ to do sth, to ~ doing sth** anfangen, etw zu tun ⊳ vi (begin) anfangen; (car) anspringen; (on journey) aufbrechen; (Sport) starten; (jump) zusammenfahren; **~ing from Monday** ab Montag

starting point [ˈstɑːrtɪŋ pɔɪnt] n (a. fig) Ausgangspunkt m

startle [ˈstɑːrtəl] vt erschrecken

startling [ˈstɑːrtlɪŋ] adj überraschend

start off vt (discussion, process etc) anfangen, beginnen ⊳ vi (begin) anfangen, beginnen; (on journey) aufbrechen

start over vi wieder anfangen

start up vi (in business) anfangen ⊳ vt (car, engine) starten; (business) gründen

starve [stɑːrv] vi hungern; (to death) verhungern; **I'm ~ing** ich habe einen Riesenhunger

state [steɪt] n (condition) Zustand m; (Pol) Staat m; **the (United) S~s** die (Vereinigten) Staaten ⊳ adj Staats-; (control, education) staatlich ⊳ vt erklären; (facts, name etc) angeben

stated [ˈsteɪtɪd] adj (fixed) festgesetzt

statement [ˈsteɪtmənt] n (official declaration) Erklärung f; (to police) Aussage f; (from bank) Kontoauszug m

state-of-the-art adj hochmodern, auf dem neuesten Stand der Technik

static [ˈstætɪk] adj (unchanging) konstant

station [ˈsteɪʃən] n (for trains, buses) Bahnhof m; (underground station) Station f; (police station, fire station) Wache f; (TV,

Radio) Sender *m* ▷ *vt* (*Mil*) stationieren

stationery [ˈsteɪʃənərɪ] *n* Schreibwaren *pl*

station wagon *n* Kombiwagen *m*

statistics [stəˈtɪstɪks] *nsing* (*science*) Statistik *f*; (*figures*) Statistiken *pl*

statue [ˈstætʃuː] *n* Statue *f*

status [ˈsteɪtəs, ˈstæt-] *n* Status *m*; (*prestige*) Ansehen *nt*

status bar *n* (*Inform*) Statuszeile *f*

stay [steɪ] *n* Aufenthalt *m* ▷ *vi* bleiben; (*with friends, in hotel*) wohnen (*with* bei); **to ~ the night** übernachten

stay away *vi* wegbleiben; **to ~ from sb** sich von jdm fernhalten

stay behind *vi* zurückbleiben; (*at work*) länger bleiben

stay in *vi* (*at home*) zu Hause bleiben

stay out *vi* (*not come home*) wegbleiben

stay up *vi* (*at night*) aufbleiben

steady [ˈstɛdɪ] *adj* (*speed*) gleichmäßig; (*progress, increase*) stetig; (*job, income, girlfriend*) fest; (*worker*) zuverlässig; (*hand*) ruhig; **they've been going ~ for two years** sie sind seit zwei Jahren fest zusammen ▷ *vt* (*nerves*) beruhigen; **to ~ oneself** Halt finden

steak [steɪk] *n* Steak *nt*; (*of fish*) Filet *nt*

steal [stiːl] (**stole, stolen**) *vt* stehlen; **to ~ sth from sb** jdm etw stehlen

steam [stiːm] *n* Dampf *m* ▷ *vt* (*Gastr*) dämpfen

steamer [ˈstiːmər] *n* (*Gastr*) Dampfkochtopf *m*; (*ship*) Dampfer *m*

steam iron *n* Dampfbügeleisen *nt*

steam up *vi* (*window*) beschlagen

steel [stiːl] *n* Stahl *m* ▷ *adj* Stahl-

steep [stiːp] *adj* steil

steeple [ˈstiːpl] *n* Kirchturm *m*

steer [stɪər] *vt, vi* steuern; (*car, bike etc*) lenken

steering [ˈstɪərɪŋ] *n* (*Auto*) Lenkung *f*

steering wheel *n* Steuer *nt*, Lenkrad *nt*

stem [stɛm] *n* (*of plant, glass*) Stiel *m*

step [stɛp] *n* Schritt *m*; (*stair*) Stufe *f*; (*measure*) Maßnahme *f*; **~ by** Schritt für Schritt ▷ *vi* treten; **~ this way, please** hier entlang, bitte

stepbrother [ˈstɛpbrʌðər] *n* Stiefbruder *m*

stepchild [ˈstɛptʃaɪld] (*pl* **-children**) *n* Stiefkind *nt*

step down *vi* (*resign*) zurücktreten

stepfather [ˈstɛpfɑːðər] *n* Stiefvater *m*

stepladder [ˈstɛplædər] *n* Trittleiter *f*

stepmother [ˈstɛpmʌðər] *n* Stiefmutter *f*

stepsister [ˈstɛpsɪstər] *n* Stiefschwester *f*

stereo [ˈstɛrɪou, ˈstɪər-] (*pl* **-s**) *n*: **~ system** Stereoanlage *f*

sterile [ˈstɛral] *adj* steril

sterilize [ˈstɛrɪlaɪz] *vt* sterilisieren

sterling [ˈstɜːlɪŋ] *n* (*Fin*) das Pfund Sterling

stew [stuː] *n* Eintopf *m*

steward [ˈstuːərd] *n* (*on plane, ship*) Steward *m*

stewardess [ˈstuːərdɪs] *n* Stewardess *f*

stick [stɪk] (**stuck, stuck**) *vt* (*with glue etc*) kleben; (*pin etc*) stecken; (*fam: put*) tun ▷ *vi* (*get jammed*) klemmen; (*hold fast*) haften ▷ *n* Stock *m*; (*hockey stick*) Schläger *m*; (*of chalk*) Stück *nt*; (*of celery, rhubarb*) Stange *f*

sticker [ˈstɪkər] *n* Aufkleber *m*

stick out *vt*: **to stick one's tongue out (at sb)** (jdm) die Zunge herausstrecken ▷ *vi* (*protrude*) vorstehen; (*ears*) abstehen; (*be noticeable*) auffallen

stick to *vt* (*rules, plan etc*) sich halten an +*akk*

sticky [ˈstɪkɪ] *adj* klebrig; (*weather*) schwül; **~ label** Aufkleber *m*; **~ tape** Klebeband *nt*

stiff [stɪf] *adj* steif

stifle [ˈstaɪfl] *vt* (*yawn etc, opposition*) unterdrücken

stifling [ˈstaɪflɪŋ] *adj* drückend

still [stɪl] *adj* still; (*drink*) ohne Kohlensäure ▷ *adv* (*yet, even now*) (immer) noch; (*all the same*) immerhin; (*sit, stand*) still; **he ~ doesn't believe me** er glaubt mir immer noch nicht; **keep ~!** halt still!; **bigger/better ~** noch größer/besser

still life (*pl* **still lives**) *n* Stillleben *nt*

stimulate [ˈstɪmyəleɪt] *vt* anregen, stimulieren

stimulating [ˈstɪmyəleɪtɪŋ] *adj* anregend

sting [stɪŋ] (**stung, stung**) *vt* (*wound with sting*) stechen ▷ *vi* (*eyes, ointment etc*) brennen ▷ *n* (*insect wound*) Stich *m*

stingy [ˈstɪndʒɪ] *adj* (*fam*) geizig

stink [stɪŋk] (**stank, stunk**) *vi* stinken (*of* nach) ▷ *n* Gestank *m*

stir [stɜːr] *vt* (*mix*) (um)rühren

stir-fry *vt* (unter Rühren) kurz anbraten

stir up *vt* (*mob*) aufhetzen; (*memories*) wachrufen; **to ~ trouble** Unruhe stiften

stitch [stɪtʃ] *n* (*in sewing*) Stich *m*; (*in knitting*) Masche *f*; **to have a ~** (*pain*) Seitenstechen haben; **he had to have ~es** er musste genäht werden; **she had her ~es out** ihr wurden die Fäden gezogen; **to be in ~es** (*fam*) sich kaputtlachen ▷ *vt* nähen

stitch up vt (*hole, wound*) nähen

stock [stɒk] n (*supply*) Vorrat m (*of* an +*dat*); (*of shop*) Bestand m; (*for soup etc*) Brühe f; **~s and bonds** pl Aktien und Wertpapiere pl; **to be in/out of ~** vorrätig/ nicht vorrätig sein; **to take ~** Inventur machen; (*fig*) Bilanz ziehen ▷ vt (*keep in shop*) führen

stockbroker [stɒkbroukər] n Börsenmakler(in) m(f)

stock exchange n Börse f

stocking [stɒkɪŋ] n Strumpf m

stock market n Börse f

stock up vi sich eindecken (*on, with* mit)

stole [stoul] pt of **steal**

stolen [stoulən] pp of **steal**

stomach [stʌmək] n Magen m; (*belly*) Bauch m; **on an empty ~** auf leeren Magen

stomachache [stʌməkeɪk] n Magenschmerzen pl; **upset stomach** Magenverstimmung f

stone [stoun] n Stein m; (*seed*) Kern m, Stein m ▷ adj Stein-, aus Stein

stony [stouni] adj (*ground*) steinig

stood [stʊd] pt, pp of **stand**

stool [stuːl] n Hocker m

stop [stɒp] n Halt m; (*for bus, tram, train*) Haltestelle f; **to come to a ~** anhalten ▷ vt (*vehicle, passer-by*) anhalten; (*put an end to*) ein Ende machen +*dat*; (*cease*) aufhören mit; (*prevent from happening*) verhindern; (*bleeding*) stillen; (*engine, machine*) abstellen; (*payments*) einstellen; (*check*) sperren; **to ~ doing sth** aufhören, etw zu tun; **to ~ sb from doing sth** jdn daran hindern, etw zu tun; **~ it!** hör auf (damit)! ▷ vi (*vehicle*) anhalten; (*during journey*) Halt machen; (*pedestrian, clock, heart*) stehen bleiben; (*rain, noise*) aufhören; (*stay*) bleiben

stop by vi vorbeischauen

stopgap [stɒpgæp] n Provisorium nt, Zwischenlösung f

stop over vi Halt machen; (*overnight*) übernachten

stopover [stɒpouvər] n (*on journey*) Zwischenstation f

stopper [stɒpər] n Stöpsel m

stop sign n Stoppschild nt

stopwatch [stɒpwɒtʃ] n Stoppuhr f

storage [stɔrɪdʒ] n Lagerung f

store [stɔr] n (*supply*) Vorrat m (*of* an +*dat*); (*place for storage*) Lager nt; (*large store*) Kaufhaus nt; (*small store*) Geschäft nt ▷ vt lagern; (*Inform*) speichern

store owner n Geschäftsinhaber(in) m(f)

storeroom [stɔrum] n Lagerraum m

store window n Schaufenster nt

storm [stɔrm] n Sturm m; (*thunderstorm*) Gewitter nt ▷ vt, vi (*with movement*) stürmen

stormy [stɔrmi] adj stürmisch

story [stɔri] n Geschichte f; (*plot*) Handlung f; (*of building*) Stock m, Stockwerk nt

stout [staut] adj (*fat*) korpulent

stove [stouv] n Herd m; (*for heating*) Ofen m

stow [stou] vt verstauen

stowaway [stouəweɪ] n blinder Passagier

straight [streɪt] adj (*not curved*) gerade; (*hair*) glatt; (*honest*) ehrlich (*with* zu); (*fam: heterosexual*) hetero ▷ adv (*directly*) direkt; (*immediately*) sofort; (*drink*) pur; (*think*) klar; **~ ahead** geradeaus; **to go ~ ahead** geradeaus weitergehen/weiterfahren

straightaway [streɪtˈɛweɪ] adv sofort

straightforward [streɪtfɔrwərd] adj einfach; (*person*) aufrichtig, unkompliziert

strain [streɪn] n Belastung f ▷ vt (*eyes*) überanstrengen; (*rope, relationship*) belasten; (*vegetables*) abgießen; **to ~ a muscle** sich einen Muskel zerren

strained [streɪnd] adj (*laugh, smile*) gezwungen; (*relations*) gespannt; **~ muscle** Muskelzerrung f

strainer [streɪnər] n Sieb nt

strand [strænd] n (*of wool*) Faden m; (*of hair*) Strähne f ▷ vt: **to be left ~ed** (*person*) festsitzen

strange [streɪndʒ] adj seltsam; (*unfamiliar*) fremd

strangely [streɪndʒli] adv seltsam; **~ enough** seltsamerweise

stranger [streɪndʒər] n Fremde(r) mf; **I'm a ~ here** ich bin hier fremd

strangle [stræŋgəl] vt (*kill*) erdrosseln

strap [stræp] n Riemen m; (*on dress etc*) Träger m; (*on watch*) Band nt ▷ vt (*fasten*) festschnallen (*to* an +*dat*)

strapless [stræplɪs] adj trägerlos

strategy [strætədʒi] n Strategie f

straw [strɔ] n Stroh nt; (*drinking straw*) Strohhalm m

strawberry [strɔbɛri] n Erdbeere f

stray [streɪ] n streunendes Tier ▷ adj (*cat, dog*) streunend ▷ vi streunen

streak [strik] n (*of color, dirt*) Streifen m;

(in hair) Strähne f; *(in character)* Zug m

stream [striːm] n *(flow of liquid)* Strom m; *(brook)* Bach m ▷ vi strömen

streamer [striːmər] n *(of paper)* Luftschlange f

street [striːt] n Straße f

streetcar [striːtkɑːr] n Straßenbahn f

street light, street lamp n Straßenlaterne f

street map n Stadtplan m

strength [strɛŋkθ, strɛŋθ] n Kraft f, Stärke f

strengthen [strɛŋθən] vt verstärken; *(fig)* stärken

strenuous [strɛnyuəs] adj anstrengend

stress [strɛs] n Stress m; *(on word)* Betonung f; **to be under ~** im Stress sein ▷ vt betonen; *(put under stress)* stressen

stressed [strɛst] adj: **~ out** gestresst

stretch [strɛtʃ] n *(of land)* Stück nt; *(of road)* Strecke f ▷ vt *(material, shoes)* dehnen; *(rope, canvas)* spannen; *(person in job etc)* fordern; **to ~ one's legs** *(walk)* sich die Beine vertreten ▷ vi *(person)* sich strecken; *(area)* sich erstrecken *(to* bis zu)

stretcher [strɛtʃər] n Tragbahre f

stretch out vt: **to stretch one's hand/legs out** die Hand/die Beine ausstrecken, ausstrecken ▷ vi *(reach)* sich strecken; *(lie down)* sich ausstrecken

strict [strɪkt] adj *(severe)* streng; *(exact)* genau

strictly [strɪktli] adv streng; genau; **~ speaking** genauer gesagt

strike [straɪk] *(struck, struck)* vt *(match)* anzünden; *(hit)* schlagen; *(find)* finden; **it struck me as strange** es kam mir seltsam vor ▷ vi *(stop work)* streiken; *(attack)* zuschlagen; *(clock)* schlagen ▷ n *(by workers)* Streik m; **to be on ~** streiken

strike up vt *(conversation)* anfangen; *(friendship)* schließen

striking [straɪkɪŋ] adj auffallend

string [strɪŋ] n *(for tying)* Schnur f; *(Mus, Tennis)* Saite f; **the ~s** pl *(section of orchestra)* die Streicher pl

strip [strɪp] n Streifen m ▷ vi *(undress)* sich ausziehen, strippen

stripe [straɪp] n Streifen m

striped [straɪpt] adj gestreift

stripper [strɪpər] n Stripper(in) m(f); *(paint stripper)* Farbentferner m

strip search n Leibesvisitation f *(bei der man sich ausziehen muss)*

striptease [strɪptiːz] n Striptease m

stroke [strouk] n *(Med, Tennis etc)* Schlag m; *(of pen, brush)* Strich m ▷ vt streicheln

stroll [stroul] n Spaziergang m ▷ vi spazieren

stroller [stroulər] n *(for baby)* Buggy m

strong [strɒŋ] adj stark; *(healthy)* robust; *(wall, table)* stabil; *(shoes)* fest; *(influence, chance)* groß

strongly [strɒŋli] adv stark; *(believe)* fest; *(constructed)* stabil

struck [strʌk] pt, pp of **strike**

structural [strʌktʃərəl], **structurally** adj strukturell

structure [strʌktʃər] n Struktur f; *(building, bridge)* Konstruktion f, Bau m

struggle [strʌgəl] n Kampf m *(for* um) ▷ vi *(fight)* kämpfen *(for* um); *(do sth with difficulty)* sich abmühen; **to ~ to do sth** sich abmühen, etw zu tun

stub [stʌb] n *(of cigarette)* Kippe f; *(of ticket, check)* Abschnitt m ▷ vt: **to ~ one's toe** sich dat den Zeh stoßen *(on an* +dat)

stubble [stʌbəl] n Stoppelbart m; *(field)* Stoppeln pl

stubborn [stʌbərn] adj *(person)* stur

stuck [stʌk] pt, pp of **stick** ▷ adj: **to be ~** *(jammed)* klemmen; *(at a loss)* nicht mehr weiterwissen; **to get ~** *(car in snow etc)* stecken bleiben

student [stuːdənt] n Student(in) m(f); *(at school)* Schüler(in) m(f)

studio [stuːdiou] *(pl* **-s**) n Studio nt

studious [stuːdiəs] adj fleißig

study [stʌdi] n *(investigation)* Untersuchung f; *(room)* Arbeitszimmer nt ▷ vt, vi studieren

stuff [stʌf] n Zeug nt, Sachen pl ▷ vt *(push)* stopfen; *(Gastr)* füllen; **to ~ oneself** *(fam)* sich vollstopfen

stuffing [stʌfɪŋ] n *(Gastr)* Füllung f

stuffy [stʌfi] adj *(room)* stickig; *(person)* spießig

stumble [stʌmbəl] vi stolpern; *(when speaking)* stocken

stun [stʌn] vt *(shock)* fassungslos machen; **I was ~ned** ich war fassungslos *(o* völlig überrascht

stung [stʌŋ] pt, pp of **sting**

stunk [stʌŋk] pp of **stink**

stunning [stʌnɪŋ] adj *(marvelous)* fantastisch; *(beautiful)* atemberaubend; *(very surprising, shocking)* überwältigend; unfassbar

stunt [stʌnt] n *(Cine)* Stunt m

stupid [stuːpɪd] adj dumm

stupidity [stupɪdɪti] n Dummheit f
sturdy [stɜrdi] adj robust; (building, car) stabil
stutter [stʌtər] vi, vt stottern
stye [staɪ] n (Med) Gerstenkorn nt
style [staɪl] n Stil m ▷ vt (hair) stylen
styling mousse [staɪlɪŋ mus] n Schaumfestiger m
stylish [staɪlɪʃ] adj elegant, schick
subconscious [sʌbkɒnʃəs] adj unterbewusst ▷ n: the ~ das Unterbewusstsein
subdivide [sʌbdɪvaɪd] vt unterteilen
subject [sʌbdʒɪkt] n (topic) Thema nt; (in school)Fach nt;(citizen)Staatsangehörige(r) mf; (of kingdom) Untertan(in) m(f); (Ling) Subjekt nt; **to change the ~** das Thema wechseln ▷ adj: **to be ~ to** (dependent on) abhängen von; (under control of) unterworfen sein +dat
subjective [səbdʒɛktɪv] adj subjektiv
sublet [sʌblɛt] (irr) vt untervermieten (to an +akk)
submarine [sʌbmərin] n U-Boot nt
submerge [səbmɜrdʒ] vt (put in water) eintauchen ▷ vi tauchen
submit [səbmɪt] vt (application, claim) einreichen ▷ vi (surrender) sich ergeben
subordinate [səbɔrdᵊnɪt] adj untergeordnet (to +dat) ▷ n Untergebene(r) mf
subscribe [səbskraɪb] vi: **to ~ to** (magazine etc) abonnieren
subscription [səbskrɪpʃᵊn] n (to magazine etc) Abonnement nt; (to club etc) (Mitglieds)beitrag m
subsequent [sʌbsɪkwənt] adj nach(folgend)
subsequently [sʌbsɪkwəntli] adv später, anschließend
subside [səbsaɪd] vi (floods) zurückgehen; (storm) sich legen; (building) sich senken
substance [sʌbstəns] n Substanz f
substantial [səbstænʃᵊl] adj beträchtlich; (improvement) wesentlich; (meal) reichhaltig; (furniture) solide
substitute [sʌbstɪtut] n Ersatz m; (Sport) Ersatzspieler(in) m(f) ▷ vt: **to ~ A for B** B durch A ersetzen
subtitle [sʌbtaɪtᵊl] n Untertitel m
subtle [sʌtᵊl] adj (difference, taste) fein; (plan) raffiniert
subtotal [sʌbtoʊtᵊl] n Zwischensumme f
subtract [səbtrækt] vt abziehen (from von)
suburb [sʌbɜrb] n Vorort m; **in the ~s** am Stadtrand
suburban [səbɜrbən] adj vorstädtisch, Vor-

stadt-
subway [sʌbweɪ] n (Rail) U-Bahn f
succeed [səksid] vi erfolgreich sein; **he ~ed in doing it** es gelang ihm(, es zu tun) ▷ vt nachfolgen +dat
succeeding [səksidɪŋ] adj nachfolgend
success [səksɛs] n Erfolg m
successful [səksɛsfəl] adj, **successfully** adv erfolgreich
successive [səksɛsɪv] adj aufeinanderfolgend
successor [səksɛsər] n Nachfolger(in) m(f)
succulent [sʌkyələnt] adj saftig
succumb [səkʌm] vi erliegen (to +dat)
such [sʌtʃ] adj solche(r, s); **~ a book** so ein Buch, ein solches Buch; **it was ~ a success that ...** es war solch ein Erfolg, dass ...; **~ as** wie ▷ adv so; **~ a hot day** so ein heißer Tag ▷ pron: **as ~** als solche(r, s)
suck [sʌk] vt (toffee etc) lutschen; (liquid) saugen; **it ~s** (fam) das ist beschissen
Sudan [sudæn] n: the ~ der Sudan
sudden [sʌdᵊn] adj plötzlich; **all of a ~** ganz plötzlich
suddenly [sʌdᵊnli] adv plötzlich
sudoku [sudoʊku] Sudoku nt
sue [su] vt verklagen
suede [sweɪd] n Wildleder nt
suffer [sʌfər] vt erleiden ▷ vi leiden; **to ~ from** (Med) leiden an +dat
sufficient [səfɪʃᵊnt] adj, **sufficiently** adv ausreichend
suffocate [sʌfəkeɪt] vt, vi ersticken
sugar [ʃʊgər] n Zucker m ▷ vt zuckern
sugar bowl n Zuckerdose f
sugary [ʃʊgəri] adj (sweet) süß
suggest [səgdʒɛst] vt vorschlagen; (imply) andeuten; **I ~ saying nothing** ich schlage vor, nichts zu sagen
suggestion [səgdʒɛstʃᵊn] n (proposal) Vorschlag m
suggestive [səgdʒɛstɪv] adj vielsagend; (sexually) anzüglich
suicide [suɪsaɪd] n (act) Selbstmord m
suicide bomber [suɪsaɪd bɒmər] n Selbstmordattentäter(in) m(f)
suicide bombing [suɪsaɪd bɒmɪŋ] n Selbstmordattentat nt
suit [sut] n (man's clothes) Anzug m; (woman's clothes) Kostüm nt; (Cards) Farbe f ▷ vt (be convenient for) passen +dat; (clothes, color) stehen +dat; (climate, food) bekommen +dat
suitable [sutəbᵊl] adj geeignet (for für)

suitcase [sutkeɪs] n Koffer m

suite [swit] n (of rooms) Suite f; (sofa and chairs) Sitzgarnitur f

sulk [sʌlk] vi schmollen

sulky [sʌlki] adj eingeschnappt

sultana [sʌltænə] n (raisin) Sultanine f

sum [sʌm] n Summe f; (money a.) Betrag m; (calculation) Rechenaufgabe f

summarize [sʌmər, aɪz] vt, vi zusammenfassen

summary [sʌməri] n Zusammenfassung f

summer [sʌmər] n Sommer m

summer camp n Ferienlager nt

summertime [sʌmərtaɪm] n: in the ~ im Sommer

summer vacation n Sommerferien pl

summit [sʌmɪt] n (a. Pol) Gipfel m

summon [sʌmən] vt (doctor, fire company etc) rufen; (to one's office) zitieren

summons [sʌmənz] nsing (Jur) Vorladung f

summon up vt (courage, strength) zusammennehmen

sumptuous [sʌmptʃuəs] adj luxuriös; (meal) üppig

sum up vt, vi (summarize) zusammenfassen

Sun (abbr) = Sunday So.

sun [sʌn] n Sonne f ▷ vt: to sun oneself sich sonnen

sunbathe [sʌnbeɪð] vi sich sonnen

sunbathing [sʌnbeɪðɪŋ] n Sonnenbaden nt

sunblock [sʌnblɒk] n Sunblocker m

sunburn [sʌnbɜrn] n Sonnenbrand m

sunburned [sʌnbɜrnd] adj: to be/get ~ einen Sonnenbrand haben/bekommen

sundae [sʌndeɪ, -di] n Eisbecher m

Sunday [sʌndeɪ, -di] n Sonntag m; see also Tuesday

sung [sʌŋ] pp of sing

sunglasses [sʌnglæsɪz] npl Sonnenbrille f.

sunhat [sʌnhæt] n Sonnenhut m

sunk [sʌŋk] pp of sink

sunlamp [sʌnlæmp] n Höhensonne f

sunlight [sʌnlaɪt] n Sonnenlicht nt

sunny [sʌni] adj sonnig

sun protection factor n Lichtschutzfaktor m

sunrise [sʌnraɪz] n Sonnenaufgang m

sunroof [sʌnruf] n (Auto) Schiebedach nt

sunscreen [sʌnskrin] n Sonnenschutzmittel nt

sunset [sʌnsɛt] n Sonnenuntergang m

sunshade [sʌnʃeɪd] n Sonnenschirm m

sunshine [sʌnʃaɪn] n Sonnenschein m

sunstroke [sʌnstroʊk] n Sonnenstich m

suntan [sʌntæn] n (Sonnen)bräune f; to get/have a ~ braun werden/sein; ~ lotion o oil Sonnenöl nt

super [supər] adj (fam) toll

superb [supɜrb] adj, superbly adv ausgezeichnet

superficial [supɜrfɪʃʲl] adj, superficially adv oberflächlich

superfluous [supɜrfluəs] adj überflüssig

superglue [supɜrglu] n Sekundenkleber m

superior [supɪəriər] adj (better) besser (to als); (higher in rank) höhergestellt (to als), höher ▷ n (in rank) Vorgesetzte(r) mf

supermarket [supərmarkɪt] n Supermarkt m

supersede [supərsid] vt ablösen

supersonic [supərsɒnɪk] adj Überschall-

superstition [supərstɪʃʲn] n Aberglaube m

superstitious [supərstɪʃəs] adj abergläubisch

superstore [supərstɔr] n Verbrauchermarkt m

supervise [supərvaɪz] vt beaufsichtigen

supervisor [supərvaɪzər] n Aufsicht f; (at university) Doktorvater m

supper [sʌpər] n Abendessen nt

supplement [sʌplɪmənt] n (of newspaper) Beilage f ▷ vt ergänzen

supplementary [sʌplɪmɛntəri, -tri] adj zusätzlich

supplier [səplaɪər] n Lieferant(in) m(f)

supply [səplaɪ] vt (deliver) liefern; (drinks, music etc) sorgen für; to ~ sb with sth (provide) jdn mit etw versorgen ▷ n (stock) Vorrat m (of an +dat)

support [səpɔrt] n Unterstützung f; (Tech) Stütze f ▷ vt (hold up) tragen, stützen; (provide for) ernähren, unterhalten; (speak in favor of) unterstützen; he ~s the LA Galaxy er ist LA Galaxy-Fan

suppose [səpoʊz] vt (assume) annehmen; I ~ so ich denke schon; I ~ not wahrscheinlich nicht; you're not ~d to smoke here du darfst/Sie dürfen hier nicht rauchen

supposedly [səpoʊzɪdli] adv angeblich

supposing [səpoʊzɪŋ] conj angenommen

suppress [səprɛs] vt unterdrücken

surcharge [sɜrtʃardʒ] n Zuschlag m

sure [ʃʊər] adj sicher; I'm not ~ ich bin mir (nicht) sicher; make ~ you lock up vergiss/

vergessen Sie nicht abzuschließen ▷ adv:
~! klar!; ~ **enough** tatsächlich

surely [ʃʊərli] adv: ~ **you don't mean it?**
das ist nicht dein/Ihr Ernst, oder?

surf [sɜrf] n Brandung f ▷ vi (Sport) surfen
▷ vt: **to ~ the net** im Internet surfen

surface [sɜrfɪs] n Oberfläche f ▷ vi auftauchen

surface mail n: **by ~** auf dem Land-/See-
weg

surfboard [sɜrfbɔrd] n Surfbrett nt

surfer [sɜrfər] n Surfer(in) m(f)

surfing [sɜrfɪŋ] n Surfen nt; **to go ~** surfen
gehen

surgeon [sɜrdʒ³n] n Chirurg(in) m(f)

surgery [sɜrdʒəri] n (operation) Operation
f; (room) Praxis f, Sprechzimmer nt; **to
have ~** operiert werden

surname [sɜrneɪm] n Nachname m

surpass [sərpæs] vt übertreffen

surplus [sɜrplʌs, -pləs] n Überschuss m (of
an +dat)

surprise [sərpraɪz] n Überraschung f ▷ vt
überraschen

surprising [sərpraɪzɪŋ] adj überraschend

surprisingly [sərpraɪzɪŋli] adv überra-
schenderweise, erstaunlicherweise

surrender [sərɛndər] vi sich ergeben (to
+dat) ▷ vt (weapon, passport) abgeben

surround [səraʊnd] vt umgeben; (stand all
around) umringen

surrounding [səraʊndɪŋ] adj (countryside)
umliegend ▷ n: ~s pl Umgebung f

survey [n sɜrveɪ, vb sɜrveɪ] n (opinion poll)
Umfrage f; (of literature etc) Überblick m
(of über +akk); (of land) Vermessung f ▷ vt
(look out over) überblicken; (land) ver-
messen

survive [sərvaɪv] vt, vi überleben

susceptible [səsɛptɪb³l] adj empfänglich
(to für); (Med) anfällig (to für)

sushi [suʃi] n Sushi nt

suspect [n, adj sʌspɛkt, vb səspɛkt] n
Verdächtige(r) mf ▷ adj verdächtig ▷ vt
verdächtigen (of +gen); (think likely) vermuten

suspend [səspɛnd] vt (from work) suspen-
dieren; (payment) vorübergehend einstellen; (player) sperren; (hang up) aufhängen

suspenders [səspɛndərz] npl (for pants)
Hosenträger pl

suspense [səspɛns] n Spannung f

suspicious [səspɪʃəs] adj misstrauisch (of
sb/sth jdm/etw gegenüber); (causing suspi-

cion) verdächtig

SUV [ɛs yu vi] abbr (= sport utility vehicle)
SUV m, Geländewagen m

swallow [swɒloʊ] n (bird) Schwalbe f ▷ vt,
vi schlucken

swam [swæm] pt of swim

swamp [swɒmp] n Sumpf m

swan [swɒn] n Schwan m

swap [swɒp] vt, vi tauschen; **to ~ sth for
sth** etw gegen etw eintauschen

sway [sweɪ] vi schwanken

swear [swɛər] (swore, sworn) vi (promise)
schwören; (curse) fluchen; **to ~ at sb** jdn
beschimpfen

swear by vt (have faith in) schwören auf
+akk

swearword [swɛərwɜrd] n Fluch m

sweat [swɛt] n Schweiß m ▷ vi schwitzen

sweatband [swɛtbænd] n Schweißband
nt

sweater [swɛtər] n Pullover m

sweatshirt [swɛtʃɜrt] n Sweatshirt nt

sweaty [swɛti] adj verschwitzt

Swede [swid] n Schwede m, Schwedin f

Sweden [swid³n] n Schweden nt

Swedish [swidɪʃ] adj schwedisch ▷ n (language) Schwedisch nt

sweep [swip] (swept, swept) vt, vi (with
brush) kehren, fegen

· sweep up vt (dirt etc) zusammenkehren,
zusammenfegen

sweet [swit] adj süß; (kind) lieb

sweet-and-sour adj süßsauer

sweetcorn [switkɔrn] n Mais m

sweeten [swit³n] vt (tea etc) süßen

sweetener [swit̬nər] n (substance) Süßstoff m

sweet potato n Süßkartoffel f

swell [swɛl] (swelled, swollen o swelled)
vi: **to ~ up** (an)schwellen ▷ adj (fam) toll

swelling [swɛlɪŋ] n (Med) Schwellung f

sweltering [swɛltərɪŋ] adj (heat) drückend

swept [swɛpt] pt, pp of sweep

swift [swɪft] adj, **swiftly** adv schnell

swig [swɪg] n (fam) Schluck m

swim [swɪm] (swam, swum) vi schwimmen ▷ n: **to go for a ~** schwimmen gehen

swimmer [swɪmər] n Schwimmer(in) m(f)

swimming [swɪmɪŋ] n Schwimmen nt; **to
go ~** schwimmen gehen

swimming pool n Schwimmbad nt; (private, in hotel) Swimmingpool m

swimsuit [swɪmsut] n Badeanzug m

swindle [swɪnd³l] vt betrügen (out of um)

S

swine [swaɪn] *n* (*person*) Schwein *nt*
swing [swɪŋ] (**swung, swung**) *vt, vi* (*object*) schwingen ▷ *n* (*for child*) Schaukel *f*
swipe [swaɪp] *vt* (*credit card etc*) durchziehen; (*fam: steal*) klauen
swipe card [swaɪp kɑrd] *n* Magnetkarte *f*
Swiss [swɪs] *adj* schweizerisch ▷ *n* Schweizer(in) *m(f)*
switch [swɪtʃ] *n* (*Elec*) Schalter *m* ▷ *vi* (*change*) wechseln (*to* zu)
switchboard [swɪtʃbɔrd] *n* (*Tel*) Vermittlung *f*
switch off *vt* abschalten, ausschalten
switch on *vt* anschalten, einschalten
Switzerland [swɪts²rlənd] *n* die Schweiz
swivel [swɪv²l] *vi* sich drehen ▷ *vt* drehen
swivel chair *n* Drehstuhl *m*
swollen [swoʊl²n] *pp of* **swell** ▷ *adj* (*Med*) geschwollen; (*stomach*) aufgebläht
sword [sɔrd] *n* Schwert *nt*
swore [swɔr] *pt of* **swear**
sworn [swɔrn] *pp of* **swear**
swum [swʌm] *pp of* **swim**
swung [swʌŋ] *pt, pp of* **swing**
syllable [sɪləb²l] *n* Silbe *f*
symbol [sɪmb²l] *n* Symbol *nt*

symbolic [sɪmbɒlɪk] *adj* symbolisch
symbolize [sɪmbəlaɪz] *vt* symbolisieren
symmetrical [sɪmɛtrɪk²l] *adj* symmetrisch
sympathetic [sɪmpəθɛtɪk] *adj* mitfühlend; (*understanding*) verständnisvoll
sympathize [sɪmpəθaɪz] *vi* mitfühlen (*with sb* mit jdm)
sympathy [sɪmpəθi] *n* Mitleid *nt*; (*after death*) Beileid *nt*; (*understanding*) Verständnis *nt*
symphony [sɪmfəni] *n* Sinfonie *f*
symptom [sɪmptəm] *n* (*a. fig*) Symptom *nt*
synagogue [sɪnəgɒg] *n* Synagoge *f*
synonym [sɪnənɪm] *n* Synonym *nt*
synonymous [sɪnɒnɪməs] *adj* synonym (*with* mit)
synthetic [sɪnθɛtɪk] *adj* (*material*) synthetisch
syphilis [sɪfɪlɪs] *n* Syphilis *f*
Syria [sɪriə] *n* Syrien *nt*
syringe [sɪrɪndʒ] *n* Spritze *f*
system [sɪstəm] *n* System *nt*
systematic [sɪstəmætɪk] *adj* systematisch
system disk *n* (*Inform*) Systemdiskette *f*
system(s) software [sɪstəm(z) sɔftwɛər] *n* (*Inform*) Systemsoftware *f*

T

tab [tæb] n (for hanging up coat etc) Aufhänger m; (Inform) Tabulator m; **to pick up the tab** (fam) die Rechnung übernehmen

table [teɪbᵊl] n Tisch m; (list) Tabelle f; **~ of contents** Inhaltsverzeichnis nt

tablecloth [teɪbᵊlklɔθ] n Tischdecke f

table lamp n Tischlampe f

table mat n Set nt

tablespoon [teɪbᵊlspun] n Servierlöffel m; (in recipes) Esslöffel m

tablet [tæblɪt] n (Med) Tablette f

table tennis n Tischtennis nt

table wine n Tafelwein m

tabloid [tæblɔɪd] n Boulevardzeitung f

taboo [təbuː] n Tabu nt ▷ adj tabu

tacit [tæsɪt] adj, **tacitly** adv stillschweigend

tack [tæk] n (small nail) Stift m; (thumbtack) Reißzwecke f

tackle [tækᵊl] n (Sport) Angriff m; (equipment) Ausrüstung f ▷ vt (deal with) in Angriff nehmen; (Sport) angreifen; (verbally) zur Rede stellen (about wegen)

tacky [tæki] adj trashig, heruntergekommen

tact [tækt] n Takt m

tactful [tæktfəl] adj, **tactfully** adv taktvoll

tactic(s) [tæktɪk(s)] n(pl) Taktik f

tactless [tæktlɪs] adj, **tactlessly** adv taktlos

taffy [tæfi] n (sweet) Karamellbonbon nt

tag [tæg] n (label) Schild nt; (with maker's name) Etikett nt

Tahiti [təhiːti] n Tahiti nt

tail [teɪl] n Schwanz m; **heads or ~s?** Kopf oder Zahl?

taillight [teɪllaɪt] n (Auto) Rücklicht nt

tailor [teɪlər] n Schneider(in) m(f)

tailpipe [teɪlpaɪp] n (Auto) Auspuffrohr nt

tainted [teɪntɪd] adj (food) verdorben

Taiwan [taɪwɑːn] n Taiwan nt

take [teɪk] n (fam: Fin) Einnahmen pl ▷ vt (took, taken) nehmen; (take along with one) mitnehmen; (take to a place) bringen; (subtract) abziehen (from von); (capture: person) fassen; (gain, obtain) bekommen; (Fin, Comm) einnehmen; (train, taxi) nehmen, fahren mit; (trip, walk, holiday, exam, course, photo) machen; (bath) nehmen; (phone call) entgegennehmen; (decision, precautions) treffen; (risk) eingehen;

(advice, job) annehmen; (consume) zu sich nehmen; (pills) nehmen; (heat, pain) ertragen; (react to) aufnehmen; (have room for) Platz haben für; **I'll ~ it** (item in shop) ich nehme es; **how long does it ~?** wie lange dauert es?; **it ~s 4 hours** man braucht 4 Stunden; **do you ~ sugar?** nimmst du/nehmen Sie Zucker?; **I ~ it that** ... ich nehme an, dass ...; **to ~ part in** teilnehmen an; **to ~ place** stattfinden

take after vt nachschlagen +dat

take along vt mitnehmen

take apart vt auseinandernehmen

take away vt (remove) wegnehmen (from sb jdm); (subtract) abziehen (from von)

take back vt (return) zurückbringen; (retract) zurücknehmen; (remind) zurückversetzen (to in +akk)

take down vt (picture, curtains) abnehmen; (write down) aufschreiben

take in vt (understand) begreifen; (give accommodation to) aufnehmen; (deceive) hereinlegen; (include) einschließen; (show, film etc) mitnehmen

taken [teɪkən] pp of **take** ▷ adj (seat) besetzt; **to be ~ with** angetan sein von

take off vi (plane) starten ▷ vt (clothing) ausziehen; (hat, lid) abnehmen; (deduct) abziehen; **to take a day off** sich einen Tag freinehmen

takeoff [teɪkɔf] n (Aviat) Start m; (imitation) Nachahmung f

take on vt (undertake) übernehmen; (employ) einstellen; (Sport) antreten gegen

take out vt (wallet etc) herausnehmen; (person, dog) ausführen; (insurance) abschließen; (money from bank) abheben; (book from library) ausleihen

takeout [teɪkaʊt] n (meal) Essen nt zum Mitnehmen

take over vt übernehmen ▷ vi: **he took over from me** er hat mich abgelöst

takeover [teɪkoʊvər] n (Comm) Übernahme f

take to vt: **I've taken to her/it** ich mag sie/es; **to ~ doing sth** (begin) anfangen, etw zu tun

take up vt (carpet) hochnehmen; (space) einnehmen; (time) in Anspruch nehmen; (hobby) anfangen mit; (new job) antreten; (offer) annehmen

tale [teɪl] *n* Geschichte *f*

talent [tælənt] *n* Talent *nt*

talented [tælɪntɪd] *adj* begabt

talk [tɔk] *n* (*conversation*) Gespräch *nt*; (*rumor*) Gerede *nt*; (*to audience*) Vortrag *m* ▷ *vi* sprechen, reden; (*have conversation*) sich unterhalten; **to ~ to** *o* **with sb about sth** mit jdm (über etw *akk*) sprechen ▷ *vt* (*language*) sprechen; (*nonsense*) reden; (*politics, business*) reden über +*akk*; **to ~ sb into doing/out of doing sth** jdn überreden/jdm ausreden, etw zu tun

talkative [tɔkətɪv] *adj* gesprächig

talk over *vt* besprechen

talk show *n* Talkshow *f*

tall [tɔl] *adj* groß; (*building, tree*) hoch; **he is 6ft ~** er ist 1,80m groß

tame [teɪm] *adj* zahm; (*joke, story*) fade ▷ *vt* (*animal*) zähmen

tampon [tæmpɒn] *n* Tampon *m*

tan [tæn] *n* (*on skin*) (Sonnen)bräune *f*; **to get/have a tan** braun werden/sein ▷ *vi* braun werden

tangerine [tændʒərɪn] *n* Mandarine *f*

tango [tængoʊ] *n* Tango *m*

tank [tæŋk] *n*·Tank *m*; (*for fish*) Aquarium *nt*; (*Mil*) Panzer *m*

tanker [tæŋkər] *n* (*ship*) Tanker *m*; (*vehicle*) Tankwagen *m*

tanned [tænd] *adj* (*by sun*) braun

tanning bed *n* Sonnenbank *f*

tantalizing [tæntəlaɪzɪŋ] *adj* verlockend

Tanzania [tænzənɪə] *n* Tansania *nt*

tap [tæp] *n* (*for water*) Hahn *m* ▷ *vt, vi* (*strike*) klopfen; **to tap sb on the shoulder** jdm auf die Schulter klopfen

tap-dance *vi* steppen

tape [teɪp] *n* (*adhesive tape*) Klebeband *nt*; (*for tape recorder*) Tonband *nt*; (*cassette*) Kassette *f*; (*video*) Video *nt* ▷ *vt* (*record*) aufnehmen

tape measure *n* Maßband *nt*

tape recorder *n* Tonbandgerät *nt*

tapestry [tæpɪstrɪ] *n* Wandteppich *m*

tape up *vt* (*parcel*) zukleben

tap water *n* Leitungswasser *nt*

target [tɑrgɪt] *n* Ziel *nt*; (*board*) Zielscheibe *f*

target group *n* Zielgruppe *f*

tariff [tærɪf] *n* (*price list*) Preisliste *f*; (*tax*) Zoll *m*

tart [tɑrt] *n* (*fruit tart*) (Obst)kuchen *m*; (*small*) (Obst)törtchen *m*

tartan [tɑrtˀn] *n* Schottenkaro *nt*; (*material*) Schottenstoff *m*

tartar sauce [tɑrtar-] *n* Remouladensoße *f*

task [tæsk] *n* Aufgabe *f*; (*duty*) Pflicht *f*

taskbar [tæskbɑr] *n* (*Inform*) Taskbar *f*

Tasmania [tæzmeɪnɪə] *n* Tasmanien *nt*

taste [teɪst] *n* Geschmack *m*; (*sense of taste*) Geschmackssinn *m*; (*small quantity*) Kostprobe *f*; **it has a strange ~** es schmeckt komisch ▷ *vt* schmecken; (*try*) probieren ▷ *vi* (*food*) schmecken (*of* nach); **to ~ good/ strange** gut/komisch schmecken

tasteful [teɪstfəl] *adj*, **tastefully** *adv* geschmackvoll

tasteless [teɪstlɪs] *adj*, **tastelessly** *adv* geschmacklos

tasty [teɪsti] *adj* lecker

tattered [tætərd] *adj* (*clothes*) zerlumpt; (*fam: person*) angespannt

tattoo [tætu] *n* (*on skin*) Tätowierung *f*

taught [tɔt] *pt, pp of* **teach**

Taurus [tɔrəs] *n* (*Astr*) Stier *m*

tax [tæks] *n* Steuer *f* (*on auf +akk*) ▷ *vt* besteuern

taxable [tæksəbˀl] *adj* steuerpflichtig

taxation [tækseɪʃˀn] *n* Besteuerung *f*

tax bracket *n* Steuerklasse *f*

tax-free *adj* steuerfrei

taxi [tæksi] *n* Taxi *nt* ▷ *vi* (*plane*) rollen

taxi driver *n* Taxifahrer(in) *m(f)*

taxi stand *n* Taxistand *m*

tax return *n* Steuererklärung *f*

tea [ti] *n* Tee *m*; (*afternoon tea*) ≈ Kaffee und Kuchen; (*meal*) frühes Abendessen

teabag [tibæg] *n* Teebeutel *m*

teach [titʃ] (**taught, taught**) *vt* (*person, subject*) unterrichten; **to ~ sb how to dance** jdm das Tanzen beibringen ▷ *vi* unterrichten

teacher [titʃər] *n* Lehrer(in) *m(f)*

teaching [titʃɪŋ] *n* (*activity*) Unterrichten *nt*; (*profession*) Lehrberuf *m*

teacup [tikʌp] *n* Teetasse *f*

teakettle [tikɛtˀl] *n* Kessel *m*

team [tim] *n* (*Sport*) Mannschaft *f*, Team *nt*

teamwork [timwɜrk] *n* Teamarbeit *f*

teapot [tipɒt] *n* Teekanne *f*

tear[1] [tɪər] *n* (*in eye*) Träne *f*

tear[2] [tɛər] (**tore, torn**) *vt* zerreißen; **to ~ a muscle** sich einen Muskel zerren ▷ *n* (*in material etc*) Riss *m*

tear down *vt* (*building*) abreißen

tearoom [tirum] *n* Teestube *f*, Café, *in dem in erster Linie Tee serviert wird*

tear up *vt* (*paper*) zerreißen

tease [tiːz] vt (person) necken (about wegen)

tea set n Teeservice nt

teashop [tiːʃɒp] n Teestube f

teaspoon [tiːspuːn] n Teelöffel m

technical [tɛknɪkᵊl] adj technisch; (knowledge, term, dictionary) Fach-

technically [tɛknɪkli] adv technisch

technique [tɛkniːk] n Technik f

techno [tɛknoʊ] n Techno f

technological [tɛknəlɒdʒɪkᵊl] adj technologisch

technology [tɛknɒlədʒi] n Technologie f, Technik f

tedious [tiːdiəs] adj langweilig

teen(age) [tiːn(eɪdʒ)] adj (fashions etc) Teenager-

teenager [tiːneɪdʒər] n Teenager m

teens [tiːnz] npl: **in one's ~** im Teenageralter

teeth [tiːθ] pl of tooth

teetotal [tiːtoʊtᵊl] adj abstinent

telecommuting n Telearbeit f

telephone [tɛlɪfoʊn] n Telefon nt ▷ vi telefonieren ▷ vt anrufen

telephone book n Telefonbuch nt

telephone booth n Telefonzelle f

telephone call n Telefonanruf m

telephone directory n Telefonbuch nt

telephone number n Telefonnummer f

telephone pole n Telegrafenmast m

telephoto lens [tɛlɪfoʊtoʊ lɛnz] n Teleobjektiv nt

telescope [tɛlɪskoʊp] n Teleskop nt

televise [tɛlɪvaɪz] vt im Fernsehen übertragen

television [tɛlɪvɪʒᵊn, -vɪʒ-] n Fernsehen nt

television (set) [tɛlɪvɪʒᵊn (sɛt)] n Fernseher m

tell [tɛl] (**told, told**) vt (say, inform) sagen (sb sth jdm etw); (story) erzählen; (truth) sagen; (difference) erkennen; (reveal secret) verraten; **to ~ sb about sth** jdm von etw erzählen; **to ~ sth from sth** etw von etw unterscheiden ▷ vi (be sure) wissen

tell apart vt unterscheiden

telling [tɛlɪŋ] adj aufschlussreich

tell off vt schimpfen

temp [tɛmp] n Aushilfskraft f ▷ vi als Aushilfskraft arbeiten

temper [tɛmpər] n (anger) Wut f; (mood) Laune f; **to lose one's ~** die Beherrschung verlieren; **to have a bad ~** jähzornig sein

temperamental [tɛmprəmɛntᵊl] adj

(moody) launisch

temperature [tɛmprətʃər, -tʃʊər] n Temperatur f; (Med: high temperature) Fieber nt; **to have a ~** Fieber haben

temple [tɛmpᵊl] n (Anat) Tempel m; Schläfe f

temporarily [tɛmpərɛɚɪli] adv vorübergehend

temporary [tɛmpərɛri] adj vorübergehend; (road, building) provisorisch

tempt [tɛmpt] vt in Versuchung führen; **I'm ~ed to accept** ich bin versucht anzunehmen

temptation [tɛmpteɪʃᵊn] n Versuchung f

tempting [tɛmptɪŋ] adj verlockend

ten [tɛn] num zehn ▷ n Zehn f; see also eight

tenant [tɛnənt] n Mieter(in) m(f); (of land) Pächter(in) m(f)

tend [tɛnd] vi: **to ~ to do sth** (person) dazu neigen, etw zu tun; **to ~ towards** neigen zu

tendency [tɛndənsi] n Tendenz f; **to have a ~ to do sth** (person) dazu neigen, etw zu tun

tender [tɛndər] adj (loving) zärtlich; (sore) empfindlich; (meat) zart

tendon [tɛndən] n Sehne f

Tenerife [tɛnərif] n Teneriffa nt

tennis [tɛnɪs] n Tennis nt

tennis ball n Tennisball m

tennis court n Tennisplatz m

tennis racket n Tennisschläger m

tenor [tɛnər] n Tenor m

tense [tɛns] adj angespannt; (stretched tight) gespannt

tension [tɛnʃᵊn] n Spannung f; (strain) Anspannung f

tent [tɛnt] n Zelt nt

tenth [tɛnθ] adj zehnte(r, s) ▷ n (fraction) Zehntel nt; see also eighth

tent peg n Hering m

tent pole n Zeltstange f

term [tɜrm] n (in school, at university) Trimester nt; (expression) Ausdruck m; **~s** pl (conditions) Bedingungen pl; **to be on good ~s with sb** mit jdm gut auskommen; **to come to ~s with sth** sich mit etw abfinden; **in the long/short ~** langfristig/kurzfristig; **in ~s of ...** was ... betrifft

terminal [tɜrmɪnᵊl] n (bus terminal etc) Endstation f; (Aviat) Terminal m; (Inform) Terminal nt; (Elec) Pol m ▷ adj (Med) unheilbar

terminally [tɜrmɪnᵊli] adv (ill) unheilbar

terminate [tɜrmɪneɪt] vt (contract) lösen; (pregnancy) abbrechen ▷ vi (train, bus) enden

terminology [tɜrmɪnɒlədʒi] n Terminologie f

terrace [tɛrɪs] n (of houses) Häuserreihe f; (in garden etc) Terrasse f

terraced [tɛrɪst] adj (garden) terrassenförmig angelegt

terrible [tɛrɪbᵊl] adj schrecklich

terrific [tərɪfɪk] adj (very good) fantastisch

terrify [tɛrɪfaɪ] vt erschrecken; **to be terrified** schreckliche Angst haben (of vor +dat)

territory [tɛrɪtɔri] n Gebiet nt

terror [tɛrər] n Schrecken m; (Pol) Terror m

terrorism [tɛrərɪzəm] n Terrorismus m

terrorist [tɛrərɪst] n Terrorist(in) m(f)

test [tɛst] n Test m, Klassenarbeit f; (driving test) Prüfung f; **to put to the ~** auf die Probe stellen ▷ vt testen, prüfen; (patience, courage etc) auf die Probe stellen

testament n (will) Testament nt; **the Old/New T~** das Alte/Neue Testament

test-drive vt Probe fahren

testicle [tɛstɪkᵊl] n Hoden m

testify [tɛstɪfaɪ] vi (Jur) aussagen

test tube n Reagenzglas nt

tetanus [tɛtᵊnəs] n Tetanus m

text [tɛkst] n Text m; (of document) Wortlaut m; (sent by mobile phone) SMS f ▷ vt (message) simsen, SMSen; **to ~ sb** jdm simsen, jdm eine SMS schicken; **I'll ~ it to you** ich schicke es dir per SMS

textbook [tɛkstbʊk] n Lehrbuch nt

texting [tɛkstɪŋ] n SMS-Messaging nt

text message n SMS f

text messaging [tɛskt mɛsɪdʒɪŋ] n SMS-Messaging nt

texture [tɛkstfər] n Beschaffenheit f

Thailand [taɪlænd] n Thailand nt

Thames [tɛmz] n Themse f

than [ðən, STRONG ðæn] prep, conj als; **bigger/faster ~ me** größer/schneller als ich; **I'd rather walk ~ drive** ich gehe lieber zu Fuß als mit dem Auto

thank [θæŋk] vt danken +dat; **~ you** danke; **~ you very much** vielen Dank

thankful [θæŋkfəl] adj dankbar

thankfully [θæŋkfəli] adv (luckily) zum Glück

thankless [θæŋklɪs] adj undankbar

thanks [θæŋks] npl Dank m; **~!** danke!; **~ to** dank +gen

Thanksgiving (Day) ist ein Feiertag in den USA, der auf den vierten Donnerstag im November fällt. Er soll daran erinnern, wie die Pilgerväter die gute Ernte im Jahre 1621 feierten. In Kanada gibt es einen ähnlichen Erntedanktag(, der aber nichts mit den Pilgervätern zu tun hat,) am zweiten Montag im Oktober.

KEYWORD

that [ðæt] adj (demonstrative: pl those) der/die/das, jene(r, s); **that one** das da

▷ pron 1 (demonstrative: pl those) das; **who's/what's that?** wer ist da/was ist das?; **is that you?** bist du/sind Sie das?; **that's what he said** genau das hat er gesagt; **what happened after that?** was passierte danach?; **that is** das heißt

2 (relative: subj) der/die/das, die; (direct obj) den/die/das, die; (indirect obj) dem/der/dem, denen; **all (that) I have** alles, was ich habe

3 (relative: of time): **the day (that)** an dem Tag, als; **the winter (that) he came** in dem Winter, in dem er kam

▷ conj dass; **he thought that I was ill** er dachte, dass ich krank sei, er dachte, ich sei krank

▷ adv (demonstrative) so; **I can't work that much** ich kann nicht so viel arbeiten

that's [ðæts] contr of that is; that has

thaw [θɔ] vi tauen; (frozen food) auftauen ▷ vt auftauen lassen

KEYWORD

the [ðə, ði] def art 1 der/die/das; **to play the piano/violin** Klavier/Geige spielen; **I'm going to the bakery/the movies** ich gehe zum Bäcker/ins Kino; **Elizabeth the First** Elisabeth die Erste

2 (+adj to form noun) das, die; **the rich and the poor** die Reichen und die Armen

3 (in comparisons): **the more he works the more he earns** je mehr er arbeitet, desto mehr verdient er

theater [θiətər] n Theater nt; (for lectures etc) Saal m

theft [θɛft] n Diebstahl m

their [ðɛər] *adj* ihr; *(unidentified person)* sein; **they cleaned ~ teeth** sie putzten sich die Zähne; **someone has left ~ umbrella here** jemand hat seinen Schirm hier vergessen

theirs [ðɛərz] *pron* ihre(r, s); *(unidentified person)* seine(r, s); **it's ~** es gehört ihnen; **a friend of ~** ein Freund von ihnen; **someone has left ~ here** jemand hat seins hier liegen lassen

them [ðəm, STRONG ðɛm] *pron (direct object)* sie; *(indirect object)* ihnen; *(unidentified person)* ihn/ihm, sie/ihr; **do you know ~?** kennst du/kennen Sie sie?; **can you help ~?** kannst du/können Sie ihnen helfen?; **it's ~** sie sind's; **if anyone has a problem you should help ~** wenn jemand ein Problem hat, solltest du/sollten Sie ihm helfen

theme [θiːm] *n* Thema *nt*; *(Mus)* Motiv *nt*; **~ park** Themenpark *m*; **~ song** Titelmusik *f*

themselves [ðəmsɛlvz] *pron* sich; **they hurt ~** sie haben sich verletzt; **they ~ were not there** sie selbst waren nicht da; **they did it ~** sie haben es selbst gemacht; **they are not dangerous in ~** an sich sind sie nicht gefährlich; **all by ~** allein

then [ðɛn] *adv (at that time)* damals; *(next)* dann; *(therefore)* also; *(furthermore)* ferner; **from ~ on** von da an; **by ~** bis dahin ▷ *adj* damalig

theoretical [θɪərɛtɪkᵊl] *adj*, **theoretically** *adv* theoretisch

theory [θɪəri] *n* Theorie *f*; **in ~** theoretisch

therapy [θɛrəpi] *n* Therapie *f*

KEYWORD

there [ðɛr, STRONG ðɛr, ðɛər] *adv* **1: there is, there are** es *o* da ist/sind; *(there exists/exist also)* es gibt; **there are 3 of them** *(people, things)* es gibt 3 davon; **there has been an accident** da war ein Unfall

2 *(place)* da, dort; *(direction)* dahin, dorthin; **put it in/on there** leg es dahinein/dorthinauf

3: there, there *(esp to child)* na, na

thereabouts [ðɛərəbaʊts] *adv (approximately)* so ungefähr

therefore [ðɛərfɔr] *adv* daher, deshalb

thermometer [θərmɒmɪtər] *n* Thermometer *nt*

thermos [θɜrməs] *n*: **T~ bottle** Thermosflasche® *f*

these [ðiːz] *pron, adj* diese; **I don't like ~ apples** ich mag diese Äpfel nicht; **~ are not my books** das sind nicht meine Bücher

thesis [θiːsɪs] *(pl* **theses**) *n (for PhD)* Doktorarbeit *f*

they [ðeɪ] *pron (pl)* sie; *(people in general)* man; *(unidentified person)* er/sie; **~ are rich** sie sind reich; **~ say that …** man sagt, dass …; **if anyone looks at this, ~ will see that …** wenn sich jemand dies ansieht, wird er erkennen, dass …

they'd [ðeɪd] *contr of* **they had**; **they would**

they'll [ðeɪl] *contr of* **they will**; **they shall**

they've [ðeɪv] *contr of* **they have**

thick [θɪk] *adj* dick; *(fog)* dicht; *(liquid)* dickflüssig; *(fam: stupid)* dumm

thicken [θɪkən] *vi (fog)* dichter werden; *(sauce)* dick werden ▷ *vt (sauce)* eindicken

thief [θiːf] *(pl* **thieves**) *n* Dieb(in) *m(f)*

thigh [θaɪ] *n* Oberschenkel *m*

thimble [θɪmbᵊl] *n* Fingerhut *m*

thin [θɪn] *adj* dünn

thing [θɪŋ] *n* Ding *nt*; *(affair)* Sache *f*; **my ~s** *pl* meine Sachen *pl*; **how are ~s?** wie geht's?; **I can't see a ~** ich kann nichts sehen; **he knows a ~ or two about cars** er kennt sich mit Autos aus

think [θɪŋk] *(pret, pp* **thought**) *vt, vi* denken; *(believe)* meinen; **I ~ so** ich denke schon; **I don't ~ so** ich glaube nicht

think about *vt* denken an +*akk*; *(reflect on)* nachdenken über +*akk*; *(have opinion of)* halten von

think of *vt* denken an +*akk*; *(devise)* sich ausdenken; *(have opinion of)* halten von; *(remember)* sich erinnern an +*akk*

think over *vt* überdenken

think up *vt* sich ausdenken

third [θɜrd] *adj* dritte(r, s); **the T~ World** die Dritte Welt ▷ *n (fraction)* Drittel *nt*; **in ~ gear** im dritten Gang; *see also* **eighth**

thirdly [θɜrdli] *adv* drittens

thirst [θɜrst] *n* Durst *m (for* nach)

thirsty [θɜrsti] *adj*: **to be ~** Durst haben

thirteen [θɜrtiːn] *num* dreizehn ▷ *n* Dreizehn *f*; *see also* **eight**

thirteenth [θɜrtiːnθ] *adj* dreizehnte(r, s); *see also* **eighth**

thirtieth [θɜrtiəθ] *adj* dreißigste(r, s); *see also* **eighth**

thirty [θɜrti] *num* dreißig; **~-one** einunddreißig ▷ *n* Dreißig *f*; **to be in one's thirties** in den Dreißigern sein; *see also* **eight**

this [ðɪs] *adj* (*demonstrative: pl these*)
diese(r, s); **this evening** heute Abend; **this
one** diese(r, s)(da)
  ▷ *pron* (*demonstrative: pl these*) dies, das;
who/what is this? wer/was ist das?; **this is
where I live** hier wohne ich; **this is what he
said** das hat er gesagt; **this is Mr Brown**
dies ist Mr Brown; (*on telephone*) hier ist
Mr Brown
  ▷ *adv* (*demonstrative*): **this high/long** *etc*
so groß/lang *etc*

thistle [ˈθɪsᵊl] *n* Distel *f*
thong [θɔŋ] *n* String *m*
thorn [θɔrn] *n* Dorn *m*, Stachel *m*
thorough [ˈθɜroʊ] *adj* gründlich
thoroughly [ˈθɜroʊli] *adv* gründlich; (*agree
etc*) völlig
those [ðoʊz] *pron* die da, jene; **~ who** dieje-
nigen, die ▷ *adj* die, jene
though [ðoʊ] *conj* obwohl; **as ~** als ob ▷ *adv*
aber
thought [θɔt] *pt, pp of* **think** ▷ *n* Gedanke
m; (*thinking*) Überlegung *f*
thoughtful [ˈθɔtfəl] *adj* (*kind*) rücksichtsvoll; (*attentive*) aufmerksam; (*in Gedank-
en versunken*) nachdenklich
thoughtless [ˈθɔtlɪs] *adj* (*unkind*) rücksichtslos, gedankenlos
thousand [ˈθaʊzᵊnd] *num*: **one ~, a ~** tausend; **five ~** fünftausend; **~s of** Tausende
von
thrash [θræʃ] *vt* (*hit*) verprügeln; (*defeat*)
vernichtend schlagen
thread [θrɛd] *n* Faden *m* ▷ *vt* (*needle*) einfädeln; (*beads*) auffädeln
threat [θrɛt] *n* Drohung *f*; (*danger*) Bedrohung *f* (*to* für)
threaten [ˈθrɛtᵊn] *vt* bedrohen
threatening [ˈθrɛtᵊnɪŋ] *adj* bedrohlich
three [θri] *num* drei ▷ *n* Drei *f*; *see also*
eight
three-dimensional [θriˈdɪmɛnʃᵊnəl] *adj*
dreidimensional
three-piece suit *n* Anzug *m* mit Weste
three-quarters [θriˈkwɔrtərz] *npl* drei Viertel *pl*
threshold [ˈθrɛʃhoʊld] *n* Schwelle *f*
threw [θru] *pt of* **throw**
thrifty [ˈθrɪfti] *adj* sparsam
thrilled [θrɪld] *adj*: **to be ~ with sth** sich
(über etw *akk*) riesig freuen
thriller [ˈθrɪlər] *n* Thriller *m*

thrilling [ˈθrɪlɪŋ] *adj* aufregend
thrive [θraɪv] *vi* gedeihen (*on* bei); (*fig,
business*) florieren
throat [θroʊt] *n* Hals *m*, Kehle *f*
throbbing [ˈθrɔbɪŋ] *adj* (*pain, headache*)
pochend
thrombosis [θrɒmˈboʊsɪs] *n* Thrombose *f*;
deep vein ~ tiefe Venenthrombose *f*
throne [θroʊn] *n* Thron *m*
through [θru] *prep* durch; (*time*) während
+*gen*; (*because of*) aus, durch; (*up to and
including*) bis; **arranged ~ him** durch ihn
arrangiert ▷ *adv* durch; **to put sb ~** (*Tel*)
jdn verbinden (*to* mit) ▷ *adj* (*ticket, train*)
durchgehend; **~ flight** Direktflug *m*; **to be
~ with sb/sth** mit jdm/etw fertig sein
throughout [θruˈaʊt] *prep* (*place*) überall in
+*dat*; (*time*) während +*gen*; **~ the night** die
ganze Nacht hindurch ▷ *adv* überall;
(*time*) die ganze Zeit
throw [θroʊ] (**threw, thrown**) *vt* werfen;
(*rider*) abwerfen; (*party*) geben; **to ~ sth to
sb, to ~ sb sth** jdm etw zuwerfen; **I was ~n
by his question** seine Frage hat mich aus
dem Konzept gebracht ▷ *n* Wurf *m*
throw away *vt* wegwerfen
throw in *vt* (*include*) dazugeben
throw-in *n* Einwurf *m*
thrown [θroʊn] *pp of* **throw**
throw out *vt* (*unwanted object*) wegwerfen;
(*person*) hinauswerfen (*of* aus)
throw up *vt, vi* (*fam: vomit*) sich übergeben
thru [θru] *see* **through**
thrush [θrʌʃ] *n* Drossel *f*
thrust [θrʌst] (**thrust, thrust**) *vt, vi* (*push*)
stoßen
thruway [ˈθruweɪ] *n* Schnellstraße *f*
thumb [θʌm] *n* Daumen *m* ▷ *vt*: **to ~ a lift**
per Anhalter fahren
thumbtack [ˈθʌmtæk] *n* Reißzwecke *f*
thunder [ˈθʌndər] *n* Donner *m* ▷ *vi* donnern
thunderstorm [ˈθʌndərstɔrm] *n* Gewitter
nt
Thur(s) (*abbr*) = **Thursday** Do.
Thursday [ˈθɜrzdeɪ, -di] *n* Donnerstag *m*;
see also **Tuesday**
thus [ðʌs] *adv* (*in this way*) so; (*therefore*)
somit, also
thyme [taɪm] *n* Thymian *m*
Tibet [tɪbɛt] *n* Tibet *nt*
tick [tɪk] *vt* (*name*) abhaken; (*box, answer*)
ankreuzen ▷ *vi* (*clock*) ticken
ticket [ˈtɪkɪt] *n* (*for train, bus*) (Fahr)karte *f*;

(*plane ticket*) Flugschein *m*, Ticket *nt*; (*for theater, match, museum etc*) (Eintritts)karte *f*; (*price ticket*) (Preis)schild *nt*; (*raffle ticket*) Los *nt*; (*for car park*) Parkschein *m*; (*for traffic offense*) Strafzettel *m*

ticket collector *n* Fahrkartenkontrolleur(in) *m(f)*

ticket machine *n* (*for public transportation*) Fahrscheinautomat *m*; (*in parking lot*) Parkscheinautomat *m*

ticket office *n* (*Rail*) Fahrkartenschalter *m*; (*Theat*) Kasse *f*

tickle [ˈtɪkᵊl] *vt* kitzeln

ticklish [ˈtɪklɪʃ] *adj* kitzlig

tide [taɪd] *n* Gezeiten *pl*; **the ~ is in/out** es ist Flut/Ebbe

tidy [ˈtaɪdi] *adj* ordentlich ▷ *vt* aufräumen

tidy up *vt, vi* aufräumen

tie [taɪ] *n* (*necktie*) Krawatte *f*; (*Sport*) Unentschieden *nt*; (*bond*) Bindung *f* ▷ *vt* (*attach, do up*) binden (**to** an +*akk*); (*tie together*) zusammenbinden; (*knot*) machen ▷ *vi* (*Sport*) unentschieden spielen

tie down *vt* festbinden (**to** an +*dat*); (*fig*) binden

tie up *vt* (*dog*) anbinden; (*package*) verschnüren; (*shoelace*) binden; (*boat*) festmachen; **I'm tied up** (*fig*) ich bin beschäftigt

tiger [ˈtaɪɡər] *n* Tiger *m*

tight [taɪt] *adj* (*clothes*) eng; (*knot*) fest; (*screw, lid*) fest sitzend; (*control, security measures*) streng; (*time*) knapp; (*schedule*) eng ▷ *adv* (*shut*) fest; (*pull*) stramm; **hold ~** festhalten!; **sleep ~** schlaf gut!

tighten [ˈtaɪtᵊn] *vt* (*knot, rope, screw*) anziehen; (*belt*) enger machen; (*restrictions, control*) verschärfen

tile [taɪl] *n* (*on roof*) Dachziegel *m*; (*on wall, floor*) Fliese *f*

tiled [taɪld] *adj* (*roof*) Ziegel-; (*floor, wall*) gefliest

till [tɪl] *prep, conj see* **until**

tilt [tɪlt] *vt* kippen; (*head*) neigen ▷ *vi* sich neigen

time [taɪm] *n* Zeit *f*; (*occasion*) Mal *nt*; (*Mus*) Takt *m*; **local ~** Ortszeit; **what ~ is it?, what's the ~?** wie spät ist es?, wie viel Uhr ist es?; **to take one's ~ over sth** sich (bei etw) Zeit lassen; **to have a good ~** Spaß haben; **in two weeks' ~** in zwei Wochen; **at ~s** manchmal; **at the same ~** gleichzeitig; **all the ~** die ganze Zeit; **by the ~ he ...** bis er ...; (*in past*) als er ...; **for the ~ being** vorläufig; **in ~** (*not late*) recht-

zeitig; **on ~** pünktlich; **the first ~** das erste Mal; **this ~** diesmal; **five ~s** fünfmal; **five ~s six** fünf mal sechs; **four ~s a year** viermal im Jahr; **three at a ~** drei auf einmal ▷ *vt* (*with stopwatch*) stoppen; **you ~d that well** das hast du/haben Sie gut getimt

time difference *n* Zeitunterschied *m*

time limit *n* Frist *f*

timer [ˈtaɪmər] *n* Timer *m*; (*switch*) Schaltuhr *f*

time-saving [ˈtaɪmseɪvɪŋ] *adj* zeitsparend

timetable [ˈtaɪmteɪbᵊl] *n* (*for public transport*) Fahrplan *m*; (*school*) Stundenplan *m*

time zone *n* Zeitzone *f*

timid [ˈtɪmɪd] *adj* ängstlich

timing [ˈtaɪmɪŋ] *n* (*coordination*) Timing *nt*, zeitliche Abstimmung

tin [tɪn] *n* (*metal*) Blech *nt*

tinfoil [ˈtɪnfɔɪl] *n* Alufolie *f*

tinsel [ˈtɪnsᵊl] *n* ≈ Lametta *nt*

tint [tɪnt] *n* (*Farb*)ton *m*; (*in hair*) Tönung *f*

tinted [ˈtɪntɪd] *adj* getönt

tiny [ˈtaɪni] *adj* winzig

tip [tɪp] *n* (*money*) Trinkgeld *nt*; (*hint*) Tipp *m*; (*end*) Spitze *f*; (*of cigarette*) Filter *m* ▷ *vt* (*waiter*) Trinkgeld geben +*dat*

tip over *vt, vi* (*overturn*) umkippen

tipsy [ˈtɪpsi] *adj* beschwipst

tiptoe [ˈtɪptoʊ] *n*: **on ~** auf Zehenspitzen

tire [taɪər] *n* Reifen *m* ▷ *vt* müde machen ▷ *vi* müde werden

tired [taɪərd] *adj* müde; **to be ~ of sb/sth** jdn/etw satthaben; **to be ~ of doing sth** es satthaben, etw zu tun

tireless [ˈtaɪərlɪs], **tirelessly** *adv* unermüdlich

tire pressure *n* Reifendruck *m*

tiresome [ˈtaɪərsəm] *adj* lästig

tiring [ˈtaɪərɪŋ] *adj* ermüdend

Tirol [tɪˈroʊl] *see* **Tyrol**

tissue [ˈtɪʃu] *n* (*Anat*) Gewebe *nt*; (*paper handkerchief*) Tempotaschentuch® *nt*, Papier(taschen)tuch *nt*

tissue paper *n* Seidenpapier *nt*

title [ˈtaɪtᵊl] *n* Titel *m*

titter [ˈtɪtər] *vi* kichern

KEYWORD

to [tə, tu] *prep* **1** (*direction*) zu, nach; **I go to France/school** ich gehe nach Frankreich/zur Schule; **to the left** nach links
2 (*as far as*) bis
3 (*with expressions of time*) vor; **a quarter to 5** Viertel vor 5

4 (*for, of*) für; **secretary to the director** Sekretärin des Direktors

5 (*expressing indirect object*): **to give sth to sb** jdm etw geben; **to talk to sb** mit jdm sprechen; **I sold it to a friend** ich habe es einem Freund verkauft

6 (*in relation to*) zu; **30 miles to the gallon** 30 Meilen pro Gallone

7 (*purpose, result*) zu; **to my surprise** zu meiner Überraschung

▷ **with vb 1** (*infin*): **to go/eat** gehen/essen; **to want to do sth** etw tun wollen; **to try/ start to do sth** versuchen/anfangen, etw zu tun; **he has a lot to lose** er hat viel zu verlieren

2 (*with vb omitted*): **I don't want to** ich will (es) nicht

3 (*purpose, result*) um; **I did it to help you** ich tat es, um dir/Ihnen zu helfen

4 (*after adj etc*): **ready to use** gebrauchsfertig; **too old/young to ...** zu alt/jung, um ... zu ...

▷ *adv*: **push/pull the door to** die Tür zuschieben/zuziehen

toad [tʊd] *n* Kröte *f*

toadstool [tʊdstul] *n* Giftpilz *m*

toast [tʊst] *n* (*bread, drink*) Toast *m*; **a piece** *o* **slice of ~** eine Scheibe Toast; **to propose a ~ to sb** einen Toast auf jdn ausbringen ▷ *vt* (*bread*) toasten; (*person*) trinken auf +*akk*

toaster [tʊstər] *n* Toaster *m*

tobacco [təbækoʊ] (*pl* **-es**) *n* Tabak *m*

toboggan [təbɒɡən] *n* Schlitten *m*

today [tədeɪ] *adv* heute; **a week from ~** heute in einer Woche; **~'s newspaper** die Zeitung von heute

toddler [tɒdlər] *n* Kleinkind *nt*

toe [toʊ] *n* Zehe *f*, Zeh *m*

toenail [toʊneɪl] *n* Zehennagel *m*

tofu [toʊfu] *n* Tofu *m*

together [təɡɛðər] *adv* zusammen; **I tied them ~** ich habe sie zusammengebunden

toilet [tɔɪlɪt] *n* Toilette *f*; **to go to the ~** auf die Toilette gehen

toilet paper [tɔɪlɪt peɪpər] *n* Toilettenpapier *nt*

toiletries [tɔɪlətriz] *npl* Toilettenartikel *pl*

toilet roll [tɔɪlɪt roʊl] *n* Rolle *f* Toilettenpapier

token [toʊkən] *n* Marke *f*; (*in casino*) Spielmarke *f*; (*voucher, gift token*) Gutschein *m*; (*sign*) Zeichen *nt*

Tokyo [toʊkioʊ] *n* Tokio *nt*

told [toʊld] *pt, pp of* **tell**

tolerant [tɒlərənt] *adj* tolerant (*of* gegenüber)

tolerate [tɒləreɪt] *vt* tolerieren; (*noise, pain, heat*) ertragen

toll [toʊl] *n* (*charge*) Gebühr *f*; **the death ~** die Zahl der Toten

toll-free *adj, adv* (*Tel*) gebührenfrei

toll road *n* gebührenpflichtige Straße

tomato [təmeɪtoʊ] (*pl* **-es**) *n* Tomate *f*

tomato juice *n* Tomatensaft *m*

tomato sauce *n* Tomatensoße *f*

tomb [tʊm] *n* Grabmal *nt*

tombstone [tʊmstoʊn] *n* Grabstein *m*

tomorrow [təmɔroʊ] *adv* morgen; **~ morning** morgen früh; **~ evening** morgen Abend; **the day after ~** übermorgen; **a week (from) ~** morgen in einer Woche

ton [tʌn] *n* Tonne *f* (*907 kg*); **tons of books** (*fam*) eine Menge Bücher

tone [toʊn] *n* Ton *m*

tone down *vt* mäßigen

toner [toʊnər] *n* (*for printer*) Toner *m*

toner cartridge *n* Tonerpatrone *f*

tongs [tɒŋz] *npl* Zange *f*; (*curling tongs*) Lockenstab *m*

tongue [tʌŋ] *n* Zunge *f*

tonic [tɒnɪk] *n* (*Med*) Stärkungsmittel *nt*; **~ water** Tonic *nt*; **gin and ~** Gin *m* Tonic

tonight [tənaɪt] *adv* heute Abend; (*during night*) heute Nacht

tonsillitis [tɒnsɪlaɪtɪs] *n* Mandelentzündung *f*

tonsils [tɒnsəlz] *n* Mandeln *pl*

too [tu] *adv* zu; (*also*) auch; **too fast** zu schnell; **too much/many** zu viel/viele; **me too** ich auch; **she liked it too** ihr gefiel es auch

took [tʊk] *pt of* **take**

tool [tul] *n* Werkzeug *nt*

toolbar [tulbɑr] *n* (*Inform*) Symbolleiste *f*

toolbox [tulbɒks] *n* Werkzeugkasten *m*

tooth [tuθ] (*pl* **teeth**) *n* Zahn *m*

toothache [tuθeɪk] *n* Zahnschmerzen *pl*

toothbrush [tuθbrʌʃ] *n* Zahnbürste *f*

toothpaste [tuθpeɪst] *n* Zahnpasta *f*

toothpick [tuθpɪk] *n* Zahnstocher *m*

top [tɒp] *n* (*of tower, class, company etc*) Spitze *f*; (*of mountain*) Gipfel *m*; (*of tree*) Krone *f*; (*of tube, pen*) Kappe *f*; (*of box*) Deckel *m*; (*of bikini*) Oberteil *nt*; (*sleeveless*) Top *nt*; **at the top of the page** oben auf der Seite; **at the top of the league** an der Spitze der Liga; **on top** oben; **on top of** auf +*dat*; (*in addition to*) zusätzlich zu;

over the top übertrieben ▷ *adj (floor, shelf)* oberste(r, s); *(price, note)* höchste(r, s); *(best)* Spitzen-; *(pupil, school)* beste(r, s) ▷ *vt (exceed)* übersteigen; *(be better than)* übertreffen; *(league)* an erster Stelle liegen in +*dat;* **topped with cream** mit Sahne obendrauf

topic [tɒpɪk] *n* Thema *nt*

topical [tɒpɪkᵊl] *adj* aktuell

topless [tɒplɪs] *adj, adv* oben ohne

topping [tɒpɪŋ] *n (on top of pizza, ice-cream etc)* Belag *m,* Garnierung *f*

top-secret *adj* streng geheim

top up *vt* auffüllen; **can I top you up?** darf ich dir nachschenken?

tore [tɔr] *pt of* **tear**

torment [tɔrmɛnt] *vt* quälen

torn [tɔrn] *pp of* **tear**

tornado [tɔrneɪdou] *(pl* **-es)** *n* Tornado *m*

torrential [tɔrɛnʃᵊl] *adj (rain)* sintflutartig

tortoise [tɔrtəs] *n* Schildkröte *f*

torture [tɔrtʃər] *n* Folter *f; (fig)* Qual *f* ▷ *vt* foltern

toss [tɒs] *vt (throw)* werfen; *(salad)* anmachen; **to ~ a coin** eine Münze werfen

total [toutᵊl] *n (of figures, money)* Gesamtsumme *f;* **a ~ of 30** insgesamt 30; **in ~** insgesamt ▷ *adj* total; *(sum etc)* Gesamt- ▷ *vt (amount to)* sich belaufen auf +*akk*

totally [toutᵊli] *adv* total

touch [tʌtʃ] *n (act of touching)* Berührung *f; (sense of touch)* Tastsinn *m; (trace)* Spur *f;* **to be/keep in ~ with sb** mit jdm in Verbindung stehen/bleiben; **to get in ~ with sb** sich mit jdm in Verbindung setzen; **to lose ~ with sb** den Kontakt zu jdm verlieren ▷ *vt (feel)* berühren; *(emotionally)* bewegen

touchdown [tʌtʃdaʊn] *n (Aviat)* Landung *f; (Sport)* Touchdown *m*

touching [tʌtʃɪŋ] *adj (moving)* rührend

touch on *vt (topic)* berühren

touch screen *n* Touchscreen *m,* Berührungsbildschirm *m*

touchy [tʌtʃi] *adj* empfindlich, zickig

tough [tʌf] *adj* hart; *(meat)* zäh; *(material)* robust; *(meat)* zäh

tour [tʊər] *n* Tour *f (of* durch*); (of town, building)* Rundgang *m (of* durch*); (of pop group etc)* Tournee *f* ▷ *vt* eine Tour/einen Rundgang/eine Tournee machen durch ▷ *vi (on vacation)* umherreisen

tour guide *n* Reiseleiter(in) *m(f)*

tourism [tʊərɪzəm] *n* Tourismus *m,* Fremdenverkehr *m*

tourist [tʊərɪst] *n* Tourist(in) *m(f)*

tourist class *n* Touristenklasse *f*

tourist guide *n (book)* Reiseführer *m; (person)* Fremdenführer(in) *m(f)*

tourist office *n* Fremdenverkehrsamt *nt*

tournament [tʊərnəmənt, tɜr-] *n* Tournier *nt*

tour operator *n* Reiseveranstalter *m*

tow [tou] *vt* abschleppen; *(caravan, trailer)* ziehen

toward(s) [təwərd(z)] *prep:* **toward(s) me** mir entgegen, auf mich zu; **we walked toward(s) the station** wir gingen in Richtung Bahnhof; **my feelings toward(s) him** meine Gefühle ihm gegenüber; **she was kind toward(s) me** sie war nett zu mir

tow away *vt* abschleppen

towel [taʊəl] *n* Handtuch *nt*

tower [taʊər] *n* Turm *m*

town [taʊn] *n* Stadt *f*

town center *n* Stadtmitte *f,* Stadtzentrum *nt*

town hall *n* Rathaus *nt*

town house *n* Reihenhaus *nt*

towrope [touroup] *n* Abschleppseil *nt*

tow truck *n* Abschleppwagen *m*

toxic [tɒksɪk] *adj* giftig, Gift-

toy [tɔɪ] *n* Spielzeug *nt*

toy store *n* Spielwarengeschäft *nt*

toy with *vt* spielen mit

trace [treɪs] *n* Spur *f;* **without ~** spurlos ▷ *vt (find)* ausfindig machen

tracing paper [treɪsɪŋ-] *n* Pauspapier *nt*

track [træk] *n (mark)* Spur *f; (path)* Weg *m; (Rail)* Gleis *nt; (on CD, record)* Stück *nt;* **to keep/lose ~ of sb/sth** jdn/etw im Auge behalten/aus den Augen verlieren

track and field *npl* Leichtathletik *f*

trackball [trækbɔl] *n (Inform)* Trackball *m*

track down *vt* ausfindig machen

tracksuit [træksut] *n* Trainingsanzug *m*

tractor [træktər] *n* Traktor *m*

trade [treɪd] *n (commerce)* Handel *m; (business)* Geschäft *nt; (skilled job)* Handwerk *nt* ▷ *vi* handeln *(in* mit*)* ▷ *vt (exchange)* tauschen *(for* gegen*)*

trademark [treɪdmark] *n* Warenzeichen *nt*

tradesman [treɪdzmən] *(pl* **-men)** *n (shopkeeper)* Geschäftsmann *m; (workman)* Handwerker *m*

tradition [trədɪʃᵊn] *n* Tradition *f*

traditional [trədɪʃənᵊl] *adj,* **traditionally** *adv* traditionell

traffic [træfɪk] *n* Verkehr *m; (pej: trading)* Handel *m (in* mit*)*

traffic circle n Kreisverkehr m
traffic island n Verkehrsinsel f
traffic jam n Stau m
traffic lights npl Verkehrsampel f
tragedy [trædʒɪdi] n Tragödie f
tragic [trædʒɪk] adj tragisch
trail [treɪl] n Spur f; (path) Weg m ▷ vt (follow) verfolgen; (drag) schleppen; (drag behind) hinter sich herziehen; (Sport) zurückliegen hinter +dat ▷ vi (hang loosely) schleifen; (Sport) weit zurückliegen
trailer [treɪlər] n Anhänger m; (camper) Wohnwagen m; (Cine) Trailer m
trailer park n Campingplatz m für Wohnwagen
train [treɪn] n (Rail) Zug m ▷ vt (teach) ausbilden; (Sport) trainieren ▷ vi (Sport) trainieren; **to ~ as o to be a teacher** eine Ausbildung als Lehrer machen
trained [treɪnd] adj (person, voice) ausgebildet
trainee [treɪni] n Auszubildende(r) mf; (academic, practical) Praktikant(in) m(f)
traineeship [treɪniʃɪp] n Praktikum nt
trainer [treɪnər] n (Sport) Trainer(in) m(f)
training [treɪnɪŋ] n Ausbildung f; (Sport) Training nt
train station n Bahnhof m; **main ~** Hauptbahnhof m
tramp [træmp] n Landstreicher(in) m(f) ▷ vi trotten
tranquillizer [træŋkwɪlaɪzər] n Beruhigungsmittel nt
transaction [trænzækʃᵊn] n (piece of business) Geschäft nt
transatlantic [trænzətlæntɪk] adj transatlantisch; **~ flight** Transatlantikflug m
transfer [n trænsfɜr, vb trænsfɜr] n (ticket) Umsteigekarte f ▷ vi (on journey) umsteigen
transferable [trænsfɜrəbᵊl] adj übertragbar
transform [trænsfɔrm] vt umwandeln
transformation [trænsfərmeɪʃᵊn] n Umwandlung f
transfusion [trænsfyuːʒᵊn] n Transfusion f
transistor [trænzɪstər] n Transistor m; **~ radio** Transistorradio nt
transition [trænzɪʃᵊn] n Übergang m (from … to von … zu)
transit lounge [trænzɪt laʊndʒ] n Transitraum m
translate [trænzleɪt] vt, vi übersetzen
translation [trænzleɪʃᵊn] n Übersetzung f
translator [trænzleɪtər] n Übersetzer(in)

m(f)
transmission [trænzmɪʃᵊn] n (Auto) Getriebe nt
transom [trænsəm] n Oberlicht nt
transparent [trænspɛərənt, -pær-] adj durchsichtig; (fig) offenkundig
transplant [vb trænsplænt, n trænsplænt] (Med) vt transplantieren ▷ n (operation) Transplantation f
transport [n trænspɔrt, vb trænspɔrt] n (transportation) Beförderung f ▷ vt befördern, transportieren
transportation [trænspərteɪʃᵊn] n (of goods, people) Beförderung f; **public ~** öffentliche Verkehrsmittel pl
trap [træp] n Falle f ▷ vt: **to be ~ped** (in snow, job etc) festsitzen
trash [træʃ] n (book, film etc) Schund m; (refuse) Abfall m
trash can n Abfalleimer m
trashy [træʃi] adj 'niveaulos; (novel) Schund-
traumatic [trəmætɪk] adj traumatisch
travel [trævᵊl] n Reisen nt ▷ vi (journey) reisen ▷ vt (distance) zurücklegen; (country) bereisen
travel agency, travel agent n (company) Reisebüro nt
traveler [trævələr] n Reisende(r) mf
traveler's check Reisescheck m
travel insurance n Reiseversicherung f
tray [treɪ] n Tablett nt; (for mail etc) Ablage f; (of printer, photocopier) Fach nt
tread [trɛd] n (on tyre) Profil nt
tread on (trod, trodden) vt treten auf +akk
treasure [trɛʒər] n Schatz m ▷ vt schätzen
treat [triːt] n besondere Freude; **it's my ~** das geht auf meine Kosten ▷ vt behandeln; **to ~ sb to sth** jdn (zu etw) einladen; **to ~ oneself to sth** sich etw leisten
treatment [triːtmənt] n Behandlung f
treaty [triːti] n Vertrag m
tree [triː] n Baum m
tremble [trɛmbᵊl] vi zittern
tremendous [trɪmɛndəs] adj gewaltig; (fam: very good) toll
trench [trɛntʃ] n Graben m
trend [trɛnd] n Tendenz f; (fashion) Mode f, Trend m
trendy [trɛndi] adj trendy
trespass [trɛspəs, -pæs] vi: **'no ~ing'** „Betreten verboten"
trial [traɪəl] n (Jur) Prozess m; (test) Versuch m; **by ~ and error** durch Ausprobieren
trial period n (for employee) Probezeit f

triangle [traɪæŋgᵉl] n Dreieck nt; (Mus) Triangel m

triangular [traɪæŋgyələr] adj dreieckig

tribe [traɪb] n Stamm m

trick [trɪk] n Trick m; (mischief) Streich m ▷ vt hereinlegen

tricky [trɪki] adj (difficult) schwierig, heikel; (situation) verzwickt

trifle [traɪfᵉl] n Kleinigkeit f

trigger [trɪgər] n (of gun) Abzug m ▷ vt: to ~ off auslösen

trillion [trɪlyən] n Milliarde f

trim [trɪm] vt (hair, beard) nachschneiden; (nails) schneiden; (hedge) stutzen ▷ n: just a ~, please nur etwas nachschneiden, bitte

trimmings [trɪmɪnz] npl (decorations) Verzierungen pl; (extras) Zubehör nt; (Gastr) Beilagen pl

trip [trɪp] n Reise f; (outing) Ausflug m ▷ vi stolpern (over über +akk)

triple [trɪpᵉl] adj dreifach ▷ adv: ~ the price dreimal so teuer ▷ vi sich verdreifachen

triplet [trɪplɪt] n Drilling m

tripod [traɪpɒd] n (Foto) Stativ nt.

trite [traɪt] adj banal

triumph [traɪʌmf] n Triumph m

trivial [trɪviəl] adj trivial

trod [trɒd] pt of **tread**

trodden [trɒdᵉn] pp of **tread**

trolley [trɒli] n (streetcar) Straßenbahn f

trombone [trɒmboʊn] n Posaune f

troops [trups] npl (Mil) Truppen pl

trophy [troʊfi] n Trophäe f

tropical [trɒpɪkᵉl] adj tropisch

trouble [trʌbᵉl] n (problems) Schwierigkeiten pl; (worry) Sorgen pl; (effort) Mühe f; (unrest) Unruhen pl; (Med) Beschwerden pl; to be in ~ in Schwierigkeiten sein; to get into ~ (with authority) Ärger bekommen; to make ~ Schwierigkeiten machen ▷ vt (worry) beunruhigen; (disturb) stören; my back's troubling me mein Rücken macht mir zu schaffen; sorry to ~ you ich muss dich/Sie leider kurz stören

troubled [trʌbᵉld] adj (worried) beunruhigt

trouble-free adj problemlos

troublemaker [trʌbᵉlmeɪkər] n Unruhestifter(in) m(f)

troublesome [trʌbᵉlsəm] adj lästig

trout [traʊt] n Forelle f

truck [trʌk] n Lastwagen m

trucker [trʌkər] n (driver) Lastwagenfahrer(in) m(f)

trucking [trʌkɪŋ] n Transport m; (trade) Spedition f

true [tru] adj (factually correct) wahr; (genuine) echt; **to come ~** wahr werden

truly [truli] adv wirklich; **Yours ~** (in letter) mit freundlichen Grüßen

trumpet [trʌmpɪt] n Trompete f

trunk [trʌŋk] n (of tree) Stamm m; (Anat) Rumpf m; (of elephant) Rüssel m; (piece of luggage) Überseekoffer m; (Auto) Kofferraum m

trunks [trʌŋks] npl: **swimming ~** Badehose f

trust [trʌst] n (confidence) Vertrauen nt (in zu) ▷ vt vertrauen +dat

trusting [trʌstɪŋ] adj vertrauensvoll

trustworthy [trʌstwɜrði] adj vertrauenswürdig

truth [truθ] n Wahrheit f

truthful [truθfəl] adj ehrlich; (statement) wahrheitsgemäß

try [traɪ] n Versuch m ▷ vt (attempt) versuchen; (try out) ausprobieren; (sample) probieren; (Jur: person) vor Gericht stellen; (courage, patience) auf die Probe stellen ▷ vi versuchen; (make effort) sich bemühen; **try and come** versuch zu kommen

try on vt (clothes) anprobieren

try out vt ausprobieren

T-shirt [tiʃərt] n T-Shirt nt

tub [tʌb] n (for ice cream, margarine) Becher m

tube [tub] n (pipe) Rohr nt; (of rubber, plastic) Schlauch m; (for toothpaste, glue etc) Tube f

tuck [tʌk] vt (put) stecken

tuck in vt (shirt) in die Hose stecken; (blanket) feststecken; (person) zudecken ▷ vi (eat) zulangen

Tue(s) (abbr) = **Tuesday** Di.

Tuesday [tuzdeɪ, -di] n Dienstag m; **on ~** (am) Dienstag; **on ~s** dienstags; **this/last/next ~** diesen/letzten/nächsten Dienstag; **(on) ~ morning/afternoon/evening** (am) Dienstagmorgen/-nachmittag/-abend; **every ~** jeden Dienstag; **next ~/a week from ~** Dienstag in einer Woche

tug [tʌg] vt ziehen; **she tugged his sleeve** sie zog an seinem Ärmel ▷ vi ziehen (at an +dat)

tuition [tuɪʃᵉn] n (fees) Studiengebühren pl; **~ fees** pl Studiengebühren pl

tulip [tulɪp] n Tulpe f

tumble [tʌmbᵉl] vi (person, prices) fallen

tumbler [tʌmblər] n (glass) (Becher)glas nt

tummy [tʌmi] n (fam) Bauch m

tummyache [tʌmieɪk] n (fam) Bauchweh nt

tumor [tumər] n Tumor m

tuna [tunə] n Thunfisch m

tune [tun] n Melodie f; **to be in/out of ~** (instrument) gestimmt/verstimmt sein; (singer) richtig/falsch singen ▷ vt (instrument) stimmen; (radio) einstellen (to auf +akk)

tuner [tunər] n (in stereo system) Tuner m

Tunisia [tunɪʒɪə] n Tunesien nt

tunnel [tʌnºl] n Tunnel m; (under road, railway) Unterführung f

turban [tɜrbən] n Turban m

turbulence [tɜrbyələns] n (Aviat) Turbulenzen pl

turbulent [tɜrbyələnt] adj stürmisch

Turk [tɜrk] n Türke m, Türkin f

Turkey [tɜrki] n die Türkei

turkey [tɜrki] n Truthahn m

Turkish [tɜrkɪʃ] adj türkisch ▷ n (language) Türkisch nt

turmoil [tɜrmɔɪl] n Aufruhr m

turn [tɜrn] n (rotation) Drehung f; (performance) Nummer f; **to make a left ~** nach links abbiegen; **at the ~ of the century** um die Jahrhundertwende; **it's your ~** du bist/Sie sind dran; **in ~, by ~s** abwechselnd; **to take ~s** sich abwechseln ▷ vt (wheel, key, screw) drehen; (to face other way) umdrehen; (corner) biegen um; (page) umblättern; (transform) verwandeln (into in +akk) ▷ vi (rotate) sich drehen; (to face other way) sich umdrehen; (change direction: driver, car) abbiegen; (become) werden; (weather) umschlagen; **to ~ into sth** (become) sich in etw akk verwandeln; **to ~ cold/green** kalt/grün werden; **to ~ left/right** links/rechts abbiegen

turn around vt (to face other way) umdrehen ▷ vi (person) sich umdrehen; (go back) umkehren

turn away vt (person) abweisen

turn back vt (person) zurückweisen ▷ vi (go back) umkehren

turn down vt (refuse) ablehnen; (radio, TV) leiser stellen; (heating) kleiner stellen

turning [tɜrnɪŋ] n (in road) Abzweigung f

turning point n Wendepunkt m

turnip [tɜrnɪp] n Rübe f

turn off vi abbiegen ▷ vt (switch off) ausschalten; (tap) zudrehen; (engine, electric-

ity) abstellen

turn on vt (switch on) einschalten; (tap) aufdrehen; (engine, electricity) anstellen; (fam: person) anmachen, antörnen

turn out vt (light) ausmachen; (pockets) leeren ▷ vi (develop) sich entwickeln; **as it turned out** wie sich herausstellte

turn over vt umdrehen; (page) umblättern ▷ vi (person) sich umdrehen; (car) sich überschlagen; (TV) umschalten (to auf +akk)

turnover [tɜrnoʊvər] n (of staff) Fluktuation f; (Fin) Umsatz m

turnpike [tɜrnpaɪk] n gebührenpflichtige Autobahn

turntable [tɜrnteɪbºl] n (on record player) Plattenteller m

turn to vt sich zuwenden +dat

turn up vi (person, lost object) auftauchen ▷ vt (radio, TV) lauter stellen; (heating) höher stellen

turquoise [tɜrkwɔɪz] adj türkis

turtle [tɜrtºl] n Schildkröte f

tutor [tutər] n (private) Privatlehrer(in) m(f)

tux [tʌks], **tuxedo** [tʌxidoʊ] (pl -s) n Smoking m

TV [ti vi] n Fernsehen nt; (TV set) Fernseher m; **to watch TV** fernsehen; **on TV** im Fernsehen ▷ adj Fernseh-; **TV program** Fernsehsendung f

TV dinner n tiefgekühltes Fertiggericht

tweed [twid] n Tweed m

tweezers [twizərz] npl Pinzette f

twelfth [twɛlfθ] adj zwölfte(r, s); see also eighth

twelve [twɛlv] num zwölf ▷ n Zwölf f; see also eight

twentieth [twɛntiəθ] adj zwanzigste(r, s); see also eighth

twenty [twɛnti] num zwanzig; **~-one** einundzwanzig ▷ n Zwanzig f; **to be in one's twenties** in den Zwanzigern sein; see also eight

twice [twaɪs] adv zweimal; **~ as much/many** doppelt so viel/viele

twig [twɪg] n Zweig

twilight [twaɪlaɪt] n (in evening) Dämmerung f

twin [twɪn] n Zwilling m ▷ adj (brother etc) Zwillings-; **~ beds** zwei Einzelbetten

twinge [twɪndʒ] n (pain) stechender Schmerz

twinkle [twɪŋkºl] vi funkeln

twin room n Zweibettzimmer nt

twin town *n* Partnerstadt *f*

twist [twɪst] *vt (turn)* drehen, winden; *(distort)* verdrehen; **I've ~ed my ankle** ich bin mit dem Fuß umgeknickt

two [tuː] *num* zwei; **to break sth in two** etw in zwei Teile brechen ▷ *n* Zwei *f*; **the two of them** die beiden; *see also* **eight**

two-dimensional [tuːdɪmɛnʃˀnəl] *adj* zweidimensional; *(fig)* oberflächlich

two-faced [tuːfeɪst] *adj* falsch, heuchlerisch

two-piece [tuːpiːs] *adj* zweiteilig

two-way *adj:* **~ traffic** Gegenverkehr

type [taɪp] *n (sort)* Art *f*; *(typeface)* Schrift(art) *f*; **what ~ of car is it?** was für ein Auto ist das?; **he's not my ~** er ist nicht mein Typ

typeface [taɪpfeɪs] *n* Schrift(art) *f*

typewriter [taɪpraɪtər] *n* Schreibmaschine *f*

typhoid [taɪfɔɪd] *n* Typhus *m*

typhoon [taɪfuːn] *n* Taifun *m*

typical [tɪpɪkˀl] *adj* typisch *(of* für)

typing error [taɪpɪŋ ɛrər] *n* Tippfehler *m*

Tyrol [tɪroʊl] *n:* **the ~** Tirol *nt*

U

UFO [yu ɛf ou, yufou] (acr) = **unidentified flying object** Ufo nt
Uganda [yugɑndə] n Uganda nt
ugly [ʌgli] adj hässlich
UK [yu keɪ] (abbr) = **United Kingdom**
Ukraine [yukreɪn] n: ~ die Ukraine
ulcer [ʌlsər] n Geschwür nt
ulterior [ʌltɪəriər] adj: ~ **motive** Hintergedanke m
ultimate [ʌltɪmɪt] adj (final) letzte(r, s); (authority) höchste(r, s)
ultimately [ʌltɪmɪtli] adv letzten Endes; (eventually) schließlich
ultimatum [ʌltɪmeɪtəm] n Ultimatum nt
ultra- [ʌltrə-] pref ultra-
ultrasound [ʌltrəsaund] n (Med) Ultraschall m
umbrella [ʌmbrɛlə] n Schirm m
umpire [ʌmpaɪr] n Schiedsrichter(in) m(f)
umpteen [ʌmptin] num (fam) zig; ~ **times** zigmal
UN [yu ɛn] nsing (abbr) (= **United Nations**) VN, Vereinte Nationen pl
un- [ʌn-] pref un-
unable [ʌneɪbᵊl] adj: **to be ~ to do sth** etw nicht tun können
unacceptable [ʌnəksɛptəbᵊl] adj unannehmbar
unaccountably [ʌnəkauntəbli] adv unerklärlicherweise
unaccustomed [ʌnəkʌstəmd] adj: **to be ~ to sth** etw nicht gewohnt sein
unanimous [yunænɪməs] adj, **unanimously** adv einmütig
unattached [ʌnətætʃt] adj (without partner) ungebunden
unattended [ʌnətɛndɪd] adj (luggage, car) unbeaufsichtigt
unauthorized [ʌnɔθəraɪzd] adj unbefugt
unavailable [ʌnəveɪləbᵊl] adj nicht erhältlich; (person) nicht erreichbar
unavoidable [ʌnəvɔɪdəbᵊl] adj unvermeidlich
unaware [ʌnəwɛər] adj: **to be ~ of sth** sich einer Sache dat nicht bewusst sein; **I was ~ that …** ich wusste nicht, dass …
unbalanced [ʌnbælənst] adj unausgewogen; (mentally) gestört
unbearable [ʌnbɛərəbᵊl] adj unerträglich
unbeatable [ʌnbitəbᵊl] adj unschlagbar
unbelievable [ʌnbɪlivəbᵊl] adj unglaublich

unblock [ʌnblɒk] vt (pipe) frei machen
unbutton [ʌnbʌtᵊn] vt aufknöpfen
uncertain [ʌnsɜrtᵊn] adj unsicher
uncle [ʌŋkᵊl] n Onkel m
uncomfortable [ʌnkʌmftəbᵊl, -kʌmfərtə-] adj unbequem
unconditional [ʌnkəndɪʃənᵊl] adj bedingungslos
unconscious [ʌnkɒnʃəs] adj (Med) bewusstlos; **to be ~ of sth** sich einer Sache dat nicht bewusst sein
unconsciously [ʌnkɒnʃəsli] adv unbewusst
uncork [ʌnkɔrk] vt entkorken
uncover [ʌnkʌvər] vt aufdecken
undecided [ʌndɪsaɪdɪd] adj unschlüssig
undeniable [ʌndɪnaɪəbᵊl] adj unbestreitbar
under [ʌndər] prep (beneath) unter +dat; (with motion) unter +akk; **children ~ eight** Kinder unter acht; ~ **an hour** weniger als eine Stunde ▷ adv (beneath) unten; (with motion) darunter; **children aged eight and** ~ Kinder bis zu acht Jahren
underage adj minderjährig
underdog [ʌndərdɒg] n (outsider) Außenseiter(in) m(f)
underdone [ʌndərdʌn] adj (Gastr) nicht gar, durch; (deliberately) nicht durchgebraten
underestimate [ʌndərɛstɪmeɪt] vt unterschätzen
underexposed [ʌndərɪkspouzd] adj (Foto) unterbelichtet
undergo [ʌndərgou] (irr) vt (experience) durchmachen; (operation, test) sich unterziehen +dat
undergraduate [ʌndərgrædʒuɪt] n Student(in) m(f)
underground [ʌndərgraund] adj unterirdisch
underlie [ʌndərlaɪ] (irr) vt zugrunde liegen +dat
underline [ʌndərlaɪn] vt unterstreichen
underlying [ʌndərlaɪɪŋ] adj zugrunde liegend
underneath [ʌndərniθ] prep unter; (with motion) unter +akk ▷ adv darunter
underpants [ʌndərpænts] npl Unterhose f
undershirt [ʌndərʃɜrt] n Unterhemd nt
undershorts [ʌndərʃɔrts] npl Unterhose f

understand [ʌndərstænd] (irr) vt, vi verstehen; **I ~ that ...** (been told) ich habe gehört, dass ...; (sympathize) ich habe Verständnis dafür, dass ...; **to make oneself understood** sich verständlich machen

understandable [ʌndərstændəb⁰l] adj verständlich

understanding [ʌndərstændɪŋ] adj verständnisvoll

undertake [ʌndərteɪk] (irr) vt (task) übernehmen; **to ~ to do sth** sich verpflichten, etw zu tun

undertaker [ʌndərteɪkər] n Leichenbestatter(in) m(f); **~'s** (firm) Bestattungsinstitut nt

underwater [ʌndərwɔtər] adv unter Wasser ▷ adj Unterwasser-

underwear [ʌndərweər] n Unterwäsche f

undesirable [ʌndɪzaɪərəb⁰l] adj unerwünscht

undo [ʌndu] (irr) vt (unfasten) aufmachen; (work) zunichtemachen; (Inform) rückgängig machen

undoubtedly [ʌndautɪdli] adv zweifellos

undress [ʌndrɛs] vt ausziehen; **to get ~ed** sich ausziehen ▷ vi sich ausziehen

undue [ʌndu] adj übermäßig

unduly [ʌnduli] adv übermäßig

unearth [ʌnɜrθ] vt (dig up) ausgraben; (find) aufstöbern

unease [ʌniz] n Unbehagen nt

uneasy [ʌnizi] adj (person) unbehaglich; **I'm ~ about it** mir ist nicht wohl dabei

unemployed [ʌnɪmplɔɪd] adj arbeitslos ▷ npl: **the ~** die Arbeitslosen pl

unemployment [ʌnɪmplɔɪmənt] n Arbeitslosigkeit f

unemployment benefit n Arbeitslosengeld nt

unequal [ʌnikwəl] adj ungleich

uneven [ʌniv⁰n] adj (surface, road) uneben; (contest) ungleich

unexpected [ʌnɪkspɛktɪd] adj unerwartet

unfair [ʌnfɛər] adj unfair

unfamiliar [ʌnfəmɪlyər] adj: **to be ~ with sb/sth** jdn/etw nicht kennen

unfasten [ʌnfæs⁰n] vt aufmachen

unfit [ʌnfɪt] adj ungeeignet (for für); (in bad health) nicht fit

unforeseen [ʌnfɔrsin] adj unvorhergesehen

unforgettable [ʌnfərgɛtəb⁰l] adj unvergesslich

unforgivable [ʌnfərgɪvəb⁰l] adj unverzeihlich

unfortunate [ʌnfɔrtʃənɪt] adj (unlucky) unglücklich; **it is ~ that ...** es ist bedauerlich, dass ...

unfortunately [ʌnfɔrtʃənɪtli] adv leider

unfounded [ʌnfaundɪd] adj unbegründet

unhappy [ʌnhæpi] adj (sad) unglücklich, unzufrieden; **to be ~ with sth** mit etw unzufrieden sein

unhealthy [ʌnhɛlθi] adj ungesund

unheard-of [ʌnhɜrdʌv] adj (unknown) gänzlich unbekannt; (outrageous) unerhört

unhelpful [ʌnhɛlpfəl] adj nicht hilfreich

unhitch [ʌnhɪtʃ] vt (camper, trailer) abkoppeln

unhurt [ʌnhɜrt] adj unverletzt

uniform [yunɪfɔrm] n Uniform f ▷ adj einheitlich

unify [yunɪfaɪ] vt vereinigen

unimportant [ʌnɪmpɔrt⁰nt] adj unwichtig

uninhabited [ʌnɪnhæbɪtɪd] adj unbewohnt

uninstall [ʌnɪnstɔl] vt (Inform) deinstallieren

unintentional [ʌnɪntɛnʃən⁰l] adj unabsichtlich

union [yunyən] n (uniting) Vereinigung f; (alliance) Union f

Union Jack n Union Jack m (britische Nationalflagge)

unique [yunik] adj einzigartig

unit [yunɪt] n Einheit f; (of system, machine) Teil nt; (in school) Lektion f

unite [yunaɪt] vt vereinigen; **the U~d Kingdom** das Vereinigte Königreich; **the U~d Nations** pl die Vereinten Nationen pl; **the U~d States (of America)** pl die Vereinigten Staaten (von Amerika) pl ▷ vi sich vereinigen

universe [yunɪvɜrs] n Universum nt

university [yunɪvɜrsɪti] n Universität f

unkind [ʌnkaɪnd] adj unfreundlich (to zu)

unknown [ʌnnoun] adj unbekannt (to +dat)

unleaded [ʌnlɛdɪd] adj bleifrei

unless [ʌnlɛs] conj es sei denn, wenn ... nicht; **don't do it ~ I tell you to** mach das nicht, es sei denn, ich sage es dir; **~ I'm mistaken ...** wenn ich mich nicht irre ...

unlicensed [ʌnlaɪs⁰nst] adj (premises) ohne Lizenz

unlike [ʌnlaɪk] prep (in contrast to) im Gegensatz zu; **it's ~ her to be late** es sieht ihr gar nicht ähnlich, zu spät zu kommen

unlikely [ʌnlaɪkli] adj unwahrscheinlich

u

unload [ʌnlˈoʊd] *vt* ausladen

unlock [ʌnlˈɒk] *vt* aufschließen

unlucky [ʌnlˈʌki] *adj* unglücklich; **to be ~** Pech haben

unmistakable [ʌnmɪstˈeɪkəbəl] *adj* unverkennbar

unnecessary [ʌnnˈɛsəsɛri] *adj* unnötig

unobtainable [ʌnəbtˈeɪnəbəl] *adj* nicht erhältlich

unoccupied [ʌnˈɒkjʊpaɪd] *adj* (*seat*) frei; (*building, room*) leer stehend

unpack [ʌnpˈæk] *vt, vi* auspacken

unpleasant [ʌnplˈɛzənt] *adj* unangenehm

unplug [ʌnplˈʌg] *vt*: **to ~ sth** den Stecker von etw herausziehen

unprecedented [ʌnprˈɛsɪdəntɪd] *adj* beispiellos

unpredictable [ʌnprɪdˈɪktəbəl] *adj* (*person, weather*) unberechenbar

unreasonable [ʌnrˈiːzənəbəl] *adj* unvernünftig; (*demand*) übertrieben

unreliable [ʌnrɪlˈaɪəbəl] *adj* unzuverlässig

unsafe [ʌnsˈeɪf] *adj* nicht sicher; (*dangerous*) gefährlich

unscrew [ʌnskrˈuː] *vt* abschrauben

unsightly [ʌnsˈaɪtli] *adj* unansehnlich

unskilled [ʌnskˈɪld] *adj* (*worker*) ungelernt

unsuccessful [ʌnsəksˈɛsfəl] *adj* erfolglos

unsuitable [ʌnsˈuːtəbəl] *adj* ungeeignet (*for* für)

until [ʌntˈɪl] *prep* bis; **not ~** erst; **from Monday ~ Friday** von Montag bis Freitag; **he didn't come home ~ midnight** er kam erst um Mitternacht nach Hause; **~ then** bis dahin ▷ *conj* bis; **she won't come ~ you invite her** sie kommt erst, wenn du sie einlädst/wenn Sie sie einladen

unusual [ʌnjˈuːʒʊəl] *adj*, **unusually** *adv* ungewöhnlich

unwanted [ʌnwˈɒntɪd] *adj* unerwünscht, ungewollt

unwell [ʌnwˈɛl] *adj* krank; **to feel ~** sich nicht wohlfühlen

unwilling [ʌnwˈɪlɪŋ] *adj*: **to be ~ to do sth** nicht bereit sein, etw zu tun

unwind [ʌnwˈaɪnd] (*irr*) *vt* abwickeln ▷ *vi* (*relax*) sich entspannen

unwrap [ʌnrˈæp] *vt* auspacken

unzip [ʌnzˈɪp] *vt* den Reißverschluss aufmachen an +*dat*; (*Inform*) entzippen

KEYWORD

up [*prep* ʌp, *adv, adj* ʌp] *prep*: **to be up sth** oben auf etw *dat* sein; **to go up sth** (auf)

etw *akk* hinaufgehen; **go up that road** gehen Sie die Straße hinauf
▷ *adv* **1** (*upwards, higher*) oben; **put it up a bit higher** stell es etwas weiter nach oben; **up there** da oben, dort oben; **up above** hoch oben

2: **to be up** (*out of bed*) auf sein; (*prices, level*) gestiegen sein; (*building, tent*) stehen

3: **up to** (*as far as*) bis; **up to now** bis jetzt

4: **to be up to** (*depending on*): **it's up to you** das hängt von dir ab; (*equal to*): **he's not up to it** (*job, task etc*) er ist dem nicht gewachsen; (*fam: be doing*): **what is he up to?** was führt er im Schilde?; **it's not up to me to decide** die Entscheidung liegt nicht bei mir; **his work is not up to the required standard** seine Arbeit entspricht nicht dem geforderten Niveau

▷ *n*: **ups and downs** (*in life, career*) Höhen und Tiefen *pl*

upbringing [ʌpbrɪ̍ŋɪŋ] *n* Erziehung *f*

update [ʌpdˈeɪt] *n* (*list etc*) Aktualisierung *f*; (*software*) Update *nt* ▷ *vt* (*list etc, person*) auf den neuesten Stand bringen, aktualisieren

upgrade [ʌpgrˈeɪd, -grˈeɪd] *vt* (*computer*) aufrüsten; **we were ~d** das Hotel hat uns ein besseres Zimmer gegeben

upheaval [ʌphˈiːvəl] *n* Aufruhr *m*; (*Pol*) Umbruch *m*

uphill [ʌphˈɪl] *adv* bergauf

upon [əpˈɒn] *prep see* **on**

upper [ʌpˈər] *adj* obere(r, s); (*arm, deck*) Ober-

upright [ʌprˈaɪt] *adj, adv* aufrecht

uprising [ʌprˈaɪzɪŋ] *n* Aufstand *m*

uproar [ʌprˈɔːr] *n* Aufruhr *m*

upset [ʌpsˈɛt] (*irr*) *vt* (*overturn*) umkippen; (*disturb*) aufregen; (*sadden*) bestürzen; (*offend*) kränken; (*plans*) durcheinanderbringen ▷ *adj* (*disturbed*) aufgeregt; (*sad*) bestürzt; (*offended*) gekränkt; **~ stomach** Magenverstimmung *f*

upside down [ʌpsˈaɪd dˈaʊn] *adv* verkehrt herum; (*fig*) drunter und drüber; **to turn sth ~** (*box etc*) etw umdrehen/durchwühlen

upstairs [ʌpstˈɛərz] *adv* oben; (*go, take*) nach oben

up-to-date *adj* modern; (*fashion, information*) aktuell; **to keep sb ~** jdn auf dem Laufenden halten

upwards [ʌpwˈərdz] *adv* nach oben

urban [ɜrbən] *adj* städtisch, Stadt-
urge [ɜrdʒ] *n* Drang *m* ▷ *vt*: **to ~ sb to do sth** jdn drängen, etw zu tun
urgent [ɜrdʒ°nt] *adj*, **urgently** *adv* dringend
urine [yʊərɪn] *n* Urin *m*
URL [yu ɑr εl] *abbr* (= *uniform resource locator*) (*Inform*) URL-Adresse *f*
US [yu εs], **USA** *nsing* (*abbr*) (= *United States (of America)*) USA *pl*
us [əs, STRONG ʌs] *pron* uns; **do they know us?** kennen sie uns?; **can he help us?** kann er uns helfen?; **it's us** wir sind's; **both of us** wir beide
use [*n* yus, *vb* yuz] *n* (*using*) Gebrauch *m*; (*for specific purpose*) Benutzung *f*; **to make use of** Gebrauch machen von; **in/out of use** in/außer Gebrauch; **it's no use doing that** es hat keinen Zweck(, das zu tun); **it's of no use to me** das kann ich nicht brauchen ▷ *vt* benutzen, gebrauchen; (*for specific purpose*) verwenden; (*method*) anwenden

used [*adj* yuzd, *vb* yust] *adj* (*secondhand*) gebraucht ▷ *vb aux*: **to be ~ to sb/sth** an jdn/etw gewöhnt sein; **to get ~ to sb/sth** sich an jdn/etw gewöhnen; **she ~ to live here** sie hat früher mal hier gewohnt
useful [yusfəl] *adj* nützlich
useless [yuslɪs] *adj* nutzlos; (*unusable*) unbrauchbar; (*pointless*) zwecklos
user [yuzər] *n* Benutzer(in) *m(f)*
user-friendly *adj* benutzerfreundlich
use up *vt* aufbrauchen
usual [yuʒuəl] *adj* üblich, gewöhnlich; **as ~** wie üblich
usually [yuʒuəli] *adv* normalerweise
utensil [yutεns°l] *n* Gerät *nt*
uterus [yutərəs] *n* Gebärmutter *f*
utilize [yutɪlaɪz] *vt* verwenden
utmost [ʌtmoʊst] *adj* äußerst; **to do one's ~** sein Möglichstes tun
utter [ʌtər] *adj* völlig ▷ *vt* von sich geben
utterly [ʌtərli] *adv* völlig
U-turn [yutɜrn] *n* (*Auto*) Wende *f*; **to do a ~** wenden; (*fig*) eine Kehrtwendung machen

u

V

vacancy [veɪkənsi] n (job) offene Stelle; (room) freies Zimmer

vacant [veɪkənt] adj (room, toilet) frei; (post) offen; (building) leer stehend

vacate [veɪkeɪt] vt (room, building) räumen; (seat) frei machen

vacation [veɪkeɪʃ°nər] n Ferien pl, Urlaub m; (at university) (Semester)ferien pl; **to go on ~** in Urlaub fahren; **~ course** Ferienkurs m

vacationer [veɪkeɪʃ°nər] n Urlauber(in) m(f)

vaccinate [væksɪneɪt] vt impfen

vaccination [væksɪneɪʃ°n] n Impfung f; **~ card** Impfpass m

vacuum [vækyum, -yuəm] n Vakuum nt ▷ vt, vi (staub)saugen

vacuum (cleaner) [vækyum (klinər)] n Staubsauger m

vagina [vədʒaɪnə] n Scheide f

vague [veɪg] adj (imprecise) vage; (resemblance) entfernt

vaguely [veɪgli] adv in etwa, irgendwie

vain [veɪn] adj (attempt) vergeblich; (conceited) eitel; **in ~** vergeblich, umsonst

vainly [veɪnli] adv (in vain) vergeblich

valentine (card) [vælentaɪn (kard)] n Valentinskarte f

Valentine's Day [vælentaɪnz deɪ] n Valentinstag m

valid [vælɪd] adj (ticket, passport etc) gültig; (argument) stichhaltig; (claim) berechtigt

valley [væli] n Tal nt

valuable [vælyuəb°l] adj wertvoll; (time) kostbar

valuables [vælyuəb°lz] npl Wertsachen pl

value [vælyu] n Wert m ▷ vt (appreciate) schätzen

valve [vælv] n Ventil nt

van [væn] n (Auto) Lieferwagen m

vanilla [vənɪlə] n Vanille f

vanish [vænɪʃ] vi verschwinden

vanity [vænɪti] n Eitelkeit f

vanity case [vænɪti keɪs] n Schminkkoffer m

vapor [veɪpər] n (mist) Dunst m; (steam) Dampf m

variable [veəriəb°l] adj (weather, mood) unbeständig; (quality) unterschiedlich; (speed, height) regulierbar

varied [veərid] adj (interests, selection) vielseitig; (career) bewegt; (work, diet) abwechslungsreich

variety [vəraɪti] n (diversity) Abwechslung f; (assortment) Vielfalt f (of an +dat); (type) Art f

various [veəriəs] adj verschieden

varnish [varnɪʃ] n Lack m ▷ vt lackieren

vary [veəri] vt (alter) verändern ▷ vi (be different) unterschiedlich sein; (fluctuate) sich verändern; (prices) schwanken

vase [veɪs, vɑz] n Vase f

vast [væst] adj riesig; (area) weit

Vatican [vætɪkən] n: **the ~** der Vatikan

VCR [vi si ɑr] (abbr) = **video cassette recorder** Videorekorder m

VD [vi di] (abbr) = **venereal disease** Geschlechtskrankheit f

veal [vil] n Kalbfleisch nt

vegan [vigən] n Veganer(in) m(f)

vegetable [vedʒtəb°l, vedʒɪ-] n Gemüse nt

vegetarian [vedʒɪteəriən] n Vegetarier(in) m(f) ▷ adj vegetarisch

veggie [vedʒi] n (fam) Vegetarier(in) m(f), Gemüse nt ▷ adj vegetarisch

veggie burger [vedʒi bərgər] n Veggieburger m, Gemüseburger m

vehicle [viɪk°l] n Fahrzeug nt

veil [veɪl] n Schleier m

vein [veɪn] n Ader f

Velcro® [velkroʊ] n Klettband nt

velvet [velvɪt] n Samt m

vending machine [vendɪŋ məʃin] n Automat m

venetian blind [vənɪʃ°n blaɪnd] n Jalousie f

Venezuela [venəzweɪlə] n Venezuela nt

Venice [venɪs] n Venedig nt

venison [venɪs°n, -z°n] n Rehfleisch nt

vent [vent] n Öffnung f

ventilate [vent°leɪt] vt lüften

ventilation [vent°leɪʃ°n] n Belüftung f

ventilator [vent°leɪtər] n (in room) Ventilator m; **to be on a ~** (Med) künstlich beatmet werden

venture [ventʃər] n (project) Unternehmung f; (Comm) Unternehmen nt ▷ vi (go) (sich) wagen

venue [venyu] n (for concert etc) Veranstaltungsort m; (Sport) Austragungsort m

verb [vərb] n Verb nt

verbal [vərb°l] adj (agreement) mündlich; (skills) sprachlich

verbally [vərb°li] adv mündlich

verdict [vɜrdɪkt] n Urteil nt

verge [vɜrdʒ] n (of road) (Straßen)rand m;
to be on the ~ of doing sth im Begriff sein,
etw zu tun ▷ vi: **to ~ on** grenzen an +akk

verification [vɛrɪfɪkeɪʃᵊn] n (confirmation)
Bestätigung f; (check) Überprüfung f

verify [vɛrɪfaɪ] vt (confirm) bestätigen;
(check) überprüfen

vermin [vɜrmɪn] npl Schädlinge pl; (insects)
Ungeziefer nt

versatile [vɜrsətᵊl] adj vielseitig

verse [vɜrs] n (poetry) Poesie f; (stanza)
Strophe f

version [vɜrʒᵊn] n Version f

versus [vɜrsəs] prep gegen

vertical [vɜrtɪkᵊl] adj senkrecht, vertikal

very [vɛri] adv sehr; **~ much** sehr ▷ adj: **the
~ book I need** genau das Buch, das ich
brauche; **at that ~ moment** gerade in dem
Augenblick; **at the ~ top** ganz oben; **the ~
best** der/die/das Allerbeste

vest [vɛst] n (waistcoat) Weste f

vet [vɛt] n Tierarzt m, Tierärztin f

veto [vitoʊ] (pl -es) n Veto nt ▷ vt sein Veto
einlegen gegen

VHF [vi eɪtʃ ɛf] (abbr) = **very high frequency** UKW

via [vaɪə, viə] prep über +akk

viable [vaɪəbᵊl] adj (plan) realisierbar;
(company) rentabel

vibrate [vaɪbreɪt] vi vibrieren

vibration [vaɪbreɪʃᵊn] n Vibration f

vicar [vɪkər] n Pfarrer(in) m(f)

vice [vaɪs] n (evil) Laster nt; (Tech) Schraub-
stock m ▷ pref Vize-; **~ chairman** stellver-
tretender Vorsitzender; **~ president**
Vizepräsident(in) m(f)

vice versa [vaɪsə vɜrsə, vaɪs] adv umgekehrt

vicinity [vɪsɪnɪti] n: **in the ~** in der Nähe (of
+gen)

vicious [vɪʃəs] adj (violent) brutal; (malicious) gemein

vicious circle n Teufelskreis m

victim [vɪktəm] n Opfer nt

Victorian [vɪktɔriən] adj viktorianisch

victory [vɪktəri, vɪktri] n Sieg m

video [vɪdioʊ] (pl -s) adj Video- ▷ n Video
nt; (recorder) Videorekorder m ▷ vt (auf
Video) aufnehmen

video camera n Videokamera f

videocassette n Videokassette f

video clip [vɪdioʊ klɪp] n Videoclip m

video game n Videospiel nt

videophone [vɪdioʊfoʊn] n Bildtelefon nt

video recorder [vɪdioʊ rɪkɔrdər] n Videorekorder m

video store n Videothek f

videotape [vɪdioʊteɪp] n Videoband nt
▷ vt (auf Video) aufnehmen

Vienna [viɛnə] n Wien nt

Vietnam [vietnɑm] n Vietnam nt

view [vyu] n (sight) Blick m (of auf +akk);
(vista) Aussicht f; (opinion) Ansicht f, Meinung f; **in ~ of** angesichts +gen ▷ vt (situation, event) betrachten; (house) besichtigen

viewer [vyuər] n (for slides) Diabetrachter
m; (TV) Zuschauer(in) m(f)

viewpoint [vyupɔɪnt] n (fig) Standpunkt
m

vigilant [vɪdʒɪlənt] adj wachsam

vile [vaɪl] adj abscheulich; (weather, food)
scheußlich

village [vɪlɪdʒ] n Dorf nt

villager [vɪlɪdʒər] n Dorfbewohner(in)
m(f)

villain [vɪlən] n Schurke m; (in film, story)
Bösewicht m

vine [vaɪn] n (Wein)rebe f

vinegar [vɪnɪgər] n Essig m

vineyard [vɪnyərd] n Weinberg m

vintage [vɪntɪdʒ] n (of wine) Jahrgang m

vintage wine n edler Wein

vinyl [vaɪnɪl] n Vinyl nt

viola [vioʊlə] n Bratsche f

violate [vaɪəleɪt] vt (treaty) brechen;
(rights, rule) verletzen

violence [vaɪələns] n (brutality) Gewalt f;
(of person) Gewalttätigkeit f

violent [vaɪələnt] adj (brutal) brutal;
(death) gewaltsam

violet [vaɪəlɪt] n Veilchen nt

violin [vaɪəlɪn] n Geige f, Violine f

VIP [vi aɪ pi] (abbr) = **very important person** VIP mf

virgin [vɜrdʒɪn] n Jungfrau f

Virgo [vɜrgoʊ] n (Astr) Jungfrau f

virile [vɪrᵊl] adj (man) männlich

virtual [vɜrtʃuəl] adj (Inform) virtuell

virtually [vɜrtʃuəli] adv praktisch

virtual reality n virtuelle Realität

virtue [vɜrtʃu] n Tugend f; **by ~ of** aufgrund
+gen

virtuous [vɜrtʃuəs] adj tugendhaft

virus [vaɪrəs] n (Med, Inform) Virus nt

visa [vizə] n Visum nt

visibility [vɪzɪbɪlɪti] n (Meteo) Sichtweite f;
good/poor ~ gute/schlechte Sicht

visible [vɪzɪbᵊl] adj sichtbar; (evident)

sichtlich
visibly [vɪzɪbli] *adv* sichtlich
vision [vɪʒᵊn] *n* (*power of sight*) Sehvermögen *nt*; (*foresight*) Weitblick *m*; (*dream, image*) Vision *f*
visit [vɪzɪt] *n* Besuch *m*; (*stay*) Aufenthalt *m* ▷ *vt* besuchen
visiting hours [vɪzɪtɪŋ aʊərz] *npl* Besuchszeiten *pl*
visitor [vɪzɪtər] *n* Besucher(in) *m(f)*; **~'s book** Gästebuch *nt*
visitor center *n* Informationszentrum *nt*
visor [vaɪzər] *n* (*on helmet*) Visier *nt*; (*Auto*) Blende *f*
visual [vɪʒuəl] *adj* Seh-; (*image, joke*) visuell; **~ aid** Anschauungsmaterial *nt*; **~ display unit** Monitor *m*
visualize [vɪʒuəlaɪz] *vt* sich vorstelle
visually [vɪʒuəli] *adv* visuell; **~ impaired** sehbehindert
vital [vaɪtᵊl] *adj* (*essential*) unerlässlich, wesentlich; (*argument, moment*) entscheidend
vitality [vaɪtælɪti] *n* Vitalität *f*
vitally [vaɪtᵊli] *adv* äußerst
vitamin [vaɪtəmɪn] *n* Vitamin *nt*
vivacious [vɪveɪʃəs] *adj* lebhaft
vivid [vɪvɪd] *adj* (*description*) anschaulich; (*memory*) lebhaft; (*color*) leuchtend
V-neck [vinɛk] *n* V-Ausschnitt *m*
vocabulary [voʊkæbyəlɛri] *n* Wortschatz *m*, Vokabular *nt*
vocal [voʊkᵊl] *adj* (*of the voice*) Stimm-; (*group*) Gesangs-; (*protest, person*) lautstark
vocation [voʊkeɪʃᵊn] *n* Berufung *f*
vocational [voʊkeɪʃənᵊl] *adj* Berufs-

vodka [vɒdkə] *n* Wodka *m*
voice [vɔɪs] *n* Stimme *f* ▷ *vt* äußern
voice mail *n* Voicemail *f*
void [vɔɪd] *n* Leere *f* ▷ *adj* (*Jur*) ungültig; **~ of** (*ganz*) ohne
volcano [vɒlkeɪnoʊ] (*pl* **-es**) *n* Vulkan *m*
volley [vɒli] *n* (*Tennis*) Volley *m*
volleyball [vɒlibɔl] *n* Volleyball *m*
volt [voʊlt] *n* Volt *nt*
voltage [voʊltɪdʒ] *n* Spannung *f*
volume [vɒlyum] *n* (*of sound*) Lautstärke *f*; (*space occupied by sth*) Volumen *nt*; (*size, amount*) Umfang *m*; (*book*) Band *m*
volume control *n* Lautstärkeregler *m*
voluntary [vɒlənteri] *adj*, **voluntarily** *adv* freiwillig; (*unpaid*) ehrenamtlich
volunteer [vɒləntɪər] *n* Freiwillige(r) *mf* ▷ *vi* sich freiwillig melden ▷ *vt*: **to ~ to do sth** sich anbieten, etw zu tun
voluptuous [vəlʌptʃuəs] *adj* sinnlich
vomit [vɒmɪt] *vi* sich übergeben
vote [voʊt] *n* Stimme *f*; (*ballot*) Wahl *f*; (*result*) Abstimmungsergebnis *nt*; (*right to vote*) Wahlrecht *nt* ▷ *vt* (*elect*) wählen; **they ~d him chairman** sie wählten ihn zum Vorsitzenden ▷ *vi* wählen; **to ~ for/ against sth** für/gegen etw stimmen
voter [voʊtər] *n* Wähler(in) *m(f)*
voucher [vaʊtʃər] *n* Gutschein *m*
vow [vaʊ] *n* Gelöbnis *nt* ▷ *vt*: **to vow to do sth** geloben, etw zu tun
vowel [vaʊəl] *n* Vokal *m*
voyage [vɔɪɪdʒ] *n* Reise *f*
vulgar [vʌlgər] *adj* vulgär, ordinär
vulnerable [vʌlnərəbᵊl] *adj* verwundbar; (*sensitive*) verletzlich
vulture [vʌltʃər] *n* Geier *m*

W

W [dʌbᵊlyu] (*abbr*) = **west** W

wade [weɪd] *vi* (*in water*) waten

wading pool [weɪdɪŋ pul] *n* Planschbecken *nt*

wafer [weɪfər] *n* Waffel *f*; (*Rel*) Hostie *f*

wafer-thin [weɪfərθɪn] *adj* hauchdünn

waffle [wɒfᵊl] *n* Waffel *f*

wag [wæg] *vt* (*tail*) wedeln mit

wage [weɪdʒ] *n* Lohn *m*

wagon [wægən] *n* (*horse-drawn*) Fuhrwerk *nt*; (*Auto*) Wagen *m*

waist [weɪst] *n* Taille *f*

waistline [weɪstlaɪn] *n* Taille *f*

wait [weɪt] *n* Wartezeit *f* ▷ *vi* warten (*for* auf +*akk*); **to ~ and see** abwarten; **~ a minute!** Moment mal!

waiter [weɪtər] *n* Kellner *m*; **~!** Herr Ober!

waiting [weɪtɪŋ] *n*: **'no ~'** „Halteverbot"

waiting list [weɪtɪŋ lɪst] *n* Warteliste *f*

waiting room [weɪtɪŋ rum] *n* (*Med*) Wartezimmer *nt*; (*Rail*) Wartesaal *m*

waitress [weɪtrɪs] *n* Kellnerin *f*

wait up *vi* aufbleiben

wake [weɪk] (**woke** *o* **waked**, **woken** *o* **waked**) *vt* wecken ▷ *vi* aufwachen

wake up *vt* aufwecken ▷ *vi* aufwachen

wake-up call *n* (*Tel*) Weckruf *m*

Wales [weɪlz] *n* Wales *nt*

walk [wɔk] *n* Spaziergang *m*; (*ramble*) Wanderung *f*; (*route*) Weg *m*; **to go for a ~** spazieren gehen; **it's only a five-minute ~** es sind nur fünf Minuten zu Fuß ▷ *vi* gehen; (*stroll*) spazieren gehen; (*ramble*) wandern ▷ *vt* (*dog*) ausführen

walking [wɔkɪŋ] *n*: **to go ~** wandern

walking shoes *npl* Wanderschuhe *pl*

walking stick *n* Spazierstock *m*

Walkman® [wɔkmən] (*pl* **-s**) *n* Walkman® *m*

wall [wɔl] *n* (*inside*) Wand *f*; (*outside*) Mauer *f*

wallpaper [wɔlpeɪpər] *n* Tapete *f*; (*Inform*) Bildschirmhintergrund *m* ▷ *vt* tapezieren

walnut [wɔlnʌt, -nət] *n* (*nut*) Walnuss *f*

waltz [wɔlts, wɒls] *n* Walzer *m*

wander [wɒndər] *vi* (*person*) herumwandern

want [wɒnt] *n* (*lack*) Mangel *m* (*of an* +*dat*); (*need*) Bedürfnis *nt*; **for ~ of** aus Mangel an +*dat* ▷ *vt* (*desire*) wollen; (*need*) brauchen; **I ~ to stay here** ich will hier bleiben; **he doesn't ~ to** er will nicht

war [wɔr] *n* Krieg *m*

ward [wɔrd] *n* (*in a hospital*) Station *f*; (*child*) Mündel *nt*

warden [wɔrdᵊn] *n* Aufseher(in) *m(f)*; (*in youth hostel*) Herbergsvater *m*, Herbergsmutter *f*

wardrobe [wɔrdroʊb] *n* Kleiderschrank *m*

warehouse [weərhaʊs] *n* Lagerhaus *nt*

warfare [wɔrfɛər] *n* Krieg *m*; (*techniques*) Kriegsführung *f*

warm [wɔrm] *adj* warm; (*welcome*) herzlich; **I'm ~** mir ist warm ▷ *vt* wärmen; (*food*) aufwärmen

warmly [wɔrmli] *adv* warm; (*welcome*) herzlich

warm over *vt* (*food*) aufwärmen

warmth [wɔrmθ] *n* Wärme *f*; (*of welcome*) Herzlichkeit *f*

warm up *vt* (*food*) aufwärmen; (*room*) erwärmen ▷ *vi* (*food, room*) warm werden; (*Sport*) sich aufwärmen

warn [wɔrn] *vt* warnen (*of, against* vor +*dat*); **to ~ sb not to do sth** jdn davor warnen, etw zu tun

warning [wɔrnɪŋ] *n* Warnung *f*

warning light *n* Warnlicht *nt*

warranty [wɔrənti] *n* Garantie *f*

wart [wɔrt] *n* Warze *f*

wary [weəri] *adj* vorsichtig; (*suspicious*) misstrauisch

was [wəz, STRONG wʌz, wɒz] *pt of* **be**

wash [wɒʃ] *n*: **to have a ~** sich waschen; **it's in the ~** es ist in der Wäsche ▷ *vt* waschen; (*plates, glasses etc*) abwaschen; **to ~ one's hands** sich *dat* die Hände waschen; **to ~ the dishes** (das Geschirr) abwaschen ▷ *vi* (*clean oneself*) sich waschen

washable [wɒʃəbᵊl] *adj* waschbar

washbasin [wɒʃbeɪsᵊn] *n* Waschbecken *nt*

washcloth [wɒʃklɔθ] *n* Waschlappen *m*

washer [wɒʃər] *n* (*Tech*) Dichtungsring *m*; (*washing machine*) Waschmaschine *f*

washing [wɒʃɪŋ] *n* (*laundry*) Wäsche *f*

washing machine *n* Waschmaschine *f*

wash off *vt* abwaschen

washroom [wɒʃrum] *n* Toilette *f*

wash up *vi* (*clean oneself*) sich waschen

wasn't [wʌzᵊnt, wɒz-] *contr of* **was not**

wasp [wɒsp] *n* Wespe *f*

waste [weɪst] *n* (*materials*) Abfall *m*; (*wasting*) Verschwendung *f*; **it's a ~ of time** das ist Zeitverschwendung ▷ *adj* (*superfluous*)

überschüssig ▷ *vt* verschwenden (*on* an
+*akk*); (*opportunity*) vertun

wastepaper basket [wEIstpeIpər bɑskIt]
n Papierkorb *m*

watch [wɒtʃ] *n* (*timepiece*) (Armband)uhr *f*
▷ *vt* (*observe*) beobachten; (*guard*) aufpassen auf +*akk*; (*film, play, program*) sich *dat*
ansehen; **to ~ TV** fernsehen ▷ *vi* zusehen;
(*guard*) Wache halten; **to ~ for sb/sth** nach
jdm/etw Ausschau halten; **~ out!** pass
auf!

watchdog [wɒtʃdɔg] *n* Wachhund *m*; (*fig*)
Aufsichtsbehörde *f*

watchful [wɒtʃfəl] *adj* wachsam

water [wɔtər] *n* Wasser *nt* ▷ *vt* (*plant*) gießen ▷ *vi* (*eye*) tränen; **my mouth is ~ing**
mir läuft das Wasser im Mund zusammen

watercolor [wɔtərkɑlər] *n* (*painting*)
Aquarell *nt*; (*paint*) Wasserfarbe *f*

watercress [wɔtərkrɛs] *n* (Brunnen)kres-
se *f*

water down *vt* verdünnen

waterfall [wɔtərfɔl] *n* Wasserfall *m*

watering can [wɔtərɪŋ kæn] *n* Gießkanne *f*

water level *n* Wasserstand *m*

watermelon [wɔtərmɛlən] *n* Wassermelone *f*

waterproof [wɔtərpruf] *adj* wasserdicht

water-skiing *n* Wasserskilaufen *nt*

water sports *npl* Wassersport *m*

watertight [wɔtərtaɪt] *adj* wasserdicht

water wings *npl* Schwimmflügel *pl*

watery [wɔtəri] *adj* wässerig

wave [weɪv] *n* Welle *f* ▷ *vt* (*move to and fro*)
schwenken; (*hand, flag*) winken mit ▷ *vi*
(*person*) winken; (*flag*) wehen

wavelength [weɪvlɛŋθ] *n* Wellenlänge *f*; **to
be on the same ~** (*fig*) die gleiche Wellenlänge haben

wavy [weɪvi] *adj* wellig

wax [wæks] *n* Wachs *nt*; (*in ear*) Ohren-
schmalz *nt*

way [weɪ] *n* Weg *m*; (*direction*) Richtung *f*;
(*manner*) Art *f*; **can you tell me the way
to…?** wie komme ich (am besten) zu…?;
we went the wrong way wir sind in die
falsche Richtung gefahren/gegangen; **to
lose one's way** sich verirren; **to make way
for sb/sth** jdm/etw Platz machen; **to get
one's own way** seinen Willen durchsetzen; **'give way'** (*Auto*) „Vorfahrt achten";
the other way around andersherum; **one
way or another** irgendwie; **in a way** in
gewisser Weise; **in the way** im Weg; **by the
way** übrigens; **'way in'** „Eingang"; **'way

out'** „Ausgang"; **no way!** (*fam*) kommt
nicht infrage!

we [wI, STRONG wi] *pron* wir

weak [wik] *adj* schwach

weaken [wikən] *vt* schwächen ▷ *vi* schwächer werden

wealth [wɛlθ] *n* Reichtum *m*

wealthy [wɛlθi] *adj* reich

weapon [wɛpən] *n* Waffe *f*

wear [wɛar] (**wore, worn**) *vt* (*have on*) tragen; **what shall I ~?** was soll ich anziehen?
▷ *vi* (*become worn*) sich abnutzen ▷ *n*: **~
and tear** Abnutzung *f*

wear off *vi* (*diminish*) nachlassen

wear out *vt* abnutzen; (*person*) erschöpfen
▷ *vi* sich abnutzen

weather [wɛðər] *n* Wetter *nt*; **I'm feeling
under the ~** ich fühle mich nicht ganz
wohl

weather forecast *n* Wettervorhersage *f*

weave [wiv] (**wove** *o* **weaved, woven** *o*
weaved) *vt* (*cloth*) weben; (*basket etc*)
flechten

web [wɛb] *n* (*a. fig*) Netz *nt*; **the Web** das
Web, das Internet

webcam [wɛbkæm] *n* Webcam *f*

web page *n* Webseite *f*

website [wɛbsaɪt] *n* Website *f*

Wed (*abbr*) = **Wednesday** Mi.

we'd [wId, STRONG wid] *contr of* **we had; we
would**

wedding [wɛdɪŋ] *n* Hochzeit *f*

wedding anniversary *n* Hochzeitstag *m*

wedding dress *n* Hochzeitskleid *nt*

wedding ring *n* Ehering *m*

wedge [wɛdʒ] *n* (*under door etc*) Keil *m*; (*of
cheese etc*) Stück *nt*, Ecke *f*

Wednesday [wɛnzdeɪ, -di] *n* Mittwoch *m*;
see also **Tuesday**

wee [wi] *adj* klein ▷ *vi* (*fam*) Pipi machen

weed [wid] *n* Unkraut *nt* ▷ *vt* jäten

week [wik] *n* Woche *f*; **twice a ~** zweimal in
der Woche; **a ~ from Friday** Freitag in einer
Woche; **a ~ from last Friday** letzten Freitag vor einer Woche; **in two ~s' time, in
two ~s** in zwei Wochen; **for ~s** wochenlang

weekday [wikdeɪ] *n* Wochentag *m*

weekend [wikɛnd] *n* Wochenende *nt*

weekly [wikli] *adj, adv* wöchentlich; (*magazine*) Wochen-

weep [wip] (**wept, wept**) *vi* weinen

weigh [weɪ] *vt, vi* wiegen; **it ~s 20 kilos** es
wiegt 20 Kilo

weight [weɪt] *n* Gewicht *nt*; **to lose/put on
~** abnehmen/zunehmen

weightlifting [weɪtlɪftɪŋ] n Gewichtheben nt

weight training n Krafttraining nt

weighty [weɪti] adj (important) schwerwiegend

weigh up vt abwägen; (person) einschätzen

weird [wɪərd] adj seltsam

weirdo [wɪərdou] n Spinner(in) m(f)

welcome [wɛlkəm] n Empfang m ▷ adj willkommen; (news) angenehm; ~ to New York! willkommen in New York! ▷ vt begrüßen

welcoming [wɛlkəmɪŋ] adj freundlich

welfare [wɛlfɛər] n Wohl nt; (social security) Sozialhilfe f

welfare state n Wohlfahrtsstaat m

well [wɛl] n Brunnen m ▷ adj (in good health) gesund; **are you ~?** geht es dir/Ihnen gut?; **to feel ~** sich wohlfühlen; **get ~ soon** gute Besserung! ▷ interj nun; ~, I **don't know** nun, ich weiß nicht ▷ adv gut; ~ **done** gut gemacht!; **it may ~ be** das kann wohl sein; **as ~** (in addition) auch; ~ **over** 60 weit über 60

we'll [wɪl, STRONG wil] contr of **we will; we shall**

well-behaved [wɛlbɪheɪvd] adj brav

well-being [wɛlbiɪŋ] n Wohl nt

well-built adj (person) gut gebaut

well-done adj (steak) durchgebraten

well-earned [wɛlɜrnd] adj wohlverdient

well-known [wɛlnoʊn] adj bekannt

well-off [wɛlɔf] adj (wealthy) wohlhabend

well-paid [wɛlpeɪd] adj gut bezahlt

Welsh [wɛlʃ] adj walisisch ▷ n (language) Walisisch nt; **the ~** pl die Waliser pl

Welshman [wɛlʃmən] (pl **-men**) n Waliser m

Welshwoman [wɛlʃwʊmən] (pl **-women**) n Waliserin f

went [wɛnt] pt of **go**

wept [wɛpt] pt, pp of **weep**

were [wər, STRONG wɜr] pt of **be**

we're [wɪər] contr of **we are**

weren't [wɜrnt, wɜrənt] contr of **were not**

west [wɛst] n Westen m; **the W~** (Pol) der Westen ▷ adv (go, face) nach Westen ▷ adj West-

westbound [wɛstbaʊnd] adj (in) Richtung Westen

western [wɛstərn] adj West-, westlich; **W~ Europe** Westeuropa nt ▷ n (Cine) Western m

West Germany n: **(the former) ~** (das ehemalige) Westdeutschland nt

westwards [wɛstwərdz] adv nach Westen

wet [wɛt] (wet, wet) vt: **to wet oneself** in die Hose machen ▷ adj nass, feucht; **'wet paint'** „frisch gestrichen"

wet suit n Taucheranzug m

we've [wɪv, STRONG wiv] contr of **we have**

whale [weɪl] n Wal m

wharf [wɔrf] (pl **-s**) (o) (**wharves**) n Kai m

KEYWORD

what [wʌt, wɒt] adj **1** (in questions) welche(r, s), was für ein(e); **what size is it?** welche Größe ist das?

2 (in exclamations) was für ein(e); **what a mess!** was für ein Durcheinander!

▷ pron (interrogative/relative) was; **what are you doing?** was machst du/machen Sie gerade?; **what are you talking about?** wovon redest du/reden Sie?; **what's your name?** wie heißt du/heißen Sie?; **what is it called?** wie heißt das?; **what about ...?** wie wär's mit ...?; **I saw what you did** ich habe gesehen, was du gemacht hast/Sie gemacht haben

▷ excl (disbelieving) wie, was; **what, no coffee!** wie, kein Kaffee?; **I've crashed the car - what!** ich hatte einen Autounfall - was!

whatever [wʌtɛvər, wɒt-] pron: **I'll do ~ you want** ich tue alles, was du willst/Sie wollen; ~ **he says** egal, was er sagt

what's [wʌts, wɒts] contr of **what is; what has**

wheat [wit] n Weizen m

wheel [wil] n Rad nt; (steering wheel) Lenkrad nt ▷ vt (bicycle, trolley) schieben

wheelbarrow [wilbærou] n Schubkarren m

wheelchair [wiltʃɛər] n Rollstuhl m

KEYWORD

when [wɛn] adv wann

▷ conj **1** (at, during, after the time that) wenn; (in past) als; **she was reading when I came in** sie las, als ich hereinkam; **be careful when you cross the road** sei vorsichtig, wenn du über die Straße gehst/seien Sie vorsichtig, wenn Sie über die Straße gehen

2 (on, at which) als; **on the day when I met him** an dem Tag, an dem ich ihn traf

3 (whereas) wo ... doch

w

whenever [wɛnɛvər] *adv* (*every time*)
immer wenn; **come ~ you like** komm,
wann immer du willst/kommen Sie, wann
immer sie wollen
where [wɛər] *adv* wo; **~ are you going?**
wohin gehst du/gehen Sie?; **~ are you
from?** woher kommst du/kommen Sie?
▷ *conj* wo; **that's ~ I used to live** da habe
ich früher gewohnt
whereabouts [*adv* wɛərəbaʊts, *npl* wɛərə-
baʊts] *adv* wo ▷ *npl* Aufenthaltsort *m*
whereas [wɛərˈæz] *conj* während, wohinge-
gen
whereby [wɛərˈbaɪ] *adv* wodurch
wherever [wɛrɛvər] *conj* wo immer; **~ that
may be** wo immer das sein mag; **~ I go**
überall, wohin ich gehe
whether [wɛðər] *conj* ob

KEYWORD

which [wɪtʃ] *adj* **1** (*interrogative: direct,
indirect*) welche(r, s); **which one?** welche(r,
s)?
2: in which case in diesem Fall; **by which
time** zu dieser Zeit
▷ *pron* **1** (*interrogative*) welche(r, s); (*of
people also*) wer
2 (*relative*) der/die/das; (*referring to people*) was; **the apple which you ate/which is
on the table** der Apfel, den du gegessen
hast/der auf dem Tisch liegt; **he said he
saw her, which is true** er sagte, er habe sie
gesehen, was auch stimmt

whichever [wɪtʃɛvər] *adj, pron* welche(r, s)
auch immer
while [waɪl] *n:* **a ~** eine Weile; **for a ~** eine
Zeit lang; **a short ~ ago** vor Kurzem ▷ *conj*
während; (*although*) obwohl
whine [waɪn] *vi* (*person*) jammern
whip [wɪp] *n* Peitsche *f* ▷ *vt* (*beat*) peitschen; **~ped cream** Schlagsahne *f*
whirl [wɜrl] *vt, vi* herumwirbeln
whirlpool [wɜrlpul] *n* (*in river, sea*) Strudel
m; (*pool*) Whirlpool *m*
whisk [wɪsk] *n* Schneebesen *m* ▷ *vt* (*cream
etc*) schlagen
whisker [wɪskər] *n* (*of animal*) Schnurr-
haar *nt*; **~s** *pl* (*of man*) Backenbart *m*
whisk(e)y [wɪski] *n* Whisky *m*
whisper [wɪspər] *vi, vt* flüstern; **to ~ sth to
sb** jdm etw zuflüstern
whistle [wɪsəl] *n* Pfiff *m*; (*instrument*) Pfeife *f* ▷ *vt, vi* pfeifen

white [waɪt] *n* (*of egg*) Eiweiß *nt*; (*of eye*)
Weiße *nt* ▷ *adj* weiß; (*with fear*) blass; (*cof-
fee*) mit Milch/Sahne
White House *n:* **the ~** das Weiße Haus

WHITE HOUSE

Der Amtssitz des amerikanischen Prä-
sidenten liegt in der Hauptstadt
Washington D.C. und heißt das White
House. Es wurde im Jahr 1800 unter
dem Präsidenten John Adams gebaut.
Die Briten haben es 1814 abgebrandt,
aber es wurde später wiederaufgebaut
und vergrößert. 1902 gab Präsident
Theodore Roosevelt dem Gebäude
den offiziellen Namen White House.
Jedes Jahr wird es von 1,5 Millionen
Besuchern besichtigt.

white lie *n* Notlüge *f*
white meat *n* helles Fleisch
white sauce *n* weiße Soße
whitewater rafting [waɪtwɔtər ræftɪŋ] *n*
Rafting *nt*
white wine *n* Weißwein *m*

KEYWORD

who [hu] *pron* **1** (*interrogative*) wer; (*akk*)
wen; (*dat*) wem; **who is it?, who's there?**
wer ist da?
2 (*relative*) der/die/das; **the woman/man
who spoke to me** die Frau/der Mann, die/
der mit mir sprach

whoever [huɛvər] *pron* wer auch immer; **~
you choose** wen auch immer du wählst/
Sie wählen
whole [hoʊl] *adj* ganz ▷ *n* Ganze(s) *nt*; **the
~ of my family** meine ganze Familie; **on
the ~** im Großen und Ganzen
whole food *n:* **~ store** Bioladen *m*
wholeheartedly [hoʊlhɑrtɪdli] *adv* voll
und ganz
wholesale [hoʊlseɪl] *adv* (*buy, sell*) im
Großhandel
wholesome [hoʊlsəm] *adj* gesund
whole wheat *adj* Vollkorn-
wholly [hoʊlli] *adv* völlig

KEYWORD

whom [hum] *pron* **1** (*interrogative: akk*)
wen; (*dat*) wem; **whom did you see?** wen

hast du/haben Sie gesehen?; **to whom did you give it?** wem hast du/haben Sie es gegeben? **2** (*relative: akk*) den/die/das; (*dat*) dem/der/dem; **the man whom I saw/to whom I spoke** der Mann, den ich sah/mit dem ich sprach

whooping cough [huːpɪŋ kɔf] *n* Keuchhusten *m*

whose [huːz] *adj* (*in questions*) wessen; (*in relative clauses*) dessen/deren/dessen, deren *pl*; **~ bike is that?** wessen Fahrrad ist das? ▷ *pron* (*in questions*) wessen; **~ is this?** wem gehört das?

why [waɪ] *adv* warum, weshalb
▷ *conj* warum, weshalb; **that's not why I'm here** ich bin nicht deswegen hier; **that's the reason why** deshalb
▷ *excl* (*expressing surprise, shock*) na so was; (*explaining*) also dann; **why, it's you!** na so was, du bist/Sie sind es!

wicked [wɪkɪd] *adj* böse; (*fam: great*) geil
wide [waɪd] *adj* breit; (*skirt, trousers*) weit; (*selection*) groß ▷ *adv* weit
wide-angle lens [waɪdæŋgˀl lɛnz] *n* Weitwinkelobjektiv *nt*
wide awake *adj* hellwach
widely [waɪdli] *adv* weit; **~ known** allgemein bekannt
widen [waɪdˀn] *vt* verbreitern; (*fig*) erweitern
wide-open *adj* weit offen
widescreen TV [waɪdskriːn tiviː] *n* Breitbildfernseher *m*
widespread [waɪdsprɛd] *adj* weit verbreitet
widow [wɪdoʊ] *n* Witwe *f*
widowed [wɪdoʊd] *adj* verwitwet
widower [wɪdoʊər] *n* Witwer *m*
width [wɪdθ, wɪtθ] *n* Breite *f*
wife [waɪf] (*pl* **wives**) *n* (Ehe)frau *f*
Wi-Fi [waɪfaɪ] *n* Wi-Fi *nt*
wig [wɪg] *n* Perücke *f*
wiggle [wɪgˀl] *vt* wackeln mit
wild [waɪld] *adj* wild; (*violent*) heftig; (*plan, idea*) verrückt ▷ *n*: **in the ~** in freier Wildbahn
wildlife [waɪldlaɪf] *n* Tier- und Pflanzenwelt *f*
wildly [waɪldli] *adv* wild; (*enthusiastic, exaggerated*) maßlos

will [wɪl] *vb aux* **1** (*forms future tense*) werden; **I will finish it tomorrow** ich mache es morgen zu Ende
2 (*in conjectures, predictions*): **he will** *o* **he'll be there by now** er dürfte jetzt da sein; **that will be the postman** das wird der Postbote sein
3 (*in commands, requests, offers*): **will you be quiet!** sei/seien Sie endlich still!; **will you help me?** hilfst du/helfen Sie mir?; **will you have a cup of tea?** trinkst du/trinken Sie eine Tasse Tee?; **I won't put up with it!** das lasse ich mir nicht gefallen!
▷ *vt* wollen
▷ *n* Wille *m*; (*Jur*) Testament *nt*

willing [wɪlɪŋ] *adj* bereitwillig; **to be ~ to do sth** bereit sein, etw zu tun
willingly [wɪlɪŋli] *adv* gern(e)
willow [wɪloʊ] *n* Weide *f*
willpower [wɪlpaʊər] *n* Willenskraft *f*
wimp [wɪmp] *n* Weichei *nt*
win [wɪn] (**won, won**) *vt, vi* gewinnen ▷ *n* Sieg *m*
wind[1] [waɪnd] (**wound, wound**) *vt* (*rope, bandage*) wickeln
wind[2] [wɪnd] *n* Wind *m*; (*Med*) Blähungen *pl*
wind down *vt* (*car window*) herunterkurbeln
wind farm [wɪnd fɑrm] *n* Windpark *m*
wind instrument [wɪnd ɪnstrəmənt] *n* Blasinstrument *nt*
windmill [wɪndmɪl] *n* Windmühle *f*
window [wɪndoʊ] *n* Fenster *nt*; (*counter*) Schalter *m*; **~ of opportunity** Chance *f*, Gelegenheit *f*
window box *n* Blumenkasten *m*
windowpane [wɪndoʊpeɪn] *n* Fensterscheibe *f*
window-shopping *n*: **to go ~** einen Schaufensterbummel machen
windowsill [wɪndoʊsɪl] *n* Fensterbrett *nt*
windpipe [wɪndpaɪp] *n* Luftröhre *f*
windshield [wɪndʃild] *n* Windschutzscheibe *f*
windshield wiper [wɪndʃild waɪpər] *n* Scheibenwischer *m*
windsurfer [wɪndsɜrfər] *n* Windsurfer(in) *m(f)*; (*board*) Surfbrett *nt*
windsurfing [wɪndsɜrfɪŋ] *n* Windsurfen *nt*
wind up *vt* (*clock*) aufziehen; (*car window*)

W

hochkurbeln; (*meeting, speech*) abschließen; (*person*) aufziehen, ärgern

windy [wɪndɪ] *adj* windig

wine [waɪn] *n* Wein *m*

wine bar *n* Weinlokal *nt*

wineglass [waɪnglɑːs] *n* Weinglas *nt*

wine list *n* Weinkarte *f*

wine tasting [waɪn teɪstɪŋ] *n* (*event*) Weinprobe *f*

wing [wɪŋ] *n* Flügel *m*; **~s** *pl* (*Theat*) Kulissen *pl*

wink [wɪŋk] *vi* zwinkern; **to ~ at sb** jdm zuzwinkern

winner [wɪnər] *n* Gewinner(in) *m(f)*; (*Sport*) Sieger(in) *m(f)*

winning [wɪnɪŋ] *adj* (*team, horse etc*) siegreich; **~ number** Gewinnzahl *f* ▷ *n*: **~s** *pl* Gewinn *m*

win over *vt* für sich gewinnen

winter [wɪntər] *n* Winter *m*

winter sports *npl* Wintersport *m*

wintry [wɪntrɪ] *adj* winterlich

wipe [waɪp] *vt* abwischen; **to ~ one's nose** sich *dat* die Nase putzen; **to ~ one's feet** (*on mat*) sich *dat* die Schuhe abtreten

wipe off *vt* abwischen

wipe out *vt* (*destroy*) vernichten; (*data, debt*) löschen; (*epidemic etc*) ausrotten

wire [waɪər] *n* Draht *m*; (*Elec*) Leitung *f*; (*telegram*) Telegramm *nt* ▷ *vt* (*plug in*) anschließen; (*Tel*) telegrafieren (*sb sth* jdm etw)

wireless [waɪərlɪs] *adj* drahtlos

wisdom [wɪzdəm] *n* Weisheit *f*

wisdom tooth *n* Weisheitszahn *m*

wise [waɪz] *adj*, **wisely** *adv* weise

wish [wɪʃ] *n* Wunsch *m* (*for* nach); **with best ~es** (*in letter*) herzliche Grüße ▷ *vt* wünschen, wollen; **to ~ sb good luck/Merry Christmas** jdm viel Glück/frohe Weihnachten wünschen; **I ~ I'd never seen him** ich wünschte, ich hätte ihn nie gesehen

witch [wɪtʃ] *n* Hexe *f*

with [wɪð, wɪθ] *prep* **1** (*accompanying, in the company of*) mit; **we stayed with friends** wir übernachteten bei Freunden; **I'll be with you in a minute** einen Augenblick, ich bin sofort da; **I'm not with you** (*I don't understand*) das verstehe ich nicht; **to be with it** (*inf: up-to-date*) auf dem Laufenden sein; (*alert*) (voll) da sein (*inf*)
2 (*descriptive, indicating manner etc*) mit;

the man with the gray hat der Mann mit dem grauen Hut; **red with anger** rot vor Wut

withdraw [wɪðdrɔː, wɪθ-] (*irr*) *vt* zurückziehen; (*money*) abheben; (*comment*) zurücknehmen ▷ *vi* sich zurückziehen

wither [wɪðər] *vi* verwelken

withhold [wɪðhoʊld, wɪθ-] (*irr*) *vt* vorenthalten (*from sb* jdm)

within [wɪðɪn, wɪθ-] *prep* innerhalb +*gen*; **~ walking distance** zu Fuß erreichbar

without [wɪðaʊt, wɪθ-] *prep* ohne; **~ asking** ohne zu fragen

withstand [wɪðstænd, wɪθ-] (*irr*) *vt* standhalten +*dat*

witness [wɪtnɪs] *n* Zeuge *m*, Zeugin *f* ▷ *vt* Zeuge sein

witness stand *n* Zeugenstand *m*

witty [wɪtɪ] *adj* geistreich

wives [waɪvz] *pl of* **wife**

WMD [dʌbᵊlyu ɛm diː] (*abbr*) = **weapon of mass destruction** Massenvernichtungswaffe

wobble [wɒbᵊl] *vi* wackeln

wobbly [wɒblɪ] *adj* wackelig

wok [wɒk] *n* Wok *m*

woke [woʊk] *pt of* **wake**

woken [woʊkən] *pp of* **wake**

wolf [wʊlf] (*pl* **wolves**) *n* Wolf *m*

woman [wʊmən] (*pl* **women**) *n* Frau *f*

womb [wuːm] *n* Gebärmutter *f*

women [wɪmɪn] *pl of* **woman**

won [wʌn] *pt, pp of* **win**

wonder [wʌndər] *n* (*marvel*) Wunder *nt*; (*surprise*) Staunen *nt* ▷ *vt, vi* (*speculate*) sich fragen; **I ~ what/if ...** ich frage mich, was/ob ...

wonderful [wʌndərfəl] *adj*, **wonderfully** *adv* wunderbar

won't [woʊnt] *contr of* **will not**

wood [wʊd] *n* Holz *nt*; **~s** Wald *m*

wooden [wʊdᵊn] *adj* Holz-; (*fig*) hölzern

woodpecker [wʊdpɛkər] *n* Specht *m*

woodwork [wʊdwɜːrk] *n* (*wooden parts*) Holzteile *pl*; (*in school*) Werken *nt*

wool [wʊl] *n* Wolle *f*

woolen [wʊlən] *adj* Woll-

word [wɜːrd] *n* Wort *nt*; (*promise*) Ehrenwort *nt*; **~s** *pl* (*of song*) Text *m*; **to have a ~ with sb** mit jdm sprechen; **in other ~s** mit anderen Worten ▷ *vt* formulieren

wording [wɜːrdɪŋ] *n* Wortlaut *m*, Formulierung *f*

word processing [wɜːrd prɒsɛsɪŋ] *n* Textverarbeitung *f*

word processor [wɜrd prɒsɛsər] *n* (*program*) Textverarbeitungsprogramm *nt*

wore [wɔr] *pt of* **wear**

work [wɜrk] *n* Arbeit *f*; (*of art, literature*) Werk *nt*; **~ of art** Kunstwerk *nt*; **he's at ~** er ist in/auf der Arbeit; **out of ~** arbeitslos ▷ *vi* arbeiten (*at, on* an +*dat*); (*machine, plan*) funktionieren; (*medicine*) wirken; (*succeed*) klappen ▷ *vt* (*machine*) bedienen

workaholic [wɜrkəhɔlɪk] *n* Arbeitstier *nt*

worker [wɜrkər] *n* Arbeiter(in) *m(f)*

working class [wɜrkɪŋ klæs] *n* Arbeiterklasse *f*

workman [wɜrkmən] *n* (*pl* **-men**) *n* Handwerker *m*

work out *vi* (*plan*) klappen; (*sum*) aufgehen; (*person*) trainieren ▷ *vt* (*price, speed etc*) ausrechnen; (*plan*) ausarbeiten

workout [wɜrkaʊt] *n* (*Sport*) Fitnesstraining *nt*, Konditionstraining *nt*

work permit *n* Arbeitserlaubnis *f*

workplace [wɜrkpleɪs] *n* Arbeitsplatz *m*

workshop [wɜrkʃɒp] *n* Werkstatt *f*; (*meeting*) Workshop *m*

workstation [wɜrksteɪʃᵊn] *n* (*Inform*) Workstation *f*

work up *vt*: **to get worked up** sich aufregen

world [wɜrld] *n* Welt *f*

world championship *n* Weltmeisterschaft *f*

World War [wɜrld wɔr] *n*: **~ I/II, the First/ Second ~** der Erste/Zweite Weltkrieg

worldwide [wɜrldwaɪd] *adj, adv* weltweit

World Wide Web *n* World Wide Web *nt*

worm [wɜrm] *n* Wurm *m*

worn [wɔrn] *pp of* **wear** ▷ *adj* (*clothes*) abgetragen; (*tyre*) abgefahren

worn-out *adj* abgenutzt; (*person*) erschöpft

worried [wɜrid] *adj* besorgt; **be ~ about** sich *dat* Sorgen machen um

worrisome [wɜrɪsəm] *adj* beunruhigend

worry [wɜri] *n* Sorge *f* ▷ *vt* Sorgen machen +*dat* ▷ *vi* sich Sorgen machen (*about* um); **don't ~!** keine Sorge!

worse [wɜrs] *adj comparative of* **bad**; schlechter; (*pain, mistake etc*) schlimmer ▷ *adv comparative of* **badly**; schlechter

worsen [wɜrsən] *vt* verschlechtern ▷ *vi* sich verschlechtern

worship [wɜrʃɪp] *vt* anbeten, anhimmeln

worst [wɜrst] *adj superlative of* **bad**; schlechteste(r, s); (*pain, mistake etc*) schlimmste(r, s) ▷ *adv superlative of* **badly**; am schlechtesten ▷ *n*: **the ~ is over** das Schlimmste ist vorbei; **at the ~** schlimmstenfalls

worth [wɜrθ] *n* Wert *m*; **$10 ~ of food** Essen für 10 Dollar ▷ *adj*: **it is ~ $50** es ist 50 Dollar wert; **~ seeing** sehenswert; **it's ~ it** (*rewarding*) es lohnt sich

worthless [wɜrθləs] *adj* wertlos

worthwhile [wɜrθwaɪl] *adj* lohnend, lohnenswert

worthy [wɜrði] *adj* (*deserving respect*) würdig; **to be ~ of sth** etw verdienen

KEYWORD

would [wəd, STRONG wʊd] *vb aux* **1** (*conditional tense*): **if you asked him he would do it** wenn du ihn fragtest/Sie ihn fragten, würde er es tun; **if you had asked him he would have done it** wenn du ihn gefragt hättest/Sie ihn gefragt hätten, hätte er es getan

2 (*in offers, invitations, requests*): **would you like a cookie?** möchtest du/möchten Sie einen Keks?; **would you ask him to come in?** würdest du/würden Sie ihn bitte hereinbitten?

3 (*in indirect speech*): **I said I would do it** ich sagte, ich würde es tun

4 (*emphatic*): **it WOULD have to snow today!** es musste ja ausgerechnet heute schneien!

5 (*insistence*): **she wouldn't behave** sie wollte sich partout nicht anständig benehmen

6 (*conjecture*): **it would have been midnight** es mag ungefähr Mitternacht gewesen sein; **it would seem so** es sieht wohl so aus

7 (*indicating habit*): **he would go there on Mondays** er ging jeden Montag dorthin

wouldn't [wʊdᵊnt] *contr of* **would not**

would've [wʊdəv] *contr of* **would have**

wound¹ [wuːnd] *n* Wunde *f* ▷ *vt* verwunden; (*fig*) verletzen

wound² [waʊnd] *pt, pp of* **wind**

wove [woʊv] *pt of* **weave**

woven [woʊvᵊn] *pp of* **weave**

wrap [ræp] *vt* (*parcel, present*) einwickeln; **to ~ sth round sth** etw um etw wickeln

wrapper [ræpər] *n* (*of sweet*) Papier *nt*

wrapping paper [ræpɪŋ peɪpər] *n* Packpapier *nt*; (*giftwrap*) Geschenkpapier *nt*

w

wrap up vt (parcel, present) einwickeln ▷ vi (dress warmly) sich warm anziehen
wreath [riːθ] n Kranz m
wreck [rɛk] n (ship, plane, car) Wrack nt; **a nervous ~** ein Nervenbündel m ▷ vt (car) zu Schrott fahren; (fig) zerstören
wreckage [rɛkɪdʒ] n Trümmer pl
wrench [rɛntʃ] n (tool) Schraubenschlüssel m
wrestling [rɛslɪŋ] n Ringen nt
wring out [rɪŋ aʊt] (wrung, wrung) vt auswringen
wrinkle [rɪŋkᵊl] n Falte f
wrist [rɪst] n Handgelenk nt
wristwatch [rɪstwɒtʃ] n Armbanduhr f
write [raɪt] (wrote, written) vt schreiben; (check) ausstellen ▷ vi schreiben; **to ~ to sb** jdm schreiben
write down vt aufschreiben
write off vt (debt, person) abschreiben; (car) zu Schrott fahren ▷ vi: **to ~ for sth** etw anfordern
write out vt (name etc) ausschreiben;
(cheque) ausstellen
write-protected [raɪtprətɛktɪd] adj (Inform) schreibgeschützt
writer [raɪtər] n Verfasser(in) m(f); (author) Schriftsteller(in) m(f)
writing [raɪtɪŋ] n Schrift f; (profession) Schreiben nt; **in ~** schriftlich
writing paper n Schreibpapier nt
written [rɪtᵊn] pp of write
wrong [rɒŋ] adj (incorrect) falsch; (morally) unrecht; **you're ~** du hast/Sie haben unrecht; **what's ~ with your leg?** was ist mit deinem/Ihrem Bein los?; **you've got the ~ number** du bist/Sie sind falsch verbunden; **I dialed the ~ number** ich habe mich verwählt; **don't get me ~** versteh/ verstehen Sie mich nicht falsch; **to go ~** (plan) schiefgehen
wrongly [rɒŋli] adv falsch; (unjustly) zu Unrecht
wrote [rout] pt of write
WWW [dʌbᵊlyu dʌbᵊlyu dʌbᵊlyu] (abbr) = World Wide Web WWW

X

xenophobia [zɛnəfoʊbiə] *n* Ausländer-
feindlichkeit *f*
XL (*abbr*) = **extra large** XL, übergroß
Xmas [ɛksməs] *n* Weihnachten *nt*

X-ray [ɛksreɪ] *n* (*picture*) Röntgenaufnahme *f* ▷ *vt* röntgen
xylophone [zaɪləfoʊn] *n* Xylophon *nt*

Y

yacht [yɒt] *n* Jacht *f*

yachting [yɒtɪŋ] *n* Segeln *nt*; **to ~** segeln gehen

yam [yæm] *n* Süßkartoffel *f*

yard [yɑrd] *n* Hof *m*; (*garden*) Garten *m*; (*measure*) Yard *nt* (*0,91 m*)

yawn [yɒn] *vi* gähnen

yd (*abbr*) = **yard(s)**

year [yɪər] *n* Jahr *nt*; **this/last/next ~** dieses/letztes/nächstes Jahr; **he is 28 ~s old** er ist 28 Jahre alt; **~s ago** vor Jahren; **a five-~-old** ein(e) Fünfjährige(r)

yearly [yɪərli] *adj, adv* jährlich

yearn [yɜrn] *vi* sich sehnen (*for* nach +*dat*); **to ~ to do sth** sich danach sehnen, etw zu tun

yeast [yist] *n* Hefe *f*

yell [yɛl] *vi, vt* schreien; **to ~ at sb** jdn anschreien

yellow [yɛlou] *adj* gelb; **~ card** (*Sport*) gelbe Karte; **~ fever** Gelbfieber *nt*; **the ~ pages** (*pl*) die Gelben Seiten *pl*

yes [yɛs] *adv* ja; (*answering negative question*) doch; **to say yes to sth** ja zu etw sagen ▷ *n* Ja *nt*

yesterday [yɛstərdeɪ, -di] *adv* gestern; **~ morning/evening** gestern Morgen/Abend; **the day before ~** vorgestern; **~'s newspaper** die Zeitung von gestern

yet [yɛt] *adv* (*still*) noch; (*up to now*) bis jetzt; (*in a question: already*) schon; **he hasn't arrived yet** er ist noch nicht gekommen; **have you finished yet?** bist du/sind Sie schon fertig?; **yet again** schon wieder; **as yet** bis jetzt ▷ *conj* doch

yield [yild] *n* Ertrag *m* ▷ *vt* (*result, crop*) hervorbringen; (*profit, interest*) bringen ▷ *vi* nachgeben (*to* +*dat*); (*Mil*) sich ergeben (*to* +*dat*); **'~'** (*Auto*) „Vorfahrt beachten"

yoga [yougə] *n* Yoga *nt*

yogurt [yougərt] *n* Jog(h)urt *m*

yolk [youk] *n* Eigelb *nt*

KEYWORD

you [yu] *pron* **1** (*subj, in comparisons: familiar form: sg*) du; (*pl*) ihr; (*in letters*) Du, Ihr; (*polite form*) Sie; **you Germans** ihr Deutschen; **she's younger than you** sie ist jünger als du/ihr/Sie

2 (*direct object, after prep +akk: familiar form: sg*) dich; (*pl*) euch; (*in letters*) Dich, Euch; (*polite form*) Sie; **I know you** ich kenne dich/euch/Sie

3 (*indirect object, after prep +dat: familiar form: sg*) dir; (*pl*) euch; (*in letters*) Dir, Euch; (*polite form*) Ihnen; **I gave it to you** ich gab es dir/euch/Ihnen

4 (*impers: one: subj*) man; (*direct object*) einen; (*indirect object*) einem; **fresh air does you good** frische Luft tut (einem) gut

you'd [yud] *contr* of **you had**; **you would**; **~ better leave** du solltest/Sie sollten gehen

you'll [yul] *contr* of **you will**; **you shall**

young [yʌŋ] *adj* jung ▷ *n*: **the ~** *pl* (*young people*) die jungen Leute *pl*; (*animals*) die Jungen *pl*

youngster [yʌŋstər] *n* Jugendliche(r) *mf*

your [yɔr, yuər] *adj* (*sing*) dein; (*polite form*) Ihr; (*pl*) euer; (*polite form*) Ihr; **have you hurt ~ leg?** hast du dir/haben Sie sich das Bein verletzt?

you're [yɔr, yuər] *contr* of **you are**

yours [yɔrz, yuərz] *pron* (*sing*) deine(r, s); (*polite form*) Ihre(r, s); (*pl*) eure(r, s); (*polite form*) Ihre(r, s); **is this ~?** gehört das dir/Ihnen?; **a friend of ~** ein Freund von dir/Ihnen

yourself [yɔrsɛlf, yuər-] *pron* (*sing*) dich; (*polite form*) sich; **have you hurt ~?** hast du dich/haben Sie sich verletzt?; **did you do it ~?** hast du/haben Sie es selbst gemacht?; **all by ~** allein

yourselves [yɔrsɛlvz, yuər-] *pron* (*pl*) euch; (*polite form*) sich; **have you hurt ~?** habt ihr euch/haben Sie sich verletzt?; **did you do it ~?** habt ihr/haben Sie es selbst gemacht?; **all by ~** allein

youth [yuθ] *n* (*period*) Jugend *f*; (*young man*) junger Mann; (*young people*) Jugend *f*

youth group *n* Jugendgruppe *f*

youth hostel *n* Jugendherberge *f*

you've [yuv] *contr* of **you have**

yucky [yʌki] *adj* (*fam*) eklig

yummy [yʌmi] *adj* (*fam*) lecker

yuppie [yʌpi], **yuppy** *n* Yuppie *m*

Z

zap [zæp] *vt* (*Inform*) löschen; (*in computer game*) abknallen ▷ *vi* (*TV*) zappen
zapper [zæpər] *n* (*TV*) Fernbedienung *f*
zapping [zæpɪŋ] *n* (*TV*) ständiges Umschalten, Zapping *nt*
zebra [zíbrə] *n* Zebra *nt*
zero [zɪərou] (*pl* -**es**) *n* Null *f*; **10 degrees below ~** 10 Grad unter null
zest [zɛst] *n* (*enthusiasm*) Begeisterung *f*
zigzag [zɪgzæg] *n* Zickzack *m* ▷ *vi* (*person, vehicle*) im Zickzack gehen/fahren; (*path*) im Zickzack verlaufen
zinc [zɪŋk] *n* Zink *nt*
zip code [zɪp koʊd] *n* Postleitzahl *f*
Zip disk® [zɪp dɪsk] *n* (*Inform*) ZIP-Diskette® *f*

Zip drive® [zɪp draɪv] *n* (*Inform*) ZIP-Laufwerk® *nt*
Zip file® [zɪp faɪl] *n* (*Inform*) ZIP-Datei® *f*
zipper [zɪpər] *n* Reißverschluss *m*
zit [zɪt] *n* (*fam*) Pickel *m*
zodiac [zoʊdiæk] *n* Tierkreis *m*; **sign of the ~** Tierkreiszeichen *nt*
zone [zoʊn] *n* Zone *f*; (*area*) Gebiet *nt*; (*in town*) Bezirk *m*
zoo [zu] *n* Zoo *m*
zoom [zum] *vi* (*move fast*) brausen, sausen ▷ *n*: **~ lens** Zoomobjektiv *nt*
zoom in *vi* (*Foto*) heranzoomen (*on* an +*akk*)
zucchini [zukíni] (*pl* -**(s)**) *n* Zucchini *f*